Introduction to Child Development

Fifth Edition

CDEV

INTRODUCTION TO CHILD DEVELOPMENT

Fifth Edition

John P. Dworetzky
Department of Psychology
Western Washington University
Bellingham, Washington

West Publishing Company
Minneapolis/St. Paul ■ New York ■ Los Angeles ■ San Francisco

For Peter and Alex,
with all our love to Steve and Korie.

Copy Editor: Janet Greenblatt
Composition: Parkwood Composition Service
Cover Art: Diamond Doyle, Age 6

West's Commitment to the Environment

In 1906, West Publishing Company began recycling materials left over from the production of books. This began a tradition of efficient and responsible use of resources. Today, up to 95 percent of our legal books and 70 percent of our college and school texts are printed on recycled, acid-free stock. West also recycles nearly 22 million pounds of scrap paper annually—the equivalent of 181,717 trees. Since the 1960s, West has devised ways to capture and recycle waste inks, solvents, oils, and vapors created in the printing process. We also recycle plastics of all kinds, wood, glass, corrugated cardboard, and batteries, and have eliminated the use of styrofoam book packaging. We at West are proud of the longevity and the scope of our commitment to the environment.

Production, Prepress, Printing and Binding by West Publishing Company.

Special thanks to the students of The St. Paul Open School, St. Paul, Minnesota, who provided the artwork appearing on the cover and unit opening pages.

Photo credits and acknowledgments appear following the subject index.

610 Opperman Drive
P.O. Box 64526
St. Paul, MN 55164-0526

Printed in the United States of America

00 99 98 97 96 95 94 93 8 7 6 5 4 3 2 1 0

Library of Congress Cataloging-in-Publication Data

Dworetzky, John.
Introduction to child development / John P. Dworetzky.—5th ed.
p. cm.
Includes bibliographical references and index.
ISBN 0-314-01135-8
1. Child development. 2. Child psychology. I. Title.
RJ131.D93 1993
305.23′1—dc20 93-39465
CIP 

Contents in Brief

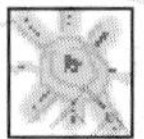

UNIT THREE

The Developing Child: Learning, Language, and Cognition 180

UNIT FOUR

The Developing Child: Social Processes 330

CONTENTS

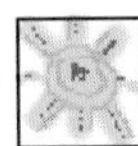

Chapter 2
Inheritance and the Biological Foundations of Development 31

UNIT TWO
Beginnings of Life: Birth and Infancy 62

Chapter 3
Conception, Prenatal Development, and Birth 65

Chapter 4
Growth, Maturation, and Individual Differences 101

Chapter 5
Neural, Sensory, and Perceptual Development 123

Chapter 6
Infant Social and Emotional Development 147

Chapter 8
Language Development 209

Chapter 9
Cognitive Development I: Historical Foundations 239

Chapter 10
Cognitive Development II: Modern Perspectives 273

Chapter 11
Intelligence and Creativity 299

UNIT FOUR

The Developing Child: Social Processes 330

Chapter 12
Socialization and Personality Development 333

Chapter 15
The Development of Morality and Self-Control 417

Chapter 16
Child Development in Other Cultures 445

Chapter 17
Children With Special Needs 469

UNIT FIVE

Adolescence 498

Chapter 18
Adolescent Physical and Cognitive Development 501

Chapter 19
Adolescent Social and Personality Development 521

PREFACE

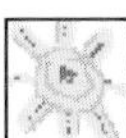

Each spring thousands of instructors, myself included, review new textbooks to see if there is one we might wish to adopt, and each spring we search for the textbook we'll never find—the one that would be just right for each and every student and still fit well with our own method of teaching. Even so, when I began writing, it was my hope to come as close to that kind of book as possible. I've therefore tried to incorporate the content and format that I think will be of most value to both professors and students, while keeping in mind that professors may have widely varying methods of teaching child development and that students will come to the course with different background and goals.

For this reason, this text attempts an integration of the popular formats used in most child development texts and holds them together with an SQ3R organization. As an author, I have been very pleased with the comments I have received from so many professors and students expressing their support for the first four editions.

Those unfamiliar with the text will find that the fifth edition continues to rely on the feedback and input from adopters throughout the United States, Canada, and overseas. Such feedback from the field has truly helped to make this a successful text, for which I am very grateful.

Because this is an introduction to child development, the basic content essential to all introductory courses has been included. At the same time, emphasis has been given to topics that have recently become important in the research literature. There is also an attempt to resolve a problem peculiar to textbooks on child development, that of whether to present material topically or chronologically. Material presented topically usually covers one topic at a time. Students obtain information about such topics as cognitive development, moral development, or social development in a single unit. Unfortunately, this approach often leaves students with a poorer sense of continuous development than does the chronological approach, in which different topics are covered in relation to different age groups. For example, the first few chapters of a chronologically based text may discuss many topics relating to infants and then, in the next chapters, may discuss the same topics as they relate to 2-, 3-, and 4-year-olds. In the next chapters, again, the same topics may be discussed in relation to school-age children, and so on. The problem with this approach is that students are exposed to major concepts piece-meal. Because of this the entire flow of the material may be disrupted. I have tried in this textbook to combine the best of both topical and chronological approaches. The material within each chapter is organized topically, while the general course of the text and the flow of each chapter from beginning to end is chronological.

As for the depth and level of the coverage of this text, I have tried to continue the example of the first four editions and present complex technical ideas in a way that will maintain interest. I hope that you, the reader, will find that the material is set down in a comprehensible, enjoyable, and interesting way.

Organization of the Textbook

As you may already have noticed in skimming through the text, the format is unusual. Each chapter is divided into sections. First there is a *Chapter Preview*, which presents an interesting fact about or perspective on the material contained within the chapter. Following the *Chapter Preview* is the *Resources* section, which provides the basic information within each chapter. Contained within the *Resources* are *At Issue* sections, which highlight and discuss important issues currently being debated in the literature or press. Following the *Resources* is the *Applications* section, in which a topic or area covered in the chapter is applied in order to solve a problem or to deal with day-to-day issues. Next is a *Summary* in which the text material is reviewed. A *For Discussion* section sometimes follows the *Summary* section; it briefly deals with an unusual topic related to the chapter content. Following this in all chapters are *Questions for Discussion,* which are meant to stimulate discussion in class or among friends or classmates who are interested in the topic. The questions are provocative and answers are not provided, since many different answers are possible. The final section is *Suggestions for Further Reading*. Students often find a particular area exciting and want to learn more. I have been careful to select books that preset new or thought-provoking material that you may enjoy. In this way you may pursue a particular area in order to do research or follow up your own interests.

Acknowledgments

It would be impossible to write a textbook without the help and cooperation of many others. I would like to thank those who kindly and generously gave their time to review this book and to provide criticism, encouragement, comments, suggestions, and ideas. I wish to express my personal appreciation to the following members of our academic community who assisted in the preparation of previous editions:

First Edition

Linda P. Acredolo
University of California, Davis

Thomas Bond
Thomas Nelson Community College, Virginia

Glendon Casto
Utah State University

Dennis Coon
Santa Barbara City College

Stephen Cooper
Glendale College, Arizona

Joseph G. Cunningham
Auburn University, Alabama

Jeffrey W. Elias
Texas Tech University

Barry Gholson
Memphis State University, Tennessee

Frances S. Harnick
University of New Mexico

Don Holmlund
College of Marin, California

Ann Husmann
El Camino College, California

Daniel W. Kee
University of Southern California

Patti Keith-Spiegel
California State University, Northridge

Candida Lutes
Texas A & M University

Richard Rees
Glendale College, Arizona

Barbara Rogoff
University of Utah

Stephen M. Saltzman
Los Angeles Valley College

Margaret Sand
San Diego State

Toni E. Santmire
University of Nebraska

Lois Pall Wandersmith
University of South Carolina

Mary Weir
Long Beach City College, California

Patricia E. Worden
California State University, Fullerton

Second Edition

Jeanne Armstrong
Lane Community College, Oregon

James A. Bard
Cleveland State University

Debra E. Clark
State University of New York at Cortland

Edward J. Forbes
Lock Haven State College, Pennsylvania

Ellen R. Green
St. Louis Community College

Laurence H. Harshbarger
Ball State University, Indiana

Seth Kunen
University of New Orleans

Robert O'Neill
University of California, Santa Barbara

William Romoser
University of Wisconsin, River Falls

J. Michael Shaner
Central Michigan University

Barbara Sommer
University of California, Davis

John E. Stone
East Tennessee State University

Third Edition

Nancy Hamblen Acuff
East Tennessee State University

Linda Baker
University of Maryland

Kathryn N. Black
Purdue University

DuWayne D. Furman
Western Illinois University

Gary W. Guyot
West Texas State University

Maury Haraway
N.E. Louisiana State

Garrett Lange
University of North Carolina

Mary W. Laurence
University of Toronto

Gene R. Medinnus
San Jose State University

Jim Stigler
University of Chicago

Fourth Edition

Connie H. Duncanson
Northern Michigan University

Louella Fong
Western Kentucky University

Jan Kennedy
Georgia Southern College

Catherine King
University of New Orleans

George P. Knight
Arizona State University

Kathleen McCormick
Ocean County College

Francine Smolucha
Moraine Valley Community College

Amye Warren-Leubecker
University of Tennessee, Chattanooga

I also wish to thank all those who contributed so much of their time and skill to the preparation of this fifth edition:

Robert Bornstein
Miami University

Rod Smith
Pensacola Junior College

H. Stuart Smith
Tidewater Community College

Jim Duffy
Memorial University of Newfoundland

Eliot J. Butter
University of Dayton

William H. Zachry
University of Tennessee

James Starzec
State University of New York—Cortland

Shirley M. Ogletree
Southwest Texas State University

Charlotte J. Patterson
University of Virginia

In addition, I'd like to express my deepest gratitude to Clyde Perlee, Jr., editor-in-chief of West's college division, for his creativity, interest, and skill. His valued friendship and professionalism have been the supports upon which this edition, as well as the other editions, have been built. I also wish to express my personal appreciation to Bill Stryker for the excellent design of this book and for his talent, patience, humor, and friendship under the most pressing of time constraints.

I also wish to thank Janet Greenblatt for her excellent copyediting, to Parkwood Composition Service for their extremely fast and skillful typesetting, and to Steve Schonebaum, Denis Ralling, and all the others at West Publishing who have had a part in preparing this textbook. A special thanks to Dr. Arleen Lewis for many of the wonderful photographs in the text and to Dr. Nancy Davis for her valuable advice and information.

John P. Dworetzky

To the Student

How to Use the Unique Features of this Textbook

This book is based on a method known as SQ3R. SQ3R is a five-step plan that was developed by Dr. Francis P. Robinson. The SQ3R method is designed to promote effective studying, and the letters S-Q-R-R-R refer to the five steps.

The First Step: Survey The S in SQ3R stands for *survey*. The first thing to do is survey the assigned chapter. Read the titles and the headings. Glance at the captions under illustrations and pictures; read the summary at the end of the chapter. This may seem like an unusual way to begin, but it is the way the SQ3R method is designed, and it's effective. Usually you read a summary in order to review what you've covered in the chapter. But in this case the *Summary* is the very first thing you should read. Although you may not understand everything, the summary will give you an overall picture of the chapter contents, and it helps us to reinforce the major points when you come to them in the chapter, once you have read the entire chapter you may, of course, reread the *Summary* in order to refresh your memory.

The Second Step: Question The Q stands for *question*. In the SQ3R method, every topic is introduced as a question, a means of increasing your interest in what you will be reading and helping you to focus on the material to come. In this text, the questions are already provided for you. Flip through the text for a moment, and you'll notice them. You may find the interjection of questions in the text obtrusive at first, but you will quickly become used to them and find that the questions help you focus your attention. You may even find that you were about to ask many of the same questions. This shows that you are concentrating on the material and that you understand what is being presented.

The Third Step: Read The first R stands for *read*. You should read the material under one heading and stop before going on to the next heading. That is, you should cover one small area within a chapter at a time. Before continuing to read, go on to step four.

The Fourth Step: Recite The second R stands for *recite*. When you recite, ask yourself questions about the material you have just read and make sure that you are able to answer them. Your student study guide* can help you in this because

*If a student study guide for this text is not available in your bookstore, a copy may be obtained through West Publishing Company, or your bookstore may be able to order one for you.

it contains questions with which you can test yourself. Once you known, by reciting, that you thoroughly understand what you have read, you can proceed to the next heading, reciting once again, before going on to the next heading, and so on.

Throughout the book you will find Learning Checks that help you to recite. If you can answer these Learning Checks correctly, you will know that you have read the material carefully and understand it. Remember, this is a textbook; it's a book for work. Don't feel uncomfortable about writing in it. It's not a complete work like *Moby Dick.* Add to it, make notes from class in the margins; fill in the answers in the Learning Checks where there are blanks; circle the answers to the multiple choice questions. Recording your answers will help you to remember the material and to catch errors.

The Fifth Step: Review *Review* is the final R in SQ3R. When you have read an entire chapter, review your notes, check through your student study guide, and look over any questions that you have written down. If possible, have someone read through the material and ask you about it. Make sure that you can answer the questions that have been posed. This is an important way of obtaining feedback.

GLOSSARY

Finally, you will find words set in boldface throughout the text. These are terms that are defined in the running glossary on each page near the first appearance of the term. If you are uncertain about the meaning of a term at later time, you can also look it up in the Glossary provided at the back of the book.

I hope that this text will provide you with a thorough introduction to child development, and that it will make you want to learn more.

John P. Dworetzky

Introduction to Child Development

Fifth Edition

UNIT ONE

FOUNDATIONS OF DEVELOPMENT

Caite Schmidt, age six

Unit Contents

CHAPTER 1

AN INTRODUCTION TO DEVELOPMENT: HISTORY AND RESEARCH

CHAPTER PREVIEW

WHO IS RIGHT?

IN THE HALLS OF Congress, concerned parents implore their elected representatives to ban violence from children's television programs. Testimony is given, and parents describe how their children have imitated the aggression they have seen on television. Television producers argue, on the other hand, that the

effect of television on children is overestimated and that many children are aggressive from time to time even if they haven't watched television.

AFTER PUTTING IN A full day at her regular school, a young girl then goes to a privately operated Learning Center, to which her parents have paid tuition. There she is taught her regular school lessons with the most modern psychological techniques, such as the use of incentives and reinforcements. She is expected to learn at a much faster rate than her peers, and this; her parents believe, will give her an important edge over other children who are less fortunate. Others argue, however, that such additional work puts too much stress on the child and may cause her to "burn out."

IN A HIGH SCHOOL health center in a disadvantaged neighborhood, a program is started to help eliminate unwanted pregnancies and sexually transmitted diseases among students. Sex education programs are conducted, and condoms are given to students without their parents' knowledge. While some applaud this action, others argue that such programs encourage sexual activity among teenagers and therefore lead to an increase in pregnancies and sexually transmitted diseases.

ON A TV TALK SHOW, parents and teachers debate the value of spanking children who disrupt the classroom. Some favor it as the only way to maintain discipline. Others argue that it may harm the child psychologically or encourage abuse.

WHO IS CORRECT in these situations, and how can you tell?

HOW MANY DEBATES can you think of that involve the development or welfare of children? For example, is it wrong for parents or teachers to spank children? How easily can someone undermine a child's self-confidence? How "normal" is it for young children to be strongly attached to their mothers? When do children start to speak, and how much of what is said to them do they actually understand? How do children acquire a sense of right and wrong? What do babies think about? When should children be expected to walk? On questions such as these, unlike questions about nuclear physics or molecular chemistry, for instance, almost everyone will have an opinion.

TRY IT. Ask friends or relatives, "Should sodium ferricyanide be mixed with ferric ammonium sulfate?"* See what they say. Then ask, "Is it wrong for parents to spank their children?" The first question is not likely to bring ready responses, except from chemists, while the second will usually provoke comment and advice. The reason for this is, of course, that people feel that they should be knowledgeable about children because they've been around them, raised a few, or can recall their own childhood, while almost no one expects to be knowledgeable about complex chemical interactions. And yet, in a very real sense, a developing child is the most complex chemical reaction known, and while common sense or general observation may tell us something about what is going on or what we might expect, scientific examination can often uncover surprises that no one, not even grandma, had ever supposed. And so, while it is true that there are thousands of commonly held and discussed opinions and beliefs about child development, it is also true that many of these are contradictory because they are often based on different people's limited experiences rather than on scientific research.

IN THIS CHAPTER, we'll look at the methods researchers use when exploring complex issues, and we'll examine ways to answer questions like those posed in this chapter preview. But first, let's take a brief look at the historical concept of childhood and the emergence of interest in infant and child development.

*Answer: Only if you wish to make Prussian blue dye.

RESOURCES

The Historical Concept of Childhood

THE DAWN OF HISTORY

> Go to school, stand before your teacher, recite your assignment, open your schoolbag, write your tablet, let the teacher's assistant write your new lesson for you. . . . Don't stand about in the public square. . . . Be humble and show fear before your superiors. (Sommerville, 1982, p. 21)

In this letter you can hear a father's concern as he writes to his son. In terms of its general content, the letter might have been written yesterday, but it wasn't. It was found in the dry sands of Egypt, where it had been undisturbed by the elements. The date: 1800 B.C.!

After reading the ancient letter, you may think that things haven't changed much in 3,800 years. But our modern, detailed understanding of childhood as a special time of development—a time unique unto itself, when foundations are built—is really quite recent. In fact, it is difficult to find a full appreciation of what we now know to be the uniqueness of childhood in writings much older than 100 years or so. Before that time, the idea of childhood as an exceptional entity unto itself simply didn't exist. One researcher has stated:

> This is not to suggest that children were neglected, forsaken, or despised. The idea of childhood is not to be confused with affection for children: it corresponds to an awareness of the particular nature of childhood, that particular nature which distinguishes the child from the adult, even the young adult. In . . . society this awareness was lacking. That is why, as soon as the child could live without the constant solicitude of his mother, his nanny, or his cradle-rocker, he belonged to adult society. (Aries, 1962, p. 128)

Prior to the twentieth century, if a society placed any emphasis on childhood, it was usually in reference to education. For children to be prepared for life, their education had to begin early; in a limited sense, then, many societies saw childhood as a time to prepare for adulthood. Even so, children were typically not thought of as having any exceptional or unique *qualities*, but rather were viewed as being *quantitatively* different, that is, as being obviously smaller and less educated than adults. It wasn't until the scientific investigations of children began in earnest that the richly unique and qualitative differences between children and adults started to become apparent.

SCIENTIFIC APPROACHES TO CHILD DEVELOPMENT

Question: When was childhood first studied scientifically?

Before any detailed understanding of childhood could begin to develop, interest in the study of children needed to be stimulated. To a great degree, some of the most stimulating thoughts concerning child development can be traced to the questions asked by philosophers. By the start of the eighteenth century, such questions were beginning to appear in abundance. For instance, the English philosopher John Locke (1632–1704) wondered if children were born *tabula rasa* (as a blank slate). According to this view, a child would be born neither "guilty" nor "good" nor any particular way at birth but rather unshaped and unmolded, and every behavior and manner that the child would come to possess would be acquired through interaction with the environment. In this way, the culture would determine what was written on the "blank slate."

A little later, support for the *tabula rasa* idea (that children were the products of their environments) grew when Captain James Cook (1728–1779) became the

Charles Darwin (1809–1882), whose concept of evolution through natural selection became the cornerstone of modern evolutionary biology.

first Westerner to discover Tahiti. He and his crew found Tahitian children to be very different from European children. For instance, no one in that culture, including the children, equated sex with guilt (as the Christian Europeans did). In the Rites of Venus, for example, young Tahitian boys and girls who had just reached puberty were brought together by the older women and taught the most enjoyable ways to have sexual intercourse. The French philosopher Jean Jacques Rousseau (1712–1778) reacted to these observations by writing in praise of "natural man." He argued that the aim of education should be to offset the corrupting influence of institutions and that children should be allowed to develop without any interference, especially from the church or state.

Throughout the eighteenth century, interest in child development grew, and speculation about how children might best develop became a topic of general interest. By the middle of the nineteenth century, however, many of the philosophical speculations about the nature of children were being replaced by a new approach.

EMPIRICAL EFFORTS

Question: What kind of approach replaced philosophical speculation?

The first **empirical** efforts to record and scientifically study the behavior of developing organisms were being made by British **naturalists,** who had developed methods for carefully observing and recording nature. These attempts to document observations systematically also marked the beginning of contemporary **developmental psychology** (as it, too, incorporates empirical methods).

The famous naturalist and founder of modern evolutionary biology, Charles Darwin (1809–1882), made a unique contribution to the understanding of the development of living creatures, humans included. In his work, he demonstrated that time was a powerful force and that given sufficient time, many important changes can occur within any given species through **evolution.**

Once the changes that occurred in living creatures became an area of interest, naturalists, including Darwin, already familiar with the development of other animal species, began to compare their data with observations of the development and behavior of children. In the following passage, you can see the kind of thorough, although sometimes informal, observational method common among the naturalists—in this case applied by Darwin to his own son:

> When nearly four months old, and perhaps much earlier, there could be no doubt, from the manner in which the blood gushed into his whole face and scalp, that he easily got into a violent passion. When eleven months old, if a wrong plaything was given him, he would push it away and beat it; I presume that the beating was an instinctive sign of anger, like the snapping of the jaws by a young crocodile just out of the egg, and not that he imagined he could hurt the plaything.

G. Stanley Hall (1846–1924), the first developmental psychologist. He pioneered investigations into many areas of child development.

THE TWENTIETH CENTURY

By the beginning of the twentieth century, American psychologist G. Stanley Hall (1846–1924) had incorporated Darwin's views into a **psychology.** Hall could thus be considered the first developmental psychologist. In fact, Hall was the first in many things. He was the first to receive a Ph.D. in psychology, and he was the founder of the American Psychological Association. He was also one of the first to study children in a laboratory, where he investigated the traditional topics of perception, learning, and memory as they applied just to children. Hall's interest in child development was extensive. While teaching at Clark University, Hall became aware of the new and dynamic theories of a Viennese psychiatrist, Sigmund Freud (1856–1939).

Freud placed tremendous emphasis on the early years of childhood as the force shaping later healthy or unhealthy personalities. Unhealthy personality, Freud argued, had its origins in childhood. These theories were introduced in the United States through Freud's books and a series of lectures he gave, at Hall's invitation, at Clark University in 1908. His lecture topics included theories of infantile sexuality and the effects of various early childhood experiences on later life. A direct result of these lectures was an upsurge of interest in children and their development.

In 1905, Alfred Binet (1857–1911), a French psychologist, developed tests designed to distinguish intellectually subnormal from normal children. These were the forerunners of modern IQ tests. By the 1920s, developmental research was growing at a rapid pace. Arnold Gesell (1880–1961), an American who held both an M.D. and a Ph.D. in psychology, began systematically comparing age-related differences of social, motor, emotional, language, and physical development among children. Longitudinal studies, in which the same individuals are periodically tested over long periods of time, were also started.

During the decades following World War I, the Swiss scientist Jean Piaget (1896–1980) investigated the **cognitive development** of children; he was to become perhaps the most influential voice in the history of developmental psychology. At the same time, in America, John Watson (1878–1958), the founder of **behaviorism,** began to lecture and write about child psychology and child-rearing practices. In response to the teachings of Freud, Binet, Piaget, Watson, and others, interest in child development grew.

World War II drew the nation's efforts and attention elsewhere, and by the end of the 1940s, research in child development had declined to half its 1938 level (Stevenson, 1968). In the 1950s, however, this downward trend reversed dramatically.

After World War II, many returning veterans began families, causing the so-called baby boom. Science was in the forefront of modern consciousness, having produced television, jet planes, and atomic power, so these postwar parents were

EMPIRICAL
Relying or based solely on experiments or objective observation.

NATURALIST
A person who studies natural history, especially zoology and botany.

DEVELOPMENTAL PSYCHOLOGY
The study of age-related differences in behavior.

EVOLUTION
The process by which plants or animals change from earlier existing forms. Darwin understood evolution to occur primarily through the processes of diversification and natural selection.

PSYCHOLOGY
The discipline that attempts to describe, explain, and predict behavior and mental processes.

COGNITIVE DEVELOPMENT
Age-related changes in behavior as they relate to perceiving, thinking, remembering, and problem solving.

BEHAVIORISM
The school of psychology that views learning as the most important aspect of an organism's development. Behaviorists objectively measure behavior and the way in which stimulus-response relationships are formed.

Attitudes toward children have changed greatly over the years. Children were previously thought of as small adults and were often expected to go to work at a very early age. These children spent 12 hours a day sorting coal by size and removing rocks and other impurities.

NATURE
In developmental research, the hereditary component of an organism's development.

NURTURE
In developmental research, the environmental component of an organism's development.

TEMPERAMENT THEORY
In developmental research, any theory that emphasizes the predisposition an individual has toward general patterns of emotional reactions, changes in mood, or sensitivity to particular stimulation. Most temperament theories view temperament as a genetic disposition.

determined to raise their children "scientifically." As a result, parental concerns and interests helped to shape the direction of developmental research, and this research, in turn, further helped to shape and guide parents to better understand their children. Along with the generally expanding interest in psychology, research in child development during the postwar years has been extensive.

Compared with that of people in centuries gone by, our current knowledge of childhood is enormous. In the chapters of this book, you will learn more about children's development than was ever known or dreamed of by our forebears. And you can use this knowledge to be a better parent, teacher, citizen, or researcher or simply to satisfy your curiosity.

Issues in Development

When empirical methods were first applied to the field of child development, a number of major issues emerged. These issues in development are still of central importance. Let's take a moment to examine them.

NATURE VERSUS NURTURE

As you sit now, reading this book, you are an excellent example of the interaction of **nature** (the effects of heredity) and **nurture** (the effects of the environment). Your human brain allows you to process and recall vast amounts of information. If you had inherited the brain of a dog or cat, no amount of training would enable you to comprehend this chapter.

If this chapter were written in Turkish, you would be unable to understand it unless through experience, or nurturance, you had come to learn Turkish. It is a combination of your inherited brain and your experience with reading the English language, as well as the experience you've gathered about the world, that enables you to understand and make use of the information in this text. All human development can be understood as an *interaction* of nature and nurture (Weisfeld, 1982).

Question: Aren't some behaviors determined mainly by genetics?

Some behaviors, such as growing physically or learning to walk, do seem to be mainly a function of the genetic component. Others, such as driving a car or reading a book, seem to be shaped primarily by the environment. It is important to remember, however, that nature versus nurture isn't a pure dichotomy. Without proper nutrition, a child's growth may be stunted, or a child's first steps may occur much later than if the child had been properly nourished. And without a powerful enough brain or the inherited physical capacity, driving a car or even reading might be impossible. It is always the interaction between the two that determines our behavior.

STABILITY VERSUS CHANGE

There is much evidence that shortly after birth, babies are different from one another (Eisenberg & Marmarou, 1981). Some cry and fret, some sleep, some are quietly active. Workers on obstetrics wards are familiar with the great range of personalities noticeable among infants within the first few days of life. Although newborns may behave very differently from one another, their own individual rates of activity and crying are quite stable and consistent during the first days of life (Korner, Hutchinson, Koperski, Kraemer, & Schneider, 1981). **Temperament theories** are based on the fact that these early infant personalities or characteristics may be consistent and stable over even greater lengths of time (Goldsmith, 1983). On the other hand, some of the most interesting changes in development may appear to occur suddenly, sometimes even unexpectedly. In this sense, development can sometimes seem to be an unstable process.

Repeated studies of the same individuals, however, have suggested that when considering the great range of human development, both elements of instability and consistency are to be found (Costa & McCrae, 1980; Thomas, Chess, & Birch, 1970).

As with the nature-nurture issue, it is important to realize that stability versus change is not a dichotomy. It is not an either-or situation; both are usually involved. In future chapters, we will look at some of these consistencies and changes.

CONTINUITY VERSUS DISCONTINUITY

Developmental researchers have debated for years whether child development can be viewed as a natural, orderly progression or whether it occurs in a series of stages, with abrupt changes occurring from one stage to the next.

Question: Isn't it more reasonable to assume that development follows an orderly progression?

Some people think that child development, and development in general, should follow a fairly linear (straight-line) progression—that is, that it should proceed at a fairly stable and steady rate and that each new development should be built on all the developments that came before.

Question: But isn't that the way children develop?

Not necessarily. Many of the most important phenomena in child development are nonlinear in nature (Roberts, 1986). For instance, when you speak of child development, are you referring to physical development? If so, which physical development? Growth of the lymphatic system, or sexual organs, or visual acuity, or body size? Or by child development do you mean cognitive development, or intellectual development, or social development, or language development, or emotional development, or sexual development, or . . . ?

Question: Wait! Wouldn't child development include all these areas?

Yes, and that's the point. Child development may occur rapidly *and* slowly, *and* it may plateau *and* even sometimes appear to reverse, all at the same time, depending on which developmental aspect you consider. Some behaviors appear to be acquired in an orderly progression; others may appear in an abrupt shift. In a word, child development is complex. A professor who was once asked whether there wasn't some aspect of child development that could be counted on to occur at a nice, simple, fixed rate replied, after giving it much thought, "birthdays!"

Figure 1.1 summarizes the three developmental issues discussed so far in this chapter. As you now know, none of these ideas is simple. No factor can be used to explain any aspect of child development without consideration of the complementary one. Nature is meaningless without nurture; it is impossible to study

Nature...Nurture	Are certain behavioral characteristics more influenced by heredity or by the environment?
Stability...Change	Are certain behavioral characteristics relatively stable over time, or do changes occur throughout the lifespan?
Continuity...Discontinuity	Can development be characterized as a steady progression, or does it occur in abrupt shifts?

FIGURE 1.1
Concept review of three major developmental issues.

EXPERIMENT
A test made to demonstrate the validity of a hypothesis or to determine the predictability of a theory. Variables are manipulated during the test. Any changes are compared with those of a control that has not been exposed to the variables of interest.

development without seeing both change and stability in the process; and although certain behaviors appear to be acquired in a relatively orderly progression, many others are not.

Research Methods

In general, those who conduct research in child development rely on scientific and empirical methods. These modern methods have replaced philosophical speculation as the mainstay of all developmental investigation. For this reason, developmental research relies on systematic and objective methods of observing, recording, and describing events.

Question: What sort of studies do developmental researchers conduct?

Table 1.1 is an outline of the six dimensions of developmental research. The developmental research discussed in this text (and, for that matter, all psychological research) will fall on one side or the other of all six dimensions (Reese & Lipsitt, 1970). If you become familiar with these dimensions, you'll find it easier to understand the research described in the chapters that follow.

Experimental Methods

Question: When scientists conduct research, how can they be sure that their findings are accurate?

One of the most convincing ways is by conducting an **experiment.** Perhaps the best way to learn how to conduct an experiment (and how not to conduct one) is to try it yourself. So, for the next few pages, let's work on one together.

First, we need an issue that is testable. If we come up with a question for which no test can be devised, we'll be out of luck.

Question: What kinds of questions are not testable?

What was the weight of Julius Caesar's liver?
How did the Neanderthals raise children?
What will the world be like in 20 years?
Is there life on Neptune?

These questions are currently untestable because no one has access to concrete observable information about these subjects, such as a soil sample from Neptune (assuming it even has soil) or child-rearing advice carved in stone by a Neanderthal. Until we have such information, there is no obvious way to answer these questions. So let's examine an issue that can be tested: Do violent programs on television cause aggressive behavior in children who view them?

Sigmund Freud believed that the desire to be violent was instinctive and that viewing violence would satisfy an instinctive urge. In other words, according to Freud, viewing violence would act as a release, or catharsis, reducing the viewer's desire to be violent.

On the other hand, contemporary social psychologist Albert Bandura has developed a social learning theory that leads to predictions contradicting Freud's catharsis hypothesis. Bandura predicts that viewing violence (especially viewing someone rewarded for being violent, as TV heroes often are) will increase the probability that the viewer will imitate the violence. Clearly, we have a disagreement—and one that can be tested.

Question: How can we conduct a test to decide who is correct?

What we need are some children, some violent programs, and some observers to watch the children's behavior and record what actually happens when the children are exposed to the shows.

TABLE 1.1

Dimensions of Developmental Research

DIMENSIONS OF RESEARCH	DESCRIPTION
Descriptive vs. Explanatory	Descriptive research describes only *what* has occurred, while explanatory research attempts to explain *how* something has occurred, that is, what caused it. Descriptive research is often a good way to begin, as it is generally less subject to error. A caveman describing what has occurred during a thunderstorm might say, "There was a bright flash of light followed by a terrible loud rumble," and he would be accurate. The same caveman attempting to be explanatory might say, "The Great God Zog has decided to go bowling." As you can see, the caveman is in trouble already. Descriptions, of course, can be inaccurate. The more objective they are, however, the more accurate they are likely to be; for example, the people standing in a given room can be objectively counted. The more subjective descriptions are, though, the more likely they are to be open to misinterpretation; for example, how many children in a particular school would you describe as happy? In this case, the description is open to personal interpretation and is more likely to be inaccurate. For this reason, developmental researchers often begin with objective descriptions and then, through careful experimental research, begin to examine cause-and-effect relationships in the hope that they may eventually be able to explain how and why the events they have described are occurring.
Naturalistic vs. Manipulative	When conducting naturalistic research, researchers refrain from interacting with the subjects of their observations in order to examine behavior in a natural setting. Careful, detailed records of the observations are kept. Naturalistic research can be conducted in an informal or structured manner, although the more informal the observations, the more chance there is that bias or inaccurate observations and interpretations will result. Parents who simply watch their children are engaged in informal naturalistic observation. In a more structured naturalistic observation, the behaviors observed are clearly defined beforehand, and careful reports are kept. During manipulative research, experimenters purposely expose their subjects to different situations and observe the effects caused by this exposure. This kind of research often can be carefully controlled in a laboratory setting, allowing close and careful observations of each studied behavior.
Historical vs. Ahistorical	If research is fundamentally dependent on past events, it is considered historical research; if not, it is called ahistorical. For example, a study concerned with the effects of a particular therapy for abused children would be historical because a previous history of child abuse would be an important factor, while a study concerned with the effects of brightly colored blocks on an infant's vocalizations would be ahistorical because there would be no particular interest in the infant's experience or history.
Theoretical vs. Serendipitous	Research designed to investigate a particular theory is called theoretical research, while research designed simply to investigate phenomena without regard to theoretical speculation is called serendipitous, or atheoretical.
Basic vs. Applied	Basic research advances knowledge; applied research advances already developed technology. Once the basic knowledge has been gathered, applied research is concerned with assembling it for a particular purpose. The space program is a good example of applied research, as most of the basic knowledge about rockets, aerodynamics, and space had been gathered beforehand. The search for a cancer cure, however, is an example of basic research. No one is certain of the fundamental causes of cancer, so our basic knowledge of biology must be expanded before the next major application of technology can occur. Thus, basic research is the foundation on which applied research can be built. Although it often may seem that basic research is valueless because it appears to have no immediate application, it is essential for any science and technology that knowledge be expanded.
Single Subject vs. Group	In single-subject research, the behavior and behavior changes of only one person at a time are of interest, while in group research, the researcher looks at group averages, ignoring whether those averages accurately reflect the behavior patterns of any given individual within the group.

SELECTING SUBJECTS

First, we'll select some children. What kinds of children shall we use? Older? Younger? Boys? Girls?

Question: How about 6-year-old boys and girls?

All right, but when we publish our results, we won't be able to say anything about 4-, 8-, or 10-year-olds.

Question: Then should we get children of many ages and backgrounds?

Given adequate time and sufficient research funds, this would be a good idea because there is always a risk if we generalize beyond our sample. If we run a study on little boys, for instance, we must be very cautious about generalizing our findings to little girls (and unless we have a sound reason for doing so, we shouldn't attempt it). Psychologists, like all scientists, should be careful not to go beyond their data unless they specifically state that they are speculating.

Well, I see we now have a room full of children aged 5 through 10. What's next?

Question: Should we show them some violent programs?

Fine. Which ones?

Question: How about some of those violent Saturday morning cartoons?

Good idea, but how can we tell which ones are violent? As a matter of fact, after showing the cartoons, how will we decide if the children are being aggressive?

DEFINITIONS AND RELIABILITY

Do we all agree on what aggression is? Is a good salesperson aggressive? Are all murderers aggressive? Is it good for a football player to be aggressive? Obviously, aggression has come to mean many different things, and before we can study it—and perhaps conclude that watching TV violence causes it—we must be able to define it. If aggression means something different to everyone who reads our findings, we will have succeeded only in making the issue more confusing.

If a tree falls in the forest and there isn't a creature about to hear it, does it make a noise? Perhaps you've heard this famous question before, but do you know the answer? It depends totally on how you define noise. If you define noise as the production of sound waves, the answer to the question will be yes. If you define noise as the perception of sound waves by a living creature, the answer will be no. The only reason that this question can cause an argument in the first place is that people are often unaware that they are using different definitions of noise. How would you define aggression to avoid that kind of confusion in our experiment?

Question: How about defining aggression as any act that damages property or physically hurts another person?

If you use this definition, how would you classify someone who accidentally stepped on your toe or a sniper who fired at a crowd and missed everyone?

Question: Then how about defining aggresion as any act committed with the intention of damaging property or hurting another person?

Although intentions aren't easy to observe, let's try this definition. It fits what most people would call aggression. We must also agree on a definition of violent cartoons: perhaps cartoons showing any act that if carried out with live actors would likely result in injury. Once we have defined both terms, we will watch a particular child after the child has viewed a violent cartoon. Your job will be to note whether aggression occurs and how often. Can you be trusted to be accurate in your observations?

Question: Even using our definition, isn't it possible that I might consider something aggressive that someone else wouldn't?

This could be a serious problem. To avoid it, we will use two or more people who will *independently* observe and measure the same child over the same period of time. The observations and measurements can then be compared, and if they are in fairly good agreement, we can conclude that it is possible to observe and record reliably the behavior in question. This technique yields what is known as **interobserver reliability.** By using the same method, we can also make sure that we agree on our definition of violence in cartoons.

Interobserver Reliability
The degree of agreement or disagreement between two or more observers who make simultaneous observations of a single event.

Control
In a controlled study, experimental or research conditions are arranged deliberately so that observed effects can be traced directly to a known variable or variables. The control is similar to the experimental subject but is not exposed to the variable.

The Control

Now that we have used interobserver reliability to ensure that we agree on definitions of aggression and violent cartoons, what should the next step be?

Question: Should we show a violent cartoon to the children and observe their aggressive behavior?

If the children are aggressive after viewing the cartoon, how will we know that it was the violence in the cartoon that was responsible? For that matter, how will we know whether the children wouldn't have been even more aggressive had they not seen the cartoon? If you asked someone, "Who won the soccer match?" and the only answer you got was that one team had scored three times, you wouldn't know whether that team had won or lost. To know, you would need the other team's score as a comparison. It's the same with an experiment. As a comparison, or **control,** we must have a second, similar group of children who do not see the violent cartoon. In fact, it is the use of a control that defines a scientific experiment.

Question: How can I decide whether the second group of children is similar to the first?

One of the most common ways to do this is simply to divide the original group of children in half. Then, in all probability, the two groups will be similar. Nonetheless, we must be careful when dividing the original group to do it randomly. By "randomly," we mean that each child has an equal chance of being placed in

Developmental researchers observe and record children's behavior to draw scientific conclusions from empirical data.

Independent Variable
In an experiment, the variable that is manipulated or treated to see what effect differences in it will have on the variables considered to be dependent on it.

Dependent Variable
In an experiment, the variable that may change as a result of changes in the independent variable.

Observer Bias
An error in observation caused by the expectations of the observer.

Subject Bias
Changes in a subject's behavior that result from the subject's knowledge of the purpose of the experiment or from the subject's awareness of being observed.

either group. For example, we might divide the children into an experimental and control group by flipping a coin. Once we have the two groups, what should the next step be?

Question: Should the experimental group see the violent cartoon while the control group sees no cartoon?

Although that might seem like the correct approach, it is important to remember that the control and experimental groups must be treated exactly the same except for the one variable we wish to measure: in this case, violence. If we show the control group no cartoon, we will fail to control for the effects of simply watching any kind of cartoon. For this reason, the experimental group should see a violent cartoon while the control group watches a nonviolent cartoon of the same length—ideally, the same cartoon with nonviolent rather than violent scenes. In this way, the effect of violence is isolated from all other effects. Anything that happens to the experimental group is *controlled for* if it also happens to the control group. In our case, everything is controlled except viewing violence, which happens only to the experimental group. If the amount of aggression observed in both groups of children is similar before they see the cartoon but different afterward, we have isolated the effect of watching violence and probably nothing else. In this way, researchers are able to separate variables one at a time and observe their effects.

A variable is any measurement that may vary, as opposed to a constant, such as the speed of light, which does not vary. Examples of variables include a person's height and weight, the outside temperature or barometric pressure, the miles per gallon obtained by a car, the rainfall in Rangoon, the number of teeth in an audience, or the number of ice cream scoops dropped on the sidewalks of Detroit each day by consequently upset children. To reiterate, in a scientific experiment, both groups share all the variables but one, and both groups are similar to each other at the beginning of the experiment; therefore, if there is a difference between the groups at the end of the experiment, the only variable responsible for the difference is most likely to be the one variable that they didn't share. Remember, variables shared by both groups are controlled. Or, putting it another way, if it starts to rain on the experimental group, your experiment won't be disrupted as long as it starts to rain on the control group, too. The variable that is manipulated—in our case how much and what kind of TV violence we show—is called the **independent variable.** The variable that may be influenced by the manipulations—in our case the amount of aggression—is called the **dependent variable.***

Observer and Subject Bias

Before continuing the experiment, we need to examine other problems that might arise. Among these are **observer bias** and **subject bias.**

Suppose that we are scornful of Freud's theories and certain that Bandura's predictions will be upheld. We may all be hoping to see more aggression occurring among the members of the experimental group. Although working independently, we might all consider certain behavior aggressive if it is exhibited by a child from the experimental group, while we might consider the same behavior nonaggressive if we observe it in a child from the control group. Our observations would be badly biased even though the interobserver reliability would have remained high because we were all in biased agreement.

Subjects can also be biased. This fact is well known to researchers who, on entering a child's home to observe the environment firsthand, are greeted by for-

*If you have trouble recalling which variable is which, just think of freedom and independence. The variable that the experimenter is "free" to manipulate is the "independent" variable.

mally dressed parents, a spotless home, the scent of furniture polish in the air, and a well-scrubbed child with slicked-down hair approaching timidly to attempt a handshake. Subjects can act differently simply because they know they are being observed.

Question: But can't we keep from making such mistakes if we are careful?

Probably not. It's very hard not to see what you expect to see. For years, in psychology labs throughout the country, students have been sent by "sly" professors to observe "bright" and "dull" rats run mazes. Students, even careful ones, have tended to report that the bright rats do better than the dull ones, even though, unknown to the students, the rats had been labeled bright or dull simply by the flip of a coin.

Question: How can we avoid any observer or subject bias in our experiment?

It's simple. The observers must not know whether the children they are observing are from the experimental group or the control group (someone else will keep track of that). The observers can't unconsciously lean toward one group or the other if they don't know which is which. Because the children are also unaware of which group they are in, our study can now be called a **double-blind experiment;** that is, neither the subjects nor the observers know who is in which group. Double-blind controlled experiments are an extremely effective research tool because they allow us to examine variables one at a time while they eliminate human bias.

DOUBLE-BLIND EXPERIMENT
A research technique in which neither the subjects nor the experimenter knows which subjects have been exposed to the experimental variable. It is used for controlling biases that may be introduced by either the subjects or the researcher.

REPLICATION
Repeating an experiment to enhance the reliability of the results.

EXPANSION
An enlargement, increase, or extension of initial research efforts.

RESULTS OF OUR EXPERIMENT

Once we have observed the levels of aggression in the children from both groups, we need to statistically analyze the data to determine whether the difference in observed aggression between the control and the experimental groups is significantly large. Assuming that the results of our hypothetical experiment are similar to those obtained by researchers who have conducted actual experiments examining the effects of television violence on children's aggression, we will find that the experimental group is significantly more aggressive (Eron, Huesmann, Brice, Fischer, & Mermelstein, 1983; Huesmann, Lagerspetz, & Eron, 1984).

Our conclusion? Viewing cartoon violence increases the probability of immediate postviewing aggression in grade school children. In addition, note that our observations fit Bandura's theory. After replicating and expanding on the experiment, we may even suggest that cartoon violence on children's television be toned down or eliminated.

REPLICATION AND EXPANSION

Now that we have completed our double-blind controlled experiment, we need to consider two valuable procedures, **replication** and **expansion.** An old rule in research states, If it hasn't happened twice, it hasn't happened. For this reason, it would be a good idea to have someone else, perhaps at another institution, replicate our study to see whether the same results are obtained. Should those results agree with ours, we will feel more confident about our own findings. Such confirmation is important because there may have been something peculiar about our particular sample of children, or perhaps an important event, unknown to us, interfered with the treatment or testing of one of the groups.

We may also wish to expand on our research. For instance, what would happen if we used live actors instead of cartoons? And would adults become aggressive in the way that children do? How long does this aggression last? As you can see, the answer we discovered in our own experiment has generated many more questions than we initially faced, perhaps all worth pursuing.

SINGLE-SUBJECT EXPERIMENT
An experiment in which only one subject participates. Generally, time is used as the control; for example, the subject's behavior changes over time in relation to the presentation and withdrawal of a variable.

CORRELATION
A relationship between two variables.

Question: According to Table 1.1, what kind of research was our study?

1. *Explanatory:* We concluded that watching violence was why aggression occurred.
2. *Manipulative:* We altered the situation so that the children were exposed to the variables that we desired them to see.
3. *Ahistorical:* We were unconcerned with the children's past history.
4. *Theoretical:* We were deciding between Freud's theoretical prediction and Bandura's.
5. *Basic:* We were advancing our knowledge rather than attempting to change the technology of the cartoon industry (although that may eventually be a result of our research).
6. *Group:* We worked with groups of children rather than concentrating on a single subject.

SINGLE-SUBJECT DESIGN

Question: How can you conduct an experiment with only one subject? You wouldn't have a control group, would you?

Single-subject experiments use time as the control, which means that we create a certain condition and see what the response is and whether the response continues as long as the condition is maintained. Examine Figure 1.2. By using time as a control, we can feel confident that it is the mother's attention that is prolonging the child's pounding of the spoon on the table.

Question: But couldn't that have been just a coincidence that the child stopped pounding after his mother no longer paid attention to him? Couldn't he have just gotten tired of pounding the spoon at the same time that she stopped paying attention?

Yes, and that's why we again had the mother pay attention to the child's behavior (the second instance of condition A) before the behavior ended.* Because the

*In some circumstances, it would obviously be unethical to return to condition A (e.g., if the child's initial behavior was dangerous).

Research has shown that children who view violence on television are more likely to be violent themselves.

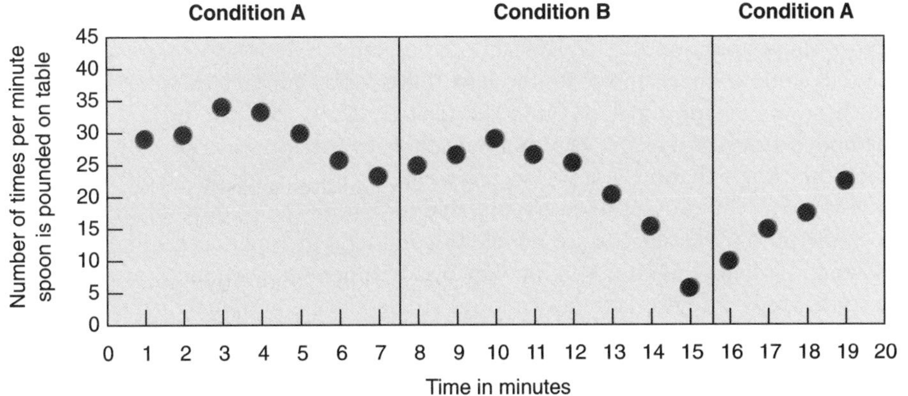

FIGURE 1.2
Example of a single-subject A-B-A experimental design. The purpose of this experiment was to find the cause of a child's unwanted behavior (spoon pounding) by introducing and withholding a possible stimulus (the mother's attention). In condition A, the mother pays attention to the child's action; in condition B, she ignores it.

spoon pounding returned to a high rate *when attention was reinstated,* we can feel more confident that attention maintained the pounding. It seems that by giving attention, withholding it, and giving it again, we are controlling the spoon-pounding rate. This is called an *A-B-A single-subject experimental design.* If you like, we can eliminate the spoon pounding again by withholding the attention (and thereby leaving us with a happy mother). An A-B-A-B design will thus be created, which will lend support to our conviction that we have isolated the cause of the spoon pounding because, once again, the behavior will change when we expect it to.

You must remember, however, to be cautious when assuming that what you have discovered about one subject will explain the behavior of any other subject. It may not.

Nonexperimental Methods

THE CORRELATIONAL METHOD

A **correlation** is defined as the relationship between two variables. For example, there is a strong correlation between height and weight. The taller one is, the heavier one tends to be, and vice versa. However, when dealing with a correlation,

In the A-B-A single-subject design, the effects of the administration and withdrawal of parental attention on spoon-pounding behavior can be measured experimentally.

CASE STUDY
An intensive study of a single case, with all available data, test results, and opinions about that individual. Usually done in more depth than studies on groups of individuals.

we must be extremely careful not to assume that a cause-and-effect relationship exists simply because the two variables go together.

Let's look at an example. By the late 1800s, army physicians were aware that the best way to stop a malaria outbreak was to move everyone to high, dry ground. Although these physicians were unaware that the disease was carried by mosquitoes, they knew that malaria was well *correlated* with altitude and moisture. Without knowing the cause, they were still able to predict the chances of an outbreak.

Sometimes psychologists are unable to conduct experiments (or, like the army doctors, perhaps they don't know which experiments to conduct), and they are forced to rely on correlational data. Such data can be extremely valuable. First, correlational data allow predictions to be made. Second, correlations are often the first clue to an important discovery. As you can imagine, doctors soon wondered what it was about damp, warm lowlands that related to malaria.

Question: Can you give another example of what you mean?

If you were to tell me that ice cream sales in a certain city had increased, I'd be able to predict that the number of drownings had also increased—and I'd be right. But this does not mean that eating ice cream makes you drown or, conversely, that drowning makes you want ice cream! If it did, this would be an example of cause and effect. The reason for the correlation between ice cream and drownings is, of course, that in summer both swimming and ice cream sales increase.

Question: You said that psychologists had to be cautious not to assume a cause-and-effect relationship when dealing with a correlation. But who would be so foolish as to think that eating ice cream would make you drown or that drowning would make you eat ice cream?

Probably no one. Suppose, though, that you are watching children at play who are being supervised by their parents. You notice that the children whose parents discipline them by yelling at them are more aggressive. What would you conclude?

Question: Wouldn't that demonstrate that parents who are verbally harsh cause their children to act out and be aggressive?

It might seem like that, but in fact, all you would have is a correlation: Parental yelling coincides with aggressive behavior in children. How do you know that the children weren't aggressive to start with and that their aggression drove their parents to yelling? You don't. To examine cause and effect, you would have to create an experiment by manipulating the variables involved. Until then, you know only that one variable is correlated with the other.

CASE STUDIES

In a **case study,** a scientist or researcher will report or analyze the behavior, emotions, beliefs, or life history of a single individual in more depth than is generally done with groups of subjects. The rigorous controls common to single-subject experimental design are not incorporated into case studies. Some of the earliest case studies of child behavior were simply informal descriptions of what the child was doing. Of course, even though baby biographies or case studies allow for the recording of a personal detailed account of one child over time, biases can still easily affect the observations.

Question: If biases cannot be eliminated or reduced, why would anyone report a case study or record a baby biography?

Sometimes a situation occurs in which it is impossible to gather data by conducting an experiment or observing a correlation. However, we can still obtain valuable information by viewing a subject carefully and reporting what we observe.

Question: Can you give an example of a case study?

A particular case of a little boy who had deaf parents was reported. The boy, however, was not deaf. His parents and all the visitors to his home communicated by using the American Sign Language for the Deaf. This was the only way, in terms of language, that the parents and visitors ever interacted with the boy.

Unfortunately, the boy had chronic asthma and was housebound. As a result, he never had a chance to interact with anyone who spoke English. But the child's parents wanted him to learn English, so they placed him before a television every day for a number of hours. By the time the child was 3 years old, he was fluent in sign language, but he still couldn't speak any English (Moskowitz, 1978).

Ethically, there is no way that such a situation could be investigated by experiment because it would be a violation of ethical principles to isolate children so that the only spoken language they heard came from television. Yet when an odd case study like that of the little boy comes along, it generates interest. Although we always take a chance in generalizing from one child to all children, it appears that for children to acquire language, two-way conversation may be necessary. Reporting of this "accidental" case study provided information that otherwise might not have been obtainable; a controlled study would not be acceptable on ethical grounds.

LEARNING CHECK

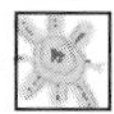

Multiple Choice

1. During the eighteenth century,
- **a.** people had no concept of childhood as separate from adulthood.
- **b.** the first empirical efforts to record and study children were made.
- **c.** philosophical speculations about the nature of children were common.
- **d.** G. Stanley Hall began developmental psychology.

2. Developmental psychology is the study of
- **a.** age-related differences in behavior.
- **b.** children.
- **c.** human psychology.
- **d.** time.

Matching

3. ___ subjects and observers are unaware which group is the experimental group and which group is the control
4. ___ applied research
5. ___ the relationship between two variables
6. ___ observer bias
7. ___ uses time as a control
8. ___ Sigmund Freud
9. ___ case study
10. ___ replication

- **a.** see what you expect to see
- **b.** catharsis hypothesis
- **c.** single-subject design
- **d.** repeating an experiment to enhance its reliability
- **e.** correlation
- **f.** double-blind
- **g.** a detailed description of an individual
- **h.** advances technology

Answers: 1. c 2. a 3. f 4. h 5. e 6. a 7. c 8. b 9. g 10. d

AT ISSUE

How Broad Is the Scope of Child Research?

Unlike the fields of mathematics and physics, which seem to be the province of a few specialists, child development interests and attracts us all. The study of child development is vast in scope, and many researchers who are not psychologists have become involved in it. The research is multidisciplinary and includes the contributions made by anthropologists, biologists, physicians, sociologists, and researchers in other social and natural sciences. Researchers wishing to grasp a full understanding of the field, therefore, must be careful not to limit themselves to exploring data developed only within one particular field. Contributions from any discipline, as long as it is scientifically gathered, can greatly enhance our knowledge of child development.

True or False

1. It is wrong for children to sleep in the same bed with their parents.
2. Adolescence is usually a time of storm and stress.
3. Homosexual behavior among adolescents is rare.
4. Babies who are held and carried by their mothers too much of the time will become spoiled and fussy.

Each of these statements is false. In fact, each was shown to be false by a researcher from a field other than developmental psychology, and each provides a brief example of the wide range of contributions. For example, statement 1 refers to something many American parents have believed for years—that it is wrong for children to share their parents' bed. But cultural anthropologists have shown that a number of cultures allow children to share their parents' bed, apparently without problems. In Japan, for example, children often share their parents' bed until they reach puberty, with the youngest child traditionally sleeping closest to his or her mother, where the child can be easily nursed. There is no evidence to indicate that this practice is harmful in any way to the children.

Cross-cultural research also helped to show that statement 2 is false. In fact, anthropologist Margaret Mead, who studied the process of "coming of age" in Samoa, demonstrated that adolescence need not be a time of storm and stress (Mead, 1928). Because of cultural factors, adolescents in Western cultures may seem to have more problems in their transition to adulthood, but there is nothing *inherent* in adolescence that makes it more turbulent. Subsequent research has shown that even adolescence in Western cultures isn't generally as stormy as most people think it is (Bachman, O'Malley, & Johnston, 1978; Offer, Ostrov, & Howard, 1981).

Statement 3 was shown to be false by Alfred Kinsey, a zoologist and expert on the sexual behavior of wasps. His pioneering research on the human sexual response helped to dispel many myths and widened our understanding of the development of sexual behavior. Kinsey discovered that many heterosexual people had homosexual experiences, and vice versa, and that homosexual experiences were common, often beginning in adolescence, with as many as 20 percent of all adults having had a homosexual encounter to the point of orgasm at some time in their lives (Kinsey, Pomeroy, & Martin, 1948; Kinsey, Pomeroy, Martin, & Gebhard, 1953).

Over the years, pediatricians have also made substantial contributions to the study of child development, particularly the study of babies and young children. Statement 4 was shown to be false by two pediatricians who performed research based on some cross-cultural observations (Hunziker & Barr, 1986). In many cultures, infants are carried for extended periods of time by their care givers. These infants often appear to be *less* "fussy" than children who do not have this close and constant physical contact.

In summary, research on child development is multidisciplinary. Many social and natural sciences other than psychology have made valuable contributions. A significant number of researchers and theorists who study development come from such diverse fields as anthropology, biology, medicine, and sociology. Without their contributions, our knowledge would be substantially diminished. Thanks to the input by researchers in other fields, developmental psychologists have expanded their research to include cross-cultural, pediatric, and demographic studies, as well as other studies once thought to be beyond the scope of child development.

Using Age as a Variable

Developmental researchers are interested in how people change over time, so it's not unusual for them to examine and compare subjects of different ages. There are two basic methods that rely on age as a variable: longitudinal and cross-sectional approaches. The **cross-sectional approach** requires that a number of subjects of different ages be measured, tested, or observed at one given time. While the **longitudinal approach** involves repeated measurements obtained from the same subject over time. It is also possible to combine both longitudinal and cross-sectional approaches.

Question: Can you give an example of how developmental researchers use these two approaches?

CROSS-CULTURAL RESEARCH
Research in which different cultures are evaluated on different behavioral dimensions, such as attachment, emotional development, and intellectual development. Its primary purpose is to isolate and distinguish the effects and influences of culture from those of other variables.

LONGITUDINAL APPROACH
A research study design in which investigators follow an individual through time, taking measurements at periodic intervals.

CROSS-SECTIONAL APPROACH
A research strategy in which investigators examine subjects of different ages simultaneously to study the relationships between age, experience, and behavior.

COHORT
A group of people all of whom possess a common demographic characteristic; for example, a group of people born at approximately the same time.

THE CROSS-SECTIONAL APPROACH

Over the years, many cross-sectional studies have been conducted. In 1970, for example, two researchers used the cross-sectional approach to investigate the development of independence in children (Rheingold & Eckerman, 1970). If you had walked into the middle of their experiment, you would have seen chairs lined up on a large lawn, spaced so that the occupants of the chairs were sitting a fair distance from one another. Sitting in each of these chairs was somebody's mother. And that somebody—namely, one of 54 different children between the ages of 12 and 60 months—was in front of each chair, attended to by the mother. To the uninitiated, it might have looked like the beginning of a children's Olympic event. Furthermore, hidden observers were watching these youngsters from behind windows at the edge of the lawn. What was actually being measured, however, was how far any given child would travel from his or her mother.

The results of the study revealed a clear relationship between the distance that the child would travel and the child's age. The average distance traveled by 1-year-olds was 6.9 meters. Two-year-olds went 15.1 meters; 3-year-olds went 17.3 meters; and 4-year-olds dared to travel an average of 20.6 meters away. Researchers Rheingold and Eckerman found that for each month of age beyond a year, a child was likely to travel about 1/3 of a meter farther. By using the cross-sectional approach, these researchers could see how children of different ages displayed different degrees of independence. As you can see, all these data could be collected in a very short time; and if the researchers had wanted, they could have included other age-groups in their study.

Question: What are the disadvantages of the cross-sectional approach?

Any group sharing a similar characteristic, such as having all been born in the same year, or all living in the same time, or all living in the same town, may be considered a **cohort.** Because these individuals were born at about the same time, they have been exposed to similar cultural and historical experiences, such as economic depression or war and can be considered to be a cohort. The cross-sectional approach can't control for the differences between cohorts. For instance, a cohort of 40-year-olds who did not grow up during the Great Depression might not, once they turned 70, be readily comparable to a similarly matched cohort of 70-year-olds who did suffer through those times. How could you say if differences between the cohorts were the result of their ages or their life experiences?

Unfortunately, the cross-sectional approach also won't tell what individual children were like when they were younger or how they later developed. It cannot be used to answer certain kinds of questions, such as, Will a very independent 2-year-old child also exhibit great independence at age 6? This is exactly the kind of problem that the longitudinal approach addresses.

TIME-LAG DESIGN
A research design in which different groups of people are measured on a characteristic or behavior when they are the same age; for example, a group of 2-year-old children is measured in one year, another group of 2-year-old children is measured in the same way in a subsequent year, and so on.

SEQUENTIAL DESIGN
A research design that combines elements of different time-dependent research approaches to control for biases that might be introduced when any single approach is used alone.

THEORY
A system of rules or assumptions used to predict or explain phenomena.

ENVIRONMENTAL THEORY
Theory that attempts to predict or explain behavior based primarily on a person's learning and past experience.

EPIGENETIC THEORY
Theory that emphasizes the interaction between the environment and a person's genetic inheritance.

THE LONGITUDINAL APPROACH

Over the years, many important studies have incorporated the longitudinal approach (Schaie & Hertzog, 1982). Among the interesting areas that have been examined by means of longitudinal research is the relationship between intelligence test scores in childhood and achievement in adult life. Generally, these studies have challenged the old belief that it isn't good to be too smart. For example, a longitudinal study conducted by Lewis Terman examined children whose intelligence scores were in the top 1 percent and followed these individuals into adulthood and old age. Terman discovered that bright children tended to become happier, more productive adults than their more average peers. (For a more detailed discussion of the Terman study, see Chapter 11.)

Question: Are there problems with longitudinal research?

Because social conditions are always changing, we can't be sure that the developmental path followed by children through the end of this century will be similar to the development of children in future generations. Another drawback to longitudinal research is that problems that interested psychologists long ago and caused them to initiate a longitudinal study may no longer be of interest; thus, by the time the study is completed, the findings may be considered of little value. Also, longitudinal research is often expensive and time consuming. Many subjects move, or drop out of the study, or become tired of repeated testing. However, the benefits of this kind of research far outweigh the drawbacks.

Question: Is it possible to eliminate some of the problems introduced when using the cross-sectional or longitudinal approaches?

Through the years, researchers have devised several ways to help eliminate some of these problems. The **time-lag design** has been used to help control for the effects of cultural variation over time. In a time-lag design, different groups of subjects are tested in different years while *age is held constant.* For example, a researcher could study 2-year-old children's abilities to perform certain tasks during a certain year, could examine a new group of 2-year-old children for the abilities to perform the same tasks in a subsequent year, and so on. This approach may give the researcher information about cultural or historical influences on performance of the task. Researchers have often combined elements of the cross-sectional, longitudinal, and time-lag designs in a **sequential design,** thus combining the different methods' strengths and lessening their drawbacks.

Figure 1.3 summarizes the cross-sectional, longitudinal, and time-lag approaches by outlining a hypothetical experiment in which all three approaches could be used to help eliminate the individual drawbacks of each. Over a five-year period, a researcher could gather information about age differences and cultural variation and could follow one group through time to see the developmental progression.

Building a Theory

Once you've begun to collect data using the methods described so far, there will come a time when it will be valuable to organize your findings.

A JIGSAW PUZZLE

Collecting data is like gathering individual pieces of a jigsaw puzzle. By itself, any one piece may be interesting, but it will fail to reveal the entire picture. To produce the entire picture, you must gather and assemble many pieces. Assembling jigsaw puzzles has a lot in common with gathering data. In putting a jigsaw puzzle together, people will usually assemble the pieces in a logical sequence. One person may work first with just the edge pieces, gathering them until the frame is assembled, while another may concentrate on sorting pieces by color or some other distinguishing characteristic. Someone gathering data or deciding which hypothesis to develop and test works in much the same way. Sometimes an important piece is found by chance, and sometimes an important piece is overlooked because a researcher has failed to see it for what it is. Both experiences are common to scientists in conducting research and gathering evidence.

At some point during the assembly of a jigsaw puzzle, the subject of the picture may suddenly start to emerge (even though many pieces are still missing). At this point, the person doing the puzzle may develop a theory about what the picture is. He or she has seen enough to recognize some sort of symmetry and believes it's now possible to determine what the entire scene will be. Even though only one wall and part of a door are showing, the puzzle doer may already know that it is a picture of a house and may then feel free to predict the existence of windows and a chimney even before these particular pieces turn up.

Similarly, when scientists have gathered enough data, they, too, may think that they see an emerging picture. This insightful view of the completed work or section of work is called a **theory.** A theory is a way of organizing data, ideas, and hypotheses to provide a more complete understanding of what the data have been indicating in piecemeal fashion. Of course, theories can be wrong. You may think you see a house as you put the puzzle pieces together, only to find out later that it is a picture of a boat in dry dock. But as Albert Einstein suggested, if your theory is correct, no matter who finds another piece of the puzzle, it will always fit perfectly! If, however, someone comes up with a puzzle piece that doesn't fit the picture you had in mind, then you will need to change your guess about the picture. In the same way, if a researcher finds a datum that doesn't fit a particular theory, the theory must be changed.

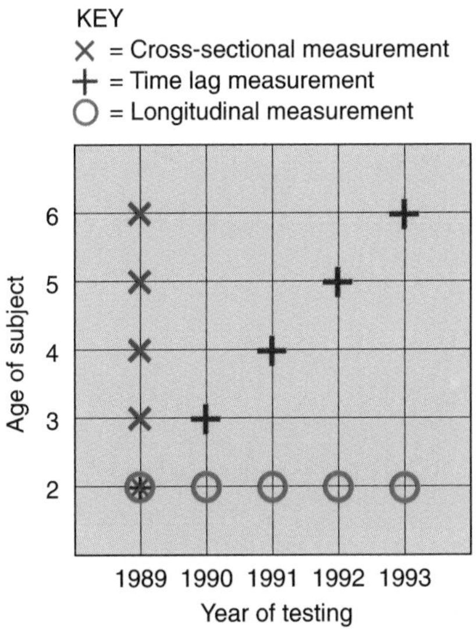

FIGURE 1.3
Hypothetical five-year experiment in which elements of the cross-sectional, longitudinal, and time-lag approaches are combined in a sequential design. In 1989, the researcher used the cross-sectional approach to measure a group of subjects of different ages; the first measurement in a five-year longitudinal study was also made at this time, as well as the first measurement of 2-year-old children for a five-year time-lag study. In 1990, another measurement was made of a different group of 2-year-old children for the time-lag study, and the longitudinal study group from 1989 (who were by then 3 years old) were again measured. In 1991, another group of 2-year-old children were measured, and the 4-year-old children in the longitudinal study were again measured. And so on. Such sequential research designs can help eliminate some of the problems and biases encountered when only one approach is used.

Theories of Human Development

There are many different theories of human development. To date, no theory has been found to be the one and only correct theory. Theories are often in conflict with one another, and there may be arguments among the supporters of the different theories. Sometimes students feel compelled to take sides. The only way to decide among these theories, however, is to conduct further research or experiments. Eventually, theories will become more accurate and our powers of prediction more acute. Throughout this text, you'll come across many developmental theories. There are theories that attempt to explain or predict behavior based primarily on a person's learning and past experience while placing less emphasis on genetics. These are called **environmental theories.** In contrast, there are theories that emphasize the interaction between the environment and a person's genetic inheritance. These are called **epigenetic theories.** Both environmental and epigenetic theories can be further divided according to the dimensions of human development on which they focus. Behavioral or cognitive theories emphasize the individual's developing abilities to learn or think, while other theories emphasize personality or social forces.

These divisions have come about for many reasons. For instance, historically it was common for European theories to be epigenetic, while American theories were more often environmental. This happened because Europeans have traditionally emphasized family ties and lines of inheritance, while Americans believe that all citizens are "created equal." Although there are many modern exceptions, this historical emphasis is still strong. This particular example is interesting because it came about for political rather than scientific reasons.

Precision
The accuracy of predictions made from a theory.

Scope Versus Precision, or It's Better to Be a Big Fish in a Small Pond

By definition, a theory is a system of rules or assumptions used to predict or explain phenomena. Predictions about human behavior can be derived from psychological theories. However, for a theory to be useful, it must lead to accurate predictions. After all, there is no point in applying a theory that yields only inaccurate predictions. If most of the predictions derived from a theory are accurate, the theory is said to have **precision.**

Consider the following: Why do astronomers have high precision in predicting eclipses (which are accurately predicted years in advance), while meteorologists have relatively low precision in predicting the weather?

The answer lies in the number and accessibility of variables that each profession must deal with. In predicting an eclipse, an astronomer must deal with only a few variables and their interactions. Because the number of variables is low, the scope of the theory of eclipses is limited, not grand. But there are so many variables involved in predicting the weather! Is it any wonder that weather prediction rapidly loses precision when predictions are made more than a few hours in advance? The scope of weather theory is vast (and the headaches of meteorologists, many). In weather theory, so many variables are interacting that it's like trying to predict where a dropped gum wrapper will end up after a hurricane has passed.

Unfortunately for psychology, the scope of human behavior is also vast in terms of the variables involved. Understanding human behavior on a grand scale is more like figuring out where the gum wrapper will wind up than like predicting an eclipse.* Human behavior is so complex that when a theory prematurely attempts explanations of a grand scope, the degree of precision lessens drastically. When the degree of precision lessens, predictions fail, which of course makes application of the theory pointless. It's only when the scope is limited (few variables involved) that the degree of precision becomes markedly high and predictions become accurate.

The work of astronomers has demonstrated that a high level of precision can be obtained when a limited number of well-understood variables are used for predictions.

Question: How does modern psychology deal with this problem?

Following World War II, a philosophical reorientation occurred throughout most of psychology, including developmental psychology. Increasingly, experiments and investigations were limited to highly specific areas so that a science high in precision (though limited in scope) might be developed. Grand theories that pretty much try to explain all of human behavior (like the theories of Freud and other early researchers) are now considered an eventual goal but not an appropriate starting point.

Question: What do modern theories hope to accomplish?

The current hope is to develop a high degree of precision *within a limited scope* (i.e, within limited and specific areas of interest) and then to examine the effects of adding new variables to slowly broaden the scope. We must thoroughly understand how the new variables interact with those that are already well understood. Then, perhaps, we can expand the scope of newly developing theories bit by bit, without losing precision. Perhaps someday, grand explanatory theories of great precision will exist from which thousands of extremely accurate predictions can be derived. Perhaps such theories will contain so much information and so many different relationships between variables that only a huge computer will be able to handle the vast number of interactions.

*It is not surprising that when astronomers begin to deal with too many variables at once, their predictions also begin to lose precision.

At first glance, it might seem that we are certain to acquire this knowledge if we continue to conduct experiments until our understanding of behavior finally becomes complete enough that we can make accurate predictions about human behavior in any given set of circumstances. After all, this kind of experimental approach has served physics well. Physicists have studied the action of fundamental particles and forces, seen how they interact under different conditions, and then made assessments about how these particles and forces can be controlled and manipulated. The development of computers, atomic power, television, and space travel bears witness to the physicists' success.

Human development, however, is more the study of complex systems than it is the study of fundamental forces. Children and adults are not uniform from one to the next in the way that electrons or protons are. They are not fundamental or elemental. They are, and will remain, complex systems interacting in a world that's never quite the same from one day to the next (Manicas & Secord, 1983). As researchers or students of child development, we must always remember that our search for knowledge is somewhat limited by the fact that no two humans are ever exactly the same. Because of this, our predictive ability will never be 100 percent or even close to it. Even so, we can develop a science that will provide us with a certain amount of predictive power that will be very useful and that will add greatly to our knowledge.

LEARNING CHECK

Multiple Choice

1. Theories
   a. are a system of rules or assumptions used to predict or explain phenomena.
   b. can be wrong.
   c. are tentative.
   d. are all of the above.

2. ______________ theories emphasize a person's learning and past experience rather than genetic forces.
   a. Epigenetic **c.** Ethological
   b. Environmental **d.** Temperamental

3. Which is most likely to lessen precision?
   a. careful measurements
   b. a large number of constants
   c. a large number of variables
   d. narrow scope

4. Modern theories aim eventually to
   a. increase precision without diminishing scope.
   b. lessen precision without diminishing scope.
   c. increase precision but eliminate scope.
   d. lessen precision while expanding scope.

Answers: 1. d 2. b 3. c 4. a

APPLICATIONS

The Ethical and Legal Aspects of Experimenting with Children

Whenever an experiment is conducted with a child as a subject, a very complex ethical and legal question arises, namely, Who gave the right to experiment on children?

Children in Experiments

In England during the 1700s, Caroline, Princess of Wales, demanded that before her children be given the new vaccine against smallpox, six charity children from St. James Parish be given the vaccine to make sure of its safety (Lasagna, 1969). Since that time, many children have been subjects in experiments.

Question: Have children been abused in modern experiments?

A prominent example of abuse occurred at the Willowbrook School in New York (an institution for the retarded), where children were purposely exposed to hepatitis so that researchers could use them to search for a cure (Mitchell, 1975).

Question: How could professionals do something like that?

They made a number of excuses. They contended, for example, that while a few might suffer, a great many would benefit, and they also claimed that most of the children in the school seemed to catch hepatitis anyway (yet no one seemed to consider closing the school as a health hazard). The truth of the matter was that these children were forced to suffer for purposes of experimentation. Researchers must be very cautious and avoid causing such suffering when conducting experiments.

Question: But how could a child be injured in a psychological experiment?

The child wouldn't be physically endangered as the children at Willowbrook were.

But psychologists may, in an experiment, manipulate physical stimuli, social situations, or other variables that may have a direct psychological effect on the child. If a psychologist presents a child with an "impossible puzzle" and, to test frustration, tells the child that most children can solve it, is the child being psychologically harmed if he breaks down and loses his self-confidence? Suppose that even after the child is told the truth about the experiment, he continues to think less of himself. Could this have a harmful effect on his future life? The use of such deception in experiments is common.

Question: Isn't it possible that the child will not suffer any real psychological harm just because he fails to solve the puzzle?

It is more than likely that the child won't be harmed by the experience. But the question remains, Should someone gamble with a child's normal development for the sake of an experiment?

Question: Then children shouldn't be used for experiments?

Not necessarily. Thousands of children have been subjects in important experiments without suffering physical or psychological injury as far as anyone can tell, and eliminating all children as research subjects would be a devastating blow to developmental research.

Ethics

Question: How can we protect children's rights while still using children as experimental subjects?

Sometimes a group of professionals will outline or describe behavior that they consider morally good and appropriate for dealing with the specific issues faced by their profession. Such professional morals are called ethics. Table 1.2 briefly outlines the major ethical principles for research with children. After examining these ethical guidelines, ask yourself whether the experiment on violence and aggression that we conducted in this chapter was unethical.

Question: Among other possible violations, we didn't obtain informed consent, did we?

That's right, we didn't. While we were busy defining our terms and considering what we might discover, no one thought to obtain informed consent from the children's parents. Now aren't you glad that it was a hypothetical experiment—and that you don't have to worry that angry parents who do not allow their children to see violent cartoons will come knocking on your office door?

The Law

You should keep in mind that ethical guidelines are only guidelines. In the United States, the final arbiter of such matters is the court. In actual practice, though, lawsuits are rarely brought against psychologists or educators for experimenting with children. Society appears content that the ethical practices outlined by the

APPLICATIONS

TABLE 1.2

Ethical Standards for Research with Human Subjects

A CHILD'S LIST OF RIGHTS

1. No matter how young the child, he or she has rights that supersede the rights of the investigator.
2. Any deviation from these ethical principles requires that the investigator seek consultation in order to protect the rights of the research participants.
3. The investigator should inform the child of all features of the research that may affect the child's willingness to participate, and the investigator should answer the child's questions in terms appropriate to the child's comprehension.
4. The informed consent of parents or of those who act *in loco parentis* (e.g., teachers, superintendents of institutions) similarly should be obtained, preferably in writing. Informed consent requires that the parents or other responsible adult be told all features of the research that may affect their willingness to allow the child to participate. The responsible adults should be given the opportunity to refuse without penalty.
5. The investigator may use no research operation that may harm the child either physically or psychologically.
6. If concealment or deception is practiced, adequate measures should be taken after the study to ensure the participants' understanding of the reasons for the concealment or deception.
7. The investigator should keep in confidence all information obtained about research participants.
8. The investigator should clarify any misconceptions that may occur during or after the research.
9. When, in the course of research, information comes to the investigator's attention that may seriously affect the child's well-being, the investigator must make all arrangements necessary to assist the child.
10. If, during the research, any previously unforeseen consequences of an undesirable nature should occur, it is incumbent upon the researcher to correct these consequences or redesign the experimental procedures.
11. When experimental treatment is believed to benefit the children, the control group should be offered the same or similar beneficial treatment.
12. Every investigator also has the responsibility to maintain the ethical standards of his or her colleagues.
13. Teachers of courses related to children should present these ethical standards to their students.
14. The research must be scientifically sound and significant.
15. The research should be conducted on animals, human adults, and older children before involving infants.

SOURCE: Adapted, in part, from the standards of the Society for Research in Child Development's Ethical Standards for Research with Children and those of the National Commission for the Protection of Human Subjects of Biomedical and Behavioral Research.

profession are adequate, while criminal statutes protect against heinous violations. However, legally there are still two very tricky issues. First, what constitutes "psychological damage" as outlined in the ethical procedures, and second, can a parent give "informed consent" for a child by proxy (given that children are probably legally incapable of giving it for themselves)?

Question: What does the law say?

Frankly, it doesn't say anything about psychological experiments (because no case of "psychological damage" caused by an experiment has been proved in court). But after a child was harmed in a medical experiment, the U.S. Supreme Court held, in *Prince v. Massachusetts* (1944), that it wasn't legal for a parent to give the child's informed consent by proxy in such a situation. The Court stated:

> Parents may be free to become martyrs themselves. But it does not follow [that] they are free, in identical circumstances, to make martyrs of their children before they have reached the age of full and legal discretion when they can make that choice for themselves.

One legal commentator has further clarified this position in the following way:

> It is essential that while humanity and science are served, the individual's rights must be protected with vigor and vigilance. If this means that certain experiments cannot be conducted, it is appropriate that they are not. Medical scientists in the laboratory are privileged to embrace an operative pragmatism during the continuum of inductive and deductive reasoning, intuition, imagination and possibly even serendipity that comprise the scientific method. Occasionally, the means and the end are blurred and may even be indistinguishable. In the clinical experiment with human subjects this facile laboratory stratagem cannot be permitted, for here the end can never justify the means if human rights and dignity are violated. There is a special meaning for the scientist in this cliché, for he above all others exults in his freedom to seek the truth of life and he is first a human, then a scientist. (Ritts, 1968, p. 638)

Psychologists, as human beings first and scientists second, must continue to conduct research with children carefully and conscientiously, placing the children's best interests above any experimental concerns. Failure to do this would be a most serious ethical breach.

SUMMARY

- Although societies prior to the twentieth century often supported education for children, children were not typically thought of as having any exceptional or unique qualities. Instead, they were viewed as being quantitatively different, that is, as being obviously smaller and less educated than adults.
- It wasn't until the scientific investigations of children began in earnest that the richly unique and qualitative differences between children and adults started to become apparent.
- During the eighteenth century, exposure to child-rearing practices in far-off lands stimulated philosophers to speculate on the nature of child development.
- Developmental psychology can trace its roots to the work of the nineteenth-century naturalists, but it wasn't until the beginning of the twentieth century that G. Stanley Hall incorporated Darwin's views into a developmental psychology.
- When empirical methods were first applied to the field of child development, a number of central issues emerged, including nature versus nurture, stability versus change, and continuity versus discontinuity.
- Psychologists and others conduct experiments to determine the effects of different variables on behavior. When experiments are conducted, terms must be carefully defined to obtain agreement among observers.
- When conducting an experiment that measures the effects of a variable, researchers use a control group as a comparison. The control and experimental groups are treated exactly the same except that the experimental group is presented with the variable one wishes to study.
- Observers may be biased by their expectations.
- Subjects in experiments may be biased by the knowledge that they are being observed.
- One way of overcoming observer and subject bias is to conduct a double-blind experiment in which neither observers nor subjects know which is the control group and which is the experimental group.
- Single subjects may be investigated experimentally by using time as a control. An A-B-A experimental design is an example of single-subject research.
- Correlational data may be useful because predictions may be derived from them. Correlations are often the first clues that a scientist has to an important discovery. Researchers must be careful, however, not to assume cause-and-effect relationships based only on correlations; correlations are often only coincidental.
- Case studies, though open to bias, often supply valuable information that might otherwise be unobtainable.
- Both longitudinal and cross-sectional methods of research use age as a variable.
- In cross-sectional studies, subjects of different ages are compared, while in longitudinal studies, the same individual is measured repeatedly over time.
- A theory is a way of organizing data, ideas, and hypotheses to provide a more complete understanding. There are many different theories of human development. Among these are environmental and epigenetic theories. Although grand scope may be an eventual goal of the study of human development, modern researchers believe that it is more important to concentrate first on obtaining a degree of precision.
- Psychologists are human beings first and scientists second and must conduct research with children carefully and conscientiously, placing the children's best interests above any experimental concerns.

QUESTIONS FOR DISCUSSION

1. Do you believe that parents should have the right to give informed consent for their children by proxy?

2. Have you ever assumed a cause-and-effect relationship concerning your friends or neighbors that might simply be correlational?

3. How might an eyewitness's testimony be biased?

4. Can you think of situations in which you may have been biased by your expectations?

5. How would you arrange an experiment to test whether aspirin really alleviates headaches?

6. Ironically, the study conducted at the Willowbrook School, in which children were deliberately exposed to hepatitis, yielded some extremely valuable medical information. It was found that hepatitis B, the worst form of hepatitis, is carried by a virus. This discovery actually helped researchers to develop a vaccine that is effective in preventing hepatitis B. In addition, none of the children in the experiment was apparently permanently injured by the exposure. Does this information, all quite true, alter your feelings about the ethics of the study?

7. Could a psychology with a high level of precision and which deals with only specific areas of limited scope be applied to the large social problems faced by our society?

SUGGESTIONS FOR FURTHER READING

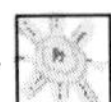

1. Aries, P. (1962). *Centuries of childhood: A social history of family life* (R. Baldick, Trans.). New York: Knopf. (Original work published 1960).
2. Deese, J. (1972). *Psychology as science and art.* New York: Harcourt Brace Jovanovich.
3. Hannah, G. T., Christian, W. P., & Clark, H. W. (Eds.). (1981). *Client rights.* New York: Free Press.
4. Keuill-Davies, S. (1992). *Yesterday's children: the antiques & history of childcare.* Chicago: Antique Collectibles.
5. Smuts, A. B., & Hagen, J. W. (Eds.). (1985). History and research in child development. *Monographs of the Society for Research in Child Development, 50* (4–5, Serial No. 211).
6. Sommerville, C. J. (1982). *The rise and fall of childhood.* Beverly Hills, CA: Sage.

CHAPTER 2

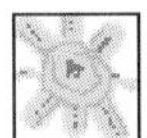

INHERITANCE AND THE BIOLOGICAL FOUNDATIONS OF DEVELOPMENT

CHAPTER PREVIEW

HOW TO BUILD YOUR OWN HUMAN BEING

THYMINE, adenine, cytosine, and guanine. Often abbreviated as T, A, C, and G, these four simple **molecules** are found abundantly in every living creature and are the basis of a larger molecule called DNA. The smaller molecules are typically linked to one another, forming a chain. For example, an A might be joined with a G, and then another G, forming AGG. Or the chain can be longer:

AATTCGCGAATCGCGATCTCGGACCAGCTCGCCA

Notice how it took nearly an entire line of this book to describe a chain consisting of 34 of these molecules. When strung together, these chains can become very long indeed. Instead of an entire line, an entire page or an entire book may be needed to describe a series!

DATELINE: June 3, 2017 The Massachusetts Institute of Technology, Boston, Massachusetts. Dr. Aaron Steymeyer, director of Biophysical Research and Development at MIT, announced in a press conference this morning that his team of scientists had accomplished a long-awaited breakthrough. The team had successfully manufactured a fertilized human egg.

NORMALLY, FERTILIZATION in humans occurs when a sperm and egg unite after sexual intercourse. But in this case, the MIT team designed and built its own sperm and egg cells using chemicals taken from the laboratory shelf. The manufactured fertilized egg will be implanted into the womb of a female volunteer, where it will develop into a blue-eyed boy. The child-to-be has further been designed to be athletic, 6′1" tall, handsome, intelligent, slow to anger, and resistant to disease. The team did not elaborate on other specifics. Of course, the child, when born, will have no real mother or father because he was created and designed by the scientists at MIT according to a complex formula. Dr. Steymeyer explained that the formula's major ingredient was a series of complex chains consisting of the base chemicals thymine, adenine, cytosine, and guanine. Dr. Steymeyer said that if written on paper, the formula would require a few hundred books, each at least a thousand pages long.

DATELINE: April 11, 2031 Athens, Greece. The International Olympic Committee announced today, "No manufactured human beings specifically designed to excel in an athletic event will be allowed to participate in the Olympic Games."

DATELINE: December 3, 2031 Washington, D.C. Jane Mohr, president of the American Bar Association, gave testimony today before the House subcommittee that is investigating ethical issues involving manufactured humans. The issue brought before the committee concerned the possibility that a manufactured child might one day become a criminal adult. Ms. Mohr said, "Unlike a 'normal' human who would usually be held responsible for his or her actions, a manufactured human who commits a crime should be recalled for repairs by the laboratory that built him or her." Sir Lawrence Arnold, the famed British psychologist and philosopher, is expected to give opposing testimony tomorrow arguing that environmental influences are responsible for criminal behavior and are therefore not the fault of the laboratory.

DATELINE: November 6, 2034 Harvard University, Boston, Massachusetts. Dr. Sol Crane, winner of this year's Nobel Prize for social affairs, has voiced his growing concern that the popularity of manufactured fertilized human eggs is steadily increasing "not because the children are certain to be free of genetic disease, or because their sex can be determined beforehand, or even because they are generally intelligent and disease resistant. The major interest seems to center on the fact that the beauty of the child can be guaranteed." Dr. Crane went on to say, "I admit to a growing fear concerning the great emphasis being placed on beauty and the increasing discrimination against the unattractive, which I attribute directly to the ability to make a child look exactly as the future parents desire."

Doubtful? Perhaps not.

YOU WOULD HAVE undoubtedly been confronted with disbelief had you suggested to anyone, in 1956, that men would be driving a car on the moon only 15 years later. In fact, in 1956, many people, including some scientists, believed that travel to the moon was at least a century away.

KEEP THIS IN MIND while you wonder if the news stories presented here could ever occur. Read this chapter—and then decide.

RESOURCES

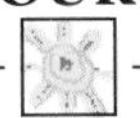

DNA—The Essence of Life

Question: How are the chemicals you mentioned in the Chapter Preview related to life?

There is evidence that these chemicals occurred quite naturally in the kind of atmosphere that existed on the earth billions of years ago. Experiments that recreate the early earth atmosphere—in which air bubbles trapped in ancient rocks serve as a guide to the chemicals present at that time—show that such chemicals readily form (Garmon, 1981). For example, among the organic precursors of life that have been discovered in these experiments is the molecule called adenine.

Adenine and the other simple substances—thymine, cytosine, and guanine—combine to form a chemical molecule known as **deoxyribonucleic acid,** or **DNA.** DNA is a unique molecule. It is sometimes called the essence of life. Every living creature—plant or animal—contains DNA in each cell of its being. Your body is made of all kinds of cells, including brain cells, liver cells, and nerve cells. Your body has about 60 trillion (60,000,000,000,000, or 60×10^{12}) cells in all, and each cell contains DNA.

In 1953, the structure of DNA was discovered by James Watson, Francis Crick, and Maurice Wilkins. For this discovery they shared a Nobel Prize.

They found that the DNA molecule is shaped like a double helix. A phosphate-sugar backbone forms the outside, and the four molecules adenine, thymine, guanine, and cytosine (known as bases) form the inside (Watson & Crick, 1953). This configuration is shown in Figure 2.1. As mentioned in the Chapter Preview, biochemists refer to the four bases by their first letters: A, T, G, and C.

A feature of DNA that makes it truly amazing is that it replicates; that is, it makes copies of itself (Figure 2.2). This one property, more than any other, distinguishes biology from chemistry.

As you continue to study DNA, you will notice that the horizontal joining of molecules in this incredible substance occurs only in certain ways. An A must join with a T (they are **A**lways **T**ogether), and a T with an A. G must join with a C, and a C with a G. However, there are no particular rules for the vertical arrangement of pairs. One strand of DNA may continue for thousands of A-T and G-C pairs, and the number of differently sequenced strands that can be made is almost infinite (Figure 2.3).

Question: How is DNA related to living things?

The DNA is arranged in a code, which is determined by the vertical sequence of the base pairs. The code is divided into sections, and each section orders the building of a sequence of proteins that determine the kind of animal or plant that will be made. Each section of code is called a **gene.** For example, a DNA code consisting of many sections, or genes, exists in each one of your approximately 60 trillion cells. Each one of your cells contains the same code (the same genes), the blueprint for your entire body. Had the DNA code in your body been different, it might have ordered the construction of a box elder beetle, a kangaroo, a great white shark, or an oak tree instead of you! Different DNA codes make different animals or plants or different varieties of the same animal or plant. You look different from a friend of yours mainly because you have a different DNA code in your cells. On the other hand, identical twins share the same or extremely similar codes.

MOLECULE
A distinct chemical unit or group of atoms that have joined together.

DEOXYRIBONUCLEIC ACID (DNA)
A chemical constituent of cell nuclei, consisting of two long chains of alternating phosphate and deoxyribose units twisted into a double helix and joined by bonds between the complementary bases of adenine, thymine, cytosine, and guanine. It is the substance that enables cells to copy themselves.

GENE
The smallest functional unit for the transmission of a hereditary trait; a section of genetic code.

FIGURE 2.1
The DNA double helix. The external backbone of the structure is formed by phosphate and sugar; the base pairs form the internal core. The completed molecule looks much like a spiral staircase with the base pairs forming the steps.

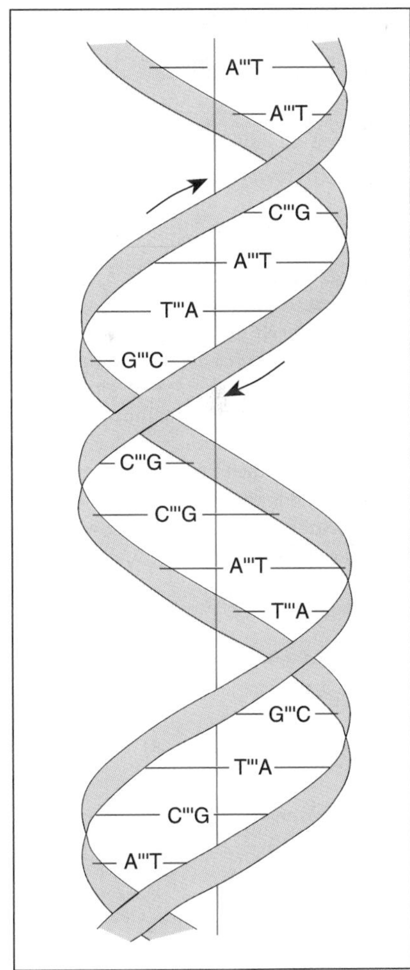

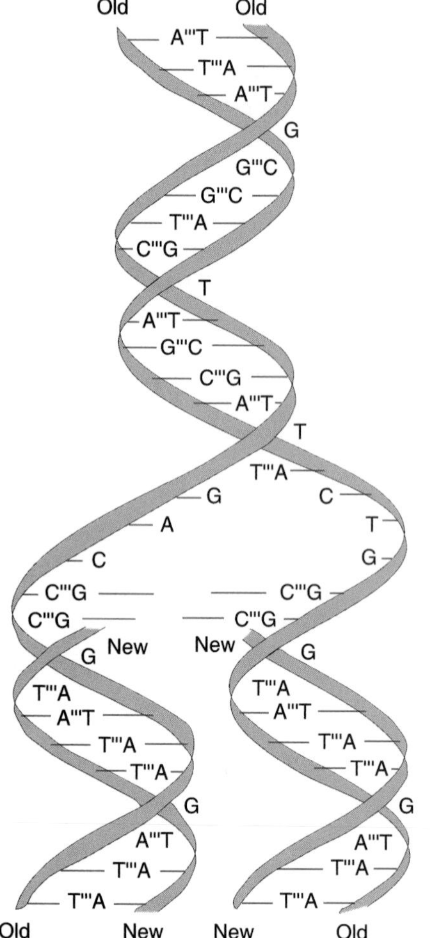

FIGURE 2.2

Replication of DNA. As the old DNA, which resides within the nucleus of the cell, begins to unzip owing to the action of certain chemicals called enzymes, free A, T, G, or C molecules floating nearby become attracted to the now unzipped single strands of the original molecule. The new binding of these free floating molecules with their counterparts on the original strands results in two new and *identical* strands of DNA, both of which are copies of the original.

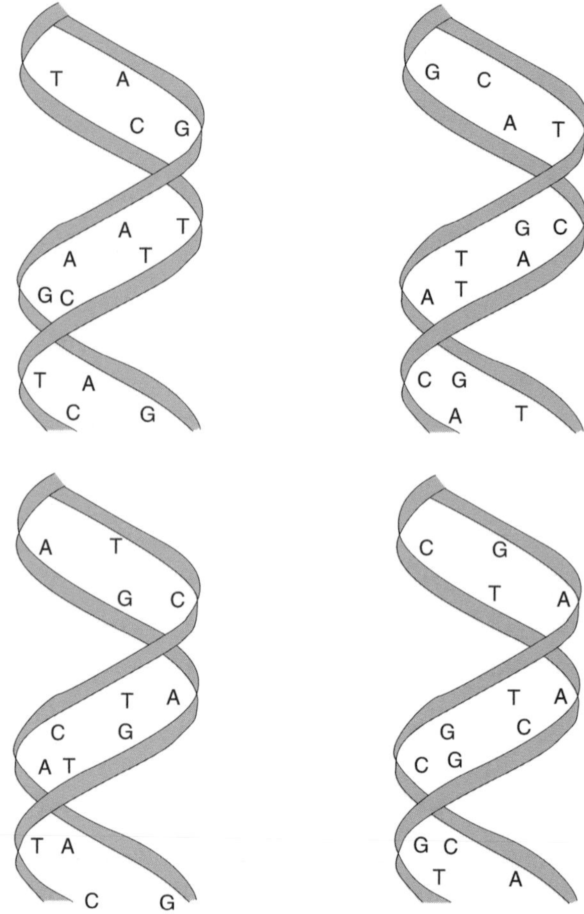

FIGURE 2.3

In a DNA sequence of only seven base pairs, 8,192 possible combinations can be made. Four of these possibilities are pictured here. Most DNA strands contain thousands of base pairs, with the result that an almost infinite number of combinations are possible.

Nature-Nurture: Cloning the Boys from Brazil

The blueprint for your entire body is contained in each cell, so it should be possible, at least in theory, to create a twin of yourself from any one of your body cells. This treated cell could be used to impregnate a volunteer woman or, perhaps in the future, an artificial womb. The cell would then develop into a fetus, and nine months later, your copy would be born. Such a copy of yourself would be called a **clone** and would be exactly the same as a twin, except that you and your clone could be years apart in age, and, in theory anyway, thousands of clones of you could be produced.

Actually, the cloning of a mammal has already been achieved. By taking cells from a developing mouse embryo, researchers were able to clone additional mice (Marx, 1981). Cloning from an embryo, however, is relatively easy, while cloning from the cells of a developed animal is still in the realm of science fiction.

A popular novel written some years back, made into a movie called *The Boys from Brazil,* used the concept of the clone as the basis for a frightening tale. In the story, an evil Nazi doctor was hiding out in Brazil, having escaped the fall of Nazi Germany over 30 years earlier. The doctor had taken some of Hitler's cells with him, which he later used to make a number of clones of Hitler. As the novel develops, we find that the Hitler clones have all reached about 10 years of age and are being raised in various countries throughout the world. The evil hope is that one of these Hitlers will eventually be able to institute a new Nazi reign.

Now that you know what a clone is, you can see that this story is perfect for examining the interaction of **nature** and **nurture.**

What if the novel were true? How frightened should we be of these Hitler clones? Would a child with all of Hitler's genes necessarily become a dictator, political leader, great orator, and mass murderer? Certainly, the child would grow up to look like Hitler (which would hardly be a social plus). He would probably also have the same intellectual capacity and similar personality traits, much as you would expect from an identical twin.

But what about the experiences that shaped the personality of Adolf Hitler? Could these be replicated? In the novel, some of Hitler's life experiences were replicated for the clones, but many others could not be. To truly re-create Adolf Hitler, wouldn't all of Hitler's experiences have to be considered as well as his genes? Couldn't someone who had Adolf Hitler's genes (nature) but who lived a different life (nurture) become a Jewish pacifist? As you will see later, learning plays a very important role.

Of course, there is no way of testing these hypotheses at present, because no human clone has yet been created, but it is interesting to think about.

CLONE
An organism genetically identical to its ancestor organism and derived from one of its cells.

NATURE
In developmental research, the hereditary component of an organism's development.

NURTURE
In developmental research, the environmental component of an organism's development.

DIFFERENTIAL REPRODUCTION
A mechanism by which organisms with favorable traits tend to reproduce in greater numbers than those with less favorable traits, resulting in an increase in favored traits in later generations.

NATURAL SELECTION
The process, first suggested by Darwin, through which those individuals of a species best adapted to their environment have a better chance of passing on their genes to the next generation than do those not as well adapted.

The Evolution of Life

Around 3.6 billion years ago, long before anyone had ever thought of cloning, forces were at work creating the first single-celled organism—the first life on this planet. It is believed that life began in the clay beds of the oceans with the creation of a stable code that, by chance, ordered up a secure protein "cell" structure that became the first single-celled organism (Dickerson, 1978).

Question: What makes a code stable?

Many things contribute to making a DNA code stable, that is, able to replicate and pass on copies of itself. Some sort of external cell membrane must be ordered by the code. (One possibility is that the first "cell membranes" were a long-lasting type of bubble that could sit quietly attached to nickel-bearing rocks for months at a time while interesting chemical reactions could proceed.) The code must also include orders creating a mechanism for obtaining energy from the environment. The first stable living cells had, by chance, developed an advantageous trait that enabled them to obtain energy through the process of fermentation. In fact, bacteria similar to those first cells are still alive today (e.g., the bacteria responsible for gangrene). Codes favored by the environment—that is, codes that are successful—continue to exist and are passed on to the next generation, while codes that are detrimental eventually die out. This happens because organisms with favorable codes tend to reproduce in greater numbers than do those with less favorable ones, and this **differential reproduction** leads to an increase in the favored codes or traits in the later generations. Supporting this assertion is the fact that far more plant and animal varieties have become extinct than have survived (Fishbein, 1976).

In the mid-nineteenth century, Charles Darwin became the founder of modern evolutionary biology when he realized that natural forces were responsible for the fact that so many creatures were well suited, or adapted, to their individual environments. Also, the creatures that had been ill suited to the environment had generally failed to reproduce or had produced few offspring, leaving few organisms to continue carrying the disadvantageous traits. Darwin called this phenomenon **natural selection.**

DIVERSIFICATION
In evolution, the great range of individual differences that exist in each species from which natural forces may select.

MUTATION
Any heritable alteration of the genes or chromosomes of an organism.

POINT MUTATION
A mutation that results in the replacement of one base pair by another within the DNA itself.

PRIMATE
Member of the most highly developed order of mammals, including humans, apes, and lemurs. Primates are marked by their large stereoscopic eyes, nails (rather than claws), opposing thumbs, and short snouts.

HOMINID
Any family of bipedal primate mammals. Includes all forms of human beings, extinct and living.

DIVERSIFICATION AND MUTATION

Natural selection is not the only force in the evolution of life. The second major force is **diversification.** For the forces of natural selection to function, there must be a great variety from which nature can select. If all the members of a given species were alike, they would all have an equal chance of succeeding or failing; but they are not all alike. Compare yourself with a close friend. Perhaps you are taller, she is shorter, you have blue eyes, she has brown. There are thousands of other differences between the two of you. Although you are both classified as members of the same species, you are distinctly different creatures. Our species has become diversified; we are not all alike.

Question: What caused diversification in the first place?

The answer lies in the biochemical phenomenon of **mutation.** Most people think of mutations in terms of gross body changes that are highly visible. However, mutations are changes that are often extremely small and that usually result in very minor alterations.

When an error is made in the translation or structure of the DNA code, a mutation has occurred. If the mutation is limited to the replacement of one base by another in the DNA itself, it is called a **point mutation** (Ayala, 1978). Such a mutation is likely to alter or change an organism in some fashion. Usually, the change is for the worse. This is because the mutation alters a successful code in a haphazard way. Although changing the code by altering just one of the bases is a terribly small change, it can have disastrous effects. For example, the change of just one base, thymine replacing guanine, in a particular section of one human gene, has been discovered to be the cause of one form of bladder cancer (Miller, 1982). On very rare occasions, however, a mutation may be beneficial. For example, mutations in the first single-celled organism, which used fermentation to acquire energy, may have eventually led to a more advanced single-celled organism, one capable of using photosynthesis to obtain energy. Any code made superior by a lucky mutation would probably be favored during natural selection and passed on to offspring. In this way, mutations initially led to the diversification of species (Stebbins & Ayala, 1985). Eventually, once many members of a particular species are established, they continue to diversify their genetic heritage by mating with one another, thus creating new variations of species members.

Question: What causes mutations?

Mutations can be induced by ionizing radiation (ultraviolet rays, X rays, or gamma rays), heat, contact with various chemicals, contact with certain viruses, and other processes. It is believed that evolution began when such mutations occurred in the offspring of the first single-celled organisms.

THE EVOLUTION OF MODERN HUMANS

Table 2.1 is a brief outline of the history of the biological evolution that eventually led to the creation of our own species.

The first single-celled bacteria, which existed 3.6 billion years ago, were capable of surviving without oxygen. This had to be the case because the early earth atmosphere contained no free oxygen. Later, bacteria evolved the capability of photosynthesis and began to release oxygen as part of the photosynthetic process. The free oxygen that now exists in our atmosphere originated during this time (Schopf, 1978).

Fifty million years ago, the first **primates** evolved. Primates are marked by their large stereoscopic eyes, nails instead of claws, opposing thumbs, and short snouts.

TABLE 2.1

The Evolution of Life

NUMBER OF YEARS AGO	EVOLUTIONARY ADVANCES
3.6 billion	Primitive one-celled organisms that obtained energy through the method of fermentation
3 billion	Sulfur bacteria that used hydrogen sulfide to conduct photosynthesis
	Single-celled organisms able to use water in photosynthesis instead of sulfur; these were the ancestors of the blue-green algae and green plants
2 billion	Oxygen atmosphere
1.6 billion	Bacteria able to use nonsulfur photosynthesis and oxygen in respiration; these bacteria could extract 19 times more energy from food than could the first primitive bacteria
1.3 billion	Cells with nuclei evolved, which concentrated genetic material, increasing, in turn, the opportunities for diversification to occur
1 billion	Multicelled organisms; plant and animal kingdoms divide
500 million	Many marine animals, corals, clams, and fish
300 million	Amphibians, ferns, spiders, insects (over 800 species of cockroach), and first reptiles
150 million	Dinosaurs and reptiles rule the land, sea, and air
	First birds evolve from smaller dinosaurs
	Modern insects (bees, moths, flies)
70 million	Dinosaurs extinct
	Marsupials and primitive mammals
	Flowering plants
	Deciduous trees
	Giant redwoods
	50 percent of North America under water; Rocky Mountains are formed
50 million	Modern birds
	The early horse (only 1 foot high)
	Ancestors of the cat, dog, elephant, camel, and other mammals
	Seed-bearing plants and small primates
1.5 million	*Homo erectus* (probable direct ancestor of modern humans)
100,000	*Homo sapiens neanderthalensis* (an extinct variety of human)
100,000	*Homo sapiens sapiens* (modern humans)

The small tree-dwelling lemur of today is very similar to the first primates of 50 million years ago (Bronowski, 1973). We, too, are primates.

Modern humans have been in existence for only 100,000 years or so (Stringer, Grun, Schwarcz, & Goldberg, 1989), an extremely brief time in evolutionary terms. However, **hominid** (humanlike) predecessors to our own species have been on this planet for at least 5 million years and perhaps for as long as 14 million years (Washburn, 1978). It all depends on how liberal one is in classifying extinct species with human characteristics as hominid.

LEARNING CHECK

1. *Nature* is a term used by developmental psychologists to refer to __________, and *nurture* is a term used to refer to __________.
2. The molecule known as the essence of life is __________.
3. DNA is shaped like a __________.
4. An exact copy of yourself made from a single cell would be called a __________.
5. It is believed that life began on earth __________ years ago.
   a. 1 million **c.** 3.6 million
   b. 3 billion **d.** 3.6 billion
6. Diversification and natural selection are two major forces of __________.
   a. mutations **c.** evolution
   b. developmental theory **d.** differential reproduction

Answers:
1. heredity, or genetics; learning, or experience **2.** DNA **3.** double helix
4. clone **5.** d **6.** c

Chromosomes and Inheritance

Throughout millions of years of evolution, genetic material has been passed from one generation to the next. Species have evolved and diversified. A genetic heritage now resides within all living creatures. It is formed within the **nucleus** of each cell.

When a certain colored stain is applied to the nucleus of a cell, small bodies within the nucleus absorb the stain and become visible. These small bodies are called **chromosomes.** In fact, the word *chromosome* means "colored body."

In a human body cell, there are 46 chromosomes arranged in 23 pairs. On the chromosomes of each cell lie the genes (made from strands of DNA), which contain the genetic code for your entire body. The number of chromosomes per cell varies from one species of plant or animal to another. It may range from as few as 4 to as many as 254 (Sinnott, Dunn, & Dobzhansky, 1958). For example, toads have 44 chromosomes in their body cells; potatoes have 48. Of the 46 chromosomes in your body cells, you inherited 23 from your father and 23 from your mother.

Human sperm or egg cells, called **gametes,** contain only 23 chromosomes each, rather than 23 pairs. During the creation of these sex cells, a special process known as **meiosis** creates gametes with only half the usual number of chromosomes (Figure 2.4). Because of this, when a human sperm and egg unite during fertilization, the next generation will also have 46 chromosomes in each body cell. (Without the process of meiosis, sperm and egg cells would have the same number of chromosomes as body cells, and when they joined during fertilization, the number of chromosomes in each cell of the new generation would be doubled.)

Once chromosomes are made visible by staining, they can be photographed. The individual chromosomes can be cut from the photograph, arranged in pairs, and placed in rows for easy inspection. Such an arrangement is called a **karyotype** (Figure 2.5). A karyotype can show a number of serious chromosomal abnormalities that are known to be associated with various disorders. The first 22 pairs of chromosomes are called the **autosomes.** The twenty-third pair is labeled separately from the others; these two chromosomes are known as **sex chromosomes.**

NUCLEUS
A central body within a living cell that contains the cell's hereditary material and controls its metabolism, growth, and reproduction.

CHROMOSOME
A thread-shaped body that is contained within the nucleus of a body cell and that determines those characteristics that will be passed on to the offspring of an organism. Chromosomes carry the genes; humans have 23 pairs of chromosomes.

GAMETE
Male or female germ cell containing one-half the number of chromosomes found in the other cells of the body.

MEIOSIS
The process of cell division in sexually reproducing organisms that reduces the number of chromosomes in reproductive cells, leading to the production of gametes.

KARYOTYPE
A photomicrograph of chromosomes in a standard array.

AUTOSOME
Any chromosome that is not a sex chromosome.

SEX CHROMOSOME
In humans, one of the two chromosomes responsible for producing the sex of the child; the X and Y chromosomes.

FIGURE 2.4
Unlike the process of mitosis, in which cells replicate, making copies of themselves, the process of meiosis leads to the creation of gametes, which have only one-half the number of chromosomes of a typical body cell.

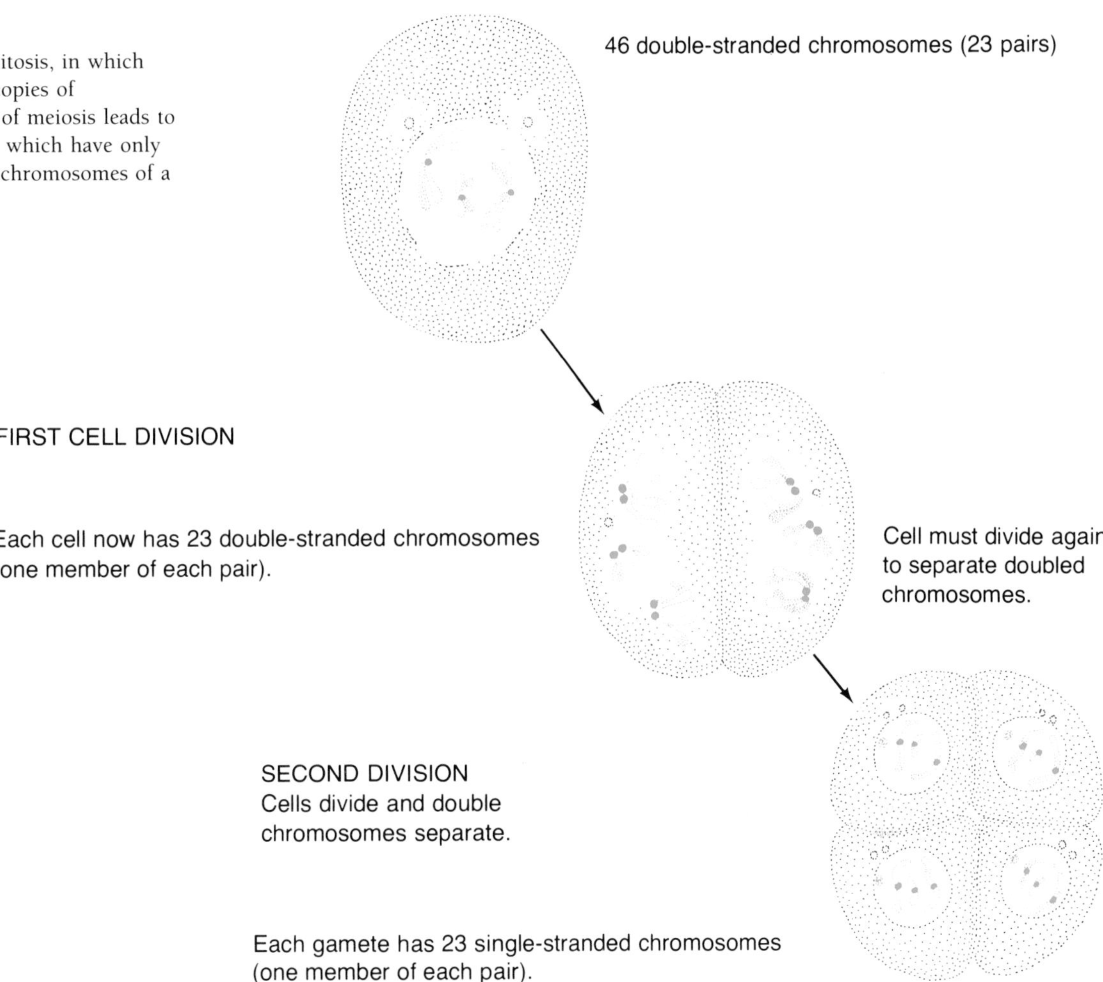

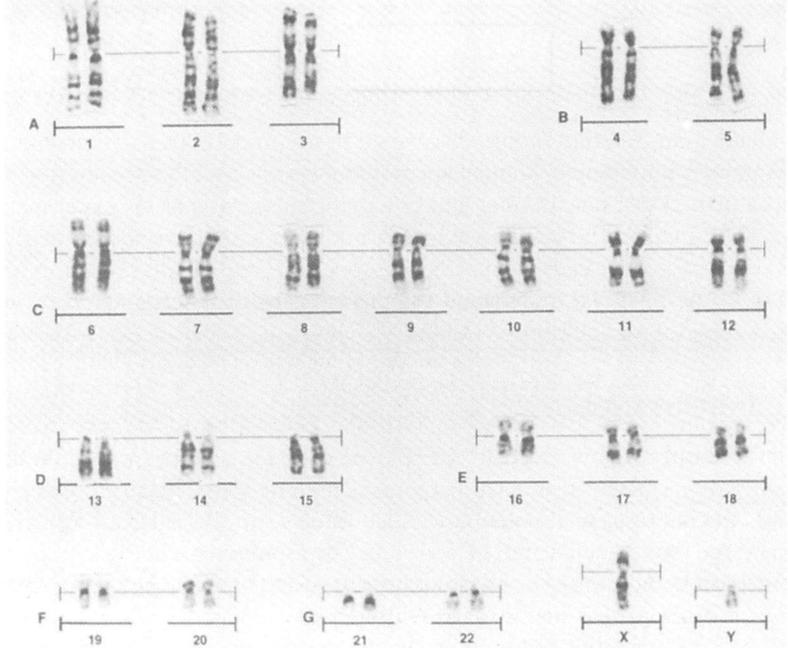

FIGURE 2.5
Humans have 23 pairs of chromosomes. In the karyotype, the pairs are matched. One member of each pair is from the mother and one from the father.

ALLELE
Any of a group of possible mutational forms of a gene.

DOMINANT
In genetics, describing a gene whose characteristics are expressed while suppressing the characteristics controlled by the other corresponding gene for that trait.

RECESSIVE
In genetics, describing a gene whose characteristics are not expressed when paired with a dominant gene.

CARRIER
In genetics, an organism that carries a particular trait in its genes and, while not expressing that trait itself, is able to pass on the trait to its offspring.

DOUBLE RECESSIVE
A condition in which both allelic pairs for a given trait are recessive and no dominant allelic gene is present to override them. In this case, the recessive trait will be expressed.

HOMOZYGOUS
Describing alleles of a gene pair that are identical.

HETEROZYGOUS
Describing alleles of a gene pair that are different.

PHENOTYPE
The observable characteristics of an organism due to inheritance.

GENOTYPE
The characteristics that an individual has inherited and may transmit to descendants, regardless of whether the individual manifests these characteristics.

Question: How are the sex chromosomes different from the autosomes?

Like the autosomes, the sex chromosomes carry many genes. The sex chromosomes are different, however, in that they also carry the genetic code that determine your sex. Interestingly, these chromosomes are shaped differently, depending on which sex code is being carried. Sex chromosomes carrying the genetic code for a girl are shaped like an X, and those carrying the code for a boy are shaped like a Y. These chromosomes are, in fact, referred to as X and Y chromosomes. As you can see, the twenty-third pair in the karyotype pictured in Figure 2.5 contains both an X and a Y chromosome.

Question: Which sex would a child with this karyotype be—male because of the Y or female because of the X?

Male. Males have an XY twenty-third pair, while females have an XX twenty-third pair. Because females are XX, they have no Y chromosomes in their cells. A woman's ovum, or egg, can contain only the X sex chromosome. Therefore, *both* boys and girls receive one X chromosome from their mother's egg. Because men are XY, their sperm cells created during meiosis may contain either an X or a Y sex chromosome. The child will inherit one or the other, which will then determine the child's sex. If a sperm carrying an X chromosome fertilizes the mother's ovum, a girl will be produced; if a sperm carrying a Y chromosome fertilizes the ovum, the child will be a boy.

There are rare cases, however, of girls who are XY and boys who are XX. They are worth mentioning here to illustrate that the Y chromosome has the effect that it usually does because it is carrying the gene that determines gender. In fact, the actual gene, discovered in 1990 (Sinclair et al., 1990), sometimes is absent from the father's Y chromosome or present on his X chromosome, causing the aforementioned rare occurrences.

Again, it is only the male who can contribute a Y chromosome, so the gender of the offspring is determined by the father's sperm. Perhaps someone should have told King Henry VIII about that before he had Ann Boleyn executed for, among other things, not having borne him a son! Still, in the sixteenth century, no one knew about the genetic mechanisms of inheritance or the natural laws that they followed.

MENDEL'S LAWS

Question: Who first became aware that inheritance followed natural laws?

Gregor Mendel, an Austrian monk, discovered in the mid-1800s the fundamental laws that govern inheritance. Mendel spent many years carefully crossing garden-variety pea plants with one another and cataloging the results of his experiments. He watched as a number of traits—such as wrinkled or smooth seeds, tall or short stalks, yellow or green seeds—appeared, disappeared, and reappeared from one generation to the next. To understand the mechanisms of inheritance, it's worth examining some of Mendel's observations.

Gregor Mendel (1822–1884).

SIMPLE INHERITANCE

Pea seeds are either yellow or green. Genes that code for seed color are inherited from both parents (even peas have parents). Different genes that can affect the same trait (in this case, seed color) are called **alleles,** or allelic genes. For every allelic gene on one chromosome of a pair, a corresponding allele exists in the same position on the other chromosome of the pair. For example, if the allelic gene for seed color were located at a particular position on a chromosome, another gene for seed color would be found in the same position on the corresponding chromosome of that pair. The letter Y (for yellow) will represent the pea allele responsible for yellow seed color, and the letter g (for green) will represent the allele responsible for green seed color. Notice in Figure 2.6 what occurs when a yellow-seeded plant is crossed with a green-seeded plant. The seed-color alleles of all the offspring are Yg.

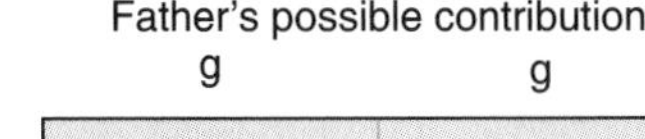

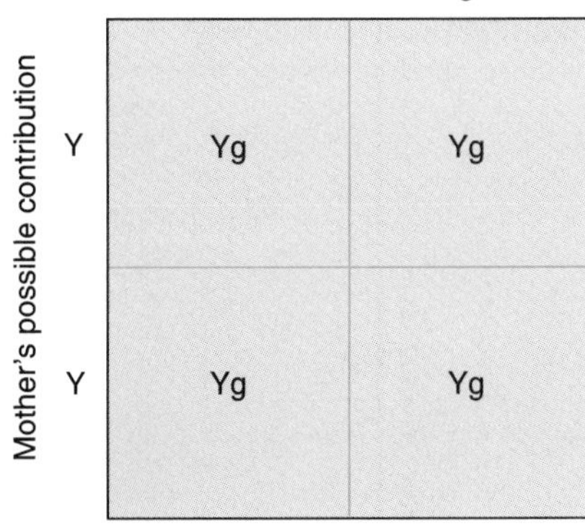

FIGURE 2.6

This diagram is called a Punnett square and shows the possible interactions or crosses between a green-seeded plant and a yellow-seeded plant. As with humans, the pea plant inherits half of its genetic material from one parent's gamete and the other half from the other parent's gamete. Remember, these gametes were created during meiosis and contain only half the usual number of chromosomes.

Question: Then will all these offspring have yellowish green seeds?

You would think so, but in fact the yellow color is controlled by a **dominant** allele, while the green color is controlled by a **recessive** allele. Dominant allelic genes are designated by capital letters, and recessive allelic genes are designated by lowercase letters. When a dominant Y allelic gene inherited from one parent and a recessive g allelic gene inherited from the other form a pair in the offspring, the genetic code in the dominant gene is turned on, while the code in the recessive gene stays off. Because of this, seeds that have Yg allelic genes are just as yellow as the seeds with YY allelic genes. The difference is that seeds with Yg alleles, even though they are bright yellow, are **carriers** of green color.

Question: If yellow is the dominant color, how could seeds ever be green?

In the next example, two plants that have yellow seeds, but that are carriers of green color, are crossed (Figure 2.7). Four kinds of offspring can result: YY, Yg, gY, and gg. When a plant inherits the **double recessive** gg, the seeds will be green. Because no dominant allelic gene is present to override the recessive ones, the recessive alleles are expressed. In fact, when Mendel ran this experiment, he discovered yellow to green seeds in a ratio of 3:1, which is exactly what is predicted by this example.

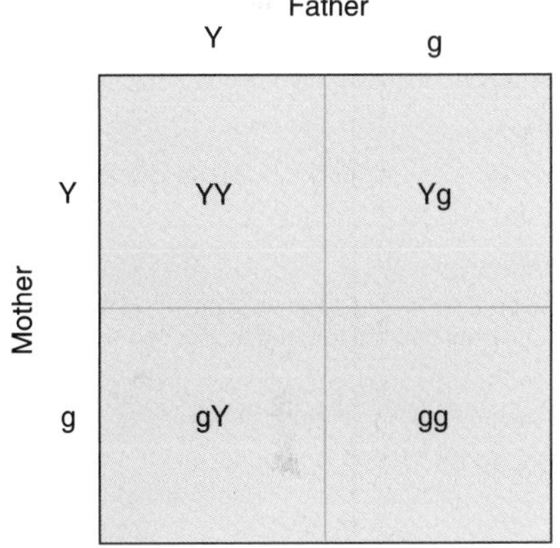

FIGURE 2.7

The recessive trait (green seed color) can be expressed only when no dominant allele is present. Because an allele for seed color is inherited from each parent, the recessive trait can be expressed only as a double recessive (gg).

When the alleles in a pair are identical, such as with YY, or gg, the pair is defined as **homozygous.** If the alleles in a pair are different, as in the case of Yg and gY (yellow seeds that carry the recessive green trait), the pair is defined as **heterozygous.** The observable characteristics of a trait (such as the actual color of the seeds) are called the **phenotype,** while the genetic composition of the organism is the **genotype.**

Table 2.2 shows the four possible offspring from the crossing of the two pea plants with genotype Yg. Notice that the first three offspring have the same appearance, or phenotype (yellow seeds), but that offspring 1 has a different genotype from offspring 2 and 3. Offspring 1 is not a carrier of the recessive green trait.

Question: Do researchers in child development really care that much about peas?

To be honest, no. Not many people do. In fact, Mendel's laws went unnoticed during his lifetime, and scientists of his day, such as Darwin, never had a chance to examine them. It wasn't until Mendel's laws were "rediscovered" in the early 1900s that his name became prominent.

TABLE 2.2

Offspring from the Crossing of Two Pea Plants with Genotype Yg

OFFSPRING	PHENOTYPE (OF SEED COLOR)	GENOTYPE (OF SEED COLOR)
1. YY	Yellow	Homozygous YY
2. Yg	Yellow	Heterozygous Yg
3. gY	Yellow	Heterozygous gY
4. gg	Green	Homozygous gg

NOTE: The first three offspring have identical phenotypes. However, offspring 1 has a different genotype from that of 2 and 3. The second and third offspring have the same phenotype and genotype (there is no difference between Yg and gY—they mean the same thing).

CODOMINANCE
Situation in which heterozygous alleles consist of two dominant genes. In such instances, both genes are expressed.

The reason, of course, for any interest at all in the pea experiments is that these simple mechanisms of inheritance also apply to many other plants and animals, including human beings.

Question: What kinds of human traits follow Mendel's laws?

In humans, eye color is inherited in this simple manner. Pigmented eyes are dominant (for convenience, let's call all pigmented eyes "brown"), and blue eyes are recessive. Using the capital letter B to represent the dominant allelic gene for brown eyes and the small letter b to represent the recessive allelic gene for blue eyes, cross two people with heterozygous brown eyes by filling in the following square:

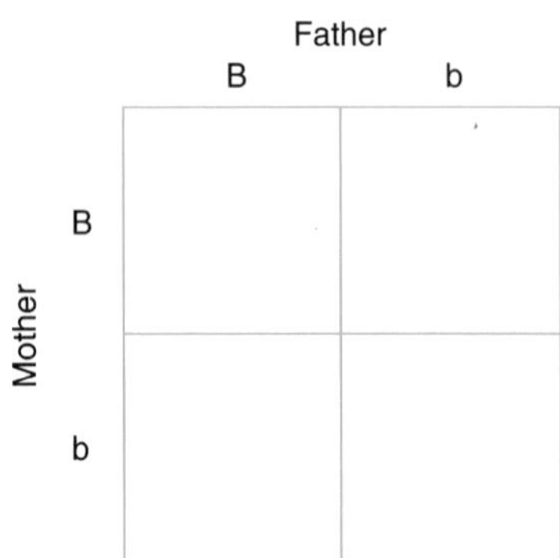

As you can see, it works just like Mendel's peas, with a 3:1 ratio of brown to blue. You should, of course, keep in mind that the 3:1 ratio is derived from an average. On the average, for every three brown-eyed children born from such a cross, one blue-eyed child should be born. But it is possible for such parents to have three or four blue-eyed children in a row, just as it is possible to have six or seven girls or boys in a row.

Question: Are parents always more likely to have brown-eyed children?

No. Suppose that both parents have blue eyes. Then they must both be homozygous double recessives (bb), which means that all their children will have blue eyes. Or if one of the parents is homozygous blue (bb) and the other is heterozygous brown (Bb), then, on the average, half their children will have blue eyes.

Question: I've heard that a person can have one brown eye and one blue eye. How can that happen?

The genes work indirectly by creating biochemistry that in turn may affect the body or its development. Sometimes a person is genetically programmed to have brown eyes, but for some reason the biochemical message fails to be correctly transmitted to one of the eyes, with the result that one eye is brown and one blue. You should understand, though, that a heterozygous genotype of Bb does not mean that one eye is supposed to be brown and one blue. Both eyes should be brown.

Question: What other human characteristics are inherited in this manner?

Hair shape, among others: Kinky is dominant, and straight is recessive. Blood types also follow Mendel's laws.

Consider the standard blood-typing system using A, B, AB, and o. A and B are dominant; o is recessive. In Figure 2.8, three examples of blood-type crosses are shown. The first is between a homozygous type A father and a homozygous type B mother. Because A and B genes are both dominant, both codes in the inherited allelic pair "turn on" and are expressed. This results in the creation of type AB

Mother \ Father	A	A
B	BA	BA
B	BA	BA

Mother \ Father	o	o
o	oo	oo
o	oo	oo

Mother \ Father	A	o
B	BA	Bo
o	oA	oo

FIGURE 2.8
Examples of blood-type crosses between parents with A, B, or O blood types. In human blood, types A and B are dominant (and exhibit codominance in type AB blood), and O is recessive.

blood in all offspring and is an example of **codominance,** where two dominant genes in one allelic gene pair express themselves simultaneously.

In the second example, two homozygous type o parents (double recessive) cross, and all offspring are type o. Because o is recessive, two parents with type o blood must have a type o child. Notice, though, that in the third example, a type A father and a type B mother could have children with any of the four blood types, as long as both parents are heterozygous, that is, as long as they are carriers of the recessive o gene.

SEX-LINKED INHERITANCE

From 1837 to 1901, Queen Victoria was the ruling monarch of Great Britain. Early in Queen Victoria's life, a mutation occurred to one of her genes. This mutation destroyed the gene's ability to make factor VIII, a substance that helps blood clot the way it should. Without factor VIII, a person will suffer classic hemophilia, or bleeder's disease. The hemophilia inherited by Queen Victoria's descendants probably began with her; no case of hemophilia existed in the royal family before her reign.

Queen Victoria (center left, foreground), shown here with some of her children, was a carrier of hemophilia. Because hemophilia is a sex-linked disorder, only her sons were at risk for the condition (their father was not hemophilic).

SEX-LINKED DISORDER
A hereditary disorder controlled by a gene carried on the sex-determining chromosome. Color blindness is an example.

MODIFIER GENE
A gene that acts on another gene and modifies the latter's effects.

PHENYLKETONURIA (PKU)
A genetic disorder marked by an inability to oxidize normally the amino acid phenylalanine. If this disorder is unchecked by a suitable diet, permanent damage is caused to the developing child's central nervous system.

All the royal descendants of Queen Victoria who suffered from hemophilia were male. This is because hemophilia is a **sex-linked disorder** inherited mostly by males. Neither Queen Victoria herself nor any of her female descendants had hemophilia; instead, they were carriers. Because of the constant hemorrhaging and dark blue bruises that appeared around the joints, these victims were referred to as "blue bloods." After a time, *blue blood* became a term that referred to anyone of royal birth.

Because the defective gene is located on the twenty-third pair of chromosomes, the sex chromosomes, the disease it causes is sex-linked. (All sex-linked disorders involve genes on the sex chromosomes.) Remember that although the sex chromosomes contain the genes that determine your sex, they also contain many thousands of other genes, among them the gene that makes factor VIII.

Question: Why is it that men can get the disease, while women are only carriers?

The Y chromosome is so named because of its shape. It is similar to an X chromosome, but it does not contain as many genes. It is as though it is missing a part. And because a part is "missing," so are many of the genes that would normally be on that part. As a result, if a woman inherits a defective hemophilic gene on the X sex chromosome that she receives from her mother, the second X sex chromosome that she inherits from her father will provide a "backup" allelic gene that is not defective. She will be a carrier, not a sufferer, of hemophilia (Figure 2.9).*

Question: Could the gene that makes factor VIII ever be defective on both of a woman's X chromosomes? And would this cause her to have hemophilia?

Yes, but this could only happen if her mother were at least a carrier of hemophilia and her father suffered from the disease. Such an occurrence is very rare.

Question: Are there other characteristics in human beings that are sex-linked?

Yes, male-pattern baldness, red-green color blindness, and many other characteristics. In the United States, approximately 8 percent of men and 0.05 percent of women are red-green color-blind. Because such characteristics as male-pattern baldness and red-green color blindness are sex-linked, grandfathers pass on these characteristics to their grandsons by way of their daughters, who are carriers. In other words, if you are a man and are wondering about your chances of having inherited male-pattern baldness, don't look at your father, but rather, look at your mother's dad. If your X chromosome came from him via your mother (a 50 percent chance) and he has male-pattern baldness, you will have inherited his hair loss pattern. If, however, your X chromosome came down from your maternal grandmother, whether or not you inherit male-pattern baldness will depend on the makeup of that chromosome, and a look at *her* father will give you a 50 percent chance of guessing what it is. It gets complicated, doesn't it?

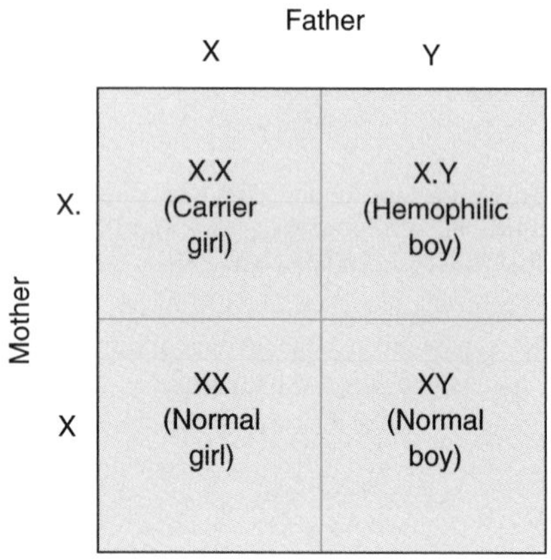

Mother \ Father	X	Y
X.	X.X (Carrier girl)	X.Y (Hemophilic boy)
X	XX (Normal girl)	XY (Normal boy)

FIGURE 2.9
Women typically do not suffer from hemophilia because when they inherit an affected *X.* chromosome from their mother, they receive an unaffected *X* chromosome from their father. Men, however, lack an effective "backup" allele because they do not have the "leg" of the *X* chromosome in which it is carried. Note that a female carrier and a normal male will produce, on the average, one normal girl, one normal boy, one carrier girl, and one hemophilic boy.

COMPLEX GENETIC INTERACTIONS

Not all genetic laws follow Mendel's principles or those of sex-linked inheritance. Many complications are possible. For instance, some genes act on other genes. Such **modifier genes** can determine how other genes express themselves. An example of the effects of modifier genes can be found in the disease **phenylketonuria (PKU).**

PKU is a genetic disorder caused by the inheritance of a double recessive (pp) and marked by an inability to oxidize normally the amino acid phenylalanine,

*Some female carriers, however, do have reduced levels of factor VIII in the blood; although one working gene is enough to spare them from hemophilia, apparently two working genes are better.

which is found in fish, dairy products, and most protein sources. If detected early enough by blood or urine tests, the disease can be controlled by eliminating phenylalanine from the diet. If the disorder is not checked by a suitable diet, however, by-products formed by the incomplete oxidation build up in the infant's body and cause permanent damage to the central nervous system. It is estimated that about 1 percent of the children institutionalized because of mental retardation suffer from PKU.

Even though this disease is caused by a double recessive, children with PKU may exhibit considerably different levels of phenylalanine, and this is where the modifier genes come in. Variations in levels are determined by modifier genes located at positions on the chromosomes different from those of the recessive genes responsible for PKU.

Question: How many complex interactions can affect the mechanisms of inheritance?

Probably hundreds, maybe thousands. Even the "simple" form of inheritance described by Mendel does not take place inviolately. For instance, it is not uncommon for the genes on identical sections of chromosomes to be expressed somewhat differently, depending on whether they are inherited from one's father or one's mother, a phenomenon known as **genetic imprinting,** (Sapienza, 1990). Some instances of genetic imprinting are striking. For example, Prader-Willi syndrome, caused by the absence of a portion of chromosome 15, leads to shortness of stature, retardation, and voracious eating. Parents of such children have to lock the refrigerator, hide pet food, and even keep edible garbage out of reach. Interestingly, if the defective chromosome 15 is inherited from the father, Prader-Willi is the result. But if the same defective chromosome 15 is inherited from the mother, the result is Angelman's syndrome, a very different disease, whose sufferers have been described as "happy puppets" because of their constant laughter and jerky movements. Why this is the case is not entirely clear, since it seems reasonable to assume that identical missing portions of the same chromosome would result in an absence of the same allelic genes. The best current guess is that modifier genes, different in the mother and father, somehow cause subtle biogenetic alterations to these areas, making seemingly identical genetic sections of chromosomes different, depending on whether they are paternal or maternal.

GENETIC IMPRINTING
The process whereby identical sections of the same chromosome will yield different phenotypic outcomes, depending on whether the chromosome was inherited from the mother or the father.

MONOSOMY
A single unpaired chromosome that is located where there should be a pair of chromosomes.

TRISOMY
A chromosomal abnormality in which a third chromosome occurs on a chromosome pair.

MULTISOMY
A chromosomal abnormality in which more than one additional chromosome is associated with a chromosome pair.

DOWN SYNDROME
A chromosomal abnormality that manifests itself in such features as a thick tongue, extra eyelid folds, and heart deformities, as well as deficient intelligence. It is caused by a trisomy of the twenty-first chromosome pair.

Inherited Disorders

Question: How might the developing biology of the individual or his or her genetic inheritance adversely affect development?

Sometimes during the formation of the sperm or ova, something goes wrong, and these gametes end up missing a chromosome or having an extra one. Such an unfortunate occurrence may result in various disorders, including **monosomies, trisomies,** and **multisomies.** Some of these disorders are outlined in Table 2.3.

DOWN SYNDROME

Of all the disorders listed in Table 2.3, perhaps the best known is a trisomy that occurs on the twenty-first autosome pair, identified by geneticists as trisomy 21. Trisomy 21 always results in **Down syndrome** (Patterson, 1987).* Children who

*Professionals generally prefer to call this condition Down syndrome rather than the commonly used Down's syndrome, arguing that the possessive form *Down's* is incorrect because Dr. John Langdon Down, who in 1866 was the first to describe the disorder, did not himself suffer from the syndrome. Still, Alzheimer's disease, Wilson's disease, Cushing's syndrome, and so on, are "professional" terms currently in use, and none of these named researchers ever suffered from the disorder they described. It appears, therefore, to have become a matter of convention as to which form to use. *Down* is currently preferred.

FRAGILE X SYNDROME
A sex-linked inherited chromosomal disorder that produces moderate retardation among males who inherit the fragile *X* chromosome. After Down syndrome, it is the most common biological cause of retardation.

have Down syndrome typically have protruding tongues, short necks, and rounded heads. They also often have webbed toes or fingers, unusual dental abnormalities, or a flat-footed clumsy gait. Although children with Down syndrome are usually affectionate and cheerful, most are sufficiently intellectually disabled to need some form of care the rest of their lives. Approximately 10 percent of institutionally retarded persons have Down syndrome.

Question: Does anyone know what causes Down syndrome?

Although no one knows exactly why Down syndrome occurs, the chances of its occurrence are known to be associated with the mother's age at the time of conception. Offspring who have Down syndrome are more common among older women. For this reason, many doctors suggest routine chromosome testing of the fetus for any pregnant woman 35 years of age or older, so that she has the option to terminate the pregnancy should Down syndrome be discovered.

Present evidence also shows that mothers who give birth before they are 20 have a higher risk of having a child with Down syndrome. The cause of Down syndrome may be related to the level of the female hormone estrogen. Estrogen levels are at their peak in women between the ages of 20 and 35. When meiosis occurs in females lacking sufficient estrogen, the meiotic division may progress too slowly. For a number of complex biochemical reasons, this may result in a trisomy in the twenty-first pair of chromosomes (Crowley, Gulati, Hayden, Lopez, & Dyer, 1979). Errors in the father's sperm may also account for 20 to 25 percent of all Down syndrome cases (Arehart-Treichel, 1979). Further research has shown that the risk of Down syndrome increases for children of fathers younger than 20 or older than 55 (Abroms & Bennett, cited in Arehart-Treichel, 1979).

Out of every 700 babies born in the United States, approximately 1 has Down syndrome (Patterson, 1987). In the United States, over 250,000 individuals have Down syndrome, and the population of victims increases by about 5,000 each year. Forty percent of these individuals have congenital heart defects, and heart

TABLE 2.3

A Selection of Chromosome Disorders That May Affect Development

TYPE	NAME	DESCRIPTION	EFFECT
Monosomy of sex chromosome 23	Turner's syndrome	Second chromosome of 23rd pair is missing (X-)	Female; short fingers, webbed neck, minimal sexual differentiation, often mildly retarded
Trisomy of sex chromosome 23	Kleinfelter's syndrome	Extra X chromosome on XY 23rd pair (XXY)	Male; female body characteristics, minimal sexual differentiation, often mildly retarded
Trisomy of sex chromosome 23	Supermale	Extra Y chromosome on XY 23rd pair (XYY)	Male; tall, acne, sometimes mildly retarded
Trisomy of sex chromosome 23	Superfemale	Extra X chromosome on XX 23rd pair (XXX)	Female; low verbal skills, short-term memory deficit
Trisomy of autosome 21	Down syndrome	Extra chromosome on autosome pair 21	Retardation; unique appearance; high incidence of heart disease, leukemia, and Alzheimer's disease
Fragility of X sex chromosome	Fragile X syndrome	X chromosome of the 23rd pair breaks easily at fragile site	Male and female; males show retardation, females are carriers
Multisomies of the sex chromosomes	(Various)	Among known forms are XXYY; XXXY; XXXYYY	Numerous severe physical and developmental impairments
Multisomy mosaics	(Various)	Rare multisomies of the autosomes	(Various)

Down syndrome is a chromosomal disorder characterized by physical abnormalities and impaired intellectual functioning.

disease is the principal cause of death. Children with Down syndrome often suffer from congenital intestinal blockages and are 30 times more likely to develop leukemia, probably because of a gene on chromosome 21 that is known to cause leukemia if improperly activated (Siwolop & Mohs, 1985). With modern medical care, fully 80 percent will live to reach their fiftieth birthday (Siwolop & Mohs, 1985). Sadly, people who have Down syndrome who survive to middle age invariably acquire Alzheimer's disease, a degenerative brain disorder. For this reason, it is believed that Alzheimer's disease may also, in some way, be associated with damage to chromosome 21 (Patterson, 1987).

Children who have Down syndrome generally have IQs in the range of 30 to 70. Approximately one-half of all children with Down syndrome who are provided with adequate educational facilities can attain reading comprehension at about the second-grade level (Turkington, 1986). They remain intellectually impaired throughout their lives.

OTHER CHROMOSOMAL ABNORMALITIES

Second only to Down syndrome as the leading cause of mental retardation is **fragile X syndrome.** It is believed to affect between 1 in 1,000 and 1 in 1,500 individuals in the general population (Barnes, 1989).

When the X chromosome of people with this syndrome is viewed under a microscope in certain conditions, it shows a distinctive narrowing at a particular location near its tip. The chromosome can easily break at this narrow point. Should the broken piece incorrectly join with other chromosomes during cell division, it can cause translocations of genetic information. Translocations scramble genetic information. Why the X chromosome in these cases is fragile is unknown.

Fragile X syndrome is a sex-linked inherited disorder. Males who receive a fragile X chromosome usually are moderately retarded. Common signs of the syndrome in males include hand flapping, hand biting, poor eye contact, and hyperactivity (Barnes, 1989). Interestingly, unlike the situation with most sex-linked disorders, fully 20 percent of males who inherit the fragile X show no signs or symptoms of the disorder but are able to pass on the disorder to their children! No one yet understands how this unusual mechanism works (Barnes, 1989).

About one-third of female carriers (whose sex chromosome pairs are composed of one normal X and one fragile X chromosome) are mildly retarded. This is similar to the situation in which some female carriers of hemophilia have been shown to have subtle signs of the disease. There are no physical abnormalities associated with fragile X syndrome in females, but these carriers are generally socially withdrawn and shy, and they often have learning disabilities, especially in math (Turner, Brookwell, Daniel, Selikowitz, & Zilibowitz, 1980; Barnes, 1989).

Gene Disorders

Enzymes can now be used to remove individual genes from cultured fetal cells extracted during pregnancy. Before this discovery, scientists were limited to observing gross chromosomal abnormalities—such as an extra or missing chromosome or a fractured or misplaced chromosome—while the condition of the thousands of genes on these chromosomes remained obscure.

Although some gene disorders are directly related to chromosome dysfunctions and are obvious when observed under a microscope (because the larger chromosomes themselves appear to be abnormal), most gene disorders are not so apparent. The defective genes that may cause a disturbance are not visible under the typical microscope and are extremely difficult to isolate and examine. Often the first steps taken to determine if heritable gene disorders are present is to examine the family tree of the parents.

Genetic Counseling Parents who are concerned about the possibility of a gene disorder in their offspring may seek help in the form of genetic counseling. Genetic counseling provides an opportunity to examine the potential for inherited disorders. As noted earlier, we are just now on the verge of actually examining the fetal genes themselves for possible defects. Such examinations are limited to special cases and are carried out at large research universities. Typically, these methods are unavailable to genetic counselors. Even if they were available, only a few genetic disorders have been isolated by these techniques; the genes controlling most disorders still go unrecognized.

Question: Then how can genetic counselors help prospective parents?

Counselors usually help by investigating the family trees of both potential parents. The counselor looks for incidences of gene disorders. Many gene disorders follow Mendel's laws of inheritance; thus, although no one can say for certain whether a child will be affected, the prospective parents can be told the chances that the disorder will occur.

Question: Even if the parents know the odds, won't they still have to gamble if they want children?

In some instances, prospective parents can take direct action based on their knowledge. For example, hemophilia is almost exclusively a male disorder; females are carriers of the disease. If medical tests determine that the prospective mother is a carrier of hemophilia, the counselor may then inform the couple that they have a 25 percent chance of producing a hemophilic male child. The other possibilities, as you will recall, each with a 25 percent probability, are a normal male, a normal female, and a female carrier. Given this knowledge, the mother may choose to have an ultrasound scan of her womb as early as 16 weeks to determine the sex of the fetus (Plattner, Renner, Went, Beaudett, & Viau, 1983). If the fetus is a male, the parents may choose to have an abortion; if a female, they would be assured that hemophilia would not manifest itself. Of course, if parents rely on this method, there is a chance that they will abort a healthy male.

Perhaps a less controversial approach would be to rely on a method of preselecting the child's sex, a technique that is currently being developed and refined. Parents in such circumstances might then be free to choose to have only daughters, which would avoid the sex-linked disorders that only sons might suffer.

Screening and Treatment of Inherited Disorders

Question: What can parents do if the disease isn't sex-linked—that is, if both boys and girls are likely to have it?

Again, the answer depends on the disease itself. If no tests are available to measure whether the disorder is present in the fetus, the genetic counselor may be limited to analyzing family trees and making odds. However, the number of fetal screening tests available is rapidly increasing. Currently, the screening and detection of **Tay-Sachs disease** provide a model program for screening tests of the future. Tay-Sachs disease, most common among the Jewish population, is devastating to the family. Infants appear normal for the first 5 months of life, but then nerve degeneration begins and death follows within 2 to 5 years.* Today, couples may be screened by use of a blood test that looks for a particular enzyme associated with Tay-Sachs disease. If both parents are carriers, there is a 25 percent chance that their infant will have Tay-Sachs (because it is a double recessive disorder). In such cases, an examination of fetal cells extracted during pregnancy will reveal if the enzyme is present.

TAY-SACHS DISEASE
A fatal double recessive genetic disorder most commonly found among the Jewish population. The disease results in death due to nerve degeneration by the time the victim reaches 5 years of age.

SICKLE-CELL ANEMIA
A sometimes fatal double recessive genetic disorder of the red blood cells that is most commonly found among the black population. The red blood cells form a sickle shape that reduces their ability to carry oxygen effectively.

Question: How many diseases such as Tay-Sachs exist?

There are over 100 such recessive genetic diseases; screening tests have been developed for a few of them. For instance, since 1988, screening tests have been used to detect fetal **sickle-cell anemia.** Sickle-cell anemia is a painful, sometimes fatal blood disease common among blacks. It is hereditary and is believed to currently affect approximately 50,000 people in the United States. Fifteen years ago, the only prenatal detection method involved drawing blood from the fetus, a dangerous technique that had a 5 percent mortality rate. Then a new technique was developed called the *blot hybridization test,* which cleaves the DNA from a fetal cell and actually provides a look at the genetic material inside (Orkin, Little, Kazazian, & Boehm, 1982).

Similarly, a blood test was developed that can isolate carriers of PKU. It is used to test individuals who are at high risk of carrying PKU because of a family history of the disorder. Normally, 1 person out of 200 is a carrier. The chances of a PKU baby are still slight, however. The probability of both parents being carriers is 1 in 200 × 200, which equals a probability of 1 in 40,000. Furthermore, because PKU is caused by a double recessive gene, such a union will produce only 1 baby in 4, on average, with the disorder. Thus, the odds of having a baby who has PKU are 1 in 4 × 40,000, or 1 in 160,000.

Perhaps someday all the recessive genetic diseases will be identified and tests will be available for each one. It should be noted that not all genetic disorders are deadly. In fact, some, like PKU, if caught in time, can even be overcome with careful diet. In fact, you may have noticed that products containing the artificial sweetener aspartame have warnings printed on them alerting those who suffer from PKU.

Question: What is the outlook for children born with chromosomal or genetic diseases that aren't fatal but that can't yet be cured?

The outlook depends greatly on the disorder in question. There are unique problems associated with many of the chromosomal or genetic disorders. Depending

*There is an exception to this time frame, however, for the very rare and less severe adult form of this disorder.

POLYGENIC INHERITANCE The control of a single characteristic or function by more than one gene.

on the problem, special medical assistance may be available, such as surgery or physical therapy. Respirators, hearing aids, or other special devices also may be necessary.

More generally, Down syndrome, fragile *X* syndrome, damage caused by PKU, or damage created by a wide range of genetic disorders share common ground, often including intellectual disability. Meeting the needs of the intellectually disadvantaged depends largely on the degree of retardation and its cause. Children with biogenetic disorders such as Down syndrome or with damage caused by PKU are viewed, realistically, as limited in terms of what they can accomplish. However, with modern teaching techniques, improved medical services, and significant community support, many children with biogenetic intellectual dysfunctions are leading lives of greater quality and happiness than previously was thought possible.

It is hoped that specific defective genes can one day be repaired in living people. Certain viruses are known to have the ability to insert their own genetic codes into live human DNA. This is how these viruses survive—by latching on to us in this most fundamental way. Researchers are now working to make use of such viruses. First, the code of the virus is altered to make it harmless. Then new genetic material—say, the healthy code absent from the cells of sufferers of cystic fibrosis (an inherited and debilitating lung disease)—is added to the code of the virus. The virus can then be used to penetrate the affected person's genetic code, where it then implants the attached healthy code to the defective section of DNA, thereby overcoming the inherited illness (Montgomery, 1990). Early efforts along these lines have been very promising and offer hope that heritable disorders now regarded as incurable will eventually be overcome.

The Evolution of Behavior

You are a product of several billion years of evolution. Your body has been shaped by the forces and stresses of those times. This process constitutes the foundation of anthropological studies and evolutionary biology. However, evolution also plays an important role in developmental psychology because the tendency to behave in certain ways can be inherited. Behavior, too, can be shaped by the forces of evolution (Plomin, 1990).

Salmon return to the stream in which they were spawned in order to reproduce. This behavior is passed on from one generation to the next and is therefore "in the genes."

POLYGENIC INHERITANCE

Sometimes genes work together to determine more than one characteristic. This is referred to as **polygenic inheritance** and is another example of the possible complexities that can affect our heredity. Genes involved in polygenic inheritance don't typically show the simple pattern of dominance and recessiveness. Sometimes they work to modify each other, as in PKU, and sometimes their combination results in a totally different characteristic. Intellectual capacity is an example of a characteristic determined by many genes. In fact, most human behaviors that may have an important genetic component are polygenic in nature. Or, as psychologist Robert Plomin has put it, "Unlike characteristics that Mendel studied in the edible pea such as smooth versus wrinkled seeds, most behaviors and behavior problems are not distributed in 'either/or' dichotomies—we are not either smooth or wrinkled, psychologically," (Plomin, 1990, p. 183).

There are many examples of polygenically inherited behavior in nonhuman species. For example, dogs often turn round and round in the same spot before they lie down; all healthy cats bathe themselves with their tongues; robins build nests without benefit of blueprints; and salmon return to the same stream in which they were spawned.

Question: Are these behaviors therefore "in the genes"?

Yes. Just as the bodies of these creatures have evolved through the processes of diversification and natural selection, so have many of their behavior patterns. These behaviors, or the tendency to behave in certain ways, are inherited. They are carried in the genes and passed on from one generation to the next.

Question: What kinds of behaviors are in human genes?

All healthy human beings are born with a number of reflexive behaviors. Among these are coughing, swallowing, blinking, and breathing. However, our inheritance may also shape and control behaviors through more subtle genetic mechanisms. Two such mechanisms have become of increasing interest to developmental researchers: canalization and sensitive periods.

CANALIZATION
The process by which behaviors, due to genetic predisposition, are learned extremely easily, almost inevitably. The more canalized a behavior is, the more difficult it is to change or alter.

INNATE
Inborn; referring to the hereditary component of a physiological or behavioral trait.

CANALIZATION

An inherited mechanism that may have an important influence on the development of human behavior is **canalization.*** A behavior is said to be canalized not by whether the behavior is learned or **innate,** but by the fact that it is learned very easily, almost with certainty, because of our genetic heritage. Washburn and Hamburg (1965) described the phenomenon as follows:

> What is inherited is ease of learning rather than fixed instinctive patterns. The species easily, almost inevitably, learns the essential behaviors for its survival. So, although it is true that monkeys learn to be social, they are so constructed that under normal circumstances this learning always takes place. Similarly human beings learn to talk, but they inherit structures that make this inevitable, except under the most peculiar circumstances.

Behaviors may be weakly or strongly canalized. Strongly canalized behaviors are almost inevitable; they are also highly resistant to the effects of the environment. Conversely, weakly canalized behaviors are highly subject to environmental influences. Figure 2.10 shows the genetic-environmental landscape, which demonstrates the forces of canalization, as depicted by C. H. Waddington (1957).

In a classic experiment that demonstrated the phenomenon of canalization, Garcia and Koelling (1966) allowed thirsty rats to drink saccharine-flavored water from a tube. Whenever the rats drank the water, lights were turned on and a tone sounded. In the first part of the experiment, the rats were exposed to a strong dose of X rays while they drank. Because of the X rays, the rats became nauseated about an hour after they had consumed the liquid. Garcia and Koelling discovered that the nausea taught the rats to avoid the sweetened water but not to fear or avoid the lights and tone. In the second part of the experiment, an electric shock (instead of X rays) was administered to different rats when they drank. Under the new circumstances, the rats learned to fear the lights and tone, but their desire to drink the sweetened water wasn't noticeably affected. It was as though drinking and nausea were "naturally" paired, while lights and sound went "naturally" with a shock.

Perhaps you've had a similar experience. If you accidentally burned your tongue while eating pizza, it would probably have little effect on your desire for that food, even if the burn were very painful. If, however, you happened to eat pizza and then coincidentally contracted a good case of stomach flu, your desire for such cooking might forever be demolished, and it probably wouldn't help much to realize that the food did not, in fact, cause the nausea!

FIGURE 2.10
C. H. Waddington developed this interesting "landscape" to demonstrate the effects of genetic and environmental influences on a child's development. The ball in the photograph represents the child. The channels in the landscape depict the typical directions along which most children will develop (in reality, of course, there are many more possible pathways than are shown in this simple representation). Although all children are different from one another, they do develop in many remarkably similar ways (ways represented by the channels); after all, they are genetically members of the same species.

Although the "blowing winds" of environment (e.g., losing a parent or changing to a new school) may push a child from one channel to another, it takes an extreme environmental wind to force development out of the channels altogether. (*Source:* Adapted from Waddington, 1957)

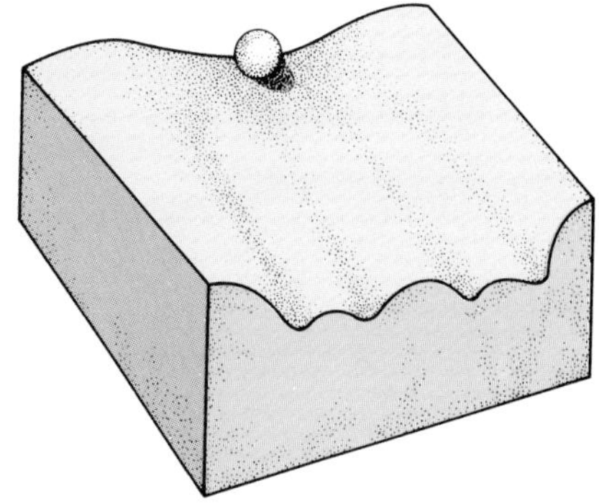

*Some researchers prefer the term *preparedness.*

AT ISSUE

Breaking the Code

For centuries, the "holy grail" of biology was to find the essence of life, that is, to discover what it was that made biology different from chemistry. The answer, of course, was DNA, finally uncovered in 1953.

The next great goal in biology—mapping the human genome, that is, creating a complete guide to the location of every single gene on each of the human chromosomes is now underway. In the Chapter Preview, you saw a string of 34 bases of A, T, G, and C run together. But the actual code for a human being is estimated to be just a bit longer—about 3 billion bases long, actually. Just imagine trying to pinpoint 3 billion A, T, G, and C bases in their exact order and at their exact locations!

In 1986, when the project was first considered possible, it was estimated that it might take the better part of 50 years to complete. By 1989, however, new breakthroughs in mapping techniques allowed researchers to complete in a single day work that used to take months. Once that fundamental step had been made, James Watson, the discoverer of DNA who initially headed the human genome project, asked Congress for more funds, saying, "I have stuck my reputation on getting [an initial general map of all the chromosomes and their genes] done in five years" (Roberts, 1989, p. 424). It is now expected that the complete map, that is, the entire code for a human being, with its *complete* sequence and *exact* order, will be ready by the year 2005 at a cost of about $3 billion. And success may come even sooner because the United States is not the only nation in the race for gene technology; Japan and Great Britain are also making a national effort, and many other labs throughout the world are helping as well. In fact, to avoid overlapping research efforts, Watson has suggested that individual countries be responsible for breaking the code of specific chromosomes. The first such breakthrough came in late 1992 when American researchers produced the first complete maps of two human chromosomes, number 21 and the Y chromosome (Vollrath et al., 1992). Although these chromosomes have now been mapped, the genes described on their surfaces remain mostly shrouded in mystery. As an analogy, you might imagine researchers trying to decipher an alien language. Once the chromosomes are mapped the dictionary of alien words will be complete insomuch as all of the words (genes) will be known, but the definitions of most of the words (what the genes actually do) will remain to be discovered.

Breaking the human code offers tremendous benefits. Once we know the entire code, we will be able to track down the genes that cause diseases like PKU, Huntington's disease, and Alzheimer's disease. But the effort is not without its detractors. Some have argued that if the purpose of the project is to promote good health, the money could be better spent. For example, consider the fact that the greatest threats to children are environmental rather than genetic. For this reason, the case is put that the $3 billion might be better spent to feed and house children or to fight child abuse and neglect than to discover the causes of the genetic disorders that afflict far fewer children (Paul, 1991).

But the effort to map the human genome is being made despite such arguments—in no small part because other nations are also making the effort, and it is feared that

From an evolutionary standpoint, such a built-in, or canalized, tendency makes sense. If an animal were startled while eating a certain food, there would be no survival benefit in forever avoiding that food. But if an animal became sick after eating a certain food, there would be a definite advantage to learning rapidly to avoid that food. The latter behavior can be said to be canalized. And an animal that innately avoided bad food would be more likely to pass this valuable tendency on to its offspring.

Question: What important human behaviors may be canalized?

Human beings seem to learn to use tools with great ease. You drive a car, operate a television, or use a stove. Are you able to deal with these complexities simply because you have a powerful learning brain or because using tools may have given

AT ISSUE

failure on the part of the United States to proceed may mean that important discoveries and their salable technological spin-offs may be lost to other nations.

In a less commercial vein, there is the wonder of having the knowledge—to know the chemical formula for a human being. The pure romance of this thought will also draw us forward into the new world that the code will reveal. With such knowledge, we will eventually be able to settle the long-argued issue of nature versus nurture because we will finally discover what, in fact, the genes do control.

What kind of a world will it be for you or your children after the code is broken? We can't know for sure, but you will probably be called on to make decisions you may never have thought about before. What's more, there may be many problems created by breaking the code as well as benefits won. For instance, one thing that breaking the code will show for certain is that we are *not* all created equal. Take a moment to consider the following situations:

> Ellen spent four years completing her PhD in industrial and chemical engineering. Now, wincing as a company doctor draws a few drops of blood for her preemployment physical, she can hardly contain her excitement about the job she's been offered at one of the country's foremost metallurgical research institutes.
>
> Two days later the phone call comes. "You are perfectly healthy," the young doctor says. "But tests have revealed that you harbor a gene that can result in decreased levels of a blood enzyme, glucose-6-phosphate dehydrogenase. Without the enzyme's protection, you have a slightly increased risk of developing a red blood cell disease if you come into contact with certain chemicals in our laboratory."
>
> "I'm sorry," he says. "The job has been offered to someone else."
>
> When Frank married at age 31, he decided to take out a life insurance policy. A swimmer and avid racquetball player with no previous hospitalization, he felt certain that his low premiums would be a worthy investment for his family.
>
> Weeks later, after a routine physical exam, he was shocked by the insurance company's response. Sophisticated DNA testing had revealed in Frank's tissues a single missing copy of a so-called RB anti-oncogene and minor variations in two other genes. Computer analysis showed that the molecular misprints more than tripled his risk of getting small-cell lung cancer by age 55. His application was rejected (Weiss, 1989, p. 40).

As you can see, bit by bit, as scientists break the code, lawmakers will come face to face with a distinctly twenty-first-century problem: *genetic discrimination.* Now is the time to begin thinking about this and other social problems that might be created by our new-found knowledge. If we begin to deal with these issues now instead of waiting until the problems are upon us, the transition into the next century might be considerably smoother. Whatever our future, one thing is certain: Once we break the code, the world will never be the same.

earlier hominids a natural advantage? If the latter is the case, then a specific tendency to learn to use tools easily may have been inherited. Incidentally, anthropologists have never discovered a human culture that did not use tools of some sort.

In our species, the use of language may be canalized. Suppose that two infants were left alone on a desert island and somehow managed to stay alive and healthy. Do you think that when the infants grew up they would invent a complex language that would include a grammar structure and a vocabulary of thousands of words? It may surprise you, but most developmental psychologists believe that this would happen. Language seems to come so naturally to all members of our species that we may be genetically canalized for its acquisition. Which language we speak is, of course, a function of our experience (nurture), but the fact that we speak language may be human nature.

SENSITIVE PERIOD
A time during which a particular organism is most sensitive to the effect of certain stimuli.

SENSITIVE PERIODS

A **sensitive period** is defined as a time during an organism's development when a particular influence is most likely to have an effect.

Question: Does this mean that there could be times in our lives when we are genetically primed to respond to certain influences and other times when those influences would have little or no effect?

That is essentially what is meant by a sensitive period. As you read other chapters, you may notice that observations of human development often suggest the existence of such sensitive periods. For example, much attention has been given to sexual roles and preferences, but how are they formed? They seem to be shaped early. A study of individuals who desired sex-change operations found that most of these people felt that they had been "trapped in the wrong-sexed body" for as long as they could remember (Stoller, 1976). Is this because there is a genetically programmed sensitive period, lasting perhaps a few months, during which a child is extremely influenced by, and easily attracted to, various sexual stimuli? The answers to such questions are not known; it would be exceptionally useful if they were.

Question: Why would it be valuable to know?

If scientists knew which sensitive periods exist in our species, then we would be alert to them and could ensure that children and adults would be in a position to profit from them when they occurred.

For instance, in Chapter 1, we discussed the effects on children's behavior of viewing violent TV programs. Research has indicated that there is a sensitive period for children who view such violence. This sensitive period seems to occur between the ages of 8 and 9 years. During this time, the effect of viewing television violence appears to be especially influential in directing a child's behavior (Eron, Huesmann, Brice, Fischer, & Mermelstein, 1983). If they were aware of this sensitive period, parents and educators might be especially cautious about exposing 8- and 9-year-olds to violent television programs.

LEARNING CHECK

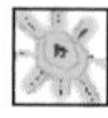

Matching (An answer may be used more than once.)

1. ___ sex cells (sperm and ova)
2. ___ the actual genetic composition of an organism
3. ___ the readily observable inherited characteristics of an organism
4. ___ 23 pairs in each body cell
5. ___ genes depicted by capital letters
6. ___ created by meiosis
7. ___ all of the chromosomes except the twenty-third pair
8. ___ identical allelic pairs
9. ___ nonidentical allelic pairs
10. ___ blue eyes and green seeds but not brown eyes and yellow seeds

a. chromosomes
b. dominant genes
c. autosomes
d. gametes
e. homozygous
f. genotype
g. heterozygous
h. double recessives
i. phenotype

11. Some genes affect how other genes express themselves. They are called _______________ genes.
- **a.** pleiotropic
- **b.** modifier
- **c.** dominant
- **d.** sex-linked

12. When the ability to learn a behavior easily has been inherited, the behavior is said to be _______________ .

13. It may be that humans have sensitive periods during which they are more susceptible to a particular _______________ .

14. Trisomy 21 is also known as _______________ .
- **a.** Down syndrome
- **b.** Turner's syndrome
- **c.** fragile X syndrome
- **d.** Kleinfelter's syndrome.

15. Down syndrome
- **a.** is not a chromosomal disorder
- **b.** is more common among children born to older mothers
- **c.** is caused by high levels of estrogen in the mother during pregnancy
- **d.** is not related to the father's age.

Answers:
1. d **2.** f **3.** i **4.** a **5.** b **6.** d **7.** c **8.** e or h **9.** g **10.** h **11.** b **12.** canalized
13. stimulus (or influence) **14.** a **15.** b

APPLICATIONS

Eugenics: Selectively Breeding Human Beings

In 1883, Sir Francis Galton, a cousin of Charles Darwin, coined the term *eugenics* and attempted to begin a scientific movement concerned with the selective breeding of human beings. According to this new science, selected human beings would be mated with each other in an attempt to obtain certain traits in their offspring, much the way that animal breeders work with champion stock. The eventual goal of eugenics was to create a better human race.

Galton believed that intelligence was inherited, along with many "civilized" behavior patterns. He believed that the upper class of his day best represented these "inherited" traits, and although his hope was to improve the lot of the common people, the thrust of his argument seemed to be that the English upper class was truly better bred. Such a concept was believed by the English aristocracy. The idea that learning and experience might play an important role in determining the behavior patterns of the upper, middle, or lower class seemed ridiculous. Nineteenth-century England simply wasn't ready for such democratic notions. In fact, in 1912, when George Bernard Shaw wrote the play *Pygmalion* (later rewritten as the musical *My Fair Lady*), the plot was quite revolutionary because it was about a professor of language *teaching* a street urchin to pass as a lady of great breeding.

From time to time, various groups and sects have incorporated selective breeding into their social doctrine. For example, a nineteenth-century commune at Oneida, New York, begun by John Humphrey Noyes, tried specific breeding with humans, but the commune's efforts were not well documented (Sussman, 1976). Perhaps the most organized and horrifying efforts to carry out a eugenics program were made in Germany during World War II. The leaders of the Nazi Third Reich devised a plan that, in their view, would ensure the continuance and eventual numerical superiority of the Nordic, or German, bloodline. The leaders of the SS (the *Schutzstaffel* elite guard), under Reichsfuhrer Himmler, arranged for babies of "pure stock" to be kidnapped from overrun nations and brought to the German heartland. There the children were placed in luxurious *lebensborn* centers, where they were to be raised according to the ideals of the Nazi high command.

In addition, special houses, or maternity homes, were set aside by the Gestapo so that the SS soldiers, who had already been selected for their light features, height, and robust physique, could impregnate specially selected women who had such physical characteristics as blue eyes, blonde hair, and wide hips. These women were to bear the children of the future master race (Hillel & Henry, 1976). All "inferior" humans, especially Jews, retarded children or adults, and any individual with genetic defects, were to be destroyed; and so, along with 6 million Jewish victims, many ill and retarded people were also murdered.

Sir Francis Galton (1822–1911)

Nazi "scientific" texts concerned with genetics make interesting reading; they are filled with horrifying misconceptions about human inheritance.

Negative Eugenics

Negative eugenics is a process of elimination. Thousands of pregnancies are monitored each year, and fetuses found to have serious genetic disorders are often aborted. In this way, parents practice negative eugenics by eliminating defective genes (Miller, 1981). Some people, however, argue that abortion is not a moral or justifiable means to control the spread of genetic disease. The debate over this issue continues.

There are, however, other methods of eliminating unwanted genes besides abortion, possibly by compulsory sterilization or by controlling the right to reproduce. Many argue that because the state has the right to quarantine individuals to prevent the spread of infectious diseases, the state should also have the right to prevent the spread of defective genes.

Question: But who would decide who should be sterilized and who allowed to have children?

APPLICATIONS

As a citizen of this country and, in a sense, of the world, you may be the one to decide. The following facts are offered without comment:

A. Laws have been suggested that would require people with IQs (intelligence quotients) below 75 to be sterilized.

1. IQ tests measure only limited aspects of a person's ability.

2. Approximately 80 percent of people with IQ scores below 75 are physically normal and have no history of brain or genetic damage (Liebert, Poulos, & Marmor, 1977).

3. IQ scores may change or vary by as much as 40 points or more during one's lifetime (Skeels, Updegraff, Wellman, & Williams, 1938).

B. A number of years ago, thousands of people in North Carolina were sterilized by law because they were examined and found to be mentally defective by the North Carolina State Eugenics Board (Coburn, 1974).

1. During the 1960s, 63 percent of those sterilized in North Carolina were black, although blacks constituted only 24 percent of North Carolina's population.

2. Black children tend to score from 10 to 15 points lower on IQ tests than do white children (Kennedy, 1969).

3. Many IQ tests have been criticized for asking "white" questions, that is, questions that are easier for white children to answer because of their cultural background (see Chapter 12) (Kagan, 1973).

4. Black children raised in white homes tend to score higher on IQ tests than do black children raised in black homes (Scarr & Weinberg, 1976).

C. A majority of states have had, at one time or another, statutes that allow eugenic measures for controlling the incidence of congenital defects. Many states currently have such laws.

1. Some years back, the Illinois state legislature considered a proposal to disallow marriage licenses to Illinois citizens who are carriers

During World War II, some babies were kidnapped by the German SS from overrun nations and placed in *lebensborn* centers (as shown in this rare photo of an actual center), where they were to be raised according to Nazi ideals.

APPLICATIONS

of genetic disorders or diseases that would lead to birth defects.

2. Robert Todd Lincoln, U.S. secretary of war from 1881 to 1885, might never have been born had such a law been in effect during the nineteenth century. His father, a citizen of Illinois, apparently suffered from Marfan's syndrome, a serious and slowly debilitating genetic disease of the body's connective tissue, which causes a weakening of the aorta and thus heart problems and also results in elongated fingers, toes, and a generally ugly appearance. But then some people are able to endure in spite of their genetic hardships, as did Robert Todd Lincoln's father, Abraham Lincoln, the sixteenth president of the United States (Schwartz, 1978).

Positive Eugenics

Positive eugenics places the emphasis on creative rather than weeding-out processes. With positive eugenics, selected women would be fertilized with the best sperm.

Question: Who would decide which sperm or egg is best?

That's the catch. What kind of man or woman represents the best? Mr. Universe, Miss America, a movie star, a Nobel Prize winner? Or if the best seed were to belong to the most socially respectable people, what about "ex-cons" such as Cervantes, Thoreau, Gandhi, and Martin Luther King?

In 1980, in Escondido, California, a millionaire named Robert Graham decided to begin a sperm bank for couples who might need help conceiving a child (Garelik, 1985). His intention also was to practice positive eugenics in a big way. He decided that sperm donated to his bank should be collected only from winners of the Nobel Prize! If the sperm were then given only to women who could prove that their IQ was in the top 1 percent, then the Nobel sperm bank, so the argument went, could be used to improve the lot of humanity by creating children of outstanding intelligence.

The first hitch occurred when only two Nobel winners agreed to donate sperm. One of these men remained anonymous. The other was William Shockley, who had received his Nobel Prize for codevelopment of the transistor. Shockley was also well known, however, for his controversial view that whites have a natural intellectual superiority to blacks. Going on record as refusing to donate, by the way, were a number of men who had received Nobel Prizes for their work in genetics and related fields.

Some argued that the idea of such a sperm bank smacked of biological elitism. Vance Packard pointed out that J. J. Thompson, a Nobel Prize winner who had discovered the electron, had a mother who couldn't find her way from her home to the railway station, which was about two blocks away! In fact, many illustrious men and women of great intelligence have parents who, on the surface at least, show no particular signs of genius. Although genetics, of course, does play a role in the inheritance of intellectual capacity, environment, it is often argued, may be even more important.

The next problem for Robert Graham's sperm bank occurred when women who applied for his program discovered that the sperm available from Nobel Prize winners was from men well into their 70s. Sperm from men that old are much more likely to contain mutations and genetic defects. None of the women felt comfortable being inseminated by a man in his mid-70s, Nobel Prize winner or no. In response to this, Graham created a new sperm bank with donations from young men of exceptional IQ and achievement.

The first woman to be impregnated through the new bank was Joyce K. She gave birth to a baby girl, Victoria, in 1982. It was only then that the operators of the sperm bank discovered that she and her second husband had lost the custody of two children by her first marriage after being accused of abusing them. On the heels of this scandal, she and her husband sold an interview to the *National Enquirer* in which they described expectations for Victoria that were quite extravagant (Garelik, 1985). Interestingly, Graham's response to all this was that although it "may have been a social blunder, it wasn't a genetic one." He added that Ms. K. had "an IQ of 130 or 140" (Garelik, 1985, p. 81).

Many geneticists have expressed concern about possible undue expectations and unrealistic desires placed on a child by parents who may now believe that they have a preordained "Einstein" on their hands. Such pressures could be psychologically or socially detrimental, regardless of the child's capacity for intelligence.

Question: How do most people react to eugenics programs?

Roger McIntire, a psychologist, once proposed that anyone who couldn't pass a course in parenting at a community college should be injected with a substance that would prevent reproduction. The antidote, it was argued, should be given only after both parents-to-be passed the course. He received hundreds of letters that, as he noted, ranged from "right on" to "*Seig Heil*" (Packard, 1977). What do you think?

SUMMARY

- The influences exerted on human beings by nature (heredity) and nurture (experience) are of major concern to developmental researchers.
- Among the molecules that formed from the early earth atmosphere was DNA, the essence of life. DNA is made of a double strand twisted to form a helix, and it replicates (makes copies of itself). Different DNA codes make different plants or animals or different varieties of the same animal or plant. Every cell in your body contains the same DNA code, a blueprint for your entire body. In theory, a copy of yourself could be cloned from any one of your body cells.
- The internal chemical structure of DNA consists of a series of bases made from adenine-thymine and cytosine-guanine pairs. Each particular section of a code is called a gene.
- The first life on this planet was probably a single-celled organism created in the clay beds of the oceans by a combination of chemicals. From this first life, all other life evolved.
- Evolution is defined as a combination of the processes of diversification and natural selection. Diversification of life began initially when mutations occurred to the first single-celled organism. These mutations led to different forms of life. Forms with favorable traits were able to reproduce in greater numbers and were thereby selected by nature. In the nineteenth century, Charles Darwin discovered this process of natural selection; his theories profoundly altered the conceptions that we had held of ourselves as "unchanging." Developmental psychology has its roots in Darwin's discovery.
- Although modern humans have been in existence for only 100,000 years, through fossil records we can trace the roots of early humans (hominids) back at least 5 million years and perhaps, some argue, as far as 14 million years.
- Genes are located in the nucleus of each cell on small bodies called chromosomes. Each human body cell contains 23 pairs of chromosomes. Because of the process of meiosis, sex cells, called gametes, contain only 23 chromosomes rather than 23 pairs.
- The first 22 chromosome pairs are called autosomes. The twenty-third pair contains the genetic code that determines your sex; consequently, the chromosomes in this pair are known as sex chromosomes. Sex chromosomes are shaped like either an X or a Y, depending on which sex code is carried.
- Gregor Mendel discovered the simple laws of inheritance, including the concepts of homozygosity and heterozygosity, dominance and recessiveness, and phenotypes and genotypes. Many human characteristics, such as eye color and blood type, are inherited according to these principles.
- The Human Genome Project has as its ambitious goal the mapping of the human genome, that is, creating a complete guide to the location of every single gene on each of the human chromosomes.
- Some principles of inheritance follow different rules. In the case of sex-linked inheritance, a disorder or trait tends to be carried by women and expressed in men.
- Other complex genetic interactions include the effect of modifier genes, which control the expression of other genes.
- Sometimes during the formation of sperm or ova, something goes wrong, and these gametes may end up missing a chromosome or having an extra one. Such an occurrence may result in various disorders, including monosomies, trisomies, and multisomies.
- Down syndrome is a chromosome disorder that results from a trisomy on the twenty-first pair of autosomes. It causes physical abnormalities and impaired intellectual functioning and may be related to the age of the mother or father at the time of the child's conception.
- Second only to Down syndrome as the leading cause of mental retardation is fragile *X* syndrome, caused by narrowing at a particular location on the *X* chromosome and the consequent ease with which the chromosome loses a piece that may then join with another chromosome during cell division.
- Although some gene disorders are directly related to chromosome dysfunctions, most gene disorders cannot be so easily traced.
- Couples who are concerned about the possibility of bearing children who have a gene disorder can seek help through genetic counseling.
- Developmental researchers are interested in evolution because behaviors can be inherited.
- Canalized behaviors are those that, because of genetic inheritance, are learned extremely easily, almost inevitably, except under the most peculiar circumstances.
- Sensitive periods are times during an organism's development when a particular influence is most likely to have an effect. Thus, humans may be genetically primed to respond, or learn rapidly, during certain periods.
- Eugenics refers to the selective breeding of human beings. According to this science, selected humans would be mated with each other in an attempt to obtain certain traits in their offspring, much the way that animal breeders work. Positive eugenics places the emphasis on creative rather than weeding-out processes. Negative eugenics is a process of eliminating defective genes, for example, by abortion.

FOR DISCUSSION

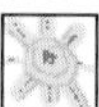

ALIEN LIFE

Literally, there are more stars in the known universe than there are grains of sand on all of the beaches in the world, and most astronomers believe that perhaps half these stars have planets in orbit about them. Exobiologists (biologists who study the possibility of life on other worlds) believe that many of these planets may be very much like our own earth. If this is so, then many of these other worlds may also have generated life. No one knows exactly what this life would be like or even if it would be based on DNA.

If aliens do exist, and if they happened to tune into earth, they would be able to determine our existence (though not our intelligence!) by our radio and television programs because the signals of these programs usually continue out into space after they have been broadcast.

With the reverse possibility in mind, scientists are at this moment eagerly searching for life on other worlds. In New Mexico, a huge bank of radio telescopes costing many millions of dollars is being used in part to search for television or radio messages from other planets. The project is known as SETI (the search for extraterrestrial intelligence). Finding intelligent life elsewhere in the universe would no doubt be the greatest discovery of our time. The alternative, perhaps a sad one, is that in this great and massive universe, through some strange twist of chemical fate, we are completely alone.

The Very Large Array (VLA), the biggest radio telescope in the world. One of its many functions has been to assist in the search for extraterrestrial intelligence (SETI).

QUESTIONS FOR DISCUSSION

1. Can human beings ever be "at odds with nature"? We are a product of nature, so isn't everything we do "nature's way"?
2. Can you conceive of a humane eugenics program that would be just and that would improve the human race? What problems do you immediately encounter?
3. What problems might arise if all eugenics efforts were forever abandoned?
4. Could *we* be aliens? Some scientists believe that life may have started somewhere other than on earth and that our planet was "seeded." Such notable biochemists as Francis Crick and Leslie Orgel believe that such "panspermia" theories merit serious consideration (Crick, 1981).
5. If you could change human genes, how would you alter them? What improvements in our species would you like to see? Are you sure that the kinds of behavior you have chosen are genetic and not learned?
6. From which people would you like to take cells to make clones? Why? Have you considered the consequences of nurture?
7. What kinds of questions might a genetic counselor ask of parents who were worried that their next child might suffer from a genetic disease?
8. Have you inherited any of your parents' personality or behavioral characteristics? How could you know whether these characteristics were inherited or learned?
9. In many states, it is difficult for an adopted child to obtain information about his or her biological parents from state agencies because most of these parents want to remain anonymous. Should such information be made available to the adopted child? Why or why not?
10. The concept of sociobiology was advanced by Harvard zoologist Edward Wilson. Sociobiologists believe that most human acts, even the most altruistic, are ultimately selfish ways of passing on and maintaining one's genes. They argue that parents have a genetic "investment" in their children and will make sacrifices for them to protect this investment. Children, on the other hand, have no such genetic investment in their parents. In this sense, it is argued, children are born selfish in terms of how they act toward their parents (Lumsden, 1984). Sociobiologists believe that this difference is behind the frequent conflict between parents and children. What do you think?

SUGGESTIONS FOR FURTHER READING

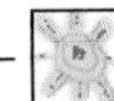

1. Bishop, J. E., & Waldholz, M. (1991). *Genome: The story of the most astonishing scientific adventure of our time—the attempt to map all the genes in the human body*. New York: Touchstone Books.
2. Kevles, D. J. (1985). *In the name of eugenics*. New York: Knopf.
3. Kevles, D. J. & Hood, L. (eds) (1992). *The code of codes: Scientific & social issues in the human genome project*. Cambridge, MA: Harvard Univ. Press.
4. Pierce, B. A. (1990). *The family genetic sourcebook*. New York: Wiley.
5. Swift, D. W. (1990). *SETI pioneers: Scientists talk about their search for extraterrestrial intelligence*. Tucson: University of Arizona Press.
6. Watson, J. (1968). *The double helix*. New York: Atheneum.
7. White, F. (1990). *The SETI factor: How the search for extraterrestrial intelligence is revolutionizing our view of the universe and ourselves*. New York: Walker.
8. Wills, C. (1991). *Exons, introns, and talking genes: The science behind the human genome project*. New York: Basic Books.
9. Wingerson, L. (1990). *Mapping our genes. The genome project and the future of medicine*. New York: Dutton.

UNIT TWO

BEGINNINGS OF LIFE: BIRTH AND INFANCY

Vera Lee, age seven

Unit Contents

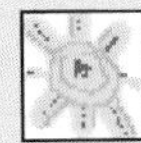

CHAPTER 3

CONCEPTION, PRENATAL DEVELOPMENT, AND BIRTH

CHAPTER PREVIEW

THE LAMAZE METHOD

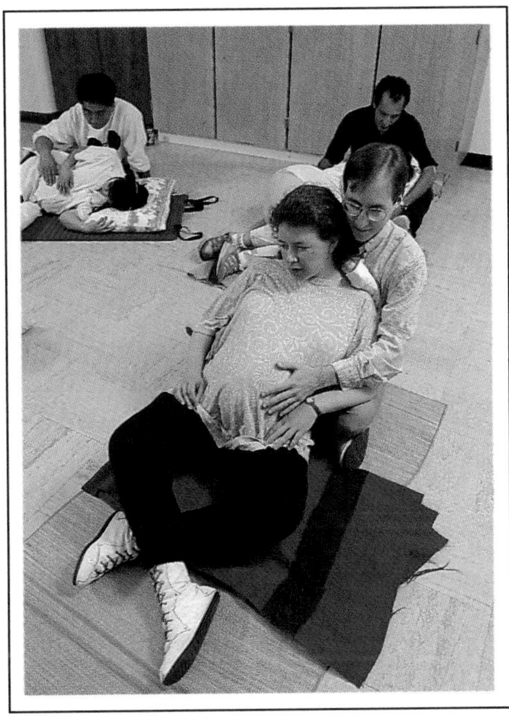

THIS WILL BE her first child. As they wheel her into the delivery room, she is, quite naturally, a little afraid. The father, preferring the traditional role, waits patiently in the outer room. He has two boxes of unopened cigars—one with pink wrappers that say "It's a girl!" and another with blue wrappers that announce "It's a boy!" He's prepared.

AS THE LABOR continues, the pain becomes more intense. She has told the doctors that she doesn't want drugs for the pain, but now she changes her mind. For a brief second she laughs, as she recalls comedienne Carol Burnett's comment on labor pains: "If you want to know what labor feels like, just grab your lower lip and pull it up over your face." Her laughter is cut short by another surge of pain; she asks for an analgesic.

ON THE OTHER SIDE OF the world, a woman in a hut, surrounded only by other women, squats in order to give birth to her first child. In this position, she is helped by gravity. She hopes that it won't hurt much. The other women have assured her that it won't be too painful. The baby is born. Although tired and exhausted, the mother holds her newborn, smiles broadly, and agrees that it didn't hurt as much as she had expected (Mead & Newton, 1967).

DO MOTHERS WHO haven't been properly prepared for birth have more trouble because they often expect it to be very painful? In the 1940s, Fernand Lamaze, an obstetrician, introduced the Lamaze method of childbirth to the West. His method was based on a turn-of-the-century Russian procedure called psychoprophylaxis. The technique is designed to help a woman relax and control her muscular responses and breathing to ease the birth process at each stage.

During the 1950s, another European obstetrician, Grantly Dick-Read, championed the Lamaze method as useful for childbirth. Today there are many variations of the Lamaze technique. Most include the father as a partner throughout the pregnancy. He assists with exercises to improve respiration and relaxation and provides valuable companionship, which can help the mother feel more relaxed and confident. Such companionship has been shown to reduce the length of labor and help lessen fetal distress (Sosa, Kennell, Klaus, Robertson, & Urrutia, 1980). In this way, the father can play an active role in the birth.

Although there have been few controlled experiments to indicate that the Lamaze method is superior to unaided childbirth, the method may reduce the need for drugs during delivery. As you will see, the use of anesthetics and drugs during labor can occasionally cause problems, and any method that can help to lessen their use is valuable.

In this chapter, we'll take a look at the birth process, the development of twins, and the creation of test-tube babies. We will also examine the process of conception and the development of the embryo and fetus, including conditions that may be harmful to their development.

RESOURCES

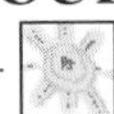

Mammals—including humans—have evolved in such a way as to require both a mother and a father for conception. Who knows. Perhaps people could just as easily have evolved to self-fertilize like some fungi or to fission like bacteria (although both arrangements sound uninviting and may evoke some rather unpleasant mental images). But the complex mammalian arrangement of mixing genes from two parents to produce an offspring appears to have evolved because it leads to diversification, and diversification gives a species better chances of surviving the natural selection process.

The evolution of sex has ensured the diversification of species.

CONCEPTION
The moment at which the sperm penetrates the ovum and the ovum becomes impervious to the entry of other sperm.

FALLOPIAN TUBES
The pair of slender ducts leading from the uterus to the region of the ovaries in the female reproductive system.

Conception

Fertilization, or **conception,** occurs when a father's sperm cell joins with a mother's egg cell, called an ovum. The ovum is much larger than the sperm. The sperm is microscopic, while the ovum is about half the size of the period at the end of this sentence.

Conception typically takes place within one of the **fallopian tubes,** which are part of the female reproductive system (Figures 3.1 and 3.2). Sometimes, though not often, an ovum is fertilized before it enters a fallopian tube or after it enters the uterus. Prior to fertilization, the egg releases a fluid that attracts the sperm (Ralt, et al., 1991). The instant that a sperm penetrates an ovum, a special reaction occurs that immediately makes the ovum impervious to other sperm (Wassarman, 1987).

Question: What are the chances that a woman will become pregnant following intercourse?

The probabilities vary from couple to couple, depending on the fertility of the woman and the sperm production of the man. If we assume that both partners are healthy, the one variable that seems the most influential is the woman's age. In France, researchers studied thousands of women who were made pregnant by artificial insemination because their husbands were sterile. This was an ideal way to study the effects of maternal age on the chances of pregnancy, because the amount of sperm given and the timing of its delivery were held constant. It was found that the chances of becoming pregnant over a period of 12 menstrual cycles were 73 percent for women aged 25 years or younger, 74 percent for women aged 26 to 30, 61 percent for women 31 to 35, and 54 percent for women over age 35 (Federation CECOS, Schwartz, & Mayaux, 1982).

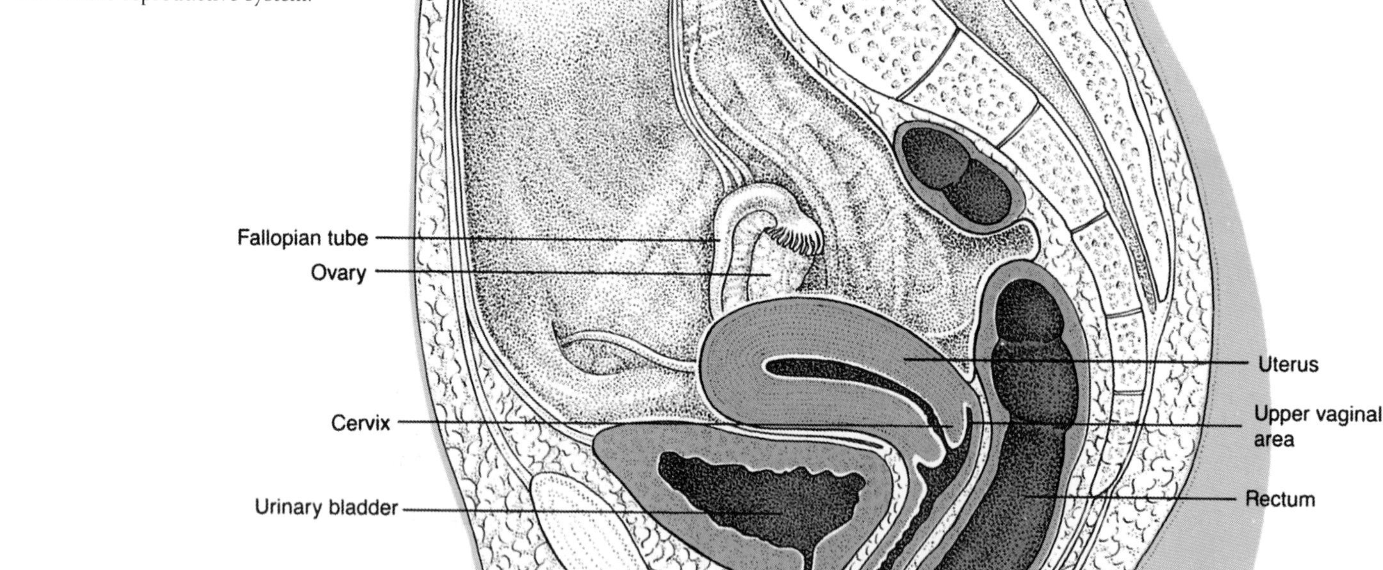

FIGURE 3.1
The female reproductive system.

The primary reason why older women conceive less frequently is that they often fail to ovulate. This most likely is due to changes in hormone levels associated with aging and the simple fact that the body's metabolism tends to slow down as we get older (Silber, 1980).

Another common reason why older women may have trouble conceiving is scarred or blocked fallopian tubes from past infections or **endometriosis** (which may also affect younger women, but not as often). The chances of conception also decrease with paternal age, but much less significantly.

The chances of conception are also influenced by the woman's ratio of body fat to lean tissue. Loss of fat owing to diet or exercise can lead to infertility, which is restored once the fat is regained (Frisch, 1988). This particular mechanism probably evolved because of the survival advantages of preventing pregnancy during stressful times.

ENDOMETRIOSIS
A pathological condition in which bits of the endometrial lining of the uterus invade the body cavity and periodically bleed during a woman's monthly cycle. The disorder is found more often in women over 30 and may interfere with fertility by producing scar tissue that can damage or block the fallopian tubes.

ZYGOTE
The fertilized ovum that results from the union of a sperm and egg.

BLASTOCYST
A stage of development during the period of the ovum when the embryo consists of one or several layers of cells around a central cavity, forming a hollow sphere.

The Period of the Ovum

The ovum, once fertilized, is called a **zygote.** Assuming that fertilization has occurred in a fallopian tube, it usually takes 3 to 4 days for the zygote to make its way to the uterus. By the time it reaches the uterus, the zygote has become a fluid-filled sphere called a **blastocyst.** The blastocyst may float unattached in the uterus for approximately 48 hours.

An inner cell mass then forms to one side of the interior of the blastocyst (see Figure 3.2). This mass will begin to differentiate into two layers. The outside layer, or *ectoderm,* will later form the skin, teeth, hair, nails, and nervous system of the fetus. The inner layer, or *endoderm,* will eventually develop most of the body organs. At a later time, a *mesoderm,* or middle layer, will develop, eventually creating the muscles, skeletal system, and circulatory system.

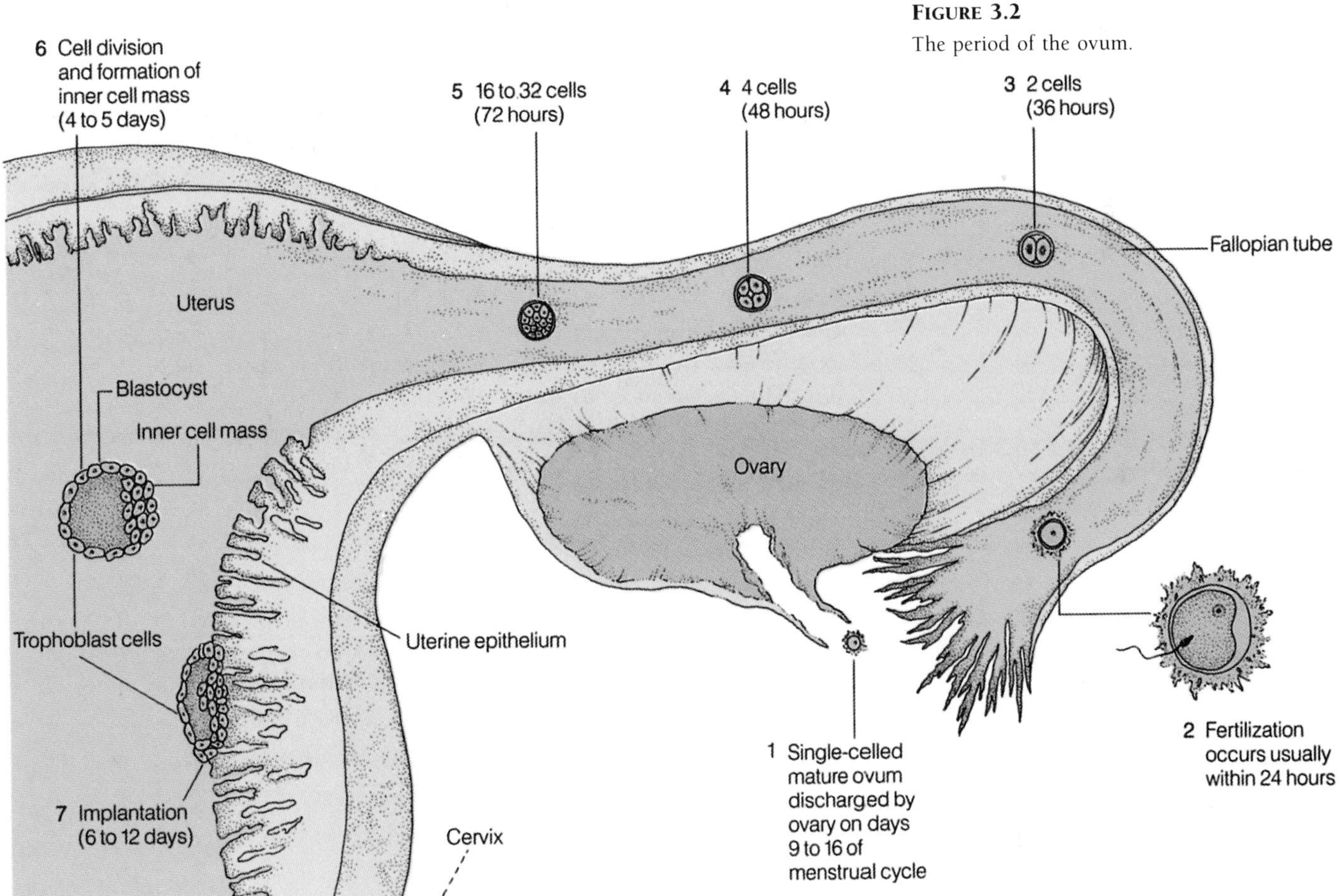

FIGURE 3.2
The period of the ovum.

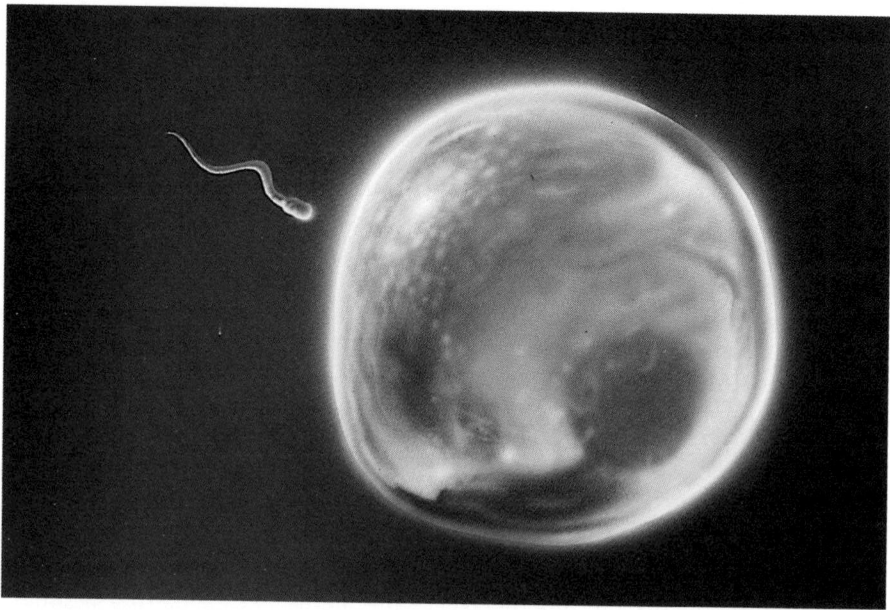

Conception will occur when the sperm cell penetrates the ovum.

Once the blastocyst enters the uterus (which, at this time, has about the capacity of a thimble), it attaches itself to the uterine wall, and a series of complex connections between the blastocyst and the mother's body begin to form. The **trophoblast,** which is the external cellular layer of the blastocyst, produces fine spindlelike structures that penetrate the uterine epithelium, or lining, and begins to develop nurturing connections with the mother's body.

The time from conception until the blastocyst is attached within the uterus, or womb, is called the **period of the ovum;** it lasts approximately 2 weeks.

The Period of the Embryo

The **period of the embryo** lasts from the time of the blastocyst's attachment to the uterine wall until the first occurrence of ossification (the formation of solid bone) in the embryo. This period usually lasts from 2 weeks following fertilization to the eighth week.

Once implantation has occurred, the trophoblast plays a very important role. It sends signals to the mother's body that "a baby is forming," which in turn triggers a protective "dampening" response from her, preventing her antibodies, which normally fight foreign invaders such as bacteria, from attacking the newly forming embryo (Kajino, McIntyre, Faulk, Cai, & Billington, 1988).

Interestingly, about 1 out of every 300 women spontaneously abort because their immune system does, in fact, attack the embryo. Researchers have discovered that such an occurrence is most likely if the father is genetically similar to the mother. In such a case, the trophoblast, which is a combination of the father's and mother's genes, will appear only slightly different from the mother's own body cells. This similarity may result in the failure of the mother's immune system to distinguish the trophoblast as different from the mother. If that happens, the mother's immune system may miss the initial "a baby is forming" message because the message is too weak. If that message is not received, the mother's immune system will attack when it finally detects that something foreign is forming, which then may lead to an infection and a spontaneous abortion.

Question: Is there anything that can be done for couples who have this problem?

Doctors have been successful at helping such couples to have children by inoculating the woman with cells from her husband, thereby sensitizing her to her husband's body cells, which in turn makes her more sensitive to the trophoblast's "a baby is forming" message (Silberner, 1986).

It should also be pointed out that not all antibodies that reach the embryo are a threat. Certain antibodies from the mother, a type known as immunoglobulins, are actively carried from the mother to the embryo by special molecules that act somewhat like miniature ferryboats (Simister & Mostov, 1989). Once the immunoglobulins reach the embryo, they help protect it by providing disease resistance—a kind of before-birth inoculation (Beaconsfield, Birdwood, & Beaconsfield, 1980).

During the period of the embryo, cellular division continues at a very rapid rate, and cellular specialization occurs.

Question: What do you mean by cellular specialization?

Although each cell in a body carries the DNA blueprint for the entire body, during cellular specialization, or *differentiation,* different portions of the DNA code in each cell become active, while other portions go dormant, depending on which kind of cell (skin cell, blood cell, etc.) is to be created. The forces that determine how cells differentiate, or specialize, are not fully understood. This specialization of cells, however, becomes apparent as skin, hair, sensory organs, a cartilage skeleton, a nervous system, a digestive system, a circulatory system, and other internal organs develop (Table 3.1).

TROPHOBLAST
The outer layer of cells by which the fertilized ovum is attached to the uterine wall and through which the embryo receives its nourishment.

PERIOD OF THE OVUM
Time from conception until the zygote is first attached within the uterus, about 2 weeks following conception.

PERIOD OF THE EMBRYO
Time from the attachment of the zygote to the uterine wall until the first formation of solid bone in the embryo, from about 2 to 8 weeks following conception.

TABLE 3.1

The Development of the Embryo and Fetus*

TIME ELAPSED SINCE CONCEPTION	STAGE
4 weeks	The embryo is approximately 1/5 inch in length. A primitive heart is beating. The head and tail are established. The mouth, liver, and intestines begin to take shape.
8 weeks	The embryo is now about 1 inch in length. For the first time, it begins to resemble a human being. Facial features, limbs, hands, feet, fingers, and toes become apparent. The nervous system is responsive, and many of the internal organs begin to function.
12 weeks	The fetus is now 3 inches long and weighs almost 1 ounce. The muscles begin to develop and sex organs are formed. Eyelids, fingernails, and toenails are being formed. Spontaneous movements of the trunk can occasionally be seen.
16 weeks	The fetus is now about 5 inches long. Blinking, grasping, and mouth motions can be observed. Hair appears on the head and body.
20 weeks	The fetus now weighs about 1/2 pound and is approximately 10 inches long. Sweat glands develop, and the external skin is no longer transparent.
24 weeks	The fetus is able to inhale and exhale and could make a crying sound. The eyes are completed, and taste buds have developed on the tongue. Fetuses born as immature as this have survived.
28 weeks	The fetus is usually capable by this time of living outside the womb, but would be considered immature at birth.
38 weeks	The end of the normal gestation period. The fetus is now prepared to live in the outside world.

*NOTE: Obstetricians count "weeks of pregnancy" from the beginning of a woman's cycle because there is often no way to determine exactly when conception occurred. Embryologists, however, typically describe the developing embryo or fetus by the number of weeks since conception. For this reason, to determine the number of weeks pregnant a woman would be from this table, add 2 weeks. In other words, 28 weeks since conception equals 30 weeks pregnant.

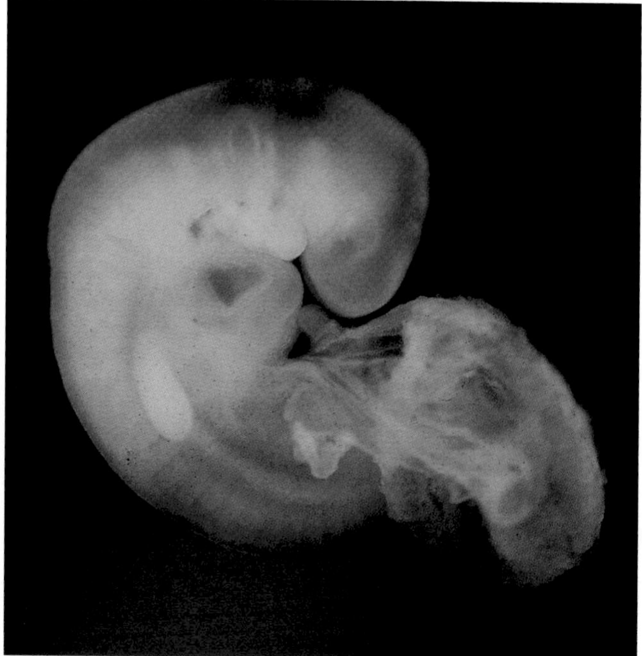
4-week-old embryo

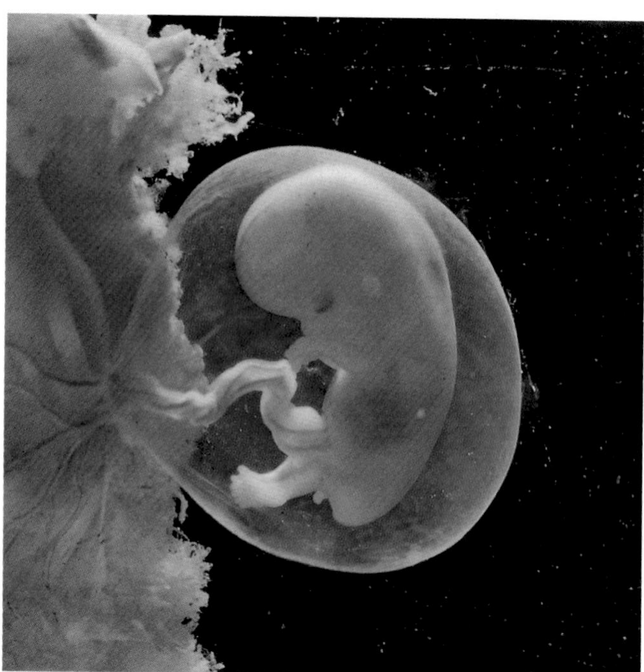
3-month-old fetus

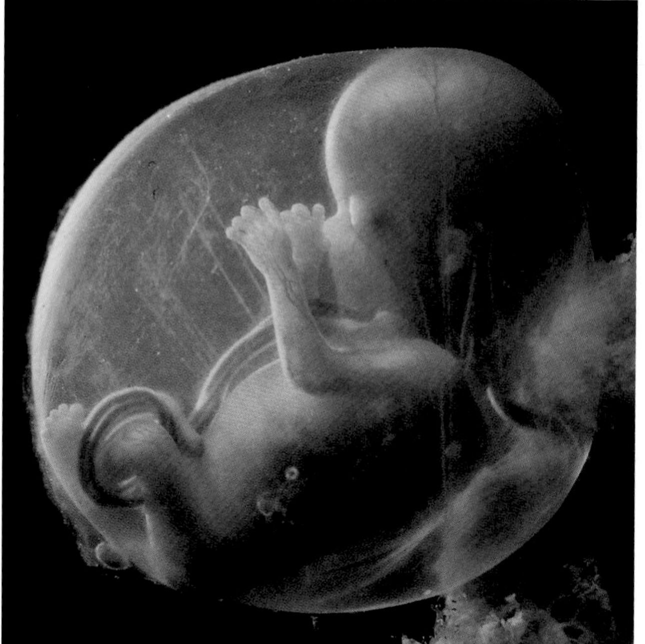
4-month-old fetus

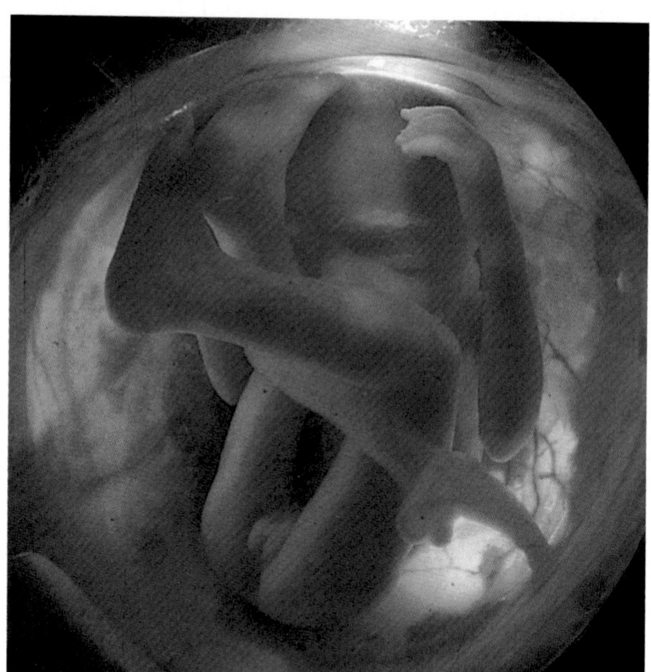
5-month-old fetus

By the fourth week following conception, a tiny vessel destined to become the heart begins to pulse, even though the embryo is only a little larger than an adult's thumbnail. By 2 months, the embryo is approximately 1 inch long and is beginning to resemble a human being. As the embryo grows, additional life-supporting auxiliary structures continue to develop. Among these are the **umbilical cord** and **placenta,** which maintain the connection with the mother's body. It is through these structures that the embryo obtains nutrients and expels wastes. The umbilical cord consists of major blood vessels that pass through the placenta en route to and from the mother's body. The placenta consists of a number of semipermeable membranes that allow only molecules of relatively small size to pass. For this reason, the red blood cells of the mother and those of the unborn infant never mix prior to birth. This separation of blood is essential because the mother's blood type may be different from—and incompatible with—that of the embryo. Moreover, nutrients and wastes can pass through the placental barrier, so a shared bloodstream is unnecessary.

Research has shown that the spontaneous abortion rate is relatively high during the period of the embryo. Approximately 31 percent of all pregnancies end in spontaneous abortion (Wilcox, et al., 1988). About two-thirds of the time, the women who undergo spontaneous abortion are unaware that they were ever pregnant, because the spontaneous abortion may seem to be nothing more than an unusually heavy flow during menstruation.

Question: Do women who have spontaneous abortions have something wrong with them?

It is assumed that the spontaneously aborted embryos are usually abnormal in some way. But there is no assumption that there is something wrong with the women, because 95 percent of women who have spontaneous abortions eventually have normal pregnancies.

UMBILICAL CORD
The flexible, cordlike structure connecting the fetus at the navel with the placenta. This cord contains the blood vessels that nourish the fetus and remove its wastes.

PLACENTA
A vascular, membranous organ that develops during pregnancy, lining the uterine wall and partially enveloping the fetus. The placenta is attached to the fetus by the umbilical cord.

FETUS
The unborn child from the eighth week of conception to the time of live birth.

PERIOD OF THE FETUS
Time from the first formation of bone in the embryo until birth, generally from 8 weeks following conception until birth.

The Period of the Fetus

From the time of ossification (approximately 8 weeks after conception) until birth, the developing prenatal organism is called a **fetus.** The **period of the fetus** is marked by continued and rapid growth of the specialized systems that emerged during the embryonic phase. Cellular differentiation is quite well advanced by the time ossification begins. As the fetus develops, the muscular and nervous systems grow at great speed. Often, before the twentieth week following conception, the mother is able to feel the fetus move. By the fifth month, reflexes such as swallowing or sucking occur.

By the end of the sixth month, the fetus is a little over 1 foot long and weighs almost 2 pounds. Its skin is thin and there is, as yet, no underlying layer of fat. Fingerprints are visible. The eyelids have developed and are functional. As the fetus grows, it becomes more active.

FIGURE 3.3
Ultrahigh-frequency sound scans have proved to be a valuable aid. Ultrasound scans can spot fetal cerebral bleeding and its complications and can identify other abnormal difficulties that may be a sign of developmental problems. Ultrasound scanning, however, may not be completely without risk. Some researchers have argued that ultrasound, in theory at least, may affect fetal cells because of the heat generated by the sound waves. Although no fetal damage directly attributable to ultrasound scans has been documented, the National Institutes of Health have recommended that ultrasound not be used simply for demonstration purposes, to ascertain the sex of the child, or to obtain pictures of the fetus, unless there is a medical reason for doing so.

By the end of the seventh month of pregnancy, a layer of fat is deposited beneath the skin of the fetus. The fetus can also easily respond to stimuli. Should a bright light be surgically passed into the womb, the fetus will close its eyes and perhaps block the light by shading its eyes with its hands. During this time, ultrahigh-frequency sound scans (Figure 3.3) of a pregnant woman's womb may produce a moving image of the fetus hiccuping or even sucking its thumb! The most sensitive of these scanners can resolve objects as small as 1 millimeter in length, enabling physicians to see detail as fine as the pupil of the fetus's eye. A fetus born at this time has a good chance of surviving.

By the end of the eighth month, the fetus is about 18 inches long and weighs about 5 pounds. Development of the brain is especially rapid. Most systems are mature, but the lungs may still need more time in the womb. By the end of the ninth month, the fetus becomes less active probably because it is feeling confined. The lungs are mature. The fetus's length is about 20 inches and the weight approximately 7.5 pounds. The infant is now ready to be born.

LEARNING CHECK

Multiple Choice

1. In human beings, diversification is due mainly to
- **a.** the interaction between the sperm and egg
- **b.** mutations
- **c.** natural selection
- **d.** none of the above

2. The period of the embryo ends
- **a.** when ossification occurs
- **b.** approximately 8 weeks after conception
- **c.** when the period of the fetus begins
- **d.** all of the above

3. The age at which physical development is far enough advanced so that the fetus could survive if it were born prematurely is approximately
- **a.** 18 weeks following conception
- **b.** 24 weeks following conception
- **c.** 28 weeks following conception
- **d.** at least 32 weeks following conception

4. Which of the following is correct?
- **a.** The mother and the infant must have the same blood type.
- **b.** The placenta consists of a number of semipermeable membranes.
- **c.** During the period of the embryo, spontaneous abortions are very rare.
- **d.** The unborn child's heart does not begin to beat until the fifth month following conception.

Answers: 1.a 2.d 3.c 4.b

Adverse Influences on Prenatal Development

A number of adverse influences can seriously harm an unborn child. Psychologists are especially interested in these potential dangers because they may seriously affect the child's psychological development or upset the family or social structure on which the child will have to depend. Unfortunately, the reaction of others to a child's handicap can often be the most damaging result of any birth defect or disability. Because many of these dangers to the unborn can be prevented by changing parental behavior or by altering the environment, it is essential that prospective parents be made aware of them.

Question: How might a parent's behavior injure an unborn child?

Often, though not always, the greatest burden lies with the mother because she has the greatest control over the intrauterine environment. Substances capable of producing fetal abnormalities are classified as **teratogens.**

TERATOGEN
Any substance capable of producing fetal abnormalities, such as alcohol or tobacco.

SMOKING

By smoking, the mother can create a dangerous environment for her unborn child. When a mother smokes, carbon monoxide levels in her blood (produced by the burning cigarette) increase rapidly. The carrier molecule that normally takes oxygen across the placental barrier to the embryo or fetus will choose carbon monoxide over oxygen whenever possible, and the unborn child will begin to suffocate. This lack of vital oxygen may result in damage to the fetus that is expressed later as a learning or memory deficit (Mactutus & Fechter, 1984).

In addition to the danger from the carbon monoxide, there is the threat of the 3,000 or so other chemicals in the smoke that enter the mother's body. One of the most serious of these is nicotine, an extremely powerful stimulant. Nicotine is a vasoconstrictor: It causes constriction of the capillaries in the mother's body. This, in turn, further deprives the fetus of oxygen by reducing blood flow.

Maternal smoking may also affect the ability of the fetus's lungs to grow and mature. Children born to smoking mothers were found, even at the age of 5 years, to have lungs with significantly less capacity than children born to nonsmoking mothers (Tager, Weiss, Munoz, Rosner, & Speizer, 1983). Women who smoke also have a 40 percent greater chance of having a tubal pregnancy in which the fertilized egg becomes implanted in one of the fallopian tubes rather than in the uterus (Stergachis, Scholes, Daling, Weiss, & Chu, 1991). If not treated in time, this condition can result in a rupture of the tube—a serious medical emergency.

But the most damning evidence against cigarette smoking by pregnant women was first brought to light almost 20 years ago by the U.S. Collaborative Perinatal Project. Using data collected from a sample of 50,000 pregnancies at 12 medical centers, the survey discovered that smoking during pregnancy increases the

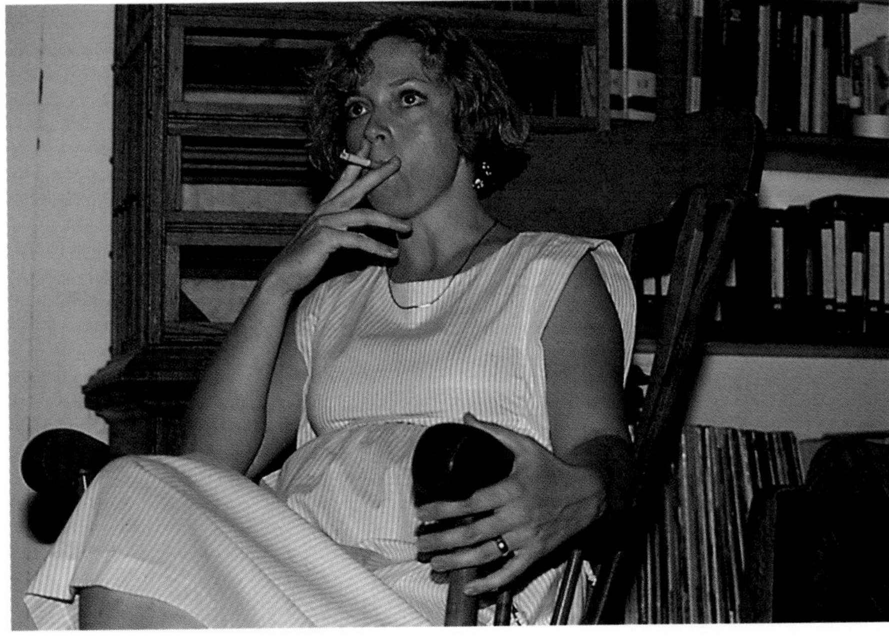

When a pregnant woman smokes, she exposes the fetus to carbon monoxide, nicotine, and thousands of other chemicals. Smoking is associated with low birth weight, which in turn is correlated with high rates of infant mortality.

FETAL ALCOHOL SYNDROME
A disorder suffered by some infants whose mothers have ingested alcohol during the prenatal period. It is characterized by facial, limb, or organ defects and reduced physical size and intellectual ability.

chance of the placenta's separating from the womb too soon and causing a miscarriage. It also discovered that smoking may contribute to the malformation of the heart or other organs in the fetus, again possibly leading to a miscarriage (Himmelberger, Brown, & Cohen, 1978). The project further revealed that cigarette smoking increases the risk of fatal birth defects as well as the possibility of sudden infant death (crib death) following a successful birth (Naeye, Ladis, & Drage, 1976). Furthermore, it was discovered that women who smoked at least 30 cigarettes per day had twice the chance of giving birth to a baby of low birth weight (Niswander & Gordon, 1972). Low birth weight, in turn, has been associated with many negative outcomes, including high infant mortality and low IQ (Broman, Nichols, & Kennedy, 1975). Over the years, many more studies have further supported these earlier findings.

Question: Is there any increased risk to the fetus if the father smokes?

If the father smokes, he may cause the mother to become a *passive smoker;* that is, she will be living in the smoky environment that he has created. This may be a hazard to the fetus. Research has shown that infants born to nonsmoking mothers who lived in a home with smokers during their pregnancies had significantly high levels of nicotine in their blood, a finding that could have been obtained only because of exposure to tobacco smoke (Greenberg, Haley, Etzel, & Loda, 1984).

Also, smoking can affect sperm production. A significantly greater number of abnormal sperm were found among men who smoked than among nonsmokers (Evans, Fletcher, Torrance, & Hargreave, 1981). Abnormally shaped sperm are less likely to reach the ovum and fertilize it. This may help explain why men who smoke generally have higher rates of infertility than those who don't.

All in all, the overwhelming majority of evidence gathered since 1935, when the effects of nicotine on the fetus were first reported (Sontag & Wallace, 1935), indicates that smoking during pregnancy has a high potential to cause harm.

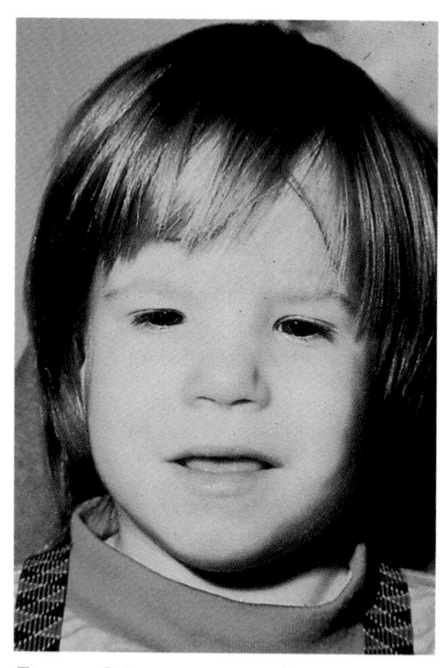

FIGURE 3.4
A child with fetal alcohol syndrome. The characteristic facial features include a small head circumference, a low nasal bridge, a short nose, a thin upper lip, and epicanthic folds of the eyelids. Intellectual deficiency also is common.

ALCOHOL

You probably already realize that a pregnant alcoholic may not be doing her unborn child much good. However, there is evidence that even a relatively small intake of alcohol can endanger the embryo or fetus (Clarren & Smith, 1978; Streissguth, Barr, & Martin, 1983).

Keep in mind that something that may not be dangerous to the mother may do considerable harm to the unborn child; that is, a safe dosage for a mother may be a huge dose for an embryo or fetus. Think of the embryo or fetus in terms of what it is—the most complex chemical reaction known. With this way of thinking, you might consider it a poor idea to dump unnecessary chemicals on it, alcohol included, while it is developing.

Question: If a mother drinks excessively while pregnant, what might happen to her child?

Such children may suffer from **fetal alcohol syndrome,** which is associated with facial, limb, or organ defects (Figure 3.4). Furthermore, many are only 80 percent of normal size or are intellectually retarded. In addition, they may exhibit abnormal behavior patterns, such as irritability, short attention span, social withdrawal, poor concentration, impulsiveness, or failure to consider the consequences of their actions (Coles, Smith, Fernhoff, & Falek, 1985; Streissguth et al., 1991). This legacy continues to follow them into adulthood, often making it impossible for them to have close personal relationships or, in many cases, even hold a job (Streissguth et al., 1991).

Alcohol consumed during pregnancy has also been found to affect adversely the developing brain of the fetus. The brain weight of the affected fetus is generally lower, and specific areas in the brain may be adversely affected (Diaz & Samson, 1980; West, Hodges, & Black, 1981). By the age of 4, children of mothers who drank moderately during pregnancy (on average, three drinks a day) are three times more likely to have subnormal intelligence test scores than are matched peers whose mothers had not consumed alcohol while pregnant (Streissguth, Barr, Sampson, Darby, & Martin, 1989). In fact, 4-year-olds have been found to be progressively more affected in direct relationship to the amount their mothers drank during pregnancy·(Barr, Streissguth, Darby, & Sampson, 1990), showing that there probably is no safe limit of alcohol consumption for pregnant woman.

Alcohol can also damage the muscles of the fetus, which may help explain the weakness so often evident among those infants who suffer from fetal alcohol syndrome (Adickes & Shuman, 1982). Alcohol can also cause the umbilical cord to constrict, cutting off needed oxygen to the fetus (Altura et al., 1982).

Question: How much alcohol can a pregnant mother safely consume?

Research has indicated that even a small amount taken each day—such as one can of beer, or one glass of wine, or 2 ounces of 86-proof alcohol—could be a hazard (Mills, Graubard, Harley, Rhoads, & Berendes, 1984).

Binge drinking may also be dangerous. A woman may produce a child with fetal alcohol syndrome if she consumes a significant amount of alcohol only once during her pregnancy. Alcohol consumption needn't be continuous or often for damage to occur (Sulik, Johnston, & Webb, 1981). In 1981, the Food and Drug Administration published the surgeon general's advisory to American doctors, which stated that women should totally abstain from all alcohol during pregnancy. No absolutely safe level of alcohol consumption for pregnant women has been identified (Kruse, 1984).

Question: But aren't there many mothers who smoked or drank during their pregnancies, even to excess, and who later gave birth to normal, healthy children?

Most women who drink, even heavily, during pregnancy do not give birth to children with fetal alcohol syndrome (Abel, 1984; Kopp & Kalar, 1989). The reports of the dangers of smoking or drinking are based on averages. You have to play the odds. Similarly, there were soldiers who fought all the way through World War II without ever being injured; that doesn't mean the war was safe. It appears that the more chances you take, the greater the danger. Furthermore, risk factors often have multiplicative effects. For instance, one study has reported that the chance of a growth-retarded infant was doubled if the mother either drank or smoked during pregnancy. However, if she both drank *and* smoked, the risk quadrupled (became four times as great) (Sokol, Miller, & Reed, 1980).

CAFFEINE

The threat posed by caffeine to the unborn child is not clear. Initial results showed lower birth weight among infants whose mothers had been heavy coffee drinkers throughout their pregnancies (Watkinson & Fried, 1985). Other researchers, however, have found no harmful effects from caffeine consumption during pregnancy (Kurppa, Holmberg, Kuosma, & Saxen, 1983). Some of this confusion may come from the difficulty in guessing caffeine exposure by the number of cups of coffee or tea pregnant women consume. Researchers have found that caffeine levels vary greatly depending on the brand of coffee or tea and the method of brewing (Stavric et al., 1988). To be on the safe side, then, pregnant women should probably avoid caffeine until the issue has been further clarified.

OTHER DRUGS

Alcohol and nicotine are drugs, of course, and so is caffeine. But there are many other drugs introduced into the embryonic or fetal environment that may cause damage.

Question: What kinds of drugs?

Many illicit drugs and many quite legal ones. Space prohibits a detailed analysis of all of them, but it may be beneficial to look at a few. Many drugs are able to cross the placental barrier and have a direct effect on the unborn child. In one study, mothers who were heavy users of marijuana during their pregnancy (four Jamaican marijuana cigars per day) had newborns whose cries were abnormal, indicating some form of neurological dysfunction (Lester & Dreher, 1989). Mothers addicted to heroin or cocaine will give birth to infants similarly addicted. After birth, these infants actually go through withdrawal, which may be life-threatening. Also, the number of babies born to mothers addicted to cocaine has been steadily growing in the United States. Often these babies are premature, born jittery, and extremely fragile (Figure 3.5). These babies are also more likely to have lower birth weight, shorter body length, and smaller head circumference than unexposed infants (Lester et al., 1991).

Many other common drugs, such as tranquilizers, antibiotics, and anticonvulsants, can seriously affect the unborn child. Researchers have concluded that pregnant women should even avoid taking aspirin (which is an anticoagulant, a substance that hinders blood clotting) because of the danger of creating blood disorders in the fetus (Eriksson, Catz, & Yaffe, 1973).

Some antibiotics, especially tetracycline and streptomycin, have also been found to cause damage to the embryo or fetus (Howard & Hill, 1979). Of course, antibiotics (and other drugs, perhaps) may still be useful during a pregnancy because they may stop a disease that is more likely than the antibiotic to have a devastating effect on the fetus. Sometimes drugs are necessary, and good prenatal care requires that all factors be weighed.

It should be pointed out that only a few substances are teratogenic compared with the number of substances to which a woman may be exposed; in this sense, teratogenic substances are relatively rare (Heinonen et al., 1977). It's important

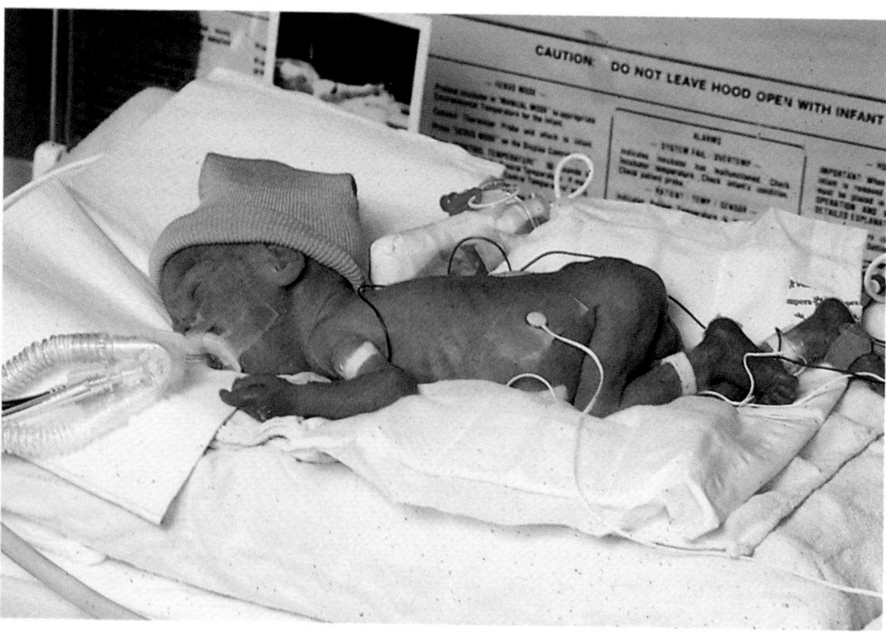

FIGURE 3.5
Babies born to mothers who used cocaine prenatally are often premature, jittery, and extremely fragile. Withdrawal can last up to 1 month after birth.

to mention this fact, because when you read a chapter like this one, filled with discussions of teratogens, it may appear that everything in the environment might be harmful, when in fact we probably need to be alert to only a limited number of substances.

Question: How many drugs is a pregnant woman likely to encounter?

The unfortunate fact remains that a majority of pregnant women use some drugs, many self-prescribed and self-administered. The drugs commonly used that have the potential to cause harm include cough remedies, barbiturates, antihistamines, antacids, cold medicines, vitamins (in excess), pain relievers, and illicit drugs. Physicians and psychologists have frequently expressed concern over this state of affairs because the effects of most drugs on an embryo or fetus are unknown. One study found that the average number of drugs consumed by women during pregnancy was 11 (Doering & Stewart, 1978).

Question: Which drugs can a pregnant woman feel safe in taking?

The use of any drug is a trade-off between the value of the drug, even an aspirin, and the potential danger of taking it. For this reason, it is probably not too conservative to advise a pregnant woman against taking any drug whatsoever unless absolutely necessary.

Interestingly, potential fathers may also need to be careful about the drugs they use. Studies have shown, for instance, that cocaine will bind directly to live sperm without deforming or slowing the sperm down (Yazigi, Odem, & Polakoski, 1991). This implies that a cocaine-covered sperm may well be able to fertilize an egg. It is believed that such a union might have a higher probability of causing damage to an embryo than a union between an egg and an unadulterated sperm. Other drugs may similarly be able to bind with sperm. Studies concerning this new area of research, which until recently had not been seriously considered, are just now getting under way.

ANESTHESIA AND ANALGESIA

During the few hours prior to birth, while the fetus is still attached to the respiratory and circulatory system of the mother, it is not uncommon for anesthetics or analgesics to be given to the mother to ease obstetrical pain. These painkillers may cross the placental barrier and cause a depression of the central nervous system in the fetus, making the fetus prone to anoxia (oxygen deprivation) and thereby creating a potential source of dangerous complications. Many infants who were born of mothers who received painkilling medication show no adverse effects (Horowitz et al., 1977); but because of the possible unwanted consequences, obstetricians and anesthesiologists use painkilling medications judiciously during delivery and often monitor fetal oxygen levels during labor via sensors passed to the scalp of the fetus through the birth canal.

ENVIRONMENTAL HAZARDS

During the last decade, people have become increasingly aware of the potential dangers from environmental hazards such as radiation or pollution.

Chemical Waste Inadequately managed chemical wastes can pervade an environment and make it unhealthy. Scientists believe that such industrial wastes may affect the developing fetus. Of course, pregnant women should not drink contaminated water or live in neighborhoods suspected of being contaminated, if they can avoid doing so. Contact with contaminated water may lower a man's sperm count as well.

TOXOPLASMOSIS
A disease of humans, dogs, cats, and certain other mammals, caused by a parasitic microorganism that affects the nervous system. The disorder is especially damaging to an embryo or fetus.

While it's easy to give such advice, a family with limited resources may find it difficult to move away or otherwise avoid local pollution. In some areas of the world, especially sections of industrialized eastern Europe, pollution is so severe that its harmful legacy may last for years, even after it is cleaned up. Data are only now being gathered for these areas, and the results, when released, are expected to be discouraging.

Heavy Metals Heavy metals, such as cadmium, mercury, and lead, have also been found to cause damage to the unborn (Klink, Jungblut, Oberheuser, & Siegers, 1983). In small amounts, they can be quite harmful to the fetus. This is especially true of lead (Bellinger, Leviton, Waternaux, Needleman, & Rabinowitz, 1987).

Lead is often found as a contaminant of lead water pipes in older houses, *and* it is also found in newer homes where newly applied lead solder leaches into the copper piping. The problem is so widespread that it is probably a good idea to have your family's water periodically tested for heavy metals. (Many such test kits are currently on the market, and many city or county governments will conduct such tests in your home for the asking or for a minimal fee.) If there is a problem and bottled water is not a reasonable alternative, the water should be run for a few minutes or so before drinking to help eliminate contaminants that may have accumulated in the water that was sitting in the pipe. Lead is also commonly ingested by the use of improperly glazed ceramic or clay dishes, mugs, or cups. This is especially a problem with imported, old, or homemade items, which often contain hundreds of times more lead than is now considered safe.

Lead has also been found in the dust of old houses where lead-based paint was used and in the air from automobile exhausts, although the latter has been reduced significantly since the introduction of unleaded gasoline. In addition, both cadmium and lead are found in cigarette smoke (Klink, Jungblut, Oberheuser, & Siegers, 1983) and can pass directly through the placenta to the fetus (Huel, Everson, & Menger, 1984).

Heat Over the last 20 years, hot tubs and spas have become very popular. Hot tubs and Jacuzzi spas are designed for recreational bathing. Their temperatures are generally raised to between 100° F (38° C) and 106° F (41° C). Very hot water surrounding the womb of a pregnant woman may rapidly increase the temperature of the fetus to a point at which damage to its central nervous system may occur. It has been found that as few as 15 minutes in a spa or hot tub at 102° F (39° C) or 10 minutes at 106° F (41° C) is sufficient to cause fetal damage. These studies were made after it was found that some women gave birth to malformed babies after spending from 45 minutes to 1 hour in hot tubs (Harvey, McRorie, & Smith, 1981).

Radiation Pregnant women in contact with X rays or radioactive materials must also be extremely cautious. As you can well imagine, given the rapid cell division occurring in the zygote, embryo, or fetus, disruption by ionizing radiation can be especially hazardous. Any woman who even suspects that she may be pregnant should inform her doctor before undergoing any tests or therapies that subject her to radiation.

PATHOGENS

Many disease processes can also threaten the unborn child. Here are the ones that cause the most concern.

Toxoplasmosis One of the many common infections caused by microscopic parasites is **toxoplasmosis;** it is often found in humans and other mammals.

About 35 percent of all adults have contracted toxoplasmosis at one time or another. In adults, the infection usually runs a mild course. However, it has a devastating effect on an unborn child's nervous system, often resulting in retardation, epilepsy, or blindness. Every year in the United States, about 1 in 1,000 infants is born with congenital toxoplasmosis, making it a more common threat to the fetus than German measles, syphilis, or PKU.

About half of infected mothers will pass on the parasite to their offspring. At birth, the infant often appears healthy because the devastating effects appear later (from a few months to as long as 9 years after birth).

A test for prenatal toxoplasmosis has been developed (Daffos et al., 1988), but it is expensive and not always readily available. If a woman is found to be infected, however, antibiotics can often control the disease and keep it from reaching the fetus. Should the fetus become infected, treatment in the womb with antibiotics has also been successful. The best treatment, however, is to avoid the parasite in the first place. The best way for the pregnant woman to do that is to avoid contact with animal fecal matter (most often encountered while gardening or changing kitty litter) and never to eat rare or undercooked meat.

Viruses A virus is typically a segment of nucleic acid (such as DNA) surrounded by a protein coating. When viruses enter the body, they often invade cells, multiply, and rupture the cell they have invaded. From there, they continue to spread unless stopped by the body's defenses. Maternal contact with the **rubella** virus (German measles) can be disastrous for the fetus, especially during the first 3 months of pregnancy. Apparently, the virus interrupts some early development. Although the mother suffers only the mild symptoms of the disease, the fetus may be born intellectually impaired, deaf, or blind. Contact with the virus later in the pregnancy does not usually result in such severe damage.

Cytomegalovirus, a virus that can infect the female genital tract, is extremely common in the United States; 82 percent of American women carry antibodies for the virus, indicating contact at some time in their lives. By the mid-1970s, cytomegalovirus was known to be responsible for approximately 3,700 cases of fetal brain damage per year in the United States (Stagno et al., 1977).

Genital **herpes** is a common venereal disease. For adults, it is more a painful annoyance than a threat to health. For newborns, however, it can be extremely dangerous. One-third of newborns who contract either the herpes I or herpes II virus die, and another one-fourth suffer brain damage (Sullivan-Bolyai, Hull, Wilson, & Corey, 1983). Most affected infants acquire the disease from their mother at birth, when they pass through her birth canal. Fortunately, most women infected with herpes do not infect their offspring. An obstetrician who is aware that the mother has the infection can often avoid infection of the newborn by performing a **Cesarean section.** The herpes virus, however, can invade the mother farther than the birth canal and may cross the placental barrier into the amniotic fluid. In such cases, which are relatively rare, Cesarean section will not be effective in avoiding infection of the infant (Silberner, 1985).

The effects of many other viruses on the unborn child, although undoubtedly important, are not as well understood. As was noted in Chapter 2, sometimes a virus can enter a cell and, rather than multiply, attach its own genetic code to that of the cell's. Such viruses are called **slow viruses** because they may take years to become active or have an effect. A number of disorders that may affect prenatal development or that may lead to mental retardation are now believed to be the result of slow viruses.

Perhaps the most deadly viral infection to which the fetus might be exposed is the one that causes **AIDS,** a lethal immune system disorder. This virus is thought to cross the placenta of infected mothers and infect the fetus. Of women who are infected, the chances of their babies being similarly infected is about 50 percent.

RUBELLA
A viral infection, commonly known as German measles, that has a serious effect on an unborn child, especially if contracted by the mother during the first trimester.

CYTOMEGALOVIRUS
A common virus to which a majority of American women have been exposed at some time in their lives. An active infection in a pregnant mother may cause harm to the unborn child.

HERPES
A disease caused by a number of viruses that can attack the skin or mucous membranes. Genital herpes is difficult to treat and can harm an infant who is born to a mother whose herpes is in an active stage.

CESAREAN SECTION
A surgical incision through the abdominal wall and uterus, performed to extract a fetus.

SLOW VIRUS
A virus that may take years to produce symptoms. Slow viruses have been implicated in some forms of mental retardation.

AIDS (ACQUIRED IMMUNE DEFICIENCY SYNDROME)
A human retrovirus type HIV, which is transmitted sexually through the exchange of bodily fluids or by shared needle use among infected IV (intravenous) drug abusers. The disease may also be passed by infusion of unscreened blood or blood products. Once the disease process occurs, the immune system fails and death follows. The virus may infect an unborn child by crossing the placental barrier of an infected mother.

Babies who are infected this way are "born dying" and usually succumb during infancy or early childhood.

Rh FACTOR INCOMPATIBILITY

Sometimes the disease process may be caused by genetics rather than external pathogens. One such example is Rh protein factor incompatibility. Rh stands for rhesus, the species of monkey in which this protein factor was first discovered. Eighty-five percent of the population is Rh positive; that is, the factor exists in their blood. Positive is a dominant trait, while negative is recessive. People who are Rh negative are therefore double recessives (see Chapter 2).

Question: What kinds of problems can occur because of the Rh factor?

A problem may occur only if the father is Rh positive and the mother is Rh negative. If their union produces an Rh positive baby, the fetus will possess the Rh factor that the mother does not have. There is generally no difficulty with the first baby, but when it is born, if its blood mixes with the mother's during birth, which is quite common, the mother's body reacts to the infant's foreign Rh factor by creating antibodies as a defense. If another child is conceived and if it, too, is Rh positive, the mother's body, having been sensitized by the first birth, may recognize her own fetus as foreign and begin to attack it. This is one of the few instances in which the mother's antibodies may attack the fetus. If, through a blood test, physicians are aware of the problem ahead of time, they may use drugs to minimize any damage from Rh incompatibility.

MATERNAL DIET

Malnourishment, as a single variable, is quite difficult to separate out from generally poor prenatal care, poor sanitation, and lack of adequate shelter (Stechler & Halton, 1982). For example, many studies conducted immediately following World War II strongly indicated that malnourished pregnant women were more likely to give birth to infants who were underweight and at greater than normal risk for developmental disorders. Unfortunately, as is so often the case in naturalistic research, it was impossible to separate the effects of malnourishment from those of the stresses of war. Nonetheless, malnourishment by itself appears to have a deleterious effect on a developing embryo or fetus. Women who were starved during World War II typically gave birth to underweight infants, and of these infants who were girls, they, too, once adults, gave birth to underweight infants, even though they themselves received proper nourishment (Diamond, 1990). In this way, the malnourishment of the grandmother during pregnancy is a legacy passed on even to her grandchildren.

Even when studies control for premature birth, they indicate that malnourished mothers tend to have children who weigh less at birth. Malnourishment doesn't necessarily mean starvation, either. Some maternal diets, while containing sufficient calories, are lacking in important nutrients and vitamins. One study of over 20,000 pregnant women in Boston revealed that diets low in folic acid resulted in underweight babies (Diamond, 1990). For this reason, it is advisable for pregnant women to take vitamin supplements.* Vitamin supplements taken during pregnancy have also been shown to significantly reduce the probability of birth defects (Fackelmann, 1991).

---

*If you are pregnant, be sure that your doctor approves of your choice of vitamin supplements before you take any (some supplements are better than others in terms of content and dosage). Your doctor will probably supply you with vitamins especially formulated for pregnant women.

EMOTIONAL STRESS

It is extremely difficult to evaluate the effects of maternal emotional stress on the developing fetus because it is so hard to eliminate this one factor from all the others associated with women under stress, such as malnutrition, poor health, or drug use (Stechler & Halton, 1982). It is known that stress in the mother stimulates the production of adrenaline, which causes capillary constriction and diverts the blood flow from the uterus to other organs of the body. Sufficient stress over enough time might conceivably deprive the fetus of needed oxygen and cause damage in that way.

Question: Are stressed mothers more likely to have problems with their pregnancies?

In one of the few carefully controlled studies to isolate anxiety as a central factor during pregnancy, it was found that mothers who were most anxious were significantly more likely to give birth to premature infants or infants of low birth weight than were mothers who were less anxious (Lobel, Dunkel-Schetter, & Schimshaw, 1992).

Some preliminary studies have also associated job-related stress in pregnant women with low birth weight in their infants (Katz, Jenkins, Haley, & Bowes, 1991). Low birth weight is a major factor in infant mortality.

As was noted in the Chapter Preview, birth complications seem to be lessened by the supportive companionship of a close friend or spouse during labor. In fact, one study reported that labor time for mothers who were presumably less anxious because they were supported by a companion was less than half that of women in the control group, who received no such support. The control group's mean length of labor was 19.3 hours; the experimental group's mean length of labor was only 8.7 hours (Sosa, Kennell, Klaus, Robertson, & Urrutia, 1980).

Question: With so many things that can go wrong, pregnancy sounds frightening. Is there really a need to be so concerned?

The purpose of discussing the dangers faced by an unborn child is not to make you overly concerned about pregnancy. After all, most pregnancies go well. The purpose is to alert you to the need for reasonable care. Parents will often spend more time in preparing the baby's new room than they will in discovering the few precautions they might observe to ensure their future baby's physical health and psychological well-being. By being cautious, you lessen the probability of encountering or creating physical or developmental handicaps that can disrupt the child's life or interfere with the early relationships between child and care giver.

Detection of Prenatal Defects

Question: If something is wrong with the developing embryo or fetus, is there any way to know?

Although it is not possible to know for sure if the embryo or fetus is healthy, there are ways to discover a number of serious problems prior to birth. When a woman is between the fourteenth and sixteenth weeks of a pregnancy, **amniocentesis** may be performed to examine the chromosomes of the fetus developing within her. The process involves inserting a hollow needle into the woman's abdomen, through which some of the amniotic fluid that surrounds the fetus is drawn out (Figure 3.6). Body cells shed by the fetus are usually drawn out with the fluid. These cells are then incubated and stained so that the chromosomes can be examined easily. Another method for obtaining this chromosomal information is called **chorionic villi sampling (CVS).** In this technique, fetal cells are

AMNIOCENTESIS
A medical procedure wherein fetal cells are removed from the amniotic sac at about the sixteenth week of pregnancy by use of a syringe. The technique is used to screen for genetic and chromosomal abnormalities.

CHORIONIC VILLI SAMPLING
A technique in which a few cells are removed from the chorionic sac that surrounds the embryo via the use of a plastic catheter inserted through the vagina. The cells may then be examined for chromosomal or genetic disorders.

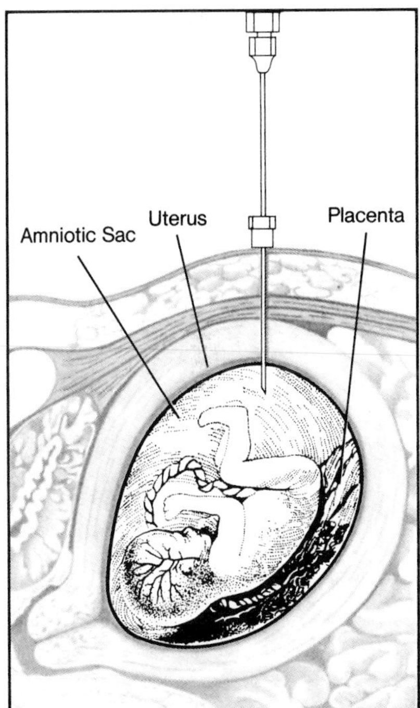

FIGURE 3.6
Amniocentesis may be performed to examine fetal cells for disease or life-shortening disorders. During the procedure, a hollow needle is inserted through the uterus into the amniotic sac surrounding the fetus. Fluid containing fetal cells is withdrawn through the needle.

removed through the birth canal without use of a needle at about the tenth week of pregnancy (eighth week since conception). Such techniques are most often used when it is suspected that a chromosomal disorder may exist in the fetus.

Many inherited and noninherited disorders can affect the fetus. The karyotype obtained (see Chapter 2) will also reveal the sex of the child-to-be. There are risks involved in the use of these techniques, however, as both amniocentesis and CVS can cause miscarriage. For CVS, the risk is about 1 to 2 percent and for amniocentesis, the risk is about 0.5 percent. CVS has an advantage of providing results much earlier, when an abortion is easier and safer, but amniocentesis can provide somewhat more information about the fetus. For this reason, doctors often will weigh the risks and benefits before recommending either procedure (Figure 3.7).

Within the next few years, however, a new technique should remove all of the risk from this kind of assessment. The new technique is called *flow cytometry with fluorescent in situ hybridization*, or "flow with FISH" for short. It appears that an extremely small amount of fetal blood will normally leak into the mother's bloodstream, but not enough to cause her body to react (there is only about 1 fetal blood cell present for every 20 million maternal blood cells). With this new technique, a blood sample is taken from the mother's arm and processed through a flow cytometer, which uses a beam of laser light to sort blood cells thousands of times more rapidly than any lab technician with a microscope could hope to do.

The fetal blood cells are then given the FISH treatment; that is, they are chemically tagged with a fluorescent dye that highlights the chromosomes when they are exposed to ultra-violet light. The technique is experimental, but it appears to work well (Price et al., 1991) and has already diagnosed one case of trisomy 18, which causes severe mental retardation, in a blood sample taken from a pregnant volunteer. The first full clinical trials of the technique should be ready to begin by 1994.

Question: What causes chromosomal disorders?

Sometimes during meiosis something goes wrong, and the gametes formed may end up having missing or extra chromosomes. Such an unfortunate occurrence may result in the various kinds of disorders discussed in Chapter 2. Should the fetus be found to be severely defective, its parents might choose to abort the pregnancy. Women who are pregnant and in their 30s or 40s should know that only chromosome-related birth defects (which account for about one-quarter of

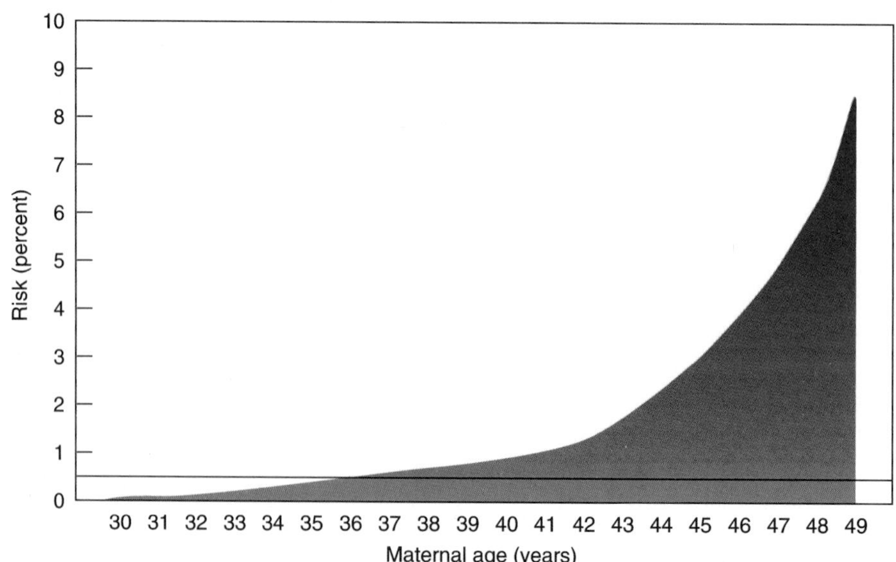

FIGURE 3.7

Maternal risk of producing a trisomy 21 Down syndrome child (see Chapter 17) among mothers of different ages. (Down syndrome is the most common cause of mental retardation, accounting for 10 percent of all retarded children.) The dark line drawn at the .5 percent risk level represents the chance of accidentally producing a miscarriage through use of amniocentesis. As you can see, by the maternal age of 36 years, the mother's risk of producing a Down syndrome child outweighs the risk posed by amniocentesis. Many physicians, however, advocate the use of amniocentesis for all women 35 or older, because many other chromosomal disorders besides Down syndrome can be detected by amniocentesis. (*Source:* Adapted from Fuchs, 1980)

all birth defects) increase in likelihood with maternal age. The vast majority of birth defects are no more likely for older mothers than for younger ones (Baird, Sadovnick, & Yee, 1991).

Parental Planning

By planning when to have children and how many to have, couples may lessen the chances of birth defects. The World Health Organization has provided the following advice for parents:

1. Women who bear children should be in their 20s. (Chromosomal abnormalities are least likely to occur in this age range, probably because hormone levels are higher than at other ages.)
2. Men who father children should be between 20 and 55 years of age. (Chromosomal abnormalities are least likely to occur to children fathered by men in this age range.)
3. Pregnancies should be at least 2 years apart (to give the woman's body a chance to recover).
4. Women should limit themselves to five births (to limit wear and tear on the uterus).
5. Women should seek competent prenatal care from the moment they realize they are pregnant.

Labor and Delivery

For 9 months, the unborn child has been developing within the womb. Now the fetus is prepared to make an exit. **Birth** in human beings typically occurs 270 days after conception, near the end of a full 9 months. Shortly before birth (typically a few weeks for first births but sometimes only a few hours for later pregnancies), the fetus usually rotates into a head-downward position. This movement is referred to as **lightening** because it releases pressure on the mother's abdomen.

For women giving birth for the first time, **labor** will usually last between 12 and 24 hours, with an average of 14 hours. However, for women who have given birth before, labor usually averages only 6 hours.

BIRTH
The passage of a child from the uterus to outside the mother's body.

LIGHTENING
The rotation of the fetus into a head-downward position prior to birth.

LABOR
The physical efforts of childbirth; parturition.

First Stage

Question: What are the first signs of labor?

Labor is commonly divided into three stages that typically overlap each other. During the first stage, which lasts, on the average, about 13 hours for a woman having her first child, uterine contractions begin. These contractions are usually spaced from 10 to 20 minutes apart. Initially the contractions are gentle, but they tend to become more powerful and sometimes uncomfortable.

Question: When should the mother go to the hospital?

Some mothers prefer not to use hospital facilities and instead give birth at home, usually with a midwife or physician present to help with the delivery. However, from 10 to 15 percent of deliveries do require special help. For this reason, unless complete facilities can be made available in the home, doctors usually recommend that mothers be in the hospital within a few hours after the beginning of labor.

Second Stage

The second stage of labor usually lasts about 90 minutes. During this stage, the cervix opens sufficiently and the baby begins to move down the birth canal. At this point, if the mother has been well prepared, she may use her abdominal

Birthing Bar
A horizontal bar, often placed across the birthing bed, which is used to help a woman in labor take a squatting position to facilitate delivery.

Catecholamines
Hormones that can affect the sympathetic nervous system; they are secreted by the medulla of the adrenal glands.

Breech Birth
A vaginal delivery during which the buttocks or feet of the fetus appear first.

Shoulder Presentation
During birth, the presentation of the shoulder first, rather than the head.

muscles to help push the baby along. This second stage of labor may often be shortened considerably by having the mother give birth in a vertical position, for example, by using a bed or room especially designed to include a **birthing bar** (Figure 3.8). When the mother is upright, gravity helps the baby move down the birth canal. Although the second stage of labor usually takes about 90 minutes, the average time in an upright position is only 30 minutes (Clark & Gosnell, 1981). At the end of the second stage of labor, the baby is born.

Birth

During birth, the human fetus is forced through the birth canal under extreme pressure and is intermittently deprived of oxygen. During this time, the baby secretes the hormones adrenaline and noradrenaline, collectively classified as **catecholamines,** at levels that are higher than they are likely to be at any other time throughout his or her life (Lagercrantz & Slotkin, 1986). Adrenaline helps open up the lungs, dry out the bronchi, and thus achieve the switch from a liquid to an air environment. Noradrenaline, which is especially prevalent, slows the heartbeat, enabling the fetus to withstand fairly lengthy oxygen deprivation. Babies delivered by Cesarean section, which we will discuss shortly, are brought out of the mother surgically and do not pass through the birth canal. Interestingly, these infants often have respiratory problems. One reason for such problems might be that the infant has not benefited from the usual stress of birth (Lagercrantz & Slotkin, 1986)!

Question: Are all babies born in the head-first position?

About 97 percent of babies are born in the head-first position (Figure 3.9). However, 2.4 percent are born rump first; this is called a **breech birth.** During a breech birth, great care must be taken to avoid damage to the baby's head, which is the largest and most difficult part of the infant's body to pass through the birth canal. An even rarer occurrence is the **shoulder presentation.** This occurs in only 1 birth out of 200. The shoulder presentation is extremely dangerous because the baby must be forced by the attendants into a breech position. This forcing can rupture the uterus, which may cause the death of the infant and severe hemorrhaging in the mother.

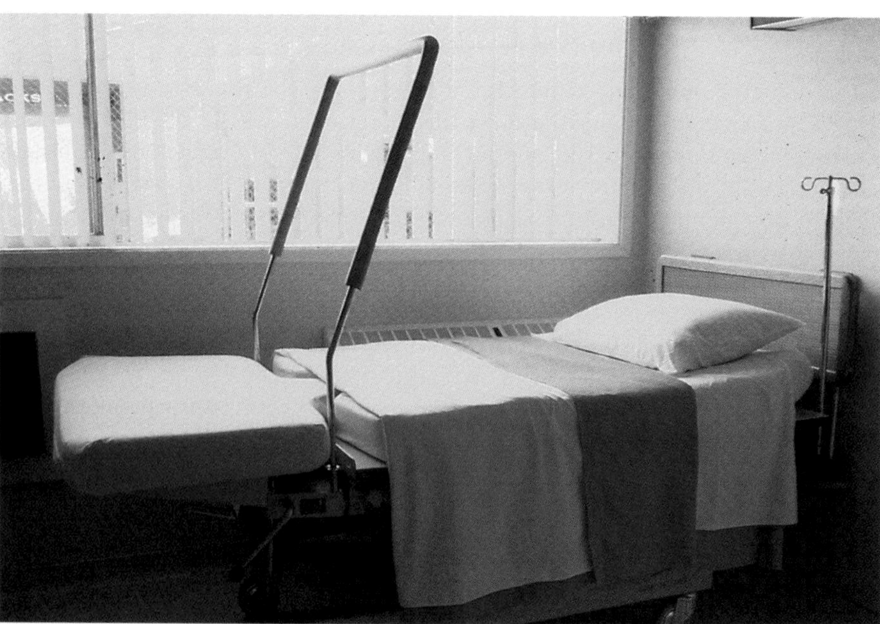

Figure 3.8

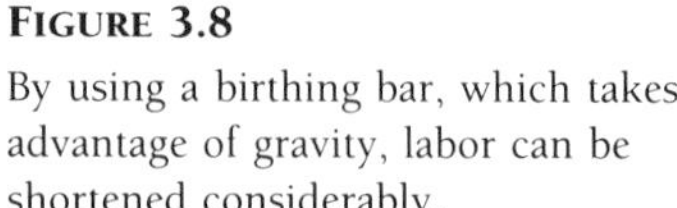

By using a birthing bar, which takes advantage of gravity, labor can be shortened considerably.

Another dangerous problem that can occur during birth is **anoxia.** Anoxia can occur if the placenta detaches prematurely, if the umbilical cord is pinched or tangled, if the infant's head is injured to the point of hemorrhaging, or if the mother has been too heavily sedated during labor. If there is a problem during birth, the child may be removed from the uterus by Cesarean section. Approximately 23 percent of all births in the United States are Cesarean sections (Entwisle & Alexander, 1987). In this procedure, the mother's abdomen is opened surgically and the baby is removed without passing through the vaginal canal. The surgical incision is then closed as it would be after any other surgical procedure.

Anoxia
A pathological deficiency in oxygen.

Whenever possible, obstetricians use special surgical incisions in the uterus so that a woman who has had one Cesarean section may later deliver babies vaginally. With the old Cesarean technique (when a vertical incision was used), once the incision was made and the uterine wall weakened, it was necessary to have any future babies also delivered by Cesarean. It should be noted, however, that women giving birth vaginally for the first time should expect labor to last as long as a typical first-time labor, regardless of how many babies they may have previously had by Cesarean section (Chazotte, Madden, & Cohen, 1990). In addition, some obstetricians have recommended that Cesarean sections not be used routinely if breech birth or labor problems begin. They argue that breech births for low-weight babies, especially if the obstetrician is skilled, may present no difficulty and that abnormal labor of and by itself is not sufficient cause for a Cesarean section. When it is necessary, however, Cesarean section can be a lifesaver for both infant and mother.

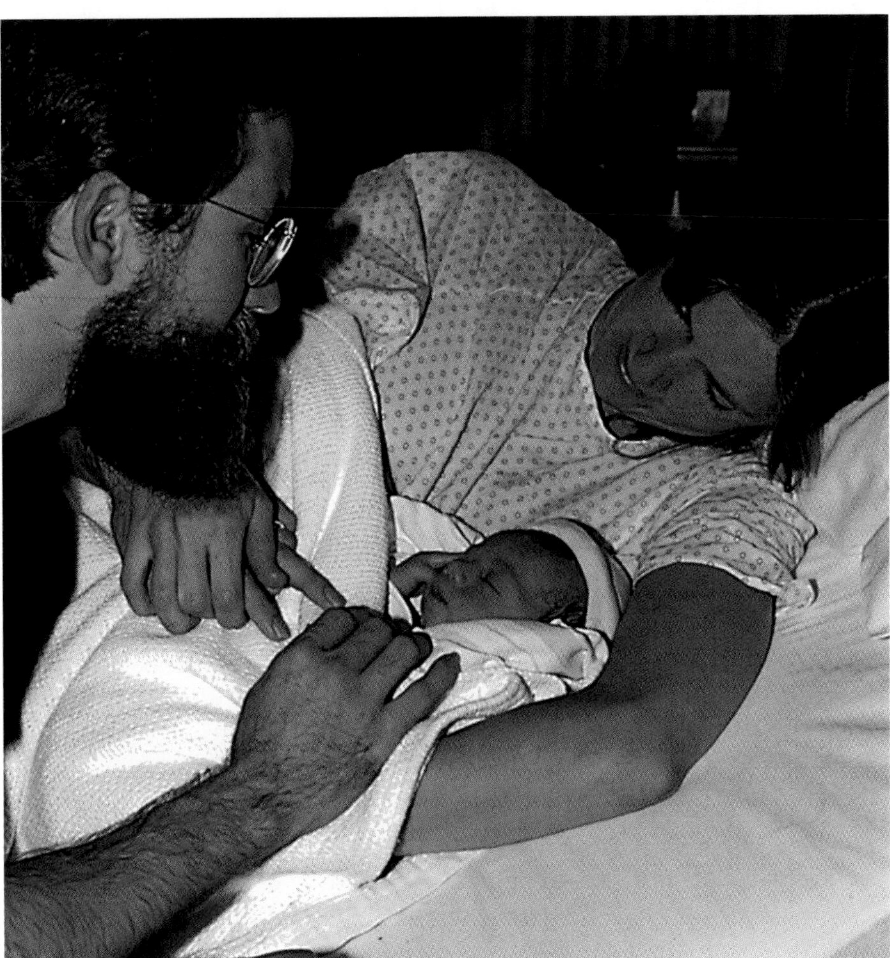

When the father or other caring companion is present during delivery, the mother's anxiety may be reduced and the length of labor shortened.

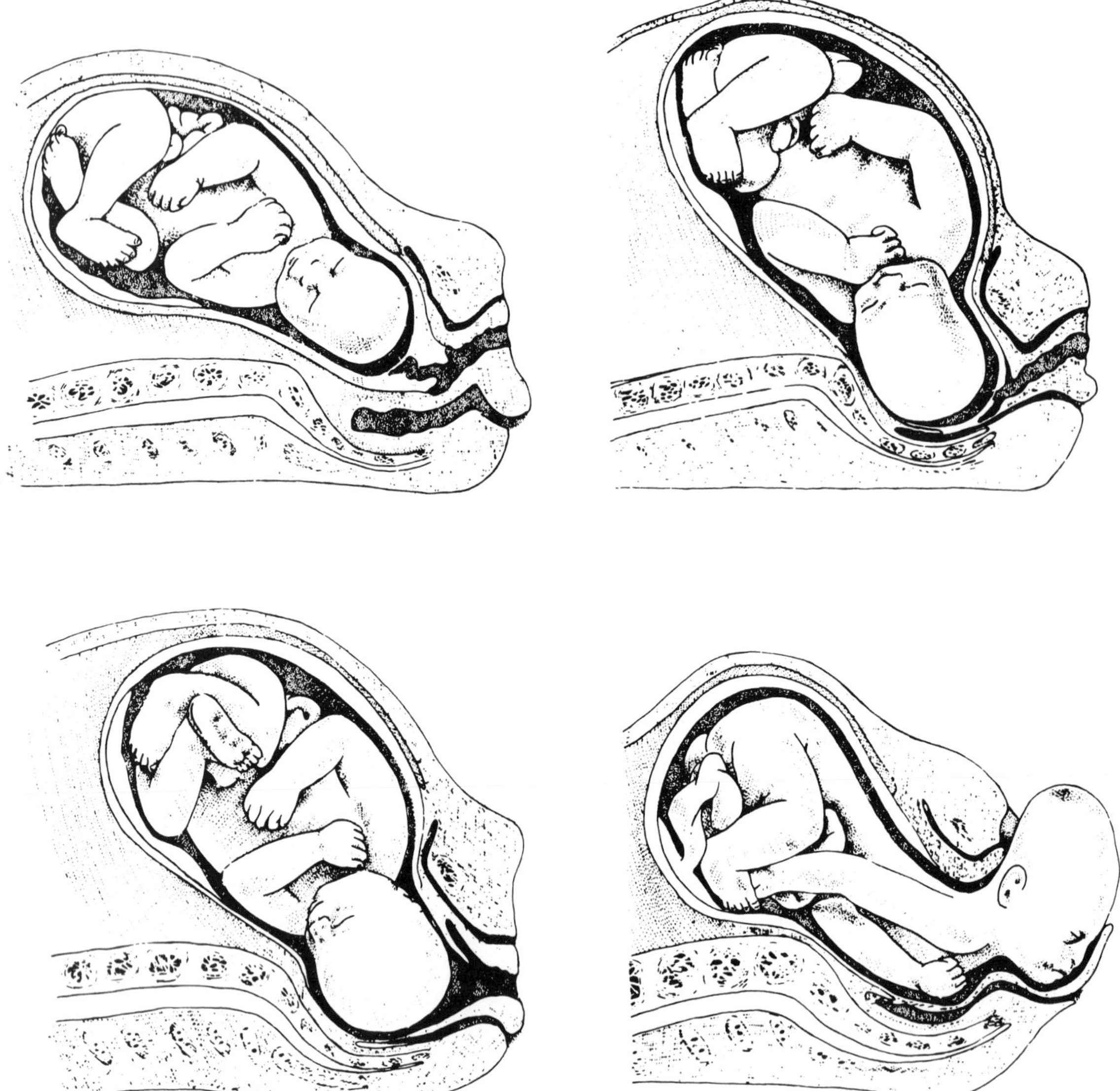

FIGURE 3.9
Ninety-seven percent of babies are born in the head-first position. The fetus's skull is soft and pliable, which helps the head to pass through the birth canal.

THIRD STAGE

Following the exit of the infant, the third stage of labor occurs, during which the placenta is expelled. The placenta and other expelled materials are called the *afterbirth*.

Multiple Births

Sometimes the newborn has company, a twin brother or sister. Sometimes, although less often, the newborn is just one of a crowd—triplets, quadruplets, or more.

Question: How do multiple births occur?

By examining Figure 3.10, you can see that many possible combinations can result in a multiple birth.

Question: What causes a zygote to split?

No one is quite certain why this occurs. Researchers are coming closer to an answer, however, and drugs that can trigger twinning were developed some time ago (Kaufman & O'Shea, 1978). Because these drugs have dangerous side effects, they are unavailable for other than experimental purposes.

A number of factors affect the probability of a multiple birth. Such a birth is more common among mothers between the ages of 35 and 39 years and among mothers who have a family history of multiple births. In addition, the more children a woman has had previously, the more likely she is to have a multiple birth in her current pregnancy.

Unlike identical twins, who develop from the splitting of a single zygote, fraternal twins result from the fertilization of two distinctly separate ova. Fraternal twins are no more alike than siblings, and they needn't be the same sex. To emphasize this point, it is interesting to consider that fraternal twins don't even have to have the same father. A few years ago, researchers described a fairly active young woman who had a double ovulation and managed to get each ovum fertilized by a different man in the space of a few hours (Terasaki et al., 1978). Having twins sired by two fathers is referred to as **superfecundity.** Although the first reported case was in 1810 (it was apparent because one father was black and the other white), it is quite rare in humans.

SUPERFECUNDITY
Having multiple offspring sired by more than one father.

The Newborn Infant

THE APGAR AND BRAZELTON ASSESSMENTS OF NEONATES

The Apgar Assessment Scale (Table 3.2) is typically administered to all infants 1 minute after delivery and again after 5 minutes. The scale was devised by Virginia Apgar and measures heart rate, reflex irritability (by facial expression), muscle tone, breathing, and body skin color (Apgar, 1953). Each of the five scales may be rated as 0, 1, or 2; the maximum score is 2 for each of the five scales, for a total of 10 points. A score of 7 or higher is typically obtained by 90 percent of all infants. Generally, an infant with a score of 4 or less is in need of immediate medical assistance. The Apgar score is a fairly good indicator of later neurological or muscular difficulties. Infants found by 1 year of age to have neuromuscular or developmental problems often had low Apgar scores at birth.

TABLE 3.2

Apgar's Scoring Chart for Newborn Infants*

	SCORE**		
SIGN	0	1	2
Heart rate	Absent	Slow (<100)	>100
Respiratory effort	Absent	Weak cry; hypoventilation	Good; strong cry
Muscle tone	Limp	Some flexion of extremities	Well flexed
Reflex irritability (response of skin stimulation to feet)	No response	Some motion	Cry
Color	Blue; pale	Body pink; extremities blue	Completely pink

*Evaluation 60 seconds after complete birth of infant disregarding the cord and placenta.
**Source of 10 indicates infant in best possible condition.

SOURCE: Apgar, Holaday, James, Weisbrot, & Berrien, 1958, p. 1988.

TWINS

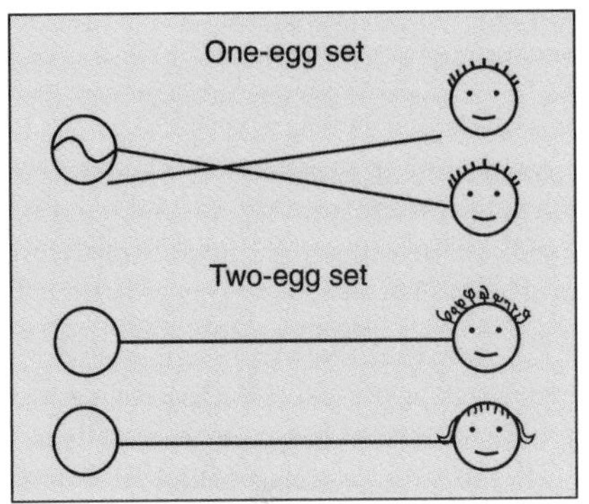

TRIPLETS

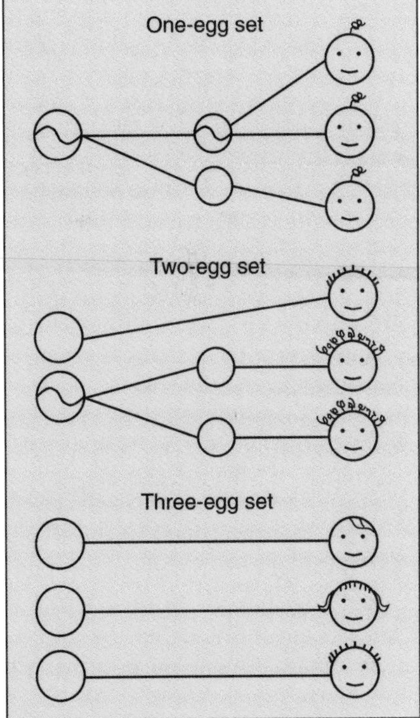

FIGURE 3.10
Fraternal offspring result when two or more ova are fertilized separately. Identical offspring result when one zygote splits, or fissions, into two identical zygotes.

AT ISSUE

Infant Mortality

At the beginning of the twentieth century, average life expectancy in the United States was approximately 49 years; it was considerably lower in most other countries. At first glance, one might think that this statistic means that people were reaching the age of 49 years and then dying of old age. Instead, this figure, compared to the present estimate of about 76 years average longevity, reflected the high mortality of infants. In 1910, infant mortality (defined as death during the first year of life) in the United States was a shocking 12.4 percent—or 124 deaths per 1000 live births. A growing emphasis on sanitation and the conquest of a number of deadly childhood diseases through inoculation helped the infant mortality rate in the United States to drop to 4.7 percent by 1940 and to 1.31 percent by 1971. The decline continued until it reached a low of .98 percent in 1989.

The United States now stands a sorry twentieth among all nations of the world for infant mortality, far behind the leaders, Finland and Japan, which have rates of approximately 0.6 percent. Why did this happen? Here are some of the theories for the higher comparative rate of infant mortality in the United States today:

1. The increasing rate of teenage pregnancy (10 percent of all teenage girls become pregnant in any given year, twice the teen pregnancy rate of countries such as Sweden, Canada, and Great Britain).
2. The increased use of tobacco, alcohol, and other drugs among pregnant young women.
3. The advent of advanced technology that may be keeping infants alive just long enough to be counted in the infant mortality statistics, when they previously would have not survived birth.
4. The racial mixture in the United States (minorities have almost twice the infant mortality rate as do non-minorities in the United States).

This last idea, that racial differences somehow account for the higher U.S. infant mortality, can be dispelled by observing that the mortality rate for white American infants is generally higher than for white European infants. The same comparison holds true for U.S. blacks versus European blacks (Miller, 1985).

The problem, instead, seems to be mostly one of birth weight. If birth weight is matched among U.S. and European infants, mortality rates are equal. In other words, the problem seems to be that U.S. babies are being born smaller and lighter. This strongly implies that the problem lies in prenatal care. As you recall, smoking, drinking, drug use, poor nutrition, stress, and other factors can contribute to low birth weight, the one factor most responsible for high rates of infant mortality.

It has been argued that the increase in the U.S. infant mortality rate has been caused by budget cuts at the national and local levels—cuts deemed necessary to help reduce the massive budget deficit. This, in turn, has made education and medical support for pregnant women less available, resulting in lower birth weights and higher infant mortality. In general, when education and medical support for pregnant women are increased, mortality rates decrease (even during economic recessions). In fact, France lowered its infant mortality rate by paying women to engage in quality prenatal care. One researcher has argued that to help bring infant mortality rates down, we need

> . . . assured access to comprehensive prenatal care, guaranteed maternity leaves for all working pregnant women and recent mothers, job protection during the leave and cash benefits equal to a significant portion of wages during the leave. These measures can be promoted on the basis of humanitarian concern, social equality, cost-effectiveness and even national security to the extent that it will depend on a coming generation, both vigorous and productive. (Miller, 1985, p. 37)

It does indeed appear that such programs could be cost-effective. This is an important consideration in these days of tight budget constraints. The Federal Office of Technology Assessment has estimated that intensive care for infants on the average costs more than $13,000 per patient. Routine prenatal care, which could greatly reduce the number of infants requiring intensive care, costs only about $350 per patient. The federal government has estimated that providing good prenatal care would save the United States $360 million per year (Budetti, as cited by Miller, 1985). Attempts to save money by cutting back on prenatal care or financial support for pregnant women may be penny-wise but pound-foolish.

The Brazelton Neonatal Behavioral Assessment Scale is also a popular assessment device with a long and valuable history (Brazelton, 1990). It yields scores on 27 nine-point behavioral scales and 17 reflex scales. The assessment also includes such things as the infant's response to a human voice or face and to being touched or cuddled. The scale is more difficult and time consuming to administer than the Apgar, but it is especially valuable in assessing which infants may need special care and what kind of care they require.

PREMATURE INFANT
An infant who weighs less than 5.5 pounds at birth and who was carried less than 37 weeks.

PREMATURE BIRTH

In the United States, approximately 7 percent of all infants are born weighing less than 5.5 pounds. By definition, **premature infants** weigh less than 5.5 pounds and are born before 37 weeks of pregnancy have been completed (i.e., before 35 weeks since conception have passed). These infants account for 65 percent of the deaths among newborns. In the United States, approximately $2 billion is spent every year caring for low-birth-weight infants. Infants who are carried to full term but weigh less than 5.5 pounds are referred to as "small for gestational age."

As a general rule, the lower the birth weight of a newborn, the greater the risk of its death. An underweight baby is approximately 40 times more likely to die during the first month of life than is a full-term, full-weight baby. Premature infants often have severe difficulty breathing, are more susceptible to infection, and have feeble reflexes.

The problems that premature infants face may last far beyond the first few weeks of life. Among the possible later problems that may be encountered are lower intelligence, learning difficulties, hearing and vision impairment, and physical awkwardness. Not all premature infants have eventual difficulties; in fact, the majority develop quite normally and are not discernible from their full-term peers (Greenberg & Crnic, 1988).

Interestingly, some of the low-birth-weight infants who were found to differ from their full-term peers may owe at least some of these differences to a parental bias against premature infants, which in turn disrupts the normal development of the parent-child relationship. In one study, for example, mothers were shown a videotape of infants with whom they were not familiar. Those infants labeled

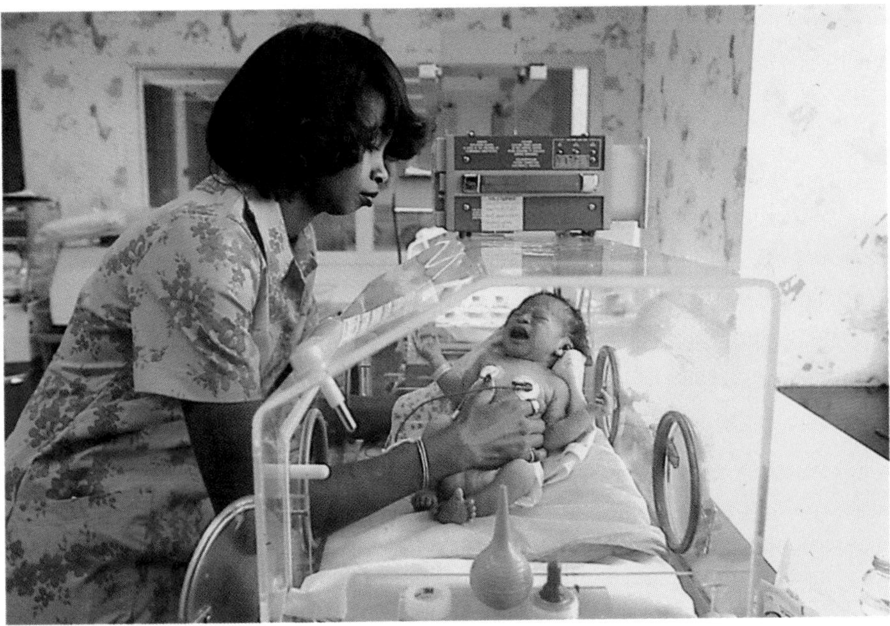

Incubators help provide a carefully controlled and monitored environment for premature infants and those born with life-threatening disorders.

"premature" (although they were really full term) received a more negative rating from the mothers than the infants labeled "full term" (Stern & Hildebrandt, 1984). When mothers were given a chance to hold and have contact with unfamiliar babies labeled "premature," they touched them less, rated them as smaller, gave them more immature toys to play with, and called them less cute than infants that were labeled "full term." Again, the infants were identical in age; only the labels given to them were different (Stern & Hildebrandt, 1986).

Mothers of preterm babies may also feel somewhat dejected when comparing their infants with full-term babies. For instance, a 4-month-old prematurely born infant may appear to lag behind a 4-month-old full-term infant. Because the 4-month-old preterm was born after only 7 months of gestation, however, the infant is only 11 months past conception and should, in all fairness, be compared to a 2-month-old full-term baby, who is also 11 months past conception! Sometimes, parents of premature infants don't consider this and may think of their babies as lagging behind when in fact they are not. For this reason, it is often helpful for hospital staff to spend time encouraging parents to feel comfortable and confident with their premature infant. In fact, such intervention in conjunction with a few additional home visits by encouraging nurses has been found to aid parents to stimulate the development of their premature infants significantly (Rauh, Achenbach, Nurcombe, Howell, & Teti, 1988).

Question: Is there any way to tell which premature infants will eventually develop problems?

One interesting measure of a premature infant's potential for future problems is the consistency the infant shows in sleep-awake states over a number of weeks (Trotter, 1980). Infants with the greatest consistency in their sleep-wake states are much less likely to develop serious problems later than are infants who show inconsistent patterns (Figure 3.11).

An infant's state can be conveniently recorded by a pressure-sensitive mattress in the infant's crib that monitors its movements. In this way, a doctor may be alerted to an infant with inconsistent states and can keep that baby under closer observation during later development than would normally be necessary. For instance, during initial tests with this monitor, doctors were twice alerted by a premature infant's inconsistency and were able, through close monitoring, to prevent death from a cessation of breathing.

Over the years, the range of techniques designed to improve care for premature infants has grown dramatically. With modern incubators and monitoring capabilities, many more premature infants are surviving than ever before. One of the most surprising ways to help a premature infant is simply to gently touch and handle the infant. As little as 45 minutes of touching per day has been shown to help infants in incubators gain weight 47 percent faster than control infants who received stimulation other than touching or handling (Field et al., 1986).

Question: What about infants who go full term but who have low birth weight?

These infants are also at high risk. Low birth weight, more than any other variable, is correlated with high infant mortality. The relationship between prematurity, low birth weight, and infant mortality, is shown in Figure 3.12.

Breast Feeding

For many years in the United States and other industrialized nations, breast feeding was considered simply "not modern." Formula and baby bottles were thought of as less confining and more scientific. During the last 20 years, however, an explosion of research has supported the idea that breast feeding is valuable for the health and safety of the infant.

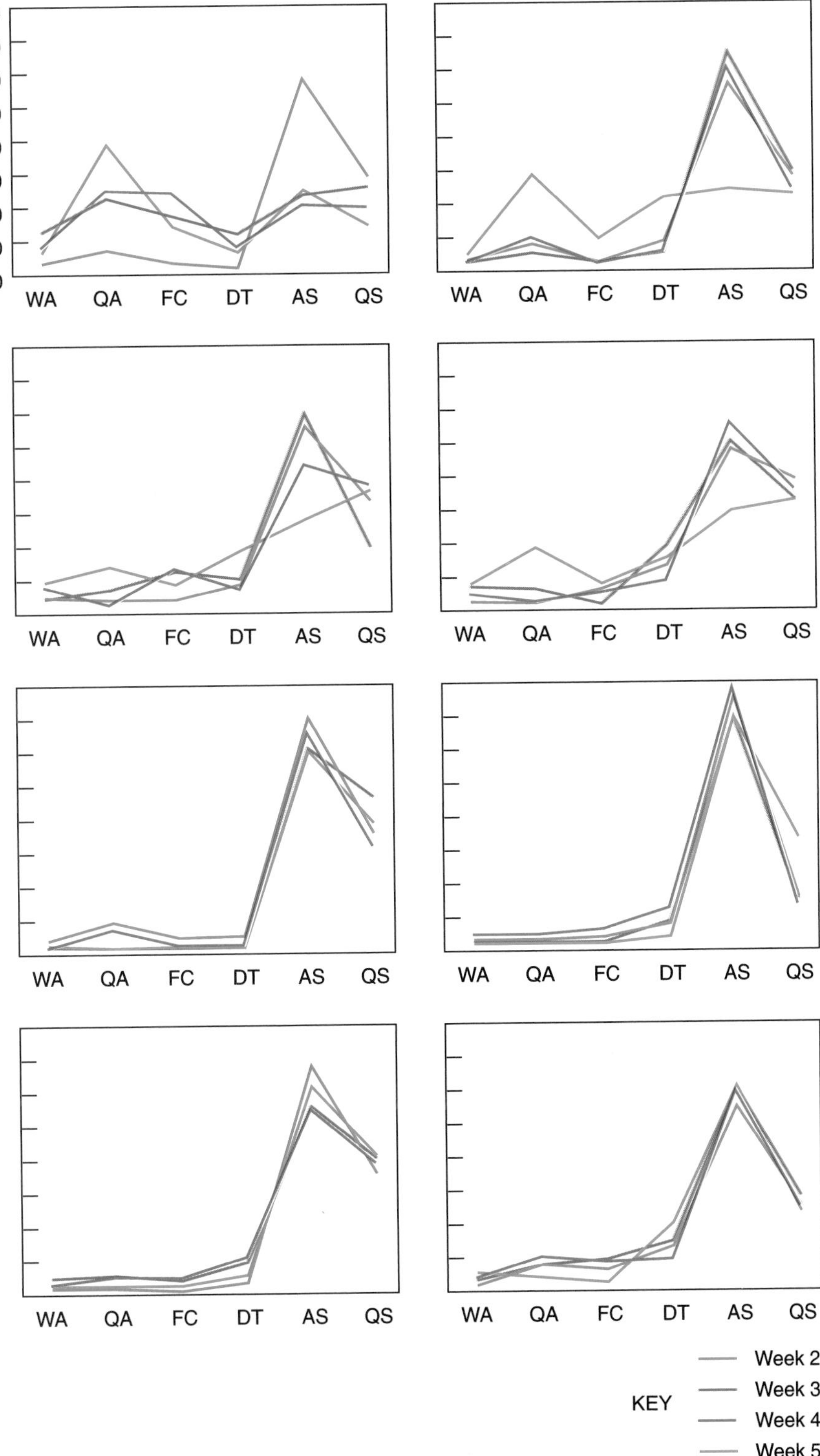

FIGURE 3.11
Researcher Evelyn Thoman and her colleagues measured the percentage of time infants spent in each of six states: waking active (WA), quiet alert (QA), fuss or cry (FC), drowse or transition (DT), active sleep (AS), or quiet sleep (QS). These measurements were taken once a week for 4 weeks. As you can see, the four infants in the top two rows (a–d) had many inconsistencies; they later developed serious problems. Those infants measured in the bottom two rows (e-h) had consistent patterns; they developed normally. (*Source:* Trotter, 1980, p. 234)

Question: But aren't properly prepared baby formulas as good for infants as breast milk?

Although at first glance it may appear so, careful examination of the differences between breast-fed and bottle-fed babies indicates that breast feeding has many

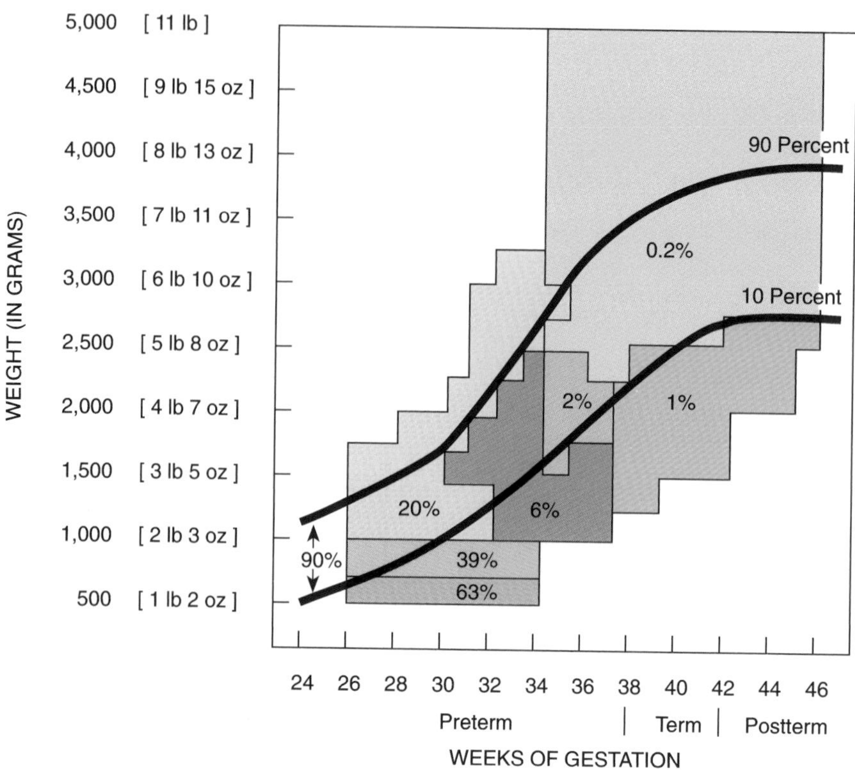

FIGURE 3.12
Newborn mortality risk by birth weight and gestational age based on 14,413 live births at the University of Colorado Health Sciences Center during 1974–1980. As you can see, infants who were carried full term and who weighed at least 6 pounds (2,725 grams) had the lowest mortality rate (0.2 percent). Mortality rate began to increase dramatically among infants whose birth weight was lower or whose gestation was shorter. Eighty percent of all babies born fell between the 90 percent and 10 percent curves on the graph. (*Source:* Koops, Morgan, & Battaglia, 1982, p. 972)

benefits. For instance, mothers who have premature infants generally produce milk with a high protein and fat content, which is valuable to the low-weight infant. It's as though the mother's body adjusts itself to the specific needs of the infant (Carpenter, 1981). In addition to the health and safety advantages it confers, breast nursing may help to establish a close and affectionate mother-infant bond (Marano, 1979).

Most research shows that breast feeding provides important nutrients and resistance to disease not provided by formulas.

Other researchers (Jelliffe & Jelliffe, 1977) have presented evidence that strongly supports what the proponents of natural nursing have been saying all along—that our species did not evolve in symbiosis with Jersey cows and that denying a baby its mother's milk may be denying it vital nutrients as well as antibodies that help fight disease. The Jelliffes demonstrated, with complex chemical analysis, that except for water and lactose, human and cow milk had little in common. Even the attempts at making formulas did not go far enough. For example, human milk had higher levels of the amino acids taurine and cystine than the formulas did. Taurine is absorbed by the infant's brain and plays a crucial role in neural development.

Human milk also contains a wide range of substances that provide the infant with disease resistance. For instance, white blood cells pass directly from the mother's milk into the infant's intestine, where they confer immunity against many organisms that might cause gastrointestinal infections. These infections are a major cause of infant mortality throughout the world (Short, 1984). Human breast milk also kills intestinal parasites that formula or cow's milk do not affect (Gillin, Reiner, & Wang, 1983) and helps the infant's own immune system to develop. Furthermore, breast-fed children are less likely to develop food allergies (Bellanti, 1984), coughs, respiratory difficulties, or diarrhea (Palti, Mansbach, Pridan, Adler, & Palti, 1984) than are bottle-fed ones. And breast-fed babies may be less prone to subsequent obesity (Kramer, 1981).

LEARNING CHECK

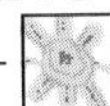

Matching

1. ___ drinking during pregnancy
2. ___ babies born to women addicted to heroin
3. ___ smoking during pregnancy
4. ___ substances capable of producing fetal abnormalities
5. ___ temperature-induced fetal damage
6. ___ parasitic infection that can affect fetus's nervous system
7. ___ a mild disease in adults; often fatal for infants
8. ___ mother's antibodies may attack the fetus
9. ___ 14 hours on the average
10. ___ 6 hours on the average
11. ___ 10 to 20 minutes
12. ___ 30 to 90 minutes
13. ___ 3 to 5 minutes
14. ___ 270 days

a. teratogens
b. hot tubs
c. herpes virus
d. toxoplasmosis
e. increases levels of carbon monoxide in the mother's blood
f. Rh factor incompatibility
g. go through withdrawal at birth
h. fetal alcohol syndrome
i. length of the average pregnancy
j. length of labor for first delivery
k. amount of time to journey down the birth canal
l. length of time between uterine contractions at the beginning of labor
m. length of labor for women who have previously given birth
n. length of time between uterine contractions near the end of labor

True or False

15. More than any other variable, low birth weight is associated with infant death.
16. In the United States, less than 1 percent of all infants are born prematurely.
17. Most baby formulas supply the same amino acids as does human milk.

Answers:
1. h 2. g 3. e 4. a 5. b 6. d 7. c 8. f 9. j 10. m 11. l 12. k 13. n
14. i 15. True 16. False 17. False

APPLICATIONS

A Brave New World

The Industrial Revolution began in earnest with the development of the steam engine. Suddenly, people had great power anywhere it was needed, power beyond what muscles could provide. Since then, we have discovered more sources of power. We actually learned how to fly—even beyond the earth. And we learned how to direct many of the forces of nature.

The Industrial Revolution is still going on, but now we are about to enter a new phase. No longer content merely to harness nature's forces, we are about to alter nature itself. Our medical and genetic knowledge will lead us to worlds undreamed of only a generation ago. In fact, some of these new worlds are already upon us.

Test Tube Babies and Beyond

In modern clinics, doctors often use fertility drugs to get multiple ovulations in order to implant more than one zygote at once in the hope that at least one will develop. This has made success rates much higher than they had been earlier, about 23 percent at the best clinics, compared to about 30 percent for natural fertilization. It is also now possible to screen the embryo before implantation for genetic or chromosomal defects (rather than through amniocentesis at a later time during the pregnancy), thus increasing the chances that only healthy embryos are implanted (Handyside et al., 1989). It is expected that by 1994 there will be a population of over 4,000 test-tube babies.

In 1985, a new technique called GIFT (gamete intrafallopian transfer), or low tubal transfer, was developed. In GIFT, eggs are retrieved from the woman, mixed with the man's sperm, and immediately placed inside a fallopian tube. This enables the period of the ovum to continue in its natural environment, allowing the embryo to develop further before implanting in the uterus. This technique provides hope for couples who are infertile because of problems such as low sperm counts or partially blocked fallopian tubes. It has a success rate of 30 percent or higher, which is about the same as that of natural fertilization. GIFT usually costs less than in vitro fertilization, in which the sperm and egg are joined outside of the body and then replaced into the womb. Babies born of this latter procedure are often referred to as "test tube babies."

Taken as a whole, the aforementioned techniques appear to simply overcome difficulties that couples have conceiving and do not in themselves seem "revolutionary." But they did open a new world because in 1983 the University of California reported achieving pregnancies among infertile women who received donor ova from other women. Owing to this technique, the women who gave birth to the infants were, for the first time ever, not the biological mothers!

In 1984, a further step was taken at the University of California to help a woman who was capable of becoming pregnant but unable to carry a fetus. In this case, after fertilization had taken place and the embryo was formed, the embryo was removed and implanted in another woman who was prepared with hormone administration to receive it. The embryo then grew to term and was born a healthy baby boy, thereby completing the first embryo transplant in humans. This, of course, is different from surrogate parenting, in which a woman agrees to carry a child for a couple, a child born of *her own ovum* and donated sperm; a woman carrying an embryo transplant is *unrelated* to the child to whom she will give birth.

You can imagine the legal questions that arise. Our system was not designed for this. Who is the legal mother—the biological mother or the one who gave birth to the child? Does the biological mother have the right to control the behavior of the "carrier" mother to ensure a healthy prenatal environment? Could the carrier mother charge for the service? As the law in the United States stands now, such an act might be considered the selling of a child, which is certainly not legal. Eventually, the law and public attitudes will

Howard and Georgeanna Jones, who began an infertility clinic in Virginia and who produced America's first test-tube baby.

APPLICATIONS

need to adjust to this new mode of human reproduction.

Gender Preselection

Another great change that will soon be upon us is that of gender preselection, the ability to choose the sex of the offspring beforehand.

Question: Why would anyone want to develop such a technique?

Scientists have a ready answer: Dairy farmers want female calves, while beef farmers want male calves. In fact, researchers intend to use a gender preselection technique to save the U.S. livestock industry about $700 million every year (Pinkel et al., 1985). The important fact is that sperm carrying the *Y* chromosomes (male) swim slightly faster than those carrying the *X* chromosomes (female). If a sample of sperm is continuously passed through a viscous protein, such as the albumin in egg white, the faster, *Y*-carrying sperm will eventually be somewhat separated from the *X*-carrying sperm. In humans, this technique has been shown to be effective in selecting the sex of the child 80 percent of the time, as opposed to the 50 percent one would expect by chance.

Question: Why is it being done with humans?

Because there are important medical advantages for families in which there are genetic sex-linked diseases, such as hemophilia or Duchenne's muscular dystrophy. Such couples might avoid the expression of these diseases by choosing to have only girls.

Some critics have expressed great concern about the widespread use of preselection techniques, however. They fear that because most individuals express a desire to have a boy or at least to have a boy first (Maranto, 1984), the percentage of males to females in the population could become skewed by a predominance of males. Some people have argued that this would eventually result not only in fewer women, but also in fewer first-born women and in poorer women, because wealthier couples would opt to use the technology and thus would be more likely to have sons than would less wealthy families. Should the technology become widespread, a predominance of sons might be especially likely in countries such as the People's Republic of China or India. In China, heavy fines are imposed by the government on couples who have more than one child; in India, because of the tradition of dowries, daughters are a financial burden; in both countries, sons are especially desired. Of course, it can be argued that a preponderance of sons might be one way for China, India, or most of the world, for that matter, to eventually get a grip on its overpopulation problems.

What do you think? Would you like to have the freedom to choose? Consider how you would feel if you and your spouse had had three girls (or three boys) in a row. How many drawbacks or benefits, in addition to those we've discussed, can you think of?

The Artificial Womb

Among the most controversial events that may be in the offing sometime next century is the creation of an artificial womb. Sophisticated incubators are currently able (with luck and a lot of hard work) to keep alive premature infants who are born after only 22 weeks of gestation and weigh less than 1 pound! With an artificial womb, a zygote would be able to develop in a laboratory from conception to "birth." Such a womb would allow for total control of the prenatal environment, which would, in theory, anyway, ensure the safe development of the fetus.

Socially, the development of a completely artificial womb would eliminate the mother's special biological role and leave her and the father as parental equals in every sense; each would contribute only the raw genetic material for the child. Furthermore, parents who so desired could have all their children at once, eliminating the age separation of almost 1 year that now exists between nontwin siblings.

Question: What implication does this research have for the future?

Techniques such as in vitro fertilization, gender preselection, and the artificial womb may be only the first applications of a new biotechnology revolution. To some, this may seem a fearful prospect, to others, one that would furnish greater happiness and freedom. However, if history has taught us anything, we should know that the effects of such new procedures probably will be different from anything we might predict. As Ronald Ericsson, who developed the filtering sperm-sorting technique for gender preselection, has said, "It's mind-boggling to think of the possible impact. . . . Actually, the world will never be the same."

SUMMARY

- For fertilization to occur in human beings, both a man and a woman are required. This arrangement ensures diversity in our species, which in turn gives our species a greater chance of surviving the natural selection process.
- Fertilization occurs when a sperm penetrates an ovum. This typically takes place in a fallopian tube, which is part of the female reproductive system.
- During the period of the ovum, lasting approximately 2 weeks following fertilization, the fertilized ovum, called a zygote, becomes attached to the wall of the uterus.
- The period of the embryo is marked by the rapid growth and development of the unborn child and lasts from the time the zygote attaches to the uterus until the formation of solid bone in the embryo, which occurs approximately 8 weeks following conception. From this point until birth, the unborn child is known as a fetus. By 28 weeks after conception, the fetus is well enough developed to survive a premature birth.
- A number of external influences may cause serious damage to the unborn child. Prospective parents can often avoid these dangers by altering their own behavior, so it is important that they be made aware of the possible threats to the embryo or fetus. Among these dangers are behaviors that the mother may engage in, such as smoking, drinking, using drugs, and eating inadequately. Potential fathers must be careful not to expose themselves to dangers that may affect their sperm.
- Other hazards that may affect the embryo or fetus include parasites, viruses, ionizing radiation, and emotional stress.
- Birth in human beings typically occurs 270 days after conception. The majority of babies are born in a head-first position following the onset of labor, which is marked by uterine contractions.
- Multiple births occur when more than one ovum is fertilized (fraternal offspring) or when a zygote splits (identical offspring).
- In the United States, approximately 7 percent of all infants are born weighing less than 5.5 pounds. As a general rule, the lower the birth weight of a newborn, the greater the risk of death.
- Within the last few years, data have indicated that breast feeding is superior to bottle feeding and that bottle feeding may deny infants vital nutrients.
- Techniques such as in vitro fertilization and gender preselection may be only the first applications of a new "technology of conception" that could have a tremendous effect on the family and society in general.

QUESTIONS FOR DISCUSSION

1. What ethical considerations do you believe should be emphasized in conducting research on novel means of human fertilization?

2. Do you think that it would be better for a fetus to develop within an artificial womb?

3. What are your thoughts about abortion? Do you believe, for example, that severe fetal damage caused by rubella should influence a decision concerning abortion?

4. What advantages and disadvantages might there be in being able to choose to have twins or triplets rather than the usual one child at a time?

5. In India, boys are often valued more than girls, and amniocentesis has become widespread. In one province, only one of thousands of abortions following amniocentesis was that of a male fetus. How do you feel about the use of abortion as a tool for gender selection?

SUGGESTIONS FOR FURTHER READING

1. Bryan, E. (1992). *Twins, triplets, & more: From pre-birth through high school—what every parent needs to know when raising two or more.* New York: St. Martin's Press.
2. Clegg, A., & Woollett, A. (1983). *Twins: From conception to five years.* New York: Van Nostrand Reinhold.
3. Graham, J. (1991). *Your pregnancy companion: A month-by-month guide to all you need to know before, during, and after pregnancy.* New York: Penguin Books.
4. Kolata, G. (1990). *The baby doctors: Probing the limits of fetal medicine.* New York: Delacorte.
5. Lansdown, R., & Yule, W. (Eds.). (1986). *Lead toxicity: History and environmental impact.* Baltimore: Johns Hopkins University Press.
6. Manginello, F. P., & DiGeronimo, T. F. (1991). *Your premature baby: Everything you need to know about the childbirth, treatment, and parenting of premature infants.* New York: Wiley.
7. Nachtigall, R., & Mehren, E. (1991). *Overcoming infertility: A practical strategy for navigating the emotional, medical, and financial minefields of trying to have a baby.* New York: Doubleday.
8. Nobel, E. (1991). *Having twins: A parent's guide to pregnancy, birth & early childhood* (2nd ed.). Boston: Houghton Mifflin Co.
9. Norwood, C. (1980). *At highest risk: Environmental hazards to young and unborn children.* New York: McGraw-Hill.
10. Rich, L. A. (1991). *When pregnancy isn't perfect: A layperson's guide to complications in pregnancy.* New York: Dutton.
11. Wolpert, L. (1991). *The triumph of the embryo.* New York: Oxford University Press.

CHAPTER 4

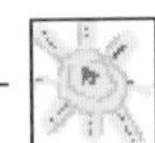

GROWTH, MATURATION, AND INDIVIDUAL DIFFERENCES

CHAPTER PREVIEW

TOILET TRAINING TWINS

BOOKS ADVISING parents how to raise children are hardly new. For centuries, parents have had at their disposal written advice given them by "experts" concerning just about every aspect of child rearing. Toilet training is one area that has always been of interest, and the following advice was provided earlier in this century:

"Training for bladder control may be begun as early as the third month. Since infants left untrained after the seventh or eighth month are conditioned with difficulty to the use of the toilet, it is important that training be started during the first six months of life, even if such training cannot be conducted in a highly systematic manner." (Scoe, 1933)

ANOTHER "EXPERT" suggested that up to the age of 6 months infants be placed on the toilet after arising, after eating, after naps, after bathing, and at bedtime (Blatz, 1928)!

Question: Is that what you're supposed to do? I never heard of anyone doing that.

THE "EXPERTS" JUST described were giving advice based on what they assumed to be true. Who knows how many parents followed this advice until a researcher named Myrtle McGraw decided to actually test the value of the advice being given.

MCGRAW TOOK TWO sets of identical twins, and in an exacting study in which frequency of urination and volume of urine were measured, one child from each set of twins was systematically given toilet training beginning at the age of 1 month (McGraw, 1940).

Question: What about each of these children's twins?

UNLIKE THEIR IDENTICAL twins, who were being trained, these boys received no toilet training at all. Month after month the training continued, and slowly the two boys receiving the training began to have some bladder control. Measurements were taken of success, and by the time the trained boys were 27 months old, their toilet training was complete.

Question: What happened to the identical twins of those boys who received no training?

THE IDENTICAL TWINS of the trained boys were then given just a couple of days of toilet training. When these newly trained boys were tested, they were found to be just as successful as their fully "trained" brothers who had received 26 months of toilet training! This finding led McGraw to state, "Concerning the inception of a training program, the results of this investigation indicate that early toilet training is, to say the least, futile" (McGraw, 1940, p. 588). In other words, until the child was neurologically ready to benefit from the training, no amount of early training would be any use at all.

IN THIS CHAPTER, we will examine predetermined biological plans of development that are relatively independent of experience, like the toilet-training example in this preview. We'll also look at the reflexes with which infants are born as well as the forces that contribute to the child's physical growth, motor development, and temperament.

RESOURCES

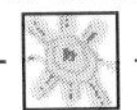

NEONATE
A newborn infant.

The Neonate

If you are among the many who are unfamiliar with **neonates** (newborns), you would probably be surprised by the appearance of a real newborn baby. Newborn infants have skin that is soft, dry, and wrinkled. They typically weigh between 6 and 9 pounds and are about 20 inches in length. The newborn's head may seem huge in proportion to the rest of its body; in fact, it accounts for fully one-fourth of the baby's length. The neonate may appear chinless (which may strike parents as strange because the infant may seem to resemble no other member of the family). In addition, the neonate's forehead is high and its nose is flat. And although the eyes may eventually be brown, most neonates' eyes are steely blue.

INFANT STATES

Newborns, like all human beings, have natural body rhythms that signal them when to sleep, eat, eliminate, or be active. Babies are individuals, so it should come as no surprise that different babies have somewhat different rhythms. For example, some newborns will sleep 11 hours a day, while others will sleep as much as 21 hours (Parmelee, Wenner, & Schulz, 1964). Yet, despite these differences, all healthy newborns exhibit the following states to one degree or another (Wolff, 1966):

1. *Crying:* Associated with strong unfocused motor activity.
2. *Waking Activity:* Frequent unfocused and sudden movements of the arms, legs, trunk, and head. Eyes are opened and alert. Breathing is irregular. General demeanor ranges from relaxed to the verge of crying.
3. *Alert Inactivity:* Infant is quiet but attentive. Eyes are open. Arm, leg, trunk, and head movements are slow and focused. Infant may spend time looking around.

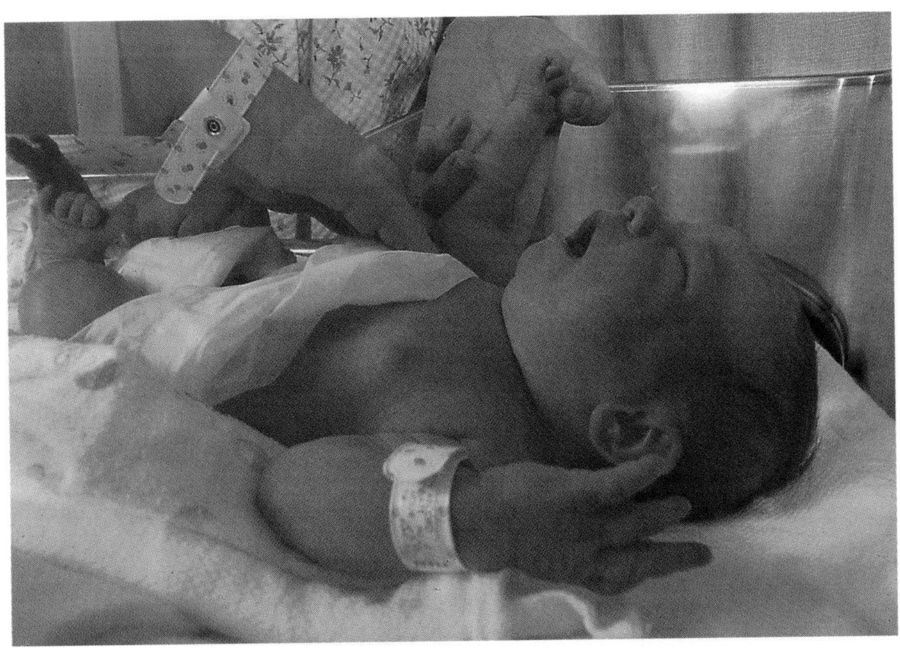

Human newborns have soft, dry, wrinkled skin. They usually weigh between 6 and 9 pounds and are about 20 inches in length. The neonate's head accounts for one-quarter its entire length. In addition, the neonate's forehead is high and its nose is flat.

REFLEX
Any unlearned response that occurs in all healthy members of a given species in the presence of an eliciting stimulus. Examples include blinking and coughing.

4. *Drowsiness:* Breathing is somewhat irregular. Eyes open and close. Reactions to stimuli are varied (smiling, startling, sucking, etc.). Occasional bursts of motor activity. Eyes are unfocused and glassy when open.
5. *Irregular Sleep:* Motor activity includes occasional arm and leg movements and some general stirring. Eyes may move rapidly beneath closed lids. Mouth movements and facial expressions are common. Breathing is slightly rapid and irregular.
6. *Regular Sleep:* Infant is very still; breathing is deep and regular. Eye movements are unobserved, and facial muscles are in repose.

A PASSIVE BABY?

From the turn of the century until the 1950s, the newborn was considered by many to be a helpless creature who was handed to the world like a lump of clay ready to be molded and shaped. The newborn was not thought to be competent in any sense of the word. Babies were generally considered helpless and *passive*. They cried, they wet, they ate, they slept, they possessed some simple reflexes, and that was about it.

However, beginning in the 1960s, there was a sudden surge of research concerning the capabilities of infants. Researchers found, for instance, that throughout infancy, babies will *initiate* social interactions and play an *active* role in maintaining and developing their parents' responses (Restak, 1982).

Question: At what age do infants first demonstrate this sociability?

This sociability begins only moments after the infant is out of the womb. Newborns will look about, and they will turn their heads in response to a voice as though they are searching for its source. Newborns seem especially attracted to faces and show an interest in them. This behavior, in turn, helps to initiate reciprocal interest from the one receiving the infant's gaze (see Figure 4.1). As you read more about newborns, you may be surprised to find how many interesting abilities and competencies they have.

The Neonate's Repertoire of Reflexes

A large number of **reflexes** can be elicited in newborns (see Table 4.1). It can safely be assumed that these responses are unlearned and are a result of the child's "nature," because all healthy neonates exhibit them.

Question: Why do these reflexes exist in newborns?

Many reflexes have apparently evolved because they have a survival value. Coughing, sucking, blinking, crying, and rooting all help the neonate survive. These reflexes are built in; they are needed immediately.

Question: What about reflexes that don't seem to have any survival value?

The common assumption is that they once served a function. When our evolutionary ancestors carried their children, the grasp reflex may have helped babies cling to their mother's hair. A Moro reflex (the extension of the arms upon sudden loss of support) in such a baby may have had the advantage of preventing spinning during a fall, which would have allowed for a more controlled drop and landing. Of course, human mothers don't rely on the ability of their babies to cling to their hair (and quickly learn to keep their hair away from baby's surprisingly powerful grip), and dropping from almost any height would be more than a newborn could handle, regardless of whether he or she were spinning. It seems most likely that many of these reflexes have outlived their usefulness in human beings but continue to exist simply because the environment has never selected against them.

Sucking is one of the reflexive behaviors in the neonate's repertoire. If pacifiers are given, neonates will spend about half of their time sucking, regardless of the amount of milk they are given (Koepke & Barnes, 1982).

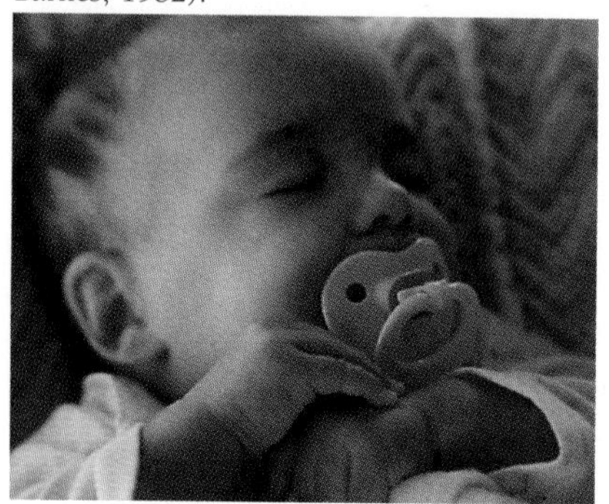

FIGURE 4.1
Newborns seem especially attracted to faces. This facilitates early social interaction between infants and their care givers.

TABLE 4.1

Some Neonatal Reflexes

REFLEX	ELICITING STIMULUS	RESPONSE	DEVELOPMENTAL DURATION
Babinski	Gentle stroke along sole of foot from heel to toe	Toes fan out, big toe flexes	Disappears by end of first year
Babkin	Pressure applied to both palms while baby is lying on its back	Eyes close and mouth opens; head returns to center position	Disappears in 3–4 months
Blink	Flash of light, or puff of air delivered to eyes	Both eyelids close	Permanent
Diving	Sudden splash of cold water in the face	Heart rate decelerates, blood flows mostly to brain and heart	Becomes progressively weaker with age
Knee jerk	Tap on patellar tendon	Rapid extension of the leg at the knee	Permanent
Moro	Sudden loss of support	Arms extend, then are brought toward each other; lower extremities are extended	Disappears in about 6 months
Palmar grasp	Rod or finger pressed against infant's palm	Baby grasps object	Disappears in 3–4 months
Rage	Both hands placed on side of alert infant's head and its movement restrained; infant's mouth blocked with cheesecloth or covered for 10 seconds	Baby cries and struggles	Disappears in 2–4 months
Rooting	Object lightly brushes infant's cheek	Baby turns toward object and attempts to suck	Disappears in 3–4 months
Sucking	Finger or nipple inserted 2 inches into mouth	Rhythmic sucking	Disappears in 3–4 months
Walking	Baby is held upright and soles of feet are placed on hard surface; baby is tipped slightly forward	Infant steps forward as if walking	Disappears in 2–3 months

MATURATION
A genetically programmed biological plan of development that is somewhat independent of experience. Maturation is highly correlated with, and dependent on, the growth and development of the nervous system.

PROBABILISTIC EPIGENESIS
Literally, the direction in which growth will probably go. The term is often used when discussing physical or cognitive development; it represents what typically occurs in the development of most individuals, but not in the development of all individuals.

As many of the reflexes become weaker or disappear, higher brain functions and learning take over to provide the baby with any of the needed responses. In fact, pediatricians often use these disappearing reflexes as markers of healthy neurological development and are concerned when an infant maintains these reflexes too long after birth. Interestingly, following neurological damage from injury or disease, some of these reflexes may reappear, even in adults. For instance, a positive Babinski response (a totally uncontrollable flexing and fanning of the toes when the sole of the foot is stroked) in an adult is generally considered a serious sign of underlying disorder.

The Forces of Maturation

An infant's reflexes are a product of its biology; reflexes are inherited. Any organism's biology will influence the direction of its development, and human beings are no exception. The term used to describe a genetically determined biological plan of development, one relatively independent of experience, is **maturation.** It is important to understand, however, that human development is not solely a function of biology; a person's biological heritage will typically direct, rather than totally determine, his or her development. The term that researchers use to describe this concept is **probabilistic epigenesis.**

Human growth seems to be mainly a function of maturation, and its development follows a probable path. The same can be said for motor development. For instance, it is known that approximately 93 percent of all humans will develop a preference for the right hand. It appears that handedness is due to our genetic arrangement rather than to our experience (Longstreth, 1980).

Question: But how do you know that hand preference isn't due to experience or to parental pressure on children to be right-handed?

If handedness were due only to experience, we would expect either that no preference would develop, as is the case with most other primates, or, if one did, that

Children can demonstrate complex motor behaviors at an early age, but only after they are maturationally capable.

the odds would be 50–50 whether it would be right or left. Moreover, even in cultures where there is no pressure to be right-handed, about 93 percent of the children become right-handed anyway. Also, careful observation of ancient objects cut by tools and sharp implements indicates that our species has had this right-hand preference for over 50 centuries (Coren & Porac, 1977).

Perhaps the most convincing evidence that handedness is mostly biologically controlled comes from the examination of ultrasound images of infants in the womb. While looking at these images, researcher Peter Hepper kept track of fetuses who were sucking their thumbs (a common occurrence in the womb). He noted *which* thumb they were sucking and discovered that 94.6 percent of the time it was the right thumb (Hepper, Shahidullah & White, 1990). The womb is such a uniform environment, with little or no opportunity for cultural or parental pressure, that we have to say that the development of handedness appears to be the result of biological maturation rather than of experience or learning.

Both physical growth and motor development have a number of things in common. Among these are that both appear to be largely a function of maturation—that is, of nature rather than nurture—and that they are the most commonly discussed aspects of infant development among parents, simply because they are so readily observable.

Actually, things that seem readily observable often aren't. For years, researchers and physicians assumed that physical growth in infants and young children progressed at a fairly steady rate of roughly ½ millimeter per day. Any "growth spurts" were thought to occur during puberty. However, when researcher Michelle Lampl very carefully measured infants and toddlers on a daily basis, she discovered that there would be long periods of no observable growth (sometimes as long as 2 months), and then suddenly the infant or toddler would grow. During these growth spurts, infants or toddlers typically became excessively sleepy, hungry, or fussy and then, within just a 24-hour period, grew from between ¹⁄₁₀ to almost ½ of an inch (Lampl, Veldhuis & Johnson, 1992)! At a rate like that, you can't help but wonder if the creaky sound parents occasionally hear in the house at night isn't the kid growing! This kind of development is called **saltatory growth.** Very early results also indicate grade school children and adolescents may also be growing in a saltatory manner (Lampl, Veldhuis & Johnson, 1992). Such findings help to emphasize that development is rarely a linear process.

SALTATORY GROWTH
Literally, growth by leaping. Growth that occurs in "spurts" or sudden leaps.

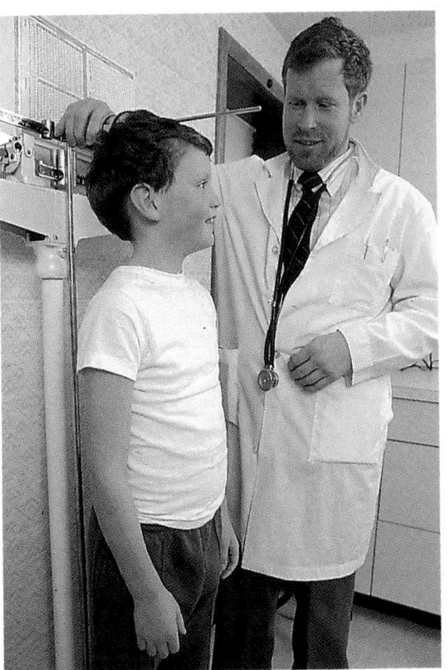

Children grow in a saltatory manner. During such spurts, they may gain from between ¹⁄₁₀ to almost ½ inch within a period of just 24 hours.

Physical growth also tends to be a decelerating process. As you can see from Table 4.2, the rate of physical growth is incredibly rapid immediately following conception and *decelerates* very quickly thereafter. Again, if human growth were a fairly linear progression—that is, if the rate of human growth during the first 3 months following your conception were maintained—by the time you were 20,

TABLE 4.2

The Deceleration of Growth during Prenatal Development

AGE	WEIGHT (IN OUNCES)	PERCENTAGE INCREASE
Conception	0.00000002	
4 weeks	0.0007	3,499,900
8 weeks	0.035	4,900
12 weeks	0.6	1,614
16 weeks	3	400
20 weeks	8	166
24 weeks	22	175
28 weeks	28	27
32 weeks	34	21

2 months (fetal)
5 months (fetal)
Newborn
2 years
6 years
12 years
25 years

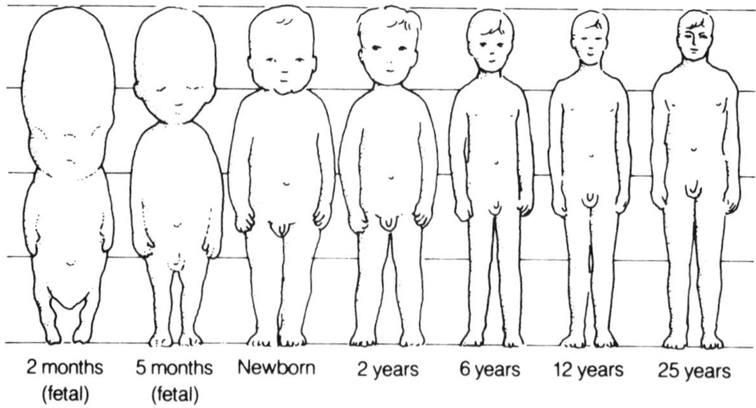

FIGURE 4.2
Changes in body form associated with age. (*Source:* Jackson, 1929, p. 118)

you'd weigh considerably more than all the planets of the solar system combined, with the sun thrown in for good measure!*

Changes in the relative sizes of different body parts also take place during growth. The change in the ratio of head to body length is an interesting example of this aspect of growth (see Figure 4.2).

In Figure 4.3, you can see how aspects of a child's motor development also appear to follow a maturational plan. Just as individual babies differ, so, too, do individual rates of motor development. Some infants proceed quickly, while others lag behind. Some develop rapidly in one area and simultaneously are slow in another. Like the story of the tortoise and the hare, some infants may race ahead of their peers only to be equaled or overtaken later.

*Based on a rate at which each cell becomes 25 billion cells every 3 months.

FIGURE 4.3
Selected motor milestones from the Denver Developmental Screening Test. The bottom end of the bar represents the age at which 25 percent of the sample could perform the task; the top end represents the age at which 90 percent could. (*Source:* Adapted from Frankenburg & Dodds, 1967, p. 186)

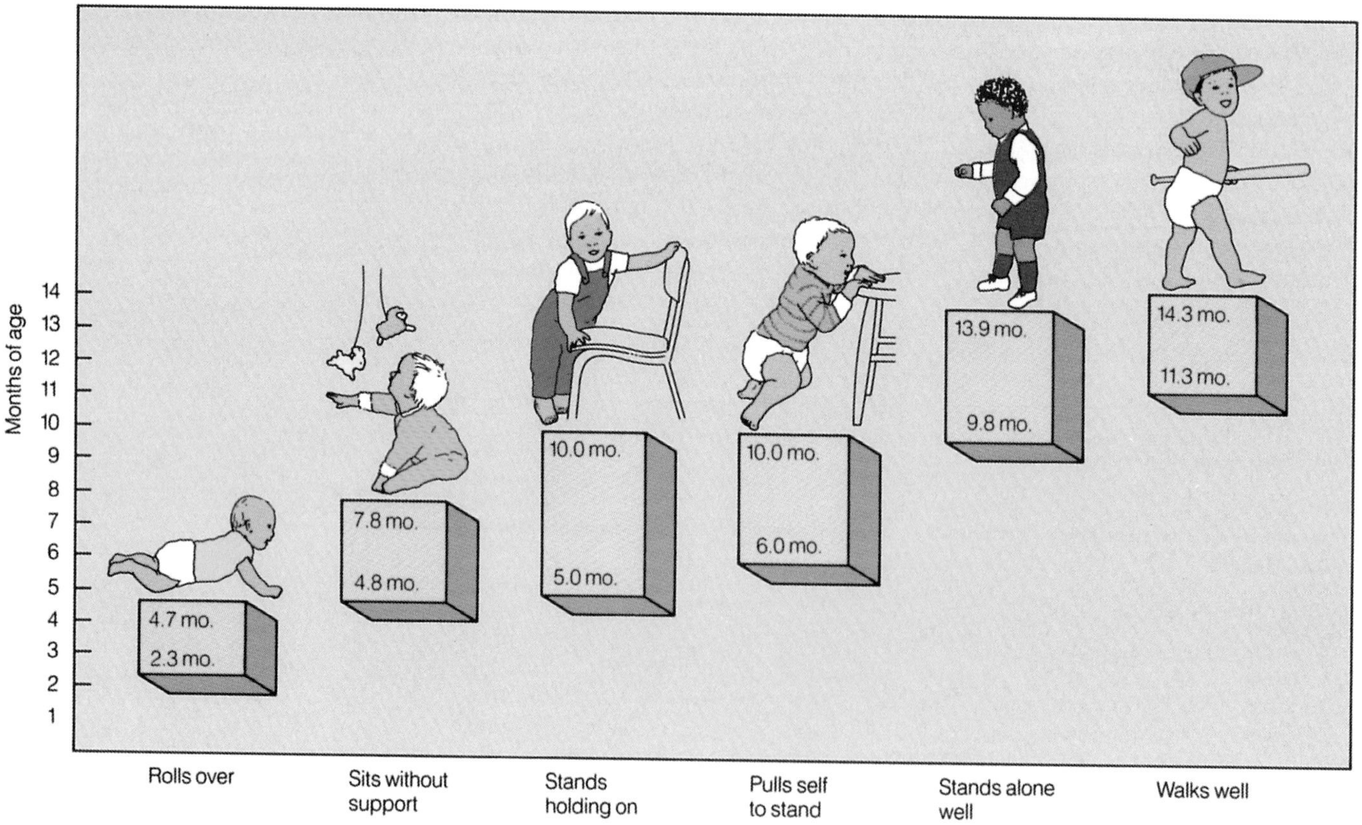

Months of age
14
13
12
11
10
9
8
7
6
5
4
3
2
1
4.7 mo.
2.3 mo.
7.8 mo.
4.8 mo.
10.0 mo.
5.0 mo.
10.0 mo.
6.0 mo.
13.9 mo.
9.8 mo.
14.3 mo.
11.3 mo.
Rolls over
Sits without support
Stands holding on
Pulls self to stand
Stands alone well
Walks well

Parents often place great importance on the speed of their child's physical and motor development. But they should not be too elated or too concerned if their infant is several months ahead of or several months behind the published norms. Sometimes a 6-month-old will learn to sit by him- or herself and then seem, from the parents' point of view, to develop no further for 4 or 5 months. The frustrated parents may wonder why their baby doesn't stand or crawl—surely a child must learn to crawl before the child can walk—only to have the child suddenly stand up and toddle off somewhere after 5 months of failing to advance much beyond sitting. Babies are individuals, and they *will* do things their own way, at their own speed.

Question: Then in terms of the rates of physical growth or motor development, environmental experience is of no importance?

Because physical growth and motor development appear to be mainly a function of maturation (Gesell, 1928), the environment may seem to play a small role. Yet environmental experiences can have an important bearing on maturational development. For example, although a child's physical growth appears to be biologically determined, proper nutrition is a very important environmental experience that can have a direct effect. With proper nutrition, the predetermined biological plan can unfold, allowing the child to reach his or her full predetermined physical potential. But without good nutrition, the child's maturation may be severely hindered.

LEARNING CHECK

Multiple Choice

1. The average neonate weighs between ______ and ______ pounds and is approximately ______ inches in length.
   a. 6 and 9; 20 **c.** 6 and 10; 25
   b. 4 and 10; 20 **d.** 6 and 9; 30
2. During the first half of the twentieth century, most researchers considered the newborn to be
   a. active. **c.** competent.
   b. passive. **d.** independent.
3. The fanning out of the toes when the sole of an infant's foot is stroked is an example of the ______ reflex.
   a. palmar grasp **c.** Moro
   b. Babinski **d.** walking
4. Handedness in humans appears to be a function of
   a. maturational forces. **c.** chance reinforcement.
   b. learning. **d.** social pressure.
5. The term used to refer to a predetermined biological plan of development is
   a. growth. **c.** learning.
   b. maturation. **d.** all of the above.

Answers: 1. a 2. b 3. b 4. a 5. b

The Strange Case of the Walking Newborn

Environmental influences other than nutrition may also affect maturational development. One of the neonate's built-in behaviors is a walking reflex. If held by the hands in an upright posture and placed so that the soles of the feet touch a solid surface, the newborn will walk forward in the direction led. Along with

AT ISSUE

The Genetics of Behavior

Carefully observing and studying behavior for the relative influences of nature and nurture, and examining how they interact, is the study of **behavioral genetics.** Behavioral genetic studies can become quite complex, but the following story will give you a feel for the kinds of issues raised by this type of investigation.

There is a hunter-gatherer tribe in Paraguay called the Ache (Kaplan & Dove, 1987). Curiously, Ache children are about one full year behind their 3-year-old American or African counterparts in terms of motor development. In fact, the Ache appear to show the slowest motor development of any children ever tested, and yet, by later childhood, their motor development is indiscernible from that of American or African children.

Nurture may be one possible contributor to this apparent lag. Until recently, Ache infants were treated in a special way by their mothers. Because the Ache used to move camp so often when they foraged, mothers and children were almost always in uncleared or partially cleared spaces. In the forest, children under 3 were rarely observed to travel more than 1 meter from their mothers and spent from 80 to 100 percent of their time in direct tactile contact with their mothers. As researchers Kaplan and Dove point out,

> It is quite common to observe mothers pulling their children back to their laps when they begin to crawl out of reach. It is also interesting to note that this reluctance on the part of parents is mirrored in the behavior of their offspring. When young children are allowed to explore their environment, they do so very tentatively; they may venture a meter or two before hurrying back to their parents and jumping into their laps and then beginning the process again. (Kaplan & Dove, 1987, p. 194)

Although the slower motor development of Ache infants might *possibly* be owing to nurture, there might be another reason. It might also be that over thousands of years, any Ache children who happened to develop motor skills early were more likely to get lost (by walking into the forest), hurt, or even attacked by predators than were those who stayed close to their mothers. If this is true, the late motor development we see today may have come about through the natural selection of slowly maturing infants, that is, through nature.

Although it is difficult to separate the relative contributions of nature and nurture, the Ache tribe may offer us some hints. Over the last few years, the tribe has abandoned its centuries-old practice of foraging and has taken up agriculture. Parents are no longer very concerned about keeping their infants close to them because they now live in the relative safety of open spaces and have permanent homes. And yet, the latest Ache infants, who are being raised in the new way, are just as delayed in their motor development as their predecessors. Furthermore, infants who have only one Ache parent (owing to a marriage outside of the tribe) develop motor skills at a rate somewhat between the slow rate for Ache children and the average rate typical of most other children (Kaplan & Dove, 1987). These data indicate the possibility of a strong genetic predisposition for slow motor development among Ache infants, probably as a result of natural selection favoring those infants who didn't wander.

Most efforts in behavioral genetics have found that there is a genetic influence on many behaviors, often one that is significant and substantial, but that the role of the environment is a powerful modifying influence (Plomin, 1990). The basic theme of nature and nurture is *interaction.*

Ache children have the slowest rate of motor development recorded among a healthy population. This rate of development may reflect the natural selection process.

many other of the neonate's early reflexes, the walking reflex disappears at about 2 or 3 months of age.

For years, developmental researchers found this reflex only mildly interesting, albeit an amusing one for the camera. Almost every discussion of the reflex included the comment, "This is reflexive walking and is not related to the voluntary walking in which the child will later engage."

However, if a neonate is made to practice the reflexive walk 12 minutes per day (four 3-minute sessions), some odd things happen. First, the reflex lasts longer than usual. Second, the voluntary walking that will eventually occur will begin much sooner than expected (Andre-Thomas & St. Dargassies, 1952; Zelazo, Zelazo, & Kolb, 1972).

Question: Why should practice at reflexive walking make voluntary walking occur sooner?

Somehow, reflexive walking *is* related to later voluntary walking, and practice seems to accelerate the maturational readiness to walk. One possibility is that both "reflexive" *and* "voluntary" walking are really different aspects of a single development, namely, the unfolding of a maturational plan that will enable the infant to walk. The reason that there seem to be two distinct kinds of walking is that there is a period during which infants can do neither (approximately from 3 to 8 months of age). This lack of continuity, or disappearance of any walking ability, does make it seem as though there are two kinds of walking. However, it turns out that although infants are unable to walk upright during the ages of 3 to 8 months, they continue to develop the walking sequence while kicking in a lying position. The kind of kicking that infants do while lying down is indistinguishable in terms of neuromuscular activation from either "form" of walking. It's just that between the ages of 3 and 8 months, infants don't have the leg strength to move their growing mass while in the upright position. As further support for this assertion, it has been found that 7-month-old infants will show all the movements associated with walking if their weight is supported somewhat while their feet are placed on a moving treadmill (Thelen, 1986). Careful examination of treadmill walking indicates that self-sustained walking gradually comes about as the legs slowly stop flexing, allowing the legs to stretch back far enough to elicit the full bilateral alternating response required for self-sustained walking (Thelen & Ulrich, 1991). In this sense, then, the development of walking is relatively continuous and without interruption, and any practice may accelerate it (Thelen & Fisher, 1982). Early walking, however, provides no long-term advantage and it is pointless to encourage it or try to accelerate its development. The same is true for very simple behaviors, such as bladder control. As you recall from the Chapter Preview, early practice in that instance had no discernible effect. What we can say, however, is that experiences tend to be viewed more as accelerators or decelerators of growth or motor development than as their cause (Bertenthal & Campos, 1987).

Question: Would you give an example of what you mean by accelerators or decelerators?

American children today typically walk on their own a few months earlier than they were observed to do 60 years ago. For that matter, children in different countries tend to walk for the first time at different ages (Hindley, Filliozat, Klackenberg, Nicolet-Meister, & Sand, 1966), and the rate and steadiness at which their walking develops may also differ (Hennessy, Dixon, & Simon, 1984). How might experience account for these different rates and average ages at which children first walk?

Question: Could these differences be due to differences in nutrition?

BEHAVIORAL GENETICS
The interdisciplinary science that focuses on the interaction of nature and nurture—that is, on the interaction of what is inherited and what is acquired—and how that interaction affects behavior.

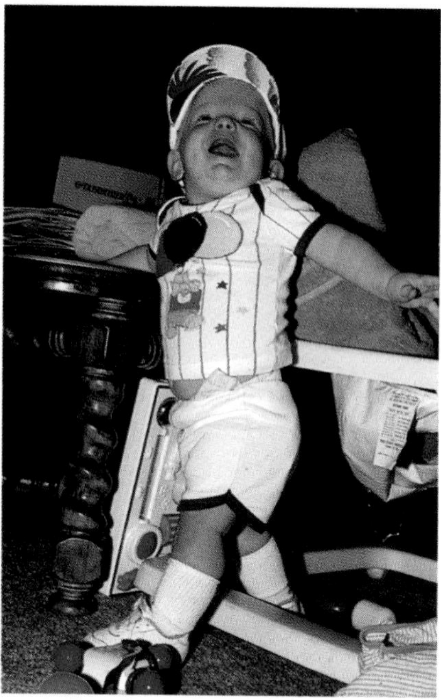
Differences in temperament emerge early in life.

It's possible. After all, American children 60 years ago were growing up during the Great Depression and may not have had sufficient nourishment. And certainly, the adequacy of nutrition varies from one country to the next. Today's accelerated rate might also be influenced by parents who are eager to see their children walk. Such parents might encourage their children to try just as soon as they are able. In contrast, parents of 60 years ago, who often had larger families, might have been considerably less excited about the first steps of their fourth, fifth, or sixth child and so have encouraged these children less. Even the introduction of wall-to-wall carpeting may have played a role! Perhaps when babies of 60 years ago tried to take their first steps, they found landing on hardwood floor punishing enough to deter their efforts for a time.

Because of such possible environmental influences, motor developments may occur at a slightly faster (accelerated) or slower (decelerated) rate than we might expect—*but only within maturational limits.* Because of the rate of maturational development, it is impossible—regardless of the kind of nutrition, coaxing, or carpeting—to get a 4-month-old to walk on his or her own.

Question: If that is true, then should children be kept from ballet or tennis lessons or any other similar activity until they are maturationally ready?

No, not really. Although a child may not be maturationally able to engage in certain motor responses, there is no reason why the child shouldn't enjoy attempting to imitate older children or adults. Younger children may also have a lot of fun at "ballet" or "tennis," even though they can't actually dance or play well; and by having fun playing at these activities when they are young, they may come to be highly motivated to continue them when they are maturationally ready.

Individual Differences and Temperament Theories

Although the human infant doesn't appear to possess a fully integrated personality in its first few days of life, people have observed that newborns do exhibit considerable differences in temperament. As we discussed in Chapter 1, there is much evidence that babies are different from one another just after birth. Some babies are fussy, some have a high activity level, and some seem to do nothing but sleep. Temperament theories consider the possibility that these early infant personalities or traits may be consistent or stable over great lengths of time.

Question: How would you define temperament?

Although researchers argue over which components of infant personality should be included, any definition would encompass the ideas that

> temperament consists of relatively consistent, basic dispositions inherent in the person that underlie and modulate the expression of activity, reactivity, emotionality, and sociability. Major elements of temperament are present early in life, and those elements are likely to be strongly influenced by biological factors. As development proceeds, the expression of temperament increasingly becomes more influenced by experience and context. (Goldsmith et al., 1987, p. 524)

Some babies are "easy"; some babies are "difficult"; and some babies are "cool."

THE NEW YORK LONGITUDINAL STUDY

In the late 1950s, two physicians, Alexander Thomas and Stella Chess, began what came to be called the New York Longitudinal Study. With their colleagues, they followed 140 children from birth to adolescence. They were initially interested in infant reactivity, but soon came to believe that they were, in fact, empirically documenting differences in temperament. In 1968, they first described their subjects in terms of "easy" or "difficult" temperaments (Thomas, Chess, & Birch, 1968, 1970).

Question: How did the researchers define "easy" and "difficult"?

The differences between easy and difficult infants and children are outlined in Table 4.3. These personality dimensions were obtained through interviews with parents, observation of infants and children, and other measures. As you can see, easy infants adapt readily to new situations, are approachable, respond with low or mild intensity, exhibit pleasant moods, and have regular body rhythms.

Question: Do all infants fall into one or the other category?

Some of the infants studied fell between the dimensions of easy and difficult. Such infants are often referred to as "slow-to-warm-up" babies. Other infants were too inconsistent to categorize, exhibiting "mixtures of traits that did not add up to a general characterization" (Thomas, Chess, & Birch, 1970, p. 105). Among the infants studied, the researchers found that 40 percent were easy, 15 percent slow to warm up, 10 percent difficult, and 35 percent inconsistent.

The categories shown in Table 4.3 were criticized for a number of reasons. First, fully one-third of the children couldn't be clearly classified. Second, further research showed that a number of the temperament categories tended to overlap each other (Sanson, Prior, & Kyrios, 1990). And finally, it was argued that parents and other raters of temperament sometimes showed bias in their observations.

However, it has since been shown that individuals who are classified according to some of these categories and who are at the extremes of a particular temperament quality do tend to display such qualities consistently over time (Kagan, Reznick, & Gibbons, 1989; Kagan & Snidman, 1991). For example, a child who doesn't cry much with wet diapers at 2 months of age is also less likely to fuss when a shirt is pulled over the child's head at 2 years of age. Follow-up studies at 5 and 10 years also show a certain stability of these traits. Some studies have found that such stable temperaments may even continue into adulthood (Carey & McDevitt, 1978; Lerner, Palermo, Spiro, & Nesselroade, 1982), although culture and social variables do exert increasing influence on temperament over the life span (Goldsmith et al., 1987).

GOODNESS OF FIT

Question: Do difficult children have more problems adjusting to the world than easy children do?

That's a hard question to answer. When researchers are faced with this kind of question, they usually refer to what they call "goodness of fit" (Sprunger, Boyce, & Gaines, 1985).

Question: What do researchers mean by "goodness of fit"?

"Goodness of fit" refers to how suitable a particular child's temperament is to his or her environment. One of the most dramatic examples of the goodness-of-fit concept comes from a study of easy and difficult infants among the Masai, an African tribe of nomadic warriors. In the early 1980s, this tribe, along with many other tribes in Africa, suffered the effects of a severe drought and famine. Developmental researchers had already taken initial measurements of which infants were easy and which were difficult and later, in their follow-up after the calamity, were shocked to discover that most of the easy infants had died, while almost all of the difficult children had survived (deVries & Sameroff, 1984)! After looking very carefully for possible differences that might account for these findings, it was observed that the Masai encouraged boldness, outspokenness, and assertiveness in their children and infants—qualities more typical of a difficult temperament. Furthermore, Masai mothers would breast feed their infants on demand, and it was discovered that the difficult infants, who by their very temperament were fussier and louder, were being fed more often. It was a perfect example of the

TABLE 4.3

Stability of Temperaments over Time

TEMPERAMENTAL QUALITY	RATING	2 MONTHS	1 YEAR	10 YEARS
Rhythmicity	Regular	Has been on 4-hour feeding schedule since birth. Regular bowel movement.	Naps after lunch each day. Always drinks bottle before bed.	Eats only at mealtimes. Sleeps the same amount of time each night.
	Irregular	Awakes at a different time each morning. Size of feedings varies.	Will not fall asleep for an hour or more. Moves bowels at a different time each day.	Food intake varies. Falls asleep at a different time each night.
Approach-withdrawal	Positive	Smiles and licks washcloth. Has always liked bottle.	Approaches strangers readily. Sleeps well in new surroundings.	Went to camp happily. Loved to ski the first time.
	Negative	Rejected cereal the first time. Cries when strangers appear.	Cries when placed on sled. Will not sleep in strange beds.	Severely homesick at camp during first days. Does not like new activities.
Adaptability	Adaptive	Was passive during first bath, now enjoys bathing. Smiles at nurse.	Was afraid of toy animals at first, now plays with them happily.	Likes camp, although homesick during first days. Learns enthusiastically.
	Not adaptive	Still startled by sudden, sharp noises. Resists diapering.	Continues to reject new foods each time they are offered.	Does not adjust well to new school or new teacher; comes home late for dinner even when punished.
Intensity of reaction	Mild	Does not cry when diapers are wet. Whimpers instead of crying when hungry.	Does not fuss much when clothing is pulled on over head.	When a mistake is made in a model airplane, corrects it quietly. Does not comment when reprimanded.
	Intense	Cries when diapers are wet. Rejects food vigorously when satisfied.	Laughs hard when father plays roughly. Screams and kicks when temperature is taken.	Tears up an entire page of homework if one mistake is made. Slams door of room when teased by younger brother.
Quality of mood	Positive	Smacks lips when first tasting new food. Smiles at parents.	Likes bottle; reaches for it and smiles. Laughs loudly when playing peekaboo.	Enjoys new accomplishments. Laughs when reading a funny passage aloud.
	Negative	Fusses after nursing. Cries when carriage is rocked.	Cries when given injections. Cries when left alone.	Cries when he cannot solve a homework problem. Very "weepy" if he does not get enough sleep.

KEY

	EASY CHILD	SLOW-TO-WARM-UP CHILD	DIFFICULT CHILD
Rhythmicity	Very regular	Varies	Irregular
Approach-withdrawal	Positive approach	Initial withdrawal	Withdrawal
Adaptability	Very adaptable	Slowly adaptable	Slowly adaptable
Intensity of reaction	Low or mild	Mild	Intense
Quality of mood	Positive	Slightly negative	Negative

SOURCE: Thomas, Chess, & Birch, 1970, pp. 108–109.

squeaky wheel getting the grease—or, in this case, the milk. Other studies have shown that children with difficult temperaments are far less likely to develop behavioral difficulties if they are reared in environments that are culturally accepting of the behaviors associated with being difficult (Korn & Gannon, 1983; Lerner, 1984).

Question: In most industrialized Western environments, is it better for a child to be easy?

Again, that's very difficult to say. It does appear that the kinds of behaviors exhibited by difficult children may be related to more significant behavior problems in childhood (Lee & Bates, 1985; Earls & Jung, 1988); and there is evidence that difficult children may be at greater risk for psychiatric disorders during adolescence (Maziade et al., 1985) and that they tend to face more daily stress, often as the result of their own behavior (Wertlieb, Weigel, Springer, & Feldstein, 1988). But none of this necessarily means that it is better if the child is easy or worse if the child is difficult. Sometimes difficult behavior can have a value for the child even though most Western parents say that they would prefer a child who is easy.

The Masai people encourage boldness, outspokenness, and assertiveness in their infants and children. Although such qualities are considered "difficult" in Western culture, these same qualities better fit the demands of the harsher environment in which the Masai live.

Question: How could it be an advantage for a child in Western culture to be difficult?

In one study, for example, it was found that difficult infants from upper- and middle-class families, when tested later at age 4, were obtaining intelligence test scores that were 20 IQ points higher than their matched easy counterparts (Maziade, Cote, Boutin, Bernier, & Thivierge, 1988). The researchers who conducted the study noted that the parents of the difficult children were stimulating them more (talking to, interacting with, and attending to them) in an attempt to deal with their behavior. They add, "Such parents would stimulate the difficult infant more than the extremely easy infant, who is more readily left to himself. Such special stimulation would favor more rapid development" (Maziade, Cote, Boutin, Bernier, & Thivierge, 1988, p. 342). Of course, it is too early to know whether this difference would be sustained over time or provide any lasting advantage. In fact, there is evidence that in the school system, it might be the easy children who have an advantage because they are better able to attend to tasks and concentrate (Palisin, 1986). As you can see, defining "goodness of fit" is not a simple task.

Environmental Influences on Temperament

Even if there are biologically determined differences in individual temperaments, this doesn't always mean that such traits will continue, or, if such traits do continue, that they are the result of a biological constitution.

Question: Are there any reasons, other than biological ones, that could explain the long-term stability of temperament?

Consider the following: It has been found that mothers who feel that their babies are difficult are less responsive to their infants and less sensitive to changes in their babies' emotional states (Donovan, Leavitt, & Balling, 1978; Klein, 1984). It may be, then, that babies who *initially* have difficult temperaments cause problems or strife between themselves and their parents (Sirignano & Lachman, 1985). Such a situation may in turn lead to a cycle of heavy-handed parental discipline and child rebellion that may, in theory, continue for *environmental* reasons long after any biologically determined temperamental predisposition has ceased to directly influence the child's personality. In other words, whether a baby continues to be easy or difficult throughout childhood may be due to the way the parents initially react to their child's temperament.

Some children may be "born shy" in the sense that shyness may be partially determined by inheritance.

To address this problem, researchers conducted a study in which they made a special effort to control for the possibility that environmental factors determine temperament. In their study, they examined many different combinations of pairs of siblings, some adopted and some not, some who were identical twins and some who were fraternal twins. The results showed that identical twins were the siblings who were most alike in temperament. But most telling was that biological siblings (who share about 50 percent of their genes with each other) were more similar in temperament than adopted siblings (unrelated biologically) who were living together in the same family. These results "indicate substantial genetic influence on infant temperament" (Braungart, Plomin, DeFries, & Fulker, 1992, p. 45).

THE SEARCH FOR INNATE COMPONENTS

In their New York Longitudinal Study, Chess and Thomas suggested that certain components of temperament may be innately determined. Researchers interested in behavioral genetics have since attempted to isolate these hypothetical innate factors; along the way, they have made some interesting discoveries that support the idea that temperament has innate components.

For example, it has been discovered that the activity levels of 4- to 8-year-old children can be predicted with considerable accuracy by knowing the activity levels they showed as neonates. In other words, the more active someone was as a newborn, the more active he or she is likely to be as a child (Korner et al., 1985). Such findings as these imply a constitutional predisposition involving activity level because there has been so little time, or opportunity, for the environment to shape activity levels in a newborn.

Further support for the existence of innate components of temperament comes from the observation that identical twins are about twice as likely to share the same fears as are fraternal twins (Rose & Ditto, 1983). Along these lines, it has also been shown that 2-year-old children who were inhibited or withdrawn exhibited faster and more stable heartbeats when confronted with novel stimuli than did outgoing children (Kagan, Reznick, Clarke, Snidman, & Garcia-Coll, 1984). This last study by Jerome Kagan and his colleagues was the first to show a clear-cut association between a temperamental characteristic (approach-withdrawal) and a physiological function (heart rate) (Chess & Thomas, 1986a). In a follow-up study, Kagan discovered that the withdrawn children at age 8 years continued to be withdrawn in unfamiliar social situations and to exhibit faster and more stable heartbeats when stressed, while the outgoing children continued to be spontaneous, talkative, and interactive in new social situations (Kagan, 1989).

It is worth emphasizing, however, that even if susceptibility to anxiety or inhibition is inherited, such predispositions are still likely to be modifiable by environmental influence (Rowe & Plomin, 1981). For instance, approximately one-third of all shy children are able to overcome their shyness by adulthood. Perhaps, with proper intervention, even a greater number could be successful. Clearly, individual differences are a function of the interaction of nature and nurture. As the child encounters the environment, innate predispositions and experience will interact to provide the child with a unique and integrated personality. This is why most researchers agree that the view best supported by the data is an interactionist one, namely, that temperament and environment interact and affect one another.

LEARNING CHECK

True or False

1. Infants are temperamentally alike until about the age of 1 year.
2. Experience may affect maturational development by accelerating or decelerating it, but only within limits.
3. Babies are alike at birth. Individual differences first appear by about 4 months of age.
4. Children must crawl before they can walk.

Answers: 1. F 2. T 3. F 4. F

APPLICATIONS

Preventing SIDS

On an early spring morning, a mother walks into the nursery to check on her 3-month-old baby. The infant had been suffering from a mild cold and had seemed to be getting better. But the child is still and does not appear to be breathing; in fact, the infant has tragically become one of the 7,000 infants who die each year in the United States of SIDS (sudden infant death syndrome), or crib death.

Question: Does anyone know what causes SIDS?

Historically, such deaths have been blamed on smothering by a pillow or blanket or even the careless movements of the infant's sleeping mother. But research has since demonstrated that smothering by a person or pillow is rarely the cause of crib death. All that we really know for sure is that something causes a failure in the central nervous system (CNS). Whether there is some factor that disrupts the CNS, or whether the CNS in SIDS victims is immature for some reason, remains to be learned. A number of possible suggestions and discoveries have been made, however, that may someday hold the key to our understanding of SIDS. Let's take a look at some of these.

Learning Disability

Because a high proportion of SIDS victims have mild colds at the time of death, researchers have begun to consider respiratory failure or weakening of the breathing response as a prime suspect. But the question remains: Why should a mild cold or stuffy nose cause a child to stop breathing altogether?

Some years ago, while investigating more than 70 SIDS cases, Lewis Lipsitt discovered some common threads among the SIDS group that he did not find in matched control groups. He discovered that compared with the control group, the victims were usually of low birth weight, had mothers who were anemic during pregnancy, and had been born after a shorter second stage of labor (Lipsitt, McCullagh, Reilly, Smith, & Sturner, 1981). He further noticed that compared with the control group mothers, the mothers of SIDS victims were more likely to be smokers, ill, less educated, of lower socioeconomic status, and living in more crowded conditions. It appeared, then, that nutritional and health factors associated with smoking, poverty, and illness could be having a direct bearing on the incidence of a breathing failure, known as sleep apnea. *Apnea* is a condition in which a person experiences a temporary cessation of breathing. Sleep apnea in an infant might result in crib death, but no one knows whether apnea is a cause of SIDS or simply associated with it; that is, no one knows whether SIDS victims die *of* apnea or simply die *with* apnea.

Lipsitt views such SIDS- and apnea-associated characteristics as possible contributors to a "learning disability" in infants.

Question: What does Lipsitt mean by a learning disability?

As we have discussed in this chapter, neonates are born with a number of reflexes. Among these is a built-in defensive reflex that helps protect them from breathing blockages. This can be demonstrated by placing a cloth over a neonate's mouth for 10 seconds to cause a partial breathing blockage. By doing this, a physician should trigger a rage reflex in the neonate that includes crying or struggling. This reflex can often aid the infant to eliminate a breathing blockage.*

*Only trained medical personnel should attempt to elicit this reflex because cutting off the air of an "at-risk" infant may lead to apnea or some other problem that will require intervention.

An infant at high risk for sudden death is monitored in a hospital. Such monitoring can often save an infant's life if the infant suddenly stops breathing.

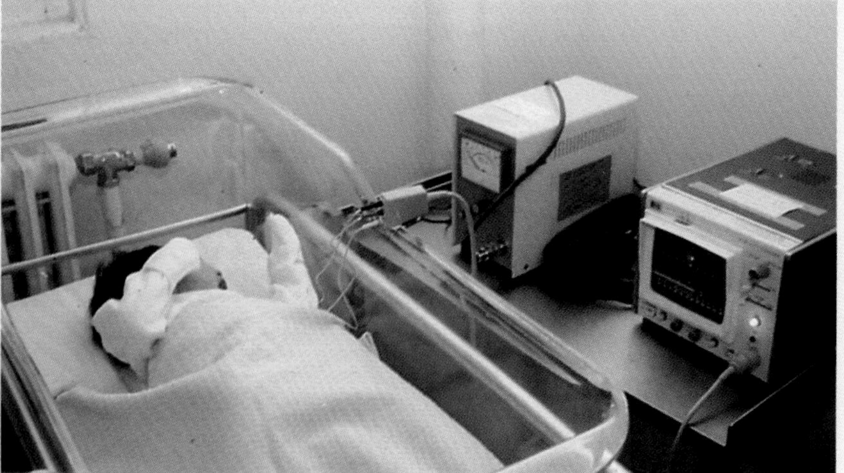

APPLICATIONS

As you may recall, many of the neonate's early reflexes become weak and disappear between the ages of 2 and 4 months. Similarly, the rage reflex becomes weak or disappears between the ages of 1 and 4 months, and learned struggling responses must replace the reflex to protect an infant who may suffer from a breathing blockage such as those caused by colds or stuffy noses.

Lipsitt argues that the crib death victims may have had a learning disability, perhaps due to poor prenatal care, which hindered their ability to *learn* the struggling necessary to survive a breathing blockage once reflexive struggling no longer occurred. This may explain why crib death is so rare in infants over 8 months of age; by then, they are likely to have developed learned responses that can help them overcome a respiratory blockage. It would also explain why most victims of SIDS are between 1 and 4 months old (see Figure 4.4). The infants at risk during these ages are old enough that they lose their rage reflex but young enough that they have not yet developed a learned method of struggling.

Physiological Defects

Question: Are there any physical problems that might cause SIDS?

Over 20 years ago, researcher Alfred Steinschneider first argued that SIDS infants have poorly developed brain mechanisms for coping with an apneic episode. He pointed out that autopsies of SIDS victims often revealed the pathological signs of long-term hypoventilation (inadequate respiratory exchange of air). Chronic hypoventilation in infants leads to underdeveloped body organs and small body size of a markedly different nature from the underdevelopment caused by infection or disease.

It was also found that infants who died of SIDS, when compared with infants who died from other causes, had a strikingly higher level of a brain neurotransmitter called dopamine (Perrin et al., 1984). High levels of dopamine decrease the rate of respiration.

Somewhat more recently, it was discovered that SIDS victims had higher than normal levels of infant hemoglobin in their blood (Giulian, Gilbert, & Moss, 1987). Hemoglobin is used by the body to transport oxygen to the tissues. Normally, after a few months, infant hemoglobin is replaced by adult hemoglobin, which is better able to carry oxygen. Perhaps this replacement is not happening fast enough in SIDS victims, and they are slowly starved of oxygen. Researchers are now looking at the possibility of developing a blood test that might give warning as to which infants are most likely to become SIDS victims. Of course, the high levels of infant hemoglobin in SIDS

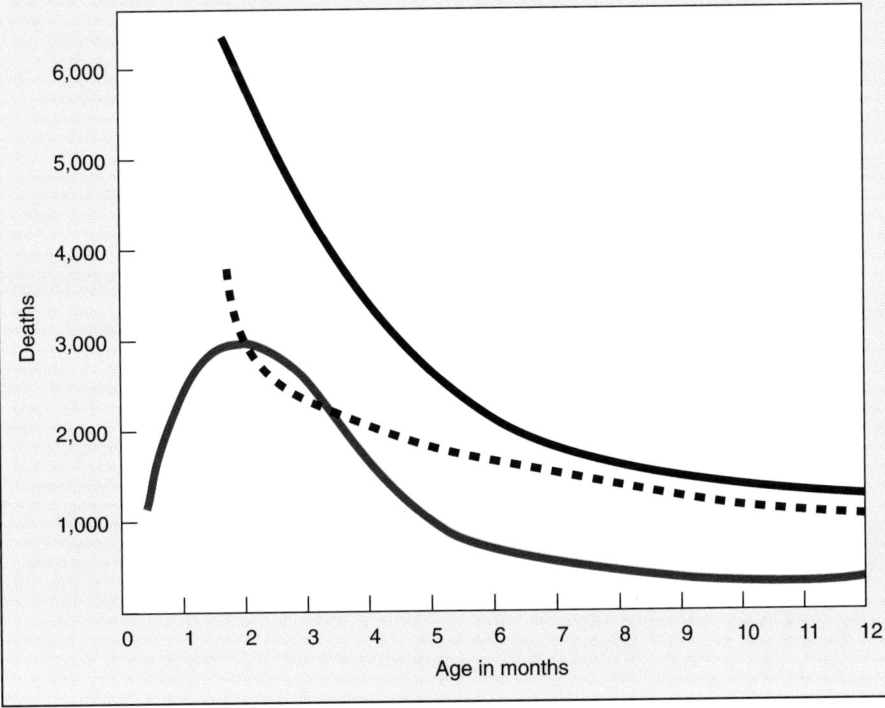

FIGURE 4.4
Infant deaths in the United States from sudden infant death syndrome (SIDS) *(colored curve)* and from all other causes *(broken curve)*. The solid black curve shows the total number of deaths of infants between the ages of 10 weeks and 12 months. SIDS is the most frequent cause of death of infants between the ages of 1 month and 1 year, and in babies 3 months of age, it exceeds all other causes. For example, approximately 1,000 5-month-old infants die each year from SIDS *(colored curve)*, and 2,000 (from all other causes *(broken curve)*, with a total of 3,000 infant deaths *(solid black curve)*. *(Source:* Naeye, 1980, p. 58)

APPLICATIONS

victims might be a result of SIDS rather than a cause.

Question: Could SIDS be an inherited problem?

Evidence to date indicates that it is probably not solely a genetic problem. This is supported by the finding that the incidence of SIDS among identical twins is the same as among fraternal twins. However, we have known for some time that SIDS does seem to run in families (Schiffman, Westlake, Santiago, & Edelman, 1980), and many researchers believe that some infants may be born with a genetic predisposition to respond to environmental experiences in a way that might lead to SIDS.

Infant Botulism

It is now believed that at least 5 percent of crib deaths, and perhaps a much greater percentage, are due to infant botulism, an acute food poisoning caused by ingestion of botulin. In 1975, the first known case of infant botulism was reported in New Jersey (Arnon, Midura, Clay, Wood, & Chin, 1977). Botulin is a toxin produced by a spore-forming bacterium. Botulism results in a nerve paralysis that may be life-threatening.

From time to time, you've probably heard of outbreaks of botulism; they are generally the result of improperly canned or preserved foods. Babies are especially susceptible to the effects of the toxin.

Question: How does the toxin affect an infant?

Affected infants appear to be "floppy" and listless. Physicians often refer to the victims of infantile botulism as "floppy babies" because of the nerve weakness caused by the toxin. As you can imagine, botulism toxin decreases a person's respiratory drive, which, in combination with the learning disability described by Lipsitt, or with apnea, could be fatal.

Suffocation

In the last few years 37 infants have died of SIDS while sleeping on infant bean-bag cushions. The babies were found with their faces buried in the soft cushions. The thought that these infants had smothered seemed odd, however, because it has been known for years that infants will turn their heads or struggle if they are unable to breathe and that such actions should have been sufficient to get their faces out of the cushions on which they were resting. But still, the deaths did look suspiciously like smothering.

Curious as to how smothering might occur under such circumstances, researchers tested the infant cushions with rabbits. The rabbits also buried their faces in the cushions when they slept, but were still able to breathe. Even so, all of the rabbits were dead within three hours. Autopsies showed that they had, in fact, suffocated (Kemp & Thach, 1991).

Question: If the infants or rabbits couldn't breathe, why didn't they struggle?

What appears to have happened is that both the infants and rabbits who died had made a pocket in the cushions with their faces deep enough for them to still breathe, but also sufficient enough to collect their exhaled carbon dioxide. After inhaling rebreathed air long enough, levels of carbon dioxide in the blood became dangerous and eventually lethal. The infants didn't struggle because their air wasn't cut off; they died breathing lethal levels of carbon dioxide.

Following these findings the Consumer Product Safety Commission requested that retailers remove the infant cushions from their shelves. The Commission also put out a warning for the owners of almost one million of the cushions sold in the U.S. to avoid using them with infants. The same dangers probably exist for any mattress or surface that is soft enough for an infant to make a rebreathing pocket with his or her face. For this reason, a number of SIDS deaths might be avoided by using a mattress or sleeping surface that is not too soft. How many SIDS deaths are the result of this unusual kind of suffocation is unknown, but about one third of SIDS victims are found face down and many of these infants may have died in this fashion.

Other Causes

Keep in mind that SIDS infants are probably not a homogeneous group. "SIDS" is just a description of what happens. It may have many different causes and may in fact eventually be discovered to be a number of different diseases. For instance, SIDS may sometimes be related to the levels of certain vitamins in the body.

Evidence that supports the idea that excessive heat may be involved in SIDS has come from England, where researchers noticed similarities between SIDS victims and heatstroke victims. The investigators noted that many SIDS babies "were judged to have been excessively clothed or covered at the time of death" (Stanton, Scott, & Downham, 1980).

Question: Whether crib death is caused by a learning disability, slow oxygen deprivation, botulism, or even something else, is there anything that can be done to prevent it?

APPLICATIONS

By applying the knowledge gained from the research in this area, parents or care givers of infants can help to some degree, especially by avoiding botulism. Although infant botulism may be due to spores already in the infant's intestines at birth, there may also be external sources ingested by the infant. Researchers have pinpointed honey as a possible source of enough toxin to harm a young infant. Physicians are now recommending that infants not be fed honey. Raw agricultural products also can be a source of spores, and it might be a good idea if all vegetables and fruits are peeled or well cooked before they are given to an infant. Furthermore, any unclean objects (such as a dropped pacifier) should be kept out of an infant's mouth until they have been washed off; one researcher even found botulism spores in the dust of a vacuum cleaner used in the house of an infant botulism victim (Marks, 1978).

Question: What should be done if an infant is thought to be at risk for SIDS?

Any infant that is considered at risk must be watched closely. In one of the first studies conducted along these lines, the staff at Massachusetts General Hospital in Boston examined 260 babies who were judged to be at high risk for SIDS (because they had had serious prior episodes of breathing failure). These infants were then connected to electronic monitors that emitted a loud tone when breathing stopped. Of the 260 infants, 156 eventually suffered severe breathing weakness and caused the monitor to sound its alarm, which, in turn, brought immediate help. It was judged that without the monitors, all but 4 of the 156 infants who suffered breathing weakness would have become crib death victims ("Preventing Crib Deaths," 1979).*

*A number of U.S. companies now make such monitors for home use. If you are considering the use of such a monitor, be sure that both the monitor and its use are approved jointly by you and your physician because some monitors are known to be of poor quality or ineffective. You should also be aware that because so little is known about SIDS, there are not as yet any national standards to help you or your physician decide which infants are at risk or who should use a monitor. Many professionals believe that because of the considerable stress that monitor use places on a family, only infants who have already had a serious bout of respiratory failure should be placed on a monitor. It's not a simple decision.

SUMMARY

■ Neonates (newborns) typically weigh between 6 and 9 pounds and are about 20 inches in length. Their skin is soft, dry, and wrinkled. Their head appears large, accounting for one-quarter of the baby's length.

■ During the first half of the twentieth century, infants were generally viewed as helpless and passive. Research during the 1960s and 1970s helped do away with the view of the infant as a passive individual.

■ Newborns exhibit a number of reflexes. Many of these reflexes serve vital functions, while others perhaps once did but no longer do.

■ *Maturation* is a term used to describe a biological plan for development that is relatively independent of experience. Both physical growth and motor development appear to be largely due to the forces of maturation. Still, it may be that certain antecedent experiences are necessary for the development of some growth or motor development. Unless every experience can be controlled for in experiments, it will probably never be possible to answer such nature-nurture questions fully.

■ Behavioral geneticists attempt to determine the relative contributions of nature and nurture as they affect behavior. The Ache of Paraguay are offered as an interesting example of this kind of work.

■ Parents should be aware of individual differences between children and not be too elated or concerned should their child be a few months ahead of or behind the published norms.

■ Temperament theories are based on the fact that early personalities or traits are fairly stable over time. Thomas, Chess, and Birch (1970) have identified a number of these traits and have found them to be stable over the first 10 years of life.

■ More important than whether a child's temperament is easy or difficult may be how well it is suited to his or her environment. Researchers refer to this as "goodness of fit."

■ Although temperament does seem to be determined in part by biological factors, the environment can play an important role in shaping and altering it.

■ Predisposition toward anxiety or shyness may be innate. Even so, the environment may influence these traits.

■ Although no one really knows what causes SIDS (sudden infant death syndrome), the suspected cause is a failure of the respiratory system. A number of possible contributing causes have been hypothesized, including botulism, learning disability, and a poor level of adult hemoglobin. To date, some success at preventing SIDS has been achieved by the use of respiration monitors for infants thought to be at risk.

QUESTIONS FOR DISCUSSION

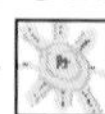

1. In what sense is the human infant a competent individual?
2. In some countries, such as Iran, children are eventually forced to become right-handed. Does this mean that in these children, maturation does not play a role in the development of handedness?
3. Do you think that easy children have an "easier" life? Do you think that easy children develop effective coping skills? What problems might easy children encounter?

SUGGESTIONS FOR FURTHER READING

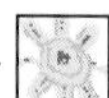

1. American Academy of Pediatrics. (1991). *Caring for your baby and young child: Birth to age 5.* New York: Bantam.
2. Buss, A. H., & Plomin, R. (1984). *Temperament: Early developing personality traits.* Hillsdale, NJ: Erlbaum.
3. Caplan, F. (1973). *The first twelve months of life.* New York: Grosset & Dunlap.
4. Maurer, D., & Maurer, C. (1988). *The world of the newborn.* New York: Basic Books.
5. Stoppard, M. (1990). *The first weeks of life.* New York: Ballantine.

CHAPTER 5

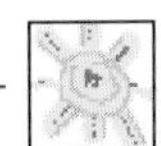

NEURAL, SENSORY, AND PERCEPTUAL DEVELOPMENT

CHAPTER PREVIEW

A DR. SEUSS STORY

PARENTS ENJOY reading to their children, and children especially like to have stories read to them. Among the favorites are the enduring stories of Dr. Seuss. It should come as no surprise, then, to discover that over 150 children observed in a study in North Carolina deliberately tried to get their mothers to read a Dr. Seuss story to them when they could. But perhaps you'd be surprised to learn that these children's ages ranged from 2 to 3.

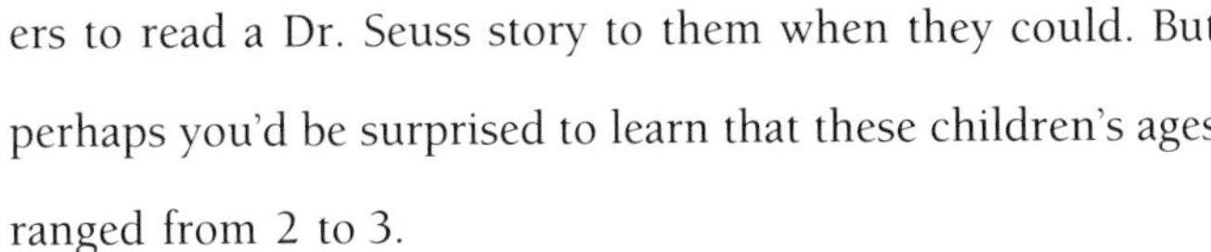

Question: What's so surprising about 2- or 3-year-olds asking their mothers to read them a Dr. Seuss story?

I MUST NOT HAVE made myself clear. The children weren't 2 to 3 years old; they were 2 to 3 *days* old. In the experiment, the babies were put in bassinets, and small, loose-fitting headsets were placed over their ears. A special nipple was placed in their mouths. If the infants sucked at a selected rate, a tape of their own mother's voice reading a Dr. Seuss story would be played. If the sucking rate deviated from the selected rate, a different woman's voice would continue with the story.

REGARDLESS OF whether the selected rate was fast or slow, at least 85 percent of the infants showed a preference for their own mother's voice over that of a stranger and adjusted their sucking rate to maintain their mother's voice on the earphones. The infants also began new sessions at the correct sucking rate, which demonstrates the presence of a functioning memory (DeCasper & Fifer, 1980).

Question: But how could babies know which voice was their mother's?

THE HUMAN EAR is developed and functional about 7 months after conception (Birnholz & Benacerraf, 1983), so the fetus probably listens to its mother's voice during the last 2 months of the pregnancy, perhaps learning the sound of the voice while it is still in the womb. Possibly, also, the infant has rapidly learned to recognize his own mother's voice during the first 1 or 2 days following birth.

Question: Is there any way to tell whether the infants learned their mother's voice before or after they were born?

THE STUDY WAS run a second time, this time with fathers instead of mothers. All the fathers in the experiment were presented with their baby daughters at birth and talked to them as often as possible, sometimes as much as 10 hours. From after birth to the time of the study, each baby heard only her father's voice. The babies, only 2 or 3 days old, once again were equipped with the earphones and the special nipple that allowed them to choose to hear their own father or a stranger read Dr. Seuss. The babies showed no preference for one voice over the other (Kolata, 1984). This was the first study to show that the infants' reaction probably was a result of their having had more experience hearing their mother's voice—which, of course, implies that they heard it while in the womb. In fact, after listening to their own father's voice for a few weeks, the infants preferred it to that of a stranger.

IN THIS CHAPTER, we will investigate the development of the infant's nervous system and also look at the basic sensory and perceptual abilities of infants. And, as you have already discovered, you may find some surprises along the way.

RESOURCES

The Nervous System of the Neonate

The human nervous system includes the brain, spinal cord, and peripheral nerves. As far as we know, there is nothing in this world more complicated. The creative and intellectual power associated with the human nervous system is unchallenged by any other species. Yet, despite all this power, there is nothing quite as helpless as a human infant. This has led many to wonder,

> What is the Meaning of Infancy? What is the meaning of the fact that man is born into the world more helpless than any other creature, and needs for a much longer season than any other living thing the tender care and wise counsel of his elders? (Fiske, 1883/1909, p. 1)

Of course, no one is sure of the answer, but many believe that the human brain requires extra time to take in the vast amount of information it will need before it no longer depends on "the tender care and wise counsel of its elders" (Greenough, Black, & Wallace, 1987). It may be, then, that other species move on to adulthood at a faster rate because they have evolved in a way that allows them to get by with less, while our species takes its time, all the while training, shaping, and developing its massive brain.

Question: Is an infant's nervous system very developed at birth, or is an infant born with a nervous system that is mostly immature?

A detailed answer will probably require the information that researchers will gain during the next century, but we do have the beginnings of an answer now.

To start with, we have to break the question into two areas of inquiry. First, is the structure of the newborn's nervous system developed or immature, and second, is the organization of the nervous system similar or dissimilar to that of an adult's? As you might have expected, research has shown that the nervous system of the newborn is less mature than your own. Readouts from an **electroencephalogram (EEG),** which measures electrical brain activity by recording wave pulses on paper, show a considerable degree of immaturity in newborns. The dendrites (parts of the **neuron,** or nerve cell, that help to receive and sometimes send nerve messages) are noticeably underdeveloped in newborns. This is especially true within the central structures of the brain. In newborns, portions of neurons of the **central nervous system (CNS),** down which neural messages typically travel, are not yet myelinated (Morell & Norton, 1980). The newborn's nervous system is still growing.

Question: What do you mean by myelinated?

This term refers to the development of the **myelin sheath,** a covering consisting of a white fatty substance that grows around the **axon** of the nerve cell. The myelin sheath acts as an insulator and aids in nerve conductivity. The myelin also helps provide nutrition for the nerve cells. Without the right amount of myelin, your body would be incapable of many functions, such as crawling or bowel and bladder control. In fact, the crippling disease multiple sclerosis, which strikes many young adults each year, involves the scarring of the myelin sheath, resulting in weakness and a lack of coordination.

Question: Are you saying that infants lack strength or coordination because they have an immature nervous system?

To a degree, yes. A great deal of the infant's maturation can be directly tied to a rigid timetable of neural growth (Chugani & Phelps, 1986). For example, it has

EEG (ELECTROENCEPHALOGRAM)
A recording of the changes in the brain's electrical potentials. The recording is made by attaching electrodes to various positions to the scalp and amplifying the electrical output coming from the brain. EEG analysis can show a number of systematic changes within the brain that occur during various activities.

NEURON
A nerve cell. The basic unit of the nervous system.

CENTRAL NERVOUS SYSTEM (CNS)
All nerves encased in bone, including the brain and spinal cord.

MYELIN SHEATH
A white fatty covering on neural fibers that serves to channel and increase the transmission speed of impulses along those fibers.

AXON
The long process of a neuron that transmits impulses away from the cell body.

AT ISSUE

Are Two Brains Better Than One?

A little later in this chapter, we will be examining the ability of the infant to sense the world and to perceive what's in it. Sensing and perceiving are activities that you and I do without thinking. You see an object and know that it is red and round. You hear a sound and know that it came from behind you. Your friend touches your hand, and you feel the touch. All this is possible because of the way in which your nervous system is organized. The organization of your nervous system also determines how you think and reason; within its organization is held all that you know and believe.

But how much neural organization was already in place at the time of your birth? Was *any* of it present? Or was there only neural chaos at first, unstructured and unformed, to be shaped only at a later time by your learning and experience? These very questions have interested philosophers for centuries. Much of the work concerning perception that you will read about in this chapter is rooted in philosophical nature-nurture debates. For instance, are we born with the ability to perceive depth, or is it acquired through experience?

Question: Which view is correct?

Research with humans has shown that in most situations, neither philosophical position is totally correct. In other words, both views are partly right. This conclusion is the result of many years of perceptual research and, more recently, a better understanding of how the central nervous system is organized.

There appear to be two separate organizational systems in the newborn's brain (Greenough, Black, & Wallace, 1987). The first organizational system is called the **experience-expectant system.** Through evolution, the experience-expectant system is, to a degree, "prewired," which enables it to make quick sense of aspects of the environment that are common to all members of the species. This does not mean that learning and experience are never involved in this system, only that certain perceptions or actions are very likely to be acquired quickly and with little or perhaps no learning necessary. It is the experience-expectant system that is thought to underlie the mechanisms of canalization, or sensitive periods.

Question: How does the experience-expectant system work?

Infants actually have *more* brain neurons than they will eventually possess as adults (Greenough, Black, & Wallace, 1987). In an experience-expectant system, some neurons will become stronger, while others will remain unstrengthened. The unstrengthened neurons are weeded out of the infant's CNS; that is, they die, leaving behind a certain organization of living neurons.

Question: What determines whether a neuron will become stronger or die?

Whether a neuron in this system is strengthened or left to die appears to depend on the infant's exposure to certain stimuli, presumably the common stimuli all healthy babies are likely to encounter (e.g., an edge, a round thing, a figure with a background, the sound of a human voice, or the feel of something smooth). As long as the necessary stimulation is encountered, the experience-expectant neural system will rapidly develop to deal with it.

Question: What happens if the necessary stimulation is not received?

Remember, we are talking here about stimulation common to all healthy members of a species, not some particular personal experience, so such failures would be

EXPERIENCE-EXPECTANT SYSTEM
A neural model of the central nervous system that pictures the CNS as containing structures that are prepared, or "prewired," to rapidly respond to, or make sense of, experiences that are common to all members of the species. The portion of the CNS that is not experience-dependent.

been observed that human infants, regardless of their culture, begin to smile at about the same age, an occurrence that may be directly related to the amount of myelin that the infant possesses.

Question: When is the newborn's nervous system fully developed?

Some nerve fiber systems develop myelin rapidly, while others take more time. In fact, some parts of the brain aren't fully myelinated until the child reaches puberty.

Question: What about the way in which the newborn's nervous system is organized? Is it like an adult's?

AT ISSUE

quite rare. However, researchers may have answered this question in the laboratory. Through experiments aimed at improving our understanding of blindness and sight, researchers have shown that if animals are denied certain visual experiences during a critical period early in their development, such as the chance to ever see a vertical edge, they often fail to recover the denied function. In contrast, such deprivation in an adult animal rarely has any long-term effect. It is assumed, then, that exposure to certain phenomena is needed for the experience-expectant system to develop, but that once the system is in place, it is pretty well set.

Interestingly, some computers have even been developed along these same lines. Unlike most computers, these machines have no built-in memory. Instead, the computer strengthens or weakens its circuits based on the experiences it encounters. Computers like these, that learn from experience, are even called *neural networks* by computer designers because they mimic the hypothesized human experience-expectant system (Allman, 1986).

Question: You said that there were two hypothesized systems. What's the second one?

The second system is called the **experience-dependent system.** In this system, we see the active formation or loss of neural connections throughout the life span in response to experiences. Infants, therefore, will acquire these connections slowly over time as the result of learning and experience and will continue this process throughout life. It is interesting to note that until recently, it was believed that neural connections were pretty well set by adulthood and that any additional changes were the result of the strengthening or weakening of fixed connections. But there is a growing body of evidence that shows that the creation of completely new neural connections and the disconnections of old neural links are ongoing lifelong processes in response to experience (Reynolds & Weiss, 1992). "Use it or lose it" is a phrase often heard today among brain scientists.

Question: Why are there two systems? Couldn't all the infant's development be handled by the experience-expectant system?

Probably not. There are too many personal experiences that individuals are likely to encounter in life (e.g., the language they speak, the customs they learn, the books they read). If the brain ever evolved so as to be expectant of *every possible experience* that a person might encounter (rather than just the ones that all people come across), we would have some rather odd problems indeed. For instance, we might need a 500-pound brain at birth just to hold the neurons required for the monumental lifelong weeding-out process that such an experience-expectant system would require—lifelong because people are always being exposed to something new. Needless to say, the head needed to hold such a brain would make a Cesarean section something of a requirement, would make nodding "yes" a dangerous activity, and would put hats out of the economic reach of most people.

Whether our depiction of what's going on inside the infant's brain is correct remains to be seen. Research will certainly find it to be more complex than described here. Already there is much agreement that both experience-expectant and experience-dependent systems overlap to a considerable degree, and whether a neural system is experience-expectant or experience-dependent is seen more as a tendency than as a rigid mode of operation. Whatever we discover, it's bound to increase our understanding of infants and all human development.

This, of course, is our other area of inquiry, and one about which we know far less, if only because it's more difficult to study the organization of entire nervous systems than it is to study the structure of nerves or individual nerve cells. The evidence we do have, however, indicates that the organization of the newborn's nervous system is very different from that of an adult's (see At Issue).

EXPERIENCE-DEPENDENT SYSTEM
A neural model of the central nervous system that pictures the CNS as containing structures that are flexible and prepared to incorporate information that is unique to each individual member of a species. The portion of the CNS that is not experience-expectant.

Methods of Sensory and Perceptual Research

It is believed that through the process of natural selection, human sensory and perceptual systems evolved in a way that enable infants to make rapid sense of their world. Although infants are not born with fully developed sensory and per-

SINGLE-STIMULUS PROCEDURE
A methodological procedure for measuring an infant's sensation and perception. An infant's current state is noted (condition A). Then a single stimulus is presented to the infant (condition B) and any measurable changes in the infant's behavior are noted. The procedure can be made experimental by creating a single-subject A-B-A design. This is accomplished by withdrawing the stimulus (return of condition A) and again noting changes in the infant's behavior.

PREFERENCE METHOD
A methodological procedure for measuring an infant's sensation and perception. Two stimuli are presented to the infant simultaneously. Any preference the infant shows for one stimulus rather than the other is taken as a sign that the infant is able to discriminate between the two stimuli. The investigator must control for such factors as right or left hand or near or far preferences.

HABITUATION METHOD
A methodological procedure for measuring an infant's sensation and perception. A stimulus is presented to the infant until habituation occurs. A second stimulus is then presented. Any increased response from the infant is taken as a sign that the infant can discriminate between the stimuli.

ceptual abilities, their sensory and perceptual systems appear to be associated with an experience-expectant neural organization and therefore develop rapidly.

Over the past few decades, researchers have worked hard to discover the rate at which basic sensory and perceptual skills become available to infants. To accomplish this, a number of pretty ingenious experimental designs have been developed.

EXPERIMENTAL DESIGNS

The designs used to study the development of infants' neural, sensory, and perceptual abilities range from very simple to highly complex. Of the many experimental designs that researchers use, the three most common are the single-stimulus procedure, the preference method, and the habituation method.

The **single-stimulus procedure** is perhaps the simplest. In this method, a single stimulus is shown to the infant, and the infant's reactions—such as eye movement, vocalization, reaching, or changes in facial expression—are recorded. The stimulus may then be withdrawn and presented again, and each time the infant's reactions are noted.

When using the **preference method,** researchers present two stimuli to the infant simultaneously. They note whether the infant displays a preference for one stimulus over the other. Indications of preferences may include spending a longer time looking at one stimulus, looking at it sooner, looking at it more often, or reaching for the preferred object. The very fact that an infant may prefer one stimulus over another lets researchers know that the infant can discriminate between the two stimuli. As you can imagine, this valuable technique enables researchers to determine many of the limits and sensitivities of an infant's sensory or perceptual ability.

With the **habituation method,** infants are presented one of two stimuli often enough so that they become "bored" with it, or, as the researchers say, habituated to it. Once habituation has occurred and the infant's response to the presentation of the first stimulus is minimal, the second stimulus is presented. If the second, or novel, stimulus regains the child's attention as measured by heart rate, visual fixation, or other indications, the researchers know that the infant has recognized the second stimulus as different from the first. Like the preference method, the habituation method allows researchers to determine the range and sensitivity of many infant sensory or perceptual abilities.

Besides these three common methods, other ways of exploring the infant's perceptual or sensory capabilities are often used. For instance, researchers may rely on the infant's ability to learn to respond differently in the presence of different stimuli. This was the technique used in the experiment reported in the Chapter Preview, where researchers determined that 2- to 3-day-old infants could discriminate their mother's voice from that of a stranger as demonstrated by their differential rates of sucking. Researchers may even rely on the infant's own reflexes to determine whether the infant is sensitive to a particular stimulation. You'll discover this later when we discuss visual acuity.

METHODOLOGICAL PROBLEMS

Although some of the techniques we've just described enable researchers to make many discoveries about infant neural, sensory, and perceptual development, they can be tricky to use. Just consider some of the difficulties that can befall an unwary researcher.

If you should decide to use the preference method, for instance, and present two stimuli to an infant, you should be aware that most infants have a natural preference for looking at things on their right side. This preference exists even in newborns and has been known for some time (Turkewitz, Moreau, & Birch,

1966). For this reason, should an infant look at the object on the right slightly more than the object on the left, it would probably indicate *no* preference! Should the infant look at both objects for the same amount of time, it would probably indicate a preference for the one on the left!

A second and perhaps more important methodological problem concerns the infant's state when being tested. The results that you might get with an alert infant can be very different from those obtained with an infant who is slightly drowsy or less alert (Williams & Golenski, 1979; Acredolo & Hake, 1982), a discovery that was made a little over 20 years ago. In most studies conducted before 1970, researchers simply weren't aware that the infant's state of alertness was a major consideration, which may help explain why so many of the results obtained before 1970 have been contradicted.

OPTOKINETIC NYSTAGMUS
Involuntary lateral motion of the eyes in response to the transverse passage of a series of vertical lines.

VISUAL SACCADE
The uneven and halting motions of the eyes as they track across edges and differing contrasts, as occurs when a person reads printed words on a page.

The Basic Sensory Abilities of the Infant

We know that infants can see, hear, taste, smell, and react to touch. But exactly how developed are these senses at birth? How does learning affect them? And what sensory maturational plans are likely to unfold as the infant develops?

As students soon discover, there appears to be no overall philosophy encompassing sensory research. Most of the research is basic, and much of it is serendipitous. If you are a person with considerable curiosity, it may be a rewarding area of study because it offers many challenges and demands for ingenious solutions.

VISION

Did you know that the average 2-week-old neonate has visual acuity of 20/800 (Fantz, Ordy, & Udelf, 1962)?* When you have your eyes checked, the examiner can ask you for feedback about what you see. From your answer, the acuity of your vision can be determined. But 2-week-old infants can't give verbal feedback. You can't ask the infant to cover one eye and read the chart.

Question: Then how were researchers able to determine that a two-week-old's vision is 20/800?

The only responses that can be examined in an infant so young are reflexes or well-canalized learned behaviors (see Chapter 2) such as sucking or head turning. A reflex, the **optokinetic nystagmus,** is used to determine visual acuity.

Question: What kind of a reflex is an optokinetic nystagmus?

Have you ever watched people's eyes closely when they read? Their eyes don't flow smoothly over the words; instead, they skitter or jump across the letters. Such motion is called a **visual saccade.** By passing a series of fine vertical stripes past a neonate's eyes, such a saccade, or optokinetic nystagmus, can be elicited. The nystagmus occurs because the eye reflexively attempts to focus on each stripe that moves through the visual field. If the black vertical lines on the white paper are made finer and finer, the paper will eventually appear gray. Researchers investigating the infant's visual acuity simply continue to use finer gradations of striping until the nystagmus no longer occurs because the neonate can no longer sense the individual stripes. In this way, visual acuity can be determined.

Question: Does it bother infants that their view of the world is blurry?

The typical subject encountered by developmental researchers. Zzzzzzz.

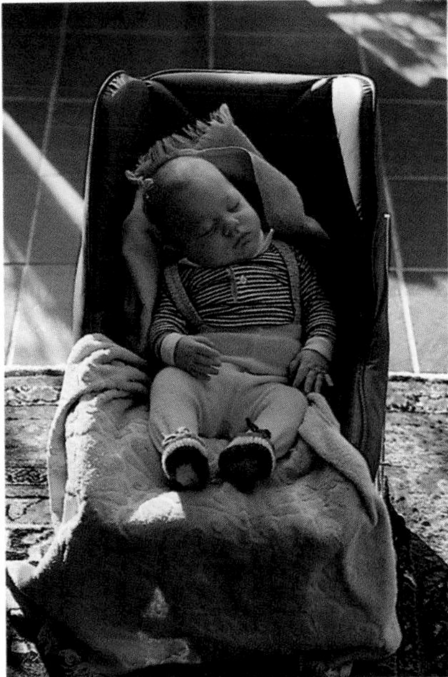

*An adult with 20/800 vision would be able to identify from a distance of 20 feet a letter that a person with good vision (20/20) could identify from a distance of 800 feet. Needless to say, if your vision were 20/800, you'd need glasses just to find the front door. Fortunately, by 5 or 6 months, the infant's vision has usually improved to about 20/70.

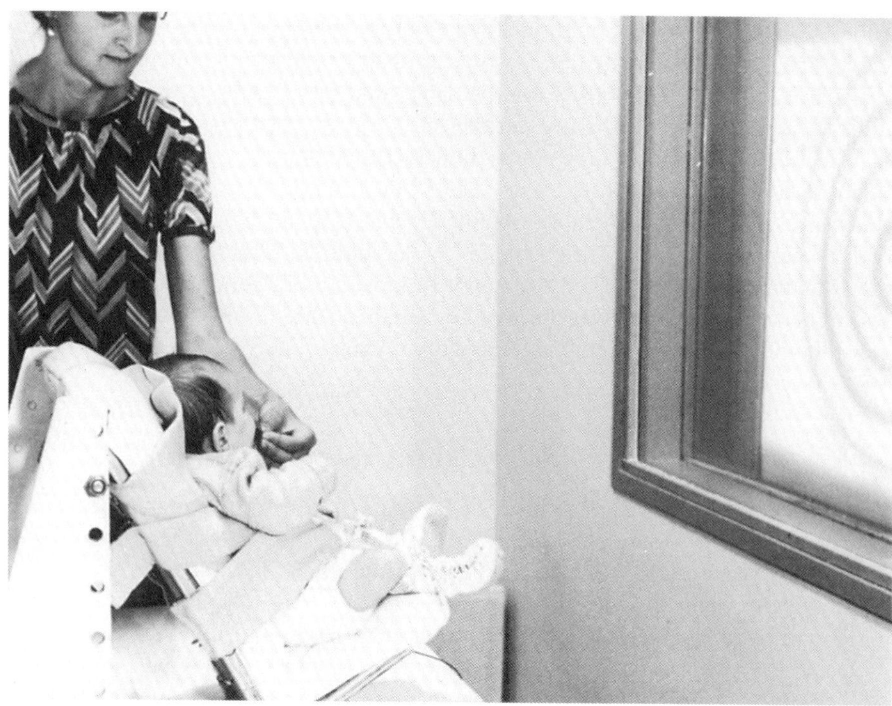

Infant learning to operate the focus on a projector by using Kalnins and Bruner's apparatus.

There's no way of asking newborns if they enjoy their view of the world. However, just like you and me, infants do like to have as clear an image as possible.

Question: How can you tell?

Infants 1 to 3 months old will learn to operate the focus on a projector to make a picture clearer (Kalnins & Bruner, 1973). The focus is connected directly to a nipple and arranged so that appropriate sucking rates will focus the blurred picture.

When we examine reflexive responses of infants (such as optokinetic nystagmus), or measure their ability to discriminate through learned responses (such as between a fuzzy and a clear picture), or use the experimental designs discussed earlier, we are recording the parameters of infant vision. We now know, for instance, that babies are sensitive to changes in brightness (from examining the pupillary reflex); that they can detect movement as early as 2 or 3 days after birth (from measuring changes in sucking rates or heart rates as objects are moved through their visual field) (Finlay & Ivinskis, 1984); and that they have the capacity to follow a moving object within the first few days of life (as measured by the tracking of the infant's eyes as they follow a red disk).

Question: When does an infant's vision become as good as an adult's?

It is generally agreed that visual acuity improves rapidly and comes within adult ranges at about 6 months to 1 year of age. In fact, a progressive sensitivity to the kinds of fine stripes used to elicit optokinetic nystagmus has been noted as infants age from 1 to 3 months (Banks & Salapatek, 1981).

Visual acuity of 20/20 is considered good, but whether an infant ever has 20/20 vision depends a great deal on the genes that determine the eventual shape of the infant's eyes. Remember that there are always individual differences among infants or, for that matter, people in general. Some infants may develop 20/20 vision by 6 months of age, while others never attain that level of acuity. Some children or adults may even have superior vision of 20/15.

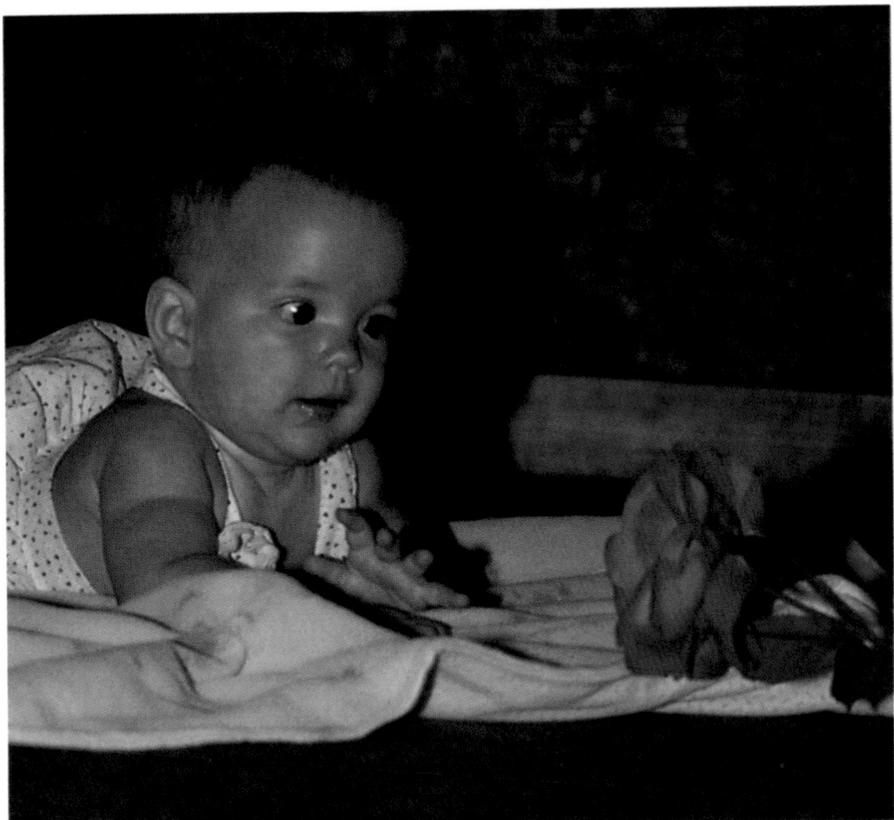

Although infants younger than 6 months don't yet have the visual acuity of adults, their vision is good enough to provide an interesting picture of the world.

Such differences appear to be due to the fact that much of an infant's eventual sensory ability depends directly on inheritance. This is also true for other species. A falcon typically has visual acuity of 20/1! This means that from a distance of 20 feet away, a falcon could respond to a dot on the wall that you couldn't see until you were within at least 1 foot of the wall. Of course, through evolutionary necessity, superior visual acuity has been naturally selected for in falcons. In evolutionary terms, humans never needed that degree of visual acuity. (When was the last time you had to get your dinner by diving from a great height to snatch a running field mouse?)

As a general rule, infant senses continue to become more refined and sensitive during the first 2 to 6 months of development (Acredolo & Hake, 1982).

AUDITION

An infant's sense of hearing is functional prior to birth (Birnholz & Benacerraf, 1983). Many pregnant women have reported that their unborn babies seem to move in response to loud sounds, such as car horns or running bath water. And the research cited in the Chapter Preview indicates that the infant might well be listening to its mother's voice while still in the womb.

As in the case of vision, auditory sensory abilities are tested by examining the infant's responses to different stimuli. For instance, changes in an infant's heart rate will occur when the baby is exposed to sudden alterations of pitch or volume.

Immediately following birth, the newborn's auditory canals often are filled with fluid. Because of this, the newborn's hearing for the first couple of days may be slightly impaired. After the second or third day, however, the neonate's hearing appears to be quite efficient. In fact, audition is initially dominant to vision (vi-

NASOFACIAL REFLEX
A facial expression that is a reflexive response to an olfactory stimulation not processed by the cerebral cortex.

sion, as you recall, takes about 6 months to reach optimal levels of performance). Supporting this is the evidence that up until about the age of 6 months, infants show greater responsiveness to auditory stimuli than they do to visual stimuli (Lewkowicz, 1988). As a general rule, auditory sensitivity improves continuously from infancy through the preschool period and well into the school years (Trehub, Schneider, Morrongiello, & Thorpe, 1988). Keep in mind, too, that auditory sensitivity can also decrease over the life span. For instance, many older adults do not hear as well as school children do.

Some of the most exciting research in this area includes the findings that newborns are *specifically* reactive to human voices and to vowel sounds (Clarkson & Berg, 1983). This may indicate a genetic predisposition favoring the sound of the human voice—especially the kinds of sounds later needed for language.

OLFACTION

The sense of smell also is well developed in the newborn. To measure the infant's reaction to odors, an infant polygraph, called a stabilimeter, is typically used. The stabilimeter measures the infant's breathing rate and may also measure heart rate, blood pressure, or changes in the electrical potential on the surface of the skin. As cotton swabs dipped in various substances are passed under the infant's nose, any bodily reaction to the presence of an odor will be detected by the stabilimeter. Researchers have discovered that infants are able to sense the odors that adults can sense; odors that adults can't smell, infants can't smell either. In fact, infants have such a well-developed sense of smell that they are capable of some very subtle discriminations. For example, in one study it was found that breast-fed infants were able to discriminate their mother's scent from that of other adults. The researchers presented to each infant gauze pads worn in the underarm by the infant's mother and strangers and measured the infant's duration of orientation to each odor (Cernoch & Porter, 1985).

Question: Do babies like some odors better than others?

While it's not always easy to tell what infants like or dislike, responses to odors usually provide a pretty good indication because infants almost always make pleasant or unpleasant facial expressions in the presence of pleasant or unpleasant odors. In fact, these expressions occur even in infants whose higher cortical brain areas have been damaged, which suggests that this kind of facial expression does not require higher cortical processing. For this reason, some researchers have referred to such odor-induced expressions as **nasofacial reflexes** (see Figure 5.1). But to answer your question: Butter and banana odors got high marks, vanilla was greeted positively or with some indifference, fishy odor was usually rejected, and the odor of rotten eggs got a unanimous thumbs down (no surprise there) (Steiner, 1977, 1979).

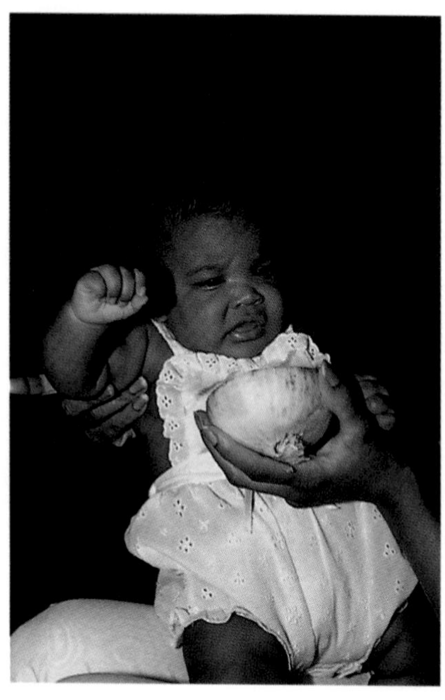

FIGURE 5.1
A nasofacial reflex induced by the strong odor of onion.

Question: Then do infants express the same likes and dislikes for odors that adults express?

Often, but not always. Babies don't seem to dislike some odors that adults generally hate (a full diaper is one example). But by about the age of 3, the odor preferences of children and adults are found to be remarkably alike (Schmidt & Beauchamp, 1988).

TASTE

The stabilimeter is also used to measure the infant's sense of taste. We know that newborns appear to respond to the four basic tastes to which adults respond (sweet, salty, sour, and bitter), because it has been found that neonates can discriminate among sugar, salt, lemon juice, and quinine (Cowart, 1981; Harris, Thomas, & Booth, 1990).

Sweet is especially preferred by infants. The presence of sweetness can even have a soothing effect. In one study, for example, newborns from whom blood was drawn for testing were soothed by the administration of a few drops of sweetened water. These newborns cried less in the presence of the sweet water than matched infants who were given either a pacifier or unsweetened water (Smith, Fillion, & Blass, 1990). By the time children are 4 or 5 years old, they often show a preference for salty foods as well as sweet foods. Whether children will eventually develop a desire for extra sugar or salt on their food is very dependent on their early experience. Children who are given extra salt or sugar tend to desire the levels to which they have become accustomed (Sullivan & Birch, 1990). Parents who may wish to teach their children to use less salt or sugar should therefore eliminate early overexposure to salt or sugar. Of course, since just about every snack food in America is loaded with one or the other, keeping preschoolers from eating too much salt or sugar should be quite a feat!

Question: Why do babies, or adults for that matter, even have a sense of taste? Does it serve any purpose?

It appears that taste evolved mainly as a protective measure. Animals use taste to avoid as well as to approach food. Safe fruits and vegetables are often sweet, while poisonous ones tend to be bitter. This may be why animals such as humans and dogs, which are omnivorous (meaning they will eat almost anything), evolved a sensitivity to sweetness, while cats, which are carnivores (meat eaters), never evolved such a sensitivity. That's why when you open up something sweet, your cat won't care (and will probably doze off), while your dog will crash about doing every trick he knows (and thereby confirming the cat's already strongly held belief that dogs have no class).

Question: You said that infants can identify the four basic tastes (sugar, salt, sour, and bitter). But are all the many flavors they enjoy just mixtures of these four?

With the exception of an early attraction to sweet, most of the infant's enjoyment of food is due to the sense of smell. It's the same for adults. If you plug your nose and close your eyes, you'll be unable to discriminate among pieces of onion, raw potato, and raw apple! The many different flavors that people enjoy are therefore mostly a function of the nose rather than of the taste buds.

Babies are very sensitive to touch and are easily soothed when being held and caressed.

TOUCH

It is easy to show that newborns are sensitive to touch. They will readily emit reflexive responses when one touches their palms (grasping reflex), the soles of their feet (Babinski reflex), or their cheeks (rooting reflex). In fact, most research involving touch in infants has relied on eliciting reflexes. Using such techniques, it has been demonstrated that full-term newborns are sensitive to strong tactile stimulation as well as to mild stimulation. Newborns are also sensitive to pain. Furthermore, female infants tend to be more sensitive to touch than males (which continues to be true even among adults) (Pick & Pick, 1970).

Exploring touch in detail, however, can be quite a complex task because "touch" really includes many senses. For instance, there are different neural receptors for heat, warmth, cold, dull pain, sharp pain, deep pressure, vibration, and light touch and even some that fire only when a touch stimulus starts or stops (Miller, 1983). Touch is also often "confounded"; that is, its effects are often difficult to understand in a "pure" sense. For example, infants and children usually like to be hugged and affectionately touched by those they love. But in such an instance, studying the effects of touching or the lack of it is confounded by the social component of the interaction. Love without touching and touch without loving are very different. And affectionate touching may be more than simply a combination of touching and love; it may be an experience or affect in its own right.

Even though touch may have great importance, especially in a social sense, "minor senses" such as touch tend to receive little attention, generally because they are overshadowed by work on vision or hearing. As a result, what you usually discover in reviewing the research concerning touch are lots of interesting bits of information that no one has really tried to fit into any kind of overall picture. For example, in one study, researchers gave 6-month-olds a vial of warmed colored liquid and let them handle it until they became habituated to it. Then a warmed vial of a *differently colored* liquid was presented. The infants showed little renewed interest. However, when the originally colored liquid was presented at a *different temperature,* the infants acted as though they had received a completely novel stimulus (Bushnell, Shaw, & Strauss, 1985). This shows that for 6-month-olds, anyway, a slight temperature difference can be of overriding interest, even more so than a visual change.

Question: How would a finding like that be related to the broader context of infant development?

Perhaps this is a good place to reiterate that research on the sensory system of the neonate is often basic and serendipitous. Explanations of the information are often not yet available and may require a greater understanding of the human nervous system before they can be found. For the time being, most developmental sensory research is directed at discovering the parameters of sensory abilities among neonates and determining how these abilities change as the child ages.

LEARNING CHECK

Multiple Choice

1. The human central nervous system is fully myelinated by the time a person reaches
   a. 1 year of age. **c.** puberty.
   b. school age. **d.** birth.
2. An infant is shown a stimulus until bored with it; then a new stimulus is presented and the infant's response is noted. This is called
   a. the preference method. **c.** the single-stimulus procedure.
   b. the habituation method. **d.** the reflex method.
3. Optokinetic nystagmus is
   a. a reflex. **c.** an involuntary movement of the eyes.
   b. a visual saccade. **d.** all of the above.
4. Infants are able to hear sounds
   a. while still in the womb.
   b. that no adult can hear.
   c. because of a fluid within their auditory canals.
   d. only if the sounds are intense and loud.
5. Which of the following is correct?
   a. Infants have a better sense of smell than do adults.
   b. Infants prefer sweet foods.
   c. A stabilimeter measures an infant's pupillary reflex.
   d. Taste is the sense used to discriminate among an apple, an onion, and a potato.

Answers: 1. c 2. b 3. d 4. a 5. b

Perceptual Abilities of the Infant

Gathering information about the parameters of an infant's senses is interesting, but sometimes the senses and their integration are examined from a functional standpoint.

Question: What do you mean by functional?

The senses appear to have evolved because of the functions they serve. They receive stimuli and then send this information to the brain. This defines **sensation.** However, once the brain receives information from these sensory inputs, the sensations must be interpreted. This defines **perception.**

SENSATION
The result of converting physical stimulation of the sense organs into sensory experience.

PERCEPTION
The ordering principle that gives coherence and unity to sensory input. Although sensory content is always present in perception, what is perceived is influenced by set and prior experience; thus, perception is more than a passive registration of stimuli impinging on the sense organs.

SIZE CONSTANCY
The learned perception that an object remains the same size, even though the size of the image it casts on the retina varies with its distance from the viewer.

OBJECT CONSTANCIES

Size Constancy

Question: Sensation refers to the input from the senses, but what the brain makes of this input is perception?

Exactly. For example, when you look at your parked car as you are walking away from it, your visual sensory system sends a message to your brain. First, the image of the car is projected through the lens of each eye onto an area at the back of the eye called the *retina.* As you walk away (still looking at your car), the image projected onto the retina gets smaller and smaller as you get farther from your car. When this happens, are you shocked? Do you cry out, "My car is shrinking!"? No, you aren't upset at all. Although the sensory image of your car is shrinking rapidly, you don't *perceive* that your car is changing size. Instead, you perceive that your car is simply becoming more distant. Because of your *experience,* you have learned that objects don't grow or shrink as you walk toward or away from them. You have learned that their size remains the same. Even when you are five blocks from your car and it seems no larger than your fingernail, you perceive that it is still your car and that it hasn't actually changed size. This learned perception is known as **size constancy.**

Question: Given that size constancy is learned, is it possible that some people don't learn it?

Yes, this could happen. Mr. B was a 52-year-old cataract patient who had been blind since birth. When his sight was restored through surgery, he had difficulty adjusting to all the new sensory input. One day he was found trying to reach out and touch some toy cars; the trouble was that he was reaching way out of a fourth-floor window and the cars weren't toys—they were real (and 40 feet below!) (Gregory, 1970).

Even people who have been able to see all their lives may have limited size constancy as a result of their particular experience. Pygmies live in dense rain forests and are not often exposed to wide vistas and distant horizons. One particular pygmy, removed from his usual environment, was convinced that he was seeing a swarm of insects when he was actually looking at a herd of buffalo at a great distance. When driven toward the animals, he was frightened to see the insects "grow" into buffalo and was sure that witchcraft was responsible (Turnbull, 1961).

Question: Do researchers have any idea at what age infants begin to acquire size constancy?

Size constancy appears to begin to be formed in infants of about 5½ months of age (Yonas, Granrud, & Pettersen, 1985). In one interesting experiment, 5- and 7-month-old infants had a patch placed over one eye to eliminate the depth cues

SHAPE CONSTANCY
The learned perception that an object remains the same shape, despite the fact that the shape of the image it casts on the retina may vary depending on the viewing angle.

POSITION CONSTANCY
The learned perception that even though the subject moves, all the objects in the environment stay stationary and maintain their positions relative to each other.

that two eyes create. The only distance cue was size. They then were shown photographs of large and small faces. To adults, who of course possess size constancy, only the large face would look near enough to touch. The small face, because of size constancy, would not be seen as *small* but rather as *distant*.

The 5-month-old infants reached for both the large and small faces equally when presented with the photographs. But the 7-month-old infants reached far more often for the large face, which indicates that they had size constancy; they seemed to react to the small face as though it were beyond reach (Yonas, Pettersen, & Granrud, 1982).

Question: Couldn't it be that 7-month-old infants have a preference for big faces?

You're starting to sound like a perceptual researcher. To control for this, the infants were tested again without their eye patches. When using both eyes, the 7-month-olds didn't prefer the larger face but reacted to both equally, presumably because two eyes provided the information that both photographs were equally distant.

Shape Constancy Researchers have also been concerned with the development of shape constancy.

Question: What is shape constancy?

Shape constancy is demonstrated in Figure 5.2. As you can see, the form, or shape, of an object is perceived to remain constant even though the shape projected onto the retina may change. A door may appear rectangular when closed and thus viewed straight on, or it may appear trapezoidal when partially opened and thus viewed from an angle, but we do not perceive the door as changing shape from a rectangle to a trapezoid. Instead, we perceive the door to be opening.

In one experiment, the habituation method was used to demonstrate shape constancy in infants as young as 12 weeks of age (Caron, Caron, & Carlson, 1979). The infants were habituated to either a square or a trapezoid presented at different angles, but not face on. The trapezoid would sometimes cast the retinal image of a square, and vice versa (see Figure 5.3). After habituation—that is, after the infants were no longer interested in seeing the object—a square or trapezoid was presented face on. Infants who had habituated to a square that cast a trapezoidal shape on the retina because of its angle of presentation showed immediate interest in a real trapezoid. And infants who had seen a trapezoid presented at an angle so that it projected a square onto the retina showed immediate interest in a real square. This showed that the infants became habituated to the real shape of the object and not to its retinally projected shape.

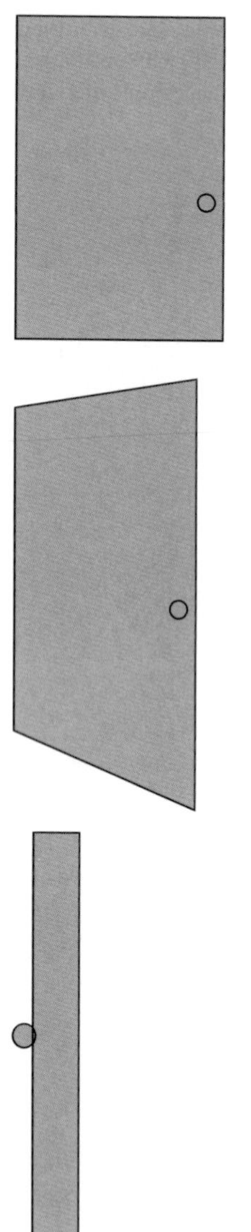

FIGURE 5.2
Although the shape of a door's image cast on the retina can change drastically, the door is not perceived to change shape. Instead, it is perceived to be a rectangular door that is opening.

Position Constancy Picture the following. You are standing at the entrance of your living room. When you look about the room, you see all the familiar furniture and other objects in it. Now imagine that you walk across the room to the other side. Do you become lost, or do you still know where everything in the room is?

Question: Of course I still know where everything is. How could I get lost when I cross my living room?

You're right. It's not too likely that you'd get lost. One of the reasons that you wouldn't get lost is that you have **position constancy:** You understand that even though *you* move, all the objects and landmarks in your living room and the walls of that room stay stationary, and the relative positions of the objects and walls remain constant. Because of position constancy, you can easily use any landmark in the room to tell you where everything else will be, even after you move. We do this so unconsciously and so simply that we are hardly ever aware of it. Infants,

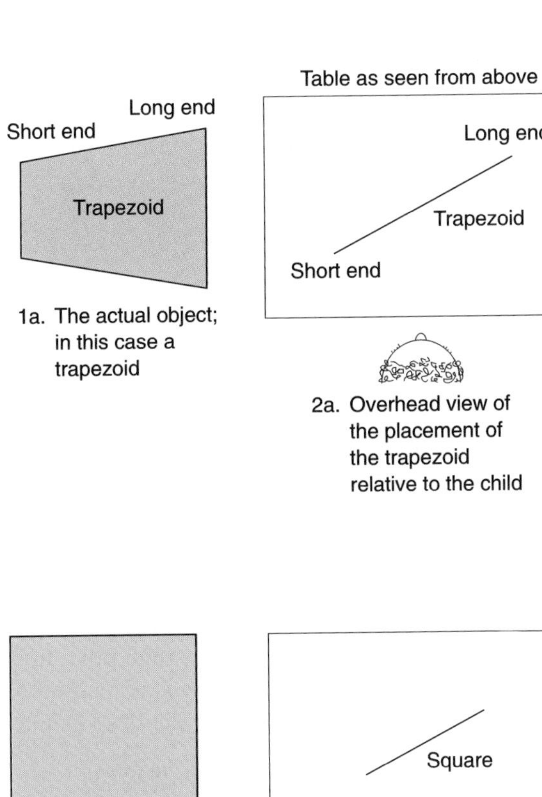

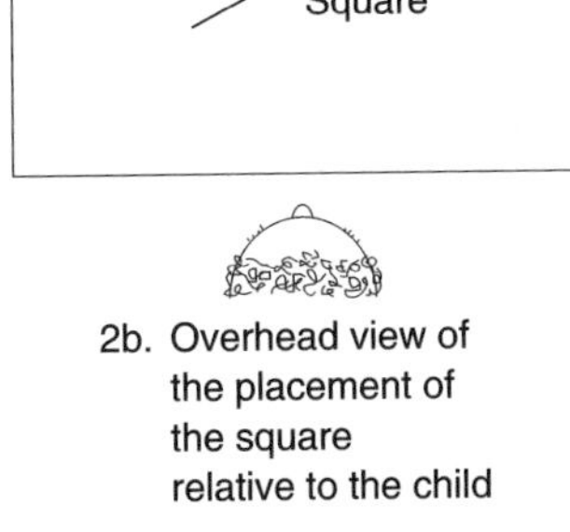

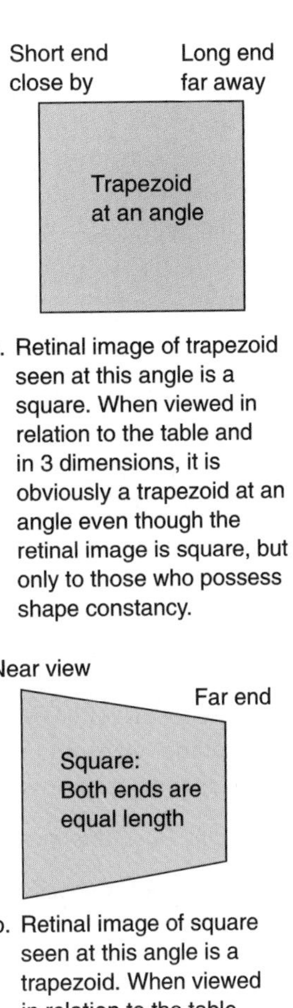

Figure 5.3
Caron, Caron, & Carlson's 1979 experiment in which they demonstrated shape constancy in infants.

however, and especially those younger than 6 months, typically show a failure of position constancy. Such an infant who had learned, let's say, to look to the right to see an event might still anticipate the event by looking to the right even after having been turned so that the event can now be seen only by looking to the left (Acredolo & Evans, 1980). An older infant would know to look to the left after having been moved.

As with size constancy, the first signs of position constancy seem to appear in infants of about 6 months (Keating, McKenzie, & Day, 1986), but it may not become really developed until between 10 and 15 months of age. This indicates that the full development of position constancy may require that the infant gain locomotion experiences through crawling and walking (Bertenthal & Campos, 1987).

Many perceptual developments may be well canalized; they seem to be learned very rapidly and early and follow a clear line of probabilistic epigenesis. Another way of saying this is that perceptual development is neurologically grounded in experience-expectant systems. Of course, if humans were organized so that such learning were difficult or required a long time, the world would be a terribly confusing place for much of our existence (as it is, it's confusing enough!). Fortunately, our sensory and perceptual systems appear to be ready to make quick sense of the world shortly after we arrive in it.

Visual Cliff
An apparatus constructed to study depth perception in humans and other animals. It consists of a center board resting on a glass table. On one side of the board, a checkered surface is visible directly beneath the glass; on the other side, the surface is several feet below the glass, thus giving the impression of a drop-off.

Depth Perception

Exactly which perceptual abilities are innate, which are due to maturation, which are due to learning, and which are due to a combination of these factors is often the basis of inquiries into perceptual development. Investigating the development of a mechanism for avoiding a sharp drop-off or cliff presents some interesting problems and provides a good example of the kind of work that developmental researchers conduct while examining perception.

Almost 35 years ago, Gibson and Walk (1960) constructed a device known as the **visual cliff** (see Figure 5.4). Infant animals, including humans, were placed on the center board between the shallow and the deep sides. Glass covered the surface and prevented any creature from actually falling off the cliff.

Baby animals of many species were tested on the cliff, and the results demonstrated that they possessed innate depth perception. Newborn chicks, whose first visual experience was on the cliff, refused to cross onto the deep side. Kittens, puppies, piglets, and various other infant animals also refused to venture onto the deep end. Baby mountain goats (a species that would have an exceptional reason for possessing a strong cliff-edge avoidance) similarly refused to venture onto the deep side, and if pushed in that direction, collapsed their front legs beneath themselves. Gibson and Walk and many other researchers also demonstrated that human infants were much more easily coaxed over onto the shallow side than onto the deep side (although some infants were willing to crawl onto the deep side).

Question: Does this mean that a tendency to avoid cliffs is innate in humans?

Unfortunately, the results of research with humans were not as clear-cut as with other species. Unlike baby chicks, kittens, or mountain goats, human infants aren't precocious in terms of motor development. Infants are typically unable to crawl (a prerequisite behavior for testing cliff avoidance) until they are about 6 months old. It has been suggested that by the time human infants are tested on the visual cliff, they have already *learned* to avoid drop-offs (Campos, Hiatt, Ramsay, Henderson, & Svejda, 1978). Campos and his colleagues noticed that precrawling infants of 2, 3, and 5 months of age showed only heart rate deceleration when placed on the glass over the deep side. This reaction is generally taken to be a

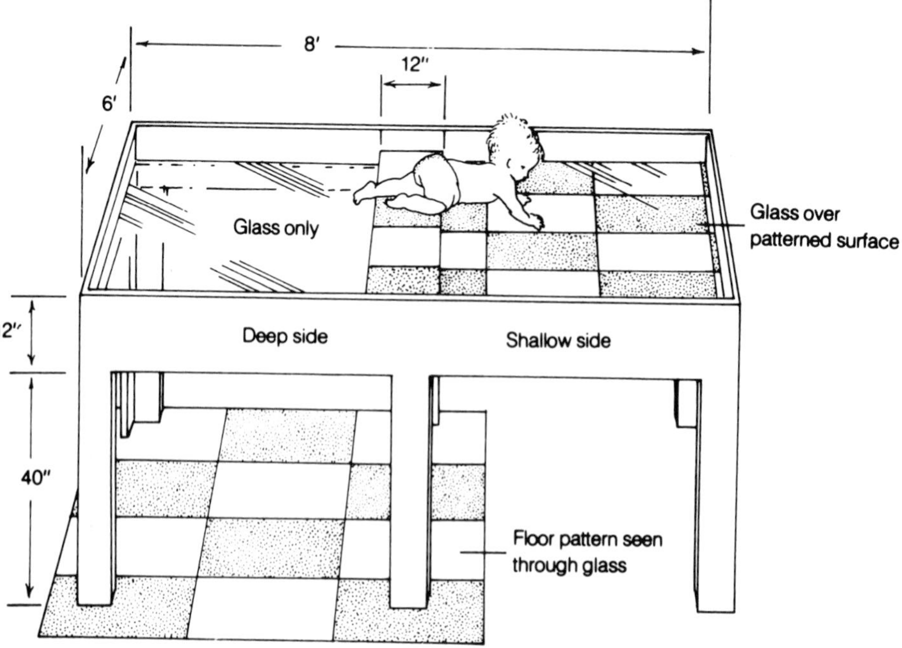

Figure 5.4
The visual cliff.

FIGURE 5.5
Two dolls of equal size are placed the same distance away from the infant, with one doll slightly higher than the other. Infants with depth perception should perceive the higher doll as more distant. Younger infants were found to reach for the two dolls about equally, while older infants reached far more often for the lower, or "nearer," doll. Experience with crawling had no effect on the infants' preferences. (*Source:* Arterberry, Yonas, & Bensen, 1989)

sign of interest, not fear (Richards, 1987). The implications are that the infants had not yet come to fear the cliff edge and that they would probably learn such avoidance behavior later.

Another researcher (Rader, 1979) argued that cliff avoidance is a genetically inherited predisposition, although the genetic program on which the avoidance is dependent doesn't function until it is maturationally triggered when the infant reaches about the age of 6 months. If this were the case, then fear of a drop-off would be innate but would *not* be present at birth.

Question: Does crawling at an early age facilitate the onset of depth perception?

If that were true, it would indicate that locomotion was an important component of the onset of depth perception (which, as you recall, was a concern of researchers working with the visual cliff). In one study, infants between 5 and 7 months of age were shown two identical objects placed on a grid that would give the illusion of depth to any infant possessing depth perception (see Figure 5.5). In general, the 7 month-old infants showed depth perception by reaching more often for the "nearer" object, while 5 month-old infants did not. Infants who had the most experience crawling, however, were *no more likely* to show depth perception than were infants with little crawling experience (Arterberry, Yonas, & Bensen, 1989).

Another important cue that has aided researchers in their investigations of depth is *overlap*. Look around you. Things that are closer naturally overlap (block your view of) things that are farther away. As an object near to you moves in front of one that's farther away, the edge of the nearby object blocks your view of the distant object. This depth cue is so strong that it even allows you to perceive depth in flat (two-dimensional) images, such as the photographs in this textbook.

In one interesting experiment, researchers used the generation of a random dot display on a computer screen to simulate overlap. As one field of dots moved across the flat screen, it appeared to delete (block out) another field of dots (see Figure 5.6). Infants as young as 5 months showed a reaching preference for the apparently "nearer" field of dots (Granrud et al., 1984). This study indicated that depth perception, like size and position constancy, develops in infants when they are between 5 and 6 months of age.

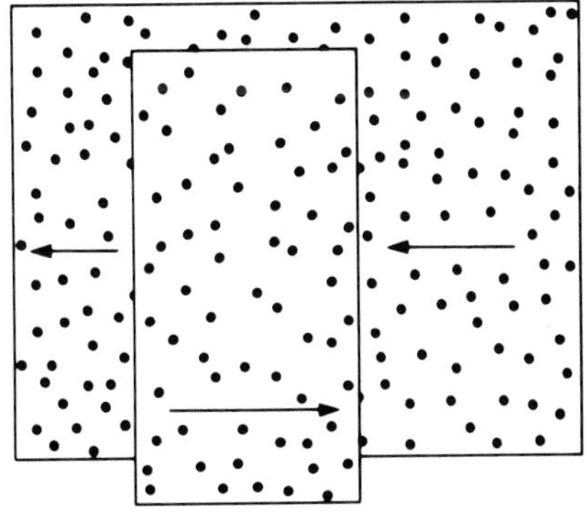

FIGURE 5.6
A random series of dots was generated on a computer screen. The pattern, of course, was two-dimensional. A field of these dots was then moved from left to right and appeared to overlap the remaining dots as it traveled. Infants perceived this field as being closer to them. The apparent overlap was the only cue that could have provided this three-dimensional illusion on a two-dimensional surface. (*Source:* Granrud et al., 1984, p. 1631)

PATTERN AND FORM PERCEPTION

Infants can also readily perceive forms and patterns. In experiments using the habituation technique, even newborn babies were found to discriminate readily among triangles, squares, crosses, and circles (Slater, Morison, & Rose, 1983). Newborns are also able to make even finer visual discriminations and can differ-

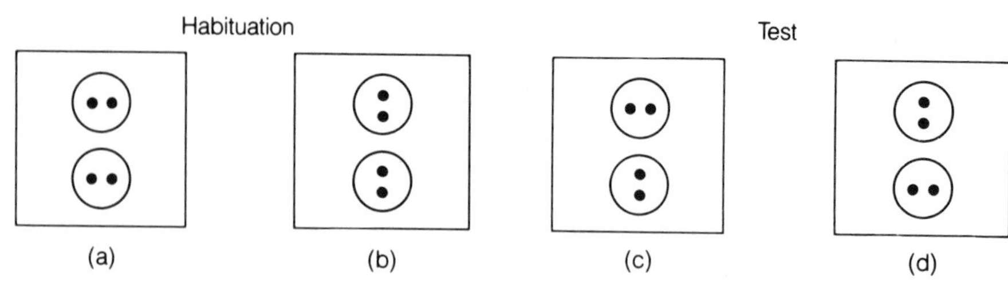

FIGURE 5.7

Newborns received successive exposures to each of two stimuli (a) and (b) until habituation occurred (i.e., the newborn's attention and interest in the stimuli had become minimal). Then the test stimuli (c) and (d) were presented. The infant's interest and attention dramatically increased, demonstrating that the newborn was able to tell that the stimuli presented in the habituation condition had now changed. It is impressive that newborns can make such subtle discriminations. (*Source:* Adapted from Antell, Caron, & Myers, 1985, p. 943)

entiate small circles that contain a subtle arrangement of dots (Antell, Caron, & Myers, 1985) (see Figure 5.7).

As children become older, their scanning of internal features and objects becomes more complex and detailed. By the age of 3 months, infants show a marked preference for viewing faces (Dannemiller & Stephens, 1988) (see Figure 5.8). Surprisingly, infants even show a preference for the faces of adults and infants whom raters had scored as attractive over the faces of those considered less attractive (Langlois, Ritter, Roggman, & Vaughn, 1991)! This is especially interesting because it had always been assumed that a preference for attractiveness was the result of gradual exposure to cultural forces such as peers, parents, or television. This study, however, points to the possibility of an innate factor in the appreciation of aesthetic beauty or perhaps shows that there is a preference for some sort of facial symmetry, curvature, or angle that is associated with attractiveness.

Question: At what age can infants tell the difference between their mother's face and that of a stranger?

By 1 month of age, infants apparently acquire enough information to be able to discriminate between their mother's face and a stranger's face (Maurer & Salapatek, 1976). By about 6 or 7 months of age, infants clearly are able to distinguish individuals by their faces (Caron, Caron, & Myers, 1982).

FIGURE 5.8

These computer-generated faces and patterns were used to test the preference that 3-month-olds have for viewing faces. Unlike earlier studies, this study incorporated the use of computer-generated images instead of photographs of real faces. In the past, when photographs of real faces were used (Fantz, 1961), it was argued that the preference that infants showed for viewing the faces might really be only a preference for contrast or complexity rather than a preference for the human face. To control for these other variables, the computer-generated faces shown in this figure were developed. For complexity, the infant has a choice of other forms (C and D) that are as complex as the faces (A and B). If high contrast is important, then face A should be preferred to the negative face B. The experiment showed, however, an equal preference for faces A and B over shapes C and D, indicating that it was, in fact, the aspect of "human face" that infants found attractive. (*Source:* Dannemiller & Stephens, 1988, p. 212)

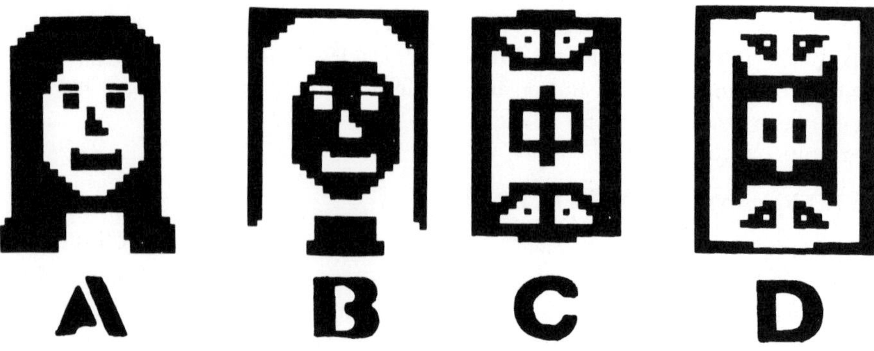

BIOLOGICAL MOTION PERCEPTION

BIOLOGICAL MOTION PERCEPTION An ability that enables humans to make perceptual sense easily and quickly of live objects in motion.

Most organisms have evolved special mechanisms that are sensitive to the motion of living objects. Such ability is often referred to as **biological motion perception** (Johansson, von Hofsten, & Jansson, 1980). Live objects in motion have distinctive ways of moving. In one study, a subject had tiny lights attached to his joints (elbows, knees, wrists, etc.) and was then placed into a darkened room where he could be observed by others who were unaware of what they were looking at. As long as the subject stood still, it was impossible for the observers to tell that they were looking at a human being (Johansson, 1973). And yet, in only one-fifth of a second after the subject moved, the observers knew what they were looking at because of the motion of the lights (Cutting, Proffitt, & Kozlowski, 1978). Because we are such social creatures, so dependent on or threatened by others, our perceptual mechanisms appear to have evolved such that they let us recognize the human form rapidly in many different circumstances.

Question: At what age do infants first show biological motion perception?

Using the habituation method, researchers have found sensitivity to biological motion perception in infants as young as 3 months (Bertenthal, Proffitt, Spetner, & Thomas, 1985).

AUDITORY PERCEPTION

Question: Have perceptual experiments dealing with the other senses been conducted?

Although research on visual perception dominates the field, perception involving the minor senses and auditory perception have also been studied. Consider, for example, the fact that when you hear a sound, you actually sense it twice, once in each ear. We have evolved so that we have the ability to perceive the sound as occurring only once, and we use the difference in the time for the two sounds to reach us to localize the source (unless its source is equally distant from both our ears). In other words, although your senses send two messages at different times to the brain, you perceive only one sound, but you are able to localize it.

Question: Is this ability innate?

There is only one way to find out: Make a sound to one side of a newborn and see if the infant attempts to respond in the direction of the sound. This is what Michael Wertheimer did in 1961. He tested a newborn girl in a delivery room by sounding a clicker to the right side and then to the left side of the infant. The baby responded by turning to the right when the clicker sound came from the right, and to the left when the sound came from the left. Wertheimer was surprised to discover that the infant also looked in the direction of the sound, as though she expected to see something! Just seconds after birth, the newborn's visual and auditory senses already were integrated (Wertheimer, 1961). Similar results have been confirmed under more stringent testing conditions (Muir & Field, 1979).

As infants develop, their ability to localize the source of a sound steadily improves (Morrongiello, Fenwick, & Chance, 1990). By 6 months of age, a baby can orient its head toward the source of a sound with no more than a 12-degree error, and by 18 months, the error is reduced to a very small angle of only 4 degrees (Morrongiello, 1988). This is all the more amazing when you consider that as the infant grows, its head size enlarges, making the distance between the ears greater and greater. This means that the infant's brain has to continuously recalibrate the meaning of the time delay between receiving a sound in one ear and receiving it in the other (Clifton, Gwiazda, Bauer, Clarkson, & Held, 1988)! By the age of 7 months, infants sitting in the dark are also able to tell whether

CROSS-MODAL TRANSFER
A recognition of an object as familiar when it is perceived with a sense other than that previously used when exposed to the object.

an object making noise is within their grasp or too far away to reach (Clifton, Perris, & Bullinger, 1991). Again, this is accomplished by perceiving the angle made between the object making the sound and the ears. Near objects yield wider angles than distant ones, and they are also louder.

Sensory and Perceptual Integration

As Wertheimer discovered, some perceptual integration exists at birth. Testing the ability to locate the source of a sound, however, is not the only way to investigate the integration of auditory and visual perception. One researcher demonstrated auditory-visual integration in 4-month-old infants by using an ingenious method (Spelke, 1979). She showed these infants two films simultaneously but presented the soundtrack of only one of the films. In this experiment, the 4-month-old infants demonstrated a significant preference for watching the film that corresponded to the soundtrack being played. In a later study, 4-month-old infants were shown two bouncing objects, one of which bounced in synchrony with a sound. The infants preferred the object that was in synchrony (Spelke, 1981).

In yet another study, 5-month-old infants were shown a movie of a car driving toward and then away from them. In one condition, the sound grew louder as the car approached and softer as it receded, which is as it should be. In the other condition, the sound was mismatched; it got louder as the car was going away and softer as the car approached. The infants showed a preference for looking at the properly matched film, indicating that they already had an understanding that a visual that is increasing in size should be associated with a sound whose volume is also increasing (Walker-Andrews & Lennon, 1985).

Further evidence of sensory integration has been obtained from research on older infants (about 6 months of age), who demonstrated what has been called **cross-modal transfer.** In a typical cross-modal transfer experiment, an infant is allowed to touch and handle, but not see, a particular object. Then this object and a new object with which the infant has never had contact are presented *visually*. Infants as young as 6 months of age often show habituation toward an object they are seeing for the first time but have felt before! This implies that the infant can recognize the object visually from tactile contact with it (Rose & Orlian, 1991). There is some evidence that certain forms of cross-modal transfer may even be possible by 4 months of age (Mendelson & Ferland, 1982).

Question: Is cross-modal transfer based on an experience-expectant neurology the way other perceptual abilities appear to be?

Yes, it is believed that cross-modal transfer is based on an experience-expectant rather than an experience-dependent neurological system. This belief is based on the fact that it appears to be very difficult to *teach* infants unusual cross-modal associations (Bahrick, 1988), such as the volume of a sound being inversely proportional to its distance (the closer a sound source gets, the harder it becomes to hear). And yet, infants do clearly show many cross-modal transfers, demonstrating that perceptual associations found in the real world (as opposed to unusual ones found only in a laboratory) are often easily acquired. Also, cross-modal transfer is readily acquired by other species, such as apes (Savage-Rumbaugh, Sevcik, & Hopkins, 1988), implying a fairly broad natural selective process favoring the acquisition of such perceptions. In fact, monkeys that show poor cross-modal transfer are also more likely to show poor cognitive development when they are older (Gunderson, Rose, & Grant-Webster, 1990). With this in mind, researchers are currently investigating cross-modal transfer tests in children as a possible predictor of later cognitive and intellectual development.

Infants even show a cross-modal transfer reaction that may indicate an innate predisposition for mathematical comprehension. For example, in one study,

7-month-old infants were shown two slides, one to their left and one to their right. One slide showed two objects (e.g., a ribbon and a pipe), and the other showed three objects (e.g., a coin purse, a ring box, and a feather). When the slides were presented, a drum was beaten either two times or three times; the duration of the drum beats was the same from start to finish whether two or three beats were sounded. When infants heard two beats of the drum, they tended to look at the slide that showed two objects; when they heard three beats, they tended to look at the slide that showed three objects (Starkey, Spelke, & Gelman, 1983).

Perceptual research is detailed, involved, and voluminous. Entire texts have been written solely on the development of sensory and perceptual systems in infants. Because of the nature of this text, however, we cannot fully examine all the research here. Nonetheless, perhaps you have obtained some feeling for the kind of research that is conducted in these areas. Perhaps, too, you have come to appreciate that the infant's neurological development appears to be greatly responsible for the infant's sensory and perceptual development and that the infant is born equipped to organize his or her world and to deal with the experiences that will be gained through interaction with it.

LEARNING CHECK

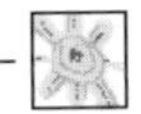

Fill-in-the-Blank

1. *Sensation* refers to the input from the senses, but what the brain makes of it is called ______________ .
2. When you walk away from an object, it doesn't appear to be shrinking; rather, you perceive that it is farther away than it was. This is an example of ______________ .
3. Wertheimer discovered that only a few seconds after birth, a newborn's ______________ and ______________ senses are integrated.
4. After feeling an object, an infant reacts to her first visual presentation as though she is familiar with the object. This demonstrates ______________ .
5. The hypothesized neural system associated with the acquisition of personal experiences unique to each individual is called ______________ .
6. The ability to recognize the motion of living objects is called ______________ .

Answers: **1.** perception **2.** size constancy **3.** visual, auditory **4.** cross-modal transfer **5.** experience-dependent **6.** biological motion perception

APPLICATIONS

The Value of Infant Walkers

One of the most important developmental milestones in an infant's life occurs when the infant acquires the ability to move from one place to another. As we have discovered in this chapter, many of the infant's perceptual advancements appear to be timed to coincide with the development of locomotion.

Infants first achieve locomotion by crawling, rolling, scooting, and even, sometimes, walking. For years, researchers have noted that this newly acquired locomotion has a positive effect on other aspects of development.

Question: Would you give an example?

Locomotion provides the infant with certain experiences that in turn further development (Kermoian & Campos, 1988). For instance, it has been well documented that babies who are able to crawl or walk spend more time near adults, usually their parents. This, in turn, leads to further social contact and interaction (Green, Gustafson, & West, 1980).

Infants who locomote also explore more, and as they go from place to place, typically see and manipulate many objects. Often, when infants first encounter new objects, parents spend extra time naming the object and telling the child about it; detailed discussions may evolve from the baby's exploration. One study noted that

> the mothers talked not only about the toys the babies have encountered but also about such minor details as the cracks between the vinyl squares of the floor and its cleanliness, details brought to their attention by the exploratory activities of their infants. (West & Rheingold, 1978, p. 214)

Such findings also imply that locomotion may be helpful for the acquisition and development of language.

Locomotion also changes the infant's visual perspective. The interaction of changing visual perspective and locomotion may play an important role in perceptual development by helping to organize the infant's understanding of the surrounding world (Acredolo, 1978). As you recall, infants rapidly acquire position constancy once they begin to move about on their own.

Considering all these effects, locomotion can be viewed as a general reorganizer of the infant's experiences (Gustafson, 1984) and an action that should foster the development of neural experience-expectant systems.

Question: Are infants who walk early, then, at an advantage over those who walk late?

FIGURE 5.9
This baby really enjoys getting around in her soft, inflatable walker.

Based on the research we've just discussed, it would seem reasonable to assume that the babies who aren't locomoting relatively early could be missing some of the important experiences obtained by infants who get around.

To test this hypothesis, researchers placed infants between the ages of 6 and 10 months in "walkers" and observed the babies' experiences (Gustafson, 1984). Walkers are devices that support infants on wheels such that their feet just touch the ground. By pushing with their feet, babies can propel themselves wherever they wish to go, as long as there are no obstacles or barriers in the way and the surface is relatively flat (see Figure 5.9). Some manufacturers have claimed that the walkers benefit the infant by accelerating development.

Question: Is the claim true?

Gustafson discovered that nonlocomoting infants who were now getting around in walkers soon encountered the typical experiences of locomoting infants, namely, closer adult contact, greater social interchange, generation of more language by parents, and adjustment to a continually changing visual perspective.

By the end of the study, in terms of the experiences they shared, nonlocomoters in walkers were much more like their locomoting peers than like their nonlocomoting peers who had no walkers. This study might tempt one to say that infants who locomote early have special social, cognitive, and perceptual advantages.

Question: Then babies who would normally walk later are helped by the walkers?

APPLICATIONS

If this is so, then the walkers afford valuable experiences for nonlocomoting infants. Researchers such as Gustafson, however, point out that although it is true that locomotion reorganizes an infant's world, it is not necessarily true that infant walkers are beneficial.

Question: If walking is so valuable, and walkers help infants get around, how could walkers not be beneficial?

Recall from Chapter 4 that the practice of reflex walking generally enables infants to walk at an earlier age; also recall that this practice has no long-term advantage. Furthermore, healthy infants who are late to start walking quickly catch up to their early walking peers. Similarly, early locomoting infants who may have particular social, cognitive, language, and perceptual experiences as a result of their early locomotion don't seem to hold any long-term advantage over peers who are late locomoters.

All healthy children will eventually locomote and gain the experiences that such movement affords. Any early advantage appears to be lost, just as was the case for the toilet-trained twins in the Chapter 4 Preview. It is important to keep such considerations in mind. Parents are so often delighted when their child crawls or talks at an early age and, conversely, dismayed if their child is a little late walking or talking. In general, neither reaction is justified. As the maturational plan for development unfolds, there is a great range of individual differences. Children who reach certain maturational goals early are typically indistinguishable a few years later from peers who reached those goals at a slower pace.

Question: Should parents give their infants a walker?

Probably not. In 1992, both the American Medical Association and the American Academy of Pediatrics argued that infant walkers should be banned. Walkers, they pointed out, are a leading cause of infant injury in the United States. Infants in walkers are simply too likely to fall down stairs or roll up against hot ovens or fireplaces. If, however, parents really wish to purchase a walker for their infant, it is important that it should be a safe walker (one that does not tip over easily or have sharp edges) that they can keep in a safe environment, which means an environment free from stairs or any other hazard. Parents shouldn't think, however, that they are depriving their infant of an important experience if they don't provide a walker.

SUMMARY

- The newborn's nervous system is relatively immature compared with that of an adult. Much of an infant's development is directly related to the rate of myelination throughout the nervous system. Myelination is usually completed by puberty.
- Many of the sensory parameters of infants have been measured by examining reflexes, by conditioning well-canalized learned behaviors, or by investigating habituation or preferences.
- Infant neural organization appears to operate according to two systems. The experience-expectant system responds to stimuli that the species is likely to encounter, while the experience-dependent system responds to the unique learning and experience of each individual.
- Using optokinetic nystagmus, researchers are able to measure the visual capacity of newborn babies and have determined that visual acuity comes within adult ranges when infants are about 6 months to 1 year of age.
- Although an infant's sense of hearing is functional prior to birth, auditory sensitivity increases steadily until the child reaches approximately 12 to 13 years of age.
- The sense of smell is also well developed in the newborn. Infants have such an acute sense of smell that they are capable of very subtle discriminations.
- Infants appear to respond to the same four basic tastes to which adults respond.
- It has been demonstrated that full-term newborns are sensitive to strong tactile stimulation as well as to mild stimulation.
- *Sensation* refers to the input from the senses, but what the brain makes of it is called *perception*. Infants appear to be biologically organized to acquire many perceptions, such as size, shape, and position constancy.
- Experiments using the visual cliff have indicated that fear of sudden drop-offs or cliffs does not occur in humans until they reach about 6 months of age.
- Many perceptual abilities appear to be tied directly to the infant's rate of maturation. Among these abilities are pattern and form perception.
- Biological motion perception is the ability to respond to the motion of living objects. It appears to begin developing in humans when they are about 3 months of age.
- Studies with newborns have demonstrated that sensory integration already exists just seconds after an infant's birth. Further sensory and perceptual integration appears to depend on the maturation of the infant's nervous system.
- Other evidence of perceptual integration in infants comes from experiments concerning cross-modal transfer. In such experiments, infants exposed to a stimulus through only one sensory mode will later show familiarity toward the stimulus when it is presented to them through other sensory modes.
- All healthy children will eventually locomote and gain the experiences that such movement affords. Any early advantage appears to be lost. Children who reach certain maturational goals early are typically indistinguishable a few years later from peers who reached those goals at a slower pace.

QUESTIONS FOR DISCUSSION

1. Why do you think it was once a common belief that babies were born blind?
2. Our senses act as filters; there are many things to which we are not sensitive. We can't see X rays, hear dog whistles, or smell carbon dioxide. Why do you think our senses are so selective?
3. Some researchers were surprised by the discovery that size constancy develops so early in infancy. What evolutionary advantages do you think there might be in developing size constancy at about the time we are able to crawl?

SUGGESTIONS FOR FURTHER READING

1. Maurer, D., & Maurer, C. (1988). *The world of the newborn.* New York: Basic Books.
2. Stern, D. N. (1990). *Diary of a baby: What your child sees, feels, and experiences.* New York: Harper-Collins.

CHAPTER 6

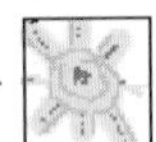

INFANT SOCIAL AND EMOTIONAL DEVELOPMENT

CHAPTER PREVIEW

CHECK WITH MOM

IN A LABORATORY, researchers place a 1-year-old baby on a visual cliff. This visual cliff, however, is a little different from the one described in Chapter 5. In this case, there's only one drop-off, and it's neither shallow nor deep but somewhere in between. The baby begins to crawl, stops in front of the drop-off, and looks down. It's the kind of drop-off that makes you think, "If I were that baby, would I try it or not?"

DIRECTLY ACROSS from the baby, on the other side of the visual drop-off, is the baby's mother. She's been instructed to stand still and maintain an expression of fear on her face. The baby looks down at the drop, up at her mother, and then back down at the drop. Once again she looks at her mother, and refuses to crawl any farther.

LATER, ANOTHER baby is placed on the cliff. This baby's mother is told to look happy and interested. The baby crawls to the edge of the drop and looks down. He looks at his mother, looks back down again, and crawls across.

IN THIS EXPERIMENT, most of the infants who saw fear on their mothers' faces refused to cross, while those who saw happy, encouraging mothers crossed over the drop (Sorce, Emde, Campos, & Klinnert, 1985). If the drop-off was removed and the visual cliff made flat, the infants crawled about without checking first with their mothers. In the ambiguous situation with the drop-off, however, the babies looked to their mothers for cues about what to do. Looking for cues in this fashion is called **social referencing**, and the emotion that the mother showed was an important communication for her infant. Infants will actively search for emotional cues, not just from their mothers but from any familiar adult who happens to be present (Klinnert, Emde, Butterfield, & Campos, 1986).

IN THIS CHAPTER, we will examine the social and emotional ties formed between infants and their parents. We'll pay special attention to the relationship between infant and mother, and we'll discuss how theorists believe that this important attachment forms. We'll also look at the special relationship that infants have with their fathers. We'll examine six stages of social-emotional development. Finally, we'll explore the development of the emotions themselves.

RESOURCES

Social Ties

We humans are social creatures. We live within communities and families; we form social and emotional ties with one another. Such ties are essential for newborns because babies rely on their parents or others for basic needs. During this time of helplessness, infants come to know their parents socially and form attachments to them.

SOCIAL REFERENCING
The use of emotional signals or cues from others as a guide for one's own behavior in ambiguous situations.

ATTACHMENT
An especially close affectional bond formed between living creatures.

EARLY THEORIES OF ATTACHMENT

The mechanism of **attachment,** especially between the infant and her mother, has been intensely debated and investigated by developmental theorists, and the theoretical orientation of most researchers over the years has changed.

Question: What do you mean by a change in theoretical orientation?

During the first decade of this century, the famous Viennese psychiatrist Sigmund Freud proposed that the mother-infant relationship was an extremely important one and that it determined the quality of the child's later social relationships, even into adulthood. In Freud's view, the infant was dependent on the mother and formed an attachment because the mother provided for the infant's basic biological needs, especially during nursing. In the United States, as learning theory grew in popularity during the first half of this century, a similar view of attachment was adopted. Learning theorists argued that the infant learned attachment because attachment was associated with the fulfillment of primary biological needs. In other words, the infant learned through experience that by becoming attached to its parents, it would have its biological needs gratified.

The Freudian view and the learning theory view on this issue were so close that many writers argued that the only difference was the choice of terminology used to describe the phenomenon (Beller, 1957; Sears, Maccoby, & Levin, 1957).

Question: Then is attachment acquired because it results in the fulfillment of biological needs?

This was once thought to be the case; as noted, however, our theoretical orientation has changed. To understand the modern view and to explore why our thoughts about attachment have changed, let's take a look at the work of researcher Harry Harlow.

MONKEY LOVE

As you recall, both Freud and the learning theorists believed that nursing led to the formation of strong attachments between infant and mother because attachment was associated with the satisfaction of biological needs. But research with rhesus monkeys conducted by Harry Harlow and his associates cast doubt on this speculation (Harlow & Suomi, 1970).

In a series of widely publicized experiments begun about 40 years ago, Harlow and his colleagues separated rhesus monkeys from their mothers at an early age and placed them with artificial surrogate mothers (see Figure 6.1). One surrogate was made of wire; the other was covered with terry cloth and possessed a more rhesus-looking face. Both "mothers" could be equipped with baby bottles placed through a hole in the chest, which allowed nursing to take place. Regardless of which mother provided food, the baby rhesus spent as much time as possible cuddling and hugging the cloth mother. Even rhesus monkeys fed by only the

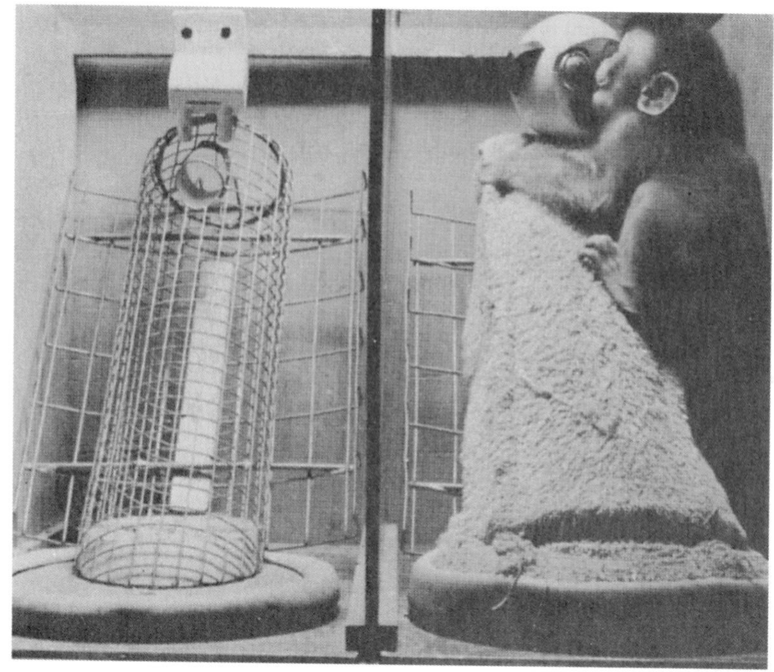

FIGURE 6.1

Baby rhesus monkey with its surrogate cloth mother. The wire mother is also shown.

wire mother formed strong attachments to the cloth mother and spent most of their time hugging it.

Question: Isn't that just because cloth feels better than wire?

That was the first response of the researchers to these findings—that "contact comfort" was more important than nursing in the formation of attachments. But Harlow went further than this interpretation. Do you remember those plastic insects called "cooties" that you could buy in the store and assemble (see Figure 6.2)? Harlow discovered that baby rhesus monkeys are generally terrified of cooties. After all, they are about the same size as a baby monkey and they do look scary. Harlow found that when a baby rhesus was placed in a room with a cootie and a cloth surrogate mother, the infant would run to the surrogate mother and cling to its body. The baby monkey would then become relaxed and calm; apparently, it felt safe. At this point the baby monkey would often begin to use the "mother" as a safe base of operations from which to explore the environment. Harlow even captured on film one monkey infant who, after a few daring attempts, found the courage to run up to the cootie, pull off one of its antennae, and run back to the surrogate mother.

Interestingly, the baby monkeys did not show similar attachment to just a soft piece of terry cloth left lying on the floor. There was something special about "mother" beyond nursing or contact comfort.

Question: Could these attachments be instinctive?

There may be instinctive components to these attachments. For instance, such attachments are easier to form with objects that appear similar to real mothers. But without early experience, the attachment won't occur. Baby rhesus monkeys raised without a surrogate or real mother will not run to a surrogate mother when faced with a fear stimulus like a cootie, but will simply curl up and shake with fear or try to run as far away as possible.

Such early attachments in rhesus monkeys are formed quickly and are long-lasting. Baby rhesus monkeys raised with cloth mothers and then separated from them for six months will respond eagerly the instant they are reunited, rushing to the cloth mothers and clinging to them.

Other researchers found that with human subjects, too, that attachment is more than just dependence on someone who fulfills biological needs. For instance, infants may become attached to other infants their own age (Schaffer & Emerson, 1964). Attachment may develop even if an infant is seriously mistreated by the one to whom he or she is becoming attached (Rosenblum & Harlow, 1963). Infants also respond readily to others in social situations in which they have never received food or contact comfort (Brackbill, 1958; Rheingold, Gewirtz, & Ross, 1959). Furthermore, infants do not become passive and unresponsive once all their biological needs have been taken care of; they continue to be social and show attachment (Gewirtz, 1961).

THE INTRAORGANISMIC PERSPECTIVE

Question: What is the current view of infant attachment?

Developmental researchers do not all agree on one view. In recent years, however, the most accepted theoretical orientation has been toward an **intraorganismic perspective.** In this view, attachment is not merely an outward manifestation of a learned or acquired behavior pattern; rather, it is dependent on an internal or intraorganismic organization.

INTRAORGANISMIC PERSPECTIVE
The theory, first espoused by Bowlby, that infants possess innate mechanisms that foster and promote the development of attachment. Such mechanisms are believed to have been naturally selected, as they have survival value.

Question: What do you mean by intraorganismic organization?

In this case, *intraorganismic organization* means that the infant is biologically organized or ready to form attachments to care givers (Ainsworth, 1973; Bowlby, 1969). In other words, attachment to others is thought to be based on an experience-expectant neurological system (see Chapter 5). This makes sense because contact with others is an experience that our species would be almost certain to have; therefore, it would be economical for our neurology to have evolved in a way that would "expect" such contact to occur. And in terms of evolution, organisms who are innately predisposed to form attachments to care givers are more likely to survive than those who don't form such attachments. In this sense, parents or adult care givers are seen as *intrinsically* attractive to an infant.

Question: Are there any data that support the view that attachments can be inherited?

FIGURE 6.2
The dreaded cootie.

Ethology
The study of behavior from a biological point of view, characterized by the study of animals in their natural environments.

Imprinting
As used by ethologists, a species-specific bonding that occurs within a limited period early in the life of the organism and that is relatively unmodifiable thereafter.

Critical Period
A specific time during an organism's development when certain experiences will have an effect and after which the effect can no longer be obtained through exposure to the experience.

Imprinting

Throughout this century, research on inherited behavior has attracted great interest, especially in Europe. People who specialize in this area of research are called ethologists, and their field of study is called **ethology.** Ethologists usually conduct naturalistic observations, and they are also interested in learned behavior.

Ethology traces its experimental roots to nineteenth-century zoology. In an early ethological experiment conducted in 1873, D. A. Spalding discovered that baby chicks tended to follow the first moving object that they saw, usually the mother hen. This tendency seemed to exist either at birth or shortly thereafter. Spalding speculated that the tendency to follow was probably innate, because it helped the chicks to survive, keeping them with the mother. Spalding wanted to be sure that the behavior was not learned—that is, acquired through experience—so he covered the chicks' heads with hoods immediately after they were hatched, before they opened their eyes. When the hoods were removed a few hours later, the chicks followed the first object that crossed their field of vision, regardless of what the object was. This result demonstrated that the tendency was not learned, because experience could not have played a role.

Research in this new field began to grow significantly after Konrad Lorenz published a paper in 1937 describing the *following response.* As part of his study, Lorenz actually made certain that he was the first moving object that some newborn goslings saw. From that time on, the goslings followed "mama" Lorenz everywhere he went, even swimming. It seemed to Lorenz that the first object to move past these goslings was "stamped into" the animals' brains as the object to be followed. Lorenz called this stamping phenomenon **imprinting.** He also observed that imprinting could occur only during a **critical period** lasting from hatching until about 2 days later. The most effective imprinting occurred approximately 14 hours after hatching. If the chicks were more than 2 days old when they saw their first moving object, imprinting was not observed to occur.

Ethologists and other researchers believe that such inherited behavior must serve a function. The following response has the obvious function of keeping the chick or gosling close to its mother. Offspring that don't stay close to the mother will have less chance of surviving and passing on their genes.

Question: Has imprinting been demonstrated in human beings?

Young ducklings followed "mama" Lorenz wherever he went because they had been allowed to imprint on him.

Although infants generally become attached to parents or care givers and sometimes show changes in the strengths of their attachments, there appears to be no particular period that is most important in determining their first attachment figure, the way there is with baby geese or chicks (Reed & Leiderman, 1983). In this sense, imprinting has not been found to occur in humans. Modern ethologists, however, argue that this does not preclude the possibility that infants are still genetically predisposed to form attachments. In their view, even without critical periods, there is an innate drive in humans to form attachments that is as strong as the motivational forces of mating or eating (Bowlby, 1982a). The debate concerning the strength and quality of infant–care giver attachments continues (see At Issue).

BOWLBY AND CONTEMPORARY ATTACHMENT THEORY

One of the most important proponents of the intraorganismic perspective is researcher John Bowlby, whose paper, "The Nature of the Child's Tie to His Mother" (Bowlby, 1958), has been considered by many to mark the beginning of contemporary attachment theory (Joffe & Vaughn, 1982).

Question: How did Bowlby view attachment?

Before Bowlby's work, most researchers who studied attachment concentrated on a few specific behaviors, such as how long a child cried after his mother left a room. These behaviors would be counted and sometimes observed for changes over a period of years. Bowlby, however, did not view attachment as consisting of a few behaviors that might be counted and measured in the laboratory, such as how long a child clings to his mother; rather, he saw attachment in a much broader sense. Bowlby believed that attachment was an *entire way of interacting* with others, incorporating many different behaviors at different times. The importance of such behaviors is that they serve and maintain social attachment. Thus, Bowlby argued that researchers must examine a very wide range of attachment behaviors in each individual they study. To make this advantage clear, consider that a 1-year-old child who demonstrates avoidance by turning away from his mother may continue to demonstrate this same avoidance when he is 1½ years old, *but this time* by paying little attention to the mother when she returns from a short absence. Researchers examining only one kind of behavior (such as turning away) would have missed the continuity that is afforded when the *purpose* of behavior is considered rather than just the specific behavior itself. To examine the long-term development of a mode of attachment, many behaviors must be examined for the continuity of purpose.

Question: How is Bowlby's view intraorganismic?

Bowlby emphasized that any infant evolutionarily adept at surviving is rapidly prepared to make attachment a major mode of interaction. Infants not predisposed to some kind of attachment are simply less likely to survive. His view is intraorganismic because he saw much of attachment as stemming from *within* the infant.

Question: How did Bowlby explain a mother's attachment to her infant?

He saw it in exactly the same way. Any mother who did not feel attachment for her infant would be less likely to care for him. Her infant, then, might very well die from neglect and not pass on her genetic predispositions for a low level of attachment.

From the intraorganismic perspective, infant smiles are *intrinsically* satisfying to parents, infant cries are *intrinsically* distressing, and the interaction between parent and child is all that is necessary to foster attachment. In other words:

John Bowlby

AT ISSUE

The Mother-Infant Bond

In 1972, John Kennell and Marshall Klaus thought that there might be a sensitive (though perhaps not critical) period immediately following birth when a special bond formed between the infant and mother during skin-to-skin contact. Although such a bond might not be as obvious as the kind we see during imprinting, they argued that it would still be one that fostered a special relationship and that a disruption of that bond might leave the infant at a lasting disadvantage (Klaus et al., 1972).

Kennell and Klaus conducted a detailed study to investigate the importance of these first few minutes or hours of contact between a mother and her infant. Twenty-eight healthy mothers with normal full-term infants were divided into two groups. The first group was given more hours of contact (16 hours altogether) with their infants during the first 3 days after birth than was the second group (Kennell et al., 1974). A significant difference was noted between the two groups of mothers when they returned to the hospital 1 month later. During the babies' feeding, the extra-contact mothers cuddled and soothed their babies more and had more eye contact with them.

After 2 years, five mothers randomly selected from each group were reexamined. The extra-contact mothers still showed differences when compared to the less-contact mothers. The conclusion was that the 16 extra hours of contact during the first 3 days of life were still having an effect on the mothers' behavior 2 years after the birth! How the mothers reacted to their infants in turn affected the way the infants responded to their mothers.

These findings, many of which are contained in Klaus and Kennell's *Maternal-Infant Bonding* (1976), led many researchers to conclude that this bond should be encouraged (Klaus & Kennell, 1976; Kennell, Voos, & Klaus, 1979). As a result, many hospitals began changing their procedures. In fact, the hospital procedure of giving the

Because of the bonding research, hospitals changed their practices to encourage closer mother–infant contact during the first hours and days of life.

> Attachment behavior is regarded as a class of social behavior equivalent in importance to that of mating or parental behavior and is deemed to have a function specific to itself. The origins of attachment are, therefore, not to be found in feeding per se but in mother-infant interaction, and no reference to "needs" or "drives" is required. Attachment behavior is simply regarded as that which occurs when certain behavioral systems [the infant-mother interaction] are activated. Such species characteristic behaviors as smiling and crying are presumed to possess a signaling function that serves to activate maternal behavior and bring the adult into proximity to the child. (Joffe & Vaughn, 1982, p. 193)

Question: Did Bowlby believe that learning plays any role in attachment?

He agreed that learning certainly has an effect; infants are not born knowing to whom they should become attached, and infants can become as attached to adopted parents as they can to biological ones. In his view, infants have a pre-

AT ISSUE

baby to the mother immediately after birth while encouraging her to hold and stroke the infant can be traced, in part, to the bonding research of Kennell and Klaus.

Kennell and Klaus's findings did not go unchallenged, however. The first major criticism of the bonding research was a fairly obvious one, namely, that parents of adopted children feel as close to their kids as any biological parent does—that they do not feel at all distant or "unbonded." This last observation led researchers to conclude that "the initial post delivery bonding, as described by Klaus and Kennell (1976) and others, which is obviously not part of the adoption experience, does not appear to be necessary for the formation of a healthy family relationship" (Singer, Brodzinsky, Ramsay, Steir, & Waters, 1985, p. 1550). These authors argued, therefore, that whatever the early mother-infant bond was, missing it was something that could easily be overcome.

Intrigued by this observation, researchers Chess and Thomas, well known for their work on temperament (see Chapter 4), decided to examine the bonding research on their own. After doing so, they argued that Kennell and Klaus's research design had methodological flaws. They concluded that the idea of a unique type of relationship between mother and child due to skin-to-skin contact immediately after birth was unfounded (Chess & Thomas, 1982, 1986b).

Following this, researchers looking at other cultures discovered that motherly affection wasn't any greater in societies that encouraged early mother-infant body contact, that a father's involvement with his child was no greater if he were allowed to attend the child's birth, and that maternal affection or bonding was not greater in societies that encouraged early nursing (Lozoff, 1983).

In the light of these new findings, Kennell and Klaus agreed that it would be unlikely for the life-sustaining mother-infant relationship to be dependent on any one process such as bonding (although they still believed the bonding effect to be a real one) and that there probably were many other "fail-safe" routes to attachment (Kennell & Klaus, 1984).

Other researchers have concluded that the bonding model is oversimplified and in fact no longer useful (Svejda, Pannabecker, & Emde, 1982; Myers, 1984). One researcher presented the general consensus this way:

> The bonding hypothesis caught the fancy of the public in the 1980s; it is invoked in child custody disputes and has promoted changes in obstetrical practices. Given these far-reaching implications, it is especially important to note that the existence of a critical period for bonding is not supported by the most relevant data. (Hay, 1986, p. 153)

The bonding issue continues to flourish, however, because so many hospitals still encourage what they believe to be "bonding" even though research has failed to show a real benefit to be derived from immediate skin-to-skin contact between mother and infant. This attitude may lead to problems if, because of some medical emergency or other valid reason, the infant and mother can't be brought together directly following birth. The mother, if she knows about the supposed importance of bonding, may then feel that she has missed out on something crucial by not being able to "bond" with her baby (Chess & Thomas, 1986b). Still, a number of welcome humanitarian hospital reforms were brought on by this research; these days, parents are encouraged to participate fully in the birth and to become immediately involved with their newborn, which is something that most parents enjoy and appreciate.

disposition toward attachment, but the actual attachment depended on the *experience* they had with the different people to whom they became attached.

Question: According to Bowlby, how does the development of attachment proceed?

Bowlby viewed the attachment system as becoming well organized sometime during the second half of an infant's first year of life. By then, the attachment system is already building on earlier behaviors (Bowlby, 1969, 1973, 1982b). For instance, shortly after birth, babies do certain things that might be seen as helping to promote attachment, such as smiling, crying, touching, and following their parents with their eyes. A little later, the infant may display these behaviors *as part of an actual attachment* by smiling, touching, or especially looking toward a familiar person rather than just anyone (Brooks-Gunn & Lewis, 1981).

ATTACHMENT-EXPLORATION BALANCE
Term used by Ainsworth to describe the interplay between the child's desire to be attached and the child's need to explore the environment.

SECURE-BASE PHENOMENON
Term used by Ainsworth to describe the child's tendency to use the attachment figure as a secure base of operations from which to explore the environment.

By the time the baby is able to crawl at about 6 to 8 months of age, she usually makes an *active* attempt to maintain closeness to the person to whom she has become attached. The baby also begins to demonstrate an awareness of the absence of that person (Bell, 1970). During this time, babies will typically become very upset whenever the mother or primary care giver leaves. After the child passes the age of about 18 months, her attachment, especially to the mother, becomes even more complex. At this time, the child may begin to form what are often called "internal working models" of the relationships between the child and the care givers (Main, Kaplan, & Cassidy, 1985; Pipp & Harmon, 1987).

Question: What is meant by an internal working model?

An *internal working model* in this case refers to the child's memories of the attachment relationship, memories on which he can draw to determine what he can expect from care givers (primarily the mother) in different situations. Such an internal working model also helps the child to develop an appraisal of the relationship. For instance, if the child is rejected or abused when attempting to obtain comfort from his parents during stressful situations, he is likely "to develop not only an internal working model of the parent as rejecting but also one of himself or herself as not worthy of help and comfort" (Bretherton, 1985, p. 12). Clearly, the *quality* of attachment between child and parent may play a crucial role in a child's development.

THE DYNAMICS OF HUMAN ATTACHMENT

Question: Has anyone ever investigated the quality of attachment?

Mary Ainsworth, who trained with John Bowlby, conducted some of the most interesting, careful studies of human attachment during infancy and childhood. Ainsworth investigated two interesting concepts. One she calls the **attachment-exploration balance** (the balance between the child's need for attachment and his desire to explore the environment); the other she refers to as the **secure-base phenomenon** (the child's use of the attachment figure, generally the mother, as a secure base of operations from which to explore, much as Harlow's rhesus monkeys used the terry cloth mother as a safe base of operations). Both of these concepts are used to account for the fact that attachment can be disrupted by the infant's desire to explore. Because even the most attached infants are driven to explore, Ainsworth abandoned the idea of proximity to the attachment figure as the main way of measuring attachment and began to study situations in which the child felt either secure or insecure.

Mary Ainsworth

Question: What kinds of studies did Ainsworth conduct?

Ainsworth's studies are superior to most others in their scope. They have included a 1-year longitudinal investigation of infant attachments in the home, as well as a 20-minute laboratory test known as the *strange situation*, in which 10- to 24-month-old infants are placed in a situation where they are exposed to a gradually increasing amount of stress. The strange situation demonstrates individual differences in the quality of attachment, and it makes possible an assessment of the variables that determine the quality of infant attachment.

Question: How is the strange situation arranged?

The strange situation is arranged in the following way. A mother and her young child enter the experiment room. The mother places her child on a small chair surrounded by toys and then takes a seat on the other side of the room. A short time later, a stranger enters the room, sits quietly for a moment, and then tries to engage the child in play. At this point, the mother abruptly leaves the room.

In a short while, the mother returns and plays with the child, and the stranger leaves. Then the mother exits once more, leaving the child completely alone for 3 minutes. Then the stranger returns. A few minutes later, the mother returns and the stranger leaves. All these comings and goings may read like a scene from a Marx Brothers movie, but Table 6.1 will clarify the sequence. Everything that occurs during these 20-minute periods is recorded by an observer who sits behind a one-way mirror.

As you can see, the organization of the strange situation places the child in a number of circumstances designed to measure his or her sense of security and attachment. It is worth noting that one advantage of the strange situation is that it allows observers to quantify many ways in which an infant can demonstrate attachment, instead of measuring only proximity to the mother. This is in agreement with Bowlby's plea (mentioned earlier) that researchers see attachment in more global terms.

Although earlier studies of separation concentrated on how much infants cried when abandoned or how they reacted to spending time alone, Ainsworth and her associates concentrated on the infant's reaction to the return of the mother. By using a number of observational techniques, they were able to identify three attachment reactions of differing quality.

The first, **secure attachment,** was the most common, accounting for about 65 to 70 percent of children studied. Babies exhibiting this response gave their returning mothers a happy greeting and approached them or stayed near them for a time. The second kind of reaction, **anxious/resistant attachment,** accounted for about 10 to 15 percent of children. Infants who respond in this way approach their mothers, cry to be picked up, and then squirm or fight to get free, as though they aren't sure what they want. The third kind, **anxious/avoidant attachment** (a rather paradoxical term), accounted for about 20 percent of children; it is demonstrated by infants who don't approach their returning mothers or who actively avoid them.

Question: Are the kinds of attachments that infants show stable over time?

They have been found to be fairly stable over time (Waters, 1983; Main & Cassidy, 1988), but they can change. For instance, in one study, infants were observed at 12 months and then again at 18 months of age. Over the 6-month period, changes in the mother's behavior were found to coincide with changes in the infant's attachment. Young mothers who initially had anxious/resistant or anxious/avoidant infants but who, through experience, learned to be more competent and caring for their infants eventually had securely attached infants; furthermore, securely attached infants whose mothers became more irritable and tense owing to

SECURE ATTACHMEMT
Most common form of attachment observed by Ainsworth. Securely attached children respond happily to their mother's return, greet her, and stay near her for a while.

ANXIOUS/RESISTANT ATTACHMENT
A form of attachment observed by Ainsworth in which children approach their returning mothers, cry to be picked up, and then struggle to be free. Their behavior is ambivalent; they appear to wish to approach and avoid their mothers simultaneously.

ANXIOUS/AVOIDANT ATTACHMENT
A form of attachment observed by Ainsworth in which children do not approach—and in fact actively avoid—their returning mothers.

TABLE 6.1

The Strange Situation

EPISODE	ACTORS PRESENT IN ROOM	ACTION
1	Child, mother	Mother and child enter room
2	Child, mother, stranger	Stranger enters
3	Child, stranger	Mother exits
4	Child, mother	Mother returns and stranger exits
5	Child alone	Mother exits
6	Child, stranger	Stranger returns
7	Child, mother	Mother returns and stranger exits

Securely attached babies tend to show greater competence in early childhood.

various circumstances eventually became anxious/resistant or anxious/avoidant (Egeland & Farber, 1984).

Question: Why would infants show different qualities of attachment?

It is generally assumed that anxious/avoidant and anxious/resistant attachments are weak attachments, while secure attachments are strong ones (Bretherton, 1985). Supporting this assertion are data showing that babies who are forming secure attachments will get "in tune" with the person to whom they are becoming attached. Their heart rate will become more stable in that person's presence (Izard et al., 1991), and their interactions with that person will become smooth and well timed (Isabella & Belsky, 1991); the same cannot be said for anxious/avoidant and anxious/resistant babies.

If what we are seeing, then, is strength of attachment, it becomes reasonable to wonder whether the way mothers treat anxious/avoidant or anxious/resistant infants is different from the way mothers treat securely attached infants.

Question: How do mothers treat babies who show anxious/avoidant or anxious/resistant attachment, and how is it different from the way mothers treat securely attached infants?

Mothers of anxious/avoidant infants tend to respond to their infants' cries and demands only when they are in the mood to do so, often ignoring the infants at other times. They also appear to be less sensitive than other mothers to their infants' requests or needs (Smith & Pederson, 1988) and often state that they disliked physical contact with their infants (Ainsworth, Blehar, Waters, & Wall, 1978; Main & Weston, 1982). Infants who are anxious/avoidant may be that way because they expect to be rebuffed rather than comforted in the strange situation. To avoid a rebuff, they may turn away from the person who has been unresponsive in the past.

Anxious/resistant attachment, on the other hand, is not related to rejection but rather to inconsistency by the mother during the infant's first year of life (Ainsworth, Blehar, Waters, & Wall, 1978). Anxious/resistant infants may react the way they do simply because they don't know what to expect because the adult's behavior has been so inconsistent and unreliable in the past. Supporting this idea is the observation that anxious/resistant infants engage in social referencing (just like the ambivalent infants on the visual cliff, as described in the Chapter Preview) more than secure or anxious/avoidant infants do (Dickstein, Thompson, Estes, Malkin, & Lamb, 1984).

Mothers who are the most accessible, consistent, and sensitive and who respond most to their babies' cries and signals have securely attached babies (Isabella, Belsky, & von Eye, 1989) and appear to enjoy their babies more than do mothers with less securely attached infants (Pederson et al., 1990). Interestingly, this kind of maternal sensitivity can be promoted by just encouraging the mother to have more physical contact with her baby, which in turn increases the chances that the baby will become securely attached (Anisfeld, Casper, Nozyce, & Cunningham, 1990). Securely attached infants require *less* proximity and physical contact as they grow older than do anxious/resistant or anxious/avoidant infants (Clarke-Stewart & Hevey, 1981). This might imply that infants who are securely attached have learned to trust and count on the adult who has responded correctly and quickly in the past to their needs or desires.

Until these findings were uncovered, it was commonly believed that infants who were coddled or hugged whenever they cried or showed fear would become dependent. As it turns out, just the opposite happens! Secure babies are more likely to develop independence (Sroufe, 1983).

Question: Why do some mothers behave one way toward their infants, while other mothers behave differently?

No one knows for sure. Each mother is an individual and as such has her own personality and beliefs that come into play when she interacts with her child. And of course, each has her own environment filled with various stressors and supports. However, some studies have provided a few clues that hint at an answer. For example, it was found that mothers of children who showed secure attachment typically recalled from their *own* childhood that they had felt secure and that attachments to others had been important to them. On the other hand, mothers of anxious or insecurely attached children often recalled feelings of rejection, hurt, or neglect from their childhood (Crowell & Feldman, 1988). It may be, then, that mothers have developed their own internal working models about what attachment between child and mother is, or should be, and this understanding is reflected in their relationships with their own children. Their children, in turn, then use the working models provided by their mothers to form their own ideas of what attachment means and respond accordingly (Crowell & Feldman, 1991).

Question: You say that the mother's behavior seems to shape the child's quality of attachment. But couldn't infants of different temperaments be shaping their mothers to behave in different ways?

Because attachment is a two-way street, because it is an interaction, it's probably true that both temperament and the mother's behavior play a role in the formation of attachments. Temperament has been found to be related to a child's score in the strange situation. For instance, it was found that children who were temperamentally more fearful and who reacted to change with greater intensity showed more distress when separated from their mothers. This, in turn, was associated in the strange situation with resistance to the mother when she returned (Thompson, Connell, & Bridges, 1988).

Other observations also point to temperamental components in the formation of attachments. It has been found that the infant's behavior at 3 months of age is generally a better predictor of later attachment than is the behavior of the infant's mother (Lewis & Feiring, 1989). For example, regardless of how mothers acted toward their infants, it was found that 3-month-olds who preferred to play with toys rather than people were more likely to show avoidant behavior toward their mothers at 1 year of age (Lewis & Feiring, 1989).

On the other hand, while certain temperaments are associated with a *lack* of secure attachment, no temperament measure has been found to be associated *with* the formation of secure attachments (Vaughn, Lefever, Seifer, & Barglow, 1989). This indicates that environmental experiences may play a more important role than temperament in the formation of attachments, especially secure ones.

Further highlighting the play of environmental factors in the formation of attachments is cross-cultural research incorporating the strange situation. As it turns out, research conducted in other cultures has produced different results in the strange situation than Ainsworth obtained with her original American samples. For instance, among children who grew up on Israeli kibbutzim (collective farms) and also among Japanese children, there were higher percentages of anxious/resistant attachment in the strange situation. And among a sample of children from northern Germany, anxious/avoidant attachment was the most common form (see Table 6.2).

Question: Why are the results from different cultures so varied?

The way that children in different cultures initially interpret the strange situation is a product of their experiences (Sagi, Van IJzendoorn, & Koren-Karie, 1991). For example, it has been noted that children on a kibbutz generally are raised communally and not directly by their parents. In that sense, the strange situation might really have been "strange" to them because they weren't used to that kind of interaction with their mother. In fact, in this instance, a better choice for the

TABLE 6.2

The Distribution of Infants across Cultures by Mode of Attachment Demonstrated during the Strange Situation

	TYPE OF ATTACHMENT		
COUNTRY	**Secure**	**Anxious/ Resistant**	**Anxious/ Avoidant**
United States	71%	12%	17%
Japan	68%	**32%**	0%
Israel	62%	**33%**	5%
N. Germany	40%	11%	**49%**

SOURCE: Adapted from Sagi, Van IJzendoorn, & Koren-Karie, 1991.

role of parent in the strange situation might have been the child's *metapelet* (care provider on the kibbutz), because attachments don't have to form with the parent but may just as well form with a grandmother, nurse, nonrelative, or, in the case of the metapelet, with anyone who fulfills the role of regular care giver.

Japanese children may have shown more anxious/resistant attachment in the strange situation because they were especially upset at being left alone with a stranger, since that is something that Japanese mothers never do. Differences in German data probably reflect the cultural values of northern Germany that teach parents to keep a certain interpersonal distance from their children.

While these suggestions have received some support, it's probably too early in our research to make the jump from a few samples and results to a description of whole cultures. In fact, when all the scores of studies throughout the world involving the strange situation are examined, one discovers that the variation of results *within* cultures is 1½ times greater than the variation of results *between* cultures (Van IJzendoorn & Kroonenberg, 1988). Moreover, many American samples give results very different from Ainsworth's original results, often resembling the Israeli, German, or Japanese findings.

Question: How come American results can be so different from one study to the next?

The many American samples were quite diverse and included many different populations from different socioeconomic strata and ethnic backgrounds.

Question: Then what can we say about these diverse data?

When examining all these studies, we can say that secure attachment is usually the most common form of attachment exhibited. And we can say that whatever is happening, it appears to be strongly influenced by environmental forces. Beyond this, we have to be extremely cautious (Van IJzendoorn & Kroonenberg, 1988).

THE FLEXIBILITY OF HUMAN ATTACHMENT

Most models of human attachment focus on the importance of a primary caregiver, usually the mother. But recent cross-cultural studies of the Efe, a forest-dwelling tribe in Africa, have raised questions about the assumption that a primary caregiver is necessary for healthy attachment and human development.

Question: How are Efe children raised?

Efe babies and toddlers spend about half of their time away from their mothers in the care of many older children and adults. Infants are commonly breast fed by any available woman who is able. Three-year-olds are away from their mothers 70% of the time. Contact with fathers stays at about roughly 8% during the child's early years.

The infants and toddlers are not left alone, but are usually carried by an older child or adult throughout the day and when set down, are typically within earshot of about 10 tribe members. It is not surprising, therefore, that unlike children in other cultures, the Efe children form strong and close emotional attachment to many members of the tribe and have no primary caregiver as such (although some Efe children may, on occasion, show preferences for certain tribe members). The Efe children appear to develop quite well within this arrangement (Tronick, Morelli, & Ivey, 1992).

Question: Is this mode of child rearing comparable to modern day care arrangements?

No, not really. Efe infants see the same caregivers each day while there is often considerable turnover at modern day care centers. Also, children who attend day care leave their homes each day to go to day care and can experience the contrast between the two arrangements. Efe children are all raised the same way and know no other arrangement. The important finding concerning the Efe children is not that it is a vindication of day care (we will discuss day care in greater detail in the Application section), but rather that it is possible for infants and toddlers to form very strong emotional attachments to many caregivers at once, and that they are not limited to one primary caregiver by some innate biological organization, but rather, most often become attached to a primary caregiver probably because of culture.

Early Attachment and Later Development

Question: Does the kind of attachment that a child shows in infancy have any lasting consequences?

Securely attached infants (at least most of the ones from American studies) have been found to be more likely to explore their environments (Joffe, 1980) and to tolerate a moderate amount of separation from their mothers (Jacobson & Wille, 1984). Because they can tolerate some separation from their mothers, securely attached infants also feel more comfortable exploring, and when faced with something new, such as a toy or a game, will persist in examining it. They are also often encouraged by their mothers in a happy and joyful way to play and explore, which further encourages these children to expand their experiences (Rheingold, Cook, & Kolowitz, 1987). This persistence in exploring and experiencing often provides children with an opportunity to master the new things they have encountered (Frodi, Bridges, & Grolnick, 1985). Not surprisingly, children who exhibit such mastery in infancy tend to show greater competence in early childhood (Sroufe, 1983; Messer et al., 1986); and the persistence and confidence they gain as infants have been shown to have lasting benefits, as reflected in the schoolwork of these same children at age 12 years (Estrada, Arsenio, Hess, & Holloway, 1987).

Insecurely attached children, once they reach school, show various problems, depending on their gender. Boys who are insecurely attached tend to be more assertive, aggressive, controlling, disrupting, and attention seeking than securely attached boys, while girls tend to be more dependent and compliant than their securely attached peers (Turner, 1991).

Attachment and Social Relationships

Question: Does the kind of attachment that a child shows in infancy affect later social relationships?

Researcher L. Alan Sroufe conducted one of the more detailed investigations of personal competence and peer approval among children; the study was known as the Minnesota Preschool Project (Sroufe, 1983). Since that time, other data have also supported Sroufe's findings.

Sroufe and his co-workers developed objective measures for observing positive, negative, and inappropriate emotional reactions in preschool children. Using this technique, they designed a rating of "social competence," a score derived by subtracting the number of inappropriate and negative social-emotional interactions demonstrated by each child from the number of the child's appropriate and positive interactions. The children who were described by the researchers as securely attached at 15 months of age tended to have the highest scores and by the age of 3½ years were more likely to be peer leaders in the preschool. They tended to be involved in social relationships and actively engaged in their environments, to be well liked by their peers, and to enjoy sharing good feelings and thoughts with others (Park & Waters, 1989). They also often rewarded their peers for behaving in these ways. In other words, they demonstrated greater personal competence and peer approval (Waters, Wippman, & Sroufe, 1979).

On the other hand, low-ranked children generally were not liked or admired by their peers and were referred to by their teachers in such terms as "unpredictable," "a loner," or "a chronic whiner" (Bower, 1985). Other studies have shown the same sort of classifications for school-age children who had not shown secure attachment as infants (Cohn, 1990).

Attachment quality can also affect sibling relationships. In families with two children, if both were securely attached, there was less hostility and rivalry between siblings than if one or both of the siblings were not securely attached (Teti & Ablard, 1989).

All of these data, however, are correlational (not causal), in that we can state only that high levels of positive behaviors and emotions are correlated with peer approval, acceptance, and early secure attachment, while less desired outcomes are associated with insecure forms of attachment. Again, it may be a third variable that is causing both secure attachment and positive outcomes.

ATTACHMENT THERAPY

Question: If being securely attached at an early age is so important, is there any way to intervene and alter an insecure attachment to make it a secure one?

That has been attempted and with some success. In one experiment, a group of 100 relatively poor mothers who had recently immigrated from Mexico or Central America were studied along with their 1-year-old toddlers. This group was chosen because they were "considered at risk for disorders of attachment because recent Latino immigrants face a high incidence of depression and anxiety as a result of poverty, unemployment, and cultural uprootedness" (Lieberman, Weston, & Pawl, 1991, p. 200).

Toddlers classified as anxious/resistant or anxious/avoidant (63 percent of the children tested) were randomly separated into an experimental and control group. Securely attached toddlers functioned as a second control group. The experimental group received weekly 1½-hour visits from a bilingual, bicultural therapist who provided information to the mother about child development and who helped her to express her worries and concerns about being unsettled. The therapist also helped the mother to understand her toddler's needs and to see the child's actions as more benign than she might otherwise. For example, it might be pointed out that a 1-year-old who is getting into everything isn't being spiteful and isn't a bad boy, but rather is exploring his environment in a very natural way for his age and is simply too young to fully control himself.

Question: Was the therapeutic intervention successful?

After two years of intervention it was impossible to distinguish the children in the experimental group from the securely attached children in the control group. In comparison, the anxious/resistant and anxious/avoidant control group children showed little or no improvement over the two years (Lieberman, Weston, & Pawl, 1991). These results indicate that therapeutic intervention can change an anxious attachment into a secure one. The question, then, becomes whether such change will have any long-term benefit.

Question: But aren't securely attached children more likely to succeed and do well in school?

This is true, but the long-term benefits associated with secure attachment may not be *caused* by secure attachment. Researcher Michael Lamb and his colleagues have pointed out that even though there does seem to be some sort of connection between attachment quality and later behavior, the relationship is most likely only a reflection of something more general; according to Lamb, that something is family stability.*

In stable families, attachment is more secure and children tend to be more successful in terms of their social-emotional development. Supporting this assumption is the fact that predictions of future behavior based on findings in the strange situation are more likely to be correct for children who are from stable families, especially those that have stable child-care arrangements. In this view, the results from the strange situation *and* the child's later development simply reflect the more general influence of family and child-care stability, which in turn gives rise to secure attachment and later social acceptance (Lamb, Thompson, Gardner, Charnov, & Estes, 1984). If this view is correct, then increasing secure attachment through therapeutic intervention may not have long-term benefit unless it also increases family and child-care stability. It will be very interesting to compare those children who received intervention with those who did not once they are in school, so that we might see if the intervention did produce a long-term benefit. If it did, the next question will be, Why did it? Did it have an effect on family stability, or was there something about secure attachment alone that made a difference? As with most research, one question often leads to another.

THE FATHER'S ROLE

Because of the growing interest of researchers in what goes on in the entire family, scientists have increased their focus on the importance of other family members or care givers, especially fathers. In the past, fathers were shortchanged. Ainsworth and just about every other researcher before 1970 ignored fathers. Happily, however, fathers have attracted more attention since then.

One reason for the growing interest in the father's role during infancy is that fathers have been participating increasingly in the feeding, care, and stimulation of their infants (Parke & Tinsley, 1981). This change, which has occurred in many Western industrialized nations, has come about for a number of reasons, the foremost of which is the growing number of working mothers. Also important is the conscious effort on the part of many people to alter or abolish sex stereo-

*This assertion highlights a point that was made in Chapter 1. There it was noted that a correlation between increased ice cream sales and increased drownings should not lead us to believe that there is a causal connection between these two variables. Instead, both increases were caused by a third factor—summer. In the same way, the correlation between attachment and later social success may be accounted for by a third factor that is causally related to both—family stability. Whenever you find a strong correlation between two events, it's a good idea to ask yourself whether a third factor could be causing the two events you have observed.

types, which in turn affects the *traditional* roles of "mother" and "father." Even though more than 50 percent of American mothers work, however, these sex role stereotypes are still strong. It has been found that on average, mothers spend 121 hours with their infants for each 26 hours spent by fathers (Cowan & Cowan, 1987). As one group of researchers stated, "Mothers more frequently responded to, stimulated, expressed positive affection toward, and took basic care of their infants, while fathers spent more time reading or watching TV" (Belsky, Gilstrap, & Rovine, 1984, p. 702). The same has been found in other Western industrialized nations, such as Israel (Greenbaum & Landau, 1982) and Sweden (Frodi, Lamb, Hwang, & Frodi, 1982). The Swedish study is especially interesting because the difference between mother and father involvement was evident in both traditional and nontraditional families. Fathers are simply less likely to be the primary care giver, and this holds true across a great range of paternal ages, from teenage fathers to much older ones (Lamb & Elster, 1985).

Question: Are mothers, in some natural way, more capable of caring for an infant?

Except for the obvious ability to breast feed, it has been found that fathers who voluntarily assume child-care duties are just as competent with their infants as mothers are (Parke, O'Leary, & West, 1972; Parke & Tinsley, 1981). Such competent nurturant behavior on the part of fathers has been found among members of all socioeconomic classes (Parke & O'Leary, 1976; Parke & Sawin, 1975) and in many countries (Parke, Grossman, & Tinsley, 1981). The fact that fathers can function as well as mothers in the care of their infants, however, doesn't necessarily mean that they will do so regularly (Frodi, Lamb, Hwang, & Frodi, 1982; Belsky, Gilstrap, & Rovine, 1984). That both fathers and mothers appear to accept the mother's role as primary care giver seems to be culturally and socially motivated behavior. Probably it is an offshoot of the mother's anatomical functions of carrying, giving birth to, and breast feeding the baby.

Question: Is there any way to predict which fathers will be most involved with their infants?

The attitudes that both parents express before a child's birth concerning how much the father should be involved generally predict how active a role the father will take with his infant (Palkovitz, 1984). Interestingly, when fathers are alone with their infants, they are far more likely to assume the role of primary care giver and tend to their infant's needs than they are when the mother is present (Palkovitz, 1980).

Research has shown that children especially appreciate the father's role as playmate.

Question: Does this mean that fathers are just sort of backup care givers, or do they have a special role?

Fathers have been found to spend more time than mothers do playing with their infants (Kotelchuck, 1976). This playmate role on the part of fathers also has been observed in other countries (Richards, Dunn, & Antonis, 1977). Furthermore, there is a difference in the quality of play of mothers and fathers. Fathers are more likely to be arousing and physical (tossing the baby in the air, for example), while mothers tend to be quieter in their vocalizations and to engage in more structured play activities, playing conventional games, such as peekaboo or pattycake (Clarke-Stewart, 1980).

Infants also react differently to the different ways their parents play with them. Generally, babies respond more positively to the father's play (Lamb, 1977). By the time an infant reaches 2½ years of age, this appreciation of the father as a playmate becomes more apparent. In one study, 2½-year-old children were given an opportunity to choose either their father or mother in a play situation; more than two-thirds of the children chose to play with their father first (Clarke-Stewart, 1977).

Question: Then, for infants, the mother is the attachment figure and the father the playmate?

John Bowlby once described the distinction between playmate and attachment figure. He noted that while playmates are approached by infants who are in a positive mood, attachment figures are approached by infants who are frightened or under stress (Bowlby, 1982b). In this sense, mothers and fathers are *both* attachment figures *and* playmates for the infant. It's just that generally, the mother is the *primary* attachment figure, while the father is the *preferred* playmate.

This view of father as playmate and mother as care giver is probably based on culture and tradition and is certainly not the case for every family. Studies from Norway, Sweden, and Australia have shown that the traditional arrangement is not universal and is dependent on the working arrangements of the parents and other factors, such as the health of the infant and the organization of the family (Gronseth, 1975; Russell, 1980; Radin & Harold-Goldsmith, 1989).

Emotion is such an important part of social situations that it's hard to consider it separately. For this reason, researchers like to speak about social-emotional development.

Question: Can infants become as attached to their fathers as they are to their mothers?

There is no doubt that by the time attachment is well developed, the child has a clear understanding that mother and father are different individuals in that they behave differently. In fact, in the strange situation, infants often show different kinds of attachment to their fathers and mothers, and these differences remain stable for some time (Main & Weston, 1981; Bridges, Connell, & Belsky, 1988). But how attached the infant is to the father and whether that attachment is as great as that between infant and mother is difficult to measure. Unfortunately, the criteria used in research to define attachment are often different from one study to the next. The general consensus, however, is that attachment between infant and father can be as strong as that between infant and mother; the strength of the former depends on how responsive the father is to the infant's signals.

Although fathers can be as responsive as mothers, again, this does not mean that they necessarily *will* be. How responsive a father is appears to depend on whether he perceives himself to be a care giver (Zelazo, Kotelchuck, Barber, & David, 1977; Palkovitz, 1984).

Many important questions about fathering remain, but we do have some answers, some of which we have already discussed. We can add that infants form attachments to both mothers and fathers at about the same age (during their first year of life) and that although infants do generally prefer their mothers to their fathers, this is probably because the mother in her cultural role is the primary care giver (Lamb, 1981). This preference for the mother may change or even be reversed if fathers come to be more responsible for the direct care of their infants.

LEARNING CHECK

Matching

1. ____ Are more likely to feed or clean their infants
2. ____ Theoretical viewpoint that attachment is dependent on internal organization
3. ____ Looks to others' emotional expressions for information
4. ____ Child uses attachment figure as location from which to explore the environment

a. secure-base phenomenon
b. secondary-drive theory
c. strange situation
d. imprinting
e. internal working model
f. fathers
g. intraorganismic perspective
h. social referencing
i. mothers

5. ___ Research paradigm used by Ainsworth and colleagues to assess the quality of infant attachment
6. ___ Baby geese follow the first moving object they see
7. ___ Memories on which a child can draw to determine what to expect from care givers
8. ___ Are more likely to be playmates to their children

Answers: 1. i 2. g 3. h 4. a 5. c 6. d 7. e 8. f

Social-Emotional Development

It has been said that our emotions are what make us most human. We rage, we laugh, we cry, we fear, and we love. To be without emotions is to be unfeeling, perhaps "inhuman." Having feelings is an important part of being human.

Everyone has emotions, even infants. Babies smile and laugh, show fear, and, as you have seen, form loving attachments. Parents often report that the first smile from their baby is a magical moment that seems instantly to create a closer and more meaningful bond. Emotions are so important in forming our social bonds and attachments that researchers often use the term *social-emotional* development to emphasize the intertwining of the social and emotional dimensions of human behavior.

Question: Besides helping to form a closer bond between parent and child, what purpose do emotions serve? Why might they have evolved in the first place?

No one is certain why emotions exist, but many researchers believe that it is because emotions serve important functions. Charles Darwin was the first to espouse this view in his book *The Expression of the Emotions in Man and Animals* (Darwin, 1872/1967). According to this view, emotions perform two valuable services. First, they motivate us. For example, although you might *logically* decide to get out of the way of a speeding car, you're more likely to do it if you're scared than if you don't particularly feel one way or the other about it; and if you do

Young infants show discrete emotional expressions.

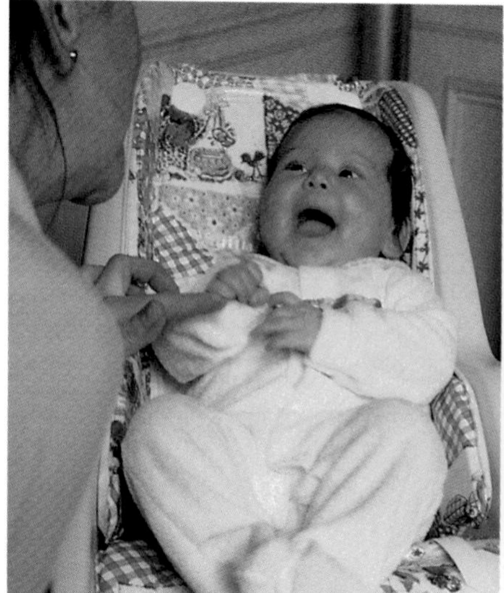

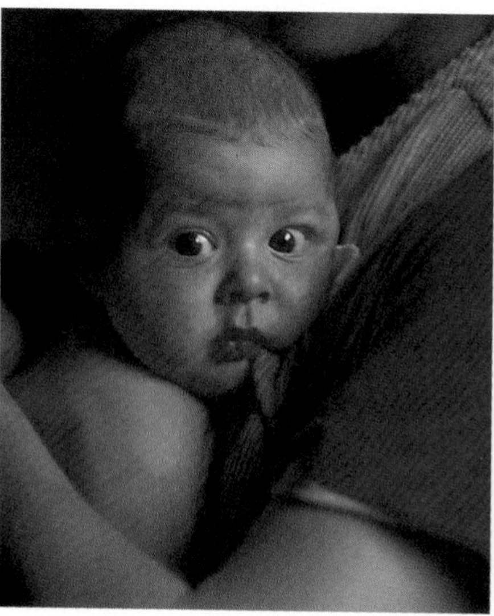

run, you are more likely to live and pass on the genes for this strong motivational mechanism: the ability to feel afraid. Second, emotions help us to communicate our desires and wishes to others. By looking at others—that is, by engaging in social referencing—we can often sense what others want us to do because we perceive how they feel.

Similarly, emotions motivate infants and also help them to interact. Remember how the infants on the visual cliff in the Chapter Preview relied on their mothers' expression for information about whether crossing over the cliff edge was safe. The interpersonal communication provided by facial expressions endows emotion with an important social aspect. In this way, emotion becomes involved in the social process.

Question: Does social-emotional development progress in a particular way?

There are certain milestones that appear to be common to children everywhere; there is a sequence of social-emotional development. While Chief of the Clinical Infant and Child Development Research Center at the National Institute of Mental Health, physician Stanley Greenspan, integrated the research of many other scientists with his own observations. He outlined social-emotional development in a series of six distinct stages that occur during the first 4 years of life (Cordes, 1985; Greenspan & Greenspan, 1985). You will notice that many of Greenspan's stages overlap. There is a great range of individual differences among infants, so some infants enter certain stages at different ages, but the stages follow the same *sequence* for all infants. Let's take a moment to examine these stages so that you car fully appreciate the unfolding of social-emotional development. Notice the importance of *emotion* in relation to the *social* context in each of the stages.

GREENSPAN'S SIX STAGES

Stage 1: Self-Regulation and Interest in the World (Birth to 3 Months) After 9 months of peace and quiet in the womb, the infant suddenly finds itself in a world filled with stimulation. The first emotional task facing an infant is to handle the sudden shock of all this excitement. During these first months, infants must learn to become calm despite the bombardment of sensations and to rely on their senses. Infants who take these steps begin to calm down and sleep regularly. They show interest when they see or hear something new; they enjoy being touched and like being moved about in space.

Stage 2: Falling in Love (2 to 7 Months) Once an infant has become interested in the sights and sounds during stage 1, the infant begins to take a very special interest in the people around him or her. Those to whom infants are becoming attached become the most attractive, enjoyable, and exciting of all individuals. Greenspan calls this "falling in love," and in a sense, he is correct. Now that they are calm and able to pay attention, infants at stage 2 look eagerly into faces, and their emotions during this time are most expressive when the attachment figure (mother, father, care giver) is involved.

Stage 3: Development of Intentional Communication (3 to 10 Months) At stage 3, it is as though the baby says, "Love alone is not enough—I now want a dialogue" (Greenspan & Greenspan, 1985, p. 4). The infant begins to show emotion and expression *in response* to the attachment figure's emotions and expressions, and when the infant makes a response, he or she may look toward the attachment figure for a further response. For instance, the infant may vocalize in response to the mother's voice, or a smile from the father may beget a smile from the infant. It is quite common for infants to spontaneously woo their parents and try to make them smile.

Stage 4: Emergence of an Organized Sense of Self (9 to 18 Months) During stage 4, the infant takes the emotional dialogue further and integrates the small social-emotional interactions of stage 3 into complex patterns.

Question: Would you give an example of such a complex pattern?

In stage 3, a thirsty infant might attempt to communicate thirst simply by an emotional display such as crying. By stage 4, however, the infant might take its mother by the hand and lead her to a glass or point to the water. The child also shows a more complete sense of self as the originator and organizer of social-emotional interaction. Such complex interactions can also foster attachment. For example, a child who wants to be closer to his or her father may tug on his hand and motion to be picked up.

At this time, children also show greater emotional sophistication. They seem better able to understand what others want by listening to the tones of their voices or by observing their gestures. These children may also know how to make others react emotionally; that is, they may know what to do to make others laugh or make them angry.

Stage 5: Creation of Emotional Ideas (18 to 36 Months) By stage 5, the child is able to imagine for the first time and to conceive of images and events in his or her "mind's eye." Cognitive psychologists call this *object permanence;* the child understands that even if an object is out of sight, it can still exist in the mind. Interestingly, children younger than 18 months don't seem to possess complete object permanence; for them, out of sight is typically out of mind (see Chapter 9).

A 2½-year-old child in stage 5, might cry in the middle of the night because "there's a monster in my closet." The emotional fear stimulus in this case is actually the child's imagination.* By engaging his or her imagination, a child in this stage can pretend to play and interact emotionally with others. This is an important emotional development, because now the child can react to emotional thoughts and imaginative experiences as well as to the actual experiences that occur in the child's world.

During stage 5, the child also begins to develop the idea that in particular situations, emotions can have a *function* (to motivate or communicate). By listening to the way children speak about emotions, we can obtain some understanding of the development of these emotional ideas. Table 6.3 provides a few examples of statements obtained from children during stage 5 and specifies the emotional ideas that each is expressing.

Stage 6: Emotional Thinking: The Basis for Fantasy, Reality, and Self-Esteem (30 to 48 Months) During stage 6, children begin to understand the way that

*Then again, perhaps it's best not to look in the closet (Stephen King, 1978, 1980, 1981, 1982, 1984, 1986, 1987, 1989, 1990, 1992, 1993).

TABLE 6.3

Examples of Emotional Ideas of Stage 5 Children

CHILD'S STATEMENT	EMOTIONAL IDEA
"Grandma mad [because] I wrote on wall."	One's behavior can cause emotion in another.
"I cry [so] lady pick me up and hold me."	One's emotion can motivate another person.
"I not cry now. I happy."	Certain emotions go with particular situations.

SOURCE: Adapted from Bretherton, Fritz, Zahn-Waxler, and Ridgeway, 1986, pp. 534–535.

emotions work. They can then learn to use this information to develop a better understanding of the world.

Question: What does it mean to understand the way that emotions work?

Children begin to understand, through experience with their own emotions and those of others, certain things about the emotions themselves. For example, children by this age already know which facial expressions should go with which emotions (Russell & Bullock, 1986), and they can describe things about emotions that we as adults know to be true, such as that an emotion will lose strength with the passage of time (Harris, Guz, Lipian, & Man-Shu, 1985). During stage 6, children not only show a deeper understanding of emotion; they also come to realize how their thoughts, feelings, and behavior all can be related to consequences. Children also come to know that "emotion words" are not only useful for labeling their own or someone else's feelings but are also valuable for suggestion or for manipulation of the behavior of others. Table 6.4 provides a few examples of this more sophisticated emotional thinking as expressed in children's statements. As you can see, by stage 6, children have gained a more mature understanding of emotion and its functions. These insights allow the beginning of the self-regulation of emotions and social behavior that enables children to act in socially appropriate ways in the company of peers and adults; this, in turn, can build children's self-esteem.

DISCRETE EMOTIONS THEORY
A view of emotional development that has as its central premise that all basic emotions are present and functional in newborns or very shortly after birth.

THE DEVELOPMENT OF EMOTIONS

Question: Are infants born with a full array of emotions, or do the emotions develop over time?

This issue is central to our understanding of emotional development, and it remains unresolved. Twenty-five or thirty years ago, most textbooks stated, rather matter-of-factly, that newborns started out by showing only arousal or quiescence. They went on to say that it wasn't until babies were between about 1 and 6 months of age that they displayed weak, less specifically defined emotional states, such as pleasure, wariness, or rage. And it was only older infants, those older than about 6 months of age, who showed distinct emotions, such as joy, fear, or anger. Emotions, therefore, became more differentiated and obvious as infants grew older, and more specific terms were used to denote these emotions as they developed (see Table 6.5). It was also assumed that infants were being socialized, to a great degree, about how to be emotional in certain circumstances. This view of emotional development is still popular today, but it is no longer the only view.

Challenging this long-held assumption is the **discrete emotions theory.** Researchers espousing this view believe that *all* the basic emotions are present in newborns and that as the infants age, they become better able to express these

TABLE 6.4

Some Emotional Concepts of Stage 6 Children

CHILD'S STATEMENT	EMOTIONAL IDEA OR CONCEPT
"If you go on vacation again, I'll cry."	Emotional reaction may influence the future behavior of others.
"He's sad. He'll be happy when his daddy comes home. His daddy comes home soon."	Future events may change current emotional states.
"He cried because he wanted me to go away."	Others may use emotion to manipulate us.

SOURCE: Adapted from Bretherton, Fritz, Zahn-Waxler, and Ridgeway, 1986, p. 536.

TABLE 6.5

The Development of Some Basic Human Emotions*

MONTH	PLEASURE-JOY	WARINESS-FEAR	RAGE-ANGER
0	Endogenous smile	Startle/pain	Distress due to: covering the face, physical restraint, extreme discomfort
1	Turning toward	Obligatory attention	
2			
3	Pleasure		Rage (disappointment)
4	Delight Active laughter	Wariness	
5			
6			
7	Joy		Anger
8			
9		Fear (stranger aversion)	
10			
11			
12	Elation	Anxiety Immediate fear	Angry mood, petulance
18	Positive valuation of self-affection	Shame	Defiance
24			Intentional hurting
36	Pride, love		Guilt

*The age specified is neither the first appearance of the affect in question nor its peak occurrence; it is the age when the literature suggests that the reaction is common.

SOURCE: Adapted from Sroufe, 1979, p. 473.

emotions in a way that others can see clearly, which explains the earlier assumptions about the gradual development of emotions (Campos, Barrett, Lamb, Stenberg, & Goldsmith, 1983). Supporting this assertion is a study that shows that infants only 10 weeks old can discriminate their mother's different emotional states. In this study, a mother would face her baby and say, "You make me (happy, sad, angry)," and match her voice to her facial expression. The infant typically acted as though the mother's actions had meaning, and the infant would react.

Question: How did the infants react?

The happy mothers produced happiness in their infants. Babies exposed to angry exhibitions eventually turned away and stopped looking. Those exposed to sad exhibitions appeared to suck their lips and tried to sooth themselves (Haviland & Lelwica, 1987). The researchers concluded that the mother's demeanor and emotional behavior were triggering the corresponding emotions in her infant. As you can see, this view is quite different from one that supposes that infants have undifferentiated affective states at first and only experience the full range of emotions once they are older.

This alternative view of emotional development also places a stronger emphasis on the biology and maturation of emotion. Support for a strong biological influence in the development of emotions comes from a number of sources. For instance, it has been observed that facial musculature of both full-term and premature newborns is fully developed and functional at birth (Ekman & Oster, 1979), so infants can make many of the same expressions that an adult can (Oster & Ekman, 1978). Newborns can smile slightly, knit their brows, or appear to pout and cry. And if you give them something that tastes awful, they look disgusted (Camras, 1988).

Central to the discrete emotions theory is the idea that the same basic emotions are common to all people and that they are produced early in infancy or are present at birth, having been brought forth by the maturation of the nervous system. One example of evidence for the maturational development of emotion comes from the work of Mel Konner, a Harvard biological anthropologist who has studied the onset of smiling among the !Kung San tribe in the Kalahari Desert in Africa. The !Kung San are one of the last hunter-gatherer tribes in the world. Konner observed more than 60 !Kung infants, and despite the great cultural and environmental differences between the !Kung and industrialized Western cultures, he discovered no differences in the onset and development of smiling (Greenberg, 1977). Konner believes that like motor and physical development, much of emotional development is directly tied to a maturational timetable of neurological growth.

Question: With all these findings, why hasn't the discrete emotions theory replaced the earlier view of gradual emotional development?

The discrete emotions theory hasn't been fully accepted because no one has yet found a convincing way to show that young infants acting in what appear to be complex emotional ways actually *feel* the emotions they are displaying. For example, although a baby might smile back at her mother and act in a happy way when her mother acts happily, how can we know if the baby *feels* happy? Perhaps she is only imitating the mother's facial expression. Some researchers are considering trying to uncover physiological changes that happen during emotions in adults and children and then looking for similar results in young infants. Such findings would help to indicate that a similar emotional process is going on in both infants and older humans. Until then, however, it remains an open question as to how rich a young infant's emotional experience is compared with older infants and children.

The infant's first faint smile is related to activity in the central nervous system, and this "reflex smile" is replaced by the familiar "social smile" at about 3 or 4 weeks of age.

SEPARATION ANXIETY
Fear of being separated from the care giver; a form of anxiety that usually manifests itself in children between the ages of 7 and 30 months. Separation anxiety usually is strongest at 18 months of age.

STRANGER ANXIETY
A fear of unfamiliar individuals that most infants develop around 6 months of age.

The very existence of biological or maturational components to emotion, however, does not prove that emotions are discrete and present at birth. Other alternatives are possible and are being actively investigated. For example, one researcher, attempting to find emotional correlates with the electrical activity of infants' brains, noticed that the only emotional activity associated with EEG readings in infants was the initial decision to approach or withdraw from a stimulus (Fox, 1991). Perhaps infants require experience with the environment before these two basic orientations can begin to differentiate into discrete emotional states. If that is the case, human emotions may develop according to the chart shown in Figure 6.3.

Question: But doesn't this finding conflict with the research showing that 10-week-old infants show discrete emotions?

This research doesn't necessarily conflict with those findings. First, as we mentioned, the 10-week-old infants in that study may have just been imitating their mothers without really having yet developed discrete emotions. Second, of course, is the possibility that emotions do develop as shown in Figure 6.3, but become discretely differentiated *before* 10 weeks of age.

Separation Anxiety Sometimes emotional development has been used to help assess the overall development of the child. Because of the variability in the onset of emotions, however, this manner of assessment has become less popular. Still, it is not uncommon to hear of certain emotional stages that children are expected to pass through. One such "stage" is referred to as **separation anxiety.** Separation anxiety is the fear expressed by the child when he or she is left alone by the parent or care giver. Children between 9 and 30 months will often show anxiety at being left, even if the parent is just in another room (sometimes even if the parent is still in view). They will cry and try to regain contact with the parent or care giver. Separation anxiety is often used to explain the clinging, following behavior of toddlers who may seem driven to be near the adult to whom they have become attached. This anxiety usually reaches its peak at about 18 months of age and declines steadily thereafter. Separation anxiety, however, is often quite variable. Infants who are separated from their primary care givers on a daily basis often become quite used to the separations and stop reacting to them (Field, 1991a). Some children express separation anxiety far more than others, and some children may express it strongly on one day but not on the next.

Separation anxiety is assumed to have evolved because of the survival value involved in keeping close contact with the care giver.

Fear of Strangers Another emotion that has been of particular interest to developmental researchers is the fear of strangers, which, like separation anxiety, appears to be a universal phenomenon that develops in infants of about the same age worldwide, regardless of their cultural backgrounds.

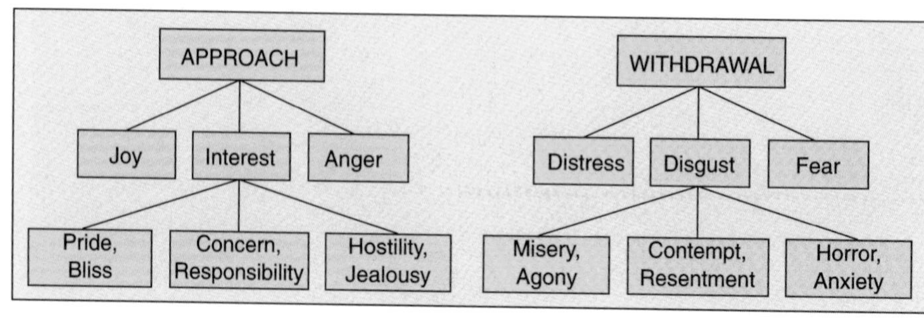

FIGURE 6.3
The possible development of emotions as indicated by Fox's research. Beginning with a mode of responding along a very basic approach-withdrawal continuum, the child eventually develops a refined set of responses, all stemming from the original two of approach and withdrawal. (*Source:* After Fox, 1991)

Table 6.6 shows the onset of fear of strangers in a group of infants. As you can see, this fear first appears in some babies as early as 4 months of age, but usually begins at about the age of 6 months.

As with separation anxiety, **stranger anxiety,** as this fear of strangers is called, isn't a clear-cut phenomenon. For many years, for example, it has been known that 9- to 13-month-old infants who have been exposed to only a limited number of adults will often show a strong fear of strangers, while similar infants who have been exposed to many different strangers aren't nearly as likely to be frightened (Collard, 1968). This might mean that infants who react positively to strangers have simply become used to them. Any dog owner can tell you that even the noisiest of dogs will stop barking at strangers if constantly surrounded by them. Perhaps such habituation also occurs in our own species.

Furthermore, fear of strangers is not an extremely reliable phenomenon. Infants who are clearly afraid of strangers on one day will, only a few days later, appear not to be frightened by them at all. At a later time, these same infants may once again manifest fear in the presence of a stranger (Shaffran & Decarie, 1973).

TABLE 6.6

Age of Onset of Fear of Strangers in a Group of Children

AGE (IN WEEKS)	PERCENTAGE OF CHILDREN AFFECTED AT EACH AGE
21–24	0
25–28	16
29–32	25
33–36	32
37–40	11
41–44	6
45–48	3
49–52	0
53–78	5

SOURCE: Adapted from Schaffer and Emerson, 1964.

Question: Are babies afraid of strangers because of the way the strangers look, or is it something that the strangers do?

Some have suggested that the baby is reacting only to strange behavior, not to unfamiliar people. Research by Rafman has indicated that this may be the case. When strangers are trained to behave like the infant's mother, fear appears to subside (Rafman, 1974). Then again, other studies have shown that although the fear subsides, it doesn't immediately disappear, as it would if the infant were actually with his or her mother (Klein & Durfee, 1976).

Question: Are there any theories to explain why infants often develop a fear of strangers?

Ethological theory provides an interesting explanation: Perhaps some genetic program maturationally turns on when an infant reaches about 6 months of age, and this program tells the infant that unfamiliar people should now be feared. From an ethological point of view, this would make sense, because there would be survival value in avoiding strangers once you were old enough to get around on your own. "Don't talk to strangers" is a caution probably as old as our species. In this view, fear of strangers has evolved as a protective mechanism.

Social learning theory places emphasis on what we learn from other people and is rarely concerned with inherited predispositions. Proponents of this position

Prior to 6 months of age, babies show a general wariness of the unknown or unfamiliar (or perhaps a big nose and a bad haircut).

propose that stranger anxiety occurs because when an unfamiliar adult enters the scene, the parents usually have to interact with the stranger at some length. In other words, by the age of 6 months, babies may have *learned* that the appearance of an unfamiliar adult is a signal that the mother is going to pay less attention to the baby. Supporting this view is the fact that infants rarely show stranger anxiety to children (who usually appear on the scene to play with other children and therefore don't take the mother's attention away from the infant) but, rather, tend to smile at them (Lewis & Brooks, 1974; Lenssen, 1975). For this reason, babies may come to dislike adult strangers, while still smiling at unfamiliar children. In a further attempt to resolve this issue, one researcher even presented infants with an unfamiliar midget (Lewis, 1975). Interestingly, the infants responded with a prolonged stare; perhaps they were trying to decide whether the midget was an adult or a child! Of course, both social learning theory and ethological theory may be correct in their interpretation of stranger anxiety; they are not mutually exclusive.

LEARNING CHECK

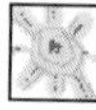

Multiple Choice

1. Unlike those who argued that newborn infants showed only arousal or quiescence, proponents of the discrete emotions theory argue that
   a. all the basic emotions are present in the newborn.
   b. newborns show only arousal but not quiescence.
   c. infants have no emotions until they are 6 months old.
   d. anger comes first, then wariness and rage.

2. Infants exposed to many adults are
   a. less likely to fear strangers.
   b. more likely to fear strangers.
   c. never going to fear strangers.
   d. likely to fear strangers at an earlier age.

3. Greenspan uses the expression "falling in love" to refer to
   a. the closer bond between mother and father after the baby is born.
   b. the time when the infant first becomes attached to someone.
   c. the mother's new love for her infant following the first true smile.
   d. the time when the child can first express affection verbally.

4. According to Greenspan, the development of emotional thoughts and ideas first occurs in stage
   a. 1 **b.** 2 **c.** 4 **d.** 5

Answers: 1. a 2. a 3. b 4. d

APPLICATIONS

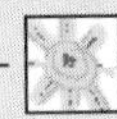

Is Day Care a Good Idea?

Human babies are not precocious. They must be cared for. Infants may need a care giver for a number of years before they can survive unaided. For this reason, if for no other, it is very much in an infant's best interests to form a strong attachment to a primary care giver rapidly. As you recall, John Bowlby developed a theory (Bowlby, 1969, 1973) that emphasized the reciprocal nature of such care giver arrangements. He thought that both infants and their mothers are biologically primed to form special attachments to each other.

If what Bowlby theorized is correct, what happens if we disrupt this very special arrangement between infant and mother and place the infant in a day-care center each day? Is the infant flexible enough to learn to adapt to this situation, or will there be some serious consequences? This issue is an important one, because in the United States, more than 50 percent of mothers of children under 6 are working (see Figure 6.4). In other industrialized nations, a large portion of married women with preschool children are also working, even in countries such as Japan, where mothers have traditionally stayed home with their children. A great number of infants around the world are therefore affected.

For years, developmental researchers studied day care; the general consensus early on was that day care had no effect, one way or the other, on the quality of the infant's attachment to the mother (Belsky & Steinberg, 1978; Farran & Ramey, 1977). Most of these early studies, however, were conducted with infants in high-quality day-care centers, usually at universities. This is not the day-care setting that most infants encounter. Psychologist Jay Belsky examined infants in more typical day-care settings. He concluded that babies who spent more than 20 hours per week with nonmaternal care during the first year of life were more likely to show anxious/avoidant attachment to their mothers than were other babies (Belsky, 1986, 1988). Other researchers have made similar observations and have suggested that infants left in day care might be showing anxious/avoidant attachment because they perceive the mothers' daily abandonment as rejection (Barglow, Vaughn, & Molitor, 1987). As you recall, insecure attachment is associated with problems as the infant matures. According to Belsky, "We've identified a window of vulnerability. Now we have to figure out what conditions open it and which shut it" (Wallis & Ludtke, 1987, p. 63).

Some researchers have questioned these findings, however. One of the main criticisms is that Belsky used the strange situation to measure infant attachment. Infants in day care have much more experience with separations and strangers than do those who aren't in day care, and this may affect their performance in the strange situation (Thompson, 1988). Belsky's own research, however, indicates that this is not the case (Belsky & Braungart, 1991). A stronger criticism comes from researcher Michael Lamb, who points out that while it may be true that day-care infants often show more anxious/avoidant attachment, these findings are all based on the strange situation, whose very validity can be questioned (Lamb & Sternberg, 1990). Perhaps, as Lamb and others have argued, other measures should be used to assess the infant's social and emotional well-being, including the long-term effects of day-care quality.

Question: What determines the quality of day care?

FIGURE 6.4

The percentage of working mothers of children under 6 years of age was increasing since 1960 until it leveled off in 1986. It appears that about 45 percent of women with young children will stay at home with their children barring extreme circumstances and that the growing trend for mothers of young children to work outside the home has peaked. Still, because the majority of mothers with young children work outside the home, many preschoolers require some form of nonparental care (*Source:* Adapted from Wallis, Hull, Ludtke, & Taylor, 1987; *Statistical Abstract of the United States,* 1991)

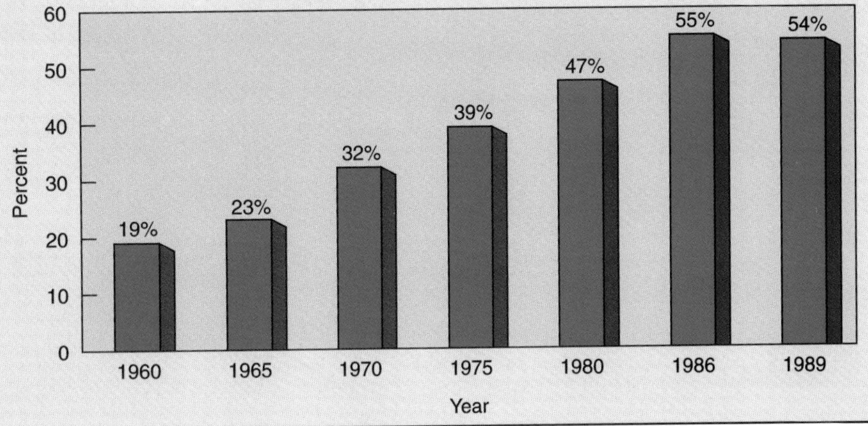

APPLICATIONS

It's hard to say. The greatest difficulty in understanding the issue of day-care quality is that there is such a great range of what we call "day care." Care may be provided in licensed or unlicensed facilities and even in informal family day-care arrangements. For example, one adult on a particular block may take in others' children for profit, in a sense serving as a group baby-sitter. Some states have standards for day care, but most do not. In a number of states, the accepted caregiver-to-infant ratio is 1:10. You can't help but wonder how one caregiver could rescue 10 infants from a fire.

In addition to health and safety standards, many other variables affect the quality of the day-care environment. Unfortunately, longitudinal studies assessing the long-term consequences of different variables in day care are few and far between, and the results we have are highly tentative.

Question: Do we know anything about what constitutes quality day care?

The federal government once developed standards (the Federal Interagency Day Care Requirements, or FIDCR) for day-care centers in terms of child ratios, group size, and teacher training, but they were never implemented. Even so, it has been found that children in day-care facilities meeting those standards were more likely to show secure attachment and to be more competent with peers than children in day-care facilities not meeting the FIDCR standards (Howes, Phillips, & Whitebook, 1992).

These standards were based on earlier findings of what high-quality day care would include. In terms of language, social, and intellectual development, children in day-care centers were found to do better if they were in small groups (18 or fewer) of children the same age or older (Roupp et al., 1979; Miller & Greenberg, 1985). The most effective teachers, not surprisingly, had the highest education level and the most training in child development. Day-care providers who spoke to the child at an appropriate level and who had conversations with the child often helped to foster language development significantly more than did caregivers who devoted most of their verbal interaction to speaking at an adult level with other staff members (McCartney, 1984). This same kind of involved verbal interaction between caregiver and child was also found to foster successful social development among day-care children (Phillips, McCartney, & Scarr, 1987). Teachers with better training were more likely to become involved with children in this way.

Children who were enrolled in low-quality day care (day-care centers that did not meet the previously mentioned standards) at an early age (1 to 2 years) were found in kindergarten to be more distractible, less considerate, and less able to work at a task than children who had entered low-quality day care at a later age or who had been enrolled in a high-quality day-care facility (Howes, 1990). In contrast, the more time that preschool children spent in high-quality day care, the more likely they were to receive positive ratings in leadership, popularity, attractiveness, and assertiveness once they entered grade school than were children who had spent less time in high-quality day care (Field, 1991b). Perhaps most interesting is a Swedish study showing that children enrolled in high-quality day care before the age of 1 performed better in school (when measured at ages 8 and 13) than did their counterparts who had entered day care at a later age (Andersson, 1992). Although some of these results may be related to the fact that families who can afford high-quality day care may be quite different from families who cannot (Pence & Goelman, 1987),

Day-care centers often differ greatly one from another. Parents considering placing their children in a day-care center should investigate it thoroughly beforehand.

APPLICATIONS

all of these data taken collectively do seem to indicate that the quality of day care is an important factor, probably more so than the age at which the child enters a day-care facility.

Question: What about home day-care arrangements that are informal or unlicensed?

Little research has been done in that area, but one study indicated that there probably are no significant differences as long as the caregivers have experience, interact with the children, and provide them with some structure by giving them things to do (Stith & Davis, 1984)—in other words, by creating a high-quality home-care or unlicensed day-care environment. Of course, the results of this limited study do not mean that unlicensed day-care centers are as good as licensed ones. Unlicensed centers may run the range from excellent to dangerous. (Of course, the same may be true of licensed centers; presumably, however, this is less likely.) Another study did find that children in day-care situations fared better in terms of language, social, emotional, and intellectual development than did those left alone with individual baby-sitters (Miller & Greenberg, 1985).

Question: Do the infants ever form stronger attachments to day-care providers than to their parents?

In general, research has shown that there are no differences between home-reared and day-care infants in terms of the infants' attachments to their mothers. Furthermore, day-care infants don't usually come to prefer the members of the day-care staff over their mothers, although the day-care staff are preferred to strangers (Farran & Ramey, 1977; Etaugh, 1980).

As was noted, however, day-care centers differ from one another, and much more research is needed before we can know the full effects of day-care arrangements.

Question: Assuming I were a parent, what could I do to ensure adequate day care for my children?

Unfortunately, because of financial constraints and geographical location, parents will often accept a day-care facility that does not meet their own personal standards simply because they have little choice to do otherwise (Gravett, Rogers, & Thompson, 1987). Even if this is the case, there are some things you can do. First and foremost, get to know the day-care center you are considering. Several studies have found that parents who have chosen a day-care center spend very little time there and interact with the caregivers only occasionally, usually when they are dropping off or picking up their children (Powell, 1977, 1978; Zigler & Turner, 1982). Instead, it's a good idea to spend time getting to know the day-care staff personally. As a consumer, feel free to ask questions about their backgrounds, training, and licensing. Be suspicious of any day-care center that won't let you spend time observing the caregivers at work. See how the staff interacts with the children. Is the staff alert and prepared for medical and safety emergencies? Your questions and pressure may help turn a borderline facility into an acceptable one.

Day-care centers with some structure—that is, those that provide children with things to do—tend to be superior. Ask what kinds of games, activities, and toys are available for the children. Look at the staff-to-child ratio. Is the center well enough staffed to be able to consider the individual requirements of your child? Are there regular mealtimes and nap times? Is the place clean? Are children's toilet needs taken care of promptly and hygienically? Are all injuries, bumps, and bruises explained in detail and in writing? These are all concerns you might have. Be a careful consumer and shop around. If there is nothing nearby, consider that there may be others in your neighborhood who would also like to use a more distant day-care facility. Perhaps by getting together with them and car pooling, it might be possible to accommodate the greater distance by taking turns driving the children to the day-care center. Finally, if you are disappointed with the day-care facilities available in your area, you might investigate initiating changes in licensing or practice through your local or state government officials.

Question: What about the news stories I've heard concerning child abuse in some day-care centers?

Although there have been a few scary headlines of sexual or other forms of child abuse in day-care centers, direct physical abuse is rare. Of much greater concern are questions such as: Are social interactions available (will the child be alone or ignored)? Will the child get a hot, nutritious lunch? Is there adequate fire protection? Generally speaking, high-quality day care can be very valuable and beneficial because it allows both parents to work, and a family with a higher income may provide a more stress-free and happy environment for its children. There is no question that a child will fare better spending part of the day with a high-quality care giver than spending the whole day with a depressed or frustrated parent. So don't be afraid to use day care; just use a good dose of common sense when choosing a facility.

SUMMARY

■ The theoretical orientation taken by researchers toward attachment has changed significantly over the years. Initially, attachment was assumed to occur because the mother provided for the infant's basic needs. This view was eventually replaced by the intraorganismic perspective, which sees attachment-seeking behavior as being generated from innate mechanisms in the presence of appropriate environmental stimulation.

■ The first major rejection of the Freudian and learning theories came with the work of Harry Harlow, who investigated the attachment that rhesus monkeys formed with surrogate mothers. Harlow discovered that much more than nursing and the satisfaction of primary biological needs was involved.

■ The idea of an innate attachment mechanism stems from the work of the ethologists. Konrad Lorenz demonstrated the phenomenon of imprinting, an innate attachment mechanism evidenced during a critical period soon after birth.

■ John Bowlby, a proponent of the intraorganismic perspective, viewed the attachment system as becoming well organized sometime during the second half of the infant's first year of life. After the age of about 18 months, the child may begin to form internal working models of the relationships between him- or herself and caregivers.

■ Attachment does not occur in isolation. To investigate such interactions as the attachment-exploration balance and the secure-base phenomenon, Mary Ainsworth devised the strange situation. This experimental design offers many situations or circumstances in which to measure attachment and exploration.

■ Ainsworth has identified three kinds of attachment: secure, anxious/resistant, and anxious/avoidant. These forms of attachment appear to be fairly stable over time and may have predictive value in determining the child's social development and behavior throughout life.

■ Michael Lamb and others have pointed out that children's reactions in the strange situation may reflect something more general than quality of attachment, probably family stability.

■ Since 1970, research concerning the father's role has increased dramatically. Although fathers are less likely to be primary care givers, they have a special role to play. Fathers are more likely to be arousing and physical with their children and to be their children's preferred playmate.

■ Emotions are so important in forming our social bonds and attachments that researchers often use the term *social-emotional development* to emphasize the intertwining of the social and emotional dimensions of human behavior. Emotions motivate infants and also help them to interact in communication.

■ Stanley Greenspan has outlined six stages of social-emotional development: (1) self-regulation and interest in the world, (2) falling in love, (3) development of intentional communication, (4) emergence of an organized sense of self, (5) creation of emotional ideas, and (6) emotional thinking.

■ There is a debate among those who study emotion as to whether the infant has limited emotional capacity at first or a full range of emotional capabilities.

■ Many specific issues concerning emotions have attracted investigators' attention. Among these are why infants fear strangers.

■ Day care has become an issue of growing concern because so many families now have both parents working outside the home. In general, high-quality day care does not harm toddlers or older children, although there is still some concern about the effects on infants. Parents should be cautious when choosing a day-care facility because these facilities vary greatly.

QUESTIONS FOR DISCUSSION

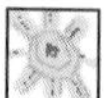

1. How might an unlearned fear of strangers have been naturally selected for in infants?

2. How subjective do you think appraisals of infants' facial expressions are? Could adults be reading too much into them?

3. Do you think that "attachment" is an adequate way of measuring infant "love"?

4. Would you say that the baby rhesus monkey "loves" its cloth mother? Harlow did.

5. If you were considering leaving your infant in a day-care center, what would be your major concerns? Why?

6. Except for breast feeding, do you think that a mother's position as care giver of an infant is biologically different from a father's?

Suggestions for Further Reading

1. Emde, R. N., & Harmon, R. J. (1982). *The development of attachment and affiliative systems.* New York: Plenum.
2. Greenspan, S., & Greenspan, N. T. (1985). *First feelings: Milestones in the emotional development of your baby and child.* New York: Viking.
3. Greenspan, S., & Greenspan, N. T. (1989). *The essential partnership: How parents & children can meet the challenges of childhood.* New York: Viking Penguin.
4. Izard, C., Kagan, J., & Zajonc, R. (Eds.). (1984). *Emotions, cognition and behavior.* New York: Cambridge University Press.
5. Lusk, D., & McPherson, B. (1992). *Nothing but the best: Making day care work for you & your child.* New York: Teacher's College Press.
6. Reed, G. (1992). *Where are we coming from?: Day-care positives & negatives.* New York: Vantage.
7. Shell, E. R. (1992). *A child's place: A year in the life of a day care center.* Boston: Little Brown.
8. Thorman, G. (1989). *Day care—An emerging crisis.* Springfield, IL: Charles C. Thomas Publishing.

UNIT THREE

THE DEVELOPING CHILD: LEARNING, LANGUAGE, AND COGNITION

Allison Spears, age 7

UNIT CONTENTS

CHAPTER 7

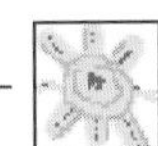

LEARNING

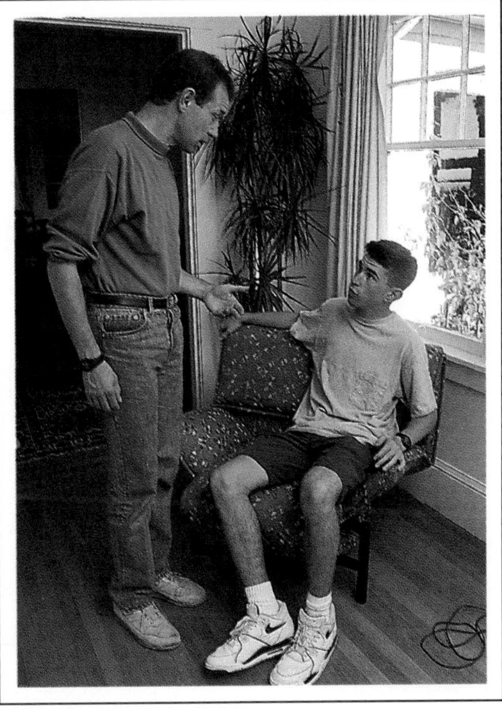

CHAPTER PREVIEW

THE PROBLEMS WITH SPANKING

ONCE UPON A TIME there was a nation—an industrialized, democratic Western nation—that took great interest in the health and welfare of its citizens, especially its children. One day the lawmakers of this land listened to psychologists describing the dangers and unfortunate aftereffects of a popular method being used by some parents and schools to control children's behavior—spanking. The psychologists argued that spanking should be abolished for a number of reasons:

1. All too often, the adult administering the spanking became overly emotional and inflicted physical damage on the child. Such child abuse has been demonstrated among parents of all educational and income levels. Although actual torture of children is rare, most abuse began with an intent to spank.

2. Sometimes children become used to spanking, so that the adults have to be more and more severe to have any effect.

3. Through the process of classical conditioning, the parent became paired with pain, with the result that the parent came to elicit a fear response from the child.

4. Through instrumental learning, children were often reinforced in such a way that they would generally avoid the parents, lie, or run away from home.

5. According to research on punishment, mild spankings usually had only a temporary effect.

6. Additional research on instrumental learning had demonstrated that many nonphysical techniques were highly successful in controlling and modifying children's behavior.

7. Many well-behaved children and adults had never been spanked or hit by either of their parents (so much for "spare the rod, spoil the child").

8. Finally, and most devastatingly, came the testimony concerned with spanking and social learning. One father stated that he realized that something was wrong when he said, as he was spanking his 5-year-old for having hit his 2-year-old brother, "This will teach you not to hit someone smaller than you." By watching others (social learning), children who were spanked were apparently learning that physical force is an appropriate response when you are frustrated with someone; that it's all right to hit people; and that spanking is something that parents are supposed to do (which may help explain why so many child abusers were themselves abused as children).

AFTER REVIEWING THE evidence, the legislators of this land passed a law making it illegal for anyone, including parents, to spank or even verbally abuse a child. Although they realized that the law would be almost impossible to enforce, the lawmakers believed that it would help make everyone aware of the problem and impress on them that spanking was wrong.

BY THE WAY, if you think that this fairy-tale Chapter Preview is too fanciful, you had better take up your protest with the Swedish government; it was they who passed this law.

IN THIS CHAPTER, we will examine the different aspects of learning and the ways that learning can affect the behavior of children, adults, and even other species.

RESOURCES

Reflexes and Instincts

The study of learning is the study of the acquired behaviors that come to be a relatively permanent part of our repertoire. Many behaviors, however, are not acquired but are inherited.

Question: Are you referring to a phenomenon such as imprinting, which we discussed in Chapter 6?

Imprinting is only one example of numerous innate behaviors. Ethologists and psychologists are also interested in fixed-response patterns. A **fixed-response pattern** is a complex inherited behavior that is triggered by a particular **stimulus** (something that can be sensed) called, because of its function, a **releaser stimulus,** or sign stimulus. The reactions themselves are known as **species-specific behaviors** because they are peculiar to particular species. For example, dangling a worm above a baby robin is a releaser stimulus for the fixed-response pattern of chirping, opening the mouth, tipping back the head, and fluttering the wings. On the other hand, holding a worm in the palm of the hand beneath the baby robin's beak will not provoke this response because this action is not a releaser stimulus for such a fixed-response pattern.

FIXED-RESPONSE PATTERN
A species-specific response pattern that is presumed to have survival value for the organism and is elicited by a releaser stimulus.

STIMULUS
Anything that can be sensed, for example, visible light or audible sound.

RELEASER STIMULUS
A stimulus that sets off a cycle of instinctive behavior; also called a sign stimulus.

SPECIES-SPECIFIC BEHAVIOR
Inherited behavior characteristic of one species of animal.

Question: Do humans have fixed-response patterns?

Scientists are doubtful about the existence of fixed-response patterns in our species. Certainly, human beings have a number of inborn behaviors, such as blinking, coughing, swallowing, hiccuping, and sucking. But these behaviors are usually considered simple *reflexes* and not truly comparable with the complex fixed-response patterns found in other species.

Question: Don't women have a maternal instinct?

Such an instinct does appear to exist in other animals—for instance, in cats. All healthy female cats build some form of nest before giving birth, and after delivery they lick the afterbirth off the kittens, stimulate them, and nurse them. But human responses are not so fixed from one mother to another. Some mothers nurse, others don't; some mothers want their babies, others don't; some mothers cuddle their children, others are distant. In evolutionary terms, however, the idea of a human maternal instinct seems plausible. Human babies require a great deal of care before they are able to survive on their own, and it would be an advantage if the sight of a human baby were a releaser stimulus for a pattern of instinctive maternal care, comforting, and protection. Indeed, many ethologists and psychologists note that people tend to be attracted to small, cuddly, babylike animals and believe that this babyish quality may be a releaser stimulus for a parental attraction (see Figure 7.1) (Alley, 1981; Lorenz, 1943). After all, if people didn't find their babies attractive, the next generation might not survive.

As you recall from Chapter 6, researchers who have applied an ethological perspective have argued that such instinctive interaction is an important feature of attachment. Even so, psychologists cite the general rule that the more advanced a species is on the evolutionary scale, the less its behavioral patterns seem to be rigidly fixed by the genes.

The Importance of Learning

Question: Why didn't we evolve to rely only on species-specific behaviors? Couldn't we have inherited all the valuable behaviors we needed with fixed-response patterns? Why did learning develop?

FIGURE 7.1
Comparison of visual features provided by morphological characteristics of infantile and adult forms of four different species: human, rabbit, dog, and bird. Whereas the infantile characteristics seem to release parental responses, the adult ones do not. (Adapted from Lorenz, 1943)

As with fixed-response patterns, the ability to learn has a survival value. In this sense, the ability to learn has been inherited. But unlike fixed-response patterns, which are rigid and resistant to change, learning allows great flexibility in behavior. An animal that can learn is not restricted to a fixed-response pattern but can take into account changes that occur in the immediate environment and can respond to them. This argument is reminiscent of the reasoning as to why the infant's brain can not depend solely on an experience-expectant neurology. Obviously, creatures with the ability to learn are far more flexible and, as such, more likely to survive, procreate, and pass on the tendency to learn. No two members of any species need adapt in exactly the same way, because different experiences can give rise to different learning.

Kinds of Learning

Learning is defined as a relatively permanent change in behavior that is the result of experience. There are three main ways, according to **behavior theory,** in which we learn. The first is through the association of stimuli—that is, changing your reaction to one stimulus because of its association with another. Second, there is learning through the association of a response and its consequence—that is, learning through rewards and punishments (learning because of the rewarding or punishing consequences that follow a particular behavior). This is known as instrumental learning. Third, there is learning through observation of what others do, usually called social learning. Regardless of the kind, all learning is still defined as a relatively permanent change in behavior brought about by practice or experience.

LEARNING THROUGH THE ASSOCIATION OF STIMULI

Classical Conditioning—Does the Name Pavlov Ring a Bell? During the 1890s, the Russian physiologist Ivan Pavlov reported an experiment of an associative learning process. He had been investigating digestion in dogs and had been trying to understand why his dogs often began to salivate *before* they received food. This reaction seemed to occur when a **contiguous association** was made between the presentation of food and another stimulus, such as seeing someone in the laboratory open the cupboard where the dog food was kept. Other researchers had observed this phenomenon but had either considered it a nuisance or ignored it. Pavlov, however, became seriously interested in this learning process and began to investigate it systematically.

Question: What kind of experiments did Pavlov conduct?

Pavlov's Experiments In a series of well-known experiments, Pavlov decided to *pair* a stimulus (food) that would elicit an unlearned response (salivation) with a stimulus (bell) that did not elicit salivation and was therefore neutral at the beginning of the experiment. Because no learning is required to make dogs salivate when they are given meat, meat is referred to as an **unconditioned stimulus (US),** and the reflex response of salivating is referred to as an **unconditioned response (UR).** Pavlov took the stimulus that did not cause salivation in dogs (a bell) and began to pair it systematically with the presentation of food. He would ring the bell, immediately present the food (US), and observe the salivation (UR). After the bell and the food had been paired, or contiguously associated, Pavlov was able to cause salivation without giving food; ringing the bell was enough. The dogs associated food with the bell, and they would salivate. The bell had become a stimulus to which the dogs responded in a predictable way. For this reason, the bell is referred to as a **conditioned stimulus (CS),** and the response it elicits is called a **conditioned response (CR)** (see Figure 7.2). The process by which the bell obtained the power to elicit the conditioned response is called **reinforcement.** The unconditioned stimulus (the meat) reinforced the conditioned stimulus (the bell) by being associated with it. The more the two were paired, the more the meat reinforced the bell (gave the bell power to elicit the CR—salivation). This form of learning is referred to as **classical conditioning.**

In Pavlov's day, it was thought that simply contiguously associating two stimuli would cause conditioning to occur. This is not necessarily the case. In the experiment with Pavlov's dogs, for instance, many other stimuli besides the bell were associated with the food: the harness to which the dogs were attached, the leather straps that held their front legs, the scaffolding that held the harness, the elevated table on which they stood, the saliva collection tube, and so on. None of these stimuli, however, when presented to the dogs, caused salivation the way that the bell did, although they, too, had been associated with food many times. There was something special about the bell. As it turned out, the presentation of the food in this case was contingent (dependent) on the presentation of the bell. The other stimuli (the harness, table, etc.) were often present when *no* food was given. The bell, on the other hand, *never* rang when food was not presented. The fact

BEHAVIOR THEORY
A view that behavior can be explained as the result of learning and experience and that an understanding of internal events or constructs such as the mind are unnecessary.

CONTIGUOUS ASSOCIATION
The occurrence of two events in time such that they are temporally associated. In conditioning, the presentation of two or more stimuli within a certain time frame or the presentation of a stimulus within a certain time following a response.

UNCONDITIONED STIMULUS (US)
A stimulus that normally evokes an unconditioned response, such as the food that originally caused Pavlov's dogs to respond with salivation.

UNCONDITIONED RESPONSE (UR)
A response made to an unconditioned stimulus; for example, salivation in response to food.

CONDITIONED STIMULUS (CS)
In classical conditioning, a previously neutral stimulus that through pairing with an unconditioned stimulus acquires the ability to produce a similar response.

CONDITIONED RESPONSE (CR)
A learned response similar to a reflex but elicited by a conditioned stimulus owing to the previous association of the conditioned stimulus with an unconditioned stimulus.

REINFORCEMENT (IN CLASSICAL CONDITIONING)
Any increase in the ability of a conditioned stimulus to elicit a conditioned response owing to the association of the conditioned stimulus with another stimulus (typically an unconditioned stimulus). In the classical conditioning process, a stimulus is reinforced.

CLASSICAL CONDITIONING
An experimental learning procedure in which a stimulus that normally evokes a given reflex is continually associated with a stimulus that does not usually evoke that reflex, with the result that the latter stimulus will eventually evoke the reflex when presented by itself.

that the animal learned to associate the bell with the food implies that the animal was using the bell to predict when food would arrive.

As a result of these observations, learning theorists now believe that such **contingency detection** by an organism is as important as the contiguous association of stimuli in explaining why conditioning occurs (Rescorla, 1969).

CONTINGENCY DETECTION
The process by which an organism discriminates between stimuli that are present only when the US is presented and those that are present both when the US is presented and when it is not. The result is that the organism can rely on the sensing of the stimulus that is present only when the US is presented to predict that the US will soon appear.

STIMULUS GENERALIZATION
The process by which once a stimulus has come to elicit or cue a response, similar stimuli may also elicit or cue the response, although not usually as effectively.

Question: Does classical conditioning occur in humans?

Yes, in children, adults, and even infants (Fitzgerald & Brackbill, 1976).

The Case of Little Albert Perhaps the classic example of such conditioning is the case of Little Albert, published by John Watson and Rosalie Rayner in 1920. Although there have been some criticisms of the methodology used by Watson and Rayner, the case is an interesting one historically and illustrative of the classical conditioning process in humans.

Watson and Rayner tested Albert B., a healthy 11-month-old boy, by systematically exposing him to a white rat, a rabbit, a dog, a monkey, various masks, cotton wool, and even a burning newspaper. As Watson noted, "at no time did this infant ever show fear in any situation" (Watson & Rayner, 1920, p. 2). The two researchers found, however, that making a very loud noise by striking a steel

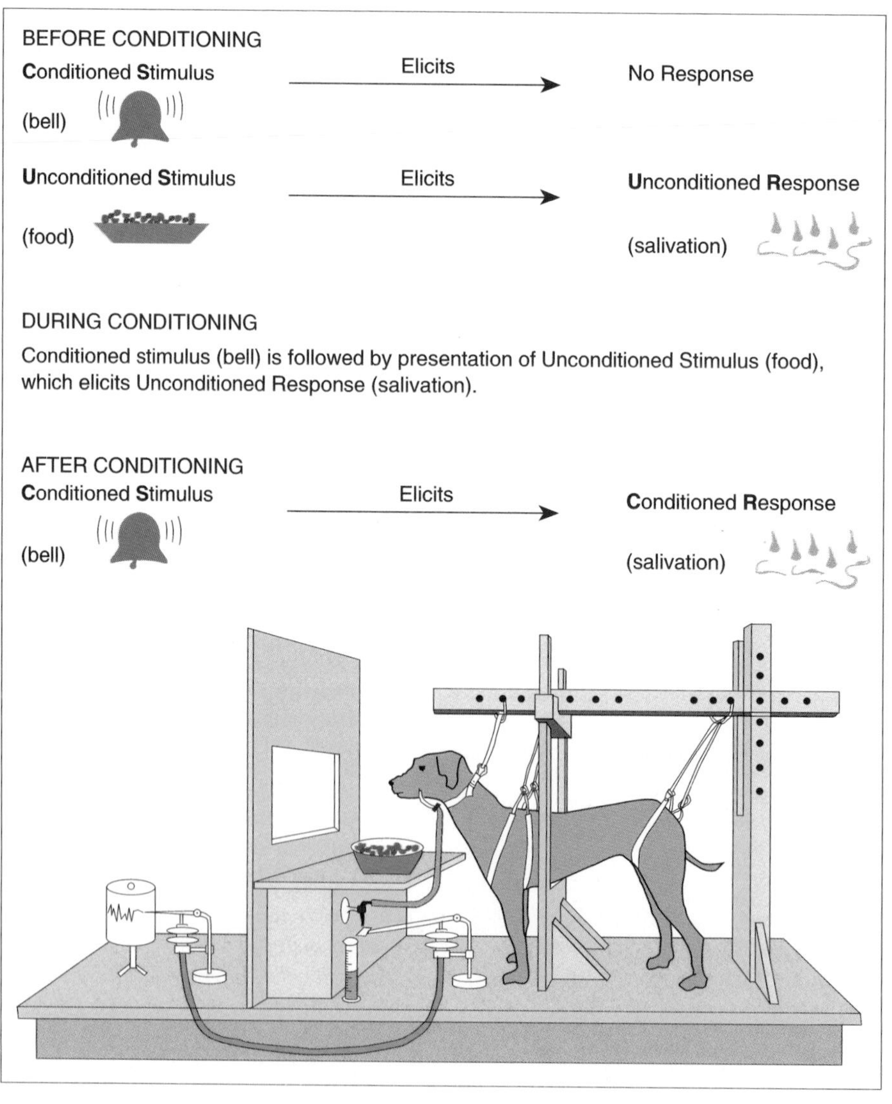

FIGURE 7.2
The paradigm used by Pavlov to condition a dog to salivate at the sound of a bell.

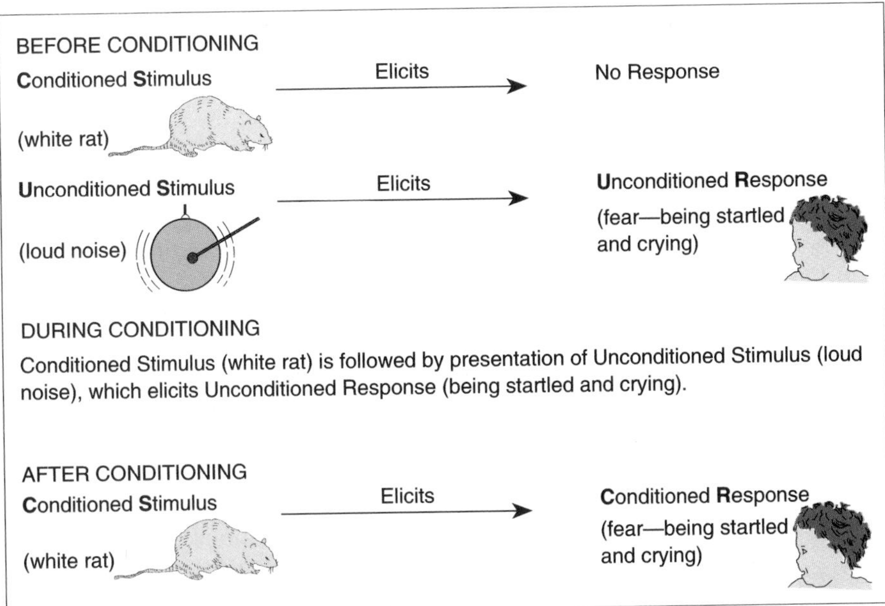

FIGURE 7.3
The paradigm used by Watson and Rayner to condition Little Albert to fear a rat.

rod with a hammer (US) startled baby Albert and made him cry (UR). Next, the researchers paired the loud gong with the white rat that Albert had previously seen. Whenever Albert touched the rat (CS), the loud gong would be struck (US), which would startle Albert and cause him to cry (UR) (see Figure 7.3). Eventually, Albert would start to cry as soon as he saw the rat. In Watson's words:

> The instant the rat was shown, the baby began to cry. Almost instantly he turned sharply to the left, fell over on left side, raised himself on all fours and began to crawl away so rapidly that he was caught with difficulty before reaching the edge of the table. (Watson & Rayner, 1920)

In addition, Albert's fears generalized to related objects, such as a rabbit, a dog, a white cotton ball, and even a Santa Claus mask (probably because of the white beard), but not to dissimilar objects, such as blocks. This **stimulus generalization**

An extremely rare photograph of John Watson (in Santa mask) with assistant, Rosalie Rayner, as they conditioned Little Albert.

COUNTERCONDITIONING
A technique used by behavioral therapists to eliminate unwanted behavior through new associations, extinction, or punishment, while promoting the acquisition of more appropriate behavior in place of the old.

EXTINCTION
In classical conditioning, the elimination of the power of the conditioned stimulus to elicit a conditioned response. Classical extinction will occur if the conditioned stimulus is repeatedly presented without being reinforced through further association with the unconditioned stimulus.

probably occurred because Albert had associated the loud noise with the characteristics possessed by the rat—white, live, legged, and furry—that he subsequently saw in other objects as well.

Question: Would all children react like Little Albert?

Not all children can be conditioned as Little Albert was. Consider H. B. English's attempt in 1929 to replicate Watson and Rayner's findings. English tested a 14-month-old girl placed in a high chair. A wooden duck was presented to her, and as in the earlier experiment, a steel gong was struck from behind the child. After 50 pairings, the child remained wholly unafraid of the duck. English wrote, "The writer must express surprise—and admiration—at the child's iron nerves" (English, 1929, p. 222). English then decided to try a 2-pound steel mallet on the gong to obtain the fear response, but the child remained unafraid of the duck, although other faculty members throughout the building complained of the noise. English knew that the child was able to hear. He also knew that she was capable of fear, because she had previously developed a fear of boots for an unknown reason. Why, then, had the duck failed to become a conditioned stimulus?

On further investigation, English discovered that the girl had three older brothers who kept up a screaming, banging racket throughout her house. Apparently, she had become *habituated* to loud noise, that is, she became used to it, and the noise no longer functioned as an unconditioned stimulus for her. As any parent with three boys can confirm, there are times when even a 2-pound steel mallet striking a gong will go unnoticed! Then again, perhaps such older brothers make for iron-nerved little sisters.

Question: Is it ethical to try to create what amounts to a phobia in children by placing them in such experiments?

By today's standards, these experiments clearly would violate ethical procedures. Watson and Rayner had discussed ways in which to cure Albert of his experimentally induced fears. They thought that by offering Albert candy or his favorite food in the presence of the white rat, they might create a positive association and thereby **countercondition** him. Alternatively, they considered stimulating Albert's erogenous zones in the presence of the rat to help alter his associations. A third idea was simply to show Albert the rat again and again, without pairing it with the gong, until he finally became used to it—a process known as **extinction.***

Unfortunately, the researchers never had a chance to try any of their plans because Albert's mother moved away, taking him with her. It does appear, however, that before Watson and Rayner ever began their experiment, they knew that Albert was going to have to leave early and that they would probably never have a chance to undo any learned fear response that they might produce. Yet they conducted the experiment anyway (Harris, 1979). Of course, Little Albert was not the only human ever to be classically conditioned; millions of children are daily conditioned in this way as they interact with their environment. Any pediatrician who has given a child an injection (US) can attest to this fact. The child's screaming fit (CR) the next time he or she enters the office (CS) is a good indication that classical conditioning plays a role in fear responses.

Affective Conditioning In addition to classical conditioning, in which a new stimulus obtains the power to elicit a response, associative experiences can also lead to the formation of emotions, beliefs, and attitudes. Changing or creating emotions, beliefs, or attitudes by associating stimuli with one another is called

*Extinction is not the same as habituation. Extinction occurs through repeated presentation of the conditioned stimulus alone, while habituation occurs through repeated presentation of an unconditioned stimulus.

affective conditioning. In the mid-1940s, Kenneth Clark held a black doll and a white doll in his hands and asked the following questions of young white children living in the South:

> "Which doll looks like you?"
> "Now tell me which doll is the good doll?"
> "Which doll is the bad doll?"

AFFECTIVE CONDITIONING
An associative learning process in which emotional appraisals of a stimulus are altered by pairing the stimulus with one or more other stimuli that already have an emotional effect. Attitudes and beliefs often are influenced by affective conditioning.

These children knew that the white doll looked like them. Most of them also indicated that the white doll was the "good" doll and the black doll was the "bad" one, that the white doll was "nice" and the black doll was "dirty" or "ugly" (Clark & Clark, 1947). How had these southern white children learned to make such associations? During the decades of racial prejudice that had come before, darker skin had become associated with poverty and with being "inferior," not just in the South but generally throughout the United States. The white children had learned to attribute these characteristics to black people.

This racist attitude is what the white children had been taught; it is also what the black children had been taught. The black children had been raised in the same general environment, the same country. They, too, had seen that the whites had better, and they had worse. And as the Clarks discovered in further research, a majority of black children *also* chose the white doll as the good one and the black doll as the bad one! Perhaps these environmental teachings were best expressed by a 12-year-old black child, Tommy, when he said hopefully, "One day I'll wake up and be white!" (Chethik, Fleming, Mayer, & McCoy, 1967, p. 74).

During the 1960s, when the phrase "black is beautiful" became well known, many people didn't understand what was meant by it. It really wasn't difficult to understand; it was simply another association, this one long overdue, pairing "black" with "beautiful." Still, the consciousness raising of the 1960s did not overcome racial conditioning. In the 1970s, for instance, researchers found that children as young as 3 would still readily pick white dolls and drawings of white children as more desirable than their black counterparts, (Spencer & Horowitz, 1973) and, more recently, the same results have been found among American Indian children (Spencer & Markstrom-Adams, 1990).

In an experiment conducted by researchers Nunnally, Duchnowski, and Parker (1965), elementary school children were asked to play a game involving a spinning arrow that could end up pointing at any of three nonsense syllables (GYQ, ZOJ, and MYV). The game was arranged so that one syllable paid a 2-cent reward, another cost a 1-cent fine, and the last brought no loss or gain. These three syllables meant nothing to the children at the beginning of the experiment. After allowing the children to play the game for some time, the researchers showed them three stick figures that were identical, except that one of the three nonsense syllables was placed below each figure. The children were then asked questions such as, "Which is the friendly boy?" or "Which is the mean boy?" (Sound familiar?) The stick figure associated with the positive nonsense syllable, the one that yielded a 2-cent gain, was almost always chosen as the "friendly boy," whereas the figure paired with the syllable that was associated with the fine was almost always identified as the "mean boy."

In another study that showed the same principles at work, Staats and Staats (1958) asked college students to look at one word while pronouncing another. Without being aware of the purpose of the experiment, the students were maneuvered into pairing pleasant words or unpleasant words with a particular name (Tom or Bill) or a certain nationality (Swedish or Dutch). In a short time, subjects revealed obvious differences in attitudes toward these names and nationalities, simply because they had been paired with positive or negative words.

Question: What happens if a single stimulus is paired with both something positive and something negative?

LAW OF EFFECT
Thorndike's principle that responses associated with pleasant consequences tend to be repeated, while those associated with discomforting consequences tend to be eliminated.

If this happens, the individual for whom the associations have been made may tend to feel neutral toward the stimulus. If the associations are strong ones, the person may feel both learned aspects of the stimulus simultaneously, giving rise to bittersweet memories or feelings—an apt description for the sensations encountered.

LEARNING CHECK

Fill-in-the-Blank

1. ____________ is defined as a relatively permanent change in behavior brought about by practice or experience.

2. Repeating a CS again and again without pairing it with the original US leads to ____________ .

3. Classical conditioning was first investigated in detail by ____________.

4. Salivating to a ringing bell is considered a CR because such salivation is ____________ .

True or False

5. Stimulus generalization occurred in Little Albert because he associated the loud noise with characteristics possessed by the rat.

6. In classical conditioning, responses are reinforced.

7. Associative experiences can lead to the formation of emotions, beliefs, and attitudes through affective conditioning.

Answers: **1.** Learning **2.** extinction **3.** Ivan Pavlov **4.** learned **5.** True **6.** False **7.** True

Learning Through the Association of Responses and Stimuli

THE LAW OF EFFECT

About the time that Pavlov was studying the behavior of dogs, an American psychologist, E. L. Thorndike, was observing the behavior of cats. Thorndike would deprive a cat of food for some time and then place it inside a puzzle box, a container from which escape is possible if the animal happens to trip a latch that opens the door (see Figure 7.4). Food was placed outside the box in plain view of the cat. Eventually, the cat would accidentally hook a claw onto the wire loop or step on the treadle that pulled the latch, and the door to the box would open. The cats came to appreciate this way of escaping, and each time they were put into the box, they released themselves sooner (see Figure 7.5).

Thorndike's observations of such trial-and-error learning led him to consider that the consequences of an act were an important factor in determining the probability that the action would occur. His thesis was this:

> Any act which in a given situation produces satisfaction becomes associated with that situation, so that when the situation recurs, the act is more likely than ever before to recur also. Conversely, any act which in a given situation produces discomfort becomes disassociated from that situation, so that when the situation recurs, the act is less likely than before to recur. (Thorndike, 1905, p. 202)

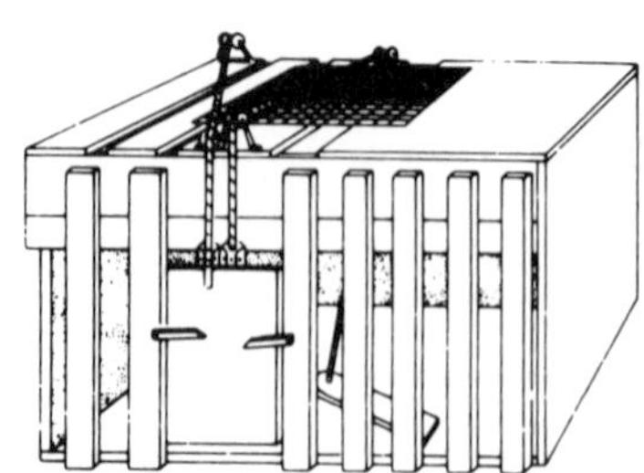

FIGURE 7.4
The puzzle box similar to that used by Thorndike in 1898. (*Source:* Bitterman, 1969, p. 445)

Thorndike's explanation, known as the **law of effect,** is one of the cornerstones of instrumental learning. Much of what you've learned in life has been acquired through instrumental learning.

Because instrumental responses are maintained or changed depending on the consequences that follow a response, when you respond to something, the response is strengthened if the consequence is pleasant and weakened if the consequence is aversive. In this way, you (and members of other species) learn because of the outcomes of different behaviors.

OPERANT CONDITIONING Skinner's term for changes in behavior that occur as a result of consequences that reinforce or punish emitted responses. These responses are classified according to how they operate on the environment. They are in turn shaped by further environmental experiences. Also known as instrumental learning.

OPERANT CONDITIONING

In classical conditioning, a particular stimulus elicits a response (in Pavlov's experiments, a bell elicited salivation). In instrumental learning, however, the response is followed by a consequence that may strengthen or weaken the response. In instrumental learning, *responses* are strengthened or weakened; in classical conditioning, *stimuli* are strengthened or weakened. In Thorndike's day, behaviorists were very concerned with analyzing the muscular responses that constituted behaviors, the way physicists might analyze a billiard shot, to determine exactly which event led to or caused the next. Because of this, it was quite natural in the case of instrumental learning to ask, What elicits the initial instrumental response? For example, what made Thorndike's cats step on the escape treadle? Which stimulus triggered it? Was it the sight of the treadle, the view of the cage bars, or something else in the cage? It's not at all clear, the way it is in classical conditioning (e.g., the bell caused the salivation). To make matters more confusing, Thorndike's cats didn't always use exactly the same response to escape. Sometimes they'd press the treadle with their left paw, sometimes with the right. Sometimes they'd just rub against it. Should each of these be considered a different response? Did each have its own eliciting stimulus?

Partly to steer clear of the complexities of building a theory of instrumental learning on a convoluted maze of stimulus-response connections, B. F. Skinner argued that *any* lever press, whether with the left paw, right paw, or body, could be considered the *same* response because *it had the same effect on the environment:* It provided the cat with an escape from the box. Skinner used the term **operant conditioning** to refer to the learning of instrumental responses that shared the same effect on the environment rather than the same muscular motions. These

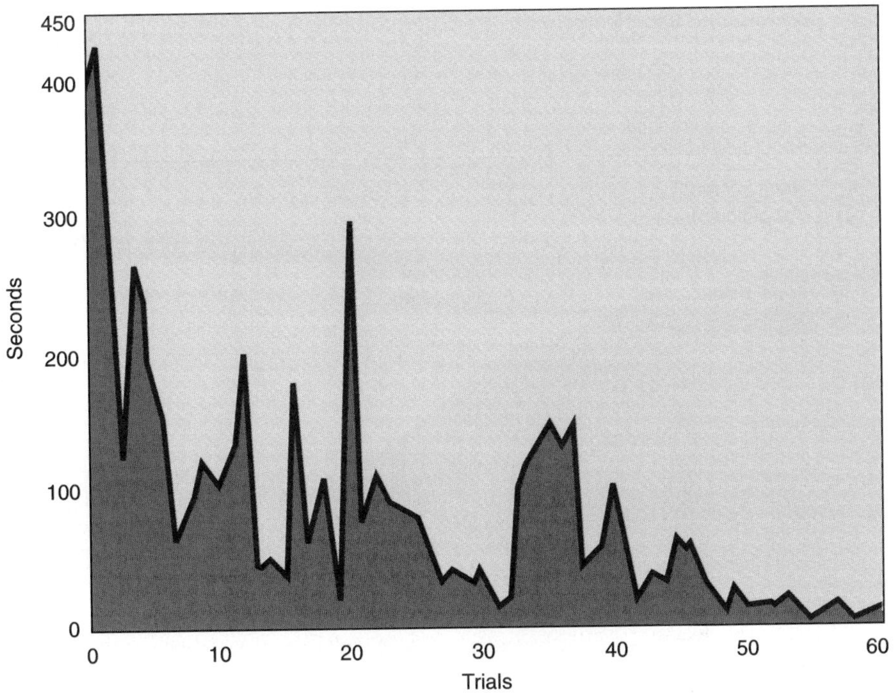

Seconds: 0, 100, 200, 300, 400, 450
Trials: 0, 10, 20, 30, 40, 50, 60

FIGURE 7.5
The graph shows the gradual decline in the amount of time necessary for one animal to release itself from the Thorndike puzzle box in successive trials. This is one of the earliest learning curves in the experimental study of conditioning. Notice, however, that the curve is not completely smooth but has marked fluctuations. Smooth learning curves usually result when many learning curves are averaged out. (*Source:* Bitterman, 1969, p. 446)

OPERANT
Skinner's term for any emitted response that affects the environment. Operants are classified or grouped not according to the particular muscular combinations involved in creating the response but according to their effect on the environment. Thorndike's cats used the same operant when they pressed the treadle that opened their cage, regardless of which paw or muscles they used.

REINFORCEMENT (IN OPERANT CONDITIONING)
An event that strengthens the response that preceded it. Operant (instrumental) conditioning is a process by which a response is reinforced.

operants, Skinner argued, can be made stronger if they are followed (as Thorndike had originally suggested) by a reinforcing consequence. In this view, a response is initially emitted for unknown reasons. The *probability* that the response will be emitted *again,* however, can be predicted by the organism's past experience with the effect of that response on the environment. Responses that had pleasant consequences are more likely to be repeated in similar circumstances, while responses that produced unpleasant consequences are less likely to be repeated.

For our purposes, instrumental learning and operant conditioning are synonymous, and the terms will be used interchangeably.

Reinforcement and Extinction The strength of an operant response can be measured by its resistance to extinction, that is, by how long it takes for the behavior to return to its original rate once the pleasant consequence following the behavior no longer occurs (see Figure 7.6). It is generally correct that to strengthen an operant response, the response should be rewarded. In ordinary language, however, "reward" denotes things such as money, candy, or praise, and something commonly considered a reward will not always strengthen an operant response. Suppose, for example, that you had a toothache. Although you might normally consider chocolate candy a reward, in this case, being given a piece probably wouldn't strengthen your desire to have a second piece. For this reason, psychologists prefer to speak of **reinforcement** rather than reward.

An Ex Post Facto Deductive System, or a 20-Pound Bird Seed Dropped on a Pigeon Is Not a Reinforcer *A particular stimulus cannot be considered a reinforcer until its effect on a behavior has been observed.* This describes an ex post facto deduction (a deduction made after the fact), a self-correcting arrangement that prevents a researcher from attributing reinforcing qualities to a stimulus until it has been tried. The need for such a precaution is an important reason why those engaged in behavioral research or behavior modification chart behavior (see Figure 7.7). Interestingly, once a behavior has been measured and charted in different circumstances, it is often possible to determine with considerable accuracy *beforehand* which consequences will, or will not, function as reinforcers (Timberlake & Farmer-Dougan, 1991). Although not technically an ex post facto approach, such knowledge beforehand can save time when setting up a behavior modification program and can also provide a greater ability to predict behavior in different circumstances.

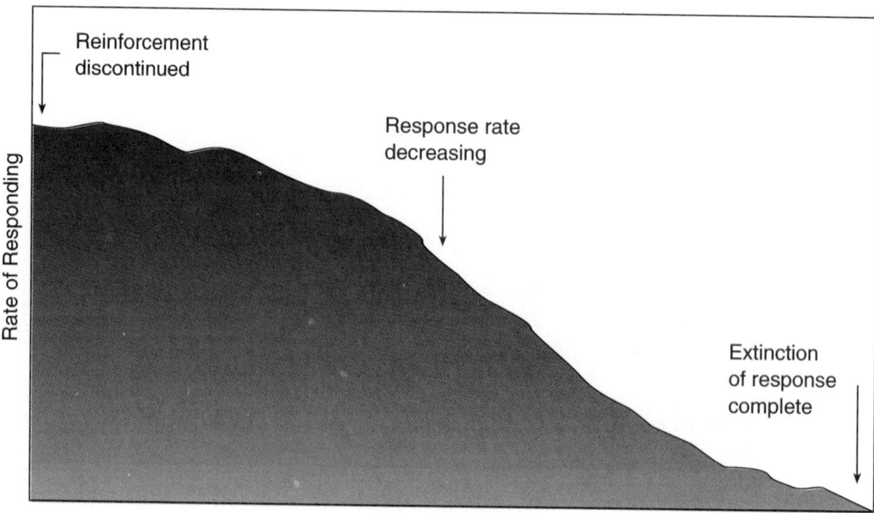

FIGURE 7.6
Once a response is no longer reinforced, it will undergo extinction. Slowly over time, the response occurs less and less until it reaches the level it held before reinforcement.

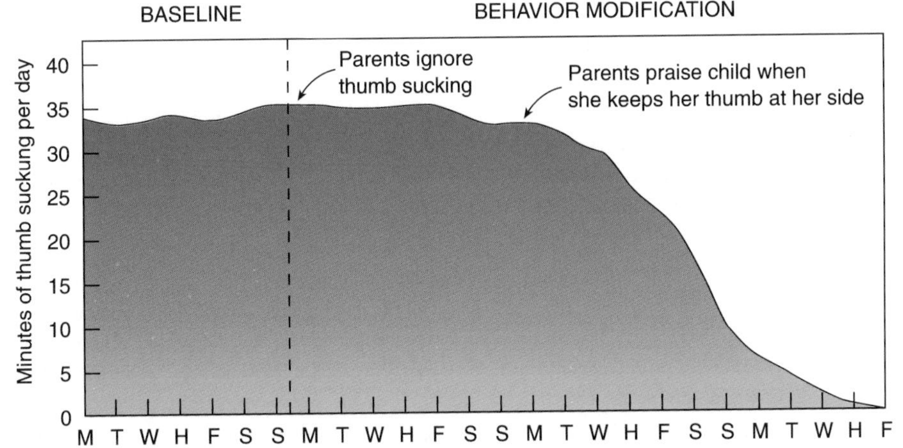

FIGURE 7.7
This chart shows a child's daily rate of thumb sucking as the behavior is modified and terminated. First, the initial rate of responding is measured; this is known as the baseline. The parents then attempt to eliminate thumb sucking by ignoring the behavior (and thereby removing what they assumed might be the reinforcer). This fails, indicating that parental attention is not the reinforcer maintaining thumb sucking. The reinforcer remains unknown, but it is not always necessary to know the reinforcer to stop a behavior. As you can see, praising the child when she is *not* thumb sucking is, in this case, successful. Charting behavior helps show the effects that various consequences of a stimulus can have on a behavior.

A Short Review of What You've Learned about Learning Is crying an unlearned reflex, a classically conditioned response, or an instrumentally learned response? Consider the question carefully before answering.

By now you may realize that crying is potentially any one of these three. If a baby cries (UR) because it is stuck with a pin (US), the crying has not been learned and therefore is considered a reflex. If a child cries (CR) at seeing a dentist's chair (CS), the crying may be the result of the chair's having been associated with pain in the past, in which case the crying can be said to be classically conditioned. Finally, if a child cries to get ice cream, the crying is serving a purpose and is instrumental (see Figure 7.8).

Shaping In operant conditioning, a response must occur before it can be reinforced. It is impossible to strengthen a behavior that in fact never occurs, and forgetting this can sometimes lead to difficulty. I once observed a father trying to get his 2-year-old son to "hand Daddy the newspaper." The child's response was "No!" This particular father, however, was a psychology graduate student and decided to obtain his newspaper by using the principle of **shaping,** reinforcing successive approximations toward a particular final response.

The father began by dividing the child's future paper-fetching response into a series of substeps:

1. Looking at the paper
2. Walking toward the paper
3. Grasping the paper
4. Carrying the paper toward the father
5. Releasing the paper once it is in the father's hand

Because the child did occasionally look at the paper (a behavior must first occur before it can be reinforced), the first step in the shaping sequence could be reinforced. The father took a fairly safe gamble and assumed that his praise would function as a reinforcer for his son. The following events illustrate the shaping of the child's response.*

*Parents sometimes get nervous when their actions are to be described in a textbook. This father was no exception. He asked that if I used this example (I have), I include his statement (I am) that he was only curious about shaping when he did this. He assured me that he has no intention of training his child to be a compliant slave and that he (the father) really does fetch his own paper and stuff most of the time—honest!

SHAPING
A method of modifying behavior by reinforcing successive approximations toward the goal behavior.

FATHER: Jimmy, please bring me the paper.
JIMMY: *(Glances about, does not look at the paper)* No.
FATHER: *(Looking at paper)* Jimmy, please bring me the paper.
JIMMY: *(Looking at paper)* No.
FATHER: *(Hugging Jimmy)* Good boy, Jimmy! You looked at the paper. Now bring me the paper.
JIMMY: *(Seems confused at first, smiles, looks at paper)* No.
FATHER: Please bring me the paper, Jimmy.
JIMMY: *(Looking at paper)* No.
FATHER: *(Withholding affection from voice, calmly repeats request)* Jimmy, please bring me the paper.
JIMMY: *(Looks at paper, seems confused, walks away from it; then, looking at it, takes a few steps toward it)* No.
FATHER: *(Hugging Jimmy)* Good boy! You looked at it and you walked toward it. Now get the paper.
JIMMY: *(Smiles, walks over to paper, touches it)* No.
FATHER: *(Again hugs Jimmy) Good boy. You touched the paper. Now bring it to me.*
JIMMY: *(Picks up the paper, carries it to his father)* No.

Notice that Jimmy persisted in saying no even as he complied with his father's request. To an adult, a "no" following a request is a refusal, a negation. To Jimmy, apparently, the word was a sound that he had learned to make following a request—a sound that brought him attention—but the complete meaning of it was obviously unclear to him.

Question: Can shaping work on adults, too?

Very effectively and in thousands of ways. A simple experiment can demonstrate this point. A particular teacher may never lecture from the corner of a room, so this response cannot be reinforced. But 10 or so well-trained students scattered about a class may be able to use shaping to alter this state of affairs. These students should be careful to pay attention, smile, and take notes when the teacher makes any move toward a chosen corner of the room but to appear bored or uninterested when the teacher heads in the other direction. Some instructors will change their behavior without any awareness of what's happening and will end up lecturing from the corner.*

*Caution: The use of such techniques on your instructor may be hazardous to your grade.

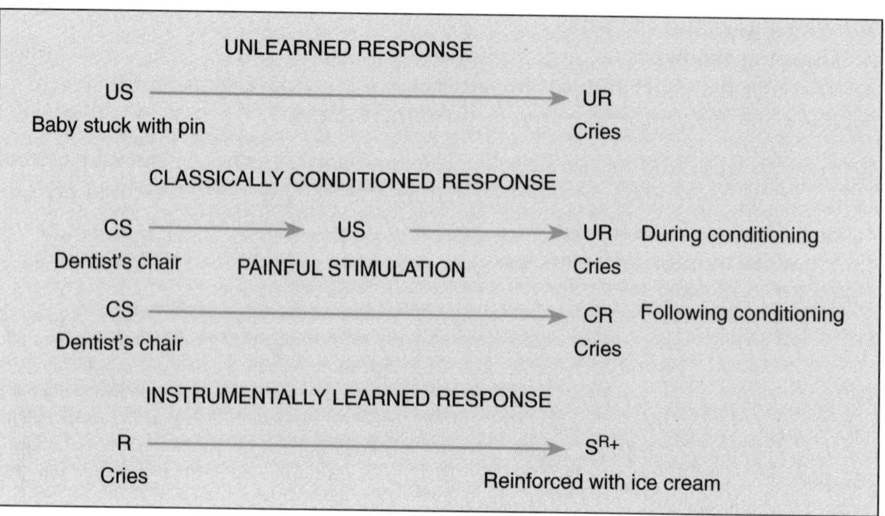

FIGURE 7.8
Crying can be an unlearned reflex, a classically conditioned response, or an operantly conditioned response. If a baby cries (UR) when stuck with a pin (US), the crying is a reflex. If a child cries (CR) at seeing a dentist's chair (CS), the crying is classically conditioned. (Notice, too, that this kind of crying is not operant because it does not help the child obtain or avoid the chair.) Finally, if a child cries (R), because last time in the same circumstances the child received ice cream or avoided homework by crying, the crying has been operantly conditioned. A reinforcing stimulus consequences is depicted as S^{R+}.

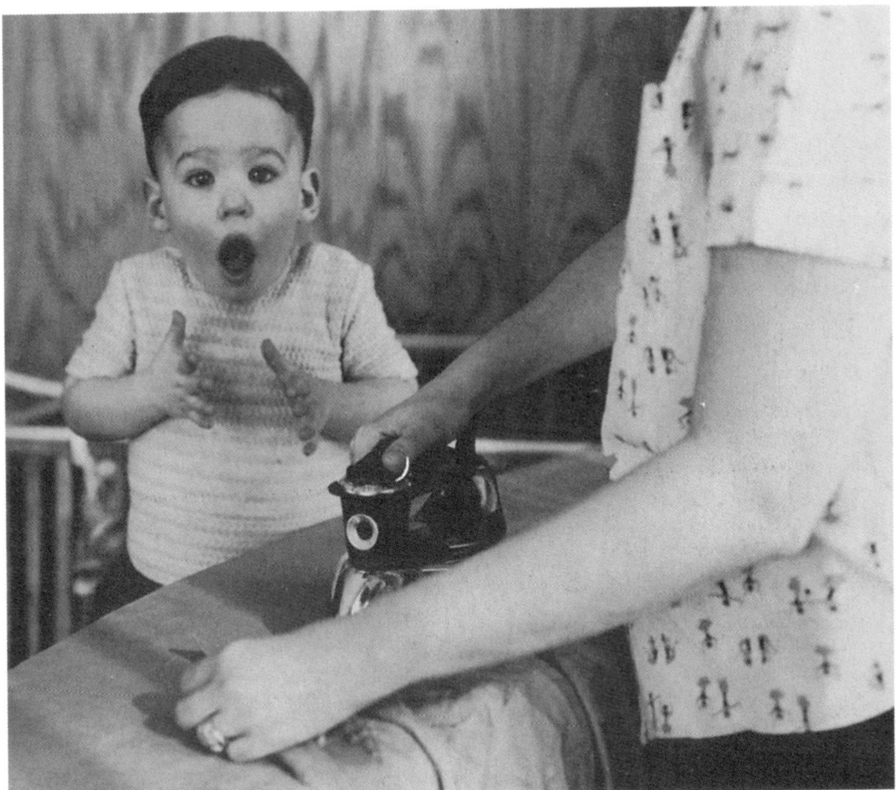

Because touching the hot iron was painful, the next time the child sees the iron the probability that he will touch it is reduced. Therefore, touching the iron has been punished.

Conditioning in Early Infancy

Question: When can an infant's behavior first be conditioned?

For the last 50 years, this issue has been hotly debated; it hasn't yet been settled to everyone's satisfaction. Over 35 years ago, there were reports of successful classical conditioning of the fetus. However, these early reports suffered from methodological problems and were not replicable. Although some people have argued that it might not be possible to obtain classical conditioning in newborns, there is evidence that such conditioning is possible (Fitzgerald & Brackbill, 1976). But the responses that have been successfully conditioned are most often those involving the autonomic nervous system, such as heart rate and respiration, rather than complex muscular behaviors, such as reaching or sucking.

There is less debate concerning the modification of young infants' behavior through operant conditioning. Newborns have been taught to change their rates of sucking to obtain milk (Sameroff, 1968). And as you recall from the Chapter 5 Preview, this was the technique used by DeCasper when he trained neonates to respond to their mother's reading of a Dr. Seuss story.

Question: Why are developmental researchers so interested in learning?

Learning is largely responsible for the great diversity of observed human behavior; for this reason, developmental researchers have become interested in the environmental surroundings or experiences of individuals over time. In fact, some researchers have taken the extreme behavioral position of considering the environment as the sole agent responsible for the great range of observed human behavior. For example, a famous quote by John B. Watson, whom you recall worked with Little Albert and who is often referred to as the father of behaviorism, has been reprinted many times (Horowitz, 1992) and goes as follows:

SOCIAL LEARNING
Learning by observing the actions of others.

MODEL
In social learning theory, anyone who demonstrates a behavior that others observe.

> Give me a dozen healthy infants, well-formed, and my own specified world to bring them up in and I'll guarantee to take any one at random and train him to become any type of specialist I might select—doctor, lawyer, artist, merchant-chief, and even yes, beggarman and thief, regardless of his talents, penchants, tendencies, abilities, vocations and race of his ancestors. (Watson, 1924/1970, p. 104)

This statement by Watson reflected the concept of *tabula rasa* proposed in the eighteenth century by the eminent philosopher John Locke. To Locke, the mind of the newborn was like a *tabula rasa* ("blank tablet"), a fresh marble surface on which environment and experience could chisel a unique pattern. Today, modern understanding of heredity and genetic mechanisms, as well as our knowledge of how infants actively interact with their environment, lead researchers to reject the idea that learning is *solely* responsible for behavior or that the infant is a passive recipient of experience. In fairness to Watson, however, most books don't mention that his famous quote continues:

> I am going beyond my facts and I admit it, but so have the advocates of the contrary and they have been doing it for many thousands of years. Please note that when this experiment is made I am to be allowed to specify the way the children are to be brought up and the type of world they have to live in. (Watson, 1924/1970, p. 104)

Social Learning

You have seen that an individual can learn by experiencing associations between stimuli or as a result of the reinforcing or punishing consequences that may follow behaviors. Now we will investigate a third possibility—learning through observation of another's behavior, or **social learning.**

OBSERVATION AND IMITATION—MONKEY SEE, MONKEY DO

Question: Why is learning by observing another person's behavior considered a third kind of learning?

Albert Bandura and several of his colleagues at Stanford University have argued that social learning is a distinct kind of learning that requires new principles to be understood. Bandura, Ross, and Ross (1963) demonstrated their thesis in an experiment now considered by many to be a classic. They asked nursery school children to observe an adult **model** striking a large inflated Bobo doll with a mallet. The model also hit, kicked, and sat on the doll. During the assault, the model said a number of unusual sentences, probably unlike any the children had heard before. Neither the model nor the observing children were directly reinforced at any time during the session.

Later, after the model had gone, the children were secretly observed as they played in a toy-filled room with the Bobo doll. For comparison, other children who had not seen the model's behavior were also allowed to interact with the doll. The results of the experiment clearly demonstrated that the children who had observed the model were far more likely to be aggressive, in imitation of the model's behavior, than were the other children. Furthermore, many of the children who had observed the model also imitated the model's unusual verbal statements. These results would not have been predicted by associative or instrumental learning theories, inasmuch as the imitation seemed to be occurring without reinforcement.

Question: But why would a child continue to imitate a behavior when the imitation is not reinforced?

No one is quite sure, although it does seem to happen, which is one reason why some researchers view social learning as a distinctly different kind of learning.

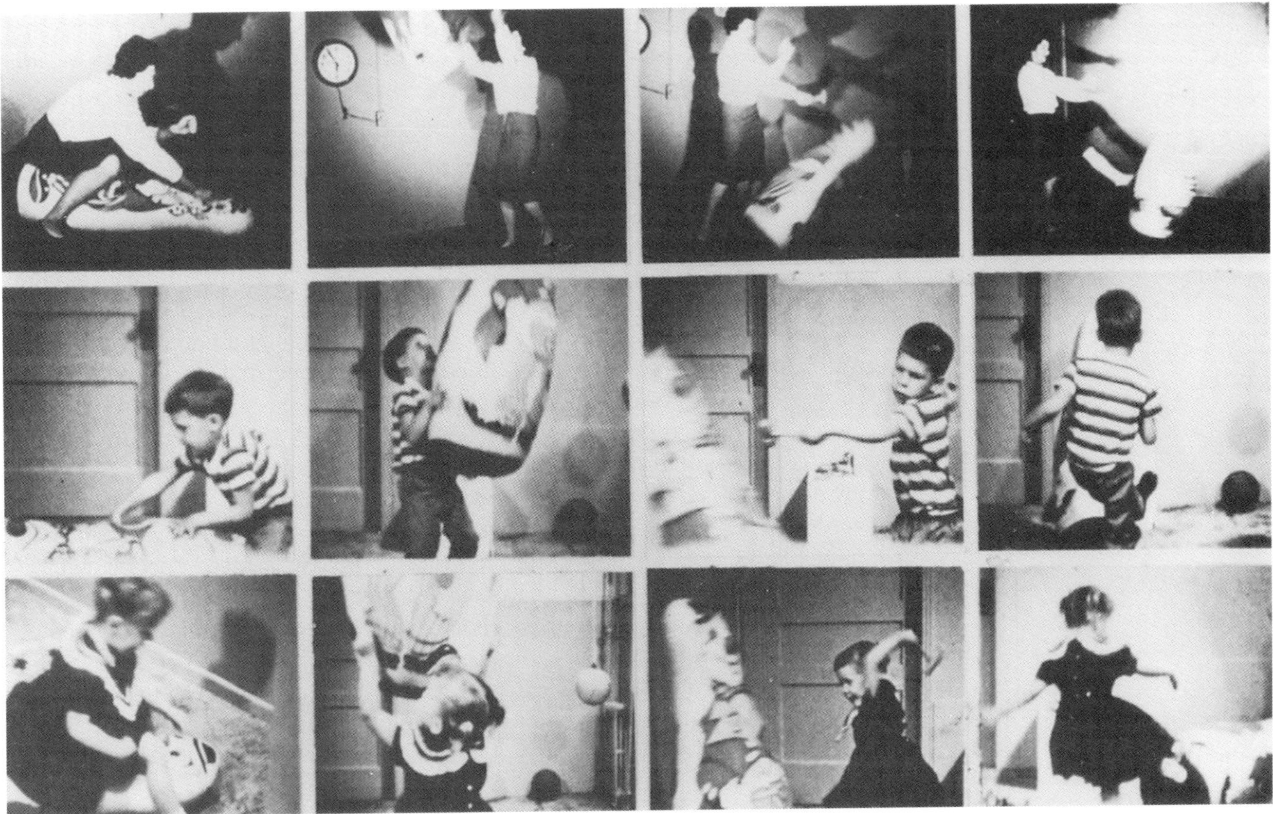

After observing an adult model being aggressive, children in Bandura, Ross, and Ross's 1963 experiment showed similar aggressive behaviors.

In our species, learning by imitating another's behavior is an easy thing to do, and the imitation of others occurs often except under the most unusual circumstances. This ease of learning defines, as you will recall, a well-canalized behavior, one that is easily learned because the forces of natural selection have favored it. In fact, it seems quite reasonable that the ability to imitate certain behaviors would be well canalized. If you consider that learning by trial and error can be extremely time consuming or even dangerous, you can see how valuable it would be to learn by imitating the successful behavior of another person. If our learning were restricted to what we could gain through classical or operant conditioning, our ability to master our world would be severely limited. Albert Bandura emphasizes this point in the following description of a driving instructor attempting to teach a student to operate a car strictly by using the principles of reinforcement:

> As a first step our trainer, who has been carefully programmed to produce head nods, resonant hm-hms, and other verbal reinforcers, loads up with an ample supply of candy, chewing gum and filter-tip cigarettes. A semi-willing subject, who has never observed a person driving an automobile, and a parked car complete the picture. Our trainer might have to wait a long time before the subject emits an orienting response toward the vehicle. At the moment the subject does look even in the general direction of the car, this response is immediately reinforced and gradually he begins to gaze longingly at the stationary automobile. Similarly, approach responses in the desired direction are promptly reinforced in order to bring the subject in proximity to the car. Eventually, through the skillful use of differential reinforcement, the trainer will teach the subject to open and to close the car door. With perseverance he will move the subject from the back seat or any other inappropriate location chosen in this trial-and-error ramble until at length the subject is shaped up behind the steering wheel. It is unnecessary to depict the remainder of the training procedure beyond noting that it will likely prove an exceedingly tedious, not to mention an expensive and hazardous enterprise. (Bandura, 1962, pp. 212–213)

Thus, there is a potential survival value in imitating others' successful behavior. This survival value is especially conspicuous for our species because we are not precocious creatures; we need care givers from birth until years later when we are able to care for ourselves. (See At Issue.)

Question: Wouldn't other species, even precocious ones, also benefit from social learning because of its survival value?

Yes, and such social learning has been demonstrated in other species. Dachshund puppies learned to pull a food cart sooner when they saw other puppies doing it than when they didn't observe such behavior (Adler & Adler, 1977). Bottle-nosed dolphins learned to pull a rope into their pool by watching other dolphins (Adler & Adler, 1978). Three sea lions learned to pull a rope into the center of their cage after they had watched a fourth learn the task by the shaping method (Adler & Adler, 1977). Rats learned by observing rat leaders who were the first to discover the best route through a cage door (Konopasky & Telegdy, 1977). Another study demonstrated that naive mice learned to copulate sooner by watching other mice do so (Hayashi & Kimura, 1976). And just in case you have formed the opinion that social learning is the province of more advanced species, such as mammals, it should be noted that such learning has also been documented in invertebrates (creatures without backbones). For example, when an untrained octopus (yes, you can train an octopus) watched another octopus learn to select from two objects, it was able to learn the same task faster than untrained octopuses that had not had the chance to observe a fellow creature learn the task (Fiorito & Scotto, 1992).

PERFORMANCE VERSUS ACQUISITION

Question: Then learning can take place simply by observation of another person, in the absence of reinforcement?

It does appear that learning can take place simply by observing another person's behavior. However, reinforcement can be important in social learning. Consider a second experiment conducted by Bandura in 1965. In this study, one group of young children watched as a model was rewarded with juice and candy for being aggressive, while another group of children on a different occasion observed the same model being chastised for the same aggressive behavior. The results of the experiment indicated that the consequences following the model's behavior were important in determining whether the children would imitate the model. The children who observed the model receiving the juice and candy for aggressive behavior became, in turn, more aggressive. But the children who observed the model being disciplined for aggressive behavior rarely imitated the aggression.

Question: You said that social learning is special because reinforcement is not needed for learning to take place. But doesn't Bandura's 1965 experiment indicate that reinforcement is necessary?

It may seem so at first glance. However, the problem can be resolved by considering the distinction between the *performance* of a behavior and the *acquisition* of a behavior. Whether the model's behavior was reinforced or punished did affect whether the children would imitate the model. However, when the children who had seen the model disciplined for aggression were offered reinforcers for demonstrating what the model had done, they were quite able, under these new circumstances, to recall and demonstrate the model's behavior, even though they had not spontaneously imitated the model at first. This experiment showed, therefore, that children who observed a model being disciplined for aggressive behavior were unlikely to imitate (perform) the behavior but that they did learn (acquire) the behavior and could imitate it at a later time if the reinforcing and punishing contingencies changed.

AT ISSUE

Baby See, Baby Do?

As you have already discovered, imitating another person is an important way to learn information about the world. In 1977, Andrew Meltzoff and M. Keith Moore reported that infants as young as 12 to 20 *days* could imitate an adult model who stuck out his tongue, opened his mouth, or did a number of other things (Meltzoff & Moore, 1977). This was not the first time that such findings had been reported, but in the past, the results were inconsistent and the research designs were thought to be poor. Meltzoff and Moore, however, argued that their results were clear and conclusive: Imitation was so basic to our species that infants displayed it just after birth.

To understand the significance of this claim, you must first consider that for newborns to be able to imitate facial expressions and actions (having never even seen themselves in a mirror), they must be able to take the perception of a tongue stuck out and imitate it. To do this, they must somehow "know" which actions are required to create a copy of the expression they are seeing! Pretty impressive stuff—if it's true.

Other researchers immediately began to conduct studies of their own in which they attempted to get infants to imitate a model. The results weren't very exciting and went the way that detractors of the original study had predicted: Meltzoff's and Moore's findings were not supported (Jacobson, 1979; McKenzie & Over, 1983). The original report had attracted attention overseas, but studies there also failed to document infant imitation (Neuberger, Merz, & Selg, 1983).

Undaunted, Meltzoff and Moore returned to the laboratory, this time with infants less than 4 days old who, the researchers argued, clearly imitated an open mouth expression and tongue protrusion (Meltzoff & Moore, 1983). One of the young imitators was only 42 minutes old! The experiment was recorded on videotape. What was going on? Certainly, Meltzoff and Moore weren't making this up. Why were they getting results that other scientists weren't?

Soon new clues emerged, clues suggesting that the effect may be sensitive to certain variables but not to others. For example, the next important studies in this area were conducted with infants 4 to 21 weeks old. The researchers made two interesting discoveries. First, the infants were successful at imitating only tongue protrusion or mouth opening, whereas they did not imitate hand gestures, such as opening a hand. Second, only the *youngest* infants,

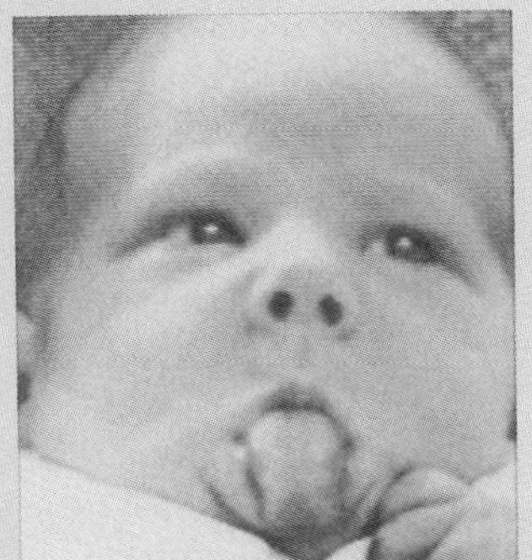

A 3-month-old baby imitates facial expression of an adult.

those who were 4 to 6 weeks old, would imitate (Abravanel & Sigafoos, 1984; Fontaine, 1984)! These findings, especially that the imitation is limited to very young infants who imitate only certain actions and who cannot, for instance, imitate emotional expressions (Kaitz, Meschulach-Sarfaty, Auerbach, & Eidelman, 1988), have led some researchers to argue that these babies are displaying not true social imitation but rather some kind of hitherto undiscovered reflex.

Meltzoff and Moore stood by their guns, however, and a study from Italy helped explain the different findings among researchers. In this study, 4-day-old infants were found to imitate tongue protrusion *and* hand opening and closing, *but only if the models were in motion!* If the model simply stood there with his tongue stuck out or with his hand opened, the infants did not imitate (Vinter, 1986).

Further support then came from overseas in a study conducted with newborns in Nepal who were less than 1 hour old. This study confirmed Meltzoff and Moore's original findings (Reissland, 1988).

Meltzoff and Moore have also shown that young infants will imitate head turning and that they can remember what they have seen long enough to imitate it at a later time (Meltzoff & Moore, 1989).

These studies may give you some idea of what an ongoing controversy in the research literature is like. This particular issue remains controversial. Why is it necessary that motion occur for imitation to take place? How does a newborn infant know what to do to imitate an expression? The research in this area is, of course, basic research; it is continuing.

What does this experiment tell you about the old Hollywood notion that it's all right to show the "bad guys" being violent as long as they are caught and jailed at the end?

TELEVISION AND AGGRESSION*

After Bandura's Bobo doll studies in the early 1960s, people began to be more interested in the effects of television on aggression. As you recall, Bandura demonstrated that children who observe aggression are more likely to imitate aggression. Thus, if television puts children in a position to see aggressive behavior, television programming may be promoting aggression in children. We considered this hypothesis in Chapter 1. Now let's see what other researchers have discovered.

A significant relationship has been found between the amount of violence in children's favorite television programs and the amount of aggressiveness that children display (McIntyre & Teevan, 1972). Among adolescents, it has been found that boys who have gotten into serious fights at work or school and have hurt someone severely enough to require medical attention were more likely to have watched violent television programs than were other adolescents (Robinson & Bachman, 1972). Two researchers (Dominick & Greenberg, 1972) have stated that "the greater the level of exposure to television violence, the more the child was willing to use violence, to suggest it as a solution to conflict, and to perceive it as effective" (p. 329).

Question: Do these studies prove that watching aggression on television causes children to behave aggressively?

As you may have noticed, all these studies were correlational, not experimental. Thus, it may be that children who are aggressive to begin with are attracted to aggressive television programs. If this is the case, the television would not be the cause of their aggression.

To test such a hypothesis, researchers have carried out experimental studies investigating the possibility that television could cause aggression. In one study, 4- and 5-year-old boys from a Sunday school were the subjects. Half the children watched a 2½-minute color sound movie in which an adult model committed aggressive acts against a human clown. The children were then allowed to play in a room with some toys and a live clown. The children who had seen the film engaged in significant physical aggression against the clown, whereas none of the other children were aggressive. The children who had seen the aggressive film also showed increased aggression against toys and other articles in the room (Hanratty, Liebert, Morris, & Fernandez, 1969). Similar results have been obtained with girls as subjects (Hanratty, 1969).

On the other hand, researchers have examined trends in violent crimes, burglary, and auto theft and have found no consistent relationship between the pattern of these crimes and the advent of television and its subsequent expansion into almost every household in the United States (Hennigan et al., 1982), which indicates that violent crime has root causes far beyond mere exposure to television.

Question: Is there any way to ensure that children who are exposed to violence on television will not be affected by it in a negative way?

One way to help eliminate aggressive responses after a child has viewed violence may be to set clear-cut behavior rules and to help the child discriminate between the make-believe of television and the reality of his or her actions. Rewarding children for calm, gentle, and affectionate behavior may also help undermine any of the detrimental effects of viewing violence. In one study, preschoolers who,

*We will cover television and its effects in much greater detail in Chapter 14.

before watching violence, were trained to be gentle and affectionate with one another were less affected by the aggressive actions they saw than would have been expected (Marton & Acker, 1981).

BEHAVIORISM
The school of psychology that views learning as the most important aspect of an organism's development. Behaviorists objectively measure behavior and the way in which stimulus-response relationships are formed.

BEHAVIOR MODIFICATION
A set of procedures for changing human behavior, especially by using behavior therapy and operant conditioning techniques.

I Think; Therefore, I'm Complicated

Early in this century, John B. Watson argued that any science of behavior must be based on observable events rather than on inferred ones. Watson believed that this would limit the biased and subjective assessments of behavior that he thought were plaguing psychology. His arguments were quite popular in the United States and helped to formulate a particularly American psychology called **behaviorism.**

Behaviorists intended to develop a strong and powerful science based on their acquired knowledge of observable stimuli and responses. They argued that through the scientific manipulation of the environment, a technology of **behavior modification** could be developed. According to behaviorists, as long as you could predict the responses, knowing what went on inside an organism's head was unnecessary.

Although this radical approach has produced volumes of valuable research showing how the environment controls and contributes to behavior, it is nonetheless a limited perspective. Humans do think, however unobservably. In other words, the way you internally organize and process information can modify your behavior. People aren't like computers; we are not simply the sum of our inputs. As Albert Bandura has stated, to exclude thinking from any theory of learning would be like attributing "Shakespeare's literary masterpieces to his prior instruction in the mechanics of writing" (Bandura, 1978, p. 350).

Question: Isn't Bandura a behaviorist?

Social learning theory has its roots in behaviorism, but philosophically, social learning theory maintains that there is an interaction between environment and thought (Bandura, 1978). Social learning theorists and many other learning theorists are beginning to incorporate the complexities of internalized thought processes into their research. In later chapters, we will examine this cognitive research and how it relates to behavior.

Learning Check

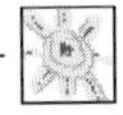

Fill-in-the-Blanks

1. A particular stimulus cannot be considered a reinforcer until its effect on a ______________ has been observed.
2. Learning by observing another is known as ______________ learning.
3. Social learning appears to be well canalized because of its ______________ value.
4. Whether a model is rewarded or disciplined following a behavior may affect whether an observer will ______________ the behavior.
5. Observers may ______________ a behavior simply by watching someone else model it.
6. Social learning involves an ______________ between environment and thought.
7. Children who watch violent television programs are ______________ likely to display aggression afterward.

Answers: 1. behavior or response 2. social 3. survival 4. perform or imitate 5. acquire or learn 6. interaction 7. more

APPLICATIONS

Behavior Modification

Or How Ya Gonna Keep 'Em Down on the Beach After They've Seen *Jaws III?*

A technology of behavior modification has developed from learning theory. Table 7.1 lists some of the operant techniques used in behavior modification. The following are just two applications among many, of this technology.

Overcoming Fear of Dogs

Children may come to fear many things. Sometimes the fears are reasonable; other times they are out of proportion to any real danger. One of the most intense fears that a child may develop beyond rational proportion is a fear of dogs. Such a fear may become exaggerated for many reasons. Children may actually have seen someone bitten or may have been bitten themselves. Occasionally, all it takes is a dog's loud bark or threatening growl. Sometimes the fear occurs because the child senses excessive fear in someone else, such as a parent. Whatever the reason, once the fear is acquired, it can become more intense than is warranted.

To help children overcome an unrealistically intense fear of dogs, Albert Bandura and his colleagues at Stanford University organized a behavior modification treatment based on social learning theory. In this treatment, young children who showed an extreme fear of dogs when actually confronted with one were allowed to watch a fearless child of their own age initiate play with a dog. At each stage of the treatment, the fearless model came closer to the dog than before, until finally the model played inside a closed playpen with the dog (Bandura & Menlove, 1968).

By watching a fearless child approach a dog in slow, successive stages without any adverse consequences, fearful children could be coaxed into following the model's lead. Little by little, the fearful children approached the dog. They were asked

> to approach and to pet the dog, to release her from a playpen, to remove her leash, to feed her dog biscuits, and to spend a fixed period of time alone in the room with the animal. The final and most difficult set of tasks required the children to climb into the playpen with the dog and, after having locked the gate, to pet her and to remain alone with the animal under the con-

TABLE 7.1

Operant Techniques Used in Behavior Modification

TECHNIQUE	DESCRIPTION
Positive reinforcement	Providing a reinforcer following an appropriate response
Negative reinforcement	Removing an aversive stimulus following an appropriate response
Punishment	Providing an aversive stimulus following an inappropriate response
Extinction	Removing the reinforcer that is maintaining the inappropriate response
Positive reinforcement of incompatible response	Reinforcing the behavior that is incompatible with the inappropriate response (e.g., reinforcing telling the truth, which is incompatible with lying)
Time-out from positive reinforcement	Essentially producing boredom following an inappropriate behavior by removing the opportunity to engage in any reinforcing activities for a brief time (usually a few minutes)
Altering response effort	Structuring the environment in such a way that inappropriate responses are more difficult to make or appropriate responses are easier to make
Token economy	Providing tokens (generalized secondary reinforcers) for appropriate behaviors; tokens may later be redeemed for specific reinforcers unique to each person's taste
Response cost	Imposing fines for inappropriate behavior (often used in conjunction with token economies)
Negative practice	Forcing repetition of an inappropriate behavior (e.g., yelling) until it finally becomes aversive to engage in the behavior

APPLICATIONS

A girl who was afraid of dogs watched a film of a model (top row) engaging in interactions with dogs. The girl then fearlessly interacted with dogs herself (bottom row).

fining, fear-arousing conditions. (Bandura, 1969, p.177)

Question: Were the fearful children willing to do this?

Of the children who observed the model play with the dog, 67 percent were able to stay alone with her in the playpen. As a control, Bandura used fearful children who had not seen the model play with the dog. Only an extremely small percentage of these children were willing to join the dog in the playpen.

Question: Did the children's fears eventually return, or had the children overcome their problem?

In a follow-up study, the researchers discovered that the original fear expressed by the children had not returned; thus, the behavior modification program had been successful (Bandura & Menlove, 1968).

Toilet Training in Less Than a Day

Using models as a behavior modification technique is usually incorporated into more comprehensive modification programs that often include both associative and instrumental learning. A good example of such a comprehensive behavior modification program is described in the book *Toilet Training in Less Than a Day*, by Nathan Azrin and Richard Foxx (1974).

Question: Toilet train a child in less than a day? You've got to be kidding.

Although we can all sympathize with parents for whom toilet training turns out to be a three-year siege, it does appear that toilet training can be accomplished in under 24 hours by making use of the learning principles that have been described in this chapter. To see how this is possible, let's examine some of the techniques used in the toilet-training program developed by Azrin and Foxx. As you'll discover, these techniques take both physical and environmental aspects into consideration:

1. The authors recommend that no attempt be made to train children much younger than 24 months. Children younger than this usually do not have the muscle development necessary for bladder and bowel control.
2. A learning environment should be created in which the child and parent are together, without distraction, for the whole day. In this way, all their energies may be devoted to learning and to strengthening the new behavior.
3. The behavior to be developed is specifically defined; that is, the child will go to the potty-chair when the time arises, lower his or her training

APPLICATIONS

pants, urinate or defecate, wipe where appropriate, raise the training pants, remove the plastic pot from the potty-chair, empty its contents into the toilet, flush the toilet, and return the plastic pot to the potty-chair.

4. The authors give a number of tips for making many of these behaviors easier to accomplish. They suggest, for example, using large, loose training pants because they are easier to raise and lower.

5. Instrumental learning is achieved as the child's appropriate behaviors are reinforced through lavish praise and the administration of large amounts of juice or soda. Drinking liquid makes urination more likely, giving the child more chances to learn the desired response; remember, a behavior must occur before it can be reinforced.

6. The technique of modeling is incorporated in an ingenious way by making use of a doll that wets. At the beginning of the Azrin and Foxx program, before anything else, the child is required to toilet train the doll! In this way, the child observes as the doll models the desired behavior and then sees that the doll is immediately rewarded for its good behavior with praise and juice (administered to the doll in a special baby bottle that refills the doll's reservoir).* This is an effective technique because a model, even a doll, is more likely to be imitated if the observer sees the model's behavior reinforced.

*Dolls such as these are available in most toy stores.

SUMMARY

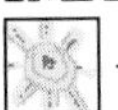

- A fixed-response pattern is a complex inherited behavior triggered by a particular stimulus called a releaser stimulus or sign stimulus. The reactions themselves are known as species-specific behaviors.
- The capacity to learn appears to have been inherited because of its survival value.
- Learning may be defined as a relatively permanent change in behavior brought about by practice or experience.
- Learning may occur when one stimulus is associated with another; through the association of a response and its consequences, such as learning through rewards and punishments; or through observation of what others do, called social learning.
- Among the associative learning processes is classical conditioning, first described in detail by the Russian physiologist Ivan Pavlov. In classical conditioning, a new stimulus (a conditioned stimulus, or CS) acquires the power to elicit a response because the CS has been paired, or associated, with an unconditioned stimulus (US) that originally produced the reflex. A response elicited by a CS is called a conditioned response (CR) because it is learned.
- Various beliefs and attitudes may also be learned through associative experiences.
- The most important principle of instrumental learning is Thorndike's law of effect, which states that a behavior that has been successful in helping an organism obtain something pleasant will be strengthened, whereas a behavior that leads to something unpleasant will be weakened.
- Reinforcement theory is based on an ex post facto deductive system. This means that a particular stimulus cannot be considered a reinforcer until its effect on a behavior has been observed.
- In instrumental learning, a response must occur before it can be reinforced. New responses that have not yet occurred can be created by shaping, that is, reinforcing successive approximations of the final response desired.
- Social learning (learning by observing another's behavior) appears to function according to principles that are different from those of other learning processes. Social learning can occur and be maintained in the absence of any obvious reinforcers.
- Imitation of another organism, especially of the same species, appears to be a well-canalized behavior (one that is easily learned) because of the great survival value inherent in learning by imitating the successful behavior of others.
- Although it is not required, reinforcement can play an important role in social learning. The consequences shown to follow a model's behavior can determine whether an observer will perform (imitate) the behavior but not whether an observer will acquire (learn) the behavior.
- Children who view violence on television display more aggressive behavior than do their peers who are not exposed to violent programs.
- Social learning is considered an interaction between environment and thought, not just a function of environmental input.
- A technology of behavior modification has developed from learning theory.

QUESTIONS FOR DISCUSSION

1. What ethical considerations are encountered by researchers who wish to conduct research similar to Watson and Rayner's study of Little Albert?
2. How have past associations from films made you feel about stimuli such as great white sharks, the shower at the Bates Motel, the name Freddy Kruger, or deformed men called Igor who work night shifts in old castles?
3. After a man calling himself D. B. Cooper had successfully bailed out of a passenger jet over Oregon with thousands of dollars in ransom money, a rash of similar hijacking attempts followed in rapid succession. Do you think that there was a connection between the original hijacking and the ones that followed?
4. According to social learning theory, what special responsibility does the news media have in reporting and covering such events as snipings, kidnappings, or hijackings?
5. Who are the models you admire most, and how have they affected your behavior?

SUGGESTIONS FOR FURTHER READING

1. Azrin, N., & Foxx, R. (1974). *Toilet training in less than a day*. New York: Simon & Schuster.
2. Davey, G., & Cullen, C., Eds. (1988). *Human operant conditioning & behavior modification*. New York: Wiley.
3. Krumboltz, J. D., & Krumboltz, H. B. (1972). *Understanding and hanging children's behavior*. Englewood Cliffs, NJ: Prentice-Hall.
4. Packard, V. (1977). *The people shapers*. Boston: Little, Brown.
5. Patterson, G. R. (1976). *Living with children: New methods for parents and teachers*. Champaign, IL: Research Press.
6. Skinner, B. F. (1971). *Beyond freedom and dignity*. Des Plaines, IL: Bantam.

CHAPTER 8

LANGUAGE DEVELOPMENT

CHAPTER PREVIEW

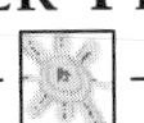

CATEGORICALLY SPEAKING

DO YOU LIKE to type? I won't blame you if you say no. I don't like it either. In fact, considering the length of this book, I wish I had one of those "speakwriters" that scientists have been working on—the kind you simply talk into and it types what you say! Unfortunately, they're not available yet because computers have a terrible time distinguishing the same word when spoken by different people.

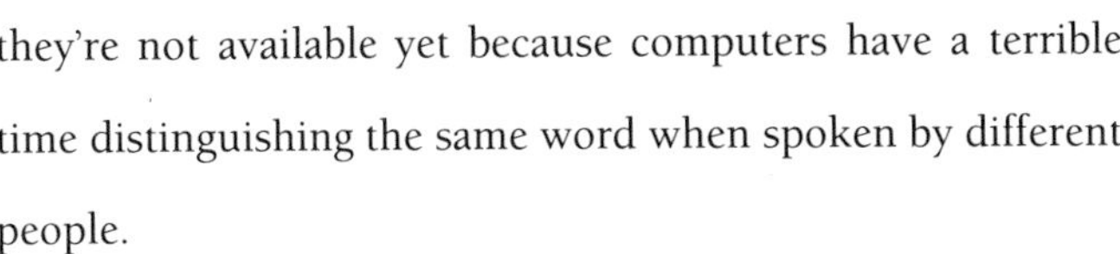

Question: Why do computers have that problem?

Have you ever heard of "voiceprint identification"? It's based on the fact that no two people have exactly the same voice. The way I say "tomato" and the way you say "tomato" sound completely different to a computer. Perhaps the onset of my voice is a little more rapid than yours, or perhaps we differ in our inflections or in which **phones** we use. In general, inexpensive machines programmed to "understand" one person's speech are typically unable to understand anyone else's.

Question: Why don't people have the same problem that computers do?

That's the crucial question. How come babies don't grow up able to understand only their mothers? How is it that they can also understand their fathers, or strangers, or siblings, or anyone else speaking their language? The answer may lie in an inborn mechanism for the perception of spoken words.

IN A SERIES OF experiments already considered to be classics, researcher Peter Eimas (1985) examined what it is that infants hear when they listen to a spoken language. The infants in the experiments were given a special pacifier to suck, and their rates of sucking were recorded. A word was then spoken by a computer. In this instance, the word *bin* was repeatedly said to the infant. When the infant first heard the computer say "bin," the sucking rate increased, indicating that the infant had noticed a change in the environment. After a short time of listening to "bin," the infant became habituated to it (see Chapter 5). Then suddenly the voice changed from "bin" to "pin," and the infant immediately reacted, showing that the infant had perceived the switch in sound from one letter to the other.

NEXT, THE COMPUTER simply said "bin" differently, changing intonation, voice onset, or length of voicing, so that it imitated the way different people might say the word *bin*.

Question: Did the baby's sucking rate change this time, too?

No, the baby did not react! It's as though the baby treated different individual voices as *not* different, while perceiving a change in letter sounds as very different. Eimas argues that this occurs because infants perceive language sounds, called **phonemes,** in categories. To an infant, *bin* is *bin,* no matter who is saying it, but *bin* is not *pin.* The baby easily does what most computers find impossible to do. This has led Eimas and others to conclude that babies are genetically "prewired" for language recognition. Eimas even refers to this ability as **phoneme constancy,** classifying it as a perceptual constancy (see Chapter 5).

IN MUCH THE SAME manner, infants as young as 2 months old treat basic vowel sounds as distinct categories, even though they might hear these few basic vowel sounds spoken hundreds of different ways by different speakers (Marean, Werner, & Kuhl, 1992).

BY ABOUT 6 MONTHS of age, infants will also have expanded these distinct categories to especially include the speech sounds of the language to which they are being exposed. For example, in one study, 6-month-olds listened to a stereo speaker play the English long *ee* sound as in *free.* Then subtle changes in the sound were made, as might occur if different people were saying the sound. The infants were trained to look at the speaker if they heard a change in sound (when they did so correctly, they were rewarded with the sight of a toy bear). The speaker also played subtle variations of the Swedish sound *y,* as in the Swedish word *fy.* (The sound can be made by forming your lips in the shape of an *o* and saying the English long *ee* sound; there is no such sound in English.) The infants exposed to English were more aware of subtle changes in the *Swedish sounds* than in the English sounds, while Swedish infants were more aware of changes in the English sounds (Kuhl, Williams, Lacerda, Stevens, & Lindblom, 1992). These results imply that the infants are already learning to categorize the variations of sounds from their own language into categories to be treated as identical—and they are doing this before ever speaking their first words.

THIS ABILITY TO TAKE the tremendous variety of speech sounds, which are different for each person speaking, and perceive them within category groupings is what makes language perception and production possible. And while it is true that a few extremely elaborate and expensive computers are making some small strides in this same direction, babies have it down pat!

IN THIS CHAPTER, we'll take a closer look at the amazing language capacities of infants, investigate the normal sequence of language acquisition in children, and discuss some of the theories and heated debates that have been generated by the language research of the last few years.

RESOURCES

What Is Language?

Question: Isn't language the same as communication?

Have you ever seen a dog carry its leash over to its master and drop it at his feet? The meaning is clear, but language isn't necessary. In this way, dogs can communicate, but they don't have language. A language requires the use of signs or symbols within a **grammar**—that is, within a structure of rules that determines how the various signs or symbols are to be arranged. Language also allows the use of signs or symbols within a grammar to create novel constructions.

Question: What do you mean by a novel construction?

If a myna bird says, "Candy is dandy, but liquor is quicker," you know that the bird is simply imitating someone who has been reading Ogden Nash poems aloud. Myna birds don't use English to express meanings; they only mimic the sounds they have heard. Although the sentence the myna spoke was made with English words and was grammatically correct, the myna is not said to have language. Ogden Nash, on the other hand, as the originator of the statement (a novel construction), has proved his language capability.

The Prelinguistic Period

Newborn infants don't possess language, of that we are sure. But as infants grow, they gradually develop language in a step-by-step sequence. Interestingly, this sequence of language acquisition is quite similar among children throughout the world.

Question: When do infants begin to acquire language?

Some researchers believe that the rudiments of language acquisition are present within 72 hours after birth. Evidence for this comes from the apparent vocal "dialogues" engaged in by mothers and their newborns.

Question: What do you mean by "dialogues"?

For example, researchers in one study analyzed the vocal interactions between mothers and their 3-day-old infants (Rosenthal, 1982). They discovered that the duration and kind of infant vocalization seemed to depend on the presence or absence of the mother's voice. What the mother said and when she said it were in turn affected by the sounds the infant made. Infants also move their hands and body differently in the presence of their mothers than in the presence of an equally active doll, indicating a social understanding of their interactions (Legerstee, Corter, & Kienapple, 1990). Other researchers have found similar "conversations" (Keller & Scholmerich, 1987). In fact, they are quite common. Although the newborn has no words to say, this reciprocal pattern of exchange is not too different from one aspect of adult conversation, inasmuch as the mothers and their newborn infants seem to take turns "speaking" (Bateson, 1975).

Question: Couldn't it just be that infants make noises every once in a while and their mothers respond to these sounds, so that it seems as though they're taking turns speaking but really aren't?

Some researchers have suggested that the infant may be making vocalizations in a rhythmic way that sets a pace for the mother to follow (Kaye, 1977). But further

PHONES
The smallest units of vocalized sound that do not affect meaning but can be discriminated. (Derived from the Greek word *phone*, meaning "voice" or "sound.") Phones are often responsible for regional and foreign accents. For example, someone from Boston might pronounce the word *car* differently than someone from Dallas.

PHONEMES
The smallest units of speech that can affect meaning. For instance, the only difference between *mat* and *bat* is the phoneme sounds *m* and *b*. These two sounds are phonemes because they affect meaning; a mat is certainly not a bat. Phonemes are typically composed of phones. Some languages use more phonemes than others.

PHONEME CONSTANCY
A perceptual ability that develops in infancy in which a phoneme, although spoken or pronounced differently by different individuals, is perceived as a single entity regardless of speaker.

GRAMMAR
A set of rules that determines how sounds may be put together to make words and how words may be put together to make sentences.

investigation reveals that infant vocalizations don't continue in the same way if the mother doesn't hold up her end of the "conversation" (Schaffer, 1977).

PHONATION STAGE
A stage of language acquisition that develops between birth and 2 months of age. During this stage, infants often make comfort sounds composed of quasi vowels.

GOOING STAGE
A stage of language acquisition that typically occurs between the ages of 2 and 4 months. During this stage, infants combine the quasi vowels from the phonation stage with harder sounds that are precursors of consonants.

CRYING

For years, parents have claimed that they can tell if their newborn babies are afraid, hungry, or bored by the way the baby cries. Until recently, most developmental researchers argued that parents were being biased by information other than cries, information from the environment that gave them hints about what the newborn might be feeling. However, carefully controlled studies using tape recordings of babies' cries without the presence of other cues have supported what parents have been saying all along—that they really can tell (Hostetler, 1988; Zeskind & Marshall, 1988). Even a newborn's cry, it seems, has some communicative value.

Some researchers, however, believe that neither social dialogue nor crying can be considered the beginning of real language. Many animals that never acquire language engage in social interaction or make sounds that have some communicative value. Instead, it is argued, language acquisition doesn't truly begin until the infant shows evidence of having acquired the first language-like sounds.

THE FIRST LANGUAGE-LIKE SOUNDS

Question: What would be considered the first language-like sounds?

Even that is difficult to say. Between birth and 2 months of age, babies are in the **phonation stage** of language acquisition. During this stage, infants often make what are called "comfort sounds." These are "quasi-vowel" sounds ("quasi" because they are not as full or rich as vowel sounds made later). Quasi vowels are made from phones. That is why this period is called the phonation stage.

"Gooing" might be a better example of a first language-like sound. Between the ages of 2 and 4 months, infants are usually in what is called the **gooing stage.** Young infants typically say "goo," or something similar, by combining the quasi vowels from the phonation stage with harder sounds that they have acquired, sounds that are the precursors of consonants.

Question: Why is the **g** *sound in "goo" considered a consonant precursor rather than a consonant?*

Even when infants are only a few days old they engage their mothers in "conversations."

It is referred to as a precursor because when adults attempt to imitate infant gooing sounds, their renditions are quite different; adults' consonants are harder and richer. The reason that an adult's sounds differ from those of a young infant may be that a young infant's developing skull and oral cavity differ from an adult's. Anthropologists comparing the sizes of the skulls and oral cavities of adults and infants have uncovered some evidence that infants before 6 months of age may be physically incapable of making the kinds of sounds necessary for spoken language (Lieberman, Crelin, & Klatt, 1972). One of the reasons for this inability may be that the young infant's larynx, or voice box, is very high in the throat. Because of this positioning, newborns are actually able to drink and breathe at the same time! This, in turn, helps them during nursing. As infants grow, the larynx moves lower in the throat, creating the large vocal cavity required for language production. (This lowering of the larynx also makes our species more likely to choke on food, a price we must pay for the ability to speak.)

Question: Then it is because the infant's skull and mouth grow and change shape that the infant is able to make real language sounds?

Perhaps. Further development of the nervous system also may be needed before an infant is capable of articulation. Interestingly, no one is certain of exactly which neurological or physical prerequisites are necessary for language. However, we do know that infants between the ages of 4 and 7 months typically begin to produce many new sounds, which is why this time is called the **expansion stage.**

Question: What kinds of new sounds are produced?

These new sounds include yells, whispers, growls, squeals, and, every parent's favorite, the **raspberry.** Also during this time, the first fully formed vowels appear. Mature syllables during the expansion stage are rare. As the infant's phonetic repertoire grows, parents become aware that the infant has begun to "babble."

Between the ages of 7 and 10 months, babbling greatly increases as the infant begins to produce syllables and duplicated sequences such as "dadada" or "mamama." This is known as the **cononical stage.** Interestingly, babies who can hear soon begin to babble cononical syllables, whereas deaf babies, who also babble, do not (Oller & Eilers, 1988). This finding tells us that even very early on, experience with sound has affected the language acquisition of hearing infants. Interestingly, deaf infants who are exposed to sign language also babble, they just do it manually! That is, they babble with their hands, starting out with the basic shapes they have seen adults use and progressing to make various combinations of hand shapes until they say their first signed word at about 1 year of age (Petitto & Marentette, 1991). Apparently, the brain develops language capability in a very similar way regardless of the mode of expression.

Question: Then when infants first start to babble, you can't tell the difference between the babbling of an infant who has been exposed to English and one exposed to Japanese?

When babbling first appears, no differences can be detected. However, sometime between about 4 and 10 months of age, infants begin to show a preference for the phonemes common to the language they have been hearing and eventually will learn. In one study, the babbling of 6- to 10-month-old infants who came from different language backgrounds was presented to adults from different language communities. The adults were required to judge which infants came from which language background. Although they found it difficult, most judges were able to tell (deBoysson-Bardies, Sagart, & Durand, 1984).

Following the cononical stage, infants increasingly narrow their use of phonemes, mainly to the ones they will be using in the language they will eventually learn. This is known as the **contraction stage** and generally occurs between 10

EXPANSION STAGE
A stage of language acquisition that typically occurs between the ages of 4 and 7 months. During this stage, infants produce many new sounds and rapidly expand the number of phonemes they use, giving rise to babbling.

RASPBERRY
In foodstuffs: a rather tasty fruit; a type of berry. In social discourse: an explosive sound caused by the rapid expulsion of air from the mouth. The expelled air vigorously vibrates the lips (especially the lower lip), which have been deliberately placed in a configuration so as to make contact with and surround the protruded tongue. Considered unrequired in most social circumstances. (For an exception, see "Sporting events.")

CONONICAL STAGE
A stage of language acquisition that typically occurs between the ages of 7 and 10 months and is typified by an increase in babbling and the production of cononical syllables (made of consonant and vowel sounds of certain intensities). Duplicated sequences such as "dadada" or "mamama" also mark this stage.

CONTRACTION STAGE
A stage of language acquisition that typically occurs between the ages of 10 and 14 months. It is so named because during this time, infants begin to narrow their phoneme production to the phonemes common to the language to which they are exposed. During this stage, infants also acquire the pacing and rhythm of their language.

and 14 months of age. Now, infants also are beginning to acquire the pacing and rhythm of their language. At this time, the phonemes an infant chooses to speak in conjunction with the rhythm, pacing, and length of babbled utterances can be so uncannily like the actual language (except that real words are not spoken) that parents swear that their baby has just said a totally intelligible sentence—it's just that they somehow missed what the infant said (and it drives them crazy trying to get their baby to say it again).

Question: How do infants specifically acquire the phonemes of their language? What causes the contraction stage to occur?

It appears that feedback is necessary before phonetic contraction can begin. Infants learn to imitate what they hear.

Question: Wait a minute. Infants don't hear babbling, they hear language. If they imitated what they were hearing, wouldn't they speak in sentences instead of babbling?

We are able to discriminate or recognize individual words only because they have been associated with particular objects, actions, or circumstances. Until these associations have been made—that is, until these different sounds have meanings—any of us would discern only the phones and phonemes. Suppose that you were suddenly transported to a foreign land where everyone spoke an unfamiliar language. You wouldn't be aware of distinct words. Everything that was said would sound like gibberish to you. After a short time, though, you might become aware of some aspects of the language. Perhaps you'd become aware of the spacing, when sounds begin and when they end. You might also become aware of the rhythm and tone changes or the differences among the phonetic sounds. Unfortunately, that's not much to go on when you want to communicate. It probably wouldn't be too long before you felt helpless, or even childlike. However, in time you probably could imitate the sounds—that is, you could learn to sound like the native speakers without actually saying a single word of their language.

Question: How could you do that?

It's easy; you've probably heard it done many times. Comedians such as Sid Caesar and Robin Williams are able in this way to "speak" many languages. You can probably tell which language you are hearing by listening to the sound of it, even

If parents motivate their children to interact with picture book stories, as the stories are being read, their children's overall language development will be substantially boosted.

though you are unfamiliar with any of the words. French simply doesn't sound like Russian, and neither sounds like Swahili.

The Linguistic Period

Infans is a Latin word meaning "without speech" or "not speaking." The word *infant* is derived from *infans*. It seems logical, then, to consider the first spoken word uttered by a child as the point at which infancy has come to an end.

First Words

Question: When do children usually speak their first word?

When my son Christopher was 7 months old, he looked right at me and said, "dada." Naturally, I assumed that he was showing an inherited intellectual gift by saying his first word at an early age. Oddly, he then looked out the window and said, "dada," and right after that, he looked at the dog and said, "dadadada." On hearing of Christopher's first word (and what he did afterward), my colleagues concluded that the precocious first word was no more than a combination of the cononical stage and parental pride bias. (What nerve!) So, unless you'll take my word about Christopher at 7 months (he looked right at me when he said it!), we will have to yield to studies in which two or more observers heard a child use the same first word appropriately at least two times before they would call it a real "first word." Such studies have shown that first words generally occur between 10 and 17 months, at an average age of 13.6 months (Bloom & Capatides, 1987).

The first words spoken usually relate directly to certain objects or actions (Benedict, 1979). Although generalizing from an adult's experience to a child's is often speculative, you might imagine yourself living in a foreign land, as we discussed earlier. Like a child, you might first acquire words that you could pair directly with some tangible object or obvious action. Children seem to acquire basic nouns and verbs first, such as *mama, wa-wa* (water), or *go*; they learn abstract words later.

The first basic nouns that children use tend to follow the "three bears rule."

Question: What is the three bears rule?

It is simply that a child is most likely to learn a basic noun such as *dog* before learning a subordinate noun such as *collie* or a superordinate noun such as *mammal*. It's called the three bears rule because, as in the story of *Goldilocks and the Three Bears*, the category "mammal" is *too large* and the category "collie" is *too small*, while the category "dog" is *just right* (Gleitman & Wanner, 1984).

Question: Why do children acquire words according to the three bears rule?

Basic words, such as *dog* or *chair*, are perceptually accessible; they don't require abstract cognitive skills to comprehend. Children are simply more likely to be aware of what is easiest to perceive. That seems to be a fairly straightforward explanation for why children acquire basic words first, rather than the more abstract superordinate words.

Why they first acquire basic words rather than subordinate words isn't as obvious. The reason might have to do with the fact that as children acquire language, they continue to organize their experiences into categories in much the same way that they did when hearing their first verbal sounds (recall from the Chapter Preview Peter Eimas's discovery that infants treated all variations of *bin* as identical members of one "bin category"). For example, in one study, 9-month-old infants were habituated to drawings of different kinds of birds (a parakeet, hummingbird, and hawk). None of these infants knew the word *bird* or were very familiar with birds. After habituation, the infants were shown drawings of two *different* birds (a robin and a toucan) and one familiar bird (the hummingbird, which was used as a control). The infants also saw a horse (see Figure 8.1). When tested, the habituated infants reacted to the new kinds of birds as though they were no different from the birds they had already seen. They treated all new birds as though they were all the same—all members of a "bird" category. They reacted strongly to the horse, however, realizing that it was something very different (Roberts, 1988).

This study indicates that infants appear to form basic categories even before they are able to speak. For this reason, the basic category "dog" might be perceptually accessible, while the subordinates "collie" or "poodle" are not readily sorted out or attended to. This tendency to organize perceptions into categories is probably based on an experience-expectant neural process. In other words, it may be the child's nature to do it that way.

Question: When do children learn to use the subordinate?

Preliminary research has indicated that when children are given a new name for something *that they already know by a name,* they will treat the new name as a subordinate. For example, in one study, two different-looking toy dogs were shown to 2-year-olds who already knew that both animals were dogs. One dog was then labeled a "fep." Rather than deciding that both animals were now feps or that one should now be called by the proper name Fep, the children appeared to conclude that the one given a new name was a "fep" kind of dog (Taylor & Gelman, 1989). This level of sophistication, shown even by preschoolers, is remarkable when you consider that bilingual preschoolers, like their monolingual counterparts, will readily reject the idea that an object should have two common names unless one is considering a superordinate or subordinate category of that object, but *will* readily accept that the same object is called by different names in different languages (Au & Glusman, 1990).

Question: When do children acquire superordinate or abstract words?

Words that are more abstract are acquired after basic nouns and verbs. The first abstract words tend to be adjectives, such as *red, tall,* or *big.* Later, terms that are more abstract are acquired, such as the spatial referents *in, on,* and *between.* Finally, children acquire superordinate classifications and other very abstract words, such as *freedom* or *tangential,* items that philosopher Bertrand Russell called "dictionary words" because we learn their definitions verbally rather than by their relationships to real objects. Use of dictionary words among children younger than 5 years is rare, so you can imagine the shock one father received when his 3-year-old daughter, while looking at the clouds lazily drifting by, sighed and

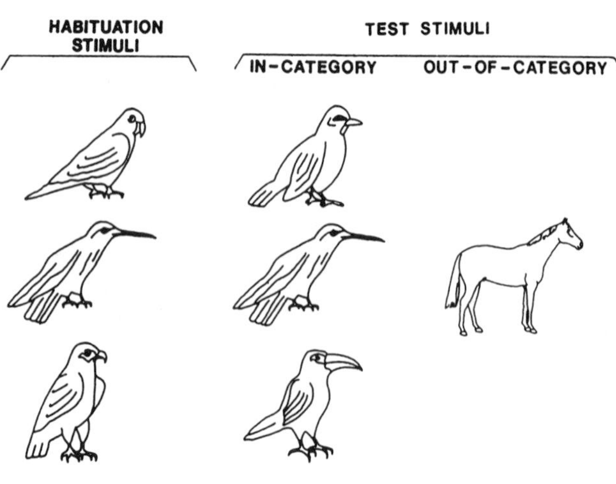

FIGURE 8.1
The stimuli used in Roberts' experiment in which he demonstrated the tendency of 9-month-old infants to perceive differing objects within categories. Following habituation to the habituation stimuli, the infants in the experiment showed no significant increase in response to any of the in-category test stimuli but did show a marked response to the out-of-category stimulus (horse).

said, "When I'm older, I'll be free." He recovered from his shock when she added, "I mean four" (Whitehurst, 1982, p. 379).

ONE-WORD STAGE
The universal stage in language development in which children's speech is limited to single words.

THE ONE-WORD STAGE

The average 1½-year-old child speaks about four or five words. At first, the child will separate words from sentences by listening for emphases. This is why a giraffe might be referred to by a young child as "raf" or an elephant as "e-fant" (Gleitman & Wanner, 1984). The child speaks these new words that he or she is mastering individually rather than putting them together to form a sentence. Thus, this period of language acquisition is called the **one-word stage.** In fact, the child's first "word" is most likely to be expressed in a kind of personal sign language (Acredolo & Goodwyn, 1985).

Question: How can infants learn a sign language?

Infants appear naturally to make specific motions or hand responses—such as an open hand, closed fist, or pointed finger—to variations in the voices they hear as early as 9 weeks of age (Fogel & Hannan, 1985). Of course, such early actions aren't examples of a real sign language, but they show an early tendency to involve the hands in a systematic way during exposure to language. By 1 year of age, however, infants commonly show real "sign" words we can all understand, such as "come here" or "go away," when they wish to communicate their desires through gestures (Goldin-Meadow & Morford, 1985). Gesturing of this kind is a typical rather than a rare phenomenon and is, along with the first spoken words, clearly part of the effort to communicate (Acredolo & Goodwyn, 1988).

Question: When children say their first words, aren't they usually just mimicking something they've heard?

Children at the one-word stage may at first only repeat a word that they have heard. But soon it is obvious that they intend to communicate—if only with single

"Beats me!"

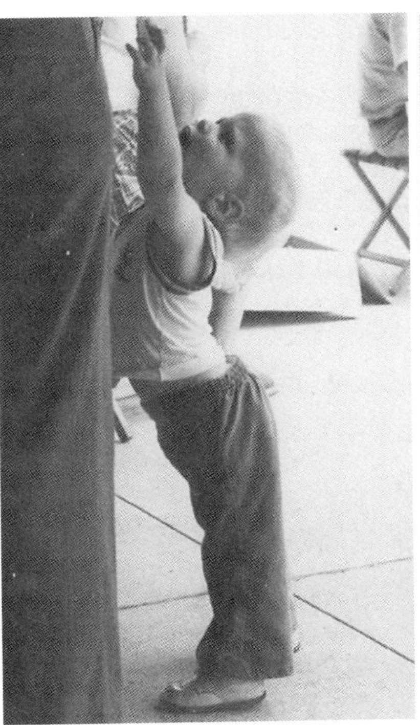
"Pick me up."

"Get me out of here."

NAMING
A development of early childhood in which the child begins pointing out objects and calling them by name. It is considered a special development because it appears to be intrinsically reinforcing and satisfying to humans and seems to occur only in our species.

words. By the time children have a vocabulary of 100 words or more, there is logic behind their choice of words. They usually choose a word that names or points out something new in a particular situation. Later in the one-word stage, they begin to use a chosen word to ask for things (Greenfield & Smith, as cited in Moskowitz, 1978).

Naming Children often know what a word means before they are able to say it. In one study, special equipment was used to measure the direction of 13-month-old infants' glances while the infants listened to an adult say the name of an object. Many objects were present, only one of which was being named. The researchers discovered that these infants, although unable to say the word they heard, were commonly looking at the object being named (Thomas, Campos, Shucard, Ramsay, & Shucard, 1981). (When my son Christopher was 13 months old, he would go get the toy I named and bring it to me without any other coaching, even though he couldn't yet say the name of the toy. Did I tell you that he said "dada" at a *very* early age?)

In another study, brain waves in 14-month-old infants showed distinct differences when words that the infants had learned were deliberately mismatched with objects that the infants had previously associated with particular names (Molfese, Morse, & Peters, 1990). This finding indicates that during the naming process, the brain learns to match objects with names and reacts in a measurable neurological way when a mismatch is perceived.

Once **naming** does start, it is a very important way of acquiring words.

Question: When does the naming process begin?

Because naming must first begin with the focusing of attention, it is said that the rudiments of the naming process may be found in infants as young as 1 month, with sustained eye contact between infant and parent. By about 4 months of age, infants look at objects simply because parents are looking at them (Bruner, 1983). A little later, the parent can get the child to look by just pointing. It is very difficult to get a dog or even a chimpanzee to do the same thing. Have you ever tried to get a dog to look at something by pointing at it? The dog will look at your finger, not where you are pointing. But young children are different. They usually realize that you are directing their attention. Because of this, by the time the child acquires his or her first words, it's very easy for a parent to direct the child's attention to particular objects. As children come to realize that different objects can have names, they begin to pay more attention to those objects (Baldwin & Markman, 1989). This sets the stage for more naming and is a major step in language acquisition.

Pronunciation Interestingly, children often mispronounce the first words that they use. The following is a short conversation between Harvard Professor Roger Brown and a young child (Brown, as cited in Moskowitz, 1978):

CHILD: Fis.
BROWN: Fis?
CHILD: *(Correcting Brown)* Fis!
BROWN: *(Confused)* Fis?
CHILD: Fis!!
BROWN: Fish?
CHILD: Yes, fis.

Although the child couldn't say the word, she obviously knew what it should have sounded like. Surprisingly, when adults present children with a choice between the correct pronunciation of a word and the way the child has been pronouncing the word, the child typically knows that the adult pronunciation is correct (Kuczaj, 1983). Children hear the correct pronunciation and apparently know the correct pronunciation. It's just that when they speak, they tend to simplify what they've heard.

Question: Why do they simplify it? Why don't they just repeat what they hear?

No one is certain. It may be that the speech and language centers in the brains of younger children simply aren't developed enough to make pronunciation easy. It may be that the mouth, palate, and vocal apparatus—which are not fully comparable to an adult's until the child is about 6 years of age—are too immature for good pronunciation (Pappas, 1983; Ostry, Feltham, & Munhall, 1984).

Overextension It is also interesting that when children first use a word, they may understand it to mean something more than you do. In this way, children often overextend the meanings of words. Researchers have examined hundreds of such overextensions in detail. For example, one child was told that the bright, round object in the night sky was called the moon. The child pointed at the moon and called it "mooi." The next few times she said "mooi," however, occurred when she saw a cake and later when she saw round marks on a window. She appeared to have overextended the meaning of *moon* to include any round shape. In another example, a child was told that the sound he heard the rooster make in the morning was called crowing. He called it "koko." The next time he said "koko" was when he heard a tune played on a violin. Later he used the word to describe any music. He apparently had overextended the meaning of *crowing* to include all musiclike sounds (Moskowitz, 1978).

Question: Why do children often overextend the meaning of words?

It really isn't surprising that they do when you think about the task that a child faces when acquiring language. Consider the fact that the average English-speaking high school graduate has a vocabulary of about 40,000 words. If you add in all the names of people and places he or she knows, as well as idiomatic expressions, the number doubles to about 80,000 (Miller & Gildea, 1987). If you figure that this individual has been learning words for about 16 years (since the age of 1), that comes to about 5,000 words a year, or 13 new words each and every day of the young graduate's life! Children with very large vocabularies may acquire words at even twice that rate! No wonder that there is overextension. With a demand to learn at that rate, the only workable strategy would be to grab a word any way you can, get a rough idea of what it means, and go on. The details can wait until later.

Interestingly, when children do nail down a word's definition, they often do it surprisingly quickly. Researchers refer to this ability as **fast mapping.** In a classic study of fast mapping, Susan Carey and Elsa Bartlett (1978) showed 3-year-olds two cafeteria trays, one painted blue, the other olive. The trays were identical in every other way. The children knew what blue was, but most of them called the olive tray either green or brown. The researchers then assigned a nonsense name (*chromium*) for olive. In casual conversation, each child was asked, "Hand me the chromium tray. Not the blue one, the chromium one." Typically, the child would pause, and pointing to the olive tray, ask, "This one?" The experimenter would say, "Yes, that one. Thank you."

One week later, without further guidance, the children were asked to name the colors. Even though they had forgotten the word *chromium,* they *didn't* call the olive tray brown or green. They already knew that the color they were seeing had its own name. Just one exposure had begun the process of reorganizing their color lexicons. Since that experiment was conducted, even children as young as 2 years old have been found able to nail down the correct definitions of words in short order when the words are placed in a context that compels the children to attend

FAST MAPPING
The ability of children to rapidly narrow down the correct meaning of a word.

SYNTAX
The body of linguistic rules that makes it possible to relate a series of words in a sentence to the underlying meaning of that sentence; that is, the rules governing word order in a language (sentence structure).

PHONOLOGY
The study of how sounds (phonemes and phones) are put together to make words.

to a word's limited meaning (Heibeck & Markman, 1987). And preschoolers were found to fast map new words and acquire pretty good ideas as to the words' meanings just from watching television (Rice & Woodsmall, 1988)—which, of course, is not news to parents.

Question: If the trays hadn't been exactly the same shape or size, couldn't the children have gotten confused and thought that chromium referred to something other than color?

That's true, they might have. Even you might. For instance, suppose I said to you, "Please pass me the cup—not the red cup, but the ecru one." You would know that I meant not the red cup but the other cup, but what is ecru? Is it a color, a shape, a style, the name of the manufacturer? Who could tell? In fact, in one study, children were told, "Pass me the gombe block, not the red one or the green one, but the gombe one." They passed the right block all right, but assumed that gombe was a shape and not a color because all of the blocks looked different (Au & Laframboise, 1990).

Eventually, children do map out most of the definitions of the words they know and bring their usage into line with adults' usage. But how can they do that when it is so easy to become confused? The answer appears to lie in the way that many parents, adults, and older children correct younger children when they mislabel an object. The adult or older child tends to refute the child's label and replace it with the correct one. For instance, if the child says, "The ball is yellow," it is common for the listener to say, "It's not yellow, it's orange" (Au & Laframboise, 1990).

This kind of feedback is responsible, in part, for the speed of fast mapping.

First Sentences

Question: When do children first speak in sentences?

Logically, you might assume that they speak their first sentence when they say two words—a noun and a verb—one following the other. But it may be that "sentences" already exist in the one-word stage.

Question: How could that be possible?

Well, not a true sentence, actually, because that would require a verb and a noun. But it is possible that children in the one-word stage possess an understanding of syntax.

Question: What is syntax?

Perhaps this is a good place to make a short excursion into the world of linguistic terms. The **syntax** of a language refers to the rules that describe how words may be put together to form sentences.

Question: I thought that the term grammar *referred to the rules that describe how words may be put together to make sentences.*

Grammar is a broader term than *syntax;* it includes both syntax and phonology. **Phonology** is the study of how sounds (phonemes and phones) are put together to make words.

Question: What did you mean before when you said that children in the one-word stage might have a knowledge of syntax?

Single words, as spoken in the one-word stage (one word per line), may show evidence of an early attempt at syntactic structure when read vertically. Consider the following conversation between psycholinguist Ronald Scollon and Brenda, a child in the one-word stage (Scollon & Bloom, as cited in Moskowitz, 1978):

BRENDA: Ka. Ka. Ka. Ka. *(Car)*
SCOLLON: What?
BRENDA: Go. Go.
SCOLLON: *(Undecipherable)*
BRENDA: Baish. Baish. Baish. Baish. Baish. Baish. Baish. Baish. Baish. *(Bus)*
SCOLLON: What? Oh, bicycle? Is that what you said?
BRENDA: Na. *(Not)*
SCOLLON: No?
BRENDA: Not.
SCOLLON: No. I got it wrong.

HOLOPHRASE
A possible semantic statement made by children in the one-word stage when they utter single words. A holophrase is a single-word "sentence," that is, a one-word utterance that may be interpreted to contain the semantic content of a phrase.

Here Brenda never says more than one word at any given time, which, of course, defines a child in the one-word stage. Still, can we discover an attempt to arrange or structure a "sentence" by reading Brenda's words vertically from top to bottom? Was Brenda saying that hearing the car reminded her that she'd been on the bus the day before and not on the bicycle? What do you think?

As recently as the late 1960s, linguists generally agreed that children in the one-word stage were learning only the names of various objects, actions, or concepts, not syntactic rules. But investigation of the way children order their single-word utterances is turning up evidence that these children already are forming hypotheses about how to put words together to make sentences. In light of these findings, many researchers have begun to use the term **holophrase** to describe these single-word utterances. A holophrase is a one-word "sentence" (Molfese, Molfese, & Carrell, 1982).

Question: How many single words do children usually master before they say a real sentence?

Figure 8.2 illustrates the extremely rapid acquisition of vocabulary in young children. Most children have mastered over 200 words by the time they begin to speak in true sentences. Children's acquisition of words at this time is truly extraordinary. Very often, they will recall and use words that they have heard only

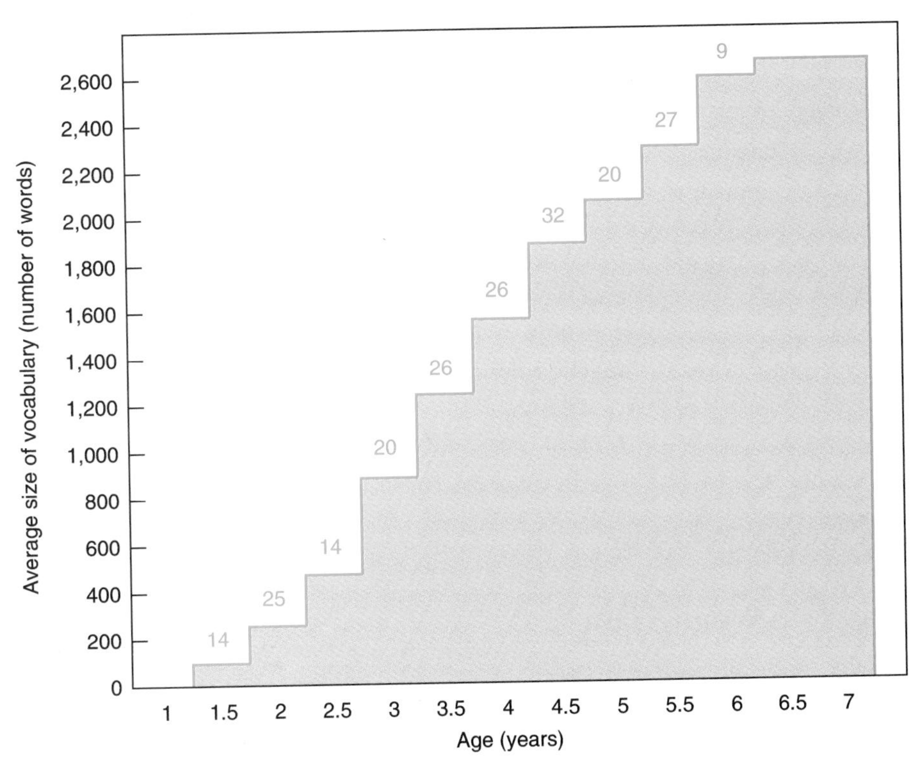

FIGURE 8.2
Typical acquisition of vocabulary in children. Children's average vocabulary size increases rapidly when they are between the ages of $1\frac{1}{2}$ and $6\frac{1}{2}$ years. The number of children tested in each sample age group is shown in color. (Data are based on work done by Madorah E. Smith of the University of Hawaii, as presented by Moskowitz, 1978)

DUO
A two-word utterance made by children during the two-word stage.

TWO-WORD STAGE
The universal stage of language development in which children's expressions are limited to two-word utterances.

once (sometimes to the horror of the parent, considering what the word could be) (Dickinson, 1984).

Question: What most influences how quickly a child's vocabulary will grow?

It was commonly assumed that the child's capacity to learn was the most important factor, but research has shown otherwise. The two major factors are gender and the amount of time that parents spend talking with their children (Huttenlocher, Haight, Bryk, Seltzer, & Lyons, 1991). Not surprisingly, parents who spend more time conversing with their children have youngsters who develop vocabulary at a faster rate. Also, girls acquire vocabulary at a faster rate than boys, even though parents haven't been found to talk more to their daughters than to their sons. Why this occurs is not known.

LEARNING CHECK

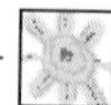

Multiple Choice

1. Language requires
a. the use of signs or symbols.
b. a grammar.
c. the ability to create novel constructions.
d. all of the above.

2. The smallest units of speech that can affect meaning are called
a. phonemes. **b.** consonants. **c.** accents. **d.** phones.

3. Place the following stages in the correct chronological order:
a. cononical. **b.** gooing. **c.** expansion. **d.** phonation.

True or False

4. *Infans* is Latin for "speech."

5. Different accents are based on different phones and phonemes.

6. Normal healthy infants sometimes don't speak their first words until 16 months of age.

7. Often it is difficult to assess a child's language awareness.

Matching

8. ___ Phoneme
9. ___ Grammar
10. ___ Syntax
11. ___ Phonology
12. ___ Goo
13. ___ *Infans*

a. A sound commonly made by 3-month-old infants by combining a precursor consonant with a quasi-vowel
b. "Without speech"
c. The study of how sounds are put together to make words
d. The rules for putting words together to make sentences
e. *m* in "mat" and *b* in "bat"
f. The rules for constructing words and sentences

Answers:
1. d **2.** a **3.** d, b, c, a **4.** False **5.** True **6.** True **7.** True **8.** e **9.** f **10.** d
11. c **12.** a **13.** b

THE TWO-WORD STAGE

By the time children are between 18 and 20 months of age, they have usually begun to utter two-word statements, called **duos.** During this stage (referred to as the **two-word stage**—what else?), children rapidly learn the value of language for expressing concepts and especially the power of language to aid them in communicating their desires to others. At this time, it is not unusual for more than 1,000 new two-word statements to appear monthly (Braine, 1963)! Such two-word utterances enable children to make use of many of the descriptive forms found in language—nominative ("that house"), possessive ("daddy book"), and action ("kitty go"). Throughout the two-word stage, children have a chance to practice these language forms before attempting to expand them. The two-word stage is a universal phenomenon, as shown in Table 8.1.

TELEGRAPHIC SPEECH
Pattern of speech that develops following and including the two-word stage, in which English-speaking children rely on a grammar of strict word order to convey their meaning and do not use conjunctions, prepositions, or other function words.

GRAMMATICAL MORPHEMES
Words or parts of words that help add meaning to a sentence and that are acquired by children generally between the ages of 2½ and 5 years. Conjunctions, prepositions, suffixes, and prefixes are examples of grammatical morphemes. Morphemes are the smallest language units to have meaning and cannot be broken down into smaller meaningful units.

TELEGRAPHIC SPEECH

Question: When do children enter the three-word stage?

Oddly, they don't. Unlike the one-word and two-word stages, which appear to be universal among children, there is no specific three-word stage. Instead, following the two-word stage, children spend the next few years creating many short sentences. Roger Brown at Harvard University has referred to children's sentences during the two-word stage and just after as **telegraphic speech.**

Telegraphic speech is really an apt term. When people send telegrams, at so many cents per word, they want to be brief and to the point; unnecessary words are excluded. Children's telegraphic speech, during the two-word stage and after, is quite similar. A famous example of telegraphic speech can be found in the old Tarzan films. Johnny Weismuller believed that because Tarzan was just getting the hang of English after having lived with the apes for so long, he would speak in a certain way. The speech pattern Weismuller chose in portraying Tarzan was a telegraphic one—that is, rich in important words such as nouns and verbs ("Jane go now," "Boy home soon," "Tarzan help Cheetah"). As you can see, function words are missing; there are no tenses, plurals, conjunctions, articles, prepositions, and so forth. This is typical of telegraphic speech.

To arrange their expressive statements, children during this stage often adopt a grammar of rigid word order. In this rigid word order, the subject is usually placed before the verb, just as it is in normal English word order.

Question: Why do children in the telegraphic stage use a rigid word order?

Without **grammatical morphemes**—for example, conjunctions, prepositions, and suffixes such as *ing* or the plural *s*—many of the more subtle meanings of a language are difficult to convey. Although children who rely on telegraphic speech make some use of the grammatical morphemes they hear to comprehend what is said to them (Gerken, Landau, & Remez, 1990), they generally don't use them

TABLE 8.1

The Two-Word Stage: The Same the World Over

FUNCTION OF UTTERANCE	ENGLISH	GERMAN	RUSSIAN	FINNISH	SAMOAN
Locate, name	There book	Buch da (Book there)	Tasya tam (Tasya there)	Toussa Rina (There Rina)	Keith lea (Keith there)
Demand, desire	More milk	Mehr milch (More milk)	Yesche moloko (More milk)	Anna Rina (Give Rina)	Mai pepe (Give doll)
Indicate possession	My shoe	Mein ball (My ball)	Mami chashka (Mama's cup)	Täti auto (Aunt car)	Lole a'u (Candy my)
Question	Where ball	Wo ball (Where ball)	Gdu papa (Where papa)	Missä pallo (Where ball)	Fea Punafu (Where Punafu)

SOURCE: Liebert, Poulos, & Marmor, 1977, p. 250, as adapted from Slobin, 1970.

in their own speech, at least not at first. Because of this, English-speaking children have to rely greatly on word order to make sure that their own meaning is clear, although they may also rely heavily on inflection and emphasis to understand the meanings of sentences (Weist, 1983).

Language and Meaning

Even from this early language use, it is obvious that the development of grammar and semantics (the meaning in the language) are closely allied. English-speaking children are trying to find a way to link the words together to express a meaning, and rigid word order often allows them to communicate a particular meaning effectively. For example, if your 3-year-old child suddenly informs you, "Kitty follow Ann home," you know from the word order that (a) *Kitty* is the subject, (b) *follow* was the action taken, and (c) *Ann* is about to begin imploring you to keep the cat (such is a parent's life). You can tell that young children use rigid word order to express meanings by performing an experiment. Take your 3-year-old child aside and explain to her, using a *passive* sentence, that "Ann was followed home by the kitty." An interesting thing will happen. A 3-year-old using telegraphic speech and rigid word order will typically ignore such words as *was* or *by* and will only notice that *Ann* came first in the sentence, *follow* came second, and *kitty* came last. The interpretation, as explained by children of this age who hear such passive sentences, would likely be that Ann is now following the cat (Slobin, 1966). Because you and I use function words, we are able to understand that the statement "*Ann* was *followed* home by the *kitty*" does not mean "Ann follow kitty." Although we sometimes rely on word order to express our meaning, we don't rely on it exclusively.

Question: How do you know that children are trying to express meaning with their word order? Maybe children of this age just have a tendency to string words together in a rigid way.

Evidence that children of this age use syntactic structure in an attempt to convey meaning, rather than simply showing a tendency to use rigid word order, comes from examining the acquisition of languages other than English in which the use of a rigid word order does *not* help convey meaning. For example, the Japanese language relies on the use of subjects, objects, and verbs, yet the word order is highly flexible because of the use of small Japanese phonemes called *particles,* which are inserted at different places in the sentence to indicate a word's grammatical role, whether it is a subject, object, or verb. Japanese children in the telegraphic stage, unlike their English-speaking counterparts, show no interest in using a rigid word order; instead, they seem to focus on the position of a particle within a sentence (Hakuta, 1982). It seems, therefore, that a child's early attempts at syntactic use and comprehension are centered on the *semantic* value inherent within the grammatical structure, not on any particular desire to use a rigid word order (Akiyama, 1985). These differences also are observed when considering Western languages. For instance, whereas American children rely on word order to convey and understand meaning, Italian children rely primarily on semantic cues. In one study, American and Italian children were presented with the sentence, "The pencil kicked the cow." The majority of American children chose the pencil as the subject of the sentence (as dictated by word order), whereas most of the Italian children chose the cow (dictated by the fact that pencils don't kick, and therefore a kicking pencil is meaningless) (Bates et al., 1984).

Grammatical Morphemes

Question: How do children acquire the grammatical morphemes that adults use?

Findings indicate that children throughout the world acquire grammatical morphemes in the same general order, although at different rates (deVilliers & de-

Villiers, 1973). In Table 8.2, you will see 14 grammatical morphemes used in the English language, given in the general order in which children acquire them. This sequence of acquisition is so pervasive that even children who are hard of hearing or who have language disorders acquire these grammatical morphemes in this same order (Khan & James, 1983; Brown, 1984).

Question: Why do children learn grammatical morphemes in this order?

Researchers aren't certain, although the order may have to do with the complexity of each task. Return for a moment to that foreign land to which you were sent earlier in this chapter. Once you had acquired single words and then two-word phrases and had begun to string them together in a clipped, telegraphic manner, you, too, would slowly begin to acquire grammatical morphemes. But in what order? The answer might be that you would learn the simplest and most obvious ones first. This may be exactly what children do. They learn the easiest and most obvious rule first and then simply begin to apply it.

Other researchers have argued that it's not complexity that determines the order of acquisition, but functionality (MacWhinney, 1978). In other words, the order of acquisition is determined by how much function each grammatical morpheme serves; the ones providing the child with the most value or function are learned first. For example, expressing plurals and locations is more useful in day-to-day conversation than using a copula (you may have even gotten through the whole day without feeling a deep need to use one).

For some time it was assumed that the child's language needed a syntactic structure on which grammatical morphemes could be built. The idea here was that a child needed a certain level of comprehension to grasp the meaning of any of the grammatical morphemes, a comprehension level that included a syntax (i.e., the ability to form a sentence). As you will notice, all 14 of the grammatical morphemes in Table 8.2 have a semantic structure, or meaning; each carries information. However, careful examination has found that the plural may be used correctly by children in the one-word stage, when they may say, for instance, "dogs" when they clearly mean more than one dog (Mervis & Johnson, 1991).

TABLE 8.2

Fourteen English Grammatical Morphemes

FORM	MEANING	EXAMPLE
1. Present progressive: *ing*	Ongoing process	He is sitt*ing* down.
2. Preposition: *in*	Containment	The mouse is *in* the box.
3. Preposition: *on*	Support	The book is *on* the table.
4. Plural: *s*	Number	The dog*s* ran away.
5. Past irregular: e.g., *went*	Earlier in time relative to time of speaking	The boy *went* home.
6. Possessive: *'s*	Possession	The girl*'s* dog is big.
7. Uncontractible copula *be:* e.g., *are, was*	Number; earlier in time	*Are* they boys or girls? *Was* that a dog?
8. Articles: *the, a*	Definite/indefinite	He has *a* book.
9. Past regular: *ed*	Earlier in time	He jump*ed* the stream.
10. Third person regular: *s*	Number; earlier in time	She run*s* fast.
11. Third person irregular: e.g., *has, does*	Number; earlier in time	*Does* the dog bark?
12. Uncontractible auxiliary *be:* e.g., *is, were*	Number; earlier in time; ongoing process	*Is* he running? *Were* they at home?
13. Contractible copula *be:* e.g., *'s, 're*	Number; earlier in time	That*'s* a spaniel.
14. Contractible auxiliary *be:* e.g., *'s, 're*	Number; earlier in time; ongoing process	They*'re* running very slowly.

SOURCE: Clark & Clark, 1977; based on Brown, 1973.

Question: How do you know that they understand the rule and are not simply repeating the word dogs?

In 1958, J. Berko demonstrated this by asking children to answer the question posed in Figure 8.3. The children correctly answered, "Wugs," a clear demonstration that they had learned the plural rule, because they obviously had never before heard the word *wugs.* In fact, children often are not aware that they have acquired these rules. And now we see that even children in the one-word stage are able to grasp some of these rules. To know so much and yet be able to say only one word at a time brings us back to the concept of a holophrase. Although children in the one-word stage may be able to only say single words at a time, their comprehension is clearly much broader than single-word utterances might suggest.

IRREGULAR WORDS

English, like many other languages, contains a number of words that are exceptions to the rule. Children's early attempts to handle these words give us clues to their acquisition of grammar rules. Parents are sometimes dismayed to hear their young child switch from "Mommy go" to "Mommy goed." At first it sounds as though the child is regressing and is becoming less competent. Actually, the child has advanced and is now using the past regular by adding the suffix *ed.* It's not the child's fault that the past tense of *go* is *went. Go* is simply an irregular English word. Frankly, it is hard to argue with the child's logic. Why shouldn't it be *goed* instead of *went?* Children during this time make many similar errors. *One foot—obviously two foots; one man—two mans;* and going in the other direction, although it is a less common error, *many clothes—one clo.* Such overregularization—that is, applying the rule in each and every case—demonstrates the rapid acquisition of the general rules of grammar. The exceptions are acquired later.

Question: But why do children make overregularizations in the first place? That is, why don't they just learn the exceptions like they learn other words?

They do learn the exceptions like they learn regular words. In fact, if adults use a particular irregular word often enough, the child will be far less likely to overregularize it (Marcus et al., 1992). What appears to happen is that the child learns grammar rules and irregular exceptions to those rules separately. For instance, imagine a child who wishes to refer to *feet.* First, she will search her memory for the right word. If she has heard the irregular word *feet* often enough she will, in fact, use that word, which is why older children almost never overregularize an irregular word. If, on the other hand, she hasn't heard the exception applied correctly often enough, she will come up with the less complex word *foot,* and then apply the plural rule which yields *foots* (Marcus et al., 1992).

FIGURE 8.3
An example of the "wugs" used by Berko in her study of the acquisition of language rules. (*Source:* Berko, 1958, p. 154)

THE DEVELOPMENT OF SYNTACTIC SKILLS

Beginning with the holophrase, children acquire the rules and knowledge necessary to construct utterances with a growing complexity of syntax. Table 8.3 provides a synopsis of the acquisition of a child's syntactic skills. The second column, MLU (which stands for "mean length of utterance"), is simply the average number of words that a child uses during each utterance at any given time. You may also notice that the example "kitty in basket" (between the ages of 2½ and 3 years) is an instance of telegraphic speech.

Question: Given that children eventually learn the rules of grammar, wouldn't Tarzan have done so, too? After all, he listened to Jane a lot, and she spoke very well.

Edgar Rice Burroughs, the author of the Tarzan books, certainly thought so. As his readers know, Tarzan was depicted as an extremely well-spoken man, who eventually became fluent in many languages. And as you have pointed out, he listened to Jane and she spoke quite well, which brings us to our next topic: caretaker speech.

CARETAKER SPEECH*

Until about the age of 3 years, children learn to construct their language according to their parents' usage. After this time, peers also become important models. Interestingly, adults who interact with children restructure their language for the children's benefit, often quite unconsciously (Blewitt, 1983). This restructured language is called **caretaker speech,** and it differs in a number of ways from the language generally used by adults to communicate with one another. Caretaker speech is characterized by short, simple sentences. The sentences are usually said in a relatively high-pitched voice, with the highest pitches used for emphasis (Fernald & Mazzie, 1991), and often with exaggerated inflections and intonations

CARETAKER SPEECH
A speech pattern used in addressing others who are obviously less competent in their speech than is the speaker. Universally applied, caretaker speech is characterized by short, simple sentences, simple vocabulary, a relatively high-pitched voice, and exaggerated inflections. It should not be confused with baby talk, which refers only to the simplification of individual words, such as saying "wa-wa" for water.

*Also known as "motherese" or "caregiver speech."

TABLE 8.3

The Development of Syntactic Skills

AGE (IN YEARS)	MLU	SYNTACTIC SKILLS	EXAMPLES
1½ to 2½	1.5	One-word utterances, called *holophrases,* and two-word utterances, called *duos.* The children can express basic semantic relationships, such as:	
		Recurrence	*More ball.*
		Nonexistence	*All gone ball.*
		Attribution	*Big ball.*
		Possession	*My ball.*
		Nominations	*That ball.*
		Agent-action	*Adam hit.*
		Agent-action-object	*Adam hit ball.*
2½ to 3	2.25	Grammatical morphemes are added, such as:	
		Present progressive inflection	*I walking.*
		Locative prepositions	*Kitty in basket.*
		Plurals	*Two balls.*
		Possessive	*Adam's ball.*
		Past	*It broke.*
		Verb inflections	*He walks.*
3 to 3½	2.75	Auxiliary verbs	*I am walking.* *I do like you.*
		Negative particles	*I didn't do it.* *This isn't ice cream.*
		Yes–no questions	*Will I go?* *Do you want it?*
		Wh questions	*What do you have?* *Where is the doggie?*
3½ to 4	3.25	Sentence clauses	*You think I can do it.* *I see what you made.*
4 to 5	3.75	Conjunctions of two sentences	*You think I can, but I can't.* *Mary and I are going.*
> 5	> 4	Reversible passives	*The truck was chased by the car.*
		Connectives	*I am going to go although I don't want to.*
		Indirect object–direct object constructions	*The man showed the boy the friend.*
		Pronominalization	*He knew that John was going to win the race.*

SOURCE: Whitehurst, 1982, p. 371.

(Ratner & Pye, 1984). The vocabulary is simple, and individual words are sometimes simplified by reducing their phonetic complexity. Caretaker speech appears to be a universal phenomenon. It is just as likely to occur, for instance, whether the adult interacting with an infant is speaking English, German, or Mandarin Chinese (Grieser & Kuhl, 1988). Caretaker speech is also richer in information than the kind of speech adults direct toward each other. In one experiment, for instance, five different types of comments were made either to infants or to other adults. The comments reflected a bid for attention, approval, prohibition, comfort, or playing peek-a-boo (since peek-a-boo isn't an adult interaction, answering the telephone and starting a conversation was substituted for adults). The comments were then electronically filtered to remove all but the intonation. No individual words could be discerned. The resulting tone patterns associated with these comments are shown in Figure 8.4. Interestingly, when subjects were asked to distinguish the five categories based on intonation alone, they were only able to do so if listening to the infant-directed speech patterns, because they were able to rely

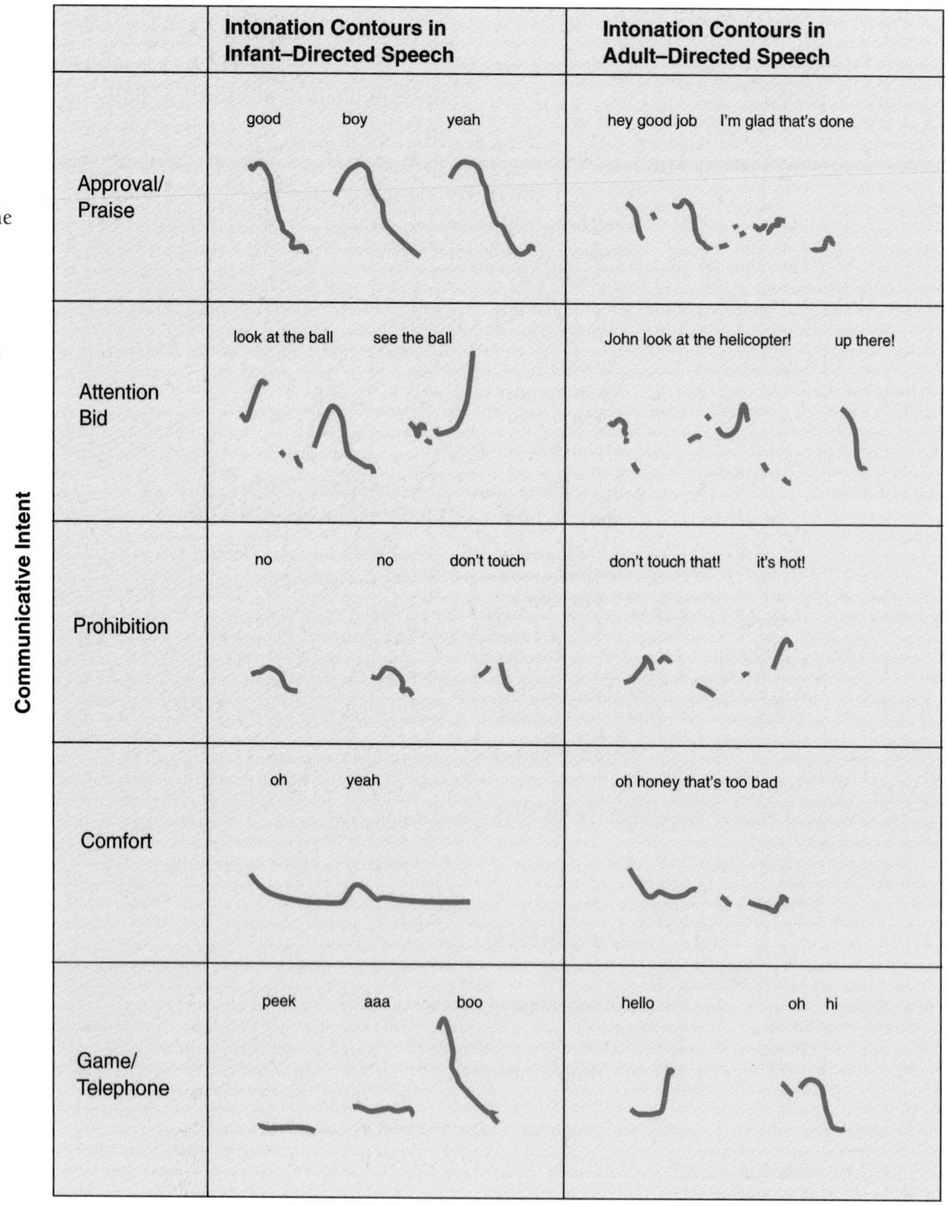

FIGURE 8.4

In Anne Fernald's experiment, five different types of comments were made either to infants or to other adults. The comments reflected a bid for attention, approval, prohibition, comfort, or game/telephone. The comments were electronically filtered, removing all but the intonation. When subjects were asked to distinguish the five categories based only on intonation, they were able to do so only for the infant-directed speech patterns. (*Source:* Fernald, 1989, p. 1501)

Communicative Intent

	Intonation Contours in Infant–Directed Speech	Intonation Contours in Adult–Directed Speech
Approval/ Praise	good boy yeah	hey good job I'm glad that's done
Attention Bid	look at the ball see the ball	John look at the helicopter! up there!
Prohibition	no no don't touch	don't touch that! it's hot!
Comfort	oh yeah	oh honey that's too bad
Game/ Telephone	peek aaa boo	hello oh hi

on the tonal content of the caretaker speech that had been used when talking to the infants (Fernald, 1989). This study shows that caretaker speech is rich in additional tonal information, like a melody accompanying words, which helps to communicate the speaker's intentions more clearly than adult-directed speech.

As you can imagine, caretaker speech enables the child to grasp the language more easily. Returning for a moment to the foreign country you visited at the beginning of this chapter, you would no doubt have found it helpful if the local friends you acquired had adjusted their speech for you, so that their sentences were shorter, simpler, and less involved than the speech they used with their native friends. Indeed, you might readily do the same for a friend of yours who is just learning English. Even young children may adjust their speech to the level of the person to whom they are speaking (Dunn & Kendrick, 1982a). Consider a conversation held by the same 4-year-old child, first with an adult and then with a 2-year-old.

> **A.M. to adult:** You're supposed to put one of these persons in, see? Then one goes with the other little girl. And then the little boy. He's the little boy and he drives. And then they back up. And then the little girl has marbles. . . . And then the little girl falls out. And then it goes backwards.
>
> **A.M. to 2-year-old child:** Watch, Perry, watch this. He's backing in here. Now he drives up. Look, Perry. Look here, Perry. Those are marbles, Perry. Put the men in here. Now I'll do it. (Shatz & Gelman, 1973)

As you can see, the 4-year-old adjusted his speech so that the 2-year-old would be more likely to understand what was being said.

Parents engaging in caretaker speech help their children to acquire language. Parents and older children regularly adjust their speech to a level just slightly above that of the younger child to whom they are speaking. Correcting a child's grammar in slow, easy steps also can help the child to focus on and acquire the next language advances (Goldstein, 1984; Rondal, 1985).

Question: Isn't it bad to use baby talk or caretaker speech? Won't that just encourage the child to speak that way?

Many years ago, it was argued by some people that "common sense" shows that if you use baby talk, then baby talk is what the infant will learn. Even so, people continued to use baby talk or caretaker speech, either through their own natural inclination or because the baby wouldn't pay attention to them if they didn't. They took comfort in the fact that baby talk had been used by parents for centuries, yet it was *not* what babies eventually learned. Furthermore, parents simply don't keep using baby talk after the child gets older and wants to hold a more sophisticated conversation. For these reasons, researchers have adopted the view that the use of baby talk by parents is harmless and probably beneficial.

Parents or care givers also provide important guidance by correcting semantic aspects of a child's language.

Question: What do you mean by semantic aspects of a child's language?

This refers to correcting the child's understanding of what words *mean*. Although parents will often correct or shape their children's grammar (Bohannon & Stanowicz, 1988), they will also spend time correcting semantic comprehension (Brown & Hanlon, 1970; Ninio & Bruner, 1978). For instance, if a child looks at a lighthouse and calls it a farmhouse, the parent is likely to correct the child. This kind of parental correction, or feedback, may be invaluable for semantic acquisition.

Question: What would happen if parents never used caretaker speech and didn't adjust their conversations when they interacted with their child?

Because caretaker speech is a universal phenomenon, we have few chances of examining what might happen. Without caretaker speech, children might be unable to acquire language. You will recall the case study of the hearing child of deaf parents, who learned sign language but never learned to speak English, even though he was exposed to the television set daily (see Chapter 1). This is not surprising. Do you think that you could learn Turkish by watching old Turkish movies on TV? Perhaps you'd catch a phrase or two, perhaps even a few words, but without caretaker speech or the opportunity to interact in conversations, you might be lost forever among the strange phonemes.

Question: Why is caretaker speech universal?

This is a nature-nurture question that has not been resolved. We do know that the presence of the infant or child is important. Even an experienced parent is unable to produce fully adequate caretaker speech if the child isn't present (Snow, 1972). Furthermore, nonparents who have little experience with infants will engage in caretaker speech that is as rich in quality as parents possess (Jacobson, Boersma, Fields, & Olson, 1983). We also know that as the child's world and interests expand, the parents adjust their caretaker speech to keep just slightly ahead of the child's abilities (Molfese, Molfese, & Carrell, 1982). But whether adults change their behavior in these ways owing to a biological propensity or because they are shaped by the child's positive reaction to caretaker speech is unknown (Jacobson, Boersma, Fields, & Olson, 1983).

Nativists, who believe that it is human nature to acquire language, argue that the presence of a child is a sign stimulus that increases the rate of caretaker speech among those present. Learning theorists, on the other hand, argue that when a person is interacting with a child, that person is quickly "persuaded," as a function of shaping, to adjust his or her speech, because the younger child attends more closely to simpler sentences. Learning theorists argue that for the same reason, caretaker inflections may be the result of shaping. For instance, a higher-pitched voice, as a contrasting stimulus, attracts the child's attention and therefore reinforces the care giver. Theories of language acquisition are ripe with such nature-nurture questions. (See At Issue.)

The Function of Grammar

How do children learn to express themselves through language? Can you recall from your own childhood how you learned to express what you wanted to say? In fact, are you even aware of how you currently go about deciding how to express yourself? Suppose that you are working in the hot sun and are becoming thirsty. How do you express a desire for a glass of water? How do you tell your friend on the job that you think it's time to take a break and get a drink? How do you express your meaning in a structured sentence?

Question: I just say, "Let's take a break and get a drink of water." Isn't it just as simple as that?

Was that simple? How did you come up with that sentence? Did you just string the words together? Were some words more important than others? Could you have strung them together differently?

When you put together that sentence, "Let's take a break and get a drink of water," did you begin by searching your entire vocabulary until you struck upon the contraction *let's,* which you then decided was the best first word? A language computer might perform that way. Then did you go through another search for the next word and finally choose *take?* No, you didn't. People don't sort through their vocabularies before speaking each word, as a machine might. People build the structure or syntax of a sentence to express a meaning, and they do this before they begin to speak.

Question: How can you know that people form their sentences before they begin to speak them?

We can obtain clues about the way people organize syntax to express their meaning by examining **spoonerisms.** Spoonerisms are rather interesting transpositions named after William A. Spooner (1844–1930), an English clergyman well known for accidentally making such rearrangements. No doubt you've occasionally committed a spoonerism yourself. I think of a theater usher who recently baffled my friends and me when he asked, "Would you like me to sew you to your sheets?" Everyone soon realized that he had meant to say, "Would you like me to show you to your seats?" What this spoonerism demonstrates, though, is that the usher had to have had the word *seats* in mind (the tenth word in the sentence) before he ever said *show* (the sixth word), or how could he have gotten them confused? People prepare their syntactic structures before they say them; they don't simply link one word to the next (Motley, 1985).

Question: How would a child, then, choose a starting place for building a sentence?

That's not an easy question to answer. Language theorists have debated and wondered about this for years. There are those who believe that children use some as-yet-unknown processing system to go from the meaning they wish to express to the syntax they use. Noam Chomsky (1957), a well-known and respected linguist, has proposed the existence of a **language acquisition device,** or LAD, that has evolved in our species to handle the interaction between syntax and semantics. This is akin to the innate grammar addressed by Derek Bickerton when he planned to study the development of creole in children. Others, like Henrietta Lempert (whom we shall discuss in a moment), place greater emphasis on semantic aspects as a driving force behind syntactic structure.

Question: What do you mean when you say that some semantic aspect might drive the formation of syntax?

Earlier, we used the active sentence "Kitty follow[ed] Ann home," and then we used the passive voice, "Ann was followed home by the kitty." Both sentences really say the same thing. It makes you wonder why there should even be a passive voice. What's the point of having two ways to say the same thing? I wonder how the passive form got started. I have this fleeting image of a caveman one day announcing to his friends, "This new thing—the passive voice—has been invented by me. With it, we can be amused and our enemies will be confused!" But odds are it didn't happen that way. Instead, the passive voice (as just one of many examples of our grammar) seems to have evolved from our need to express ourselves.

Researcher Henrietta Lempert believes that the way constructions such as the passive voice may have gotten started, and the reason children find them useful to acquire, has to do with the need to express a particular *topic*—not with some rule of grammar.

Question: What do you mean when you stress topic, rather than grammar, as the motivation for using the passive voice?

Consider the following incident: A bus hit a dog. If it were your dog and you wanted to talk about what happened to your dog, *your dog* would be the topic of concern. You would start your statement with "My dog." But then where do you go? My dog—what? You can't say, "My dog hit the bus"; that's not what happened. Instead, you are forced to say, "My dog *was hit by the bus*"—the passive voice.

SPOONERISM
An unintentional transposition of sounds in a sentence, for example, "People in glass houses shouldn't stow thrones." Named for the English clergyman William A. Spooner (1844–1930), who was well known for such errors.

LANGUAGE ACQUISITION DEVICE (LAD)
As hypothesized by Noam Chomsky a neural structure inborn in every healthy individual that is preprogrammed with the underlying rules of a universal form of grammar. Once the child is exposed to a particular language, he or she selects from the complete set of rules with which he or she was born only those rules required by the language he or she will be speaking. Most psychologists and linguists currently find the idea interesting, but agree that a proof is doubtful because it is so difficult to find ways to demonstrate the existence of such a hypothesized device.

AT ISSUE

Children and the Origins of Language

One of the longest ongoing debates concerning language development involves whether language is basically a learned phenomenon or whether we, as a species, are biogenetically "prewired" for its acquisition. In fact, research concerning this debate is thousands of years old.

Question: What kind of research concerning language acquisition was conducted thousands of years ago?

According to the ancient Greek historian Herodotus, in the seventh century B.C. the Egyptian pharaoh Psamtik the First had two newborns raised in silence to see what language they would eventually come to speak. The Egyptians didn't know quite what to make of the "language" that the children eventually spoke, but concluded that it sounded something like Phrygian, although it obviously wasn't.

Other attempts were made throughout history—by Frederick II of Sicily, James IV of Scotland, and Akbar, emperor of India from 1556–1605, to name the most notable. The reports concluded that children not exposed to language either failed to learn any language or spoke a gibberish of some sort. Frederick II was especially disappointed by these results because he had hoped that the children in his experiment, left undisturbed by exposure to common language, would come to speak the pure language that God had intended them to speak—which Frederick assumed to be Latin, although others had argued that it would be Greek.

Akbar, however, noted that all his little victims had turned out mute. He was pleased with this result because he had said all along that exposure to language was a requirement for its acquisition. Fortunately, none of the other emperors of India who followed him were interested in replicating or building on his "research."

Today, of course, we know that children must have contact with a particular language before they can be expected to speak it and that Latin won't spring from the mouth of anyone not exposed to it. But modern researchers still wonder if our childhood isn't a special time during which we apply a natural inborn grammar to the words we hear for the first time and if, in fact, children aren't the ones responsible for the creation of new languages.

Question: What do you mean by an "inborn grammar," and how can children be responsible for the creation of new languages?

Let's look at these questions one at a time. First, consider the case of a 13-year-old girl found wandering the streets of a California city in 1970. She was lost because she had escaped from an abusive parent who had kept her in total isolation since she was 18 months old. She was unable to speak a single word—because she didn't know any. Like the children experimented on by Akbar, she had not been exposed to any language (Berreby, 1992). After years of rehabilitation, the girl became a functioning adult. Her intelligence scores were adequate so long as the tests given were nonverbal intelligence tests—tests that don't require a verbal answer. In spite of her remarkable recovery, her language was limited to that of a 2-year-old. As far as complex adult language was concerned, she just never caught on to it. Because it is unethical to conduct the kind of experiment tried by Akbar and various other rulers throughout history, we typically find that case studies like this one form the basis for many of our modern assumptions concerning language formation. Because of this case and others like it, researchers wonder if experience with some sort of grammar during childhood isn't a prerequisite for mature language acquisition.

Question: Why would a child need to use a grammar during childhood to speak a language fully as an adult?

Many researchers believe that humans have evolved a language capacity that includes a brain equipped, perhaps at birth, with a form of rudimentary grammar (Chomsky, 1957). Even more controversial is the idea that children naturally impose this inborn grammar early in their development, somehow laying down the neurological groundwork on which the grammar of their own language can be built. The idea, then, is that through corrections and modeling, parents reshape this inborn grammar until the children eventually come to learn the *specific grammar* of the language that their family is speaking.

Question: Is there any way to tell if children are using an inborn grammar early on in their development?

There may be. There have been many times and places in history in which peoples of different languages have been thrown together. In Hawaii, for example, there is even the term *four-blood,* which refers to someone whose grandparents are each from a different heritage and culture. For centuries, plantation workers in different parts

AT ISSUE

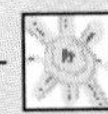

of the world often found themselves brought together by circumstances. Germans worked with Chinese, French with Vietnamese, and Portuguese with just about everybody. Sometimes, especially on plantations in French Guiana, as many as 12 groups might be working together, each speaking a different language. To get by, people often tried to get a handle on one another's language by picking up a few hundred words and sayings from each other. This approach led to the creation of a "broken" English, French, Japanese, and so forth, known as **pidgin.** For example, to express "They put the body in the ground and covered it with a blanket, and that was all," someone speaking pidgin English was recorded as saying, "Inside dirt and cover and blanket, finish" (Berreby, 1992, p. 47). With a little effort, you might understand what this person was saying, especially if you know the context, but it certainly isn't clear, acceptable English.

But people could usually get by with pidgin while working with others in the fields and then speak their native tongues at home. What makes a confluence of different language speakers so interesting, however, is how their children interact. The children typically enrich pidgin by combining many of the words from the languages they use while playing together and then apply a grammatical structure to it. This newly emerging "language," known as a **creole,** may explain how new languages and dialects get started: The children create them!

Question: Is the creole that forms a new language based on an inborn grammar?

That's the big question. Some say that it is. Creole "languages" throughout the world appear to be formed by the children of people with different native tongues who come together, usually at the borders of nations speaking different languages. Different creole "languages" also have many points in common. Some argue, however, that most creoles have common antecedents, often Portuguese or African, and that these commonalities among creole "languages" are reflective of common linguistic roots rather than genetic ones. And yet, we have to ask, could it be that creole tongues have much in common because they are reflecting a natural grammar we have all inherited? Researchers like linguist Derek Bickerton believe that even if it isn't so, children's creole is directly based on the deep grammatical structure within us all.

Question: Is there any way to find out if creole grammar, or some other form of grammar, is inborn?

In 1978, Derek Bickerton actually found an uninhabited island 300 miles east of the Philippines for an experiment that might address this question. He received a grant to populate the island with six young families, each speaking a language very different from the others. Wells were to be dug and homes built for the experiment, which was to last one year. The idea was to give the six families, including their children, 200 made-up words for different objects and actions, thereby creating a common pidgin that the families could use. Then the children would play together each day and their creole, if they in fact created one, would be examined.

Question: What were the results?

Some felt that the experiment might not be ethical because it required isolating the children for experimental purposes. The legacy of Akbar was still on people's minds five centuries later, and with good reason. Medical facilities and other emergency services were many hours away from the island—which would have virtually marooned the children who were to participate in the experiment. Thus, the National Science Foundation withdrew the grant. Not to be deterred, however, Derek Bickerton is trying again with new funding and a less isolated location on an estate in Europe, where eight families, two each of Greek, Flemish, Basque, and Hungarian speakers, will be living.

Question: Do you think that his experiment will uncover evidence of an innate grammar?

I think that Bickerton gave the best answer to that question when he said,

> Whether my hypotheses are supported or not, I don't much care. What I do care about are the things that we shall know for the first time. I want to discover things. And I think we're going to have some fun. (Berreby, 1992, p. 53)

Lempert demonstrated in experiments that children of 2 to 5 years could acquire such forms of expression as the passive voice, *especially* if the topic were, like the dog in our example, animate and live (Lempert, 1989). Live and animate things attract children's attention and are likely to become main topics for them. On the other hand, the children had great difficulty understanding the passive voice if the topic was inanimate and stationary (Lempert, 1984, 1989). The passive voice, then, was easy for the children to learn if their main interest was to express a

PIDGIN
A simplified form of speech typically derived from a mixture of two or more languages. It has as its basis a rudimentary form of grammar and vocabulary and is generally used for communication between people speaking different languages.

CREOLE
A mixture of language that develops when groups speaking different languages have prolonged contact. Typically, the basic vocabulary of the dominant language is combined with the grammar of a subordinate language, creating an admixture (a mingling within a mixture) of words and grammar that becomes in itself a new subordinate and creolized language.

particular topic. As in our example, they placed the topic first in the sentence, which in turn necessitated use of the passive voice. When it was used simply as a grammatical form without an attractive topic up front in the lead position, children had difficulty understanding the passive voice. Perhaps our grammar works that way. We start with a central topic and then try to build from it. This, in turn, may lead to a series of complicated grammatical forms, all of which have a use, namely, to support the topic. Such an assumption is incredibly difficult to demonstrate, however, and no one knows for sure whether this approach is correct (Bock, 1990).

As you've come to appreciate, language and language acquisition are anything but simple. It may be many years before we fully understand how language develops in humans. But the work has begun, and future results promise to be interesting.

LEARNING CHECK

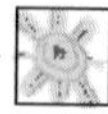

Multiple Choice

1. A 2-year-old child is most likely to be
a. in the one-word stage. **c.** using function words.
b. in the two-word stage. **d.** none of the above.

2. "Jane go now" is an example of
a. telegraphic speech.
b. rigid word order.
c. a sentence that lacks grammatical morphemes.
d. all of the above.

3. If you are speaking to 3-year-old children and you restate your sentence in the passive form,
a. they no longer understand the words.
b. they cannot imitate what you have said.
c. they often assume that the meaning has changed.
d. they usually realize that the meaning has not changed.

4. When a child switches from "Daddy do it" to "Daddy doed it,"
a. the child is regressing.
b. the child is advancing in language competence.
c. the child has not been listening carefully to you.
d. it is because the past of *do* is regular.

5. It appears that creole is first formed by the ____________ of a culture.
a. children **c.** English speakers
b. pidgin-speaking adults **d.** leaders

Matching

6. ____ MLU
7. ____ Duos
8. ____ Spoonerisms
9. ____ Grammatical morphemes
10. ____ Caretaker speech

a. The smallest language units to have meaning
b. Unintentional transpositions of sounds in a sentence
c. Characterized by short, simple sentences, a relatively high-pitched voice, and exaggerated inflections
d. The average number of words that a child uses during each utterance
e. Two-word utterances

Answers: 1. b 2. d 3. c 4. b 5. a 6. d 7. e 8. b 9. a 10. c

APPLICATIONS

Strike When the Iron Is Hot

Earlier in this chapter, we discussed the importance of naming as a major step in the acquisition of language. But whether a child will learn a new name for something often depends on his or her motivation. For example, let's consider an experiment conducted by Marta Valdez-Menchaca and Grover Whitehurst (1988). In this experiment, English-speaking preschool children were divided into an experimental group and a control group. Then both groups of children were taught the Spanish names of some attractive toys that were out of reach. The children were then told that if they wanted to play with any of the toys, they would have to ask for them by their Spanish names.

When the children were first taught the Spanish names for the toys, however, the two groups were treated differently. Children in the experimental group were taught the Spanish name of a toy only when they expressed an interest in playing with it. Children in the control group were told the Spanish names of the toys just as often, but at random times.

The results were revealing. Children in the experimental group learned the new words at a faster rate and remembered more of them than did children from the control group. The best way to teach children new names for objects, then, is to "strike when the iron is hot," that is, to engage them in naming when they show an interest in the object to be named.

Question: But does it really matter? Wouldn't children eventually learn the names of things anyway, even if their parents or teachers didn't pay special attention to the times when the children were most interested and motivated to learn?

No doubt any healthy child would eventually learn the names of things. The main point being made by the experiment is not that there is a way to accelerate children's acquisition of names, but rather that children's motivation plays an important role in the acquisition of language.

In fact, the motivational aspect of language acquisition goes beyond just the learning of names for things. To illustrate, consider another experiment conducted by Grover Whitehurst and his colleagues (1988). In this second experiment, it was demonstrated that if parents motivate their children to interact with picture book stories as the stories are being read, their children's overall language development will be substantially boosted. When carrying out this experiment, the researchers gathered 30 middle-class parents and their 2- to 3-year-old children. Half the children were placed in an experimental reading program, conducted in their own homes, for 1 month. The other half served as controls.

In the experimental group, one of the parents, most often the mother, was given a one-hour training session in which she was taught a special way to read to her child. Unlike most parents who might simply read a story straight through, she was taught to stop from time to time and ask open-ended questions, often beginning her question with the word *what.* She was also instructed not to ask questions that could simply be answered with a yes or no, or by pointing, or by giving a simple name. For example, "Who's that?" is a poor question because it simply requires the child to give a name. A far better question would be "There's Eeyore. What's happening to him?" This effective question requires the child to elaborate about the story. Parents were also asked to expand on the answers that their children gave by providing alternative explanations or by asking progressively more challenging questions.

Parents in the control group read stories to their children in their usual way. Children in both groups were read to just as often—about eight times a week.

At the beginning of the study, children in both groups did not differ in their language ability. This is, of course, what one would expect because the children had been assigned to one group or the other randomly. But after only 1 month with the new reading technique, children in the experimental group were 8½ months ahead of the control group children on a standard measure commonly used to assess verbal expression (the Illinois Test of Psycholinguistic Abilities, which requires children to tell the experimenter as much as possible about various objects) and 6 months ahead on another standard measure commonly used to test vocabulary (the Expressive One Word Picture Vocabulary Test). This all seems to have occurred as the consequence of a change of parental reading style, itself the result of nothing more than a simple one-hour training session!

Question: Are these results long-lasting, or will the control group children soon catch up?

After 9 months had passed, the chil-

Applications

dren from both groups were tested once again. The results showed that the experimental group children still maintained a 6-month advantage over the children from the control group.

Question: Do you think that the advantage will be maintained over longer periods of time and that the advantage is an important one?

Further follow-up studies have yet to be conducted, so it is not known if the advantage will continue. However, there are correlational data that show that reading to children is associated with literacy and high teacher ratings of oral language skill as well as with reading comprehension (Wells, 1985). It has also been shown that children who are exposed to interactive reading at age 2½ are among the most advanced in language development at age 4½ (Crain-Thoreson & Dale, 1992).

Question: Then something as simple as reading picture books to children, especially in a way that encourages them to think and express themselves, might have important long-term effects?

From the little that we now know, it's really too early to say. But it's not too difficult to imagine that something as seemingly simple as reading stories with children in an interactive way could have profound effects. From Whitehurst's research, we know that the reading experience is likely to help children advance considerably in terms of language and vocabulary skills. Consider, then, a possible snowball effect following this experience, in which these children's thought skills develop faster (because they have more words to use to help them form thoughts) and their interest in reading grows stronger (because reading has been associated with the fun of actively engaging with their parents).

As a result, these children decide to read more often. Reading is a very good way for children to become exposed to new vocabulary and ideas (Miller & Gildea, 1987), which in turn might well expand further the cognitive abilities they will need to perform well in school. Next, because they are cognitively advanced compared to their peers, these children succeed in their schoolwork, earning the praise of teachers and parents, which in turn gives them confidence to accept new challenges and progress further. All this from eight hours per week of interactive reading with their parents when they were little!

Of course, I'm not saying that this is what would happen or that it would be as simple as I've made it sound. Many more experiments and more data are needed before we can fully know the long-term value of such an experience. But it does seem possible, even probable, given the value of reading in our society, that it could all happen in just the way I've described. The point is that such interaction with children might be a great help and requires little effort, so it's worth a try.

SUMMARY

- A language requires the use of signs and symbols within a grammar. A language also allows novel constructions to be created by manipulation of the various signs and symbols within the grammatical structure.
- There is evidence for the existence of vocal "dialogues" between mothers and their newborns within 72 hours following birth.
- Language acquisition may begin when the infant acquires the first language-like sounds. An infant's gooing sounds seem vowel-like, although the sounds differ considerably from the vowel-like sounds produced by adults, probably because of the differences between infant and adult skull and oral cavities.
- Infants progress through a number of stages during their acquisition of language. These are the phonation stage (0 to 2 months), the gooing stage (2 to 4 months), the expansion stage (4 to 7 months), the cononical stage (7 to 10 months), and the contraction stage (10 to 14 months). Babbling begins with the onset of phonetic expansion. During the contraction stage, infants often imitate the tones and inflections of the language to which they have been exposed.
- Infants perceive language sounds in categories. To an infant, a phoneme is a phoneme, no matter who is saying it, even when there is a change of intonation, voice onset, or length of voicing. The ability to perceive that the phoneme remains the same even with these changes is known as phoneme constancy.
- By 1 year of age, children often have begun to speak their first words. This developmental period is known as the one-word stage. The first words that children acquire usually are concrete nouns, and these tend to follow the "three bears rule."
- The child's first "word" is most likely to be expressed in a kind of personal sign language. Even deaf children typically develop their own sign language, which further supports the probability that language acquisition is prewired into our species.
- Naming is a very important way of acquiring words. By the time the child has acquired his or her first words, it's easy for a parent to direct the child's attention to particular objects. As the child comes to realize that different objects can have names, this sets the stage for a major step in language acquisition.
- Even though young children may have difficulty pronouncing certain words, they are often aware that the adult pronunciation is the correct one. This discrepancy may occur because the child's vocal apparatus is not fully comparable to an adult's until the child is about 6 years of age.
- Careful examination of the way children in the one-word stage order their single words indicates that children are already forming hypotheses about how sentences are constructed. For this reason, many researchers refer to single-word utterances as holophrases. A holophrase is a one-word "sentence."
- After the one-word stage, children enter the two-word stage. Both the one-word and two-word stages appear to be universal among children. During the two-word stage, the child may utter over 1,000 new statements every month.
- Interestingly, children don't enter a three-word stage, but, instead begin to use telegraphic speech; that is, they form sentences without using function words. They learn grammatical morphemes later, in a specific sequence that is probably dependent on the difficulty of mastering each rule.
- Both adults and children engage in caretaker speech, which appears to be a universal way of addressing other people whose language competence is less than one's own. Such speech helps children to understand what is being said and to learn how to use more advanced forms of the language.
- Children may be the ones responsible for the formation of new languages. Creole is an example of the possible influence that children may have on language formation.
- Spoonerisms give a clue to the way people organize their syntax to express their meaning. People prepare their syntactic structures before they say them; they don't simply link one word to the next. Many researchers believe that the first focus of a sentence is the topic at hand and that certain aspects of grammar derive from the need to emphasize a topic.
- Reading picture books with children in an interactive way has been found to increase children's vocabulary and descriptive verbal skills and may promote later school achievement.

QUESTIONS FOR DISCUSSION

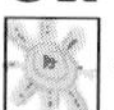

1. If you had no language, how do you think this would affect your thought processes?
2. Would an Italian baby learn Italian in the same way as an American college student taking an Italian language class? What differences would there be? After five years, who would know more Italian?
3. Do you think that you could restructure the language class so that the college student in question 2 would be sure to win the "race"? How would you make the class different?
4. Eskimo children have a better recall of what kind of snow was on the ground the day before than do children from warmer climes. Eskimo languages also include many more words for different kinds of snow than languages used in warmer places. What do these two statements tell us about language and memory? If the Eskimos had no language, do you think that they would still remember the kind of snow that fell the day before better than would someone from a southern climate, simply because the Eskimos have learned to pay more attention to things that are meaningful in their culture?
5. We know that it is beneficial to engage young children in an interactive dialogue while reading to them. Do you think that it might also help young children to develop their thought skills if parents spent time engaging them in an interactive dialogue about the television programs that they watched together? Do you think that it could help older children?

SUGGESTIONS FOR FURTHER READING

1. Baron, N. S. (1992). *Growing up with language: How children learn to talk.* Reading, MA: Addison-Wesley.
2. Bickerton, D. (1990). *Language and species.* Chicago, IL: University of Chicago Press.
3. Hulit, L. M., & Howard, M. R. (1992). *Born to talk: An introduction to speech & language development.* New York: Macmillan.
4. Miller, P. J. (1982). *Amy, Wendy, and Beth: Learning language in South Baltimore.* Austin, TX: University of Texas Press.
5. Terrace, H. S. (1979). *Nim.* New York: Knopf.
6. Wang, W. S-Y. (Ed.). (1990). *The emergence of language: Development and evolution.* New York: W. H. Freeman.

CHAPTER 9

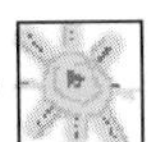

COGNITIVE DEVELOPMENT I: HISTORICAL FOUNDATIONS

CHAPTER PREVIEW

THE DAWNING OF CONSCIOUSNESS

THE SENSE OF BEING conscious, of residing inside your body, seeing through your eyes, hearing through your ears; the sense of self-awareness; the sense that you exist. When did you first develop it? When did you become aware that you were alive, that you were you, and that on each passing day when you awoke, you would still be you?

YOU WALK INTO A bathroom and see yourself in a mirror. There you are, it's you all right, as usual. You notice that somehow a smudge of ink has gotten onto your forehead. You wipe it off.

A SMALL SMUDGE of rouge is put on a 5-month-old infant's nose, and she is placed before a mirror. She glances at the reflection in the mirror and at objects in the room; she doesn't seem to realize what the reflection is.

A SMALL SMUDGE of rouge is placed on the nose of a 12-month-old child, and he is placed before a mirror. He reaches out and tries to touch the reflection. He looks behind the mirror. (Is he looking for the baby in the reflection?) He doesn't seem to realize who the baby with the spot on his nose is (Brooks-Gunn & Lewis, 1975).

A 20-MONTH-OLD child with a smudge of rouge on her nose is placed before a mirror. She looks at the reflection, reaches her hand to her face, and rubs her nose (Amsterdam, 1972). She is aware; she knows that it is her reflection and that she is seeing herself. Sometime between the ages of 1 and 2 years, children become aware of themselves; they become conscious of being living creatures.

IN A LABORATORY, researchers wonder whether monkeys or baboons ever develop such self-awareness. The animals' foreheads are marked with a colored dye, and they are given prolonged exposure to mirrors. After viewing themselves in the mirrors for thousands of hours, they still apparently fail to realize that they are viewing their own reflections (Benhar, Carlton, & Samuel, 1975; Gallup, 1977).

THE RESEARCHERS try again, this time with great apes, animals closer to humans on the evolutionary scale than are monkeys or baboons. A chimpanzee and an orangutan are marked on their faces with an unobtrusive application of dye while they are anesthetized. After being exposed to mirrors for a relatively short time, both apes respond alike; they look at the reflection, bring their hands to their faces, and rub the marks (Gallup, 1977). They are consciously aware; they know who they are. This series of classic experiments was the first to clearly show conscious awareness in other species.

IN THIS CHAPTER, we will examine the important cognitive theories that laid down the foundations on which our modern understanding of cognition has been built. As you have already seen from this Chapter Preview, you will discover some surprises along the way.

RESOURCES

Cognition

The term **cognition** refers to internal mental processes, in other words, anything that is going on inside one's "mind." For the first 50 years of psychology's history, the minds of infants or young children were generally ignored. Most psychologists believed that this was a reasonable approach because whatever infants or young children were thinking about, it couldn't be too important. The American psychologist James Mark Baldwin was an exception to this belief. Even before the turn of the century, Baldwin had outlined a theory that described infants' and children's cognitive development as progressing through stages (Baldwin, 1894). When describing cognitive development, Baldwin coined the terms *circular reaction, accommodation,* and *adaptation,* important concepts still much in use.

COGNITION
An extremely broad term that refers to pretty much anything that goes on inside your mind, including attention, perception, memory, language formation and development, reading and writing, thinking, problem solving, intelligence, creativity, imagination, expectation, intention, belief.

Owing to the rise of behaviorism, Baldwin's work went largely unnoticed in the United States. He did, however, travel to France, where he spent some time working. There, some of his writings were translated into French and read by a young man who found them so stimulating that he decided to pursue Baldwin's ideas further. That young man was the Swiss scientist Jean Piaget, and the study of cognitive development has never been the same since.

Jean Piaget

Jean Piaget affected developmental psychology perhaps more than anyone else (Beilin, 1992). Piaget was not initially trained as a psychologist; he was a biologist and naturalist. By the time he was 21 years old, he had published over 20 scientific papers on mollusks.

Question: Was Piaget interested in development before he read Baldwin's work?

Yes, Piaget's interest initially developed as a result of his biological observations. Piaget noticed that when large mollusks were taken from lakes and moved to small ponds, they underwent structural changes because of the reduced wave action in the ponds. Piaget understood this to mean that the mollusks had inherited a structure that was flexible; they would adapt, within limits, to the environment into which they were placed. After being exposed to Baldwin's work, Piaget became curious about the structure of the child's mind. Then, while helping to administer some test questions to children to earn some extra money, Piaget noticed that older children seemed to have adapted their thought processes so that they could deal differently with the questions than could younger children. This observation led him to the remarkable conclusion that older children, rather than simply knowing more than younger children, actually thought differently about problems. Piaget wondered if this could be evidence that their brains were flexibly adapting to their environments through experience by altering their underlying cognitive structures in some global way, much as the mollusks had adapted to the ponds. This led him to study cognition in human beings. Piaget worked in this area for many decades and contributed greatly to our knowledge, becoming one of the most widely read and respected psychologists of our time.

Jean Piaget (1896–1980)

Piaget's Stages of Cognitive Development

In Piaget's view, cognitive development was the combined result of the maturation of the brain and nervous system and the experiences that help individuals adapt

SCHEME
A basic unit of cognition. The comprehension an infant has about different aspects of his or her world at any given moment as pertains to actions. Piaget believed that infants develop schematic outlines (or maps) of what the world is like and maintain these outlines in their memories enabling them to organize their world into such action categories as "Things I can touch" or "Things I can eat."

to their environments. Piaget believed that because humans are genetically similar and share many of the same environmental experiences, they can be expected to exhibit considerable uniformity in their cognitive development. In fact, he argued, predictable stages of cognitive development will occur during specific periods of a child's life (see Table 9.1).

Question: Did Piaget believe that all children develop by advancing through these stages?

Yes. According to Piaget, cognitive development in all children will follow the outline given in Table 9.1. However, intellectually impaired children may develop at a slower rate or may fail to reach the higher stages.

As you may have already noticed by looking at Table 9.1, infants don't think in the same way that adults do. (In fact, you may have had this figured out before you saw Table 9.1.) Adult thinking is based on the use of symbols, language, and logic. As adults, we can imagine the future and remember the past in the form of mental images, such as pictures "in the mind's eye," or symbols, such as the words in our language. We can even imagine things that haven't happened or things we wish would happen. Adolescents, of course, also have these abilities, and children even as young as 2 years have certain symbolic abilities. Young infants, according to Piaget, don't appear to possess mental images or symbolic skills.

Question: Then does the infant know anything—or think about anything?

Piaget argued that at the beginning, during the sensorimotor period, an infant's "thoughts" are based on her physical actions. When an infant recognizes her rattle and reaches for it, she is showing a *sensorimotor* understanding of her environment because she is able to sense the rattle and reach for it. Piaget used the term **scheme** to describe this basic unit of cognition. A scheme is the action equivalent of a concept. With it, the infant can organize her world into categories, such as *things I can touch* or *things I can eat.* An infant relying on sensorimotor schemes, Piaget argued, is qualitatively different in her cognitive ability from children or adults.

TABLE 9.1

Piaget's Stages of Cognitive Development
SENSORIMOTOR PERIOD (0–2 YEARS)
Stage 1 (0–1 month): reflex activity Stage 2 (1–4 months): self-investigation Stage 3 (4–8 months): coordination and reaching out Stage 4 (8–12 months): goal-directed behavior Stage 5 (12–18 months): experimentation Stage 6 (18–24 months): problem solving and mental combinations
PREOPERATIONAL PERIOD (2–7 YEARS)
Preconceptual stage (2–4 years): emergence of symbolic functions, syncretic and transductive reasoning, and animism
Intuitive stage (4–7 years): centers on one aspect at a time, egocentrism
PERIOD OF CONCRETE OPERATIONS (7–11 YEARS)
Logical operations applied to concrete problems
Identity, reversibility, and decentration obtained
PERIOD OF FORMAL OPERATIONS (11+ YEARS)
Can solve hypothetical problems, make complex deductions, and test advanced hypotheses
Can analyze the validity of different ways of reasoning (the foundation of science)

Question: Was Piaget saying that the cognitive differences outlined in Table 9.1 occur because adults know more than children do?

Not really. According to Piaget, it's not a simple matter of children knowing less (a quantitative difference). Piaget argued that children are not simply adults who know less and, conversely, that adults are not simply knowledgeable children. For instance, older children are capable of thoughts that are, quite literally, beyond the conceptual abilities of younger children. Piaget believed that this is because older children have more extensive cognitive development: They have broader experiences, and they process the information in a qualitatively more sophisticated way, almost as though they had a different kind of brain than that possessed by younger children.

ADAPTATION

During cognitive growth, children continue to adapt to their environments. **Adaptation** is a favorite term in biology and describes an organism's ability to fit in with its surroundings. Borrowing from Baldwin, Piaget argued that children adapt in two ways—through **assimilation** and **accommodation.**

Assimilation Piaget stated that "assimilation is the integration of external elements into evolving or completed structures" (Piaget, 1970, p. 706). Assimilation, then, is the act of taking in information and perceptions in a way that is compatible with your current understanding of the world.

Question: What do you mean by "taking in"?

According to Piaget, we have all developed cognitive structures based on our experience. By "cognitive structures," Piaget was referring to the total mental facility that one has to process, comprehend, or organize information at any given time. Anything we perceive that is new can be assimilated and interpreted *only by the cognitive structures we currently possess.*

Accommodation Whenever we assimilate information or perceptions into our understanding of the world, such additional data, according to Piaget, may affect underlying cognitive structures and alter them. Such alteration is called accommodation.

Question: Would you give an example of what you mean?

If a little girl sees a squirrel and says "kitty," she has assimilated the new object (squirrel) into the cognitive structures that already contained "kitty" but did not contain squirrel. The child has assimilated, or fit, her new perception into her current understanding. Her understanding didn't change; she simply took the new information and made it fit. Any information that didn't fit was overlooked, denied, or distorted, so that she perceived the new object to be what she already knew or understood, more or less pounding a square block into a round hole. Quite often, though, children actively take notice of the discrepancies between the objects they see and their current understanding of those objects, or such discrepancies are pointed out by someone else. For example, the child's mother may correct her and say, "No, dear, that's a squirrel," and may point out the differences between a squirrel and a cat. The child may react by observing the discrepancies between the squirrel and her mental picture of a cat and then *accommodate* the squirrel into her cognitive structures. Her understanding has developed further, so that it now includes both squirrel and cat. Through the process of accommodation, cognitive structures change or develop further.

By bringing new objects into categories they already possess (assimilation) or by creating a new understanding of something (accommodation), children adapt

ADAPTATION
A term used by Piaget to describe the mechanism through which schemes develop as a result of adjustment to changes; such adjustment occurs through the processes of assimilation and accommodation.

ASSIMILATION
Piaget's term for the act of taking in information and perceptions in a way that is compatible with the person's current understanding of the world.

ACCOMMODATION
Piaget's term for the process in which a person adjusts or changes his or her cognitive structures to incorporate aspects of an experience not currently represented in them.

Research now shows that even infants and young toddlers may learn to imitate what they see on television.

EQUILIBRIUM
Term used by Piaget to describe a hypothetical goal state achieved through an innate drive that forces a person actively to pursue cognitive adaptation. In this view, children have a natural inclination toward cognitive development.

OBJECT PERMANENCE
Term used by Piaget to refer to the individual's realization that objects continue to exist even though they are not presently sensed.

to their environments. Even infants, when first reaching for objects, go through such an assimilation and accommodation process as they learn to adjust their reach and grasp to touch new objects. For instance, an infant may reach for a new object using the same-size grasp that successfully obtained an earlier object (*assimilation*). If he fails, he may adjust his grasp to *accommodate* the new object's size. His reaching and grasping scheme has now further *adapted* to his environment.

Question: Why do children adapt cognitively to their environments?

No one knows for certain. Piaget believed that there is an innate force that drives children from within to actively pursue cognitive adaptation. In this view, humans desire cognitive **equilibrium,** or balance. For example, when a child feels comfortable with the way she thinks—that is, when she is able to assimilate most of what she finds in her environment into her existing cognitive structures—she feels satisfied and is considered in equilibrium. However, when she becomes aware of the failings of any of her thought strategies, she experiences disequilibrium. The conflict that arises during disequilibrium, when cognitive structures are unable to comprehend external events, throws the child off balance. This leaves her feeling uncomfortable, and until she acquires a more sophisticated approach for accommodating new information, her equilibrium will not return. In this way, Piaget argued, the struggle to resolve discrepancies between one's current understanding of the world and what one observes is the force that eventually propels a child upward through the stages of cognitive development outlined in Table 9.1 (Block, 1982).

Before we discuss the stages in detail, there are a few things to keep in mind. The ages given for each period and stage are *only approximate.* A child does not, for example, advance from the sensorimotor to the preoperational period by simply having a second birthday. All children advance through each stage in the order and sequence described. Children are never observed to skip a stage, although sometimes, while leaving one period or stage and entering another, a child may exhibit cognitive aspects typical of both periods or stages. The stages are universal; they are observed to occur in all human beings.

THE SENSORIMOTOR PERIOD (0–2 YEARS)

Question: How did Piaget view the cognitive world of the newborn?

Piaget saw it as a world of the present. There are no dreams of the future or memories of the past. The newborn has no information that could serve as a basis for thought. Piaget argued that newborns don't think; they only behave. Nonetheless, this behavior without thought—or reflex activity, as Piaget called it—is the foundation on which all cognitive advances eventually will be built (through the processes of assimilation and accommodation). The first of Piaget's four periods of cognitive development is the sensorimotor period, which is characterized by a lack of fully developed object permanence.

Question: What do you mean by object permanence?

Object permanence refers to the ability to represent an object, whether or not it is actually present. Piaget believed that object permanence is necessary before problem solving or thinking can be carried out internally—that is, carried out by using mental symbols or images.

Lack of object permanence, then, means *lack of mental representations!* Look around you. Do you see a redwood tree? Unless you live in a fairly scenic California setting and are sitting next to a window, you probably don't. But can you mentally represent the redwood tree to yourself, even though one isn't actually present? You can do this in a number of ways. You can picture a redwood tree in your "mind's eye" (if you know what the tree looks like), or you can think of the letter symbols REDWOOD TREE, or you can remember the sound of the words "redwood tree." Or you might actually depict a redwood tree with your hands, by trying to mimic its shape to hold on to that object mentally, even though it's out of sight. The point is that you can keep any object "permanent," even when it is absent, by using these techniques. Without mental sounds, images, symbols, or depictions to represent an object, you would be unable to think of it, because you would have no internal way of representing it. In other words, without object permanence, "out of sight, out of mind."

Just imagine what it would be like if you couldn't use mental representations—if you couldn't think! Actually, imagining it is impossible, because imagining it requires thought! We are so advanced beyond the first stages of the sensorimotor period that we can barely grasp the idea of having no thoughts at all, of reacting only to external events. And yet, Piaget argued that during the first two stages of the sensorimotor period, an infant is unable to think.

According to Piaget, it isn't until the third stage that it becomes apparent that some thought processing is occurring, but object permanence is still not fully developed until the end of stage 6, the final stage in the sensorimotor period (see Table 9.1). By definition, once object permanence is fully developed, the child leaves the sensorimotor period. Indeed, Piaget chose the term *sensorimotor* because most of the child's thinking during this period is based, as we have noted, on schemes of overt actions in response to what the child senses (*sensori* = stimulus; *motor* = physical action).

Question: When does object permanence first begin to develop?

The best way to observe the onset of object permanence in infants is to examine each of the six stages of the sensorimotor period in turn.

Stage 1, Reflex Activity (0–1 Month) This stage involves a systematic and increasingly less awkward use of natural reflexes. In Piaget's words, this is a time of **reflex exercise.** However, accommodation can be observed even during this early stage, for example, when the infant distinguishes the mother's nipple from the surrounding skin areas and localizes it.

Stage 2, Self-Investigation (1–4 Months) During this stage, the infant begins to display a class of behaviors known as *circular reactions.* A circular reaction consists first of

> stumbling upon some experience as a consequence of some act, and second, of trying to recapture the experience by re-enacting the original movements again and again in a kind of rhythmic cycle. The importance of circular reactions lies in the fact that it is the sensorymotor device par excellence for making new adaptations, and of course new adaptations are the heart and soul of intellectual development at any stage. (Flavell, 1963, p. 93)

During this second stage, the circular reactions observed are of a particular type, called **primary circular reactions.** Primary circular reactions are simple repetitive acts that center on the infant's own body and include thumb sucking, hand clasping, and foot grabbing. That's why this stage is referred to as a time of self-investigation.

Stage 3, Coordination and Reaching Out (4–8 Months) During this stage, **secondary circular reactions** appear. These differ from primary circular reactions in that they no longer center on the infant's own body; instead, the infant "reaches out" to manipulate objects discovered in the environment. Also during this time, a number of coordinations occur that serve to integrate previously isolated be-

REFLEX EXERCISE
Piagetian description of the first stage of the sensorimotor period, during which the infant's reflexes become smoother and more coordinated.

PRIMARY CIRCULAR REACTIONS
Simple repetitive acts that center on the infant's own body and include thumb sucking and foot grasping; characteristic of the second stage of the sensorimotor period.

SECONDARY CIRCULAR REACTIONS
Circular reactions characteristic of the third stage of the sensorimotor period, in which the child reaches out to manipulate objects discovered in the environment.

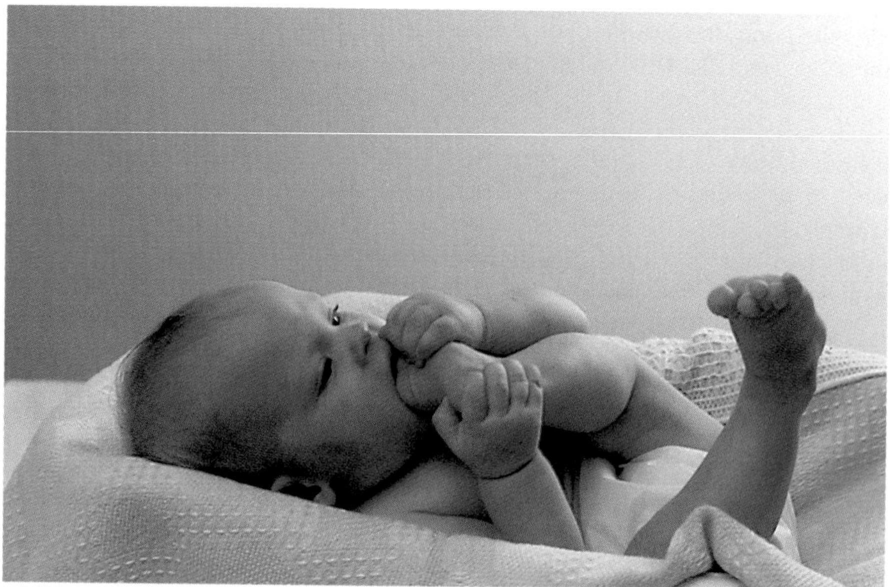

Primary circular reactions are simple repetitive acts that center on the infant's own body, such as thumb sucking, hand clasping, or foot grabbing.

haviors. For example, an infant will shake a rattle in order to hear it or reach for a ball in order to grasp it. Object permanence, however, has still not emerged.

Question: How can you tell?

As John Flavell observed of an infant in the coordination and reaching-out stage,

> His behavior in this situation also testifies to the immaturity of his object concept; if a sufficient fraction of the object shows from behind the screen, he reaches for it; if this fraction is then made to decrease, the reaching hand abruptly drops. More generally, it is characteristic of this stage that the child makes no attempt to retrieve an object manually once it has disappeared from view (e.g., by being covered with a cloth), in spite of the fact that such activity would by this age be well within his physical capabilities. (Flavell, 1970, p. 1010)

Stage 4, Goal-Directed Behavior (8–12 Months) During this stage, children integrate and adapt their schemes to attain specific goals. Techniques stumbled on that were successful in obtaining something in one situation may now be generalized to new situations. For the first time, children begin to display purposeful sequential behavior designed to achieve a desired end. Infants accomplish this by integrating previously separate schemes into one overriding scheme (action concept) that controls the sequencing of these once-isolated schemes into a single goal-oriented effort.

For example, an infant may purposely move one object out of the way to reach another or may open something for the purpose of obtaining what's inside. Once, while observing his infant son Laurent, Piaget noted the exact moment when Laurent first exhibited the goal-directed behavior characteristic of stage 4. The infant was 7 months and 13 days old when, for the first time, he moved his father's interposing hand aside to obtain a match box. Previously, when Piaget had played this blocking game with Laurent, the infant, although apparently interested in the match box, had never made an attempt to move the blocking hand aside (Piaget, 1952).

Question: Does object permanence begin to appear during stage 4?

Yes, by this time children begin regularly to search for objects that they see disappear. Later in stage 4, as infants continue to develop a system for representing objects that are no longer present, they will even search for an object several minutes after it has been covered or otherwise hidden.

Question: Doesn't this demonstrate that object permanence is fully developed?

At first glance it may appear to be fully developed, but you need only play a simple game with a 10-month-old child who is in stage 4 to discover the serious deficiencies that still exist in the child's object permanence. To play this game, you will need two cloths. Place the infant in front of the cloths and then place something that the infant wants beneath one of them. What do you think the infant will do?

Question: Because there is purposeful goal-directed behavior during stage 4, won't the infant pull the cloth off the object and then reach for the object?

Probably. Now play the game a few more times, each time placing the object under the same cloth. Then play the game once more, only this time, after you've placed the object under the usual cloth, clearly remove it, right in front of the infant's eyes, and place it under the other cloth. Now what will the infant do?

Question: Look under the other cloth?

Surprisingly, most infants won't. They'll look where they most often found the object in the past rather than where they last saw it. Although children in stage 4 have some object permanence, it is not fully developed. (As you can see, 10-month-old babies make a terrific audience for would-be magicians who have not yet perfected their sleight-of-hand technique.)

Stage 5, Experimentation (12–18 Months) During the fifth stage, **tertiary** (third-order) **circular reactions** appear. Unlike secondary circular reactions, wherein an infant tries to recapture an external event in a repetitive and mechanical way, in tertiary circular reactions, children begin to experiment actively with things to discover how various actions will affect an object or outcome. As an example of tertiary circular reactions, consider an experimenting toddler sitting in her high chair dawdling over her oatmeal. She drops a handful over the side of the high chair. Then she does it again, this time with more force, and seems to delight in the splat. Then she repeats her actions, only this time she releases the blob gently. She learns that (1) things fall down, not up; (2) the force of the throw determines the radius of the splat; and (3) you can make an interesting pattern on the floor with oatmeal. Whereas stage 4 children can reach goals only by using actions that already exist in their repertoires as a result of accidental

TERTIARY CIRCULAR REACTIONS
Circular reactions characteristic of the fifth stage of the sensorimotor period, in which the child actively experiments with things to discover how various actions affect an object or outcome.

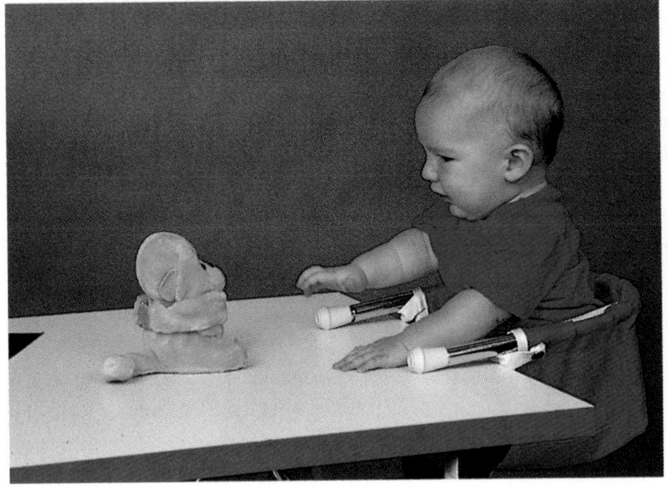

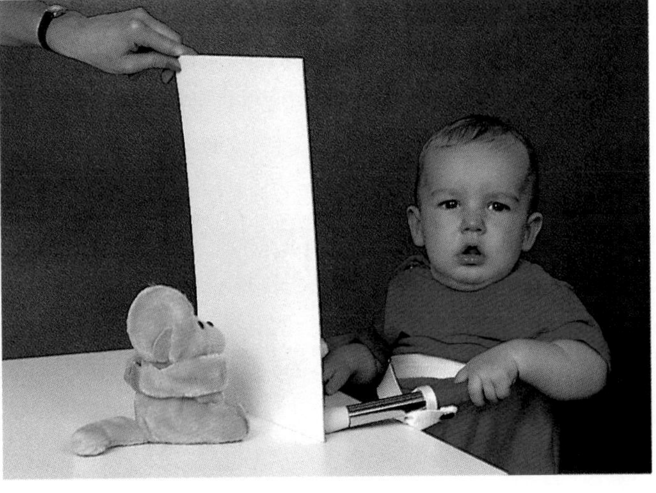

For infants in the sensorimotor period, "out of sight" is often "out of mind."

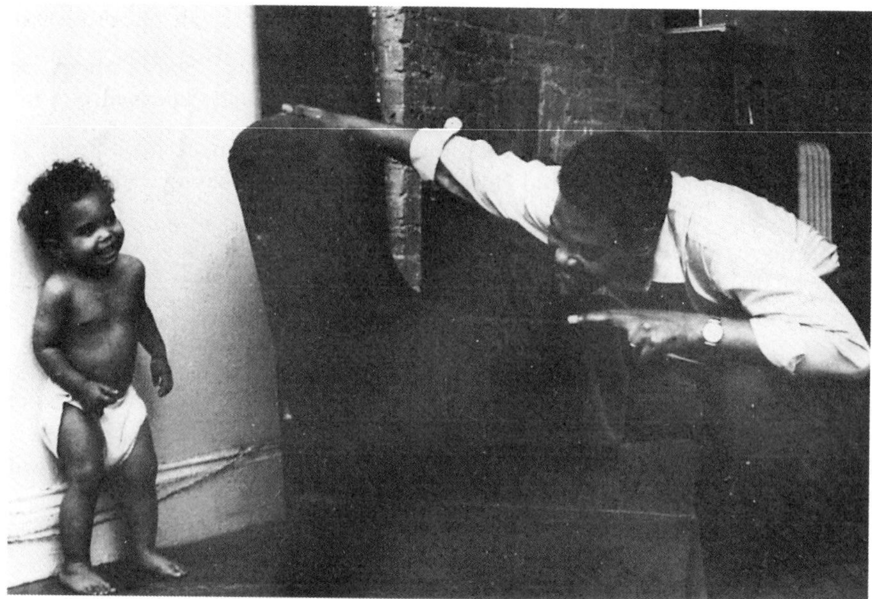

A sense of object permanence is useful in a game of hide and seek.

discovery, stage 5 children will *actively* build their schemes through this kind of experimentation.

The beginning of tertiary circular reactions is evidence that the child is developing an appreciation of cause-and-effect relationships. Many researchers argue that this comprehension of cause and effect also is reflected in the child's language development (Bates, Camaioni, & Volterra, 1975; Molfese, Molfese, & Carrell, 1982; Sugarman, 1977). Children's attempts to tell adults things or to give adults commands are believed to be built on their early notions of cause and effect. After all, before the child would make a deliberate attempt to communicate, he or she would need to "know" that different verbal efforts would result in different effects. Such linguistic efforts are not apparent in children before stage 5.

Question: Stage 5 doesn't begin until children reach 12 months of age. What about children who are saying words, pointing at objects, and making declarations when they are only 10 months old?

Now is a good time to reiterate that these stage ages are only approximate. Some infants will even show evidence of stage 5 acquisition by the age of 8 months (Harding & Golinkoff, 1979).

Question: Why do some children enter a stage earlier than others?

Such individual differences are probably due, in part, to the child's inheritance or biology. But the speed at which the child progresses through the sensorimotor period also depends on the child's environment. If the child has a mother who provides a stimulating environment and who is highly communicative, the child will progress through the sensorimotor period at a slightly faster pace than might be otherwise expected (Chazan, 1981). Interestingly, if children are provided with an enriched environment that helps accelerate their progress through the sensorimotor period, their verbal requests will begin earlier—but still at the onset of stage 5 (Steckol & Leonard, 1981).

Question: Does object permanence improve during stage 5?

A child searching for an object hidden from sight under a cloth will now look for the object where he or she last saw it rather than where the child has found it most often.

Question: Would Piaget have said that object permanence was complete at this point?

Not yet. If a stage 5 child observes you picking up an object and closing your hand about it so that it is no longer visible, then watches as you first place your hand in your pocket, then remove it, and finally appear to carry the object over and deposit it in a hiding place, the stage 5 child seems to be able to "see" only part of what has happened. When asked to find the object, the child will search for the object in your hand and may even look in your pocket, but will not search further by looking in the final hiding place. Piaget referred to this as a *failure to fully infer invisible displacements,* which does not occur if object permanence is fully developed.

Stage 6, Problem Solving and Mental Combinations (18–24 Months) During this time, problem solving can be accomplished by mental combinations of signs, symbols, or images; the child no longer needs to depend on physical exploration and manipulation of the environment. This ability to think, for that's what it is, can lead to sudden insightful solutions that make little use of the kinds of trial-and-error exploration observed in stage 5. For example, a stage 6 child might set his juice glass down on the floor to have both hands free to open a door, and after looking at the door and the juice glass, "realize," through a mental image of the door opening, that the juice glass is in the way. The stage 6 child might then decide to move the glass to a safer place before attempting to open the door. Even so, this child is still in the sensorimotor period and will often need a certain scheme to aid him in his understanding. He might be seen to mimic the opening and closing of the door with his hands or his mouth as a way of physically hanging onto the "realization" that he has. But thinking has begun to emerge.

The fact that children of this age are beginning to think may also help explain why they begin to develop self-awareness at about the same time. As you will recall from the Chapter Preview, it is between the ages of 1 and 2 that children first become aware of themselves—the time frame that also corresponds with the onset of internalized manipulations and thought.

Question: At the end of stage 6, then, the child finally infers invisible displacement and obtains a fully developed object permanence?

Yes. According to Piaget, it is during this stage that children develop a full understanding that objects continue to exist even after they have disappeared from sight or have been moved by hidden displacement.

THE STAGES IN REVIEW

As you can see, the sensorimotor period is a time when many cognitive changes occur. To help you organize the information that has been covered so far, let's examine the following record of the cognitive development of a baby girl named Samara as she progresses through the sensorimotor period.

- **Stage 1: reflex activity**
Samara reflexively grasps at just about everything, especially her mother. Other reflexes become smoother and more efficient.

- **Stage 2: self-investigation**
Primary circular reactions appear as Samara repetitively sucks her fingers and clasps her hands and feet.

- **Stage 3: coordination and reaching out**
Secondary circular reactions appear as Samara goes beyond her mother to reach

Great ape and human infants display similar reaching out at about the same age. Of course, as human infants develop, their cognitive abilities will far surpass those of the great apes.

for and manipulate other objects not associated with her body. The first signs of object permanence are observed.

- **Stage 4: goal-directed behavior**
Samara combines behaviors in sequence to achieve specific goals.

- **Stage 5: experimentation**
Tertiary circular reactions appear. Samara begins to experiment actively with objects.

- **Stage 6: problem solving and mental combinations**
Samara can solve problems through insight and use of mental symbolism. Object permanence becomes fully developed.

As researchers observed Samara progress through the sensorimotor period, they became more and more astounded.

Question: Why were they surprised to observe an infant progressing through the sensorimotor period?

Because Samara wasn't human. She was an orangutan baby! Actually, this was the first documentation of the similarity in cognitive development between our species and another. Although Samara passed through the six stages of the sensorimotor period at a different rate from that usually observed in humans—with stages 3 and 4 each arriving 2 months earlier than they would in a human infant, and stages 5 and 6 arriving later—she did pass through all of Piaget's stages, and in the correct sequence. Incidentally, so did 35 other orangutan, gorilla, and chimpanzee babies who were observed (Chevalier-Skolnikoff, 1979, 1983).

These findings indicate that the sensorimotor period is not unique to our species, and they emphasize the biological aspects of Piaget's cognitive theory. Piaget's theory is an epigenetic one (emphasizing both inheritance and environment). Piaget stressed that in addition to the adaptations accomplished through assimilation and accommodation, cognitive development is also closely related to the maturation of cognitive structures within the brain and nervous system. Although there are many similarities between ourselves and the great apes, we are different—perhaps only because our cognitive development is greater, and thus our capabilities are greater.

LEARNING CHECK

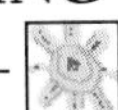

Multiple Choice

1. Which of the following depicts the correct chronological order of Piaget's stages of cognitive development?
   a. sensorimotor, preoperational, concrete, formal
   b. sensorimotor, concrete, formal, preoperational
   c. concrete, sensorimotor, formal, preoperational
   d. sensorimotor, concrete, preoperational, formal
2. In Piaget's view, cognitive development results solely from the development of the brain and nervous system.
   a. true **b.** false
3. According to Piaget,
   a. accommodation occurs through the processes of adaptation and assimilation.
   b. assimilation occurs through the processes of accommodation and adaptation.
   c. adaptation occurs through the processes of accommodation and assimilation.
4. Piaget argued that adults are not simply knowledgeable children; rather, adults are capable of thoughts beyond the conceptual abilities of children.
   a. true **b.** false
5. According to Piaget's stage theory, which of the following statements is *false?*
   a. Children may sometimes skip a stage.
   b. The ages assigned to each period or stage are only approximate.
   c. Children possess cognitive schemes.
   d. Sometimes children may exhibit aspects of both the stage they are leaving and the one they are entering.
6. The sensorimotor period is characterized by
   a. the lack of fully developed object permanence.
   b. a learning theory paradigm.
   c. conceptual thinking.
   d. eight stages.

Match the events in the left-hand column with the stage or period in which they first occur.

7. ___ Secondary circular reactions
8. ___ Coordination and reaching out
9. ___ Experimentation
10. ___ Tertiary circular reactions
11. ___ First sign of object permanence
12. ___ Reflex activity
13. ___ Problem solving and mental combinations
14. ___ Primary circular reactions
15. ___ Ability to infer invisible displacements
16. ___ Goal-directed behavior
17. ___ Self-investigation

a. Stage 1
b. Stage 2
c. Stage 3
d. Stage 4
e. Stage 5
f. Stage 6

} Sensorimotor period

Answers:
1.a 2.b 3.c 4.a 5.a 6.a 7.c 8.c 9.e 10.e 11.c 12.a 13.f
14.b 15.f 16.d 17.b

CONCEPT
An abstract idea based on grouping objects by common properties.

PRECONCEPTS
Immature concepts held by children in the preoperational stage.

SYNCRETIC REASONING
A type of reasoning used by preconceptual children, in which objects are classified according to a limited and changing set of criteria.

The Preoperational Period (2–7 Years)

The major distinction between the sensorimotor and preoperational periods is the degree of development and use of internal images and symbols. The development of thought, as represented by the establishment of object permanence, marks the dividing line between the sensorimotor and preoperational periods.

As the preoperational period sets in, the child demonstrates greater and greater use of symbolic functions. Language development increases dramatically, and imaginative play becomes more apparent as children spend much of their time engaging in make-believe. Piaget argued that another important difference seen during this period is that children can imitate another's behavior after some time has passed, implying that they now have a way of symbolically remembering behavior originally observed in a model. All these actions suggest an internal cognitive mediation between incoming stimuli and later responses.

Question: Why is this period called preoperational?

Children's intellectual development during this period is called preoperational because the children haven't acquired the logical operations or rules of thought characteristic of later periods of cognitive development. The first part of the preoperational period is called the preconceptual stage; the second part is called the intuitive stage.

Preconceptual Stage (2–4 Years) One of the most valuable ways that thinking can be organized is by forming concepts. A **concept** may be defined as the relationship between, or the properties shared by, the objects or ideas in a given group. If you have the concept of boat, you can recognize something as a boat even though it may look different from all the other boats you've ever seen. A new boat can be included within the concept because it has qualities that are common to the entire class of objects we call boats. It has a hull; it floats in water; and it's used for transport. Because our concept of boat is highly developed, we are able to tell not only what this new object is (a boat) but also what distinguishes it from other boats. We see the qualities that place it within our conceptual understanding of boat, but we also see qualities that make it unique. Children, however, as they begin to symbolize their environments and develop the ability to internalize objects and events, first develop immature concepts, which Piaget called **preconcepts.** For instance, a preconceptual child may have a general idea that winged, flying objects found in trees are birds or that wheeled, doored objects found on streets are cars and still not have sufficient grasp of the conceptual class to isolate and distinguish characteristics unique to any member of that class. In other words, it is common for 3-year-old children to refer to every car as "Daddy's car" or to believe that every Santa Claus they encounter on a Christmas shopping trip is the one and only Santa. (Of course, as adults, you and I know that there is only one Santa and that the others are just helpers.)

During the preconceptual stage, children's reasoning processes are limited to two kinds of reasoning: syncretic and transductive.

Question: What did Piaget mean by syncretic reasoning?

Syncretic reasoning refers to the method by which preschoolers tend to sort and classify objects. When disparate things are classified syncretically, they are organized according to a limited and changing set of criteria. A preconceptual 3-year-old child placed before a group of different objects might organize them syncretically in the following manner: The boat goes with the other boats because they are boats. This glove goes with the boat because they are both green. This block goes with that block because they are blocks, and the blocks go with the boat because they can fit on the deck.* When the child is asked the question, "Does the glove go with the block?" a common syncretic answer is, "No, the blocks go with the glove 'cause they fit inside."

Syncretic reasoning may occur in part because the child's conceptual understandings are not fully developed. The child isn't necessarily wrong in saying that glove and blocks go together, but in this case the reasoning is syncretic because the child has classified the objects according to a limited or changing set of criteria ("'cause [the blocks] fit inside"). An adult with a fully developed conceptual understanding might easily have placed a glove and a block together, and when asked why, answered, "because they are both manufactured items." Such an advanced classification scheme relies on highly organized and fixed sets of conceptual criteria.

TRANSDUCTIVE REASONING
A type of reasoning used by preconceptual children, in which inferences are drawn about the relationship between two objects based on a single attribute.

ANIMISTIC THINKING
A kind of thinking common to children in the preconceptual stage, in which inanimate objects, especially those that move or appear to move, are believed to be alive.

Question: Besides syncretic reasoning during the preconceptual stage, you also mentioned transductive reasoning. What is transductive reasoning?

Transductive reasoning involves drawing an inference about the relationship between two objects based on a single attribute. This kind of reasoning doesn't generally lead to correct conclusions, although occasionally it may. For example, if A has four legs and B has four legs, then A must be B and vice versa. If A happens to be a cat and B a dog, a transduction based on legs alone obviously will lead to a faulty conclusion. Transductive reasoning appears to occur because the child's emerging preconcepts are limited to only a few conceptual attributes; in other words: Mommy went to the hospital and had a baby—so when Daddy goes to the hospital, he'll have a baby.

Transductive reasoning can also lead to animistic thinking.

Question: What is animistic thinking?

Animistic thinking is the belief that inanimate objects are alive. Consider the following conversation between Piaget and a preconceptual child (Piaget, 1960, p. 215):

PIAGET: Does the sun move?
CHILD: Yes, when one walks it follows. When one turns around it turns around too. Doesn't it ever follow you too?
PIAGET: Why does it move?
CHILD: Because when one walks, it goes too.
PIAGET: Why does it go?
CHILD: To hear what we say.
PIAGET: Is it alive?
CHILD: Of course, otherwise it wouldn't follow us, it couldn't shine.

In this case, the child has attributed life to the sun because it appears to move, which is a quality of most living objects.

Intuitive Stage (4–7 Years) The latter portion of the preoperational period is called the intuitive stage because children's beliefs are generally based on what they *sense* to be true rather than on what logic or rational thought would dictate.

Question: Would you give an example of intuitive thinking?

Piaget once described a problem in which three beads were placed in a narrow, hollow cardboard tube. The tube was held in front of a child so that a blue bead

*Now that I think about it, things in my garage are sorted in much the same way. Unfortunately, I can't claim to have been 3 years old when I did it.

EGOCENTRISM
Thought process characteristic of children in the preoperational period in which they view their perspective as the reference point from which they, as well as all others, view the world.

CONSERVATION
The principle that quantities such as mass, weight, and volume remain constant regardless of changes in the appearance of these quantities and that such changes in appearance can be undone, thereby regaining the original state by reversing any operations that had been performed. The concept of conservation encompasses the concepts of identity, decentration and reversibility.

IDENTITY
In Piagetian theory, a deep understanding that two objects will remain identical in some elemental way even though one of the objects may have its appearance altered in some dramatic way.

was on the bottom, a yellow bead was in the middle, and a red bead was on top. Even though the child couldn't see through the tube, he knew the order of the beads because he could remember the order in which they had been dropped into the tube. If the tube were turned upside down, the child might still be able to give the correct order of the beads from top to bottom if he could imagine how they might look in the upside-down tube. An intuitive child answers this problem by relying on his or her ability to imagine the position of the beads rather than by applying any logical operations.

Question: What do you mean by logical operations?

Suppose that you watch three beads dropped into a tube. Like the child, you know that the blue bead is on the bottom, the yellow bead is in the middle, and the red bead is on top because you can remember the order in which they were placed in the tube. Suppose, now, that the tube is turned vertically 29½ times. Which color bead would be on top? You know that it's the blue bead, but how? Did you imagine the column of beads going through 29½ turns? Or did you apply a logical rule about full turns and half turns? You probably concluded that any number of whole turns would bring the red bead back to the top position, whereas any number of whole turns plus a half turn would bring the blue bead to the top position. This kind of logical operation is generally beyond the ability of intuitive children. Instead, they rely more on their senses and imagination. Piaget also argued that during this time, the reasoning of intuitive children is further limited because they tend to be **egocentric,** or conceptually self-centered (Gzesh & Surber, 1985).

THE PERIOD OF CONCRETE OPERATIONS (7–11 YEARS)

Operations are logical rules. Preoperational children, Piaget argued, do not rely on logic or logical operations to form their conclusions. Children in the period of concrete operations, though, are able to use such logical rules to deal with problems. How children acquire a logical understanding of the world is not clear, but they seem to do it rather abruptly.

Question: Is it just that children begin to guess at the logic?

Not really. Preoperational children, who can't comprehend the logic of concrete operations, will, as soon as they enter the next stage, suddenly see these logical operations as self-evident and unmistakable (Miller, 1986). This finding supports the idea that the child has moved into a *qualitatively* new and more advanced stage—that of concrete operations. The child, however, is limited to the concrete, to the world she has directly experienced. She is not yet able to comprehend the completely hypothetical—to compare what is with what may be.

Identity and Decentration Piaget stated that the onset of **conservation** marks the end of the preoperational period and the beginning of concrete operations. The major difference between the preoperational and concrete periods is that children are beginning to use logical operations and rules rather than intuition. This change is viewed as a shift from reliance on perception to a reliance on logic, and, as you will come to appreciate, it is a giant leap.

During the period of concrete operations, children's thought processes become more competent, flexible, and powerful as they come to understand and apply identity, decentration, and reversibility.

Question: What do you mean by the ability to apply identity?

Identity refers to the ability to grasp the fact that the amount of a material does not change unless something is added or taken away from it, even though its form or distribution may change. For example, both a preoperational and concrete operational child presented with two identical glasses of water will realize that they are equally full. But suppose that we pour the water from one of the glasses into a dish while both children watch. The preoperational child most likely will say, when comparing the dish of water with the remaining glass, that there is now less water in the dish because it is at a lower level than the water in the glass (see Figure 9.1). The concrete operational child, however, will know that the amount of water is the same as before. He will understand that no water has been added or taken away. Another way of saying this is that he is able to break away from centering his attention on one aspect of the problem (e.g., how tall the column of water looks) and *decenter* his attention so he can now conserve quantity (one aspect), even though the shape has altered (another aspect). **Decentration** enables the child to conserve. In this way the identity of the water as comprising a particular amount is maintained.

DECENTRATION
In Piagetian theory, the cognitive ability to break out of the frame of thought that causes one to focus on only one aspect of a changing situation.

REVERSIBILITY
In Piagetian theory, the ability, obtained during concrete operations, to understand that actions that affect objects, if reversed in sequence, will return the objects to their original state.

HORIZONTAL DECALAGE
Term used by Piaget to describe the onset and order of different conservation abilities.

Reversibility Another way we can solve the problem posed in Figure 9.1 is to imagine that the water from the dish is being poured back into the glass. This action would bring us right back to where we began, and it is one way of proving that the dish held the same amount of water as was originally in the glass. We are using the concept known as **reversibility**—the ability to imagine or conceive of doubling back, or reversing, what we have just done. The ability to reverse operations in your mind is another key aspect of the concrete operational period. Preoperational children have a terrible time with this seemingly simple way of thinking.

As an example, consider the following 4-year-old preoperational child who is having difficulty with the "rule of reversal" (Phillips, 1969, p. 61). He is asked, "Do you have a brother?" He says, "Yes." Then he is asked, "What's his name?" He replies, "Jim." But when asked, "Does Jim have a brother?" he says, "No."

The Horizontal Decalage Figure 9.2 outlines the many different kinds of conservations that children acquire during the period of concrete operations. The ages given are only approximate and vary, depending on the method employed to test the particular conservation (Baer & Wright, 1974). Piaget used the term **horizontal decalage** to refer to the fact that some conservations are mastered before others. It's fascinating to observe children dealing with conservation tasks before the horizontal decalage is complete. For instance, a child who has grasped conservation of substance may realize that a ball of clay rolled into the shape of a hot dog still has the same *amount* of clay as when it was a ball. But since conservation of weight is farther along the horizontal decalage, the same child may fail a conservation of weight test. For example, if the child is shown two clay

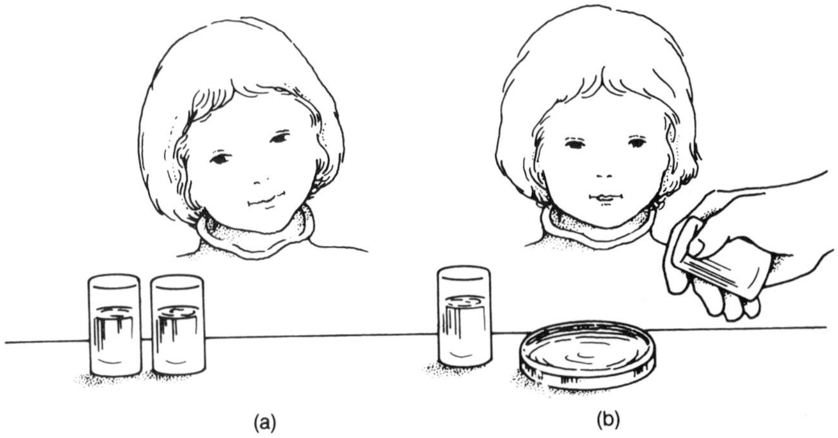

(a) (b)

FIGURE 9.1
Testing a child for the ability to conserve.
(a) The child agrees that glasses A and B contain the same amount of water.
(b) Water from one of the glasses is poured into a dish. The child doesn't realize that the dish and the remaining glass contain the same amount of water—that is, the child is unable to conserve one aspect (amount) when another aspect (height of water column) changes. This inability is typical of children in the preoperational stage.

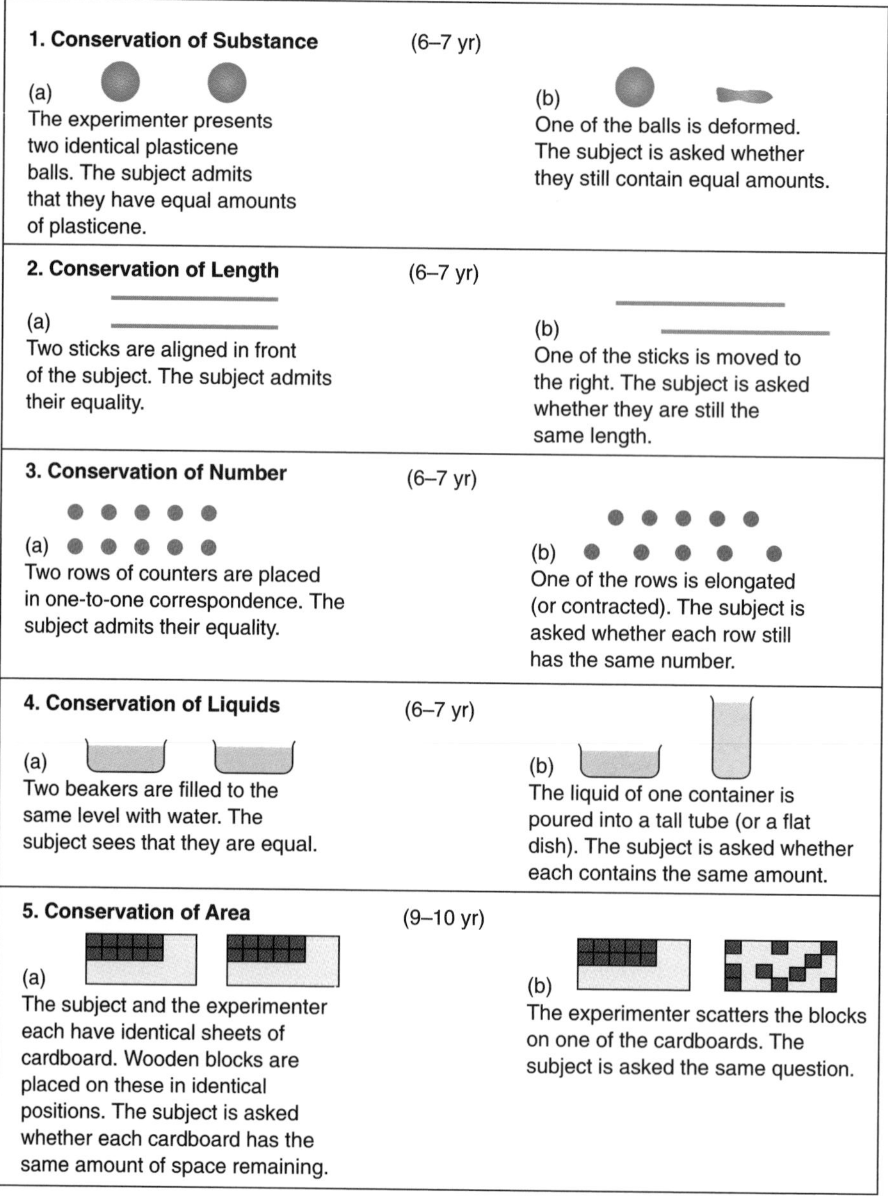

FIGURE 9.2
Some of the many kinds of conservation tasks investigated by Piaget. The ages at which the conservations are generally first obtained are shown in parentheses. (*Source:* Lefrancois, 1983, p. 327)

balls and watches as they are weighed on a balance scale, the child sees that they weigh the same. But then suppose that one of the clay balls is rolled out into a hot dog shape. If the child is asked whether the rolled-out clay still weighs the same as the ball, the child may not know the answer. Although this child *can* conserve substance, he is unable, as of yet, to conserve weight, and although the child knows that the *amount* of clay has remained the same despite the change in shape, he does not realize that the two pieces of clay still *weigh* the same!

Seriation Besides conservation and reversibility, children in the period of concrete operations are able to engage in three other important logical operations. The first of these is understanding serial position. In Figure 9.3, you will see the falling-stick cards. Children in the period of concrete operations are able to place these cards in correct sequence—quite an advance over preoperational children, who can't order objects according to a particular dimension, such as height, length, or size.

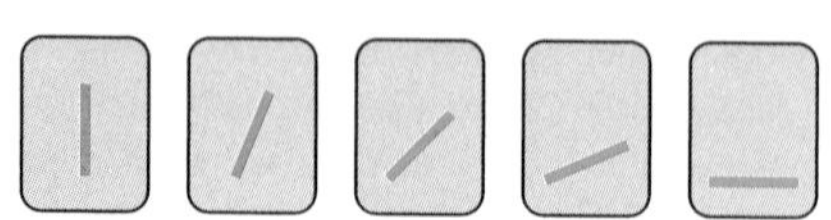

FIGURE 9.3
The falling-stick cards represent a temporal, or time, order when placed in the correct sequence. Preoperational children seem unable to comprehend this kind of ordering.

Classification The second additional acquisition is the ability to deal with classes of objects. Unlike a younger, preoperational child, the average 8-year-old child would be able to answer the following class inclusion question: In a bunch of flowers with two yellow daisies and six red roses, are there more roses or flowers? This new-found ability to sort subclasses from the original class and to understand that they are not two equal items but that, instead, one is part of the other is an important cognitive advance. When combined with an understanding of serial order, the ability to classify according to groups and subgroups can enable the child to attain the third important acquisition: the concept of number.

Numeration

Question: Don't children understand numbers before they reach school age?

Although preoperational children can count and relate numbers to certain objects, their understanding of numbers is quite limited (Halford & Boyle, 1985). Before they enter the period of concrete operations, children generally have a poor grasp of the ordinal relationships among numbers (Michie, 1985). Once they obtain an understanding of serial order and classification, however, children begin to comprehend the sequence of numbers as well as classes and subclasses of numbers. For example, during the period of concrete operations, a child will come to understand that a group of six is made from three subgroups of two. As you can see, this kind of understanding forms the foundation on which concepts such as multiplication and division can be built.

THE PERIOD OF FORMAL OPERATIONS (11+ YEARS)

Piaget noted time and again that unlike children in the concrete operational period, who are still limited, adolescents and adults are able to apply logical rules to situations that violate principles of reality.

Question: What is an example of this difference?

Ask children limited to concrete operations what it would be like if people had tails. You will find that the answers you receive generally will center on literal descriptions of where the tail would be or how funny it would look; or the reply might be that people don't have tails, or that they might hang from trees if they did. The children will stay within the boundaries of what they have actually seen an animal or cartoon character do with a tail. Their ability to imagine beyond the concrete to situations or actions never seen before is limited.

Question: How would older children in the formal operational period respond to the same question?

The ability to form hypotheses beyond anything ever seen or experienced before becomes apparent. If you ask children who have advanced beyond concrete operations what it would be like if people had tails, they might respond that lovers could secretly hold tails under the table, or that people would leave elevators in a great hurry, or even that dogs would know when you were happy.

As you can see from this simple example, adolescents and adults are able to perceive abstract relationships far beyond the real and concrete. During the period of formal operations, individuals acquire the ability to make complex deductions, analyze ways of reasoning, and solve problems by systematically testing hypothetical solutions. The period of formal operations will be examined in greater detail in Chapter 18.

Piaget's Influence on Education

In 1957, the Soviet Union launched *Sputnik,* the first artificial satellite, and the United States wondered why its own scientists hadn't done it first. The nation's attention turned to its educational system. Something had to be done.

AT ISSUE

Children's Understanding of Adoption

One of the most difficult tasks facing adoptive parents is what and when to tell their adopted children about their status. Most adoption agencies and adoption experts strongly recommend that a child be told early in life, generally between the ages of 2 and 4 years, that he or she has been adopted. The typical suggestion is that parents start with the basic adoption facts and build on them with more and more information until the child comes to deal with and understand what it means to be adopted (Mech, 1973).

Alan is adopted; he is 5½ years old. He knows that he is adopted. Listen, as he discusses adoption with a researcher (Brodzinsky, Singer, & Braff, 1984, p. 873):

ALAN:	Adoption means you go to try to get a baby, and if you can't, you can't.
RESEARCHER:	Where do you get the baby that you adopt?
ALAN:	From your vagina or your tummy.
RESEARCHER:	Whose vagina or tummy?
ALAN:	The baby's mommy.
RESEARCHER:	Is the baby adopted?
ALAN:	Yes . . . cause the mommy has it now. It came out of her.
RESEARCHER:	Are all babies adopted?
ALAN:	Yep.
RESEARCHER:	If a man and a woman want to be parents, what do they have to do?
ALAN:	Adopt a child.
RSEARCHER:	Is there any other way of becoming a parent—a mommy or daddy—besides adopting?
ALAN:	I don't know.

The idea of telling children early that they are adopted and then building on this knowledge is based on the theory that children's knowledge results from a continuous and progressive accumulation of facts. As you know, Piaget's findings do not support this assertion. In the Piagetian view, children progress through different cognitive stages, and these stages are qualitatively different. Cognitive theorists who have studied Piaget and his work have therefore drawn a different conclusion about how to tell children that they are adopted. These theorists agree that children should be told that they are adopted, but add that they should be *retold* at each of the different cognitive stages, because at each stage they will have a different understanding of what "adoption" means. Alan, in our earlier example, is typical; very few 6-year-old children who are told that they are adopted understand the difference between adoption and birth or that these can be different paths toward parenthood. They also understand little about the adoption process or the reasons for adoption (Brodzinsky, Singer, & Braff, 1984). Once children enter concrete operations, their understanding of the different aspects of adoption grows; in adolescence, with formal operations, they reach a sophisticated and abstract appreciation of the adoption process.

Question: Should parents then wait until the child is older before trying to explain adoption?

The issue here really isn't whether parents should tell children early that they are adopted; adoption experts, as well as cognitive theorists, generally agree that they should. It is more the unrealistic expectations that parents may have concerning the effects of their explanations on a young child. For instance, when the parent of a 4- or 5-year-old girl quite comfortably says, "My child knows she is adopted," we have to ask if the parent realizes that the child has an extremely limited understanding of adoption. Does the parent realize that when the child reaches concrete operations, it might be good to describe once again, *from the start,* that she is adopted and what adoption means? Researchers have noted that a false sense of security after telling a young child, and the child's apparent comfort and acceptance of the information, "may well lead to a premature termination of the disclosure process—a factor that presumably could place the child, and parents, at risk for future adjustment problems" (Brodzinsky, Singer, & Braff, 1984, p. 877). The emphasis, then, is on telling and *retelling* the child about her adoption at each of the successive stages of cognitive development, so that at each stage the child can understand what adoption means as best as she is cognitively able to do so.

At just about this time, American psychologist John Flavell was busy translating the work of Jean Piaget into English. Suddenly, Americans "discovered" and embraced work that had been known in some parts of the world for 30 years.

Question: How did Piaget's work influence American education?

One could easily write a text on that topic—and many good ones have been written. However, given our space limitations, let's look at a simple outline of the major effects.

Teachers were encouraged to:

1. Gear education to the child's current stage of development. *Result:* Significant reorganization of class curricula.
2. Be oriented toward the spontaneous and creative aspects of learning: "Every time we teach a child something, we prevent him from discovering it on his own" (Piaget, 1964). *Result:* Former heavy emphasis on direct, structured teaching is reduced; creativity and flexibility are emphasized; the idea that structure inhibits creativity grows (although this assertion has been strongly challenged—see Chapter 10).
3. Broaden the focus of children's interest so that the children can apply their operational structures to many topics. *Result:* Curriculum opens, and many elective or special courses become available for grade schoolers.
4. Encourage children to expand at their own level of cognitive development rather than be accelerated through it. *Result:* Former practice of allowing fast or bright students to skip grades is discouraged.

Criticisms of Piaget

Without a doubt, Jean Piaget contributed immeasurably to our knowledge of cognitive development in children. His theories have had a wide influence on education and psychology. Nonetheless, a number of researchers have criticized some of Piaget's assumptions.

THE LEARNING THEORY REBUTTAL

Ever since Piaget outlined his theory of cognitive development, researchers have been stimulated to investigate the way children's thinking develops. Piaget viewed the young child as a naturally inquisitive being who adapted to his or her surroundings by developing cognitive—or mental—structures in a stagelike process. At each stage, Piaget argued, the child was able to handle a more sophisticated logic. Such a view is an example of an **organismic-structural approach.** The root metaphor for this approach is the growing biological organism (Reese & Overton, 1970). In this view, a child will grow mentally according to the biological dictates of the species and will develop into a final adult form following a biologically preordained pattern of development. This, of course, is why Piaget argued that the stages of cognitive development were universal: They were part of our biological heritage and were to be found in all people.

Throughout the years, however, there have been some strong arguments against Piaget's view, especially among researchers in the United States.

Question: How did American researchers view cognitive development?

Throughout the mid-twentieth century, the learning theorist's view was paramount among American psychologists. Proponents of behaviorism, such as John Watson and B. F. Skinner, took a **mechanistic-functional approach** to explain a child's cognitive development. The root metaphor for this approach is the machine (Reese & Overton, 1970). In this view, development does not occur from within,

ORGANISMIC-STRUCTURAL APPROACH
An approach to the understanding of cognitive development that takes as its metaphor the growing biological organism. Environmental influences on cognitive development are considered minor, with only extreme environmental forces having any appreciable effect on biological structure or development.

MECHANISTIC-FUNCTIONAL APPROACH
An approach to the understanding of cognitive development that takes the machine as its metaphor. Environmental influences on cognitive development are considered major, since machines don't change from within but must be added to from without.

as in a living organism, but rather occurs from *without* by "adding on" to the basic machine. In other words, cognitive development is the result of *learning* (the principles of which were discussed in Chapter 7).

Question: But didn't Piaget also believe that learning was important?

Piaget drew a distinction between development and learning. Piaget believed that the kinds of learning that the learning theorists had demonstrated in children, through their conditioning experiments, were the equivalent of teaching the children "circus tricks" (Piaget, 1952). For example, Piaget argued that children didn't advance *developmentally* when they learned to recite the alphabet—they simply learned to recite the alphabet. Learning theorist B. F. Skinner, on the other hand, countered by stating that the stages of development that Piaget had observed were nothing more than an illusion based on the kinds of questions that Piaget had asked and the tasks that he had set for the children. Skinner argued that children actually developed according to the principles of cumulative learning, that is, in an orderly and regular *quantitative*, not qualitative, way (Skinner, 1969).

In 1970, researcher Robert Gagné outlined cognitive development from the learning theorist's point of view. His description provides a good example of "cumulative learning" as applied to cognitive development. Let's take a moment to examine Gagné's description and also to try our hand at a problem that will show how learning theorists view cognitive development.

Gagné described complex cognitive skills as the product of a hierarchy of more elementary skills obtained through prior experience and learning. According to this view, complex skills can be acquired easily and quickly as long as the *simpler* prerequisite skills already have been mastered (Keil, 1981). The prerequisite skills required for drawing a square, for example, would be holding a pencil, drawing straight lines of equal length, and making right angles. Such prerequisite skills directly affect the way we think about problems.

Question: What is an example of how the prerequisite skills and rules I have acquired may have affected my thinking?

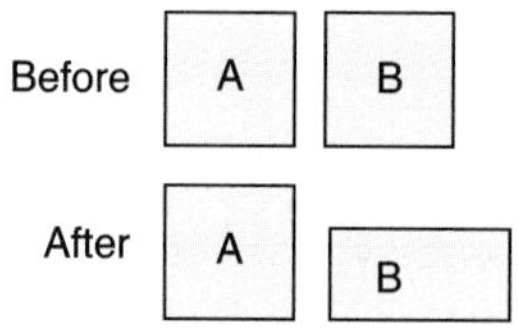

Before A B

After A B

Because you're an adult, you'll have no problem with the following conservation task, although a preoperational child would be hard pressed to deal with it. For the sake of the example, work through the problem anyway. The two square windows labeled "before" (windows A and B) are equal in size; they both contain the same amount of glass. Let's subtract 2 feet from the height of window B, but add 2 feet to its width. Now which window contains more glass, A or B?

Question: Don't A and B still have the same?

Do they? It's a good thing you don't sell glass for a living. Window A now contains more! Interestingly, preoperational children tend to answer this "pseudo-conservation" problem correctly; college students and developmental psychologists are likely to get it wrong. Try it again with numbers. To obtain the area of a rectangle or a square, you multiply the length by the width; in the case of windows A and B before the change, both areas are, let's say, 6 by 6 feet, or 36 square feet. After the change, window A is still 6 by 6 feet, or 36 square feet, but window B is now 8 by 4 feet, or 32 square feet!

*Question: Why did I get it wrong?**

You used the wrong rule to process what you perceived. You assumed that if we took 2 feet from the height of the window but added 2 feet to its width, nothing would be gained or lost; therefore, the area would still be the same. Don't feel too

*If you didn't get it wrong, feel free to sell glass for a living.

bad about it; it's not that uncommon for adults to rely more on context than logic or previous knowledge to conceptualize the best way to solve a problem (Winer, Craig, & Weinbaum, 1992). You did the same. You organized your thinking based on what you knew about conservation problems from your earlier reading of this chapter. You conserved when you shouldn't have! You forgot to recall that an area is an *interaction* of length and width. Of course, now that I've explained it to you, you understand it. Or do you?

Question: To get the area, you multiply the length by the width. Isn't that correct?

Do you truly *understand* now? Or are you simply applying one more rule to handle the information in a better way? Does this make you *qualitatively* different from a preoperational child?

Question: But I understand how to obtain the right answer, and the preoperational child doesn't. Isn't that an important difference?

But did you get the right answer? Actually, all you got was *an* answer—one that is useful in day-to-day experience. However, if you acquire further experiences, such as mastering Einstein's general theory of relativity, you will find that a window of 8 by 4 feet does not have an area of exactly 32 square feet! Because of the curvature of space-time due to the mass of the glass in the window frame and the mass of universe surrounding it, the total area of the glass will be ever-so-slightly greater than 32 square feet (Clark, 1971).

Question: I don't understand. How can that make sense?

It would make sense, perfectly good sense, if you had mastered Einstein's experience for handling information. The point is that there may be no "right" answer. There may be only more and more complex experiences that you learn to apply to earlier knowledge. To a learning theorist, the cognitive changes that occur throughout your entire adult life as you acquire more useful experiences are every bit as important as the cognitive advances that occur during your childhood. Each advance refines your ability to deal with your experiences.

The debate, then, boiled down to this: Were there universal discontinuous stages, as Piaget had suggested—stages that were structurally similar and common to all people, regardless of their culture and activity? Or, as learning theorists argued, was development continuous—without stages, with no particular sequence of development—and diversified among people as a *function* of their previous learning and conditioning? Concerning these questions, American learning theorists had many debates with Piaget and his followers (who were known collectively as the Geneva school, after the city of Geneva, Switzerland, where Piaget lived and conducted his research).

Question: Piaget had the results of observations and experiments on his side. What proof did the learning theorists offer to support their view?

Learning theorists mostly tried to show in experiments that the stages didn't exist and that there were no universal consistencies in cognitive development.

ASSAULTING STAGE THEORY

Question: How could someone design experiments that would show that stages didn't exist?

First, it's necessary to specify the requirements *for* a stage theory. To demonstrate convincingly that stages of cognitive development *do* exist, it's necessary to show that each stage is a structured whole unto itself (Piaget, 1957). The shift from one stage to another must be abrupt, as though some catalyst had suddenly changed all the diverse schemes in the mind (Fischer & Bullock, 1981). These sudden changes should occur "across the board," that is, in a given child at the same time, regardless of which task is being investigated. For example, when the stage of concrete operations is reached, defined according to Piaget by the ability to conserve, conservation should occur "across the board" on every conservation task given the child.

Question: Earlier in this chapter, you mentioned the horizontal decalage concerning concrete operations and showed that concrete operations occur when children are different ages, depending on the task involved. Doesn't that go against this last requirement for a stage theory?

It does indeed. The horizontal decalage frustrated Piaget, and some argue that he was never able to explain it adequately (Fischer & Silvern, 1985). Learning theorists jumped on this exception, which they saw as a flaw in Piaget's theory (Fischer, 1980; Bruner, 1983). Furthermore, learning theorists pointed to other experiments that also appeared to call Piaget's views into question.

Reexamining Piaget's Assertions

Question: Which experiments ran counter to Piaget's theory?

The kinds of experiments that raised the most serious challenges were ones that called into question Piaget's basic assumptions about the underpinnings of each of the four periods. There are scores of good studies from which to choose, so let's take a moment and quickly survey a few examples.

As you recall, the sensorimotor period is characterized, according to Piaget, by a lack of fully developed object permanence. Piaget argued that it was because of this lack of object permanence that infants younger than about 8 or 9 months generally fail to even look for an object after it has been hidden (Piaget, 1964). If strong object permanence could be demonstrated in young infants ("out of sight, out of mind," remember?), Piaget's theory might not be a very helpful place to turn for a satisfactory explanation.

Question: Has object permanence been demonstrated in young infants?

In an ingenious study, Renée Baillargeon (1987) demonstrated object permanence in infants only 3½ to 5½ months old. In her study, she used the habituation method to accustom infants from both the experimental and control groups to the movement of a solid screen that was attached to a table as the screen rotated up and away from the infant, raising up to its full height at 90 degrees and then continuing on over to once again lie flat on the table after a full 180 degrees of rotation (see Figure 9.4). Once the infants from both groups had habituated to the movement of the screen, the infants from the experimental group observed a box being placed in a location that would make it impossible for the screen to rotate more than 112 degrees without hitting the box (see Figure 9.5). In this condition, the infants would first see the box, then watch as the screen was first raised up to 90 degrees (blocking the infants' view of the box—out of sight, out of mind?), then rotated away until it struck the out-of-view box at an angle of 112 degrees (which should come as a surprise if the infant had forgotten that the box was there). The neat trick in this experiment was that for half of the infants in the experimental group, the box was secretly removed via a trap door when the screen was up at the 90-degree angle so that the screen would continue on for its full 180 degrees (just what the infants were used to seeing—what they had been habituated to). In this last situation, however, an adult, who would be expecting the screen to hit the box, would probably ask, "Hey, where'd the box go?" Interestingly, when the infants watched this same situation, they stared at the screen *significantly longer* when the box seemed to disappear than when the screen

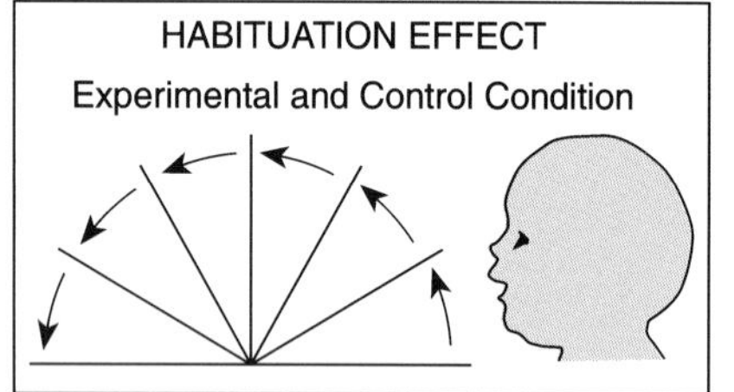

FIGURE 9.4
The apparatus used by Renée Baillargeon to habituate infants in both her experimental and control groups to the action of a moving screen. The infants were allowed to observe a screen raise up in front of them, reach its highest point at an angle of 90 degrees, and then continue on over once again to lie flat on the tabletop, having completed a rotation of 180 degrees. Both groups of infants observed the same stimulation repeatedly until they became "bored" with it. (*Source:* Baillargeon, 1987, p. 656)

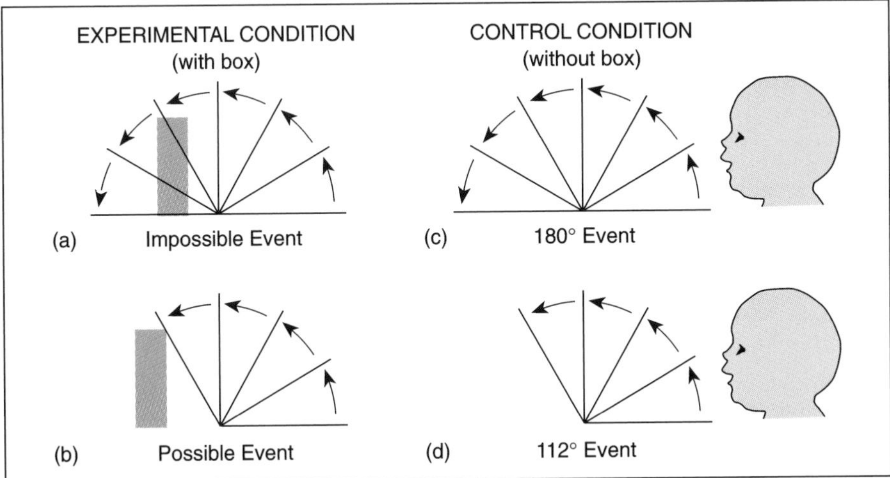

FIGURE 9.5

Infants in the experimental group observed a box placed in a location where it would be struck by the screen should the screen be rotated in the manner in which it had previously been during habituation. Half the experimental group infants were exposed to condition (a), in which the box was secretly lowered through a trap door when the screen had rotated to an angle of 90 degrees. The screen then continued to move the full 180 degrees, a seemingly impossible event to an observer who possessed object permanence, considering the location at which the observer would assume the box to be. The other half of the infants in the experimental group observed the screen strike the out-of-sight box at an angle of 112 degrees, condition (b).

No box was used with the control infants. They either observed a 180-degree rotation (c), as they had seen during the habituation event, or they saw the screen rotate 112 degrees and stop for no apparent reason (d). Of the four conditions, only condition (a) generated prolonged staring from the infants, indicating that these infants were aware that something strange had happened, something that they could not think strange unless they possessed object permanence. (*Source:* Baillargeon, 1987, p. 656)

struck the box. Infants in the control group were observed to see if they, too, would stare at the 180-degree rotation longer than the 112-degree rotation (which would have indicated that infants in the experimental group had looked longer at the 180-degree rotation probably because they had simply found it to be more interesting than the 112-degree motion), but the results showed that the control group infants *did not* look longer at the 180-degree rotation.

Now ask yourself, how could the babies in the experimental group have been aware that the 180-degree rotation was something unusual and pay more attention to it—especially after they had been habituated to it—unless, like you or I would have, they had expected the screen to hit the box, the box that was out of sight but apparently *not* out of mind. In follow-up studies, Baillargeon and her colleague Julie DeVos (1991) further demonstrated object permanence in 3½ month old infants using similar methods.

Other studies have also shown that there is more going on in the infant's mind than Piaget's theory might indicate. Among the more interesting of these are Andrew Meltzoff's studies of delayed imitation. Meltzoff investigated the ability of 14-month-olds to imitate simple behaviors a full week after having seen an adult demonstrate them (Meltzoff, 1988a). In Meltzoff's first experiment, infants watched adults perform a number of simple tasks, such as pulling apart a plastic dumbbell-shaped toy, pushing a hinged flap over the top of a box, pushing a button to make a beeping sound, shaking an egg that rattled, and bouncing a stuffed bear about by a string attached to its head. A novel act was also performed that the infants were not likely to have seen before; the experimenter bent forward and touched a plastic panel on top of a box with his forehead, which caused a bulb to light.

One week later, all but one of the infants imitated at least three of the actions when given the same toys to play with. The same could be said for only 3 out of the 24 infants in the control group. In addition, the novel act was imitated by 8 infants from the experimental group and none of the infants from the control group!

Meltzoff then went on to conduct another experiment similar to the one just described, only this time he used infants who were only 9 months old (about the age that Piaget noted that infants wouldn't even look for a hidden object, presumably because they had no object permanence). Meltzoff found that 9-month-olds in his experiment were able to imitate what they had seen even after a 24-hour delay. This led Meltzoff to conclude,

> The findings demonstrate that there exists some underlying capacity for deferring imitation of certain acts well under 1 year of age, and thus that this ability does not develop in a stagelike step function at about 18–24 months as commonly predicted. (Meltzoff, 1988b, p. 217)

Once again, we see that the underpinning of the sensorimotor period, namely the idea of a steady and stagelike movement toward object permanence, has been called into serious question.

Adding to this impressive body of work, Meltzoff went on to show that 14-month-olds can imitate actions 24 hours after they have seen them depicted *on television* (Meltzoff, 1988c). This last finding has implications for parents who wish to control which programs their children view. They might now want to extend that supervision to include even their infants!

Let's take a quick look at another example of research that has questioned Piaget's assumptions about the underlying properties of his stages. If you look back at Figure 9.2 you'll see an example of conservation of length (example 2). Study it for a moment. Piaget argued that preoperational children fail to conserve in this example because they don't have a *conceptual* understanding of length. Figure 9.6 shows two sticks like Piaget used next to five very interesting boxes. The children in the experiment we're about to discuss were considered preoperational and were between 3½ and 5½ years old. They were shown sticks of different lengths and asked which ones would fit into each of the boxes "just right"; that is, which sticks would not be so long that they didn't fit or so short that they fit loosely. The children were able to tell which sticks went into which boxes "just right" without difficulty.

Next, as in the classic Piagetian experiment, two sticks of equal length were laid side by side. All the children agreed that the two sticks were the same length. Then one stick was pushed forward. Just as Piaget had discovered many years earlier, the children now said that the one that had been moved forward was longer. But—and this is the interesting part—the experimenter then asked the children to point to the box into which the stick that hadn't been moved would fit. The children correctly identified the middle box. Then the children were asked to point to the box into which the stick that had been moved would fit, and they again correctly identified the middle box (Schiff, 1983)! Obviously, the children could not have made the correct choice unless they possessed a *conceptual* understanding of length from which they could derive that the stick had *not,* in fact, gotten longer when it was moved. William Schiff, who conducted this experiment, argues that children in the traditional Piagetian task fail not because they don't

FIGURE 9.6

The boxes and sticks used by William Schiff to investigate "preoperational" children's conceptual understanding of length. (*Source:* Schiff, 1983, p. 1499)

have a conceptual understanding of length but because they don't understand the question, "Which one is longer?"

Question: In what way were the children misunderstanding the question?

Maybe they understood the researcher to mean, "Which stick has been moved farther away from you?" In that case, the distance from the child to the end of the stick that had been moved *was* longer. Whatever the reason for the mistake, it's not that the children didn't understand the *concept* of length during the preoperational period, contrary to what Piaget suggested.

These are just a few examples of the hundreds of studies that have shown that children's behavior often fails to conform to Piaget's idea of well-defined stages (Carey, 1985; Gelman & Baillargeon, 1983; Keil, 1981).

In addition to the research that undermines Piaget's stages of development, some scientists have launched attacks on his work on theoretical grounds.

Question: What do you mean by theoretical grounds?

Look again at Table 1.1 (page 11) and you will see the research dimension labeled "descriptive vs. explanatory." Piaget's cognitive theory has aspects of both. It is descriptive, and it often attempts to be explanatory. As a *descriptive* endeavor, Piaget's theory is masterful. For over 50 years, Piaget and his colleagues recorded the responses of thousands of children throughout the world to various cognitive tasks. There can be no question that Piaget observed the way children respond to these tasks at different points in their development or that there are many similarities in the way children develop throughout the world. The difficulty with Piaget's theory usually occurs when an attempt is made to synthesize these descriptive observations into an explanation. Such a synthesis usually involves inductions—that is, making the jump to general principles from specific observations. This is the aspect of Piaget's work that has been criticized most often: Piaget may have made some premature inductions based on limited data.

Question: What do you mean by a premature induction?

A well-known fable from India describes how a number of blind men who knew nothing about elephants were led to one and asked to describe the animal by feeling it with their hands. The blind man who grabbed the tail said that the elephant was like a rope. The man who touched one of the elephant's legs disagreed, arguing that the elephant was like a tree. A third man holding the trunk said that the first two were both wrong; the elephant was like a snake. The last man laughed and wondered how the others could be so wrong. He had both hands against the elephant's side, and he said that the elephant was obviously like a wall.

The lesson is clear. One must be careful not to generalize prematurely when dealing with specific findings. Notice that all the blind men had given accurate descriptions but had failed to arrive at an inductive picture of the entire creature because each made a premature attempt, based on incomplete information.

As a description of a complex matter—the development of thought—Piaget's theory is unequaled. There is no question about the accuracy of what Piaget observed; as noted, his findings have been confirmed repeatedly. However, explanations of *why* cognitive development progresses as it does are not as clear.

It has also been argued that it is not clear exactly how the stages were initially selected (Fischer & Silvern, 1985). For instance, why should the ability to conserve be considered a great cognitive leap marking the start of a stage? Surely, a stage of cognitive development could just as well be based on the dynamic advances that occur during language development (see Chapter 8) or something equally interesting.

Question: But isn't the onset of conservation when children first begin to use logical operations?

Learning theorists argue that it depends on which tasks you examine. Our discussion of language development in Chapter 8 mentioned that children use the symbols and rules of grammar in a logical way quite competently throughout the period that Piaget called *pre*operational. A good stage theory, as was noted, should show each stage to be a *qualitatively structured whole* encompassing a wide range of different tasks and abilities (or, as psychologists like to say, *domains*). Because children can handle the *logical operations* of *grammar* when they are 3 or 4 years old, but can't handle the *logical operations* of *conservation* until they are 6 or 7, it can be argued that the onset of logical operations is not showing itself to be part of a *qualitatively structured whole across domains.*

These attacks on Piaget's theory give strength to the mechanistic-functional approach. Piaget addressed these concerns by considering each separate task along the decalage, including language, as a different domain (Beilin, 1992). In this way, each task was in accordance with Piaget's theory in that children approached each one (grammar development, conservation of weight, seriation) first in a sensorimotor way, then in a preoperational way, then in a concrete operational way, and finally in a formal operational way. Learning theorists saw this as the creation of hundreds of substages that, when lined up along a graph, began to approach a steady "learning curve" of gradual acquisition of knowledge that learning theorists had envisaged all along. Piaget countered that within each domain, no matter how many domains there were, the stages were clear, showing an abrupt shift from one to the next.

In the next chapter, we will examine how some researchers have attempted to integrate both the organismic-structural and mechanistic-functional approaches into a single coherent view of cognitive development. We'll also see how interesting areas, such as the development of egocentrism and animism, have been studied in greater detail, and we'll look at efforts by the students of Piaget to update and advance his influential theory.

LEARNING CHECK

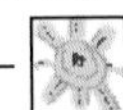

Multiple Choice

1. According to Piaget, among the abilities mastered *during* the period of concrete operations is
   - **a.** object permanence.
   - **b.** understanding of serial order.
   - **c.** syncretic reasoning.
   - **d.** all of the above.
2. According to Piaget, which is *not* a quality of concrete operational thought?
   - **a.** thinking in terms of abstractions and the hypothetical
   - **b.** reversing operations
   - **c.** classifying groups
   - **d.** understanding number concepts
3. According to the latest research concerning the development of object permanence,
   - **a.** object permanence does not begin until about 2 years of age.
   - **b.** object permanence is present at birth.
   - **c.** infants as young as $3\frac{1}{2}$ months have shown convincing evidence of object permanence.
   - **d.** none of the above; Piaget never discussed the exact age at which object permanence begins.
4. According to Piaget, which of the following cognitive abilities is *not* commonly found in the preoperational period?
   - **a.** syncretic reasoning
   - **b.** reversing operations
   - **c.** transductive reasoning
   - **d.** animistic thinking
5. A good stage theory
   - **a.** should be supported by a majority of researchers.
   - **b.** should argue for development in some domains but not all domains.
   - **c.** should be submetarepresentational.
   - **d.** should show the shift from one stage to another abruptly and "across the board."

Matching

6. ____ Organismic-structural approach
7. ____ Jean Piaget
8. ____ Mechanistic-functional approach
9. ____ Robert Gagné
10. ____ Renée Baillargeon

- **a.** Complex cognitive skills obtained through experience via a hierarchy of more elementary skills
- **b.** Root metaphor is the growing biological organism
- **c.** Criticized for making premature inductions
- **d.** Root metaphor is the machine
- **e.** Possible object permanence in infants as young as $3\frac{1}{2}$ months of age

Answers: 1. b 2. a 3. c 4. b 5. d 6. b 7. c 8. a or d 9. a 10. e

APPLICATIONS

Why Children Stop Believing in Santa Claus, or "Daddy, Based on Your Midnight ETA for Santa, I Don't See How Only Eight Reindeer Can Handle the Fuel-to-Load Ratio"

Let's take a moment to examine Piaget's theory as it might be applied to an interesting problem—namely, why children stop believing in Santa Claus. Because children throughout the world progress through periods of cognitive development in a specific order, and because each period is said to define the child's cognitive abilities, studying each stage of their children's cognitive development might help parents to understand changes in their children's thinking, such as why they stop believing in Santa Claus.

Question: But wouldn't that only be true if Piaget's theory is correct?

Once again, it is helpful to remember that Piaget's *descriptive* data are generally undisputed, although there are a few exceptions. The explanatory nature of his theory is what is typically debated. Thus, we are probably on fairly safe ground when we describe a child as being in, say, the stage of concrete operations, if by that we mean that the child will most likely approach certain problems in a certain way and will most likely perceive the world with certain limitations. *Why* the child thinks as he or she does is another matter, and there we may agree or disagree with Piaget's assessment. The point is that the "stages," whether they exist or not, can still function surprisingly well as descriptive terms. They can, of course, also function as explanatory terms, but with advised caution, considering that there are many unresolved issues concerning the data that Piaget's work has generated.

Santa Claus and a "true believer."

But let's get back to our important issue. Do you remember when you stopped believing in Santa?* I do. I recall that there was this one day shortly before Christmas when something seemed all wrong to me about the whole idea of Santa Claus. I suddenly began to wonder how Santa could possibly get all the toys that I wanted, along with the toys that I knew my friends wanted, not to mention the toys that all of the rest of the kids in the world wanted, into one sleigh. Conservation had struck with a vengeance. My mother recalled when it happened because I wandered about for days worried about this knotty problem that Santa faced and how it was likely to influence my Christmas.

Have you ever wondered what kind of thinking is required to believe in Santa Claus? Look again at Table 9.1, and you will see why children in the period of concrete operations—children capable of conserving—would come to doubt Santa's existence.

Can you see how a child who conserves amount will realize that for

*Assuming you ever believed in Santa.

APPLICATIONS

every child in the world to receive at least one gift, the number of toys must be at least equal to the number of children? Any child who has seen that seven or eight packages can just barely fit into the trunk of the car will be as perplexed as I was. How can Santa put all those presents in one sack (or even two or three)? Furthermore, a child engaging in concrete operations, who can understand the temporal sequence of events, will begin to wonder how Santa can visit every house in the world on one night. As you can see, even if the mean kid on your block hadn't told you that there was no Santa Claus, you'd probably have deduced it sooner or later on your own. I had just turned 6 when I found out. I suppose that was pretty old to finally get the picture. It probably took that long because the older kids on my street were kind and didn't say anything, and all my friends were just as gullible as I was.

I was proud after I found out, though. I felt as if I had accomplished some kind of mental breakthrough into the secret world of adults. Unfortunately, I had a touch of horizontal decalage. By the following March, I knew full well that there was no Santa, and was still proud of knowing that fact, but was happily waiting for the Easter Bunny to arrive. Maybe parents shouldn't lie to their kids in the first place. I still feel bad about the Easter Bunny, which had seemed quite a reasonable concept at the time. I wasn't ready for the truth about that, but my parents broke it to me rather than have me get much older and embarrass them. I suppose I had to grow up. There was no way to hold onto my old concepts once I had advanced cognitively, or was there?

Question: You mean that there might be a way for a cognitively advanced child to continue to believe in Santa Claus—and still be normal?

Yes, there is a way, and examining it will help you have an even better understanding of the logic behind Piaget's theory. It would be possible to maintain the Santa myth if you solved the child's dilemma. Parents sometimes try to accomplish this with statements such as, "Santa can do all these things because he has many helpers," or "Santa uses magic." Interestingly, if peers and other adults support the myth and supply such answers, the child may continue to believe. There are many cultures in which superstitions or myths, certainly as wild as the Santa Claus one, are firmly believed by even the adult members. This distinction is important. The fact that we develop more complex cognitive reasoning doesn't necessarily mean that we develop the ability to distinguish truth from fiction. To answer the question, Why do children stop believing in Santa Claus?, we must admit that it is *not* because children develop cognitively; it is because members of the society confess to the myth when a conserving child begins to chip away at it. If peers, parents, and other adults supported the myth and provided answers *satisfactory for the child's cognitive level,* Santa could be expected to survive the onslaught of concrete and even formal operations. (The Easter Bunny, too!)

SUMMARY

- Cognitive theory emphasizes the ability to think and the development of thought processes.
- The most prominent of the cognitive theorists was the Swiss scientist Jean Piaget, who developed a stage theory that emphasizes the interaction between biological development and experience.
- Piaget believed that because humans are genetically similar and share many of the same environmental experiences, they can be expected to exhibit considerable uniformity in their cognitive development. He outlined this uniformity in his four basic periods: the sensorimotor, preoperational, concrete operational, and formal operational periods.
- Piaget believed that children adapt to their world through the processes of accommodation and assimilation. Through this adaptation, Piaget argued, children develop schemes that help them to organize the world about them.
- The first of Piaget's cognitive periods, the sensorimotor period, is characterized by the lack of fully developed object permanence. This period is divided into six stages. All six stages have been observed to occur among the great apes, which further supports the importance of biological and genetic variables in the development of human cognition.
- During the preoperational period, children engage in syncretic and transductive reasoning. Piaget argued that they also have a tendency to be egocentric. The preoperational period is marked by a failure to engage in logical operations.
- Children in the period of concrete operations develop the abilities of identity, conservation, decentration, and reversibility. In addition, concrete operational children acquire the abilities of seriation, classification, and numeration.
- During the period of formal operations, children break free of the need for tangible representations gathered by their senses and become able to use their thoughts to form hypotheses beyond the real and to reason scientifically.
- Jean Piaget contributed immeasurably to our knowledge of cognitive development in children. His theories have had a wide influence on education and psychology. Nonetheless, a number of researchers have criticized some of Piaget's assumptions.
- Piaget viewed the young child as a being who adapted to his or her surroundings by developing cognitive—or mental—structures in a stagelike process. Such a view is an example of an organismic-structural approach. The root metaphor for this approach is the growing biological organism. Proponents of behaviorism, such as John Watson and B. F. Skinner, took a mechanistic-functional approach to explain a child's cognitive development. The root metaphor for this approach is the machine.
- Robert Gagné has outlined cognitive development from the learning theorist's "cumulative learning" point of view. Gagné described complex cognitive skills as the product of a hierarchy of more elementary skills obtained through prior experience and learning.
- Renée Baillargeon demonstrated object permanence in infants only 3½ to 5½ months old. Other studies, such as those by Andrew Meltzoff, have also shown that there is more going on in the infant's mind than Piaget's theory might indicate. Many other studies have also shown that children's behavior often fails to conform to Piaget's idea of well-defined stages.
- Some scientists have launched attacks against Piaget's stage view based on theoretical grounds. They have argued that it is not clear exactly how the stages were initially selected and that each stage often fails to show itself to be a qualitatively structured whole encompassing a wide range of different tasks and domains.

QUESTIONS FOR DISCUSSION

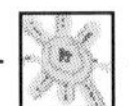

1. Do you think that there might be a cognitive stage beyond formal operations? For example, do you believe that Einstein was thinking in a way qualitatively beyond the abstractions of formal operational thought?

2. How might you apply your knowledge of Piaget's stages of cognitive development in arranging a program of education for children between the ages of 2 and 12 years? Why do you suppose that algebra isn't usually taught until the ninth grade, when the average student is 13 or 14 years old?

3. If you ask a 1-year-old child, "Where's Mommy?" he may actually leave his mother's side to go look for her where he most often finds her (Bower, 1979). What does this tell you about the child's concept of mother? Consider stage 4 of the sensorimotor period.

4. Would you feel comfortable drinking orange juice from a clean, unused bedpan? Concrete operational children (who knew what a bedpan was) didn't mind, as long as the bedpan was clean and unused. Adults, on the other hand, couldn't easily overcome their disgust (Rozin, Fallon, & Augustoni-Ziskind, 1985). How might the ability to hypothesize, which occurs in formal operations, explain the adults' revulsion?

SUGGESTIONS FOR FURTHER READING

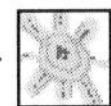

1. Flavell, J. H., Miller, P. H., & Miller, S. A. (1993). *Cognitive Development* (3rd ed.). Englewood Cliffs, NJ: Prentice Hall.
2. Howe, M. L., & Pasnak, R., Eds. (1992). *Emerging themes in cognitive development.* New York: Springer Verlag.
3. Keil, F. (1992). *Concepts, kinds & cognitive development.* Cambridge, MA: MIT Press.
4. Perkins, D. (1992). *Teaching children how to think: New strategies for parents & teachers.* New York: Free Press.
5. Sutherland, P. (1992). *Cognitive development today: Piaget and his critics.* New York: Taylor & Francis.

CHAPTER 10

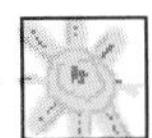

COGNITIVE DEVELOPMENT II: MODERN PERSPECTIVES

CHAPTER PREVIEW

REMEMBRANCE OF THINGS PAST

HAVE YOU EVER found something that suddenly brought to mind memories of things long ago? Perhaps you came across an old photograph, or a flower pressed between the pages of a book, or something that reminded you of where you were and what had happened on a particular day—memories that you were surprised you still had. Memories like these are known as *redintegrated memories*—memories that you couldn't have recovered without a reminder. The reminder—perhaps a photograph or an old letter—acts like a key, opening a door in your mind that had been closed.

A 6-MONTH-OLD infant is placed in a comfortable reclining position inside her playpen. A colorful liner is draped all around the playpen; it is bright yellow and has green squares on it. Next, a mobile with wooden figures and jingling bells is hung over the playpen, and a satin ribbon is attached to the mobile and then gently fastened to the baby's ankle. Pretty soon the baby realizes that she can make the mobile move and jingle if she kicks her leg. It's a fun game and she kicks more and more.

The next day the baby is again placed in the playpen, and the mobile is attached like before. Only this time the colors of the playpen liner are reversed; the new liner is green with yellow squares. With this new liner in place, the baby is once again set up with her mobile—but she doesn't kick. She acts like she doesn't know what the mobile is or how it works. It is like she has forgotten everything. If the original yellow liner with green squares is put back in place, however, the baby remembers the game and begins kicking (Rovee-Collier, Schechter, Shyi, & Shields, 1992)!

Question: What happened? Why did the baby forget when the liner was changed?

The baby apparently came to associate a certain location and its surroundings with the new kicking game she had learned. In the same way that the old photo brought back your "lost" memories, so the sight of the original liner brought back the baby's memories of the mobile game. With the original yellow liner with green squares, she was able to use the sight of her surroundings to redintegrate her memory of the mobile game. If, however, she was placed in surroundings that were different, she had no key to enable her to tap into her memory of the mobile game and she simply couldn't recall it! Even the sight of the mobile wasn't enough of a clue unless the surroundings were the same as when she first learned the game.

IN ALL, 85 BABIES were tested this way. The researchers discovered that if the original liner was changed in some minor way, kicking continued. (Apparently, these minor changes were not enough to disrupt access to the memory.) But if the original liner of yellow with green squares was changed more drastically, say, to yellow with green stripes or circles, kicking dropped off drastically. And if the liner was totally removed for the second test, kicking declined or stopped in that case, too.

EVEN 3-MONTH-OLDS showed these effects. For example, a 3-month-old who was trained to move the mobile in the kitchen, but who was then moved to the bedroom, stared blankly at the mobile as though he had never seen it before. Similarly, a 3-month-old trained to move the mobile in his crib, but then moved to a lower portable crib, didn't seem to have a clue about what the mobile was.

These kinds of experiences aren't surprising to memory researchers who work with adults. Perhaps you have had the experience of thinking about something in one room and then forgetting it later, only to find that you can often get the lost thought back by returning to the room in which you first had the thought. But researchers were quite stunned to find similar effects in young infants because it had been generally assumed that the possession and storage of organized memories required the presence of language or symbolic thought.

Question: How do researchers now think of infant memory?

Carolyn Rovee-Collier, who was the senior researcher in this series of interesting experiments, says that she believes that the surrounding contextual information in the infant's world acts like an "attention gate," giving the infant access to memories associated with the particular context. Babies, then, are learning very early something that is generally true, namely, that certain things often happen in certain places. For this to occur without language or mature symbolic thought indicates that memories created directly from the senses (from what has been seen, smelled, felt, tasted, or heard) are directly tied into memories for learned events without the need for language or complex symbolic thought.

IN THIS CHAPTER, we'll see how the field of cognitive development has matured and grown since the days of Jean Piaget and his supporters. We will see how modern researchers have delved as never before into specific areas of cognitive development, such as infant memory. We will also see how a Russian theory more than half a century old has recently created quite a stir, how a former student of Piaget is continuing to build and modify the master's stage theory, and how the advent of the modern computer has led to a different way to look at cognitive development. And finally, we will take a close look at some of the inquiries made by modern cognitive researchers.

RESOURCES

The history of child development is rich with the thoughts and ideas of many scholars and researchers. Sometimes the work of one person will have a great influence; Jean Piaget is a case in point. This next story, however, is about someone who died in relative obscurity many years ago, but who might yet have an important influence on the history of child development.

Between the ages of one and two children become consciously aware that they have a self.

The Social-Cognitive Theory of Lev Vygotsky

The Russian Lev Vygotsky, a critic of Piaget's, has been receiving much attention lately. It is somewhat odd, because he died of tuberculosis at the age of 37 in 1934.

Following his death, Vygotsky's work remained little known outside the Soviet Union because it had been banned by Stalin. During this time, many of Vygotsky's colleagues secretly continued to pursue the work that he had begun. However, even after Stalin's death, Vygotsky's work remained unknown to most Western scholars because English translations of his efforts were rare. All these circumstances help to explain why he remained relatively obscure for more than half a century.

Happily, the collapse of the Soviet Union has opened up a greater dialogue with Russian researchers, who are still elaborating on Vygotsky's work and who are both willing and able to discuss their efforts openly. In addition, English translations of Vygotsky's work are becoming more common.

Question: Why is Vygotsky's theory called "social-cognitive"?

In Chapter 7, we discussed the social learning theory of Albert Bandura. As you recall, Bandura argued that much of children's behavior is shaped by social exposure—that is, that children learn how to act by watching people model different behaviors. In Chapter 9, we looked at Jean Piaget's cognitive theory, in which he argued that the child's mind develops through interaction with the environment. Vygotsky's theory encompasses both these domains, emphasizing the social *and* the cognitive aspects of development. Both these motifs run throughout his work and can be found in the themes that underlie his intricate and encompassing theory. These themes are the influence of culture, especially the predominant role of language, and what Vygotsky called the zone of proximal development.

CULTURE, LANGUAGE, AND THOUGHT

In Vygotsky's view, each person is born with a set of elemental cognitive functions, such as the ability to attend, perceive, and remember. These abilities are unlearned. Each person's culture then transforms these elemental abilities into higher cognitive functions, largely through social interaction, especially through the teaching and use of language.

Question: How can the acquisition and use of language lead to the creation of higher cognitive functions?

Vygotsky argued that it is language that makes thought possible. He further argued that language eventually comes to govern behavior. He supported his argument by describing three types of speech—external, egocentric, and internal—which make up the stages of language-thought development.

In the first stage of "language-thought," called external speech, thinking comes from a source external to the child. Typically, the source will be an adult's speech directing the child in some way. For example, a child might be scribbling and his

ZONE OF PROXIMAL DEVELOPMENT
In Lev Vygotsky's cognitive theory, any and all activities that a child is almost able to perform or is able to perform with a little help.

mother might ask, "What are you drawing?" The child might reply, "A doggie." His mother might then ask, "Where's the tail?" and so on, directing the child's thoughts (Smolucha, 1988, p. 3).

In the next stage, called egocentric speech, the mother's speech is no longer required. The child now speaks out loud as a way of thinking. For example, while drawing, he might now be heard to say aloud, "This is a doggie. Here's his tail."

Question: How did Vygotsky know that this shift from external to egocentric language was related to thinking?

He conducted a number of experiments to test his assumptions. According to Piaget, the way children talked to themselves out loud (egocentric speech) was not social and was not related to problem solving but was simply an expression of the child's egocentric thought. Vygotsky was familiar with Piaget's view on this issue, and it stimulated him to test it. In experiments, Vygotsky discovered that children's egocentric speech increased in direct proportion to the amount of thought required of them to solve a problem (Vygotsky, 1934/1962). This finding, since replicated by American researchers (Berk, 1986; Kohlberg, Yaeger, & Hjertholm, 1968), demonstrated that egocentric speech is directly tied to the thought process, not what Piaget had supposed it to be.

By about the age of 6 or 7, children rely on what Vygotsky called internal speech and have fully internalized their thought processes. For example, a child might think to himself, "What should I draw? I know, I'll draw a picture of my dog" (Smolucha, 1988, p. 3).

Another important aspect of cognitive development, according to Vygotsky, is the **zone of proximal development.** According to this view, at each level or stage, individuals are prepared to be responsive to a particular environment and the people in it. A collaboration then occurs between one's cognitive structures and the environment. In this way, different experiences and cultures can shape a child's naturally developing cognitive processes, which then create a particular way of thinking about one's world. As an analogy, think of the developing child as a building under construction. Adults provide children with a *scaffolding* that helps direct and nurture their cognitive development. Thus, adults provide children with the kinds of special support needed for accomplishing what would normally be beyond a child's ability. In other words, adults guide children to discover gradually what adults already know (Radziszewska & Rogoff, 1991). Adults provide similar kinds of scaffolding for one another when they help each other develop different cognitive skills and ways of thinking.

Question: What is a specific example of scaffolding?

Let's look at a cultural example, although families and individuals also shape cognitive development. One study found that illiterate adults in the African nation of Liberia had a very difficult time when they tried to organize, categorize, and sort pictures of geometric shapes, such as differently colored triangles and squares. According to Piaget, this sort of task should be quite simple for someone who has achieved concrete operations, but these adults were confused by it and couldn't decide where to begin. When these same adults were given bowls containing many different kinds and colors of rice, an important food in their country, they quickly organized them into sensible and reasonable categories (Irwin & McLaughlin, 1970).

In a follow-up to that study, American undergraduates given the same pictures of differently colored geometric shapes had no trouble sorting or categorizing them into meaningful groups. When given the many bowls of rice, however, the undergraduates showed the same bewilderment and hesitation that the illiterate adults in Liberia had shown when faced with the geometric shapes (Irwin, Schafer, & Feiden, 1974). These findings support Vygotsky's view in that the scaffolding of each culture appears to have shaped its members' thinking and thought processes along different lines based on what is important to each culture.

As you might imagine, the concept of a zone of proximal development and the idea of scaffolding are having an impact on American education. While Piaget saw the drive toward cognitive development as stemming mainly from within the child, Vygotsky emphasized the spoken interaction between the child and his or her teacher, parent, or culture as the force that drives the child forward toward higher levels of thinking that might not be achieved independently. If you recall Piaget's quote—"Every time we teach a child something, we prevent him from discovering it on his own"—you'll see immediately how diametrically opposed Piaget's ideas are to Vygotsky's.

Vygotsky's ideas are stimulating research in the areas of language and teaching cognitive skills. His views will no doubt continue to stimulate research for many years to come. One can only wonder what might have been if Vygotsky had worked in a free society and had, like Piaget, lived well into his 80s.

M
In Juan Pascual-Leone's theory of cognitive development, the amount of mental capacity, or power, available for cognitive tasks. The greater the M available, the greater the number of schemes that can be mentally examined and manipulated at a given time, and the more advanced the cognitive skill and level of the individual.

Meanwhile, Back in Geneva . . .

During his lifetime, Piaget was his own greatest revisionist (Block, 1982). He changed old ideas for new and reorganized his thinking many times. It should come as no surprise that while Piaget's theory was being undermined by the recent interest in Vygotsky's work as well as by those who were arguing that cognitive development was continuous and not stagelike, a student of Piaget's named Juan Pascual-Leone was busy revising Piaget's stage theory so that it could withstand these latest assaults.

Question: What was Pascual-Leone's approach?

Pascual-Leone built on Piaget's ideas that the individual adapts schemes through assimilation and accommodation (see Chapter 9) and that children develop through distinct cognitive stages (Pascual-Leone, 1976, 1984; Pascual-Leone & Smith, 1969). For Pascual-Leone, however, the main thrust of cognitive theory was centered not on qualitatively different ways of thinking, as Piaget suggested, but rather on mental capacity, or mental power, depicted by the symbol **M.** M refers to the number of schemes that a child can attend to or mentally work with at a given time. The idea that the *amount of processing capacity available* is responsible for most, and perhaps all, cognitive advances is appealing because of its simplicity. In this view, cognitive development progresses as M increases. In other words, the more schemes, ideas, or concepts that we can attend to at a given time, the more we can compare, contrast, and examine them. With an M of only *a*1, you would be as limited as a young child. (The *a* in this instance refers to the M power needed to focus attention on a given task and to store the instructions given concerning the task; 1 means that there is enough M power left over to attend to one additional scheme.) With an M of *a*7, however, you could make thousands of comparisons and thereby handle complex logic, because you could attend to seven schemes at once (and thereby compare scheme 1 with scheme 2, 1 with 3, 1 with 4, and so on; 2 with 3, 2 with 4, 2 with 5, and so on). The amount of M, or processing capacity, was presumed by Pascual-Leone to be the result of neurological development. The ability to make so many comparisons would be required for the tasks of formal operations (Case, 1985). It's like a juggler throwing balls in the air. Each time a new ball—or a new M integer—is added, the juggler has stepped up the difficulty of the performance by one stage.

Question: Has Pascual-Leone's view been well accepted?

Pascual-Leone's improvement of Piaget's theory explains quite well one of the discoveries made by learning theorists who were attacking Piaget's stage view, namely, the ability of preoperational children to handle concrete operational tasks if the tasks are made simpler. For example, recall Piaget's classic conservation problem that begins with two identical glasses of water, one of which is then poured into a dish (see Chapter 9). The child is asked the question, "Which contains more, or are they the same?" As you recall, preoperational children usually fail this test, announcing that the remaining glass now has more water. If, however, we fill the two glasses equally with beads instead of water and allow a preoperational child to count each bead as we fill the glasses, the child is less likely to fail the conservation task when the beads from one glass are poured into a differently shaped container (Bower, 1979).

As you might imagine, this kind of finding presented some problems for Piaget's theory, because it implies that preoperational children can, after all, understand the *logic* of conservation, and whether they succeeded when given a conservation task really depended on nothing more than variations in the task's complexity. In Pascual-Leone's theory, such problems no longer pose a difficulty. According to the concept of M, once any task is simplified, the child should be able to understand it at a lower cognitive level because the child would need to juggle fewer schemes at one time to master the problem.

Pascual-Leone's advance on Piaget's theory brought new life and support for stage theories of cognitive development (Case, 1985). Even so, there were plenty of unanswered questions. For instance, how do we define schemes precisely enough to count them? The term *scheme* represents a concept that cognitive psychologists have about how the units of thought can be organized, but counting schemes requires a more precise definition. Furthermore, although Pascual-Leone has argued that a child's M power is too limited during the preoperational stage to handle the concepts necessary for concrete operations, he has been unable to explain how the same child is able to handle the logic and rules of language (Case, 1985), which, you may recall from Chapter 8, "preoperational" children do quite well. Pascual-Leone's improvements on Piaget's theory leave these and other questions unanswered.

Question: Then which is the best way to view cognitive development: as progressing in stages or as developing in a continuous fashion?

Debate concerning this question has been considerable. Some theorists believe that there is a way to construct a theory that contains elements of both views and also comes closer to describing and explaining most of the diverse data gathered in the field (see At Issue).

LEARNING CHECK

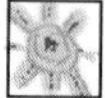

1. ____ External speech
2. ____ Scaffolding
3. ____ Scheme
4. ____ Lev Vygotsky
5. ____ A reconciliation of the Geneva learning theorist debate
6. ____ Juan Pascual-Leone
7. ____ Probabilistic epigenesis

a. A concept about how the units of thought can be organized
b. The first stage of "language-thought"
c. The typical or most probable development
d. The idea that cognitive development occurs in a universal stagelike progression and in a continuous way
e. Adults helping to direct and nurture the child's cognitive development
f. The idea that the main factor in a child's cognitive development is mental power (M)
g. Postulated a zone of proximal development

Answers: 1. b 2. e 3. a 4. b, c, or g 5. d 6. a or f 7. c

Information Processing

ARTIFICIAL INTELLIGENCE
A computer simulation of human cognitive ability and performance.

The information-processing approach is yet another way of looking at cognitive development. This particular approach is not generally considered a theory, but rather is thought of as a useful approach to the study of the field. At the center of this approach is the idea that the human intellect may function like a computer. In this view, both the human and the computer are seen as information-processing systems.

One reason that developmental researchers became interested in using the computer as a model for the human intellect was Piaget's emphasis on the growth of *logic* as the centerpiece of his theory. Although Piaget discussed the acquisition of logic and its development, he never dealt with the way it might be operating or combining to produce the performance of a given individual (Siegler & Richards, 1982). Researchers thought that by closely examining computers and the way they "think," they might find important parallels in human development. The idea, then, was to develop a model that, unlike Piaget's approach, offered a definite, exactly articulated description of the series of cognitive operations that humans perform when solving problems. After all, computers have memories and solve problems in very particular ways. It therefore seems reasonable to assume that humans might solve problems in a similar way.

Question: But has anyone ever developed a computer that can solve problems in the same way that humans do?

As far back as 1958 (the Dark Ages, by modern computer standards), Allen Newell and his colleagues developed a special problem-solving logic for their computer (Newell, Shaw, & Simon, 1958). They fed in a sequence of elementary logic problems and *compared* the results with solutions given by human subjects. The computer and the human subjects performed equally well. The computer even made many of the same errors that the humans did! To the shock of just about everyone, the fit between computer and human was remarkably good (Case, 1985).

Since that time, progress in **artificial intelligence** has continued at a rapid pace. Nobel laureate Herbert Simon, who was one of Newell's colleagues during those early years, believed that it was perfectly reasonable to assume that someday computers would be able to think like people. Although no one has ever claimed that computers and humans are the same, the computer does provide a model of cognitive development that stimulates research. Prior to the advent of the computer, areas of current interest, such as attention and memory, had been given little consideration by either Piaget or learning theorists.

SELECTIVE ATTENTION

The ability to pay attention is an important part of computer function and human cognition. But when computers were first given the job of paying attention to the sights or sounds that were about them, it was immediately apparent that the computer was even less competent than the average newborn. The computer simply had no way to organize or deal with the tremendous amount of stimuli that it found in sights and sounds. To create programs that enabled computers to sort meaningful from extraneous stimuli required a monumental effort. Only now are special computers just able to "recognize" faces or spoken words. It is hoped that as we discover the way to "teach" computers to pay attention, we may find out how we humans do it.

Question: How important for human cognitive development is the ability to attend?

Acquiring the ability to attend selectively to the relevant features of any object is absolutely crucial. Without that ability, we would be overwhelmed by extraneous stimuli and thus unable to attend to what is important. Every day we are bom-

AT ISSUE

All the World's a Stage—Unless, of Course, It's Continuous

The experiments and observations of supporters of both the organismic-structural and mechanistic-functional approaches (see Chapter 9) have been extensive and varied. In fact, a number of researchers have come to the conclusion that in a sense, both views are correct!

Question: But how can both views be correct? How can there be both stages and no stages in cognitive development?

Perhaps there can be both; perhaps cognitive development occurs in a universal stagelike progression, with each stage having a structural organization, *and* develops in a continuous way, with people showing differing individual cognitive development, depending on their learning histories and culture (Fischer & Silvern, 1985). It may be possible to integrate the two approaches if we look at it in the following way.

Piaget and other stage theorists may have demonstrated what is *typical* under usual environmental and organismic conditions, that is, what is *probable*. But there can always be variations. When modern theorists talk about stages of cognitive development, they often use the term *probabilistic epigenesis* to refer to the fact that stages describe only the typical or most probable development. In fact, researchers currently like to use the word *level* instead of *stage,* because stage has a rigid, inflexible connotation. Table 10.1 outlines the *levels* of cognitive development that best represent a consensus among most researchers (Fischer & Silvern, 1985).

Question: If both the mechanistic-functional and organismic-structural approaches have merit, then the environment must be viewed as being just as important as structural stages or levels. How do the two operate together? How do they interact?

Lev Vygotsky has provided us with a fine conceptual example in his description of the zone of proximal development, in which he argued that at each level or stage of development, individuals are prepared to be responsive to a particular environment and the people in it. In this way, different experiences and cultures can shape a child's naturally developing cognitive processes.

Question: What about the idea that the stages underlying cognitive development are mainly the result of genetics or biological maturation?

Evidence gathered from investigations of the great apes has indicated that cognitive development, at least during the sensorimotor period, may be closely tied to genetics and biological maturation. It may also be that infants and young children develop cognition in a more stagelike and universal manner because much of their development may be directly tied to neurological maturation (Fischer, 1987; Thatcher, Walker, & Giudice, 1987), whereas older children and adults may develop in a less stagelike and less universal manner because learning and individual experiences come to play a greater role in their cognitive processing (Lerner, 1984; Scarr & McCartney, 1983). In this approach, an interactionist view might eventually emerge that explains early cognitive development in terms of strong stages while explaining later cognitive development in terms of weak stages or levels. Future research may eventually help us understand more fully what role learning and biology play in the cognitive development of human beings.

Question: Where does our understanding of cognitive development rest today?

The general consensus (and there certainly are exceptions) is that there is an interaction between human beings and their environment and that we cannot assume that cognitive development comes mostly from within the organism or mostly from exposure to the environment. Both elements interact in a complex and complete way, resulting in important differences *and* similarities among people, cultures, and the way human cognition develops.

SELECTIVE ATTENTION
The process of discriminating one stimulus from multiple stimuli and attending to it.

barded by stimuli. We have no hope of processing all of it. If, in achieving our goals, we want to use the information we obtain, we have to focus our attention on the stimuli that have the most meaning for us. Such **selective attention** is essential for memory, problem solving, and thought as well as for perception.

An important information-processing theory in this area was developed by Eleanor Gibson. The theory is mainly concerned with the ability of infants and children gradually to learn to focus their attention on the important distinctive features of any object.

AT ISSUE

TABLE 10.1

A General Consensus of the Levels of Cognitive Development

COGNITIVE LEVEL	DESCRIPTION	AVERAGE AGE OF CHILD AT FIRST APPEARANCE
1. Sensorimotor actions	Adaptation of single action (child looks at a face; grasps a rattle)	2–4 months
2. Sensorimotor relations	Differentiation of a means from an end (child moves object aside to reach for toy)	7–8 months
3. Sensorimotor systems	Organization of schemes into a cognitive system—actions and events no longer are treated as unrelated or isolated (child knows that a rattle will make the same noise regardless of which action is used to shake it); actions also unified to make first words	11–13 months
4. Representations	Symbolization of objects, events, and people independent of any particular action by the child (child displays rapid growth of language; pretend play)	18–24 months
5. Simple relations of representations	Coordination of two or more ideas in a single skill (child can take the perspective of another and relate it to his or her own; can perform simplified versions of Piaget's concrete operations tasks)	4–5 years
6. Concrete operations	Combination of multiple representations to form complex constructs (child understands the constructs of conservation, seriation, classification, and numeration and is able to complete Piaget's standard tasks for concrete operations)	6–8 years
7. Early formal operations	Generalization from the concrete to construct abstract or hypothetical ideas (child is able to understand the concepts of justice, liberty, personality, conformity)	10–12 years
8. Relations of abstract generalizations	Coordination of abstractions (child can deal with relational concepts, such as liberal or conservative; can create new abstract ideas; is able to complete most of Piaget's formal operations tasks)	14–16 years
9. ???	Continuation of cognitive development clearly continues after the age of 16 years (Kitchener, 1982), but it is not yet certain that such development meets the criteria for a new level of cognitive development.	

SOURCE: Adapted from Fischer & Silvern, 1985, pp. 633–636.

Question: What is a distinctive feature?

A **distinctive feature** is any portion of an object that can be discriminated from any other portion. Take a look at the test depicted in Figure 10.1. How good are you at isolating the distinctive features? One of the reasons that your cognitive abilities are superior to those of a child is that you are more skilled at attending to the relevant features of an object. In fact, the older that children are, the more skilled they are at attending to such relevant distinctive features (Day, 1975). For instance, in one experiment, while 2- and 4-year-old children watched "Sesame Street," researchers carefully recorded the children's attentiveness. They observed that younger children were easily distracted, often looking away from the television. The older children, on the other hand, were better able to attend to the program and spent more time concentrating on its relevant aspects (Anderson & Levin, 1976).

DISTINCTIVE FEATURE
Gibson's term for that portion of an object that can be discriminated from other portions.

Some researchers argue that children 6 years of age or older are far superior to 2- or 4-year-old ones at recognizing distinctive features because they use the sys-

FIGURE 10.1

Attending to pertinent distinctive features requires systematic observation—a skill that children acquire slowly as they develop. In this test, the children are asked to find the object from the group that matches the top sample. (*Source:* Kagan, Rosman, Day, Albert, & Phillips, 1964, p. 22)

tematic techniques and logic common to the concrete operations level to conduct their visual searches and scans of objects. Using sensitive devices that record and measure the refraction of light from the cornea of the eye (a good indicator of where someone is fixing his or her gaze), researchers have discovered that the scanning techniques of 6- to 9-year-old children are systematic (Vurpillot & Ball, 1979), whereas those of younger children are not (Hale, 1979; Vurpillot & Ball, 1979). In Gibson's view, cognitive advances are furthered when children learn how to handle relevant information without being sidetracked or overwhelmed by stimuli that are not pertinent.

Interestingly, the time it takes people to process information decreases exponentially throughout childhood and adolescence at a rate clearly defined by a mathematical function (Kail, 1991).* For example, when comparing different tasks, such as pressing a button when a light flashes, tapping a button as rapidly as possible, moving 10 pegs in a pegboard from one row to another, or rapidly judging whether two pictures are the same or not, processing time decreases with age at the same rate. The fact that so many different tasks show decreasing processing time as children age and that these decreases occur *at the same rate across the board* implies the existence of a general mechanism for speeded processing of information (Kail, 1991).

THE DEVELOPMENT OF MEMORY

Memory is also an important part of computer function and human cognition. The power of a computer often is measured by its memory capacity. The more memory a computer can access, the more it can do. And as you recall, Pascual-Leone's theory is based on the argument that much the same is true of humans. Without a memory, a computer wouldn't be able to do much; neither would a human being. The information-processing view makes use of such an analogy and incorporates the language used to describe computer memory. In this view, new-

*For those interested in the mathematics, the developmental changes in processing times are defined by an exponential function of the form $Y = a + be^{-cx}$, where a represents asymptotic processing time set to the mean of the adult control groups, $b + a$ defines the intercept, e is the base of natural logarithms, x is age, and c, which represents the rate of change, or decay parameter, is set at 0.334 (Kail, 1988).

borns are born with "memory banks," except that theirs are made of developing brain tissue, not silicon chips. And although infants aren't programmed with information simply by being fed prepackaged data, they **encode** much of what their senses record.

Because of their biological organization, infants do have some perceptual understanding of their earliest sensations. As you recall, newborns can track a moving object with their eyes and can orient themselves in the direction of a sound (see Chapter 4). In a very limited way, then, newborns can innately engage in selective attention. Soon after birth, infants actively attend, thus beginning the process of encoding information from the environment, placing it in their memories for later retrieval. Experiments have shown that infants by 3 months of age already display the **storage** of different distinctive features. For instance, special operant conditioning experiments have shown that 3-month-old infants will forget the color of an object before they forget many of its other features (Fagen, 1984). One of the implications of this research, of course, is that the object's color must have been encoded into the memory *as a distinctive feature,* or how could it have been forgotten separately? So, even in an infant at the young age of 3 months, memory for selective features is already building—which, of course, is vital for the child's survival. And as you recall from the Chapter Preview, these selective features in the environment can in turn be associated with learned tasks and can be used to help recall these tasks from memory (Rovee-Collier, Schechter, Shyi, & Shields, 1992).

By the time infants are 6 months old, they can encode memories that can last for a very long time. For example, in one experiment, 2½-year-old children were retested for a memory of a task they had been trained to do when they were only 6 months old (reaching out in the dark for a rattle they could hear). Children who had had the experience as infants learned faster than control children who had not had such a previous experience (Perris, Myers, & Clifton, 1990).

As children grow older, their memories become more effective. However, not all memory abilities develop at the same rate. Certain components of memory may even be fully developed by the time children are 5 years old.

Question: You mean that in some instances, a 5-year-old can remember as well as an adult?

There are certain memory tasks that a 5-year-old child can do as well as an adult (Kail & Hagen, 1982). For instance, there appears to be little developmental difference between children and adults in the ability to judge recency (Brown, 1973). In one study, subjects were shown two pictures one after the other and were asked to state which picture they had seen first; 5-year-old children performed as well as adults. In fact, by using the habituation method, researchers have shown that even 11-month-old infants are aware of the sequence of two events and can recall, just as adults and children, which of two events came first (Bauer & Mandler, 1992).

SCRIPTS

Question: But isn't it true that an adult would most likely remember what he did during a whole day, and in what sequence, better than a 5-year-old would?

Probably. Of course, what interests cognitive researchers is *why*. At the moment, researchers aren't sure, but it may have to do, in part, with scripts.

Question: What is a script?

A **script** is a hypothetical cognitive structure that encompasses people's knowledge of the *typical* events in everyday experience (Abelson, 1981). By using the scripts you have come to know through experience, you can fill in what you may have

MEMORY
The complex mental function of recalling what has been learned or experienced.

ENCODE
In memory, to organize a stimulus input into an acceptable form for storage.

STORAGE
In memory, the placement of information within the nervous system such that the individual can retrieve it at a later time.

SCRIPT
In cognitive study, one's knowledge of the appropriate events that should occur in a particular social setting and of how one might carry them out. This includes knowledge of who is expected to do what to whom as well as when, where, and why. A script would include such typical behaviors as those expected of a person going to a restaurant or movie.

forgotten with what you think probably happened; you'll just fill in the blank spots, often without being aware that you are doing so, with information based on the common everyday events to which you have become accustomed. It is a valuable ability, because any events you can't recall you can *assume* based on a script—and be right most of the time. Children, on the other hand, with their limited knowledge and experience of the world, may be less successful at developing scripts.

Question: If children had greater experience with the world, would they seem better able to recall events?

In one study, children were given a detailed story about two boys who had lunch at a McDonald's restaurant. The entire lunch was described in a sequence that was familiar to all children who have been to a McDonald's. Later, when the children were asked to identify which words from a list were also in the story (words such as "wagon," "hamburger," "teddy bear," or "pie"), their memory was extremely accurate (Mistry & Lange, 1985). In this instance, the children were probably helped by their strong and clear script for a visit to a McDonald's. For example, if a child couldn't remember "hamburger," he might *assume* from his script that a hamburger was probably among the words associated with McDonald's. Children of the same age who were given a less structured story about a picnic in the park were less likely to recall the words on the list, although the same list of items was mentioned.

Question: Why were the children less likely to recall the list when the words were in the picnic story?

A script of what happens in the park is less structured than a script of what happens in a McDonald's. Each visit to McDonald's is fairly similar (providing a strong script of what is typical), whereas one trip to the park might vary quite a bit from another such trip (and so the script is weak because it's not certain what a park visit entails).

Further evidence for the use of scripts in recall comes from the fact that as memories fade, instead of completely forgetting something, children often replace the missing memory with a "recollection" of what they *assume* must have hap-

In Mistry and Lange's study, children had excellent memories of what they had done at McDonald's, presumably because their script of a McDonald's visit helped them fill in experiences they may have forgotten.

pened based on their scripts of day-to-day experience (Myles-Worsley, Cromer, & Dodd, 1986). With this in mind, however, it should be said that children's memory may sometimes be faultier when they use scripts because they may "fill in" things that never happened to them, but were simply typical of the script (Hudson, 1990).

Scripts also help children remember, or reconstruct, memories they can share. Young children who have similar scripts are more likely to have conversations about these events and share recollections with each other, which in turn facilitates important social interactions and the formation of friendships (Furman & Walden, 1990).

REHEARSAL
A technique for memorizing information in which an item is repeated over and over so that it is not lost from memory. This behavior may eventually result in storage of the item in the long-term memory.

The Development of Memory Strategies

Successful memory storage and access are important aspects of both computer function and human cognition. We adults possess some knowledge about the problems we are likely to encounter when we put information into our memories or try to retrieve it. Because there can be problems, we often try various strategies to help us remember information.

Question: When do children first learn to use specific memory strategies?

Children as young as 2 years of age engage in simple strategies to remember the existence of a hidden object, such as pointing toward where they last saw it, looking at the hiding place, or talking about it. Such behavior may be evidence of a very early attempt to retain what must be remembered (DeLoache, Cassidy, & Brown, 1985). As children become older, they attempt more formal memory strategies. One of the most common of these strategies is **rehearsal,** which is repeatedly going over material for the purpose of helping memory. Although rehearsal may seem to be an obvious strategy for aiding memory, it is not commonly observed in children until they reach about 8 years of age (Lovett & Flavell, 1990).

In a study in which 5-, 7-, and 10-year-old children were shown seven pictures and asked to remember three specific ones, only 10 percent of the 5-year-old children made some attempt to rehearse at least once, whereas 25 percent of the 7-year-olds and 65 percent of the 10-year-olds regularly rehearsed (Flavell, Beach, & Chinsky, 1966).

Question: Why don't children younger than 9 or 10 years commonly realize that they should rehearse something if they want to have a better memory of it?

In general, researchers have discovered that 5- and 6-year-old children are unlikely to use memory strategies to help them recall or encode information. At first, it was believed that children of that age simply didn't realize that memory tasks require some kind of special activity or effort. More recently, however, researchers have found that these children are able successfully to rehearse and memorize information if they are given extra time to do it *and* if they are able to observe visually all the information while they rehearse (Ornstein, Medlin, Stone, & Naus, 1985). This finding indicates that younger children *are* aware that they must do something special to memorize (Baker-Ward, Ornstein, & Holden, 1984; Wellman, 1983).

A lack of motivation also may be responsible for the failure of younger children to perform well on memory tasks in the laboratory. For instance, until children are exposed to such school-type memorization as learning a list, they may not see why it would be important to do so. In support of this assertion are observations made outside the laboratory that preschoolers have extremely good memories for stories (Mandler, 1983) and social or family events.

Question: When do children first demonstrate mature memorization strategies?

METAMEMORY
One's knowledge of how best to use one's memory.

METACOGNITION
All the skills and abilities that encompass one's knowledge and understanding about one's own cognitive and thinking abilities; what one knows about one's own cognition and thinking processes.

Mature strategy efforts appear when children are about 10 years of age (Hasselhorn, 1992). We can thus say that between ages 5 and 10 years, children are beginning to develop **metamemory;** that is, they are becoming aware that their memory works in certain ways and that certain efforts are required to use it effectively (Fabricius & Wellman, 1983). However, children as young as 4 years of age can make effective use of certain memory strategies if carefully instructed about how to incorporate them (Lange & Pierce, 1992).

Question: Are memory and memory strategies solely dependent on maturation for their development?

Experience also can play a strong role in the development of memory and memory strategies. In one study, Michelene Chi compared the abilities of 10-year-old children with those of college students to recall positions of chess pieces on a board. The college students did not have an unfair advantage, because they were chess beginners, whereas the 10-year-old children were chess masters. In this instance, the children were far superior to the adults in recalling the positions of the pieces (Chi, 1978). When the same children and adults were asked to memorize a series of random numbers with which neither had any special experience, the adults' scores were superior.

The first signs of metamemory appear when a child realizes that had she used a particular memory strategy earlier she would be able to remember something now.

Question: Do computers make use of a metamemory, or is metamemory strictly a human attribute?

Computers can have a metamemory of sorts. They often incorporate what are called *executive programs* (programs that oversee and control other programs). H. A. Simon (who, with Allan Newell, developed the problem-solving computer we discussed earlier) applied executive programs to his problem-solving computer. From time to time, the program reorganized the computer's knowledge, allowing the computer to process information at a higher level (Simon, 1962). As an extremely simple example, the computer program might find "$32 \times 25 - {}^{14}/_{2}$" and replace it with "793," because these two terms refer to the same thing. This action now leaves the computer with more M power, or memory space, for other data. In much the same way, once a new problem has become routine for you, you might replace "Take my laces, make an X, bring one under and pull it tight, now make a loop, . . ." with "Tie my shoe." Simon intended to show how an information-processing system could work in logical stages like those Piaget had outlined for human cognitive development. When the executive program reorganized itself, the entire program appeared to show a sudden improvement in power, much like the stage advances observed by Piaget. Perhaps something akin to this does occur in humans. Perhaps, from time to time during development, a cognitive restructuring takes place in which all current knowledge is reorganized and somehow better integrated. Such changes might be responsible for the different universal levels of cognitive development we see.

METAMEMORY AND CULTURE

Question: Do children throughout the world show the same development of metamemory as they grow older?

Surprisingly, they don't, which raises an interesting point. It appears that certain experiences are necessary before the child begins to emerge as a memory strategist. Some researchers have concluded that the most important experience is exposure to formal schooling (Cole & Scribner, 1977). These researchers argue that because schools place such a heavy emphasis on the ability to memorize, children begin to acquire memorization strategies by necessity so that they can succeed in school. Evidence for this also comes from cross-cultural studies showing that German children are better memory strategists than their same-age American counterparts primarily as a result of the emphasis on memory strategy found in German schools (Carr, Kurtz, Schneider, Turner, & Borkowski, 1989).

Although advances in memory skills and cognitive development may occur because children are exposed to a formal schooling that requires them, such advances may also be stimulated in any situation in which the advanced skill becomes *needed*. For example, let's look at the mathematical proficiency of children who have had no formal schooling but who nonetheless require such skills to survive. Geoffrey Saxe (1988) studied Brazilian children who were between the ages of 10 and 12 and who made a living as street vendors. Not too surprisingly, he found them to have mathematical skills far superior to street children who didn't sell for a living. This example provides another illustration of what is meant by social scaffolding and further supports the idea that cognitive development cannot be viewed out of its specific environmental context.

Children who are street vendors, but who have little or no formal education, show remarkable memory and mathematical skills.

Other memory tasks besides the kind of list memorization required by most schools—tasks such as the everyday chore of recalling the location of objects or remembering incidents—seem to be independent of schooling. In such everyday cases, educated children and uneducated children do equally well (Rogoff & Waddell, 1982). In fact, it appears that people encode some memories, such as whether an object was to the right or left, so automatically that they can recall them even though they made no active effort to remember them (Park & James, 1983). Such "automatic" encoding is even found among children as young as 3 or 4 years of age and may even develop much earlier (Hazen & Volk-Hudson, 1984).

Furthermore, automatically encoded memories appear to be independent of memory strategies. For example, one study tested the recall abilities of schooled and unschooled children and adults in Morocco (Wagner, 1978). The schooled children were far superior to the unschooled children and unschooled adults. But when tested on a recognition task, such as whether they had seen a particular object, all groups showed equal scores, regardless of schooling. Exactly how schooling influences metamemory and which experiences are the most important for children to develop their memory remain a mystery for future researchers to solve.

Metacognition

The information-processing metaphor of the mind as a computer is an interesting model, but it has some obvious limitations. To begin with, the model can't adequately explain why change occurs, that is, why human cognition is a developing rather than a static phenomenon. Perhaps a more important failing of the model is that however you look at it, computers aren't human. They can't think for themselves.

Unlike computers, there is something unique and mysterious about human beings. We are consciously aware, and we deliberately exercise control over many of our own thoughts, thereby demonstrating **metacognition,** the ability to think about thought. This observation isn't new, of course. Even Lev Vygotsky, writing so many years ago, deemed these two human aspects, self-awareness and deliberate control of thought, to be what made cognition so uniquely human (Vygotsky, 1934/1962).

Question: What causes us to have self-awareness?

That is perhaps the greatest philosophical question of all time, and no one so far has an even remotely satisfying scientific answer. All the world's great religions have addressed the issue and refer to a soul or spirit. And until fairly recently, self-awareness was believed to be a uniquely human attribute. But as you read in the Chapter 9 Preview, the great apes may share this quality with us.

Question: Why might apes share this attribute with our species?

The data indicating that great apes also pass through a sensorimotor period and develop object permanence (see Chapter 9) may help explain why they share a sense of self-awareness with our species. Perhaps once a creature begins thinking to itself by using internal representations of objects (object permanence), it suddenly becomes aware that it has a self. Maybe that's why the child and great apes described in the Chapter 9 Preview recognized their own reflection when they looked in a mirror. This may also explain why young infants don't know what the mirror is reflecting. Their object permanence has not developed sufficiently for them to engage in the kinds of internal thinking that may be necessary before a sense of self-awareness can develop.

Once self-awareness develops, thought becomes possible as we begin to mull things over in our minds.

Question: How do researchers study metacognition?

The typical approach is to examine the strategies used by children or adults when they try to purposefully reorganize their thinking.

Question: Would you give an example of what you mean?

Researchers have discovered that an important difference in memory effectiveness between children and adults may be due to the different ways they organize the information contained in their memories (Cox, Ornstein, Naus, Maxfield, & Zimler, 1989). In one study of the memories of fourth graders and adults, researchers found that the adults tended to organize information in ways that made access and recall much easier (see Figure 10.2). Once the researchers observed how the adults and fourth graders clustered nouns given to them, they prepared new lists incorporating these clusters. They then gave the fourth graders the adults' clusters to memorize (in other words, the children were given the nouns grouped as the adults had clustered them). For example, the children might have been given *flower, seed, tree, apple,* and *wheat* as one group and *cabin, tent, room,* and *window* as another group. The adults, on the other hand, were given the fourth graders' clusters to memorize. Afterward, both the fourth graders and the adults were asked to recall the nouns. When the fourth graders used the adults' clustering strategies, their memory for the nouns significantly improved compared to when they used their own clusters. Conversely, adult scores fell significantly when they were forced to use the fourth graders' clustering techniques as opposed to their

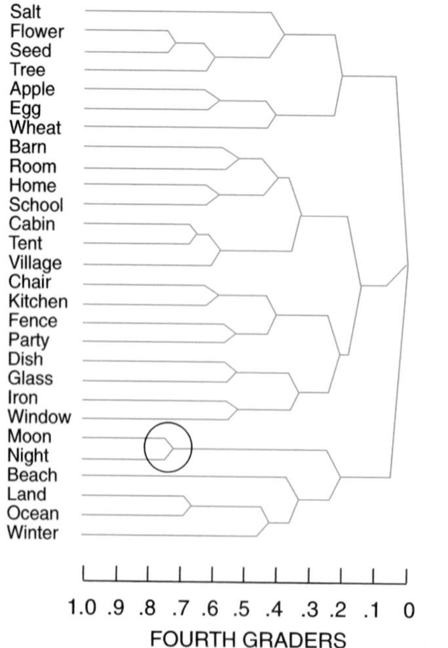

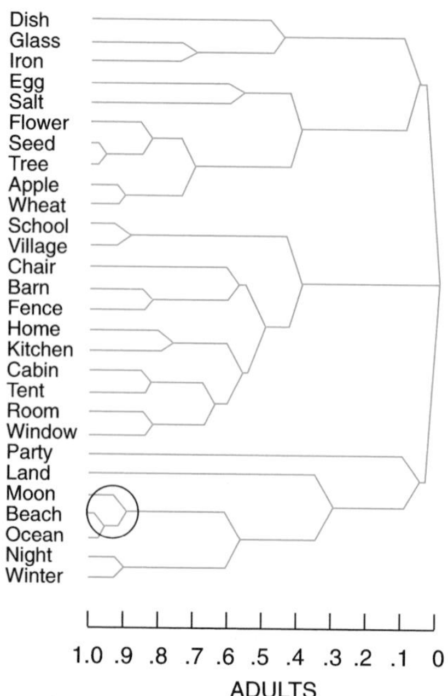

FIGURE 10.2

Ways in which fourth graders and adults organized nouns they were required to remember. For instance, 70 percent of the fourth graders associated *moon* and *night* (circled area), whereas 90 percent of the adults associated *moon, beach,* and *ocean* (circled area). In other words, 70 percent of the fourth graders who remembered *moon* were also more likely to remember *night,* while 90 percent of the adults who remembered *moon* were also likely to remember *beach* and *ocean.* These associations were plotted according to the probability of recall. Thus, if a child recalled *barn,* there was a 50 percent probability that he or she also would recall *room.* The adults' organization facilitated better recall. (*Source:* Liberty & Ornstein, 1973, p. 177)

own (Liberty & Ornstein, 1973). Although the fourth graders' scores (even when using adult clusters) were never as high as the adults', and the adults' scores never fell as low as the fourth graders', the differences indicated that fourth graders had been using an inferior organization strategy and could benefit cognitively by using adult approaches to organization. Interestingly, it has also been shown that once children have been taught to use advanced sorting strategies, they will often apply their new metacognitive skills to other tasks, enabling them to increase their success—and providing us with a nice example of how scaffolding can foster the development of metacognition (Cox, Ornstein, Naus, Maxfield, & Zimler, 1989).

And the Research Continues . . .

As you have no doubt noticed, much of what we have discussed in Chapters 9 and 10 has focused on theoretical considerations, such as whether cognitive development occurs in a stagelike fashion or in a more continuous way or even in a way that might combine both approaches. We've examined ways to approach the understanding of cognitive development, viewing it through the eyes of Piaget, Vygotsky, learning theorists, and computer modelers. But in so presenting the information, I may have done you a disservice. Something may have been lost as you came to understand the current scope of cognitive developmental research.

Question: What did you leave out?

In the day-to-day world of the researcher, there is often more concern for a detailed analysis of a particular area of interest than there is in settling theoretical disputes. In a textbook such as this one, it is necessary to provide a theoretical overview so that you, the student, can see the "big picture." Unfortunately, in so doing, you lose a feel for much of the fun and excitement that research in the field offers for those who go exploring. So for the remainder of this section, let's take a closer look at several researchers who are simply digging into cognitive development, looking only to find out more about the things that have captured their interest. And while you may discover that there are some theoretical angles in these studies, you will see that the main thrust is that of basic research, that is, the pursuit of knowledge for its own sake and the fun of satisfying one's curiosity.

EGOCENTRISM

Fairly early in his career, Piaget argued that egocentrism was common to the preoperational period, occurring most often among the youngest children in the period and becoming less common just prior to the onset of concrete operations. Piaget assumed that as egocentrism diminished over the preoperational period, children were developing the conceptual understanding that others are different human beings and possess different viewpoints. Considering all the attention that egocentrism received in America,* it is interesting that egocentrism wasn't a major point of interest for Piaget; in fact, until late in his career, he rather ignored the preoperational period to concentrate on the other three periods of cognitive development (Beilin, 1992). Piaget even dropped the use of the term *egocentric* early on because he felt it was too often misunderstood to mean selfish or self-centered (Beilin, 1992).

However, curiosity about egocentrism among American researchers did help spawn a series of fascinating investigations concerning how and when children

*American psychologists, especially learning theorists eager to prove Piaget wrong, conducted many experiments showing that preoperational children were often not egocentric (e.g., 4-year-olds typically understand that someone else will not know a secret unless it has been shared with them). Many conducted these studies based on the misunderstanding that Piaget had claimed that preoperational children were *always* egocentric in their responses, something that Piaget never said (Beilin, 1992).

COPY THEORY OF KNOWLEDGE
A theory that helps explain the occurrence of egocentrism among preoperational children. It holds that preoperational children act as though knowledge is not subjective but instead lies within objects; thus, all persons who are in line of sight of an object, regardless of orientation or experience, receive the same copy image of that object as the child does.

come to understand that others may have views and ideas different from their own. Let's take a look at some of these interesting experiments.

In the first of these experiments, a three-dimensional head of a witch was utilized (nothing special—just the typical three-dimensional head of a witch that you'd find in most homes). The head was then placed on a table between 4-year-old children and an adult observer. The witch faced the children; the observer could only see the back of the witch's head. When the children were asked what the observer saw, they gave egocentric answers; they argued that the observers, too, could see the witch's face. Interestingly, when the witch's head was split down the middle and the front of the head was separated from the back by a small distance, the children's egocentrism disappeared! In this arrangement, the children seemed to understand that while they could see the witch's face, the observer could see only the back of the witch's head (Masangkay et al., 1974).

The Copy Theory of Knowledge

Question: Why did separating the witch's head change the child's understanding of the observer's perspective?

Attempts to explain this phenomenon led to the development of the **copy theory of knowledge** (Chandler & Boyes, 1982)—that preoperational children act as though any object within an individual's *line of sight* projects a common copy of itself into the observer's mind. Another way of saying this is that the child behaves as though knowledge is not symbolic, having developed within an observer, but instead is a real property of objects and that anyone within line of sight of an object will somehow be bombarded with all the information that object has to offer.

In a demonstration of such reasoning, John Flavell and his colleagues at Stanford University placed a drawing of a turtle on a table in front of 4- and 5-year-old children (see Figure 10.3). An observer sat on the opposite side of the table. From the observer's point of view, the turtle appeared upside down, whereas from the child's viewpoint, it appeared right side up. The children's initial reactions were egocentric. They believed that the observer also saw the turtle in the same orientation as they did. However, when a thin screen was placed on the picture of the turtle, bisecting it top from bottom, the children immediately realized that while they could see the feet, the observer could see only the back of the turtle (Flavell, Everett, Croft, & Flavell, 1981). The line of sight along which "objective" knowledge could travel was broken.

This demonstration also explains why separating the witch's head changed the child's understanding of the observer's perspective. As long as the head was viewed as one object and the child saw that the observer was in the line of sight of that object, the child believed that the observer saw exactly what the child saw, that

FIGURE 10.3
Flavell's egocentrism experiment. In the first situation, the child believes that the observer sees exactly what the child sees. In the second situation, a thin screen bisects the turtle, and the child realizes that the observer can see only what is in direct line of sight—that is, the turtle's back.

is, the witch's face. As soon as the head was separated and the child saw *two* objects, one of which was eclipsed by the other, the child understood that the observer could see only the object in direct line of sight, that is, the back of the witch's head.

Children's Understanding of False Beliefs Researchers have known for some time that 3-year-old children have great difficulty understanding that someone else may hold a belief that is false about something that they themselves know to be true. This failure implies that children of this age do not possess a "theory of mind"; that is, they don't grasp that others think differently and therefore come to different conclusions than they themselves might. To better understand this phenomenon, consider the following: A 3-year-old child and a woman named Ellie (an assistant to the experimenter) are shown two flowers, a big one and a small one. Both agree which is which. Ellie then leaves the room. Next, the experimenter raises a screen that will block Ellie's view of the flowers when she returns. The small flower is then removed, leaving only the big flower behind the screen where the child and the experimenter can see it. Upon her return, Ellie is asked whether she thinks that they have a big or small flower behind the screen that is blocking her view. Ellie says, "I can't see the flower. Hmm. *I don't think* you have a big flower over there. I *think* you have a flower that is *not* big" (Flavell, Flavell, Green, & Moses, 1990, p. 923).

Children who are 4 or 5 years old, like those used in the bisected turtle experiment, will generally realize that Ellie cannot see the flower because her line of sight to it is broken and, because of what she said, will state that Ellie believes that it is the small flower that is hidden, even though it isn't. But among the group of 3-year-olds, two-thirds of them said that Ellie believed that it was the *big* flower that was behind the screen because that is what they themselves could see. They held onto this belief in spite of what Ellie had said. They held onto the egocentric idea that Ellie, too, somehow knew what they themselves knew—that the big flower was present even though Ellie had said that she believed them to be hiding the small one.

This experiment helps to show how knowledge, as described by the copy theory, develops between the ages of 3 and 5. But much more interesting was another experiment with Ellie and the flowers. In this version, 3-year-olds and Ellie were shown a large colorful flower and a sad-looking dried-up little flower. They were asked which was prettier. All of the children said that the big colorful flower was prettier. Ellie, however, made the opposite judgment and said that she thought that the little dried flower was the pretty one. Then the experimenter asked the critical question: "Ellie can choose just one flower to keep. Which flower will she choose to take home and keep?" (Flavell, Flavell, Green, & Moses, 1990, p. 925).

Question: What did the children decide?

Ninety-one percent of the children said that Ellie would pick the little dried flower! When it came to a matter of values or taste, the 3-year-olds seemed to know that other people have different desires, likes, and dislikes, than they themselves do. When it comes to a matter of fact, such as which flower is present, rather than which is prettier, they tend to be much more egocentric.

Question: Why does this difference occur?

No one is really sure. The best guess is that somehow children come to have an earlier understanding of desire than they do of knowledge (Flavell, Flavell, Green, & Moses, 1990). They seem to learn early that people have different likes and dislikes. Interestingly, under the right circumstances, even 3-year-olds can show a grasp of others' knowledge. In one study, 3-year-olds were asked to play a hide-and-seek game and to make it hard for someone else to find the treasure they were hiding. In this case, even 3-year-olds took steps such as hiding evidence of where they had been or producing false trails—both acts designed to lead others to false beliefs about what they themselves know to be true (Hala, Chandler, & Fritz, 1991).

Question: Then is it correct to say that children by the age of 3 have a "theory of the mind" in that they can understand thought from the perspective of another?

It is probably correct to say that by the age of 3, children are beginning to form a theory of the mind, but their understanding is limited and will continue to grow and develop. For instance, the idea that the mind of another person is part of that person, like an arm or leg, is more complex and not understood by children until they reach a later age. For example, consider one interesting experiment in which children were asked how it would be for them if their brains were switched with those of another child. Although they were instructed as to the process of such an operation, children much younger than 7 were hard pressed to grasp that after such a switch they would still be themselves but residing in someone else's body (Johnson, 1990).

ANIMISM AND ARTIFICIALISM

Piaget believed that children in the preoperational stage of cognitive development could not distinguish between self-generated and externally caused movement. He assumed that preoperational children believed that any object in motion was alive, that is, was animate. Piaget also argued that preoperational children showed a high degree of artificialism; that is, they believed that naturally occurring events were caused by people.

Modern researchers have discovered, however, that animism in young children is not as common or as clear-cut as Piaget had thought (Bullock, 1985). In Piaget's initial investigations, he asked children about inanimate entities such as the sun or the wind, which are not as clearly inanimate to children as are things such as rocks or chairs. Had he chosen objects more obviously inanimate, he would have found less animism. For instance, in one study, only 9 percent of 3-year-old children thought that vehicles were alive, even though vehicles move, and only 13 percent of them thought that dead animals were alive, even though they looked like their living counterparts (Dolgin & Behrend, 1984).

Rochel Gelman and her colleagues wondered how it is that children come to know whether or not an object is living. Among adults, the distinction as it pertains to daily life is so obvious that we rarely stop to consider it:

> Without reflecting on it, adults constantly make use of their implicit knowledge about the differences between animate and inanimate objects. When we fold up our umbrellas and put them in the closet, we fully expect them to be there the next time we need them. We do not expect them to have changed size or position, to have grown, eaten, fallen asleep, and so forth. (Massey & Gelman, 1988, p. 307)

To investigate how this understanding develops, Gelman examined natural kinds of objects, such as tigers, gold, cactus, and water—natural in the sense that they are found in nature and are not manufactured in the way that chairs, gloves, and cars are.

Gelman discovered that when she showed 3- and 4-year-old children these natural kinds of objects, the children typically classified them according to conceptual categories. By classifying the objects in this way, the children were then able to infer that objects of a kind would share unforeseen properties. In one instance, children were told certain properties about a black beetle and then also shown a picture of a leaf. When next shown a picture of a leaf bug (an insect that looks very much like a leaf), the children chose to infer that the leaf bug would share the same attributes as applied to the *categorically similar* black beetle but not to the *perceptually similar* leaf.

Results such as these have shown that, "by age 4, children can override perceptual similarity to make inferences on the basis of category membership" (Gelman & Markman, 1987, p. 316). Even 2-year-olds will organize objects in a similar fashion, placing together those that are categorically similar rather than perceptually similar, but only if the objects are obvious members of a particular category. For example, although different-looking birds (eagles, pigeons, and owls) might be organized into one category by a 2-year-old, the child might not include a bird like a penguin or a dodo, because these birds don't clearly look like birds. In all likelihood, 2-year-olds are less inclusive in their categorizations than are 3- or 4-year-olds because the younger children are less able to attend to the distinctive features that determine members of a given category (Gelman & Coley, 1990). Older children, for instance, are more likely to include a penguin as a bird because they are better able to pick out the more subtle distinctive features that penguins have in common with other birds, such as wings.

Even infants 10 to 13 months old will correlate certain distinctive features as belonging together. For example, in one study, infants of this age were habituated to pictures of two types of imaginary animals. Among these imaginary animals, the ones that had feathers for tails also had ears, while those that had furry tails had antlers. When shown new animals, the infants reacted only when the correlation between distinctive features that they had learned was violated, that is, if the new animal with a furry tail was now shown with ears, or if a new animal with a feathered tail now was seen to have antlers (Younger, 1990).

In applying these discoveries to the problem of animism, Gelman has pointed out that her research has also highlighted how very rapidly young children appear to acquire knowledge about *shared characteristics*, including the characteristics that enable animation to occur. In Gelman's view, children seem to have a bias toward focusing on the cause of an object's movement, often showing an interest in the insides of live things as they search for shared characteristics for a clue to explain animation. For instance, Gelman reports that young children will usually describe the innards of animate objects as having or containing blood, bones, food, or organs, while they will state that they don't know what is inside an inanimate object or that its inside has the same "stuff" as its outside does (Denton, 1987). For example, 3- and 4-year-olds tend not to classify metallic robots as animates, even though the robots can move, and give as reasons that the robots are "too shiny" or "not squishy."

Question: Why do children show a bias toward focusing on the cause of an object's movement?

Gelman believes that the bias is an innate one, perhaps based on an experience-expectant neural system (see Chapter 5). In terms of evolutionary survival and natural selection, it would make sense for our species to have evolved a rapid way of learning what was and what wasn't animate. Perhaps that is why, when you ask a preschooler, "Can statues walk?" the child will ignore the fact that the statue might look like a living thing and say, "No, because it doesn't have real feet, it's stone inside."

Building on these discoveries, researchers Susan Gelman and Kathleen Kremer (1991) examined children's understanding about how things originate. They asked interesting questions of 4-year-olds to test for artificialism. Examples of the kinds of questions they asked were, How did the sun begin? Why do leaves turn color? and Why do tigers have stripes? They also asked questions like, How do chairs begin? Why do houses change color? and Why do shirts have stripes? In general, 4-year-olds were aware that human agency is not involved in the first three cases, while it is in the latter three. As you can tell, we've come a long way since Piaget, but still have much to learn.

There are many more studies in this area, all of interest. It's too bad that space prohibits a closer look at more of them, but perhaps these few have given you a better idea of the kinds of detailed research that investigators conduct on a day-to-day basis.

NEW THEORETICAL APPROACHES

Sometimes an entire area that has been well studied can be seen again in a fresh light. Recently, some researchers have begun to look at cognitive development in a new way. Rather than thinking of the cognitively immature child as lacking something possessed by older children, some are arguing that cognitive immaturity is in itself highly adaptive (Bjorklund & Green, 1992). In this view, the preoperational period, for example, would not just be considered a time when children can't conserve or use logical operations, but rather as a valuable time during which children's cognitive immaturity provides them with important benefits. For instance, it has been shown that preoperational children's poorly developed metacognition leads them to overrate their abilities. But that, in turn, may motivate them to keep trying because they are unaware of how little they really know (Bjorklund & Green, 1992). If they had a more advanced metacognition, they might lose their self-confidence. Although this idea may seem farfetched at first, it is interesting to consider that we may have evolved a slowly developing metacognitive ability through natural selection because it was adaptive not to dampen motivation too early!

Continuing in this vein, research has also shown that children are better able to remember things if the things they are trying to remember are related to themselves (Pratkanis & Greenwald, 1985). Perhaps, then, egocentrism evolved because it aids memory by forcing the young child to relate most everything to herself!

If this adaptive view of immature cognition is correct, then perhaps we shouldn't try to accelerate cognitive development. Maybe children receive numerous benefits from the lengthy time they spend at each level. Why, for example, is a preoperational child better equipped to master a second language than an adult? Perhaps it is because each level is a special time when certain abilities are laid down, and as such, it shouldn't be rushed by parents or educators interested in giving a child a "head start" by academically pushing him forward. It might be very interesting, then, to reexamine cognitive immaturity, not in the light of what young children can't do, but rather in the light of what benefit such immaturity might have for them. Such research is now under way (Bjorklund & Green, 1992).

Whether there is merit to this view or the many others that are sure to follow, researchers interested in child development will continue to explore human cognition. After all, it is the essence of the human experience.

LEARNING CHECK

Fill-in-the-Blank

1. In a sense, the child, like the computer, is an information ______.

2. Acquiring the ability to attend selectively to the ______ features of any object is crucial to cognitive development.

3. The power of a computer is often measured by its ______ capacity.

4. ______ refers to the knowledge one possesses about how to operate one's memory.

5. ______ refers to the knowledge one possesses about one's own thought processes.

6. A ______ is a hypothetical cognitive structure that encompasses people's knowledge of the ______ events in everyday experience.

Answers:

1. processor **2.** distinctive **3.** memory **4.** Metamemory **5.** Metacognition

6. script; typical, common, or usual

APPLICATIONS

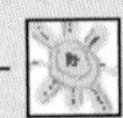

Speak Softer, I Can't Understand You

"A mother watches as a neighbor's child darts across a busy street; she then sees her own child about to imitate this act. The mother shouts, 'Don't cross the street!' " (Saltz, Campbell, & Skotko, 1983, p. 461). Instead of stopping, however, the child looks at her mother, smiles, and continues into the street at an even faster rate than before. Luckily, she isn't injured, but her mother feels extremely frustrated by the child's behavior. Not only did the child disobey but also seemed actually to become more disobedient at the mother's command.

Such a reaction in 2- to 4-year-old children is well known to both teachers and parents. The adult shouts at the child to stop an action, perhaps something dangerous, such as running into the street, and this seems only to make the child continue the action all the more enthusiastically.

Question: Isn't it just that children of that age are trying to test the limits and see what they can get away with?

That commonsense explanation for the behavior has been offered for many years. However, if we carefully examine the behavior of children 2 to 4 years of age when they are receiving shouted negating instructions (such as "Don't do this!" or "Stop doing that!"), a very different picture emerges. The fact is, the child may not be processing the verbal commands in the way that his mother intended.

Here, again, we are glad to see the growing contribution of Russian research. Russian psychologist A. R. Luria studied the language-processing capabilities of children under 5 years of age. He concluded that shouted negating instructions are likely to have exactly the opposite effect from what speakers desire because of the way children cognitively process the instructions (Luria, 1961, 1969). In fact, Luria's research indicates that the best way to get a child to cease a particular action is by using a soft voice. If this is true, it certainly contradicts what adults appear to believe—that the best way to get a child's attention and obedience, especially in a serious situation, is to shout.

Question: What is it about shouted negating statements that children younger than 5 years have difficulty understanding?

According to Luria, there are two problems with shouted commands such as "Don't cross the street!" or "Don't pull the dog's tail!" The first is the volume of the command. The louder it is, the less likely it is to be obeyed. The second is that these sentences contain a compound structure consisting of two opposing ideas; namely, "don't" (the negating or negative idea) and "cross the street" or "pull the dog's tail" (positive actions).

Question: Why is high volume a problem?

Both Russian and American researchers have discovered that the ability of children to respond to verbal controls intended to inhibit their behavior is something that develops gradually (Fuson, 1979). As Luria has argued, until such time as language becomes "decontextualized"—that is, until the child can separate the meaning of words from the perceptual context in which they are spoken—context always will play an important role, sometimes a confounding one. If the child is unable to separate the meaning of "don't go into the street" from the perception of shouting, there may be a conflict. For example, Luria and other researchers have discovered that exciting visual or auditory stimulation occurring in conjunction with the onset of muscular activity helps to stimulate that muscular activity, much as cheering would. Once a child begins an action, shouting or any other perceptual stimulation is likely to make the child act more vigorously rather than to negate his actions. The child hears the *loudness* of the shouting voice and interprets it as would a football or soccer player who hears the roar of the crowd. The meaning of what's spoken is ignored, and the "go, go, go" feeling obtained from the volume is what matters.

Question: How might the compound structure of the statement also confuse children?

Compound statements may provide too much information for the child to process. She may understand "Don't go into the street!" as "Go into the street!" Realizing that the "don't" makes a negated statement may require more complex information processing than 2-, 3-, or 4-year-old children can handle (Saltz, Campbell, & Skotko, 1983). Simply saying "Stop!" would be more effective.

Question: Is there experimental evidence that supports Luria's theory?

A number of experiments have supported Luria's conclusions (Fuson, 1979). In one study (Saltz, Campbell, & Skotko, 1983), 3- and 4-year-

APPLICATIONS

old children were compared with 5- and 6-year-old children in a game situation similar to Simon Says. The children were told that they were going to play a game to see how well they could follow instructions. They were given 15 positive commands, such as "Clap your hands," and 15 negative commands, such as "Don't touch your toes." In each condition, the experimenter modeled the behavior, even if it was negative (i.e., she touched her toes even if the command was "*Don't* touch your toes"). The commands were given in a soft, medium, or loud voice.

The results of the experiment are shown in Figure 10.4. As you can see, with a soft-spoken command, the younger and older children were about equally likely to respond correctly. The interesting effect occurred, however, when the command was shouted. For older children, the average number of errors was zero. Shouting the word "don't" before "touch your toes" seemed to function as an attention-getter and made the older children aware that this was a verbal negation of a command. The older children were far enough advanced semantically for the command to inhibit the behavior that was consistent with the visual cues (seeing the model act). In other words, even though the experimenter bent down and touched her toes, shouting "Don't touch your toes!" inhibited the behavior of all the 5- to 6-year-old children. The younger children, on the other hand, were quite different. They made *more* errors when the command was shouted than they did when it was spoken softly. This indicates that the younger children perceived the loudness of the shout more than they comprehended its semantic content. As predicted by Luria's theory, the loudness of the shout, even though it was a command *not* to do something, spurred the children on.

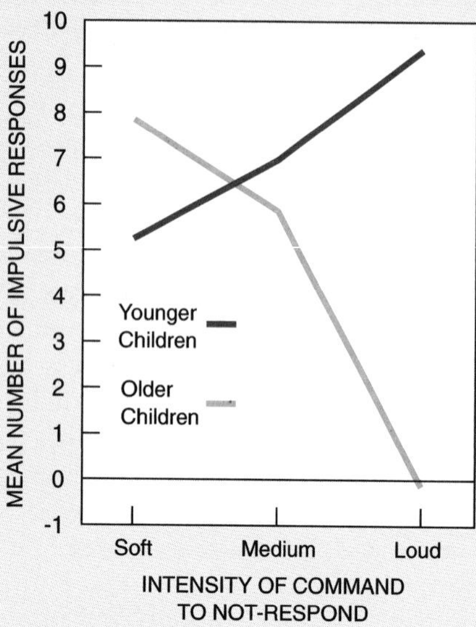

FIGURE 10.4

The results of Saltz, Campbell, and Skotko's 1983 test of A. R. Luria's theory that younger children (3- and 4-year-olds) would be more likely to respond incorrectly to a shouted negated command than would older children (5- and 6-year-olds). As you can see, as the loudness of the commands increased, the younger children made more errors, whereas the older children made fewer errors. (*Source:* Saltz, Campbell, & Skotko, 1983, p. 463)

SUMMARY

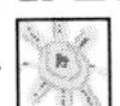

- Lev Vygotsky argued that children always possess a zone of proximal development, which is sensitive to cultural and environmental influences. In this sense, cognitive development may be shaped by culture, language, and experience.
- Juan Pascual-Leone revised Piaget's stage theory to explain the discrepancies that learning theorists had demonstrated. For Pascual-Leone, the main factor of a child's cognitive development is mental power (M). M refers to the number of schemes that a child can attend to at a given time.
- Although Pascual-Leone's improvement of Piaget's theory is valuable and explains many experimental findings, it is still not able to explain language acquisition or to provide a precise enough definition of schemes to allow them to be counted.
- An interactionist reconciliation combines both the organismic-structural approach and the mechanistic-functional approach.
- A general consensus is that cognitive development occurs through "soft stages" or levels and that Piaget had demonstrated with his stages what was most typical of cognitive development.
- The information-processing view uses the computer as a model for understanding cognitive development. This perspective emphasizes selective attention and memory as important factors in cognitive development.
- As selective attention develops, children become better able to attend to the distinctive features in an environment.
- The notions of memory strategies and memory organizations may help to explain the differences in memory power between adults, older children, and younger children.
- Scripts help individuals reconstruct memories based on typical experiences.
- Metamemory is most likely to develop in cultures that provide formal schooling.
- Metacognition is the ability to think about thought. The typical approach for studying metacognition is to examine the strategies used by children or adults when they purposefully try to reorganize their thinking.
- The copy theory of knowledge may help to explain egocentrism. This is the argument that during the early development of social role taking, the child's cognitive understanding of others' perspectives is presymbolic. The child behaves as though knowledge resides within objects and that all objects within direct line of view project a copy of themselves to the observers.
- Piaget assumed that preoperational children believed that any object in motion was animate. However, animism in young children is not as common or as clear-cut as Piaget thought.
- By classifying objects according to kind, children are able to infer that objects of a kind share unforeseen properties. Even infants can override perceptual similarity to make inferences on the basis of category membership.
- Children appear to have an innate bias toward focusing on the cause of an object's movement and often show an interest in the insides of living things as they search for a clue to explain animation.
- Some cognitive researchers are examining cognitive development in a new way. They are examining cognitive immaturity not in the light of what young children can't do, but rather in the light of what adaptive benefit such immaturity might have for them.
- Soviet psychologist A. R. Luria studied the language-processing capabilities of children under 5 years of age. He concluded that shouted negating instructions are likely to have exactly the opposite effect from what speakers desire because of the way children cognitively process the instructions.

QUESTIONS FOR DISCUSSION

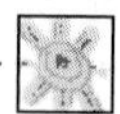

1. Researchers at the Johns Hopkins University studied 131 college students who were 12 and 13 years old and found that the children were maintaining a grade point average of 3.59 (A). There have been no reports of 8-year-old children attending regular college classes. Do you think that this is because 8-year-olds haven't reached the level of formal operations, or because they haven't lived long enough to gain the information-processing capabilities needed for college classes, or both? Might there be (as yet undiscovered) teaching techniques that could prepare an 8-year-old child for college?

2. How has your reading of the last few chapters affected your own metacognition?

3. How might a child's cognitive development be affected if he or she were raised in a one-parent family? (Consider scaffolding.)

4. How might the fields of neurology and cultural anthropology further our understanding of cognitive development?

SUGGESTIONS FOR FURTHER READING

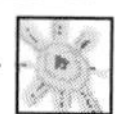

1. Dreyfus, H. L., & Dreyfus, S. E. (1986). *Mind over machine: The power of human intuition and expertise in the era of the computer.* New York: Free Press.
2. Flavell, J. H., Miller, P. H., & Miller, S. A. (1992). *Cognitive development* (3rd ed.). Englewood Cliffs, NJ: Prentice-Hall.
3. Siegal, M. (1992). *Knowing children: Experiments in conversation & cognition.* Hillsdale, NJ: Erlbaum.
4. Sternberg, R. J. (Ed.). (1984). *Mechanisms of cognitive development.* New York: Freeman.
5. Sutherland, P. (1992). *Cognitive Development Today: Piaget & His Critics.* New York: Taylor & Francis.

CHAPTER 11

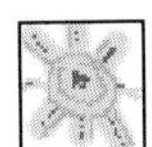

INTELLIGENCE AND CREATIVITY

CHAPTER PREVIEW

SMART IS AS SMART DOES

IN THE SUMMER OF 1942, psychologist Seymour Sarason was working at the Southbury Training School for the Mentally Retarded, a school in Connecticut. Among Sarason's many jobs was giving various intelligence examinations to the handicapped students. One of the tests he commonly used was the Porteus Mazes Test. This test demanded no spoken response; rather, it simply required those taking it to trace their way through a series of printed mazes with a pencil. Perhaps you have come across similar puzzles; some are very easy, while others can be quite complicated. Many of the handicapped students at the school, however, weren't able to do even the simplest puzzle. This came as a great surprise to Sarason.

Question: Why was he surprised that mentally retarded students had difficulty doing an intelligence test?

He was surprised because a number of the students who failed his mazes had previously broken out of the institution and had successfully negotiated the woods of the Connecticut countryside in an effort to return to their homes! Sarason has said, "That was when I realized that what these kids could plan on their own was in no way reflected by how they did on tests" (McKean, 1985, p. 25).

Although testing can be a powerful and helpful tool, the relationship between a test score and what is commonly thought of as intelligence is a complicated one.

IN THIS CHAPTER, we will examine the development of intelligence in children, the ways in which it is measured, and the problems faced by researchers interested in studying developmental changes in intelligence. We will also see how researchers attempt to deal with what Professor Sarason and others have discovered—that the concept of intelligence isn't always as clear or obvious as one might imagine.

INTELLIGENCE
A general term for a person's abilities in a wide range of tasks, including vocabulary, numbers, problem solving, and concepts. May also include the ability to profit from experience, to learn new information, and to adjust to new situations.

MENTAL AGE (MA)
A concept developed by Binet, used to calculate a person's IQ. Mental age is derived by comparing a person's test score with the average scores of others within different specific age-groups.

CHRONOLOGICAL AGE (CA)
A concept developed by Binet, used to calculate a person's IQ. Chronological age is actual age.

INTELLIGENCE QUOTIENT (IQ)
A quotient derived from the formula MA/CA × 100 = IQ, where MA is mental age and CA is chronological age; devised by psychologist William Stern and introduced in the United States by Lewis Terman.

RESOURCES

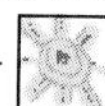

Defining Intelligence

The first scientific interest in **intelligence** and intelligence testing can be traced to the inheritance theories of Sir Francis Galton (1822–1911). Galton's studies marked not only the beginning of efforts to measure intelligence but also the start of the entire psychological testing movement. The differences among people became an important consideration, especially to anyone interested, as Galton was, in positive eugenics (see Chapter 2). After all, distinguishing different traits and measuring inferiority and superiority would be prerequisites for deciding who should be mated with whom to produce certain offspring.

Although Galton's hopes for a full-fledged eugenics movement were never fulfilled, interest in individual differences and their measurement grew. By the turn of the century, the public had come to accept the idea that science could measure psychological differences to identify superior and inferior abilities. It was a common belief at the time, even among scientists, that intelligence was mainly the product of inheritance. Little consideration was given to learning or the influence of experience, partly because much of this early work was conducted in Europe, where upper classes and royalty still claimed to be intrinsically superior, and not, as some "radicals" argued, a product of their fortunate birth into families of wealth and power. Consequently, the public readily accepted that most behaviors and attributes, including intelligence, were wholly inherited and fixed from childhood.

More recently, however, the contributions of experience and environment have received significant consideration, and a more modern view of intelligence as an *interaction* between inherited capacity and environmental influences has emerged.

Measuring Intelligence—IQ Tests

In 1905, Alfred Binet (1857–1911) and Theodore Simon (1873–1961) developed the precursor to the modern intelligence test. Its purpose was to determine which schoolchildren in the Paris school system would benefit from regular classes and which should receive special education.

Binet established which tasks or questions could be solved easily by children in each of the school grades and which were difficult for them. Carrying his research further, he developed a concept of **mental age (MA).** For example, a 5-year-old child who performed as well on the test as an average 6-year-old child would be said to have a mental age of 6. A 10-year-old child who performed only as well as an average 5-year-old child would be said to have a mental age of 5. Binet used the term **chronological age (CA)** to represent the actual age of the child.

A few years later, the German psychologist William Stern developed a formula to avoid the fractions that arose when comparing MA and CA. It yielded a score he called the **intelligence quotient,** or **IQ.** Stern's formula, MA/CA × 100 = IQ, gave a rough index of how bright or dull any child was in comparison with his or her school peers. In the case of the 5-year-old (CA = 60 months) with an MA of 72 months, the IQ is 120, quite sufficient for schoolwork. But the 10-year-old (CA = 120 months) with an MA of 60 months has an IQ of 50, which would be defined as developmentally retarded—not sufficient for regular schoolwork.

Alfred Binet.

In 1916, Lewis Terman (1877–1956) and his colleagues at Stanford University revised the original Binet-Simon intelligence scale and incorporated Stern's idea of the IQ. Their revision, known as the Stanford-Binet, became the first of the modern IQ tests. The Stanford-Binet IQ Test is used mainly to measure children's IQs, although there are adult sections on the test. Using the Stanford-Binet test, most IQ scores in a normal population fall between 85 and 115, although some are higher or lower. Figure 11.1 depicts the typical distribution of scores found in a normal population.

VALIDITY
The capacity of an instrument to measure what it purports to measure.

RELIABILITY
The capacity of an instrument to measure consistently and dependably. A reliable test will provide approximately the same score on retesting under similar conditions.

TEST VALIDITY

Question: If a child does well on an IQ test, does this mean that he is intelligent?

Although it is true that we now have IQ tests, intelligence itself has never been adequately defined, and there is some question about the **validity** of these tests. A test is said to have validity if it measures what it claims to measure; it is said to have **reliability** if it produces scores that are consistent on retesting.

Question: But do IQ tests measure intelligence as most people use the term? Are they valid?

Generally, IQ tests are a very good predictor of performance in school because they measure common skills and abilities, many of which are necessary to be successful academically. But consider the areas covered in a widely used intelligence test, the revised Wechsler Intelligence Scale for Children (WISC-R), illustrated in Figure 11.2. Ask yourself if a child who had the ability to answer the example questions correctly would coincide with what most people understand by the term *intelligence*.

As you may have already considered, many people believe that intelligence also includes such attributes as creativity, persistent curiosity, and the desire for success. But IQ tests aren't always good indicators in these areas. For instance, in an example using adults, two researchers worked with bright mathematicians whose IQs were similar, who all were about the same age, and who all had PhDs from prestigious universities. These subjects were found to have remarkable differences in *creative* output, as measured by other mathematicians (Helson & Crutchfield, 1970). IQ tests, then, are not generally a valid measure of high levels of creativity.

Question: Are there valid uses for IQ tests?

Yes. In other instances, IQ tests have been found to be valid. They are generally able to predict school success with a fairly high degree of certainty—not surpris-

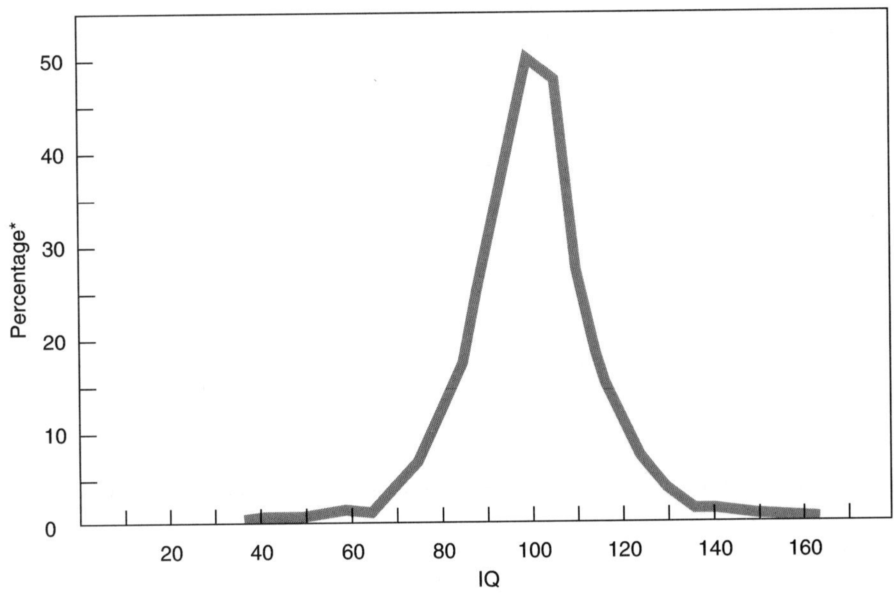

FIGURE 11.1
The standard distribution of IQ scores within the general population. The most common IQ score is 100. Approximately two-thirds of all scores fall within the IQ range of 84 to 116. *Source:* Data from Stanford-Binet Intelligence Scale (4th ed.), *Technical Manual*, 1986, p. 129. The average score for the standardization population was 99.7.
*Percentage of individuals from a normal population scoring above or below a given score.

FIGURE 11.2
Subtests of the Wechsler Intelligence Scale for Children (WISC-R).

Verbal Scale (requires a spoken response)

1. Information: 30 questions covering a wide range of general knowledge that children presumably have had an opportunity to gain simply by being exposed to the culture.

   Example: "How many dimes make a dollar?"

2. Similarities: 17 items requiring that children explain the similarity between two things.

   Example: "In what way are a finger and a toe alike?"

3. Arithmetic: 18 problems similar to those encountered in elementary school. The problems must be solved without paper or pencil.

   Example: "How much would three pieces of candy cost if each piece cost 15 cents?"

4. Vocabulary: 32 vocabulary words of increasing difficulty presented visually and orally. Children must define each word.

   Example: "What does save mean?"

5. Comprehension: 17 questions that ask children to indicate the correct thing to do under varied circumstances or why certain practices are followed.

   Example: "Why are checks signed?"

6. Digit span: 14 groups of from two to nine digits presented orally, one group at a time. After hearing a group, children must repeat it from memory. Some exercises require repetition forward, others backward.

Performance Scale

7. Picture completion: 26 pictures. In each picture something is missing. Subjects must identify the missing part.

   Example:

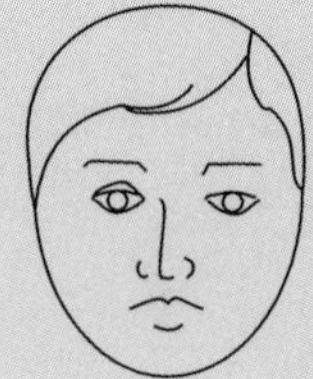

ingly, perhaps, inasmuch as this is what they originally were designed to do. And in certain instances, IQ tests are also valid for clinical assessments of children or adults who have anxiety problems or neurological and perceptual deficiencies.

FACTOR ANALYSIS

Some IQ tests are given individually, one on one, such as the Stanford-Binet or the WISC-R, whereas others are given to groups. Some IQ tests are designed to

8. Picture arrangement: 12 sets of cards. Each set contains cartoon characters performing an action. If the set of cards is placed in the proper sequence, it will depict a sensible story. Subjects must place cards from each set in the proper order.

Example: "Place the cards in the proper sequence so that they depict a sensible story." (Answer: Correct order should be 3, 1, 4, 2.)

Example:

9. Block design: 11 designs of increasing complexity must be made using four or nine blocks having sides that are white, red, or half white and half red.

Example:

10. Object assembly: Children are provided with pieces of a puzzle made of hardened cardboard. Children must decide what the pieces represent and must assemble them correctly. There are four puzzles.

Example:

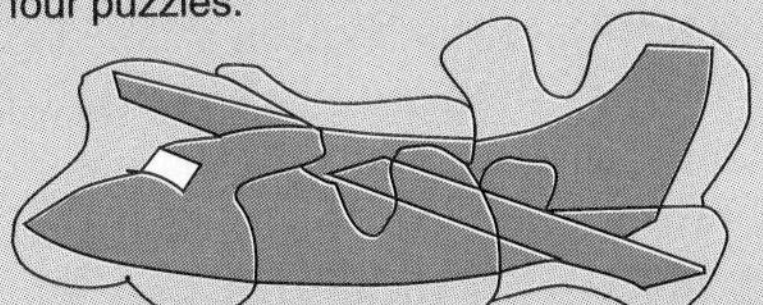

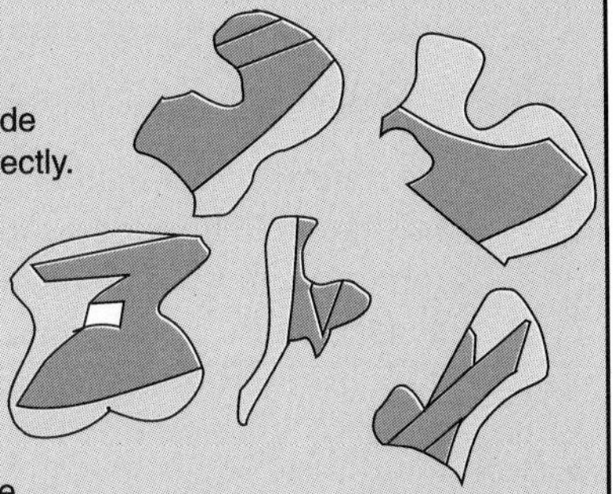

11. Coding: Five symbols are shown. Children must draw the appropriate mark within each symbol. The test is timed. Children who forget and have to look back at the example of correct marks take longer to complete the test.

Example: Correct Marks: 1 2 3 4 5

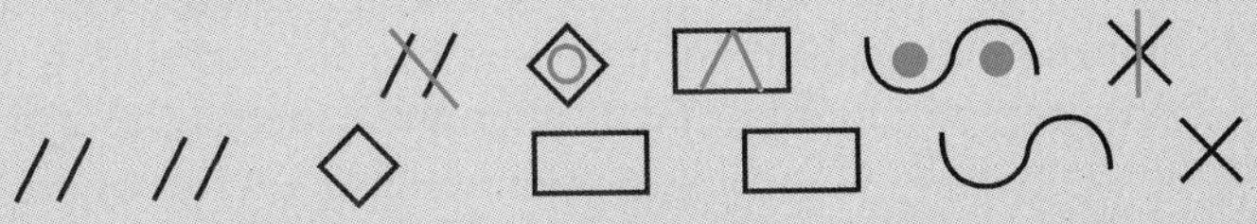

Begin: etc.

12. Mazes: Nine mazes of increasing difficulty are presented. Children must complete the mazes without going out of the paths with their pencils. The tests are timed.

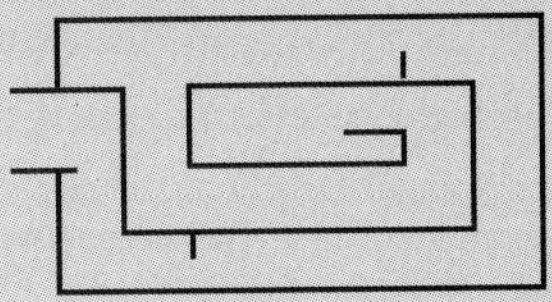

FIGURE 11.2
Continued

be taken exclusively by infants, or by children, or by adults. All the IQ tests ask different questions, and although they all are called "intelligence tests" and they all yield an IQ score, they often measure different abilities. Furthermore, some tests measure the same ability more than once and thereby give that one ability more weight in the final score. The amount of weight or emphasis given to any one ability is known as a **factor load.**

FACTOR LOAD
The weight or emphasis given to any factor or ability.

FACTOR ANALYSIS
A statistical procedure aimed at discovering the constituent components within a complex system such as personality or intelligence; enables the investigator to compute the minimum number of factors required to account for the intercorrelations among test scores.

To understand factor loading better, let's look at an example from athletics. Think of an Olympic decathlon athlete who must compete in the following 10 events:

100-meter dash
javelin (requires running start)
110-meter high hurdles
pole vault (requires running start)
400-meter run
high jump (requires running start)
1,500-meter run
discus
running long jump
shot put

Do you see any particular ability that has a heavy factor load, that is, an ability that is measured more than once?

Question: Running?

Exactly. Perhaps decathlon champions have the best all-around legs! At any rate, the decathlon is a test that is loaded with running factor. The idea of trying to balance test factors (including those in IQ tests) so that each ability is tested only once was developed by L. L. Thurstone in 1938. To accomplish this, Thurstone relied on a technique known as **factor analysis.**

Question: How does factor analysis relate to the development of intelligence?

Thurstone was a mathematician who had been hired to work in Thomas Edison's laboratory. Thurstone soon became aware that Edison seemed completely unable to comprehend mathematics. This led Thurstone to conclude that rather than a single quality called general intelligence, there must be many kinds of intelligence, perhaps each unrelated to the other. Thurstone believed that if people were intelligent in one area, this didn't necessarily mean that they would be intelligent in another. One of Thurstone's goals was to isolate social from nonsocial intelligence, academic from nonacademic intelligence, and mechanical from abstract intelligence.

Since Thurstone's day, there have been many such attempts to isolate different kinds of intelligence. One of the most exhaustive efforts was made by J. P. Guilford. Guilford developed a model of intelligence based on his factor analysis of the human intellect. Guilford proposed as many as 150 different factors, or kinds, of intelligence (Guilford, 1982). Other researchers agree with Guilford that there are different kinds of intelligence, but disagree on the number. For example, psychologist Howard Gardner at Harvard University has proposed that there are only seven different kinds of intelligence (Gardner, 1983). Gardner's categories are quite broad in terms of what most people might consider intelligence to be, including such aspects as social grace and athletic skill. The view that there are many different kinds of intelligence lies in direct contradiction to an idea proposed early in this century by Charles Spearman. Spearman argued that there was only one kind of general intelligence (*g*) and that g represented the amount of mental energy that a person could bring to bear on any given task (Spearman, 1927). A number of modern researchers also hold this view. Of course, because no one has been able to define intelligence adequately, no one is sure how many kinds of intelligence there may be—a state of affairs that plainly illustrates the difficulty of measuring intelligence (Weinberg, 1989).

Currently, this issue remains unresolved. The two camps remain. There are the *lumpers*, who believe that all intelligence stems from one general ability, and the *splitters*, who argue in favor of many separate kinds of relatively independent intelligence. There are even some who take a middle ground, arguing in favor of a hierarchical organization of specific skills stemming from one or two factors (Horn, 1986).

The Triarchic Theory of Intelligence

Question: Is there a way to construct a test that more closely measures what most people consider intelligence?

After having studied the issues of intelligence and intelligence testing for many years, psychologist Robert J. Sternberg at Yale University came to a conclusion: Intelligence tests are simply too narrow. Remember Sarason's experience, described in the Chapter Preview, that children unable to complete the simplest mazes fared far better in their attempts to escape from the institution. The test said that they couldn't find their way from point A to point B, but experience showed otherwise. Sternberg believes that there are many individuals who are "street smart" or creative but who score poorly on intelligence tests.

The Wechsler Intelligence Scale for Children includes performance tasks such as block design that do not require a verbal response from the subject.

Sternberg argues that most intelligence tests rely on problem-solving skills and cognitive abilities. In fact, if the tests commonly used by Piaget to test children's cognitive development (see Chapter 9) are assembled and given as an "intelligence" test, they correlate quite well with the Wechsler Intelligence Test (Humphreys, Rich, & Davey, 1985).

In his book *Beyond IQ* (1984), Sternberg proposed an information-processing approach to the study of intelligence, one that would encourage a step-by-step analysis of cognitive processes *and be applicable in any sociocultural context.* Toward this aim, Sternberg developed a triarchic theory of intelligence that would account for what he argues were two missing legs necessary to support the concept we call intelligence. This triarchic view of intelligence is far broader than the perspective psychologists have traditionally accepted, and it may be more in line with what most people believe intelligence to be.

The first leg of the theory, of course, includes the cognitive problem-solving and information-processing skills measured by most IQ tests. This is what Sternberg calls *componential intelligence;* the layperson might call it "book smart" or "school smart."

The second leg concerns the ability of the individual to adapt to his or her environment or culture. This is known as *contextual intelligence.* For years, people have referred to this as "street smart"; it describes the ability of a person to know the ins and outs, to know all the angles, essentially to know how to get by in a given situation. Learning how to survive and do well in the social and cultural environment is important and, after all, is an intelligent thing to do.

The third leg is *experiential intelligence.* Sternberg argues that an important part of intelligence is the ability to take a newly learned skill and make it routine. We have phrases to describe this kind of intelligence, such as "learning from your mistakes" and "capitalizing on your experiences." People with this intelligence quickly develop expertise by making their newly acquired skills routine. By so doing, the mental tasks that once required thought become almost effortless or automatic.

Sternberg has developed a test to measure these three components (The Sternberg Multidimensional Abilities Test). Perhaps this new test will be better able to predict performance and to help individuals discover their weaknesses and identify ways to correct them than standard IQ tests can. Sternberg's book *Intelligence Applied* (1986) even provides a training program, based on the author's theory, to help individuals strengthen any or all of the three forms of intelligence he identifies.

Heritability of Intellectual Capacity

When children are born, their brains, nervous systems—in fact, their entire bodies—are constructed according to instructions received from the genes they have inherited from their parents. It would seem reasonable that superior genes would provide a child with superior intellectual capacity. And researchers have, in fact, discovered that parents with high IQs tend to have children with high IQs, whereas parents with low IQs tend to have children with low IQs.

Question: Doesn't that prove that intelligence is inherited?

Not necessarily. Rich parents tend to have rich children, and parents who like tostadas and enchiladas tend to have children who like tostadas and enchiladas; it doesn't necessarily follow that these attributes are passed on via genes. Environment also can play an important role. Perhaps being raised by intelligent parents in a stimulating or intellectual home tends to increase a child's IQ.

Question: Does inheritance play any role in the development of intelligence?

Genetics determines brain structure and differences within that structure, and obviously, brain structure is related to intellectual functioning. In fact, in one study, the brain sizes of young adults who had IQs above 130 were compared with the brain sizes of matched subjects (in terms of body size, gender, etc.) who had IQs that were slightly below average (100). An extremely sensitive imaging technique was used (magnetic resonance imagining) to compare the brains of the two groups. Brain size and IQ were found to correlate +.35 (Willerman, Schultz, Rutledge & Bigler, 1991). What this typically would mean, for example, is that if we compared two women who were about the same physical size and age, we would expect the one with the higher IQ to have the larger brain. Psychologist Lee Willerman, who conducted this study, points out that those with higher IQs appeared to have more myelin in their brains, especially in areas of the brain associated with higher mental processes, which seems to account for the larger size of their brains. Young adults with lower IQs had brains that more closely resembled the less myelinated brains of older adults.

Psychologists often debate the importance of genetics in determining IQ. What you should remember is that intelligence is not strictly something children are born with—that they either have or don't—but is rather an attribute greatly determined by *interactions* among genetic inheritance, culture, and experience. This is true even in the case of something such as brain size, which at first glance may seem to depend solely on genetics. It may be, for instance, that the young adults with higher IQs in Willerman's study came from more stimulating homes where they were also provided with better nutrition. Either of these environmental factors may possibly lead to a greater production of myelin. If this were the case, larger brains to a great degree could be the result of environmental forces.

This example also helps us to understand that if some aspect of intelligence is inherited, it doesn't necessarily mean that that aspect, whatever it might be, is right there at birth and is rigidly fixed in the child and unchangeable from that point on. Because intelligence is determined by more than one gene, and because it is also a complex response to the environment, it doesn't follow Mendel's simple laws for the inheritance of traits (see Chapter 2). Richard Weinberg expressed this point when he said, "There is a myth that if a behavior or characteristic is genetic, it cannot be changed. Genes do not fix behavior. Rather, they establish a range of possible reactions to the range of possible experiences that environments can provide" (Weinberg, 1989, p. 101).

METHODS OF BEHAVIORAL GENETICS

Question: Is there any way psychologists can study genetic effects on intelligence?

There are two basic ways to study the inheritance of human intelligence. The first is the **twin design,** in which a characteristic or behavior is compared between identical twins and then between fraternal twins. The second method is the **adoption design.** Researchers who use this design study genetically related individuals who are reared apart from one another or genetically unrelated individuals who are reared together. As you can see, these designs allow the effects of nature and nurture to be separately examined. It is not uncommon for both designs to be incorporated into a single study.

TWIN DESIGN
A research design used for sorting the influence of nurture from nature. A characteristic or behavior is compared between identical twins; then the same characteristic or behavior is compared between fraternal twins.

ADOPTION DESIGN
A research design used for sorting the influence of nurture from nature. Genetically related individuals who are reared apart from one another or genetically unrelated individuals who are reared together are studied.

Question: Would you give an example of this kind of behavioral genetic research?

Consider the fact that relatives share many of the same genes, while unrelated people do not (which no doubt has some bearing on why relatives are related to each other and unrelated people aren't). Keeping this in mind, look at Table 11.1, and you'll see categories of related and unrelated people, with a correlation coefficient next to each.

Question: What is a correlation coefficient?

These correlations represent the relationship between the IQ scores of pairs of individuals within each category (the scores of two first cousins, of a parent and child, etc.).

Let's look at parents and their children to see how these correlations would be derived. Each parent and his or her child are given an IQ test. Then a computation is made that allows these test scores to be compared with each other; each parent's score is compared with his or her own child's score. The more alike these compared scores are, the closer to +1.00 the correlation coefficient will be. A high positive correlation means that the test scores of the parents and their respective children are similar. We can predict from a positive correlation that if a parent's IQ is high, his or her child's is likely to be high, or that if a parent's IQ is low, his or her child's is likely to be low also. A correlation of zero, or near zero, indicates no relationship between the two scores. If that were the case, the parent's score would tell us nothing about the child's score. A correlation approaching −1.00 indicates an inverse relationship; that is, if one score is high, the other is likely to be low, and vice versa. As you can see, the actual correlation between parents and their children is +.40, a moderate positive correlation.

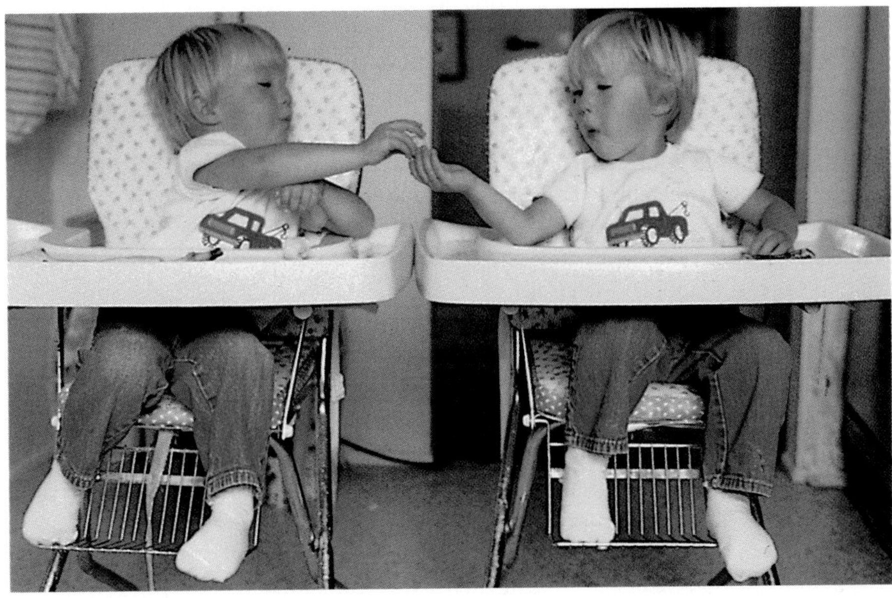

IQs of identical twins reared together are more similar than IQs of siblings reared together. Is this because twins share the same genes, or because twins are more likely to be treated the same?

TABLE 11.1

Correlations of Intelligence Test Scores*

CORRELATIONS BETWEEN INDIVIDUALS	MEDIAN VALUE
GENETICALLY RELATED PERSONS	
Identical twins reared together	.86
Identical twins reared apart	.72
Parent and child	.40
Fraternal twins reared together	.60
Siblings reared together	.47
Siblings reared apart	.24
Half-siblings	.31
Cousins	.15
UNRELATED PERSONS	
Nonbiological sibling pairs (adopted/adopted pairings)	.34
Adopting parent-offspring	.19

*Based on a study of 111 studies that reported on familial resemblances in intelligence.

SOURCE: Adapted from Bouchard & McGue, 1981, p. 1056.

One of the areas of greatest interest in Table 11.1 is the "twins reared apart" category. It is rare for identical twins to be reared apart, but when they are, it provides an ideal chance to study the IQs of two people sharing the same genes *but having different upbringing and experiences.* As you can see from the table, identical twins reared apart have an even higher correlation than do siblings reared together (Segal, 1985). In the Minnesota Study of Twins Reared Apart, one of the most extensive studies of its kind, Thomas Bouchard and his colleagues at the University of Minnesota found the correlation for IQs among identical twins reared apart to range from +.69 to +.78 (strong positive correlations), depending on the IQ test used (Bouchard, Lykken, McGue, Segal, & Tellegen, 1990). In this survey, the researchers were careful to use only identical twins who were separated at infancy and who were raised in different environments. Identical twins reared apart were also found to show many similarities other than intellectual ones, including shared aspects of personality and social attitudes. This has led Thomas Bouchard to say:

> For almost every behavioral trait so far investigated, from reaction time to religiosity, an important fraction of the variation among people turns out to be associated with genetic variation. This fact need no longer be subject to debate; rather, it is time instead to consider its implications. (Bouchard, Lykken, McGue, Segal, & Tellegen, 1990, p. 227)

Question: Does this mean that inheritance plays a greater role in the determination of IQ than the environment does?

At first glance, this result would seem to indicate that inheritance must play an exceedingly large role in the formation of intellectual capacity. However, the "twins reared apart" category is not without problems. As you might imagine, it isn't easy to find twins who have been reared apart. In earlier studies, from which much of this table was developed, "reared apart" often turned out to mean that they were living next door to one another, or that they went to the same school, or that one was with the father and the other with the mother; and because married couples tend to have similar IQs, the "reared apart" environments may have been quite alike in terms of intellectual stimulation. Therefore, the "twins reared apart" category might be contaminated (in a research sense). If so, IQ similarities between identical twins reared apart could no longer be sorted in terms of heredity or experience, and researchers began to question these earlier data (Kamin, 1974; Schwartz & Schwartz, 1974).

In an effort to overcome such problems, many rigorously sampled twins reared apart were studied for the Minnesota Study of Twins Reared Apart. These newer data tripled the current number of subjects in the "twins reared apart" category. Even so, some researchers are still concerned that there may have been some contamination of the "reared apart" category even in these new studies (Dudley, 1991). But Thomas Bouchard and his colleagues point out that they were very careful with their selections and that even if there were some contamination, there is no doubt that twins reared apart are far more alike along many dimensions than are siblings reared together and that this could not possibly be explained by shared environments (Bouchard, Lykken, McGue, Segal, & Tellegen, 1991).

THE TEXAS ADOPTION PROJECT

In one of the most detailed efforts to differentiate the effects of the environment and heredity, researcher Joseph Horn examined 300 adoptive families who had acquired their children at birth (Horn, 1983). He compared the IQs of these children with the IQs of both the adoptive mother *and* the biological mother. In all, 469 adopted children were tested. The results showed that the children's IQs were more strongly correlated with their *biological mothers'* (+.28), even though the children had never met these women, than with their adoptive mothers' (+.15), who had raised them.

Question: Then heredity is the most important factor in intelligence?

At first glance, it might appear so, but this is not the finding of the study. To begin with, the difference between correlations of +.15 and +.28 is very small, almost insignificant (Walker & Emory, 1985). Correlations that small leave much to be explained.

Question: What is left to be explained?

Given these small correlations, the statistical analysis shows us that the biological mothers' IQs accounted for (or, in statistical terms, *explained*) only about 8 percent of the scores obtained by the adopted children. The IQ scores of the adoptive mothers explained only about 2 percent of their adopted children's IQ scores.* In other words, fully 90 percent of the variables that accounted for the children's IQ scores were unaccounted for, even after the contributions of both adoptive and biological mothers had been considered.

Question: What might those unaccounted variables be?

They could include, for example, the contributions of the fathers, both biological and adoptive. Assuming that the fathers contributed as much to the children's intelligence as the mothers, however, would still leave a large percentage of the variables unaccounted for. These variables may very well have to do with the children's environment—the environment beyond that supplied by exposure to the adoptive parents. These variables might include television, school, friends, and a host of other possible factors. Joseph Horn, who conducted the Texas Adoption Project, states unequivocally that he believes that IQ can be strongly affected by environmental factors (Horn, 1985).

The Texas Adoption Project also produced a surprise when the same children were retested after a 10-year interval. The researchers running the project discovered that

> the popular view of genetic effects as fixed at birth and environmental effects as changing has got matters almost backward, at least for the trait of intelligence in this population during these developmental years. . . . Especially provocative is the finding that genes seem to continue actively contributing to intellectual variation at least into early adulthood, whereas the effect of shared family environment appears to be largely inertial after early childhood. (Loehlin, Horn, & Willerman, 1989, pp. 1000–1001)

In other words, the influence that genetics was having on intelligence *increased* as these children aged, while the effects of environment *decreased*. Other studies support these data and yield estimates showing that by age 3, while the *shared family environment* accounts for about 70 percent of IQ correlations among twins, its influence *decreases* dramatically to 30 to 40 percent in middle childhood and drops to about 20 percent by age 15 (Wilson, 1983).

Question: What! How could that be?

At first it is difficult to see how genes could have a greater effect on the expression of intelligence the older a child gets. But remember what the authors of this

---

*By squaring the correlation coefficient, you can derive what statisticians refer to as the *explained variance*. For example, Table 11.1 shows that siblings reared together have an average correlation of +.47 when their IQ scores are compared. +.47 × +.47 = +.2209, or, when rounded off, +.22, which equals 22 percent. This means that whichever variables are responsible for one sibling's IQ score, 22 percent *of those same variables* are responsible for the other sibling's test score. In other words, 22 percent of the variance has been "explained" (although we still may not know which variables, environmental or genetic, they are sharing). As you can see by using this formula, correlations such as +.28 or +.15 are really quite weak.

AT ISSUE

Birth Order and Intelligence

In 1896, Galton observed something intriguing about the order in which children were born. He noticed that an exceedingly large number of prominent British scientists were firstborn children. Since Galton's time, a number of studies have indicated that firstborn children have a distinct advantage in certain areas of development over other children (Koch, 1955). Firstborn children are more articulate and tend to score higher on intelligence tests than children born later. Firstborns also tend to be more reflective, whereas later children are more impulsive. When dealing with important choices, reflective children tend to examine a number of options and delay decisions so that they can minimize their errors. Impulsive children, on the other hand, are eager to rush to a solution when dealing with problems (Kagan, 1966).

Firstborn children also appear to have a greater need to achieve (Sampson, 1962), to be more active (Eaton, Chipperfield, & Singbeil, 1989), and to perform better academically (Altus, 1967). Firstborn children are more likely to attend college (Bayer, 1966) and have higher educational aspirations (Falbo, 1981). Interestingly, 21 of the first 23 astronauts to travel into space were firstborn children.

Question: Why would firstborn children be unique in these respects?

The meaning of these birth-order data is not clear. The answer may have something to do with the size of the family into which children are born. Perhaps firstborn children enjoy a more stimulating environment than do later children because they have the undivided attention of both parents. Supporting this interpretation is the fact that firstborn children develop language rapidly, whereas twins develop language at a slower rate, and triplets more slowly still (Davis, 1937). Research has shown that twins tend to be shortchanged by their parents because parents don't like to repeat themselves. In other words, a twin is likely to be spoken to less often because parents treat the twins as a unit rather than doubling their verbal interactions (Lytton, Conway, & Suave, 1977). Because IQ scores reflect verbal skills to a considerable degree, it would not be surprising if firstborn children tended to have higher IQ scores than twins—and they do. Furthermore, while firstborn children tend to have higher IQ scores than second children, second children also tend to have higher scores than third, third than fourth, and so on (Zajonc & Markus, 1975); in other words, children from families with many siblings tend to have poorer verbal skills (Blake, 1989).

Zajonc and Markus have developed a model of intellectual climate designed to help predict the differences among the average intelligence scores in children from large and small families (see Table 11.2). In their model, the parents are each assigned a value of 30, and the children are assigned a value equal to their chronological age. These values are added and then divided by the number of family members. For example, a firstborn child would enter an intellectual climate equal to [30 (father) + 30 (mother) + 0 (baby)] ÷ 3 = 20. A child born to a single parent would be born into an intellectual climate of (30 + 0) ÷ 2 = 15. A second child with a 6-year-old brother would be born into a family with an intellectual climate of (30 + 30 + 6 + 0) ÷ 4 = 16.5. And so on. With this formula, Zajonc and Markus found close agreement between their values of intellectual climate and the average IQ scores among children in different-sized families.

For instance, the model predicts that the birth of a baby will reduce the average intellectual climate in the home. Researchers have since found that the birth of a baby does, in fact, appear to result in a slight decrease in the IQs of older siblings (McCall, 1984). This model has also been used to explain the decline in SAT (Scholastic Aptitude Test) scores among high school students prior to 1980 and the rise in scores following that time (Zajonc, 1986). Just prior to 1980, when test scores were low, a high percentage of later-born students were taking the test. That trend is now reversing, as many of the baby boomers' firstborn children are now in high school and taking the test. The model predicts that SAT test scores should continue to rise until the year 2000, level off, and then start to decline once again. Findings such as these help to validate the model (Berbaum & Moreland, 1985; Berbaum, Moreland, & Zajonc, 1986).

Changes in the average number of siblings per family are also expected to make a difference in the years ahead (Blake, 1989). For instance, in the 1930s, less than half of all children were reared in families with three or fewer siblings, and one-quarter were reared in families with seven or more. Today, for the first time in U.S. history, three-fourths of children are being reared in families with three or fewer siblings, and only 5 percent are being reared in families with seven or more.

The Zajonc and Markus formula for intellectual climate shown in Table 11.2 was developed for a family of up to

AT ISSUE

TABLE 11.2

Zajonc-Markus Model of Intellectual Climate As Applied to a Large Family Over an 18-Year Period with Children Spaced 2 Years Apart

YEAR OF BIRTH OF CHILD	NUMBER OF CHILDREN	VALUE OF INTELLECTUAL CLIMATE: FORMULA	RESULT
1975	1	mother (30) + father (30) + baby (0) / number in family (3) =	20.0
1977	2	mother (30) + father (30) + 2 yr old (2) + baby (0) / number in family (4) =	15.5
1979	3	66 ÷ 5	13.2
1981	4	72 ÷ 6	12.0
1983	5	80 ÷ 7	11.4
1985	6	90 ÷ 8	11.3
1987	7	102 ÷ 9	11.3
1989	8	116 ÷ 10	11.6
1991	9	132÷ 11	12.0
1993	10	150 ÷ 12	12.5

10 children spaced two years apart and shows the lessening of intellectual stimulation for children reared in larger families. Of special interest is the model's prediction that in such a large family, with children spaced two years apart, the intellectual climate actually *increases* for the eighth, ninth, and tenth children. This is because, by the time these last children arrive, the older siblings are in their late teens and provide a more stimulating intellectual environment.

Question: Are the model's predictions for the increase among the later children in such large families supported by data?

It's not easy to find a great number of eighth, ninth, and tenth children. However, one large study conducted in Israel, which included almost 200,000 subjects, closely fit the predictions made by the Zajonc-Markus model (Davis, Cahan, & Bashi, 1977). The Israeli researchers found that firstborn children scored highest on cognitive and intellectual measures, whereas second, third, and subsequent children showed progressively lower scores. However, this trend reversed after the seventh child.* Eighth children were found to have higher scores than seventh, ninth higher than eighth, and tenth higher still!

Question: Could parents overcome these differences if they paid extra attention to their younger children?

Extra attention may be helpful. On the other hand, there may not be great cause for concern, because the difference between firstborn and later children on IQ tests is generally only 3 or 4 points, which, in practical terms, is not significant. In addition, the fact that firstborn children tend to be more successful may be related to many other factors besides extra parental attention or stimulation. Larger families, for example, often are of lower socioeconomic status, and a later child, who is simply more likely to come from a poorer family, is more likely to be at an economic disadvantage than is an earlier child, who is more likely to come from a financially better-off family. For this reason, later children typically are found to have fewer opportunities made available to them. You may find more firstborn children among scientists or astronauts simply because, as firstborns, they were given opportunities that those born later were denied. Finally, it should be noted that not all scientists agree that there is a real or significant birth-order effect (Grotevant, Scarr, & Weinberg, 1975). Some studies have reported finding no

*So much for Sinbad, the sailor, whose luck was said to stem from being the seventh son of a seventh son!

AT ISSUE

such effect (Galbraith, 1982; McCall & Johnson, 1972). Nonetheless, studies that include large samples of subjects generally support the theory that birth order is related to achievement motivation and IQ test scores (Belmont & Marolla, 1973; Berbaum, Markus, & Zajonc, 1982; Berbaum & Moreland, 1985).

As you can see, the birth-order effect is at best a very subtle and small one, although it is interesting. Unfortunately, in just about any bookstore, you can find books claiming all sorts of fantastic things about birth order—books that tell you that first children act this way, middle children act that way, and last-born children act still another way. Many of these books—to boost sales, no doubt—treat birth order as though it were destiny itself, making ridiculous and extravagant claims about its effects. The birth-order effects described in this text are subtle, and as far as we know, that's all there is (Ernst & Angst, 1983). Books claiming to tell how any individual child will develop based solely on birth order are nonsense and should be treated as such.

John Glenn, first American astronaut to orbit the earth, was a firstborn child. Firstborn children generally have a greater need to achieve and to perform better academically.

research said about needing to break away from the idea that genetic effects are fixed at birth, expressing themselves only then and there. Perhaps an example from another field will help to clarify this apparent paradox. Consider the effectiveness of the heart at pumping blood when a person is resting. Among a population of 20-year-olds, environmental factors (exercise, diet, etc.) may play a greater role in heart efficiency than do genetic factors. It is simply rare for a 20-year-old to have a bad heart. By the time these same people are 80 years old, however, genetic factors will probably account more for their heart efficiencies than environmental factors. If you want to live a long time, exercise and diet are important, but nothing beats a great set of genes.

Similarly, genetic influences are, for reasons yet unknown, playing a greater role in intellectual variation among children as they grow older.

Question: Then where do we stand? Are genes more important than environment, or is it the other way around?

No one really knows for certain, but the general consensus of over 1,000 psychologists is that both play a major role (Snyderman & Rothman, 1987). If you pressed me for a current assessment as it stands in the mid-90s, I would say that on average, environment and inheritance each account for about 50 percent of the differences observed in intelligence as measured by traditional tests. This still leaves great room for the effects of environment. Even with our limited understanding of intelligence, we can often boost IQ 20 to 25 points with environmental intervention (Weinberg, 1989). And with the advanced technology coming our way, we may be able to engage in genetic intervention sometime in the next century. Imagine finding the genes responsible for some of the variance of IQ and medically adjusting them in a living person to raise intelligence. Although it may sound like science fiction, there is a good chance that you will live to see it happen in your own lifetime. In fact, a few years ago, the National Institute on Child Health and Human Development awarded psychologist Robert Plomin $600,000 to head a project to search for more than 100 genetic "markers" in the blood of over 600 school children in an effort to find alleles (see Chapter 2) associated with intelligence and giftedness. Plomin says that he expects the most interesting results to come from the blood of "the really smart kids [because] the only way to get high scores is if you've got everything going for you, including the positive alleles" (Holden, 1991, p. 1352).

LEARNING CHECK

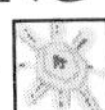

Matching

1. ____ Galton
2. ____ Thurstone
3. ____ relationship between two variables
4. ____ inverse relationship

a. correlation coefficient
b. factor analysis
c. negative correlation
d. individual differences

Multiple Choice

5. Stern's formula is
a. CA/MA × 100 = IQ **c.** CA/100 × MA = IQ
b. MA/100 × CA = IQ **d.** MA/CA × 100 = IQ

6. High factor load is
a. one ability measured many times.
b. many abilities measured once.

7. Guilford argues
a. Thurstone was wrong.
b. there are many different kinds of intelligence.
c. there is only one general intelligence.
d. factor analysis cannot be applied to intelligence.

8. One of the surprising findings from the Texas Adoption Project was that
a. IQ is unaffected by environmental factors.
b. the influence of genetics on intelligence increased as the children aged.
c. the effects of the environment increased as the children aged.
d. no other study supports their findings.

9. Intelligence may be affected by genetic differences.
a. true **b.** false

10. Environmental intervention can sometimes boost IQs by as much as 20 or 25 points.
a. true **b.** false

Answers: 1. d 2. b 3. a 4. c 5. d 6. a 7. b 8. b 9. a 10. a

IQ and Race

A serious controversy over the heritable aspects of intelligence developed immediately after researcher Arthur Jensen published an article in the *Harvard Educational Review* back in 1969. Jensen suggested that the reason whites were superior to blacks on IQ tests by an average of 15 to 18 points was probably related more to genetic variables than to the effects of experience. In other words, Jensen was saying that whites might be, in some way, naturally intellectually superior to blacks.

Question: How could anyone but a racist believe that whites would score higher on an IQ test than blacks would?

But whites do score, on average, 15 to 18 points higher than blacks. This is a fact and is not in dispute.

Question: Does this mean that Jensen was right?

Although no one disputes that whites generally score higher than blacks on IQ tests, this fact does not necessarily mean that Jensen was right. There are other

ACHIEVEMENT TEST
A test that purports to measure the knowledge gained from experience, also known as type B intelligence, or sometimes crystallized intelligence. Achievement tests are distinguished from aptitude tests, which supposedly measure aspects of intelligence that are relatively free of culture or training, sometimes called type A intelligence, or fluid intelligence. In actual practice, however, there is often very little difference between achievement and aptitude tests because it is not yet known how to test only one kind of intelligence without substantially involving the other.

CULTURE-FAIR TEST
A test supposedly free of cultural biases, usually constructed so that language differences and other cultural effects are minimized.

interpretations. For instance, psychologist Sandra Scarr conducted an adoption study in which she gathered data on the IQ scores of black children who were being raised by white families. In a study now considered a classic, Scarr discovered that the younger the black children were at the time of adoption, the closer their scores came to the white IQ averages (Scarr & Weinberg, 1976). Similarly, the IQs of poor children increased when they were adopted by affluent families (Schiff, Duyme, Dumaret, & Tomkiewicz, 1982).

The results of these and other studies strongly suggest that a child's background, experience, and culture to a great extent will influence the child's knowledge and thought processing as measured by any particular intelligence test. Different cultures teach not only different things but also different ways to think about things. Different cultures also require their children to meet different educational standards. For example, Japanese children tend to outscore white American children by about 7 IQ points (Mohs, 1982). Although a few researchers believe that this, too, may be due to genetic differences, most point to the possible effects of the superior Japanese school system (Stevenson et al., 1985). The effect of schooling cannot be too strongly stated. IQ and schooling go hand in hand: Schooling boosts IQ (Cahan & Cohen, 1989), and IQ predicts school performance mostly because IQ tests are typically filled with the kinds of questions children encounter in school. Supporting this assertion is the interesting finding that the IQs of schoolchildren tend to make a small, but measurable decline just following summer vacation (Ceci, 1991) and typically lose up to 6 IQ points for each year of missed school. Considering that year after year, Japanese schoolchildren spend many more days in school than do their American counterparts, the differences in IQ should not be surprising.

IQ AND SCHOOL PLACEMENT

In the 1970s, the landmark case of Larry P. reached the courts. Larry P. was a student in California who was placed in a special class as a result of his low score on an IQ test. In the court case, *Larry P. v. Wilson Riles,* it was argued that IQ tests should no longer be used to assign students to such "special" classes. The prosecutor maintained that a disproportionate number of African-Americans such as Larry P., as well as other minority children, had been wrongly assigned to special classes for the mentally retarded because of their IQ scores. In these classes, they were taught little. Furthermore, assignment to such a class stigmatized the students. A federal appeals court agreed, and IQ tests were no longer allowed to be used as a basis for assigning a child to a "special" class.

Question: Does this mean that schools can no longer use IQ tests

The case of Larry P. was somewhat offset by a later ruling of a federal district judge in 1980 in *PASE v. Hannon.* In that case, a federal district court judge in Illinois ruled that IQ tests could still be used to place minority students in special education classes *as long as other factors were considered* when placing the students. Some researchers believe that by balancing a test to adjust for cultural differences between blacks and whites, an IQ test may be developed that eliminates black-white differences.

THE KAUFMAN ASSESSMENT BATTERY FOR CHILDREN

The Kaufman Assessment Battery for Children (K-ABC) was developed by Alan and Nadeen Kaufman in the early 1980s, in part to eliminate black-white differences. While field-testing the K-ABC, the Kaufmans discovered that the test cuts the IQ differences between blacks and whites by 50 percent (to about 7 points) and eliminates the difference between white and Hispanic children. The Kaufmans argue that this is because the test reduces cultural and educational bias.

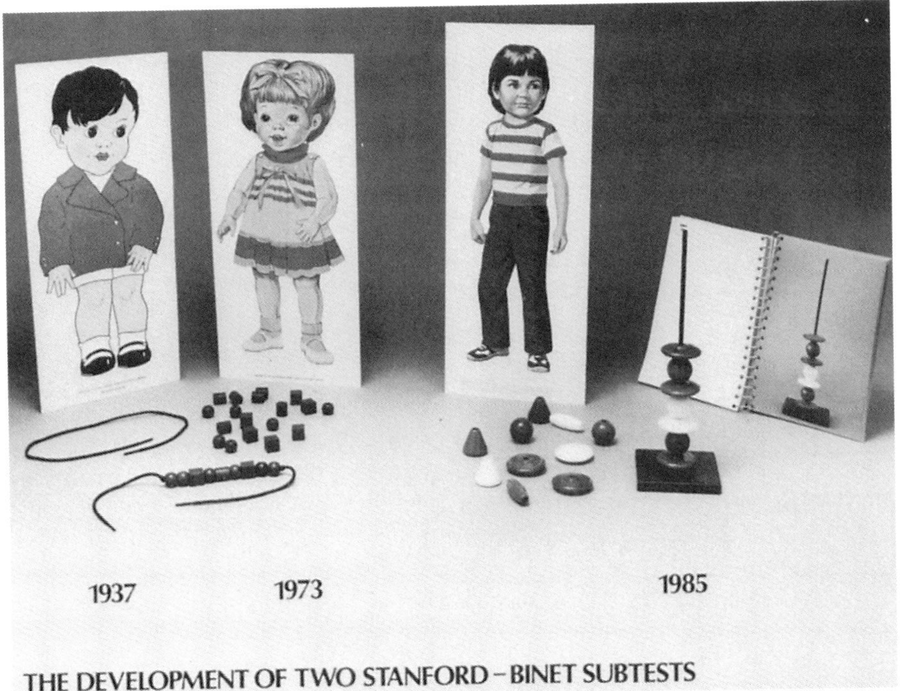

FIGURE 11.3
Several IQ tests in their subsequent revisions have also attempted to eliminate cultural bias. For example, this photograph depicts the evolution of two item types in the Stanford-Binet, the first modern IQ test developed and used in the United States. According to the publisher of the 1985 revision of the Stanford-Binet: "The card used to measure the examinee's knowledge of parts of the body illustrates an increased sensitivity to issues pertaining to ethnicity and gender. The rosy-cheeked boy used in the 1937 edition wore a short red jacket, shorts, and black patent-leather shoes. The blue-eyed girl in the 1972 edition had blond hair tied with a pretty pink ribbon. The illustration of a child in the 1985 edition is drawn with facial features, dress, and hair that minimize gender and racial characteristics. . . . The Bead Memory subtest also originated in the 1937 edition and required the examiner to create sample bead chains. The new text uses photographs as the stimuli. This eliminates a need for examiners to create sample bead chains and results in increased standardization of administrative conditions" (Riverside Publishing Company, 1983, p. 1).

Question: Does this mean that the K-ABC is a fairer and better test of children's intelligence?

Initially, there were worries that the design of the K-ABC might result in its scores concealing important differences that should be exposed. In other words, it might appear to be fairer but in fact might be hiding serious educational deficits displayed by minorities who had been victims of discrimination, poverty, and poorer schools. The K-ABC, however, has been found to correlate well with **achievement tests** (Childers, Durham, Bolen, & Taylor, 1985; Valencia, 1985), which implies that the K-ABC distinguishes those individuals who have acquired knowledge from those who haven't, while at the same time avoiding a racial bias.

The K-ABC is just now coming into wider use. Eventually, we will be able to judge whether it has actually overcome some of the cultural bias that other tests include (see Figure 11.3).

CULTURE-FAIR TESTING

Question: Is it possible to devise a test that contains absolutely no cultural bias?

Any intelligence test that makes use of language is likely to be culturally biased. Consequently, attempts have been made to produce language-free **culture-fair tests** that would be equally difficult for members of any culture. Initial efforts generally relied on pictures and nonverbal instructions, but these still tended to favor some cultures. Children in the favored cultures were simply more familiar with pictures or the requirements of certain tasks. Still, there are tests that are self-explanatory and do not require pictures of familiar objects. One of the most widely used of these "culture-fair" tests is the Raven Progressive Matrices Test. In Figure 11.4, you'll see a sample question from the Raven test. Even without instructions, you can understand what is required. In this test, too, however, people from cultures in which fill-in or matching exercises are more common may be more likely to do well than people from other cultures. To date, no one test that is completely culture fair has been developed.

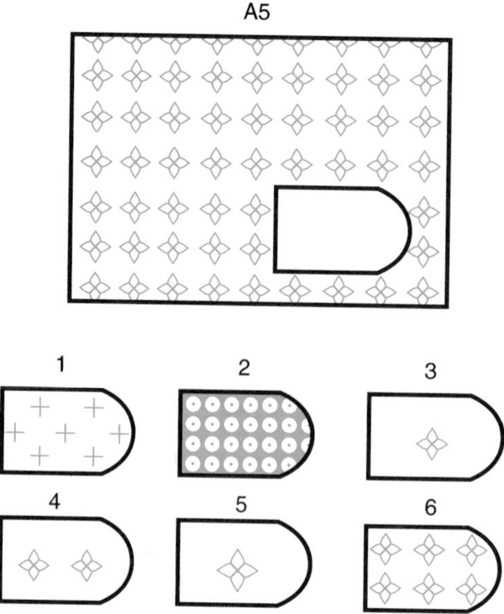

FIGURE 11.4
Sample item from the Raven Progressive Matrices Test.

IQ and Environment

We have discussed how researchers have studied inheritance in an effort to understand the influence of genes and how some of these efforts have influenced social and educational debate. Similarly, researchers have also investigated the environment in a bid to understand its effects on intelligence.

One of the largest efforts along these lines is the Rochester Longitudinal Study, begun in the 1970s. The directors of the study, Arnold Sameroff and Ronald Seifer, have followed a few hundred children from birth through adolescence. They have discovered a number of environmental factors that, they argue, account for 49 percent of the variance of the children's IQs in their sample.

Question: What kinds of environmental factors have they found to be important determiners of a child's IQ?

Sameroff and Seifer have listed 10 environmental factors, each of which they have found to account for the loss of roughly 4 to 6 IQ points (see Table 11.3). Children with six of these risk factors, for instance, were found to have IQ scores that were, on the average, 35 points below children who had no risk factors.

Question: Can we say, then, that we now understand which environmental forces are responsible for IQ?

Unfortunately, we can't. Even though, in the case of the children from the Rochester Longitudinal Study, 49 percent of the variance was explained, we can't assume that the unexplained remainder is owing to genetics alone. Furthermore, environmental factors responsible for IQ may vary greatly from one population to the next. IQ, what it measures, and the concept of intelligence are still fairly mysterious.

For example, researcher James Flynn has been examining IQ scores obtained from 14 nations around the world, all the way from the Netherlands to New Zealand, and has discovered a significant jump in IQ scores occurring from one generation to the next, gains ranging from 5 to 25 points (Flynn, 1987).

Question: Why has there been a great increase in IQ since the last generation?

No one knows. It obviously isn't genetic because the forces of natural selection couldn't have worked such a change in only 30 years. For some of the samples, at least 20 points of the increase have occurred for completely unknown reasons. The real surprise was that the greatest gains occurred on the Raven culture-fair test, which, as you recall, is purported to measure intellectual *aptitude* that is free of cultural bias.

Question: How could scores increase so dramatically in one generation on a culture-fair test if the reason weren't genetic?

Culture-fair tests probably aren't culture fair. One researcher trying to solve this dilemma has argued that so called culture-fair tests become easier if your culture has provided you with training, as many modern schools do, emphasizing intelligent guessing (which modern students exposed to multiple choice testing often raise to an art form) and speed of thought (Brand, 1987).

Another possibility, and one that does not preclude other explanations, may be that societies in the last 20 years have come to provide better environments for their disadvantaged citizens, thereby raising the lower end of their nation's IQ spectrum, which in turn raises IQ averages in general (Bouchard, Lykken, McGue, Segal, & Tellegen, 1990).

As you can see, although we have learned a great deal, the factors that influence IQ or intelligence are still far from understood.

Question: You mentioned that we can sometimes adjust the environment to deliberately boost intellectual ability. How is that done?

Project Head Start was designed in the 1960s to help disadvantaged preschool children do better in school as they grew older. At first, research results from the Westinghouse Learning Corporation and researchers at Ohio State University indicated that Head Start was making little difference in the long-term intellectual development of its children. However, researchers David P. Weikart and Lawrence J. Schweinhart released an interim report in 1980 on an 18-year study of the progress of 123 children at Perry Elementary School in Ypsilanti, Michigan. Their findings indicated that high-quality preschool education programs do benefit the disadvantaged. The Ypsilanti Project provided 12½ hours per week of education, plus 90-minute weekly home visits, to children 3 and 4 years old. Children in the enrichment program scored significantly higher on reading, math, and language achievement tests than did children in the control group. The first group also showed fewer antisocial and delinquent tendencies (Williams & King, 1980a).

An executive report released in 1986 noted that although it was not known whether all Head Start programs in the United States were producing beneficial results, such results could be achieved if the programs were adequately funded and the teachers were well trained and competent (Schweinhart & Weikart, 1986). Among the benefits are

> . . . improved intellectual performance during early childhood; better scholastic placement and improved scholastic achievement during the elementary school years; and, during adolescence, a lower rate of delinquency and higher rates of both graduation from high school and employment at age 19. (Schweinhart & Weikart, 1985, p. 547)

A 20-year follow-up study of children from two American cities who were enrolled in Head Start, preschool, or no school during the school year 1969–70 showed that although the value gained from Head Start had diminished over the years, some benefit was still observed. The benefit gained, however, was somewhat comparable to the long-term value of preschools in general. The long-term benefits were obvious when compared with those who had had no school during that year, and this was especially true of members from the lowest socioeconomic group (Lee, Brooks-Gunn, Schnur, & Liaw, 1990).

Other programs like the Ypsilanti Project have been effective (Gray & Ruttle, 1980; van Doorninck, Caldwell, Wright, & Frankenburg. 1981). A notable ex-

TABLE 11.3

Environmental Factors Known to Significantly Influence IQ Scores

1. The mother has a history of mental illness.
2. The mother has serious anxiety.
3. The mother has rigid attitudes, beliefs, and values concerning her child's development.
4. There are few positive interactions between mother and child during infancy.
5. Head of household has a semiskilled occupation.
6. The mother didn't go to high school.
7. The child is a member of a minority group.
8. The father does not live with the family.
9. The family has suffered at least 20 stressful events during the child's first four years.
10. There are four or more children in the family.

SOURCE: Adler, 1989, p. 7.

KIBBUTZ
An Israeli farm or collective, where children often are reared within groups, allowing them to receive nurturance and guidance from many different adults and older children.

ample of institutional enrichment can be found in Israel, where children with a European Jewish heritage have an average IQ of 105, whereas those with a Middle Eastern Jewish heritage have an average IQ of only 85. Yet when raised on a **kibbutz,** children from both groups have an average IQ of 115. As you can see, these environmental efforts help children to fulfill their genetic potential.

Question: Are early intervention efforts uniformly successful?

Depending on the program, how the program is implemented, and the population that receives the intervention, early intervention may produce many different results. Programs with a high academic content are generally the most successful in producing increases in IQ and achievement (Miller & Dyer, 1975; Stallings, 1975). Special programs aren't always required to give an intellectual boost. For example, good-quality day care has been found to improve the intellectual development of socioeconomically disadvantaged children (Burchinal, Lee, & Ramey, 1989).

Some curious things have been discovered, too. For instance, although a high IQ in a child is a good predictor of school success, high IQ scores brought about through early intervention are somewhat poorer predictors of school success. Apparently, it's better to have an IQ that has been high all along than to have one that has been raised. No one knows why (Miller & Bizzell, 1983). Also, in certain instances, the intervention needs to be continued for many years to be effective (Miller & Dyer, 1975; Palmer, 1972). Furthermore, depending on the program, girls will sometimes benefit more than boys, or vice versa (Datta, 1973; Dweck, Davidson, Nelson, & Enna, 1978).

In summary, there is no clear-cut answer to the question of whether a given early intervention will be effective. Many programs claim success, but their work is often hard to assess because the criteria they use to define success and to define which children are needy differ (Scarr & McCartney, 1988). The general consensus appears to be that early intervention can have lasting and valuable effects (Casto & Mastropieri, 1986; Lazar & Darlington, 1982) but that there is no guarantee that any given program with any given group of children is sure to work (Ramey, 1982; Woodhead, 1988).

Jewish children from different national backgrounds show very similar average IQ scores when raised together on a kibbutz.

Intellectual Changes Over Time

Problems arise when IQ tests are used to measure intellectual changes during a life span. In the 1930s, Nancy Bayley developed a test called the Bayley Mental and Motor Scale to evaluate infants' intellectual and motor skills. Interestingly, subjects who were measured by the Bayley test when they were 9 months of age often had very different IQs when they were retested at 5 years of age by the Stanford-Binet IQ Test. In fact, the correlation between the two IQ scores was zero (Anderson, 1939), indicating that the infants' IQ scores at 9 months of age on the one test were totally unrelated to their IQ scores at 5 years on the other test. Table 11.4 shows the correlations obtained for the children's scores at various ages with those at 5 years.

Question: Why would there be no relationship?

The correlation between 9 months and 5 years was virtually zero because tests given at different ages often measure different abilities. Tests for very young children and infants generally emphasize motor skills, whereas tests for older children tend to emphasize verbal and cognitive skills. Yet both are said to measure intelligence.

A number of other tests were then designed to assess infants' intellectual development. They included the Griffiths Test of the Abilities of Babies (Griffiths, 1954), the Cattell Test of the Measurement of Intelligence of Infants and Young Children (Cattell, 1966), and the Bayley Scales of Infant Development (Bayley, 1969). As with the Bayley Mental and Motor Scale, these tests all failed significantly to predict what the IQs would be once the children reached school age (McGowan, Johnson, & Maxwell, 1981). Although such tests have some limited utility for describing the infant's current state, they simply cannot predict intellectual changes over a long time.

As Figure 11.5 shows, IQ scores don't tend to become consistent over time or reliable until children are about 10 years old. This means that IQ scores obtained from children younger than 10 years may not be reliable; they may change considerably as the children grow up.

Question: Is it impossible, then, to develop an infant IQ test that would have scores well correlated with later intellectual performance?

Unless there were some common denominator that could be measured in infancy that was also related to IQ in childhood, it would not be possible. And for a long time, it was believed that no such denominator was likely to be found. Slowly, however, this view has begun to change (DiLalla et al., 1990).

For example, in one study, 4-month-old infants were given both repetitive and new sounds to listen to. An intelligence score was developed based on how easily they recognized a new stimulus (measured by change in heart rate) and how quickly they came to recognize a repeated stimulus as familiar. The children were followed until they were 5 years old and were then given the Stanford-Binet IQ Test. The correlation was an impressive +.60 (O'Connor, Cohen, & Parmelee, 1984), implying that 36 percent of the variables responsible for one test score (the auditory discrimination) were also responsible for the score on the Stanford-Binet at 5 years of age (.60 × .60 = .36, or 36 percent). It was assumed that in this instance, a basic memory skill had been tapped.

Similar results have been obtained with the use of a visual habituation test developed by Joseph Fagan (see Figure 11.6) (Rose, Feldman, & Wallace, 1988). This test appears to be most useful with infants who are deemed at risk for retardation due to premature birth or other reasons. This test was used on 128 infants between 3 and 7 months of age, who were then retested with the Stanford-

TABLE 11.4

Correlation Between IQ Scores of 91 Children at Various Ages (Bayley Mental and Motor Scale) and Their Scores at 5 Years (Stanford-Binet)

AGE	TOTAL CORRELATION COEFFICIENT
3 months and 5 years	.008
6 months and 5 years	−.065
9 months and 5 years	−.001
12 months and 5 years	.055
18 months and 5 years	.231
24 months and 5 years	.450

SOURCE: Adapted from Anderson, 1939, p. 204.

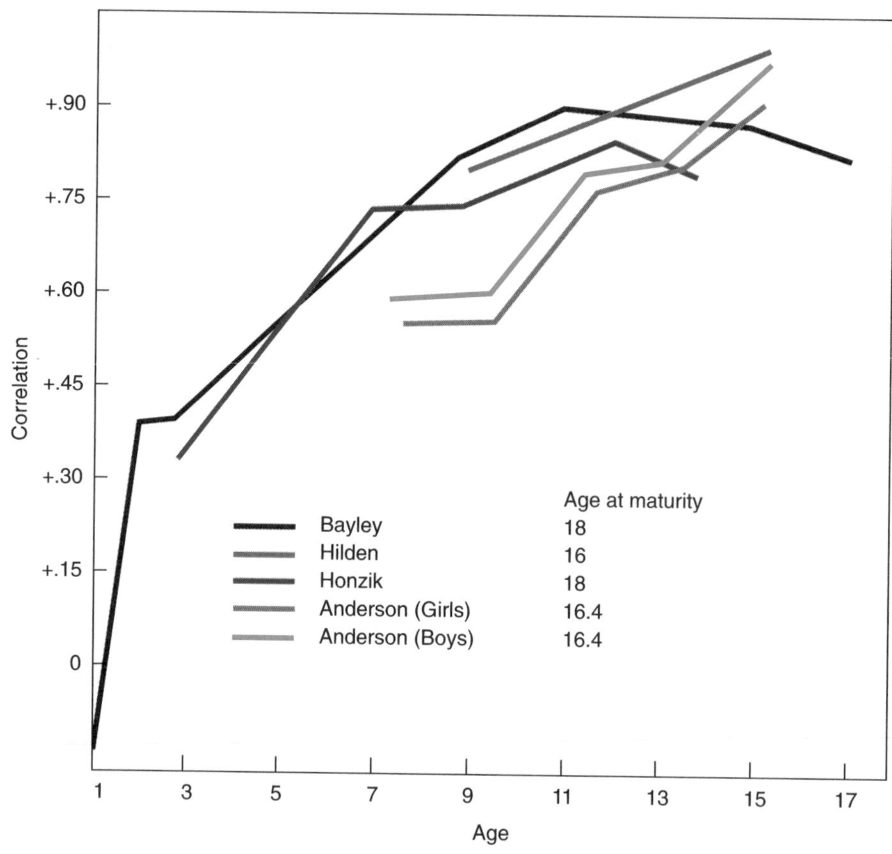

FIGURE 11.5
Correlations between children's IQ scores at various ages and their IQ scores at age of maturity, as cited by numerous studies. For example, Hilden's study found that the correlation of children's IQs at age 9 and the same children's IQs at age 16 was about +.80 (fairly stable over time). Scores below +.75 are not very stable over time. (*Source:* Bloom, 1964)

Binet at age 3 years. Fagan discovered that he was able to correctly predict 101 of the 104 children whose IQs would be within the normal range by age 3 and also predict fully half of the infants whose scores would be in the retarded range by that age (Bower, 1988). The test may also be able to predict certain memory and language abilities that are relatively independent of IQ (Thompson, Fagan, & Fulker, 1991).

TERMAN'S STUDY

Question: Are children who have high IQ scores more likely to be successful than other children?

In 1921, psychologist Lewis Terman received a grant from New York City to conduct a long-term longitudinal study of children with IQs above 140. Terman selected his 1,528 subjects from grade schools in California. Their average IQ was 150, and 80 of them possessed IQs of 170 or higher (Terman, 1925). Follow-up studies were conducted in 1922, 1927–28, 1939–40, 1951–52, 1960, 1972, 1977, and 1982. Terman strongly believed that intelligence, or giftedness, was an inherited quality. In fact, during his life, he often turned a blind eye toward any evidence that there was also a strong environmental component to IQ (Cravens, 1992). Even so, his data do tell us a lot about men who have high IQs.

Question: Why do you specify "men"? Weren't women also studied?

Because few women were encouraged during the 1920s to seek professions, most of the follow-up studies concerning professional accomplishments concentrated on the approximately 800 men included in the original selection. This is not to say that the Terman women didn't choose professions; many of them did, but

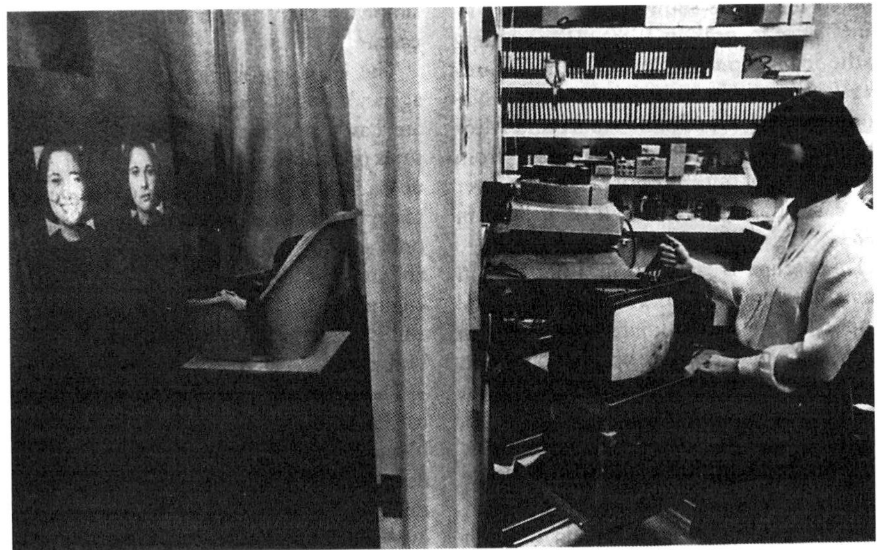

FIGURE 11.6
The baby in this photograph is looking at pictures of two faces. One of those faces he has seen before; the other is new. The researcher is measuring how long the baby looks at each of the faces. Babies who spend less time looking at the familiar face tend to have higher scores on intelligence tests when they reach school age.

there were few professional women in the average general population with whom to compare them. By 1950, at an average age of 40 years, the men had written and published 67 books, over 1,400 articles, and 200 plays and short stories, and had obtained over 150 patents. Seventy-eight of them had received a PhD, 48 an MD, and 85 an LLB. Seventy-four were university professors, and 47 were listed in *American Men of Science*. As Terman noted, "the number who became research scientists, engineers, physicians, lawyers, or college teachers, or who were highly successful in business and other fields, is in each case many times the number a random group would have provided" (Terman, 1954, p. 41).

Among the Terman women, there were also some surprises. According to Pauline Sears, who reviewed the latest data, the Terman women

> were way ahead of several trends that have only lately become true for the nation as a whole. They were quicker to join the work force. They took longer to marry and have children, and more were childless. A high proportion were in managerial positions; I suspect that because they were bright, they got ahead faster. Their brightness made another intriguing difference: the divorced women among them were happier than most, at least on our measure of satisfaction with their work pattern. Almost all the divorced women worked full time, and their work was satisfying to them. The same was true of the women who remained single. All of them worked, and they were much happier with their work than most working women are. Their satisfaction wasn't from income, either, but from the work itself. (Goleman, 1980, p. 44)

Pauline Sears's late husband, psychologist Robert Sears, was in charge of overseeing the Terman study. Robert Sears was formerly head of the psychology department at Harvard and dean of Stanford University. He also was one of the 1,528 children in Terman's original study.

Question: How are Terman's "kids" doing now?

The remaining Terman "kids" are now in their early 80s, and when last reported, compared favorably with the average person of that age: They were healthier, happier, and richer, and they had a far lower incidence of suicide, alcoholism, or divorce. These findings dispelled the myth that genius is next to insanity, because few of the Terman subjects suffered from serious behavioral disorders compared with the average populace.

Question: Why would high IQ scores be related to happiness, wealth, or the incidence of alcoholism or divorce?

A possible reason may be that the subjects in Terman's study stayed in school (probably because they were good at it, which is what a high IQ would indicate). If you stay in school long enough, and do well, you're likely to obtain an advanced degree. And generally, if you have an advanced degree, you'll earn more money. Furthermore, as social psychologists have known for a long time, people who are richer tend to be happier (perhaps that doesn't surprise you). If you are better educated, wealthier, and happier, you probably can afford better medical care, are more aware of how to take good care of yourself, and are under less stress. You are also less likely to be divorced, because happier people get divorced less often.

Question: You mentioned earlier that some of Terman's "kids" had exceptionally high IQs, over 170. Were these individuals even more successful than the rest of those in Terman's study?

One researcher studied 26 of Terman's subjects who had IQs of 180 or higher and compared them with 26 randomly selected subjects from the rest of Terman's sample. The differences found were negligible (Feldman, 1984). This finding helps to emphasize that extra IQ points needn't make an important difference, at least at the upper end of the scale. What did seem to make a difference for Terman's "kids" is that they all were at the upper end of the IQ spectrum.

Creativity

Individual differences in intellectual capacity are not the only characteristics that have attracted interest in recent years. Psychologists are also concerned about the development of **creativity.**

Defining creativity is difficult, but we all seem to have some idea of what it means. Look at the picture in Figure 11.7 and decide what it is. A fairly common but rather uncreative answer is that it looks like a broken window. But what if someone told you that it was a boat arriving too late to save a drowning witch? That's a more creative response.

The traditional way of defining creativity is by applying a set of criteria first described by P. W. Jackson and David Messick (1968). The four criteria are **novelty, appropriateness, transcendence of constraints,** and **coalescence of meaning.**

Novel, of course, means new. Something creative should be new. However, spelling *cat* Q-R-S would be new, but it wouldn't be appropriate. Jackson and Messick therefore included appropriateness as a necessary dimension. Something transcends constraints when it goes beyond the traditional. A creative idea may transcend constraints by lending a new perspective to something with which we are all familiar. An example might include Albert Einstein's idea that space can be bent, something that was later proved correct but which certainly transcended the ideas that people had at that time. Finally, the most creative ideas have meanings that coalesce over time. In other words, the depth and value of an extremely creative idea, although often not apparent at first, become more obvious as time passes. For instance, when Thomas Edison first developed the motion picture projector, many people wondered why the great genius was wasting his time on something that was obviously of little value. Only after some time did the full value of the invention become apparent.

High creative ability is poorly predicted by IQ tests. Individuals with very similar IQs often differ considerably in their creativity (Torrance & Wu, 1981).

Question: Why can't IQ tests predict creativity?

This failure of IQ tests to predict creativity was first investigated by Guilford and his colleagues back in 1957. They believed that IQ tests typically measure a kind of intelligence different from that required for creativity. Two of the factors Guilford mentioned in his model of the intellect were **convergent production** and

CREATIVITY
The ability to originate something new and appropriate by transcending common thought constraints and to create something the value of which becomes more apparent over time.

NOVELTY
A component of creativity described by Jackson and Messick. Creative objects are novel; that is, they are new.

APPROPRIATENESS
One of the four qualities of creativity defined by Jackson and Messick. Appropriate ideas are those that make sense in context.

TRANSCENDENCE OF CONSTRAINTS
According to Jackson and Messick, a component of creativity. Creative ideas transcend constraints in that they often shed new light on something familiar.

COALESCENCE OF MEANING
A component of creativity described by Jackson and Messick. The meaning of a creative thought is said to coalesce over time in that it becomes more valuable and powerful with each application.

CONVERGENT PRODUCTION
Part of Guilford's model of intelligence. A type of thinking in which an individual attempts to search through his or her knowledge and use all that he or she can find to converge on one correct answer.

DIVERGENT PRODUCTION
According to Guilford, a type of thinking in which a person searches for multiple ideas or solutions to a problem; characteristic of the creative thought process.

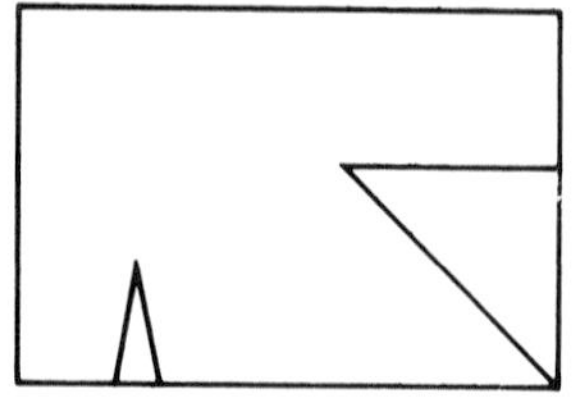

FIGURE 11.7
What do you see?

Part of being creative includes the ability to transcend constraints, that is, to make something different, something unique.

divergent production. Guilford argued that most IQ tests rely heavily on convergent production. When people use convergent production, they search their knowledge for all that they can find to help them converge on one correct answer. In divergent production, they use their knowledge to develop as many solutions as possible to a given problem. Figure 11.8 illustrates the difference between these two thought processes. Guilford argued that creativity relies more on divergent production (Guilford, 1983). If Guilford's view is accurate, then the ability to see many solutions to one problem is very different from the ability to develop one correct answer from a store of information.

Question: How are skills in divergent or convergent production acquired?

These skills appear to be acquired, at least in part, through experience. In one study, 3- and 4-year-old children were given convergent games to play, which consisted of blocks that had to be inserted into particular forms cut from a board. This group spent two-thirds of their time placing these pieces within the forms on the board. Another group of children, the divergent group, played with blocks only. Using the different block pieces, they engaged in a wide variety of activities. A third group, a control group, did not partake in either the convergent or divergent games. After this play, the divergent group performed better than the other two groups on new divergent tasks, whereas the convergent group performed better than the other two on new convergent tasks (Pepler & Ross, 1981).

Question: Are there tests that measure divergent production, and do they predict creativity?

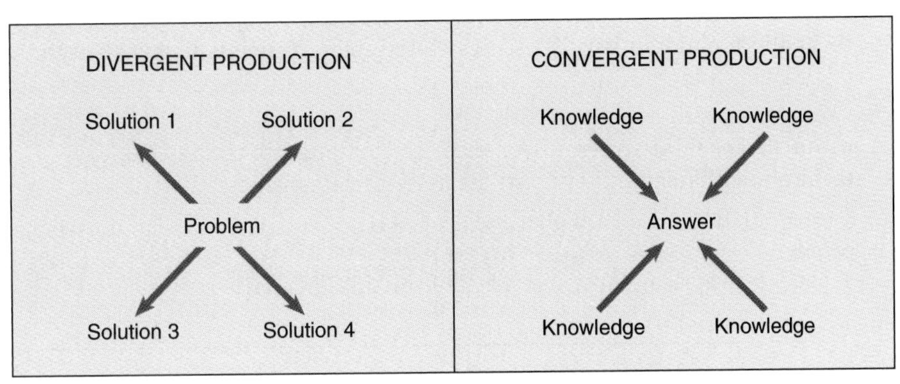

FIGURE 11.8
Divergent and convergent production.

IDEATIONAL FLUENCY
A term used by Wallach to describe an individual's ability to produce many ideas; sometimes used as a measure of creativity; correlates poorly with IQ.

MAINSTREAMING
The philosophy of keeping as many exceptional children in the regular classroom as possible rather than placing them into special classes.

Some tests have been designed to predict creativity by measuring divergent production. One such test, described by Michael Wallach (1970), employs the concept of ideational fluency. **Ideational fluency** is the ability to develop a large number of ideas appropriate to a particular task. To measure ideational fluency, researchers might ask someone to name as many uses as possible for a common object, such as a cork or a shoe, or to point out all the similarities between a train and a tractor. People with high ideational fluency produce many answers (Wallach & Kogan, 1965). Divergent production tests such as this one predict creativity much more accurately than IQ tests do. In one study of almost 500 college students (Wallach & Wing, 1969), ideational fluency was found to be well correlated with creative attainments such as receiving prizes in science contests, publishing original writing, or exhibiting artwork. Like IQ test scores, ideational fluency scores among older children appear to be fairly stable over time (Kogan & Pankove, 1972).

Some Final Thoughts on Individual Differences

Biology is not democratic. Some of us are tall, some of us are short, and some of us are no doubt better able biologically to develop skills considered to be indicators of intelligence. Inheritance and genes are important. On the other hand, as you have seen, intelligence (or whatever it is that our "intelligence" tests measure) can be dramatically affected by the environment. Intelligence might best be considered a complex interaction between genetic heritage and experience. The Terman subjects probably did well in school and therefore did well on IQ tests that asked academic types of questions because they had inherited excellent brains and nervous systems *and also* because they were stimulated at home and school to learn and to develop their cognitive and intellectual skills.

LEARNING CHECK

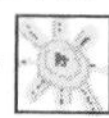

1. Culture-fair tests should not use language.
a. true **b.** false

2. IQ score differences between Hispanics and whites on the K-ABC have been found to be
a. nonexistent. **c.** slight (Hispanics higher).
b. very small. **d.** slight (whites higher).

3. IQ tests best measure
a. success in school. **c.** persistent curiosity and motivation.
b. creativity. **d.** all of the above.

4. Birth-order data have shown that
a. firstborn children tend to be more successful than children born later.
b. on the average, tenth children tend to score lower on intelligence tests than do seventh children.
c. twins develop language skills faster than others.
d. firstborn children have IQ scores that average 20 points higher than those of later children.

5. Creativity is well correlated with
a. intelligence test scores. **c.** degrees from prestigious universities.
b. ideational fluency. **d.** a career in mathematics.

6. Terman's kids showed a higher incidence of ______________ than do average people.
a. suicide **b.** happiness **c.** alcoholism **d.** divorce

Answers: 1. a 2. a 3. a 4. a 5. b 6. b

APPLICATIONS

Reaching Their Full Potential: Mainstreaming Handicapped Children

If we consider intelligence not as a quality solely the result of inheritance but rather as a fluid and changing group of abilities sensitive to environmental effects, then our understanding of bright or dull, superior or retarded, must change (see Table 11.5).

How many times have you tangled with your own intellect? Sometimes it lets you down, sometimes it doesn't. Does this make you bright, average, dull? At one time or another, every child or adult faces this problem. Incapable adults are often left to fend for themselves (which may be unfortunate). But what should we do with incapable children? If they can't match their school peers, should we label them "minimally brain damaged," "hyperactive," "emotionally disturbed," "learning disabled," or "mentally retarded" and send them for "special" education?

How many children have been given a potentially negative label, dropped out of school, and been unable to save themselves? On the other hand, some children do have serious problems and clearly require special help; we certainly can't abandon all testing and ignore them.

Question: How can this problem be solved?

In 1975, Public Law 94–142 was enacted by the U.S. Congress to deal, in part, with the fact that too many children were not being given the education to which they were entitled; instead, they were being labeled and isolated, usually as a result of a single test or because they were born with physical markers of handicaps, such as spina bifida or Down syndrome.

In an attempt to change this unfortunate trend, Public Law 94–142 stipulated that the *least restrictive* educational environment be provided to meet the handicapped child's needs. This is sometimes referred to as **mainstreaming** because every effort is made to keep the child within the regular academic class.

Question: What has been the result of mainstreaming?

As with early intervention programs, the outcome seems to depend on the type of mainstreaming program used.

TABLE 11.5

IQ Scores and Their Respective Category Labels*

SCORE	CATEGORY
130+	Very superior
120–129	Superior
110–119	Bright normal
90–109	Average
80–89	Dull normal
70–79	Borderline retarded†
50–69	Mildly retarded (if also showing adaptive dysfunction) (educable)
35–49	Moderately retarded (trainable)
20–34	Severely retarded
below 20	Profoundly retarded (custodial)

*Based on category labels in the Wechsler Adult Intelligence Scale and the American Psychiatric Association's *Diagnostic and Statistical Manual—III-R.*

†Scores that determine retardation categories may vary from state to state.

In some cases, students who have been exposed to both mainstreaming and special education perform at about the same level in both environments (Semmel, Gottlieb, & Robinson, 1979). But where mainstreaming is supported by the school district, teachers, and parents, and where careful planning has gone into selection of students for mainstreaming, then mainstreaming can be successful (Madden & Slavin, 1983).

Question: Would you give an example of successful mainstreaming?

Down syndrome is one of the most common birth defects and the leading cause of mental retardation in the United States. Children born with Down syndrome often are severely mentally handicapped. They are also commonly born with a constellation of other physical defects (see Chapter 3). In the past, many physicians told parents that there was little hope of an intellectual life for these children. In some cases, physicians have even shown considerable ignorance:

> When Mindie Crutcher was born, physicians said she would always be hopelessly retarded, that she would never sit up, never walk, never speak. "She will never know you're her mother," they told 25-year-old Diane Crutcher. "Tell relatives your baby is dead."
>
> Today, the child who would never sit up is a lively seventh-grader. The child who would never walk is the star of dance recitals. The child who would never talk or know her own mother told a symposium of physicians she was "glad Mom and Dad gave me a chance." (Turkington, 1987, p. 42)

APPLICATIONS

Mainstreaming has posed a particular challenge for children with Down syndrome, perhaps because it was so commonly believed that these children were capable of very little, but this challenge has been met by some successful mainstreaming programs. First of all, many children born with Down syndrome were institutionalized because many physicians and parents often believed that education could not possibly help. But after Public Law 94–142 was passed, many children born with Down syndrome were given educational opportunities for the first time. One institutionalized girl (with a rare and less severe form of Down syndrome), who began educational training as a result of the law, received a two-year associate's degree in early childhood education from the University of Maine (Turkington, 1987).

Researchers now believe that the *majority* of children born with Down syndrome "who are reared at home in middle- or upper-middle class families can be expected to be educable when they enter school" (Turkington, 1987, p. 44). Psychologist John Rynders and his colleagues at the University of Minnesota designed Project EDGE to improve communication skills in children with Down syndrome. The children with Down syndrome entered Project EDGE when they were 30 months old. Of the 13 children in the project, 7 are currently in educable classes or in a combination of regular and educable classes. In 1984, a follow-up study of the 13 EDGE children found that 11 of these children were reading with comprehension at or above second-grade level (Turkington, 1987), a far cry from being hopelessly retarded, never able to sit up, never able to walk, never able to speak. In 1986, Congress passed Public Law 99–457, which was designed to provide early intervention for handicapped children. This extension to Public Law 94–142 was provided so that states could begin helping handicapped children from birth, perhaps preparing these children for future regular schooling, as did Project EDGE.

Question: But are these children ever accepted by other children in the regular classroom?

Two Australian studies, carried out to examine both the academic and social progress of children with Down syndrome in the regular classroom, demonstrated that most of the children were well accepted by their peers (Hudson & Clunies-Ross, 1984; Pieterse & Center, 1984). All the handicapped children in these studies had attended some form of early intervention, such as Project EDGE, and then had been mainstreamed into the regular classroom. These studies emphasize that even though children with mental handicaps may require some form of special intervention or help, they can also do well if given the chance, and mainstreaming is one way to help them fulfill their potential. Mainstreaming also gives children in the regular classroom the opportunity to learn compassion, tolerance, and understanding, and even more important, to learn about the special potentials of handicapped children.

SUMMARY

- In 1905, Alfred Binet and Theodore Simon developed the precursor to the modern intelligence test. Its purpose was to determine which Parisian schoolchildren should receive special education.
- Binet developed the concept of mental age, or MA. By comparing mental age with chronological age, CA, Binet was able to make comparisons between children. The German psychologist William Stern developed the formula MA/CA × 100 = IQ, which yielded a rough index of how bright or dull any child was in comparison with school peers.
- A test is said to be valid if it measures what it claims to measure. IQ tests have been found to be valid for predicting school performance and in use as a tool in clinical assessment.
- The amount of weight or emphasis given to any one ability as measured on a test is called a factor load. Some IQ tests measure particular factors more than others. For this reason, the same individual may score differently on different IQ tests.
- To balance a test for factors so that each ability is tested only once, L. L. Thurstone advocated the use of a technique called factor analysis.
- According to Thurstone, Guilford, Gardner, and other factor analysts, there are many different kinds of intelligence, not just a general ability called intelligence. The debate over this issue continues today.
- Psychologist Robert Sternberg has argued that traditional IQ tests have too narrow a focus. In his triarchic theory of intelligence, Sternberg includes measures of contextual and experiential intelligence along with the traditional componential intelligence.
- Psychologists have studied the heritability of human intelligence and other characteristics by examining people who are related to one another. On the basis of current data, many psychologists agree that heredity does play a role in determining individual differences and intelligence. How important it is in comparison with environmental experiences has yet to be determined.
- Methods of behavioral genetics include the twin design, in which a characteristic or behavior is compared between identical twins and then between fraternal twins, and the adoption design, in which genetically related individuals reared apart or genetically unrelated individuals reared together are studied.
- Researchers Zajonc and Markus have developed a model of intellectual climate designed to predict differences in intelligence scores according to birth order. However, not all scientists agree that a significant birth-order effect exists.
- According to researcher Arthur Jensen, the fact that whites average 15 to 18 points higher than blacks on IQ tests is mainly the result of genetic variables. Other researchers argue that cultural bias on the tests accounts for the discrepancy.
- In one study, Scarr and Weinberg gathered data on the IQ scores of black children adopted by white families. They discovered that the younger the black children were at the time of adoption, the closer their IQs came to white averages.
- Because of past misuses of IQ test results in schools, courts have generally held that students should not be assigned to remedial classes solely on the basis of IQ test scores.
- The Kaufman Assessment Battery for Children (K-ABC) was developed to help minimize differences between minority children and whites on IQ tests.
- Attempts have been made to devise a culture-fair test, one that contains no cultural bias. Even on tests that do not use language, however, the advantage will go to people from cultures incorporating any of the skills, techniques, and concepts required by the test.
- The Ypsilanti Project and other home-based early intervention projects generally have been successful in raising the intellectual levels of the children who participated.
- Intellectual changes are difficult to measure over time. Tests measure different skills among subjects of different ages, and as a result, reliability is not always high.
- Lewis Terman initiated a study that surveyed high-IQ children for over 65 years. The Terman kids are now in their 80s, and compared with the average person of that age, are healthier, happier, and richer, and they have a far lower incidence of suicide, alcoholism, or divorce.
- Jackson and Messick judged creativity by four criteria: novelty, appropriateness, transcendence of constraints, and coalescence of meaning. High creativity by these measures is poorly correlated with IQ scores.
- Some tests have been designed to predict creativity by measuring divergent production. One such test, described by Michael Wallach, employs the concept of ideational fluency.
- Intelligence might best be considered a complex interaction between genetic heritage and experience.

Questions for Discussion

1. How would you define *gifted?* How would you discover whether your definition was valid?

2. Think of intelligent people whom you know well. What unintelligent things do they do? All of them are bound to do some unintelligent things, so why did you consider them to be intelligent people? Were you emphasizing some factors at the expense of others?

3. Did you ever consider that your class might be filled with people of tremendous potential? There might be a world-class archer, a great poet, a magnificent violinist, and a great president. However, the archer never happened to try the bow, the poet never tried writing, the violinist ignored music, and the president never ran for office. Instead, they worked at other things and weren't very good. They all think of themselves as failures, although they would have been successful if they had only tried these other things.

What argument is being made by these statements? How would the concept of a general intelligence refute this argument?

SUGGESTIONS FOR FURTHER READING

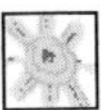

1. Blake, J., (1989). *Family size and achievement*. Berkeley: University of California Press.
2. Brody, N. (1992). *Intelligence (2nd ed.)*. Orlando, FL: Academic Press.
3. Brown, J. (1992). *The definition of a profession: The authority of metaphor in the history of intelligence testing, 1890–1930*. Princeton, NJ: Princeton University Press.
4. Chapman, P. D. (1988). *Schools as sorters: Lewis M. Terman, applied psychology, and the intelligence testing movement. 1890–1930*. New York: New York University Press.
5. Fancher, R. E. (1985). *The intelligence men*. New York: Norton.
6. Minton, H. L. (1988). *Lewis M. Terman: Pioneer in psychological testing*. New York: New York University Press.
7. Shurkin, J. N. (1992). *Terman's kids: The groundbreaking study of how the gifted grow up*. Boston: Little Brown.
8. Sternberg, R. J. (1985). *Beyond IQ: A triarchic theory of human intelligence*. New York: Cambridge.
9. Sternberg, R. J. (1986). *Intelligence applied: Understanding and increasing your intellectual skill*. New York: Harcourt, Brace, & Jovanovich.
10. Smutney, J. F., Veenker, K., & Veenker, S. (1991). *Your gifted child: How to recognize and develop the special talents of your child from birth to age seven*. New York: Ballantine.
11. Terman, L. M., & Oden, M. H. (1959). *The gifted group at midlife: Thirty-five years' follow-up of the superior child*. Palo Alto, CA: Stanford.

UNIT FOUR

THE DEVELOPING CHILD: SOCIAL PROCESSES

Izzy Wexler-Mann, age six

Unit Contents

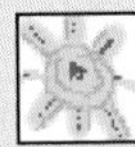

CHAPTER 12

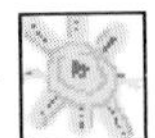

SOCIALIZATION AND PERSONALITY DEVELOPMENT

CHAPTER PREVIEW

THREE WAYS TO PARENT

THE MOTHER OF a 1-year-old boy finds that when all else fails and her infant son won't behave, she becomes frustrated enough to withdraw her love and attention from him. As the mother herself stated: "He woke up about 4:30 and began crying. Absolutely nothing would make him happy. Even when I was holding him, he was still crying and climbing all over me. Finally, after about a solid hour of crying, I succumbed to my frustration and lost patience with him. I was sitting on the sofa, holding him, and it seemed he was trying to climb up to the top of my head. Anyway, he scratched my nose with his fingernail, and it made me so angry that I very harshly put him down on the floor. He seemed really hurt and screamed much louder. All I needed at that point was more screaming, so I picked him up and carried him upstairs and put him in his bed. When I put him in bed he screamed even more, but at that point I was so angry that I just didn't want to be near him anymore. So I left him in bed and closed the door and came downstairs." (Maccoby & Martin, 1983, p. 55)

A FATHER NOTICES that his 10-year-old daughter has finished her homework in just 15 minutes. He questions her about it, and she provides some excuses. On further examination, he discovers that she has completed only part of her homework, and only in a cursory way. He loves his daughter very much, but at times like this he feels he must be firm. He sits her down and tells her that she's going to work however long it takes and that she's going to perform to his satisfaction. If she doesn't, she won't be allowed to watch television for three months, and she won't be allowed to accompany the family on a picnic she is looking forward to next Saturday. The daughter responds by offering more excuses and argues that she should be allowed to handle her own life. Her father disagrees and reasserts himself, once again stating his demands. With tears in her eyes, the daughter insists on knowing why she has to do it. "Because I'm bigger than you and I say so, that's why," answers her father.

A 7-YEAR-OLD BOY won't share his toy with his sister. Their father overhears the argument between them and intervenes. He takes the boy aside and sits him down. "That's not the way big boys behave," the father explains. He continues, "Don't you love your sister? If you love your sister, you should be willing to share things with her. Your mother and I share things with you, and sharing is something that families do. Your sister is good to you and she promises not to hurt any of your things. When I was a boy, I always shared with my brothers and sisters. Now that I'm grown up, I'm glad, because my brothers and sisters are all friends with me. Don't you like Aunt Jenny and Uncle Mark? I share with Uncle Mark. Well, someday your sister will be grown, and you'd like her to be friends with you, right?"

IN EACH OF THESE cases, a parent is trying to obtain compliance from a child. In one case, the parent has withdrawn her love; in another, he has asserted power; and in the last, the parent has tried to induce compliance through reason and example. Each of these techniques is common, and most parents eventually use all three, although they may rely more on one than another.

IN THIS CHAPTER, we will examine these parenting techniques and ways in which families socialize their children. We'll also take a look at specific areas of interest, including the effects of working mothers, divorce, and the one-parent family. In addition, we will see how a child's personality may develop as we look at the work of theorists such as Sigmund Freud and Erik Erikson.

RESOURCES

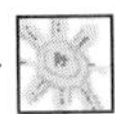

Socialization

SOCIALIZATION
The teaching process through which the beliefs, attitudes, and behavioral expectations of a culture are transmitted to children.

As soon as an infant is treated by others in a way that fosters the development of skills, attitudes, or behaviors deemed appropriate by the society, the process of **socialization** has begun. Socialization may begin as early as when someone decides to wrap a boy baby in a blue blanket or a girl baby in a pink one.

Question: Is socialization different in different cultures?

Every organized culture attempts to transmit its beliefs and values to its children. Different cultures, however, may have different attitudes and beliefs and therefore foster different behaviors in their children. These cultural differences are discussed in detail in Chapter 16.

The socialization process may also be affected by its historical context (Smuts & Hagen, 1985). Attitudes and beliefs have changed over time, and the behaviors that a society fostered in its children in the past may not be the same behaviors promoted by that society today.

Question: Is socialization a lifelong process?

Unless a person is isolated from all others in the society and avoids all the society's influence, socialization will be a lifelong process. Nonetheless, because an individual is socialized does not mean that he or she is passively programmed by society. The socialization process is a reciprocal one. Individuals alter society, and society alters individuals. In fact, any child within a family is bound to have an effect on the family and on its attempts to socialize that child (Brunk & Henggeler, 1984; Maccoby & Martin, 1983).

Unfortunately, the notion that children are somehow passive and are socialized by having things done to them is a difficult one to dispel. As a result, the majority of studies dealing with socialization in the family have concerned the effects of parental behavior on children. Less is known about the effects of children on parents and their marital relations. And even less is known about the effects that third parties might have on reciprocal social interactions, as might commonly

Parents provide a stable environment in which to raise and socialize their children and, occasionally, provide raw horsepower, too.

IDENTIFICATION
In psychoanalytic theory, the process by which the child tries to imitate the behavior of parents or other heroes to share vicariously in their lives.

IMITATION
Term used by social learning theorists to describe the acquisition of observed behavior.

ADOPTION OF ROLES
Term used by anthropologists to describe the acquisition of sexual and social behavior by individuals in a given culture.

occur, for instance, when a grandfather interacts with an ongoing relationship between a mother and child (Vuchinich, Emery, & Cassidy, 1988).

Question: Do researchers working with parents and families conduct experiments?

Not usually. Most researchers studying the family collect survey data from the recollections of family members or make observations of families interacting. They rarely are able to organize experiments because it is difficult to manipulate family interactions experimentally. Thus, most child-rearing studies are correlational, and cause-and-effect relationships are very difficult to infer.

THE FAMILY AS SOCIALIZING AGENT

Until children are old enough to interact meaningfully with peers or to enter school, their families are usually the primary agents of socialization. Even after young children enter school, their families still function as the central unit in their lives. Look at Table 12.1, and you can clearly see that a parent's job is truly one of "teacher."

Question: How do parents decide what to teach?

The parents, too, are products of socialization. They have been taught what they must do within the society and that they must now pass on this knowledge to their children. Children learn from parents. The parent is an important social model for the child. Children watch their parents and often try to imitate what they see. Freud referred to this process as **identification,** social learning theorists such as Albert Bandura call it **imitation,** and anthropologists refer to it as the **adoption of roles.** Whatever it is called, the process has been observed throughout the world.

SOCIALIZATION AND DEVELOPMENTAL CHANGE

Another important dimension of the socialization process is how it changes in accordance with the child's level of development. Interestingly, one of the first to

TABLE 12.1

The Tasks of Parent and Child in the Socializing Process

PARENTAL AIM OR ACTIVITY	CHILD'S TASK OR ACHIEVEMENT
1. Provision of nurturance and physical care	Acceptance of nurturance (development of trust)
2. Training and channeling of physiological needs in toilet training, weaning, provision of solid foods, etc.	Controlling the expression of biological impulses; learning acceptable channels and times of gratification
3. Teaching and skill training in language, perceptual skills, physical skills, self-care skills to facilitate care, ensure safety, etc.	Learning to recognize objects and cues; language learning; learning to walk, negotiate obstacles, dress, feed self, etc.
4. Orienting the child to child's immediate world of kin, neighborhood, community, and society, and to child's own feelings	Developing a cognitive map of one's social world; learning to fit behavior to situational demands
5. Transmitting cultural and subcultural goals and values and motivating the child to accept them for his or her own	Developing a sense of right and wrong; developing goals and criteria for choices; investment of effort for the common good
6. Promoting interpersonal skills, motives, and modes of feeling and behaving in relation to others	Learning to take the perspective of another person; responding selectively to the expectations of others
7. Guiding, correcting, and helping the child to formulate his or her own goals, plan his or her own activities	Achieving a measure of self-regulation and criteria for evaluating own performance

SOURCE: Clausen, 1968, p. 141.

NOTE: Teaching is a major part of the parent's role. As teachers, parents impart the demands and requirements of the family and society.

investigate this interaction was Sigmund Freud (1856–1939), who presented an outline of socialization and **personality** formation that focused on the child's level of development and how it related to the child's behavior. Let's take a brief look at some of Freud's work so as to better understand how socialization might interact with the child according to the child's developmental level.

PERSONALITY
The organization of relatively enduring characteristics unique to an individual, usually revealed by the individual's reaction to his or her environment.

PSYCHOANALYTIC THEORY
The school of psychological thought founded by Freud that emphasizes the study of unconscious mental processes and psychosexual development. As a therapy, psychoanalysis seeks to bring unconscious desires into consciousness and to resolve conflicts that usually date back to early childhood experiences.

ID
In psychoanalytic theory, the reservoir of instinctive drives; the most inaccessible and primitive portion of the mind.

EGO
In psychoanalytic theory, the part of the personality that regulates the impulses of the id to meet the demands of reality and maintain social approval and esteem.

SUPEREGO
In psychoanalytic theory, the part of the personality that incorporates parental and social standards of morality.

Sigmund Freud and Psychoanalytic Theory

Sigmund Freud's theories about personality and its development in childhood were to make him one of the most influential and controversial figures of the twentieth century. He is considered the founder of **psychoanalytic theory.**

Question: What exactly is psychoanalytic theory?

Psychoanalytic theory is a system derived by Freud from his observations of his many patients; it is a system from which he attempted to make predictions and explanations of behavior. Freud constructed this system with the aid of special techniques. Among these were free association (in which the patient is asked to say the first thing that comes to mind), dream interpretation, and the analysis of slips of the tongue (e.g., "I'm a prostitute—I mean Protestant!"). Any of these techniques, Freud believed, could tap hidden thoughts or desires lying below the surface of the conscious mind.

Most psychoanalysts accept Freud's theory either totally or to a considerable degree. Because the scope of Freud's theory is encompassing (tries to explain most of human behavior), it is often considered a "grand" explanatory theory (see Chapter 1).

THE THREE-PART PERSONALITY

Question: How did Freud come to develop his theory?

Freud began by using his knowledge of biology, natural selection, and socialization to create a picture, or model, of the personality. In Freud's model, the personality is divided into three parts: the **id,** the **ego,** and the **superego.**

Question: What do these three parts represent?

Part of the socialization process is learning through imitation.

PLEASURE PRINCIPLE
The psychoanalytic postulate that an organism seeks immediate pleasure and avoids pain. The id functions according to the pleasure principle.

REALITY PRINCIPLE
According to Freud, the principle on which the ego operates as it tries to mediate the demands of the unconscious id and the realities of the environment.

PSYCHOSEXUAL STAGES
Five stages of human development postulated by Freud. All but the latency stage are centered about the stimulation of erogenous zones. The erogenous stages—oral, anal, phallic, and genital—are predominant at different times.

ORAL STAGE
According to Freud, the first psychosexual stage, in which pleasure is focused on the mouth and oral cavity.

ANAL STAGE
The second psychosexual stage according to Freud, during which bowel control is achieved and pleasure is focused on the functions of elimination.

PHALLIC STAGE
According to Freud, the third psychosexual stage, during which the child manipulates and explores his or her genitals and experiences a strong attraction for the parent of the opposite sex.

EROGENOUS ZONES
According to psychoanalytic theory, physically defined areas of the body from which is obtained the greatest psychosexual gratification. Different areas are predominant during different stages of psychosexual development.

NEGATIVE FIXATION
In psychoanalytic theory, remaining in a particular psychosexual stage of development because the id has failed to receive sufficient satisfaction.

POSITIVE FIXATION
In psychoanalytic theory, remaining in a particular psychosexual stage of development because the id has received too much satisfaction.

Freud described the id as having no objective knowledge of reality. It serves only as a ruthless, relentless engine, driving the organism toward pleasure and away from pain. It operates according to the **pleasure principle.**

The ego, as described by Freud, is the portion of the personality that must deal with objective reality if the id's desires are to be met. The ego functions according to a **reality principle.** For instance, although the id may want all the money in the bank, it is the ego that must deal with the vault, the guards, and the other *realities* of the situation.

Question: What about the idea that stealing is wrong? Isn't that a consideration?

Yes. According to Freud, that realization would be a function of the superego. Freud viewed the superego as the internal representation of social and traditional values. Because the superego develops as a result of socialization, it is not inherited or present at birth.

Of course, these hypothetical constructs (id, ego, and superego) were only designed to create a picture of biological (id), psychological (ego), and social (superego) development.

PSYCHOSEXUAL STAGES OF DEVELOPMENT

According to Freud, as the id, ego, and superego develop, the child passes through various levels of development called **psychosexual stages.** The first three stages (**oral, anal,** and **phallic**) are involved with physical satisfaction and are centered around the **erogenous zones.**

Oral Stage (Birth to Approximately 1 Year) Freud believed that during this time in a child's personality development, the greatest satisfaction is obtained by stimulation of the lips, mouth, tongue, and gums. He noted that sucking and chewing are the chief sources of an infant's pleasure. Freud believed that during this stage, socialization is fairly limited to guiding the infant to nurse and form a strong attachment with the mother.

Anal Stage (Approximately 1 to 3 Years) During this time, Freud stated, the child gains the greatest satisfaction by exercising control over the anus during elimination and retention. Freud believed that one of the most important achievements in the socialization process is toilet training.

Phallic Stage (Approximately 4 to 6 Years) According to Freud, the child's greatest pleasure during the phallic stage comes from stimulating the genitals. It is during this stage, Freud believed, that the child is socialized to identify with the same-sex parent, enabling the child to develop into a healthy, mature adult.

Question: What if this early development doesn't go smoothly? Could there be problems?

Freud thought so. He believed that it is possible to become fixated at any one of the psychosexual stages. For example, if the id doesn't receive enough satisfaction during the oral stage, Freud argued, it may be reluctant to leave that stage until enough satisfaction has been obtained. This is known as **negative fixation** and can result, according to Freud, in a manifestation of oral-stage processes later in life. On the other hand, the id may receive too much satisfaction during the oral stage; if this happens, the id may want to retain oral-stage satisfaction in later life. Freud called this **positive fixation.**

Question: How would a fixation manifest itself in later development?

According to Freud, such an individual would remain immature in social relations and might engage excessively in oral activities, such as eating, talking, and smoking. Such possibly problematic behavior in adult life, Freud argued, might be the result of negative or positive fixation during the oral stage. For example, he considered the possibility that a child whose id is not satisfied during toilet training because of the demands made by parents might seek satisfaction through undue retention. He believed that such **anal-retentive** personalities would show signs later in life, such as stinginess and selfishness.

The final two stages (latency and genital) were considered by Freud to be less important than the first three.

ANAL RETENTIVE
According to Freud, a personality type formed by fixation at the anal stage. Characteristics include stinginess, selfishness, and withholding.

LATENCY STAGE
In psychoanalytic theory, the fourth psychosexual stage, occurring between the phallic stage and puberty, during which sexual drives and feelings become lessened or nonexistent.

GENITAL STAGE
In psychoanalytic theory, the final stage of psychosexual development, characterized by the expression of heterosexual interests.

Latency Stage (Approximately 6 Years to Puberty) Freud referred to this time as the **latency stage** because he believed that the sexual drive becomes dormant from the age of 6 years until the onset of puberty. Children during this psychosexual stage, according to Freud, are free of erotic feelings and instead direct their efforts toward further socialization by acquiring cultural and social skills.

Genital Stage (Puberty to Adulthood) Freud believed that heterosexual desire awakens during the **genital stage,** and provided that no strong upsetting fixations have occurred, the child is on his or her way to a "normal" life.

Question: How do researchers currently view Freud's theory?

Psychologists owe much to Freud and his followers. Whether one agrees with psychoanalytic theory or not, Freud's work and the work of other psychoanalysts stimulated research into the interaction between socialization and development. Furthermore, some of Freud's ideas have been widely accepted by modern theorists. For instance, his contentions that we are often governed by unconscious motivations and that sexuality can be a strong force during childhood have been supported by modern research. Some of Freud's other beliefs, or those of other psychoanalysts, have not been upheld (Erwin, 1980). Among these are Freud's ideas about fixations and their lasting effects. Few modern scientists believe, for instance, that problems with toilet training are likely to lead to anal retentiveness or stinginess.

A Modern Psychoanalyst: Erik Erikson

Question: Are there any modern psychoanalysts who have an influence on developmental psychology?

Erik Erikson (1902–) is a good example. As a young student, Erikson worked with Freud, and over the years he has expanded on Freud's ideas.

Question: How does Erikson's theory differ from Freud's?

Erik Erikson (1902–).

There are three principal differences. First, Erikson places a much greater emphasis on social and cultural forces than Freud did. Freud believed that a child's socialization and personality are determined mainly by parents, considering parents primarily responsible for the child's eventual development, whereas Erikson places the child in the broader social world of parents, friends, family, society, and culture, all of which, in Erikson's view, have an impact on the child's eventual development.

Second, Erikson does not believe that failure at any particular stage necessarily has irreversible consequences akin to the fixations that Freud argued might occur. Erikson argues that setbacks at any stage can be overcome with suitable attention, care, and love more easily than Freud assumed.

Third, Erikson emphasizes the entire life span of an individual, whereas Freud placed the greatest emphasis on the first six years of life.

Question: Does Erikson also describe development in terms of psychosexual stages?

PSYCHOSOCIAL STAGES
Stages of ego development as formulated by Erikson, incorporating both sexual and social aspects.

No. Instead, Erikson chooses to emphasize the social aspects of development and views human development as a progression through eight **psychosocial stages.** These eight stages can be roughly related to Freud's psychosexual stages, but as noted, the emphasis is quite different (see Table 12.2).

Erikson argues that each of these stages represents a period in our lives when we are faced with social conflicts that must be resolved. Failure to resolve these conflicts will, Erikson argues, lead to unhealthy development.

Question: What are the eight psychosocial stages identified by Erikson?

Erikson argues that the first major conflict faced by a child—the establishment of trust rather than mistrust—occurs during the child's first year. During the first year, Erikson states, parents or primary caregivers play the major role in helping the child form a sense of basic trust. Not only should the parents feed and care for the child, but they should also work to build an affectionate and warm relationship.

After a sense of basic trust has been established, the child must develop autonomy if healthy ego and personality development are to continue. This is the beginning of the second psychosocial conflict (autonomy versus shame or doubt), which Erikson asserts develops between the ages of 1 and 3.

Question: According to Erikson, how do children develop autonomy?

Children start to develop autonomy when they are taught how to master tasks or do things for themselves. This teaches them that they are important and can manipulate their environment. Erikson believes that children who are not encouraged to develop this self-confidence may come to doubt themselves or be ashamed of their inability.

Between the ages of 3 and 5½, children who have a sense of basic trust and feel autonomous or competent may feel free to initiate their own activities. At this

TABLE 12.2

Erikson's Psychosocial Stages and Freud's Psychosexual Stages, Compared

PERIOD OF TIME	PSYCHOSOCIAL CONFLICT	DESCRIPTION OF ERIKSON'S STAGES	FREUDIAN STAGES
1. Infancy	Basic trust vs. mistrust	Parents must maintain an adequate environment—supportive, nurturing and loving—so that the child develops basic trust.	Oral
2. Years 1–3	Autonomy vs. shame or doubt	As the child develops bowel and bladder control, he or she must also develop a healthy attitude toward being independent and somewhat self-sufficient. If the child is made to feel that independent efforts are wrong, then shame and self-doubt develop instead of autonomy.	Anal
3. Years 3–5½	Initiative vs. guilt	The child must discover ways to initiate actions on his or her own. If such initiatives are successful or acceptable, guilt will be avoided.	Phallic
4. Years 5½–12	Industry vs. inferiority	The child must learn to feel competent, especially when competing with peers. Failure results in feelings of inferiority.	Latency
5. Adolescence	Identity vs. role confusion	The child must develop a sense of role identity, especially in terms of selecting a vocation and future career.	Genital
6. Early adulthood	Intimacy vs. isolation	The formation of close friendships and adult sexual relationships is vital to healthy development.	↓
7. Middle adulthood	Generativity vs. stagnation	Adults develop useful lives by helping and guiding children. Childless adults must fill this need through adoption or other close relationships with children.	↓
8. Later adulthood	Ego integrity vs. despair	An adult will eventually review his or her life. A life well spent will result in a sense of well-being and integrity.	↓

point, the third psychosocial conflict emerges (initiative versus guilt). Erikson argues that during this time, children should be encouraged to initiate activities on their own.

Sometimes, of course, the activities that a child initiates may run counter to parental or social rules of conduct. Erikson argues that the best way to deal with this problem is to forbid the inappropriate behavior but in a manner that won't make the child feel guilty. When, for example, a 5-year-old decides it would be fun to play with delicate stereo equipment, a parent should forbid the activity firmly but also gently, so as not to make the child feel guilty for having initiated the behavior. In this way, the child can develop confidence in his or her own planning without fear that almost anything initiated will be wrong.

Between the ages of about 5½ and 12, the conflict to be resolved is industry versus inferiority. During this time, according to Erikson, children should be encouraged to produce things and to complete the activities they have initiated. Through these efforts, a sense of industry is attained. The conflict between industry and inferiority becomes especially strong among schoolchildren, who are often in competition with their peers. Erikson believes that failure to be successfully industrious will lead to feelings of inferiority.

The fifth stage occurs during adolescence. During this time, Erikson states, adolescents who have a sense of basic trust in their family and themselves, who can be autonomous and feel comfortable initiating activities, and who are industrious are best able to resolve the next crisis: identity versus role confusion. "Who am I?" becomes a question of major concern. To negotiate this stage, adolescents must discover their own world philosophy, ideals, and identity.

During early adulthood, Erikson argues, the major conflict is between intimacy and isolation.

Question: By intimacy, does Erikson mean marriage and sexual intimacy?

To a degree, but also *social* intimacy. The healthy development of the young adult personality, according to Erikson, requires close interpersonal bonds with a spouse, friends, or colleagues.

Erikson describes the major conflict during middle adulthood as generativity versus stagnation.

Question: What does Erikson mean by generativity?

Generativity means expanding your love and concerns beyond your own immediate group to include society and future generations. Erikson sees an involved, active parenthood as one way to achieve generativity—but not the only way. *Stagnation,* on the other hand, refers to becoming preoccupied with your own material and physical well-being and having no concern for society or the next generation.

The last stage—ego integrity versus despair—belongs to later adulthood. By this time, anyone who has been successful in resolving the earlier psychosocial crises, according to Erikson, will be able to look back on life with a sense of accomplishment and satisfaction. Those who have lived fruitless lives filled with self-centered pursuits or lost opportunities may feel a sense of despair.

Question: Does Erikson mean, then, that during later adulthood, despair is a sign of an unhealthy personality?

In Erikson's theory, the psychosocial stages are not to be thought of as dichotomies, that is, as either one thing or the other. Instead, there is a range between any of the opposing positions at each psychosocial stage. For example, Erikson would not expect an adolescent to have either a complete identity or total role confusion. The adolescent would be somewhere in between, leaning more, it is hoped, toward the positive identity formation than the negative role confusion.

According to Erikson, a certain degree of despair would be normal and natural for persons with healthy personality development in later adulthood. As Erikson has said, "During old age the life crisis involves the conflict between integrity and despair. How could anybody have integrity and not also despair about certain things in his own life, about the human condition?" (Hall, 1983, p. 27).

Question: How do most researchers view modern psychoanalysts such as Erikson?

Some researchers think that Erikson's theory fits well the informal observations obtained from many sources and that his theory may have much to contribute as a general outline for healthy socialization and personality development. However, hard scientific proof for Erikson's theory is not easy to come by because of the difficulty of examining each of Erikson's stages under controlled laboratory conditions or by other scientific methods. Furthermore, it has been argued that Erikson's stages of development have been too subjectively determined.

Question: Is there hard scientific evidence that development has a pronounced effect on the socialization process?

The psychoanalytic theories of Freud and Erikson attempt to explain much of human behavior. For this reason, they are considered to have great scope. But as you recall from Chapter 1, such theories usually have low precision. Most modern researchers now tend to move carefully when making assertions, compiling great amounts of experimental data before they do. Table 12.3 outlines the important developmental changes that currently are assumed to have an important effect on socialization. Notice that the changes described in Table 12.3 are of a more general nature and regarded more cautiously and tentatively than those outlined by Freud or Erikson. And unlike the psychoanalytic theories, these developmental changes are more descriptive than explanatory.

Continuity Within Change

Although a child's development may greatly influence the socialization process, there tends to be a continuity in the behavior patterns of families over time (Maccoby, 1984; Wachs, 1987). In this view, what changes as the child develops is often the way in which family *continuity* is maintained. For example, parents who hug and caress their infants may, once the children are grown, continue to show this love and affection but in a nonphysical way. Parents who show their love and affection with gestures may, once the child acquires language, display their caring verbally. And so on. In other words, the *mode* of expression may change as the child develops, but the basic family patterns of interaction usually remain quite stable.

Question: If family interaction patterns tend to be stable, how can you explain that children from the same families are often very different in terms of behavior and personality?

There is no question that siblings brought up in the same family can differ considerably in behavior and personality (Scarr & Grajek, 1982). It is generally accepted that although siblings may differ in terms of personality and temperament for genetic reasons (Plomin, McClearn, Pedersen, Nesselroade, & Bergeman, 1988), family socialization must also play an important role (Hoffman, 1991). Researchers therefore assume that when siblings are very different, the parents may have treated the children in different ways (Dunn, Plomin, & Daniels, 1986; Scarr & McCartney, 1983). Although it may not be pleasant to contemplate, and parents often deny it, some children in a family are favored over others (Aldous, Klaus, & Klein, 1985; Sroufe, Jacobvitz, Mangelsdorf, DeAngelo, & Ward, 1985). Another possibility, of course, is that siblings affect each other. For instance, if you grew up with a mother, father, and a brother, consider that your brother had a very different family—your mother, your father, and *you*.

Social Regulation

One of the many functions of the socialization process is to teach children how to regulate their own behavior with an eye on eventually letting them "out of the nest" to fend for themselves.

Question: How does social regulation develop?

During the first year of a child's life, special bonds of attachment form between the child and parents. During the second year, however, this interaction undergoes a major qualitative change. At this time, socialization pressures begin in earnest (Maccoby & Martin, 1983). This increased effort by parents to socialize their children usually starts with an attempt to regulate the child's behavior. Regulation becomes necessary during the child's second year because this is when the child begins to display sufficient autonomy to interfere occasionally with parental desires. For this reason, the parents attempt to instill in the child an understanding of what is acceptable, which is, of course, an important step in the socialization

TABLE 12.3

Developmental Changes and Their Effects on Socialization

DEVELOPMENTAL CHANGE	DESCRIPTION OF CHANGE	EFFECT ON SOCIALIZATION
Physical growth	Increase in size; significant gains in motor coordination	New skills requiring greater size, strength, or motor coordination can be taught. Physical discipline and manipulation declines. Affectionate displays involve less hugging, touching, and physical contact.
Language development	Child begins to understand and use language	Entire new form of communication develops between parents and child. Guidance becomes verbal and less physical. Explanations and reasoning are used. Child can now interact more easily with members outside of the immediate family.
Impulsivity	Fairly steady decline in impulsivity throughout childhood; fewer outbursts and greater ability to postpone gratification and deal with frustration	Parents move away from discipline techniques requiring the assertion of power and rely more on reasoning and gentle persuasion. Parents expect children to control more of their own behavior.
Changes in the conceptions of others	Between the ages of 6 and 12 years, child begins to understand the desires, expectations, and probable actions of others	Appeals to fairness and reminders about parents' greater knowledge begin to replace promises of rewards and threats of punishment. Child's knowledge of parental desires makes it easier for the child to engage in persuasive counter-arguments.
Changes in the concept of the self	Child comes to realize that others' perceptions of the child affect the way the child is treated	There is a greater pressure to conform. The child begins to tailor behavior and emotional expressions to suit a given audience. Child may become more self-conscious and may, when it is thought to be self-beneficial, keep to herself opinions and thoughts private that she would otherwise have expressed.
Autonomy	Child develops a greater need to do things for herself	Child resists parental limits, guidance, and teachings to achieve control for herself.

SOURCE: Adapted from Maccoby, 1984.

process. In this way, children begin learning at an early age to regulate themselves based on their understanding of what their parents allow (Dunn & Munn, 1985; Lytton, 1980).

Question: Rather than trying to teach self-control to a preschooler, wouldn't it be better to just "babyproof" your entire house by putting away anything that the child might be able to damage or harm?

Any home should be "babyproofed" to the extent that all potential poisons, medicines, and dangerous objects should be kept well out of reach of children. It's probably not advisable, however, to babyproof the home further by taking away every object that might possibly be damaged by a young child. Most preschoolers eventually comply (although it may take some parental insistence) with requests to leave appealing objects alone. Apparently, the presence of the objects can help the child acquire his own impulse control as the child learns to leave the objects alone (Power & Chapieski, 1986). Furthermore, babyproofing a home may make it somewhat sterile, limiting the opportunities for the exploration of new and interesting things. This, in turn, may hinder the development of nonverbal competence. In fact, children from heavily babyproofed homes tend to score slightly lower on the nonverbal test items in IQ tests (Power & Chapieski, 1986).

Throughout their development, children will continue to increase their abilities for self-regulation, in large measure because of the parenting they receive.

Aspects of Parenting

Over the years, developmental researchers have examined many different kinds of parenting techniques. Building on the earlier work of Earl Schaefer (1959), Diana Baumrind (1967, 1971, 1980) has become one of the most prominent researchers in parenting styles. Baumrind has examined the interaction of two of the most important dimensions of parenting. One dimension indicates the degree

Part of the socialization process includes parental efforts to help children acquire self-regulation. Here a child is being instructed as to the limited uses of breakfast food.

of parental permissiveness. This is the **permissive-demanding dimension.** The second dimension indicates the degree of affection. This is the **accepting-rejecting dimension.** These two parenting dimensions have been observed in all human societies (Rohner & Rohner, 1981). As you might imagine, Baumrind's work has generated a great deal of research over the years.

PERMISSIVE-DEMANDING DIMENSION One of two major dimensions used by Baumrind to describe parenting; denotes the degree of parental permissiveness.

ACCEPTING-REJECTING DIMENSION One of two major dimensions used by Baumrind to describe parenting; denotes the degree of affection within the parent-child relationship.

The field created by the interaction of these two dimensions can be seen in Figure 12.1. For example, if a mother scored −60 on the accepting-rejecting dimension and −80 on the permissive-demanding dimension, her form of parenting would fall within the rejecting-demanding field and would be labeled authoritarian-dictatorial. We can study various points within four fields—accepting-permissive, accepting-demanding, rejecting-permissive, and rejecting-demanding—by examining the interaction of these dimensions.

Question: What makes parents select a particular mode of interaction?

No one knows for certain. A parent's own upbringing may have a bearing on her choices. Experiences with other parents and parental models from television or other media probably also play a role. There is even evidence that the choice of any of these dimensions, except for demanding, is influenced to a degree by the parent's genetics (Plomin, McClearn, Pedersen, Nesselroade, & Bergeman, 1988). Research also shows that once a particular mode of parenting is established, it tends to remain in place; that is, the parent is generally consistent in his mode of parenting (McNally, Eisenberg, & Harris, 1991).

ACCEPTING-PERMISSIVE

Parents who are loving and accepting and at the same time are fairly permissive create what is referred to as a democratic environment. Each child is treated as an individual and held in esteem. Although democratic parents do not allow complete freedom and do enforce rules of conduct, their children are relatively free to try new things and are encouraged to develop independently. Children raised in this kind of environment tend to be independent, outgoing, active, and assertive

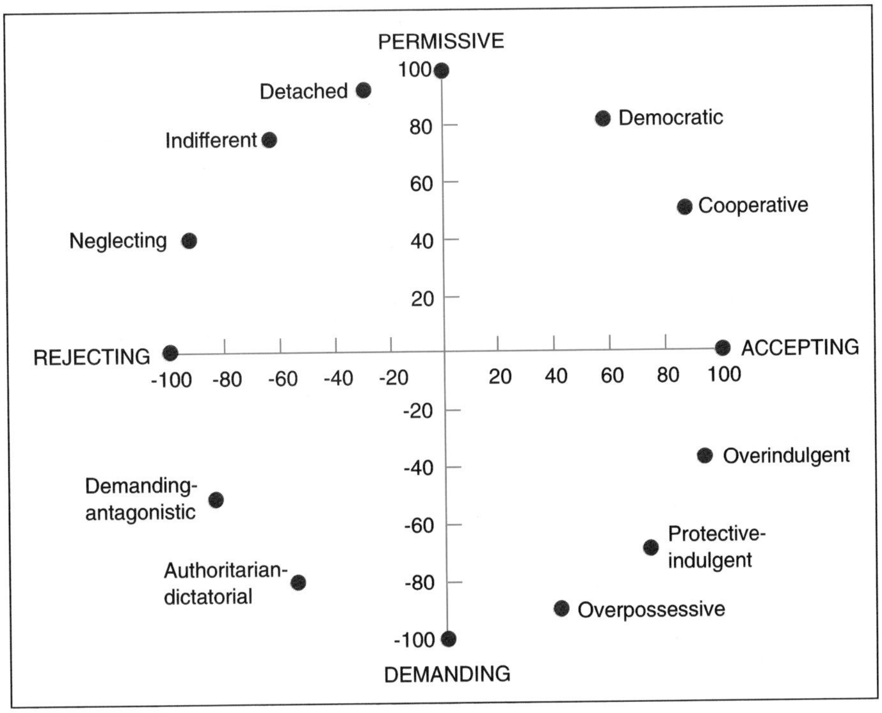

FIGURE 12.1
Modes of parenting. The interaction of two important dimensions of parenting, permissiveness and affection, describes many different environments in which children may be reared. (*Source:* After Schaefer, 1959)

(Baldwin, 1949). They are also friendly and tolerant and have a high sense of self-worth (Kagan & Moss, 1962).

Question: What do you mean when you refer to a parent as "permissive"?

Diana Baumrind has defined permissive parents as those who are tolerant, who take an accepting attitude toward their children's desires, who rarely use punishment, and who try to avoid using restrictions and controls when possible. These parents rarely demand mature behavior, such as engaging in proper manners or carrying out family assignments; they allow their children to make many of their own decisions and rarely have strict rules governing the children's time (such as when to go to bed or how much television may be watched) (Baumrind, 1967). Of course, no one functioning as a parent, by the very nature of the role, could ever be completely permissive, nor is it necessarily a good idea that one should be. All parenting requires some control over children.

Question: What happens if parents are too permissive?

Although it is true that children from loving, permissive families (those that might be considered cooperative or democratic in Figure 12.1) often do well, too much permissiveness may result in children who are immature and who have poor impulse control (Baumrind, 1967). It should also be pointed out that permissiveness is an inappropriate response if the child is engaging in excessive aggression. Researchers have observed that there is a positive correlation between permissiveness toward aggression and children's aggressive behavior toward parents and other family members (Yarrow, Campbell, & Burton, 1968).

ACCEPTING-DEMANDING

Parenting behaviors within the accepting-demanding field include not only warmth and affection but also a high degree of control. Children of such parents can sometimes be overprotected or taught to be dependent on adults. If these children become too dependent, they may be unable to stand up for themselves and may develop a sense of insecurity (Becker, 1964). Creativity can also be restricted in the accepting-demanding environment. Children of overprotective parents are generally dominated excessively and tend to be submissive, dependent,

Although democratic parents do not allow complete freedom, their children are relatively free to try new things and are encouraged to develop independently. Children raised in this kind of environment tend to be independent, outgoing, active, and assertive.

polite, and obedient, whereas children of overindulgent parents are more disobedient, rebellious, and aggressive.

Question: But can't control be beneficial?

As was noted before, parents, in the very act of parenting, must exert some control. It is the excessive or inappropriate control that may lead to overprotection. Judicious and fair control is often beneficial, however. Parents who set strict standards but who are also warm and willing to explain their reasoning to their children are referred to by Baumrind as **authoritative parents.** For instance, it has been found that boys with high self-esteem had authoritative parents who required high standards of competence and obedience and who consistently enforced these standards and rules (Comstock, 1973; Coopersmith, 1967). You may also recall the risk factors associated with lower IQ gathered from the Rochester Longitudinal Study (see Chapter 11). It has been found that even children from families with many of these risks will do well on cognitive tests as long as they "come from loving families with strict but clearly stated rules" (Adler, 1989, p. 7).

Furthermore, parents who practice judicious and fair control are more likely to provide teaching and encouragement within what Vygotsky called the child's zone of proximal development (see Chapter 10), probably because such parents are more sensitive to their children's successes and failures and are therefore more aware of the kinds of cognitive scaffolding their children require (Pratt, Kerig, Cowan, & Cowan, 1988).

Baumrind has also discovered that authoritative parenting is especially productive when it comes to raising teenagers (Baumrind, 1991). This has come as a surprise to some, who point to Erikson's contention that adolescence is a time for the formation of one's own identity, a time when one breaks away from parental demands. Baumrind agrees that while this may be true in stable social environments, in today's often unstable world of working mothers, high divorce rates, and accessible illicit drugs, adolescents do best when parents are both demanding and sensitive to their teenager's growing need for independence. Baumrind has shown in her research that adolescents from authoritative (accepting-demanding) families are less likely to abuse drugs than are those from democratic (accepting-permissive) families and are also likely to become competent, mature and optimistic. Other researchers confirm that authoritative parenting fosters academic achievement in adolescents. Adolescents who describe their parents as being democratic and warm, but at the same time firm, are more likely than other adolescents to develop positive attitudes toward their achievements and therefore do better in school (Steinberg, Elmen, & Mounts, 1989). As Baumrind points out,

> Authoritative parents are not bossy. They make it their business to know their children, how they're doing in school and who their friends are. Their control reflects a high level of commitment to the child, and they are not afraid to confront the child. (Bower, 1989a, p. 117)

REJECTING-PERMISSIVE

Rejecting parents who do not control their children's behavior are creating an environment that fosters rebellion, anger, and disharmony. Children in these settings tend to be disobedient, aggressive, and delinquent (Becker, 1964; Sears, Maccoby, & Levin, 1957). The high rate of aggression in this group may be because hostile parents so often model aggression themselves.

REJECTING-DEMANDING

Parents who are demanding but at the same time hostile, or rejecting, are referred to by Baumrind as **authoritarian parents.** These parents put forward a strict set of rules and require unquestioned obedience. Physical punishment is commonly

AUTHORITATIVE PARENTS
Parents who set strict standards, but who are also warm and willing to explain their reasoning to their children.

AUTHORITARIAN PARENTS
Parents who put forward a strict set of rules and require unquestioned obedience to them. They are both demanding and hostile. Authoritarian parents often use physical punishment to enforce the rules, and reasoned discussion with the child is rare.

POWER ASSERTION
A disciplinary technique in which caregivers use physical punishment, removal of privileges, or the threat of these actions.

LOVE WITHDRAWAL
A disciplinary technique in which caregivers express disapproval by ignoring, isolating, or expressing lack of love for the child.

INDUCTION
A disciplinary technique in which caregivers try to show the child the reasoning behind the discipline.

used by the parent to enforce the rules, and reasoned discussion with the child is rare. Children reared by rejecting, demanding parents tend to be socially withdrawn and sullen. Their friendships are marked by quarreling and shyness (Becker, 1964). Because of the high degree of control maintained by authoritarian parents, these children are unable to express their hostility outwardly and may have a tendency to turn their aggression inward. This group exhibits a high degree of self-punishment and suicide compared with the other groups.

Question: Are these modes of parenting guaranteed to create the kinds of outcomes you have described?

Not necessarily. This is perhaps a good place to point out that these findings not only are general but also are often limited to middle-class populations in Western industrialized nations. For instance, parenting within the accepting-demanding dimension is perceived by Korean children as far more loving and acceptable than parenting that falls within the accepting-permissive dimension (Rohner & Pettengill, 1985). This is probably because despite Western influence, the Korean family stresses obedience to its authority and deference to its elders. The child is viewed as a fractional part of the more significant whole—that is, the family. A Korean child treated with too much permissiveness is, unlike his or her Western counterpart, quite likely to feel rejected.

Question: What kinds of discipline do parents use to control their children?

Three distinct kinds of disciplinary practices used by parents have been described (Hoffman, 1970). These are power assertion, love withdrawal, and induction. Each of these was introduced in the Chapter Preview.

Power assertion refers to the use of physical punishment, the removal of privileges, or the threat of these actions and is commonly associated with the authoritarian parent. With this practice, some parents hope to control their children by exploiting the child's weakness and lack of power. The use of physical punishment may, however, create serious problems for the child and family because of the potential for it to become abusive.

Love withdrawal is a nonphysical attempt to discipline the child. Parents using such methods ignore or isolate their children or express lack of love for them. Parents usually resort to this technique because they are frustrated and because it does often create a high level of compliance (Chapman & Zahn-Waxler, 1981). The child becomes very willing to "behave," apparently because of the great anxiety he or she feels at the threat of loss of love. Some researchers have argued that this technique may be more harmful than physical punishment because it holds within it the constant threat of abandonment (Meyer & Dusek, 1979).

Induction is a disciplinary technique by which the parent either attempts to give the child an understanding of the reasoning behind the discipline or appeals to the child's pride or desire to be grown up. Induction is more commonly associated with the authoritative parent. For example, parents using this technique may warn a child not to tease an animal by describing how the child may be bitten or injured. Through induction, parents attempt to build children's comprehension of the perspective of others and to help children realize how their actions may affect the people around them. Parents who use induction often augment it with praise for appropriate behavior. Parents use induction more often when they want long-term compliance from their children rather than the immediate cessation of some action (Kuczynski, 1984). By the time children are about 4 or 5, parents usually begin to favor induction over distraction as a way of preventing children from engaging in some action, simply because older children are beginning to understand the parent's reasoning. Interestingly, at about the same time, children will switch from noncompliance or direct defiance to the more sophis-

AT ISSUE

Born to Be Wild: An Evolutionary Theory of Socialization

Every once in a while, a theory comes along with a broad enough sweep to take your breath away. Such a theory has been proposed by Jay Belsky and his colleagues (Belsky, Steinberg, & Draper, 1991). Essentially, their theory suggests how the process of natural selection may influence socialization. The researchers readily admit that their theory is unproved; but like any good theory, it explains a great deal and contains many features that are testable.

Question: What do they argue in their theory?

The argument is a bit shocking at first, but in many ways it does make sense. Belsky and his colleagues claim that human beings, as products of natural selection (see Chapter 2), are genetically "programmed" to a certain degree to raise and socialize offspring in a way that will provide the best chance for the continuation of their own genetic line. Of course, people aren't like insects or lower animals. Culture, religion, learning, and tradition all play a role in the procreative process. If there were an unrelenting drive to reproduce, we wouldn't be able to explain the use of birth control, or, for that matter, people who opt to have no children. What is argued in their theory is that there is an inherited tendency to socialize children in a way that fosters their reproductive fitness, that is, in a way that best ensures that the offspring will survive to maintain their gene line.

Addressing this point, Belsky, Steinberg, & Draper argue that there are two somewhat distinct paths along which reproductive fitness may travel. First, parents may make a long-term investment in their children, caring for and nurturing each child for a lengthy time and in so doing expend many resources to protect their genetic "investment." Or second, parents may expend their resources to reproduce often, giving up the time they might otherwise have spent giving special care to a few offspring to mate many times and have many children. The researchers compare these approaches by thinking in terms of quantity (low resource investment in many children) versus quality (high resource investment in fewer children).

Question: What would determine which path was the most advantageous in terms of fostering one's genetic line?

In times of upheaval—for instance, during forced migrations, when families are broken apart and resources uncertain—the quantity approach is more likely to result in the passing on of one's genes because these tend to be times of high infant mortality. Anyone who puts off having children to wait for better times or who has few children may well end up not producing at all or losing the few children that he or she does have. In other words, during such times, there is genetic safety in numbers. In stable times, however, when families can stay together and resources are more certain, the quality approach, in which fewer offspring are protected and nurtured for long periods of time, produces better results because resources (food, shelter, parental attention) can be concentrated to benefit the few and almost guarantee their survival.

Question: But what about parents who make a large personal investment in their children but who also have a dozen kids?

The major feature of the quality approach is the stable, caring family. Therefore, in very stable times with ample resources, a family with even a dozen children would still be considered following a quality approach if sufficient time was invested in each child. On the average, however, the quality approach will result in fewer births (but a greater likelihood of survival for each individual birth) than will the quantity approach. It should also be noted that the quantity approach will outproduce (in terms of live births) the quality approach. For instance, a man with many mates who expressed the quantity approach could in one lifetime father scores of children—something beyond the reach of a man and woman who had bonded together for life.

Question: How do these ideas pertain to socialization?

Belsky and his colleagues argue that during the first five to seven years of a child's life, the child comes to understand how generally trustworthy his or her parents are, how available certain resources (food and shelter) tend to be, and how much he or she can count on relationships to endure. If the family is in upheaval—if the family suffers from violence, divorce, a missing parent, or fewer resources owing to poverty—a series of genetically programmed triggers will ensue within the family that will direct the child toward the "quantity" line of reproduction! For *genetic* reasons, then, as well as environmental ones, parents in such circumstances will become harsh, rejecting, insensitive, and inconsistent toward their children. In fact, it is interesting that when times get tough, parents often turn on their children. Wouldn't you think

AT ISSUE

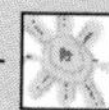

it would be the other way around—that tough times would foster extra kindness from parents?

Question: But isn't it because parents under stress become frustrated?

Yes, but Belsky argues that parents have been naturally selected to react to frustration by turning on their children! Furthermore, when parents reject their children, the children are accelerated toward early puberty!

Question: What! Why should parents who reject their children cause puberty to occur earlier in those children?

No one is sure, but it does appear to occur. Some have argued that what really happens is that *accepting* parents cause a genetic *delay* in puberty, a delay naturally selected for as a way to lessen incestuous pregnancies brought on by fathers who become too close to early-maturing daughters (Maccoby, 1991). But Belsky believes that early puberty occurs *because* the parents' behavior of rejection, triggered by hard times, helps bring on early puberty for the child as a preparation for early pregnancy, so that the child may begin down the "quantity" reproductive track! For example, daughters who are treated harshly at home are more likely to become depressed, which in turn causes them to internalize their problems, which lowers metabolism, which in turn stores fat, which in turn brings on menarche sooner (the first reproductive cycle and period). In this sense, then, harsh parenting and the resulting depression in children, aspects of family life usually considered pathological or dysfunctional, are in fact highly adaptive!* Furthermore, Belsky argues that children who come from broken or "dysfunctional" homes, or who are raised in poverty, or whose families are in upheaval, will not only strive for early pregnancy by being sexually promiscuous, but will not invest in long-term

*Researcher Robert Hinde makes the comparison that fear of the dark used to be classified as an "irrational fear of childhood." After John Bowlby's work demonstrated that such fears were probably the product of natural selection because of the survival value of children staying close to the parent during the night, children's fear of the dark was no longer seen as irrational, but as adaptive (Hinde, 1991).

FIGURE 12.2

Two pathways of reproductive development: quantitative (type 1) and qualitative (type 2). (*Source:* After Belsky, Steinberg, & Draper, 1991)

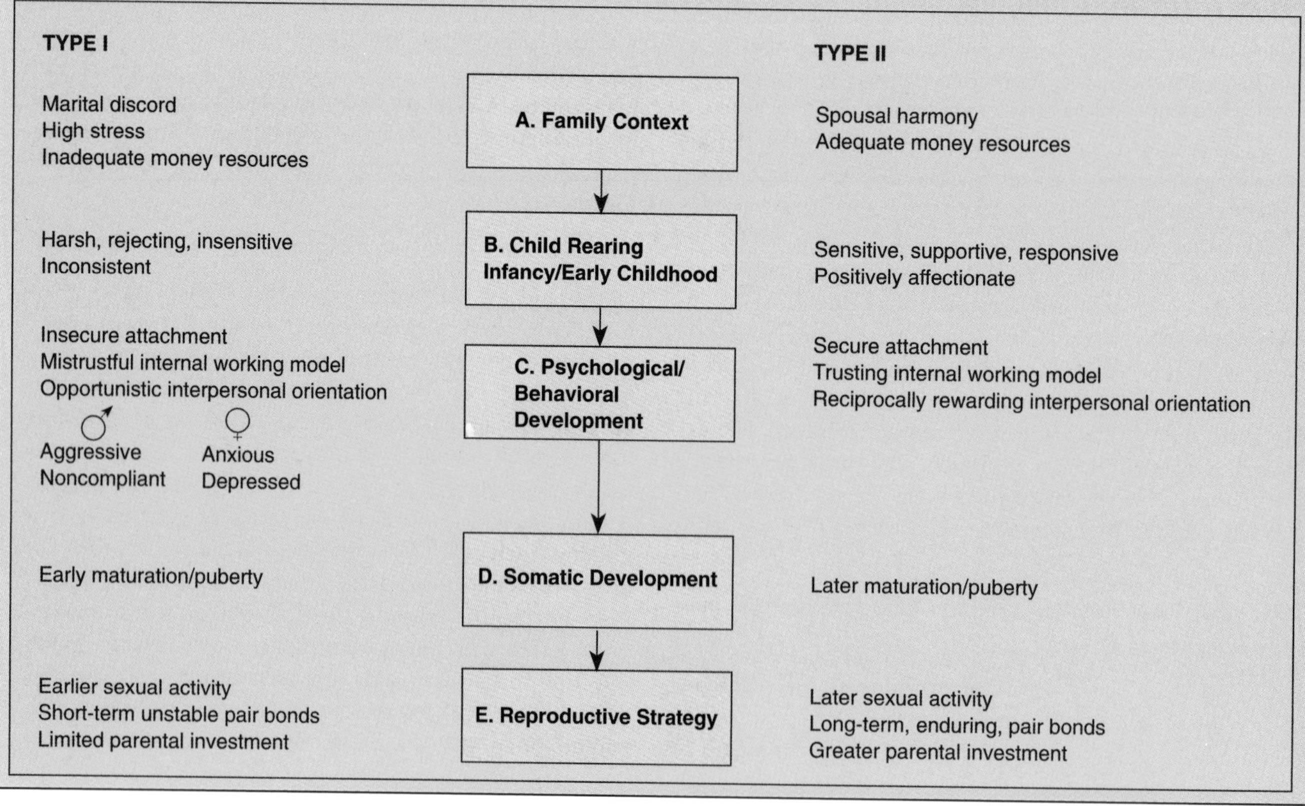

At Issue

relationships, nor will they be very interested in being close, loving parents!

Children, on the other hand, raised in stable, loving families, with sufficient resources, will find their genetic "quality" program triggered and will be more amenable to socializing processes that lead to trusting relationships, delayed sexual activity, long-term relationships, and greater parental investment (see Figure 12.2).

Question: How much of this theory is correct?

No one knows, but it explains a great deal. For example, why *are* kids who live in poverty more likely to be aggressive, sexually promiscuous individuals who fail at long-term relationships and make poor or abandoning parents? Of course, there may be other reasons, but this theory yields a potentially viable explanation—and one that is testable to a considerable degree. For instance, exactly how do parenting techniques and behaviors influence the onset of puberty? We know that harsh treatment of animals brings on early puberty and that early puberty is also associated with poverty and upheaval in humans. But to be definitive, Belsky proposes a study of identical twins reared apart to see if different parenting directly affects the timing of puberty.

Question: If this theory is correct, how might we use this information to help socialize children in a way that would be most beneficial to society as a whole?

If it does turn out that this theory is correct, or that major portions of it are, it would mean that we might be able to solve many serious social problems by finding ways to keep troubled families together while teaching them ways to interact that foster closeness and caring. If a national effort along those lines was feasible, it would, in one generation, transfer millions of children over from the quantity line to the quality line of social development simply because they had experienced a stable and loving environment during the first five to seven years of their lives. While such ideas may seem naive, the theory must be given a full examination if there is even the remotest possibility that such changes could be implemented.

ticated strategy of negotiation, also attempting to use reason (Kuczynski, Kochanska, Radke-Yarrow, & Girnius-Brown, 1987).

Exactly why a parent might choose one technique over another in any given situation is not clear. Some researchers believe that it has to do with the parent's perception of why the child is behaving as she is or of which technique will provide the best results. For instance, data indicate that parents who score low (more rejecting) on the accepting-rejecting dimension are more likely to use power-assertive disciplinary techniques, whereas parents who score high on this dimension (more loving) are more likely to use praise and induction (Becker, 1964).

Parents are more likely to use power-assertion discipline with boys than with girls (Kuczynski, 1984), probably because parents often expect boys to be harder to control. Because parents who use physical punishment are more likely to have aggressive children (Martin, 1975), it would be expected that parents who score low on the accepting-rejecting dimension would raise children who are more aggressive. According to the data, this is exactly what happens (Becker, 1964). In fact, harsh parenting techniques tend to be passed down from generation to generation. This finding suggests that modeling such parenting techniques teaches children how to act once they themselves become parents (Simons, Whitbeck, Conger, & Chyi-In, 1991). Research examining such perceptions and beliefs, however, is still in its earliest stages; too little is currently known for us to draw firm conclusions.

Question: Then how exactly should parents treat their children?

There is probably no one best way to treat children. Nonetheless, the following general guidelines are not likely to lead you too far astray, and for the most part they probably will be helpful.

1. Try not to be excessively demanding. Parents who control their children too much are often more concerned with meeting their own needs than with meeting those of their children. Although the children of such parents may grow up to be self-controlled, they may fail to develop confidence and self-assurance.
2. Try not to be extremely permissive. Be sure to reinforce responsible behavior while discouraging disruptive or immature acts. Without this feedback from you, your child may not learn to be adequately self-controlled.
3. Try to maintain a warm, accepting home where independent actions and thinking are encouraged, where rules are firm but fair, and where children know they are loved.
4. Be consistent. Don't change rules suddenly without a reason.

LEARNING CHECK

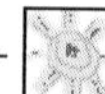

1. Socialization
   - **a.** is a lifelong process.
   - **b.** is reciprocal within families.
   - **c.** is a way of passing cultural values from one generation to the next.
   - **d.** is all of the above.
2. While working with families, researchers rarely
   - **a.** make direct observations.
   - **b.** conduct interviews.
   - **c.** conduct experiments.
   - **d.** use surveys.
3. According to Freud, what is the correct ordering of the psychosexual stages?
   - **a.** oral, anal, phallic, latent, genital
   - **b.** oral, anal, genital, latent, phallic
   - **c.** oral, anal, latent, phallic, genital
   - **d.** oral, anal, latent, genital, phallic
4. A difference between the theories of Freud and Erikson is that Freud emphasized the entire life span, while Erikson focused mainly on the first six years.
   - **a.** true **b.** false
5. It is a good idea to "babyproof" a home completely so that children aren't exposed to objects they shouldn't touch.
   - **a.** true **b.** false
6. The dimension of parenting that indicates the degree of parental permissiveness is called the ____________ dimension.
   - **a.** permissive-demanding
   - **b.** accepting-rejecting
   - **c.** discipline-independence
   - **d.** induction-demanding
7. Physical punishment is a form of ____________ discipline.
   - **a.** power-assertive
   - **b.** autonomous
   - **c.** inductive
   - **d.** love-withdrawal

Answers: 1. d 2. c 3. a 4. b 5. b 6. a 7. a

The Shifting Sands of Parenthood

When values and traditions in a culture begin to undergo rapid change, it becomes difficult to decide which attitudes and beliefs children should be taught. Changes occur to the traditional family structure that in themselves alter the way children are raised. Today, more mothers are working than ever before, families often break up through divorce and re-form with different members, and more children than at any time in our history are being reared in single-parent households. Researchers are interested in how these changes will affect the development of children, and some arresting new theories have been developed to help explain the behavior of families involved in these changes [see At Issue].

WORKING MOTHERS

For many years, our society was oriented toward an arrangement favoring a working father and a homemaker mother. Mothers who worked outside the home were considered neglectful of their children (if they didn't "have to" work) or unfortunate (if they did).

Now all of that has changed. The statistics tell the story: Beginning in 1986, the labor force included for the first time a majority of mothers whose children were not yet grown. This was double the percentage found in 1970. Nearly half of these working mothers were married women who had a child at home under 1 year of age; a majority (71 percent) of these working women held full-time jobs (Scarr, Philips, & McCartney, 1989).

Question: Why have so many women decided to enter the work force?

A single wage earner could sustain an entire family 20 or 30 years ago. Today, things are different. Many families are finding it easier to make ends meet if both husband and wife hold full-time jobs. Statistics also indicate another reason. In 1984, 1 out of 4 mothers was single; by 1993, it was 1 out of 3. The financial burden faced by these women typically requires them to work outside the home.

Question: How will these changes in maternal employment affect the children?

In all honesty, it will probably take another generation before we have the answer to that question. However, in one of the most comprehensive, long-term studies of its kind, the National Longitudinal Survey of Youth, results indicated that maternal employment during an infant's first year of life was detrimental in terms of cognitive and behavioral dimensions, regardless of the infant's gender or socioeconomic status (Baydar & Brooks-Gunn, 1991).

Results for children older than 1 year of age generally support a different outcome. Typically, data show that there are no adverse outcomes if the mother of a toddler or older child is employed. As measured by achievement on IQ, reading, arithmetic, spelling, and linguistic tests during an eight-year longitudinal study, young children of working mothers were not ordinarily adversely affected by their mother's absence (Cherry & Eaton, 1977). More recent studies have come to a similar conclusion (Gottfried & Gottfried, 1988), especially for girls (Baydar & Brooks-Gunn, 1991).

In fact, many children of working mothers have been found to be superior to the children of nonworking mothers in terms of cognitive and social development. Furthermore, although data have shown that working mothers spend about 2 hours per day less alone with their children than do nonworking mothers (Easterbrooks & Goldberg, 1985), these mothers can compensate for their absence by interacting frequently with their children when they are at home (Moorehouse, 1991). The *total* amount of time that the entire family (mother, father, and child) spends together is unaffected by maternal employment (Easterbrooks & Goldberg, 1985). Also, the stability of infant attachments to mothers and fathers appears generally to be unaffected by maternal employment (Hoffman, 1989).

In addition, if an employed mother is happy with her job and is able to provide for her child's daily needs so that she need not worry about her child's security, she may perform as a parent as well as or better than an unemployed mother. Unemployed mothers, in contrast, often find their homemaking job overly stressful because of money problems. Unemployed mothers are also more likely to be depressed if they want to work but are unable to (Hock & DeMeis, 1990). Finally, and perhaps most importantly, employed mothers tend to encourage their children to be more independent and self-sufficient from an early age (Hock, 1978).

Question: Why is it important to encourage children to be self-sufficient at an early age?

It appears that self-sufficiency may be a valuable attribute for children to acquire. Children who are encouraged to participate in household tasks and to organize and plan their daily activities often discover (as long as they are not forced to attempt tasks beyond their capabilities) that they can be successful. Such early independence training has been shown to increase achievement motivation and competence (Woods, 1972).

Question: Could the differences between children of employed and unemployed mothers stem from the fact that employed mothers are better educated?

In a study done by Birnbaum (1975), educated full-time mothers were compared with professionally employed mothers. The full-time mothers had lower self-esteem, felt less competent and less attractive, and expressed more feelings of loneliness than did their professional counterparts. Data have shown that a mother's morale is positively correlated with her effectiveness as a parent (Hoffman, 1979). However, if working fathers support nonworking mothers by providing intellectual and stimulating company and by sharing many of the child-care duties, mother-infant relations become more affectionate, competent, and sensitive (Pederson, Anderson, & Cain, 1977). One study that examined employed mothers' feelings about being separated from their firstborn infants found that mothers who chose to work were better able to cope than those who had to work but didn't want to (DeMeis, Hock, & McBride, 1986). Still, there are many exceptions. Quite a few women do find it stressful to combine the dual roles of primary care giver and employee. Such stress may offset any advantages gained from their employment (Hoffman, 1989).

Question: You mentioned earlier that maternal employment generally was not a detriment to children older than 1 year of age, especially for girls. Why would the gender of the child make a difference in his or her reaction to the mother's employment?

Employed mothers provide an incentive to children to set higher occupational and educational goals for themselves (Stein, 1973). This is especially true for daughters. Daughters of working mothers perceive the woman's role as more satisfying and women as more competent than do those of nonworking mothers (Broverman, Vogel, Broverman, Clarkson, & Rosenkrantz, 1972). Daughters, therefore, may admire their working mothers and see them as an important role model. Sons, on the other hand, are often more resentful when their mothers work. These differences appear to be especially pronounced among preschool children (Bronfenbrenner, Alvarez, & Henderson, 1984). Of course, as was said earlier, these are only general findings and cannot be applied in every instance.

In general, most of the effects that we have examined concerning working mothers are not due to employment of the mother per se, but rather to the circumstances, attitudes, and expectations that both parents experience as they relate to the mother working outside the home (Scarr, Phillips, & McCartney, 1989).

DIVORCE AND SINGLE-PARENT FAMILIES

Divorce rates in the United States have increased dramatically in the past 30 years. According to current assessments, 40 to 50 percent of marriages among young people will end in divorce. Of the children born in the last 10 years, almost 50 percent will spend an average of 5 years in one-parent households (Hetherington, Stanley-Hagan, & Anderson, 1989).

The number of single-parent families has increased more than 400 percent since 1970. As of 1990, 50 percent of all children under 18 years of age were spending some time in a single-parent household as the result of divorce or separation.

It used to be common practice following a divorce to award sole custody of the children to the mother. It was believed to be in the best interest of the children and occurred in about 90 percent of all cases. Although little was said about it, fathers often suffered severely from this practice (Meredith, 1985).

Now most states provide for an arrangement known as **joint custody.** Unlike sole custody, joint custody ensures that both parents have access to their children. It also provides the parents with an opportunity to share in the responsibility for raising the children. With joint custody, both parents can take part in important decisions, such as schooling and medical care.

JOINT CUSTODY
An arrangement in which more than one person shares legal custody of a child.

Question: Is joint custody a better arrangement for the children?

Sometimes joint custody isn't the best solution, especially when parents won't cooperate with each other (Atwell, Moore, Nielsen, & Levite, 1984). In a study of over 100 children of divorcing parents in which custody was being bitterly contested, access to both parents was often found to *increase* the children's emotional distress (Johnston, Kline, & Tschann, 1989).

On the other hand, joint custody can sometimes be a beneficial arrangement. For example, it has been found that fathers with joint custody are more likely to maintain a high degree of involvement with their children and are more likely to provide economic support (Grief, 1980; Meredith, 1985). Parents who choose joint custody generally work out agreements that better cover their children's needs than when sole custody is awarded (Phear et al., 1983).

Because 80 percent of men and 75 percent of women eventually remarry, 25 percent of all children will spend some time as a member of a stepparent family before they are 18 years of age (Hetherington, 1989). For this reason, the period of transition and disequilibrium for children following a divorce can continue for a considerable time, in that they must become accustomed to stepparents and to new environments. Sadly, of the 75 to 80 percent of divorced parents who do remarry, more than half will get a second divorce (Hetherington, 1989). Divorce rates are accelerating too quickly for longitudinal data on these changes to be available yet, and very little is known about the effects of a second divorce on children.

Question: How do children initially react to divorce?

The largest data source concerning the effects of divorce on children comes from the Virginia Longitudinal Study conducted by E. Mavis Hetherington. Hetherington discovered that, at first, most children respond with anger, fear, and shock. It is also common for children to feel guilty about or in some way responsible for the divorce and to become withdrawn and depressed (Hetherington, 1979; Kalter & Plunkett, 1984). Still, most children can adapt to a divorce within a couple of years; if the crisis is aggravated by additional stresses or conflicts, however, serious developmental disruptions may result.

Whether children fare well may depend on their past experience, their age, and the support they receive from their parents (Hetherington, 1989). Parental support often is lacking, however, because parents become so wrapped up in their own problems during a divorce that their ability to function as parents diminishes (Wallerstein, 1985; Wallerstein & Kelly, 1975, 1976, 1981).

Temperament can also play an important role in the child's ability to adjust to a divorce. Temperamentally, children labeled as "difficult" (see Chapter 4) have been found to be more vulnerable to the stress of a divorce than "easy" children (Hetherington, 1989). This may be because difficult children are more likely to elicit anger and hostility from parents who are already under considerable stress because of the divorce.

Question: What kinds of stress do children encounter during their parents' divorce?

There are many stresses associated with the divorce of one's parents (Hetherington et al., 1992). The child's bedtime and eating schedules may be disrupted. The parents' emotional state and the lessening of adult contact are likely to place stress on the child. Also, the level of income in the household usually decreases, which accounts for a significant portion of the stress children encounter following a divorce (Guidubaldi & Perry, 1985). In fact, about 45 percent of mothers who have custody of their children following a divorce report an annual income of less than $10,000 per year (Hernandez, 1988), which is well below the poverty level. Ex-husbands who fail to pay child support are often partly to blame for this state of affairs (Haskins, Schwartz, Akin, & Dobelstein, 1985).

A lower income often requires the parent to move, which in turn may cause the child to lose close friends and neighbors. In addition, the child may have to change schools or move to a neighborhood that has a higher rate of crime and delinquency (Tessman, 1978). Furthermore, if the mother is forced to take a job, the child may now feel abandoned by both parents. This is especially true for preschool children (Hetherington et al., 1982). As you can see, divorce is not a single event but a complex series of transitions requiring considerable adjustment.

Question: Do boys and girls react differently to the stress of divorce?

Generally, girls are better able to cope with the effects of divorce than boys (Guidubaldi & Perry, 1985; Hetherington, 1989). Following a divorce, boys usually have more behavior disorders and problems relating to others. The reason may be that in 90 percent of divorces that do not involve joint custody, the mother still receives custody (Hetherington, Stanley-Hagan, & Anderson, 1989). The children "lose" their fathers, and, boys are usually more attached to their fathers than girls are. The extra difficulties associated with boys may also stem in part from the fact that mothers who have custody of their sons may expect greater discipline problems from them because the fathers are absent, and they may try to forestall such problems by being stricter with them than they are with their daughters. In general, mothers tend to view their sons more negatively after a divorce than they do their daughters (Santrock & Tracy, 1978).

Girls, however, often have a more difficult time than boys do adjusting to a remarriage (Hetherington, 1989; Vuchinich, Hetherington, Vuchinich, & Clingempeel, 1991).

Question: Why would that be?

No one is sure. Hetherington has argued that it might be because

> . . . daughters in one-parent families have played more responsible, powerful roles than girls in nondivorced families and have had more positive relationships with their divorced mothers than have sons. They may see both their independence and their relationship with the mother as threatened by a new stepfather, and therefore resent the mother for remarrying. (Hetherington, 1989, p. 7)

The effect is apparently quite a strong one, because as Hetherington notes about the girls in her study whose mothers had remarried, "No matter how hard stepfathers tried, their stepdaughters rejected them" (Hetherington, 1989, p. 7). Sons, however, are more likely to view the stepfather as a source of support, a companion, and a role model (Vuchinich, Hetherington, Vuchinich, & Clingempeel, 1991).

Question: What are the long-term effects of divorce on children?

In a 10-year study of over 130 children of divorce, researcher Judith Wallerstein found that the effects of a divorce can last a long time (Wallerstein, 1984a, 1984b, 1985). Even after 10 years, the young men and women she interviewed typically perceived the divorce as the most stressful event in their lives. Many felt that they had missed something important by not growing up in a family with both parents. Many were angry because of their parents' extramarital affairs and were determined to keep such experiences away from their own future marriages. (Unfortunately, research indicates that children from divorced families are themselves more likely to become divorced.)

Although many researchers have noted that boys typically react more severely at the beginning of the divorce, Wallerstein found that after 10 years, it was the girls who seemed to face the most difficulties. Many were afraid to make a commitment and feared betrayal and rejection by men. They were more likely to become involved in sexual relationships of shorter duration, occasionally with older men. Another interesting finding was that children of divorced parents had formed closer relationships with their siblings 10 years following the divorce.

Question: Because divorce can be so stressful for children, should parents who are considering divorce make a great effort to stay together?

Years ago it was a common belief that parents should do anything to "stay together for the kids." Research has consistently shown, however, that children live more adequately in single-parent families than they do in stressful families in which parents are in continual conflict with each other (Hetherington, Cox, & Cox, 1978). Divorce in certain instances may also be helpful in putting distance between a disturbed parent and a child (Wallerstein, 1985). Also, it's been found that children, especially boys, often become more aggressive and uncontrollable many months, sometimes even years, before a separation or divorce as compared with children whose families have no desire to separate (Block, Block, & Gjerde, 1986; Cherlin et al., 1991). These findings indicate that predivorce marital stress may be having a significant influence on children's development.

Question: How are children affected by living in one-parent families?

Children may fare well in single-parent families, but the chances of problems increase. Whether children in single-parent families have adjustment problems may depend greatly on the community support services available to the parent, such as day care or financial aid.

Single parents often find it particularly helpful to be relieved of the burdens of parenting 24 hours a day or to receive added financial support to make ends meet. Any warm, structured, and predictable environment, whether a day-care center, school, or extended family, can be of great help for children suffering the turmoil of divorcing parents (Hetherington, Stanley-Hagan, & Anderson, 1989). One study even found that when medical and social services, including day care, were provided for single parents, beneficial effects were evident even a decade after the support had ended (Seitz, Rosenbaum, & Apfel, 1985); the single mothers receiving the help had children with better school attendance and were themselves more likely to be self-supporting, to attain a higher education, and to maintain a smaller family when compared to mothers in a control group who did not receive support. Furthermore, the mothers and children in the study's control group (who had not received the services) required far more financial assistance when the children reached early adolescence than did the mothers who had received help. This shows that failing to provide early help for single parents may be more costly in the long run.

CHILD ABUSE
Behavior by parents, caregivers, or others responsible for children's welfare that, through malice or negligence, results in psychological or physical injury to a child.

CHILD NEGLECT
Failure by parents, caregivers, or others responsible for children's welfare to provide reasonable and prudent standards of care for the children in their charge, thereby threatening the children's well-being.

PSYCHOLOGICAL MALTREATMENT
Mistreatment of children in a psychological way, as distinguished from physical abuse or neglect; includes verbal abuse, failure to provide warmth or love, and belittlement or berating.

CRISIS NURSERY
A place where parents may leave infants and young children for a short time until the parents are better able to deal with their stress and the danger of abuse is thus lessened.

PARENTS ANONYMOUS
An organization to help parents who abuse their children make constructive changes in their responses; uses the same intensive contact and principles as Alcoholics Anonymous.

LEARNING CHECK

Multiple Choice

1. Children of working mothers are more likely to be adversely affected if their mothers
   a. are professionals.
   b. work only for financial reasons.
   c. have high self-esteem.
   d. work part-time.
2. Judith Wallerstein discovered that the long-term consequences of divorce are most likely to adversely affect
   a. boys.
   b. girls.
   c. neither. Both girls and boys have been found to be equally vulnerable.
   d. stepchildren.
3. Which of the following children is *least* likely to show adverse effects following a divorce?
   a. a temperamentally difficult child
   b. one whose parents are contesting custody
   c. a girl whose mother has just remarried
   d. a boy whose father has custody

Answers: 1. b 2. b 3. d

Applications

Parents Under Stress: Helping to Prevent Child Abuse

Going through a divorce and raising children in a single-parent home are just two of the many stressful circumstances that families can encounter, any of which may lead to a situation that gets out of control. This loss of control may lead to child abuse and child neglect, which often are associated with such stresses (Egeland, Breitenbucher, & Rosenberg, 1980; Hay & Hall, 1981).

Child abuse has been with us for all recorded history—and, no doubt, long before that. In the United States, child abuse can be traced back to the first settlers to come ashore (Pleck, 1987). But it wasn't until the early 1960s, when researchers first coined the term *battered child syndrome* (Kempe, Silverman, Steele, Droegemueller, & Silver, 1962), that the nation's interest in the problem was aroused.

Question: What kinds of behaviors are considered child abuse?

There is no one accepted definition of **child abuse** (Emery, 1989). Although the term *child abuse* implies the physical assault or sexual abuse of a child by a parent or caregiver (Starr, 1979), defining the term can be quite tricky. Consider the following case. In 1974, a woman who had recently immigrated to England slashed the faces of her two young sons with a razor blade and then rubbed charcoal into the lacerations. When the woman was found out, she was arrested and charged with child abuse. Later, however, it was discovered that she was a member of the Yoruba tribe of Nigeria, a group that traditionally practices scarification as part of a rite of manhood. All the Yoruba boys get scarred, and the scars are then stained with charcoal. The Yorubas think it quite proper and manly (Korbin, 1977). The woman was found guilty, but considering her culture, she was given a suspended sentence. If you think that the court was too lenient, consider what anthropologist Jill Korbin has pointed out: Some cultures, including the Yoruba, find the Western practice of forcing an infant to sleep alone, away from its parents in a separate room, very cruel! As you can see, cultural factors must also be considered when defining abuse.

Occasionally, acts of omission are also incorporated in a definition of child abuse. These include failure by parents or other caregivers to provide the child with adequate food, shelter, safety, or health care. Such acts of omission are sometimes classified as **child neglect** and are more common than acts of child abuse (Wolock & Horowitz, 1984). For example, consider that in the United States, fully 40 percent of all children have not been immunized against certain common diseases, and a majority of the 5 million handicapped children in America are not receiving the help they need. Over half a million children have no home at all.

More recently, **psychological maltreatment,** such as constantly berating or humiliating a child or continuously showing resentment or coldness toward the child, has come under consideration (Garrison, 1987). Psychological maltreatment may actually be the most prevalent form of child abuse and potentially the most destructive, because in the long run, it tends to destroy the child's self-image and distort his or her relationships with other people (Hart & Brassard, 1987). Psychological maltreatment is so difficult to define, however, that it is not likely to be controllable through state intervention (Melton & Davidson, 1987). Any major effort toward prevention of psychological maltreatment will probably have to focus on public education to make people aware of the problem and teach them how to lessen it.

Question: How prevalent is child abuse?

If we include child neglect and psychological maltreatment in our definition, it is believed to be very common, although specific numbers are unknown. If we limit ourselves to the consideration of violence alone, the prevalence of child abuse is easier to calculate. In 1989, 2.4 million cases were reported in the United States alone (U.S. Advisory Board on Child Abuse and Neglect, 1990). Child abuse and neglect are so prevalent that the federal government has classified the situation as a national emergency.

Question: What kind of people abuse children?

Child abuse is seven times more likely to occur in families earning less than $15,000 per year (U.S. Advisory Board on Child Abuse and Neglect, 1990), but there is also considerable child abuse among parents who are at middle or high socioeconomic levels. Child abuse is also more common in families where parents are under stress or are unemployed (Elder, Nguyen, & Caspi, 1985) or where parents were themselves abused as children (Knutson,

APPLICATIONS

1978; Newberger & Bourne, 1978; Oliver & Taylor, 1971; Parke & Collmer, 1975). Generally, however, there are no characteristics that are especially associated with abusive parents that are not also characteristics of nonabusers (Spinetta & Rigler, 1972).

Abuse of children is rarely systematic. Abusers often are surprised at their actions and usually are remorseful. This reaction may in turn lead to a sense of guilt and worthlessness that raises the chances of another outburst of anger.

Question: How are children affected psychologically by abuse?

The psychological effects, of course, depend on the type of abuse and its severity. Among the most common findings are that abused children often come to see themselves as "bad" and often assume that their behavior legitimately merited such abuse (Dean, Malik, Richards, & Stringer, 1986). Younger abused children studied in the *strange situation* (see Chapter 6) often show such unusual patterns of behavior that can't be assessed according to the commonly used type A (anxious/avoidant), type B (secure), and type C (anxious/resistant) classifications. More than 80 percent of these children show such similar odd behaviors that they are now classified as a new group, type D (disorganized/disoriented) (Carlson, Cicchetti, Barnett, & Braunwald, 1989).

Another unfortunate outcome of child abuse is that the more children are exposed to adult anger, the more sensitized and upset they become by it (Cummings, Iannotti, & Zahn-Waxler, 1985). As an interesting example of this, consider one study in which abused and nonabused children, both from socioeconomically disadvantaged backgrounds, responded to the stress of a child of the same age. The nonabused children showed concern, sadness, and empathy; *not one* of the abused children, however, showed such a reaction. Instead, the abused children reacted to their peers' distress by engaging in disturbed behavior, such as physical attacks or displays of anger or fear (Main & George, 1985). Researchers in one study found that by the time abused children enter kindergarten, they are almost three times as likely to be aggressive and violent than nonabused children (Dodge, Bates, & Pettit, 1990). This ratio was found to hold true regardless of whether the abused children came from poor or well-to-do families or whether they came from two- or one-parent homes. The abused children continually expressed anger and incited conflict, often attributing hostile intentions to others and considering aggression as the only solution to problems. They were also more emotionally withdrawn and socially isolated than their peers.

The emotional outbursts, anger, and fear shown among abused children often fuels the cycle of abuse because abused children are more difficult to control and are more often noncompliant with their parents' requests. The parents are more likely to become angry, furthering the likelihood of abuse (Trickett & Kuczynski, 1986; Oldershaw, Walters, & Hall, 1986).

Question: What can be done to help prevent child abuse?

Among the treatment efforts currently being pursued are individual therapy, child foster care, and self-help groups such as Parents Anonymous. Parent aides, crisis nurseries, and short-term residential treatment for entire families can also play an important role.

Question: How do these therapeutic treatments work?

A **crisis nursery** is a place where a parent can bring infants and young children and leave them for a short time, until the parent is better able to deal with his or her stress and the danger of abuse is lessened. Mandatory counseling for parents is usually a condition for leaving children in a crisis nursery. Unfortunately, there are very few crisis nurseries available for those who need them. **Parents Anonymous** groups have been created by abusive parents who want to talk about their difficulties with others who share their problems (Lystad, 1975).

Question: Which is the most effective treatment?

Parents Anonymous, in conjunction with casework, generally has been the most effective at reducing abuse or neglect, but programs rarely have a success rate higher than 40 to 50 percent (Berkeley Planning Associates, 1977).

Question: You've talked about families. But don't strangers also abuse children, especially sexually?

Strangers are not usually the ones responsible for the sexual abuse of children. Family friends or relatives are much more likely to commit such crimes.

Question: But aren't about 1 million children—some of whose photos I've seen on milk cartons and the television news—reported missing each year in the United States?

Fully 90 percent of these missing children are adolescents who have

APPLICATIONS

run away from their families. Of the 10 percent remaining, a great number are children of parents who are engaged in custody battles, situations in which one parent has illegally taken custody of the child. In fact, in the United States in 1985, to choose a typical year, the FBI recorded fewer than 60 cases of a stranger's kidnapping a child (Kantrowitz & Leslie, 1986). Kidnapping by strangers is a rare phenomenon.

Question: But shouldn't we teach children to be careful about talking to strangers?

Certainly it's good to teach children to be wary of strangers to some degree. It's *also* important to teach them to recognize sexual abuse. However, inordinate attention given to kidnapped children or to telling children about how strangers might touch them in "bad" ways may actually succeed in doing more harm than good (Reppucci & Haugaard, 1989). There was even a Saturday morning cartoon in which a dog named McGruff pointed to a little girl named Jenny being coaxed into a car by a stranger and said, "If she gets into that car, you may be looking at Jenny for the last time" (Kantrowitz & Leslie, 1986, p. 62). Parents need to remain calm and to keep child safety issues in perspective. By talking to children carefully about such problems, rather than inundating them with alarming stories, parents can teach their children to be cautious rather than unnecessarily scared.

Question: What can I do to help prevent child abuse?

If you know anyone who is abusing or neglecting a child, don't hesitate to notify the police or child protection authorities in your community. In almost every case, the end result will be constructive, and both parents and children will receive help. The staff of professional agencies that deal with child abuse are usually tactful and compassionate and are concerned that every member of the family be helped. You might also make an effort to support or develop a crisis nursery for your community.

Also, if you know of an abused child and are in a position to provide emotional support for that child, you might be able to help break the cycle of violence. It has been shown that abuse becomes less likely to occur in the next generation if an abused child receives emotional support from a nonabusive adult (Egeland, Jacobvitz, & Sroufe, 1988).

Additionally, be prepared to support local and state efforts to raise funds for abuse prevention. Many states are now attempting to do this "painlessly" by establishing trust funds drawn from add-on fees to marriage or birth certificates. Check and see if your state has such a system, and if not, consider writing to your state representatives suggesting the implementation of one.

SUMMARY

- Socialization begins when an infant is treated by others in a way that fosters the development of skills, attitudes, or behaviors deemed appropriate by the society.
- Unless a person is isolated from all others in society and avoids all of society's influence, socialization will be a lifelong process.
- Most researchers studying the family collect data, but they rarely are able to organize experiments. As a result, most child-rearing studies are correlational, and cause-and-effect relationships are difficult to infer.
- Until children are old enough to interact meaningfully with peers or to enter school, their families are usually the primary agents of socialization. The parent's job is that of teacher.
- An important dimension of the socialization process is the influence brought to bear on it by the child's own development.
- Sigmund Freud believed that individuals develop by progressing through five psychosexual stages.
- Erik Erikson developed a modern psychoanalytic theory that expanded Freud's ideas to include adulthood. Erikson emphasized social processes in a larger context, encompassing friends, family, society, and culture.
- During the second year of a child's life, parents generally begin to place greater emphasis on regulating that child's behavior. Such social regulation is an important part of the socialization process. This process helps to encourage self-regulation in the child.
- Totally babyproofing a home may make it somewhat sterile, limiting the opportunities for the exploration of new and interesting things.
- Baumrind has examined four modes of parenting: accepting-permissive, accepting-demanding, rejecting-permissive, and rejecting-demanding. Each mode is likely to produce different kinds of behavior in children.
- Three distinct kinds of discipline practices used by parents have been described: power assertion, love withdrawal, and induction.
- All parents have desires and hopes for their children. How parents seek to achieve these ends can differ greatly from family to family. Researchers do not agree on which of the many child-rearing practices is best.
- Belsky's evolutionary theory of socialization incorporates the idea that harsh environments trigger a series of behaviors in parents and their children that foster goals that encourage early puberty, early pregnancy, short-term commitments, and weak parenting in children as a way of increasing the quantity of offspring in difficult times. In this view, many behaviors thought dysfunctional are, in fact, highly adaptive.
- Data have indicated that children of working mothers need not necessarily be adversely affected. Family disruption and an adverse reaction in the child are most likely to occur if the mother is less educated, if she does not wish to work but feels she has to for financial reasons, if she has a low sense of self-worth, or if she feels that she is abandoning her children.
- Divorce rates have increased dramatically in the United States in the past 30 years. Divorce creates a complex series of disorganized transitions requiring considerable adjustment by the child. Among the stresses of divorce that children must face are the disruption of bedtime and eating schedules and the lessening of adult contact, as well as the effects of the parents' emotional state.
- Unlike sole custody, joint custody ensures that both parents have access to their children. Most researchers have concluded, however, that the degree of tension and disruption that children face during a divorce is a more important indicator of later development than is the kind of custody arrangement that is selected.
- Although children may fare well in single-parent families, the chances of problems are greater than in children from two-parent homes.
- When families are placed in stressful situations, the danger of child abuse, neglect, or psychological maltreatment increases. The most effective treatments available for abusive parents include individual therapy, child foster care, and Parents Anonymous and other self-help groups.

QUESTIONS FOR DISCUSSION

1. Some researchers have argued that inconsistent discipline techniques can be worse than harsh discipline or no discipline at all. What kinds of difficulties might arise when parents are inconsistent in applying discipline?
2. What factors do you believe have contributed to the rising divorce rate in the United States? Do you think the trend will continue?
3. Of the people sampled in a large, nationwide poll, 28 percent said that neither of their parents had ever used physical force against them. How do you think these parents maintained discipline?
4. How did your parents treat you, and how might their behavior have influenced your attitudes about child rearing?
5. How might single parents compensate for their children's lack of a second role model?

SUGGESTIONS FOR FURTHER READING

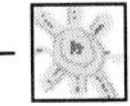

1. Bell, R. Q., & Harper, L. V. (1977). *The effect of children on parents.* Hillsdale, NJ: Erlbaum.
2. Boer, F. & Dunn, J. F. (eds.) (1992). *Sibling relationships: Developmental & clinical issues.* Hillsdale, NJ: Erlbaum.
3. Dunn, J. (1990). *Separate lives: Why siblings are so different.* New York: Basic Books.
4. Garbarino, J., Guttmann, E., & Seeley, J. W. (1986). *The psychologically battered child: Strategies for identification, assessment, and intervention.* San Francisco: Jossey-Bass.
5. Lamb, M. E. (1981). *The role of the father in child development.* New York: Wiley.
6. Lamb, M. E. (Ed.). (1982). *Non-traditional families: Parenting and child development.* Hillsdale, NJ: Erlbaum.
7. Pleck, E. (1987). *Domestic tyranny. The making of social policy against family violence from colonial times to the present.* New York: Oxford.
8. Walker, M. (1992). *Surviving secrets: The experience of abuse for the child, the adult, & the helper.* New York: Taylor & Francis.
9. Wiehe, V. R. (1992). *Working with child abuse & neglect.* Itasca, IL: Peacock.
10. Zigler, E., & Frank, M. (Eds.). (1988). *The parental leave crisis.* New Haven, Connecticut: Yale University Press
11. Hewlett, S. A. (1992). *When the bough breaks: The cost of neglecting our children.* New York, NY: HarperCollins.

CHAPTER 13

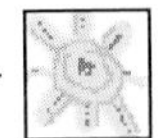

THE DEVELOPMENT OF SEXUALITY AND SEX ROLES

CHAPTER PREVIEW

FIRST WOMAN, THEN MAN

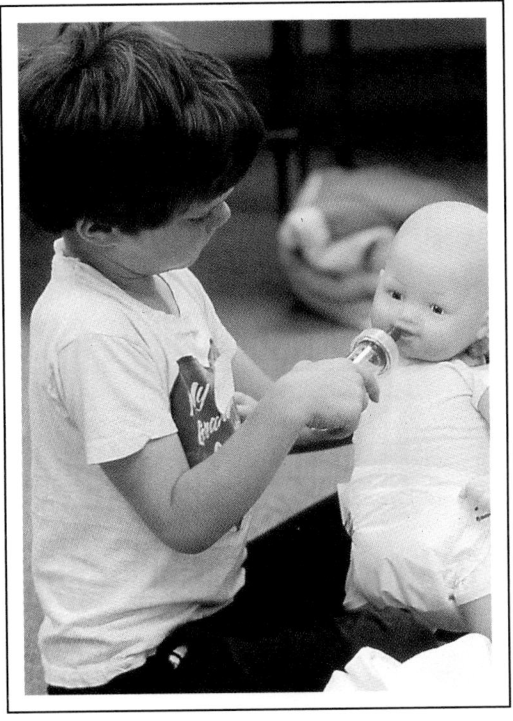

IN THE LATE 1970s, Julienne Imperato-McGinley of the Cornell University Medical College traveled to the city of Santo Domingo in the Dominican Republic, where she examined 38 boys with a peculiar genetic disorder relatively common to that area. This particular genetic disorder keeps the male hormone testosterone from undergoing a chemical transition that would, under normal circumstances, trigger the formation of male genitals while the fetus was still in the womb. This biogenetic failure keeps the male genitals from being formed during prenatal development.

Question: What happens to these boys when they are born?

Boys who suffer from this disorder look like girls at birth. They are often given girls' names and raised as girls, because the parents are unaware that they are really boys! However, owing to a further secretion of hormones at puberty, the penis, originally thought to be a clitoris, lengthens; the voice deepens; and the boy develops a muscular body. In fact, the local Spanish slang expressions for this disorder translate roughly to "penis-at-12" and "first woman, then man."

WHAT JULIENNE Imperato-McGinley found so interesting about these boys was that although the boys born with this genetic disorder had been socialized to be girls, after the physical change occurred, they easily adopted the culturally accepted male sex role in terms of their identity, occupational desires, and sexual activity.

Question: How could these boys have adjusted so easily to being male after being raised for so many years as girls?

Imperato-McGinley concluded that the boys she studied in

Santo Domingo could adjust to their sudden new male sex role because their brains had already been masculinized in the womb by hormones. She argued that inside of each "girl's" body was the brain of a boy (made male by the testosterone present before birth), which was then activated by another surge of hormone (dihydrotestosterone) during the adolescent period (Imperato-McGinley, Peterson, Gautier, & Sturla, 1979). In this way, she argued, hormones are important in determining human behavior because they sensitize the brain of the fetus in the womb to organize itself along certain lines in preparation for a later surge of hormone during puberty.

STILL, SOME ARGUE that environment may have played an important role. For example, these children may have made the transition to their different adolescent roles easily because their environment supported their new role in any number of ways. In fact, a couple of parents were even proud to discover that their daughter was really their son! As you will come to appreciate, the nature-nurture argument is often raised when studying the development of sex roles.

IN THIS CHAPTER, we will examine the biological, cognitive, and sociocultural aspects of human sexual development. We will look at the biological differences between the brains of males and females, the formation of sex roles and gender identity, and the pressure that culture can bring to bear in shaping our sexual behavior.

RESOURCES

Boys and Girls, Men and Women—The Role of Biology

"It's been said that the one thing you will never forget about a person is that person's sex" (Coon, 1986, p. 567). A person's sex greatly influences the relationships, pursuits, choices, and conflicts that he or she will face in life.

The basic anatomical differences between males and females are quite apparent, both in terms of primary and secondary sexual characteristics.

PRIMARY AND SECONDARY SEXUAL CHARACTERISTICS

Question: What are primary and secondary sexual characteristics?

The penis, scrotum, and testes of the male and the vagina, uterus, and ovaries of the female are **primary sexual characteristics.** The **secondary sexual characteristics** appear at **puberty.** In girls, these include the development of breasts and the widening of the hips; in boys, the deepening of the voice and the appearance of facial hair. In both sexes, underarm and pubic hair develops. The appearance of secondary sexual characteristics signals that the body is preparing for the capacity to reproduce. This period is reached in males at the time when the first ejaculation of sperm becomes possible and in females once **menarche** (the onset of menstruation) has occurred. These events usually take place when children are between the ages of 11 and 14 years, with girls able to reproduce on the average slightly sooner than boys. Healthy males will remain capable of reproduction throughout their lives, and healthy females will be capable until **menopause,** which signals the end of their fertile cycles.

SEX HORMONES AND CHROMOSOMES

Question: What factors are responsible for the development of sexual characteristics?

Both the primary and secondary sexual characteristics are closely related to the actions of sex hormones. **Hormones** are chemicals carried in the blood that can affect psychological and physiological development. The sex glands, called **gonads,** secrete hormones. The gonads in the female are the **ovaries,** and in the male they are the **testes.** The adrenal glands on the adrenal cortex of the kidney are also a source of sex hormone in both sexes. The female hormones are called **estrogens** and the male hormones **androgens.*** The secretion of hormones may be directed by the master gland, called the **pituitary,** which is located at the base of the forebrain. The pituitary itself is controlled by areas of the brain.

A child's genetic sex is determined at conception (see Chapter 2). If the twenty-third pair of chromosomes are both *X*, then the child will be a female. If the twenty-third pair is *XY*, then the child will be a male (with rare exception; see Chapter 2). During the development of the embryo, nature seems inclined at first to make a girl. However, if testosterone (one of the androgens) is present, as usually occurs under the direction of the *Y* chromosome, male genitals will develop in place of female ones. In this way, genes determine sex indirectly through the action of hormones.

In 1849, the German physiologist Arnold Berthold found that by castrating roosters, he could stop them from fighting with one another. When the testicles were transplanted back into the castrated birds, the birds once again began to

*Actually, all normal individuals produce both estrogens and androgens. It is the ratio of one substance to the other that affects sexual characteristics.

PRIMARY SEXUAL CHARACTERISTICS
The penis, scrotum, and testes of the male; the vagina, ovaries, and uterus of the female.

SECONDARY SEXUAL CHARACTERISTICS
Physical characteristics that appear in humans around the time of puberty and are sex differentiated but not necessary for sexual reproduction. Examples include beards in men and breasts in women.

PUBERTY
The stage of maturation in which the individual becomes physiologically capable of sexual reproduction.

MENARCHE
The first occurrence of menstruation.

MENOPAUSE
The cessation of menstruation, usually occurring when a woman is between the ages of 45 and 50 years.

HORMONES
Secretions of the endocrine glands that specifically affect metabolism and behavior.

GONADS
The sex glands that regulate sex drive and the physiological changes that accompany physical maturity; the ovaries in the female and the testes in the male.

OVARIES
Paired female reproductive glands that produce ova, or eggs, and female hormones.

TESTES
Male reproductive glands that produce spermatozoa and male hormones.

ESTROGENS
Female sex hormones, produced by the ovaries; responsible for maturation of the female sex organs, secondary sexual characteristics, and, in some species, sexual behavior.

ANDROGENS
Male hormones that regulate sexual development; produced by the testes and the adrenal cortex.

PITUITARY
A gland that is located beneath the hypothalamus and that controls many hormonal secretions; often called the "master gland" because it appears to control other glands throughout the body.

fight. The reimplanted testicles were connected not with the rooster's nervous system, but rather, with the circulatory system. This led Berthold and others to assume that something was being carried in the blood that affected behavior. That "something" was later discovered to be a sex hormone.

In 1916, a Canadian physiologist named Frank Lillie presented a paper in which he explained why some genetically normal cows, called freemartins, acted and looked like bulls. Freemartins always have fraternal twin brothers. Lillie speculated that the hormones from the testes of the male twin somehow masculinized the freemartins in the womb.

Researchers are interested in the effects of hormones on human beings because, as we have seen, hormones directly influence many behaviors in lower animals, such as aggression and sexual activity. Following Lillie's discovery about freemartins, researchers discovered that girls who had fraternal twin brothers were a little more likely to act tomboyish or to show a greater interest in what have typically been considered "male" activities, such as contact sports. Since these girls were raised with brothers their own age with whom they played, however, it was not possible to isolate the effects of their environment from any possible hormonal effects. There is a way, however, to examine the effects of hormones on a human fetus.

Occasionally a fetus may be exposed to levels of hormones that are higher than normal. For example, researchers have studied young girls who were exposed to abnormally large amounts of androgenic (male) hormones before birth. Such exposures may be caused by the therapeutic administration of synthetic hormones to the mother during pregnancy or by a disorder of the infant's own hormone secretions known as congenital adrenal hyperplasia, or CAH. CAH occurs when the fetus secretes excessive androgen from the cortex on her kidneys. Sometimes female infants with this disorder are born with partially masculinized genitals, although their gonads are female and normal.

During their preadolescence, these girls played in the rough and tumble way more commonly observed among boys and were characterized as less culturally feminine than most girls (Baker, 1980; Eccles-Parsons, 1982; Hines, 1982; Money & Ehrhardt, 1972). CAH girls also show a stronger preference for toys traditionally considered to be for boys than do matched female relatives without CAH (Berenbaum & Hines, 1992).

Similarly, two populations of boys, aged 6 and 16 years, whose mothers received large doses of estrogens (female hormones) during pregnancy, were believed to be less athletic, less assertive, and less aggressive than most boys (Ehrhardt & Meyer-Bahlburg, 1981; Yalom, Green, & Fisk, 1973). It should be stressed, however, that studies of the effects of estrogen on males generally have been correlational or poorly controlled. Therefore, many researchers believe that no definite conclusions can yet be drawn concerning the effects of estrogen on males in the womb.

Question: Can we conclude that hormones are responsible for the differences in behavior between boys and girls or men and women?

Although hormonal factors alone may account for some of the observed behavioral differences between males and females, the effects of androgynization can't be all that strong. Once girls with CAH reach adolescence and adulthood, they no longer behave differently from nonandrogynized females, and their sexual desires are just as likely to be heterosexual as are any woman's (Ehrhardt & Meyer-Bahlburg, 1981; Money & Mathews, 1982). If androgynization in the womb had given these females strong "male" inclinations, we might assume that they would take a homosexual orientation in adulthood. Furthermore, male fetuses exposed to insufficient androgen levels in the womb are just as likely to have a heterosexual orientation as any other males (Ehrhardt & Meyer-Bahlburg, 1981).

There is further evidence that biological variables, such as hormones, may not be the only ones responsible for the development of gender identity. For example, monozygotic (identical) twins share their genetic makeup as well as the same womb. Yet identical twins have been found who clearly would prefer different sexual identities. Investigators Green and Stoller (1971), studying identical 8-year-old twin boys who were anatomically normal, found that one of them unquestionably wanted to be a girl. In another study, these same researchers described a pair of identical, anatomically normal, 24-year-old women, one of whom wanted very much to be a man.

Question: But males are known to be more aggressive than females. Isn't that the result of a biological difference?

There does appear to be a biologically determined difference in aggressiveness among primates, but it is only a slight difference. Male chimps and male humans are a little more likely to engage in rough and tumble play than are the females. And if female chimps are given higher levels of testosterone, they will become as "rough and tumble" as the males (Young, Goy, & Phoenix, 1964). But this difference in the level of playful roughness would hardly seem great enough to explain the differences we see between the sexes in terms of the aggression found in our culture. Men are much more likely than women to be involved in brawls or violent crime. Is this the result of biology? Although it is true that American men are more aggressive than American women, American women are far more aggressive than English women.

In some cultures, women are very aggressive even in comparison with men. For example, among the Trobriand Islanders, researchers observed that groups of women, to foster their tribe's reputation for virility, would catch a man from another tribe, arouse him to erection, and rape him (Malinowski, 1929). This "gang rape," brutal and lacking affection, was not something that the victim cared to have recur. The Trobriand Island women and their tribe were unashamed. In fact, the rapists commonly bragged about what they had done. For a more contemporary example, we can turn to the work of Laura Cummings (1991), who has studied girls in Mexico belonging to a tough youth culture known as *Cholos*. Cummings discovered that a new female who wished to join the group was required to engage in a fistfight with an established female member and that females in rival groups often battled with other female members. These battles were just as dangerous as any engaged in by the males and included knife fights and other lethal forms of combat. Researcher Victoria Burbank, who has studied female aggression extensively, concludes that "girls and boys follow cultural dictates that can overwhelm any genetic influence on aggressive behavior" (Bower, 1991, p. 359). Culture obviously has a lot to do with fostering or suppressing aggression in both males and females.

Currently, research concerning the ability of hormones or other biological forces to directly control or determine our behavior is inconclusive. Part of the problem stems from the fact that it is very difficult to measure hormone levels in human beings. Hormone assays are very expensive, and in many instances, blood must be drawn from volunteers three or more times on the hour, leaving them with aching arms, a collapsed vein or two, and a fervent desire never again to volunteer for anything. Adding to this complication is the fact that in studies in which hormone levels were tracked over time, it has been shown that while absolute hormone levels in humans are a poor predictor of behavior, the *range of hormone fluctuation* throughout the day may be a valid predictor (Jacklin, 1989). Even so, if hormones do play an important role in our behavior, it is obviously not as strong as the one observed in lower species. If it were, we would have seen more conclusive research along the lines of Berthold's discovery that roosters completely stop fighting following castration. Actually, human males who have

SEX TYPING
The process whereby an individual incorporates the behaviors, traits, and attitudes appropriate to his or her biological sex or the sex assigned at birth.

undergone castration for testicular cancer or other disorders are often unaffected in terms of sex drive or aggression, although this may be because their brains have already been hormone sensitized in the womb and activated at puberty, something that apparently isn't the major hormone mechanism in roosters.

To summarize: In our species, hormones may, in a subtle way, play the greatest role in shaping behaviors related to gender, or perhaps learning and culture do. The point is that no one is certain. Researchers continue to debate the effects of hormones on development as well as to look for the origin of all gender differences (see At Issue).

LEARNING CHECK

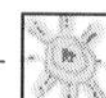

1. Differences in the ______________ have been clearly linked with differences in sexual orientation.
   a. way children are raised **c.** genes on chromosome 12
   b. hypothalamus **d.** ability to do math
2. Estrogens
   a. are controlled by the *Y* chromosome.
   b. are "male" hormones.
   c. are "female" hormones.
   d. cause the growth of facial hair.
3. Menarche refers to
   a. ejaculation. **c.** gonads.
   b. menopause. **d.** none of the above.
4. Which is not a primary sexual characteristic?
   a. scrotum **c.** ovaries
   b. pubic hair **d.** vagina
5. Girls born with CAH
   a. are characterized as being less culturally feminine than most girls are.
   b. have never been exposed to androgens.
   c. are maintained on estrogens all their lives.
   d. are born with male gonads.
6. It has been proved conclusively that males and females have different natural skills or traits.
   a. true **b.** false

Answers: 1. b 2. c 3. d 4. b 5. a 6. b

The Role of Culture

Different sexual behaviors may be shaped by social and cultural forces. Culture dictates how long skirts are, whether pants are held by belt or suspenders, who should or shouldn't wear makeup, and what is considered appropriate behavior for either gender. Each culture expects certain behaviors from its male and female members, and each culture will reinforce and model the "correct" sex role for its children. The process by which an individual incorporates the attitudes, behaviors, and traits deemed appropriate to his or her biological sex is called **sex typing.** The degree of masculinity or femininity that the child eventually displays reflects the amount of sex typing. An extremely masculine male or extremely feminine female is said to be highly sex typed.

One reason you may believe that one way is "natural" or "traditional" whereas another is not is that your culture has taught you to feel comfortable with the

AT ISSUE

Do Males and Females Show "Natural" Gender Differences or Orientations?

What causes the psychology of men and women to be different? Why do boys and girls develop different attitudes, behaviors, and sexual orientations, seemingly based on their gender? Is it mostly a matter of biology, or does the environment play a large role?

To give you a feel for just how long people have had an interest in these kinds of questions, let's look back a couple of thousand years to the great Greek philosopher Aristotle (384–322 B.C.), who said that women were "more compassionate . . . more envious, more querulous, more slanderous, and more contentious,"; of men, he said that they were "more disposed to give assistance in danger" and "more courageous" (Book IX of *The History of Animals*, Chapter 1; cited in Miles, 1935, p. 700). These he believed to be *natural* female and male traits, not characteristics that were taught or learned.

As recently as our own century, researchers made statements that equated the abilities of women with those of primitive people or children, beliefs that we today find ridiculous. Even Sigmund Freud argued that females were psychologically inferior (Horney, 1939).

But what do we actually know about real sex differences? Except for obvious anatomical differences, and the fact that one gender has the ability to give birth, what true sex differences are there?

One part of the debate has focused on the term *sex difference*. It is argued that a real sex difference exists when, for example, a rooster crows but a hen doesn't. What we observe in people, on the other hand, should be considered a *sex-related variation in ability*, because *on average*, one sex may be slightly better than the other at certain skills (Caplan, MacPherson, & Tobin, 1985). However it is defined, "sex differences" is a hot issue. And, while it is probably correct to say that we may still be a long way from having solid answers to our questions, the discoveries made so far have been intriguing.

To get some of the flavor of this ongoing debate, let's look at a few topics that have been the focus of sex differences research. The first thing that may surprise you is that the major topics in this field are very specific ones such as gender differences in spatial ability or mathematic skill, rather than broader aspects of personality, such as gender differences in emotion or aggression. Although the broader topics are often discussed, and we have already mentioned some examples in this chapter, specific skills are easier to define and measure and are, therefore, better candidates for demonstrating a clear and true biological gender difference in behavior.

Business textbooks from the 1950s often stated as a fact that women were better typists than men because of a natural superior manual dexterity. While this may have justified hiring only women for the typing pool the same texts never bothered to say why such a supposed superior dexterity shouldn't have also made women better surgeons. So what real gender differences are there?

Spatial Ability

The modern field of gender differences dates back to 1974 when Eleanor Maccoby and Carol Jacklin published *The Psychology of Sex Differences*, hoping to document thoroughly, or to dismiss many, of the beliefs concerning sex differences in behavior (Maccoby & Jacklin, 1974). They discovered that there were a few real sex differences, but they were small. Among these differences was a superior spatial ability among boys. (Spatial ability is the ability to understand how objects would appear at different angles and how they would relate to each other in a given space.) After this, many biological theories to explain these differences were proposed (Kimura, 1985).

It is interesting to note also that at this point in history, the economic and social status of women were becoming major issues. Because of this, researchers were often worried about how their findings might be misinterpreted. There was a fear among many that social justice might become the victim of any research that, even in the slightest way, showed one sex (especially women) as somehow less able than the other. This was especially true because reported gender differences were quickly picked up by the media and disseminated widely, often to an audience that made more of the typical subtle difference than was merited. For instance, at the time I was engaged to my wife and I can recall giving her advice about parking the car. When she didn't listen and did it her way, and not very well, I hastened to add that she should have deferred to my superior spatial abilities. I recall at this point that she crumpled up a piece of paper and deftly bounced it right off the end of my nose asking, "Is that good enough spatial ability for you?"

The concern over the problem of superior male spatial

AT ISSUE

ability led to an enormous amount of research in this area. Then, in a detailed critique presented in 1985, years of research supporting male superiority in spatial ability was dismissed because of faulty methodology, debatable statistics, observer bias, and failure to define adequately what was meant by "spatial ability" (Caplan, MacPherson, & Tobin, 1985). As a result, many researchers dismissed the previously held belief that males have a superior spatial ability. Others, however, tightened study protocols and definitions and continued to argue that research shows a difference in spatial ability. For example, one such study has shown that compared to unaffected females, males *and* females suffering from CAH (who were therefore exposed to testosterone in the womb) are superior at tasks that require that they find hidden patterns or make mental rotations of geometric forms or shapes (Resnick, Berenbaum, Gottesman, & Bouchard, 1986).

Finally, in 1992 researchers revived the issue of gender differences in spatial ability when it was discovered that among females at age 16, spatial ability was best predicted by how masculine the girls had rated themselves to be when they were 11 years old (e.g., how much they wished to be a boy) (Newcombe and Dubas, 1992). Perhaps this means that "masculinity," rather than maleness, is somehow associated with better spatial skills. For instance, do certain "male" activities enhance spatial skills? Or do biological variables link masculinity in either sex with increased spatial skills? No one yet knows, but research in this interesting area is continuing.

Mathematical Ability

While supposed differences in spatial ability raised a few eyebrows, the reported difference in mathematical ability caused a furor. In 1979, researchers Camilla Benbow and Julian Stanley gave the Scholastic Aptitude Test (SAT), which includes mathematical and verbal portions, to 9,927 seventh and eighth graders who had the same exposure to mathematics, regardless of sex. The boys performed significantly better than the girls on the math portion. Among those students who scored over 700 out of a possible 800, boys outnumbered girls 13 to 1 (Benbow & Stanley, 1983). Using questionnaires, the researchers found that the girls who were tested liked math as much as the boys and believed that math would be valuable in their careers (Benbow & Stanley, 1981).

In opposition, some researchers argued that these kinds of tests alone do not demonstrate in any conclusive way that the superior mathematical ability of males is due to biological or brain differences. Furthermore, even if male mathematical superiority were traced to sexually differentiated brain structures, such structures might still be the result of early childhood experience, because early experience might dictate the development of specialized brain organization. Another possibility is that girls are socialized to be afraid of math or to believe that they can't master its apparent complexities (Licht & Dweck, 1984).

Then, in 1982, the eminent Harvard neurologist Norman Geschwind (1926–1984) described a possible hormonal basis to explain math excellence in boys. Geschwind recalled that an excess of testosterone during fetal development can change the brain anatomy of rats so that the right hemisphere of their brains becomes dominant; perhaps, he argued, the same occurs in humans. Geschwind argued further, that if the right brain were dominant, there should be a greater proportion of left-handedness (Geschwind & Behan, 1982) because the brain hemispheres control the *opposite* side of the body; thus; right-hemisphere dominance would likely lead to left-handedness. Geschwind also argued that immune system disorders might also be present as a reaction to the excessive fetal testosterone levels that led to the right-hemisphere dominance in the first place.

To test Geschwind's view, Benbow and Stanley took a survey of 40,000 students for whom they had scores on the SAT mathematical portion. To their surprise, 20 percent of the mathematically gifted students were found to be left-handed (more than twice the expected number), and 60 percent had immune system disorders such as allergies or asthma (five times the expected level). In the same population of students, but among the ones whose scores were lower, left-handedness and immune system disorders were found to occur at normal rates (Kolata, 1983).

Upon further examination, however, it was concluded that Geschwind's theory of brain reorganization in the presence of excessive hormone is so complex that it is unclear how one would go about testing it or how one might develop an animal model to demonstrate some of the theory's principles (McManus & Bryden, 1991). The reason for the mathematical superiority of boys at the extreme end of the spectrum remains a mystery.

It is again interesting to note how social or political pressure might influence this kind of research. For instance, a number of researchers have pointed out that gender differences in spatial or intellectual abilities observed in the past are not as great now as they were 10 or 20 years ago (Feingold, 1988; Hyde & Linn, 1988; Jacklin, 1989). This, in turn, has led some to argue that

AT ISSUE

gender differences observed and recorded over the years must be the result of environment, because there hasn't been enough time for evolutionary developments to account for the recent narrowing of these gender differences. Others argue that a bias toward equality is skewing the research. Still others argue that many of the tests used to measure gender differences have been altered to reduce the appearance of gender differences and that the research is only showing this effect rather than a real effect. All of this has led to a growing belief that studying gender differences is far more complicated than anyone had originally envisioned and that much more will have to be discovered before a clear understanding of the nature-nurture aspects of gender differences can emerge.

Sexual Orientation

One dimension of our development is the orientation we take toward a possible sexual partner. In our culture the majority of people develop a *heterosexual* orientation. Nonetheless, a large number of people express a *homosexual* orientation, and a still larger number develop a *bisexual* orientation in which they have complete sexual experiences with members of both sexes. An extensive survey among men has shown that about one-fifth of adult males have had at least one homosexual experience, while about 6% have had homosexual contacts fairly often (Fay, Turner, Klassen, & Gagnon, 1989). Other studies indicate that women express homosexuality about 25 to 50 percent as often as men. In general, these percentages are not much different from those observed by Kinsey when he gathered data about sexual orientation in the 1940s (Kinsey, Pomeroy, & Martin, 1948) and are comparable to the data on adolescents.

This led some researchers to wonder if sexual orientation might be formed early in development. Pursuing this idea, Richard Green conducted a long-term 15-year study in which he kept track of 66 boys who were described as extremely effeminate, who liked to dress as girls, and who played with dolls (Green, 1987). As adults, 44 of these boys were homosexual or bisexual, far more than would be expected from a population of 66 boys chosen at random. This study indicates that sexual orientation might begin early in development.

A number of researchers have even argued that the crucial time for the determination of sexual orientation occurs in the womb, sometime around the second trimester (middle third) of the pregnancy (Marmor, 1985). Researchers Lee Ellis and M. Ashley Ames (1987) have stated:

> The involvement of learning, by and large, only appears to alter how, when, and where the orientation is expressed. For humans, the crucial timing appears to be between the 2nd month of [pregnancy] and about the middle of the fifth month, during which time the hypothalamic-limbic regions of the male's nervous system are permanently diverted away from their otherwise-destined female [connections and organization]. (p. 251)

Ellis and Ames believe that biochemical changes occurring in the womb may alter future sexual orientation by modifying the neural development of the fetus's brain. They argued that stress, drugs, or other influences during pregnancy might affect the environment of the womb (Ellis & Ames, 1987).

Then, in 1991, researcher Simon LeVay discovered that there were clear anatomical differences in the brain structures of homosexual and heterosexual men (LeVay, 1991). A particular cluster at the forefront of the hypothalamus, an area of the brain involved with emotions and sexual drives, was found to be consistently smaller in homosexual men and heterosexual women than in heterosexual men. LeVay's discovery fit well with earlier observations that sexual orientation was formed early in life.

The immediate effect of these findings was to remove some of the guilt and blame from among those who felt guilty about their own sexual orientation or from among those who wished to espouse blame for the sexual orientation of others. Following LeVay's discovery, the idea that sexual orientation is a free choice or that it is fostered by how one is raised, diminished.

Further support for this view comes from J. Michael Bailey and Richard C. Pillard who examined 167 pairs of male brothers, of whom 56 pairs were identical twins, 54 pairs fraternal twins, and 57 pairs unrelated adoptive brothers. In this, the largest study of its kind, they discovered that among identical twins, if one brother was homosexual, there was a 52 percent chance that the other brother would be. Among fraternal twins, the concordance was 22 percent. And among unrelated brothers, it was 11 percent (Bailey & Pillard, 1991). The national average for male homosexuality is roughly between 4 and 10 percent. The researchers concluded from these findings that sexual orientation was substantially genetic although other influences, perhaps arising in the womb, are also important.

As you have seen, research in gender differences is anything but straightforward. It certainly is engaging, however, and is likely to stay so for some time to come.

SEX ROLES
The behaviors associated with one sex or the other.

way *you* were raised. For instance, Ethel Albert found cultures in which women did the heavy work because men were thought to be too weak (Albert, 1963). Generally, this cultural assessment of men is inaccurate, because the average man is stronger than the average woman in terms of the muscle strength required to lift or push objects. Interestingly, however, in some of the cultures where women are believed to be stronger than men, the women really are stronger because they have been doing heavy work for years, while the men haven't been exercising. In fact, in such a culture, any man attempting to build his muscular strength might be considered unmasculine!

As further evidence of the influence of environment on sex typing, researchers examining the masculinity and femininity of twins have found that genetics accounts for only between 20 and 48 percent of the explained variance. In other words, how feminine or masculine a child acts according to our cultural concepts of masculinity and femininity appears to be mostly a function of the environment and how it shapes the child to behave (Mitchell, Baker, & Jacklin, 1989).

ACQUIRING SEX ROLES

See if you can solve the following riddle: A mother and her son are driving in a car when an accident occurs. The mother is knocked unconscious, and the boy receives a bad laceration on his scalp. They are rushed to a hospital. Doctors work to bring the mother around and also to stop the boy's bleeding. Suddenly, a frantic student nurse rushes in and, seeing the child, begins to cry. Another nurse says, "What's wrong?" The student nurse says, "That's my son." How is this possible?

Answer: The student nurse is the boy's father. If you didn't figure it out, it was probably because you pictured a frantic weeping student nurse as a woman. Perhaps your culture has taught you that "nurse," "frantic," and "weeping" are associated with the woman's role.

I once saw a young boy playing with a GI Joe doll. He and his friends (all male) seemed to be having a good time. They were all about 7 or 8 years old and probably well socialized into the male **sex role.*** Yet it dawned on me that they were playing with dolls, which in our culture is often considered a girl's activity. I wondered how they might reconcile this potential conflict, so, always looking to cause trouble, I approached them and said, "I thought boys didn't play with dolls!" After a few seconds of looking mortified, one of them said most emphatically, "It's *not* a doll, it's GI Joe!" Not one to let them off so easily, I said, "Yes, but it's still a doll." The owner of the doll became obviously annoyed with my ignorance, and holding the doll in front of him, pointed to the little grenades hanging from Joe's shirt pocket. "You see these," he said, "these are grenades and they're gonna blow you up." It was obvious to him that if he had a toy that could blow up an annoying child psychologist, it was a toy for boys, not for girls. (And, of course, it wasn't a doll. It was GI Joe.)

With the changing times, our perceptions of the behaviors appropriate to the sex roles change, too. In our culture just a few decades ago, the use of hair dryers, deodorant, and most jewelry was considered solely the province of women. However, as cultural attitudes shifted, it became acceptable for men to use these items.

EARLY INFLUENCES ON SEX TYPING

Question: When does a culture first begin to shape children's sex roles?

The shaping of sex roles may begin as early as birth. In a sense, it can even begin before birth as parents busy themselves preparing color schemes for a nursery or choosing clothing and nursery items for the baby.

---

*Some researchers prefer the term *gender role*. In practice, however, the two terms, *sex role* and *gender role*, should be treated as synonymous (Maccoby, 1988).

From the moment of an infant's birth, parents tend to treat boys and girls differently (Ban & Lewis, 1974; Will, Self, & Datan, 1976). Although there are few behavioral differences between male and female babies, most parents will describe their daughters as cuter, softer, or more delicate than their sons. Fathers tend to emphasize the beauty and delicacy of their newborn daughters and the strength and coordination of their newborn sons (Krieger, 1976). Both mothers and fathers treat their infants differently (Etaugh, 1983). Also, fathers interact with their sons differently than mothers (Huston, 1983). Fathers are more physical and rougher with their boy children and engage in play of a more gross motor nature (Parke & Suomi, 1980). Mothers tend to provide their sons with more verbal stimulation than they do their daughters, especially the kinds of verbal interactions thought to enhance cognitive development (Weitzman, Birns, & Friend, 1985).

In one entertaining experiment, the different reactions of mothers and fathers were made apparent. In this study, preschoolers were given stereotypical sex-typed toys to play with, including kitchen play sets, a doll house, an army war game, and cowboy outfits. Both boys and girls were given "girls' toys" to play with on one occasion and "boys' toys" on another. The children were told to play with these toys *the way girls would* (for girls' toys) *or boys would* (for boys' toys). What the experimenters were interested in was the reaction of the mother and father when they entered the room and saw which toys their children were playing with. Mothers showed little differential reaction to the toy sets. Fathers, on the other hand, showed far more negative reactions when their children were playing with the "inappropriate" toys. This was especially true if the fathers found their sons playing with "girls' toys" in the way that girls would. Fathers in these cases tended to interfere with play or show disgust (Langlois & Downs, 1980). Fathers are also more likely to offer sons toys that are stereotypically considered male, such as trucks or footballs (Jacklin & Maccoby, 1983). Mothers are also more supportive of their children's play when it involves "sex-appropriate" toys, but their reactions tend to be more subtle (Caldera, Huston, & O'Brien, 1989). Mothers generally treat boy and girl infants less differently than do fathers. For this reason, fathers, in our culture, may have a greater effect on the early learning of sex roles (Power, 1981).

Question: Why do fathers treat boy and girl infants so differently?

These differences between parental attitudes toward child rearing may be determined to a great degree by the parent's own cultural training. Fathers may perceive part of their role to be that of a guiding force in their children's sex typing. Of course, fathers alone can't be totally responsible for the child's acquisition of a sex role, if for no other reason than that children raised without fathers also acquire an understanding of gender-associated behavior.

Not only fathers and mothers but also other adults treat boys and girls differently. In one study, it was found that adults were more likely to offer a doll to a child that they thought was a girl and more likely to offer a truck to a child that they thought was a boy (Huston, 1983). In another study, observers were found to make different observations of the same infant based on whether they were told it was a boy or a girl (Condry & Condry, 1977). Many forces are at work teaching children the sex roles of the culture.

Sex Role Acquisition

Question: How and when do children acquire an understanding of sex roles?

It is more difficult to determine how they do it than when. "How" requires an explanation, whereas "when" relies mostly on description. Even so, let's begin with a look at "how."

SEX ROLE IDENTIFICATION
The degree to which a child adopts the sex role of a particular model.

Determining how children learn sex roles requires a theoretical understanding of **sex role identification.** Psychoanalytic, social learning, and cognitive theories have all addressed this question. Each predicts that a parent's behavior will have a striking effect on the child's developing sexual identity, even though each theory views the development of sex role identification and "appropriate" sex typing differently.

In Freudian, or psychoanalytic, theory, a son's identification with his father results from a drive to avoid retaliation by the father for the son's initially desiring his mother. Once identification with the father is made, the Oedipus complex, as Freud called it, is resolved and the boy adopts the father's ways as his own. According to Freud, daughters develop a female identity by resolution of the Electra complex, a more roundabout journey. A mirror image of the Oedipus complex was not possible because daughters, too, initially are attached to their mothers through nursing. Freud therefore developed the concept of penis envy, in which the girl comes to covet the male anatomy, which would provide her with something she is missing. In this way, the daughter comes to desire the father and identifies with the mother, who possesses the object of the daughter's desire.

The Freudian view of sex role identification has received little empirical support over the years (Jacklin, 1989), and his concept of penis envy has received strong attack (Horney, 1939). Most psychologists find Freud's views historically interesting but scientifically limited, and few currently refer to them or consider them when examining sex role identification. Although some people have developed a more modern psychoanalytic approach to this issue (Chodorow, 1978; Lerman, 1986), their work is viewed as quite subjective (Stoller, 1985). Instead, most researchers currently emphasize social learning theory or cognitive theory.

SOCIAL LEARNING THEORY

Social learning theory is based on the work of Albert Bandura, described in Chapter 7. In this view, children's behaviors are reinforced or punished based on what parents and society deem appropriate for the child's gender. We have already discussed how parents may differentially treat children based on gender. Parents provide different toys for their daughters than for their sons, and they encourage their children to develop sex-typed interests.

Children engage in culturally sex-appropriate behavior even before they acquire gender constancy.

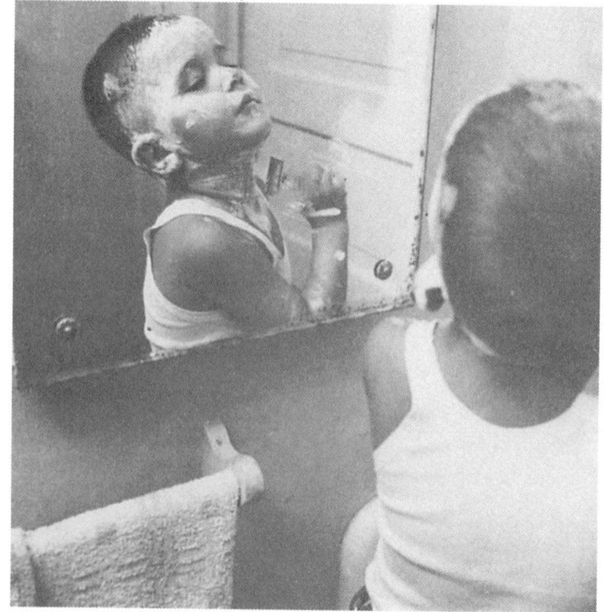

Modeling and observational learning are also considered to be important. Boys learn to observe men, and girls learn to observe women to see how they are expected to behave. Boys observe that men are portrayed more as the initiators of action. On television, for example, about 70 percent of the major characters who initiate actions in any kind of program are men. According to social learning theory, parents, television, peers, and society as a whole shape the acquisition of sex roles.

Question: It seems fairly straightforward. Children learn their sex roles by watching others and by being reinforced for certain behaviors. Correct?

Social shaping of behaviors is not necessarily that simple. All sorts of variables can affect the shaping process. These include the particular attributes of the child, the concepts previously learned by the child, how much importance the society places on gender, the attributes of the model, and how the child perceives the situation that he or she is observing (Huston, 1983). In essence, however, you have stated the basic assumption of social learning theory.

GENDER UNDERSTANDING
A person's comprehension that he or she is either a boy or a girl; usually develops in children by about the age of 3 years.

GENDER CONSTANCY
The realization that one's sex is determined by unchanging criteria and is unaffected by one's activities or behavior; usually develops in children by the age of 6 or 7 years.

THE COGNITIVE VIEW

Question: What is the cognitive view of sex role acquisition?

Lawrence Kohlberg first proposed a cognitive conceptualization of sex role acquisition way back in 1966 (Kohlberg, 1966). According to this view, a child first comes to realize that he is a male or she is a female, and this cognitive realization then guides the child to change his or her behavior to match what society deems appropriate for the gender of that child. In this view, the time at which children first become aware of their gender and its meaning is an important consideration, because cognitive theory predicts that sex typing will not begin until the child has the concept that he is a boy, or that she is a girl, and an idea of what it means to be one.

The Development of Gender Understanding

Question: When do children first become aware of their sex?

Children appear to develop a **gender understanding**—that is, to comprehend that they are boys or girls—by about the age of 3 (Thompson, 1975).

Question: Aren't children aware of their sex earlier than that?

Although a 2-year-old child may tell you that she is a girl, she may have trouble understanding who else is a girl or who is a boy or, for that matter, why she is called a girl. By the age of 3 years, however, children are better able to judge who is a girl and who is a boy. Yet 3-year-old children, whose cognitive processing is necessarily preconceptual (see Chapter 9), generally fail to understand gender constancy.

By the age of 7 years, children begin to show gender constancy in that their sex is a permanent and unchanging characteristic.

Question: What is gender constancy?

Gender constancy is the understanding that your own sex will remain constant: Once a boy, always a boy. A girl is demonstrating a grasp of gender constancy when she understands that just because she puts on a jersey and plays football, she does not turn into a boy, but is still a girl.

Question: At what age do children acquire gender constancy?

Once children come to comprehend the anatomical basis of gender distinction, which has been found to be the case in about 40 percent of a population of 3- to 5-year-olds, they will generally acquire gender constancy (Bem, 1989). Most children acquire it by the age of 7 (Emmerich & Goldman, 1972; Wehren & De Lisi,

1983). The progression from rudimentary gender understanding to the completion of gender constancy has been found to be similar in other cultures, although the final age at which gender constancy occurs may vary by a few years (Munroe, Shimmin, & Munroe, 1984). But the acquisition of gender constancy can have its costs. For instance, in one experiment, boys who had achieved gender constancy were found to play more with an uninteresting toy that was endorsed as a "boy's toy" than with a toy that was more fun (Frey & Ruble, 1992). That's rather sad and shows one of the costs of sex typing; children who acquire gender constancy may come to believe that certain fun toys, games, or activities are now out of bounds for them simply because they aren't considered sex appropriate.

Question: Once children understand which gender they are and that their gender stays constant, do they begin to develop "appropriate" sex role behaviors?

As we noted earlier, this is what Kohlberg's cognitive theory predicts, but it is not always what happens. Children engage in stereotypical sex role behaviors even *before* they are cognitively aware of their gender or its constancy. As early as 26 months of age, children are typically aware of the different things that constitute masculine and feminine dress and behavior. They already know that men shave and wear shirts and suits and that women wear blouses, dresses, and makeup. It is quite common for children as young as 2 or 3 years to show some preference for what are deemed by their culture to be sexually appropriate toys and activities (Jacklin, 1989); yet these children are often unaware that most of the toys they choose for themselves are considered more appropriate for their sex than for the opposite sex. In other words, contrary to Kohlberg's cognitive development view, children demonstrate a certain degree of sex typing *before* they have a complete understanding of which sex they are or that their sex remains constant.

Toy Selection

Question: Does this mean that the social learning view of sex role acquisition is correct?

Social learning theorists like to point to the child's selection of same-sex stereotyped toys to play with as one of the earliest manifestations of sex role acquisition. Even as early as 14 months of age, toddlers more often play with toys that are considered stereotyped for their own gender than with other toys (O'Brien & Huston, 1985), although they will readily play with both. Social learning theorists argue, of course, that parents have shaped and reinforced the toddler's choice of toys. In fact, in one study, the rooms of boys and girls between 1 and 5 years of age were examined, and it was found that parents had indeed provided their children with a far greater variety of same-sex stereotyped toys than of opposite-sex stereotyped toys (Rheingold & Cook, 1975).

Social learning theory also predicts that parents will differentially reinforce behaviors they deem sex appropriate for the gender of their child. The assertiveness of boys and girls at 13 to 14 months of age appears to be identical. However, parents tend to pay more attention to boys' assertive behaviors while attending more to girls' less intense communications (Fagot, Hagan, Leinbach, & Kronsberg, 1985). Peers also reinforce boys for being more assertive and girls for being less assertive. Peers apply strong sanctions against boys who show interest in female activities (Birns & Sternglanz, 1983). With all this pressure, it is argued, children who have adopted behaviors "appropriate" for the opposite sex soon are discouraged and begin to become sex typed.

Question: You mentioned earlier that fathers play an important role in the sex typing of children. Suppose a father shares equally with a mother in the domestic responsibilities of raising the children. Will the children be less likely to acquire stereotypical sex roles?

In one study, children's sex role attitudes were examined in relationship to the father's participation in child care and home chores. Even when fathers did not overtly display the stereotyped paternal role, the children's attitudes were barely affected; the children continued to show sex role stereotyped attitudes (Baruch & Barnett, 1986).

Question: Isn't this finding contrary to the social learning view?

Yes, and many other studies also contradict the social learning view. One study, for example, found that some children didn't necessarily care to choose same-sex stereotyped toys with which to play. According to social learning theory, this would indicate that the children had not been shaped to play with them. These same children, however, when asked to choose a sex-stereotyped toy for another child, were quite able to do so. This shows that they *knew* which toys were deemed appropriate for boys and girls; they just did not always care to play with the toys sex stereotyped for their own gender (Eisenberg, 1983).

Question: Wait a minute. If neither the cognitive nor social learning view is correct, how do we explain sex role acquisition in children?

This debate has gone on for years. It is now believed by many researchers that the two views may intertwine to create a cognitive–social learning view (Serbin & Sprafkin, 1986).

Each culture expects certain behaviors from its male and female members. Cultural expectations may change from generation to generation, however. Body building, once considered strictly the domain of men, is now considered to be an appropriate pursuit for women.

GENDER SCHEMA THEORY

In 1981, researcher Sandra Bem suggested *gender schema theory* to explain the intertwining of the two theories. In her view, as children develop, they reach a point when they are able to integrate *cognitively* all the different sex-typed behaviors they have acquired through social learning and conditioning. This cognitive integration helps to shape their attitudes and beliefs about sex roles and guides them to their own decisions about what is sex appropriate (Bem, 1981). Bem's view explains how children can show sex-typed behaviors long before they have gender constancy. The theory also explains how, bit by bit, cognitive advances can help the child organize and integrate all the information that he or she has

TABLE 13.1

The Development of Sexual Identity

THEORETICAL VIEW	INITIAL STATE	FORCE	REACTION
Psychoanalytic (boys)	Pleasure bond made with mother through nursing	Desires mother; identifies with father	Male sex typing
Psychoanalytic (girls)	Pleasure bond made with mother through nursing	Desires father; identifies with mother	Female sex typing
Social learning (boys and girls)	No differentiation of behavior with respect to gender	Differential reinforcement for and modeling of gender-specific behaviors	Shaping of culturally appropriate sex typing
Cognitive (boys and girls)	No understanding of gender	Advances in cognitive development allow an understanding of gender	Sex typing based on child's comprehension of what culture deems appropriate for his or her gender
Gender schema (boys and girls)	No understanding of gender	Slowly, through reinforcement, modeling, and cognitive development, an understanding (schema) of sex-typical behavior is acquired	The child's schema is applied to the self in varying degrees, depending on how much the child is reinforced or encouraged to behave in a manner deemed sex appropriate by his or her culture

acquired about sex roles up to that point. Supporting this view is research showing that as soon as children acquire even a very rudimentary understanding of gender, sex typing suddenly becomes more prominent as the children rapidly form gender stereotypes and alter their behavior to better fit gender expectations (Martin & Little, 1990).

Gender schema theory may also apply to the way parents help shape their children's sex typing. For instance, although it is true that parents typically reinforce the use of sex-appropriate toys, parents are more likely to do so for children they know possess gender constancy (Fagot, Leinbach, & O'Boyle, 1992).

Table 13.1 outlines the development of sexual identity according to the four theories we have discussed in this chapter. Research is currently continuing in this area at a fast pace; whether Bem's view is correct remains to be seen. Perhaps a complete understanding of children's sex typing will require an entirely new theoretical view—one not yet considered.

LEARNING CHECK

1. Children's sex roles probably begin to be shaped
  a. at birth.
  b. at about 3 years of age.
  c. at about 18 months of age.
  d. by about 6 or 7 years of age.

2. In our culture, ______________ may have a greater effect on the early learning of sex roles.
  a. mothers **c.** school
  b. siblings **d.** fathers

3. The ______________ theory states that children learn their sex roles by watching others and by being reinforced differentially for certain behaviors.
  a. Freudian **c.** cognitive
  b. social learning **d.** gender schema

4. The ______________ theory is an intertwining of the social learning and ______________ views.
  a. cognitive; gender schema **c.** Freudian; gender schema
  b. gender schema; cognitive **d.** cognitive; Freudian

5. Children appear to develop an understanding of gender by about the age of 3 years.
  a. true **b.** false

6. Children develop gender constancy
  a. at about age 6 or 7.
  b. by about 1 year of age.
  c. before they develop an understanding of gender.
  d. during adolescence.

Answers: 1. a 2. d 3. b 4. b 5. a 6. a

APPLICATIONS

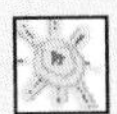

Overcoming Sex Stereotypes

Although it appears that the basic temperamental characteristics of the two sexes are similar, the roles of men and women in society are not. Almost all the nurses and secretaries are women, whereas almost all the engineers, mathematicians, and mechanics are men.

Women earn only about 60 percent as much as men, and large wage differences remain even when comparisons are made within the same occupation.

Question: But aren't things changing quickly now that so many American mothers are in the work force?

A working mother may help to alter the stereotypical sex role socialization of her child, but that is not likely. Even after 50 percent of American mothers had entered the work force, researchers found that the fantasy play of little girls was still focused on a domestic role (Connolly, Doyle, & Ceschin, 1983). There are apparently so many examples of stereotypical sex role behavior in a child's world that a mother's working role is not sufficient to overcome stereotypical sex role socialization. Little girls tended to do what little girls always have done—they played house (Birns & Sternglanz, 1983).

Question: What's wrong with little girls playing house?

Nothing. A problem may occur, however, if little boys learn that it is not their role to play house and little girls learn that it is their only role. Many people have argued that early training in such a domestic role *as the only acceptable female role* is the beginning of second-class citizenship.

Question: Aren't you stating the case a little strongly?

Perhaps, but there may be cause to worry, especially when we examine the changes in the toys themselves. For example:

> as in previous decades, girls play with dolls, pots, and toy brooms. Although boys still like blocks and vehicles, some of the traditionally male toys have changed dramatically over time, reflecting technological change. It is hard to find toy horses and bows and arrows today. Cars and trucks are still popular, but space-age toys are quickly gaining in popularity. . . . [I]n the future an additional problem will be that girls will enter high school and college with deficits in computer experience. When boys' toys change as technology progresses and girls' toys do not, it means that we are still preparing men for careers and women for domestic activities and/or low pay, low preparation jobs. (Birns & Sternglanz, 1983, pp. 246–247)

The twenty-first century is about to dawn, and there can be no doubt that computer literacy will be of extreme importance. It may even be that those people unfamiliar with or intimidated by computers will fall behind and create a new lower class of "techno-peasants." Researchers fear that a high percentage of such a class may be women.

Also important is the shaping of attitudes and emotions as they relate to the sexes. Men and women may be at a certain disadvantage if they are limited to strictly "male" or "female" emotions or attitudes. As researchers have noted,

> Nurturance, sensitivity, and compassion are ideal characteristics for physicians (mostly male) as well as for mothers, nurses, teachers, and social workers. However, passivity and dependency are not particularly valuable for mothers, nurses, or anyone else. (Birns & Sternglanz, 1983, p. 248)

Question: What can be done to overcome stereotypical sex typing?

It is possible to modify gender-stereotyped behavior to some degree (Katz & Walsh, 1991). In one study, for example, researchers observed children for a period of three years in a special open-school setting that emphasized nontraditional teaching methods. In the school, the goal was to respond to each child's individual needs and characteristics. Sex-stereotyped expectations concerning any child's interest, personality, or ability were deliberately avoided. As often as was feasible, both male and female teachers were together in the classroom and engaged in a wide range of roles and duties. The children were all together; there were no separate classes for preschoolers, kindergartners, first graders, second graders, and so on.

Although the school constituted only a portion of the children's world, and there was no way to insulate the children from sex-stereotyped experiences outside the classroom, the open-school setting provided for much more mixed-sex activity—boys and girls segregated themselves less often—than would a traditional setting. Even among children 7 years of age, when it is most common for boys and girls to associate with their own sex (Freud referred to it as the "latency period"),

APPLICATIONS

there was more boy-girl interaction and sharing of ideas, roles, and tasks (Bianchi & Bakeman, 1983). Similarly, researchers have discovered that children raised in nontraditional families that stress or model atypical gender roles (such as a mother who is a pilot or a father who does most of the cooking and cleaning in the home) are less likely to adhere to gender stereotypes, although this was more true of girls than of boys (Weisner & Wilson-Mitchell, 1990). These findings add to the evidence that it isn't necessarily the sex of the child that determines playmates and activities; rather, it may be the properties and structure of the environment.

Perhaps by deliberately structuring our environment to help avoid sex-stereotyped representations, we can all help to provide a world in which boys and girls can choose from the greatest possible range of roles and behaviors. This requires the cooperation of parents and, of course, all of society. Perhaps most people don't want to change or get away from the traditional roles; or perhaps they wish to change them only to a limited degree. It will be up to all of us in the future to make these choices and to decide what is best for our children and our society.

SUMMARY

- Imperato-McGinley observed boys with a genetic disorder that keeps the male genitals from being formed during prenatal development. At puberty, owing to an additional secretion of hormones, the male genitals do appear, and the child, previously thought to be a girl, becomes a boy.
- The penis, scrotum, and testes of the male and the vagina, uterus, and ovaries of the female are primary sexual characteristics. Secondary sexual characteristics appear at puberty and include the development of breasts in girls, the deepening of the voice and the appearance of facial hair in boys, and the appearance of underarm and pubic hair in both sexes.
- Sex hormones are responsible for the development of sexual characteristics. They are secreted by the gonads and the kidneys. The female hormones are called estrogens and the male hormones androgens.
- Researchers are interested in the effects of hormones on human beings because hormones directly influence many behaviors in lower animals, such as aggression and sexual activity.
- Occasionally, a fetus may be exposed to levels of hormones higher than normal in the womb. CAH occurs when the fetus secretes excessive androgen from the cortex of its kidneys, resulting in female infants with partially masculinized genitals.
- There appears to be a biologically determined difference in aggressiveness among primates, including human beings.
- There is a controversy over whether men and women have different natural skills or traits and whether sexual orientation is predominantly controlled by biogenetic forces.
- Different sexual behaviors may be shaped by social and cultural forces. Each culture expects certain behaviors from its male and female members.
- The shaping of sex roles may begin as early as birth. Both mothers and fathers treat their infants differently, although mothers treat boy and girl infants less differently than do fathers.
- Psychoanalytic, social learning, and cognitive theories have all addressed the question of how children acquire an understanding of sex roles.
- The Freudian, or psychoanalytic, view of sex role identification has received little empirical support over the years. Most current researchers place emphasis on other theories.
- In the social learning theory of sex role identification, children's behaviors are reinforced or punished based on what parents and society deem appropriate for the child's gender.
- In the cognitive view of sex-role identification, the cognitive realization by the child that he is a male or she is a female guides the child to change his or her behavior to match what society deems appropriate for his or her gender.
- Children develop an understanding of gender by about the age of 3 years, but they don't possess gender constancy until the age of about 7.
- Cognitive theory can't explain why children engage in stereotypical sex role behaviors even before they are cognitively aware of their gender or its constancy.
- The child's selection of same-sex stereotyped toys at a very early age supports the social learning view of sex role identification.
- Gender schema theory is an intertwining of the social learning and cognitive views of sex role identification. In this view, as children develop, they reach a point at which they are able to integrate cognitively all the different sex-typed behaviors they have acquired through social learning and conditioning.
- Perhaps by deliberately structuring our environment to help avoid sex-stereotyped representations, we can all help to provide a world in which boys and girls can choose from the greatest possible range of roles and behaviors.

QUESTIONS FOR DISCUSSION

1. Some people have argued that homosexual teachers should not be allowed to teach children because they might affect children's sexual orientations. How well fixed do you think children's sexual orientations are by the time they enter school? Do you believe that there is anything wrong with a child's adopting a homosexual orientation? Why or why not?

2. Some of the beliefs about sexual development held at the turn of the century were found to be incredibly inaccurate. Do you think there might be beliefs about sexual development held today that will seem equally foolish 50 years from now? If so, which ones and why?

SUGGESTIONS FOR FURTHER READING

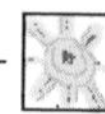

1. Basow, S. (1992). *Gender: Stereotypes & roles. (3rd ed.).* Monterey, CA: Brooks-Cole.
2. Hare-Mustin, R. T. & Marecek, J. (1992). *Making a difference: Psychology & the construction of gender.* New Haven, CT: Yale University Press.
3. Liss, M. B. (Ed.). (1983). *Social and cognitive skills: Sex roles and children's play.* New York: Academic Press.
4. Maccoby, E. E., & Jacklin, C. N. (1974). *The psychology of sex differences.* Palo Alto, CA: Stanford University Press.
5. Money, J., & Ehrhardt, A. A. (1973). *Man and woman, boy and girl.* Baltimore: Johns Hopkins University Press.
6. Turner, J. S., & Rubinson, L. (1992). *Contemporary human sexuality.* Englewood Cliffs, NJ: Prentice-Hall.

CHAPTER 14

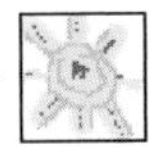

PEERS, SCHOOL, AND THE SOCIAL ENVIRONMENT

CHAPTER PREVIEW

TV OR DADDY

MOST PRESCHOOLERS spend many hours watching television. If you ask them why they watch television, they will usually tell you that it is because they like it. That is a straight enough answer, but one that leaves something to be desired.

Question: Could television really mean that much to a child?

It is difficult to tell how attached children are to things or how important things are to them. But since 4-, 5-, and 6-year-olds are old enough to understand simple questions, one limited way to find out about their feelings is to ask about them. This is exactly what one researcher did when he asked 156 preschoolers an amazing question: "Which do you like better, TV or Daddy?" (Ra, 1977).

If, as any good reporter would, you probe further and ask them why they like it, they will most often say they don't know why. Preschoolers seem pretty comfortable with the fact of liking television, whether or not they know why.

IN AN ATTEMPT to measure the depth of preschoolers' feelings about television, one researcher uncovered evidence that preschoolers may like television so much that they actually form emotional bonds with the set, in much the same way that they become attached to people (Morris, 1971).

YOU MIGHT HAVE already guessed that there probably aren't too many fathers who would like to be standing in the same room when their child answered that question! Supporting this assertion is the finding from the study that of the 156 children, 68 (44 percent) said they liked television better!

Question: Were the children asked the same question about their mothers?

Yes, and mothers were more appreciated, with only 20 percent of the children stating that they liked television better than Mommy (*only* 20 percent!)

IT MAY BE, of course, that the children's answers are not a true reflection of how they really feel. One would hope that a child would feel a greater loss over the absence of his or her father than over the loss of the television set! Even assuming this to be true, which is probably a safe assumption, the preschoolers' answers do show us that television has an impact on a child's world in an emotional way and that some kinds of attachments are formed to it.

IN THIS CHAPTER, we'll examine the influence of television and how children react to it. We'll also look at the social environment in which the child is raised and how that affects her. We'll examine the influence of schools, peers, and siblings. And along the way, we'll explore how friendships form and learn why children play.

RESOURCES

PEERS
Equals; developmentally, people who interact at about the same behavioral level, regardless of age.

The Development of Peer Relationships

Strictly speaking, **peers** are equals. Even so, children often have playmates who are 3 or 4 years older or younger than they are. For this reason, many researchers consider children to be peers so long as they are interacting at about the same behavioral level, regardless of age. Explorations of peer relationships usually focus on children of approximately the same age because these children are most likely to be interacting with one another (Roopnarine, 1981).

THE FIRST YEAR: EARLY PEER INTERACTION

Infants are individuals, and they don't all behave alike (Bronson, 1981). During the first year of life, however, certain age-related trends in peer interaction that are common to most infants can be seen.

Interestingly, some infants don't have the opportunity to interact with peers. Approximately 25 percent of 6-month-old babies have never had contact with another infant, and another 20 percent have contact with other babies only about once a week.* Among those who do interact with one another, a particular developmental sequence can be observed. This sequence is not necessarily peer specific; it is also observed in the development of infant-mother interactions. The sequence, then, is part of a more general developmental trend.

The Onset of Social Awareness

Question: How does this developmental sequence unfold?

Infants react to each other's cries and seem to be slightly aware of one another by about 3 months of age (Field, 1979; Fogel, 1979). By 6 months, they look at, smile at, and reach toward other infants (Vandell & Mueller, 1980). By 1 year of age, slightly more complex social interactions emerge (Hartup, 1983).

The Effect of Toys

Question: If infants are provided with toys to share and play with, will this accelerate social interaction?

Six-month-old infants are more likely to be social with one another when toys are present (Hay, Nash, & Pedersen, 1983). This is especially true if you provide only one toy for two infants, as this tends to bring the infants together because they have a mutual interest (Adamson & Bakeman, 1985).

Question: But wouldn't two 6-month-old infants focusing on the same toy be likely to fight over it?

Interestingly, 6-month-old infants don't tend to fight over toys, even if one baby takes a toy away from the other (Hay, Nash, & Pedersen, 1983). Instead, 6-month-old babies typically respond in the following fashion:

> At the simplest level the infants reacted to the presence of peers by touching them and touching the toys they held. Once they did so, their peers reacted in consistent ways. Although infants did not always respond actively to being touched, if they did so, they were much more likely to match their peers' overtures than to shrink from contact; fussing when touched was very rare, despite the fact that initiations were frequently

*The percentage of infant-infant contact may be much higher in non-Western societies, especially in those cultures in which extended families are common (Hartup, 1983).

By the age of 6 months, infants look at, smile at, and reach toward other infants.

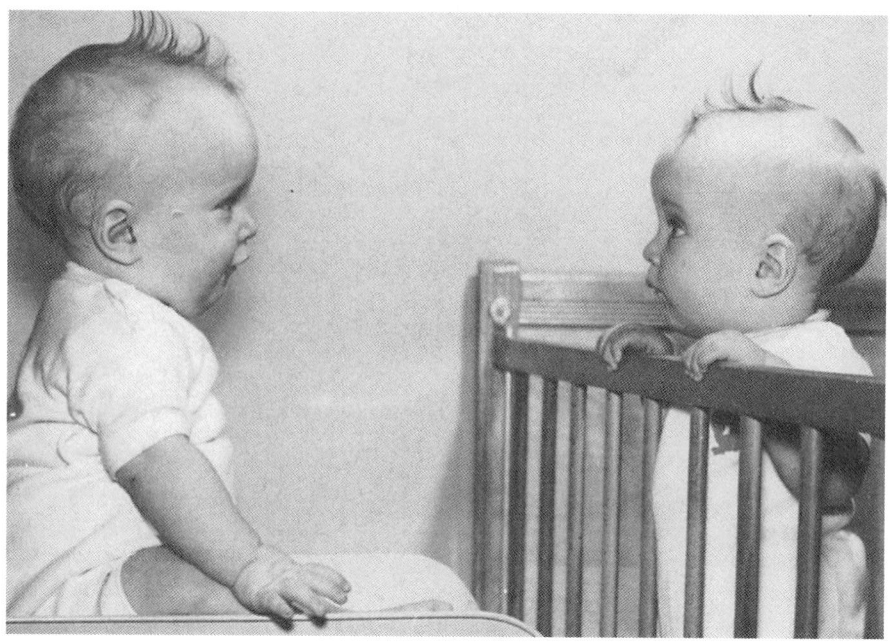

directed to the peer's hair and face and infants sometimes found themselves trapped beneath their partners. Similarly, episodes of joint toy contact typically were not accompanied by fussing or other visible signs of protest and resistance. In most cases, the original holder of a toy retained access to it without recourse to tears or the use of force. Thus, 6-month-olds' interactions featuring contact of the peer or the peer's toys, which are common themes in the conflict of older toddlers (Hay & Ross, 1982), seemed remarkably harmonious. (Hay, Nash, & Pedersen, 1983, p. 561)

THE SECOND YEAR: EMOTIONAL AND COGNITIVE CHANGES

Between the ages of 1 and 2 years, children's social skills and peer interactions are rudimentary (Hartup, 1983) but still more complex than during infancy (Eckerman, Whatley, & Kutz, 1975). In fact, children as young as 18 to 24 months have been shown to adjust their social interactions when dealing with younger or older children so as to facilitate social communication (Brownell, 1990).

Some researchers have argued that the development of peer relationships during the first year or two passes through three distinct stages (Mueller & Lucas, 1975; Mueller & Vandell, 1977). In the first stage, the *object-centered stage,* children occasionally interact with one another, but most of their attention is focused on objects or toys. During the second stage, the *simple interactive stage,* which begins at about 1½ years of age, infants respond primarily to each other and prefer social play to solitary play (see Figure 14.1). By the age of 2 years, children enter the *complementary interactive stage.* During this final stage, many complex social interchanges occur (Howes, 1987). Imitation becomes more likely, and positive social interactions often are accompanied by appropriate emotional responses, such as smiling or laughter (Mueller & Brenner, 1977).

Emotional reactions of children to one another appear to become more important during the second year as well. Although 1-year-old babies laugh and smile at each other, most of their interactions lack discernible emotional tone (Rubenstein & Howes, 1976). By the age of 2 years, however, emotions clearly become a more important part of social interaction (Mueller & Rich, 1976; Ross & Goldman, 1976). By this time, children take careful note of one another's emotional expressions and dispositions before acting or responding socially. Adults do this as a matter of course, and it is an important part of any social interaction. Further

FIGURE 14.1
By the age of $1\frac{1}{2}$ years, children engage more often in social play than in solitary play (*Source:* Eckerman, Whatley, & Kutz, 1975, p. 47)

evidence for the social influence of peers comes from the fact that by the age of 18 months, children are more likely to leave their mother's side and explore a room when a peer is present than when no peer is present (Gunnar, Senior, & Hartup, 1984).

Cognitive changes during the second year also play an important role in social interaction. As you may recall from our earlier discussion about toys, 6-month-old infants rarely show distress when a peer takes a toy away. The same interaction between children 20 months of age or older, on the other hand, *is* likely to start a fight.

Question: Why would a fight occur among older children but not among 6-month-olds?

In the Chapter Preview for Chapter 9, we discussed the dawning of consciousness. We noted that 20-month-old children probably know their own reflections and recognize their own faces, whereas younger children and infants typically do not (Amsterdam, 1972). This occurs, it is argued, because at about 20 months of age, children become aware of themselves; they become conscious of being living creatures; they develop a sense of self. In one study, researchers found that as children develop this sense of self-awareness and become able to see themselves as distinct from others, they begin to claim toys and other items as "mine" (Levine, 1983). Once they've defined "mine," they are more likely to become possessive.

Question: Do children become selfish at this age?

Not necessarily. Children of this age often share, especially if they become familiar with one another or if other children have shared with them (Levitt, Weber, Clark, & McDonnell, 1985). What has happened, however, is a basic developmental step toward becoming a social being, a step that shouldn't necessarily be equated with "selfishness." Before any mature or complex social interaction can take place, a child must have a clear understanding of "you" and "I." As children develop this awareness, their behavior with peers will follow a different pattern:

> Specifically, they would attempt to define their territory by claiming toys as *mine*, and they would comment on the other child or his possessions. These children would also show a different pattern of interaction that reflected their increased self-awareness and social awareness. They would be wary initially of a new peer in an unfamiliar setting. However, they would then try to define their boundaries by claiming toys. Once this issue appeared to be clarified, they might then express increased social interest in the other child. (Levine, 1983, p. 544)

PERSONALITY
The organization of relatively enduring characteristics unique to an individual, usually revealed by the individual's reaction to his environment.

FRIENDSHIP
Close emotional ties formed with another person through mutual preference for interaction, skill at complementary and reciprocal peer play, and shared positive affect.

Longitudinal studies have shown that throughout the second year of life, a child's social behavior becomes more consistent and predictable (Bronson, 1985). This increased stability of social behavior may indicate that by the age of 2 years, children are beginning to regulate their own behavior internally in a consistent way. Consistency of behavior in different situations marks the beginning of what psychologists call **personality.** By 2 years of age, a social person is emerging; the child has a unique personality.

THE PRESCHOOL YEARS

Most interactions among children between the ages of 2 and 5 years have been studied in day-care centers or in nursery schools. During the preschool years, both friendly and, less commonly, antagonistic social interactions emerge.

Friendships Major changes occur in children's social relationships between the age of 2 years and the time they enter school. By the age of 3 or 4 years, most children overcome their reluctance to join other children fully in play. They begin to interact with one another (Hinde, Stevenson-Hinde, & Tamplin, 1985) and form **friendships.**

Question: Do infants form friendships?

Although it's hard to imagine 8- or 9-month-old babies having friends, infants of this age have been observed, in nurseries and day-care centers, to have definite preferences for certain peers (Lee, 1973). These preferences, however, are not complex enough to be considered friendships in the general sense of the term.

Question: How do developmental researchers define friendship?

Researchers have defined *friendship* as "mutual preference for interaction, skill at complementary and reciprocal peer play, and shared positive affect" (Howes, 1983, p. 1041). As you can see, friendship involves more than just friendly interaction. Children who form friendships do many things together; most importantly, they form emotional ties with one another.

By the age of about 6 years, most children have a sufficient understanding of the distinction between themselves and others to know that others may not feel or react in the same way as they themselves do (Selman, Schorin, Stone, & Phelps,

By the time children reach the age of 2 years, fights over toys are more likely to occur because the children have developed self-awareness, which enables them to conceive of things as "mine."

1983). Because of this, grade school children are better able to predict one another's characteristics accurately (Ladd & Emerson, 1984). Compare this with preschool children, who more typically adopt another child as "best friend" in a rather one-sided way, without the mutual understandings or sharing of knowledge and feelings that older children have. These findings show that as children grow older, a shared knowledge about one another's unique characteristics helps to form and cement a friendship.

Also, as children become older, they spend more and more time with other children, especially with close friends (Howes, 1983). In fact, by the age of 7 years, the average child will begin to spend as much social time with friends and peers as with adults.

Question: What determines whether children who meet will become friends?

When children first meet, they are more likely to become friends if they are able to exchange information successfully, to establish a common-ground activity, and to manage conflicts (Gottman, 1983) (see Table 14.1). After an initial relationship

TABLE 14.1

How Children Establish an Initial Relationship

CATEGORY	EXAMPLE
Information exchange	
Success	A: What's this? B: This is my room right here. This is my farm here. Look how very, very large.
Failure	A: How come we can't get this off? B: You know, I'm gonna get the rolling pin so we can roll this.
Common-ground activity	
Success: A joint activity is successfully initiated.	A: And you make those for after we get together, okay? B: 'Kay. A: Have to make those. B: Pretend like those little roll cookies, I mean. A: And make, um, make a, um, pancake too. B: Oh, rats, this is a little pancake. A: Yeah, let's play house. B: Okay, play house.
Failure: Initiation is ignored or disagreed with; activity does not develop.	A: Let's play house. B: Nope, nope, nope, nope, nope, nope. A: Because you're coloring that brick wall? B: Yep.
Conflict	A: This is stretchy. B: No, it's not. A: Uh huh. B: Yes. A: Uh huh. B: It's dirty. A: Uh uh. B: Uh huh. A: Uh uh. B: Uh huh. A: Uh uh. B: Uh huh. A: Uh uh. It's not dirty.

SOURCE: Adapted from Gottman, 1983, pp. 27, 53–54.

Children who form friendships do many things together; most important, they form emotional ties with one another.

has been established, other processes become more important. Among these are the exploration of similarities and differences, self-disclosure, and amity (peaceful relations) (Gottman, 1983) (see Table 14.2). As soon as children become older, they improve their acquaintanceship abilities. They become more successful at exchanging information, establishing common-ground activities, resolving conflicts, and exploring differences. They also share intimate details of their lives. This last characteristic is especially true among girls (Furman, 1987). These qualities, along with the emotional exchanges, become the most important aspects of the friendship (Diaz & Berndt, 1982; Furman & Bierman, 1983).

TABLE 14.2

The Development of Friendship

CATEGORY	EXAMPLE
Similarity: Children note that they are the same.	A: Mine's almost finished. B: Mine's too.
Contrast: Children note that they are not the same.	A: I'm gonna be 5 at, in my birthday. B: Well, I'm 5 now.
Self-disclosure: Any personal statement about one's feelings that is intimate; excludes low-intimacy statements (e.g., "I love chocolate") even if they are strongly stated.	A: She didn't say anything about the dress. She said leave me alone. B: Why'd she say that? A: She doesn't love me.
Amity: Validation or approval of the other person; affirmation of the relationship; sympathy; offers of affection; wit and hilarity; or shared deviance.	A: *(kisses B)* B: Oh gosh. A: What? B: You just kissed me on the cheek. Thank you. A: I'll kiss you on the forehead. B: I'll kiss you.

SOURCE: Adapted from Gottman, 1983, pp. 54–55.

Play One of the most obvious occurrences during the preschool years is the development of **play.** Although children often may play alone, as children grow older, play becomes more a social phenomenon (Cooper, 1977; Hartup, 1983). Playing can be simple and unstructured, as in a game of hide-and-seek, or it can be more complex and structured, as in a school basketball game.

PLAY
Pleasurable activity engaged in for its own sake, with means emphasized rather than ends. Play is not usually engaged in as a serious activity and is flexible in that it varies in form or context.

EXPLORATION-PLAY-APPLICATION SEQUENCE
An ethological term describing the function of play as a bridge between the cautious exploration of the unfamiliar and its eventual application for useful purposes.

Question: How do developmental researchers define play?

Curiously, *play* has never been defined precisely. Part of the problem is that the word *play* is used to describe such diverse behaviors as adolescents assembling model ships and dogs frolicking in a yard (Vandenberg, 1978). Most people seem to know what is meant by play (Smith & Vollstedt, 1985), but researchers wish to define it. In an attempt to do so, they have tried to isolate different aspects of the behavior. It has been suggested that there are five descriptors of play and that the greater the number of descriptors that can be applied in any given situation, the more likely people are to call those circumstances play (Rubin, Fein, & Vandenberg, 1983; Smith & Vollstedt, 1985).

Question: What are the five descriptors?

1. *Intrinsic motivation:* The behavior is motivated from within; that is, it is done for its own sake and not to satisfy social demands or bodily functions.
2. *Positive affect:* The behavior appears to be pleasurable or fun to do.
3. *Nonlaterality:* The behavior is not lateral; that is, it does not follow a serious pattern or sequence, having more a pretend quality about it.
4. *Means/ends:* The means are emphasized rather than the ends; that is, there is more interest in the behavior itself than in any outcomes it may produce.
5. *Flexibility:* The behavior is not rigid. It shows flexibility in form and context and across situations.

If we use all five descriptors, we might say that a child who is manipulating toy animals in a flexible way with no apparent goal in mind, who is pretending, who is enjoying herself, and who is doing the activity for its own sake is playing. Such an activity fits all five criteria, and almost any observer would call it playing. A major league baseball player at bat, however, may fit only one or two of these criteria. For this reason, fewer people would call this activity play, although some would.

However *play* is defined, playing and playful interaction with peers seem to have an important role in the social and cognitive development of children.

Why Children Play

Question: What makes children play?

No one is certain. Social scientists generally believe that play has evolved because it has a function (Vandenberg, 1978). It may be that playing with objects, playing make-believe, and playing together at various games help children to become skilled at manipulating objects (Cheyne & Rubin, 1983) and to learn adult roles or, once they are grown, to cooperate while dealing with serious and complex tasks. Some ethologists have argued that there is an **exploration-play-application sequence** found in humans and more advanced animals (Vandenberg, 1978; Wilson, 1975).

Question: What do they mean by "exploration-play-application sequence"?

When children are confronted with a completely novel toy, they tend to explore it before playing with it (Belsky & Most, 1981; Vandenberg, 1984). It's as though they want to be sure that it is safe before they play (Weisler & McCall, 1976).

SOLITARY PLAY
The type of play that children engage in when they play by themselves.

ONLOOKER PLAY
A type of play in which the child watches other children play but does not participate.

PARALLEL PLAY
The kind of play that children engage in when they play alongside other children but do not participate directly with the other children.

ASSOCIATIVE PLAY
A type of play in which children play and share with others.

COOPERATIVE PLAY
The kind of play in which children play structured games with other children according to rules.

This same kind of exploration-before-play sequence has also been observed in chimpanzees (Loizos, 1967; Mason, 1965).

During play, the skills necessary for serious application are acquired. For example, it was discovered many years ago that chimpanzees needed to spend time playing with sticks before they could use sticks for purposeful applications such as food gathering (Birch, 1945; Schiller, 1957). Researchers have found similar play-before-application sequences while investigating children (Sylva, Bruner, & Genova, 1976; Vandenberg, 1978). Perhaps, then, play has evolved as a means of helping children practice motor and cognitive skills they may later apply.

Types of Play

Question: Is all play the same, or are there different kinds?

In what has since become a classic study of play, Mildred Parten observed 42 nursery school children between 2 and 4½ years of age while they played (Parten, 1932). Parten observed six distinct kinds of behavior in the play situation. These included unoccupied behavior, **solitary play, onlooker play** (watching others but not participating in play activity), **parallel play** (playing alongside other children but not directly interacting with them), **associative play** (playing and sharing with other children), and **cooperative play** (playing structured games with other children according to rules). After 60 one-minute observations of children's play, Parten noticed that older children spent more time in social play (associative and cooperative), whereas younger children were more likely to engage in parallel or solitary play (see Figure 14.2).

Question: Are older children who prefer solitary play maladjusted or withdrawn?

Most researchers believe that solitary play has an important function and is not usually a sign of maladjustment (Rubin, Maioni, & Hornung, 1976). About 50 percent of all solitary play involves educational activities, and an additional 25

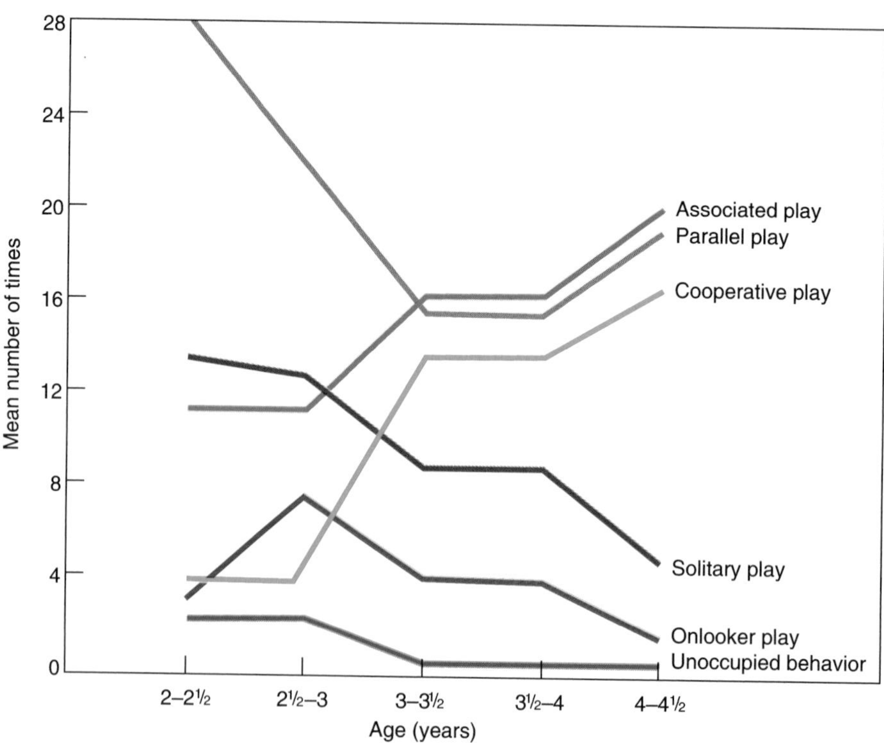

FIGURE 14.2
Developmental changes in play according to Parten's 1932 study. As children become older, the social kinds of play increase while the solitary forms of play decrease. (*Source:* Parten, 1932)

percent focuses on large-muscle activity such as dancing, spinning, hopping, or running (Moore, Evertson, & Brophy, 1974).

Question: Is parallel play an important step from solitary play toward the more social types of play?

It can be. During parallel play, children often imitate the play of other children who are near and thereby learn the established themes for play according to another. This nonverbal understanding is often an important antecedent to the verbal interaction and social coordination found later in associative and cooperative play (Eckerman, Davis, & Didow, 1989). In addition, solitary or parallel play can also be viewed as an alternative to playing with others (Harper & Huie, 1985). In fact, with the rapid growth in availability of computer and video games, solitary or parallel play among grade school children is increasing.

REALITY PLAY
Play devoid of fantasy or in which fantasy is an insignificant part; essentially, play in which an object or situation is treated as what it actually is.

FANTASY PLAY
Play in which an object, person, or situation becomes a target for fantasy and is not treated as what it actually is.

SOCIAL FANTASY PLAY
Play in which one pretends to be someone else or adopts a role other than one's own; common to children age 5 years or older.

Fantasy Play

Question: When do children first learn to pretend?

Certain cognitive abilities must be present before a child is able to pretend (see Chapter 9). Object permanence—the ability to imagine an object even though it is not presently sensed—is a basic requirement. This ability generally develops by the age of 2 years; any form of social pretend play with others is quite rare in children younger than 2 years of age (Howes, 1985).

Question: Do children begin pretend play once they have developed object permanence?

Although object permanence appears to be a prerequisite for pretending, pretend play doesn't appear all at once but emerges gradually (Pederson, Rook-Green, & Elder, 1981). Among 2-year-old children, **reality play** (play in which an object or situation is treated as what it actually is) is the most common form of play. By the age of 3 years, **fantasy play** becomes more likely, and children begin to make believe that objects or people can be things other than what they are (Field, De Stefano, & Koewler, 1982). Also by about the age of 3 years, fantasy play and social play merge to yield **social fantasy play,** where children who are playing together come to agree on fantasy themes for their play (Howes, Unger, & Seidner, 1989). It has been shown that children who engage the most in social fantasy

In parallel play, children play alongside one another but don't directly interact; during associated play, children share and interact with one another.

PEER GROUPS
Groups that develop their own set of values and goals and establish durable social relationships. Generally, each member has a specified role or status.

play are also more likely to be popular with their peers and to receive high teacher ratings of social skill than are those who do not (Connolly & Doyle, 1984). These findings may indicate that social fantasy play is meaningful for the development of important social skills (Doyle, Doehring, Tessier, de Lorimier, & Shapiro, 1992).

The Environmental Structuring of Play

Question: Do children everywhere in the world play the same way?

The trend from reality play to a more social fantasy play appears to be universal, but the kinds of play that children engage in can be quite different from culture to culture. A particular environment may place all kinds of constraints on the kind of play that children engage in, or, conversely, it may promote certain forms of play (Sutton-Smith, 1985).

For instance, in one experiment, preschoolers were placed in one of two environments that contained play materials. In one environment, the toys were aimed at large-muscle coordination. The toys were large, they encouraged action, and the environment provided a lot of room. In the second environment, the play materials were aimed at fine-muscle coordination. The toys were small and intricate (Vandenberg, 1981). In this study, the play environments strongly influenced the kinds of social play that occurred as well as the size of the play groups. Large toys encouraged the formation of big, action-oriented groups that played more roughly, whereas small and intricate toys encouraged the formation of smaller groups that tended to stay in one location and play quietly.

Perhaps a more striking example of such effects is described in Brian Sutton-Smith's *A History of Children's Play: The New Zealand Playground 1840–1950* (published in 1981). Sutton-Smith describes how, in the mid-nineteenth century, the pioneer children of early New Zealand settlers were somewhat neglected by their busy parents and were forced to invent their own toys and games. These children created a great variety of unique play activities that characterized their life and play in the isolated settlements. By the turn of the century, however, partly because of New Zealand's rapid population growth, there was a tendency for adults to make educational reforms and to organize children's play. Regulations were passed; teachers were even graded according to their ability to organize children's games. Rugby became a national game, and children were pressured to participate to develop leadership skills and discipline.

In his epilogue, Sutton-Smith describes the more recent processes by which every part of children's lives and their play have become organized for them, in school and at home, through television and by the use of commercial toys. The great variety of play that once existed is now absent, and all children engage in the same general list of expected activities. No doubt, much the same is true in the United States and in other industrialized nations.

SCHOOL-AGE CHILDREN

For the school-age child, peer relationships both in and out of school become extremely important. Being accepted by one's peers and belonging to **peer groups** are major concerns (Zarbatany, Hartmann, & Rankin, 1990).

Between the ages of 7 and 9 years, children generally form close friendships with peers of the same sex and age (Roopnarine & Johnson, 1984). After the eighth grade, however, it is not uncommon for adolescents to have friends of the opposite sex as well (Buhrmester & Furman, 1987).

The older children become, the more likely they are to share with friends (Berndt, Hawkins, & Hoyle, 1986) and the more they come to value friends according to their personal attributes. For instance, one study found that whereas

Peer groups include individuals who share similar beliefs and attitudes.

5½-year-old children might be more interested in making friends with another child who had a new game or toy, 9-year-old children were more interested in making friends with another child because "he's real nice" (Boggiano, Klinger, & Main, 1986). Throughout the school years, children also rely on their peers as important sources of information and may use peers as standards by which to measure themselves. By the age of 7 or 8 years, children tend to look to their peers as models of behavior and for social reinforcement as often as they look to their own families. Research also has shown that by the fourth grade, children have come to rely on friends as an important source of social and moral support (Berndt & Perry, 1986).

PEER ACCEPTANCE

Question: What determines which children will be popular with their peers?

The kinds of behaviors accepted or rejected by a band of children can vary greatly from one group to the next. Some peer groups reinforce aggression, whereas others promote cooperation. Peer groups may be as diverse as a gang of 13- or 14-year-old adolescents that reinforces killing and a local Boy Scout troop that reinforces social and achievement-oriented skills. Nonetheless, we can make several general statements about peer acceptance or rejection.

Among grade school children, peers who are rejected tend to behave in ways that are more aggressive and *inappropriate* than do peers who are accepted (Dodge, Coie, Pettit, & Price, 1990). Inappropriateness is an important consideration when appraising the effect of aggression because research has shown that no more than half of aggressive children are rejected by their peers. What we find, then, is that rejected children are generally those whose aggression violates the norms set by the group; it's not just that they are aggressive (Coie, Dodge, Terry, & Wright, 1991). In fact, among older children (9-year-olds), aggression in reaction to provocation, as well as some bullying, were positively correlated with higher peer status (Coie, Dodge, Terry, & Wright, 1991). The behavior of hyperactive children is also often seen as inappropriate and as proper grounds for rejection by the group (Pope, Bierman, & Mumma, 1991).

One of the most important moments determining later acceptance or rejection is the first interaction. Children who are best able to fit in and to engage in conversation with a new group *when they first meet* show skills that predict later popularity among their peers (Black & Hazen, 1990; Putallaz, 1983). Furthermore, children who have the social skills to produce humor and laughter among their peers have been found to be more academically and socially competent and to be viewed by their peers as fun to be with and as having good ideas for things to do (Masten, 1986). Also, children who have the most positive parent-child relationships tend to form the most positive friendships (Youngblade & Belsky, 1992), and children who acquire many friends are more likely to do well in school (Ladd, 1990).

Interestingly, once a child has been accepted by a group, that child is not likely to be rejected, even if he is as aggressive as peers whom the group initially rejected (Coie & Kupersmidt, 1983). A bias exists in that once a child has been accepted by his peers, aggressive and inappropriate behavior may be overlooked; but once a child has been rejected by his peers, even relatively mild behavior may be considered undesirable by those who were rejecting (Hymel, 1986). These findings underscore the importance of possessing the social skills necessary to be accepted *initially* by a peer group.

Occasionally, peers are neglected instead of being actively rejected. Neglected children tend not to display aggressive or task-inappropriate behaviors any more than do accepted peers. Neglected children, however, often are shy and rarely approach their peers in a social way (Dodge, Coie, & Brakke, 1982).

Question: What happens if children who are rejected or neglected by their peers don't find ways to be accepted?

Sometimes these children can turn to a close sibling for support, although that can't fully make up for peer rejection (East & Rook, 1992). Children who lack close sibling relationships and who fail to find peer acceptance, or who fail to learn the appropriate behaviors demanded by peers, face a loneliness in childhood that often continues into adulthood (Cassidy & Asher, 1992; Hojat, 1982; Parkhurst & Asher, 1992). Grade school teachers know that social isolation is a genuine risk of early childhood (Hymel, Rubin, Rowden, & LeMare, 1990) and that part of their job is to nip such rejection in the bud by forcing, if necessary, peer-group acceptance and tolerance. Such initial forced acceptance often develops into real acceptance as the children come to accommodate one another.

Question: What factors besides a child's behavior are important in determining peer acceptance?

Children generally prefer to be with members of their own race and sex (Schofield & Francis, 1982). Such preferences are found throughout grade school, from kindergarten (Finkelstein & Haskins, 1983) to the sixth grade (Sagar, Schofield, & Snyder, 1983).

Question: Do children prefer others of their own race because they have learned to be prejudiced?

Learned prejudice may account for racial preferences among children to a small degree, but the main factors appear to be related to social class and levels of academic achievement. Research indicates that there is more interracial acceptance among children if they meet at the same academic and social level (Schofield & Whitley, 1983).

Those who are physically attractive are also more likely to be accepted (Vaughn & Langlois, 1983). Children as young as 3 to 6 years of age show a strong preference for attractive rather than unattractive children (Dion, 1973). This inclination is especially marked among girls (Langlois & Styczynski, 1979; Vaughn & Langlois, 1983).

The physically attractive also tend to be more resistant to peer pressure (Adams, 1977). This may be because attractive children expect to be accepted as leaders, whereas unattractive children may capitulate and be followers in order to gain acceptance. Among boys, those who mature early and have a masculine build are more likely to be imitated and accepted by their peers.

A child's name may also affect peer acceptance. Through associative learning (see Chapter 7), names such as Rose or Bertha, which were popular at the turn of the century, have become unpopular. The names Scott and Jennifer, on the other hand, have become more popular.

Question: Doesn't a child's character influence whether the child will be accepted by peers?

Although name, race, sex, and physical attractiveness initially may be most important in peer acceptance of a child (Furman & Bierman, 1983), as peer relationships grow and develop, a child's character often emerges as the most important attribute in determining continued acceptance (Reaves & Roberts, 1983). For character to play an important role, however, children must first become known by their peers, and this may not be possible if they already have been rejected because of peer-group determination that their overt aspects are undesirable. Such initial rejections may have an unfortunate influence on a child's personality, and the child may become depressed or aggressive or may change in some way as to make future peer acceptance even less likely.

Siblings

Although parents are usually considered the primary agents of socialization for their young child, in most families the child also has a relationship with one or more siblings. Siblings can have a powerful effect on one another. Research indicates that siblings spend a great deal of time together, that they interact on many different levels, and that they are often deeply emotionally involved with one another (Abramovitch, Pepler, & Corter, 1982). Because siblings are of the same generation, have a common genetic heritage, and share many of the same experiences, they often have a significant effect on one another throughout their lives (Cicirelli, 1982).

Cross-cultural research has shown that even though the sibling relationship in non-Western cultures is different from that in industrialized Western nations, it is still an important one. In non-Western cultures, siblings are more commonly involved in cooperative child rearing and in day-to-day activities necessary for survival, such as defense and food gathering.

Question: Do siblings affect children in the same way as friends or peers?

In many ways, the interactions among siblings can be much like interactions among peers. In both we see a high frequency of interaction, an uninhibited emotional quality, mutual interest in one another, and evidence of imitation and attachment (Dunn, 1983). These similarities are especially evident among siblings who are close in age (Berndt & Bulleit, 1985).

Although siblings may show antagonism and rivalry, most sibling interaction is friendly and playful (Abramovitch, Corter, Pepler, & Stanhope, 1986) (see At Issue).

Fully 80 percent of the children in the United States and Britain have siblings (Dunn, 1983). Siblings often are different from one another in terms of intellectual development and personality (Rowe & Plomin, 1981; Scarr & Grajek, 1982). Researchers have been interested in what determines differences between siblings living in the same family, and a number of important factors have been noted. First, there are genetic differences. Any two siblings will share about 50 percent of the same genes, but the other 50 percent will be unique to each sibling, allowing for considerable differences in temperament and other aspects of behavior strongly influenced by genes. Another important factor is the differential treatment of siblings by their mother. Differential treatment is the rule rather than the exception; mothers simply don't treat each of their children in exactly the same way. This is not to say that one child will be treated well and another poorly, but rather that children are individuals and end up being treated as such. This differential treatment no doubt accounts for some of the difference observed between siblings raised in the same family (Stocker, Dunn, & Plomin, 1989). Some of the differences observed between siblings may also be due to the fact that siblings may create very different family environments for one another as a result of their behaviors toward one another (Daniels, Dunn, Furstenberg, & Plomin, 1985; Stocker, Dunn, & Plomin, 1989). In this sense, because siblings directly affect the family unit, they may have a greater effect than do peers, especially during a child's first 5 years.

Question: What effect do siblings tend to have on each other if the ages between them are great?

When siblings are more than a few years apart, the older siblings tend to influence younger siblings in a way that is more parentlike than peerlike, often acting as teachers and role models for their younger brothers and sisters (Brody, Stoneman, MacKinnon, & MacKinnon, 1985; Dunn, 1983).

Strong sibling relationships have been shown to exist across life spans and throughout the world. And because of shared genetic, experiential, and cultural heritage, the sibling bond can be a very powerful one indeed.

PEER GROUPS

Question: Would any group of same-aged children be considered a peer group?

Among 6- or 7-year-old children, peer groups tend to be informal and unstructured, but as children grow older, their peer groupings sometimes become more organized and formal. The different skills, powers, and abilities of group members become important distinctions. Status ordering based on characteristics such as appearance, pubertal development, athletic skill, academic achievement, or leadership ability is common (Savin-Williams, 1979).

Members of the peer group, in an effort to be admired and accepted, will attempt as best they can to conform to the standards and values of the group. Generally, conformity to peer-group standards increases with age, but a great deal

AT ISSUE

Sibling Rivalry: Fact or Fiction?

When a second-born infant joins a family, especially a family in which the firstborn is under the age of 4, there is likely to be some conflict. Over the years, terms such as *dethronement, displacement,* and *regression* have been used when describing the firstborn's reaction to the situation in which the firstborn now finds him- or herself. These terms are still used to describe a firstborn's typical reaction, although *imitation* is now considered a better descriptor than *regression;* both refer to a strategy of acting like the baby to maintain or regain parental attention (Stewart, Mobley, Van Tuyl, & Salvador, 1987).

Although it was traditionally thought that conflict was the inevitable outcome of a sibling relationship, research has shown that rivalry and conflict are not necessarily the norm. In fact, the *most* common mode of sibling interaction is often that of cooperation and helping (Abramovitch, Pepler, & Corter, 1982).

Question: When is conflict likely to occur?

Judy Dunn and her colleagues at Cambridge University closely examined sibling relationships among preschool children and came to several interesting conclusions. First, they found that the mother's behavior following the birth of a new baby was a factor in determining the presence or absence of rivalry and conflict. They also noted that it was helpful to include the older sibling in babycare activities and to refer to the baby as a person instead of simply considering the new arrival as "the baby":

> In families where the mothers discussed caring for the baby as a matter of joint responsibility and talked about the baby as a person from the early days, the siblings were particularly friendly over the next year. Most encouraging of all, our findings show that in families where the first child was interested and affectionate toward the baby, the relationship continued to be rewarding, loving, and supportive for both children—not just the first year, but over the next three years. (Dunn & Kendrick, 1982b, pp. 220–221)

The second important finding made by Dunn and her colleagues was that the sibling relationship could not be characterized as being of any one type, that such relationships showed incredible variability and complexity. Furthermore, even though siblings may seem to get along well with one another, they can still have episodes of conflict, perhaps because they are together so much of the time.

A third finding of Dunn's study was that even when the older sibling was "naughty" after the birth of the new baby, the naughty behavior was commonly directed against the mother and usually occurred when the mother was interacting with the new baby. For example, one child deliberately began to sprinkle his milk all over the sofa while his mother was interacting with his baby sister, and another child, observing a similar interaction between mother and baby, ran outside, laughing, and let down a full line of clean clothes that had been drying onto some muddy grass (Dunn & Kendrick, 1982b).

Dunn and her colleagues also found that the gender of the siblings had a bearing on whether or not there would be conflict, with opposite-gender siblings having a stormier relationship than same-gender ones. They also found that the temperament of the firstborn child may play a role in fostering conflict (Dunn, 1984). Parents have no control over gender and little control over temperament and so can modify a stormy sibling relationship only to a certain extent.

As a general rule, however, sibling relationships become less intense as children grow older. Older children report that their sibling relationships are on a more equal footing than they were previously, with a lessening of both aggression and nurturance between themselves and their siblings (Buhrmester & Furman, 1990).

In conclusion, sibling rivalry occurs, but contrary to common belief, it is not the typical way siblings interact. Sibling rivalry is not a natural or necessary aspect of every sibling relationship, and the rivalry that does exist generally diminishes with age.

depends on the tasks or behaviors demanding conformity. Older children who are certain of the position they take on an issue are less likely to be influenced by peers than are younger children. In ambiguous situations, however, when children are uncertain of their position, conformity with peers is more likely with increasing age (Hoving, Hamm, & Galvin, 1969).

ADULT VERSUS PEER INFLUENCE

The desire to interact with peers grows throughout childhood. By the age of 10 or 11 years, peer friendships are extremely important. If a child's peers exhibit values and behaviors that conflict with those espoused by the child's family, challenges to parental authority and serious family arguments may occur (Elkind, 1971). Generally, however, there is remarkable agreement between a child's peers and family members in terms of accepted values and behaviors (Douvan & Adelson, 1966; Hartup, 1970). This is probably because children are socialized first of all by their families, and they later choose playmates and friends who hold values similar to those they have been taught.

Question: In what areas are peers more likely to have a greater influence than adults?

Peers usually have a greater influence over a child's choice of friends and in situations involving challenges to authority, personal or group identity, interpersonal behavior, language fads, and clothing choices (Brittain, 1963). Peers are also more influential in shaping sexual attitudes and behaviors (Vandiver, 1972). Although adults, especially parents, are more likely to influence the child's future aspirations, academic choices, and political views, children's behaviors are usually the result of both peer and parental influence (Siman, 1977).

Parents who are warm and supportive are likely to have the greatest influence on their children. Parents who are too permissive or too punitive are usually less accessible to their children and, as a result, have less influence. When children rely on their peers excessively or acquire antisocial behaviors supported by the peer group, the reason is often disillusionment with adult wisdom, justice, or status. Children who are disillusioned with their fathers are especially susceptible to becoming highly peer oriented (Bixenstine, DeCorte, & Bixenstine, 1976).

Question: Given the strong influence that peers can have on a child's development, should parents try to exert more control over their child's choice of friends and associates?

For most parents, this is an important concern. Although much of a child's early socialization is the result of family influences, in practically every culture, peers have been found to affect strongly the development of many behaviors, ranging from aggression to cooperation and sharing (Whiting & Whiting, 1975). Parents, of course, want their children to behave in certain ways, and if parents find that their children's peers are promoting behaviors that conflict with parental values and desires, it is understandable that they may wish to control peer relationships. This is especially true when peers are modeling aggression and antisocial behaviors. There is evidence that among all the social agents in a child's life, peers are the most effective models of aggression (Cohen, 1971).

Parents face two problems when trying to control peer influence. First, as children grow older and spend less time at home, parents may find that they have less influence and that any attempts to control the child only drive the child toward a greater peer orientation. In fact, by adolescence, the average child will spend more than twice as much time with peers as with parents (Condry, Siman, & Bronfenbrenner, 1968). The second problem faced by parents who wish to control the influence of peers is that of overcontrol. Overcontrolling children by limiting their social contacts may inadvertently keep them from developing adequate social skills or the confidence to interact in groups.

LEARNING CHECK

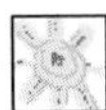

1. Many psychologists consider children to be peers, regardless of their age, if they are acting on the same behavioral level.
   a. true **b.** false
2. By the age of 7 years, the average child will spend ____________ time with peers as with adults.
   a. half as much **b.** just as much **c.** twice as much
3. Which age-group would most likely form friendships with peers of the same sex?
   a. 2- to 4-year-old children **c.** 14- to 16-year-old children
   b. 7- to 9-year-old children
4. Which of the following attitudes or values held by children are influenced more by parental opinion than by peer opinion?
   a. political views **c.** clothing choices
   b. sexual attitudes **d.** interpersonal behavior
5. Which of the following statements concerning play is true?
   a. Play is a precisely defined term.
   b. Parallel play involves more social interaction than associative play does.
   c. Play may develop according to an exploration-play-application sequence.
   d. Solitary play is a sign of maladjustment.
6. Which of the following is *not* a descriptor of play?
   a. The behavior is motivated from within.
   b. The behavior follows a pattern or sequence.
   c. The means rather than the ends are emphasized.
   d. The behavior is flexible.

Answers: 1. a 2. b 3. b 4. a 5. c 6. b

The Influence of Schools

A school serves the purpose of systematically passing on the wisdom (or prejudices) of the culture to its young. There is probably no such thing as the average school or the average student. Because of this, it is impossible to discuss *the* effect of *the* school on *the* child (Sarason & Klaber, 1985). Unquestionably, however, many attitudes, feelings, and beliefs are created, maintained, and altered by schools. Schools are a significant force, not just because they teach reading, writing, and arithmetic, but because they expose each child to new ideas, important new adult models, and greater contact with peers.

Each society also depends on its schools to produce its most important resource: the next generation of educated citizens. A decade ago, however, the National Commission on Excellence in Education reported that the United States had become a "nation at risk." Supporting its claim, the commission noted that 23 million Americans were functionally illiterate, including 13 percent of all 17-year-olds and 40 percent of minority youth, that average high school test scores had been dropping steadily over the previous 26 years, that half of gifted students failed to match their abilities in school, and that almost 40 percent of high school seniors could not draw inferences from written material, 80 percent could not write a persuasive essay, and 67 percent could not solve math problems requiring more than a few steps (Gardner, 1983).

Following that report, a growing awareness developed that something had to be done to improve American education. The government and its citizens became more interested in the effect of schooling on the development of children and demanded to know why some schools turned out well-educated, motivated children, while other schools were, for all intents and purposes, failing in this important task.

Question: Are schools really that different from one another?

All investigations in this area agree that huge differences exist among schools, and not just in the United States (Rutter, 1983). For instance, in studies conducted in Great Britain, the great range in schools was obvious. In one school, 50 percent of the pupils went on to college; in another, fewer than 9 percent did so. Delinquency rates varied from 1 percent to 19 percent, and absenteeism ranged from 6 percent to 26 percent (Power, Alderson, Phillipson, Schoenberg, & Morris, 1967; Reynolds, Jones, & St Leger, 1976; Rutter, Maughan, Mortimore, Ouston, & Smith, 1979). The range among American schools was even greater.

Question: Wouldn't these differences be because of the neighborhoods the schools serve rather than the schools themselves?

Not necessarily. Researchers have studied many pairs of schools that differ greatly in their delinquency, attendance, and college acceptance rates but that serve similar student populations in terms of intellectual characteristics and socioeconomic status (Finlayson & Loughran, 1976; Reynolds & Murgatroyd, 1977). Furthermore, a number of schools have been found consistently to turn out students who attain high levels of scholastic achievement despite the fact that these students come from inner-city neighborhoods generally associated with low achievement (Weber, 1971). All these findings indicate that different schools may provide their students with very different educations despite the neighborhood from which the students come. Schools that show superior student achievement, whether the students come from poor neighborhoods or affluent ones, tend to maintain these high standards of excellence year after year. Schools with poor performance records, regardless of neighborhood, also tend to be consistent (Rutter, 1983).

Question: What makes a successful school successful?

Successful schools generally have an academic emphasis. Academic goals are clearly stated, there's a certain degree of structure, and there are high achievement

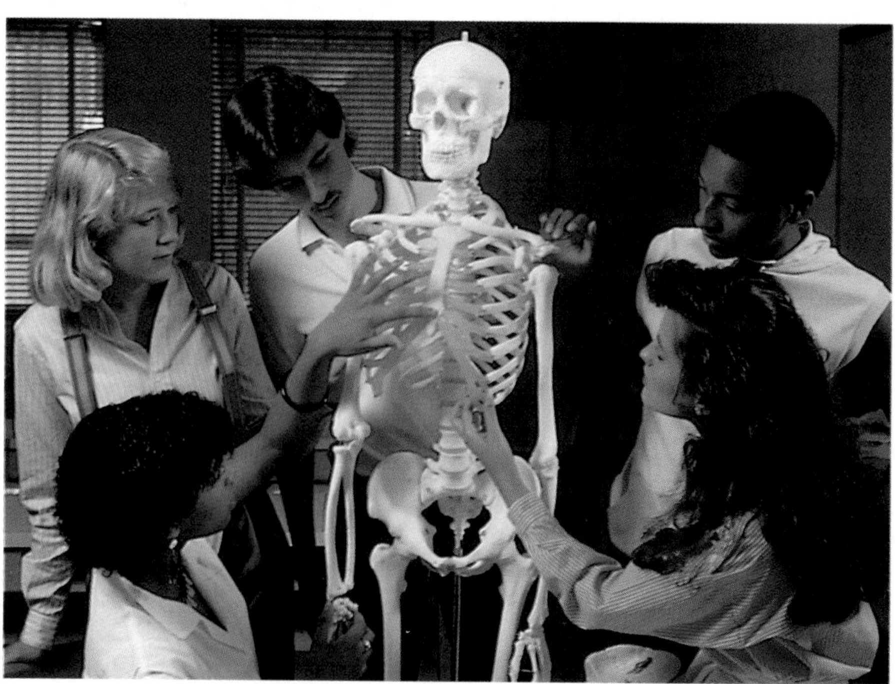

A number of schools have been found consistently to turn out students who attain high levels of scholastic achievement even though these students come from inner-city neighborhoods that are generally associated with low achievement.

expectations (Linney & Seidman, 1989). Effective schools are also characterized by regularly assigned and graded homework (Bales, 1986) and by a high proportion of time devoted to active teaching, instead of to miscellaneous activities such as calling the roll, handing out papers, setting up equipment, and disciplining students. Effective schools also have a system of checks to make certain that teachers are following the intended practices of the school. This is especially important for inexperienced teachers, who tend to be the most inefficient in classroom management (Rutter, Maughan, Mortimore, Ouston, & Smith, 1979).

Question: But don't other things, such as the age of the school or the size of classrooms, affect student achievement?

Although these things are commonly thought to matter, the age of the building and the physical size of the classrooms actually don't seem to make much difference (Rutter, Maughan, Mortimore, Ouston, & Smith, 1979). This, of course, assumes that reasonable minimal standards are met, that facilities are not completely dilapidated, and that the school has funds for rudimentary equipment.

Question: What about the number of students per class?

In a college lecture situation, the size of the class doesn't seem to matter much either (Rutter, 1983). Very large classes can be highly successful. In special classes, however, such as in a laboratory or tutorial, when it is often necessary for students to interact directly with the teacher, smaller class sizes do help (Garbarino, 1980). Overall, large classes, in contrast to small classes, generally are associated with *higher* achievement, but this is probably because popular high-quality schools tend to have larger classes rather than because of the size of the classes themselves. As a general rule, in grade schools the fewer the number of students per teacher, the better the results.

THE TEACHER

Another very important factor in school success may be the presence of just a handful of excellent and dedicated teachers. In one study (Pedersen, Faucher, & Eaton, 1978), researchers found that the children in a particular elementary school who had achieved the highest grades and who later demonstrated superior status as adults all had one thing in common—the same first-grade teacher!

Just a handful of dedicated teachers may make the difference between successful and unsuccessful schools.

Question: How could a particular first-grade teacher have an effect on children that would last into adulthood?

The simple academic material that the teacher presented obviously would have little effect on the children once they had become adults. However, it has been shown that when children first enter school, their attitudes toward learning and the desire to achieve will undergo a major revision. As they come to know their school and teacher, they will begin to realize what is expected of them (Alexander & Entwisle, 1988). For these reasons, the first teacher or two do have a unique responsibility to help students set their sights on goals and to instill confidence in the student, both for the current year and for the future. Here, the teacher may make a lasting contribution. Think of the few teachers you've had in your life whom you greatly admired and respected. They taught you more than just the academic material. They taught you to do your best, to have confidence in yourself, to set high standards, and then to attain them. Or, perhaps most important, they made you want to stay in school and continue to learn.

Question: Is it the teacher's personality that makes the difference, or is it what the teacher does in class?

Most of the research indicates that it is what the teacher does in the classroom—that is, how and what he or she teaches—rather than personality that makes the difference (Linney & Seidman, 1989). Perhaps such teachers, more than anything else, determine whether a school will be successful.

SCHOOL AND SOCIAL CLASS

Question: Are children from low socioeconomic classes at a disadvantage in school?

Children from low socioeconomic classes have severe disadvantages. Before such children ever enter school, they often have become victims of poverty and are suffering from poor health or inadequate family care, which has a direct adverse effect on their academic performance, which in turn makes it more likely that they will drop out of school (Cairns, Cairns, & Neckerman, 1989). Many economically disadvantaged children do not receive sufficient food, sleep, or stimulation (see Figure 14.3). The extent of this problem is highlighted by the discovery that one way to improve the grades of impoverished children by as much as 2 to 6 percent is simply to provide them with a nutritious breakfast once they arrive at school (Meyers, Sampson, Weitzman, Rogers, & Kayne, 1989).

Another problem associated with poverty is that while some disadvantaged families are supportive of high academic achievement and good grades (Greenberg & Davidson, 1972), many belittle their children's efforts toward scholastic success and encourage early employment as a more responsible choice. In addition, many schools in lower-class neighborhoods are so pressed for funds that school activities and school-supported programs must be cut back or eliminated. Such schools also have problems attracting the best teachers because of the crowded conditions and the high incidence of violence. In almost every lower-class neighborhood, schools spend more to repair the damage done by vandals than to buy textbooks. Teachers in these schools often expend a disproportionate amount of time on custodial and disciplinary tasks at the expense of teaching. Given these factors, it is not surprising to find substantial differences in academic achievement among children of different socioeconomic backgrounds. Greater national attention is required to solve this problem. Although it will be expensive, the costs of doing nothing are much greater. Ignorance is always more costly than education.

PARENTS

Most researchers believe that although the teacher is an extremely important influence on the child's educational development, parents are even more important. Parents set and model academic standards for their children. They are a source of encouragement or discouragement. In fact, one study has found evidence that

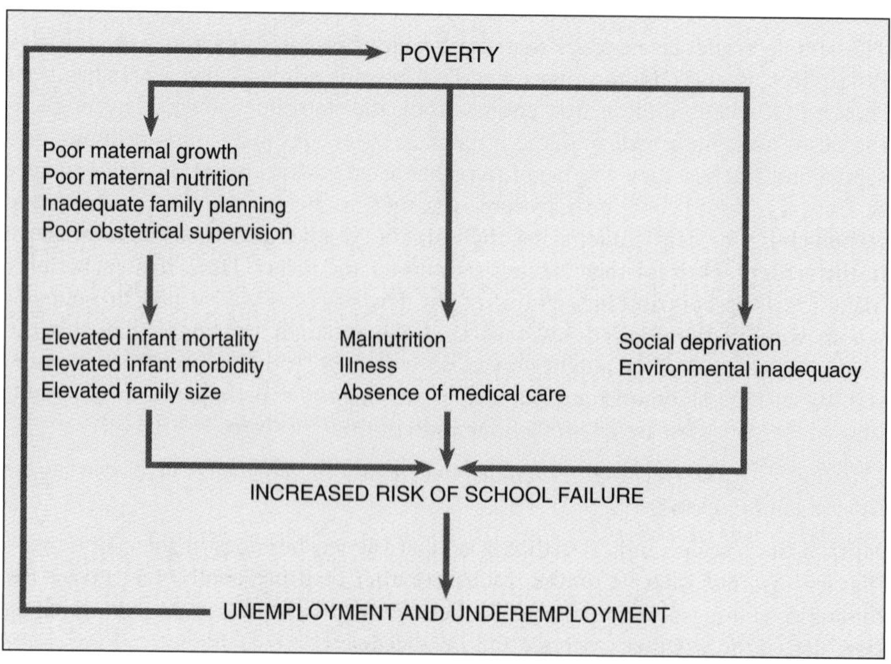

FIGURE 14.3
Children from low socioeconomic classes face a vicious cycle of poverty that can have a devastating effect on their school performance. (*Source:* Birch & Gussow, 1970, p. 268)

Unsuccessful schools generally fail to maintain high achievement expectations for their students or to state academic goals clearly.

a parent's appraisal of his child's ability has an even greater effect on determining the child's self-appraisal than does feedback from actual schoolwork (Phillips, 1987). Parents also enforce, or fail to enforce, school attendance, completion of homework, and respect for the educational system. Furthermore, when parents take an active interest in their children's daily activities at school and keep abreast of their children's academic performance, their children are more apt to receive better grades and have less conduct problems than are other children (Crouter, MacDermid, McHale, & Perry-Jenkins, 1990). When intelligent, caring parents are combined with a good school, the combination is likely to produce results. As a demonstration of this, consider an interesting study conducted in Paris in which children from disadvantaged backgrounds were placed for adoption and raised in well-to-do families. These children's school performance over many years was found to be significantly superior to similar children who were not adopted and who were raised in the poorer neighborhood and went to poorer schools (Duyme, 1988). This study also helps to deemphasize the idea that genetic differences may be the prime factor in the failure of disadvantaged students, because different environments were all that accounted for the differences in the French children's academic development.

The Influence of Television

> To put the matter most boldly: Children, at least those in the United States, are growing up in an environment in which babies and toddlers must not only process the shapes, contours, and objects of their own rooms or decode and imitate the sounds and gestures of the adults or siblings around them; they must also relate to a small box on which figures leap, dance, laugh, scream, destroy each other, and urge purchases of food and toys. (Singer, 1983, p. 815)
>
> By the time American children are 18 years old, they have spent more time watching television than in any other activity than sleep. Moreover, their experiences with television begin long before exposure to school or, in many cases, any socialization agent other than the family. (Huston, Wright, Rice, Kerkman, & St. Peters, 1990, p. 409)

Question: What do children learn from television, and how does it affect them?

No one has the full answer to that question. The effect must be considerable, however, because by the time the average person is 18 years old, she has logged 3 hours watching television for every 2 hours spent in school! American children between the ages of 5 and 13 years have been found to spend more time watching television than they spend participating in any other waking activity (Huston & Wright, 1982; Liebert & Sprafkin, 1988). And even children as young as 3 or 4 spend about 2 to 4 hours a day watching television (Huston, Wright, Rice, Kerkman, & St. Peters, 1990). Parents also report having lost some control over their children's viewing habits, and this is confirmed by research showing that the average child views television 6½ hours a week more than his parents wish him to (Sarlo, Jason, & Lonak, 1988). Television is so wide ranging in its content that it probably has both detrimental and beneficial effects on children (Liebert & Sprafkin, 1988; Singer & Singer, 1983a).

Television has changed the way we live and has influenced family life. Just having a television set in the house affects family interaction patterns. Although families spend time together watching television, they spend less time than they used to directly engaging in activities with one another. Some have joked that you can spot a television-oriented family because none of the conversations among family members ever lasts longer than the average commercial. As never before, children can isolate themselves for hours in front of the tube.

Question: Before TV was invented, couldn't children have done the same thing with books?

True. But whereas books excluded preschoolers and infants, television doesn't. To the dismay of some people, television is far more popular than books ever were. Television competes for the role of socializing agent with parents, school, and peers. Children spend a huge amount of their time in front of the TV. For instance, approximately 25 percent of all sixth to tenth graders surveyed were found to be viewing at least 5½ hours of television on any given school day (Lyle & Hoffman, 1972). Moreover, as many as 25 percent of sixth graders sampled were still watching television at 11:30 P.M. Such high percentages may indicate that these children are being socialized by television at the expense of family or school. In fact, one-third of parents surveyed more than three decades ago stated that one of television's major uses is as a baby-sitter (Steiner, 1963). Twenty years following this survey, parents still stated that one of television's major advantages is that it keeps the kids occupied—it is a baby-sitter (Singer & Singer, 1983a).

Question: What about programs such as "Sesame Street"? Aren't they good for children to see?

The idea behind "Sesame Street" was to give preschool children the basic knowledge and cognitive skills they would need in elementary school. Unfortunately, "Sesame Street" has not had as great an effect as originally hoped, although children can benefit from watching it, especially in areas such as vocabulary development (Rice, Huston, Truglio, & Wright, 1990). "Sesame Street" has also spawned some interesting criticism.

Question: What kind of criticism could "Sesame Street" merit?

The show borrowed its format of rapid pace and fast action from the late-1960s show "Laugh-In." Some researchers have voiced concern that the rapid action and high level of entertainment found on "Sesame Street" may predispose children to expect all learning experiences to be rapid and entertaining. It has been suggested, therefore, that children used to "Sesame Street" may develop a short attention span, one that is long enough only to follow rapid changes. "Sesame Street," then, may be doing a disservice by preparing children for a different kind of learning than they will later be required to experience (Lesser, 1977; Singer & Singer, 1983b). It is difficult to prove this assertion, however, because other variables that might account for shorter attention span in children who watch the show cannot be controlled. In fairness, "Sesame Street" has been shown to be a good medium for teaching children academic material (Rice, Huston, Truglio, & Wright, 1990).

On the other hand, "Mr. Rogers' Neighborhood," another PBS children's program, and "Here's Humphrey," a similar television program in Australia, were shown to increase interpersonal prosocial behaviors in preschoolers, although the effect was short-lived (Friedrich & Stein, 1973; Stein & Friedrich, 1972; Singer & Singer, 1976; Tower, Singer, Singer, & Biggs, 1979).

Most important, however, is the finding that such children's programs are most effective in teaching preschoolers if parents or teachers interact with children as they watch the programs (Friedrich, Stein, & Sussman, 1975; Singer & Singer, 1974). If an adult calls a child's attention to the significant features of a program and discusses some of the content, the child is much more likely to benefit. This finding fits well with Gibson's theory of distinctive features (see Chapter 10), inasmuch as it may well be necessary for an adult to help a less experienced child discriminate the important points in a program. Perhaps such active participation—discussing as often as possible the various aspects of the program and helping the children interpret and understand the important information (Rubinstein, 1983)—would be the best way for parents to handle their children's exposure to television.

Unfortunately, research shows that parents don't usually watch television with their children and that there isn't very much parental control or supervision over what the children watch (St. Peters, Fitch, Huston, Wright, & Eakins, 1991).

Question: If we combine the findings of all the research conducted over the past 40 years, what can we say about the effects of television on children?

Perhaps it's best to summarize those data by placing them into two categories: influences that are well documented and influences we suspect to be occurring.

Documented Influences

Heavy viewing of violent programs has been associated consistently with aggression in both children and adults (Liebert & Sprafkin, 1988; Pearl, Bouthilet, & Lazar, 1982; Rubinstein, 1983). In general, *heavy* television viewing is associated with poor school achievement (Rubinstein, 1983). Heavy viewing is also associated with poorer reading comprehension (Singer & Singer, 1983a). Interestingly, for children of lower socioeconomic status, heavy TV viewing has been associated with *higher* reading comprehension and *higher* scholastic achievement. Television viewing, therefore, appears to have a leveling effect, often raising the abilities of disadvantaged children while lowering the abilities of children with higher socioeconomic status (Gerbner, Gross, Morgan, & Signorielli, 1980; Morgan & Gross, 1982). Heavy television viewing is associated with poorer language usage (Singer & Singer, 1983b) and appears to inhibit the development of imagination.

Question: How might television viewing inhibit development of imagination?

Children who are heavy viewers of television do not need to engage in as much self-generated imaginative thinking, because the television provides fantasies. Instead of making up stories and imaginative encounters, children who are heavy watchers often reenact by rote the stories they have seen. It thus appears that imagination is somewhat dampened by heavy television viewing (Singer, 1982).

Television also influences children's concepts of sex role stereotypes. Children who watch more television tend to view the male and female roles in a more stereotypical fashion (Williams, 1986), although the more recent trend toward showing female TV characters in traditional male roles (lawyer, police officer, private detective) has increased girls' interest in these professions as acceptable careers for females (Wroblewski & Huston, 1987).

Television also shapes what is called "world knowledge": By being exposed to television, children form attitudes and beliefs about their world. This is a good thing only insofar as TV reflects reality. To the extent that it doesn't, this exposure can cause problems. For example, children who are heavy viewers of television, especially of graphic action shows, such as police dramas, tend to view the world as a mean and scary place and as more dangerous than it really is (Rubinstein, 1983). Television instills a certain paranoia in these children and may tend to make them more fearful and less trusting of others.

Question: How do you know that these data indicate a cause-and-effect relationship and not just something peculiar about heavy television viewers?

There have been many controlled experiments conducted over the years that support the findings that have been discussed. And there are other ways to approach the problem. One of the most interesting cases studied was a small town in Canada in 1973 that had no television. This town was not particularly isolated, but it was in a geographical "blind spot" where microwave transmissions and cable simply couldn't reach. In all other aspects, it was a normal North American community. For the sake of anonymity, let's call the town Notel.

In 1973, it was finally possible to bring television to Notel. This provided an opportunity for researchers to enter the town, make observations, take naturalistic data, and compare their findings with data collected from the same people after two years of television viewing. The scientists found that television generally affected the viewers in a negative way.

Question: In what ways was the effect of television on this population "negative"?

One way was through displacement: When you're watching television, you can't be doing something else. The number of hours people spent participating in outdoor activities, community events, and sporting games decreased. After two years of watching television, children were found, relative to their age-mates, to have poorer reading skills and to score lower on tests of creative thinking. Aggressive behavior increased, and sex stereotyping became more extreme, as girls and boys became more strongly sex typed (Williams, 1986).

SUSPECTED INFLUENCES

Young children don't watch television in the same way that older children or adults do. They simply are unable to attend to an entire plot line or story with full comprehension (Anderson, Lorch, Field, Collins, & Nathan, 1986). This has led researchers to suspect that TV producers who argue that violence is all right as long as justice and morality triumph in the end are overlooking the fact that younger children may see the violence but miss the just or moral conclusion. It is also suspected that exposing children to greater amounts of television violence may lead them to behave apathetically when they observe real violence (Rubinstein, 1983).

Television may also be sending subtle messages about health practices. On the good side, it must be said that very little smoking occurs on programs today. TV characters, however, are far more likely to consume alcohol than to gulp down soft drinks. Furthermore, very few TV characters buckle up their seat belts while driving, and many of them exceed speed limits and drive recklessly. It is suspected that modeling these behaviors may influence children (Rubinstein, 1983).

Question: Doesn't television viewing have its good side?

Television may be providing a great deal of *good* information and exposure for children. For the first time, children, no matter how rural or distant from major centers their homes are, are growing up with exposure to events on the entire planet. Television may thus broaden the horizons and stimulate the curiosity of millions of children who would not otherwise have known what the world might hold for them.

Studies have also shown that children can acquire good nutritional habits from television programs designed to teach such habits (Campbell, 1982) and that children can learn to help others or to give to charities from watching such behavior modeled on TV. They can also learn to cooperate, to share, and to be imaginative under certain conditions, all from being exposed to particular TV shows (Pearl, Bouthilet, & Lazar, 1982). Appropriate television programming can enhance friendliness and generosity. It can help children learn to delay gratification as well as to overcome fears of strange and unusual situations (Rubinstein, 1983). So, TV certainly has its "good side."

In fact, it's still not that easy to say exactly which is television's good or bad side. In a very intensive review of the effects of television on children (Anderson, 1989), a number of surprises were uncovered showing that we still have much to learn.

Question: What sort of surprises?

Although school-age children might spend many hours in front of the television, careful observation shows that they only spend about two-thirds of that time actually watching. The rest of the time is devoted to other activities. During these times, children often monitor the television, waiting for something that might catch their interest, which in itself might be a cognitively enriching activity in that it requires a certain amount of attention and information processing.

Television also doesn't seem to interfere that much with homework. It seems that children who do their homework get it done in spite of the presence of a television set in the house, while those who don't do their homework tend not to do it anyway, even if the television is turned off.

Question: Considering what we do know about the effects of television, how can I help put it to good use?

The best way is to cast your consumer vote by watching programs you deem appropriate and by purchasing the products associated with those programs. Sending letters to the networks describing the kinds of programming you prefer can also be helpful. Also important is to select the programs that you and your family watch with some care as to content. Of course, you can't keep children away from every show you don't want them to see, and perhaps you don't need to as long as you take the time to discuss in detail what the children have seen and what it means in terms of the real world. Let them know what is pretend and what isn't, what is really acceptable and what isn't. Let them benefit from your experience.

LEARNING CHECK

Matching

1. ____ The successful school often
2. ____ A "nation at risk" refers to
3. ____ "Sesame Street"
4. ____ "Mr. Rogers' Neighborhood" and "Here's Humphrey"
5. ____ Heavy viewing of violent television programs
6. ____ Notel's getting television

a. helped increase interpersonal prosocial behaviors in preschoolers.

b. increased violent behavior among watchers.

c. was related to poorer reading skills in children and more extreme sex stereotyping.

d. has not had a significant effect on disadvantaged preschoolers.

e. has good and dedicated teachers.

f. American students' having low levels of achievement.

Answers: 1. e 2. f 3. d 4. a 5. b 6. b or c

APPLICATIONS

"All That Glitters . . ."

The average American 19-year-old has spent more total time just watching TV commercials than a full-time employee spends on the job during an entire year! Commercial TV is very much part of our environment.

Adults tend to assume, falsely or not, that they are in control of their behavior and that TV commercials don't have much effect unless the adults allow them to. Because of this belief, most of the concern about commercial television has focused on children's television, or "kidvid," as it is known in the advertising industry. The majority of kidvid ads are for toys, cereals, and candy and other food snacks. On a typical Saturday morning, for instance, 40 percent of commercials advertise sugar-laden breakfast foods. One ad executive was quoted in *Advertising Age* as stating, "If you truly want big sales you will use the child as your assistant salesman. He sells, he nags, until he breaks down the sales resistance of his mother or father" (Packard, 1977, p. 134).

Congress, spurred by powerful lobbying organizations such as Action for Children's Television, has been investigating how commercial television attempts to alter children's emotions or attitudes toward a particular product.

Question: How do advertisers get children to want their products?

The process relies heavily on the principles of associative learning (see Chapter 7). For example, associations are made between a product and a favored cartoon character: Fred Flintstone says, about a sugared breakfast food, "CoCo Pebbles are CoCo-moko good." Associations are also made between a child's use of a product and a resulting gleeful hysteria (called "super-joy" in the ad trade) exhibited by the actors portraying parents. And toys may be associated with exciting music and interesting animations that often are hard for a child to replicate in the home (Greer, Potts, Wright, & Huston, 1982). Another advertising technique, begun in the 1980s and disturbing to many parents, is to create children's programs that are, in essence, advertisements. This is done by making available for sale toy versions of the cartoon characters and the objects used on the program.

Advertisers spend hundreds of millions of dollars every year in an effort to get children to want certain products.

These are but a few examples. Keep in mind that advertisers spend about $500 million per year systematically working to shape the attitudes of preschoolers. Judging by the sale of sugared snacks and foods, as well as the volume of the toy market, such campaigns are successful.

Furthermore, children, especially those younger than 5 years, can be terribly misled by TV advertisements. They simply do not process what they see in the same way as you or I might.

Question: What is it about TV commercials that children don't understand?

Generally, children younger than 5 years often fail to make the distinction between what may *appear* to be real and what is *actually* real. In other words, they don't know that what you see is not always what you get (Flavell, 1986).

Question: In what ways do children fail to understand the distinction between appearance and reality?

For many years, John Flavell and his colleagues at Stanford University have been experimenting with children's understanding of what is real and what is not. Often, Flavell will give the child a brief lesson in the appearance-reality distinction by introducing the child to a Charlie Brown puppet inside of a ghost costume. Flavell will explain that although Charlie Brown "looks like a ghost to your eyes right now," the puppet is "really and truly Charlie Brown," which means that "sometimes things look like one thing to your eyes when they are really and truly something else" (Flavell, 1986, pp. 39, 42). After this lesson, the child may be shown an object that looks like a rock; however, when it is picked up and felt, it is obviously a sponge! Or the child may first be shown a red car, then shown the red car again through a blue filter, which makes the car appear black. After these experiences, most 6-year-old children will realize that the rock is really a sponge and that the red car is still red even though it's been covered by a blue filter. Children 3 or 4 years old, on the other hand, will typically argue that the sponge is a

APPLICATIONS

FIGURE 14.4
Illustration of the manipulation of protagonist's appearance and behavior. (*Source:* Hoffner & Cantor, 1985, p. 1067)

rock when it's not being felt and that the car seen through the filter is really and truly black. Even in simpler tests, 3- and 4-year-old children often show a surprising inability to realize that looks can be deceiving.

These younger children also rely very strongly on appearances to decide about the goodness of something they've seen. In one experiment, children were presented with two versions of a story. One group was given the "kind" version, in which a woman picks up a cat gently and pets it, then adds that she wishes people, too, would visit her. Then she feeds the cat some cream. In the "cruel" version, the woman grabs the cat by the neck, shouts at it, and adds that she's glad that people are smart enough to stay away from her home. Then she threatens to starve the cat and throws it down the basement stairs. At the end of the story, the researcher tells the children that at this point the woman has noticed that there are children hiding under her table who do not belong in her home. The question then is, "What will happen next?" Will the children be asked to stay and have milk and cookies, or will the woman grab them and throw them into a closet (Hoffner & Cantor, 1985)? As a further manipulation, the children are shown two versions of the woman in the kind story and two versions of the woman in the cruel story. In one version the woman is middle-aged and plump; in the other, she is old and witchlike (see Figure 14.4). The researchers referred to the two portrayals as "attractive" and "unattractive."

Children aged 3 to 5 years generally agreed that the attractive woman would ask them to stay and have milk and cookies, while the unattractive woman would throw them into a closet, *regardless* of how the woman had treated the cat. Children aged 6 to 10 years, on the other hand, disregarded the woman's looks and considered only her behavior (Hoffner & Cantor, 1985). Once again, we have evidence that children under 5 years rely strongly on appearance to determine what is good or desirable.

Question: What does this say about children and television commercials?

The failure of young children to make appearance-reality distinctions, as well as their reliance on liking whatever looks attractive, makes the job of advertisers that much easier. It is easy to sucker young children into believing, through super-joy or glitz,

APPLICATIONS

that their parents will love them more or that they will be much happier if they have a certain toy or breakfast food.

Question: What's wrong with children's wanting candy and toys?

Every child likes an occasional sweet, and a childhood without toys does sound bleak. However, when children become powerfully indoctrinated and their daily caloric intake comes to consist overwhelmingly of sugar, the results may be an increased incidence of tooth decay and poor nutrition. In fact, this is what appears to be happening throughout the United States.

Although toys are not inherently bad, children often are led by commercial advertisers to believe that they must possess certain toys because of the great benefit they'll derive from owning them. Some parents testify to the frustration of seeing their child receive an abundance of Christmas presents and then finding that the child feels hurt and abandoned because he did not receive Moe, the Flying Bald Giant from Mars.

Question: What can be done to lessen the indoctrination of young children?

It has been argued that commercials should be banned from all children's television. Such legislation has been before Congress on and off for the last two decades, but has yet to be enacted. In the end, it is the public who must decide what will or will not be allowed on television. Perhaps knowing how susceptible children are to the manipulation of advertisers—how younger children are unable to tell the difference between glitter and gold—will help us to decide.

SUMMARY

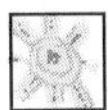

■ During the first year of life, there are certain age-related trends in peer interaction that are common to most infants. Infants at 3 months are slightly aware of each other; at 6 months, they look at, smile at, and reach toward other infants; by 1 year, they engage in more complex social interaction.

■ Between the ages of 1 and 2 years, children's social skills and peer interactions remain at a rudimentary level, but the amount and complexity are greater than during infancy. Some people have argued that peer relationships during the first 2 years pass through the object-centered stage, the simple interactive stage, and the complementary interactive stage.

■ Cognitive changes during the second year also play an important role in social interaction. Once a child has self-awareness, the child is more likely to understand the concept of "mine" and is therefore more likely to become possessive with toys.

■ By the age of 3 or 4 years, most children overcome their reluctance to join fully other children in play, and they begin to form friendships. Children are more likely to form friendships if they are able to successfully exchange information, manage conflicts, and establish a common-ground activity.

■ One of the most obvious occurrences during the preschool years is the development of play. Play can be simple and unstructured, or it can be complex and structured.

■ It has been suggested that there are five descriptors of play; the greater the number of descriptors that can be applied in any given situation, the more likely people are to call those circumstances play. The descriptors are (1) intrinsic motivation, (2) positive affect, (3) nonlaterality, (4) means/ends, and (5) flexibility.

■ Social scientists generally believe that play has evolved because it has a function. Some researchers have argued that there is an exploration-play-application sequence found in humans and some advanced animals.

■ Parten observed six distinct kinds of behavior in the play situation. They were unoccupied behavior, solitary play, onlooker play, parallel play, associative play, and cooperative play. Older children spent more time playing socially; younger children were more likely to engage in parallel or solitary play.

■ Once children have acquired the concept of object permanence, at about the age of 2 years, the stage is set for them to begin to engage in fantasy play.

■ The trend from nonsocial reality play to a more social fantasy play appears to be universal, but the kinds of play that children engage in can be quite different from culture to culture.

■ Between the ages of 7 and 9 years, children generally form close friendships with peers of the same sex. During this time, children begin to rely on their friends to provide important information and standards of behavior.

■ For the school-age child, peer relationships both in and out of school become extremely important. Being accepted by one's peers and belonging to peer groups become major concerns.

■ Many factors affect whether an individual is accepted by her peer group. Children are more likely to be accepted if they are attractive and successful and have high status according to group standards. Later on, a child's character often emerges as the most important attribute in determining continued acceptance.

■ In many ways, interactions among siblings can be much like interactions among peers. These similarities are especially evident among siblings who are close in age.

■ Peer groups are not just groups of same-aged children. Peer groups develop their own sets of values and goals, and they establish durable social relationships. As a rule, each group member has a certain role or status.

■ Parents who are warm and supportive are most likely to have the greatest influence on their children's choice of peers. Parents who are too permissive or too punitive usually are less accessible to their children and as a result have less influence.

■ A school serves to pass on systematically the wisdom (or prejudices) of the culture to its young. Schools are a significant force because they expose each child to new information, important new adult models, and increased contact with peers.

■ Huge differences exist among schools. The presence of just a handful of excellent and dedicated teachers may be a very important factor in successful schools.

■ Television has changed the way we live and has influenced family life. There is evidence that children may be considerably influenced by television.

■ Heavy viewing of violent programs has been associated consistently with increased aggression in both children and adults. Heavy viewing is also associated with poor school achievement and with poor reading comprehension. But television's effects are not always negative. Studies have shown that children can acquire good nutritional habits and can learn to help others by watching television.

■ Children, especially those younger than 6 years, can be terribly misled by TV advertisements. They fail to make the distinction between what may *appear* to be real and what is *actually* real.

QUESTIONS FOR DISCUSSION

1. Which of your peers influenced you most during your childhood? How do you think you may have affected them?
2. Were you ever placed in conflict between the desires of your parents and those of your friends? Who had the most influence? Why?
3. Do you think that television commercials should be banned from children's television? Why or why not?
4. The efforts of commercial television to get children to like broccoli or other such vegetables haven't been too successful. What does this indicate about the limits of the power of advertising?
5. Can you recall one or two teachers who had an important effect on your life? What qualities made them special?

SUGGESTIONS FOR FURTHER READING

1. Adams, R. S., & Biddle, B. J. (1970). *Realities of teaching.* New York: Holt.
2. Comstock, G., & Paik, H. (1991). *Television and the American child.* San Diego, CA: Academic Press.
3. Leder, J. M. (1991). *Brothers and sisters: How they shape our lives.* New York: St. Martin's Press.
4. Liebert, R. M., Sprafkin, J. N., & Davidson, E. (1982). *The early window: Effects of television on children and youth.* Elmsford, NY: Pergamon.
5. Pepler, D. J., & Rubin, K. H. (Eds.). (1982). *The play of children: Current theory and research.* New York: Karger.
6. Rubin, Z. (1980). *Children's friendship.* Cambridge, MA: Harvard University Press.
7. Smith, P. K. (1984). *Play in animals and humans.* New York: Blackwell.

CHAPTER 15

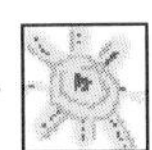

THE DEVELOPMENT OF MORALITY AND SELF-CONTROL

CHAPTER PREVIEW

"LEAD ME NOT INTO TEMPTATION"

HAVE YOU EVER tried to diet? Quit smoking? Save money? Or watch TV only after you've studied? Good luck! It isn't easy to resist immediate gratification in exchange for a long-term advantage. Some people can do it. We like to say that they have willpower.

TWO RESEARCHERS once gathered a group of kindergartners together to investigate willpower in young children. The children were asked to make some drawings. When they were finished, they were offered candy for having done such a good job. But before they took the candy, they were told that if they wanted to give up candy today and wait until tomorrow, they could have twice as much. Before the children decided which they would prefer, they were asked what they thought a "dumb kid" and a "smart kid" would do in the same situation. Most of the children said that a dumb kid would take the candy today, whereas a smart kid would wait until tomorrow and get twice as much. Yet even after making this statement, most of the children went ahead and took the candy rather than wait (Nisan & Koriat, 1977).

IT IS UNLIKELY THAT these children thought of themselves as "dumb kids." They knew the intelligent thing to do; it's just that for some reason, they couldn't bring themselves to do it. Is there any one of us who hasn't done the same thing at one time or another?

IN THIS CHAPTER, we'll investigate ways to teach children how to delay gratification and acquire self-control. We'll also look at the development of prosocial behaviors such as altruism, helping, and sharing; the development of moral values; and the control of aggression.

PROSOCIAL BEHAVIOR
Behavior that benefits other people and society.

ANTISOCIAL BEHAVIOR
Behavior that shows little or no concern for other people and little sense of right and wrong.

COOPERATION
Working together toward a common end or purpose.

RESOURCES

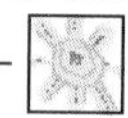

Prosocial Behavior

Prosocial behavior is the opposite of **antisocial behavior.** Prosocial behaviors benefit others and society. During our lives, we are often encouraged to be prosocial. We are asked to cooperate, to help, and to share. How children come to acquire prosocial behaviors and how these behaviors are maintained have become areas of increasing interest to developmental researchers.

COOPERATION

When two or more people work together for their mutual benefit, they are cooperating. **Cooperation** is a prosocial behavior, because societies would not be possible without cooperative efforts. Researchers showed little interest in cooperation until Azrin and Lindsley demonstrated in their classic study that direct reinforcement could increase cooperation among children (Azrin & Lindsley, 1956).

Question: As children grow older, don't they usually learn on their own to be cooperative?

Children often are spontaneously cooperative. In our society, however, and in others, individual competition often is reinforced. This is especially true for boys. In fact, by the time they reach high school, boys show strong positive correlations between competitiveness and a sense of self-worth and almost no correlation between cooperativeness and a sense of self-worth (Ahlgren, 1983). Sometimes, the desire for competition can be so intense that it interferes with the need for cooperation. Such irrational competition can spoil the success that cooperation might bring.

Question: Would you give an example of what you mean?

M. C. Madsen and his associates conducted an experiment that clearly depicts this problem. They discovered that in certain cases, cooperation *declines* as children grow older and that competition may become the most common mode of responding, even when it cannot possibly lead to success.

In his experiment, Madsen had children of the same age sit across from each other at opposite ends of a small table (see Figure 15.1). Narrow gutters ran down the length of the table on both sides. The table surface was arched so that a marble placed anywhere on the table would roll immediately into the nearest gutter. Embedded in the tabletop in front of each child was a cup. To start the game, a marble was placed into a free-sliding marble holder in the center of the table. The marble holder prevented the marble from running into a gutter. Each child had a string attached to one end of the marble holder. For a child to score, he need only pull his string and cause the marble holder to pass over his cup. The marble would then drop into the cup, and he would have succeeded. However, if both children pulled their strings simultaneously, the marble holder would come apart, and the marble would roll into the gutter.

Question: What did Madsen discover when he had children play the game?

Madsen found that cooperation was common among 4- and 5-year-old children. During the first 10 trials, the children usually would negotiate and arrange that each received about half of the marbles. However, when Madsen tested school children in the second through fifth grades, he found their desire to compete to be so strong that a majority of them failed to obtain a single marble (Madsen,

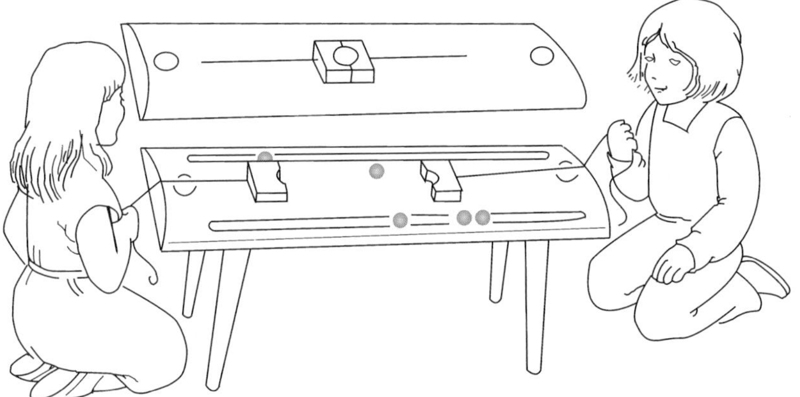

Figure 15.1
Marble-pulling apparatus used by Madsen and his colleagues to measure the extent of cooperation and competition among children. (Adapted from Madsen, 1971)

1971). In a later study, some of the children were so competitive that they argued that it was impossible to get a marble! One child pointed out that success might be possible "if I could play alone" (Kagan & Madsen, 1971, p. 38). Other studies have also supported the fact that older children tend to be more competitive (Herndon & Carpenter, 1982).

Question: Why are older children so much more competitive?

The answer appears to be in the child's experience and learning. Cross-cultural research supports this supposition. When Madsen examined children from different backgrounds, he obtained different results. His data indicate that a strong competitive outlook is more likely to develop among older children in urban surroundings. For instance, it was observed that city-dwelling Israeli children were more competitive than were Israeli children raised on a kibbutz (Madsen, 1971; Shapira & Madsen, 1974). American children were generally most competitive, regardless of their race, sex, or background, perhaps because competition is so emphasized in American society (Madsen & Shapira, 1970; Nelson & Madsen, 1969). And more recently it has been shown that children reared in family environments in which competition is emphasized tend to be more competitive (Monsaas & Engelhard, 1990).

Question: Couldn't it just be that urban children and older children tend to be more familiar with these kinds of games and that they know that such games usually require competitive strategies?

In 1981, M. C. Madsen took his game to Papua, New Guinea, where he used it to test two different groups of children. One group of children belonged to an intact rural tribe, whereas the other group lived in a more heterogeneous urban setting. Neither group was particularly familiar with similar games of any kind. The results were in keeping with Madsen's earlier studies in that the children from the rural tribe demonstrated more cooperation, whereas those from the urban setting were more competitive (Madsen & Lancy, 1981).

Question: What is the best way to teach children to cooperate?

A number of things can be done to teach children the value of cooperation. Spencer Kagan has suggested that creating a "we" rather than an "I" atmosphere can make it easier for children to conceive of themselves working with rather than against other children (Kagan & Madsen, 1971). Mexican American children, more than Anglo-American children, perceive their parents as expressing this kind of "we" attitude in the home (Knight, Kagan, & Buriel, 1982). This may help explain why Mexican American children are generally more cooperative, whereas Anglo-American children tend to be more competitive (Knight, Kagan, & Buriel, 1981, 1982).

Two factors are important in helping. This child shows both—she has the skill to help effectively, and she has empathy for her friend who needs help.

EMPATHY
An insightful awareness and ability to share the emotions, thoughts, and behavior of another person.

Modeling cooperative behavior can also help children choose cooperation as a primary method for dealing with problems when competition wouldn't be beneficial (Liebert, Sprafkin, & Poulos, 1975). The long-term effectiveness of such modeled cooperation, however, may be age related. For instance, in one study in which cooperation was modeled for 6- and 8-year-old children, both groups of children were significantly more cooperative immediately following the modeling than the control group was. Seven weeks later, however, only the 8-year-old children maintained significantly more cooperation, whereas the effect of the observed modeling on the 6-year-old children had apparently worn off (Sagotsky, Wood-Schneider, & Konop, 1981). For the modeling of cooperation to be effective, then, it should be modeled often, especially for younger children.

Still another way of teaching children to be more cooperative is to guide them through cooperative ventures so they can see for themselves the value of working together. Through firsthand experience, as children come to appreciate how their prosocial actions can help others and how others can come to depend on their behavior, they begin to develop a greater sense of social responsibility. In turn, this growing sense of social responsibility tends to foster further prosocial behavior (O'Connor & Cuevas, 1982).

Question: But isn't competition sometimes healthy and beneficial?

Certainly there are times when competition is the most beneficial strategy. Competition becomes a problem only when it is inappropriate or when it interferes with cooperative efforts that are essential for the development of a society. The race among many nations to obtain nuclear weapons and other means of mass destruction perhaps provides the most striking example in which further competition is an inappropriate strategy and cooperation is essential, in this case for the well-being of millions of people.

HELPING

Cooperating with someone is not the same as helping that person. When people help, they provide services, skills, or information necessary to others. The most extensive studies of helping in children have been conducted by psychologist Ervin Staub.

Question: What determines whether one child will help another?

Staub's hypothesis is that two factors are important in helping. The first is to possess the skills or knowledge needed to help effectively; the second is to have **empathy** with the person in need (Staub, 1978). If this hypothesis is correct, it should be possible to foster helping in children by teaching the necessary skills and by training them to empathize.

Question: Is it generally true that grade school children, especially those in higher grades, are more likely to offer help to someone in need than younger children are?

Yes, generally this is the case (Ladd, Lange, & Stremmel, 1983; Peterson, 1983), especially if the help involves sharing or generosity (Barnett, King, & Howard, 1979).

Question: When older children give help, is it because they know they have better helping skills, or is it because they have developed greater empathy?

Research indicates, as Staub has suggested, that both are important factors (Radke-Yarrow, Zahn-Waxler, & Chapman, 1983). Let's take a moment to examine the influence of each.

Knowing How to Help Offering help to another is not an uncommon behavior among children. Even very young children willingly provide assistance. In studies conducted in a laboratory that simulated a home environment, children between 18 and 30 months of age were observed while parents and other adults performed some common household chores. The researchers noted that the children promptly and spontaneously helped the adults during most of the tasks (Rheingold, 1982). Interestingly, the offer of cooperation and helping from toddlers has been observed to increase greatly at about the time that children first become aware that there is a distinction between themselves and others (Brownell & Carriger, 1990). You may recall our discussion of the dawning of conscious awareness in the preview for Chapter 9; it would seem reasonable that once children understand that there is a difference between themselves and others that they might grasp the idea that others could possibly need something at a particular moment that they themselves didn't need—such as help.

Even young children will show a willingness to offer help. Younger children, however, are less likely than older children to know how to help.

Question: Couldn't the toddlers in these studies just have been imitating the adults without really knowing that they were "helping"?

Evidence gathered during the research indicates that the children showed more than just simple imitation. They often added appropriate behaviors that the adults had not modeled. Furthermore, they said things that indicated that they knew what the goals of the tasks were and how they were helping. For instance, the older children made such statements as, "I'm going to pick up these books" and "I'm all through with my little broom" (Rheingold, 1982, p. 119). Even the youngest children made appropriate statements while they worked, such as "Sandy sweep," "fold clothes," and "all clean" (Rheingold, 1982, p. 119). This willingness among preschoolers to help is also found in their pretend play, during which they often take on the imaginary role of someone about to render help or aid (Bar-Tal, Raviv, & Goldberg, 1982).

Question: But didn't you agree earlier that grade school children were more likely to help than preschoolers?

Grade school children are more *likely* to help than are younger children. But this doesn't seem to be because grade school children are more *willing* to help; younger children are willing. Rather, the difference seems to be because older children have greater knowledge and skills that facilitate their deciding when and how to help. Initial knowledge and skills about the requirements of helping (such as knowing your own attributes, the attributes of the one to be helped, the demands of the task, and the intervention techniques required) can be used to determine the difficulty of a task and the appropriateness of different helping strategies (Barnett, Darcie, Holland, & Kobasigawa, 1982). In other words, older children are more likely than younger children to be familiar with the circumstances in which others need help and with the methods for providing that help (Ladd, Lange, & Stremmel, 1983). Children are more likely to help when they know how and when to help (Pearl, 1985). The same is true of adults. In fact, the best way to teach helping behavior to children, especially young children between ages 2 and 7 years, is to have them role-play or act out the kinds of helping that they might be able to offer another (Staub, 1971). In this way, they come to learn how best to help and which situations require them to help.

The Development of Empathy As you may recall, Staub suggested that it takes more than skills and knowledge to motivate a child to help; a child's empathy—that is, the aroused feelings over someone else's distress—can also be a motivating factor. Telling children about the value of empathy and explaining how it would benefit another person (a technique known as induction) is likely to initiate helping behavior in children, but generally only among those who are 7 years of age or older (Howard & Barnett, 1981).

Question: If induction is more successful with older children, does this mean that empathy develops as children grow older?

It has been argued that empathy does not come into being suddenly but develops over a number of years. Researcher Martin Hoffman has observed four stages of empathy development (Hoffman, 1979) (see Figure 15.2). As you can see, each of the four stages roughly corresponds to Piaget's stages of cognitive development (see Chapter 9).

The first stage of empathy, according to Hoffman, occurs during early infancy. Babies appear to be aware if someone in their immediate vicinity is in distress (Yarrow & Waxler, 1977). However, the infant has no awareness of which particular person it may be (Sagi & Hoffman, 1976). In the second stage, or person-permanence stage, the older infant will know that someone is in distress *and* be able to locate that individual. Still, the infant or young child does not seem to understand that the person in distress has inner feelings or thoughts that may be different from his own. In the third, or role-taking, stage, the child demonstrates an increasing ability to respond to others' inner states. The fourth stage emerges in late childhood and is achieved when a child's understanding of another's emotional responses is synthesized with a "mental representation of the other person's general life experiences" (Hoffman, 1977, p. 300).

Question: What are the important differences between Hoffman's hierarchy of empathy development and Piaget's stages of cognitive development?

There are some major differences. To begin with, Hoffman's stages of empathy development, unlike Piaget's stages of cognitive development, are not qualitatively different one from another. Empathy, as a quality, may occur at any age. Accord-

FIGURE 15.2
Hoffman's hierarchy of empathy development. (*Source:* After Hoffman, 1979)

	DESCRIPTION	EXAMPLE	PIAGET'S STAGES OF COGNITIVE DEVELOPMENT
DISTRESS REACTION	Child responds to another's distress. Shows no indication of knowing which particular person is in distress.	11-month-old sees another child fall and begin to cry, looks as if she, too, is going to cry, then hides her head in her mother's lap and sucks her thumb.	Sensorimotor period (0–2): Reflex reactions.
PERSON PERMANENCE	Child knows someone is in distress and knows who that person is, but is unaware that the other person may have needs different from his own and therefore may respond inappropriately.	2-year-old sees another child fall and begin to cry, brings his own mother to comfort the other child, even though that child's mother is also present.	Preoperational period (2–7): Object permanence obtained; egocentrism common.
ROLE TAKING	Child responds appropriately to another's distress because he is able to imagine himself in the other's position.	7-year-old child comforts his friend who is sad because he lost his lunch money, and shares a sandwich with him.	Concrete operations (7–11): Egocentrism ends; conservations obtained.
COMPREHENSIVE EMPATHY	Child becomes aware of distress within the larger life experience. Empathy develops for chronic as well as acute situation.	12-year-old collects money for a charity to help alleviate the distress of those less fortunate than she.	Formal operations (11+): Able to deal with the hypothetical.

ing to Hoffman, advancing cognitive development only modifies the expression of empathy—it doesn't create it (Radke-Yarrow, Zahn-Waxler, & Chapman, 1983). Second, Hoffman argues that the more primitive forms of empathetic arousal are not replaced in the course of development. They can occur throughout life. For instance, the emotional distress reaction felt by the 11-month-old child seeing another child fall, as depicted in Figure 15.2, may also be felt by a 30-year-old adult, although the adult no doubt will continue from that initial point to a more complex empathetic reaction. Nothing similar to this is found in Piaget's stages of cognitive development. For instance, no normal and healthy 30-year-old would still show instances of a lack of object permanence, as is common in the sensorimotor stage.

A final, and perhaps major, difference concerns the amount of research supporting each theory. Piaget's theory has been with us for many years, and the descriptive research supporting it is voluminous. In contrast, Hoffman's theory of empathy development is still relatively new, and many exceptions and modifications may be forthcoming.

Question: Would you give an example of an exception to Hoffman's theory?

Hoffman argues that comprehensive empathy, during which the child becomes aware of the stress within the larger life experience, begins in late childhood or early adolescence. Some naturalistic data, however, do not support this assertion. For instance, in one study, it was noted that a 4-year-old boy, when told about the death of his friend's mother, said sadly, "You know, when Bonnie grows up people will ask her who was her mother and she will have to say 'I don't know.' You know, it makes tears come to my eyes" (Radke-Yarrow, Zahn-Waxler, & Chapman, 1983, p. 493). This statement appears to be a fairly comprehensive empathetic response. Even children as young as 2 have been observed to show empathy for others (usually their mothers) and to show some sensitivity to even unfamiliar persons (Zahn-Waxler, Radke-Yarrow, Wagner, & Chapman, 1992). Because of such findings, some researchers have argued,

> More systematic data are needed on children's empathy in real-life situations before we have a good understanding of how far empathic distress arousal extends for children at various developmental levels, how empathy is molded and moderated by cognitions, how empathy enters into prosocial behavior in later childhood and adolescence. (Radke-Yarrow, Zahn-Waxler, & Chapman, 1983, p. 493)

Empathy and Prosocial Behavior

Question: Can Hoffman's hierarchy of empathy development help explain why induction works best with children older than 7 years?

Hoffman's description of the development of empathy in childhood may help explain such findings. Hoffman's hierarchy tells us that 5-year-old children, for instance, who are in the second, or person-permanence, stage, although able to understand that another person is in distress, may not fully realize *why* that person is in distress. For this reason, to discuss with them how helping can better the distressed person's life (induction) may not be as effective as it would be with an older, third- or fourth-stage child, who has role-taking ability, the ability to take another person's perspective. With younger children, it may be best to act out helping and to teach them when helping is appropriate.

Question: How can you be sure that the reason induction works for children who are 7 years or older is their role-taking ability?

It seems reasonable that induction would work only on those children who were capable of role taking, because induction calls attention to the plight of others.

To examine this issue experimentally, researchers divided 18 middle-class 7-year-old boys and girls into two groups, depending on their ability to role-take. High role takers (those found to be most able to understand the feelings of others) were placed in one group, while those lower in role taking were placed in the other. Each child was then videotaped while teaching kindergartners how to make caterpillars with paper, glue, scissors, and crayons. Researchers observed and recorded 16 categories of prosocial behavior. High role takers were found to show greater empathy with the kindergartners struggling to make their caterpillars and were more likely to offer help than were the low role takers (Hudson, Forman, & Brion-Meisels, 1982). These results indicate that children who are high role takers, independent of age, are more likely to be sensitive to another's distress and therefore are more likely to help. As you recall from Chapter 9, such role taking is closely tied to a child's cognitive development.

Interestingly, children who are role takers are more likely to help another child in distress when there is an adult present to evaluate their behavior than when no adult is present. This appears to occur because role takers, who are able to understand the stress of another child, also can take the role of the adult who is watching and realize that the adult will be pleased if the child tries to help (Froming, Allen, & Jensen, 1985).

Question: Then will children who express the most empathy be the most likely to help?

There is some evidence that the children who express the most empathy are the most likely to offer help or cooperation (Buckley, Siegel, & Ness, 1979; Marcus, Telleen, & Roke, 1979), whereas those expressing the least empathy are most likely to be delinquent (Ellis, 1982). Surprisingly, though, most researchers have found that a child's level of empathy is often a poor predictor of prosocial behavior (Chapman, Zahn-Waxler, Cooperman, & Iannotti, 1987; Radke-Yarrow, Zahn-Waxler, & Chapman, 1983).

Question: Why doesn't a child's level of empathy always correlate well with prosocial behavior?

No one is quite certain. Part of the problem may be that different studies have sometimes used different definitions of "empathy" (Eisenberg-Berg & Lennon,

In the role-taking stage of empathy development, the child demonstrates an increasing ability to respond to others' inner states.

1980). Some definitions rely heavily on cognitive changes, others on affective changes. Only in the last decade have serious attempts been made to create a uniform definition. Another reason for the occasional failure of levels of empathy to predict prosocial behaviors may be that other variables often affect children's willingness to help. Although helping increases with the intensity of a child's empathy, children who find the observed distress too severe may focus on their own "empathetic distress" rather than on the plight of the victim (Barnett, Howard, Melton, & Dino, 1982; Hoffman, 1979). Furthermore, children often behave differently in different situations. For example, children respond "more empathetically to others of the same race or sex and . . . to others perceived as similar in abstract terms (e.g., similar 'personality traits')" (Hoffman, 1979, p. 963). If these additional factors are not taken into account, predictions of prosocial behavior based on a child's measured level of empathy are not likely to be accurate.

META-EMOTION
One's knowledge about one's own emotions.

Meta-Emotion **Meta-emotion** refers to one's knowledge about his or her own emotions. Researchers have begun to examine how a child's understanding of his own emotions may influence the development of empathy. Although researchers have just scratched the surface of this area, some interesting speculations and findings have been forthcoming.

Part of having empathy for others is the ability to put oneself in the other person's shoes, that is, to know and understand other people's experiences. This is, of course, what Hoffman meant by role taking. Perhaps to have empathy for another person requires that you yourself, at some time, need the empathy of others. With this in mind, it has been argued that childhood illnesses may be one of the more interesting forces behind role taking as it concerns the development of empathy. Oddly, illnesses may have a beneficial effect on behavior and development because they provide a child with experiences that require the help and empathy of other people, which may in turn teach the child to understand what it is like to be in need and to understand how others must feel when they are in a similar situation (Parmelee, 1986).

Children also acquire greater meta-emotion when they come to understand that previous emotional experiences may affect the way that they or someone else assesses a current situation. In one study, children of different ages and college students were told stories that included a description of an earlier emotional experience. One story was as follows:

> This is a story about a boy named Pat. One day Pat picked up his gerbil, and the gerbil bit him, and it hurt. The next day in school, Pat's teacher said, "Pat, it's your turn to feed the gerbil." (Gnepp & Gould, 1985, p. 1455)

The subjects were then asked how Pat would feel after having heard the request. Kindergartners generally thought that Pat would be happy, considering only the immediate circumstances. Second graders were somewhat more likely to realize that the previous emotional experience would make Pat feel frightened. Fifth graders were more likely still to realize that the earlier experience would affect the boy, and college students understood immediately (let's hope so!) (Gnepp & Gould, 1985).

Another important concept incorporated within meta-emotion is the ability to generate strategies that can help to change emotions. In general, 5-year-old children attempt to help other children feel better after something sad has happened by providing material goods; as one young child said, "I would give her some toys" (McCoy & Masters, 1985, p. 1221). Older children, however, are more sophisticated. By the age of 10 years, children often attempt to mediate cognitive processing of emotions with verbal interventions, such as, "Tell him it's not worth thinking about" (McCoy & Masters, 1985, p. 1221).

Future discoveries concerning the development of meta-emotion will no doubt

ALTRUISM
Behavior that benefits someone other than the actor, with little or no apparent benefit for the actor.

help researchers to better understand prosocial behavior and the development of empathy.

SHARING AND ALTRUISM

"Most children in middle childhood will verbally, if not behaviorally, support the principle that one should aid the needy" (Bryan, 1970, p. 61). Both sharing and **altruism** are prosocial behaviors. How these behaviors develop and how they can be encouraged have become the focus of a large amount of research.

Question: What is the difference between sharing and altruism?

Children share whenever they give some of what they have to another person. However, sharing may or may not be altruistic. Altruism takes into consideration the motive behind the act. An altruistic act is one that is not motivated by self-interest. Sometimes children share altruistically; at other times, they share for reasons of self-interest (e.g., to avoid punitive action or to obtain a future good). When children are governed by self-interest, adults often find it necessary to structure the contingencies in the children's environment in a way that will ensure sharing or fairness. Consider the mother whose two children constantly argued about who would get the "larger half" of the apple or the "larger half" of the doughnut. Her solution was to alter the external contingencies to make the children share equally. She instructed the first child to divide the food in two and then gave the second child first choice as to which piece she wanted. From that day on, food was always divided right down the middle—unless the children were alone, in which case the older child got all the apple if the younger child did not threaten to tell. As you can see, this is not altruism. Still, many children will share when no adult is around to make them do so, and they also will share even when there is no chance that their actions will be reciprocated.

Psychologists and others are interested in altruistic behavior, especially among older children and adults, because most often it appears to be controlled by internalized systems of self-reward and morality (Peterson, 1982). These internalized systems may, in turn, have developed after long exposure to altruistic individuals, especially parents (Clary & Miller, 1986). In many cases, intrinsic motivation has been found to be superior to extrinsic motivation in creating and maintaining prosocial behavior.

Question: Would you give an example of how prosocial behavior may be intrinsically motivated?

In one experiment, researchers attempted to teach fifth graders not to litter and to help clean up after others. The children were divided into two groups. The first group was told each day for eight days that they should be neat and tidy, and the reason this behavior would be good for them was explained. The second group was told, for the same number of days, that they *were* neat and tidy people. Littering and cleanliness were measured on the tenth and fourteenth days. The differences were considerable. The children in the first group, who were motivated extrinsically, were far less likely to help clean up than were the children in the second group, who had begun to think of themselves as neat and tidy and who wanted to maintain this positive attitude (intrinsic motivation) (Miller, Brickman, & Bolen, 1975).

Question: How can intrinsically motivated sharing and altruism be developed in children?

Both role playing and empathy are important, just as they are in promoting helpful behavior. In one study, researchers found that 6-year-old children who had been trained through role playing were more likely than other children to share with

Children often share with each other without being pressured to do so.

a needy child, even though they were not given extrinsic rewards for doing so (Iannotti, 1978).

The degree of a child's intrinsic motivation is also related to age and experience. As older children develop more competence and a greater sense of responsibility, they come to understand better the needs of others and the benefit that their giving may bring. These greater feelings of competence and responsibility may be one of the reasons that sharing and altruism increase during late childhood and early adolescence (Peterson, 1983). By the age of 9 years, nearly all children are willing to share (Green & Schneider, 1974).

Question: Can modeling affect how much children will share?

Modeling can affect sharing. Children who view a generous model usually will share more than children who do not view a model (Lipscomb, Larrieu, McAllister, & Bregman, 1982), and children who view a stingy model will share least of all (Ascione & Sanok, 1982). Understanding sharing or other prosocial behaviors is a complex task. Many factors besides role playing, empathy, and modeling can be influential (Hampson, 1981). For example, sharing can be increased by asking children to think happy thoughts (Isen, Horn, & Rosenhan, 1973; Moore, Underwood, & Rosenhan, 1973), by asking them to share (Bryan, 1975), or by providing them with more than they think they deserve (Olejnik, 1976).

Sharing also can be influenced strongly by culture. In one study conducted in Israel, two groups of children were asked to share with other children based on how much work the other children had done. One group comprised 10-year-old city children raised in Jerusalem; the other group consisted of 10-year-old children who had been raised on an Israeli kibbutz (a collective in which sharing is strongly emphasized). The city children shared based on how much work other children produced. The kibbutz children, however, shared even with those children who produced little, as long as the other child tried hard (Nisan, 1984).

Question: I've heard that girls are more sharing and altruistic than boys. Is that correct?

This belief is common. Most people think that girls are much more sharing and altruistic than boys are. Researchers have found, however, that the difference between boys and girls is *extremely* slight (in favor of girls being more altruistic and sharing) or nonexistent (with no difference between the sexes) (Shigetomi, Hartmann, & Gelfand, 1981; Zarbatany, Hartmann, Gelfand, & Vinciguerra, 1985). In any case, no research has ever supported the popular belief that girls are overwhelmingly more sharing and altruistic than boys.

Question: Could it be that this popular belief is based on a real sex difference that existed many years ago but that does not exist today—that today girls are becoming more like boys?

This doesn't seem to be the case. The first study along these lines was conducted well over half a century ago (Hartshorne, May, & Maller, 1929). Those researchers discovered, as have modern researchers, that although girls were only slightly more likely to help or to share than boys were, girls had far greater reputations for altruism than boys did. The researchers concluded that "a sex prejudice may be at work" (Hartshorne, May, & Maller, 1929, p. 156). It appears that more than 60 years later, the same prejudice is still at work!

Question: In biological terms, wouldn't altruism run against our natural grain? Isn't giving without receiving in conflict with "survival of the fittest"?

At first glance, it may appear that altruistic acts should run contrary to our "natural grain" because it would seem reasonable to assume that natural selection would choose against any creature with a propensity to give without receiving. Depending on species and circumstances, however, selfishness may not necessarily aid in procreation. The animal kingdom is filled with examples of selfless altruistic behavior, behavior that often helps a species pass on its genes to the next generation. Birds risk their lives and sometimes die to attract attention away from the nest. Among baboons, zebras, moose, and wild dogs often there are "stubborn, doomed guardians, prepared to be done in first in order to buy time for the herd to escape" (Thomas, 1982, p. 58).

Human beings, too, evolved in societies and groups, and it would be reasonable to assume that altruism in our species may be canalized (Rushton & Sorrentino, 1981) (see Chapter 2). In this sense, then, altruism may be acquired easily by our species because of our genetic inheritance. It should be emphasized that even if altruism exists to a degree because nature has selected in favor of it, the effects of our society's teachings, our own experiences, and the individual differences that exist among members of our own species also appear to play extremely important roles in determining the presence of altruism. These biological and social learning views are not incompatible, and both probably help explain the existence of altruism (Rushton & Sorrentino, 1981; Sharabany & Bar-Tal, 1982).

LEARNING CHECK

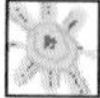

Multiple Choice

1. In Madsen's marble experiments designed to measure cooperation, it was discovered that
   a. older children generally were more cooperative than younger children.
   b. urban children generally were more cooperative than rural children.
   c. cooperation is always preferred over irrational competition.
   d. young children often were spontaneously cooperative.
2. Creating a "we" rather than an "I" atmosphere
   a. has been suggested as one way of fostering cooperation.
   b. has been suggested as one way of fostering competition.
   c. has been found to be an ineffective way of fostering cooperation.
   d. has been shown to foster cooperation more effectively than modeling or reinforcement does.

3. Which of the following is *false*?
   a. Induction generally fails with high role takers.
   b. Girls have a greater reputation for altruism than boys.
   c. Even 2-year-old children are willing to offer help.
   d. Altruism may be canalized in our species.
4. According to Hoffman, if a child is able to show empathy by responding appropriately to another's distress, but is unable to relate the distress to the person's larger life experience, the child is in the ____________ stage of empathy.
   a. role-taking
   b. person-permanence
   c. comprehensive empathy
   d. distress-reaction
5. Which experience is able to increase children's desire to share?
   a. observing a model who shares
   b. being asked to share
   c. thinking happy thoughts
   d. all of the above

Answers: 1.d 2.a 3.a 4.a 5.d

Self-Control and Delay of Gratification

SELF-CONTROL
The ability to control one's own actions despite the external pressures of the immediate situation.

Whenever children or adults control their own actions despite the external pressures of the immediate situation, they are exhibiting **self-control.** Self-control first appears during the second year of life. Its acquisition and consolidation are considered by many researchers to represent a major developmental milestone (Vaughn, Kopp, & Krakow, 1984). The very term means to have control over yourself, instead of allowing other things to control you. People who have self-control appear to rely on internalized value and reward systems. They can behave appropriately without being forced by external pressures, they can ignore immediate gratification in favor of long-term goals, and they may adhere to personal standards of moral behavior in the face of opposition.

In fact, Walter Mischel has kept track of the children he studied in experiments testing the ability to delay gratification. In a 10-year follow-up, he and his colleagues found that children from original studies who were best able to delay gratification when rewards were visible were rated as more intelligent, attentive, goal oriented, and able to concentrate than were the children who were unable to put off the immediate gratification (Mischel, Shoda, & Rodriguez, 1989). The children who were best able to delay gratification were also, as adolescents, the ones with the best academic scores and highest tolerance for frustration. In fact, the researchers discovered that the longer a child was ably to delay gratification in preschool, the higher her SAT scores were in high school (Shoda, Mischel, & Peake, 1990)! Of course, these data are correlational, and it might be that there is something about children who can delay gratification that later serves them well in terms of academic achievement. Keeping this in mind, it would be interesting to see if children who at first could not delay gratification but were later taught to do so would also show benefits 10 years later.

Question: How can children develop the ability to put off an immediate reward for a greater, long-term goal?

The first step is for the child to examine his own behavior by considering why he should wait for the greater reward. As you may recall from the Chapter Preview, most children will agree that this is "what a smart kid would do." The second step is somewhat more difficult, as any of us can attest, and that is to find some method or strategy for passing the time until the long-term goal is reached. Both of these steps are influenced by different factors (Mischel, 1974). If children see that the value of the long-term goal is great and that achieving it is within their skills and capabilities, most of them will express a desire to wait (Mischel & Staub,

NEGATIVE IDEATION
A method for delaying gratification by imagining unpleasant stimuli associated with the desired goal or object.

POSITIVE IDEATION
Imagining pleasant consequences or associations with a desired goal or object; generally a poor strategy for delaying immediate gratification.

1965). As mentioned in the Chapter Preview, however, acting on that desire and successfully delaying gratification may be difficult.

Question: What is the best way to delay immediate gratification?

In 1970, Mischel and Ebbe Ebbesen hypothesized that children would be better able to wait for a reward if they could spend their time looking at it. This way, they could see what they would receive if they waited. An experiment was conducted to test this hypothesis. Children aged 3 to 5 years were asked which they preferred—cookies or pretzels. After expressing a preference, each child was told to remain in the room alone until the experimenter returned, whereupon the child would receive the preferred food. The child was also told that by ringing a bell, he could call the experimenter back into the room anytime before the wait was over. In that case, however, only the nonpreferred food would be provided. The children were then placed alone in the room in one of four conditions. Children in the first condition could see both the preferred and the nonpreferred food. Children in the second and third conditions looked at either one or the other of the foods, and children in the last condition could see neither food (Mischel & Ebbesen, 1970).

Question: Were the children who could see both foods able to wait the longest?

No. Exactly the opposite occurred. Even though the children were aware that they would receive only the nonpreferred food if they called the experimenter back into the room, most of them weren't able to last even 1 minute! Children who could see either one or the other of the foods were able to wait about 5 minutes before they gave in and accepted the nonpreferred food. The average wait among children who were unable to view either food was 11 minutes. Of the children in this last group, 75 percent waited the full 15 minutes until the experimenter returned to the room.

Question: How did the children who were successful pass the time?

A number of them developed their own distraction techniques. Some talked to themselves, some sang songs, and some even invented games. The kinds of delaying strategies that children use and their effectiveness appear to follow an age-related progression that is tied to the child's cognitive development (Mischel & Mischel, 1979). As children are able to deal with stimuli in a more abstract manner, often they can transform the stimuli in a way that can facilitate delay (Mischel, 1974; Mischel & Moore, 1980; Moore, Mischel, & Zeiss, 1976).

Question: Would you give an example of how children's delay strategies follow a developmental progression?

Consider the plight of the preschoolers who could view both foods. They didn't last long before they wanted something to eat—even though they could have only the nonpreferred food. Generally, preschoolers in this kind of situation make waiting more difficult by using a poor delaying strategy. They focus their attention on what they shouldn't have (Yates & Mischel, 1979). By the third grade, however, children have become aware of some effective delay strategies. For example, some children advocate not looking at the reward. In an experiment using marshmallows, one 7-year-old child stated, "If she's looking at them all the time, it will make her hungry . . . and she'd want to ring the bell" (Mischel, 1979, p. 751). Some children made waiting easier by reminding themselves over and over again that if they waited they would receive the big reward, but if they didn't wait they would receive only the small one. Others even used **negative ideation** to delay their desire for the marshmallows. "Think about gum stuck all over them" (Mischel, 1979, p. 751). A small number, however, still argued in favor of **positive ideation** as a good delay strategy: "The marshmallow looks good and fluffy" (Mischel, 1979, p. 751). That didn't work too well.

By the time children reach sixth grade, their strategies may be fairly sophisticated. For instance, some of the older children used the effective delay strategy of thinking of the marshmallows as round or white (neutral attributes) instead of sweet or fluffy (positive attributes).

As children grow older, they appear to become increasingly aware of effective delay rules. A child developmentally shifts from thinking about positive attributes of the temptation, to distractions, to self-reminders about the contingencies, and finally to thoughts about neutral or negative attributes (Mischel, 1979).

Question: Can children learn self-control from watching other people model it?

Models can strongly influence whether children will take immediate rewards or delay gratification. In one experiment, fourth- and fifth-grade children were divided into two groups. Children who advocated accepting a small reward immediately over receiving a big one later were assigned to the first group, and those who advocated waiting were assigned to the second group. Members from each group were then exposed to one of three conditions. In the first condition, children watched a live adult model behave in a way opposite to what the children had advocated. When the model acted in front of the children who had advocated waiting, he would model not waiting, and vice versa. In the second condition, children in both groups read written arguments against the position they had taken. In the final condition, the control condition, the children in both groups simply were shown a series of paired objects unrelated to their positions. Among both groups of children—those who preferred to wait for a larger reward and those who did not—exposure to either a live adult model or to written arguments caused a majority to change their stance so as to agree with the model or written argument. The changes in the children's attitudes were still present a month later (Bandura & Mischel, 1965).

Other researchers have similarly found that reasoning and objective arguments can help a child change his choice, especially if the child is trying to delay immediate gratification (Nisan & Koriat, 1984). Perhaps children who are trying to delay gratification are looking for good reasons to help them do, as the children in the Chapter Preview said, what a smart kid would do.

The Development of Moral Thought

The development of empathy and self-control appears to be linked to cognitive growth. The extent of a child's cognitive development may also affect moral judgment. Piaget argued that moral judgments are dependent on cognitive development. This position is supported by the finding that problem solving and the ability to take the role of others are positively correlated with cognitive development (Kurdek, 1978). Both these abilities are necessary before a child can make sophisticated moral decisions.

PIAGET'S APPROACH TO MORAL DEVELOPMENT

Question: Which cognitive factors did Piaget think determine moral development?

In 1932, Jean Piaget published *The Moral Judgment of the Child.* Up until that time, morality generally had been an issue debated by philosophers who concerned themselves mainly with adult behavior. Rarely had the moral development of children been discussed; when it had been, moral development generally was considered a process of socialization in which adults taught children what was right or wrong and through which children slowly acquired adults' moral standards (Durkheim, 1925). Piaget, however, broke with the idea that moral development was due solely to socialization and argued instead that a child's cognitive development was most responsible for developmental changes in moral thinking

MORALS
The attitudes and beliefs that people hold that help them determine what is right and wrong.

PRECONVENTIONAL LEVEL
According to Kohlberg, a level of moral development in which good and bad is determined by the physical or hedonistic consequences of obeying or disobeying the rules.

CONVENTIONAL LEVEL
According to Kohlberg, the level of moral development in which the individual strives to maintain the expectations of family, group, or nation, regardless of the consequences.

POSTCONVENTIONAL LEVEL
According to Kohlberg, the level of moral development characterized by self-chosen ethical principles that are comprehensive, universal, and consistent.

(Piaget, 1932). In his book, Piaget supplied the following foundation on which modern moral theory is based.

1. No subject's reaction to any moral situation or dilemma can be fully understood without considering the subject's current scheme (this statement is in keeping with Piaget's cognitive theory). This idea broke away from the behaviorists' view that the external force of socialization was most important.
2. The process of socialization is not totally discounted as a factor in moral development. The child's *first* experiences with social rules typically are commands handed down by authorities who deserve respect, usually parents. The child behaves as though these social rules are fixed in nature, as are the laws of physics. At this point, the child does not know yet that social rules are agreed-on instruments designed to structure cooperation. Later, as children play together and come to arrangements and agreements, they begin to understand that rules are based on social contracts that encourage mutual cooperation and respect. This new understanding changes the child's schemes in a qualitative way.
3. These two moralities, "fixed-law" morality and "social-contract" morality, involve different principles and dynamics, each organized in a unique way. Although Piaget referred to the two moralities as stages of morality, he did not argue that they were clear-cut and distinct stages, as is the case with the stages in his theory of cognitive development. Rather, the two moralities are extremes on a developmental scale, and children develop by progressing from one extreme to the other through all the gradations between (Carroll & Rest, 1982).

Question: Is there experimental evidence supporting Piaget's suppositions?

Although many refinements have been added to Piaget's speculations, research generally has supported his view. Piaget himself conducted an experiment in which two groups of children (one group approximately 5 years old and the other group approximately 10 years old) each were told two stories. In one story, a boy attends a dinner party and accidentally breaks 15 cups. In the second story, a boy breaks a cup while trying to steal jam from a cupboard. Piaget then asked the groups of children which child was naughtier. The younger children responded that the one who broke 15 cups had been naughtier. Piaget argued that this response was because of their "fixed-law" morality—that is, the fixed law that "thou shalt break no cups" had been violated 15 times. The 10-year-old children, on the other hand, said that the child who had broken one cup while attempting to steal jam had been naughtier. They based their conclusions on a more socially oriented morality, in which justice plays a key role. In this morality, laws are not rigidly fixed, and other qualities, including intentions (to harm or to steal) and a sense of fairness (accidents can happen to anyone), prevail. Similarly, other researchers have found that younger children tend to measure immoral actions by harm done, whereas older children are more concerned with intent (Ferguson & Rule, 1982).

Lawrence Kohlberg (1927–1987)

KOHLBERG'S MORAL STAGE THEORY

The attitudes and beliefs held by children and adults that help them determine what is right and wrong are called **morals.** If moral judgments and thinking are tied to cognitive development, as Piaget believed, then it may be that moral reasoning does progress through a series of developmental stages as the child develops. As with developmental changes in empathy and delay of gratification, developmental changes in moral reasoning have attracted the attention and interest of researchers.

Building on Piaget's work (Piaget, 1932), Lawrence Kohlberg postulated three levels of moral development: the **preconventional,** the **conventional,** and the **postconventional.** Within each level are two stages. According to Kohlberg's theory, moral development begins with preconventional thinking, in which children obey to avoid punishment, and ends with the development of a sense of universal justice.

Question: How did Kohlberg determine which stage of moral development a person is in?

Kohlberg devised a test to measure moral development. Subjects are presented with a moral dilemma, and the reasoning they use as they resolve it determines how advanced their moral development is. Table 15.1 gives an example of one of

TABLE 15.1

Presentation of a Moral Dilemma with Answers Graded According to Kohlberg's Six Stages of Moral Development

In Europe a woman was near death from cancer. One drug might save her, a form of radium that a druggist in the same town had recently discovered. The druggist was charging $2,000, 10 times what the drug cost him to make. The sick woman's husband, Heinz, went to everyone he knew to borrow the money, but he could only get together about half of what it cost. He told the druggist that his wife was dying and asked him to sell it cheaper or let him pay later. But the druggist said "No." The husband got desperate and broke into the man's store to steel the drug for his wife. Should the husband have done that? Why?

Level	Stage	Pro	Con
Preconventional	Punishment and obedience orientation (physical consequences determine what is good or bad).		
	Stage 1	*Pro* He should steal the drug. It isn't really bad to take it. It isn't like he didn't ask to pay for it first. The drug he'd take is only worth $200, he's not really taking a $2,000 drug.	*Con* He shouldn't steal the drug. It's a big crime. He didn't get permission, he used force and broke and entered. He did a lot of damage, stealing a very expensive drug and breaking up the store, too.
	Instrumental relativist orientation (what satisfies one's own needs is good).		
	Stage 2	*Pro* It's all right to steal the drug because she needs it and he wants her to live. It isn't that he wants to steal, but it's the way he has to use to get the drug to save her.	*Con* He shouldn't steal it. The druggist isn't wrong or bad, he just wants to make a profit. That's what you're in business for, to make money.
Conventional	Interpersonal concordance or "good boy–nice girl" orientation (what pleases or helps others is good).		
	Stage 3	*Pro* He should steal the drug. He was only doing something that was natural for a good husband to do. You can't blame him for doing something out of love for his wife, you'd blame him if he didn't love his wife enough to save her.	*Con* He shouldn't steal. If his wife dies, he can't be blamed. It isn't because he's heartless or that he doesn't love her enough to do everything that he legally can. The druggist is the selfish or heartless one.
	"Law and order" orientation (maintaining the social order, doing one's duty is good).		
	Stage 4	*Pro* You should steal it. If you did nothing you'd be letting your wife die, it's your responsibility if she dies. You have to take it with the idea of paying the druggist.	*Con* It is a natural thing for Heinz to want to save his wife, but it's still always wrong to steal. He still knows he's stealing and taking a valuable drug from the man who made it.
Postconventional	Social contract—legalistic orientation (values agreed upon by society, including individual rights and rules for consensus, determine what is right).		
	Stage 5	*Pro* The law wasn't set up for these circumstances. Taking the drug in this situation isn't really right, but it's justified to do it.	*Con* You can't completely blame someone for stealing, but extreme circumstances don't really justify taking the law into your own hands. You can't have everyone stealing whenever they get desperate. The end may be good, but the ends don't justify the means.
	Universal ethical-principle orientation (what is right is a matter of conscience in accord with universal principles).		
	Stage 6	*Pro* This is a situation which forces him to choose between stealing and letting his wife die. In a situation where the choice must be made, it is morally right to steal. He has to act in terms of the principle of preserving and respecting life.	*Con* Heinz is faced with the decision of whether to consider the other people who need the drug just as badly as his wife. Heinz ought to act not according to his particular feelings toward his wife, but considering the value of all the lives involved.

SOURCE: Description of Kohlberg's stages from Shaver & Strong, 1976. Dilemma and pro and con answers from Rest, 1968.

these moral dilemmas. For each stage, actual answers have been provided that demonstrate the kinds of reasoning involved. The headings above each set of answers describe, in general terms, the quality of moral reasoning that defines each stage.

Before his death, Kohlberg revised his methods for scoring these interviews. This revision has proved to be a powerful improvement over his older technique. With these new methods, Kohlberg and others have examined the data collected over the years from the use of the moral interview. This extensive new review of the data strongly supports Kohlberg's position that moral thinking progresses sequentially through a series of stages (Carroll & Rest, 1982; Colby, Kohlberg, Gibbs, & Lieberman, 1983; Fischer, 1983; Saltzstein, 1983; Snarey, Reimer, & Kohlberg, 1985; Walker, de Vries, & Bichard, 1984). As with Piaget's cognitive theory of development, individuals assessed by Kohlberg sometimes were between stages, leaving one stage and entering the next. Advances in moral thinking, though, always proceeded sequentially, never skipping a stage, and never backing up. The data supported this hypothesis for all stages of moral development except stage 6. It was not possible from the data to make a clear distinction between stages 5 and 6 (Colby, Kohlberg, Gibbs, & Lieberman, 1983). For this reason, stage 6 has been dropped from current assessment procedures.

Question: Does this mean that stage 6 doesn't exist?

The data fail to support stage 6 as distinguishable from stage 5. This doesn't necessarily mean that a more sensitive interview instrument couldn't make the distinction. Stage 6 may exist; it's just that current assessment methods have not verified this.

Question: According to Kohlberg's theory, do children in the more advanced stages of development behave better?

It's not a matter of "good" or "bad" behavior. Each stage in Kohlberg's theory is value-free. What determines a child's position in the stages is not whether the child chooses "right" or "wrong" according to some value system, but the moral *reasoning* he uses in making the choice.

According to Kohlberg's theory, each stage builds on the previous stage. More advanced stages of moral development encompass earlier stages and reorganize them in a way that provides the child with new criteria and perspectives for making moral judgments (Hoffman, 1979). Kohlberg assumed that all children begin at the first stage and progress through each stage without skipping any of them.

Question: Do all individuals eventually reach the highest stages?

As with Piaget's cognitive theory, in which there is no assurance that the period of formal operations will be reached, Kohlberg argued that many children may never reach the final stage. In fact, most people do not appear to develop beyond stage 4 (Shaver & Strong, 1976).

Question: How do children advance through the stages?

Kohlberg argued that children advance to a higher stage of moral development when they are exposed to moral reasoning slightly more advanced than their own. According to Kohlberg's theory, this places the child in a cognitive conflict that is resolved by acceptance of the more advanced moral reasoning. Experiments with children have indicated that exposing them to moral reasoning that is one or two levels above their own is a strong inducement for them to advance to the next higher stage (Walker & Taylor, 1991a). Often, parents are the ones who provide the child with exposure to a more advanced level of moral reasoning (Walker & Taylor, 1991b).

Question: Is there a limit to how quickly children can advance through the moral stages?

Because moral development appears to be tied to cognitive development, it is reasonable to expect that certain cognitive abilities must exist before advances in moral development can occur. Studies have indicated that the period of concrete operations (see Chapter 9) is a prerequisite to stage 3 moral reasoning, and the period of formal operations (see Chapter 18) is a prerequisite to stage 5 moral reasoning (Kohlberg & Gilligan, 1971). Such cognitive development, however, does not ensure that these moral stages will be reached.

CRITICISMS OF KOHLBERG'S THEORY

Question: Has Kohlberg's theory been well accepted?

Although Kohlberg's theory presents a well-organized depiction of how moral development may occur, it has been criticized.

Moral Development and Moral Behavior Perhaps the most serious problem with Kohlberg's theory of moral development is that it correlates poorly with moral behavior. What people say they will do and what they actually will do are often two very different things (Kurtines & Greif, 1974). With this in mind, some researchers have argued that the approach that Kohlberg took when examining moral development may have been a poor one. Instead, it is argued, Kohlberg should have considered that moral life can be understood best by studying the behaviors that arise from actual experiences and then analyzing those experiences rather than spending his time examining the verbal responses given to hypothetical moral dilemmas (Vitz, 1990).

Furthermore, whether a person will choose to behave in a moral way often depends more on the immediate situational forces than on the person's level of moral reasoning. For instance, people are more likely to act in a moral way if the moral imperative requires that they *not do* something (e.g., steal money for food) rather than if it requires that they *do* something (e.g., give food to the hungry) (Kahn, 1992). Of course, the fact that moral behavior often is situationally dependent doesn't necessarily mean that moral reasoning doesn't progress through stages, as Kohlberg suggests, but it does indicate that fostering high levels of moral reasoning might not help create moral behaviors. Some researchers have argued that Kohlberg's theory is culturally biased in favor of Western ideas of what is morally "advanced" (Huebner & Garrod, 1991). Other people have concluded that Kohlberg's theory is an accurate description of moral development through childhood and adolescence but that it is not a valid way to measure moral development among adults (Gibbs, 1979). Still others have criticized Kohlberg for ignoring the powerful effect that emotions often have on determining our moral judgments (Shweder, 1981).

Women and Moral Development Kohlberg's original sample, on which most subsequent analyses and reanalyses have been made, consisted solely of white lower- and middle-class males. This has led to one of the most interesting criticisms of Kohlberg's work by one of his colleagues, Carol Gilligan, who has argued that women typically approach moral problems differently than men (Gilligan, 1982).

Gilligan states that women, more often than men, will focus on the interpersonal aspects of morality and on minimizing suffering. These assertions have come from interviews made by Gilligan with many women who were facing interpersonal crises. In this view, the moral development of women can better be understood as a morality of mercy and caring, which leads women, more often than

AT ISSUE

Do Preschoolers Show Moral Sensitivity?

Kohlberg's work supports the idea that preschool children are in the preconventional stages of moral development (stages 1 and 2). In this preconventional world, good is what is rewarded or what satisfies one's own needs; bad is what is punished or fails to satisfy one's needs. If this is true, and preschoolers have progressed no further than this, it would seem reasonable to assume that they would show a considerable insensitivity to others.

For quite some time, however, some researchers have believed that preschoolers are morally more sensitive than such an assessment would lead one to think (Radke-Yarrow, Zahn-Waxler, & Chapman, 1983). They have pointed out that most measurements of preschoolers' moral development have been made by using the standard Kohlberg approach, that is, by asking the preschoolers what their judgments are concerning hypothetical dilemmas. But what if it is too difficult for such young children to comprehend fully the moral dilemma when it is abstractly presented? If that is the case, then preschool children might behave in a more morally advanced way when in a real moral dilemma than when given a hypothetical one.

To test this hypothesis, 4-year-old children's moral actions were examined in a famous game called The Prisoner's Dilemma (Matsumoto, Haan, Yabrove, Theodorou, & Carney, 1986). The name of the game derives from a set of choices presented to two prisoners. The children in this study, however, were given a very simplified version of the game to play.

When the game was presented, two children were seated across from each other. The children were given two cards each, a blue one and a red one. There were four possible outcomes, depending on which cards the children chose to play (red-red, red-blue, blue-red, blue-blue). The outcomes of their choices to play either blue or red were shown to the children at all times and explained in detail before and during the game, so that the children were sure to understand the consequences of their actions (see Figure 15.3).

To begin the game, child 1 plays either a red or blue card. What's interesting is what child 2 can do after child 1 has played her card. If child 1 played a red card, child 2 might also play a red—in which case they each win a penny. Child 2 can also make the choice that most benefits himself: He can play a blue card, in which case he gets 2 pennies and child 1 gets nothing. The children then continue to play, taking turns. However, by playing through this game a few times in your mind, you can see that it is designed so that the greatest gains are obtained through cooperation, or sharing. Attempts to be highly competitive usually lead to low rewards for both players because of excessive blocking by the player who goes second or the refusal of the player who goes first to offer a red card after being betrayed once too often.

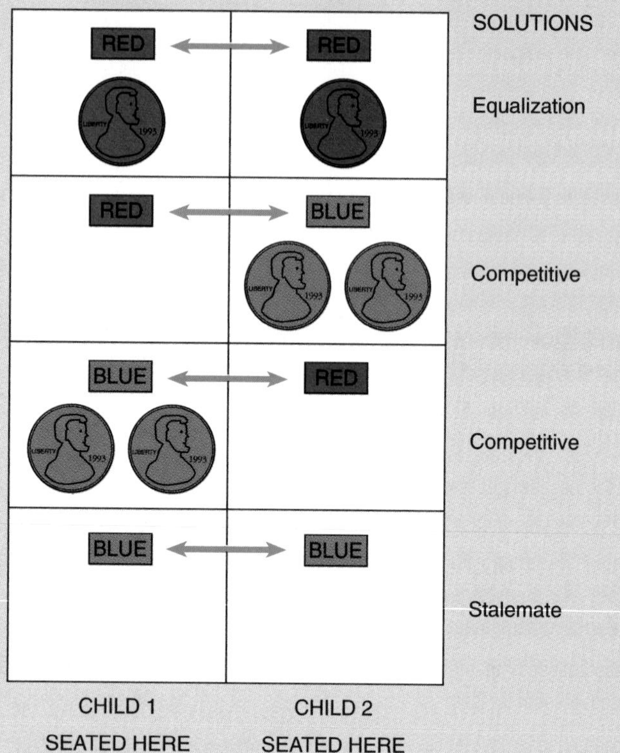

FIGURE 15.3
The four possible outcomes of the simplified Prisoner's Dilemma game. Child 1 plays first. The possibilities include equalization, in which the children each benefit; stalemate, in which both are blocked from reward; and the two possible competitive outcomes. (*Source:* Matsumoto, Haan, Yabrove, Theodorou, & Carney, 1986, p. 665)

In one case, after child 2 had betrayed his playmate and taken all the reward for himself a few times, child 1

AT ISSUE

was overheard to say, "Hey! You're not letting me win pennies!" Even if children who were losing said nothing (which was most of the time), their emotional expressions showed their distress. The question then is this: Would a preschooler busily winning pennies sense what he was doing to the other child? To the researchers' surprise, preschoolers, especially if they were friends, did show a moral sensitivity to one another's feelings and changed their behavior in a way that was considered "more moral" in response to those feelings. They tended to restructure their play so that the other child got pennies too, even when they clearly understood that they didn't have to. Their response was almost always to let the other child obtain pennies even if it meant giving up some themselves. This kind of interpersonal concordance is more in line with Kohlberg's conventional third stage, which is generally associated with older children and adults. By simplifying the procedures and investigating more carefully, researchers have come to the conclusion that preschoolers may be more morally sensitive than had been previously supposed.

Interestingly, this sensitivity may even have been inherited through the process of natural selection. Researchers using computer simulations of The Prisoner's Dilemma have found that when it is applied to animals in the wild, those creatures that share and cooperate with others have a better chance of surviving over the long term than do those that take a totally selfish approach (Nowak & Sigmund, 1992). At first glance, this finding appears to be counterintuitive, and in fact, the computer programs did show that the most selfish animals were better off in the short run. But it wasn't long before the tide turned as the "suckers" became so decimated that the "exploiters" could no longer benefit from them. Once that happened, "generous" animals were at an advantage. Perhaps, then, a certain amount of sharing, cooperation, and altruism is canalized in our species and others because, over the long term, they provide a survival benefit.

men, to consider the concrete issues of who is being hurt, what has happened each step of the way, and how help can be forthcoming. Kohlberg, Gilligan argued, presented his moral dilemmas with a male bias, stating them as an exercise in logic, a cold balancing act devoid of a morality of caring for others (Vitz, 1990). If gender differences do play an important role, then Kohlberg's work could hardly be considered a model of "human" moral development.

Question: Then what can we conclude from Kohlberg's research?

If we wish to be extremely conservative and not speculate beyond the data that have been gathered, we may conclude that "it now seems that Kohlberg's first five stages can be accepted as a legitimate description of the development of moral judgment in . . . white lower- and middle-class males" (Fischer, 1983, p. 98) and that "for a limited range of situations an individual can gradually develop the ability to apply a single type of reasoning" (Fischer, 1983, p. 104). Of course, because Kohlberg was creating a theory, it is proper to speculate, to try to form a greater whole from the component parts that the data present, and from this organization to extract a greater meaning. Whether the sequential development of moral reasoning that Kohlberg discovered will eventually be considered an important part of a child's development remains to be seen. For the moment, it certainly is intriguing.

LEARNING CHECK

Multiple Choice

1. Mischel and Ebbesen found that young children were most able to delay immediate gratification if
  a. they could view both the preferred and nonpreferred foods.
  b. they could view only the preferred food.
  c. they could view only the nonpreferred food.
  d. they could view neither food.

2. Which would be a poor strategy for helping delay gratification?
  a. thinking of the neutral attributes of the temptation
  b. engaging in distraction
  c. thinking of the positive attributes of the temptation
  d. using reminders about contingencies

3. According to Kohlberg, moral development begins with
  a. stage 2.
  b. preconventional thinking.
  c. solving moral dilemmas.
  d. all of the above.

4. "Good boy–nice girl" orientation is distinctive of ____________ moral reasoning.
  a. stage 1 **b.** stage 3 **c.** stage 4 **d.** stage 6

5. The ____________ is thought to be a prerequisite to stage 3 moral reasoning.
  a. sensorimotor period
  b. preoperational period
  c. period of concrete operations
  d. period of formal operations

Answers: 1. d 2. c 3. b 4. b 5. c

Applications

Controlling Aggression and Violence

Many researchers believe that aggression is primarily a learned behavior.

Over the years, many attempts have been made to explain violence and aggression (Parke & Slaby, 1983). One of the oldest, and at one time the most popular of these explanations, suggests that aggression, or violence, is the inevitable result of being blocked or frustrated in an attempt to achieve a desired goal (Dollard, Doob, Miller, Mowrer, & Sears, 1939). This came to be known as the *frustration-aggression hypothesis.*

A second theory, drawn from ethology, argues that aggression or violent behavior in humans is related to the fixed-response patterns of aggression found in lower animals. This theory embodies the argument that aggression is a natural response to specific situations, rather than a learned response (Hinde, 1975; Lorenz, 1966).

A third theory, based on physiological determinants, holds that aggression and violence come as the result of different levels of hormones or neurotransmitters in the brain (Mednick, Pollock, Volavka, & Gabrielli, 1982).

A fourth explanation, derived from learning theory, is that aggression and violent behavior are acquired by observing aggressive models, by being reinforced for aggression, and by having pleasant stimuli associated with aggression (Bandura, 1977).

Question: Which theory is correct?

A strict interpretation of the frustration-aggression hypothesis generally has been rejected. Some people react to frustration by becoming aggressive, but aggression isn't an *inevitable* response to frustration (Berkowitz, 1965). Reactions to frustration appear to depend on the individual and the specific situation.

To be frustrated—to be unable to attain your goal—is aversive and can result in psychological pain or depression. It is now realized that people who are anguished or depressed are more likely to become violent or aggressive. In this sense, as one of many causes of psychological anguish, frustration can lead to aggression (Berkowitz, 1983).

As for the other theories, although there may be innate patterns of aggressive behavior in lower animals, the evidence for such species-specific aggression in humans is weak.

Although specific brain structures are involved in aggressive behavior, and neurochemical and hormonal imbalance occasionally are related to acts of violence, the evidence that aggressive people are physiologically different from nonaggressive people is still tentative.

Most researchers believe that human aggression is primarily the result of learning, especially social learning (Eron, 1980). Children who observe aggression in others are more likely to act aggressively in imitation of that behavior, especially if the models are rewarded for being aggressive (Bandura, Ross, & Ross, 1963). One of the more interesting studies to demonstrate this fact examined the development of aggression among children from two neighboring communities of Zapotec Indians. These two communities had significantly different levels of adult aggression. It was found that chil-

APPLICATIONS

dren from the group in which adults modeled aggression more often became more aggressive, whereas children from the group in which aggression was less often modeled were considerably less aggressive (Fry, 1988).

The aggression that children imitate is also likely to generalize to other situations and across types. For instance, children who are aggressive at home are also likely to be aggressive at school, and children who are physically aggressive are also likely to be verbally aggressive (Lefkowitz, Eron, Walder, & Huesmann, 1977).

Although aggression may come readily into play because of our biological heritage, the things that make us aggressive appear to derive mostly from the experience we gain by watching or interacting with other people (Hall & Cairns, 1984). Through experience, we may also learn to become angry when presented with certain stimuli or situations. Although our capacity to be emotional is innate, the situations that make us emotional may depend a great deal on our learning and experiences. It has been shown that a child's knowledge both of the consequences of her actions, and of her ability to be effectively aggressive are important factors in whether or not she will choose to be aggressive (Perry, Perry, & Rasmussen, 1986).

Question: How can aggression be controlled or lessened?

Inappropriate behavior that has been learned often can be unlearned. Better still if it were never taught in the first place. Perhaps one way to help control aggression is to model less of it. Efforts along this line have concentrated on reducing television violence. During the 1970s, members of the American Medical Association, the American Psychological Association, parent-teacher associations, and Action for Children's Television argued in favor of less aggression on television. Levels of violence, however, were not diminished.

Another method might be to socialize children differently so that they are less likely to imitate aggressive models. Children who view television violence are more likely to be aggressive than other children are, and almost all the increase in aggressive behavior among children who view violence comes from changes in the behavior of boys. Girls rarely react to television violence with aggression; in fact, they often show a decrease in aggressiveness (Schuck, Schuck, Hallam, Mancini, & Wells, 1971).

Question: Why are boys more likely to imitate aggression and violence than girls?

This may be due to the early training girls receive to regard physical aggression and violence as undesirable behaviors. In our society, girls are reinforced less often for aggressive behavior than boys are (Hokanson & Edelman, 1966). Girls may be trained to be so nonaggressive that they do not identify with aggressive models and are not affected by them.

In our society, aggression is more tolerated in boys. In one study, 175 men and women watched two children play roughly in the snow. The children were dressed in snowsuits, which disguised their gender. The observers were then asked to rate the amount of aggression they saw. If the observers had been told that these were two boys playing, they saw less aggression than if they thought these were two girls or a girl and a boy (Condry & Ross, 1985). This indicates that the same behavior is accepted as nonaggressive when observed in "boys," but is called aggressive when seen in "girls." This implies that boys are allowed to play more roughly than girls are before they are considered to have "stepped over the line" and behaved aggressively. This kind of social pressure no doubt helps girls to be nonaggressive.

Question: But aren't some girls taught to be aggressive?

Some girls are taught to be aggressive, and they can be just as aggressive as any boy. Learned aggression seems to depend not on a child's gender, but on the child's experience. Just as girls can learn to be aggressive or violent, boys should be able to learn not to be aggressive or violent. Perhaps our society can discourage all its members from turning to aggression as a means of solving problems. In the words of Leonard Eron:

> If we want to reduce the level of aggression in society, we should also discourage boys from aggression very early on in life and reward them too for other behaviors; in other words, we should socialize boys more like girls. Here is where the women's liberation movement has it all wrong. Rather than insisting that little girls should be treated like little boys and given exactly the same opportunities for participation in athletic events, Little League activities, and the like, as well as in all other aspects of life, it should be the other way around. Boys should be socialized the way girls have been traditionally socialized, and they should be encouraged to develop socially positive qualities such as tenderness, sensitivity to feelings, nurturance, cooperativeness, and aesthetic

APPLICATIONS

> appreciation. The level of individual aggression in society will be reduced only when male adolescents and young adults, as a result of socialization, subscribe to the same standards of behavior as have been traditionally encouraged for women. (Eron, 1980, p. 251)

Others counter that such efforts might not succeed because it may be that the different amounts of aggression among boys and girls are biologically determined (Tieger, 1980) or that training an entire society to be passive (if such a thing even could be done) might be inherently dangerous in terms of that nation's ability to defend itself.

Question: Are there techniques besides modeling and retraining that may be effective in controlling aggression?

Many different methods have been investigated. Among these are training people in the use of humor to defuse their anger (Mueller & Donnerstein, 1977), teaching new techniques for handling stress to reduce the buildup of anger (Novaco, 1978), helping to create a greater awareness of the harmful effects of aggression (Baron, 1971), providing training to increase empathy and role taking in children (Feshbach & Feshbach, 1982), modifying family aggression (Patterson, 1982), and encouraging social and legal organizations to become more involved with children at an earlier age (Seidman, Rappaport, & Davidson, 1980).

Aggression and violence continue to be a major problem for our society. Hopefully we will someday find a way to curb these behaviors or redirect them in a constructive manner.

SUMMARY

- Prosocial behavior is the opposite of antisocial behavior. Prosocial behavior benefits others and society. During our lives, we are often encouraged to be prosocial.
- Cooperation is a prosocial behavior. Children are often spontaneously cooperative. In our society, however, and in others, individual competition is so often reinforced that children's efforts to surpass others sometimes interfere with the need for cooperation. Such irrational competition can spoil the success that cooperation can bring.
- Staub's hypothesis is that there are two important factors involved in helping. The first is to possess the skills or knowledge needed to help effectively, and the second is to empathize with the person in need.
- Induction is an effective technique when used with older children. Role playing is the most effective method for getting young children to help.
- It has been argued that empathy for another does not come into being suddenly, but rather develops over a number of years. Hoffman has observed four stages of empathy development: distress reaction, person permanence, role taking, and comprehensive empathy.
- There is some evidence that the children who express the most empathy are the most likely to offer help or cooperation, but surprisingly, researchers occasionally have found a child's level of empathy to be a poor predictor of prosocial behavior. Part of the problem may be that different studies have used different definitions of empathy and that other variables also may affect children's willingness to help.
- Both sharing and altruism are prosocial behaviors. Sharing may or may not be altruistic. Altruistic acts are not motivated by self-interest. Altruistic behavior is most likely among children who are intrinsically motivated, who have more empathy, and who observe altruistic models.
- Children most able to delay gratification have developed techniques that effectively help them to do so. As children grow older, they appear to become increasingly aware of effective delay rules. The child developmentally shifts from thinking about positive attributes of the temptation, to distractions, to self-reminders about the contingencies, and finally to thoughts about neutral or negative attributes of the temptation.
- Jean Piaget stated that moral judgments depend on cognitive development. He believed that no subject's reaction to any moral dilemma or situation can be fully understood without considering the subject's current scheme. He argued that two moralities, those based on fixed laws and those based on social contracts, involve different principles and dynamics. He argued that the two moralities are extremes on a developmental scale and that children develop by progressing from one extreme to the other.
- Building on Piaget's work, Lawrence Kohlberg postulated three levels of moral development: the preconventional, the conventional, and the postconventional. Within each level are two stages. According to Kohlberg, moral development begins with preconventional thinking, in which children obey to avoid punishment, and ends with the development of a concern for reciprocity among individuals and a sense of universal justice.
- Kohlberg argued that children advance to a higher stage of moral development when they are exposed to moral reasoning slightly more advanced than their own.
- Although Kohlberg's theory presents a well-organized depiction of how moral development may occur, it has been strongly criticized for a number of reasons. Perhaps the most serious disadvantage is that it correlates poorly with observed moral behavior.

QUESTIONS FOR DISCUSSION

1. In what ways might Kohlberg's theory of moral development be biased in favor of Western ideas of what is or isn't morally advanced?

2. Can you find parallels between Hoffman's hierarchy of empathy development and Piaget's theory of cognitive development? For example, how might person permanence be related to egocentrism or comprehensive empathy be related to formal operations?

3. Have you ever successfully postponed obtaining something you really wanted in order to obtain a greater long-term goal? What techniques did you use to pass the time while you waited? If you failed, what might you have done to help yourself succeed?

SUGGESTIONS FOR FURTHER READING

1. Eisenberg, N. (1992). *The caring child.* Cambridge, MA: Harvard University Press.
2. Eisenberg, N., & Mussen, P. (Eds.). (1989). *The roots of prosocial behavior in children.* New York: Cambridge University Press.
3. Henry, R. M. (1983). *Psychodynamic foundations of morality.* New York: Karger.
4. Lickona, T. (1983). *Raising good children: Helping your child through the stages of moral development.* New York: Bantam.
5. McGinnis, E., Goldstein, A. P., Sprafkin, R. P., & Gershaw, N. J. (1984). *Skillstreaming the elementary school child: A guide for teaching prosocial skills.* Champaign, IL: Research Press.
6. Moyer, K. E. (1976). *The psychobiology of aggression.* New York: Harper & Row.
7. Rushton, J. P., & Sorrentino, R. M. (Eds.). (1981). *Altruism and helping behavior: Social, personality, and developmental perspectives.* Hillsdale, NJ: Erlbaum.
8. Tappan, M. B., & Packer, M. J. (Eds.). (1991). *Narrative and storytelling: Implications for understanding moral development.* San Francisco: Jossey-Bass.

CHAPTER 16

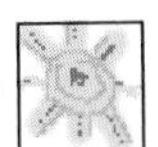

CHILD DEVELOPMENT IN OTHER CULTURES

CHAPTER PREVIEW

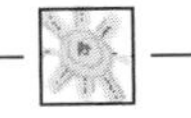

CULTURE AND PERSONALITY

AS THE SECOND World War entered its final days in Asia, thousands of Japanese living in a captured part of China called Manchuria were forced to flee from the advancing Russian army. Attacked by angry Chinese, suffering from extreme hunger and cold, Japanese parents were often forced to leave their children behind. They did this to save the children from the hardships of the escape or because the adults could not flee quickly enough with their children in tow. As a result, over 2,500 Japanese children were left behind, usually with childless Chinese couples who offered to adopt them and raise them as their own.

AFTER THE WAR, the Japanese parents were unable to look for their children because of the Chinese civil war and the closing off of contact with Japan following the rise of Mao Tse-Tung. It wasn't until 1981, 36 years after the war had ended, that the Japanese government was able to persuade the Chinese government to facilitate contact between the war orphans and their parents.

BY THIS TIME, most of the "orphans" were middle-aged, had Chinese spouses, and had teenage children of their own. Still, almost all of them took the opportunity to travel with their families to Japan to find their Japanese parents and relatives. Relying mostly on memories of their family names and locations, they began the search. Of those who were older than 9 at the time of the separation, 77.5 percent were reunited with their families. Of those who were younger than 5, whose memories were less complete, only 31.3 percent were successful (Tseng, Ebata, Miguchi, Egawa, & McLaughlin, 1990).

As the orphans' search became news, both Japanese researchers in Tokyo and American researchers in Hawaii realized that it presented a unique opportunity to do a cross-cultural investigation of how culture affects children during their formative years and how that influence may be reflected later in life. These researchers were especially interested because they knew that both Japanese and Chinese cultures encouraged distinctly different behaviors in their members. There are well-documented cultural differences between the Japanese and Chinese (Doi, 1962; Lebra, 1976; Yang, 1986). The researchers wondered if the orphans were likely to have retained a higher proportion of the traits most encouraged by Japanese culture, such as those concerned with interpersonal relations, temperament, attitude toward work, and manners. Or would having lived in China for all those years have lessened the traits more typical of Japanese culture? In other words, they were asking an old question: How much of personality is formed in childhood? This was a unique chance to find out.

Question: What did the researchers discover?

To their surprise, the orphans retained many of the attitudes and personality characteristics more common to the Japanese, even though many had been exposed to Japanese culture for less than 7 years of their 40 plus years of life. This finding does suggest that personality traits may be acquired early in life and then remain fairly resistant to change thereafter (Tseng, Ebata, Miguchi, Egawa, & McLaughlin, 1990). Because of this research, the old adage "As the twig is bent, so grows the tree" takes on greater importance.

Question: Couldn't it be that these results reflect something in the genes of the Japanese children? That is, couldn't the personality traits shown by the Japanese orphans have been the result of genetics rather than early cultural experience?

Although the researchers didn't rule out genetic influences (especially where temperament was concerned—see Chapter 4), many studies of adopted infants from other cultures have shown the environment to be a forceful molder of personality. This study, however, was the first chance to investigate a large group of children raised for a few years in one culture and then transferred to another for the remainder of their childhood and many years of their adulthood. To be able to see the initial effect of the first culture so clearly tells us something about early childhood as a special time of personality formation.

This study helps to reinforce the idea that there is no such thing as a neutral culture. We perceive things differently, depending on our experience and on what our culture has taught us. For this reason and others, it would be misleading to present a text on child development without considering how other cultures influence development. As you study the different experiences of children in other cultures and the effects of these experiences, you will begin to see how adaptive and diverse our species can be.

In this chapter, we will examine how culture can affect children's behavior and development. We'll take a close look at children in Japan, the former Soviet Union, New Guinea, and Uganda and compare them with children in the United States and western Europe.

RESOURCES

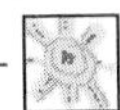

Cross-Cultural Research

How flexible is our species? How many different ways can we develop? How tied is our development to biological maturation? Studying the development of infants, children, and adults in other cultures will help us to answer these questions. Too often, we think that our culture is the only culture, that the way we raise our children is the only way to raise children. As cross-cultural researchers have noted:

> Much of what we were able to say about children in the past was based on information gathered only from white middle-class Western children. Cross-cultural studies have helped to remedy this deficiency by providing information about child development in diverse cultures and in a variety of settings. Indeed, we cannot consider child development in its broad context unless we know how children grow and develop in environments and cultures different from those in which much of our research has already been conducted. . . . Only recently has the field of child development become international in scope and less ethnocentric in its theories and research. (Wagner & Stevenson, 1982, p. vii)

Cross-cultural researchers face special problems. They often have to adjust to life in another culture without the benefits of their friends and family. Local residents may be distrustful of researchers, equating well-dressed outsiders with intrusive government officials. Locals speak a different language, have different norms concerning everyday interpersonal interaction, and are participants in long-term networks in which outside researchers have no place. Some local residents may have a status in the community that might be threatened by research results (Triandis & Brislin, 1984).

Other difficulties can arise that are unique to cross-cultural research. Translation has often been particularly fraught with problems. One language may have a word denoting a concept that does not occur in another language. Translation from one language to another may be difficult when the underlying behavior discussed carries a different connotation, either positive or negative. For instance, Phillips had trouble translating the sentence beginning "Sometimes a good quarrel is necessary because . . ." into the Thai language. This was because to the Thai, it was *inconceivable* that a quarrel could ever have a good purpose (Phillips, 1960).

Another problem occurs when only a single method is used to measure the variables under study. Consider the following example. A child is sitting at a table, stubbornly refusing to eat his vegetables. The child's mother finally says, "All right, then, you don't have to eat it" (Azuma, Kashiwagi, & Hess, 1981). American mothers were told of this exchange in a developmental psychology class, and one of these mothers stated that she would have said the same thing to her child "because I don't think that the child must eat particular kinds of food. There are other things which I can offer" (Azuma, 1986, p. 4). Researchers studying the dinner conversation, who were coding the interchange between the mother and child, also agreed that the mother must not have felt very strongly that the child should eat the vegetables. They were wrong. And although it may not seem obvious, they had missed something important. The child in the example was Japanese, and the mother's statement that he didn't have to eat the vegetables was a very powerful threat designed to make the child obey her. Implicit in the threat was the idea, "We have been close together. But now that you want to have your own way, I will untie the bond between us. I will not care what you do. You are not a part of me any longer" (Azuma, 1986, p. 4). Such a threat (e.g., "I don't care what you eat anymore") is very effective among Japanese children because they have been taught from a very early age to be extremely close to their mothers and to prize this closeness.

Researchers who looked at only what the mother had said and did not consider the statement's cultural context reached erroneous conclusions about whether the mother wished her child to eat the vegetables and about which techniques the mother was using to get her child to obey her. It is especially important to use as many methods and techniques as possible (Webb, Campbell, Schwartz, & Sechrest, 1966) to ensure accurate measurement in cross-cultural situations. Too often, those who conduct studies in other cultures, although well trained in research methods, have an inadequate understanding of the culture they are observing, which in turn can lead them to false conclusions. To help address this issue, those who conduct cross-cultural studies have begun to rely on trained researchers who are members of (or have significant experience with) the culture they are studying.

Many benefits can be gained from cross-cultural research. They include the ability to expand and fine-tune theories, to increase the range of variables beyond what is obtainable in any one study, to unconfound variables that occur together in any one culture, and to study how general principles are affected by contextual factors (Triandis & Brislin, 1984). Let's look at each of these benefits in turn.

THEORY EXPANSION

One of the most important benefits of cross-cultural research is its ability to expand and fine-tune theories. Only after being tested across cultures can a theory be said to be robust (Triandis & Brislin, 1984). For example, Piaget's theory (see Chapter 9) has been tested in other cultures to help separate biological from cultural variables. It has been found through this research that how quickly children enter concrete operations depends considerably on the language they speak (Sevinc & Turner, 1976) and on the kind of experiences their culture provides them. For example, children from pottery-making families in Mexico are much better at conserving quantity than are other Mexican children (Price-Williams, Gordon, & Ramirez, 1969).

INCREASING RANGE OF VARIABLES

Because culture shapes behavior, the range of behaviors in any one culture might be limited. By studying the same behaviors in other cultures, researchers can examine a greater range and diversity of variables as determinants of a specific behavior.

Question: Would you give an example of what you mean?

Suppose that researchers were interested in the relationship between the age at which a child is first weaned and some personality trait. If the researchers looked in the United States only, they would probably find a narrow range of ages at which children were weaned, usually under 1 year. If they looked at a number of different cultures, however, the researchers would find some cultures in which the "proper" weaning age was up to 5 or even 6 years of age! The researchers could therefore increase the age range of their subjects and thereby improve the quality of their results.

UNCONFOUNDING VARIABLES

In certain instances, while it is often difficult to separate possible biological variables from cultural ones, cross-cultural research may afford us the chance of doing so.

Question: How can you separate biological and cultural variables?

One method of separating these variables is to study members of a group who live in the culture of their birth and to compare them with members who have moved into another culture. For example, researchers studying the excellence of the Japanese student have also examined Japanese children who were raised and educated outside Japan and who then returned to Japan in their teens (Minoura, 1984). These returning children had many more adjustment problems in school than did their counterparts who had grown up in Japan and had been raised in the Japanese culture.

STUDYING THE BEHAVIOR IN CONTEXT

One of the advantages of cross-cultural research occurs when researchers work in cultures different from their own.

Question: How could that be beneficial?

According to psychologists Triandis and Brislin (1984, p. 1008):

> Researchers can often see aspects of the social context that may be influencing people's behaviors, perhaps because those aspects contrast with—and thus stand out so sharply against—what is similar in the researchers' own culture. Cross-cultural studies, then, can lead to more insights into how general principles are affected by contextual factors.

As you can see, there are many benefits to be obtained from studying child development in other cultures. The ability to generalize beyond one culture to find those aspects of development that are similar around the world helps us to understand more clearly the respective roles of nature and nurture in determining behavior.

The Culture as Teacher

Culture teaches. Through cultural research, we can see the massive power and effect of learning on development. Consider the following study in which children from two West African tribes were compared. One tribe was agricultural, whereas the other formed a merchant society. When researchers evaluated the mathematical skills of the children (ages 5 to 10 years), they discovered that among the children of the agricultural tribe, only those with formal schooling possessed basic mathematical skills. Among the children of the merchant society, however, *all* the children, even the unschooled, possessed basic mathematical skills. Because the mathematical skills of counting and comparing were of intrinsic value to the merchant society (whereas they were of little value to the agricultural tribe), the children raised in the merchant society acquired those skills as a matter of course (Posner, 1982).

Schools can differ greatly from culture to culture, and children can acquire the skills and values of their culture without formal schooling. In some cultures, children learn only by imitating adult models. Among the Cantalense of Guatemala, children are given miniature versions of the tools and implements used by the adult members of their society. These children are rarely instructed what to do with the tool (which may be a miniature broom or a corn-grinding stone) or how to handle it. The learning is simple enough to be acquired through observation and imitation alone.

Similarly, the Ojibwa Indians of Canada, who mostly trap and hunt game, pass on their culture to their children only through observational learning. From the time the Ojibwa children are old enough to follow and imitate parents who are engaged in daily activities, the children begin to take on adult tasks and responsibilities. The boys imitate their fathers' trapping and fishing, and the girls their mothers' cooking and sewing. As you can see from these examples, the power of a culture to teach and influence the development of a child extends far beyond any structured or formal schooling it provides (see At Issue).

AT ISSUE

The Development of Minority Children

Most textbooks about child development generally focus on white, middle-class, American children. Occasionally, poor children are studied or perhaps children from other cultures, but the emphasis still tends to be on white, middle-class, children.

Question: Why isn't there a greater emphasis on minority children in developmental textbooks?

Partly because our child development data base is centered mainly on white, middle-class children. This is because the majority of the U.S. population of children are white and middle class and also because so many subjects in experiments are tied in one way or another to university populations simply because they are easily accessible. These tend to include children of students or faculty, children living near the university, and children in university day care, who tend to be white and middle class by an even larger percentage than the general population.

Minority children, however, constitute a very rapidly growing segment of the American population, and by the year 2000, they will have become the new majority of young people (Spencer, 1990). Any field such as child development will have to fully consider all members of the population before it can make the general claim of studying the development of children.

Question: Why should there be a special emphasis on minority children? Shouldn't all children be studied together? After all, doesn't highlighting majority/minority differences just further the idea that minority children are somehow different?

The problem is that minority children often are different for interesting *cultural* reasons (McLoyd, 1990). One of the most controversial issues concerning these differences is the fact that for years minority children were simply compared with Anglo-American children by using the development and behavior of the white children as some sort of norm by which to measure all others. Researchers have referred to this as the *Eurocentric bias,* meaning a view that regards as normal the development of children from European heritage who, in logical extension of the bias, should therefore become the standard with whom all other children should be compared (Spencer, 1990). The Eurocentric view in child development, it is argued, fosters the tendency to ignore important cultural differences that might affect how a child develops (McLoyd, 1990).

Modern researchers in the United States are beginning to examine minority children in earnest and to consider the cultural distinctions that make African Americans, Asian Americans, Hispanic Americans, native Americans, and other minority groups different from one another, as well as different from Anglo-Americans. Even distinctions within each of these groups are considered. For instance Asian Americans may well trace their cultural roots to very different origins (Korea, Japan, China, Vietnam, etc.), and children influenced by each of these cultures may in turn develop in a somewhat different way.

There are also commonalities among minority children and their families that make them special. For instance, minority families typically are younger, more extended, and more likely to be poor than are majority families (Spencer, 1990). Each of these differences might affect a child in meaningful ways. These distinctions, therefore, are important because a general view of "people as people" overlooks the unique cultural circumstances and in-

The Effect of Culture

From time to time throughout this textbook, we have examined the role that culture can play in shaping specific behaviors.

In the rest of this chapter, we will look at four different cultures, focusing on each one's general attributes and its methods for bringing up children. In this way, you can obtain more of a "feel" for the powerful effect that culture has on children's personality and behavior. We will take a closer look at the children of Japan, the former Soviet Union, the Fore (a New Guinea tribe), and the Ik (an African tribe).

Question: Why are these four cultures of special interest?

AT ISSUE

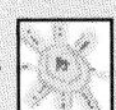

fluences that are brought to bear on the development of many minority children.

Question: What kinds of discoveries have modern researchers made concerning the development of minority children?

The discoveries are as diverse and as varied as are the subjects of the investigations. Let's examine a few of these studies so that you might have a better idea of the research in this growing area and its implications.

We mentioned that minority families are more likely to raise their children in poverty than are majority families. For many historical and social reasons, this is especially true of African American families. Studies investigating the effects of poverty on children's development have shown that level of income is one of the best predictors of later competence among African American children. The more poverty a child faces, the lower is his or her level of competence concerning school, peer relations, and conduct (Patterson, Kupersmidt, & Vaden, 1990). The level of poverty among African American families is also associated with parent effectiveness. Parents in greater poverty have been found to be less effective. They tend to be less supportive, less consistent, and less involved (McLoyd, 1990). While often having devastating effects on the development of children from any cultural background, poverty is, in terms of overall percentages, of special concern for many minorities. Because of this growing interest, we can expect, someday soon, to obtain a better understanding of the effects of poverty on children's development.

We have also mentioned that minority families are more likely to be extended. As a result, there are more studies now being conducted than ever before concerning the influence of grandparents, aunts and uncles, and cousins. One study found a significant parental involvement by grandmothers in African American families (Pearson, Hunter, Ensminger, & Kellam, 1990). However, involvement in child rearing by extended family members has also been found to be quite complex. For instance, sometimes grandparents fill in for parents because parents are absent. Other times, the extended family resides together. So while there is an emphasis on extended family among most minorities, the interactions and relationships may be quite different from one family to the next. They are not homogeneous (Tolson & Wilson, 1990). As a direct result of this growing interest, however, we can expect to see more research on the complexities of the extended family and how such families affect child development.

Also important are studies that compare minority groups to examine various stereotypes. Why, for example, is it commonly expected that Asian American children will do well in school, while African American children are expected to do poorly (Slaughter-Defoe, Nakagawa, Takanishi, & Johnson, 1990)? Researchers addressing such a stereotype will first ask, Is it true? And if it is, they will try to uncover the variables responsible for the difference; they will compare the environments of children from both minority groups in the hopes of isolating important factors that might affect school performance, such as the presence of the father in the home or expectations of the family.

By having such diversity from which to draw, researchers are expanding our understanding of the full range of child development. The only way that the field of child development can grow and continue to be relevant is if it encompasses the development of all children, not just a select group.

We will examine the children of Japan for several reasons. First, there has been much research in child development in Japan in recent years because

> several studies have shown Japanese children as a group to be among the highest achievers in international comparisons of educational attainment. Also, a number of studies (Caudill & Weinstein, 1969; Doi, 1981; and Lebra, 1984) suggest that the Japanese child-rearing culture provides a natural experiment that may suggest alternatives to the western model of child-rearing practices. . . . A less mentioned, but equally important reason for studying child development in Japan, is that the country is undergoing rapid and drastic sociocultural change. (Azuma, 1986, pp. 3–4)

We will study the former Soviet Union because it was one of the two great superpowers and because in terms of military force, there still remain within some of the republics of the former superstate, enough weapons to destroy the world. These republics are still in turmoil, and the way in which they raised their children may give us a clue as to the future of these now independent states.

Question: Why are we studying the other two cultures?

The other two cultures are included not only because they provide a stark contrast to most Western industrialized nations, but also because both were studied as they underwent drastic cultural change as a result of contact with other cultures. Knowledge of how such change can take place is invaluable these days, as the world keeps shrinking as a result of improved communication among cultures.

The Children of Japan

The average Japanese family provides an envelope of security for its children. Unlike most American children, who sleep in their own beds, Japanese children traditionally sleep with their parents. This is in sharp contrast to American infants. Dr. Spock even advised American parents "not to take a child into the parents' bed for any reason" (1968, p. 169). Among "child care experts in the United States, it is [still] assumed that the proper sleeping arrangement for infants and parents is separate" (Morelli, Rogoff, Oppenheim, & Goldsmith, 1992, p. 604). In Japan, however, the youngest child sleeps closest to his mother, where he can be easily nursed. Even toddlers share their parents' bed and sometimes even older children well into middle childhood.

During the day, infants are carried on their mothers' back, where they maintain their close contact. Because of the demands of work, the average Japanese father usually is absent for most of the week. He typically plays with the children on Sunday, taking them to their favorite places and playing their games with love and enthusiasm.

Question: How do such close family relationships affect the children's development?

Researchers who studied attachment in Japanese and American infants found several differences. Japanese infants were much more likely to show distress when their mothers left them (Miyake, Chen, & Campos, 1985). Japanese mothers were much more likely to stay in close physical contact with their children.

The Japanese family provides an envelope of security for its children.

The physical closeness between Japanese parents and their children is so great compared with the American experience that some researchers refer to the Japanese relationship as "skinship" rather than kinship (Douglas, 1978). Some non-Western psychologists have come to believe that such early experience results in a lifelong need to belong or be a member of a group (Doi, 1973). The Japanese use the word *amae* to express their family or group dependency. *Amae* is considered to be neither a good nor a bad arrangement; still, it is in stark contrast to the Western tradition of fostering independence in children. Takeo Doi, in his classic book *The Anatomy of Dependence* (1973), argued that such family closeness leads to a desire among Japanese offspring to continue the intimate relationship beyond the family and to extend *amae* to relationships with peers and superiors. Doi believed that *amae* resulted in a society oriented toward group activities and structured to include a very specific vertical social organization. Japan, Doi argued, reflects that "groupness." Unlike Western children, who often meet with strict limitations in early childhood but enjoy increasing freedom in later years, Japanese children typically encounter relatively few sanctions in early childhood but face an increasing number of social regulations as they approach adulthood (Douglas, 1978). Children are considered mature in Japan when they develop the capacity for *ittaikan,* to feel at one with persons other than the self (Weisz, Rothbaum, & Blackburn, 1984).

One possible reason for the academic superiority of Japanese students is that they often spend extra hours in special cram schools, called *juku,* to study for exams.

Question: How are children treated in the Japanese school system?

A pecking order is established by use of rigorous school examinations. Children must begin the competitive road toward success or failure, sometimes as early as kindergarten, by facing these examinations. The work is often demanding. The children are faced with 7 hours of classes each weekday and a half day on Saturday—240 days a year. Twice a year, they must take examinations to be promoted to the next grade. In addition, many students spend extra hours at special cram schools, called *juku,* to prepare for exams. The Japanese students call this examination ritual *shiken jigoku,* or "examination hell." Following this rigorous training, 90 percent of Japanese students graduate from the twelfth grade, as opposed to only 75 percent of U.S. students. Unlike U.S. students, Japanese students, when they are ready to take their college entrance examinations, are prepared to pass tests in foreign grammar, calculus, statistics, and probability. Also unlike the West, if a Japanese student is successful throughout school and gains entrance to a university, his future is almost ensured. Japanese companies, in which there is great group cohesion, will sponsor a student through college and guarantee the student a job when he graduates. The company then becomes the "family," and the student can expect to spend his entire life working for only one organization.

Question: What happens to children who fail?

Children who fail or whose behavior is at odds with the accepted group practice almost assuredly will not be given another chance to succeed. To fail in school means to be cast out of "the family." The intense pressure can lead to serious disorders associated with anxiety and fear. The Japanese refer to this pressure as *shinkeishitsu.* For this and other cultural reasons, the suicide rate among Japanese college students is high compared with that of other cultures. And Japanese universities aren't particularly consoling to students who don't succeed. One university sent this message to a student who failed the entrance examination: "You cannot go on living unless you are tough" (McGrath & Levenson, 1982, p. 80).

For Japanese children, then, the world becomes more structured and group oriented as they grow older. Pressures to succeed and to belong become intense, and the close ties with family and community remain strong.

The Children of the Former Soviet Union

In Russia today, as was the case in the former Soviet Union, a very large section of the working population is made up of women with young children. In the past, to care for these children and to provide for their schooling, the former soviet state had a nationwide organization of nursery schools.

Question: Were the former Soviet nursery schools like American day-care centers?

Both the Soviet nursery schools and American day-care centers served a custodial function, but there were few other similarities. To begin with, Soviet nursery schools started education and social indoctrination early. Infants were assigned to group playpens, where they were in immediate contact with five, six, or seven other infants of their own age. The intention was to create an experience that would lead to feelings of collective belonging rather than a sense of individuality (Ispa, 1981). However, unlike the closeness fostered among the Japanese, this group orientation was centered on peers rather than on family.

In these nursery schools, one "upbringer" was assigned to every four infants. The playpens were elevated so that the infants were at eye level with their teachers. The teacher's job was to begin the infants' stimulation and training as early as possible. Emphasis was placed on self-reliance. Infants were expected to be bowel and bladder trained by 18 months of age.

Question: How effective was this early training?

Evaluating its effectiveness is difficult. Among the children who were raised in this system and who are now grown, it is hard to assess which of their behaviors is due to early experiences and which to later experiences. Although Soviet nurseries provided effective care giving, the belief that group playpens fostered collective feelings or that early bowel and bladder control led to self-reliance is debatable.

When the system was in force (and many Russian day-care arrangements and schools still use the old methods, albeit with far less indoctrination), the children's upbringing was extremely controlled, with emphasis on the development of language and social skills. There was a strong regard for the "communist morality," as can be seen in a list of objectives outlined by the former Soviet Academy of Pedagogical Sciences (see Table 16.1). You will notice that the goals for 7- to

Organized peer group activity plays an important role in the socialization of children in the former Soviet Union.

TABLE 16.1

The Academy of Pedagogical Sciences Program for the Upbringing of School Children

AGES 7–11	AGES 16–18
Communist Mortality	
Sense of good and bad behavior	Collectivism, duty, honor, conscience
Truthfulness, honesty, kindness	Development of will, patience, perseverance
Atheism: science vs. superstition	Communist attitude toward work and public property
Self-discipline	Socialist humanism
Diligence in work, care of possessions	Soviet partriotism and proletarian internationalism
Friendship with classmates	
Love of one's own locality and the motherland	
Responsible Attitude Toward Learning	
Interest and striving for knowledge and skill	Understanding of the social significance of education
Industry in study	Perseverance and initiative in learning
Organizing intellectual and physical work	Increasing one's power of intellectual work (learning to plan one's work better, development of good work habits, self-criticism)
Striving to apply one's knowledge and ability in life and work	
Cultured Conduct	
Care, accuracy, neatness	Assimilation of norms of socialist community life
Courtesy and cordiality	Good manners and standards of behavior
Proper behavior on the street and in public places	
Cultured speech	
Bases of Aesthetic Culture	
Understanding of the beautiful in nature, in the conduct of people, and in creative art	Aesthetic appreciation of nature, social life, and works of art
Artistic creativity	Artistic creativity
Physical Culture and Sports	
Concern for strengthening and conditioning one's body	Maximizing the development of physical skills
Sanitary-hygienic habits	Mastering the rules of personal and social hygiene and sanitation
Preparation for sports and athletics	Training and participation in sports
	Mastering hiking and camping skills

SOURCE: Bronfenbrenner, 1970.

11-year-old children were more concrete than were those for 16- to 18-year-old adolescents. For instance, compare "friendship with classmates" with "socialist humanism," or "love of the motherland" with a comprehension of proletarian internationalism. These differences are reminiscent of Piaget's distinctions between concrete and formal operations (see Chapter 9). The collective aspect of the peer group and the emphasis on national devotion was encouraged throughout grade school and beyond.

Question: Did this emphasis affect Soviet children in a way that would make them develop differently from Western children?

During the reign of the Soviet Union, Urie Bronfenbrenner (1970) and his colleagues tested Russian children in a series of experiments. Bronfenbrenner interviewed 150 12-year-old children from four nations (the Soviet Union, what was then West Germany, Great Britain, and the United States) under three different conditions. In the first condition, the students were told that research was being conducted by a scientific foundation and that their responses to the researcher's questions would be kept completely confidential. Their friends, family, and teachers would not be able to see the results, and all data would be turned into group averages. In the second condition, the children were asked to participate again, only this time they were told that the results would be posted next to their names and shown at a special parent-teacher meeting. In the last condition, or peer condition, the students were presented with a series of tasks and told that only their peers would see the results.

In all three conditions, the Soviet children displayed far less antisocial behavior than their age-mates from other nations. Furthermore, in the peer condition, Soviet and American children behaved quite differently. When it was known that only the other children would see the results of their work, the American children were far more likely to misbehave. The Soviet children, on the other hand, showed the same control and discipline in the peer condition as they did when they expected the results to be viewed by their parents or teachers.

Among Soviet children, then, the world was centered around peers and national pride. There was emphasis on an egalitarian communist ethic, supposedly fostered by early peer and communal contact. Children and adolescents were expected to support the social system, and peer pressures were directed toward this end.

Question: How might this early experience influence the future of Russia?

It is, of course, impossible to know. However, some have expressed concern that the Russian people may be prone to follow a dictator owing to their past history and collective experiences (Smith, 1990). In Russia today, many individuals are having a very difficult time converting to a capitalist economy simply because they don't know how to behave as individuals. They are often unable to begin small enterprises, or large ones for that matter, because they lack initiative and are unable to do things for themselves. Many among them continue to wait for someone to organize them into collective groups and give them orders (Smith, 1990).

While it may be true that communism is dead in Russia, fascist regimes may yet be in the offing. If times become hard, if there is a successful military coup, and if Russia reverts to its 1,000-year old history, the people will almost certainly look for someone to collectivize their consciousness and bring them together. How much will their collective upbringing have mattered in such a case? It may well be that years of childhood experience, during which nursery nannies, teachers, and local and national bosses organized infants, children, and adolescents into cohesive forces, might play a role in forming that nation's future. Perhaps such early experiences will foster dictatorships; we can't know for sure. Hopefully, the experiences that Russians are now having as adults will somehow counter their lock-step childhoods. We can only wait and see, perhaps giving the Russians aid or advice whenever possible.

LEARNING CHECK

Multiple Choice

1. Which of the following is *not* one of the benefits of cross-cultural research?
   - **a.** It allows us to expand on theories.
   - **b.** It restricts the range of variables.
   - **c.** It unconfounds variables.
   - **d.** It allows us to study the behavior in context.
2. Amae refers to
   - **a.** "skinship."
   - **b.** fear and anxiety.
   - **c.** *shinkeishitsu.*
   - **d.** the Japanese school system.
3. Children in the former Soviet Union were raised to
   - **a.** be peer oriented.
   - **b.** have feelings of collective belonging.
   - **c.** be self-reliant.
   - **d.** all of the above.
4. In Bronfenbrenner's study, the children who displayed the least antisocial behavior when they knew their work would be shown to their parents and teachers were ______________ children.
   - **a.** West German
   - **b.** English
   - **c.** American
   - **d.** Soviet

Answers: 1. b 2. a 3. d 4. d

The Children of the Fore

The Fore (pronounced For′-ay) are a tribe that was isolated in the interior of New Guinea until their first contact with the outside world in the middle of the twentieth century. When discovered, they had no knowledge of currency, metal, or cloth. Their child-rearing practices were unique.

Anthropologist E. Richard Sorenson first visited the Fore in 1963, and he returned many times. The most striking aspect of the Fore noted by Sorenson was the absence of leaders. The society was totally egalitarian. The complete lack of a vertical structure, or pecking order, included even the children. Infants were allowed to walk about at will and do whatever they wished (it seemed that no one ever thought it necessary to give them permission). Infants almost never cried. There appeared to be no generation gap.

Question: Didn't the children get into things they shouldn't have?

Sorenson certainly thought so. The Fore children, some only toddlers, played with sharp stone axes, knives, and even fire. During the many months that Sorenson was with the Fore, he never saw a child warned away from these objects. Interestingly, Sorenson never saw any of the children get hurt.

Sorenson also observed that older children generally were amused by the desires of younger ones and usually submitted to them. Sibling rivalry appeared to be nonexistent. The members of the tribe all cooperated with each other. Friendship was considered more important than kinship. Daily activities were never scheduled, and no social demands were ever made. The environment made demands, of course, and the Fore comfortably met them.

Question: How did the Fore care for their infants?

Young babies were always with their mothers. Mothers and infants engaged in a great deal of physical contact. The mothers never set their infants aside, even

Fore children were raised in an indulgent atmosphere with close contact with peers and parents.

while preparing food or carrying heavy loads. As a result of so much touching and sharing, the Fore children learned to communicate well through a language of subtle body cues.

Once babies began crawling, they would explore anything that attracted their attention. They would visit nearby objects and people, and once able to walk, they would make short excursions with their peers.

Question: How was it that none of the infants ever got hurt while handling dangerous objects?

Sorenson believes that the vast amount of tactual stimulation and handling between the infants and their mothers helped the Fore children develop motor coordination, so that by the time they were first able to grasp and manipulate dangerous objects, there was less chance of mishap. Of course, the Fore didn't have to contend with the dangers of traffic, backyard swimming pools, firearms left lying about, delicate electrical appliances, or even rocky cliffs. In their environment, permissiveness was suitable; in others, it obviously isn't.

Fore children, like the children in other cultures, used their mothers as a base of operations from which to explore the world. However, the egalitarianism of the community was such that the children were just as content to use anybody else's mother who happened to be nearby. Because Fore children were allowed to move about freely, they had ample opportunity to observe many different adults engaged in work. In this way, the children learned to imitate different adult activities.

An interesting result of this relaxed upbringing and characteristic imitation of observed behavior was that the Fore children immediately adopted the new ways that they saw when they were discovered by the outside world. The next generation of the Fore readily accepted steel, salt, medicine, cloth, laws, government, religion, and money. In fact, until contact with the outside world, the Fore didn't even have a name for themselves. In 1957, an Australian patrol officer accidentally referred to them as the Fore, which is actually the name of a neighboring tribe, and rather than point out that they had no name, they accepted it.

Question: What became of the Fore?

In the 1960s, a road was opened to their village, and they soon began to roam hundreds of miles from their homeland. Many of the Fore adolescents went to work for coffee plantations. Some were impressed by the success of the European planters, and rather than work for them, took some coffee plants back to the interior. After a few years, the Fore tribe, which a generation earlier had never heard of money, was collecting earnings of $250,000 a year from its coffee crop! The Fore used the money to build better roads, which could accommodate four-wheel drive Jeeps. Another effect of the money was that the Fore ceased to be a tribe of equals. Community housing vanished, and family housing began. Children (as heirs) began to belong distinctly to somebody. Toddlers no longer had free access to their mothers' breasts, because the women had begun to wear blouses. Considerable frustration, anger, aggression, withdrawal, and even selfishness were observed for the first time among the Fore children. Sorenson has said, "One of the great tragedies of our modern time may be that most of these independent experiments in living are disappearing before we can discover the implications of their special expressions of human possibility" (Sorenson, 1977, p. 114).

The Fore have shown us how great an effect life experiences and learning can have on human development. In just one generation they changed so thoroughly as to defy belief.

The Ik: A Culture in Disintegration

In the late 1960s, anthropologist Colin Turnbull went to Africa to study the Ik of Uganda. The Ik were a hunter-gatherer tribe that had been forced by the Ugandan government to move and to take up agriculture. They were starving in the arid land in which they had been relocated. Their culture had been horribly disrupted, and their behavior had become inhumane and shocking. The Ik are worth studying because they tell us that parenting or being humane is not necessarily "natural" to our species. In the Ik, we see again how flexible our species is. This time, however, we view the darker side.

The forced migration of the Ik disrupted their family units. The family as a social kinship ceased to exist. Previously, the Ik had shown kindness, affection, and charity. Now, in the new environment, kindness, affection, and charity were dangerous qualities. When one is hungry, charity with food can be fatal.

When Turnbull visited the seven Ik villages, he found that the Ik had become harsh and cruel. Anyone who fell or was injured while walking along the steep trails was greeted with shrieks of laughter. Children as young as 2 or 3 years were forced out of their parents' huts to fend for themselves. Many begged to sit in their parents' doorway for shelter. Although they often were allowed to do this, they were forced away if they lay down or fell asleep. The old were left to starve. The Ik had learned to dismiss love. They actually referred to love as idiotic and dangerous.

Question: What happened to the young Ik children?

Unable to survive as individuals until about the age of 13 years, the young children congregated into bands. There was a junior band of children 3 to 7 years of age and a senior band of children approximately 8 to 12 years of age. The children formed temporary alliances with age-mates as protection against attack by other children or adults. The weakest soon died. Occasionally, a strong child leader emerged; but this child was often destroyed by the other children out of fear or hatred.

Turnbull recounts the story of Lobin, the last and oldest of the Ik ritual priests. Although revered in other days, when Lobin became ill from hunger, bands of roving Ik children turned on him. They danced before him and teased him, tripped him and taunted him. Lobin's own grandson crept up behind the old man and beat him on his bald head with a stick. Turnbull tried to feed Lobin, but he refused to eat. After being without food for four days and without water for two, Lobin asked his family for help. They told him to go away. He began to cry. He begged his son to let him die indoors. But his son refused because if Lobin died indoors, his son would have to give him a funeral and feed the mourners. Lobin was forced to stay outdoors that night—where he died.

Turnbull has said,

> The Ik teach us that our much vaunted human values are not inherent in humanity at all but are associated only with a particular form of survival called society and that all, even society itself, are luxuries that can be dispensed with. (Turnbull, 1973, p. 56)

LEARNING CHECK

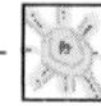

Matching

1. ___ Wandering groups of peers
2. ___ Parental rejection
3. ___ Nursery schools
4. ___ Egalitarian
5. ___ Culture that underwent a drastic change
6. ___ Aggression and selfishness as newly acquired attributes
7. ___ Professional upbringers

a. Fore
b. Ik
c. Neither Fore nor Ik
d. Both Fore and Ik

Answers: 1. d 2. b 3. c 4. a 5. d 6. d 7. c

APPLICATIONS

My First Impressionism

What child hasn't learned to draw a stick figure or make a triangle shape above a rectangle shape to draw a house? What child hasn't learned to draw a box on two circles to make a car? All of us are familiar with these kinds of children's pictures. Look at the two drawings in Figure 16.1. They were drawn by American children and are typical representations of the kinds of drawings children often make.

Question: Do the kinds of things that children draw follow a particular developmental sequence as they get older?

It has been a common belief among researchers that they do. Some IQ tests even rely on such progressions to determine a child's intellectual ability. As psychologist Howard Gardner pointed out,

> According to the emerging consensus, a child begins making marks during the second year of life, at first enjoying the motor sensations of banging marker on paper, but soon coming to prize instead the contrasts between the dark scribbled lines and the white surface. The contriving of certain geometric forms—circles, crosses, rectangles, triangles—coupled with an increasing proclivity to combine these marks into more intricate patterns is a fundamental development of the third and fourth years of life, . . . and indeed a pivotal moment occurs some time during the third, fourth, or fifth year of life: the child for the first time produces a recognizable depiction of some thing in the world—in most cases the ubiquitous "tadpole man" who stands for everyman. (Gardner, 1980, p. 10)

Is this view correct? Do children worldwide follow the same developmental sequence observed in American children? Are these drawings universal, or can the power of culture influence even this most fundamental of childhood abilities?

To provide an answer to these questions, Alexander Alland, an anthropologist at Columbia University, extensively examined the drawings of children from six different cultures. In his book *Playing with Form: Children Draw in Six Cultures* (Alland, 1983), he described the striking differences he discovered. Although his work is mostly descriptive, it also provides some interesting speculations about why children in different cultures produce different kinds of drawings.

Examine Figure 16.2, where you'll see two typical drawings made by Japanese children. At first, you may be struck by the fact that these drawings are more detailed and sophisticated than the drawings made by the American children. This may be especially surprising to you because the Japanese children who drew these were actually younger than the American children whose drawings were shown in Figure 16.1! Alland points out that this observation is typical when Japanese and American drawings are compared. He

FIGURE 16.1
Drawings by American children, ages 5 years, 7 months (left) and 5 years, 11 months (right). (*Source:* Alland, 1983, pp. 164, 168)

APPLICATIONS

believes that the difference occurs because Japanese children learn at an early age to manipulate and use art materials. Alland points out that Japanese kindergartners are well supplied with art instruction and materials and that they learn to put together paper shapes and designs that help them learn about complex shapes and perspectives. Also, the Japanese children often are able to create artistically interesting pictures that reflect their individuality and national culture. Notice the red sun in both drawings; the choice of color was perhaps influenced by the rising red sun found on the Japanese flag. As Alland has stated, "Viewed against their age mates in the United States, . . . Japanese children appear to make more complete, more interesting, and more harmoniously structured pictures" (Alland, 1983, p. 154).

FIGURE 16.2
Drawings by Japanese children, ages 5 years (top) and 5 years, 2 months (bottom). (*Source:* Alland, 1983, pp. 149, 152)

APPLICATIONS

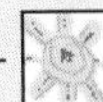

Both the Japanese and American drawings stand in stark contrast with the kinds of drawings made by French children (see Figure 16.3). French children tend to take a long time and to make very complex designs. These abstract designs often are filled with large units of color. Rarely do French children depict houses or cars.

Question: Are French children taught to express "modern art"?

Actually, the French children in Alland's sample had had little exposure to art technique. They weren't trying to imitate "modern art."

Question: Why are the drawings by the French children so different?

Alland believes that part of the difference is due to the longer attention span of these children. French parents often encourage their children to sit quietly for long periods, especially during mealtime or in the presence of adults. Sitting for a long time without any specific purpose in mind may be a general requirement for the kinds of designs the French children produced. It takes time to fill in an entire page with a colorful design. Of course, this explanation is only speculative. As was noted earlier, this research is descriptive. We can see that children *do* draw different pictures in different cultures. Culture appears to have an effect. Why this occurs, however, is not fully understood. Let's look at some more examples.

FIGURE 16.3
Drawings by French children, ages 3 years, 11 months (top) and 3 years, 6 months (bottom). (*Source:* Alland, 1983, pp. 177, 174)

Applications

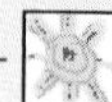

Ponape is a Pacific island in Micronesia. Drawings made by Ponapean children look extremely different from any we've seen so far (see Figure 16.4). The children tend to start in one particular place on the paper and to draw abstract connected designs outward from the initial mark. The drawings are almost always in one color, and pages rarely are filled. Alland noticed that these children were very shy, had no previous drawing experience, and seemed insecure in the unfamiliar situation of drawing a picture. Perhaps their limited drawings reflect their hesitancy and unfamiliarity.

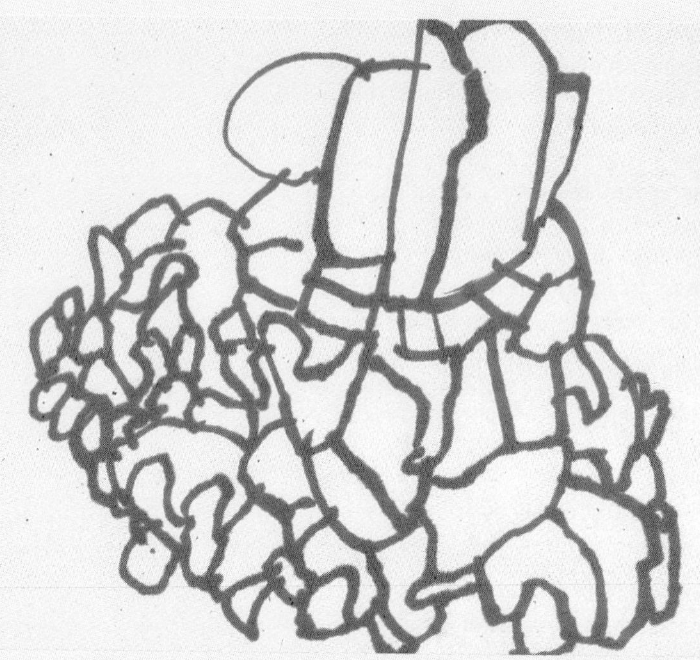

Figure 16.4
Drawings by Ponapean children, ages 5 years (top) and 4 years (bottom). (*Source:* Alland, 1983, pp. 81, 78)

APPLICATIONS

Bali, like Ponape, is an island in the Pacific Ocean. Balinese culture, unlike Ponapean culture, is rich in color. The Balinese love color, and they incorporate it in the flowers they wear, the cloth they weave, and their art. Balinese children's drawings reflect this experience. The children generally used three or more colors, and often used all the colors offered. Balinese children tended to fill the entire page with hundreds of small marks, and as they worked, the marks got progressively smaller (see Figure 16.5). Even when they used realistic forms, they still tended to fill the page with hundreds of beautiful colorful marks.

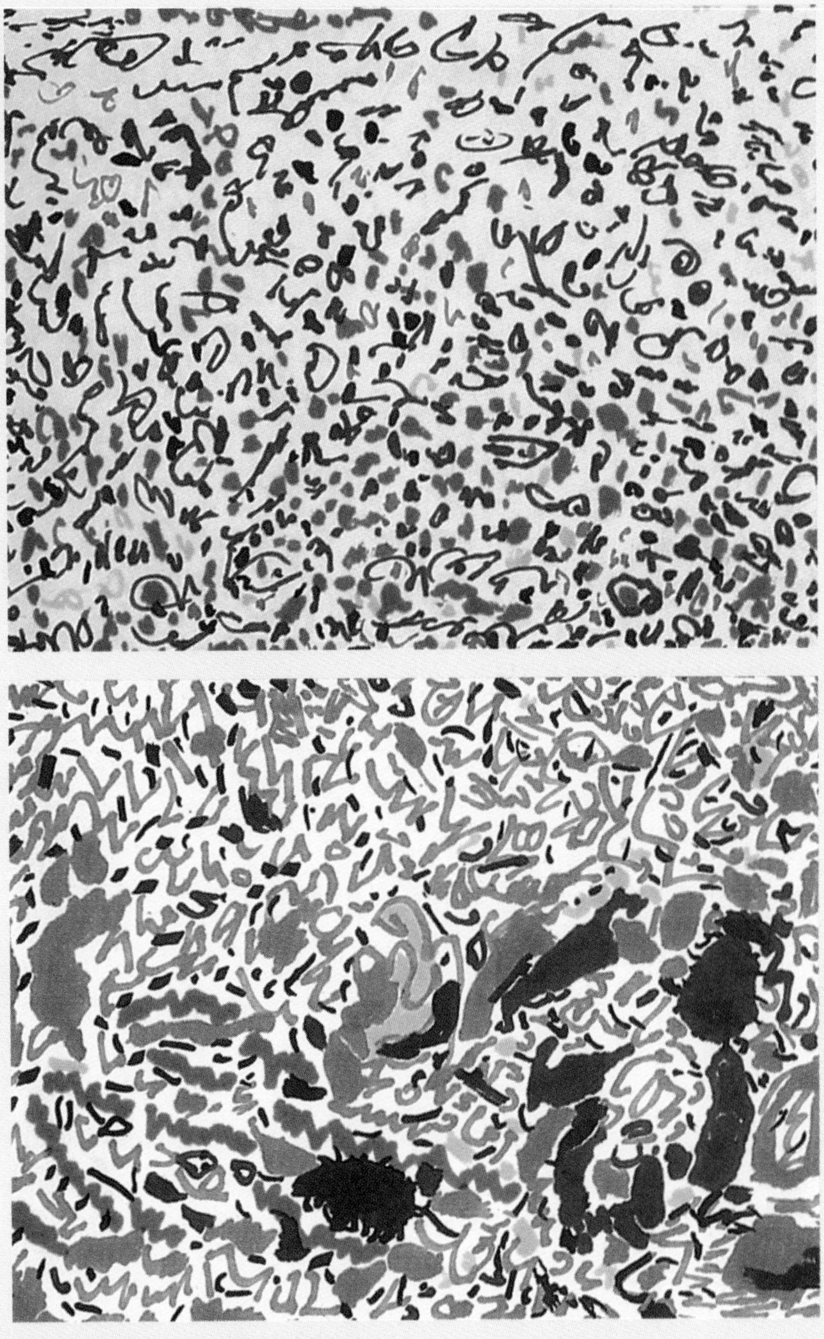

FIGURE 16.5

Drawings by Balinese children, ages 3 years, 3 months (top) and 4 years, 1 month (bottom). (*Source:* Alland, 1983, pp. 38, 44)

APPLICATIONS

The final set of drawings, shown in Figure 16.6, were made by the children of Taiwan. Like the children of Bali, the children of Taiwan tended to fill the page with many marks. But these marks appear more as self-contained units. The Taiwanese made moderate use of color.

Question: Have Taiwanese children had any particular experiences that would tend to make them draw this way?

Again, no one is certain, but the explanation may have a great deal to do with the fact that most Taiwanese children by the age of 5 years are already being trained to draw Chinese characters. You'll notice that the drawing on the bottom shows Arabic numerals, which may reflect the child's interest in schoolwork and writing. The small boxes may be the beginning representations of Chinese characters. In the drawing on the top, early forms of Chinese characters are already apparent. In this case, then, the culture has taught the child to blend language and art. In fact, while learning to recognize Chinese characters, the children are taught to paint them with brushes.

As you can see, there appear to be no obvious standard developmental sequences in children's drawings. What children draw, what they find important or beautiful appears to depend greatly on what their culture teaches and what they see in the world around them.

FIGURE 16.6
Drawings by Taiwanese children, ages 5 years, 3 months (top) and 5 years, 6 months (bottom). (*Source:* Alland, 1983, pp. 122, 123)

SUMMARY

- Different cultural experiences can affect the way a person perceives or thinks about things. Almost all the developmental aspects of human beings can be affected to some extent by culture.
- Many benefits can be gained from cross-cultural research. They include the ability to expand theories, to increase the range of variables, to unconfound variables, and to study how general principles are affected by contextual factors.
- Through cultural research, we can see the massive power and effect of learning on development. Even when formal schooling is not available, children learn what the culture deems appropriate.
- The Japanese family provides an envelope of security for its children. The physical closeness is so great that the Japanese have a word for it—*amae*. Some non-Western psychologists believe that such early experience results in a lifelong need to be a member of a group.
- Most Japanese students who finish college will work for one company for the rest of their lives; their company becomes a family to them. The danger of failure in or rejection from this family-society often places great pressure on the children to succeed in school, occasionally leading to serious disorders caused by fear or anxiety. The Japanese refer to this pressure as *shinkeishitsu*.
- In contrast, children in the former Soviet Union were raised to be peer oriented rather than family oriented. In Soviet nursery schools, there were four children to each adult upbringer. An early emphasis was placed on collective belonging and self-reliance.
- In experiments, Soviet children were found to be as well controlled and well behaved for peers as they were for parents and teachers. These findings contrasted markedly with the observations of children from West Germany, England, and the United States.
- The children of the Fore were raised in a unique way and were allowed complete freedom. The conditions in their society were such that this child-rearing technique worked well. However, the Fore were changed drastically by contact with the outside world. Their experience shows how dramatic the effect of environment and learning can be and how extremely flexible our species is.
- The example of the Ik also highlights the flexibility of our species. As their culture disintegrated, they demonstrated that even our most "human" behaviors are greatly a product of culture.

QUESTIONS FOR DISCUSSION

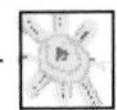

1. Do you or any of the members of your family have behaviors that can be traced to a particular cultural heritage? Which behaviors are these, and why do you attribute them to a certain culture?

2. "Very few wives would gladly share their husbands with another woman." Can you guess why this is a culturally biased statement?

3. If you had to move to Japan permanently and to raise a family there, would you change your child-rearing methods? Should Vietnam refugees or native Americans change their child-rearing techniques so that their children will be more like most Americans? Why or why not?

SUGGESTIONS FOR FURTHER READING

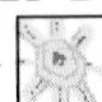

1. Fried, M., & Fried, M. H. (1980). *Transitions: Four rituals in eight cultures*. New York: Norton.
2. Munroe, R. H., Munroe, R. L., & Whiting, B. B. (Eds.). (1981). *Handbook on cross-cultural human development*. New York: Garland.
3. Sarason, S. (1990). *The challenge of art to psychology*. New Haven: Yale University Press.
4. Stevenson, H., Azuma, H., & Hakuta, K. (Eds.). (1986). *Child development and education in Japan*. New York: Freeman.
5. Wagner, D. A., & Stevenson, H. W. (Eds.). (1982). *Cultural perspectives on child development*. New York: Freeman.
6. Whiting, B. B., & Edwards, C. P. (1988). *Children of different worlds*. Cambridge, MA: Harvard University Press.

CHAPTER 17

CHILDREN WITH SPECIAL NEEDS

CHAPTER PREVIEW

SOMETHING WAS WRONG

SCHIZOPHRENIA IS A severe mental disorder. Those who suffer from it commonly experience serious disturbances of emotion and thought. They often become withdrawn, show inappropriate emotional responses, suffer from hallucinations, or express strange thoughts or beliefs. The disease commonly makes its first appearance in early adulthood.

DRS. ELAINE WALKER and Richard Lewine have been looking for early warning signs that might put a person at risk for schizophrenia. In their experiment, they had a large number of observers watch home movies of families interacting with one another (Walker & Lewine, 1990). The films had been made more than 25 years ago and were typical of the kind that most families take. Each family (there were five altogether) had two or three children, and each film covered a time span of at least five years. In each family, one of the children later became schizophrenic. None of the parents was schizophrenic, nor was any of the siblings, who, at the time of the experiment, were all healthy and at least 25 years of age. No schizophrenia had been reported in any of the children seen in the home movies until early adulthood. In fact, none of the parents ever reported seeing any sign of the impending disaster.

Question: What were the observers looking for in the home movies?

They were told only that one of the children from each family later became schizophrenic. The observers, among whom were students and other nonprofessionals, were given no criteria on which to base a judgement. They were simply told to watch the films and try to decide from what they saw which child it would be. To everyone's amazement, the observers were right 80 percent of the time, far more than chance alone would have predicted.

Question: What had the observers seen?

The children in the film all seemed normal, except perhaps one might not keep eye contact as long as another, or maybe one had a goofy grin, nothing unusual for normal children. But because the observers had to choose, they picked the child who seemed a little different. Of course, many normal children seem "a little different" and go on to be perfectly healthy adults; in fact, most do. But for this group of children, untrained observers were able to tell, just by watching, that something was wrong.

IN THIS CHAPTER, we'll investigate children who have special needs, and we'll study disorders that may impair child development. Some of these disorders have important biological components associated with them, while others are more a function of environmental experiences—or the lack of them. Any of these disorders or problems may leave a child in need compared with his or her peers.

RESOURCES

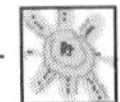

Developmental Psychopathology

Over many years, researchers have gathered a great wealth of information about the range and diversity of child development in this culture and in others. In the first 16 chapters of this textbook, we have examined many of their findings. Because of the vast amount of information that researchers have acquired about child development, it is becoming more and more possible to predict instances when development is likely to diverge from normal paths and follow a route that may result in a child's suffering a handicap or hardship. The emerging field of **developmental psychopathology** is the study of abnormal development and the factors that may make it likely to occur (Cicchetti, 1984).

More specifically, developmental psychopathology may be defined as "the study of abnormal behavior within a context of measuring the effects of genetic, ontogenetic [individual biological development], biochemical, cognitive, affective [emotional], social, or any other ongoing developmental influence on behavior" (Rolf & Read, 1984, p. 9). Many genetic, ontogenetic, biochemical, cognitive, affective, and social factors are known to have a strong influence in causing development to follow an abnormal path. For example, we have already discussed any number of genetic and chromosomal disorders that may lead to problems, giving particular attention to Down syndrome (see Chapter 2). In this chapter, let's examine some of the diverse influences that may result in abnormal development. You will see that although some devastating disorders remain shrouded in mystery, researchers are beginning to unravel others.

SCHIZOPHRENIA
A term used to describe a number of functional psychoses that are characterized by serious thought disturbances, withdrawal, inappropriate emotional response or lack of emotional response, hallucinations, and delusions.

DEVELOPMENTAL PSYCHOPATHOLOGY
The study of the development of abnormal behavior that has been brought about by genetic, ontogenetic, biochemical, cognitive, affective, or social influences.

Disorders with Probable Genetic Involvement

A number of serious disorders that may occur in childhood are thought to be tied to genetic abnormalities of some sort, although they do not follow the laws of inheritance described in Chapter 2. Three of the most studied are schizophrenia, depression, and learning disability. There is a great need for advancing our understanding in these areas. It has been estimated through population sampling that as many as 22 percent of all American children have disorders, requiring treatment, including emotional, behavioral, and temperamental disorders (Costello et al., 1988), and that many of these disorders are linked in one way or another to inheritance.

SCHIZOPHRENIA

Schizophrenia is a serious disorder affecting as many as 1 million people in the United States and many millions more throughout the world. About one-half of all the mental hospital beds in the United States are occupied by persons assessed as schizophrenic. Although schizophrenia is typically a disorder of young adults, it can begin in childhood. Schizophrenia in childhood has its most devastating developmental effects on the child's ability to monitor and test reality (Foley, Johnson, & Raye, 1983) and on her ability to initiate and maintain interactions with peers and other socially important individuals (Asarnow & Sherman, 1984).

Contrary to common belief, being schizophrenic does not mean having more than one personality. Rather, schizophrenia involves a breakdown of integrated personality functioning. Emotions become flat and distorted. Thought, language, and behavior become bizarre and disturbed. These bizarre behaviors are commonly accompanied by delusions and hallucinations. As a result, schizophrenics often see things or hear voices that are not there.

AT ISSUE

A Delicate Balance

Baby Doe was born in April 1982 with Down syndrome. His digestive tract was also blocked, so that he could not be fed in the normal way. His parents refused to consent to the corrective surgery needed and asked the hospital to withhold food and water from the baby. The hospital asked the state court to intervene, but the court refused, arguing that the parents had made a treatment decision that was reasonable. Six days later the baby died.

In October 1983, Baby Jane Doe was born. She suffered from spina bifida, a birth defect in which the vertebrae do not fuse into a backbone and a bulge, or cyst, containing part of the spinal cord pokes through an opening in the back. The baby also suffered from hydrocephalus (a building up of fluid around the brain). Without surgery to repair the spinal opening and install a shunt to draw off the fluid from the brain, the baby would be severely retarded, and even with such help, she would probably be handicapped for life. Her parents asked that no extraordinary measures, including surgery, be taken to save the baby's life.

On the eleventh day of Baby Jane Doe's life, the U.S. Department of Health and Human Services sued the hospital in an effort to require the surgery. The court, on the other hand, sided with the parents, arguing that only Congress, not the executive branch, had the power to take such a step to support the baby.

But who should have the right to decide whether to withhold medical treatment from a baby with birth defects? Should it be the parents, or the doctors, or the state government, or some branch of the federal government?

Ronald Reagan, who at the time was President of the United States, became concerned when he heard the plight of Baby Jane Doe. He sent a memo to his cabinet officer in charge of the Department of Health and Human Services. That department then issued its first *Baby Doe regulations*. Among other things, the regulations required hospitals to post a sign that said in part, "Discriminatory Failure to Feed and Care for Handicapped Infants in this Facility is Prohibited by Federal Law" (Hoving, 1986, p. 51). Along with the sign was a 24-hour toll-free hot line that individuals could call anonymously if they believed a violation was occurring. Attempts were also made by the Department of Health and Human Services to protect infants under the Civil Rights Act. Here it was argued that any decision to withhold treatment from an infant because he had Down syndrome, for instance, would be just as wrong as a decision not to treat an infant because he was black. This view was not supported by the courts, however. In 1986, the U.S. Supreme Court held in the case of *Bowen v. The American Hospital Association* that it was not legal to require hospitals to post the Baby Doe signs.

Many individuals agreed with the Court in that they supported the view that no one but parents and physicians are in a position to understand thoroughly the individual circumstances and to know what should be done. It was further suggested that the determination to protect and save every single handicapped child, no matter how severe the handicap, would place a devastating burden on many families, particularly because the government often does not provide financial support for the parents or hospitals—the ones who must care for a severely handicapped child. Also, the quality of the handicapped child's life was considered. Would the child be saved only to be faced with a life of pain and anguish that would end prematurely?

On the other hand, many people believe that someone needs to protect the children who are born with obvious handicaps and that parents, doctors, and hospitals aren't always the best advocates. The brief filed in the Bowen case by the American Association on Mental Deficiency asserted that "parents of handicapped children still consistently report that health care providers misinformed them about the nature of their child's handicapping condition and the prospect for the child's development, education and future" (Hoving, 1986, p. 52). As for Baby Jane Doe, no shunt was provided to draw off the fluid that, under pressure, was damaging her brain. Only a dressing was placed over the spinal protrusion in her back. As a result, she was, no doubt, more severely damaged by her condition than she might have been had she undergone the surgery.

The bizarre behaviors associated with schizophrenia may range in severity from surprisingly mild to completely incapacitating. Impairment of an individual may vary considerably throughout his development as well.

Question: What causes schizophrenia in children?

No one is certain what the cause of schizophrenia is, and there are many theories about it. However, studies of the incidence of schizophrenia among identical and fraternal twins have indicated a possible hereditary component to schizophrenia. For instance, among a large population in Norway, it was found that if one *identical* twin had schizophrenia, there was a 38 percent chance that the other would also have it. Among *fraternal* twins, the chance was only 10 percent (Kringlen, 1967). Similar findings have been obtained in the United States (Gottesman & Shields, 1972). A case reported at the National Institutes of Mental Health even told of schizophrenia in all the members of a set of identical quadruplets (Rosenthal & Quinn, 1977).

In 1962, Harvard psychiatrist Seymour S. Kety and his colleagues investigated the background of 33 schizophrenics in Copenhagen. These 33 schizophrenics had been adopted and raised by foster families. Kety examined the foster parents and the biological parents and blood relatives of the schizophrenics. He found that the incidence of schizophrenia among the *biological* relatives of the 33 schizophrenics was five times greater than that among the adopted relatives. Furthermore, among the biological relatives, the chance of schizophrenia was eight to ten times higher among brothers, sisters, and parents and only two to three times higher among more distant relatives. This finding indicates that not only is someone with schizophrenia in her family more likely to become schizophrenic, but also the likelihood increases in direct proportion to how close the relative is genetically to the offspring (Greenberg, 1980).

Question: Is there any way to tell which children are likely to become schizophrenic?

To date there is no adequate way to predict who will develop schizophrenia. As noted in the Chapter Preview, some attempts are under way to identify children who are at high risk for developing schizophrenia, but the results at best are tentative.

DEPRESSION

DEPRESSION
A feeling of sadness and sometimes of total apathy. Guilt or the inability to cope with problems, frustration, or conflict are often behind the depression, possibly influenced by chemical imbalances and heredity.

The term **depression** describes a wide range of emotional lows, from sadness to a severe suicidal state. All children feel unhappy at one time or another, and sadness can be quite natural as long as there is a reason for it. Clinical depression, however, is a lasting and continuous state of depression without obvious cause. A mood of unhappiness and apathy prevails. Depressed children usually regard themselves in a negative way and blame themselves for things that have gone wrong. Their formerly favorite activities bore them, and they show little interest in socializing with others (Carlson & Cantwell, 1982). Other common signs of depression in children include sleep difficulties, excessive fatigue, cognitive impairment, agitation, changes in attitude toward school, physical complaints, and changes in appetite (Poznanski, Mokros, Grossman, & Freeman, 1985). Depending on the child's age and how depression is defined, it is estimated that between 1 and 6 percent of all children suffer from serious depression (Alper, 1986).

Question: How old do children have to be before they are capable of showing a serious depression?

There may not be any minimum age. Serious depressive disorder has been found to exist in children of all ages (Kovacs, 1989), including preschoolers (Kashani, Holcomb, & Orvaschel, 1986) and infants (Field et al., 1988). In most cases, the onset of depression appears to occur after a period of significant stress.

Clinical depression in children is a lasting and continuous state of depression without obvious cause. The tendency to become depressed has been found to run in families.

Question: What kind of genetic links are there to depression?

In 1962, psychiatrist Kety investigated the possibility of a genetic link to depression. Kety studied 85 adoptees with emotional disorders, primarily major depression. These individuals had not been reared by their biological parents. Kety reported a significant concentration of depression in the adoptees' *biological* relatives, finding that the relatives were three times more likely to suffer from depression than were members of the adopted families. Among all the family members in the study, both biological and adopted, there were 18 reported suicides. The fact that 15 of these suicides were among the biological relatives of the depressed group suggests the possibility of a genetic factor in depression and suicide. More recent studies have provided further support for the hypothesis that childhood depression is associated with a family history of depression (Livingston, Nugent, Rader, & Smith, 1985).

Question: Is serious depression inherited then?

Although there may be a strong inheritance component, many depressed children have no obvious family history of the disorder (Cadoret, O'Gorman, Heywood, & Troughton, 1985). This implies, of course, that many forms of prolonged depression may have their basis in the environment.

Question: Some people are so severely depressed that they become suicidal. But isn't suicide among children extremely rare?

Unfortunately, no. Every year, 12,000 children between the ages of 5 and 14 years are admitted to psychiatric hospitals in the United States because of suicidal behavior. Many researchers believe that the figure could easily be 20 times that high, but that suicide attempts are disguised by the children as accidents, are concealed by parents, or, in cases where death occurs, are not acknowledged by coroners (Turkington, 1983).

Question: But don't children, especially younger children, have a poor understanding about what death is? How could you call their deaths "suicide"?

Consider the following quote: "It wasn't an accident. I figured if I died, it wouldn't hurt as much as if I lived" (Turkington, 1983, p. 15). This statement was whispered by a 5-year-old child as he lay dying in a hospital. He had deliberately run in front of a truck after telling his brother that he felt unwanted. In fact, suicidal children are more likely than others to be unwanted, abused, or neglected by their parents (Rosenthal & Rosenthal, 1984). Perhaps a child as young as this might not have a full understanding of the ramifications of his action. It really doesn't matter. The point is, he did kill himself.

Question: What can be done to prevent children from taking their own lives?

Because child suicide has been such an unspoken tragedy, researchers have few data on which to make assessments. The most common intervention focuses on teaching the child how to use more effective problem-solving skills and how to cope with his or her sadness and stress. This emphasis includes involving the entire family in an intensive therapy.

It should be noted that the majority of depressed children do not commit suicide or even attempt it. A distinction must be made between the depressed child and the suicidal child. Exactly how we make that distinction, though, remains unclear. Currently, the most telltale sign appears to be depression coupled with a rage that expresses itself generally in the form of threats directed toward oneself or others (Turkington, 1983). Children who commit suicide are also more likely to have discussed suicide, been exposed to suicide, and threatened suicide than are other children (Shafii, Carrigan, Whittinghill, & Derrick, 1985). Psychologically disturbed children and children who have shown a preoccupation with death are also at greater risk (Pfeffer, Plutchik, Mizruchi, & Lipkins, 1986).

Although the developmental disruption caused by childhood depression may have lifelong effects, it is more likely to be amenable to treatment if it is diagnosed and treated early. Children who suffer from depression and mood disorders often respond well to medication, and they don't necessarily have to continue taking the medication beyond childhood.

LEARNING DISABILITIES

A **learning disability** is defined as a learning problem that is not caused by environmental factors, mental retardation, or emotional disturbances. It is a form of intellectual handicap. Learning disabilities are typically specific disorders associated with listening, thinking, talking, reading, writing, spelling, or arithmetic. Learning-disabled children often have difficulty communicating to others what they have seen or heard (Feagans & Short, 1986).

Teachers who are aware of learning disabilities are able to tailor material to each child's needs. For instance, if a child finds it hard to process visual information, work can be modified to an auditory format that is easier for the child to comprehend.

Question: How common are learning disabilities?

It is estimated that between 3 and 5 percent of all schoolchildren show some difficulty that falls within the definition of learning disability (Van Osdol & Shane, 1982).

Dyslexia One of the most common learning disorders, one in which the ability to read is disrupted, is **dyslexia.** Children with dyslexia find it difficult to process certain information and often show signs of their disorder as early as age 2½, when their sentence length, sentence complexity, and pronunciation are found to be below average (Scarborough, 1990). As they become older and enter school, they often are unsure in which direction to write, and they frequently confuse *b*'s with *d*'s, *p*'s with *q*'s, and other similar letters. They also may have difficulty calling objects by their correct names. For instance, a cup may become a "drinking thing" (Clark & Gosnell, 1982).

LEARNING DISABILITY
A learning problem that is not due to environmental causes, mental retardation, or emotional disturbances; often associated with problems in listening, thinking, talking, reading, writing, spelling, and arithmetic.

DYSLEXIA
An impairment of reading ability, such that a person can make little sense of what he or she reads; letters or words often appear to be transposed.

ATTENTION DEFICIT DISORDER
A behavioral disorder characterized by the display of a developmentally inappropriate failure of attention and a pervasive impulsivity. Hyperactivity commonly accompanies the disorder.

Question: If a child typically reverses b's *and* d's, *is that an indication of a learning disability?*

Confirming learning disability takes knowledge, skill, and sophisticated testing. Many children reverse *b*'s and *d*'s or have difficulty in organizing their reading or writing, but this alone is not necessarily an indication of a learning disability. With a reasonable amount of teaching, many of these children correct their errors (Casey, 1986). A real learning disability, such as dyslexia, becomes evident only after the child fails to make adequate progress following normal school intervention.

Question: What causes dyslexia?

The cause is uncertain, but some areas of investigation look promising. Researchers have been exploring the possibility that particular areas of the brain are damaged or are in disruptive competition with one another. Autopsies of many dyslexics have revealed a jumbling of brain neurons as well as the occurrence of nonmyelinated neurons in locations where myelinated neurons usually are located (Clark & Gosnell, 1982).

It may be that dyslexia, or certain forms of it, are inherited. For years, it has been known that dyslexia runs in families. This is also true of a number of other learning disabilities (Pennington, Bender, Puck, Salbenblatt, & Robinson, 1982). Through the use of a highly sophisticated form of genetic analysis, researchers have found strong evidence for the existence of a dominant gene on chromosome 15 responsible for specific reading disability or dyslexia (Smith, Kimberling, Pennington, & Lubs, 1983). The findings are not completely conclusive, however, because this determination was made statistically, and the actual gene itself has not been isolated. Even so, this is fairly good evidence that such a reading disability can be inherited (Pennington et al., 1986). But even if the research were confirmed by further investigation, it would not necessarily mean that all dyslexia was linked to a genetic problem. Dyslexia may exist for many reasons; this may be just one cause.

Question: If children with dyslexia can't make sense of the letters they see, would larger print help?

Dyslexia is not caused by a *sensory* defect. It is not a vision problem. It's not just that the letters don't make sense or can't be put together to form words. Dyslexic children have difficulty making sense of any conceptual information given to them in written form. To emphasize this, consider the Japanese and Chinese languages. Both languages contain no letters and no words, instead using symbols in the form of characters. Each character stands for a thing or concept. Yet dyslexia is also reported among the Japanese and Chinese. Orthographic variables—variables associated with the shapes of the letters and the number of syllables in a word—are not that important. What is most striking is the inability to handle written conceptual information (Stevenson et al., 1982).

Even if dyslexia is shown to have deep roots in one's genes, this does not mean that the problem cannot be overcome. A number of interesting techniques are used to help dyslexics overcome their difficulties, and they have often proved very effective (Vellutino, 1987).

Attention Deficit Disorder **Attention deficit disorder** is a broad category that in practice has not been well defined (Bales, 1985). In general, children who show attention deficit disorder display inappropriate inattention and impulsivity. Such children will typically fail to finish what they start and won't seem to listen. They are often easily distracted and have difficulty concentrating on schoolwork. Children with this disorder are also impulsive. Such children may often act before thinking or may quickly change from one activity to another. They will frequently call out in class and require lots of supervision, and they may have difficulty waiting their turn in a group activity. Many children with attention deficit disorder also display **hyperactivity.** Besides showing inappropriate inattention and impulsivity, such children may also run around and climb on things excessively, have difficulty sitting, fidget a great deal, or move about more than would be expected during sleep. Hyperactive children are on the go, as if "driven by a motor."

HYPERACTIVITY
A disorder in children marked by a chronic tendency to be excessively active, to lack control, and to be unable to concentrate.

The underlying cause of the disorder is not known. Many researchers argue that it is biogenetically induced, some believe by an allergic reaction to food additives (Feingold, 1974), although double-blind studies have failed to support this idea (Mattes & Gittelman, 1981; Weiss, 1982). Close examination of the brains of hyperactive individuals does, however, typically show reduced activity in the regions of the brain responsible for motor activity and attention, giving further support for a biological cause (Zametkin et al., 1990). Hyperactive children are often treated with stimulant drugs, such as amphetamines or Ritalin. Ironically, stimulants seem to help hyperactive children lengthen their attention span and become calm. There is also evidence that hyperactivity may, in many instances, be a learned disorder—that is, taught by the environment. (In such cases, it is not properly classified as a learning disability, which, by definition, is not caused by environmental factors.) This view is supported by the fact that "hyperactivity" often can be treated as effectively with behavior modification (see Chapter 7) as it can with medication (Pelham, 1977; Wulbert & Dries, 1977).

Question: If drugs are effective, why take the time to do behavior modification?

The long-term effects of drugs such as Ritalin are relatively unknown. In some cases, the drugs have induced seizures or otherwise caused harm (Schrag & Divoky, 1975; Whalen & Henker, 1976). Some parents do not monitor their child's dosage carefully. And children who have to take their "good pill" every day often come to think of themselves as bad people (or why would they need a "good pill"?).

The problem is especially serious considering the number of children affected. Amazingly, 800,000 children (1 percent of all children in the United States between the ages of 5 and 12 years) at one time were undergoing treatment with drugs for hyperactivity (Havighurst, 1976). Moreover, most physicians once favored drugs as the first line of treatment (Barkley, 1977; Cole & Moore, 1975), and many still do. To complicate matters further, the "hyperactive" label has often been applied indiscriminately, often being used to describe children who simply become bored and begin to fidget in the classroom (Levine, Kozak, & Shaiova, 1977).

Toxic Induction of Learning Problems

Another concern has been the discovery that learning problems may be related to contact with toxic environmental substances. Amont the toxic substances thought to induce learning problems are the heavy metals, such as cadmium, mercury, and lead (Shaheen, 1984). In one of the first studies to show this, the Case Western Reserve Laboratory used a mass spectrographic analysis of hair samples taken from children and discovered that children who were having serious learning difficulties also tended to have significantly higher levels of cadmium and lead in their bodies than did children from a well-matched control group (Pihl & Parkes, 1977). Economically poor neighborhoods often have old buildings in which the wall paint and plumbing are lead based. The water and dust in old buildings frequently carry excessive amounts of toxic heavy metals. But the problem is not necessarily restricted to old buildings. Even in new buildings, copper water pipes

AUTISM
A disorder first noticed in early childhood, characterized by the inability of the person to relate to others and to respond to attempts at communication; may also be characterized by mutism, self-injury, or preoccupation with objects.

often are held together with lead solder, which can contaminate the water. Air pollution is still another source of lead contamination.

Poisoning by heavy metals, especially lead, has been found to significantly lower children's IQ scores as well as their ability to attend to schoolwork. Such effects indicate involvement with the central nervous system, although the peripheral nervous system can also be damaged (see Figure 17.1) (Bhattacharya, Shukla, Bornschein, Dietrich, & Kopke, 1988). These adverse consequences don't disappear over time. Lead poisoning during childhood will remain an intellectual deficit in adulthood (Needleman, Schell, Bellinger, Leviton, & Allred, 1990).

Question: How widespread is heavy-metal contamination?

It was first discovered a little over 10 years ago that one out of every five inner-city black children 5 years old or younger was carrying enough lead in his or her body to interfere with the ability to learn (Raloff, 1982). Children from poor families—families with incomes below $6,000 a year—showed eight to nine times as much lead content in their bodies as did children from families whose income exceeded $15,000 a year (see Table 17.1).

By 1985, with the increasing use of unleaded gasoline, the amount of airborne lead had decreased significantly (Sun, 1985). The lower levels of airborne lead are especially noticeable in congested inner-city areas, where the blood lead levels in children have decreased in direct proportion to the decrease in the use of leaded gasoline. An effort is now under way to eliminate all lead from gasoline.

The Centers for Disease Control now recommend the testing of all children under the age of 6 and estimate that fully one-fifth of them will have blood lead levels in excess of 10 micrograms per deciliter of blood, the new (and lower) level now considered a cutoff for lead danger. Unfortunately, the test most commonly used measures lead indirectly and often gives an inaccurate reading, causing about half of the children with lead poisoning to be overlooked. As of the writing of this text, however, an effort was under way to require direct lead testing of the blood of all children under the age of 6. While the direct lead test is more expensive, it is quite accurate.

Early Infantile Autism

Approximately 1 child out of every 2,500 suffers from a disorder known as early infantile **autism.** No one yet understands the cause of autistic behaviors in children, so you should realize that the term *autism* is a general one; it may be that numerous unrelated disorders are responsible for autistic behaviors. Like schizophrenia, depression, and learning disability, autism is perhaps best thought of not as a single disease but as a constellation of observable behaviors that appear to be uniquely related (Newsom & Rincover, 1981).

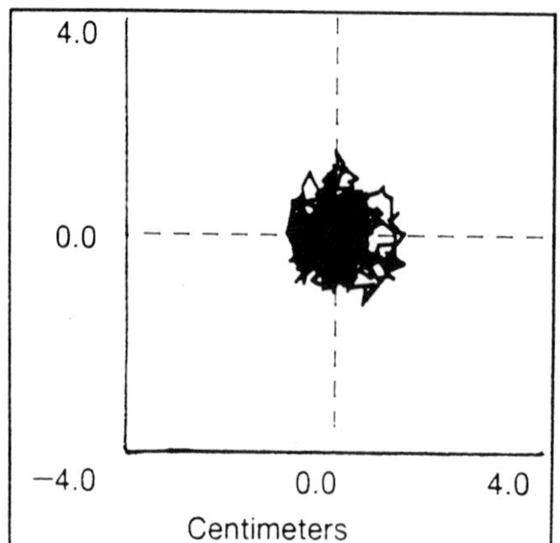

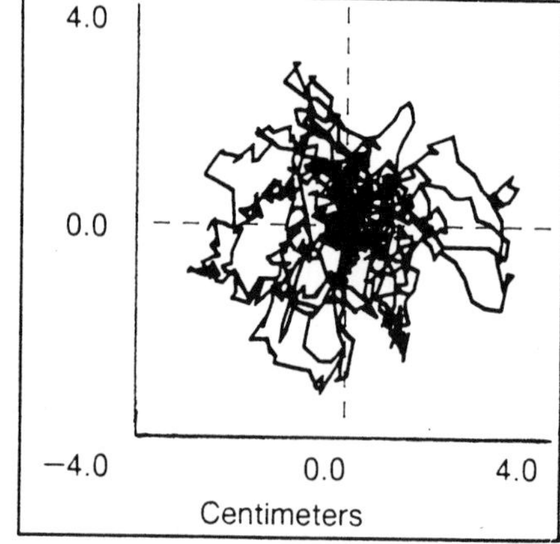

FIGURE 17.1
Plots showing the sway in posture of two 6-year-old children as they stood on a pressure sensitive platform tall and straight with their eyes closed. To read this chart, imagine in each case that you are looking straight down at a child and watching the trace made by the child's center of gravity as it moves about in relation to the swaying of the child's body. The child on the left swayed little. This child's blood lead level was 9.6 micrograms per deciliter of blood volume, which is just below the Center for Disease Control's cutoff for concern. The lead level of the child on the right was 42 micrograms per deciliter of blood volume. This child has obvious problems keeping balance. The results seen here are typical of the peripheral nervous system problems shown by children with lead poisoning. (*Source:* Bhattacharya, Shukla, Bornschein, Dietrich, & Kopke, 1988)

TABLE 17.1

U.S. Children (6 Months to 5 Years Old) with Blood Lead Levels of at Least 30 Micrograms per Deciliter

DEMOGRAPHIC VARIABLE	RACE		
	ALL (%)	WHITE (%)	BLACK (%)
Gender			
Both	4.0	2.0	12.2
Male	4.4	2.1	13.4
Female	3.5	1.8	10.9
Annual Family Income			
Under $6,000	10.9	5.9	18.5
$6,000 to $14,999	4.2	2.2	12.1
$15,000 or more	1.2	0.7	2.8
Urbanization			
Urban (1 million persons or more)	7.2	4.0	15.2
Urban: city center	11.6	4.5	18.6
Urban: city noncenter	3.7	3.8	3.3
Urban (under 1 million persons)	3.5	1.6	10.2
Rural	2.1	1.2	10.3

SOURCE: National Health and Nutrition Examination Survey, 1981.

Question: What behaviors might a child display that would be labeled autistic?

Autistic behaviors include being aloof and physically unresponsive to caregivers (Bender, 1955). Because autistic children usually lack social skills, they appear to be profoundly alone or isolated (Wing, 1977). This characteristic is reflected in the word *autism* (the root *auto* means "self"). Another characteristic is severely retarded language development. Some autistic children have no language skills at all, and others develop limited proficiency or a maddening habit, called *echolalia,* of mimicking what is said to them. Other autistic behaviors are persistent or repetitive acts, such as rocking back and forth or other hand and body motions. Yet such children usually have well-developed motor skills and rarely show signs of clumsiness or awkward motion.

Infantile autism is distinguished by the extremely early onset of autistic behaviors, indicating a disorder present from birth or very soon afterward. This feature, among others, separates autistic behaviors from constellations of behaviors typical of other psychotic disorders, such as schizophrenia.

Interestingly, autistic children usually appear physically normal, and they are often attractive. Without help, autistic children rarely improve; they become autistic adults, usually residing in institutions for the retarded or psychotic. Even with intensive intervention, autistic children generally make only very limited progress.

Question: What causes autism?

Many psychologists are beginning to believe that the cause or causes of autistic behavior involve genetic or biochemical variables to an important degree. Some data strongly suggest a genetic possibility. For example, autism is three times more common in boys than in girls (Werry, 1979), and when it appears in girls, it is more severe (Tsai, Stewart, & August, 1981). This suggests a sex-linked disorder. Of the siblings of autistic children, 15 percent have language disorders, learning disabilities, or mental retardation, compared with only 3 percent for siblings of Down syndrome children (August, Stewart, & Tsai, 1981). Siblings of autistic

Autistic children often engage in persistent or repetitive actions such as rocking back and forth, or other hand and body motions.

children also have lower IQ scores than would be expected in the general population (Minton, Campbell, Green, Jennings, & Samit, 1982), and they are 50 times more likely to be autistic themselves (Goldfine et al., 1985). Parents of autistic children, when compared with parents of Down syndrome children, are far more likely to show pronounced reading, spelling, and language difficulties (Wickelgren, 1989). Perhaps most striking is that among monozygotic (identical) twins, there is a 36 percent concordance rate of autism. In other words, if one identical twin has autism, there is a 36 percent chance that the other one will, too. Among dizygotic (fraternal) twins, the concordance rate is near 0 percent (Goldfine et al., 1985). Statistical analyses of families with multiple incidences of autism have also indicated the possibility that autism follows the patterns of a disorder caused by the inheritance of a double recessive gene (Ritvo et al., 1985). The clear pattern one might expect to emerge from the inheritance of a double recessive may not be as obvious in autism because other factors may influence how strongly the autism is expressed, which in turn might make it difficult to diagnose and identify autism adequately enough to make clear the distinct patterns of double recessive inheritance. Finally, the presence of autism in a family appears to be positively correlated with the presence of fragile *X* syndrome (Brown et al., 1982). In fact, when careful screening is conducted, approximately one autistic child in seven has been found also to have fragile *X* syndrome (Fisch et al., 1986).

Other data have provided intriguing hints that autism may involve brain chemistry. For example, it has been discovered that fenfluramine (a drug to aid people who need to lose weight), which influences brain chemicals, is effective at significantly reducing autistic behavior (Geller, Ritvo, Freeman, & Yuwiler, 1982). This does not mean, however, that the environment is not a factor. For example, some psychologists have suggested that the problem may be the result of a lack of certain environmental stimulation during an early biologically determined sensitive period (Bettelheim, 1967), although this view is rapidly being supplanted by the belief that autism is a biogenetically caused disorder.

Autism may also be related to various types of brain damage early in fetal development. In a thorough study of 233 autistic individuals with detailed medical records, it was found that fully half of these people also suffered from various rare diseases early in life. The disorders included odd bacterial and viral infections, as well as seldom-seen congenital and enzyme disorders, all of which are known to cause central nervous system damage. What this probably means is that many cases of "autism" are the result of brain damage owing to any number of different diseases (Ritvo et al., 1990).

SENSORY EXCEPTIONALITY
Technically, the possession of any sensory abilities significantly superior or inferior to those of the general population. Practically, however, the term is almost always used to denote individuals who have a visual or auditory dysfunction.

Physical and Sensory Disabilities

Physical or sensory disabilities may also place a child at a disadvantage. Among the physical problems that may require special attention are epilepsy, cerebral palsy, various birth defects, injuries caused by accidents, or physical disorders associated with illness. In each case, the emphasis is twofold. First, it is important to use the available technology to help children overcome as much of their handicap as possible before it can have too debilitating an effect on the child's development. Second, it is necessary to educate the public to meet these children's needs. For example, to assist epileptic children, the assistance available includes medication to control seizures and counseling to help them overcome the doubts, fears, and worries they may have concerning their illness. Public education is a valuable adjunct for teaching people that epilepsy is not a form of mental retardation, that it is not contagious, and that it should not keep a child from having friends or from leading a normal life.

Sensory exceptionality is a term usually applied only to those people who have visual or auditory dysfunctions. Sightless children require special assistance, especially if they must learn to read and write Braille. Nonetheless, many children who are legally blind (have vision poorer than 20/200 in both eyes) are able to benefit from magnification devices and books with large print. Many people do not realize that among children with sensory handicaps, it is the hearing-impaired child who most often experiences the greatest academic and social difficulties. Although most people consider sight a more valuable sense than hearing, hearing-impaired children suffer an additional disadvantage beyond their sensory loss: language difficulties. Because auditory feedback is essential for the development

Children with sensory handicaps can benefit from special instruction and often can succeed in the regular classroom.

of normal spoken language, hearing-impaired children are often unable to learn speech. The children who do learn to vocalize are likely to have trouble with pronunciation, pitch, and loudness control. Unfortunately, many uninformed children and adults mistakenly believe that these language problems are a sign of mental incompetence, and they limit their social contact with or totally reject those children who are unable to hear or communicate normally.

Question: What can be done to help hearing-impaired children?

Once again, the best course is a combination of public education and applied technology. The public must be made aware that a hearing loss is not synonymous with a mental deficiency. Hearing-impaired children can be integrated into society by means of hearing aids (when possible) and technological advances, such as closed-captioned television and type-and-see telephones. At the same time, people who can hear are becoming more familiar with the American Sign Language, and a larger number of hearing-impaired children are learning to lip-read and to vocalize by attending to the feedback from the vibration of their own vocal cords.

Both the visually impaired and the hearing-impaired child usually can succeed in the regular classroom. However, the addition of some special instruction is often useful.

LEARNING CHECK

Multiple Choice

1. Researchers studing home movies found
  - **a.** schizophrenia in the children they observed.
  - **b.** that observers were able to tell which children in the films later became schizophrenic.
  - **c.** that siblings were more likely to be schizophrenic.
  - **d.** a genetic link between schizophrenic parents and their offspring.

2. Half of the autistic children examined were found to have
  - **a.** no sign of autism once they became adults.
  - **b.** a double recessive genetic disorder.
  - **c.** suffered from rare diseases early in life.
  - **d.** hyperactivity.

3. Which of the following statements is true?
  - **a.** Inheritance plays no role in schizophrenia.
  - **b.** Dyslexia is an inability to understand spoken words.
  - **c.** Hyperkinesis is a form of childhood depression.
  - **d.** Children as young as 5 years have committed suicide.

4. Autism
  - **a.** is caused by a vitamin deficiency.
  - **b.** is caused by a brain allergy.
  - **c.** is caused by insufficient fenfluramine.
  - **d.** may be related to fragile *X* syndrome.

5. Lead
  - **a.** is found only in older homes and buildings.
  - **b.** may cause learning problems in those children who come in contact with it.
  - **c.** is not a problem in poorer neighborhoods.
  - **d.** is beneficial in the treatment of chromosomal abnormalities.

6. Among those with sensory handicaps, it is the ______________ who most often experience academic or social difficulties.
  a. visually impaired **b.** hearing impaired **c.** physically impaired **d.** adults

Answers: 1. b 2. c 3. d 4. d 5. b 6. b

Homelessness

On any given night in the United States, approximately 100,000 children sleep in welfare hotels, emergency shelters, cars, abandoned buildings, or parks (Bassuk, 1991). Some even sleep on the street. These are the homeless children of the richest nation on earth.

Homeless children suffer a devastating impact from the combined effects of hunger and malnutrition, health problems, lack of mental or physical care, delays in their development, psychological problems, and academic underachievement (Rafferty & Shinn, 1991).

Question: Is the main problem of homelessness lack of proper shelter?

Lack of shelter is part of it. But homelessness is far more than "houselessness." Without a home, children lose not only their shelter, but also their connection with a supportive community. This means that they often lose contact with friends and other family members as well as with church and school. The loss can be extremely felt. One homeless boy, named Robert, expressed feelings common to homeless children when he said that

> he was ugly and often thought about killing himself and would do so if he had the chance. He was not sure how he would carry out this intent but said he felt desperate enough to hold it as an idea.
>
> Robert also said he hated school. He stated that he had no friends and was bored and that he worried his classmates would discover he had no real home. Robert said he was teased by his peers and criticized by adults. He disliked the shelter and the other children there and spoke wistfully of the family's last home in a trailer. Robert was failing in school and had repeated a grade. (Bassuk, 1991, p. 71)

Homeless children like Robert face a bleak existence. In most welfare hotels or emergency shelters, people are crammed together in small spaces. There are usually no places to change or bathe infants, and there is so much noise and light that sleep is disrupted. Most homeless preschoolers, for example, are unable to take naps because of the conditions (Rafferty & Shinn, 1991).

These children are in physical danger as well, not just from people in the street, but from poor sanitation and malnourishment. Surveys have found that homeless children are three times more likely to have missed inoculations (Bassuk, 1991). Furthermore, 92 percent of families living in welfare hotels were found to have no refrigerator, and none had a stove. Children are much more likely to go hungry in such conditions (Rafferty & Shinn, 1991). In 20 out of 27 cities surveyed, emergency food programs reported turning away children because they ran out of food owing to inadequate funding. Children who are hungry and sleep-deprived are also less able to learn. Their teachers report that these children have a short attention span, are withdrawn and aggressive, and display immature behavior and poor peer interaction. Thirty percent of homeless children don't even attend school in any regular fashion (Rafferty & Shinn, 1991).

Approximately 100,000 children in the United States are homeless.

Question: Why are there so many homeless children in the United States?

Amazingly, no one is quite sure. There are numerous factors that contribute to the number of homeless children in America. Allocation of national resources accounts for some of the problem. For example, from 1960 to 1990, the number of children in the United States has stayed at a fairly constant 64 million, while the number of adults ages 18 to 64 has increased from 100 million to 152 million, and the number of elderly adults has grown from 17 million to 31 million (Fuchs & Reklis, 1992). At first glance, this might seem to indicate that there are now more adults to take care of fewer children, which might appear as a plus for children. However, as members of our society have become more isolated from one another owing to the growth of cities, the migration from small towns, the breakdown of family structure, and, to some extent, the decline of religion and church influence, adults have become less likely to take care of other people's children. As a result, these figures denote a larger adult population now competing for resources once allocated to children rather than a greater base of child support. Also, the United States has declined economically in comparison with the rest of the world over the last 30 years. This, too, limits resources available for children.

The changing cultural mores have also removed the stigma from divorce, and the number of single-parent families has increased dramatically. For example, in 1970, 1 in 10 families was headed by a woman. Twenty years later, it was more than 1 in 5 (Bassuk, 1991). In fact, single-parent families account for 34 percent of the homeless population (Bassuk, 1991).

Housing costs have also risen dramatically over the past 30 years. Rent now constitutes a much larger portion of a person's income than it used to. Because of this, any slight change in circumstances, such as an unexpected drop in pay or increased expenses, may force a family onto the street. And while government aid can often help, all the government aid currently available to the homeless, including food stamps, now buys 26 percent less per person than it did 20 years ago (Bassuk, 1991).

Question: What will happen to these children?

If we also consider the children who are living in poverty, as well as those who are homeless, we may in a very real sense be losing a significant portion of the next generation. This is especially tragic considering that it is—to look at it in a cold, blunt economic way—cost-effective to save them now. As researchers Yvonne Rafferty and Marybeth Shinn have pointed out,

> an entire generation of children faces truly unacceptable risks that jeopardize their future potential. In the long run, the monetary costs of neglecting children's needs are likely to substantially exceed the costs of combating poverty and homelessness. The human costs will be much more tragic. Our cities and the nation must develop an appropriate and effective response. (Rafferty & Shinn, 1991, p. 1177)

Question: What can be done to help?

Any solution to homelessness has to begin with permanent, affordable, and decent housing (National Alliance to End Homelessness, 1988; National Coalition for the Homeless, 1987; Partnership for the Homeless, 1989; U.S. Conference of Mayors, 1988). Of course, that alone can't solve the problem. Also needed are rehabilitation for drug and alcohol abusers, a school bureaucracy able to deal with children who often move from one place to another, education for the homeless as to their rights and services available to them, case workers who can make sure that children are given good food and proper medical care, proper government funding to meet all of these needs—in short, a nation that cares enough to spend the money needed to recover its own most precious resource, its citizens.

The Effect of Early Disadvantage

ISOLATED AT BIRTH

Many years ago, at the University of Wisconsin, an experiment was conducted in which baby rhesus monkeys were kept in small, barren cages, where different groups were socially isolated for the first 3, 6, and 12 months of their lives. During these times, the baby monkeys had no contact with their mothers or with any other monkey. These experiments continued for a number of years to discover the effects of such isolation on later development. The findings generally demonstrated that 3 months of isolation produced few long-term deficits (Griffin & Harlow, 1966) but that 6 months or more of isolation caused severe developmental disturbances.

The monkeys in the latter category began to bite themselves. They held onto themselves and rocked back and forth in an autistic way. Their emotions became bizarre, and they made strange facial grimaces. They huddled together and sometimes lashed out in rage or fear. Some of the monkeys isolated for a full year became so withdrawn that they seemed to be little more than "semianimated vegetables" (Griffin & Harlow, 1966). Furthermore, monkeys raised in isolation also showed the kinds of impairments to their immune systems commonly associated with severe stress, which in turn made them more susceptible to disease (Coe, Rosenberg, Fischer, & Levine, 1987).

In these "monkey labs," researchers investigated other important factors that related to the disadvantages of early isolation and stimulus deprivation. They discovered that the timing of the isolation was as important as its duration. Monkeys isolated later in life were not as severely affected as those whose isolation began at birth. They also discovered that females seemed to be less affected by early isolation than males were (Sackett, Holm, & Landesman-Dwyer, 1975) and that another species of monkey, the pigtail monkey, was not as severely affected by early isolation as the rhesus was (Sackett, Holm, & Ruppenthal, 1976).

This last finding was especially important because the major concern of the researchers was not necessarily to discover the effects of early experiences on the later development of monkeys but rather to generalize the monkey data to human beings. Because different monkey species react to early isolation differently, we can assume that humans might also have differing reactions. If they do, the data obtained from the rhesus studies may be of limited value in indicating how isolation might affect human children.

Although it would be unethical to attempt isolation studies with humans, the question remains: What are the effects of being reared in a deprived setting, without love or companionship? Sometimes children experience such hardships.

Would the effects of deprivation be reversible, or would the damage be permanent? Although studies with other species give us clues, our knowledge about the effects of early experience is still quite limited, although it would seem that environment and early experience can have dramatic effects. Many children, therefore, may be at a disadvantage or, for that matter, an advantage, depending on the early experiences to which they are exposed. Investigations of early human experience tend to focus on three major issues:

1. How important are early experiences, and how much of an effect do they have on a person's later life?
2. Are there critical periods during which a child must be exposed to certain stimulations or experiences or forever be at a disadvantage?
3. How "plastic" is the child? How much can a child take and still bounce back?

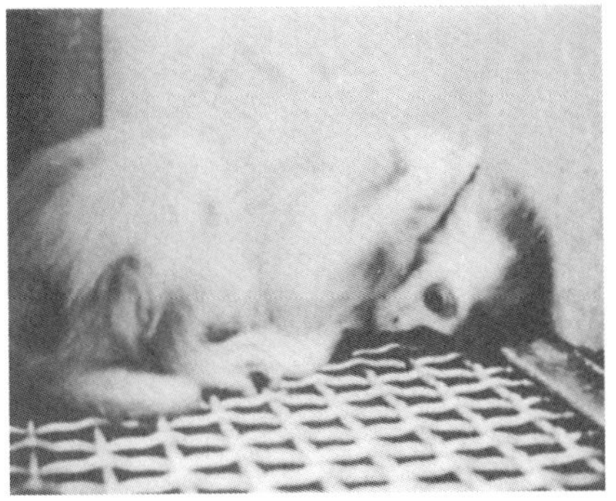

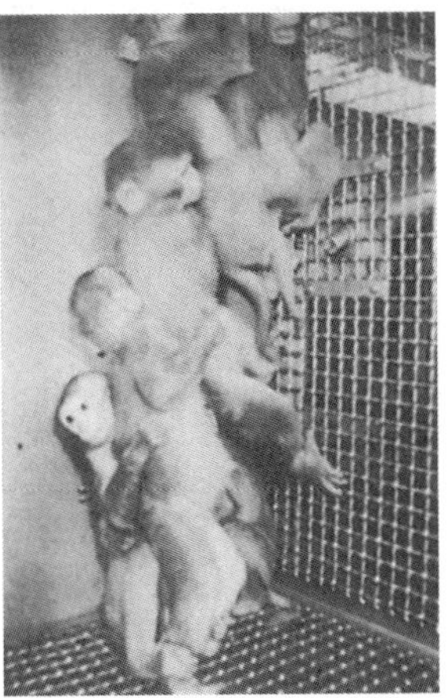

Rhesus monkeys raised in isolation often display severe development disturbances.

How much can a child endure before his or her later development will be permanently impaired?

Let's examine these issues.

THE IMPORTANCE OF EARLY EXPERIENCE

A child raised in a deprived environment with inadequate stimulation and care might fail to develop normally. This, of course, is why researchers investigated rhesus monkeys raised in isolation.

Question: Have children who have been raised in impoverished or deprived environments been investigated?

Yes. In 1945, Rene Spitz examined a number of infants who were left in a foundling home by mothers too poor to support them. The home was overcrowded, and each caregiver was forced to attend to large numbers of infants at a time. These babies were unable to observe their surroundings because the sides of their cribs were draped with white sheets to keep them quiet—the way people drape canaries at night. The babies were rarely handled. They spent so much time on their backs inside the cribs that small hollows began to develop beneath their bodies in the mattresses. The hollows eventually became so deep that the average 1-year-old child wasn't even able to turn over. The only "toys" they had were their hands and feet (Spitz, 1945).

Question: How did this early experience affect their development?

The infants were found to be developmentally retarded when compared with children in another institution who were receiving care and stimulation. In a 2-year follow-up study, Spitz noted that many of the children in the original foundling home study were still developmentally behind, even though conditions at the home had been drastically improved. He concluded that the damage to the children was probably due to lack of love and attention from a mother or close personal caregiver (Spitz, 1946). It was largely because of Spitz's discoveries that the use of foundling homes in the United States was severely curtailed and foster parent programs were begun.

Prior to World War II, foundling homes for children were common throughout the United States. Such homes provided little stimulation, and close infant–caregiver attachments were rarely formed.

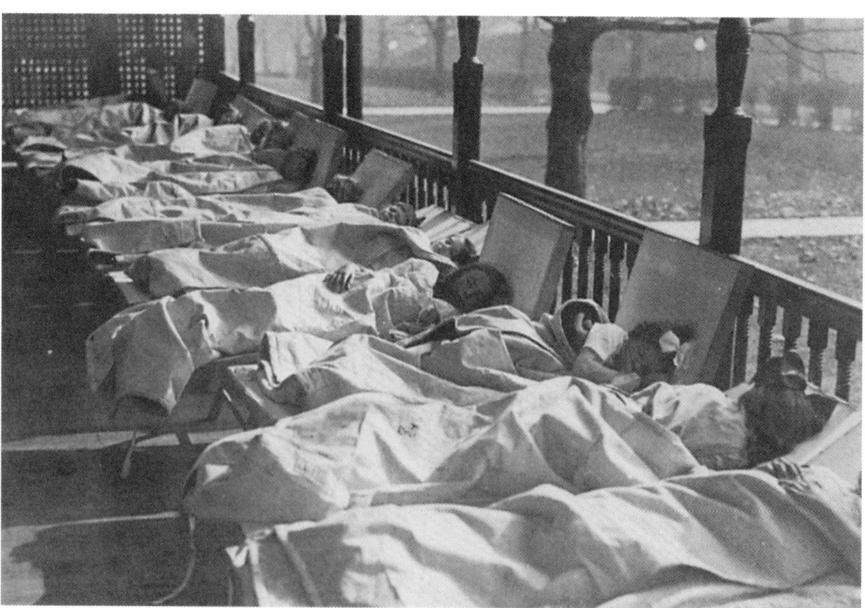

Spitz's research has not gone unchallenged, however. His findings were criticized by a number of researchers because they may have contained some methodological flaws and biases (Pinneau, 1955). Still, his observations give us an indication that severe deprivation of young children isn't likely to be beneficial.

PLASTICITY
Flexibility or adaptability. In neurophysiology the ability of brain tissue to take over the function of other brain tissue that has been damaged. In life experience, the ability to overcome the effects of early adverse experiences.

SYNAPSE
The junction at which a nerve impulse travels from one neuron to another.

PLASTICITY

The term **plasticity** refers to the flexibility of the individual in being able to maintain relatively normal development in the face of physical injury or psychological adversity. For example, during the first 5 or 6 years of childhood, the developing brain shows some remarkable plasticity. For years, neurologists have been aware that certain brain damage leads to permanent disability. But it was also known that if certain portions of the brain were destroyed while a child was still young enough, other portions of the brain might take over the functions of the destroyed portions. For example, in most right-handed people, there is a section of the brain in the left cerebral hemisphere specialized to deal with language. Should this portion of the brain be destroyed, language may be permanently lost. If injury occurs in children 6 years of age or younger, however, the right cerebral hemisphere may take over the functions of the destroyed language section of the left hemisphere. In other words, a young child's brain appears to be more flexible than that of an older child or adult.

Question: Why is a young child's brain more flexible?

For decades, this was a great mystery. However, evidence gathered in the last few years has begun to help us understand this phenomenon. The small spaces or synaptic junctions between most of the billions of neurons, or nerve cells, in the brain are of great importance, because nerve cells transfer signals by means of these spaces. Because a **synapse,** or junction, is the switching station between neurons, the larger the number of synapses, the greater the amount of information that can be transmitted. The number of synapses, their size, and their excitability can be affected by an animal's early experience. It has been demonstrated that animals raised in enriched environments tend to have greater concentrations of synapses (Rosenzweig, 1966). Moreover, an animal's ability to learn appears to be affected by the number of synapses. Researchers have long wondered whether the number of synapses in the brain or their density was related to the flexibility of a child's brain. This hypothesis appears to have been confirmed by the investigation of the human cortex conducted at the University of Chicago. Using an electron microscope, investigators discovered that synaptic density reaches its peak in humans at about 2 years of age and then declines continuously until about the age of 16 years, after which it remains relatively constant through age 72 years. Infants at 2 years of age have fully 50 percent more synaptic connections than the average adult does ("Brains: The Younger the Better," 1979). This fact may account not only for a child's ability to overcome early brain damage but also for the child's ability to rapidly learn language and acquire other skills. In this sense, then, all of childhood, especially early childhood, may be a neurologically sensitive period for learning and gaining experience.

One of the greatest concerns among investigators is whether an early experience (or lack of one) can cause permanent damage or disability. Because of this concern, the issue of plasticity—that is, whether a developmental disability can be overcome—has become a major area of study.

Both biological and environmental factors are important when considering plasticity. Studies conducted with babies who were born small for their gestational age (SGA)—that is, weighing below 1,750 grams at birth—highlight this fact. Among children raised in families of higher socioeconomic status, SGA babies generally overcome any adversity that their SGA status may have caused and catch up intellectually and cognitively with infants of normal birth weight. SGA infants raised in families of lower socioeconomic status, however, generally fail to catch up; they show scores significantly lower than those of normal-birth-weight babies (Wilson, 1985). This implies that environmental forces can help the child to overcome the adversity of being born SGA.

Occasionally, identical twins are of unequal weight at birth. Even so, a twin who is SGA almost invariably catches up to the heavier-weight twin, usually by the age of 6 years (Wilson, 1985). This indicates that the biological heritage of the infant can also play an important role in the child's ability to recover from an early deficit.

Question: How might a child be permanently disabled by early experience?

Logically, we can deduce a number of possible ways: (1) the occurrence of irreparable physical damage to a function on which later development will depend; (2) a critical period that passes without the child's obtaining the necessary experience or stimulation; and (3) a situation in which the child is kept by her culture or environment from ever obtaining the learning necessary for proper development.

In theory, no matter what happens to infants or young children, they should be able to overcome any developmental retardation or early problems if their biological mechanisms have not been damaged, if they have not missed the stimulation or experience needed during any critical periods, and if the learning experiences they may have missed are made available to them. Of course, that's only in theory.

Question: Is it easy to tell, then, by taking these three criteria into consideration, when a disability is reversible?

Unfortunately, no. How can you tell if permanent biological damage has occurred? There are probably thousands of subtle kinds of permanent biological injuries that are not observable, at least not with the techniques available today. Then there is the issue of critical periods. We don't usually know whether a child has passed through such a period without obtaining the necessary stimulation or experience, or even whether many such periods exist. However, if critical periods in early human development do exist, they must be fairly hard for a child to miss, even if the child is reared under adverse conditions.

Question: Why do you say that?

Because, as it turns out, children are often able to recover from being reared in deprived early environments. In his book *Children of the Crèche,* Dennis (1973) describes a study begun in 1959 of infants raised in a Lebanese foundling home in Beirut. There was only 1 attendant for every 10 infants. The infants were rarely handled and were unable to see out of their cribs, because sheets were draped over the sides (sound familiar?). The infants were swaddled in garments for the first 4 months of their lives, as is the Near Eastern custom, severely restricting the movement of their arms and legs. These children became developmentally retarded, as did the children Spitz observed. However, children from the Lebanese foundling home who were adopted gained back the ground they had lost during their many years in the institution and later appeared to be developmentally normal. The issue of recovery may have been clouded, however, inasmuch as it was the healthier infants who tended to be adopted.

But other studies have also indicated that early developmental deficiencies need not necessarily affect later development (Rheingold, 1961; Rheingold & Bayley, 1959). In a study of children in Guatemala, Kagan and Klein (1973) noted that the Guatemalan children generally lived in isolated, poor farm communities and spent the first year of their lives tightly clothed and confined to dark, windowless huts. The adults seldom interacted with the infants. The infants also had few toys. Adults and siblings talked and played with these babies only about one-third as often as would a similar family in an American home. Although these children at first were developmentally retarded by our standards, by the time they reached adolescence, they had become developmentally equal to American children in a variety of perceptual and cognitive tasks.

These findings demonstrate considerable plasticity in children; that is, even given adverse conditions, children appear under some circumstances to be able to bounce back. The ability to overcome early adverse environments also argues somewhat against the notion that critical periods play a large role in our development.

Other researchers, however, believe that institutionally raised children may miss the chance to form significant attachments or bonds with adults because they rarely have a chance to be with particular adults for any length of time. These researchers have found that such children behave differently from children not reared in institutions and in school seek more attention and are more restless, disobedient, and unpopular (Rutter & Garmezy, 1983). Even among institutionally reared children who have been adopted as early as age 4 years and who have formed close attachments to their foster parents, such behavioral differences are still apparent (Rutter & Garmezy, 1983). Like the children of the crèche, though, these adopted children are less developmentally retarded when compared with children who remained in institutions.

LEARNED HELPLESSNESS
Giving up, even though success is possible, because of previous experience in which success was impossible.

LEARNING AND EARLY EXPERIENCE

Sometimes a child misses an important learning experience because the environment fails to provide it. Some children may even end up in environments that will never provide the necessary experiences. To this extent, such children will be permanently disabled. But children who are fortunate enough eventually to receive the necessary experiences may be able to recover.

Question: What sort of early learning experience might a child miss that would inhibit his development?

There are many possible examples. Two of the most important are the failure to develop self-reliance in terms of manipulating the environment and the failure to engage with others socially. Let's look at each of these in turn.

Learned Helplessness It is possible through experience to learn to become helpless. Dogs trained to avoid a shock by jumping from one side of a box to the other soon gave up jumping when the shock was applied to both sides, because jumping from one side to the other no longer helped the dogs to escape (Seligman & Maier, 1967). Interestingly, the dogs never again bothered to try to avoid the shock. Even when the shock in the far side of the box was turned off, the dogs simply stayed where they were and took the shock when it came. They never discovered that the far side was now safe because they never again explored it. This is an example of **learned helplessness.** The dogs simply gave up trying to escape. Animals will also generalize this learned helplessness to new situations. When placed in water-filled mazes, rats that had learned helplessness in a previous situation gave up swimming and would have drowned if not rescued. Rats who had not previously learned to be helpless completed their swim and reached safety (Altenor, Kay, & Richter, 1977).

Question: Has learned helplessness been demonstrated in infants or children?

Learned helplessness has been observed in human infants. Two researchers (Watson & Ramey, 1969, 1972) placed a rotating mobile above the heads of three groups of infants. They placed a pressure-sensitive pillow beneath the heads of the infants in the first group. By moving their heads, these infants could open and close circuits that made the mobile turn. These infants had control over this aspect of their environment. The infants in the second group were given no control; their pillows were not connected to the mobile. As a result, their mobiles remained stationary. The third group of infants were also given no control, but in this case, the mobiles turned randomly. (The third variation served as a control to make sure that the infants who did learn to move their heads against their pillows were doing so because they had *control* over their environment and not simply because they were watching a turning object.) After a daily exposure of 10 minutes for a period of 14 weeks, the infants in the first group learned to turn their heads to make the mobile move.

Question: But wouldn't you expect infants to learn to move their heads to make the mobile turn?

Yes. But there's more. The most interesting aspect of these experiments was how *lack of control* affected the later behavior of the second and third groups of infants. The researchers gave the second and third groups of infants the mobiles once again, but this time both groups were given control over the movement of the mobiles. Even after extensive training, these infants failed to learn to operate the mobile the way the first group of infants had! Like the rats who gave up trying to escape because their early attempts had failed, the second and third groups of infants had learned to be helpless; they had learned not to expect their behavior to have any effect on the mobile. As a result, once they were given real control, they never seemed to appreciate the link between their head movements and the mobile's turning. As with the rats that transferred their helplessness to the water maze, such learned helplessness in infants can also transfer to new situations (Finkelstein & Ramey, 1977).

As you can imagine, children in institutions or other situations where they are given little opportunity to manipulate their environment and are always having things done to them or for them may quickly learn not to bother to try. It's interesting that one of the earliest findings of this kind came from the U.S. Office of Education (Coleman et al., 1966), where it was noted that minority group members who believed that they were controlled by their environment rather than the other way around were more likely to fail at school. Often when children encounter failure in school, they begin to believe themselves to be "failures," thereby lessening their efforts to succeed, making future failure even more likely, and maintaining a vicious cycle. This is especially true of older children (Heyman, Dweck, & Cain, 1992). It's a sad paradox that early experiences may be helping children learn not to learn.

The concept of learned helplessness may also play an important role in parent-child relationships. One study found that mothers who believed that they were dealing with a "difficult" infant or who had previously been exposed to infants that they could not make stop crying were far less likely to attempt to soothe a crying infant who *would* respond than were mothers who had not had such previous "helplessness" training (Donovan & Leavitt, 1985).

Shyness If at an early age a child fails to learn how to engage with others socially or becomes fearful of approaching others, the child may become withdrawn or shy. A vicious cycle can rapidly develop, whereby the child structures his or her environment so as to minimize potential social contact (Moskowitz, Schwartzman, & Ledingham, 1985). Such a condition, if unaltered, may easily continue into adulthood (Caspi, Elder, & Bem, 1988). In surveys it has been found that over 80 percent of Americans have considered themselves at one time or another to be shy and that fully 10 percent—over 20 million Americans—have said that they

Shy children are at a disadvantage because their social contact with others is often quite limited.

are shy (Zimbardo, 1979). Similarly, a survey of over 500 third- through sixth-grade children found that 10 percent of them felt lonely, left out, and shy about approaching others (Asher, Hymel, & Renshaw, 1984).

Both children who have learned not to learn—that is, learned to be helpless—and children who are shy and withdrawn have a particularly serious disadvantage because their behaviors are likely to prevent exposure to the kinds of experiences that might help them eliminate their helplessness or shyness. These children, once of school age, are often labeled as learning disabled or emotionally disturbed. The particular label is often unimportant. What is important is whether they receive the kinds of experiences necessary to help them overcome their disabilities. Such children may as well be considered permanently disabled if their environment never provides the necessary experiences to help them overcome their difficulties.

Retraining

Question: Isn't there some way that schools or public institutions can help?

Public Law 94–142, which was passed by Congress back in 1975, in part requires that children with certain disabilities—for example, being especially withdrawn or apparently unable to learn—be given extensive opportunities to obtain the kinds of experiences they need to overcome their handicaps, while still being maintained in the classroom. In other words, the school becomes more than just an academic setting; it becomes an environment for retraining. Helpless children are taught that they can, after all, manipulate their environment to a greater extent than they believed possible. And withdrawn children are encouraged to become involved with other children. Once these children have been taught how to approach others and how to interact with them, their involvement with peers increases, they are more likely to be accepted, and they begin to perceive themselves as capable and competent in social situations (Bierman & Furman, 1984).

The school system also works with other children similarly handicapped by their early experiences. Before this law was enacted, a common practice was for such children to be placed in separate classes or institutions for the handicapped. Today, through the use of peer modeling, reinforcement, and group involvement in the regular classroom, children who have learned self-defeating behaviors because of their early experiences are being helped.

LEARNING CHECK

Multiple Choice

1. Permanent developmental disability may be caused by
   a. biological damage.
   b. missed critical periods.
   c. a culture that fails to provide needed experience.
   d. all of the above.
2. The "children of the crèche"
   a. suffered permanent disability.
   b. were all adopted.
   c. made significant recoveries.
   d. lived in Guatemala.
3. Plasticity
   a. doesn't occur in children under 6 years of age.
   b. can't help a child overcome early adversity.
   c. is the ability of the individual to be flexible.
   d. is related to toxic induction of learning disorders.
4. Learned helplessness
   a. is found only in humans because it requires thinking.
   b. was an experimental artifact and not a real phenomenon.
   c. is not generalized to new situations.
   d. may occur during infancy in humans.
5. Shyness
   a. is rarely a problem among adults.
   b. is not a serious problem among children.
   c. should be ignored because a child will grow out of it.
   d. is a problem that demands early attention.

Answers: 1.d 2.c 3.c 4.d 5.d

APPLICATIONS

Overcoming Adverse Early Experiences

The Therapist Monkeys

As you have already discovered, rhesus monkeys raised in total isolation for the first 6 months of their lives developed bizarre social and emotional behaviors. In 1972, Stephen Suomi and Harry Harlow demonstrated that the effects of 6 months of isolation could be overcome by pairing the abnormal isolated monkeys with normal monkeys. Previous attempts to pair such isolated animals with normal peers had failed because normal monkeys of the same age tended to overwhelm the helpless and withdrawn isolates. This time, however, the researchers attempted to pair the 6-month-old isolates with normal 3-month-old monkeys because younger monkeys were more likely to be social without also being aggressive.

In this experiment, four 6-month-old male isolates served as "patients," and four normal 3-month-old females were the "therapists." Individual "therapy sessions" were arranged between a patient and a therapist for 6 hours per week. Group therapy between more than one patient and more than one therapist was also held. After 6 months of therapy, the patients and therapists were indistinguishable in their behaviors. As the researchers put it:

> The primary finding of this experiment was that monkeys reared in total social isolation for the first 6 months of life exhibited significant recovery of virtually all behavior deficits across all testing situations after appropriate therapeutic treatment. Reversal of the isolation syndrome to an equivalent degree over such a range of situations had not been previously achieved or approached via any experimental procedures. (Suomi & Harlow, 1972)

In 1973, Harlow and Novak were successful in treating rhesus patients who had been isolated for the first 12 months of their lives by placing them with 4-month-old therapists.

Similar results have also been found with monkeys of other species (Reite, Kaemingk, & Boccia, 1989).

The Skeels Study

Question: Have there been similar attempts with human children to overcome early deprivation?

One of the best-known attempts was the Skeels study begun in the 1930s. Skeels specifically set out to discover if the debilitating effects of early institutionalization on children could be overcome by placing them in a better environment where care givers could stimulate them and provide themselves as models of appropriate behaviors. To conduct this experiment, Skeels arranged with an overcrowded, understaffed orphanage to have one-half of its children sent to another institution.

The institution that Skeels chose was the Glenwood State School for retarded adult women, where ages ranged from 18 to 50 years. The two environments were very different from each other. The Glenwood State School was certainly an enriched environment compared to the orphanage. At the Glenwood State School, the children were able to engage in one-to-one relationships with adults. Even though the adults were intellectually deficient compared with average adults, they were intellectually superior to the children from the orphanage.

The average age of the 13 children sent to the Glenwood State School was 19 months, and their average IQ was 64.* The average IQ of the 12 children who stayed behind in the orphanage was 87, so Skeels had actually picked the *most* deficient of the orphans to place in the Glenwood School. The effects on these orphans of moving to the less deprived environment were striking. The average gain in IQ, after only 18 months in the new institution, was 29 points.

At the Glenwood State School, the children were placed in open, active wards with the older and relatively brighter inmate women. The attendants at the school and the inmate women became fond of the children placed in their charge. They often played with them, and the different wards compared children to see which had the best and brightest.

Skeels was excited by these initial improvements, but he wondered if they would last, so he began a series of follow-up studies. His first follow-up study was conducted 2½ years later. Eleven of the 13 children originally transferred to the Glenwood school had been adopted, and their average IQ was now 101. The 2 children who had not been adopted were reinstitutionalized and lost their initial gain. The contrast group, the 12 children who had not been transferred to Glenwood, had remained

*Normal IQ scores average 100. Scores below 70 are usually considered in the retarded range.

APPLICATIONS

institutional wards of the state and now had an average IQ of 66 (an average decrease of 21 points).

In 1966, Skeels again examined these subjects, who had now become adults. The differences were stunning. In the experimental group—those people raised in the Glenwood School—he found no deficits that he could trace to their early experiences in the orphanage. The differences in terms of occupations and marriage history between the experimental and the contrast group are shown in Table 17.2. Although the Skeels study has been criticized for methodological flaws (that IQ tests given to 19-month-old infants are not reliable and similar objections) (Longstreth, 1981), there is no overlooking the fact that the members of the experimental group, judging by their occupations, were not seriously disadvantaged by their early experiences to the point that they could not be included within the normal range of vocational success. As these findings indicate, early deficits can be overcome. As Skeels has said, "It seems obvious that under present-day conditions there are still countless infants born with sound biological constitutions and potentialities for development well within the normal range who will become mentally retarded and noncontributing members of society unless appropriate intervention occurs" (Skeels, 1966).

TABLE 17.2

Comparison of the Experimental and Contrast Groups in the Skeels Study—Occupations of Subjects and Spouses

CASE NO.	SUBJECT'S OCCUPATION	SPOUSE'S OCCUPATION	FEMALE SUBJECT'S OCCUPATION PREVIOUS TO MARRIAGE
Experimental Group			
1[a]	Staff sergeant	Dental technician	. . .
2	Housewife	Laborer	Nurse's aide
3	Housewife	Mechanic	Elementary school teacher
4	Nursing instructor	Unemployed	Registered nurse
5	Housewife	Semiskilled laborer	No work history
6	Waitress	Mechanic, semiskilled	Beauty operator
7	Housewife	Flight engineer	Dining room hostess
8	Housewife	Foreman, construction	No work history
9	Domestic service	Unmarried	. . .
10[a]	Real estate sales	Housewife	. . .
11[a]	Vocational counselor	Advertising copy writer	. . .
12	Gift shop sales[c]	Unmarried	. . .
13	Housewife	Pressman-printer	Office-clerical
Contrast Group			
14	Institutional inmate	Unmarried	. . .
15	Dishwasher	Unmarried	. . .
16	Deceased	. . .	. . .
17[a]	Dishwasher	Unmarried	. . .
18[a]	Institutional inmate	Unmarried	. . .
19[a]	Compositor and typesetter	Housewife	. . .
20[a]	Institutional inmate	Unmarried	. . .
21[a]	Dishwasher	Unmarried	. . .
22[a]	Floater	Divorced	. . .
23	Cafeteria (part time)	Unmarried	. . .
24[a]	Institutional gardener's assistant	Unmarried	. . .
25[a]	Institutional inmate	Unmarried	. . .

SOURCE: Skeels, 1966. [a]Male [b]B.A. degree [c]Previously had worked as a licensed practical nurse.

SUMMARY

■ Developmental psychopathology is the study of abnormal development and the factors that may make it likely to occur. Many genetic, ontogenetic, biochemical, cognitive, affective, and social factors are known to have a strong influence in causing development to follow abnormal paths.

■ Schizophrenia is a serious disorder affecting as many as 1 million people in the United States and many millions more throughout the world. Schizophrenia in childhood has its most devastating developmental effects on the child's ability to monitor and test reality and on her ability to initiate and maintain interactions with peers and other socially important individuals. It is possible that there is a hereditary component to schizophrenia.

■ Depressed children usually regard themselves in a negative way and blame themselves for things that have gone wrong. Other signs of depression in children include sleep difficulties, cognitive impairment, agitation, changes in attitude toward school, physical complaints, and changes in appetite. There is a possible hereditary component to depression.

■ A learning disability is defined as a learning problem that is not caused by environmental factors, mental retardation, or emotional disturbances. It is a form of intellectual handicap.

■ One of the most common learning disorders is dyslexia, in which the person's ability to read is disrupted.

■ Attention deficit disorder is a broad category that in practice has not been well defined. Children who have attention deficit disorder are characterized by inattention and impulsivity; they often also display hyperactivity.

■ Learning problems may be related to contact with toxic environmental substances, such as lead.

■ Early infantile autism is a disorder marked by linguistic and social deficit. Its cause is unknown, although most researchers believe that it is probably tied to biogenetic factors.

■ *Sensory exceptionality* is a term usually applied to people with visual or auditory handicaps. In addition to the sensory loss, other problems may occur, such as the language difficulties common to the hearing impaired.

■ Homeless children suffer a devastating impact from the combined effects of hunger and malnutrition, health problems, lack of mental or physical care, delays in their development, psychological problems, and academic underachievement.

■ Investigations into the effect of early disadvantage on children have tended to focus on the following major issues: (1) How important are early experiences, and how much of an effect do they have on a person's later life? (2) Are there critical periods during which a child must be exposed to certain stimuli or experiences or forever be at a disadvantage? (3) How plastic is the child? How much can a child take and still bounce back?

■ The term *plasticity* refers to the flexibility of the individual in being able to maintain relatively normal development in the face of physical injury or psychological adversity. During the first 5 or 6 years of life, the developing brain shows remarkable plasticity.

■ Both biological and environmental factors are important in determining whether a disability can be overcome.

■ Sometimes a child misses an important learning experience because the environment fails to provide it. Some children may even end up in environments that will never provide the necessary experiences. Two of the most important experiences that a child might miss are the failure to develop self-reliance in terms of manipulating the environment and the failure to engage with others socially.

QUESTIONS FOR DISCUSSION

1. How have your early experiences shaped your life? Do you believe that you were in any way permanently disabled by any of them? If so, why do you think the disability is not reversible?
2. In what way might living in a very poor neighborhood teach individuals to be helpless?
3. How might learned helplessness hinder an individual who is offered an opportunity to improve? What special help might such an individual need?
4. Can you think of a number of instances in which being shy only leads to becoming more shy? What special help might you offer a shy child or adult?
5. Do you believe that you control your environment or that it's the other way around? How do these beliefs affect your behavior?

SUGGESTIONS FOR FURTHER READING

1. Cicchetti, D., & Schneider-Rosen, K. (Eds.). (1984). *Childhood depression.* San Francisco: Jossey-Bass.
2. Cottle, T. J. (1990). *Children's secrets.* Reading, MA: Addison-Wesley.
3. Kellerman, J. (1981). *Helping the fearful child: A parent's guide to everyday and problem anxieties.* New York: Norton.
4. Kryder-Coe, J. M., Salamon, L. M., & Molnar, J. M. (Eds.). (1991). *Homeless children and youth: A new American dilemma.* New Brunswick, NJ: Transaction Publishers.
5. Louv, R. (1990). *Childhood's future.* Boston: Houghton Mifflin.
6. McMahon, R. J. & Peters, R. D. V. (Eds.). (1985). *Childhood disorders: Behavioral-developmental approaches.* New York: Brunner/Mazel.
7. Meadow, K. (1980). *Deafness and child development.* Berkeley: University of California Press.
8. Morgan, S. M. (1981). *The unreachable child: An introduction to early childhood autism.* Memphis, TN: Memphis State University Press.
9. Moss, R. A., & Dunlap, H. H. (1990). *Why Johnny can't concentrate: Coping with attention deficit problems.* New York: Bantam.
10. Wachs, T. D., & Gruen, G. E. (1982). *Early experience and human development.* New York: Plenum.
11. Whalen, C. K., & Henker, B. (Eds.). (1980). *Hyperactive children: The social ecology of identification and treatment.* New York: Academic Press.

UNIT FIVE

ADOLESCENCE

Jonathon Baker, age eight

UNIT CONTENTS

CHAPTER 18

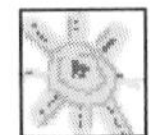

ADOLESCENT PHYSICAL AND COGNITIVE DEVELOPMENT

CHAPTER PREVIEW

ALGEBRA AND FORMAL OPERATIONS

WHEN I WAS IN the ninth grade, my cognitive development must have been coming along a little slowly. At the age of 13, before I was well enough along toward formal operations to deal with abstractions, I had the misfortune of running into algebra. I can remember the previous year, seeing the older kids in the hallway with math books that had covers showing letters being multiplied by numbers. I remember wondering how that was possible. I asked my father if it was hard, and he asked me, "How many numbers are there?" I said that there must be a zillion. And he said, "Well, how hard can letters be, there are only 26 of them." A solid picture of a small group of finite letters seemed simple enough to deal with, and so I entered algebra class with confidence.

THE INSTRUCTOR BEGAN by placing an x on the board. I remember thinking that it seemed to me he had passed up a lot of the alphabet and didn't have very far to go, but that was all right. I raised my hand and asked him what x was. I wanted something concrete. He said, "x is an unknown." In my notebook I wrote, "$x = ?$" I liked that. I decided that whenever he used an x, I would use a question mark because it would make everything easier. After a while, he wrote a y on the board. I raised my hand and asked what y was. He replied that it, too, was an unknown. So I wrote in my notebook, "$y = ?$" It didn't take an Einstein to figure out that if $x = ?$ and $y = ?$, then x must equal y, because they were both question marks. So I raised my hand and volunteered, "Then $x = y$!" The instructor said, "Well, that can happen sometimes, but it usually doesn't." I don't remember much more about that instructor, but I do remember my friend John, who sat next to me in class. He and I spent the rest of that year talking about less confusing things.

THE SECOND TIME I took algebra I think I had the same instructor; at least he looked familiar. This time when he said that *x* was an unknown and *y* was an unknown, it seemed very clear to me that this meant that they could be anything—equal to each other or not equal to each other. By that time, abstract thinking didn't seem so foreign to me. I didn't know it then, but I was slowly entering what Piaget called the period of formal operations and was beginning to be able to handle abstract concepts.

IN THIS CHAPTER, we'll examine the physical and cognitive changes that mark the period of adolescence. We will also see how these changes can affect feelings, attitudes, and behavior.

RESOURCES

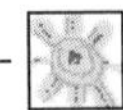

Physical Growth

Behind each maturational change lies the development of essential cells within the brain and body. Most aspects of a child, including emotions, skills, and aptitudes, are related directly or indirectly to her body structure. Feelings about body image underlie many social interactions. This is especially true during adolescence, when many obvious physical changes occur (Chumlea, 1982). Psychologists are aware of how physical growth and development affect a person's emotions and behavior. In fact, if most people had a better understanding of the physical changes that take place during adolescence, they would better understand an adolescent's feelings and behavior. For instance, most people know that girls mature earlier than boys do, but few people give much thought to the fact that adolescents of the same age may be either prepubescent or physically mature (see Figure 18.1). Yet the timing of physical development can profoundly affect adolescents and their interactions with peers and the school environment.

Question: How can early or late physical maturity affect an adolescent's feelings and behavior?

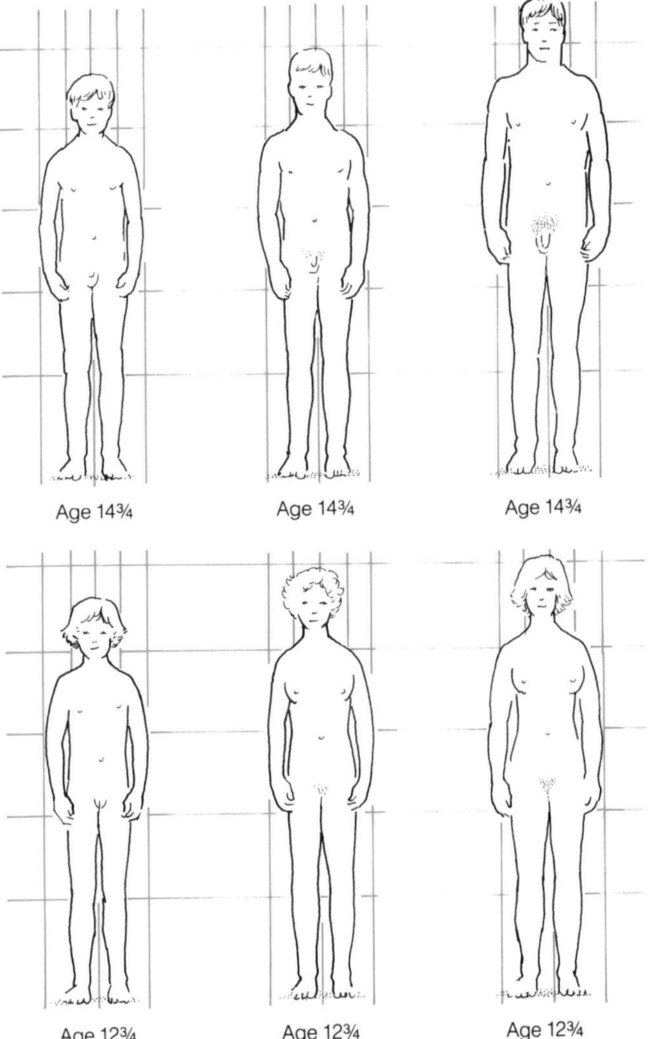

FIGURE 18.1

Differing degrees of pubertal development at the same chronological age. Upper row: three boys all age 14¾ years. Lower row: three girls all age 12¾ years. (*Source:* Adapted from Tanner, 1969)

Because girls begin their growth spurt a year or two sooner than do boys, there is an awkward time when they are taller than boys their own age.

Maturing before your friends do can be lonely. Often there is a sense of being separated from peers by some barrier, some obvious alteration that has made an important difference. Also, adults may unconsciously expect greater maturity from a physically advanced adolescent because his appearance begins to be more adult-like than childlike. However, emotional maturity develops more slowly than physical maturity, and many adolescents, especially those who are physically mature at an early age, may have difficulty living up to the new demands made of them. This, in turn, can lead to disappointment, doubt, and insecurity.

Among boys, however, early maturation can have its advantages. An appearance of being more "mature," thanks to the development of a visible sexual characteristic, such as a beard, can enhance a boy's status in his peer group. Early physical maturation can also enhance athletic ability, which often leads to increased status among peers, members of the opposite sex, and adults. However, the desire among boys to be physically mature and to excel in sports can sometimes lead to dangerous behavior. Among high school students, for instance, it has been found that 1 out of every 15 males has taken anabolic steroids (Buckley et al., 1988). The boys obtained these drugs, mostly illegally, from coaches, gym employees, body-builders, doctors, veterinarians, and pharmacists. These hormones increase muscle mass but at the same time place the body under considerable stress. Serious heart disease and behavioral changes are associated with their continued use. Many of these boys began their use before the age of 15.

In general, girls find early maturity more stressful than boys do (Nottelmann & Welsh, 1986; Petersen, 1979). Although a girl may find herself suddenly attractive to older males, she often lacks the emotional maturity to deal with the situations that may result.

Question: Do girls who mature early also gain status among their peers?

Generally, girls who mature early are given higher social status by their peers; the increased status, however, is markedly less than that enjoyed by boys who mature early. This may be because of the greater emphasis given by boys to athletic ability. But as girls participate more and more in athletic events formerly restricted to boys, girls maturing earlier will find their social status enhanced by athletics, just as boys do.

Late maturity among boys can be very stressful. Besides being teased and verbally ridiculed by more physically mature age-mates, boys who mature late often fear that they may never develop further or grow taller. These factors can lead to a negative self-image that can continue even after physical maturity has been reached (Siegel, 1982).

Girls who mature late share many of the same problems. They may fear that they will remain flat-chested or that boys won't like them. And if boys don't like them, they may be left out of activities considered important by their peers. Such physically immature girls tend to be less socially mature. Nonetheless, in terms of current standards of physical attractiveness, girls who mature late may have an advantage, becoming generally taller and slimmer as adults than those who mature early.

PUBERTY
The stage of maturation in which the individual becomes physiologically capable of sexual reproduction.

GROWTH SPURT
The time during puberty in which an adolescent's growth undergoes a marked acceleration.

Puberty and the Growth Spurt

At the beginning of adolescence, a number of physical changes occur. These changes are controlled by genetics and hormones. One change is the development of sexual maturity, which occurs during a period called **puberty.** It has been found that the hormone *melatonin,* which is secreted by the pineal gland, is responsible for the onset of puberty. As puberty nears, melatonin concentrations show a marked decrease (Waldhauser et al., 1984).

At the onset of puberty, the testes or ovaries enlarge. During puberty, the reproductive system matures, and sexual characteristics such as facial hair or breast enlargement emerge. At this time, the adolescent's growth undergoes a marked acceleration. Height and weight increase dramatically, and body proportion changes. This occurrence is known as the **growth spurt.** The growth spurt lasts for 2 to 3 years and begins in girls about 2 years earlier than it does in boys (see Figure 18.2). As you can see, the rate of growth in centimeters per year declines from birth through age 10 years in girls and through age 12 years in boys. This trend reverses during the growth spurt, when the rate of growth accelerates. During the growth spurt, the legs grow more rapidly than other parts of the body do,

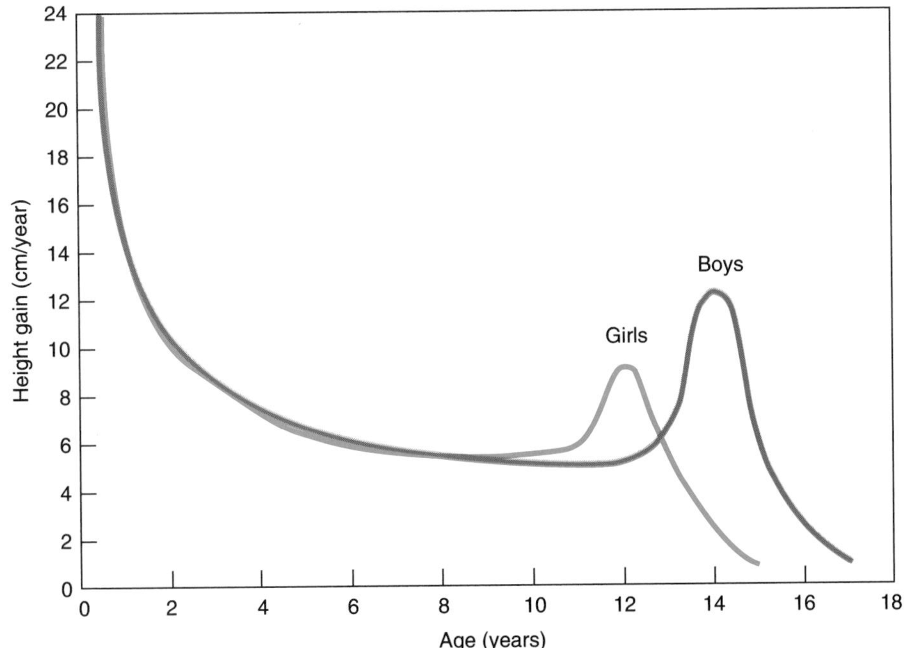

FIGURE 18.2
Typical growth curves for boys and girls. As you can see, height gain declines from a rate of about 24 centimeters (9½ inches) per year just after birth until the years of puberty, when the curve again accelerates. This growth spurt occurs earlier for girls. (*Source:* Tanner, Whitehouse, & Takaishi, 1966)

MENARCHE
The first occurrence of menstruation.

SECULAR TREND
The tendency during the last century for children to mature and grow taller at a younger age.

which often gives the adolescent a disproportional appearance. It sometimes takes a while to become accustomed to a body of new proportions. Perhaps this is one of the reasons adolescents occasionally appear clumsy.

Boys usually reach their full height between the ages of 18 and 20 years, whereas girls reach this plateau between the ages of 16 and 17 years (Roche & Davila, 1972). Other physical changes that may occur include the development of acne, caused by the activity of sebaceous glands beneath the skin, and the vocal changes that sometimes embarrass maturing boys when their voices suddenly drop an octave in midspeech.

Question: Why do some children enter puberty earlier than others?

Many factors may be involved. In past years, the onset of puberty and the completion of growth typically occurred at a later age than they do now. For example, in 1880, the average male didn't reach full height until sometime between the ages of 23 and 25 years, and the average female didn't reach full height until she was approximately 19 or 20 years old (Tanner, 1968).

THE SECULAR TREND

Further evidence that children are now maturing earlier comes from data indicating that the average age of **menarche** (onset of menstruation) is getting lower. The range of nonpathological onset of menstruation is between 9 and 16 years of age (Bullough, 1981). Today, the average age of menarche is 12.3 to 12.6 years, a year or two below some previously reported averages (Bullough, 1981). This decrease in the age of menarche, together with the corresponding tendency of children to mature and grow taller at an earlier age, is known as the **secular trend.** It is believed that the secular trend is the result of improved diet, sanitation, and medical care.

Question: Is the secular trend likely to continue?

There is evidence that the secular trend has reached its biological limit. For the first time, the most recent generation to reach adulthood has been found to average the same height and onset of puberty as the generation just before it.

Young ballet dancers and gymnasts often show delay of menarche and sexual characteristics.

EXERCISE AND MENARCHE

More and more evidence has been gathered that strenuous exercise can delay menarche. Researcher Michelle Warren has discovered that young ballet dancers usually have their first menstrual period about 3 years later, on the average, than age-matched controls. Among the dancers, menarche didn't occur until they were an average of 15.4 years old (Warren, 1980).

Question: Couldn't the reason for the delay in menarche be that young ballet dancers are generally lighter and have less body fat than other girls?

At first, some researchers believed that this was a possibility and that menarche might be triggered when a child reached a certain proportion of height and weight. However, when the ballet dancers were measured after menarche, they were found to be heavier and to have more body fat than the younger nondancers who had *also* reached menarche. Further evidence relating exercise to delayed menarche comes from the fact that the dancers generally experienced their first menstrual period when they were not exercising because of vacation or injury. Exactly why vigorous exercise should postpone menarche is unknown, but it is suspected that it may be the body's way of postponing childbearing during times of stress. It has also been found that exercise not only can delay menarche but, when it is strenuous, can lead to a disruption of the menstrual cycle (Bullen et al., 1985). Again, this may be the body's way of postponing childbearing until the mother is better able to handle a pregnancy.

MUSCLE DEVELOPMENT AND STRENGTH IN ADOLESCENCE

During puberty, as muscle growth increases, there is a corresponding increase in strength. From measurements of changes in power during this period, it has been found that girls increase their strength by about 45 percent (Faust, 1977), whereas boys increase theirs by about 65 percent. Following puberty, boys continue to gain in strength (see Figure 18.3).

Males also have an advantage over females in their ability to sustain effort. Their larger hearts and lungs help to supply needed oxygen to the muscles. In addition, during puberty, boys develop greater amounts of oxygen-carrying hemoglobin through the action of testosterone. In practical terms, these differences are slight, however, and many women are able to increase their muscular endurance substantially by engaging in the kinds of bodybuilding exercises that once were considered solely the province of men. Following puberty, the average male can bench press (raise a weight above his chest while lying on his back) about 1.7 times as much weight, relative to his own body weight, as the average female can. However, the average female athlete, after about 6 months of weight training, can bench press 150 pounds, considerably more than the average untrained male (Douglas & Miller, 1977).

Question: If girls exercise with weights after puberty, won't they become muscular?

Following puberty, boys secrete about 30 to 200 micrograms of testosterone each day, compared with about 5 to 20 micrograms a day in girls. Because testosterone is necessary for the extensive muscle growth that occurs with exercise, girls do not develop much muscle tissue in response to strenuous exercise. After 6 months of weight training, a girl's flexed biceps are not likely to have increased by more than 1/4 of an inch. And yet her arm strength will have grown considerably (Douglas & Miller, 1977). No one fully understands the relationships between muscle mass and strength. Although girls do not have the muscle mass possessed by most boys, they can approach a boy's strength.

Question: Is there a difference in muscle strength between boys and girls before puberty?

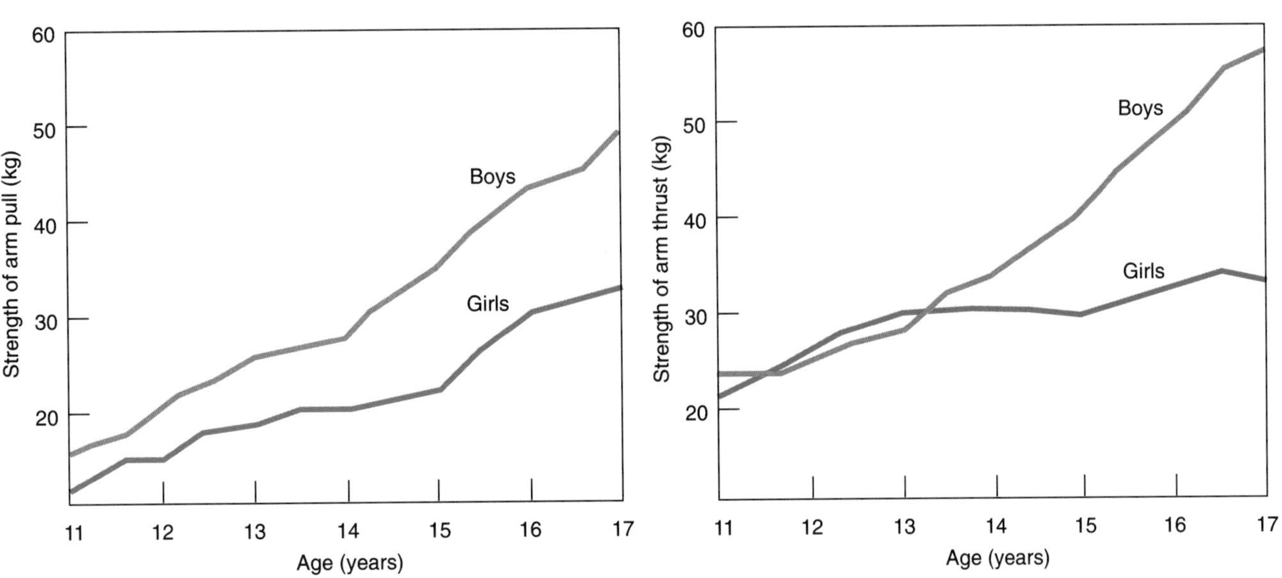

FIGURE 18.3
Strength of arm pull and arm thrust in children from ages 11 to 17 years. Mixed longitudinal data, 65 to 93 boys and 66 to 96 girls in each group. (*Source:* Tanner, 1962; data from Jones, 1949)

Many young women are able to increase their muscle strength substantially through weight-training exercises, once thought to be solely the province of men.

Data indicate that boys are only slightly stronger than girls before the age of 12 years (Malina, 1978). Between the ages of 12 and 17 years, boys tend to become progressively stronger than girls (Malina, 1979).

Nutrition and Its Effects

A considerable amount of energy is required to maintain the rapid growth rate characteristic of adolescence. This energy can be measured in terms of kilocalories. A kilocalorie, more commonly called a calorie, is a measurement of food energy. Adolescents consume a lot of calories, and a lot of food. Adults are sometimes surprised at how much food an adolescent can put away without becoming overweight.

Of course, good nutrition is essential for proper development. Malnourished adolescents may suffer from delayed puberty and poor physical growth. Although hunger and starvation in the United States are minimal compared with that in other nations, many American adolescents are not adequately nourished. Adolescents are more prone than adults to consume inordinate amounts of carbohydrates or junk food and to engage in fad diets. When I was about 15, I had a good friend who wanted to lose about 12 pounds so that he could improve in gymnastics. A normal diet didn't seem interesting enough to him, so he began a kind of Zen microbiotic transcendental diet (or something like that). At any rate, it seemed to me that for the next three weeks he ate only brown rice and cherries. I suppose he was lucky that he was healthy to start with, and I must admit he did get thin. He also got mean and sick (he's better now).

Self-Imposed Malnourishment

A growing number of children in the United States are underweight and underdeveloped because of self-imposed malnourishment caused by an obsessive fear of "becoming fat," (see At Issue). Such deliberate undereating is believed to be responsible for approximately 7 percent of the stunted growth and delayed puberty found in underdeveloped children. These children, who habitually skip meals, often eat as little as one-third of what they need.

Question: Why are these children so afraid that they'll become overweight?

Sometimes, children have parents who are preoccupied with slenderness and who often express concern about the child's figure and caution him or her about "becoming fat" (Pugliese, Lifshitz, Grad, Fort, & Marks-Katz, 1983). Because children especially need to fill their nutritional requirements, any dieting for the control or avoidance of childhood obesity should be handled only under a doctor's care. Children who undereat for considerable lengths of time may never be able to make up their lost growth.

Obesity

Obesity results when the number of calories stored is greater than the number used or passed by the body. It has been determined that the prevalence of obesity (where a person is 20 percent above appropriate weight) has increased by 39 percent among 12- to 17-year-old adolescents during the past two decades (Kolata, 1986).

Question: Why are there more obese teenagers now than before?

One hypothesis is that television has played an important role. It seems that children who watch large amounts of television are more likely to be overweight, perhaps because they tend to consume more of the kinds of foods they see in

AT ISSUE

The Pursuit of Thinness

During adolescence, children become more preoccupied with their body image. This may lead to some strange eating habits. The following case study illustrates what can happen to teens who become so concerned about their weight that they resort to bizarre weight control regimens:

> The first vomiting period perpetuated itself into a five-year-long habit in which I had daily planned and unplanned binges and self-induced vomiting sessions up to four times daily. I frequently vomited each of the day's three meals as well as my afternoon "snack" of three or four hamburgers, four to five enormous bowls of ice cream, dozens of cookies, bags of various potato chips, packs of Swiss cheese, two large helpings of french fries, at least two milkshakes, and to top it off, an apple or banana followed by two or more pints of cold milk to help me vomit more easily.
>
> During the night, I sneaked back into the kitchen in the dark so I would not risk awakening any family member by turning on the light. . . . Every night I wished that I could, like everyone else, eat one apple as a midnight snack and then stop. . . . Then I tiptoed to the bathroom to empty myself. Sometimes the food did not come up as quickly as I wanted; so, in panic, I rammed my fingers wildly down my throat, occasionally making it bleed from cutting it with my fingernails. Sometimes I would spend two hours in the bathroom trying to vomit, yet there were other nights when the food came up in less than three minutes. (Muuss, 1986, p. 261)

This case study illustrates a growing problem in the United States. Approximately 1 to 2 percent of the U. S. population either starve themselves or binge on food and then use laxatives or induce vomiting in an effort to remain slender.

Those people who starve themselves are said to be suffering from *anorexia nervosa,* which is characterized by "progressive and/or significant weight loss, alternate binge eating and dieting with avoidance of any 'fattening' foods, amenorrhea [absence of menstruation], hyperactivity and compulsive exercising patterns, and preoccupation with food and nutrition" (Lucas, 1977, p. 139). In severe cases of anorexia, death from starvation or other health problems associated with it (such as heart disorders) may occur. It has been estimated that as many as 20 percent of the people who have the disease eventually die from it (Brumberg, 1985). Anorexics are often extremely emaciated and dangerously underweight, even though they may still report that they feel "fat" and need to lose just a little more weight. Different sources estimate that there are between 150,000 and 500,000 anorexics in the United States (Brumberg, 1985).

Regular purging *without* weight loss is called *bulimia* and is approximately four times as common as anorexia. Bulimics may suffer from dental and digestive problems brought on by the incessant vomiting they induce following their binges, all in an effort to keep from gaining weight. They are also often anxious and depressed over their bizarre and secretive habit. Bulimics, like anorexics, tend to be adolescent females. They may be less likely to receive help for their problem because outwardly, at least, they may appear perfectly normal.

It's hard for some people to understand why anyone would want to follow every meal of the day with the disgusting experience of vomiting or how anyone who looked like she just stepped out of a concentration camp could insist that she needs to lose weight. Psychologists and physicians have searched for physical causes to explain these disorders. There is evidence of hypothalamic dysfunction in anorexics, although it has not been determined whether this dysfunction is a cause or merely an effect of the disease (Casper, 1984; Gold, Pottash, Sweeney, Martin, & Davies, 1980). Thyroid disease may account for a small minority of cases. There is also evidence that the physical mechanism that signals satiation in bulimics may be faulty, thus allowing them to continue to eat large quantities of food without feeling "full" (Geracioti & Liddle, 1988). Moreover, there is evidence that hormones may play a role because levels of the hormone vasopressin are found to be higher in bulimic than in nonbulimic women (Demitrack et al., 1992).

Another hint about the cause of these disorders is that males rarely have them. Adolescent females account for 90 to 95 percent of all cases of anorexia and bulimia, which has also led researchers to look for possible social or environmental causes. In our culture, there is great pressure on women to be slender and attractive. Adolescent females, especially those who have low self-esteem or who come from families in conflict (Grant & Fodor, 1986; Johnson & Flach, 1985), often try to emulate their vision of the slender models depicted on television and in magazines. This may be a way for them to show their control and to increase their sense of self-worth. One study demonstrated that adolescent girls in competitive environments that emphasize weight and appearance face

AT ISSUE

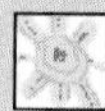

more pressure to have the "thin" ideal body (Brooks-Gunn, Burrow, & Warren, 1988). And girls who attend schools in which social acceptance into a clique or group is highly valued tend to be less satisfied with their body weight than are girls who attend less cliquish schools (Richards, Boxer, Petersen, & Albrecht, 1990).

Some researchers have argued that it is essential that society decrease the pressure it places on adolescents to have a certain body physique in order to be loved and admired. Many bulimics and anorexics may indeed be casualties of the pursuit of thinness. On the other hand, the American emphasis on being slender may help some people to maintain suitable weight and avoid obesity. Perhaps if the emphasis were more on the weight appropriate for good health than on what would look best in chic clothes, it would help remove some of the pressure to be inordinately thin.

commercials and also because they tend to be less active than children who don't watch as much television (Dietz & Gortmaker, 1985; Palumbo & Dietz, 1985). Fast foods generally have more of their calories in fat than in protein or carbohydrates. Research has shown that fat calories are far more likely to be stored than are calories from other sources. For this reason, 400 calories of french fries are actually more fattening than 400 calories of plain baked potato (Miller, Lindeman, Wallace & Niederpruem, 1990).

It has also been shown that obesity is mostly determined by inheritance (Grilo & Pogue-Geile, 1991).

Question: How does inheritance affect obesity?

Children inherit different numbers of fat cells, and the number they inherit determines, in part, how well their bodies will store fat. Children from families in which parents or other family members are overweight may be able to store excess food more efficiently than other children do and may therefore be considered genetically obese. For example, among the Pima Indians in Arizona, a farming tribe for the last 2,000 years, the vast majority are extremely obese. Their obesity begins in childhood. By the time they are 35, about half of the population have diabetes. It appears that through natural selection, the Pimas' bodies are prepared for a famine. However, in the food-rich United States, body preparation for a famine may no longer be an advantage.

During adolescence, obesity can present severe problems because of adolescents' preoccupation with self-image. Overweight adolescents may be socially isolated. Often, the social isolation is self-imposed out of fear of ridicule. Adolescents who are teased because of their obesity often take comfort by eating more, which perpetuates the cycle.

LEARNING CHECK

Multiple Choice

1. Early physical maturity is
- **a.** generally more stressful for boys than for girls.
- **b.** more likely to occur among girls who exercise strenuously.
- **c.** often associated with high status among boys.
- **d.** none of the above.

2. The growth spurt
   a. generally lasts 2 to 3 years.
   b. begins about 2 years sooner in girls than in boys.
   c. is a period of accelerated growth.
   d. all of the above.
3. The incidence of obesity among adolescents
   a. has decreased in recent years.
   b. may be related to heavy television viewing.
   c. is not a serious problem.
   d. is not determined in any way by genetics.

True or False

4. On average, boys are only slightly stronger before puberty than girls are.
   a. true b. false

Answers: 1.c 2.d 3.b 4.a

Cognitive Development in Adolescence

In most individuals, the ability to reason and to think probably becomes fully developed during adolescence. Erik Erikson (1968) has described adolescence as a time of identity crisis when the questions "Who am I?" and "What is my role in life?" become dominant themes. Without the cognitive changes that occur, it would not be possible for adolescents to consider such complex philosophical questions.

Question: What cognitive changes occur in adolescence?

First, the adolescent becomes capable of dealing with the logic of combinations, which requires the simultaneous manipulation of many factors, either singly or in conjunction. Second, the adolescent becomes able to use abstract concepts to make thought more flexible. Third, the adolescent becomes able to deal with the hypothetical as well as the real (Piaget & Inhelder, 1969). According to Piaget, this last step is the most advanced form of cognition, and it defines formal operations.

THE LOGIC OF COMBINATIONS

In 1958, Inhelder and Piaget presented a chemistry problem to a number of children and adolescents of different ages. The subjects were shown four containers (A, B, C, and D), each of which contained a different colorless liquid. They were then shown a separate container and were told that it contained a catalyst, or activating agent. It was explained that the catalyst in combination with one or more of the other liquids would produce a yellow mixture. The subjects were then asked to discover which combination or combinations would produce the colored liquid. How would you solve this problem? Many of the subjects began by examining what happened when a mixture was made from some of the contents of all five containers. This first attempt did not produce a yellow liquid. This was a simple enough place to start, but where would you go from there?

Figure 18.4 shows the correct strategy. As you can see, there are only four possible combinations of the catalyst (1) with only one of the unknown liquids (A, B, C, or D): 1 with A, 1 with B, 1 with C, and 1 with D. Then you need only progress through the other possible combinations of three (1 with A and B, 1 with A and C, etc.), four, and five substances to test every possibility. The combinations that will produce the yellow liquid are circled in the figure.

FIGURE 18.4
A chemistry problem requiring a logical analysis of combinations.

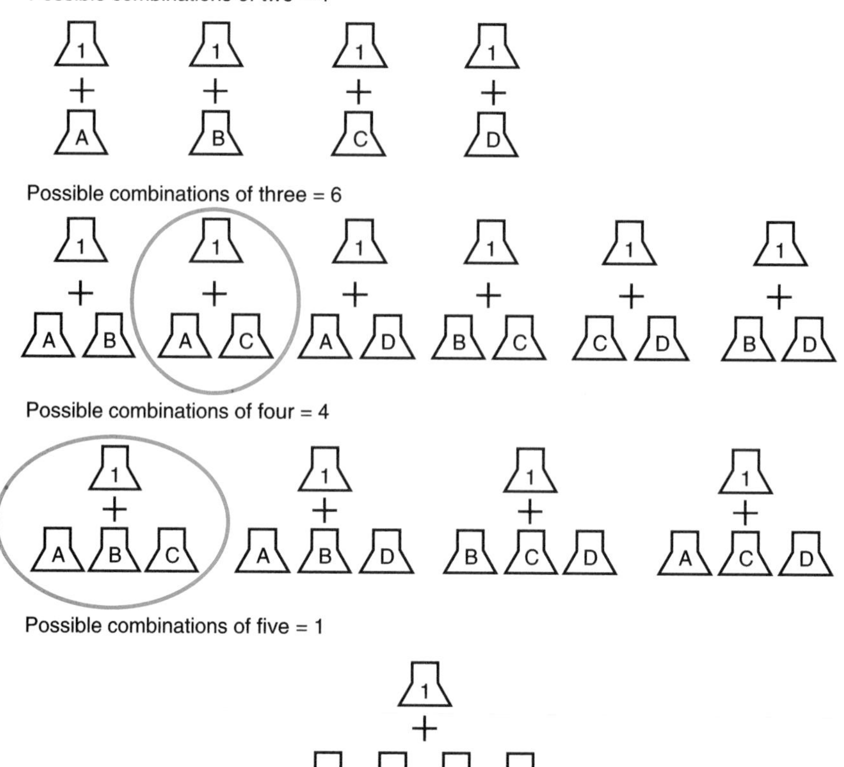

Key
1 = potassium iodide
A = diluted sulfuric acid
B = water
C = oxygenated water
D = thiosulfate

Children who have not begun to enter the period of formal operations use less sophisticated reasoning and attack the problem with a hit-or-miss strategy. This ineffective approach leads them to repeat combinations they have tried before or to overlook some of the possible combinations. As young adolescents begin to develop formal operations thinking, they become capable of examining combinations systematically in a scientific way.

This ability to examine combinations logically has also been demonstrated by Inhelder and Piaget in their famous pendulum problem. A pendulum can be created by suspending a weight from a string and allowing the weight to swing free. In the pendulum problem, the subject is asked to determine which of four factors affects the rate at which the weight will swing. The four possibilities are the force of the initial push that you give the weight, the amount of weight suspended from the string, how far out you pull the weight before you let it go, and the length of the string. The subjects are allowed to experiment with the pendulum to determine which of these variables affects the *rate* of the swinging (how many complete swings per unit of time the pendulum makes).

Adolescents who are able to examine logically the possible combinations discover that only the length of the string affects the rate at which the pendulum swings. Once the length of the pendulum string is set, each completed swing (once back and forth) takes the same amount of time regardless of how fast or slow the pendulum swings (because a faster swinging pendulum has farther to travel). This is why pendulums make good timepieces; even as they slow down, their *rate* stays constant. Children who have not yet attained formal operational thinking attempt to manipulate the different variables in a hit-or-miss fashion, just as they do when presented with the chemistry problem.

Question: Why is the ability to examine combinations logically an important advance in cognitive development?

The scientific method and all scientific reasoning depend on the ability to manipulate variables and combinations of variables independently of one another, covering all the possible combinations and sequences. In fact, solving the chemistry problem or the pendulum problem requires this kind of scientific reasoning.

USE OF ABSTRACT CONCEPTS

As cognition becomes more developed, it becomes possible for adolescents to use and manipulate abstract concepts. For instance, how are a pair of scissors, a shoehorn, and a table knife alike? They may all be made of metal, and they all have a functional use. In one experiment, this question was posed to children in the fourth grade and to adolescents in the ninth grade. One-half of the children in each group were given only the names of the objects, while the other half actually

As adolescents begin to acquire formal operations thinking, they come to understand the logic of combinations and are able, for the first time, to think scientifically.

saw the objects. As expected, the ninth graders were able to think of more similarities than the fourth graders were. However, the ninth graders were just as successful whether or not they could see the objects, whereas the fourth graders' success was markedly improved by being able to look at the three objects (Elkind, Barocas, & Johnsen, 1969).

Preadolescent thinking appears to depend substantially on concrete perceptions. Adolescents, however, can analyze the logic of a statement without becoming tied to its concrete properties. In a series of experiments, adolescents and preadolescents were asked to judge whether certain statements were true, false, or impossible to know (Osherson & Markman, 1974–75). The subjects were told that the experimenter had hidden a poker chip in his hand and that "either this chip is green, or it is not green." Most of the preadolescents thought that it was impossible to judge because they could not see the hidden chip. The adolescents, however, were able to deal with the concept of green abstractly. They realized that something must either be a particular color or not be that color. The adolescents realized that the statement had to be true. For that matter, everything in the universe is either green or not green. Preadolescents have trouble comprehending such an abstraction. This is one of the reasons why educators usually wait until children reach adolescence before they seriously present them with abstractions such as algebra, as described in the Chapter Preview.

USING AND UNDERSTANDING THE HYPOTHETICAL

By the time adolescents have reached the age of 15 years, they are often capable of the most advanced cognitive thinking (Niemark, 1982).

Question: How do advanced cognitive abilities affect an adolescent's view of the world?

As cognitive processes mature, the adolescent comes to respond to the world and its institutions with a more encompassing view (see Figure 18.5). In part, this is because of the adolescent's ability to develop abstract hypothetical ideas. The adolescent's concepts of morality become more philosophical. Religious and political views often undergo considerable analysis and change during this time. Adolescents who have treated religion in concrete terms may begin to ask questions

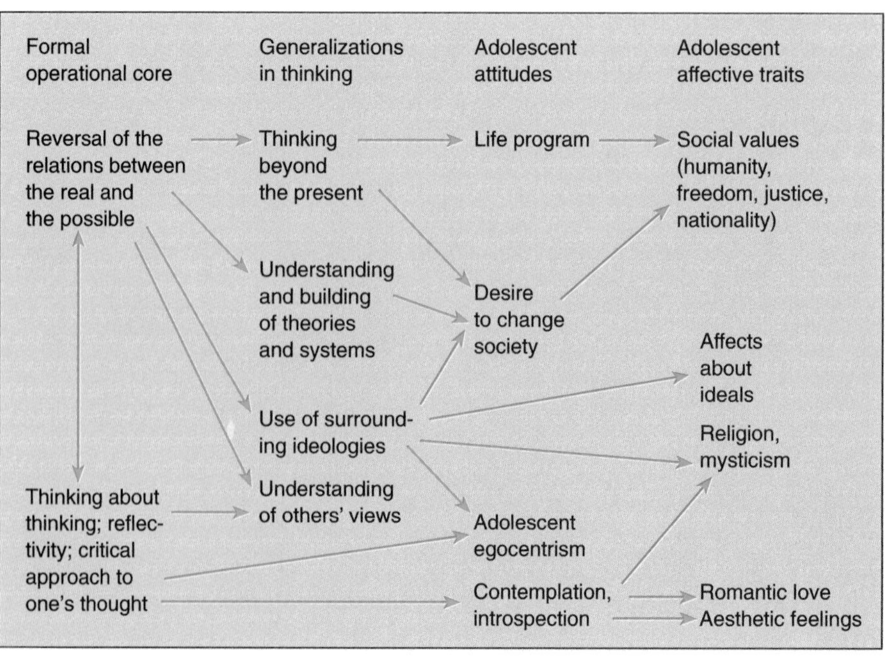

FIGURE 18.5
Model relating formal operations to the characteristics of adolescence. (Adolescent egocentrism is discussed in the Applications section.) (*Source:* Blasi & Hoeffel, 1974, p. 345)

about the nature of morality or religion, and their beliefs may become more mature and personal (Kuhlen & Arnold, 1944). During the transition into the formal operations period, the adolescent begins to view political institutions as governed by general principles. Older adolescents often are capable of considering the hypothetical potential outcomes of decisions made by governments. The development of political ideology is closely tied to the cognitive development that occurs during adolescence. In one study, adolescents who demonstrated advanced moral and cognitive development were found generally to be the most politically active (Haan, Smith, & Block, 1968).

Question: Is it rare for an adolescent not to reach the period of formal operations?

It's not uncommon for individuals to fail to reach the period of formal operations during adolescence or even during adulthood (Blasi & Hoeffel, 1974). In fact, cross-cultural studies generally find that among rural and non-Western societies, the majority of adolescents fail to complete the development of formal operations (Ashton, 1975; Glick, 1975). In the United States, a comprehensive longitudinal study of adults and adolescents found that only 30 percent of adults attained formal operations (Kuhn, Langer, Kohlberg, & Haan, 1977). In one of the most detailed studies of formal operations, a researcher examined children in the sixth, eighth, tenth, and twelfth grades, whose ages were between 11 and 18 years. Each child was given a total of 10 different tasks, each of which had been used by Inhelder and Piaget to demonstrate formal operational thinking. Among these 10 tasks was the pendulum problem described earlier. Interestingly, only about 2 percent of the subjects who were able to perform at the formal operational level on one task were able to do so on all tasks. Almost all the subjects showed inconsistency in their ability as they moved from one task to the next (Martorano, 1977). Subjects who used advanced formal operational thinking to solve one problem often were found to use rudimentary forms of concrete operational thinking in solving another problem.

Question: Why would adolescents who think formally when solving one task think concretely when solving another?

These results demonstrate the complexity of measuring advanced cognitive processes. Some psychologists have argued that if advanced human cognition is closely tied to maturational changes, as Piaget suggested, then evidence for these developmental changes should be more apparent from cross-cultural research. The fact that adolescents in Western cultures are better able to solve problems designed to measure formal operational thinking has been thought by some scientists to indicate a cultural bias in the testing. There is evidence to support the argument that specific experience can improve an adolescent's ability to solve formal operational problems (Danner & Day, 1977; Siegler & Liebert, 1975).

Question: How could specific experiences help someone think abstractly?

Gottfried Wilhelm von Leibnitz (1646–1716) was a famous German philosopher and a brilliant mathematician. Leibnitz is credited by many with independently developing calculus. People in Leibnitz's day liked to gamble, just as they do today. Dice were particularly popular. Fortunately (or unfortunately, whichever way you see it), gambling houses weren't always successful, because no one knew how to calculate the odds of throwing particular numbers on dice. Leibnitz was approached by "businessmen" who wanted his help in calculating the odds of any given throw. For instance, if three dice were used, what would be the odds of rolling a 3—that is, three 1s? Again, using three dice, how much harder would it be to roll a 3 than a 4? And so on. Leibnitz worked on this problem for over 20 years, and he finally decided it could not be solved! Interestingly, though, many college students, some with no college math at all, can figure out the odds

It has been suggested that minds like Einstein's are one or two levels beyond formal operations thinking.

of throwing a 3 with three dice, and they can figure out how much harder it would be than throwing a 4 (Bower, 1979).*

Question: Why couldn't a great mathematician solve a simple probability problem?

Undoubtedly, Leibnitz would have been capable of the mathematics involved if he had ever thought of *probability*. But Leibnitz had never been exposed to probability theory, and no one else in his day had either. Leibnitz spent most of his time trying to understand how dice might bounce when they struck a surface! The idea of odds never crossed his mind. When adolescents are asked to solve formal operational tasks such as the pendulum problem, they may rely on previous exposure to the general concepts of the scientific method. Perhaps children in non-Western cultures who haven't had such experiences are unable to solve the pendulum problem, and are unable to understand it when it is explained to them, because they have not had enough exposure to the general principles involved. After all, until Galileo solved the pendulum problem, no one had. This is an information-processing view of advanced cognitive thinking.

Question: If experiences determine cognitive development to a great extent, can it be assumed that there is a stage beyond formal operations?

Piaget believed that there wasn't. Piaget argued that any cognitive advance beyond formal operations was not qualitatively significant but rather was "mere window dressing." Some researchers, however, believe that there may be qualitative advances in cognitive development beyond formal operations (Commons, Richards,

*The odds of rolling a 3 (1, 1, 1) with three dice are $\frac{1}{6} \times \frac{1}{6} \times \frac{1}{6}$, or $\frac{1}{216}$ (1 chance in 216 throws). The odds of rolling a 4 with three dice are three times more likely, because there are three ways to do it (1, 1, 2) (1, 2, 1) (2, 1, 1), or 1 chance for every 72 throws.

& Kuhn, 1982). These researchers refer to such post–formal operational thinking as systematic and metasystematic reasoning. Systematic reasoning, they argue, relies on the ability to build operations on operations, such as would be required to build entire abstract representational systems from the hypothetical constructs generated by formal operational thinking. Metasystematic reasoning would be the next step beyond systematic reasoning. According to these researchers, an example of metasystematic reasoning can be found in Einstein's general theory of relativity. Such an ability allows entire systems to be built on each other. However, whether such reasoning is "qualitatively" different from what Piaget considered to be formal operations is still debatable. For this to be demonstrated, further research would have to show that the cognitive advance required for systematic and metasystematic reasoning depends on, and is separate from, the cognitive advance to formal operations. It may be that future research will show that such post–formal operational abilities exist.

LEARNING CHECK

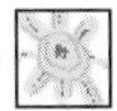

1. Advances in cognitive skill during adolescence may include acquiring the ability
   - **a.** to analyze combinations logically.
   - **b.** to deal with abstract concepts.
   - **c.** to deal with the hypothetical.
   - **d.** all of the above.
2. The ability to deal logically with combinations is necessary for scientific reasoning.
   a. true **b.** false
3. Leibnitz probably was unable to solve the dice problem because
   - **a.** he was incapable of formal operational thinking.
   - **b.** he had never been exposed to the concept of probability.
   - **c.** he was not a skilled mathematician.
   - **d.** none of the above; Leibnitz solved the dice problem.
4. Non-Western adolescents are less likely to be able to solve problems requiring formal operational thinking than are Western adolescents.
   a. true **b.** false
5. During adolescence, concepts of morality, religion, and politics generally become more concrete.
   a. true **b.** false

Answers: 1. d 2. a 3. b 4. a 5. b

APPLICATIONS

Adolescent Egocentrism: Understanding Adolescents Even Though They May Not Understand You

By the time children enter adolescence, they are well beyond the egocentrism of preschoolers, and yet they still demonstrate a kind of egocentrism.

Question: How are adolescents egocentric?

Adolescents aren't egocentric in the same way preschoolers are. Adolescents are certainly aware that others may have perspectives different from their own and that the sun doesn't shine to light their path. (Preschoolers often say that the sun shines "so I can see.") An adolescent is far from that kind of egocentrism. However, as children enter adolescence, the limits of their judgment and logic make them susceptible to another kind of egocentrism: They may become deeply involved with themselves.

Initially, as adolescents become able to deal with abstractions, they also become capable of thinking in greater detail about the thoughts of others. They form hypotheses about what others may be thinking (Elkind, 1967). As Elkind has said, "It is this capacity to take account of other people's thoughts . . . which is the crux of adolescent egocentrism" (Elkind, 1967, p. 1029). The adolescent believes, "If I'm thinking about me, they must be thinking about me" (Looft, 1971). Adolescents may also discover conflicting thoughts and behaviors in themselves because, for the first time, they are able to compare the different ways they may behave in school, with their friends, with their family, and in their romantic relationships (Harter & Monsour, 1992). This may not only leave adolescents unsure what others think of them, but make them unsure even of what they think of themselves!

I can recall first being concerned in this way about what other people were thinking when I was 12 years old and was playing with my friends who were 10 and 11. I had toy hand grenades loaded with caps that would go off when the grenades hit the ground. My two friends had a metal replica of a 50-caliber machine gun that weighed a ton. With this arsenal, we decided to go across to a vacant city lot and destroy every imaginary foe in sight. As we were winning the war, I noticed a young couple walking down the street past where we were playing. My friends continued the attack undaunted, and perhaps a few months earlier I would have, too. But now, for the first time, I felt embarrassed. I hid my grenades and walked about nonchalantly, inspecting the bits of weedy botany growing about the lot until the couple had passed. After they had gone, we successfully assaulted the one lump of remaining high ground. Now that I look back at it, I doubt that the young couple really would have given much thought to whether I was too old to play "army," but at the time I was sure I was the most important thing on their minds.

Because of this egocentrism, adolescents often place an inordinate emphasis on acne blemishes, physical features, and size. They may think that their parents, friends, teachers, and siblings are as concerned about them as they are themselves. A further consequence of this egocentrism is that an adolescent often feels that he is "on stage," playing to an "imaginary audience" (Adams & Jones, 1981; Elkind & Bowen, 1979; Gray & Hudson, 1984). "Because he believes he is of importance to so many people, he comes to regard himself, and particularly his feelings, as something special and unique" (Elkind, 1967, p. 1031). This sense of being unique becomes obvious when adolescents make statements to parents or other adults such as, "You can't possibly know how I feel" or "You just can't understand how much I love him" (Elkind, 1978).

Question: When does adolescent egocentrism diminish?

All of us are concerned about ourselves to some degree, and many of us wonder from time to time what others may think of us. However, most of us are aware that others have their own lives and concerns and that we are not on stage everywhere we go. Most of us are no longer as egocentric as we may have been during adolescence (Enright, Lapsley, & Shukla, 1979). This lessening of egocentrism, or decentering, as it is called, appears to occur when formal operations finally become established (Elkind, 1967). Through social interactions and objective analysis of our own thoughts, we come to realize that although we may be important to some, we are not the center of everyone's attention.

APPLICATIONS

Question: Is there any way to help adolescents not to become excessively egocentric?

It may be helpful for adolescents to discuss their feelings in detail with many different peers and adults. In this way, they may be better able to evaluate their own position and to understand positions different from their own. Perhaps the best way for adolescents to overcome their egocentric thoughts and feelings is to develop a genuine, intimate relationship with another. This, more than anything, may foster mature interpersonal relations (Elkind, 1967; Looft, 1971; Piaget, 1967).

SUMMARY

- Almost every aspect of a child, including emotions, skills, and aptitudes, is related directly or indirectly to body structure. Psychologists are aware of how physical growth and development affect a person's emotions and behavior.
- Adolescents of the same age may be prepubescent or physically mature. Level of development can profoundly affect adolescents and their interactions with peers and the school environment.
- At the onset of puberty, the testes or ovaries enlarge. During puberty, the reproductive system matures, and sexual characteristics develop. At this time, the adolescent's growth undergoes a marked acceleration. Boys usually reach their full height between the ages of 18 and 20 years, whereas girls reach this plateau between the ages of 16 and 17 years.
- The decrease in the age of menarche, along with the corresponding tendency of children to mature and grow taller at an earlier age, is known as the secular trend. It is believed that the secular trend is the result of improved diet, sanitation, and medical care. Increasing evidence indicates that strenuous exercise can delay menarche and disrupt the normal menstrual cycle.
- During puberty, as muscle growth increases, there is a corresponding increase in strength. Measurements of changes in strength during this period show that girls increase their strength by about 45 percent, whereas boys increase theirs by about 65 percent.
- During adolescence, obesity can present severe problems because adolescents often are preoccupied with self-image. Overweight adolescents may be socially isolated. Often, the social isolation is self-imposed out of fear of ridicule.
- During adolescence, children become more preoccupied with their body image. This, in turn, may lead to self-imposed starvation (anorexia nervosa) or a cycle of binging and purging (bulemia).
- A number of cognitive changes occur in adolescence. First, the adolescent becomes capable of dealing with the logic of combinations, which requires the simultaneous manipulation of many factors either singly or in conjunction. Second, the adolescent becomes able to use abstract concepts to make thought more flexible. Third, the adolescent becomes able to deal with the hypothetical as well as the real.
- As cognitive processes mature, the adolescent comes to respond to the world and its institutions with a more encompassing view. The adolescent's concepts of morality become more sophisticated, and religious and political views often undergo change.
- By the time children enter adolescence, they are well beyond the egocentrism of preschoolers, yet they still demonstrate a kind of egocentrism.

QUESTIONS FOR DISCUSSION

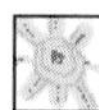

1. Because cognitive development appears to be completed by the time adolescents are about 15, should 16- and 17-year-olds be given the vote?
2. Do you think that other factors besides changes in cognitive development may contribute to adolescent egocentrism? For example, how might the emphasis in TV commercials on appearance affect an adolescent's concern with self?
3. Can you recall specific instances from your adolescence when your thinking underwent a change? How might this change have related to your cognitive development?

SUGGESTIONS FOR FURTHER READING

1. Elkind, D. (1981). *Children and adolescents: Interpretive essays on Jean Piaget* (3rd ed.). New York: Oxford University Press.
2. Graydanus, D. E. (1991). *Caring for your adolescent: Ages 12 to 21*. New York: Bantam.
3. Kaplan, L. J. (1984). *Adolescence: The farewell to childhood*. New York: Simon & Schuster.
4. Klausmeier, H. J., & Allen, P. S. (1978). *Cognitive development of children and youth: A longitudinal study*. New York: Academic Press.
5. Santrock, J. W. (1990). *Adolescence* (4th ed.). Dubuque, IA: Brown.
6. Stein, P., & Unell, B. (1986). *Anorexia nervosa: Finding the lifeline*. Minneapolis: CompCare.

CHAPTER 19

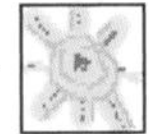

ADOLESCENT SOCIAL AND PERSONALITY DEVELOPMENT

CHAPTER PREVIEW

RITES DE PASSAGE

IN SOME CULTURES, there is no social period of adolescence. There are only childhood and adulthood. In such cultures, when a child enters puberty, it is a sign that he or she has become an adult. In many groups and tribes throughout the world, the social change from childhood to adulthood happens in a single day. For instance, a boy might be summoned by his elders, along with other children his age, and taken to a place where a ceremony is conducted that marks his passage into adulthood. Such a ceremony is called a *rite de passage*, or rite of passage. The ceremony is often stressful. A tribe in the South Pacific requires that boys leap from a 100-foot-high platform built in a tree, with nothing to protect them but some 90-foot-long vines tied to their feet. Many of the boys said that it was scary, but that it was exhilarating, too. Western observers of this practice went on to invent bungee jumping!

AMONG THE MANDAN, a now-extinct American plains Indian tribe, boys had their pectoral muscles pierced with sharp sticks and then were suspended by ropes attached to the sticks (as depicted in the film *A Man Called Horse*). The boys who could last the longest were thought of as the most manly. Among the Australian aborigines, a boy is held by his sponsor while circumcision is performed with a sharp stone tool. In each case, the ceremony represents a transition to adult status.

Question: In the Jewish religion, when a boy turns 13, he goes through a bar mitzvah ceremony to mark his passage into adulthood. Would this be considered a rite de passage?

Traditionally, the bar mitzvah was a *rite de passage*, but as it's practiced today, it isn't. In a real *rite de passage,* the child's social environment would change radically, as though he were going from night to day. He would leave his village as a child, treated as such by his mother and the other adults, but when he returned, he would have the full status of an adult and would be treated as an adult. In our culture, after a boy is bar mitzvahed, he goes right back to school and nobody expects that he will immediately vote, drive a car, or be married.

FOR OUR CHILDREN, the transition to adulthood is marked by many separate changes over the period of adolescence. A 12-year-old girl may be allowed to wear nylons and makeup, a 16-year-old may be allowed a driver's license, an 18-year-old may marry or vote, and in many states individuals must be 21 years old to drink alcohol legally. The transition is slow. For this reason, adolescents often count smoking, drinking, driving, and sexual activities as indications of adult status.

IN THIS CHAPTER, we'll examine the social world of adolescence in our society and see how personality can be shaped during the transition from childhood to adulthood.

RESOURCES

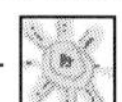

The Emergence of Adolescence

In 1904, G. Stanley Hall published the first scientific study of adolescence. His ideas were published in a two-volume work titled, curiously enough, *Adolescence,* and they had a tremendous influence on subsequent thought concerning the subject. Hall saw adolescence as a period of *storm and stress.* He believed the adolescent period to be full of many changes in direction and swings in mood; a time of turbulence and turmoil.

Question: Why is adolescence considered by so many to be a period of conflict and stress?

Think of all the changes that an adolescent must face. Adolescence is a time when self-concept and attitudes may alter considerably (Harter & Monsour, 1992; McKinney & Moore, 1982). Adolescents must deal for the first time with sexual relationships, the choice of a career, political decisions, economic alternatives, and a host of other "adult" tasks. As Erik Erikson has pointed out, there is an important struggle to establish an identity during adolescence. With so many major conflicts and decisions to face, it's no wonder that the journey from puberty to adulthood is turbulent—quite unlike the more gentle and serene adult years. This is why the adolescent . . . wait a minute! The "more gentle and serene adult years"! Is that right? Let's start again. Adolescence is a time of unusual turbulence and conflict (so far, so good) unlike—when?

Question: Actually, can't life at any time or age become turbulent and filled with conflict?

Now that you mention it, life's problems don't end when one turns 20. In fact, when's the last time you told a 40-year-old "Don't worry" and she listened to you?

Actually, the conclusion of an 8-year nationwide study conducted at the University of Michigan of 2,000 adolescent males as they went from tenth grade to the age of 20 years was that adolescence was fairly benign. The study revealed that self-concept, outlook on life, and a number of other attitudes were well formed by the time adolescents entered tenth grade. Moreover, when the subjects were retested at age 20, their attitudes were found not to have undergone the dramatic changes that might be expected following a turbulent adolescence (Bachman, O'Malley, & Johnston, 1978). Others have confirmed these findings (Offer, Ostrov, & Howard, 1981; Savin-Williams & Demo, 1984). According to one group of researchers,

> The most dramatic . . . findings are those that permit us to characterize the model American teenager as feeling confident, happy, and self-satisfied—a portrait of the American adolescent that contrasts sharply with that drawn by many theorists of adolescent development, who contend that adolescence is pervaded with turmoil, dramatic mood swings, and rebellion. (Offer, Ostrov, & Howard, 1981, pp. 83–84)

Question: What about all those hormones that hit during adolescence? Don't they cause upset and stress?

The surge in hormones during the adolescent period doesn't in itself appear to cause undue stress (Buchanan, Eccles, & Becker, 1992), although it is difficult to separate cultural forces from hormonal ones that might, for example, encourage adolescent boys to be aggressive.

Question: Then why has adolescence been singled out as a time of stress?

ROLE CONFUSION
A consequence of the failure to establish a sense of identity during Erikson's fifth psychosocial stage. Without a sense of identity, the individual will be confused about his or her role in society and will find it difficult to form a life philosophy or create a stable base on which to build a career or have a family.

There certainly are stresses associated with being an adolescent, but we might be hard pressed to say for sure that these stresses are more severe than those a person encounters during other times. Even so, although adolescence may not generally be a time of unusual turbulence, *some* adolescents may have a particularly difficult time coping with the changes that occur. There is a great range and diversity of adjustment patterns during adolescence (Boxer, Gershenson, & Offer, 1984).

There may also be specific stresses associated with adolescence that are qualitatively different from the stresses of adulthood.

A Changing Philosophy

Question: What kinds of stresses would be qualitatively different?

As an adolescent develops cognitive skills, he or she is confronted for the first time with the overwhelming complexities and abstract qualities of the world. Suddenly, nothing is simple. Religious values, political values, social concepts, and questions about personal identity seem to encompass endless hypothetical possibilities from which the adolescent is expected by parents and society to draw conclusions and adopt a life philosophy. During our adult years, we have time to organize and make sense of this confusion. We adopt a philosophy. We take political, social, and moral positions and incorporate them into our identity. In this sense, adulthood would have a stability that is not immediately available to the adolescent.

Our culture demands that adolescents handle a number of developmental tasks. As we have discussed, sexual relationships must be faced. Social maturity in dealings with both sexes is expected. The adolescent's own masculine or feminine role must be realized and adjusted to his or her satisfaction. And the adolescent must come to terms with his or her physical development. Our culture also expects adolescents to achieve emotional independence from parents and other adults. Decisions about whether to marry or have children become more pressing. Adolescents are expected to develop a philosophy and moral ideology as well as to achieve socially responsible behavior.

Choosing a Career

Pursuing a career choice is an essential part of adolescent development. Researchers Inhelder and Piaget have stated, "The adolescent becomes an adult when he undertakes a real job" (Inhelder & Piaget, 1958, p. 346).

Question: Why did Piaget believe that accepting a vocation is such a major step from adolescence to adulthood?

Piaget argued that once adolescents have entered formal operations, their newly acquired ability to use the hypothetical allows them to create ideal representations. Piaget believed that the existence of such ideals, without the tempering of reality, rapidly leads adolescents to become intolerant of their nonidealistic world and to press for reform and change in a characteristically idealistic and adolescent way. Piaget has said,

> True adaptation to society comes automatically when the adolescent reformer attempts to put his ideas to work. Just as experience reconciles formal thought with the reality of things, so does effective and enduring work, undertaken in concrete and well-defined situations, cure dreams. (Piaget, 1967, pp. 68–69).

Of course, youthful idealism often may be a valid response to the ills of society, and no one likes to give up her dreams. Perhaps, taken slightly out of context, as it is here, Piaget's quote seems a little harsh. What he was emphasizing, however, is the way reality can modify and shape idealistic conceptions. Some people refer

An adolescent's first job has a way of bringing the "real world" into sharp focus.

to such modification as "maturity." Piaget argued that attaining and accepting a vocation is one of the best ways to modify idealized conceptions and to mature.

As careers and vocations become less available during times of inflation, lowered productivity, or rising unemployment, adolescents may be especially hard hit. Difficult economic times may leave many adolescents confused about their role in society. For this reason, government job programs as well as community interventions that provide summer and vacation jobs not only provide economic relief but also, in the view of many developmental researchers, help to stimulate needed adolescent ego development (Vondracek & Lerner, 1982).

Question: What about adolescents who take part-time jobs during the school year rather than during the summer? Are they at an even greater advantage?

Actually, no. In fact, just the opposite is true. Adolescents who held part-time jobs during the school year were found to have poorer grades, greater psychological and physical stress, more drug and alcohol use, and greater delinquency. They did not show any benefits from their added work experience, such as increased self-reliance or self-esteem (Steinberg & Dornbusch, 1991). While summer jobs and vocational training may stimulate adolescent ego development, for most adolescents, school is a full-time job. Taking on what amounts to a second job during the school year is not advisable.

A CRISIS OF IDENTITY

Question: How else (besides through vocational choice) does an adolescent discover his own identity?

According to Erik Erikson, the adolescent is faced with the task of developing an acceptable, functional, and stable self-concept. Those adolescents who succeed, Erikson argues, will establish a sense of identity, and those who fail will suffer **role confusion.** Erikson has said that the sense of identity is experienced as a sense of self as distinct from others. The most obvious concomitants of a sense of identity are "a feeling of being at home in one's body, a sense of 'knowing where one is going,' and an inner assuredness of anticipated recognition from those who count" (Erikson, 1968, p. 165). In other words, the adolescent needs

FORECLOSURE
The failure of an adolescent to explore and discover a self-identity; the unquestioning acceptance and adoption of the identity demanded by parents or other important adults.

IDENTITY DIFFUSION
A problem faced by some adolescents who find themselves committed to few goals or values and are apathetic about searching for their own identity.

NEGATIVE IDENTITY
A development among some adolescents in which the identity adopted is the opposite of what parents and society had desired or expected.

MORATORIUM
The time during which an adolescent is searching for an identity.

to maintain a meaningful connection with the past, establish relatively stable goals for the future, and keep up adequate interpersonal relationships in the present to feel that he has an identity. As Erikson has said, "The adolescent needs to integrate a conscious sense of individual uniqueness" with an "unconscious striving for a continuity of experience" (Erikson, 1968, p. 165).

Many other psychologists have found the concept of identity to be a valuable tool for understanding adolescent psychosocial development. Research and case studies have indicated that the resolution of the identity crisis depends greatly on the adolescent's society, family, and peer groups. Ideally, adolescents achieve their new identity by abandoning some of the values and aspirations set for them by their parents and society while at the same time accepting others. A number of investigations have found that a mature adolescent identity is more likely to be achieved when there is a mutual redefinition of the parent-child relationship (Grotevant & Cooper, 1985), that is, when both parents and children share their own perspectives in a mutually supportive way (Powers, Hauser, Schwartz, Noam, & Jacobson, 1983). Occasionally, the adolescent fails in this task, which results in the formation of a premature identity. This identity may develop when an adolescent hasn't actively questioned alternatives and has made a commitment to a particular identity too early. This **foreclosure** often occurs when the adolescent accepts the beliefs or expectations of parents or others before having a chance to explore on her own.

Other adolescents may experience **identity diffusion** and find themselves committed to few goals or values and apathetic about searching for their own identity. And some individuals may even adopt a **negative identity,** one that is opposite to what they were expected to adopt. An adolescent who is still in the process of searching for an identity is said to be in **moratorium.**

Question: Would you give an example of what may happen when an adolescent fails to develop her own identity?

The following case study illustrates how family, peers, future goals, and other forces can create role confusion.

LINDA C.—A CASE OF ROLE CONFUSION.

Linda C. was successful in high school. She was well liked by other people and maintained a B average. She was the second child in a fairly strict Italian Catholic family. Her brother Thomas was 1 year older than she was.

Her two closest girlfriends in school were sexually active and had steady boyfriends. Linda felt a great deal of peer pressure to find a boy to "go with," so she developed a relationship with a boy in her class, a relationship that was sexual but excluded intercourse because she believed that it was wrong outside of marriage.

Linda's father was an alcoholic. Often, she was embarrassed by her father's drinking. For example, she was very upset when her boyfriend arrived one day to see her father drunkenly falling down the stairs. She thought that her father's behavior reflected on her.

Linda was determined to go to college and make a better life for herself than the one her family provided. Her father, however, believed that girls shouldn't go to college, and he spent his savings to finance his son at a private university. Linda's brother had been a poor student in high school, and eventually he failed at college, having spent the family's savings. Linda, still determined, decided when she was 19 years old to attend night school.

She had been much influenced by reading about Madame Curie in high school, and she decided to become a physicist. She took physics and math classes. She was the only woman in many of her classes; the other students were mostly employees of an aerospace company who were taking classes to help advance their careers. Linda was attractive and had several admirers who accompanied her for coffee during class breaks.

Unexpectedly, her high school boyfriend, with whom she had been going steady for 4 years, left to take up with her best friend. Linda's father's alcoholism became more severe, and Linda spent more time at school to escape from her family. She fell in love with a 54-year-old draftsman in her class who talked kindly to her and made her feel wanted. She began a sexual relationship with him. Later she discovered that he was married and had three children (all older than she). She ended the relationship. Her grades suffered; she failed her courses.

During this time, Linda continued to live at home. She quit night school, but found that her days and nights were still turned around. She slept until 3 P.M. and walked her German shepherd until dawn. She gained weight and became less attractive; men stopped approaching her. She thought it was just as well. She continued to stay at home. Her parents tolerated her, hoping that she eventually would marry. She took some boring night jobs and couldn't seem to adjust her sleep schedule. She didn't like going out on her own. She had no close friends. To placate her parents, she began to do volunteer work for the church, where, for the first time, she felt she had found her identity. She gained more weight, worked longer hours for the church, and lived at home. She gave up paying jobs, with her parents' permission, so that she could devote even more time to the church. She did not want to become a nun, because her parents wanted grandchildren. The more her father drank, the more he referred to her lack of a husband. She remained at home until she was 28, at which time she took her own life.

Question: You wouldn't consider Linda's adolescence and later life normal, would you?

Statistically, no. Most adolescents and young adults don't commit suicide. However, an alarming number do.

Question: How did Linda fail to form a coherent identity?

Consider the problems that Linda had with her "identity." She had one boyfriend and few girlfriends. It was the fashion to go steady and pay total attention to your partner instead of to friends of the same sex. Part of her identity, then, was that she was this boy's girlfriend. Many women find that their identity after marriage is that of Mrs. John Jones, no first name or last name of their own, just "Mrs." Eventually, Linda's "girlfriend" identity was rejected by her boyfriend.

Then there was Linda's identity as a sexual woman. She found herself torn between the desires of church and family and those of peer group and boyfriend. "Everything but intercourse" was her solution. Then her boyfriend left her for her best friend, who was more sexually willing. That must have intensified the conflict she experienced between competing values.

Was she physically attractive or not? At different times she held the identity of sexually attractive or nonattractive. She never achieved emotional independence from her parents. She failed to develop a career identity or goal for work. She tried to develop an ideology within the church, but she did this mostly to placate her parents. Linda had failed most of the developmental tasks that an adolescent faces. At 28, she was emotionally still an adolescent.

ADOLESCENT SUICIDE

Question: Linda committed suicide. Do many adolescents kill themselves?

Many more than you might assume. Suicide is one of the leading causes of death among adolescents. Since 1965, the rate of suicide among adolescents and young

Adolescent suicide has increased in the last decade. Many adolescents who commit suicide first give an indication that suicide is on their mind.

adults ages 15 to 24 years has more than doubled (see Figure 19.1). Every year in the United States, approximately 2,000 adolescents between the ages of 15 and 19 take their own lives, and every year about 250,000 adolescents attempt suicide. Because many attempts go unreported, there is reason to believe that this figure is conservative. One interviewer discovered that 65 percent of all college students had at one time or another thought of suicide with sufficient intensity to contemplate the means (Mishara, 1975).

Interestingly, the majority of adolescent suicides occur among those who are currently using alcohol or other drugs (Fowler, Rich, & Young, 1986; Rich, Sherman, & Fowler, 1990). It is difficult, however, to determine whether the drugs contribute directly to the suicide or whether they, like the act of suicide itself, are simply related to depression and poor impulse control.

Depression and poor impulse control are both considered common precursors to suicide and may be considerably influenced by genetics and brain chemistry (Gross-Isseroff, Dillon, Israeli, & Biegon, 1990). It is possible, then, that there may be an inherited predisposition toward suicide and that someday, medical testing will be able to determine individuals who are at risk.

The increase in suicide rate among teenagers is an international phenomenon; from the 1950s to the 1980s, suicide rates in most European countries also increased (McClure, 1986; Sainsbury, Jenkins, & Levey, 1980).

Question: Are females more likely to commit suicide than males?

Among teenagers who commit suicide, the ratio of boys to girls is about 4 or 5 to 1 (Holden, 1986). This is because males tend to use means that are immediately lethal, such as shooting or hanging, in contrast to females, who tend to favor means that are less violent and take more time, such as poison or gas. Girls are therefore more likely to be rescued and so are more likely to make an unsuccessful suicide attempt—at a ratio that has been estimated at anywhere from 2:1 to 8:1 (Holden, 1986).

Question: Are there any ways to know if an adolescent might be about to attempt suicide?

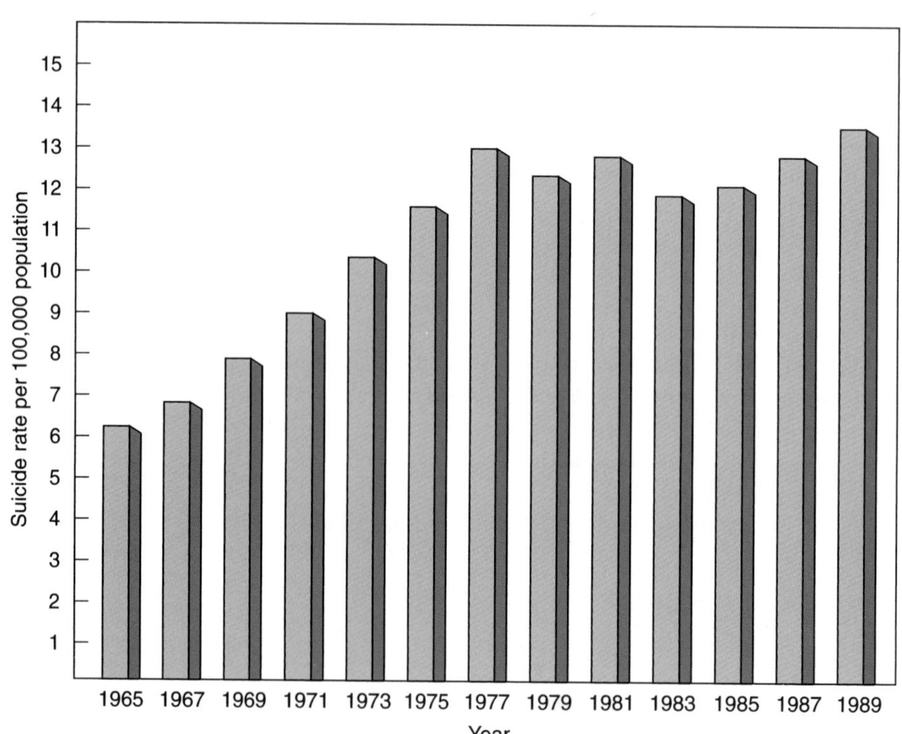

FIGURE 19.1

Rates of suicide per 100,000 population among adolescents and young adults ages 15 to 24 years, 1965 to 1987. There was a sharp increase throughout the 1960s and early 1970s that leveled out in the late 1970s and early 1980s. (*Source:* National Center for Health Statistics)

A number of signs may warn of a potential suicide. The first is an adolescent's failure to achieve in school, a sign that should be heeded, especially in students who have better-than-average ability. Of those adolescents who have committed suicide because of perceived school failure, only 11 percent were actually in serious academic difficulty (Jacobs, 1971). The second sign is an adolescent's withdrawal from social relationships. Suicidal adolescents often feel unwanted by their families or parents (Rosenkrantz, 1978). Rejection by teachers and peers can also contribute to social withdrawal. Another indication may be the termination or failure of a sexual relationship. Many adolescents fearful of venturing into sexual relationships become overly attached to the one boyfriend or girlfriend with whom they feel comfortable. And one study found that adolescents who were less able to cope with the stresses of life and who had difficulty dealing with their angry and sad feelings were more likely to attempt suicide (Khan, 1988).

The most powerful and consistent warning signs, however, are expressions of hopelessness—that life isn't worth living and that suicide is a way out. For this reason, any attempts at suicide, however mild, must be taken seriously. Any jokes about suicide, however lightly made, should alert people to a possible risk. Almost every adolescent who commits suicide first gives an indication at one time or another that suicide is on his mind. In fact, concerned parents can probably best identify a teenager at risk by simply asking him or her about feelings of hopelessness or thoughts of suicide (Swedo et al, 1991). (See At Issue.)

LEARNING CHECK

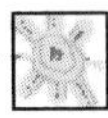

1. According to Erikson, a major task of adolescence is to establish an identity.
   a. true **b.** false
2. Which of the following goals are considered developmental tasks of adolescence?
   a. achieving social maturity with both sexes
   b. coming to terms with one's own physical development
   c. attaining emotional independence from parents
   d. all of the above
3. The formation of a premature identity is known as
   a. foreclosure. **c.** identity diffusion.
   b. negative identity. **d.** moratorium.
4. Approximately ____________ adolescents attempt suicide each year in the United States.
   a. 5000 **b.** 50,000 **c.** 100,000 **d.** 250,000
5. A large number of suicides among adolescents may be incorrectly listed as
   a. murders. **c.** automobile accidents.
   b. natural deaths. **d.** none of the above.

Answers: 1. a 2. d 3. a 4. d 5. c

The Peer Group

Adolescent peer groups may be of different sizes and may be devoted to different interests. Adolescents often belong to more than one peer group at a time. Such peer groups may consist of a few close friends of the same sex or a larger group of both sexes who hang out together. Peer groups provide an important social structure for most adolescents and can serve many other functions (Brown, Eicher,

AT ISSUE

Is Suicide Contagious?

In a 12-month period beginning in February 1983, seven teenagers in the town of Plano, Texas, committed suicide. In February 1984, five boys, all from neighboring New York counties, killed themselves. In one 5-day period in 1986 in Omaha, Nebraska, three teenagers from the same suburban high school took their own lives. In March 1987, four teenaged boys and girls killed themselves with carbon monoxide by allowing their car to run in an airtight garage in Bergenfield, New Jersey. The day after the bodies were discovered in Bergenfield, two teenaged girls were found dead under similar circumstances in Illinois (Wilentz, Gorman, & Hull, 1987). Such clusters of suicides have been documented in several other places in the United States as well (Leo, 1986).

Question: Why would suicides occur in clusters?

Researchers believe that imitation may play an important role in suicide clusters (Fox, Manitowabi, & Ward, 1984; Gould & Shaffer, 1986). The simple knowledge that a suicide has occurred may make some teenagers more likely to commit suicide. In fact, it has been known for years that suicides reach a peak just after a nationally publicized suicide, especially if the person who died was famous. Publicizing suicides could therefore be dangerous, an idea that is counter to the traditional wisdom that thoughts of suicide should be brought into the open, discussed, and dealt with. Perhaps this wisdom does hold when professionals are present to deal with the feelings generated by talk of suicide. But what about the disturbed adolescent, alone in his or her room, who hears about another teen who just committed suicide? Could it put an idea in this young person's head that must now be dealt with alone?

Imitative suicide may be more common than we know. One researcher who carefully studied automobile fatalities discovered that such deaths increased by an average of 9.12 percent following well-publicized suicides (Phillips, 1977). This is especially important because it implies that some deaths listed as accidents may really have been suicides.

Researchers studying the relationship between nationally televised news or feature stories about suicide and the fluctuations in suicide rates among American teenagers, both before and after the publicity, found a significant correlation between suicide rates for teenagers and news stories about suicide (Phillips & Carstensen, 1986). They noted that suicides increased as much after general-information suicide features as after stories about specific suicides. They concluded:

> The findings of this study strongly suggest that televised news stories about suicide trigger a significant rise in teenage suicides; that the more publicity the news story receives, the greater is the increase in teenage suicides; and that news stories providing general information about suicide are just as dangerous as specific stories. In view of these findings, educators, policy makers, and journalists may wish to consider ways of reducing public exposure to stories, both general and specific, about suicide. (Phillips & Carstensen, 1986, p. 689)

Question: How can imitative suicides be prevented?

The major U.S. television networks attempted to overcome this problem by producing educational programs that depicted fictional suicides. Some of these programs focused on the teenager who committed suicide, others on the family left behind. They were produced, once again, with the idea that bringing more information about suicides into the open might help prevent them. In many cases, the networks worked with suicide prevention centers, provided hot-line numbers for teenagers to call if they felt troubled after viewing the program, and offered educational materials and teachers' guides for use in classrooms across the country.

The results of studies analyzing *fictional* accounts of suicide have been mixed. One study (Gould & Shaffer, 1986) concluded that even these fictional stories could increase teenage suicide rates. A subsequent study that replicated and expanded Gould and Shaffer's analysis concluded that there was no such increase (Phillips & Paight, 1987).

More research needs to be conducted to determine whether *any* stories or programs about suicide among teenagers can help to inhibit rather than to provoke the act. Obviously, some elements in such broadcasts can provide help for troubled teens and their parents. Researchers need to determine what these elements are and how to apply them carefully to decrease the rate of suicide among teenagers (Davidson, Rosenberg, Mercy, Franklin, & Simmons, 1989).

& Petrie, 1986). They can be sources of ready companionship and adventure and providers of standards against which to compare oneself. As a result, a peer group can be a powerful influence.

To become or to stay a member of a desired peer group, adolescents need to appear desirable. They also need certain social skills. Adolescents who lack social skills or who are deemed socially undesirable by their peers may find themselves living a lonely or isolated existence, and eventually they may be adversely affected by the experience. To avoid rejection, adolescents may go to extremes to please their peer group. They may radically change their dress, appearance, or behavior, or they may adopt the group's jargon. Adolescents who attempt to adjust to a group that has views or values opposed to those held by their families may experience considerable conflict and stress (P. R. Newman, 1982).

Question: How much power does a peer group have to shape and change an adolescent's behavior?

A peer group may function as a reference for adolescents (Petersen & Taylor, 1980). Adolescents often resolve differences between themselves and their peer group by changing their behavior to match the group's norms. The group can influence susceptible teenagers either to perform or to avoid misconduct (Brown, Clasen, & Eicher, 1986). It has been shown, however, that peers are less likely to encourage misconduct than they are other types of behavior (Brown, Lohr, & McClenahan, 1986).

There are some important exceptions to conformity with the group's norms, however. For instance, how adolescents first evaluate themselves may have a great bearing on which peer group or peer-group behaviors they find most important and desirable (Eisert & Kahle, 1982). One study discovered that college students (mean age 18.95 years) who evaluated themselves as having high self-esteem chose groups to join and to emulate that were composed of students of high socioeconomic status (Filsinger & Anderson, 1982). This is not just a one-way street, however; the groups with whom adolescents choose to compare themselves can in turn directly affect an adolescent's self-evaluation. No doubt, the students who associated and became friends with high-status peers found their own self-esteem enhanced.

Peers can have an enormous influence on adolescent behavior, particularly in such areas as dress, general appearance, and adoption of special slang or jargon.

Question: Which carries more weight with an adolescent, peer values or parental values?

In a study of over 18,000 adolescents between the ages of 12 and 17 years, researchers asked questions about the degree to which adolescents valued their mothers', fathers', and friends' opinions (Curtis, 1975). Among adolescents at every age, the advice of parents was more valued than was the advice of friends. Among 12-year-old adolescents, parental opinions far outweighed advice offered by friends. By the age of 17 years, however, although teenagers still valued parental opinions more, they placed friends' opinions a close second.

Another study found that the more that adolescents are removed from adult supervision after school, the more susceptible they are to peer pressure to engage in antisocial activities (Steinberg, 1986). This is especially true among those who were rejected by their peers during childhood or who are failing academically (Dishion, Patterson, Stoolmiller, & Skinner, 1991).

Question: Are adolescents and parents often in conflict?

Although it can be exasperating to be an adolescent and contend with your parents, or to be a parent and contend with your adolescent, researchers have found that both parents and adolescents typically share the same views on sex, war, drugs, religion, law enforcement, and politics (Lerner & Weinstock, 1972; Weinstock & Lerner, 1972).

Question: Is the influence of the adolescent peer group a worldwide phenomenon, or is it found mostly in Western cultures?

The influence of the adolescent peer group seems to be a worldwide phenomenon (B. M. Newman, 1982). In almost every culture, adolescents congregate for companionship and adventure. The way the society views the adolescent peer group, however, quite often differs from one culture to the next. For instance, in American society, adolescent peers may more often seem to ignore or deviate from the values of the culture, whereas in other countries, such as Switzerland or Iran, adolescent peer groups are viewed as actively supporting and maintaining allegiance to the society's norms.

Drug Use and Abuse

The use of drugs by adolescents has decreased dramatically in all categories over the past 15 years, with one exception, the use of tobacco, which has remained steady (see Table 19.1). Recent educational efforts and peer pressure have apparently made a considerable difference. As one researcher has noted,

> Ten years ago, students would brag about how drunk or stoned they got. It's no longer "in" to talk that way. Ten years ago kids who went to what would be called a "sober" party would have been really considered nerdy. They would be ashamed of it. Now that's one of the "in" things to do. Popular kids go to "sober" parties. . . . There are still the addicts, of course, but they're not the "in" kids anymore. (Peck, as cited by Freiberg, 1991, p. 28)

However, despite the improved outlook, drug use among adolescents remains a serious problem, and drugs remain readily accessible, even in elementary schools.

Question: Why are some adolescents attracted to drugs?

For some adolescents, drug use provides an element of excitement and daring. Some find peer acceptance by using drugs or by demonstrating a comprehensive knowledge of street drugs and their effects. For others, selling drugs is a quick way to be admired and to make money. However, peer pressure to use drugs is

TABLE 19.1

Drug Use Among High School Seniors (1991)

CATEGORY	1991 %	PEAK YEAR %
Used illicit drugs at least once	62.2%	70.5% in 1986
Used illicit drug in previous month	15.1%	40% in 1979
Used alcohol during past month	54.0%	72.1% in 1978
Used marijuana in previous month	13.8%	37.1% in 1978
Used cocaine within the last year	3.5%	19.7% in 1986
Used crack within the last year	1.5%	3.2% in 1986
Used amphetamines during the previous month	3.2%	15.8% in 1981
Used PCP within the last year	1.4%	7.0% in 1979
Used cigarettes daily		Rate remaining steady since 1980
Used cigarettes during the past month	28.3%	Rate remaining steady since 1980

SOURCE: Adapted from Johnston, Bachman, & O'Malley, 1992.

only one of 17 major correlates associated with adolescent drug use (see Table 19.2). Each of the 17 factors appears to correlate somewhat separately and independently with drug use.

Question: What do you mean when you say that these factors correlate somewhat separately and independently with drug use?

Each of the factors shown in Table 19.2 is somewhat independent of the others. Each factor carries its own impact, and each time a factor is added to the mix, the chances of drug use will increase (Hawkins, Catalano, & Miller, 1992). By isolating the factors associated with drug use, hopefully we will be able to address each factor in an effort to lower the incidence of drug abuse. It should also be noted that adolescents who use drugs owing to one particular factor may be more likely to curtail use than would those taking drugs for different reasons. For example, adolescents who use drugs because their friends are using them are more likely to give up drugs in adulthood than are adolescents who take drugs for physiological reasons (Kandel & Raveis, 1989).

How involved someone is with drugs, and how long he or she has been taking them, also play an important role. For instance, longitudinal studies indicate that those who briefly experimented with drugs (primarily marijuana) during their adolescence were fairly well adjusted as adults, while those who used drugs frequently as adolescents showed signs of maladjustment later on, including alienation from others, poor impulse control, and emotional distress (Shedler & Block, 1990).

Question: Which are the most commonly used drugs?

The drugs most commonly used by adolescents are alcohol, tobacco, and marijuana (see Table 19.1). Alcohol use and abuse can be a serious problem among adolescents—or any group, for that matter. In a national survey of over 17,000 high school seniors conducted by the University of Michigan, nearly three out of every five students admitted to drinking alcohol within the previous month, and one out of every three acknowledged consuming five or more alcoholic drinks in a row within the prior two weeks (Johnston, Bachman, & O'Malley, 1992).

During the 1980s the use of cocaine by adolescents became a serious problem.

TABLE 19.2

Factors Associated with the Incidence of Adolescent Drug Use

FACTOR ASSOCIATED WITH DRUG USE	HOW FACTOR WOULD INCREASE THE PROBABILITY OF ADOLESCENT DRUG USE
Laws and norms	Drug is legal; use is socially acceptable
Availability	Drug is readily available
Extreme economic deprivation	Living in poor or overcrowded conditions
Neighborhood disorganization	Neighborhood has poor surveillance, mobile residents, and high rates of adult crime
Physiological factors	Is genetically prone to addiction; shows sensation-seeking behavior and has low impulse control
Family drug use	Family members model drug use
Poor or inconsistent parenting	Lack of maternal involvement; inconsistent discipline; low parental aspirations for children
Family conflict	Comes from a broken home; family members often fight
Low bonding to family	Is not close to parents; finds parents cold and untrustworthy
Early and persistent behavior problems	Has shown tendency to be aggressive and antisocial from as early as age 5
Academic failure	Is truant, placed in a special class, drops out of school, or has failing grades
Little commitment to school	Not interested in education; does not expect to attend college
Peer rejection in grade school	Child is aggressive, shy, or withdrawn and has few or no friends
Association with drug-using peers	Has many friends who use drugs
Alienation and rebelliousness	Rejects dominant values of society; low religiosity; often delinquent
Personal attitude	Believes using drugs is okay
Early onset of drug use	Tries drugs for the first time before the age of 15

SOURCE: Adapted from Hawkins, Catalano, & Miller, 1992.

Question: What determines whether an adolescent will drink?

Peer use of alcohol is the most powerful predictor of adolescent alcohol use, at least in the United States. The general rule is, if your friends drink, you are likely to drink. In other countries, patterns of alcohol use often differ. For instance, one study in Israel found that the most powerful predictor of adolescent alcohol use was parental use (Adler & Kandel, 1982).

Although most adolescents keep their drinking under control, the number of adolescent alcoholics is alarming. Four percent of high school seniors state that they are daily users of alcohol (Johnston, Bachman, & O'Malley, 1992). These data are also from the University of Michigan survey, and like the other data compiled from that survey, they did not include the 30 percent of adolescents who have dropped out of high school. It is suspected that alcohol and other drug use among dropouts is at higher rates than found among adolescents who remain in school. Alcohol use among adolescents can also be a fatal choice. Alcohol is believed to be responsible for between 30 and 50 percent of all vehicular deaths among teenagers.

About one-fifth of high school seniors reported being daily cigarette smokers (see Table 19.1). Cigarette smoking by adolescents is the only area of drug use that has not declined since the University of Michigan began tracking high school drug use in the late 1970s. For many researchers, this is the saddest part of the story because tobacco use is among the most deadly of addictions. Smoking is known to be a major cause of heart disease, cancer, stroke, and emphysema—four of the leading causes of death in the United States. Perhaps the most shocking statistic of all is that in the twentieth century, smoking has killed more people than war.

Question: What determines whether a teenager will smoke?

Parents and siblings have a considerable influence on teenagers' smoking habits. If a parent or older sibling smokes, the chances that the teenager will smoke are 1 in 5. If neither the parents nor older siblings smoke, the odds become less than 1 in 20. In general, adolescents who have friends who smoke are more likely to smoke. The single most reliable predictor of continued smoking by teenagers has been their own statement that they believed that they would still be smoking in 5 years.

Some adolescents who fear the health effects of smoking have taken to chewing tobacco. Chewing tobacco, however, poses hazards in the form of oral cancer and dental damage. Publicizing these dangers more widely might make greater numbers of adolescents aware that chewing tobacco is not a safe alternative to smoking.

After alcohol and tobacco, marijuana was found to be the most widely used illicit drug among high school seniors. Other abused drugs include amphetamines, cocaine, and hallucinogens such as LSD or PCP (see Table 19.1).

Sex and the Adolescent

"Sex is exciting."
"It's a way to show your love."
"It's a way to prove yourself."
"Everyone else is doing it."
"It's okay for boys but not for girls."
"Sex is wrong."

Many of these attitudes or beliefs are held by teenagers. In our culture, "children" of 13 years of age often are physically capable of having children of their own but are not capable emotionally or economically of maintaining and supporting a family.

Every society has standards that define acceptable and unacceptable sexual behaviors among its members. Traditionally, the majority of American adults have not condoned premarital sex among adolescents. At the turn of the century, 75 percent of all women under the age of 20 years were virgins. Since then, however, American sexual attitudes toward adolescent sexuality and dating have become more permissive (Rubinson & de Rubertis, 1991). Following the "sexual revolution" of the 1960s, only 45 percent of all women under the age of 20 were virgins. During the same time, the number of virgin males under the age of 20 dropped from approximately 50 percent to 15 percent (Reiss, 1976; Sorensen, 1973).

Nevertheless, it would be an error to assume that the majority of teenagers are capriciously engaging in sexual relations with many partners. Table 19.3 describes the sexual behaviors engaged in by a group of college-aged males and females. As

Adolescents must learn to deal with physical maturity and their own sexual desires.

SEXUALLY TRANSMITTED DISEASES (STDS)
Diseases that are primarily transmitted through sexual intercourse.

you can see, intercourse was engaged in by a majority only when they considered themselves to be in love with one person.

Teenagers often think of sexual partners as future marriage partners. Furthermore, it is common for a teenage boy and girl to latch onto each other instantly. As a result, some adolescents live as pseudomarried couples and eventually may marry without ever getting to know other potential partners—all because they've learned to feel safe with their "first love" and because "sex" and "marriage" are so often paired. Unfortunately, early marriages have a poor track record compared with marriages of more experienced or mature couples.

SEXUALLY TRANSMITTED DISEASES

One of the more unfortunate results of an increase in sexual activity among adolescents is the resultant increase in **sexually transmitted diseases (STDs).** These diseases are primarily transmitted through sexual contact and include chlamydia, gonorrhea, syphilis, venereal warts, genital herpes, and AIDS. Some of these diseases, such as chlamydia, gonorrhea, and syphilis, are treatable with drugs—although if left untreated, they can cause extensive damage to the reproductive system and even death, in the case of syphilis. Venereal warts, herpes, and AIDS, because they are caused by viruses, are more difficult to treat. AIDS, of course, is invariably fatal, although adolescents rarely die from it because the period from the time of infection to the full-blown symptoms of the disease can be many years. However, since so many individuals are first diagnosed with AIDS in their 20s, it is assumed that many were infected in their teens. Unfortunately, although use of condoms is up among sexually active teens, it remains low (21 to 37 percent) among those teens at highest risk (IV drug users, homosexuals, and those with many partners per year).

Question: Can anything be done to stop the spread of AIDS among teens?

Education seems to be the best hope. This is especially true for those teens at highest risk. In one study, researchers provided intensive education for 450 runaways and gay male youths in five New York City shelters (Rotheram-Borus, Koopman, Haignere, & Davies, 1991). When first admitted to the program, 21 percent of the teens were engaging in high-risk behavior, defined as having 10 or more sexual encounters with three or more partners during the past three months while at the same time being inconsistent concerning condom use. After six months of education conducted in 15 sessions, none of the original 21 percent fit

TABLE 19.3

Percentage of College-Aged Males and Females Reporting Specific Sexual Behaviors

SEXUAL BEHAVIOR	GENDER	DATING WITH NO PARTICULAR AFFECTION	DATING WITH AFFECTION BUT NOT LOVE	DATING AND BEING IN LOVE	DATING ONE PERSON ONLY AND BEING IN LOVE	ENGAGED
Light petting	M	25	50	81	92	94
	F	8	26	59	88	98
Heavy petting	M	18	33	68	81	88
	F	6	19	42	82	93
Intercourse	M	15	18	49	63	74
	F	4	11	32	68	81
Oral sex	M	10	32	59	78	82
	F	2	11	24	59	66

SOURCE: Adapted from Roche, 1986, p. 110.

the high-risk profile. In her testimony before congress, Rotheram-Borus recommended setting up "HIV [the AIDS virus] prevention programs in shelters, foster care, group homes and other social agencies." (Youngstrom, 1991, p. 39).

LEARNING CHECK

Which of the following statements are correct?

1. Adolescents usually are members of only one peer group at a time.
2. Sexually transmitted diseases rarely occur among adolescents.
3. Cocaine use among high school students is increasing.
4. Marijuana smoking among high school students is increasing.
5. Recent data indicate that adolescent males are more likely to be virgins than are adolescent females.

Answers: None is true.

APPLICATIONS

Preventing Teenage Pregnancy

> Before the baby came, her bedroom was a dimly lighted chapel dedicated to the idols of rock 'n' roll. Now the posters . . . have been swept away and the walls painted white. Angela Helton's room has become a nursery for 6-week-old Corey Allen. Angie, who just turned 15, finds it hard to think of herself as a mother. "I'm still just as young as I was," she insists. "I haven't grown up any faster." Indeed, sitting in her parents' Louisville living room, she is the prototypical adolescent, lobbying her mother for permission to attend a rock concert, asking if she can have a pet dog and complaining she is not allowed to do anything. The weight of her new responsibilities is just beginning to sink in. "Last night I couldn't get my homework done," she laments with a toss of her blond curls. "I kept feeding him and feeding him. Whenever you lay him down, he wants to get picked up." In retrospect she admits: "Babies are a big step. I should have thought more about it."
>
> The rhythm of her typing is like a fox trot, steady and deliberate. It is a hot summer day in San Francisco, and Michelle, a chubby black 14-year-old, is practicing her office skills with great fervor, beads of sweat trickling down her brow. She is worried about the future. "I have to get my money together," she frets. "I have to think ahead." Indeed she must. In three weeks this tenth-grader with her hair in braids is going to have a baby. "I have to stop doing all the childish things I've done before," she gravely resolves. "I used to think, 10 years from now I'll be 24. Now I think, I'll be 24, and my child will be 10." (Wallis, Booth, Ludtke, & Taylor, 1985, pp. 78–79)

If the present trend continues, it is estimated that almost 40 percent of today's 14-year-old girls will have been pregnant at least once before the age of 20. One of the unfortunate consequences of teenage pregnancy arises from the higher risk of medical complications faced by pregnant teenagers and their babies. Teenage mothers, who are often under more stress than mothers better able to cope with pregnancy, are also more likely to become child abusers. Pregnancy is also the most common reason that adolescent girls leave school, which means that teen mothers tend to have far less promising educational or economic futures than do their counterparts who delay parenting (Subramanian, 1990). Furthermore, although rates of pregnancies among teenagers have increased in many other countries, the United States leads by a large margin (see Figure 19.2). The tragedy is that few of these teenagers are in a position to provide a stable family environment or to care for their infants. In our society, they are children with children.

The major difference affecting the pregnancy rate among teenagers between the United States and other countries appears to be the level of contraceptive use. The Alan Guttmacher Institute, which conducted a comparative study of pregnancy rates among teenagers in six nations throughout the world, concluded, "It is likely that the United States has the lowest level of contraceptive practice among teen-agers of all six countries" (Adler, Katz, & Jackson, 1985, p. 90).

Question: But that study was conducted in 1985. Hasn't condom use among teenagers increased since then

FIGURE 19.2

Pregnancy rates per 1,000 teenage females in selected countries. (*Source:* The Alan Guttmacher Institute, 1985)

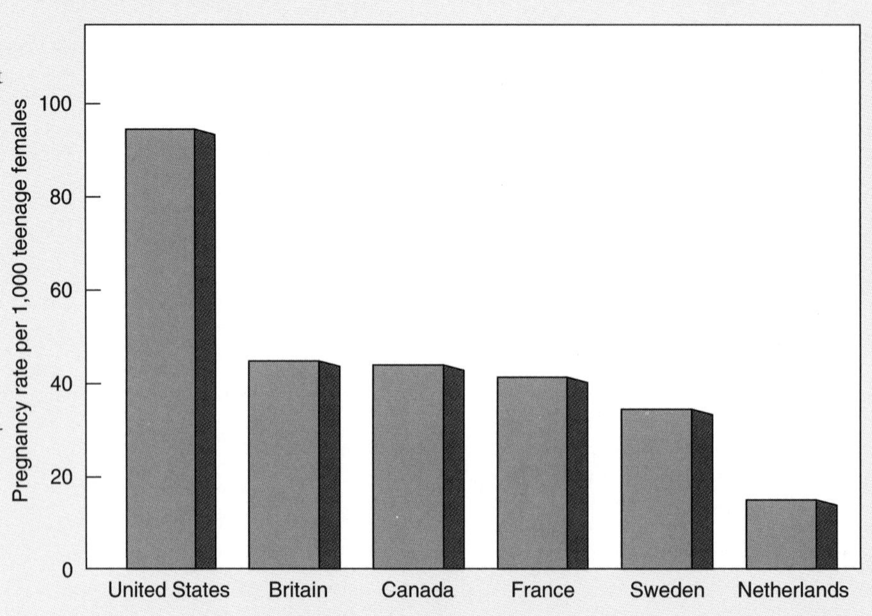

APPLICATIONS

because of AIDS, and hasn't that reduced the rate of teen pregnancy?

While it is true that condom use has increased some, the number of adolescents who don't use condoms or any contraception remains at an alarming level. In general, the rate of teen pregnancy has not declined since 1985 because more teens are sexually active now and begin sexual activity at an earlier age than they did in 1985.

It is also difficult to assess the rate of condom use among adolescents. The largest study concerning this matter, the National Survey of Adolescent Males, has found in a 10-year follow-up that the rate of condom use among adolescents ages 17 to 19 had increased from 21 percent in 1979 to 58 percent in 1988 (Landers, 1990). But again, in 1979, 67 percent of males 17 to 19 reported being sexually active, but by 1988, 75 percent were sexually active. The use of condoms or other contraceptives also appears to be far less frequent among teens ages 13 to 16 (Youngstrom, 1991).

Question: Why don't teenagers use birth control methods more often?

There are a number of reasons. Some teenagers have religious or moral objections to the use of contraceptives. Some are fearful that birth control methods may be unsafe, or they believe that the risk of AIDS in their case is minimal (because, for instance, their partner "looks healthy"). Furthermore, many teenagers know amazingly little about sexual reproduction. Still, others simply believe that sex should be unplanned, or spontaneous.

Question: Why do teenagers often want sex to be spontaneous, or unplanned?

If the present trend continues, researchers have estimated that about 40 percent of today's 14-year-old girls will have been pregnant at least once before the age of 20.

If you feel guilty, it's easier to convince yourself that you just "got carried away" and weren't aware of what was happening. It can be hard to convince yourself of that if you've spent a minute or so in technical preparation.

Question: Couldn't it just be that stopping to use contraceptives isn't very romantic?

In some cultures, "technical" prenuptial arrangements are considered part of the romance. However, our associative learning has been such that many forms of contraception appear to us to be unromantic. After all, many of us were raised to believe that sex was an embrace, a kiss, and a camera pan to the breakers of the surf (with, of course, full orchestration). At times, expectation and realism can seem far apart.

Question: Which teenage girls are most likely to become pregnant?

Careful investigation has found that there are four major risk factors. The girls most at risk are those who begin sexual activity at an early age, who are depressed, whose mothers are depressed, or whose mothers have left home within the past 15 months (Horwitz, Klerman, Kuo, & Jekel, 1991). Hopefully, girls who fit this profile will receive extra counseling concerning bearing and raising children at an early age.

Question: Is abortion a good solution?

Whether to have an abortion is, among other things, a moral decision that an individual must make for herself (or, when the father is a party to the decision, himself). Many teenagers prefer to keep their children whether they are able to care for them or not. Astonishingly, among those young women who choose abortion, the New York Planned Parenthood Society has found that many return for a second, third, fourth, or even fifth abortion.

Question: What is a good solution then?

One possible solution is to develop programs to educate teenagers. Some schools have set up on-campus health clinics that are authorized to dispense contraceptives to students who have parental permission. Unfortunately, not enough sex education programs are available in high schools, and many of the available programs don't discuss the kinds of issues we have been addressing here; instead, they tend to be courses in "plumbing" (a relentless pursuit of the fallopian tubes).

In 1987, the National Academy of Sciences Panel on Early Childbearing recommended programs to help re-

APPLICATIONS

duce teenage pregnancy. They recommended that these programs increase the options available to teenagers, such as improving school performance, providing employment opportunities, and providing role models. The panel also recommended that sex education programs be explicit and include information on contraception. The panel also recommended changes in the media—that programs glorifying sex be discouraged and that advertisements for contraceptives be available.

There is also a need for effective counseling and support programs for pregnant teenagers. One of the first such programs was developed by Janet Hardy and Theodore King at the Johns Hopkins Medical Institution in Baltimore. In this program, medical and psychological services are offered to pregnant teenagers. Classes are conducted from the first prenatal visit through labor and delivery, and, most important, they continue for three years after delivery. The relationship between the staff and teenage mothers is close and supportive ("One Solution," 1979).

Question: Has the Johns Hopkins program been successful?

Among teenage mothers enrolled in the program, 85 percent returned to school and only 5 percent became pregnant again within one year of delivery. The mothers in the program also had statistically fewer premature deliveries, medical complications, or unhealthy babies. Among teen mothers who weren't in the program, only 10 percent returned to school, and 47 percent became pregnant again within one year of delivery ("One Solution," 1979). As you can see from these data, the Johns Hopkins program was successful. This program is now used as a model for developing a nationwide program for preventing pregnancy among teenagers.

SUMMARY

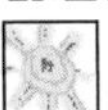

- Teenagers may seem to be a distinct and special group with special problems and needs, but their status may be more a function of culture and economics than of age.
- During adolescence, individuals must deal for the first time with sexual relationships, the choice of a future career, political decisions, economic alternatives, and a host of other "adult" tasks.
- As adolescents develop cognitive skills, they are confronted for the first time with the overwhelming complexities and abstract qualities of the world. Sexual relationships must be faced. Social maturity in dealings with both sexes is expected. The adolescent's own masculine or feminine role must be realized and adjusted to his or her satisfaction. The adolescent must come to terms with his or her physical development. Our culture expects adolescents to achieve emotional independence from parents and other adults. Decisions about whether to marry or whether to have children become more pressing. Pursuing a career choice is also an essential part of adolescent development.
- According to Erik Erikson, the adolescent is faced with the task of developing an acceptable, functional, and stable self-concept. Those adolescents who succeed, Erikson argues, will establish a sense of identity, and those who fail will suffer role confusion.
- Suicide is one of the leading causes of death among adolescents. Since 1965, the rate of suicide among adolescents and young adults ages 15 to 24 years has more than doubled. Every year in the United States, approximately 2,000 adolescents between the ages of 15 and 19 take their own lives, and every year about 250,000 adolescents attempt suicide. Females are more likely to attempt suicide than males are, but males are more likely to actually kill themselves.
- Adolescent peer groups may be of different sizes and may be devoted to different interests. Peer groups provide an important social structure for most adolescents. Such groups can be sources of ready companionship and adventure and can provide standards for adolescents.
- Some adolescents gain peer acceptance by using drugs or by demonstrating a comprehensive knowledge of street drugs and their effects. The drugs most commonly used by adolescents are tobacco, alcohol, and marijuana. In the last 15 years, drug use among high school students has declined, except for the use of tobacco, which has remained constant.
- American attitudes toward adolescent sexuality and dating have become more permissive. Nevertheless, it would be an error to assume that the majority of teenagers are capriciously engaging in sexual relations with many partners.
- One of the more unfortunate results of an increase in sexual activity among adolescents is the resultant increase in sexually transmitted diseases.
- Researchers have estimated that if the present trend continues, about 40 percent of today's 14-year-old girls will have been pregnant at least once before the age of 20. Programs to help prevent teenage pregnancy have been developed.

QUESTIONS FOR DISCUSSION

1. What are the implications for families and society if more and more unwed teenagers wish to keep their babies?
2. Was your adolescence benign? If not, was it more stormy than other times in your life have been?
3. What circumstances have influenced your identity development?
4. How can parents help their teenagers deal with the conflicts of adolescence?

SUGGESTIONS FOR FURTHER READING

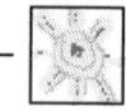

1. Adelson, J. (1985). *Inventing adolescence: The political psychology of everyday schooling.* New Brunswick, NJ: Transaction Books.
2. Gilligan, C. (1990). *Making connections: The relational worlds of adolescent girls at Emma Willard School.* Cambridge, MA: Harvard University Press.
3. Graydanus, D. E. (1991). *Caring for your adolescent: Ages 12 to 21.* New York: Bantam.
4. Group for the Advancement of Psychiatry, Committee on Adolescence. (1986). *Crises of adolescence: Teenage pregnancy, impact on adolescent development.* New York: Brunner/Mazel.
5. Hauser, S. T., Powers, S. I., & Noam, G. G. (1991). *Adolescents and their families: Paths of ego development.* New York: Free Press.
6. McAnarney, E. R. (1983). *Premature adolescent pregnancy and parenthood.* Orlando, FL: Grune & Stratton.
7. Offer, D., Ostrov, E., & Howard, K. I. (1981). *The adolescent: A psychological self-portrait.* New York: Basic Books.
8. Offer, D., Ostrov, E., Howard, K. I., & Atkinson, R. (1988). *The teenage world: Adolescents' self-image in ten countries.* New York: Plenum.
9. Simmons, R. G. (1987). *Moving into adolescence.* Hawthorne, NY: Aldine de Gruyter.
10. Youniss, J., & Smollar, J. (1985). *Adolescent relations with mothers, fathers, and friends.* Chicago: University of Chicago Press.

GLOSSARY

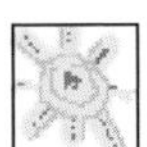

ACCEPTING-REJECTING DIMENSION One of two major dimensions used by Baumrind to describe parenting; denotes the degree of affection within the parent-child relationship.

ACCOMMODATION Piaget's term for the process in which a person adjusts or changes his or her cognitive structures to incorporate aspects of an experience not currently represented in them.

ACHIEVEMENT TEST A test that purports to measure the knowledge gained from experience, also known as type B intelligence, or sometimes crystallized intelligence. Achievement tests are distinguished from aptitude tests, which supposedly measure aspects of intelligence that are relatively free of culture or training, sometimes called type A intelligence, or fluid intelligence. In actual practice, however, there is often very little difference between achievement and aptitude tests because it is not yet known how to test only one kind of intelligence without substantially involving the other.

ADAPTATION A term used by Piaget to describe the mechanism through which schemes develop as a result of adjustment to changes; such adjustment occurs through the processes of assimilation and accommodation.

ADOPTION OF ROLES Term used by anthropologists to describe the acquisition of sexual and social behavior by individuals in a given culture.

ADOPTION DESIGN A research design used for sorting the influence of nurture from nature. Genetically related individuals who are reared apart from one another or genetically unrelated individuals who are reared together are studied.

AFFECTIVE CONDITIONING An associative learning process in which emotional appraisals of a stimulus are altered by pairing the stimulus with one or more other stimuli that already have an emotional effect. Attitudes and beliefs often are influenced by affective conditioning.

AIDS (ACQUIRED IMMUNE DEFICIENCY SYNDROME) A human retrovirus type HIV, which is transmitted sexually through the exchange of bodily fluids or by shared needle use among infected IV (intravenous) drug abusers. The disease may also be passed by infusion of unscreened blood or blood products. Once the disease process occurs, the immune system fails and death follows. The virus may infect an unborn child by crossing the placental barrier of an infected mother.

ALLELE Any of a group of possible mutational forms of a gene.

ALTRUISM Behavior that benefits someone other than the actor, with little or no apparent benefit for the actor.

AMNIOCENTESIS A medical procedure wherein fetal cells are removed from the amniotic sac at about the sixteenth week of pregnancy by use of a syringe. The technique is used to screen for genetic and chromosomal abnormalities.

ANAL RETENTIVE According to Freud, a personality type formed by fixation at the anal stage. Characteristics include stinginess, selfishness, and withholding.

ANAL STAGE The second psychosexual stage according to Freud, during which bowel control is achieved and pleasure is focused on the functions of elimination.

ANDROGENS Male hormones that regulate sexual development; produced by the testes and the adrenal cortex.

ANIMISTIC THINKING A kind of thinking common to children in the preconceptual stage, in which inanimate objects, especially those that move or appear to move, are believed to be alive.

ANOXIA A pathological deficiency in oxygen.

ANTISOCIAL BEHAVIOR Behavior that shows little or no concern for other people and little sense of right and wrong.

ANXIOUS/AVOIDANT ATTACHMENT A form of attachment observed by Ainsworth in which children do not approach—and in fact actively avoid—their returning mothers.

ANXIOUS/RESISTANT ATTACHMENT A form of attachment observed by Ainsworth in which children approach their returning mothers, cry to be picked up, and then struggle to be free. Their behavior is ambivalent; they appear to wish to approach and avoid their mothers simultaneously.

APPROPRIATENESS One of the four qualities of creativity defined by Jackson and Messick. Appropriate ideas are those that make sense in context.

ARTIFICIAL INTELLIGENCE A computer simulation of human cognitive ability and performance.

ASSIMILATION Piaget's term for the act of taking in information and perceptions in a way that is compatible with the person's current understanding of the world.

ASSOCIATIVE PLAY A type of play in which children play and share with others.

ATTACHMENT-EXPLORATION BALANCE Term used by Ainsworth to describe the interplay between the child's desire to be attached and the child's need to explore the environment.

ATTACHMENT An especially close affectionate bond formed between living creatures.

ATTENTION DEFICIT DISORDER A behavioral disorder characterized by the display of a developmentally inappropriate failure of attention and a pervasive impulsivity. Hyperactivity commonly accompanies the disorder.

AUTHORITARIAN PARENTS Parents who put forward a strict set of rules and require unquestioned obedience to them. They are both demanding and hostile. Authoritarian parents often use physical punishment to enforce the rules, and reasoned discussion with the child is rare.

AUTHORITATIVE PARENTS Parents who set strict standards, but who are also warm and willing to explain their reasoning to their children.

AUTISM A disorder first noticed in early childhood, characterized by the inability of the person to relate to others and to respond to attempts at communication; may also be characterized by mutism, self-injury, or preoccupation with objects.

AUTOSOME Any chromosome that is not a sex chromosome.

AXON The long process of a neuron that transmits impulses away from the cell body.

BEHAVIOR THEORY A view that behavior can be explained as the result of learning and experience and that an understanding of internal events or constructs such as the mind are unnecessary.

BEHAVIOR MODIFICATION A set of procedures for changing human behavior, especially by using behavior therapy and operant conditioning techniques.

BEHAVIORAL GENETICS The interdisciplinary science that focuses on the interaction of nature and nurture—that is, on the interaction of what is inherited and what is acquired—and how that interaction affects behavior.

BEHAVIORISM The school of psychology that views learning as the most important aspect of an organism's development. Behaviorists objectively measure behavior and the way in which stimulus-response relationships are formed.

BIOLOGICAL MOTION PERCEPTION An ability that enables humans to make perceptual sense easily and quickly of live objects in motion.

BIRTH The passage of a child from the uterus to outside the mother's body.

BIRTHING BAR A horizontal bar, often placed across the birthing bed, which is used to help a woman in labor take a squatting position to facilitate delivery.

BLASTOCYST A stage of development during the period of the ovum when the embryo consists of one or several layers of cells around a central cavity, forming a hollow sphere.

BREECH BIRTH A vaginal delivery during which the buttocks or feet of the fetus appear first.

CANALIZATION The process by which behaviors, due to genetic predisposition, are learned extremely easily, almost inevitably. The more canalized a behavior is, the more difficult it is to change or alter.

CARETAKER SPEECH A speech pattern used in addressing others who are obviously less competent in their speech than is the speaker. Universally applied, caretaker speech is characterized by short, simple sentences, simple vocabulary, a relatively high-pitched voice, and exaggerated inflections. It should not be confused with baby talk, which refers only to the simplification of individual words, such as saying "wa-wa" for water.

CARRIER In genetics, an organism that carries a particular trait in its genes and, while not expressing that trait itself, is able to pass on the trait to its offspring.

CASE STUDY An intensive study of a single case, with all available data, test results, and opinions about that individual. Usually done in more depth than studies on groups of individuals.

CATECHOLAMINES Hormones that can affect the sympathetic nervous system; they are secreted by the medulla of the adrenal glands.

CENTRAL NERVOUS SYSTEM (CNS) All nerves encased in bone, including the brain and spinal cord.

CESAREAN SECTION A surgical incision through the abdominal wall and uterus, performed to extract a fetus.

CHILD NEGLECT Failure by parents, caregivers, or others responsible for children's welfare to provide reasonable and prudent standards of care for the children in their charge, thereby threatening the children's well-being.

CHILD ABUSE Behavior by parents, caregivers, or others responsible for children's welfare that, through malice or negligence, results in psychological or physical injury to a child.

CHORIONIC VILLI SAMPLING A technique in which a few cells are removed from the chorionic sac that surrounds the embryo via the use of a plastic catheter inserted through the vagina. The cells may then be examined for chromosomal or genetic disorders.

CHROMOSOME A thread-shaped body that is contained within the nucleus of a body cell, and that determines those characteristics that will be passed on to the offspring of an organism. Chromosomes carry the genes; humans have 23 pairs of chromosomes.

CHRONOLOGICAL AGE (CA) A concept developed by Binet, used to calculate a person's IQ. Chronological age is actual age.

CLASSICAL CONDITIONING An experimental learning procedure in which a stimulus that normally evokes a given reflex is continually associated with a stimulus that does not usually evoke that reflex, with the result that the latter stimulus will eventually evoke the reflex when presented by itself.

CLONE An organism genetically identical to its ancestor organism, and derived from one of its cells.

COALESCENCE OF MEANING A component of creativity described by Jackson and Messick. The meaning of a creative thought is said to coalesce over time in that it becomes more valuable and powerful with each application.

CODOMINANCE A situation in which heterozygous alleles consist of two dominant genes. In such instances, both genes are expressed.

COGNITION An extremely broad term that refers to pretty much anything that goes on inside your mind, including attention, perception, memory, language formation and development, reading and writing, thinking, problem solving, intelligence, creativity, imagination, expectation, intention, and belief.

COGNITIVE DEVELOPMENT Age-related changes in behavior as they relate to perceiving, thinking, remembering, and problem solving.

COHORT A group of people all of whom possess a common demographic characteristic; for example, a group of people born at approximately the same time.

CONCEPT An abstract idea based on grouping objects by common properties.

CONCEPTION The moment at which the sperm penetrates the ovum and the ovum becomes impervious to the entry of other sperm.

CONDITIONED STIMULUS (CS) In classical conditioning, a previously neutral stimulus that through pairing with an unconditioned stimulus acquires the ability to produce a similar response.

CONDITIONED RESPONSE (CR) A learned response similar to a reflex but elicited by a conditioned stimulus owing to the previous association of the conditioned stimulus with an unconditioned stimulus.

CONONICAL STAGE A stage of language acquisition that typically occurs between the ages of 7 and 10 months and is typified by an increase in babbling and the production of cononical syllables (made of consonant and vowel sounds of certain intensities). Duplicated sequences such as "dadada" or "mamama" also mark this stage.

CONSERVATION The principle that quantities such as mass, weight, and volume remain constant regardless of changes in the appearance of these quantities, and that such changes in appearance can be undone, thereby regaining the original state by reversing any operations that had been performed. The concept of conservation encompasses the concepts of identity, decentration, and reversibility.

CONTIGUOUS ASSOCIATION The occurrence of two events in time such that they are temporally associated. In conditioning, the presentation of two or more stimuli within a certain time frame or the presentation of a stimulus within a certain time following a response.

CONTINGENCY DETECTION The process by which an organism discriminates between stimuli that are present only when the US is presented and those that are present both when the US is presented and when it is not. The result is that the organism can rely on the sensing of the stimulus that is present only when the US is presented to predict that the US will soon appear.

CONTRACTION STAGE A stage of language acquisition that typically occurs between the ages of 10 and 14 months. It is so named because during this time, infants begin to narrow their phoneme production to the phonemes common to the language to which they are exposed. During this stage, infants also acquire the pacing and rhythm of their language.

CONTROL In a controlled study, experimental or research conditions are arranged deliberately so that observed effects can be traced directly to a known variable or variables. The control is similar to the experimental subject but is not exposed to the variable.

CONVENTIONAL LEVEL According to Kohlberg, the level of moral development in which the individual strives to maintain the expectations of family, group, or nation, regardless of the consequences.

CONVERGENT PRODUCTION Part of Guilford's model of intelligence. A type of thinking in which an individual attempts to search through his or her knowledge and use all that he or she can find to converge on one correct answer.

COOPERATION Working together toward a common end or purpose.

COOPERATIVE PLAY The kind of play in which children play structured games with other children according to rules.

COPY THEORY OF KNOWLEDGE A theory that helps explain the occurrence of egocentrism among preoperational children. It holds that preoperational children act as though knowledge is not subjective but instead lies within objects; thus, all persons who are in line of sight of an object, regardless of orientation or experience, receive the same copy image of that object as the child does.

CORRELATION A relationship between two variables.

COUNTERCONDITIONING A technique used by behavioral therapists to eliminate unwanted behavior through new associations, extinction, or punishment, while promoting the acquisition of more appropriate behavior in place of the old.

CREATIVITY The ability to originate something new and appropriate by transcending common thought constraints and to create something the value of which becomes more apparent over time.

CREOLE A mixture of language that develops when groups speaking different languages have prolonged contact. Typically, the basic vocabulary of the dominant language is combined with the grammar of a subordinate language, creating an admixture (a mingling within a mixture) of words and grammar that becomes in itself a new subordinate and creolized language.

CRISIS NURSERY A place where parents may leave infants and young children for a short time until the parents are better able to deal with their stress and the danger of abuse is thus lessened.

CRITICAL PERIOD A specific time during an organism's development when certain experiences will have an effect and after which the effect can no longer be obtained through exposure to the experience.

CROSS-CULTURAL RESEARCH Research in which different cultures are evaluated on different behavioral dimensions, such as attachment, emotional development, and intellectual development. Its primary purpose is to isolate and distinguish the effects and influences of culture from those of other variables.

CROSS-SECTIONAL APPROACH A research strategy in which investigators examine subjects of different ages simultaneously to study the relationships between age, experience, and behavior.

CROSS-MODAL TRANSFER A recognition of an object as familiar when it is perceived with a sense other than that previously used when exposed to the object.

CULTURE-FAIR TEST A test supposedly free of cultural biases, usually constructed so that language differences and other cultural effects are minimized.

CYTOMEGALOVIRUS A common virus to which a majority of American women have been exposed at some time in their lives. An active infection in a pregnant mother may cause harm to the unborn child.

DECENTRATION In Piagetian theory, the cognitive ability to break out of the frame of thought that causes one to focus on only one aspect of a changing situation.

DEOXYRIBONUCLEIC ACID (DNA) A chemical constituent of cell nuclei, consisting of two long chains of alternating phosphate and deoxyribose units twisted into a double helix and joined by bonds between the complementary bases of adenine, thymine, cytosine, and guanine. It is the substance that enables cells to copy themselves.

DEPENDENT VARIABLE In an experiment, the variable that may change as a result of changes in the independent variable.

DEPRESSION A feeling of sadness and sometimes of total apathy. Guilt or the inability to cope with problems, frustration, or conflict are often behind the depression, possibly influenced by chemical imbalances and heredity.

DEVELOPMENTAL PSYCHOLOGY The study of age-related differences in behavior.

DEVELOPMENTAL PSYCHOPATHOLOGY The study of the development of abnormal behavior that has been brought about by genetic, ontogenetic, biochemical, cognitive, affective, or social influences.

DIFFERENTIAL REPRODUCTION A mechanism by which organisms with favorable traits tend to reproduce in greater numbers than those with less favorable traits, resulting in an increase in favored traits in later generations.

DISCRETE EMOTIONS THEORY A view of emotional development that has as its central premise that all basic emotions are present and functional in newborns or very shortly after birth.

DISTINCTIVE FEATURE Gibson's term for that portion of an object that can be discriminated from other portions.

DIVERGENT PRODUCTION According to Guilford, a type of thinking in which a person searches for multiple ideas or solutions to a problem; characteristic of the creative thought process.

DIVERSIFICATION In evolution, the great range of individual differences that exist in each species from which natural forces may select.

DOMINANT In genetics, describing a gene whose characteristics are expressed, while suppressing the characteristics controlled by the other corresponding gene for that trait.

DOUBLE RECESSIVE A condition in which both allelic pairs for a given trait are recessive and no dominant allelic gene is present to override them. In this case, the recessive trait will be expressed.

DOUBLE-BLIND EXPERIMENT A research technique in which neither the subjects nor the experimenter knows which subjects have been exposed to the experimental variable. It is used for controlling biases that may be introduced by either the subjects or the researcher.

DOWN SYNDROME A chromosomal abnormality that manifests itself in such features as a thick tongue, extra eyelid folds, and heart deformities, as well as deficient intelligence. It is caused by a trisomy of the twenty-first chromosome pair.

DUO A two-word utterance made by children during the two-word stage.

DYSLEXIA An impairment of reading ability, such that a person can make little sense of what he reads; letters or words often appear to be transposed.

EEG (Electroencephalogram) A recording of the changes in the brain's electrical potentials. The recording is made by attaching electrodes to various positions to the scalp and amplifying the electrical output coming from the brain. EEG analysis can show a number of systematic changes within the brain that occur during various activities.

EGO In psychoanalytic theory, the part of the personality that regulates the impulses of the id to meet the demands of reality and maintain social approval and esteem.

EGOCENTRISM Thought process characteristic of children in the preoperational period, in which they view their perspective as the reference point from which they, as well as all others, view the world.

EMPATHY An insightful awareness and ability to share the emotions, thoughts, and behavior of another person.

EMPIRICAL Relying or based solely on experiments or objective observation.

ENCODE In memory, to organize a stimulus input into an acceptable form for storage.

ENDOMETRIOSIS A pathological condition in which bits of the endometrial lining of the uterus invade the body cavity and periodically bleed during a woman's monthly cycle. The disorder is found more often in women over 30 and may interfere with fertility by producing scar tissue that can damage or block the fallopian tubes.

ENVIRONMENTAL THEORY Theory that attempts to predict or explain behavior based primarily on a person's learning and past experience.

EPIGENETIC THEORY Theory that emphasizes the interaction between the environment and a person's genetic inheritance.

EQUILIBRIUM Term used by Piaget to describe a hypothetical goal state achieved through an innate drive that forces a person actively to pursue cognitive adaptation. In this view, children have a natural inclination toward cognitive development.

EROGENOUS ZONES According to psychoanalytic theory, physically defined areas of the body from which is obtained the greatest psychosexual gratification. Different areas are predominant during different stages of psychosexual development.

ESTROGENS Female sex hormones, produced by the ovaries; responsible for maturation of the female sex organs, secondary sexual characteristics, and, in some species, sexual behavior.

ETHOLOGY The study of behavior from a biological point of view, characterized by the study of animals in their natural environments.

EVOLUTION The process by which plants or animals change from earlier existing forms. Darwin understood evolution to occur primarily through the processes of diversification and natural selection.

EXPANSION STAGE A stage of language acquisition that typically occurs between the ages of 4 and 7 months. During this stage, infants produce many new sounds and rapidly expand the number of phonemes they use, giving rise to babbling.

EXPANSION An enlargement, increase, or extension of initial research efforts.

EXPERIENCE-EXPECTANT SYSTEM A neural model of the central nervous system that pictures the CNS as containing structures that are prepared, or "prewired," to rapidly respond to, or make sense of, experiences that are common to all members of the species. The portion of the CNS that is not experience-dependent.

EXPERIENCE-DEPENDENT SYSTEM A neural model of the central nervous system that pictures the CNS as containing structures that are flexible and prepared to incorporate information that is unique to each individual member of a species. The portion of the CNS that is not experience-expectant.

EXPERIMENT A test made to demonstrate the validity of a hypothesis or to determine the predictability of a theory. Variables are manipulated during the test. Any changes are compared with those of a control that has not been exposed to the variables of interest.

EXPLORATION-PLAY-APPLICATION SEQUENCE An ethological term describing the function of play as a bridge between the cautious exploration of the unfamiliar and its eventual application for useful purposes.

EXTINCTION (IN CLASSICAL CONDITIONING) The elimination of the power of the conditioned stimulus to elicit a conditioned response. Classical extinction will occur if the conditioned stimulus is repeatedly presented without being reinforced through further association with the unconditioned stimulus.

FACTOR LOAD The weight or emphasis given to any factor or ability.

FACTOR ANALYSIS A statistical procedure aimed at discovering the constituent components within a complex system such as personality or intelligence; enables the investigator to compute the minimum number of factors required to account for the intercorrelations among test scores.

FALLOPIAN TUBES The pair of slender ducts leading from the uterus to the region of the ovaries in the female reproductive system.

FANTASY PLAY Play in which an object, person, or situation becomes a target for fantasy and is not treated as what it actually is.

FAST MAPPING The ability of children to rapidly narrow down the correct meaning of a word.

FETAL ALCOHOL SYNDROME A disorder suffered by some infants whose mothers have ingested alcohol during the prenatal period. It is characterized by facial, limb, or organ defects and reduced physical size and intellectual ability.

FETUS The unborn child from the eighth week of pregnancy to the time of live birth.

FIXED-RESPONSE PATTERN A species-specific response pattern that is presumed to have survival value for the organism and is elicited by a releaser stimulus.

FORECLOSURE The failure of an adolescent to explore and discover a self-identity; the unquestioning acceptance and adoption of the identity demanded by parents or other important adults.

FRAGILE X SYNDROME A sex-linked inherited chromosomal disorder that produces moderate retardation among males who inherit the fragile X chromosome. After Down syndrome, it is the most common biological cause of retardation.

FRIENDSHIP Close emotional ties formed with another person through mutual preference for interaction, skill at complementary and reciprocal peer play, and shared positive affect.

GAMETE Male or female germ cell containing one-half the number of chromosomes found in the other cells of the body.

GENDER UNDERSTANDING A person's comprehension that he or she is either a boy or a girl; usually develops in children by about the age of 3 years.

GENDER CONSTANCY The realization that one's sex is determined by unchanging criteria and is unaffected by one's activities or behavior; usually develops in children by the age of 6 or 7 years.

GENE The smallest functional unit for the transmission of a hereditary trait; a section of genetic code.

GENETIC IMPRINTING The process whereby identical sections of the same chromosome will yield different phenotypic outcomes, depending on whether the chromosome was inherited from the mother or the father.

GENITAL STAGE In psychoanalytic theory, the final stage of psychosexual development, characterized by the expression of heterosexual interests.

GENOTYPE The characteristics that an individual has inherited and may transmit to descendants, regardless of whether the individual manifests these characteristics.

GONADS The sex glands that regulate sex drive and the physiological changes that accompany physical maturity; the ovaries in the female and the testes in the male.

GOOING STAGE A stage of language acquisition that typically occurs between the ages of 2 and 4 months. During this stage, infants combine the quasi vowels from the phonation stage with harder sounds that are precursors of consonants.

GRAMMAR A set of rules that determines how sounds may be put together to make words and how words may be put together to make sentences.

GRAMMATICAL MORPHEMES Words or parts of words that help add meaning to a sentence and that are acquired by children generally between the ages of 2½ and 5 years. Conjunctions, prepositions, suffixes, and prefixes are examples of grammatical morphemes. Morphemes are the smallest language units to have meaning and cannot be broken down into smaller meaningful units.

GROWTH SPURT The time during puberty in which an adolescent's growth undergoes a marked acceleration.

HABITUATION METHOD A methodological procedure for measuring an infant's sensation and perception. A stimulus is presented to the infant until habituation occurs. A second stimulus is then presented. Any increased response from the infant is taken as a sign that the infant can discriminate between the stimuli.

HERPES A disease caused by a number of viruses that can attack the skin or mucous membranes. Genital herpes is difficult to treat and can harm an infant who is born to a mother whose herpes is in an active stage.

HETEROZYGOUS Describing alleles of a gene pair that are different.

HOLOPHRASE A possible semantic statement made by children in the one-word stage when they utter single words. A holophrase is a single-word "sentence," that is, a one-word utterance that may be interpreted to contain the semantic content of a phrase.

HOMINID Any family of bipedal primate mammals. Includes all forms of human beings, extinct and living.

HOMOZYGOUS Describing alleles of a gene pair that are identical.

HORIZONTAL DECALAGE Term used by Piaget to describe the onset and order of different conservation abilities.

HORMONES Secretions of the endocrine glands that specifically affect metabolism and behavior.

HYPERACTIVITY A disorder in children marked by a chronic tendency to be excessively active, to lack control, and to be unable to concentrate.

ID In psychoanalytic theory, the reservoir of instinctive drives; the most inaccessible and primitive portion of the mind.

IDEATIONAL FLUENCY A term used by Wallach to describe an individual's ability to produce many ideas; sometimes used as a measure of creativity; correlates poorly with IQ.

IDENTIFICATION In psychoanalytic theory, the process by which the child tries to imitate the behavior of parents or other heroes to share vicariously in their lives.

IDENTITY In Piagetian theory, a deep understanding that two objects will remain identical in some elemental way even though one of the objects may have its appearance altered in some dramatic way.

IDENTITY DIFFUSION A problem faced by some adolescents who find themselves committed to few goals or values and are apathetic about searching for their own identity.

IMITATION Term used by social learning theorists to describe the acquisition of observed behavior.

IMPRINTING As used by ethologists, a species-specific bonding that occurs within a limited period early in the life of the organism and that is relatively unmodifiable thereafter.

INDEPENDENT VARIABLE In an experiment, the variable that is manipulated or treated to see what effect differences in it will have on the variables considered to be dependent on it.

INDUCTION A disciplinary technique in which caregivers try to show the child the reasoning behind the discipline.

INNATE Inborn; referring to the hereditary component of a physiological or behavioral trait.

INTELLIGENCE A general term for a person's abilities in a wide range of tasks, including vocabulary, numbers, problem solving, and concepts. May also include the ability to profit from experience, to learn new information, and to adjust to new situations.

INTELLIGENCE QUOTIENT (IQ) A quotient derived from the formula $MA/CA \times 100 = IQ$, where MA is mental age and CA is chronological age; devised by psychologist William Stern and introduced in the United States by Lewis Terman.

INTEROBSERVER RELIABILITY The degree of agreement or disagreement between two or more observers who make simultaneous observations of a single event.

INTRAORGANISMIC PERSPECTIVE The theory, first espoused by Bowlby, that infants possess innate mechanisms that foster and promote the development of attachment. Such mechanisms are believed to have been naturally selected, as they have survival value.

JOINT CUSTODY An arrangement in which more than one person shares legal custody of a child.

KARYOTYPE A photomicrograph of chromosomes in a standard array.

KIBBUTZ An Israeli farm or collective where children often are reared within groups, allowing them to receive nurturance and guidance from many different adults and older children.

LABOR The physical efforts of childbirth; parturition.

LANGUAGE ACQUISITION DEVICE (LAD) As hypothesized by Noam Chomsky, a neural structure inborn in every healthy individual that is preprogrammed with the underlying rules of a universal form of grammar. Once the child is exposed to a particular language, he or she selects from the complete set of rules with which he or she was born only those rules required by the language he or she will be speaking. Most psychologists and linguists currently find the idea interesting but agree that a proof is doubtful because it is so difficult to find ways to demonstrate the existence of such a hypothesized device.

LATENCY STAGE In psychoanalytic theory, the fourth psychosexual stage, occurring between the phallic stage and puberty, during which sexual drives and feelings become lessened or nonexistent.

LAW OF EFFECT Thorndike's principle that responses associated with pleasant consequences tend to be repeated, while those associated with discomforting consequences tend to be eliminated.

LEARNED HELPLESSNESS Giving up, even though success is possible, because of previous experience in which success was impossible.

LEARNING DISABILITY A learning problem that is not due to environmental causes, mental retardation, or emotional disturbances; often associated with problems in listening, thinking, talking, reading, writing, spelling, and arithmetic.

LIGHTENING The rotation of the fetus into a head-downward position prior to birth.

LONGITUDINAL APPROACH A research study design in which investigators follow an individual through time, taking measurements at periodic intervals.

LOVE WITHDRAWAL A disciplinary technique in which caregivers express disapproval by ignoring, isolating, or expressing lack of love for the child.

M In Juan Pascual-Leone's theory of cognitive development, the amount of mental capacity, or power, available for cognitive tasks. The greater the M available, the greater the number of schemes that can be mentally examined and manipulated at a given time, and the more advanced the cognitive skill and level of the individual.

MAINSTREAMING The philosophy of keeping as many exceptional children in the regular classroom as possible rather than placing them into special classes.

MATURATION A genetically programmed biological plan of development that is somewhat independent of experience. Maturation is highly correlated with, and dependent on, the growth and development of the nervous system.

MECHANISTIC-FUNCTIONAL APPROACH An approach to the understanding of cognitive development that takes the machine as its metaphor. Environmental influences on cognitive development are considered major, since machines don't change from within but must be added to from without.

MEIOSIS The process of cell division in sexually reproducing organisms that reduces the number of chromosomes in reproductive cells, leading to the production of gametes.

MEMORY The complex mental function of recalling what has been learned or experienced.

MENARCHE The first occurrence of menstruation.

MENOPAUSE The cessation of menstruation, usually occurring when a woman is between the ages of 45 and 50 years.

MENTAL AGE (MA) A concept developed by Binet, used to calculate a person's IQ. Mental age is derived by comparing a person's test score with the average scores of others within different specific age groups.

META-EMOTION One's knowledge about one's own emotions.

METACOGNITION All the skills and abilities that encompass one's knowledge and understanding about one's own cognitive and thinking abilities; what one knows about one's own cognition and thinking processes.

METAMEMORY One's knowledge of how best to use one's memory.

MODEL In social learning theory, anyone who demonstrates a behavior that others observe.

MODIFIER GENE A gene that acts on another gene and modifies the latter's effects.

MOLECULE A distinct chemical unit or group of atoms that have joined together.

MONOSOMY A single unpaired chromosome that is located where there should be a pair of chromosomes.

MORALS The attitudes and beliefs that people hold that help them determine what is right and wrong.

MORATORIUM The time during which an adolescent is searching for an identity.

MULTISOMY A chromosomal abnormality in which more than one additional chromosome is associated with a chromosome pair.

MUTATION Any heritable alteration of the genes or chromosomes of an organism.

MYELIN SHEATH A white fatty covering on neural fibers that serves to channel and increase the transmission speed of impulses along those fibers.

NAMING A development of early childhood in which the child begins pointing out objects and calling them by name. It is considered a special development because it appears to be intrinsically reinforcing and satisfying to humans and seems to occur only in our species.

NASOFACIAL REFLEX A facial expression that is a reflexive response to an olfactory stimulation not processed by the cerebral cortex.

NATURAL SELECTION The process, first suggested by Darwin, through which those individuals of a species best adapted to their environment have a better chance of passing on their genes to the next generation than do those not as well adapted.

NATURALIST A person who studies natural history, especially zoology and botany.

NATURE In developmental research, the hereditary component of an organism's development.

NEGATIVE IDENTITY A development among some adolescents in which the identity adopted is the opposite of what parents and society had desired or expected.

NEGATIVE IDEATION A method for delaying gratification by imagining unpleasant stimuli associated with the desired goal or object.

NEGATIVE FIXATION In psychoanalytic theory, remaining in a

particular psychosexual stage of development because the id has failed to receive sufficient satisfaction.
NEONATE A newborn infant.
NEURON A nerve cell. The basic unit of the nervous system.
NOVELTY A component of creativity described by Jackson and Messick. Creative objects are novel; that is, they are new.
NUCLEUS A central body within a living cell that contains the cell's hereditary material and controls its metabolism, growth, and reproduction.
NURTURE In developmental research, the environmental component of an organism's development.

OBJECT PERMANENCE Term used by Piaget to refer to the individual's realization that objects continue to exist even though they are not presently sensed.
OBSERVER BIAS An error in observation caused by the expectations of the observer.
ONE-WORD STAGE The universal stage in language development in which children's speech is limited to single words.
ONLOOKER PLAY A type of play in which the child watches other children play but does not participate.
OPERANT CONDITIONING Skinner's term for changes in behavior that occur as a result of consequences that reinforce or punish emitted responses. These responses are classified according to how they operate on the environment. They are in turn shaped by further environmental experiences. Also known as instrumental learning.
OPERANT Skinner's term for any emitted response that affects the environment. Operants are classified or grouped not according to the particular muscular combinations involved in creating the response but according to their effect on the environment. Thorndike's cats used the same operant when they pressed the treadle that opened their cage, regardless of which paw or muscles they used.
OPTOKINETIC NYSTAGMUS Involuntary lateral motion of the eyes in response to the transverse passage of a series of vertical lines.
ORAL STAGE According to Freud, the first psychosexual stage, in which pleasure is focused on the mouth and oral cavity.
ORGANISMIC-STRUCTURAL APPROACH An approach to the understanding of cognitive development that takes as its metaphor the growing biological organism. Environmental influences on cognitive development are considered minor, with only extreme environmental forces having any appreciable effect on biological structure or development.
OVARIES Paired female reproductive glands that produce ova, or eggs, and female hormones.

PARALLEL PLAY The kind of play that children engage in when they play alongside other children but do not participate directly with the other children.
PARENTS ANONYMOUS An organization to help parents who abuse their children make constructive changes in their responses; uses the same intensive contact and principles as Alcoholics Anonymous.
PEER GROUPS Groups who develop their own set of values and goals and establish durable social relationships. Generally, each member has a specified role or status.
PEERS Equals; developmentally, people who interact at about the same behavioral level, regardless of age.
PERCEPTION The ordering principle that gives coherence and unity to sensory input. Although sensory content is always present in perception, what is perceived is influenced by set and prior experience; thus, perception is more than a passive registration of stimuli impinging on the sense organs.
PERIOD OF THE OVUM Time from conception until the zygote is first attached within the uterus, about 2 weeks following conception.
PERIOD OF THE EMBRYO Time from the attachment of the zygote to the uterine wall until the first formation of solid bone in the embryo, from about 2 to 8 weeks following conception.
PERIOD OF THE FETUS Time from the first formation of bone in the embryo until birth, generally from 8 weeks following conception until birth.
PERMISSIVE-DEMANDING DIMENSION One of two major dimensions used by Baumrind to describe parenting; denotes the degree of parental permissiveness.
PERSONALITY The organization of relatively enduring characteristics unique to an individual, usually revealed by the individual's reaction to his environment.
PHALLIC STAGE According to Freud, the third psychosexual stage, during which the child manipulates and explores his genitals and experiences a strong attraction for the parent of the opposite sex.
PHENOTYPE The observable characteristics of an organism due to inheritance.
PHENYLKETONURIA (PKU) A genetic disorder marked by an inability to oxidize normally the amino acid phenylalanine. If this disorder is unchecked by a suitable diet, permanent damage is caused to the developing child's central nervous system.
PHONATION STAGE A stage of language acquisition that develops between birth and 2 months of age. During this stage, infants often make comfort sounds composed of quasi vowels.
PHONEME CONSTANCY A perceptual ability that develops in infancy in which a phoneme, although spoken or pronounced differently by different individuals, is perceived as a single entity regardless of speaker.
PHONEMES The smallest units of speech that can affect meaning. For instance, the only difference between *mat* and *bat* is the phoneme sounds *m* and *b*. These two sounds are phonemes because they affect meaning; a mat is certainly not a bat. Phonemes are typically composed of phones. Some languages use more phonemes than others.
PHONES The smallest units of vocalized sound that do not affect meaning but can be discriminated. Derived from the Greek word *phone*, meaning "voice" or "sound", phones are often responsible for regional and foreign accents. For example, someone from Boston might pronounce the word *car* differently than someone from Dallas.
PHONOLOGY The study of how sounds (phonemes and phones) are put together to make words.
PIDGIN A simplified form of speech typically derived from a mixture of two or more languages. It has as its basis a rudimentary form of grammar and vocabulary and is generally used for communication between people speaking different languages.
PITUITARY A gland that is located beneath the hypothalamus, and that controls many hormonal secretions; often called the "master gland" because it appears to control other glands throughout the body.
PLACENTA A vascular, membranous organ that develops during

pregnancy, lining the uterine wall and partially enveloping the fetus. The placenta is attached to the fetus by the umbilical cord.
PLASTICITY Flexibility or adaptability. In neurophysiology the ability of brain tissue to take over the function of other brain tissue that has been damaged. In life experience, the ability to overcome the effects of early adverse experiences.
PLAY Pleasurable activity engaged in for its own sake, with means emphasized rather than ends. Play is not usually engaged in as a serious activity and is flexible in that it varies in form or context.
PLEASURE PRINCIPLE The psychoanalytic postulate that an organism seeks immediate pleasure and avoids pain. The id functions according to the pleasure principle.
POINT MUTATION A mutation that results in the replacement of one base pair by another within the DNA itself.
POLYGENETIC INHERITANCE The control of a single characteristic or function by more than one gene.
POSITION CONSTANCY The learned perception that even though the subject moves, all the objects in the environment stay stationary and maintain their positions relative to each other.
POSITIVE IDEATION Imagining pleasant consequences or associations with a desired goal or object; generally a poor strategy for delaying immediate gratification.
POSITIVE FIXATION In psychoanalytic theory, remaining in a particular psychosexual stage of development because the id has received too much satisfaction.
POSTCONVENTIONAL LEVEL According to Kohlberg, the level of moral development characterized by self-chosen ethical principles that are comprehensive, universal, and consistent.
POWER ASSERTION A disciplinary technique in which caregivers use physical punishment, removal of privileges, or the threat of these actions.
PRECISION The accuracy of predictions made from a theory.
PRECONCEPTS Immature concepts held by children in the preoperational stage.
PRECONVENTIONAL LEVEL According to Kohlberg, a level of moral development in which good and bad is determined by the physical or hedonistic consequences of obeying or disobeying the rules.
PREFERENCE METHOD A methodological procedure for measuring an infant's sensation and perception. Two stimuli are presented to the infant simultaneously. Any preference the infant shows for one stimulus rather than the other is taken as a sign that the infant is able to discriminate between the two stimuli. The investigator must control for such factors as right or left hand, or near or far preferences.
PREMATURE INFANT An infant who weighs less than 5.5 pounds at birth and who was carried less than 37 weeks.
PRIMARY CIRCULAR REACTIONS Simple repetitive acts that center on the infant's own body and include thumb sucking and foot grasping; characteristic of the second stage of the sensorimotor period.
PRIMARY SEXUAL CHARACTERISTICS The penis, scrotum, and testes of the male; the vagina, ovaries, and uterus of the female.
PRIMATE Member of the most highly developed order of mammals, including humans, apes, and lemurs. Primates are marked by their large stereoscopic eyes, nails (rather than claws), opposing thumbs, and short snouts.
PROBABILISTIC EPIGENESIS Literally, the direction in which growth will probably go. The term is often used when discussing physical or cognitive development; it represents what typically occurs in the development of most individuals, but not in the development of all individuals.
PROSOCIAL BEHAVIOR Behavior that benefits other people and society.
PSYCHOANALYTIC THEORY The school of psychological thought founded by Freud that emphasizes the study of unconscious mental processes and psychosexual development. As a therapy, psychoanalysis seeks to bring unconscious desires into consciousness and to resolve conflicts that usually date back to early childhood experiences.
PSYCHOLOGICAL MALTREATMENT Mistreatment of children in a psychological way, as distinguished from physical abuse or neglect; includes verbal abuse, failure to provide warmth or love, and belittlement or berating.
PSYCHOLOGY The discipline that attempts to describe, explain, and predict the behavior of organisms.
PSYCHOSEXUAL STAGES Five stages of human development postulated by Freud. All but the latency stage are centered about the stimulation of erogenous zones. The erogenous stages—oral, anal, phallic, and genital—are predominant at different times.
PSYCHOSOCIAL STAGES Stages of ego development as formulated by Erikson, incorporating both sexual and social aspects.
PUBERTY The stage of maturation in which the individual becomes physiologically capable of sexual reproduction.

RASPBERRY In foodstuffs: a rather tasty fruit; a type of berry. In social discourse: an explosive sound caused by the rapid expulsion of air from the mouth. The expelled air vigorously vibrates the lips (especially the lower lip), which have been deliberately placed in a configuration so as to make contact with and surround the protruded tongue. Considered unrequired in most social circumstances. (For an exception, see "Sporting events.")
REALITY PLAY Play devoid of fantasy or in which fantasy is an insignificant part; essentially, play in which an object or situation is treated as what it actually is.
REALITY PRINCIPLE According to Freud, the principle on which the ego operates as it tries to mediate the demands of the unconscious id and the realities of the environment.
RECESSIVE In genetics, describing a gene whose characteristics are not expressed when paired with a dominant gene.
REFLEX EXERCISE Piagetian description of the first stage of the sensorimotor period, during which the infant's reflexes become smoother and more coordinated.
REFLEX A simple innate response to an eliciting stimulus.
REHEARSAL A technique for memorizing information in which an item is repeated over and over so that it is not lost from memory. This behavior may eventually result in storage of the item in the long-term memory.
REINFORCEMENT (IN OPERANT CONDITIONING) An event that strengthens the response that preceded it. Operant (instrumental) conditioning is a process by which a response is reinforced.
REINFORCEMENT (IN CLASSICAL CONDITIONING) Any increase in the ability of a conditioned stimulus to elicit a conditioned response owing to the association of the conditioned stimulus with another stimulus (typically an unconditioned stimulus). In the classical conditioning process, a stimulus is reinforced.
RELEASER STIMULUS A stimulus that sets off a cycle of instinctive behavior; also called a sign stimulus.
RELIABILITY The capacity of an instrument to measure consistently and dependably. A reliable test will provide approximately

the same score on retesting under similar conditions.
REPLICATION Repeating an experiment to enhance the reliability of the results.
REVERSIBILITY In Piagetian theory, the ability, obtained during concrete operations, to understand that actions that affect objects, if reversed in sequence, will return the objects to their original state.
ROLE CONFUSION A consequence of the failure to establish a sense of identity during Erikson's fifth psychosocial stage. Without a sense of identity, the individual will be confused about his or her role in society and will find it difficult to form a life philosophy or create a stable base on which to build a career or have a family.
RUBELLA A viral infection, commonly known as German measles, that has a serious effect on an unborn child, especially if contracted by the mother during the first trimester of pregnancy.

SALTATORY GROWTH Literally, growth by leaping. Growth that occurs in "spurts" or sudden leaps.
SCHEME A basic unit of cognition. The comprehension an infant has about different aspects of his or her world at any given moment as pertains to actions. Piaget believed that infants develop schematic outlines (or maps) of what the world is like and maintain these outlines in their memories, enabling them to organize their world into such action categories as "Things I can touch" or "Things I can eat."
SCHIZOPHRENIA A term used to describe a number of functional psychoses that are characterized by serious thought disturbances, withdrawal, inappropriate emotional response or lack of emotional response, hallucinations, and delusions.
SCRIPT In cognitive study, one's knowledge of the appropriate events that should occur in a particular social setting and of how one might carry them out. This includes knowledge of who is expected to do what to whom as well as when, where, and why. A script would include such typical behaviors as those expected of a person going to a restaurant or movie.
SECONDARY CIRCULAR REACTIONS Circular reactions characteristic of the third stage of the sensorimotor period, in which the child reaches out to manipulate objects discovered in the environment.
SECONDARY SEXUAL CHARACTERISTICS Physical characteristics that appear in humans around the time of puberty and are sex differentiated but not necessary for sexual reproduction. Examples include beards in men and breasts in women.
SECULAR TREND The tendency during the last century for children to mature and grow taller at a younger age.
SECURE ATTACHMENT Most common form of attachment observed by Ainsworth in her research. Securely attached children respond happily to their mother's return, greet her, and stay near her for a while.
SECURE-BASE PHENOMENON Term used by Ainsworth to describe the child's tendency to use the attachment figure as a secure base of operations from which to explore the environment.
SELECTIVE ATTENTION The process of discriminating one stimulus from multiple stimuli and attending to it.
SELF-CONTROL The ability to control one's own actions despite the external pressures of the immediate situation.
SENSATION The result of converting physical stimulation of the sense organs into sensory experience.
SENSITIVE PERIOD A time during which a particular organism is most sensitive to the effect of certain stimuli.
SENSORY EXCEPTIONALITY Technically, the possession of any sensory abilities significantly superior or inferior to those of the general population. Practically, however, the term is almost always used to denote individuals who have a visual or auditory dysfunction.
SEPARATION ANXIETY Fear of being separated from the caregiver; a form of anxiety that usually manifests itself in children between the ages of 7 and 30 months. Separation anxiety usually is strongest at 18 months of age.
SEQUENTIAL DESIGN A research design that combines elements of different time-dependent research approaches to control for biases that might be introduced when any single approach is used alone.
SEX-LINKED DISORDER A hereditary disorder controlled by a gene carried on the sex-determining chromosome. Color blindness is an example.
SEX ROLES The behaviors associated with one sex or the other.
SEX CHROMOSOMES In humans, one of the two chromosomes responsible for producing the sex of the child; the X and Y chromosomes.
SEX ROLE IDENTIFICATION The degree to which a child adopts the sex role of a particular model.
SEX TYPING The process whereby an individual incorporates the behaviors, traits, and attitudes appropriate to his or her biological sex or the sex assigned at birth.
SEXUALLY TRANSMITTED DISEASES (STDS) Diseases that are primarily transmitted through sexual intercourse.
SHAPE CONSTANCY The learned perception that an object remains the same shape, despite the fact that the shape of the image it casts on the retina may vary depending on the viewing angle.
SHAPING A method of modifying behavior by reinforcing successive approximations toward the goal behavior.
SHOULDER PRESENTATION During birth, the presentation of the shoulder first, rather than the head.
SICKLE-CELL ANEMIA A sometimes fatal double recessive genetic disorder of the red blood cells that is most commonly found among the black population. The red blood cells form a sickle shape that reduces their ability to carry oxygen effectively.
SINGLE-STIMULUS PROCEDURE A methodological procedure for measuring an infant's sensation and perception. An infant's current state is noted (condition A). Then a single stimulus is presented to the infant (condition B) and any measurable changes in the infant's behavior are noted. The procedure can be made experimental by creating a single-subject A-B-A design. This is accomplished by withdrawing the stimulus (return of condition A) and again noting changes in the infant's behavior.
SINGLE-SUBJECT EXPERIMENT An experiment in which only one subject participates. Generally, time is used as the control; for example, the subject's behavior changes over time in relation to the presentation and withdrawal of a variable.
SIZE CONSTANCY The learned perception that an object remains the same size, even though the size of the image it casts on the retina varies with its distance from the viewer.
SLOW VIRUS A virus that may take years to produce symptoms. Slow viruses have been implicated in some forms of mental retardation.
SOCIAL REFERENCING The use of emotional signals or cues from others as a guide for one's own behavior in ambiguous situations.
SOCIAL LEARNING Learning by observing the actions of others.
SOCIAL FANTASY PLAY Play in which one pretends to be some-

one else or adopts a role other than one's own; common to children age 5 years or older.
SOCIALIZATION The teaching process through which the beliefs, attitudes, and behavioral expectations of a culture are transmitted to children.
SOLITARY PLAY The type of play that children engage in when they play by themselves.
SPECIES-SPECIFIC BEHAVIOR Inherited behavior characteristic of one species of animal.
SPOONERISM An unintentional transposition of sounds in a sentence, for example: "People in glass houses shouldn't stow thrones." Named for the English clergyman William A. Spooner (1844–1930), who was well known for such errors.
STIMULUS Anything that can be sensed, for example, visible light or audible sound.
STIMULUS GENERALIZATION The process by which once a stimulus has come to elicit or cue a response, similar stimuli may also elicit or cue the response, although not usually as effectively.
STORAGE In memory, the placement of information within the nervous system such that the individual can retrieve it at a later time.
STRANGER ANXIETY A fear of unfamiliar individuals that most infants develop around 6 months of age.
SUBJECT BIAS Changes in a subject's behavior that result from the subject's knowledge of the purpose of the experiment or from the subject's awareness of being observed.
SUPEREGO In psychoanalytic theory, the part of the personality that incorporates parental and social standards of morality.
SUPERFECUNDITY Having multiple offspring sired by more than one father.
SYNAPSE The junction at which a nerve impulse travels from one neuron to another.
SYNCRETIC REASONING A type of reasoning used by preconceptual children, in which objects are classified according to a limited and changing set of criteria.
SYNTAX The body of linguistic rules that makes it possible to relate a series of words in a sentence to the underlying meaning of that sentence; that is, the rules governing word order in a language (sentence structure).

TAY-SACHS DISEASE A fatal double recessive genetic disorder most commonly found among the Jewish population. The disease results in death due to nerve degeneration by the time the victim reaches 5 years of age.
TELEGRAPHIC SPEECH Pattern of speech that develops following and including the two-word stage, in which English-speaking children rely on a grammar of strict word order to convey their meaning and do not use conjunctions, prepositions, or other function words.
TEMPERAMENT THEORY In developmental research, any theory that emphasizes the predisposition an individual has toward general patterns of emotional reactions, changes in mood, or sensitivity to particular stimulation. Most temperament theories view temperament as a genetic disposition.
TERATOGEN Any substance capable of producing fetal abnormalities, such as alcohol or tobacco.
TERTIARY CIRCULAR REACTIONS Circular reactions characteristic of the fifth stage of the sensorimotor period, in which the child actively experiments with things to discover how various actions affect an object or outcome.
TESTES Male reproductive glands that produce spermatozoa and male hormones.
THEORY A system of rules or assumptions used to predict or explain phenomena.
TIME-LAG DESIGN A research design in which different groups of people are measured on a characteristic or behavior when they are the same age; for example, a group of 2-year-old children is measured in one year, another group of 2-year-old children is measured in the same way in a subsequent year, and so on.
TOXOPLASMOSIS A disease of humans, dogs, cats, and certain other mammals, caused by a parasitic microorganism that affects the nervous system. The disorder is especially damaging to an embryo or fetus.
TRANSCENDENCE OF CONSTRAINTS According to Jackson and Messick, a component of creativity. Creative ideas transcend constraints in that they often shed new light on something familiar.
TRANSDUCTIVE REASONING A type of reasoning used by preconceptual children, in which inferences are drawn about the relationship between two objects based on a single attribute.
TRISOMY A chromosomal abnormality in which a third chromosome occurs on a chromosome pair.
TROPHOBLAST The outer layer of cells by which the fertilized ovum is attached to the uterine wall and through which the embryo receives its nourishment.
TWIN DESIGN A research design used for sorting the influence of nurture from nature. A characteristic or behavior is compared between identical twins; then the same characteristic or behavior is compared between fraternal twins.
TWO-WORD STAGE The universal stage of language development in which children's expressions are limited to two-word utterances.

UMBILICAL CORD The flexible, cordlike structure connecting the fetus at the navel with the placenta. This cord contains the blood vessels that nourish the fetus and remove its wastes.
UNCONDITIONED RESPONSE (UR) A response made to an unconditioned stimulus; for example, salivation in response to food.
UNCONDITIONED STIMULUS (US) A stimulus that normally evokes an unconditioned response, such as the food that originally caused Pavlov's dogs to respond with salivation.

VALIDITY The capacity of an instrument to measure what it purports to measure.
VISUAL CLIFF An apparatus constructed to study depth perception in humans and other animals. It consists of a center board resting on a glass table. On one side of the board, a checkered surface is visible directly beneath the glass; on the other side, the surface is several feet below the glass, thus giving the impression of a drop-off.
VISUAL SACCADE The uneven and halting motions of the eyes as they track across edges and differing contrasts, as occurs when a person reads printed words on a page.

ZONE OF PROXIMAL DEVELOPMENT In Lev Vygotsky's cognitive theory, any and all activities that a child is almost able to perform or is able to perform with a little help.
ZYGOTE The fertilized ovum that results from the union of a sperm and egg.

REFERENCES

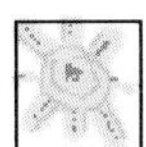

Abel, E. L. (1984). Prenatal effects of alcohol. *Drug and Alcohol Dependence, 14,* 1–10.

Abelson, R. P. (1981). Psychological status of the script concept. *American Psychologist, 36,* 715–729.

Abramovitch, R., Corter, C., Pepler, D. J., & Stanhope, L. (1986). Sibling and peer interaction: A final follow-up and a comparison. *Child Development, 57,* 217–229.

Abramovitch, R., Pepler, D., & Corter, C. (1982). Patterns of sibling interaction among preschool-age children. In M. E. Lamb & B. Sutton-Smith (Eds.), *Sibling relationships: Their nature and significance across the lifespan* (pp. 61–86). Hillsdale, NJ: Erlbaum.

Abravanel, E., & Sigafoos, A. D. (1984). Exploring the presence of imitation during early infancy. *Child Development, 55,* 381–392.

Acredolo, L. P. (1978). Development of spatial orientation in infancy. *Developmental Psychology, 14,* 224–234.

Acredolo, L. P., & Evans, D. (1980). Developmental changes in the effects of landmarks on infant spatial behavior. *Developmental Psychology, 16,* 312–318.

Acredolo, L. P., & Goodwyn, S. (1988). Symbolic gesturing in normal infants. *Child Development, 59,* 450–466.

Acredolo, L. P., & Goodwyn, S. W. (1985). Symbolic gesturing in language development. *Human Development, 28,* 40–49.

Acredolo, L. P., & Hake, J. L. (1982). Infant perception. In B. B. Wolman (Ed.), *Handbook of developmental psychology* (pp. 244–283). Englewood Cliffs, NJ: Prentice-Hall.

Adams, G. R. (1977). Physical attractiveness, personality, and social reactions to peer pressure. *Journal of Psychology, 96,* 287–296.

Adams, G. R., & Jones, R. M. (1981). Imaginary audience behavior: A validation study. *Journal of Early Adolescence, 1,* 1–10.

Adamson, L. B., & Bakeman, R. (1985). Affect and attention: Infants observed with mothers and peers. *Child Development, 56,* 582–593.

Adickes, E. D., & Shuman, R. M. (1982). Fetal alcohol myopathy-myocyte hypotrophy by morphometry. *Journal of Neuropathology and Experimental Neurology, 41,* 346.

Adler, H. E., & Adler, L. L. (1978). What can dolphins (Tursiops Truncatus) learn by observation? *Cetology, 30,* 1–10.

Adler, I., & Kandel, D. B. (1982). A cross-cultural comparison of sociopsychological factors in alcohol use among adolescents in Israel, France, and the United States. *Journal of Youth and Adolescence, 11,* 89–113.

Adler, J., Katz, S., & Jackson, T. (1985, March 25). A teen-pregnancy epidemic. *Newsweek,* p. 90.

Adler, L. L., & Adler, H. E. (1977). Ontogeny of observational learning in the dog. *Developmental Psychobiology, 10,* 267–271.

Adler, T. (1989, April). Infant is father to the child, studies show. *APA Monitor,* p. 7.

Adler, T. (1989, June). Early sex hormone exposure studied. *APA Monitor,* p. 9.

Ahlgren, A. (1983). Sex differences in the correlates of cooperative and competitive school attitudes. *Developmental Psychology, 19,* 881–888.

Ainsworth, M. D. S. (1973). The development of infant-mother attachment. In B. Caldwell & H. Ricciuti (Eds.), *Review of child development research* (Vol. 3). Chicago, Il: Univ. of Chicago Press.

Ainsworth, M. D. S., Blehar, M., Waters, E., & Wall, S. (1978). *Strange-situation behavior of one-year-olds: Its relation to mother-infant interaction in the first year and to qualitative differences in the infant-mother attachment relationship.* Hillsdale, NJ: Erlbaum.

Akiyama, M. M. (1985). Denials in young children from a cross-linguistic perspective. *Child Development, 56,* 95–102.

Albert, E. M. (1963). The roles of women: Question of values. In S. M. Farber and H. L. Wilson (Eds.), *The potential of women.* New York: McGraw-Hill.

Aldous, J., Klaus, E., & Klein, D. M. (1985). The understanding heart: Aging parents and their favorite children. *Child Development, 56,* 303–316.

Alexander, K. L., & Entwisle, D. R. (1988). Achievement in the first 2 years of school: Patterns and processes. *Monographs of the Society for Research in Child Development, 53*(2, Serial No. 218).

Alland, A., Jr. (1983). *Playing with form: Children draw in six cultures.* New York: Columbia University Press.

Alley, T. R. (1981). Head shape and the perception of cuteness. *Developmental Psychology, 17,* 650–654.

Allman, W. F. (1986, May). Mindworks. *Science 86,* pp. 23–31.

Alper, J. (1986, May). Depression at an early age. *Science 86,* pp. 44–50.

Altenor, A., Kay, E., & Richter, M. (1977). The generality of learned helplessness in the rat. *Learning & Motivation, 8,* 54–61.

Altura, B. M., Altura, B. T., Carella, A., Chatterjee, M., Halevy, S., & Tejani, N. (1982). Alcohol produces spasms of human umbilical blood vessels: Relationship to fetal alcohol syndrome (FAS). *European Journal of Pharmacology, 86,* 311–312.

Altus, W. D. (1967). Birth order and its sequelae. *International Journal of Psychiatry, 3,* 23–36.

Amsterdam, B. (1972). Mirror self-image reactions before age two. *Developmental Psychology, 5,* 297–305.

Anderson, D. R., & Levin, S. R. (1976). Young children's attention to "Sesame Street." *Child Development, 47,* 806–811.

Anderson, D. R., Lorch, E. P., Field, D. E., Collins, P. A., & Nathan, J. G. (1986). Television viewing at home: Age trends in visual attention and time with TV. *Child Development, 57,* 1024–1033.

Anderson, L. D. (1939). The predictive value of infant tests in relation to intelligence at 5 years. *Child Development, 10,* 203–212.

Andersson, B. (1992). Effects of day-care on cognitive and socioemotional competence of thirteen-year-old Swedish schoolchildren. *Child Development, 63,* 20–36.

Andre-Thomas, C., & Dargassies, St. A. (1952). *Etudes neurologiques sur le nouveau-ne et le jeune nourrisson.* Paris: Masson.

Anisfeld, E., Casper, V., Nozyce, M., & Cunningham, N. (1990). Does infant carrying promote attachment? An experimental study of the effects of increased physical contact on the development of attachment. *Child Development, 61,* 1617–1627.

Antell, S. E., Caron, A. J., & Myers, R. S. (1985). Perception of relational invariants by newborns. *Developmental Psychology, 21,* 942–948.

Apgar, V. (1953). A proposal for a new method of evaluation of the newborn infant. *Current Researches in Anesthesia and Analgesia, 32,* 260–267.

Apgar, V., Holaday, D. A., James, L. S., Weisbrot, I. M., & Berrien, C. (1958). Evaluation of the newborn infant-second report. *Journal of the American Medical Association, 168,* 1985–1988.

Arehart-Treichel, J. (1979, December 1). Down's syndrome: The father's role. *Science News,* pp. 381–382.

Arehart-Treichel, J. (1982, June 12). Fetal ultrasound: How safe? *Science News,* pp. 396–397. Aries, P. (1962). *Centuries of childhood: A social history of family life* (R. Baldick, Trans.). New York: Alfred A. Knopf. (Original work published 1960)

Arnon, S. S., Midura, T. F., Clay, S. A., Wood, R. M., & Chin, J. C. (1977). Infant botulism. *Journal of the American Medical Association, 237,* 1946–1951.

Arterberry, M., Yonas, A., & Bensen, A. S. (1989). Self-produced locomotion and the development of responsiveness to linear perspective and texture gradients. *Developmental Psychology, 25,* 976–982.

Asarnow, R. F., & Sherman, T. (1984). Studies of visual information processing in schizophrenic children. *Child Development, 55,* 249–261.

Ascione, F. R., & Sanok, R. L. (1982). The role of peer and adult models in facilitating and inhibiting children's prosocial behavior. *Genetic Psychology Monographs, 106,* 239–259.

Asher, S. R., Hymel, S., & Renshaw, P. D. (1984). Loneliness in children. *Child Development, 55,* 1456–1464.

Ashton, P. T. (1975). Cross-cultural Piagetian research: An experimental perspective. *Harvard Educational Review, 45,* 475–506.

Atwell, A. E., Moore, U. S., Nielsen, E., & Levite, Z. (1984). Effects of joint custody on children. *Bulletin of the American Academy of Psychiatry & the Law, 12,* 149–157.

Au, T. K., & Glusman, M. (1990). The principle of mutual exclusivity in word learning: To honor or not to honor? *Child Development, 61,* 1474–1490.

Au, T. K., & Laframboise, D. E. (1990). Acquiring color names via linguistic contrast: The influence of contrasting terms. *Child Development, 61,* 1808–1823.

August, G. J., Stewart, M. A., & Tsai, L. (1981). The incidence of cognitive disabilities in the siblings of autistic children. *British Journal of Psychiatry, 138,* 416–422.

Ayala, F. J. (1978). The mechanisms of evolution. *Scientific American, 239*(3), 56–69.

Azrin, N. H., & Foxx, R. M. (1974). *Toilet training in less than a day.* New York: Simon & Schuster.

Azrin, N. H., & Lindsley, O. R. (1956). The reinforcement of cooperation between children. *Journal of Abnormal and Social Psychology, 52,* 100–102.

Azuma, H. (1986). Why study child development in Japan? In H. Stevenson, H. Azuma, & K. Hakuta (Eds.), *Child development and education in Japan* (pp. 3–12). New York: W. H. Freeman.

Azuma, H., Kashiwagi, K., & Hess, R. D. (1981). *Hahaoya no taido koudo to kodomo no chiteki hattatsu* [*The effect of mother's attitude and behavior on the cognitive development of the child: A U.S.-Japan comparison.*] Tokyo: Univ. of Tokyo Press.

Bachman, J. G., O'Malley, P. M., & Johnston, J. (1978). *Adolescence to adulthood: Change and stability in the lives of young men.* Ann Arbor, MI: Institute for Social Research.

Baer, D. M., & Wright, J. C. (1974). Developmental psychology. *Annual Review of Psychology, 25,* 1–82.

Bahrick, L. E. (1988). Intermodal learning in infancy: Learning on the basis of two kinds of invariant relations in audible and visible events. *Child Development, 59,* 197–209.

Bailey, J. M., & Pillard, R. C. (1991). A genetic study of male sexual orientation. *Archives of General Psychiatry, 48,* 1089–1096.

Baillargeon, R. (1987). Object permanence in 3½- and 4½-month-old infants. *Developmental Psychology, 23,* 655–664.

Baillargeon, R., & DeVos, J. (1991). Object permanence in young infants: Further evidence. *Child Development, 62,* 1227–1246.

Baird, P. A., Sadovnick, A. D., & Yee, I. M. (1991). Maternal age and birth defects: A population study. *Lancet, 337,* 527–530.

Baker, S. W. (1980). Biological influences on human sex and gender. *Signs: Journal of Women in Culture and Society, 6,* 80–96.

Baker-Ward, L., Ornstein, P. A., & Holden, D. J. (1984). The expression of memorization in early childhood. *Journal of Experimental Child Psychology, 37,* 555–575.

Baldwin, A. L. (1949). The effect of home environment on nursery school behavior. *Child Development, 20,* 49–61.

Baldwin, D. A., & Markman, E. M. (1989). Establishing word-object relations: A first step. *Child Development, 60,* 381–398.

Baldwin, J. M. (1894). *The development of the child and of the race.* New York: MacMillan.

Bales, J. (1985, January). Attention disorders need better measures and theory. *APA Monitor,* p. 13.

Bales, J. (1986, May). What works: Consensus report gets good marks from researchers. *APA Monitor,* p. 13.

Ban, P. L., & Lewis, M. (1974). Mothers and fathers, girls and boys: Attachment behavior in the one-year-old. *Merrill-Palmer Quarterly, 20,* 195–204.

Bandura, A. (1962). Social learning through imitation. In M. R. Jones (Ed.), *Nebraska symposium on motivation: 1962* (pp. 211–269). Lincoln, Nebraska: Univ. of Nebraska Press.

Bandura, A. (1965). Influence of models' reinforcement contingencies on the acquisition of imitative responses. *Journal of Personality and Social Psychology, 1,* 589–595.

Bandura, A. (1969). *Principles of behavior modification.* New York: Holt, Rinehart, & Winston.

Bandura, A. (1977). *Social learning theory.* Englewood Cliffs NJ: Prentice-Hall.

Bandura, A. (1978). The self system in reciprocal determinism. *American Psychologist, 33,* 344–358.

Bandura, A., & Menlove, F. L. (1968). Factors determining vicarious extinction of avoidance behavior through symbolic modeling. *Journal of Personality and Social Psychology, 8,* 99–108.

Bandura, A., & Mischel, W. (1965). Modification of self-imposed delay of reward through exposure to live and symbolic models. *Journal of Personality and Social Psychology, 2,* 698–705.

Bandura, A., Ross, D., & Ross, S. A. (1963). Imitation of film-mediated aggressive models. *Journal of Abnormal and Social Psychology, 66,* 3–11.

Bandura, A., Ross, D., & Ross, S. A. (1963). A comparative test of the status envy, social power, and secondary reinforcement theories of identificatory learning. *Journal of Abnormal and Social Psychology, 67,* 527–534.

Banks, M. S., & Salapatek, P. (1981). Infant pattern vision: A new approach based on the contrast sensitivity function. *Journal of Experimental Child Psychology, 31,* 1–45.

Bar-Tal, D., Raviv, A., & Goldberg, M. (1982). Helping behavior among preschool children: An observational study. *Child Development, 53,* 396–402.

Barglow, P., Vaughn, B. E., & Molitor, N. (1987). Effects of maternal absence due to employment on the quality of infant-mother attachment in a low-risk sample. *Child Development, 58,* 945–954.

Barkley, R. A. (1977). A review of stimulant drug research with hyperactive children. *Journal of Child Psychology and Psychiatry and Allied Disciplines, 18,* 137–165.

Barnes, D. M. (1989). "Fragile X" syndrome and its puzzling genetics. *Science, 243,* 171–172.

Barnett, K., Darcie, G., Holland, C. J., & Kobasigawa, A. (1982). Children's cognitions about effective helping. *Developmental Psychology, 18,* 267–277.

Barnett, M. A., Howard, J. A., Melton, E. M., & Dino, G. A. (1982). Effect of inducing sadness about self or other on helping behavior in high- and low-empathic children. *Child Development, 53,* 920–923.

Barnett, M. A., King, L. M., & Howard, J. A. (1979). Inducing affect about self or other: Effects on generosity in children. *Developmental Psychology, 15,* 164–167.

Baron, R. A. (1971). Exposure to an aggressive model and apparent probability of retaliation from the victim as determinants of adult aggressive behavior. *Journal of Experimental Social Psychology, 7,* 343–355.

Barr, H. M., Streissguth, A. P., Darby, B. L., & Sampson, P. D. (1990). Prenatal exposure to alcohol, caffeine, tobacco, and aspirin: Effects on fine and gross motor performance in 4-year-old children. *Developmental Psychology, 26,* 339–348.

Baruch, G. K., & Barnett, R. C. (1986). Fathers' participation in family work and children's sex-role attitudes. *Child Development, 57,* 1210–1223.

Bassuk, E. L. (1991). Homeless families. *Scientific American, 265*(6), 66–74.

Bates, E., Camaioni, L., & Volterra, V. (1975). The acquisition of performatives prior to speech. *Merrill-Palmer Quarterly, 21,* 205–226.

Bates, E., MacWhinney, B., Caselli, C., Devescovi, A., Natale, F., & Venza, V. (1984). A cross-linguistic study of the development of sentence interpretation strategies. *Child Development, 55,* 341–354.

Bateson, M. C. (1975). Mother infant exchanges: The epigenesis of conversational interaction. *Annals of the New York Academy of Sciences, 263,* 101–113.

Bauer, P. J., & Mandler, J. M. (1992). Putting the horse before the cart: The use of temporal order in recall of events by one-year-old children. *Developmental Psychology, 28,* 441–452.

Baumrind, D. (1967). Child care practices anteceding three patterns of preschool behavior. *Genetic Psychology Monographs, 75,* 43–88.

Baumrind, D. (1971). Current patterns of parental authority. *Developmental Psychology, 4*(1, Pt. 2), 1–103.

Baumrind, D. (1980). New directions in socialization research. *American Psychologist, 35,* 639–652.

Baumrind, D. (1991). The influence of parenting style on adolescent competence and substance use. *Journal of Early Adolescence, 11,* 56–95.

Baydar, N., & Brooks-Gunn, J. (1991). Effects of maternal employment and child-care arrangements on preschoolers' cognitive and behavioral outcomes: Evidence from the children of the National Longitudinal Survey of Youth. *Developmental Psychology, 27,* 932–945.

Bayer, A. E. (1966). Birth order and college attendance. *Journal of Marriage and the Family, 28,* 480–484.

Bayley, N. (1969). *Manual for the Bayley Scales of Infant Development.* New York: Psychological Corporation.

Beaconsfield, P., Birdwood, G., & Beaconsfield, R. (1980). The placenta. *Scientific American, 243*(2), 94–102.

Becker, W. C. (1964). Consequences of different kinds of parental discipline. In M. L. Hoffman (Ed.), *Review of child development research* (Vol. 1). New York: Russell Sage Foundation.

Beilin, H. (1992). Piaget's enduring contribution to developmental psychology. *Developmental Psychology, 28,* 191–204.

Bell, S. M. (1970). The development of the concept of object as related to infant-mother attachment. *Child Development, 41,* 291–311.

Bellanti, J. A. (1984). Prevention of food allergies. *Annals of Allergy, 53,* 683–688.

Beller, E. K. (1957). Dependency and autonomous achievement striving related to orality and anality in early childhood. *Child Development, 28,* 287–315.

Bellinger, D., Leviton, A., Waternaux, C., Needleman, H., & Rabinowitz, M. (1987). Longitudinal analyses of prenatal and postnatal lead exposure and early cognitive development. *New England Journal of Medicine, 316,* 1037–1043.

Belmont, L., & Marolla, F. A. (1973). Birth order, family size, and intelligence. *Science, 182,* 1096–1101.

Belsky, J. (1986). Infant day care: A cause for concern. *Zero to Three, 7*(1), 1–7.

Belsky, J. (1988). The "effects" of infant day care reconsidered. *Early Childhood Research Quarterly, 3,* 235–272.

Belsky, J., & Braungart, J. M. (1991). Are insecure-avoidant infants with extensive day-care experience less stressed by and more independent in the strange situation? *Child Development, 62,* 567–571.

Belsky, J., Gilstrap, B., & Rovine, M. (1984). The Pennsylvania Infant and Family Development Project, I: Stability and change in mother-infant and father-infant interaction in a family setting at one, three, and nine months. *Child Development, 55,* 692–705.

Belsky, J., & Most, R. K. (1981). From exploration to play: A cross-sectional study of infant free play behavior. *Developmental Psychology, 17,* 630–639.

Belsky, J., & Steinberg, L. D. (1978). The effects of day care: A critical review. *Child Development, 49,* 929–949.

Belsky, J., Steinberg, L., & Draper, P. (1991). Childhood experience, interpersonal development, and reproductive strategy: An evolutionary theory of socialization. *Child Development, 62,* 647–670.

Bem, S. (1981). Gender schema theory: A cognitive account of sex typing. *Psychological Review, 88,* 354–364.

Bem, S. L. (1989). Genital knowledge and gender constancy in preschool children. *Child Development, 60,* 649–662.

Benbow, C. P., & Stanley, J. C. (1983). Sex differences in mathematical reasoning ability: More facts. *Science, 222,* 1028–1031.

Benbow, C. P., & Stanley, J. C. (1981). Mathematical ability—is sex a factor? *Science, 212,* 118.

Bender, L. (1955). Twenty years of research on schizophrenic children with special reference to those under twenty years of age. In G. Kaplan (Ed.), *Emotional problems of early childhood.* New York: Basic Books.

Benedict, H. (1979). Early lexical development: Comprehension and production. *Journal of Child Language, 6,* 183–200.

Benhar, E. E., Carlton, P. L., & Samuel, D. (1975). A search for mirror-image reinforcement and self-recognition in the baboon. In S. Kondo, M. Kawai, & A. Ehara (Eds.), *Contemporary primatology: Proceedings of the Fifth International Congress of Primatology.* Basel, Switzerland: Karger.

Berbaum, M. L., Markus, G. B., & Zajonc, R. B. (1982). A closer look at Galbraith's "closer look". *Developmental Psychology, 18,* 181–191.

Berbaum, M. L., & Moreland, R. L. (1985). Intellectual development within transracial adoptive families: Retesting the confluence model. *Child Development, 56,* 207–216.

Berbaum, M. L., Moreland, R. L., & Zajonc, R. B. (1986). Contentions over the confluence model: A reply to Price, Walsh, and Vilburg. *Psychological Bulletin, 100,* 270–274.

Berenbaum, S. A., & Hines, M. (1992). Early androgens are related to childhood sex-typed toy preferences. *Psychological Science, 3,* 203–206.

Berk, L. (1986, May). Private speech. *Psychology Today,* pp. 35–39.

Berkeley Planning Associates. (1977, December). *Evaluation of child abuse and neglect demonstration projects 1974–1977: Vol. II. Final Report.* Berkeley, Calif.: Author. (NTIS No. PB-278 439).

Berko, J. (1958). The child's learning of English morphology. *Word, 14,* 150–177.

Berkowitz, L. (1965). Some additional considerations. In L. Berkowitz (Ed.), *Advances in experimental social psychology* (Vol. 2). New York: Academic Press.

Berkowitz, L. (1983). Aversively stimulated aggression: Some parallels and differences in research with animals and humans. *American Psychologist, 38,* 1135–1144.

Berndt, T. J., & Bulleit, T. N. (1985). Effects of sibling relationships on preschoolers' behavior at home and at school. *Developmental Psychology, 21,* 761–767.

Berndt, T. J., Hawkins, J. A., & Hoyle, S. G. (1986). Changes in friendship during a school year: Effects on children's and adolescents' impressions of friendship and sharing with friends. *Child Development, 57,* 1284–1297.

Berndt, T. J., & Perry, T. B. (1986). Children's perceptions of friendship as supportive relationships. *Developmental Psychology, 22,* 640–648.

Berreby, D. (1992 April). Kids, creoles, and the coconuts. *Discover,* pp. 44–53.

Bertenthal, B. I., & Campos, J. J. (1987). New directions in the study of early experience. *Child Development, 58,* 560–567.

Bertenthal, B. I., Proffitt, D. R., Spetner, N. B., & Thomas, M. A. (1985). The development of infant sensitivity to biomechanical motions. *Child Development, 56,* 531–543.

Bettelheim, B. (1967). *The empty fortress: Infantile autism and the birth of the self.* New York: Free Press.

Bhattacharya, A., Shukla, R., Bornschein, R., Dietrich, K., & Kopke, J. E. (1988). Postural disequilibrium quantification in children with chronic lead exposure: A pilot study. *Neurotoxicology, 9,* 327–340.

Bianchi, B. D., & Bakeman, R. (1983). Patterns of sex typing in an open school. In M. B. Liss (Ed.), *Social and cognitive skills: Sex roles and children's play* (pp. 219–233). New York: Academic Press.

Bierman, K. L., & Furman, W. (1984). The effects of social skills training and peer involvement on the social adjustment of preadolescents. *Child Development, 55,* 151–162.

Birch, H. G. (1945). The role of motivational factors in insightful problem-solving. *Journal of Comparative Psychology, 38,* 295–317.

Birch, H. G., & Gussow, J. D. (1970). *Disadvantaged children: Health, nutrition and school failure.* New York: Grune & Stratton.

Birnbaum, J. A. (1975). Life patterns and self-esteem in gifted family oriented and career committed women. In M. S. Mednick, S. S. Tangri, & L. W. Hoffman (Eds.), *Women and achievement.* Washington, D.C.: Hemisphere.

Birnholz, J. C., & Benacerraf, B. R. (1983). The development of human fetal hearing. Science, 222, 516–518.

Birns, B., & Sternglanz, S. H. (1983). Sex-role socialization: Looking back and looking ahead. In M. B. Liss (Ed.), *Social and cognitive skills: Sex roles and children's play* (pp. 235–251). New York: Academic Press.

Bitterman, M. E. (1969). Thorndike and the problem of animal intelligence. *American Psychologist, 24,* 444–453.

Bixenstine, V. E., DeCorte, M. S., & Bixenstine, B. A. (1976). Conformity to peer-sponsored misconduct at four grade levels. *Developmental Psychology, 12,* 226–236.

Bjorklund, D. F., & Green, B. L. (1992). The adaptive nature of cognitive immaturity. *American Psychologist, 47,* 46–54.

Black, B., & Hazen, N. L. (1990). Social status and patterns of communication in acquainted and unacquainted preschool children. *Developmental Psychology, 26,* 379–387.

Blake, J. (1989). Number of Siblings and educational attainment. *Science, 245,* 32–36.

Blasi, A., & Hoeffel, E. C. (1974). Adolescence and formal operations. *Human Development, 17,* 344–363.

Blatz, W. E. (1928). Development and training of control of the bladder. *Genetic Psychology Monographs, 4,* 116.

Blewitt, P. (1983). Dog versus collie: Vocabulary in speech to young children. *Developmental Psychology, 19,* 602–609.

Block, J. (1982). Assimilation, accommodation, and the dynamics of personality development. *Child Development, 53,* 281–295.

Block, J. H., Block, J., & Gjerde, P. F. (1986). The personality of children prior to divorce: A prospective study. *Child Development, 57,* 827–840.

Bloom, B. S. (1964). *Stability and change in human characteristics.* New York: Wiley.

Bloom, L., & Capatides, J. B. (1987). Expression of affect and the emergence of language. *Child Development, 58,* 1513–1522.

Bock, K. (1990). Structure in language: Creating form in talk. *American Psychologist, 45,* 1221–1236.

Boggiano, A. K., Klinger, C. A., & Main, D. S. (1986). Enhancing interest in peer interaction: A developmental analysis. *Child Development, 57,* 852–861.

Bohannon, J. N., III, & Stanowicz, L. (1988). The issue of negative evidence: Adult responses to children's language errors. *Developmental Psychology, 24,* 684–689.

Bouchard, T. J., Jr., Lykken, D. T., McGue, M., Segal, N. L., & Tellegen, A. (1990). Sources of human psychological differences: The Minnesota study of twins reared apart. *Science, 250,* 223–228.

Bouchard, T. J., Jr., Lykken, D. T., McGue, M., Segal, N. L., & Tellegen, A. (1991). Response to Dudley. *Science, 252,* 191–192.

Bouchard, T. J., Jr., & McGue, M. (1981). Familial studies of intelligence: A review. *Science, 212,* 1055–1059.

Bower, B. (1985, April 27). Caution: Emotions at play. *Science News,* pp. 266–267.

Bower, B. (1988, August 27). Retardation: The eyes have it. *Science News,* p. 140.

Bower, B. (1989a, August 19). Teenagers reap broad benefits from "authoritative" parents. *Science News,* pp. 117–118.

Bower, B. (1989b, May 27). Kids talk about the "good pill." *Science News,* p. 332.

Bower, B. (1991, November 30). Females show strong capacity for aggression. *Science News,* p. 359.

Bower, T. G. R. (1979). *Human development.* San Francisco: W. H. Freeman.

Bowlby, J. (1958). The nature of the child's tie to his mother. *International Journal of Psycho-Analysis, 39,* 350–373.

Bowlby, J. (1969). *Attachment and loss* (Vol. 1). New York: Basic Books.

Bowlby, J. (1973). *Separation and loss.* New York: Basic Books.

Bowlby, J. (1982a). Attachment and loss: Retrospect and prospect. *American Journal of Orthopsychiatry, 52,* 664–678.

Bowlby, J. (1982b). *Attachment and loss: Vol. 1. Attachment* (2nd ed.). New York: Basic Books.

Boxer, A. M., Gershenson, H. P., & Offer, D. (1984). Historical time and social change in adolescent experience. *New Directions for Mental Health Services,* No. 22, 83–95.

Brackbill, Y. (1958). Extinction of the smiling response in infants as a function of reinforcement schedule. *Child Development, 29,* 115–124.

Braine, M. D. S. (1963). The ontogeny of English phrase structure: The first phase. *Language, 39*(1), 1–13.

Brains: The younger the better. (1979, August 4). *Science News,* p. 89.

Brand, C. (1987). Intelligence testing: Bryter still and bryter? *Nature, 328,* 110.

Braungart, J. M., Plomin, R., DeFries, J. C., & Fulker, D. W. (1992). Genetic influence on tester-rated infant temperament as assessed by Bayley's Infant Behavior Record: Nonadoptive and adoptive siblings and twins. *Developmental Psychology, 28,* 40–47.

Brazelton, T. B. (1990). Saving the bathwater. *Child Development, 61,* 1661–1671.

Bretherton, I. (1985). Attachment theory: Retrospect and prospect. *Monographs of the Society for Research in Child Development, 50*(1–2, Serial No. 209), 3–35.

Bretherton, I., Fritz, J., Zahn-Waxler, C., & Ridgeway, D. (1986). Learning to talk about emotions: A functionalist perspective. *Child Development, 57,* 529–548.

Bretherton, I., & Waters, E. (Eds.). (1985). Growing points of attachment theory and research. *Monographs of the Society for Research in Child Development, 50*(1–2, Serial No. 209).

Bridges, L. J., Connell, J. P., & Belsky, J. (1988). Similarities and differences in infant-mother and infant-father interaction in the strange situation: A component process analysis. *Developmental Psychology, 24,* 92–100.

Brittain, C. V. (1963). Adolescent choices and parent-peer cross-pressures. *American Sociological Review, 28,* 385–391.

Brody, G. H., Stoneman, Z., MacKinnon, C. E., & MacKinnon, R. (1985). Role relationships and behavior between preschool-aged and school-aged sibling pairs. *Developmental Psychology, 21,* 124–129.

Brodzinsky, D. M., Singer, L. M., & Braff, A. M. (1984). Children's understanding of adoption. *Child Development, 55,* 869–878.

Broman, S. H., Nichols, P. L., & Kennedy, W. A. (1975). *Preschool IQ: Prenatal and early developmental correlates.* Hillsdale, NJ: Lawrence Erlbaum.

Bronfenbrenner, U. (1970). *Two worlds of childhood: U.S. and U.S.S.R.* New York: Russell Sage.

Bronfenbrenner, U., Alvarez, W. F., & Henderson, C. R. (1984). Working and watching: Maternal employment status and parents' perceptions of their three-year-old children. *Child Development, 55,* 1362–1378.

Bronowski, J. (1973). *The ascent of man.* Boston: Little, Brown.

Bronson, W. C. (1981). *Toddlers' behaviors with agemates: Issues of interaction, cognition, and affect.* Norwood, NJ: Ablex.

Bronson, W. C. (1985). Growth in the organization of behavior over the second year of life. *Developmental Psychology, 21,* 108–117.

Brooks-Gunn, J., Burrow, C., & Warren, M. P. (1988). Attitudes toward eating and body weight in different groups of female adolescent athletes. *International Journal of Eating Disorders, 7*(6).

Brooks-Gunn, J., & Lewis, M. (1981). Infant social perception: Responses to pictures of parents and strangers. *Developmental Psychology, 17,* 647–649.

Broverman, I. K., Vogel, S. R., Broverman, D. M., Clarkson, F. E., & Rosenkrantz, P. S. (1972). Sex-role stereotypes: A current appraisal. *Journal of Social Issues, 28*(2), 59–78.

Brown, A. L. (1973). Judgments of recency for long sequences of pictures: The absence of a developmental trend. *Journal of Experimental Child Psychology, 15,* 473–480.

Brown, B. B., Clasen, D. R., & Eicher, S. A. (1986). Perceptions of peer pressure, peer conformity dispositions, and self-reported behavior among adolescents. *Developmental Psychology, 22,* 521–530.

Brown, B. B., Eicher, S. A., & Petrie, S. (1986). The importance of peer group ("crowd") affiliation in adolescence. *Journal of Adolescence, 9,* 73–96.

Brown, B. B., Lohr, M. J., & McClenahan, E. L. (1986). Early adolescents' perceptions of peer pressure. *Journal of Early Adolescence, 6,* 139–154.

Brown, J. B. (1984). Examination of grammatical morphemes in the language of hard-of-hearing children. *Volta Review, 86,* 229–238.

Brown, R. (1973). *The first language: The early stages.* Cambridge, Mass.: Harvard Univ. Press.

Brown, R., & Hanlon, C. (1970). Derivational complexity and order of acquisition in child speech. In J. R. Hayes (Ed.), *Cognition and the development of language.* New York: John Wiley.

Brown, W. T., Jenkins, E. C., Friedman, E., Brooks, J., Wisniewski, K., Raguthu, S., & French, J. (1982). Autism is associated with the fragile-X syndrome. *Journal of Autism and Developmental Disorders, 12,* 303–308.

Brownell, C. A. (1990). Peer social skills in toddlers: Competencies and constraints illustrated by same-age and mixed-age interaction. *Child Development, 61,* 838–848.

Brownell, C. A., & Carriger, M. S. (1990). Changes in cooperation and self-other differentiation during the second year. *Child Development, 61,* 1164–1174.

Brumberg, J. J. (1985). "Fasting girls": Reflections on writing the history of anorexia nervosa. In A. B. Smuts & J. W. Hagen (Eds.), History and research in child development. *Monographs of the Society for Research in Child Development 50*(4–5, Serial No. 211), 93–104.

Bruner, J. S. (1983). *Child's talk.* New York: Norton.

Brunk, M. A., & Henggeler, S. W. (1984). Child influences on adult controls: An experimental investigation. *Developmental Psychology, 20,* 1074–1081.

Bryan, J. H. (1970). Children's reactions to helpers: Their money isn't where their mouths are. In J. Macaulay, & L. Berkowitz (Eds.), *Altruism and helping behavior* (pp. 61–73). New York: Academic Press.

Bryan, J. H. (1975). Children's cooperation and helping behaviors. In E. M. Hetherington (Ed.), *Review of child development research* (Vol. 5). Chicago, IL: Univ. of Chicago Press.

Buchanan, C. M., Eccles, J. S., & Becker, J. B. (1992). Are adolescents the victims of raging hormones: Evidence for activational effects of hormones on moods and behavior at adolescence. *Psychological Bulletin, 111,* 62–107.

Buckley, N., Siegel, L. S., & Ness, S. (1979). Egocentrism, empathy, and altruistic behavior in young children. *Developmental Psychology, 15,* 329–330.

Buckley, W. E., Yesalis, C. E., III., Friedl, K. E., Anderson, W. A., Streit, A. L., & Wright, J. E. (1988). Estimated prevalence of anabolic steroid use among male high school seniors. *Journal of the American Medical Association, 260,* 3441–3445.

Buhrmester, D., & Furman, W. (1987). The development of companionship and intimacy. *Child Development, 58,* 1101–1113.

Buhrmester, D., & Furman, W. (1990). Perceptions of sibling relationships during middle childhood and adolescence. *Child Development, 61,* 1387–1398.

Bullen, B. A., Skrinar, G. S., Beitins, I. Z., von Mering, G., Turnbull, B. A., & McArthur, J. W. (1985). Induction of menstrual disorders by strenuous exercise in untrained women. *New England Journal of Medicine, 312,* 1349–1353.

Bullock, M. (1985). Animism in childhood thinking: A new look at an old question. *Developmental Psychology, 21,* 217–225.

Bullough, V. L. (1981). Age at menarche: A misunderstanding. *Science, 213,* 365–366.

Burchinal, M., Lee, M., & Ramey, C. (1989). Type of day-care and preschool intellectual development in disadvantaged children. *Child Development, 60,* 128–137.

Bushnell, E. W., Shaw, L., & Strauss, D. (1985). Relationship between visual and tactual exploration by 6-month-olds. *Developmental Psychology, 21,* 591–600.

Cadoret, R. J., O'Gorman, T. W., Heywood, E., & Troughton, E. (1985). Genetic and environmental factors in major depression. *Journal of Affective Disorders, 9,* 155–164.

Cahan, S., & Cohen, N. (1989). Age versus schooling effects on intelligence development. *Child Development, 60,* 1239–1249.

Cairns, R. B., Cairns, B. D., & Neckerman, H. J. (1989). Early school dropout: Configurations and determinants. *Child Development, 60,* 1437–1452.

Caldera, Y. M., Huston, A. C., & O'Brien, M. (1989). Social interactions and play patterns of parents and toddlers with feminine, masculine, and neutral toys. *Child Development, 60,* 70–76.

Campbell, T. (1982). *Formal cues and content difficulty as determinants of children's cognitive processing of televised educational messages.* Unpublished doctoral dissertation, University of Kansas.

Campos, J. J., Barrett, K. G., Lamb, M. E., Stenberg, C., & Goldsmith, H. H. (1983). Socioemotional development. In M. M. Haith & J. J. Campos (Eds.), *Infancy and developmental psychology.* In P. H. Mussen (Gen. Ed.), *Handbook of child psychology.* New York: Wiley.

Campos, J. J., Hiatt, S., Ramsay, D., Henderson, C., & Svejda, M. (1978). The emergence of fear on the visual cliff. In M. Lewis, & L. A. Rosenblum (Eds.), *The development of affect* (pp. 149–182). New York: Plenum Press.

Camras, L. A. (1988, April). Darwin revisited: An infant's first emotional facial expressions. In H. Oster (Chair), *Emotional expressions in infants: New perspectives on an old controversy.* International Conference on Infant Studies, Washington, DC.

Caplan, P. J., MacPherson, G. M., & Tobin, P. (1985). Do sex-related differences in spatial abilities exist? A multilevel critique with new data. *American Psychologist, 40,* 786–799.

Carey, S. (1985). *Conceptual change in childhood.* Cambridge, MA: MIT/Bradford.

Carey, S., & Bartlett, E. (1978). Acquiring a single new word. *Papers and Reports on Child Language Development* (Department of Linguistics, Stanford University), *15,* 17–29.

Carey, W. B., & McDevitt, S. C. (1978). Stability and change in individual temperament diagnoses from infancy to early childhood. *Journal of the American Academy of Child Psychiatry, 17,* 331–337.

Carlson, G. A., & Cantwell, D. P. (1982). Diagnosis of childhood depression: A comparison of the Weinberg and DSM-III criteria. *Journal of the American Academy of Child Psychiatry, 21,* 247–250.

Carlson, V., Cicchetti, D., Barnett, D., & Braunwald, K. (1989). Disorganized/disoriented attachment relationships in maltreated infants. *Developmental Psychology, 25,* 525–531.

Caron, A. J., Caron, R. F., & Carlson, V. R. (1979). Infant perception of the invariant shape of objects varying in slant. *Child Development, 50,* 716–721.

Caron, R. F., Caron, A. J., & Myers, R. S. (1982). Abstraction of invariant face expressions in infancy. *Child Development, 53,* 1008–1015.

Carpenter, G. (1981, August). The importance of mother's milk. *Natural History,* p. 6.

Carr, M., Kurtz, B. E., Schneider, W., Turner, L. A., & Borkowski, J. G. (1989). Strategy acquisition and transfer among American and German children: Environmental influences on metacognitive development. *Developmental Psychology, 25,* 765–771.

Carroll, J. L., & Rest, J. R. (1982). Moral development. In B. B. Wolman (Ed.), *Handbook of developmental psychology* (pp. 434–467). Englewood Cliffs, NJ: Prentice-Hall.

Case, R. (1985). *Intellectual development.* Orlando, FL: Academic Press.

Casey, M. B. (1986). Individual differences in selective attention among prereaders: A key to mirror-image confusion. *Developmental Psychology, 22,* 58–66.

Casper, R. C. (1984). Hypothalamic dysfunction and symptoms of anorexia nervosa. *Psychiatry Clinica of North America, 7,* 201–213.

Caspi, A., Elder, G. H., Jr., & Bem, D. J. (1988). Moving away from the world: Life-course patterns of shy children. *Developmental Psychology, 24,* 824–831.

Cassidy, J., & Asher, S. R. (1992). Loneliness and peer relations in young children. *Child Development, 63,* 350–365.

Casto, G., & Mastropieri, M. A. (1986). The efficacy of early intervention programs: A meta-analysis. *Exceptional Children, 52,* 417–424.

Cattell, P. (1966). *The measurement of intelligence of infants and young children.* New York: Psychological Corporation.

Caudill, W., & Weinstein, H. (1969). Maternal care and infant behavior in Japan and America. *Psychiatry, 32,* 12–43.

Ceci, S. J. (1991). How much does schooling influence general intelligence and its cognitive components? A reassessment of the evidence. *Developmental Psychology, 27,* 703–722.

Cernoch, J. M., & Porter, R. H. (1985). Recognition of maternal axillary odors by infants. *Child Development, 56,* 1593–1598.

Chandler, M., & Boyes, M. (1982). Social-cognitive development. In B. B. Wolman (Ed.), *Handbook of developmental psychology.* Englewood Cliffs, NJ: Prentice-Hall.

Chapman, M., & Zahn-Waxler, C. (1981). *Young children's compliance and noncompliance to parental discipline in a natural setting.* Unpublished manuscript.

Chapman, M., Zahn-Waxler, C., Cooperman, G., & Iannotti, R. (1987). Empathy and responsibility in the motivation of children's helping. *Developmental Psychology, 23,* 140–145.

Chazan, S. E. (1981). Development of object permanence as a correlate of dimensions of maternal care. *Developmental Psychology, 17,* 79–81.

Chazotte, C., Madden, R., & Cohen, W. R. (1990). Labor patterns in women with previous cesareans. *Obstetrics & Gynecology, 75,* 350–355.

Cherlin, A. J., Furstenberg, F. F., Chase-Lansdale, P. L., & Kiernan, K. E. (1991). Longitudinal studies of effects of divorce on children in Great Britain and the United States. *Science, 252,* 1386–1389.

Cherry, F. F., & Eaton, E. L. (1977). Physical and cognitive development in children of low-income mothers working in the child's early years. *Child Development, 48,* 158–166.

Chess, S., & Thomas, A. (1982). Infant bonding: Mystique and reality. *American Journal of Orthopsychiatry, 52,* 213–222.

Chess, S., & Thomas, A. (Eds.). (1986a). Cross-cultural temperament studies. In S. Chess & A. Thomas (Eds.), *Annual progress in child psychiatry and child development* (pp. 353–354). New York: Brunner/Mazel.

Chess, S., & Thomas, A. (1986b). Developmental issues. In S. Chess & A. Thomas (Eds.), *Annual progress in child psychiatry and child development* (pp. 21–26). New York: Brunner/Mazel.

Chethik, M., Fleming, E., Mayer, M. F., & McCoy, J. N. (1967). A quest for identity. *American Journal of Orthopsychiatry, 37,* 71–77.

Chevalier-Skolnikoff, S. (1979). Kids. *Animal Kingdom, 82*(3), 11–18.

Chevalier-Skolnikoff, S. (1983). Sensorimotor development in orang-utans and other primates. *Journal of Human Evolution, 12,* 545–561.

Cheyne, J. A., & Rubin, K. H. (1983). Playful precursors of problem solving in preschoolers. *Developmental Psychology, 19,* 577–584.

Chi, M. T. (1978). Knowledge structures and memory development. In R. S. Siegler (Ed.), *Children's thinking: What develops?* Hillsdale, NJ: Erlbaum.

Childers, J. S., Durham, T. W., Bolen, L. M., & Taylor, L. H. (1985). A predictive validity study of the Kaufman Assessment Battery for Children with the California Achievement Test. *Psychology in the Schools, 22,* 29–33.

Chodorow, N. (1978). *The reproduction of mothering: Psychoanalysis and the sociology of gender.* Berkeley: University of California Press.

Chomsky, N. (1957). *Syntactic structures.* The Hague: Mouton.

Chugani, H. T., & Phelps, M. E. (1986). Maturational changes in cerebral function in infants determined by 18FDG positron emission tomography. *Science, 231,* 840–843.

Chumlea, W. M. (1982). Physical growth in adolescence. In B. B. Wolman (Ed.), *Handbook of developmental psychology* (pp. 471–485). Englewood Cliffs, NJ: Prentice-Hall.

Cicchetti, D. (1984). The emergence of developmental psychopathology. *Child Development, 55,* 1–7.

Cicirelli, V. G. (1982). Sibling influence throughout the lifespan. In M. E. Lamb & B. Sutton-Smith (Eds.), *Sibling relationships: Their nature and significance across the lifespan* (pp. 267–284). Hillsdale, NJ: Erlbaum.

Clark, H. H., & Clark, E. V. (1977). *Psychology and language: An introduction to psycholinguistics.* New York: Harcourt Brace.

Clark, K. B., & Clark, M. P. (1947). Racial identification and preference in Negro children. In T. M. Newcomb, & E. J. Hartley (Eds.), *Readings in social psychology.* New York: Holt.

Clark, M., & Gosnell, M. (1981, March 2). Childbirth sitting up. *Newsweek,* p. 79.

Clark, M., & Gosnell, M. (1982, March 22). Dealing with dyslexia. *Newsweek,* pp. 55–56.

Clark, R. W. (1971). *Einstein: The life and times.* New York: World Publishing.

Clarke-Stewart, K. A. (1977, March). *The father's impact on mother and child.* Paper presented at the biennial meeting of the Society for Research in Child Development, New Orleans, Louisiana.

Clarke-Stewart, K. A. (1980). The father's contribution to children's cognitive and social development in early childhood. In F. A. Pedersen (Ed.), *The father-infant relationship: Observational studies in the family setting.* New York: Praeger.

Clarke-Stewart, K. A., & Hevey, C. M. (1981). Longitudinal relations in repeated observations of mother-child interaction from 1 to 2½ years. *Developmental Psychology, 17,* 127–145.

Clarkson, M. G., & Berg, W. K. (1983). Cardiac orienting and vowel discrimination in newborns: Crucial stimulus parameters. *Child Development, 54,* 162–171.

Clarren, S. K., & Smith, D. W. (1978). The fetal alcohol syndrome. *New England Journal of Medicine, 298,* 1063–1067.

Clary, E. G., & Miller, J. (1986). Socialization and situational influences on sustained altruism. *Child Development, 57,* 1358–1369.

Clausen, J. A. (1968). Perspectives on childhood socialization. In J. Clausen (Ed.), *Socialization and society.* Boston: Little, Brown.

Clifton, R. K., Gwiazda, J., Bauer, J. A., Clarkson, M. G., & Held, R. M. (1988). Growth in head size during infancy: Implications for sound localization. *Developmental Psychology, 24,* 477–483.

Clifton, R., Perris, E., & Bullinger, A. (1991). Infants' perception of auditory space. *Developmental Psychology, 27,* 187–197.

Coburn, J. (1974). Sterilization regulations: Debate not quelled by HEW document. *Science, 183,* 935–939.

Coe, C. L., Rosenberg, L. T., Fischer, M., & Levine, S. (1987). Psychological factors capable of preventing the inhibition of antibody responses in separated infant monkeys. *Child Development, 58,* 1420–1430.

Cohen, S. (1971). Peers as modeling and normative influences in the development of aggression. *Psychological Reports, 28,* 995–998.

Cohn, D. A. (1990). Child-mother attachment of six-year-olds and social competence at school. *Child Development, 61,* 152–162.

Coie, J. D., Dodge, K. A., Terry, R., & Wright, V. (1991). The role of aggression in peer relations: An analysis of aggression episodes in boys' play groups. *Child Development, 62,* 812–826.

Coie, J. D., & Kupersmidt, J. B. (1983). A behavioral analysis of emerging social status in boys' groups. *Child Development, 54,* 1400–1416.

Colby, A., Kohlberg, L., Gibbs, J., & Lieberman, M. (1983). A longitudinal study of moral judgment. *Monographs of the Society for Research in Child Development, 48*(1–2, Serial No. 200).

Cole, M., & Scribner, S. (1977). Cross-cultural studies of memory and cognition. In R. V. Kail, & J. W. Hagen (Eds.), *Perspectives on the development of memory and cognition.* Hillsdale, NJ: Lawrence Erlbaum.

Cole, S. O., & Moore, S. F. (1975). Stimulants and hyperkinesis: Drug use or abuse? *Journal of Drug Education, 5,* 371–379.

Coleman, J. S., Campbell, E. Q. Hobson, C. J., McPartland, J., Mood, A. M., Weinfeld, F. D., & York, R. L. (1966). *Equality of educational opportunity. Report from Office of Education.* Washington, DC: U.S. Govt. Printing Office.

Coles, C. D., Smith, I., Fernhoff, P. M., & Falek, A. (1985). Neonatal neurobehavioral characteristics as correlates of maternal alcohol use during gestation. *Alcoholism, 9,* 454–460.

Collard, R. R. (1968). Social and play responses of first-born and laterborn infants in an unfamiliar situation. *Child Development, 39,* 325–334.

Commons, M. L., Richards, F. A., & Kuhn, D. (1982). Systematic and metasystematic reasoning: A case for levels of reasoning beyond Piaget's stage of formal operations. *Child Development, 53,* 1058–1069.

Comstock, M. L. C. (1973). Effects of perceived parental behavior on selfesteem and adjustment. *Dissertation Abstracts, 34,* 465B.

Condry, J., & Condry, S. (1977). Sex differences: A study of the eye of the beholder. *Annual Progress in Child Psychiatry and Child Development, 1977,* 289–301.

Condry, J. C., & Ross, D. F. (1985). Sex and aggression: The influence of gender label on the perception of aggression in children. *Child Development, 53,* 1008–1016.

Condry, J. C., Siman, M. L., & Bronfenbrenner, U. (1968). *Characteristics of peers and adult-oriented children.* Unpublished manuscript, Cornell University.

Connolly, J. A., & Doyle, A. (1984). Relation of social fantasy play to social competence in preschoolers. *Developmental Psychology, 20,* 797–806.

Connolly, J., Doyle, A., & Ceschin, F. (1983). Forms and functions of social fantasy play in preschoolers. In M. B. Liss (Ed.), *Social and cognitive skills: Sex roles and children's play* (pp. 71–92). New York: Academic Press.

Coon, D. (1986). *Introduction to psychology: Exploration and application.* St. Paul, Minn.: West Publishing Company.

Cooper, C. R. (1977, March). *Collaboration in children: Dyadic interaction skills in problem solving.* Paper presented at the meeting of the Society for Research in Child Development, New Orleans, Louisiana.

Coopersmith, S. (1967). *The antecedents of self-esteem.* San Francisco: W. H. Freeman.

Cordes, C. (1985, March). Team maps children's emotional milestones. *APA Monitor,* pp. 32–33.

Coren, S., & Porac, C. (1977). Fifty centuries of right-handedness: The historical record. *Science, 198,* 631–632.

Costa, P. T., Jr., & McCrae, R. R. (1980). Still stable after all these years: Personality as a key to some issues in adulthood and old age. In P. B. Baltes, & O. G. Brim (Eds.), *Life-span development and behavior* (Vol. 3, pp. 65–102). New York: Academic Press.

Costello, E. J., Costello, A. J., Edelbrock, C., Burns, B. J., Dulcan, M. K., Brent, D., & Janiszewski, S. (1988). Psychiatric disorders in pediatric primary care. Prevalence and risk factors. *Archives of General Psychiatry, 45,* 1107–1116.

Cowan, C. T., & Cowan, P. A. (1987). Men's involvement in parenthood: Identifying the antecedents and understanding the barriers. In P. Berman, & F. A. Pedersen (Eds.), *Fathers' transitions to parenthood.* Hillsdale, NJ: Erlbaum.

Cowart, B. J. (1981). Development of taste perception in humans: Sensitivity and preference throughout the lifespan. *Psychological Bulletin, 90,* 43–73.

Cox, B. D., Ornstein, P. A., Naus, M. J., Maxfield, D., & Zimler, J. (1989). Children's concurrent use of rehearsal and organizational strategies. *Developmental Psychology, 25,* 619–627.

Crain-Thoreson, C., & Dale, P. S. (1992). Do early talkers become early readers? Linguistic precocity, preschool language, and emergent literacy. *Developmental Psychology, 28,* 421–429.

Cravens, H. (1992). A scientific project locked in time: The Terman genetic studies of genius, 1920s-1950s. *American Psychologist, 47,* 183–189.

Crick, F. (1981). *Life itself.* New York: Simon & Shuster.

Cronbach, L. J. (1970). *Essentials of psychological testing.* New York: Harper.

Crouter, A. C., MacDermid, S. M., McHale, S. M., & Perry-Jenkins, M. (1990). Parental monitoring and preceptions of children's school performance and conduct in dual- and single-earner families. *Developmental Psychology, 26,* 649–657.

Crowell, J. A., & Feldman, S. S. (1988). Mothers' internal models of relationships and children's behavioral and developmental status: A study of mother-child interaction. *Child Development, 59,* 1273–1285.

Crowell, J. A., & Feldman, S. S. (1991). Mothers' working models of attachment relationships and mother and child behavior during separation and return. *Developmental Psychology, 27,* 597–605.

Crowley, P. H., Gulati, D. K., Hayden, T. L., Lopez, P., & Dyer, R. (1979). A chiasma-hormonal hypothesis relating Down's syndrome to maternal age. *Nature, 280,* 417–419.

Cummings, E. M., Iannotti, R. J., & Zahn-Waxler, C. (1985). Influence of conflict between adults on the emotions and aggression of young children. *Developmental Psychology, 21,* 495–507.

Cummings, L. L. (1991, November). *Fighting by the rules: Women streetfighting in Chihuahua, Chihuahua, Mexico.* Paper presented at the annual meeting of the American Anthropological Association, Chicago, Illinois.

Curtis, R. L. (1975). Adolescent orientations toward parents and peers: Variations by sex, age, and socioeconomic status. *Adolescence, 10,* 483–494.

Cutting, J. E., Proffitt, D. R., & Kozlowski, L. T. (1978). A biomechanical invariant for gait perception. *Journal of Experimental Psychology: Human Perception and Performance, 4,* 357–372.

Daffos, F., Forestier, F., Capella-Pavlovsky, M., Thulliez, P., Aufrant, C., Valenti, D., & Cox, W. L. (1988). Prenatal management of 746 pregnancies at risk for congenital toxoplasmosis. *New England Journal of Medicine, 318,* 271–275.

Dannemiller, J. L., & Stephens, B. R. (1988). A critical test of infant pattern preference models. *Child Development, 59,* 210–216.

Danner, F. W., & Day, M. C. (1977). Eliciting formal operations. *Child Development, 48,* 1600–1606.

Darwin, C. (1967). *The expression of the emotions in man and animals.* Chicago: Univ. of Chicago Press. (Original work published 1872)

Datta, L. (1973, October). New directions for early child development programs: Some findings from research. Urbana, Ill.: ERIC Clearinghouse on Early Childhood Education. (ED 081 501).

Davidson, L. E., Rosenberg, M. L., Mercy, J. A., Franklin, J., & Simmons, J. T. (1989). An epidemiologic study of risk factors in two teenage suicide clusters. *Journal of the American Medical Association, 262,* 2687–2692.

Davis, D. J., Cahan, S., & Bashi, J. (1977). Birth order and intellectual development: The confluence model in the light of cross-cultural evidence. *Science, 196,* 1470–1472.

Davis, E. A. (1937). *The development of linguistic skills in twins, single twins with siblings, and only children from age 5 to 10 years.* Minneapolis: University of Minnesota Press, Institute of Child Welfare Series, No. 14.

Day, M. C. (1975). Developmental trends in visual scanning. In H. W. Reese (Ed.), *Advances in child development and behavior* (Vol. 10). New York: Academic Press.

Dean, A. L., Malik, M. M., Richards, W., & Stringer, S. A. (1986). Effects of parental maltreatment on children's conceptions of interpersonal relationships. *Developmental Psychology, 22,* 617–626.

deBoysson-Bardies, B., Sagart, L., & Durand, C. (1984). Discernible differences in the babbling of infants according to target language. *Journal of Child Language, 11,* 1–15.

DeCasper, A. J., & Fifer, W. P. (1980). Of human bonding: Newborns prefer their mothers' voices. *Science, 208,* 1174–1176.

DeLoache, J. S., Cassidy, D. J., & Brown, A. L. (1985). Precursors of mnemonic strategies in very young children's memory. *Child Development, 56,* 125–137.

DeMeis, D. K., Hock, E., & McBride, S. L. (1986). The balance of employment and motherhood: Longitudinal study of mothers' feelings about separation from their first-born infants. *Developmental Psychology, 22,* 627–632.

Demitrack, M. A., Kalogeras, K. T., Altemus, M., Pigott, T. A., Listwak, S. J., & Gold, P. W. (1992). Plasma and cerebrospinal fluid measures of arginine vasopressin secretion in patients with bulimia nervosa and in healthy subjects. *Journal of Clinical Endocrinology, 74,* 1277–1283.

Dennis, W. (1973). Children of the creche. New York: Appleton-Century-Crofts.

deVilliers, J. G., & deVilliers, P. A. (1973). A cross-sectional study of the acquisition of grammatical morphemes in child speech. *Journal of Psycholinguistic Research, 2,* 267–278. deVries, M. W. (1984). Temperament and infant mortality among the Masai of East Africa. *The American Journal of Psychiatry, 141,* 1189–1194.

deVries, M. W., & Sameroff, A. J. (1984). Culture and temperament: Influences on infant temperament in three East African societies. *American Journal of Orthopsychiatry, 54,* 83–96.

Diamond, J. (1990, December). War babies. *Discover,* pp. 70–75.

Diaz, J., & Samson, H. H. (1980). Impaired brain growth in neonatal rats exposed to ethanol. *Science, 208,* 751–753.

Diaz, R. M., & Berndt, T. J. (1982). Children's knowledge of a best friend: Fact or fancy? *Developmental Psychology, 18,* 787–794.

Dickerson, R. E. (1978). Chemical evolution and the origin of life. *Scientific American, 239*(3), 70–86.

Dickinson, D. K. (1984). First impressions: Children's knowledge of words gained from a single exposure. *Applied Psycholinguistics, 5,* 359–373.

Dickstein, S., Thompson, R. A., Estes, D., Malkin, C., & Lamb, M. E. (1984). Social referencing and the security of attachment. *Infant Behavior and Development, 7,* 507–516.

Diepold, J., & Young, R. D. (1979). Empirical studies of adolescent sexual behavior: A critical review. *Adolescence, 14,* 45–64.

Dietz, W. H., Jr., & Gortmaker, S. L. (1985). Do we fatten our children at the television set? Obesity and television viewing in children and adolescents. *Pediatrics, 75,* 807–812.

DiLalla, L. F., Thompson, L. A., Plomin, R., Phillips, K., Fagan, J. F., III., Haith, M. M., Cyphers, L. H., & Fulker, D. W. (1990). Infant predictors of preschool and adult IQ: A study of infant twins and their parents. *Developmental Psychology, 26,* 759–769.

Dion, K. K. (1973). Young children's stereotyping of facial attractiveness. *Developmental Psychology, 9,* 183–188.

Dishion, T. J., Patterson, G. R., Stoolmiller, M., & Skinner, M. L. (1991). Family, school, and behavioral antecedents to early adolescent involvement with antisocial peers. *Developmental Psychology, 27,* 172–180.

Dodge, K. A., Bates, J. E., & Pettit, G. S. (1990). Mechanisms in the cycle of violence. *Science, 250,* 1678–1683.

Dodge, K. A., Coie, J. D., & Brakke, N. P. (1982). Behavior patterns of socially rejected and neglected preadolescents: The roles of social approach and aggression. *Journal of Abnormal Child Psychology, 10,* 389–410.

Dodge, K. A., Coie, J. D., Pettit, G. S., & Price, J. M. (1990). Peer status and aggression in boys' groups: Developmental and contextual analyses. *Child Development, 61,* 1289–1309.

Doering, P. L., & Stewart, R. B. (1978). The extent and character of drug consumption during pregnancy. *Journal of the American Medical Association, 239,* 843–846.

Doi, T. (1962). Amae: A key concept for understanding Japanese personality structure. In R. Smith & R. Beardsley (Eds.), *Japanese culture: Its development and characteristics.* New York: Wenner Gren Foundation for Anthropological Research.

Doi, T. (1973). *The anatomy of dependence.* Tokyo: Kodansha.

Doi, T. (1981). *The structure of dependency.* New York: Kodansha International.

Dolgin, K. G., & Behrend, D. A. (1984). Children's knowledge about animates and inanimates. *Child Development, 55,* 1646–1650.

Dollard, J., Doob, L. W., Miller, N. E., Mowrer, O. H., & Sears, R. R. (1939). *Frustration and aggression.* New Haven, CT: Yale University Press.

Dominick, J. R., & Greenberg, B. S. (1972). Attitudes toward violence: The interaction of television exposure, family attitudes and social class. In G. A. Comstock, & E. A. Rubinstein (Eds.), *Television and social behavior, Volume 3: Television and adolescent aggressiveness* (pp. 314–335). Washington, D.C.: U.S. Government Printing Office.

Donovan, W. L., & Leavitt, L. A. (1985). Simulating conditions of learned helplessness: The effects of interventions and attributions. *Child Development, 56,* 594–603.

Donovan, W. L., Leavitt, L. A., & Balling, J. D. (1978). Maternal physiological response to infant signals. *Psychophysiology, 15,* 68–74.

Douglas, J. H. (1978, March 11). Pioneering a non-western psychology. *Science News,* pp. 154–158.

Douglas, J. H., & Miller, J. A. (1977, September 10). Record breaking women. *Science News,* pp. 172–174.

Douvan, E., & Adelson, J. (1966). *The adolescent experience.* New York: Wiley.

Doyle, A. B., Doehring, P., Tessier, O., de Lorimier, S., & Shapiro, S. (1992). Transitions in children's play: A sequential analysis of states preceding and following social pretense. *Developmental Psychology, 28,* 137–144.

Dreyer, P. H. (1982). Sexuality during adolescence. In B. B. Wolman (Ed.), *Handbook of developmental psychology* pp. 559–601). Englewood Cliffs, NJ: Prentice-Hall.

Dudley, R. M. (1991). IQ and heredity. *Science, 252,* 191.

Dunn, J. (1983). Sibling relationships in early childhood. *Child Development, 54,* 787–811.

Dunn, J. (1984). *Sisters and brothers.* London: Fontana.

Dunn, J., & Kendrick, C. (1982a). Siblings and their mothers: Developing relationships within the family. In M. E. Lamb & B. Sutton-Smith (Eds.), *Sibling relationships: Their nature and significance across the lifespan* (pp. 39–60). Hillsdale, NJ: Erlbaum.

Dunn, J., & Kendrick, D. (1982b). *Siblings: Love, envy, and understanding.* Cambridge, MA: Harvard University Press.

Dunn, J., & Munn, P. (1985). Becoming a family member: Family conflict and the development of social understanding in the second year. *Child Development, 56,* 480–492.

Dunn, J. F., Plomin, R., & Daniels, D. (1986). Consistency and change in mothers' behavior toward young siblings. *Child Development, 57,* 348–356.

Durkheim, E. (1925). *Moral education.* New York: Free Press.

Dusek, J. B. (1977). *Adolescent development and behavior.* Chicago: Science Research Assoc.

Duyme, M. (1988). School success and social class: An adoption study. *Developmental Psychology, 24,* 203–209.

Dweck, C. S., Davidson, W., Nelson, S., & Enna, B. (1978). Sex differences in learned helplessness, II: The contingencies of evaluative feedback in the classroom and III: An experimental analysis. *Developmental Psychology, 14,* 268–276.

Earls, F. E., & Jung, K. G. (1988). Temperament and home environment characteristics as causal factors in the early development of childhood psychopathology. In S. Chess, A. Thomas, & M. E. Hertzig (Eds.), *Annual progress in child psychiatry and child development* (pp. 373–393). New York: Brunner/Mazel.

East, P. L., & Rook, K. S. (1992). Compensatory patterns of support among children's peer relationships: A test using school friends, non-school friends, and siblings. *Developmental Psychology, 28,* 163–172.

Easterbrooks, M. A., & Goldberg, W. A. (1985). Effects of early maternal employment on toddlers, mothers, and fathers. *Developmental Psychology, 21,* 774–783.

Eaton, W. O., Chipperfield, J. C., & Singbeil, C. E. (1989). Birth order and activity level in children. *Developmental Psychology, 25,* 668–672.

Eccles-Parsons, J. (1982). Biology, experience and sex dimorphic behaviors. In W. Gove & G. R. Carpenter (Eds.), *The fundamental connection between nature and nurture: A review of the evidence.* Lexington, Mass.: Lexington Books.

Eckerman, C. O., Davis, C. C., & Didow, S. M. (1989). Toddlers' emerging ways of achieving social coordinations with a peer. *Child Development, 60,* 440–453.

Eckerman, C. O., Whatley, J. L., & Kutz, S. L. (1975). Growth of social play with peers during the second year of life. *Developmental Psychology, 11,* 42–49.

Egeland, B., Breitenbucher, M., & Rosenberg, D. (1980). Prospective study of the significance of life stress in the etiology of child abuse. *Journal of Consulting and Clinical Psychology, 48,* 195–205.

Egeland, B., & Farber, E. A. (1984). Infant-mother attachment: Factors related to its development and changes over time. *Child Development, 55,* 753–771.

Egeland, B., Jacobvitz, D., & Sroufe, L. A. (1988). Breaking the cycle of abuse. *Child Development, 59,* 1080–1088.

Ehrhardt, A. A., & Meyer-Bahlburg, H. F. L. (1981). Effects of prenatal sex hormones on gender-related behavior. *Science, 211,* 1312–1318.

Eimas, P. D. (1985). The perception of speech in early infancy. *Scientific American, 252*(1), 46–52.

Eisenberg-Berg, N., & Lennon, R. (1980). Altruism and the assessment of empathy in the preschool years. *Child Development, 51,* 552–557.

Eisenberg, N. (1983). Sex-typed toy choices: What do they signify? In M. B. Liss (Ed.), *Social and cognitive skills: Sex roles and children's play* (pp. 45–70). New York: Academic Press.

Eisenberg, R. B., & Marmarou, A. (1981). Behavioral reactions of newborns to speech-like sounds and their implications for developmental studies. *Infant Mental Health Journal, 2,* 129–138.

Eisert, D. C., & Kahle, L. R. (1982). Self-evaluation and social comparison of physical and role change during adolescence: A longitudinal analysis. *Child Development, 53,* 98–104.

Ekman, P., & Oster, H. (1979). Facial expressions of emotion. In M. R. Rosenzweig, & L. W. Porter (Eds.), *Annual review of psychology* (Vol. 30). Palo Alto, CA: Annual Reviews, Inc.

Elder, G. H., Jr., Nguyen, T. V., & Caspi, A. (1985). Linking family hardship to children's lives. *Child Development, 56,* 361–375.

Elkind, D. (1967). Egocentrism in adolescence. *Child Development, 38,* 1025–1034.

Elkind, D. (1971). *A sympathetic understanding of the child six to sixteen.* Boston: Allyn & Bacon.

Elkind, D. (1978). *The child's reality: Three developmental themes.* Hillsdale, NJ: Erlbaum.

Elkind, D., Barocas, R., & Johnsen, P. (1969). Concept production in children and adolescents. *Human Development, 12,* 10–21.

Elkind, D., & Bowen, R. (1979). Imaginary audience behavior in children and adolescents. *Developmental Psychology, 15,* 38–44.

Ellis, L., & Ames, M. A. (1987). Neurohormonal functioning and sexual orientation: A theory of homosexuality-hetereosexuality. *Psychological Bulletin, 101,* 233–258.

Ellis, P. L. (1982). Empathy a factor in antisocial behavior. *Journal of Abnormal Child Psychology, 10,* 123–124.

Emery, R. B. (1989). Family violence. *American Psychologist, 44,* 321–328.

Emmerich, W., & Goldman, K. S. (1972). Boy-girl identity task (technical report). In V. Shipman (Ed.), *Disadvantaged children and their first school experiences* (Technical Report PR-72–20). Educational Testing Service.

English, H. B. (1929). Three cases of the "conditioned fear response." *Journal of Abnormal and Social Psychology, 24,* 221–225.

Enright, R. D., Lapsley, D. K., & Shukla, D. G. (1979). Adolescent egocentrism in early and late adolescence. *Adolescence, 14,* 687–695.

Entwisle, D. R., & Alexander, K. L. (1987). Long-term effects of cesarean delivery on parents' beliefs and children's schooling. *Developmental Psychology, 23,* 676–682.

Erikson, E. H. (1950). *Childhood and society.* New York: Norton.

Erikson, E. H. (1968). *Identity, youth, and crisis.* New York: Norton.

Eriksson, M., Catz, C. S., & Yaffe, S. J. (1973). Drugs and pregnancy. In H. Osofsky (Ed.), *Clinical obstetrics and gynecology: High risk pregnancy with emphases upon maternal and fetal well being* (pp. 192–224). New York: Harper & Row.

Ernst, C., & Angst, J. (1983). *Birth order: Its influence on personality.* New York: Springer-Verlag.

Eron, L. D. (1980). Prescription for reduction of aggression. *American Psychologist, 35,* 244–252.

Eron, L. D., Huesmann, L. R., Brice, P., Fischer, P., & Mermelstein, R. (1983). Age trends in the development of aggression, sex typing, and related television habits. *Developmental Psychology, 19,* 71–77.

Erwin, E. (1980). Psychoanalytic therapy. *American Psychologist, 35,* 435–443.

Estrada, P., Arsenio, W. F., Hess, R. D., & Holloway, S. D. (1987). Affective quality of the mother-child relationship: Longitudinal consequences for children's school-relevant cognitive functioning. *Developmental Psychology, 23,* 210–215.

Etaugh, C. (1980). Effects of nonmaternal care on children. *American Psychologist, 35,* 309–319.

Etaugh, C. (1983). Introduction: The influence of environmental factors on sex differences in children's play. In M. B. Liss (Ed.), *Social and cognitive skills: Sex roles and children's play* (pp. 1–19). New York: Academic Press.

Evans, H. J., Fletcher, J., Torrance, M., & Hargreave, T. B. (1981). Sperm abnormalities and cigarette smoking. *The Lancet, I*(8221), 627–629.

Fabricius, W. V., & Wellman, H. M. (1983). Children's understanding of retrieval cue utilization. *Developmental Psychology, 19,* 15–21.

Fackelmann, K. A. (1991, July 6). Simple shield against birth defects? *Science News,* p. 141.

Fagen, J. W. (1984). Infants' long-term memory for stimulus color. *Developmental Psychology, 20,* 435–440.

Fagot, B. I., Hagan, R., Leinbach, M. D., & Kronsberg, S. (1985). Differential reactions to assertive and communicative acts of toddler boys and girls. *Child Development, 56,* 1499–1505.

Fagot, B. I., Leinbach, M. D., & O'Boyle, C. (1992). Gender labeling, gender stereotyping, and parenting behaviors. *Developmental Psychology, 28,* 225–230.

Falbo, T. (1981). Relationships between birth category, achievement, and interpersonal orientation. *Journal of Personality and Social Psychology, 41,* 121–131.

Fantz, R. L. (1961). The origin of form perception. *Scientific American, 204,* 66–72.

Fantz, R. L., Ordy, J. M., & Udelf, M. S. (1962). Maturation of pattern vision in infants during the first six months. *Journal of Comparative and Physiological Psychology, 55,* 907–917.

Farran, D. C., & Ramey, C. T. (1977). Infant day care and attachment behaviors toward mothers and teachers. *Child Development, 48,* 1112–1116.

Faust, M. S. (1977). Somatic development of adolescent girls. *Monographs of the Society for Research in Child Development, 42*(1, Serial No. 169).

Fay, R. E., Turner, C. F., Klassen, A. D., & Gagnon, J. H. (1989). prevalence and patterns of same-gender sexual contact among men. *Science, 243,* 338–348.

Feagans, L., & Short, E. J. (1986). Referential communication and reading performance in learning disabled children over a 3-year period. *Developmental Psychology, 22,* 177–183.

Federation CECOS, Schwartz, D., & Mayaux, B. A. (1982). Female fecundity as a function of age. *New England Journal of Medicine, 306,* 404–406.

Feingold, A. (1988). Cognitive gender differences are disappearing. *American Psychologist, 43,* 95–103.

Feingold, B. F. (1974). *Why your child is hyperactive.* New York: Random House.

Feldman, D. H. (1984). A follow-up of subjects scoring above 180 IQ in Terman's "Genetic Studies of Genius." *Exceptional Children, 50,* 518–523.

Ferguson, T. J., & Rule, B. G. (1982). Influence of inferential set, outcome intent, and outcome severity on children's moral judgments. *Developmental Psychology, 18,* 843–851.

Fernald, A. (1989). Intonation and communicative intent in mothers' speech to infants: Is the melody the message? *Child Development, 60,* 1497–1510.

Fernald, A., & Mazzie, C. (1991). Prosody and focus in speech to infants and adults. *Developmental Psychology, 27,* 209–221.

Feshbach, N. D., & Feshbach, S. (1982). Empathy training and the regulation of aggression: Potentialities and limitations. *Academic Psychology Bulletin, 4,* 399–413.

Field, T. (1979). Differential behavioral and cardiac responses of 3-month-old infants to a mirror and a peer. *Infant Behavior and Development, 2,* 179–184.

Field, T., De Stefano, L., & Koewler, J. H., III. (1982). Fantasy play of toddlers and preschoolers. *Developmental Psychology, 18,* 503–508.

Field, T., Healy, B., Goldstein, S., Perry, S., Bendell, D., Schanberg, S., Zimmerman, E. A., & Kuhn, C. (1988). Infants of depressed mothers show "depressed" behavior even with nondepressed adults. *Child Development, 59,* 1569–1579.

Field, T. M. (1991a). Young children's adaptations to repeated separations from their mothers. *Child Development, 62,* 539–547.

Field, T. M. (1991b). Quality infant day-care and grade school behavior and performance. *Child Development, 62,* 863–870.

Field, T. M., Schanberg, S. M., Scafidi, F., Bauer, C. R., Vega-Lahr, N., Garcia, R., Nystrom, J., & Kuhn, C. M. (1986). Tactile/kinesthetic stimulation effects on preterm neonates. *Pediatrics, 77,* 654–658.

Filsinger, E. E., & Anderson, C. C. (1982). Social class and self-esteem in late adolescence: Dissonant context or self-efficacy? *Developmental Psychology, 18,* 380–384.

Finkelstein, N. W., & Haskins, R. (1983). Kindergarten children prefer same-color peers. *Child Development, 54,* 502–508.

Finkelstein, N. W., & Ramey, C. T. (1977). Learning to control the environment in infancy. *Child Development, 48,* 806–819.

Finlay, D., & Ivinskis, A. (1984). Cardiac and visual responses to moving stimuli presented either successively or simultaneously to the central and peripheral visual fields in 4-month-olds. *Developmental Psychology, 20,* 29–36.

Finlayson, D. F., & Loughran, J. L. (1976). Pupils' perceptions in high and low delinquency schools. *Educational Research, 18,* 138–145.

Fiorito, G., & Scotto, P. (1992). Observational learning in *Octopus vulgaris*. *Science, 256,* 545–547.

Fisch, G. S., Cohen, I. L., Wolf, E. G., Brown, W. T., Jenkins, E. C., & Gross, A. (1986). Autism and the Fragile X Syndrome. *American Journal of Psychiatry, 143,* 71–77.

Fischer, K. W. (1980). A theory of cognitive development: The control and construction of hierarchies of skills. *Psychological Review, 87,* 477–531.

Fischer, K. W. (1983). Illuminating the processes of moral development. *Monographs of the Society for Research in Child Development, 48*(1–2, Serial No. 200), 97–107.

Fischer, K. W. (1987). Relations between brain and cognitive development. *Child Development, 58,* 623–632.

Fischer, K. W., & Bullock, D. (1981). Patterns of data: Sequence, synchrony, and constraint in cognitive development. *New Directions in Child Development, 12,* 1–20.

Fischer, K. W., & Silvern, L. (1985). Stages and individual differences in cognitive development. *Annual Review of Psychology, 36,* 613–648.

Fishbein, H. D. (1976). *Evolution, development, and children's learning.* Pacific Palisades, Calif.: Goodyear Publishing.

Fiske, J. (1909). *The meaning of infancy.* Boston: Houghton Mifflin. (Original work published 1883).

Fitzgerald, H. E., & Brackbill, Y. (1976). Classical conditioning in infancy: Development and constraints. *Psychological Bulletin, 83,* 353–376.

Flavell, J. H. (1963). *The developmental psychology of Jean Piaget.* Princeton, NJ: Van Nostrand.

Flavell, J. H. (1970). Concept development. In P. H. Mussen (Ed.), *Carmichael's manual of child psychology* (3rd ed.). New York: Wiley.

Flavell, J. H. (1986, January). Really and truly. *Psychology Today,* pp. 38–44.

Flavell, J. H., Beach, D. R., & Chinsky, J. M. (1966). Spontaneous verbal rehearsal in a memory task as a function of age. *Child Development, 37,* 283–299.

Flavell, J. H., Everett, B. A., Croft, K., & Flavell, E. R. (1981). Young children's knowledge about visual perception: Further evidence for the level 1-level 2 distinction. *Developmental Psychology, 17,* 99–103.

Flavell, J. H., Flavell, E. R., Green, F. L., & Moses, L. J. (1990). Young children's understanding of fact beliefs versus value beliefs. *Child Development, 61,* 915–928.

Flynn, J. R. (1987). Massive IQ gains in 14 nations: What IQ tests really measure. *Psychological Bulletin, 101,* 171–191.

Fogel, A. (1979). Peer vs. mother directed behavior in 1- to 3-month-old infants. *Infant Behavior and Development, 2,* 215–226.

Fogel, A., & Hannan, T. E. (1985). Manual actions of nine- to fifteen-week-old human infants during face-to-face interaction with their mothers. *Child Development, 56,* 1271–1279.

Foley, M. A., Johnson, M. K., & Raye, C. L. (1983). Age-related changes in confusion between memories for thoughts and memories for speech. *Child Development, 54,* 51–60.

Fontaine, R. (1984). Imitative skills between birth and six months. *Infant Behavior and Development, 7,* 323–333.

Fowler, R. C., Rich, C. L., & Young, D. (1986). San Diego suicide study: II. Substance abuse in young cases. *Archives of General Psychiatry, 43,* 962–965.

Fox, J., Manitowabi, D., & Ward, J. A. (1984). An Indian community with a high suicide rate—5 years after. *Canadian Journal of Psychiatry, 29,* 425–427.

Fox, N. A. (1991). If it's not left, it's right: Electroencephalograph asymmetry and the development of emotion. *American Psychologist, 46,* 863–872.

Frankenburg, W. K., & Dodds, J. B. (1967). The Denver Developmental Screening Test. *Journal of Pediatrics, 71,* 181–191.

Freiberg, P. (1991, April). More high school seniors say "no." *The APA Monitor,* pp. 28–29.

Frey, K. S., & Ruble, D. N. (1992). Gender constancy and the "cost" of sex-typed behavior: A test of the conflict hypothesis. *Developmental Psychology, 28,* 714–721.

Friedrich, L. K., & Stein, A. H. (1973). Aggressive and prosocial television programs and the natural behavior of preschool children. *Monographs of the Society for Research in Child Development, 38*(4, Serial No. 151).

Friedrich, L. K., Stein, A. H., & Sussman, E. (1975). *The effects of prosocial television and environmental conditions on preschool children.* Paper presented at the meeting of the American Psychological Association, Chicago, Illinois.

Frisch, R. E. (1988). Fatness and fertility. *Scientific American, 258*(3), 88–95.

Frodi, A., Bridges, L., & Grolnick, W. (1985). Correlates of mastery-related behavior: A short-term longitudinal study of infants in their second year. *Child Development, 56,* 1291–1298.

Frodi, A., Lamb, M. E., Hwang, C. P., & Frodi, M. (1982). Father-mother-infant interaction in traditional and nontraditional Swedish families: A longitudinal study. *Alternative Lifestyles, 4,* 6–13.

Froming, W. J., Allen, L., & Jensen, R. (1985). Altruism, role-taking, and self-awareness: The acquisition of norms governing altruistic behavior. *Child Development, 56,* 1223–1228.

Fry, D. P. (1988). Intercommunity differences in aggression among Zapotec children. *Child Development, 59,* 1008–1019.

Fuchs, F. (1980). Genetic amniocentesis. *Scientific American, 242*(6), 47–53.

Fuchs, V. R., & Reklis, D. M. (1992). America's children: Economic perspectives and policy options. *Science, 255,* 41–46.

Furman, L. N., & Walden, T. A. (1990). Effect of script knowledge on preschool children's communicative interactions. *Developmental Psy-*

chology, 26, 227–233.

Furman, W. (1987). Acquaintanceship in middle childhood. *Developmental Psychology, 23,* 563–570.

Furman, W., & Bierman, K. L. (1983). Developmental changes in young children's conceptions of friendship. *Child Development, 54,* 549–556.

Fuson, K. C. (1979). The development of self-regulating aspects of speech: A review. In G. Zivin (Ed.), *The development of self-regulation through private speech.* New York: Wiley.

Gagne, R. M. (1970). *The conditions of learning* (2nd ed.). New York: Holt, Rinehart, & Winston.

Galbraith, R. C. (1982). Sibling spacing and intellectual development: A closer look at the confluence models. *Developmental Psychology, 18,* 151–173.

Gallup, G. G. (1977). Self-recognition in primates. *American Psychologist, 32,* 329–338.

Garbarino, J. (1980). Some thoughts on school size and its effects on adolescent development. *Journal of Youth and Adolescence, 9,* 19–31.

Garcia, J., & Koelling, R. A. (1966). Relation of cue to consequence in avoidance learning. *Psychonomic Science, 4,* 123–124.

Gardner, H. (1980). *Artful scribbles: The significance of children's drawing.* New York: Basic Books.

Gardner, H. (1983). *Frames of mind: The theory of multiple intelligences.* New York: Basic Books.

Garelik, G. (1985, October). Are the progeny prodigies? *Discover,* pp. 45–57; 78–84.

Garmon, L. (1981, January 31). As it was in the beginning. *Science News,* pp. 72–74.

Garrison, E. G. (1987). Psychological maltreatment of children: An emerging focus for inquiry and concern. *American Psychologist, 42,* 157–159.

Geller, E., Ritvo, E. R., Freeman, B. J., & Yuwiler, A. (1982). Preliminary observations on the effect of fenfluramine on blood serotonin and symptoms in three autistic boys. *New England Journal of Medicine, 307,* 165–169.

Gelman, R., & Baillargeon, R. (1983). A review of some Piagetian concepts. In J. H. Flavell & E. M. Markman (Eds.), Ph. H. Mussen (Series Ed.), *Handbook of child psychology: Vol. 3. Cognitive development* (pp. 167–230). New York: Wiley.

Gelman, S. A., & Coley, J. D. (1990). The importance of knowing a Dodo is a bird: Categories and influences in 2-year-old children. *Developmental Psychology, 26,* 796–804.

Gelman, S. A., & Kremer, K. E. (1991). Understanding natural cause: Children's explanations of how objects and their properties originate. *Child Development, 62,* 396–414.

Gelman, S. A., & Markman, E. M. (1987). Young children's inductions from natural kinds: The role of categories and appearances. *Child Development, 58,* 1532–1541.

Geracioti, T. D., Jr., & Liddle, R. A. (1988). Impaired cholecystokinin secretion in bulimia nervosa. *New England Journal of Medicine, 319,* 683–688.

Gerbner, G., Gross, L., Morgan, M., & Signorielli, N. (1980). The "mainstreaming" of America: Violence profile No. 11. *Journal of Communication, 30*(3), 10–29.

Gerken, L., Landau, B., & Remez, R. E. (1990). Function morphemes in young children's speech perception and production. *Developmental Psychology, 26,* 204–216.

Geschwind, N., & Behan, P. (1982). Left-handedness: Association with immune disease, migraine, and developmental learning disorder. *Proceedings of the National Academy of Sciences of the United States of America—Biological Sciences, 79,* 5097–5100.

Gesell, A. (1928). *Infancy and human growth.* New York: Macmillan.

Gewirtz, J. L. (1961). A learning analysis of the effects of normal stimulation, privation, and deprivation on the acquisition of social motivation and attachment. In B. H. Foss (Ed.), *Determinants of infant behaviour* (pp. 213–298). London: Methuen.

Gibbs, J. C. (1979). Kohlberg's moral stage theory: A Piagetian revision. *Human Development, 22,* 89–112.

Gibson, E. J., & Walk, R. D. (1960). The "visual cliff." *Scientific American, 202*(4), 64–71.

Gilligan, C. (1982). *In a different voice: Psychological theory and women's development.* Cambridge, MA: Harvard University Press.

Gillin, F. D., Reiner, D. S., & Wang, C. (1983). Human milk kills parasitic intestinal protozoa. *Science, 221,* 1290–1292.

Giulian, G. G., Gilbert, E. F., & Moss, R. L. (1987). Elevated fetal hemoglobin levels in sudden infant death syndrome. *New England Journal of Medicine, 316,* 1122–1126.

Gleitman, L. R., & Wanner, E. (1984). Current issues in language learning. In M. H. Bornstein & M. E. Lamb (Eds.), *Developmental psychology: An advanced textbook* (pp. 181–240). Hillsdale, NJ: Erlbaum.

Glick, J. (1975). Cognitive development in cross-cultural perspective. In F. D. Horowitz (Ed.), *Review of child development research* (Vol. 4). Chicago, IL: Univ. of Chicago Press.

Gnepp, J., & Gould, M. E. (1985). The development of personalized inferences: Understanding other people's emotional reactions in light of their prior experiences. *Child Development, 56,* 1455–1464.

Gold, M. S., Pottash, A. L. C., Sweeney, D. R., Martin, D. M., & Davies, R. K. (1980). Further evidence of hypothalamic-pituitary dysfunction in anorexia nervosa. *American Journal of Psychiatry, 137,* 101–102.

Goldfine, P. E., McPherson, P. M., Heath, A., Hardesty, V. A., Beauregard, L. J., & Gordon, B. (1985). Association of Fragile X Syndrome with autism. *American Journal of Psychiatry, 142,* 108–110.

Goldin-Meadow, S., & Morford, M. (1985). Gesture in early child language: Studies of deaf and hearing children. *Merrill-Palmer Quarterly, 31,* 145–760.

Goldsmith, H. H. (1983). Genetic influences on personality from infancy to adulthood. *Child Development, 54,* 331–355.

Goldsmith, H. H., Buss. A. H., Plomin, R., Rothbart, M. K., Thomas, A., Chess, S., Hinde, R. A., & McCall, R. B. (1987). Roundtable: What is temperament: Four approaches. *Child Development, 58,* 505–529.

Goldstein, H. (1984). Effects of modeling and corrected practice on generative language learning of preschool children. *Hearing Disorders, 49,* 389–398.

Goleman, D. (1980, February). 1,528 little geniuses and how they grew. *Psychology Today,* pp. 28–53.

Gottesman, I. I., & Shields, J. (1972). *Schizophrenia and genetics.* New York: Academic Press.

Gottfried, A. E., & Gottfried, A. W. (Eds.). (1988). *Maternal employment and children's development.* New York: Plenum.

Gottman, J. M. (1983). How children become friends. *Monographs of the Society for Research in Child Development, 48*(3, Serial No. 201).

Gould, M. S., & Shaffer, D. (1986). The impact of suicide in television movies. *The New England Journal of Medicine, 315,* 690–694.

Granrud, C. E., Yonas, A., Smith, I. M., Arterberry, M. E., Glicksman, M. L., & Sorknes, A. C. (1984). Infants' sensitivity to accretion and deletion of texture as information for depth at an edge. *Child Development, 55,* 1630–1636.

Grant, C. L., & Fodor, I. G. (1986). Adolescent attitudes toward body image and anorexic behavior. *Adolescence, 21,* 269–281.

Gravett, M., Rogers, C. S., & Thompson, L. (1987). Child care decisions among female heads of households with school-age children. *Early Childhood Research Quarterly, 2,* 67–81.

Gray, S. W., & Ruttle, K. (1980). The family-oriented home visiting program: A longitudinal study. *Genetic Psychology Monographs, 102,* 299–316.

Gray, W. M., & Hudson, L. M. (1984). Formal operations and the imaginary audience. *Developmental Psychology, 20,* 619–627.

Green, F. P., & Schneider, F. W. (1974). Age differences in the behavior of boys on three measures of altruism. *Child Development, 45,* 248–251.

Green, J. A., Gustafson, G. E., & West, M. J. (1980). Effects of infant development on mother-infant interactions. *Child Development, 51,* 199–207.

Green, R. (1987). *The "sissy boy syndrome" and the development of homosexuality.* New Haven, CT: Yale University Press.

Green, R., & Stoller, R. J. (1971). Two monozygotic (identical) twin pairs discordant for gender identity. *Archives of Sexual Behavior, 1,* 321–327.

Greenbaum, C. W., & Landau, R. (1982). The infant's exposure to talk by familiar people: Mothers, fathers and siblings in different environments. In M. Lewiis & L. Rosenblum (Eds.), *The social network of the developing infant.* New York: Plenum.

Greenberg, J. (1977, July 30). The brain and emotions. *Science News,* pp. 74–75.

Greenberg, J. (1980, January 5). Inheriting mental illness: Nature & nurture. *Science News,* pp. 10–12.

Greenberg, J. W., & Davidson, H. H. (1972). Home background and school achievement of black urban ghetto children. *American Journal of Orthopsychiatry, 42,* 803–810.

Greenberg, M. T., & Crnic, K. A. (1988). Longitudinal predictors of developmental status and social interaction in premature and full-term infants at age two. *Child Development, 59,* 554–570.

Greenberg, R. A., Haley, N. J., Etzel, R. A., & Loda, F. A. (1984). Measuring the exposure of infants to tobacco smoke: Nicotine and cotinine in urine and saliva. *New England Journal of Medicine, 310,* 1075–1078.

Greenough, W. T., Black, J. E., & Wallace, C. S. (1987). Experience and brain development. *Child Development, 58,* 539–559.

Greenspan, S. I., & Greenspan, N. T. (1985). *First feelings: Milestones in the emotional development of your baby and child.* New York: Viking.

Greer, D., Potts, R., Wright, J. C., & Huston, A. C. (1982). The effects of television commercial form and commercial placement on children's social behavior and attention. *Child Development, 53,* 611–619.

Gregory, R. L. (1970). *The intelligent eye.* New York: McGraw-Hill.

Grief, J. B. (1980). Fathers, children and joint custody. *Annual Progress in Child Psychiatry and Child Development, 1980,* 292–304.

Grieser, D. L., & Kuhl, P. K. (1988). Maternal speech to infants in a tonal language: Support for universal prosodic features in motherese. *Developmental Psychology, 24,* 14–20.

Grieser, D. L., & Kuhl, P. K. (1989). Categorization of speech by infants: Support for speech-sound prototypes. *Developmental Psychology, 25,* 577–588.

Griffin, G. A., & Harlow, H. F. (1966). Effects of three months of total social deprivation on social adjustment and learning in the rhesus monkey. *Child Development, 37,* 533–547.

Griffiths, R. (1954). *The abilities of babies.* London: University of London Press.

Grilo, C. M., & Pogue-Geile, M. F. (1991). The nature of environmental influences on weight and obesity: A behavior genetic analysis. *Psychological Bulletin, 110,* 520–537.

Gronseth, E. (1975). Work-sharing families: Adaptations of pioneering families with husband and wife in part-time employment. *Acta Sociologica, 18,* 202–221.

Gross-Isseroff, R., Dillon, K. A., Israeli, M., & Biegon, A. (1990). Regionally selective increases in mu opoid receptor density in the brains of suicide victims. *Brain Research, 530,* 312–316.

Grotevant, H. D., & Cooper, C. R. (1985). Patterns of interaction in family relationships and the development of identity exploration in adolescence. *Child Development, 56,* 415–428.

Grotevant, M. D., Scarr, S., & Weinberg, R. A. (1975, March). *Intellectual development in family constellations ith adopted and natural children: A test of the Zajonc and Markus model.* Paper presented at the meeting of the Society for Research in Child Development, New Orleans.

Guidubaldi, J., & Perry, J. D. (1985). Divorce and mental health sequelae for children: A two-year follow-up of a nationwide sample. *Journal of the American Academy of Child Psychiatry, 24,* 531–537.

Guilford, J. P. (1982). Cognitive psychology's ambiguities: Some suggested remedies. *Psychological Review, 89,* 48–59.

Guilford, J. P. (1983). Transformation abilities or functions. *Journal of Creative Behavior, 17,* 75–83.

Gunderson, V. M., Rose, S. A., & Grant-Webster, K. S. (1990). Cross-modal transfer in high- and low-risk infant pigtailed macaque monkeys. *Developmental Psychology, 26,* 576–581.

Gunnar, M. R., Senior, K., & Hartup, W. W. (1984). Peer presence and the exploratory behavior of eighteen and thirty-month-old children. *Child Development, 55,* 1103–1109.

Gustafson, G. E. (1984). Effects of the ability to locomote on infants' social and exploratory behaviors: An experimental study. *Developmental Psychology, 20,* 397–405.

Gzesh, S. M., & Surber, C. F. (1985). Visual perspective-taking skills in children. *Child Development, 56,* 1204–1213.

Haan, N., Smith, M. B., & Block, J. (1968). Moral reasoning of young adults: Political-social behavior, family background, and personality correlates. *Journal of Personality and Social Psychology, 10,* 183–201.

Hakuta, K. (1982). Interaction between particles and word order in the comprehension and production of simple sentences in Japanese children. *Developmental Psychology, 18,* 62–76.

Hala, S., Chandler, M., & Fritz, A. S. (1991). Fledgling theories of mind: Deception as a marker of three-year-olds' understanding of false belief. *Child Development, 62,* 83–97.

Hale, G. A. (1979). Development of children's attention to stimulus components. In G. Hale, & M. Lewis (Eds.), *Attention and cognitive development.* New York: Plenum.

Halford, G. S., & Boyle, F. M. (1985). Do young children understand conservation of number? *Child Development, 56,* 165–176.

Hall, E. (1983, June). A conversation with Erik Erikson. *Psychology Today,* pp. 22–30.

Hall, G. S. (1904). *Adolescence* (Vols. 1 and 2). New York: Appleton-Century-Crofts.

Hall, W. M., & Cairns, R. B. (1984). Aggressive behavior in children: An outcome of modeling or social reciprocity? *Developmental Psychology, 20,* 739–745.

Hampson, R. B. (1981). Helping behavior in children: Addressing the interaction of a person-situation model. *Developmental Review, 1,* 93–112.

Handyside, A. H., Pattinson, J. K., Penketh, R. J., Delhanty, J. D., Winston, R. M., & Tuddenham, E. G. (1989). Biopsy of human preimplantation embryos and sexing by DNA amplification. *Lancet, 1*(8634), 347–349.

Hanratty, M. A. (1969). *Imitation of film-mediated aggression against live and inanimate victims.* Unpublished MA thesis, Vanderbilt University, Nashville, Tennessee.

Hanratty, M. A., Liebert, R. M., Morris, L. W., & Fernandez, L. E. (1969). Imitation of film-mediated aggression against live and inanimate victims. *Proceedings of the 77th Annual Convention APA,* pp. 457–458.

Harding, C. G., & Golinkoff, R. M. (1979). The origins of intentional vocalizations in prelinguistic infants. *Child Development, 50,* 33–40.

Harlow, H. F., & Novak, M. A. (1973). Psychopathological perspectives. *Perspectives in Biology and Medicine, 16,* 461–478.

Harlow, H. F., & Suomi, S. J. (1970). The nature of love-simplified. *American Psychologist, 25,* 161–168.

Harper, L. V., & Huie, K. S. (1985). The effects of prior group experience, age, and familiarity on the quality and organization of preschoolers' social relationships. *Child Development, 56,* 704–717.

Harris, B. (1979). Whatever happened to Little Albert? *American Psychologist, 34,* 151–160.

Harris, G., Thomas, A., & Booth, D. A. (1990). Development of salt taste in infancy. *Developmental Psychology, 26,* 534–538.

Harris, P. L. (1986). Bringing order to the A-Not-B Error: Commentary. In H. M. Wellman, D. Cross, & K. Bartsch (Eds.)., *Monographs of the Society for Research in Child Development, 51*(3, Serial No. 214).

Harris, P. L., Guz, G. R., Lipian, M. S., & Man-Shu, A. (1985). Insight into the time course of emotion among Western and Chinese children. *Child Development, 56,* 972–988.

Hart, S. N., & Brassard, M. R. (1987). A major threat to children's mental health: Psychological maltreatment. *American Psychologist, 42,* 160–165.

Harter, S., & Monsour, A. (1992). Developmental analysis of conflict caused by opposing attributes in the adolescent self-portrait. *Developmental Psychology, 28,* 251–260.

Hartshorne, H., May, M. A., & Maller, J. B. (1929). *Studies in the nature of character: II. Studies in service and self-control.* New York: Macmillan.

Hartup, W. W. (1970). Peer interaction and social organization. In P. H. Mussen (Ed.), *Carmichael's manual of child psychology* (3rd ed., Vol. 1, pp. 361–456). New York: Wiley.

Hartup, W. W. (1983). Peer relations. In P. H. Mussen (Ed.), *Handbook of child psychology* (4th ed., Vol. IV, pp. 103–196). New York: Wiley.

Harvey, M. A. S., McRorie, M. M., & Smith, D. W. (1981). Suggested limits to the use of the hot tub and sauna by pregnant women. *Canadian Medical Association Journal, 125,* 50–53.

Haskins, R., Schwartz, J. B., Akin, J. S., & Dobelstein, A. W. (1985). How much support can absent fathers pay? *Policy Studies Journal, 14,* 201–222.

Hasselhorn, M. (1992). Task dependency and the role of category typicality and metamemory in the development of an organizational strategy. *Child Development, 63,* 202–214.

Havighurst, R. J. (1976). Choosing a middle path for the use of drugs with hyperactive children. *School Review, 85,* 61–77.

Haviland, J. M., & Lelwica, M. (1987). The induced affect response: 10-week-old infants' responses to three emotion expressions. *Developmental Psychology, 23,* 97–104.

Hawkins, J. D., Catalano, R. F., & Miller, J. Y. (1992). Risk and protective factors for alcohol and other drug problems in adolescence and early adulthood: Implications for substance abuse prevention. *Psychological Bulletin, 112,* 64–105.

Hay, D. F. (1986). Infancy. *Annual Review of Psychology, 37,* 135–161.

Hay, D. F., & Hall, D. K. (1981). *Behavioral, psychological and developmental differences between abusive and control mother-child dyads.* Paper presented at the meeting of the Society for Research in Child Development, Boston, Massachusetts.

Hay, D. F., Nash, A., & Pedersen, J. (1983). Interaction between six-month-old peers. *Child Development, 54,* 557–562.

Hay, D. F., & Ross, H. S. (1982). The social nature of early conflict. *Child Development, 53,* 105–113.

Hayashi, S., & Kimura, T. (1976). Sexual behavior of the naive male mouse as affected by the presence of a male and a female performing mating behavior. *Physiology & Behavior, 17,* 807–810.

Hazen, N. L., & Volk-Hudson, S. (1984). The effect of spatial context on young children's recall. *Child Development, 55,* 1835–1844.

Heibeck, T. H., & Markman, E. M. (1987). Word learning in children: An examination of fast mapping. *Child Development, 58,* 1021–1034.

Heinonen, O. P., Slone, D., Shapiro, S., Gaetana, L. F., Hartz, S. C., Mitchell, A. A., Monson, R. R., Rosenberg, L., Siskind, V., & Kaufman, D. W. (1977). *Birth defects and drugs in pregnancy.* Littleton, Mass.: PSG Publications.

Helson, R., & Crutchfield, R. S. (1970). Mathematicians: The creative researcher and the average Ph.D. *Journal of Consulting and Clinical Psychology, 34,* 250–257.

Hennessy, M. J., Dixon, S. D., & Simon, S. R. (1984). The development of gait: A study in African children ages one to five. *Child Development, 55,* 844–853.

Hennigan, K. M., Del Rosario, M. L., Heath, L., Cook, T. D., Wharton, J. D., & Calder, B. J. (1982). Impact of the introduction of television on crime in the United States: Empirical findings and theoretical implications. *Journal of Personality and Social Psychology, 42,* 461–477.

Hepper, P. G., Shahidullah, S., & White, R. (1990). Origins of fetal handedness. *Nature, 347,* 431.

Hernandez, D. J. (1988). Demographic trends and the living arrangements of children. In E. M. Hetherington & J. D. Arasteh (Eds.), *Impact of divorce, single parenting, and stepparenting on children* (pp. 3–22). Hillsdale, NJ: Erlbaum.

Herndon, B. K., & Carpenter, M. D. (1982). Sex differences in cooperative and competitive attitudes in a Northeastern school. *Psychological Reports, 50,* 768–770.

Hetherington, E. M. (1979). Divorce: A child's perspective. *American Psychologist, 34,* 851–858.

Hetherington, E. M. (1989). Coping with family transitions: Winners, losers, and survivors. *Child Development, 60,* 1–14.

Hetherington, E. M., Clingempeel, W. G., Anderson, E. R., Deal, J. E., Hagan, M. S., Hollier, E. A., Lindner, M. S., & Maccoby, E. E. (1992). Coping with marital transitions. *Monographs of the Society for Research in Child Development, 57*(2–3, Serial No. 227).

Hetherington, E. M., Cox, M., & Cox, R. (1978). The aftermath of divorce. In J. H. Stevens, Jr., & M. Matthews (Eds.), *Mother-child, father-child relations.* Washington, D.C.: National Association for the Education of Young Children.

Hetherington, E. M., Cox, M., & Cox, R. (1982). Effects of divorce on parents and children. In M. Lamb (Ed.), *Nontraditional families.* Hillsdale, NJ: Erlbaum.

Hetherington, E. M., Stanley-Hagan, M., & Anderson, E. R. (1989). Marital transitions: A child's perspective. *American Psychologist, 44,* 303–312.

Heyman, G. D., Dweck, C. S., & Cain, K. M. (1992). Young chiuldren's vulnerability to self- blame and helplessness: Relationship to beliefs about goodness. *Child Development, 63,* 401–415.

Hillel, M., & Henry, C. (1976). *Of pure blood* (E. Mossbacher, Trans.). New York: McGraw-Hill. (Original work published 1975)

Himmelberger, D. U., Brown, B. W., Jr., & Cohen, E. N. (1978). Cigarette smoking during pregnancy and the occurrence of spontaneous abortion and congenital abnormality. *American Journal of Epidemiology, 108,* 470–479.

Hinde, R. A. (1975). *The bases of social behavior.* New York: McGraw-Hill.

Hinde, R. A. (1991). When is an evolutionary approach useful? *Child Development, 62,* 671–675.

Hinde, R. A., Stevenson-Hinde, J., & Tamplin, A. (1985). Characteristics of 3- to 4-year-olds assessed at home and their interactions in preschool. *Developmental Psychology, 21,* 130–140.

Hindley, C. B., Filliozat, A. M., Klackenberg, G., Nicolet-Meister, D., & Sand, E. A. (1966). Differences in age of walking for five European longitudinal samples. *Human Biology, 38,* 364–379.

Hines, M. (1982). Prenatal gonadal hormones and sex differences in human behavior. *Psychological Bulletin, 92,* 56–80.

Hock, E. (1978). Working and nonworking mothers with infants: Perceptions of their careers, their infants' needs, and satisfaction with mothering. *Developmental Psychology, 14,* 37–43.

Hock, E., & DeMeis, D. K. (1990). Depression in mothers of infants: The role of maternal employment. *Developmental Psychology, 26,* 285–291.

Hoffman, L. W. (1979). Maternal employment: 1979. *American Psychologist, 34,* 859–865.

Hoffman, L. W. (1989). Effects of maternal employment in the two-parent family. *American Psychologist, 44,* 283–292.

Hoffman, L. W. (1991). The influence of the family environment on personality: Accounting for sibling differences. *Psychological Bulletin, 110,* 187–203.

Hoffman, M. L. (1970). Moral development. In P. H. Mussen (Ed.), *Carmichael's manual of child psychology* (3rd ed., Vol. 2, pp. 261–360). New York: Wiley.

Hoffman, M. L. (1977). Personality and social development. In M. R. Rosenzweig, & L. W. Porter (Eds.), *Annual review of psychology* (Vol. 28). Palo Alto, CA: Annual Reviews, Inc.

Hoffman, M. L. (1979). Development of moral thought, feeling, and behavior. *American Psychologist, 34,* 958–966.

Hoffner, C., & Cantor, J. (1985). Developmental differences in responses to a television character's appearance and behavior. *Developmental Psychology, 21,* 1065–1074.

Hojat, M. (1982). Loneliness as a function of parent-child and peer relations. *Journal of Psychology, 112,* 129–133.

Hokanson, J. E., & Edelman, R. (1966). Effects of three social responses on vascular processes. *Journal of Personality and Social Psychology, 3,* 442–447.

Holden, C. (1986). Youth suicide: New research focuses on a growing social problem. *Science, 233,* 839–841.

Holden, C. (1991). On the trail of genes for IQ. *Science, 253,* 1352.

Horn, J. (1986). Intellectual ability concepts. In R. J. Sternberg (Ed.), *Advances in the psychology of human intelligence* (Vol. 3, pp. 35–77). Hillsdale, NJ: Erlbaum.

Horn, J. M. (1983). The Texas Adoption Project: Adopted children and their intellectual resemblance to biological and adoptive parents. *Child Development, 54,* 268–275.

Horn, J. M. (1985). Bias? Indeed! *Child Development, 56,* 779–780.

Horney, K. (1939). *New ways in psychoanalysis.* New York: Norton.

Horowitz, F. D. (1992). John B. Watson's legacy: Learning and environment. *Developmental Psychology, 28,* 360–367.

Horowitz, F. D., Ashton, J., Culp, R., Gaddis, E., Levin, S., & Reichmann, B. (1977). The effects of obstetrical medication on the behavior of Israeli newborn infants and some comparisons with Uruguayan and American infants. *Child Development, 48,* 1607–1623.

Horwitz, S. M., Klerman, L. V., Kuo, H. S., & Jekel, J. F. (1991). Intergenerational transmission of school-age parenthood. *Family Planning Perspectives, 23,* 168–172, 177.

Hostetler, A. J. (1988, July). Why baby cries: Data may shush skeptics. *APA Monitor,* p. 14.

Hoving, C. (1986). The "Baby Doe" cases. *American Bar Association Journal, 72,* 51–53.

Hoving, K. L., Hamm, N., & Galvin, P. (1969). Social influence as a function of stimulus ambiguity at three age levels. *Developmental Psychology, 1,* 631–636.

Howard, F. M., & Hill, J. M. (1979). Drugs in pregnancy. *Obstetrical and Gynecological Survey, 34,* 643–653.

Howard, J. A., & Barnett, M. A. (1981). Arousal of empathy and subsequent generosity in young children. *Journal of Genetic Psychology, 138,* 307–308.

Howes, C. (1983). Patterns of friendship. *Child Development, 54,* 1041–1053.

Howes, C. (1985). Sharing fantasy: Social pretend play in toddlers. *Child Development, 56,* 1253–1258.

Howes, C. (1987). Peer interaction of young children. *Monographs of the Society for Research in Child Development, 53*(1, Serial No. 217).

Howes, C. (1990). Can the age of entry into child care and the quality of child care predict adjustment in kindergarten? *Developmental Psychology, 26,* 292–303.

Howes, C., Phillips, D. A., & Whitebook, M. (1992). Thresholds of quality: Implications for the social development of children in center-based child care. *Child Development, 63,* 449–460.

Howes, C., Unger, O., & Seidner, L. B. (1989). Social pretend play in toddlers: Parallels with social play and with solitary pretend. *Child Development, 60,* 77–84.

Hudson, A., & Clunies-Ross, G. (1984). A study of the integration of children with intellectual handicaps into regular schools. *Australia & New Zealand Journal of Developmental Disabilities, 10*(3), 165–177.

Hudson, J. (1990). Constructive processing in children's event memory. *Developmental Psychology, 26,* 180–187.

Hudson, L. M., Forman, E. A., & Brion-Meisels, S. (1982). Role taking as a predictor of prosocial behavior in cross-age tutors. *Child Development, 53,* 1320–1329.

Huebner, A., & Garrod, A. (1991). Equilibration and the learning paradox. *Human Development, 34,* 261–272.

Huel, G., Everson, R. B., & Menger, I. (1984). Increased hair cadmium in newborns of women occupationally exposed to heavy metals. *Environmental Research, 35,* 115–121.

Huesmann, L. R., Lagerspetz, K., & Eron, L. D. (1984). Intervening variables in the TV violence-aggression relation: Evidence from two countries. *Developmental Psychology, 20,* 746–775.

Humphreys, L. G., Rich, S. A., & Davey, T. C. (1985). A Piagetian test of general intelligence. *Developmental Psychology, 21,* 872–877.

Hunziker, U. A., & Barr, R. G. (1986). Increased carrying reduces infant crying: A randomized controlled trial. *Pediatrics, 77,* 641–648.

Huston, A. C. (1983). Sex-typing. In P. H. Mussen (Ed.), *Handbook of child psychology* (4th ed., Vol. 4, pp. 388–467). New York: Wiley.

Huston, A. C., & Wright, J. C. (1982). Effects of communication media on children. In C. B. Kopp, & J. B. Krakow (Eds.), *The child: Development in a social context.* Boston: Addison-Wesley.

Huston, A. C., Wright, J. C., Rice, M. L., Kerkman, D., & St. Peters, M. (1990). Development of television viewing patterns in early childhood: A longitudinal investigation. *Developmental Psychology, 26,* 409–420.

Huttenlocher, J., Haight, W., Bryk, A., Seltzer, M., & Lyons, T. (1991). Early vocabulary growth: Relation to language input and gender. *Developmental Psychology, 27,* 236–248.

Hyde, J. S., & Linn, M. C. (1988). Are there sex differences in verbal abilities?: A meta-analysis. *Psychological Bulletin, 104*(1), 53–69.

Hymel, S. (1986). Interpretations of peer behavior: Affective bias in childhood and adolescence. *Child Development, 57,* 431–445.

Hymel, S., Rubin, K. H., Rowden, L., & LeMare, L. (1990). Children's peer relationships: Longtudinal prediction of internalizing and externalizing problems from middle to late childhood. *Child Development, 61,* 2004–2021.

Iannotti, R. J. (1978). Effect of role-taking experiences on role taking, empathy, altruism, and aggression. *Developmental Psychology, 14,* 119–124.

Imperato-McGinley, J., Peterson, R. E., Gautier, T., & Sturla, E. (1979). Androgens and the evolution of male-gender identity among male pseudohermaphrodites with 5-reductase deficiency. *New England Journal of Medicine, 300,* 1233–1237.

Inhelder, B., & Piaget, J. (1958). *The growth of logical thinking from childhood to adolescence.* New York: Basic Books.

Irwin, M. H., & McLaughlin, D. H. (1970). Ability and preference in category sorting by Mano schoolchildren and adults. *Journal of Social Psychology, 82,* 15–24.

Irwin, M. H., Schafer, G. N., & Feiden, C. P. (1974). Emic and unfamiliar category sorting of Mano farmers and U.S. undergraduates. *Journal of Cross-Cultural Psychology, 5,* 407–423.

Isabella, R. A., & Belsky, J. (1991). Interactional synchrony and the origins of infant-mother attachment: A replication study. *Child Development, 62,* 373–384.

Isabella, R. A., Belsky, J., & von Eye, A. (1989). The origins of infant-mother attachment: An examination of interactional synchrony during the infant's first year. *Developmental Psychology, 25,* 12–21.

Isen, A. M., Horn, N., & Rosenhan, D. L. (1973). Effects of success and failure on children's generosity. *Journal of Personality and Social Psychology, 27,* 239–247.

Ispa, J. (1981). Peer support among Soviet day care toddlers. *International Journal of Behavioral Development, 4,* 255–269.

Izard, C. E., Porges, S. W., Simons, R. F., Haynes, O. M., Hyde, C., Parisi, M., & Cohen, B. (1991). Infant cardiac activity: Developmental changes and relations with attachment. *Developmental Psychology, 27,* 432–439.

Jacklin, C. N. (1989). Female and male: Issues of gender. *American Psychologist, 44,* 127–133.

Jacklin, C. N., & Maccoby, E. E. (1983). Issues of gender differentiation in normal development. In M. D. Levine, W. B. Carey, A. C. Crocker, & R. T. Gross (Eds.), *Developmental-behavioral pediatrics.* Philadelphia: W. B. Saunders.

Jackson, C. M. (1929). Some aspects of form and growth. In W. J. Robbins, S. Brody, A. F. Hogan, C. M. Jackson, & C. W. Greed (Eds.), *Growth.* New Haven, CT: Yale University Press.

Jackson, P. W., & Messick, D. (1968). Creativity. In P. London, & D. Rosenhan (Eds.), *Foundations of abnormal psychology.* New York: Holt.

Jacobs, J. (1971). *Adolescent suicide.* New York: Wiley.

Jacobson, J. L., & Wille, D. E. (1984). Influence of attachment and separation experience on separation distress at 18 months. *Developmental Psychology, 20,* 477–484.

Jacobson, J. L., Boersma, D. C., Fields, R. B., & Olson, K. L. (1983). Par-

alinguistic features of adult speech to infants and small children. *Child Development, 54*, 436–442.
Jacobson, S. W. (1979). Matching behavior in the young infant. *Child Development, 50*, 425–430.
Jelliffe, D. B., & Jelliffe, E. F. P. (1977). Current concepts in nutrition: "Breast is best": Modern meanings. *New England Journal of Medicine, 297*, 912–915.
Jensen, A. R. (1969). How much can we boost IQ and scholastic achievement? *Harvard Educational Review, 39*, 1–123.
Joffe, L. S. (1980). *The relation between mother-infant attachment and compliance with maternal commands and prohibitions*. Unpublished doctoral dissertation, University of Minnesota.
Joffe, L. S., & Vaughn, B. E. (1982). Infant-mother attachment: Theory, assessment, and implications for development. In B. B. Wolman (Ed.), *Handbook of developmental psychology* (pp. 190–207). Englewood Cliffs, NJ: Prentice-Hall.
Johansson, G. (1973). Visual perception of biological motion and a model for its analysis. *Perception and Psychophysics, 14*, 201–211.
Johansson, G., von Hofsten, C., & Jansson, G. (1980). Event perception. *Annual Review of Psychology, 31*, 27–63.
Johnson, C., & Flach, A. (1985). Family characteristics of 105 patients with bulimia. *American Journal of Psychiatry, 142*, 1321–1324.
Johnson, C. N. (1990). If you had my brain, where would I be? Children's understanding of the brain and identity. *Child Development, 61*, 962–972.
Johnston, J. R., Kline, M., & Tschann, J. M. (1989). Ongoing postdivorce conflict: Effects on children of joint custody and frequent access. *American Journal of Orthopsychiatry, 59*, 576–592.
Johnston, L. D., Bachman, J. G., & O'Malley, P. M. (1992, January 15). *Most forms of drug use decline among American high school and college students*. Ann Arbor, Michigan: University of Michigan News and Information Services.

Kagan, J. (1966). Reflection-impulsivity: The generality and dynamics of conceptual tempo. *Journal of Abnormal Psychology, 71*, 17–24.
Kagan, J. (1973). What is intelligence? *Social Policy, 4*(1), 88–94.
Kagan, J. (1979). Family experience and the child's development. *American Psychologist, 34*, 886–891.
Kagan, J., & Klein, R. E. (1973). Cross-cultural perspectives on early development. *American Psychologist, 28*, 947–961.
Kagan, J., & Moss, H. A. (1962). *Birth to maturity*. New York: Wiley.
Kagan, J., Reznick, J. S., & Gibbons, J. (1989). Inhibited and unhibited types of children. *Child Development, 60*, 838–845.
Kagan, J., Reznick, J. S., Clarke, C., Snidman, N., & Garcia-Coll, C. (1984). Behavioral inhibition to the unfamiliar. *Child Development, 55*, 2212–2225.
Kagan, J., Rosman, B. L., Day, D., Albert, J., & Phillips, W. (1964). Information processing in the child: Significance of analytic and reflective attitudes. *Psychological Monographs*, (Whole No. 578).
Kagan, J., & Snidman, N. (1991). Temperamental factors in human development. *American Psychologist, 46*, 856–862.
Kagan, S., & Madsen, M. C. (1971). Cooperation and competition of Mexican, Mexican-American, and Anglo-American children of two ages and four instructional sets. *Developmental Psychology, 5*, 32–39.
Kahn, P. H., Jr. (1992). Children's obligatory and discretionary moral judgments. *Child Development, 63*, 416–430.
Kail, R. (1988). Developmental functions for speeds of cognitive processes. *Journal of Experimental Child Psychology, 45*, 339–364.
Kail, R. (1991). Processing time declines exponentially during childhood and adolescence. *Developmental Psychology, 27*, 259–266.
Kail, R., & Hagen, J. W. (1982). Memory in childhood. In B. B. Wolman (Ed.), *Handbook of developmental psychology*. Englewood Cliffs, NJ: Prentice-Hall.
Kaitz, M., Meschulach-Sarfaty, O., Auerbach, J., & Eidelman, A. (1988). A reexamination of newborns' ability to imitate facial expressions. *Developmental Psychology, 24*, 3–7.
Kajino, T., McIntyre, J. A., Faulk, W. P., Cai, D. S., & Billington, W. D. (1988). Antibodies to trophoblast in normal pregnant and secondary aborting women. *Journal of Reproductive Immunology, 14*, 267–282.
Kalnins, I. V., & Bruner, J. S. (1973). The coordination of visual observation and instrumental behavior in early infancy. *Perception, 2*, 307–314.
Kalter, N., & Plunkett, J. W. (1984). Children's perceptions of the causes and consequences of divorce. *Journal of the American Academy of Child Psychiatry, 23*, 326–334.
Kamin, L. J. (1974). *The science and politics of IQ*. Potomac, MD: Erlbaum.
Kandel, D. B., & Raveis, V. H. (1989). Cessation of illicit drug use in young adulthood. *Archives of General Psychiatry, 46*, 109–116.
Kantrowitz, B., & Leslie, C. (1986, March 10). Teaching fear. *Newsweek*, pp. 60–63.
Kaplan, H., & Dove, H. (1987). Infant development among the Ache of Eastern Paraguay. *Developmental Psychology, 23*, 190–198.
Kashani, J. H., Holcomb, W. R., & Orvaschel, H. (1986). Depression and depressive symptoms in preschool children from the general population. *American Journal of Psychiatry, 143*, 1138–1143.
Katz, P. A., & Walsh, P. V. (1991). Modification of children's gender-stereotyped behavior. *Child Development, 62*, 338–351.
Katz, V. L., Jenkins, T., Haley, L., & Bowes, W. A. Jr. (1991). Catecholamine levels in pregnant physicians and nurses: A pilot study of stress and pregnancy. *Obstetrics & Gynecology, 77*, 338–342.
Kaufman, M. H., & O'Shea, K. S. (1978). Induction of monozygotic twinning in the mouse. *Nature, 276*, 707–708.
Kaye, K. (1977). Towards the origins of dialogue. In H. R. Schaffer (Ed.), *Studies in mother-infant interactions*. New York: Academic Press.
Keating, M. B., McKenzie, B. E., & Day, R. H. (1986). Spatial localization in infancy: Position constancy in a square and circular room with and without a landmark. *Child Development, 57*, 115–124.
Keil, F. C. (1981). Constraints on knowledge and cognitive development. *Psychological Review, 88*, 197–227.
Keller, H., & Scholmerich, A. (1987). Infant vocalizations and parental reactions during the first four months of life. *Developmental Psychology, 23*, 62–67.
Kemp, J. S., & Thach, B. T. (1991). Sudden death in infants sleeping on polystyrene-filled cushions. *New England Journal of Medicine, 324*, 1858–1864.
Kempe, C. H., Silverman, F., Steele, B., Droegemueller, W., & Silver, H. (1962). The battered child syndrome. *Journal of the American Medical Association, 181*, 17–24.
Kennedy, W. A. (1969). A follow-up normative study of Negro intelligence and achievement. *Monographs of the Society for Research in Child Development, 34*(2, Serial No. 126).
Kennell, J. H., Jerauld, R., Wolfe, H., Chesler, D., Kreger, N. C., McAlpine, W., Steffa, N., & Klaus, M. H. (1974). Maternal behavior one year after early and extended post-partum contact. *Developmental Medicine and Child Neurology, 16*, 172–179.
Kennell, J. H., & Klaus, M. H. (1984). Mother-infant bonding: Weighing the evidence. *Developmental Review, 4*, 275–282.
Kennell, J. H., Voos, D. K., & Klaus, M. H. (1979). Parent-infant bonding. In J. Osofsky (Ed.), *Handbook of infant development* (pp. 786–798). New York: Wiley Interscience.
Kermoian, R., & Campos, J. J. (1988). Locomotor experience: A facilitator of spatial cognitive development. *Child Development, 59*, 908–917.
Kety, S. S., Rosenthal, D., Wender, P. H., Schulsinger, F., & Jacobsen, B. (1978). The biologic and adoptive families of adopted individuals who become schizophrenic: Prevalence of mental illness and other characteristics. In L. C. Wynne, R. L. Cromwell, & S. Matthysse (Eds.), *The nature of schizophrenia: New approaches to research and treatment*. New York: Wiley.
Khan, A. U. (1988). Heterogeneity of suicidal adolescents. In S. Chess, A. Thomas, & M. E. Hertzig (Eds.), *Annual progress in child psychiatry and child development* (pp. 675–686). New York: Brunner/Mazel.
Khan, L. M. L., & James, S. L. (1983). Grammatical morpheme development in three language disordered children. *Journal of Childhood Com-*

munication Disorders, 6, 85–100.

Kimura, D. (1985, November). Male brain, female brain: The hidden difference. *Psychology Today,* pp. 50–58.

Kinsey, A. C., Pomeroy, W. B., Martin, C. E., & Gebhard, P. H. (1953). *Sexual behavior in the human female.* Philadelphia: Saunders.

Kinsey, A., Pomeroy, W., & Martin, C. (1948). *Sexual behavior in the human male.* Philadelphia: Saunders.

Klaus, M. H., Jerauld, R., Kreger, N. C., McAlpine, W., Steffa, M., & Kennell, J. H. (1972). Maternal attachment: Importance of the first postpartum days. *New England Journal of Medicine, 286,* 460–463.

Klaus, M. H., & Kennell, J. H. (1976). *Maternal-infant bonding.* St. Louis: Mosby.

Klein, P. S. (1984). Behavior of israeli mothers toward infants in relation to infants' perceived temperament. *Child Development, 55,* 1212–1218.

Klein, R. E., & Durfee, J. T. (1976). Infants' reactions to unfamiliar adults versus mothers. *Child Development, 47,* 1194–1196.

Klink, F., Jungblut, J. R., Oberheuser, F., & Siegers, C. P. (1983). Cadmium- und Bleikonzen-trationen im Fruchtwasser von rauchenden und nicht-rauchenden Gravida. [Cadmium and lead concentrations in the amniotic fluid of pregnant smokers and non-smokers.] *Geburtshilfe Fraunheilkd, 43,* 695–698.

Klinnert, M. D., Emde, R. N., Butterfield, P., & Campos, J. J. (1986). Social referencing: The infant's use of emotional signals from a friendly adult with mother present. *Developmental Psychology, 22,* 427–432.

Knight, G. P., Kagan, S., & Buriel, R. (1981). Confounding effects of individualism in children's cooperation-competition social motive measures. *Motivation and Emotion, 5,* 167–178.

Knight, G. P., Kagan, S., & Buriel, R. (1982). Perceived parental practices and prosocial development. *Journal of Genetic Psychology, 141,* 57–65.

Knutson, J. F. (1978). Child abuse as an area of aggression research. *Journal of Pediatric Psychology, 3,* 20–27.

Koch, H. L. (1955). The relation of certain family constellation characteristics and the attitudes of children toward adults. *Child Development, 26,* 13–40.

Koepke, J. E., & Barnes, P. (1982). Amount of sucking when a sucking object is readily available to human newborns. *Child Development, 53,* 978–983.

Kogan, N., & Pankove, E. (1972). Creative ability over a five-year span. *Child Development, 43,* 427–442.

Kohlberg, L. (1966). A cognitive-developmental analysis of children's sex-role concepts and attitudes. In E. E. Maccoby (Ed.), *The development of sex differences* (pp. 81–173). Stanford, Calif.: Stanford Univ. Press.

Kohlberg, L., Yaeger, J., & Hjertholm, E. (1968). Private speech: Four studies and a review of theories. *Child Development, 39,* 691–736.

Kolata, G. (1983). Math genius may have hormonal basis. *Science, 222,* 1312.

Kolata, G. (1984). Studying learning in the womb. *Science, 225,* 302–303.

Kolata, G. (1986). Obese children: A growing problem. *Science, 232,* 20–21.

Konopasky, R. J., & Telegdy, G. A. (1977). Conformity in the rat: A leader's selection of door color versus a learned door-color discrimination. *Perceptual & Motor Skills, 44,* 31–37.

Koops, B. L., Morgan, L. J., & Battaglia, F. C. (1982). Neonatal mortality risk in relation to birth weight and gestational age: Update. *Journal of Pediatrics, 101,* 969–977.

Kopp, C. B., & Kalar, S. R. (1989). Risk in infancy. *American Psychologist, 44,* 224–230.

Korbin, J. (1977). Anthropological contributions to the study of child abuse. *International Child Welfare Review,* No. 35, 23–31.

Korn, S. J., & Gannon, S. (1983). Temperament, cultural variation and behavior disorder in preschool children. *Child Psychiatry and Human Development, 13,* 203–212.

Korner, A. F., Hutchinson, C. A., Koperski, J. A., Kraemer, H. C., & Schneider, P. A. (1981). Stability of individual differences of neonatal motor and crying patterns. *Child Development, 52,* 83–90.

Kotelchuck, M. (1976). The infant's relationship to the father: Experimental evidence. In M. E. Lamb (Ed.), *The role of the father in child development.* New York: Wiley.

Kovacs, M. (1989). Affective disorders in children and adolescents. *American Psychologist, 44,* 209–215.

Kramer, M. S. (1981). Do breast-feeding and delayed introduction of solid foods protect against subsequent obesity? *Journal of Pediatrics, 98,* 883–887.

Krieger, W. G. (1976). Infant influences and the parent sex by child sex interaction in the socialization process. *JSAS Catalogue of Selected Documents in Psychology,* 6(1), 36 (Ms. No. 1234).

Kringlen, E. (1967). *Heredity and environment in the functional psychosis: An epidemiological-clinical twin study.* Oslo: Universitsforlaget.

Kruse, J. (1984). Alcohol use during pregnancy. *American Family Physician, 29,* 199–203.

Kuczaj, S. A. (1983). "I mell a kunk!"—evidence that children have more complex representations of word pronunciations which they simplify. *Journal of Psycholinguistic Research, 12,* 69–73.

Kuczynski, L. (1984). Socialization goals and mother-child interaction: Strategies for long-term and short-term compliance. *Developmental Psychology, 20,* 1061–1073.

Kuczynski, L., Kochanska, G., Radke-Yarrow, M., & Girnius-Brown, O. (1987). A developmental interpretation of children's noncompliance. *Developmental Psychology, 23,* 799–806.

Kuhl, P. K., Williams, K. A., Lacerda, F., Stevens, K. N., & Lindblom, B. (1992). Linguistic experience alters phonetic perception in infants by 6 months of age. *Science, 255,* 606–608.

Kuhlen, R. G., & Arnold, M. (1944). Age differences in religious beliefs and problems during adolescence. *Journal of Genetic Psychology, 65,* 291–300.

Kuhn, D., Langer, J., Kohlberg, L., & Haan, N. S. (1977). The development of formal operations in logical and moral judgment. *Genetic Psychology Monographs, 95,* 97–188.

Kurdek, L. A. (1978). Perspective-taking as the cognitive basis of children's moral development: A review of the literature. *Merrill-Palmer Quarterly, 24,* 3–28.

Kurppa, K., Holmberg, P. C., Kuosma, E., & Saxen, L. (1983). Coffee consumption during pregnancy and selected congenital malformations: A nationwide case-control study. *American Journal of Public Health, 73,* 1397–1399.

Kurtines, W., & Greif, E. B. (1974). The development of moral thought: Review and evaluation of Kohlberg's approach. *Psychological Bulletin, 81,* 453–470.

Ladd, G. W. (1990). Having friends, keeping friends, making friends, and being liked by peers in the classroom: Predictors of children's early school adjustment? *Child Development, 61,* 1081–1100.

Ladd, G. W., & Emerson, E. S. (1984). Shared knowledge in children's friendships. *Developmental Psychology, 20,* 932–940.

Ladd, G. W., Lange, G., & Stremmel, A. (1983). Personal and situational influences on children's helping behavior: Factors that mediate compliant helping. *Child Development, 54,* 488–501.

Lagercrantz, H., & Slotkin, T. A. (1986). The "stress" of being born. *Scientific American, 254*(4), 100–107.

Lamb, M. E. (1977). The development of parental preferences in the first two years of life. *Sex Roles, 3,* 495–497.

Lamb, M. E., (Ed.). (1981). *The role of the father in child development* (2nd ed.). New York: Wiley.

Lamb, M. E., & Elster, A. B. (1985). Adolescent mother-infant-father relationships. *Developmental Psychology, 21,* 768–773.

Lamb, M. E., & Sternberg, K. J. (1990). Do we really know how day care affects children? *Journal of Applied Developmental Psychology, 11,* 351–379.

Lamb, M. E., Thompson, R. A., Gardner, W. P., Charnov, E. L., & Estes, D. (1984). Security of infantile attachment as assessed in the "strange situation": Its study and biological interpretation. *The Behavioral and Brain Sciences, 7,* 127–171.

Lampl, M., Veldhuis, J. D., & Johnson, M. L. (1992). Saltation and stasis: A model of human growth. *Science, 258,* 801–803.

Landers, S. (1990, April). Sex, condom use up among teenage boys. *The APA Monitor,* p. 25.

Lange, G., & Pierce, S. H. (1992). Memory-strategy learning and maintenance in preschool children. *Developmental Psychology, 28,* 453–462.

Langlois, J. H., & Downs, A. C. (1980). Mothers, fathers, and peers as socialization agents of sex-typed play behaviors in young children. *Child Development, 51,* 1237–1247.

Langlois, J. H., Ritter, J. M., Roggman, L. A., & Vaughn, L. S. (1991). Facial diversity and infant preferences for attractive faces. *Developmental Psychology, 27,* 79–84.

Langlois, J. H., & Styczynski, L. (1979). The effects of physical attractiveness on the behavioral attributions and peer preferences in acquainted children. *International Journal of Behavioral Development, 2,* 325–341.

Lasagna, L. (1969). Special subjects in human experimentation. *Daedlus, 98,* 449–462.

Lazar, I., & Darlington, R. (1982). Lasting effects of early education: A report from the Consortium for Longitudinal Studies. *Monographs of the Society for Research in Child Development, 47*(2–3, Serial No. 195).

Lebra, T. S. (1976). *Japanese patterns of behavior.* Honolulu: University of Hawaii Press.

Lee, C. L. (1973, August). *Social encounters of infants: The beginnings of popularity.* Paper presented at the meeting of the International Society for the Study of Behavioral Development, Ann Arbor, Michigan.

Lee, C. L., & Bates, J. E. (1985). Mother-child interaction at age two years and perceived difficult temperament. *Child Development, 56,* 1314–1325.

Lee, V. E., Brooks-Gunn, J., Schnur, E., & Liaw, F. (1990). Are Head Start effects sustained? A longitudinal follow-up comparison of disadvantaged children attending Head Start, no preschool, and other preschool programs. *Child Development, 61,* 495–507.

Lefkowitz, M. M., Eron, L. D., Walder, L. O., & Huesmann, L. R. (1977). *Growing up to be violent.* New York: Pergamon.

Lefrancois, G. R. (1983). *Of children.* (4th ed.). Belmont, CA: Wadsworth.

Legerstee, M., Corter, C., & Kineapple, K. (1990). Hand, arm, and facial actions of young infants to a social and nonsocial stimulus. *Child Development, 61,* 774–784.

Lempert, H. (1984). Topic as starting point for syntax. *Monographs of the Society for Research in Child Development, 49*(5, Serial No. 208).

Lempert, H. (1989). Animacy constraints on preschool children's acquisition of syntax. *Child Development, 60,* 237–245.

Lenssen, B. (1975). *Infants' reactions to peer strangers.* Paper presented at the meeting of the Society for Research in Child Development, Denver, Colorado.

Leo, J. (1986, February 24). Could suicide be contagious? *Time,* p. 59.

Lerman, H. (1986). *A mote in Freud's eye: From psychoanalysis to the psychology of women.* New York: Springer.

Lerner, R. M. (1984). *On the nature of human plasticity.* New York: Cambridge Univ. Press.

Lerner, R. M., Palermo, M., Spiro, A., & Nesselroade, J. R. (1982). Assessing the dimensions of temperamental individuality across the life span: The Dimensions of Temperament Survey (DOTS). *Child Development, 53,* 149–159.

Lerner, R. M., & Weinstock, A. (1972). Note on the generation gap. *Psychological Reports, 31,* 457–458.

Lesser, H. (1977). *Television and the preschool child.* New York: Academic Press.

Lester, B. M., Corwin, M. J., Sepkoski, C., Seifer, R., Peucker, M., McLaughlin, S., & Golub, H. L. (1991). Neurobehavioral syndromes in cocaine-exposed newborn infants. *Child Development, 62,* 694–705.

Lester, B. M., & Dreher, M. (1989). Effects of marijuana use during pregnancy. *Child Development, 60,* 765–771.

LeVay, S. (1991). A difference in hypothalamic structure between heterosexual and homosexual men. *Science, 253,* 1034–1037.

Levine, E. M., Kozak, C., & Shaiova, C. H. (1977). Hyperactivity among white middle-class children: Psychogenic and other causes. *Child Psychiatry and Human Development, 7,* 156–168.

Levine, L. E. (1983). Mine: Self-definition in 2-year-old boys. *Developmental Psychology, 19,* 544–549.

Levitt, M. J., Weber, R. A., Clark, M. C., & McDonnell, P. (1985). Reciprocity of exchange in toddler sharing behavior. *Developmental Psychology, 21,* 122–123.

Lewis, M. (1975). *The meaning of fear.* Paper presented at the meeting of the Society for Research in Child Development, Denver, Colorado.

Lewis, M., & Brooks, J. (1974). Self, other and fear: Infants' reactions to people. In M. Lewis, & L. Rosenblum (Eds.), *The origins of fear* (pp. 195–227). New York: Wiley.

Lewis, M., & Feiring, C. (1989). Infant, mother, and mother-infant interaction behavior and subsequent attachment. *Child Development, 60,* 831–837.

Lewkowicz, D. J. (1988). Sensory dominance in infants: 1. Six-month-old infants' response to auditory-visual compounds. *Developmental Psychology, 24,* 155–171.

Liberty, C., & Ornstein, P. A. (1973). Age differences in organization and recall: The effects of training in categorization. *Journal of Experimental Child Psychology, 15,* 169–186.

Licht, B. G., & Dweck, C. S. (1984). Determinants of academic achievement: The interaction of children's achievement orientations with skill area. *Developmental Psychology, 20,* 628–636.

Lieberman, A. F., Weston, D. R., & Pawl, J. H. (1991). Preventive intervention and outcome with anxiously attached dyads. *Child Development, 62,* 199–209.

Lieberman, P., Crelin, E. S., & Klatt, D. H. (1972). Phonetic ability and related anatomy of the newborn and adult human, Neanderthal man, and the chimpanzee. *American Anthropologist, 74,* 287–307.

Liebert, R. M., Poulos, R. W., & Marmor, G. S. (1977). *Developmental psychology.* Englewood Cliffs, NJ: Prentice-Hall.

Liebert, R. M., & Sprafkin, J. (1988). *The early window: Effects of television on children and youth* (3rd ed.). New York: Pergamon Press.

Liebert, R. M., Sprafkin, J. N., & Poulos, R. W. (1975). Selling cooperation to children. In W. S. Hale (Ed.), *Proceedings of the 20th Annual Conference of the Advertising Research Foundation* (pp. 54–57). New York: Advertising Research Foundation, Inc.

Linney, J. A., & Seidman, E. (1989). The future of schooling. *American Psychologist, 44,* 336–340.

Lipscomb, T. J., Larrieu, J. A., McAllister, H. A., & Bregman, N. J. (1982). Modeling and children's generosity: A developmental perspective. *Merrill-Palmer Quarterly, 28,* 275–282.

Lipsitt, L. P., McCullagh, A. A., Reilly, B. M., Smith, I. M., & Sturner, W. Q. (1981). Perinatal indicators of sudden infant death syndrome: A study of 34 Rhode Island cases. *Journal of Applied Developmental Psychology, 2,* 79–88.

Livingston, R., Nugent, H., Rader, L., & Smith, G. R. (1985). Family histories of depressed and severely anxious children. *American Journal of Psychiatry, 142,* 1497–1499.

Lobel, M., Dunkel-Schetter, C., & Scrimshaw, S. C. (1992). Prenatal maternal stress and prematurity: A prospective study of socioeconomically disadvantaged women. *Health Psychology, 11,* 32–40.

Loehlin, J. C., Horn, J. M., & Willerman, L. (1989). Modeling IQ change: Evidence from the Texas Adoption Project. *Child Development, 60,* 993–1004.

Loizos, C. (1967). Play behavior in higher primates: A review. In D. Morris (Ed.), *Primate ethology.* London: Weidenfeld & Nicholson.

Longstreth, L. E. (1980). Human handedness: More evidence for genetic involvement. *Journal of Genetic Psychology, 137,* 275–283.

Looft, W. R. (1971). Egocentrism and social interaction in adolescence. *Adolescence, 6*(24), 485–494.

Lorenz, K. (1943). Die angeborenen Formen moglicher Erfahrung. *Z. Tierpsychologie, 5,* 235–409.

Lorenz, K. (1966). *On aggression.* New York: Harcourt Brace.

Lorenz, K. (1937). Uber die Bildung des Instinkbegriffes. *Naturwissenschaften, 25,* 289–300, 307–318, 324–331.

Lovett, S. B., & Flavell, J. H. (1990). Understanding and remembering: Children's knowledge about the differential effects of strategy and task variables on comprehension and memorization. *Child Development, 61,* 1842–1858.

Lozoff, B. (1983). Birth and "bonding" in non-industrial societies. *Developmental Medicine & Child Neurology, 25,* 595–600.

Lucas, B. (1977). Nutrition and the adolescent. In P. L. Pipes (Ed.), *Nutrition in infancy and childhood* (pp. 132–144). St. Louis: Mosby.

Lumsden, C. J. (1984). Parent-offspring conflict over the transmission of culture. *Ethology & Sociobiology, 5,* 111–129.

Luria, A. R. (1961). *The role of speech in the regulation of normal and abnormal behavior.* London: Pergamon Press.

Luria, A. R. (1969). Speech development and the formation of mental processes. In M. Cole, & I. Maltzman (Eds.), *Handbook of contemporary Soviet psychology.* New York: Basic Books.

Lyle, J., & Hoffman, H. R. (1972). Children's use of television and other media. In E. A. Rubinstein, G. A. Comstock, & J. P. Murray (Eds.), *Television and social behavior, Vol. 4, television in day-to-day life: Patterns of use.* Washington, D.C.: U.S. Government Printing Office.

Lystad, M. H. (1975). Violence at home: A review of the literature. *American Journal of Orthopsychiatry, 45,* 328–345.

Lytton, H. (1980). *Parent-child interaction: The socialization process observed in twin and singleton families.* New York: Plenum.

Lytton, H., Conway, D., & Suave, R. (1977). The impact of twinship on parent-child interaction. *Journal of Personality and Social Psychology, 35,* 97–107.

Maccoby, E. E. (1984). Socialization and developmental change. *Child Development, 55,* 317–328.

Maccoby, E. E. (1988). Gender as a social category. *Developmental Psychology, 24,* 755–765.

Maccoby, E. E. (1991). Different reproductive strategies in males and females. *Child Development, 62,* 676–681.

Maccoby, E. E., & Jacklin, C. N. (1974). *The psychology of sex differences.* Stanford, Calif.: Stanford Univ. Press.

Maccoby, E. E., & Martin, J. A. (1983). Socialization in the context of the family: Parent-child interaction. In P. H. Mussen (Ed.), *Handbook of child psychology* (4th ed., Vol. IV, pp. 1–101). New York: Wiley.

Mactutus, C. F., & Fechter, L. D. (1984). Prenatal exposure to carbon monoxide: Learning and memory deficits. *Science, 223,* 409–411.

MacWhinney, B. (1978). The acquisition of morphophonology. *Monographs of the Society for Research in Child Development, 43*(1–2, Serial No. 174).

Madden, N. A., & Slavin, R. E. (1983). Mainstreaming students with mild handicaps: Academic and social outcomes. *Review of Educational Research, 53,* 519–569.

Madsen, M. C. (1971). Developmental and cross-cultural differences in the cooperative and competitive behavior of young children. *Journal of Cross-Cultural Psychology, 2,* 365–371.

Madsen, M. C., & Lancy, D. F. (1981). Cooperative and competitive behavior. Experiments related to ethnic identity and urbanization in Papua New Guinea. *Journal of Cross-Cultural Psychology, 12,* 389–408.

Madsen, M. C., & Shapira, A. (1970). Cooperative and competitive behavior of urban Afro-American, Anglo-American, Mexican-American, and Mexican village children. *Developmental Psychology, 3,* 16–20.

Main, M., & Cassidy, J. (1988). Categories of response to reunion with the parent at age 6: Predictable from infant attachment classifications and stable over a 1-month period. *Developmental Psychology, 24,* 415–426.

Main, M., & George, C. (1985). Responses of abused and disadvantaged toddlers to distress in agemates: A study in the day care setting. *Developmental Psychology, 21,* 407–412.

Main, M., Kaplan, N., & Cassidy, J. (1985). Security in infancy, childhood, and adulthood: A move to the level of representation. *Monographs of the Society for Research in Child Development, 50*(209, Serial No. 209), 66–104.

Main, M., & Weston, D. R. (1981). The quality of the toddler's relationship to mother and to father: Related to conflict behavior and the readiness to establish new relationships. *Child Development, 52,* 932–940.

Main, M., & Weston, D. R. (1982). Avoidance of the attachment figure in infancy: Descriptions and interpretations. In C. M. Parkes & J. Stevenson-Hinde (Eds.), *The place of attachment in human behavior* (pp. 31–59). New York: Basic Books.

Malina, R. M. (1978). Growth of muscle tissue and muscle mass. In F. Falkner, & J. M. Tanner (Eds.), *Human growth* (Vol. 2). New York: Plenum.

Malina, R. M. (1979). Secular changes in growth, maturation, and physical performance. *Exercise and Sport Science Reviews, 6,* 203–255.

Malinowski, B. (1929). *The sexual life of savages.* New York: Harcourt Brace.

Mandler, J. M. (1983). Representation. In J. H. Flavell, & E. M. Markman (Eds.), *Handbook of child psychology* (Vol. 3, pp. 420–494). New York: Wiley.

Manicas, P. T., & Secord, P. F. (1983). Implications for psychology of the new philosophy of science. *American Psychologist, 38,* 399–413.

Marano, H. (1979, October 29). Breast or bottle: New evidence in an old debate. *New York Magazine,* pp. 56–60.

Maranto, G. (1984, October). Choosing your baby's sex. *Discover,* pp. 25–27.

Marcus, G. F., Pinker, S., Ullman, M., Hollander, M., Rosen, T. J., & Xu, F. (1992). Overregularization in language acquisition. *Monographs of the Society for Research in Child Development, 57*(4, Serial No. 228).

Marcus, R. F., Telleen, S., & Roke, E. J. (1979). Relation between cooperation and empathy in young children. *Developmental Psychology, 15,* 346–347.

Marean, G. C., Werner, L. A., & Kuhl, P. K. (1992). Vowel categorization by very young infants. *Developmental Psychology, 28,* 396–405.

Marks, R. G. (1978, February). Infant botulism. *Current Prescribing,* pp. 67–75.

Marmor, J. (1985, October). Homosexuality: Nature vs. nurture. *Harvard Medical School Mental Health Letter,* pp. 5–6.

Martin, B. (1975). Parent-child relations. In F. D. Horowitz (Ed.), *Review of child development research* (Vol. 4). Chicago: Univ. of Chicago Press.

Martin, C. L., & Little, J. K. (1990). The relation of gender understanding to children's sex-typed preferences and gender stereotypes. *Child Development, 61,* 1427–1439.

Marton, J. P., & Acker, L. E. (1981). Television provoked aggression: Effects of gentle, affection-like training prior to exposure. *Child Study Journal, 12,* 27–43.

Martorano, S. C. (1977). A developmental analysis of performance on Piaget's formal operations tasks. *Developmental Psychology, 13,* 666–672.

Marx, J. L. (1981). More about cloned mice. *Science, 212,* 145.

Masangkay, Z. S., McCluskey, K. A., McIntyre, C. W., Sims-Knight, J., Vaughn, B. E., & Flavell, J. H. (1974). The early development of inferences about the visual percepts of others. *Child Development, 45,* 357–366.

Mason, W. A. (1965). The social development of monkeys and apes. In I. DeVore (Ed.), *Primate behavior: Field studies of monkeys and apes.* New York: Holt.

Massey, C. M., & Gelman, R. (1988). Preschooler's ability to decide whether a photographed unfamiliar object can move itself. *Developmental Psychology, 24,* 307–317.

Masten, A. S. (1986). Humor and competence in school-aged children. *Child Development, 57,* 461–473.

Matsumoto, D., Haan, N., Yabrove, G., Theodorou, P., & Carney, C. C. (1986). Preschoolers' moral actions and emotions in prisoner's dilemma. *Developmental Psychology, 22,* 663–670.

Mattes, J. A., & Gittelman, R. (1981). Effects of artificial food colorings in children with hyperactive symptoms. *Archives of General Psychiatry, 38,* 714–718.

Maurer, D., & Salapatek, P. (1976). Developmental changes in the scanning of faces by young infants. *Child Development, 47,* 523–527.

Maziade, M., Caperaa, P., Laplante, B., Boudreault, M., Thivierge, J., Cote, R., & Boutin, P. (1985). Value of difficult temperament among 7-year-olds in the general population for predicting psychiatric diagnosis at age 12. *American Journal of Psychiatry, 142,* 943–946.

Maziade, M., Cote, R., Boutin, P., Bernier, H., & Thivierge, J. (1988). Temperament and intellectual development: A longitudinal study from infancy to four years. In S. Chess, A. Thomas, & M. E. Hertzig (Eds.), *Annual progress in child psychiatry and child development* (pp. 335–349). New York: Brunner/Mazel.

McCall, J. N., & Johnson, O. G. (1972). The independence of intelligence from family size and birth order. *Journal of Genetic Psychology, 121,* 207–213.

McCall, R. B. (1984). Developmental changes in mental performance: The effect of the birth of a sibling. *Child Development, 55,* 1317–1321.

McCartney, K. (1984). Effect of quality of day care environment on children's language development. *Developmental Psychology, 20,* 244–260.

McClure, G. M. G. (1986). Recent changes in suicide among adolescents in England and Wales. *Journal of Adolescence, 9,* 135–143.

McCoy, C. L., & Masters, J. C. (1985). The development of children's strategies for the social control of emotion. *Child Development, 56,* 1214–1222.

McGowan, R. J., Johnson, D. L., & Maxwell, S. E. (1981). Relations between infant behavior ratings and concurrent and subsequent mental test scores. *Developmental Psychology, 17,* 542–553.

McGrath, E., & Levenson, T. (1982, March 15). The test must go on. *Time,* pp. 80–81.

McGraw, M. B. (1940). Neural maturation as exemplified in achievement of bladder control. *Journal of Paediatrics, 16,* 580–590.

McIntyre, J. J., & Teevan, J. J. (1972). Television violence and deviant behavior. In G. A. Comstock, & E. A. Rubinstein (Eds.), *Television and social behavior, Vol. 3: Television and adolescent aggressiveness* (pp. 383–435). Washington, D.C.: U.S. Government Printing Office.

McKean, K. (1985, October). Intelligence: New ways to measure the wisdom of man. *Discover,* pp. 25–41.

McKenzie, B., & Over, R. (1983). Young infants fail to imitate facial and manual gestures. *Infant Behavior and Development, 6,* 85–95.

McKinney, J. P., & Moore, D. (1982). Attitudes and values during adolescence. In B. B. Wolman (Ed.), *Handbook of developmental psychology* (pp. 549–558). Englewood Cliffs, NJ: Prentice-Hall.

McLoyd, V. C. (1990). The impact of economic hardship on black families and children: Psychological distress, parenting, and socioemotional development. *Child Development, 61,* 311–346.

McManus, I. C., & Bryden, M. P. (1991). Geschwind's theory of cerebral lateralization: Developing a formal, causal model. *Psychological Bulletin, 110,* 237–253.

McNally, S., Eisenberg, N., & Harris, J. D. (1991). Consistency and change in maternal child-rearing practices and values: A longitudinal study. *Child Development, 62,* 190–198.

Mead, M. (1928). *Coming of age in Samoa.* New York: Morrow

Mead, M., & Newton, N. (1967). Cultural patterning of perinatal behavior. In S. A. Richardson, & A. F. Guttmacher (Eds.), *Childbearing: Its social and psychological aspects* (pp. 142–244). Baltimore: Williams & Wilkins.

Mech, E. V. (1973). Adoption: A policy perspective. In B. Caldwell & H. Ricciuti (Eds.), *Review of child development research* (Vol. 3). Chicago: Univ. of Chicago Press.

Mednick, S. A., Pollock, V., Volavka, J., & Gibrielli, W. F. (1982). Biology and violence. In M. E. Wolfgang, & N. A. Weiner (Eds.), *Criminal violence.* Beverly Hills, CA: Russell Sage.

Melton, G. B., & Davidson, H. A. (1987). Child protection and society: When should the State intervene? *American Psychologist, 42,* 172–175.

Meltzoff, A. N. (1988a). Infant imitation after a 1-week delay: Long-term memory for novel acts and multiple stimuli. *Developmental Psychology, 24,* 470–476.

Meltzoff, A. N. (1988b). Infant imitation and memory: Nine-month-olds in immediate and deferred tests. *Child Development, 59,* 217–225.

Meltzoff, A. N. (1988c). Imitation of televised models by infants. *Child Development, 59,* 1221–1229.

Meltzoff, A. N., & Moore, M. K. (1977). Imitation of facial and manual gestures by human neonates. *Science, 198,* 75–78.

Meltzoff, A. N., & Moore, M. K. (1983). Newborn infants imitate adult facial gestures. *Child Development, 54,* 702–709.

Meltzoff, A. N., & Moore, M. K. (1989). Imitation in newborn infants: Exploring the range of gestures imitated and the underlying mechanisms. *Developmental Psychology, 25,* 954–962.

Mendelson, M. J., & Ferland, M. B. (1982). Auditory-visual transfer in four-month-old. *Child Development, 53,* 1022–1027.

Meredith, D. (1985, June). Mom, dad and the kids. *Psychology Today,* pp. 62–67.

Mervis, C. B., & Johnson, K. E. (1991). Acquisition of the plural morpheme: A case study. *Developmental Psychology, 27,* 222–235.

Messer, D. J., McCarthy, M. E., McQuiston, S., MacTurk, R. H., Yarrow, L. J., & Vietze, P. M. (1986). Relation between mastery behavior in infancy and competence in early childhood. *Developmental Psychology, 22,* 366–372.

Meyer, W. J., & Dusek, J. B. (1979). *Child psychology.* Lexington, Mass.: Heath.

Meyers, A. F., Sampson, A. E., Weitzman, M., Rogers, B. L., & Kayne, H. (1989). School breakfast program and school performance. *American Journal of Diseases in Children, 143,* 1234–1239.

Michie, S. (1985). Development of absolute and relative concepts of number in preschool children. *Developmental Psychology, 21,* 247–252.

Miles, C. (1935). Sex in social psychology. In C. Murchinson (Ed.), *Handbook of social psychology.* Worcester, Mass.: Clark Univ. Press.

Miller, C. A. (1985). Infant mortality in the U.S. *Scientific American, 253*(1), 31–37.

Miller, G. A., & Gildea, P. M. (1987). How children learn words. *Scientific American, 257*(3), 94–99.

Miller, J. A. (1981, October 31). Update on Tay-Sachs screening. *Science News,* p. 282.

Miller, J. A. (1982, November 13). Spelling out a cancer gene. *Science News,* pp. 316–317, 319.

Miller, J. A. (1983, February 26). Wiretap on the nervous system. *Science News,* pp. 140–143.

Miller, J. A., & Greenberg, J. (1985, June 15). Preschool day care: Which type is best? *Science News,* p. 376.

Miller, L. B., & Bizzell, R. P. (1983). Long-term effects of four preschool programs: Sixth, seventh, and eighth grades. *Child Development, 54,* 727–741.

Miller, L. B., & Dyer, J. L. (1975). Four preschool programs: Their dimensions and effects. *Monographs of the Society for Research in Child Development, 40*(5–6, Serial No. 162).

Miller, R. L., Brickman, P., & Bolen, D. (1975). Attribution versus persuasion as a means for modifying behavior. *Journal of Personality and Social Psychology, 31,* 430–441.

Miller, S. A. (1986). Certainty and necessity in the understanding of Piagetian concepts. *Developmental Psychology, 22,* 3–18.

Miller, W. C., Lindeman, A. K., Wallace, J., & Niederpruem, M. (1990). Diet composition, energy intake, and exercise in relation to body fat in men and women. *American Journal of Clinical Nutrition, 52,* 426–430.

Mills, J. L., Graubard, B. I., Harley, E. E., Rhoads, G. G., & Berendes, H. W. (1984). Maternal alcohol consumption and birth weight. *Journal of the American Medical Association, 252,* 1875–1879.

Minoura, Y. (1984). *Kodomo no ibunka taiken: Jinkaku keisei katei no shinri-jinruigaku-teki kenkyu* [Children's experience of other cultures: A psycho-anthropological study of the process of personality formation]. Tokyo: Shisaku-sha.

Minton, J., Campbell, M., Green, W. H., Jennings, S., & Samit, C. (1982). Cognitive assessment of siblings of autistic children. *Journal of the American Academy of Child Psychiatry, 21,* 256–261.

Mischel, W. (1974). Process in delay of gratification. In L. Berkowitz (Ed.), *Advances in experimental social psychology* (Vol. 7). New York: Academic Press.

Mischel, W. (1979). On the interface of cognition and personality. *American Psychologist, 34,* 740–754.

Mischel, W., & Ebbesen, E. B. (1970). Attention in delay of gratification. *Journal of Personality and Social Psychology, 16,* 329–337.

Mischel, W., & Mischel, H. N. (1979, March). *The development of children's knowledge of self-control.* Paper presented at the meeting of the Society for Research in Child Development, San Francisco.

Mischel, W., & Moore, B. (1980). The role of ideation in voluntary delay for symbolically presented rewards. *Cognitive Therapy & Research, 4,* 211–221.

Mischel, W., Shoda, Y., & Rodriguez, M. L. (1989). Delay of gratification in children. *Science, 244,* 933–938.

Mischel, W., & Staub, E. (1965). Effects of expectancy on working and waiting for larger rewards. *Journal of Personality and Social Psychology, 2,* 625–633.

Mishara, B. L. (1975). The extent of adolescent suicidality. *Psychiatric Opinion, 12,* 32–37.

Mistry, J. J., & Lange, G. W. (1985). Children's organization and recall of information in scripted narratives. *Child Development, 56,* 953–961.

Mitchell, A. M. (1975). Experimentation on minors: Whatever happened to Prince v. Massachusetts? *Duquesne Law Review, 13,* 919–936.

Mitchell, J. E., Baker, L. A., & Jacklin, C. N. (1989). Masculinity and feminity in twin children: Genetic and environmental factors. *Child Development, 60,* 1475–1485.

Miyake, K., Chen, S., & Campos, J. J. (1985). Infant temperament, mother's mode of interaction, and attachment in Japan: An interim report. In I. Bretherton, & E. Waters (Eds.), Growing points of attachment theory and research. *Monographs of the Society for Research in Child Development, 50*(1–2, Serial No. 209).

Mohs, M. (1982, September). I.Q. *Discover,* pp. 18–24.

Molfese, D. L., Molfese, V. J., & Carrell, P. L. (1982). Early language development. In B. B. Wolman (Ed.), *Handbook of developmental psychology* (pp. 301–322). Englewood Cliffs, NJ: Prentice-Hall.

Molfese, D. L., Morse, P. A., & Peters, C. J. (1990). Auditory evoked responses to names for different objects: Cross-modal processing as a basis for infant language acquisition. *Developmental Psychology, 26,* 780–795.

Money, J., & Ehrhardt, A. A. (1972). *Man and woman, boy and girl.* Baltimore, MD: Johns Hopkins.

Money, J., & Mathews, D. (1982). Prenatal exposure to virilizing progestins: An adult follow-up study of twelve women. *Archives of Sexual Behavior, 11,* 73–83.

Monsaas, J. A., & Engelhard, G., Jr. (1990). Home environment and the competitiveness of highly accomplished individuals in four talent fields. *Developmental Psychology, 26,* 264–268.

Montgomery, G. (1990, March). The ultimate medicine. *Discover,* pp. 60–68.

Moore, B. S., Mischel, W., & Zeiss, A. (1976). Comparative effects of the reward stimulus and its cognitive representation in voluntary delay. *Journal of Personality and Social Psychology, 34,* 419–424.

Moore, B. S., Underwood, B., & Rosenhan, D. L. (1973). Affect and altruism. *Developmental Psychology, 8,* 99–104.

Moore, N. V., Evertson, C. M., & Brophy, J. E. (1974). Solitary play: Some functional considerations. *Developmental Psychology, 10,* 830–834.

Moorehouse, M. J. (1991). Linking maternal employment patterns to mother-child activities and children's school competence. *Developmental Psychology, 27,* 295–303.

Morell, P., & Norton, W. T. (1980). Myelin. *Scientific American, 242*(5), 88–118.

Morelli, G. A., Rogoff, B., Oppenheim, D., & Goldsmith, D. (1992). Cultural variation in infants' sleeping arrangements: Questions of independence. *Developmental Psychology, 28,* 604–613.

Morgan, M., & Gross, L. (1982). Television and educational achievement. In D. Pearl, L. Bouthilet, & J. Lazar (Eds.), *Television and behavior: Ten years of scientific progress and implications for the eighties* (Vol. 2). Washington, DC: U.S. Government Printing Office.

Morris, N. S. (1971). *Television's child.* Boston: Little, Brown.

Morrongiello, B. A. (1988). Infants' localization of sounds along the horizontal axis: Estimates of minimum audible angle. *Developmental Psychology, 24,* 8–13.

Morrongiello, B. A., Fenwick, K. D., & Chance, G. (1990). Sound localization acuity in very young infants: An observer-based testing procedure. *Developmental Psychology, 26,* 75–84.

Moskowitz, B. A. (1978). The acquisition of language. *Scientific American, 239*(5), 92–108.

Moskowitz, D. S., Schwartzman, A. E., & Ledingham, J. E. (1985). Stability and change in aggression and withdrawal in middle childhood and early adolescence. *Journal of Abnormal Psychology, 94,* 30–41.

Motley, M. T. (1985). Slips of the tongue. *Scientific American, 253*(3), 116–127.

Mueller, C., & Donnerstein, E. (1977). The effects of humor-induced arousal upon aggressive behavior. *Journal of Research in Personality, 11,* 73–82.

Mueller, E., & Brenner, J. (1977). The origins of social skills and interaction among playgroup toddlers. *Child Development, 48,* 854–861.

Mueller, E., & Lucas, T. (1975). A developmental analysis of peer interaction among toddlers. In M. Lewis, & L. Rosenblum (Eds.), *Friendship and peer relations.* New York: Wiley.

Mueller, E., & Rich, A. (1976). Clustering and socially-directed behaviors in a playgroup of 1-yr-old boys. *Journal of Child Psychology and Psychiatry, 17,* 315–322.

Mueller, E., & Vandell, D. (1977). Infant-infant interaction. In J. Osofsky (Ed.), *Handbook of infant development.* New York: Wiley Interscience.

Muir, D., & Field, J. (1979). Newborn infants orient to sounds. *Child Development, 50,* 431- 436.

Munroe, R. H., Shimmin, H. S., & Munroe, R. L. (1984). Gender understanding and sex role preference in four cultures. *Developmental Psychology, 20,* 673–682.

Muuss, R. E. (1986). Adolescent eating disorder: Bulimia. *Adolescence, 21,* 257–267.

Myers, B. J. (1984). Mother-infant bonding: The status of this critical-period hypothesis. *Developmental Review, 4,* 240–274.

Myles-Worsley, M., Cromer, C. C., & Dodd, D. H. (1986). Children's preschool script reconstruction: Reliance on general knowledge as memory fades. *Developmental Psychology, 22,* 22–30.

Naeye, R. L. (1980). Sudden infant death. *Scientific American, 242*(4), 56–62.

Naeye, R. L., Ladis, B., & Drage, J. S. (1976). Sudden infant death syndrome: A prospective study. *American Journal of Diseases of Children, 130,* 1207–1210.

National Alliance to End Homelessness. (1988). *Housing and homelessness.* Washington, DC: Author.

National Coalition for the Homeless. (1987). *Broken lives: Denial of education to homeless children.* Washington, DC: Author.

Needleman, H. L., Schell, A., Bellinger, D., Leviton, A., & Allred, E. N. (1990). The long-term effects of exposure to low doses of lead in childhood: An 11-year follow-up report. *New England Journal of Medicine, 322,* 83–88.

Nelson, L., & Madsen, M. C. (1969). Cooperation and competition in four-year-olds as a function of reward contingency and subculture. *Developmental Psychology, 1,* 340–344.

Neuberger, H., Merz, J., & Selg, H. (1983). Imitation bei Neugeborenen-eine kontroverse Befundlage. *Zeitschrift fur Entwicklungspsychologie und Padagogische Psychologie, 15,* 267–276.

Newberger, E. H., & Bourne, R. (1978). The medicalization and legalization of child abuse. *American Journal of Orthopsychiatry, 48,* 593–607.

Newcombe, N., & Dubas, J. S. (1992). A longitudinal study of predictors of spatial ability in adolescent females. *Child Development, 63,* 37–46.

Newell, A., Shaw, J. C., & Simon, H. A. (1958). Elements of a theory of human problem solving. *Psychological Review, 65,* 151–166.

Newman, B. M. (1982). Mid-life development. In B. B. Wolman (Ed.),

Handbook of developmental psychology (pp. 617–635). Englewood Cliffs, NJ: Prentice-Hall.

Newman, P. R. (1982). The peer group. In B. B. Wolman (Ed.), *Handbook of developmental psychology* (pp. 526–536). Englewood Cliffs, NJ: Prentice-Hall.

Newsom, C., & Rincover, A. (1981). Autism. In E. J. Marsh, & L. G. Terdal (Eds.), *Behavioral assessment of childhood disorders*. New York: Guilford Press.

Niemark, E. D. (1982). Adolescent thought: Transition to formal operations. In B. B. Wolman (Ed.), *Handbook of developmental psychology* (pp. 486–502). Englewood Cliffs, NJ: Prentice-Hall.

Ninio, A., & Bruner, J. (1978). The achievement and antecedents of labelling. *Journal of Child Language, 5,* 1–15.

Nisan, M. (1984). Distributive justice and social norms. *Child Development, 55,* 1020–1029.

Nisan, M., & Koriat, A. (1977). Children's actual choices and their conception of the wise choice in a delay-of-gratification situation. *Child Development, 48,* 488–494.

Nisan, M., & Koriat, A. (1984). The effect of cognitive restructuring on delay of gratification. *Child Development, 55,* 492–503.

Niswander, K. R., & Gordon, M. (Eds.). (1972). *The collaborative perinatal study of the National Institute of Neurological Diseases and Stroke: The women and their pregnancies.* Washington, DC: U.S. Government Printing Office.

Nottelmann, E. D., & Welsh, C. J. (1986). The long and the short of physical stature in early adolescence. *Journal of Early Adolescence, 6,* 15–27.

Novaco, R. (1978). Anger and coping with stress. In J. Foreyt, & D. Rathjen (Eds.), *Cognitive behavior therapy, theory, research and procedures.* New York: Plenum.

Nowak, M. A., & Sigmund, K. (1992). Tit for tat in heterogeneous populations. *Nature, 355,* 250–253.

Nunnally, J. C., Duchnowski, A. J., & Parker, R. K. (1965). Association of neutral objects with rewards: Effect on verbal evaluation, reward expectancy, and selective attention. *Journal of Personality and Social Psychology, 1,* 270–274.

O'Brien, M., & Huston, A. C. (1985). Development of sex-typed play behavior in toddlers. *Developmental Psychology, 21,* 866–871.

O'Connor, M., & Cuevas, J. (1982). The relationship of children's prosocial behavior to social responsibility, prosocial reasoning, and personality. *Journal of Genetic Psychology, 140,* 33–45.

O'Connor, M. J., Cohen, S., & Parmelee, A. H. (1984). Infant auditory discrimination in preterm and full-term infants as a predictor of 5-year intelligence. *Developmental Psychology, 20,* 159–165.

Offer, D., Ostrov, E., & Howard, K. I. (1981). *The adolescent: A psychological self-portrait.* New York: Basic Books.

Oldershaw, L., Walters, G. C., & Hall, D. K. (1986). Control strategies and noncompliance in abusive mother-child dyads: An observational study. *Child Development, 57,* 722–732.

Olejnik, A. B. (1976). The effects of reward-deservedness on children's sharing. *Child Development, 47,* 380–385.

Oliver, J. E., & Taylor, A. (1971). Five generations of ill-treated children in one family pedigree. *British Journal of Psychiatry, 119,* 473–480.

Oller, D. K., & Eilers, R. E. (1988). The role of audition in infant babbling. *Child Development, 59,* 441–449.

One solution to teen pregnancies. (1979, April 21). *Science News,* p. 264.

Orkin, S. H., Little, P. F. R., Kazazian, H. H., Jr., & Boehm, C. D. (1982). Improved detection of the sickle mutation by DNA analysis. *New England Journal of Medicine, 307,* 32–36.

Ornstein, P. A., Medlin, R. G., Stone, B. P., & Naus, M. J. (1985). Retrieving for rehearsal: An analysis of active rehearsal in children's memory. *Developmental Psychology, 21,* 633–641.

Osherson, D. N., & Markman, E. (1974–75). Language and the ability to evaluate contradictions and tautologies. *Cognition, 3*(3), 213–226.

Oster, H., & Ekman, P. (1978). Facial behavior in child development. *Minnesota Symposia on Child Psychology, 11,* 231–276.

Ostry, D. J., Feltham, R. F., & Munhall, K. G. (1984). Characteristics of speech motor development in children. *Developmental Psychology, 20,* 859–871.

Packard, V. (1977). *The people shapers.* Boston: Little, Brown.

Palisin, H. (1986). Preschool temperament and performance on achievement tests. *Developmental Psychology, 22,* 766–770.

Palkovitz, R. (1980). Predictors of involvement in first-time fathers. *Dissertation Abstracts International, 40,* 3603B-3604B. (University Microfilms No. 8105035)

Palkovitz, R. (1984). Parental attitudes and fathers' interactions with their 5-month-old infants. *Developmental Psychology, 20,* 1054–1060.

Palmer, F. H. (1972). Minimal intervention at age two and three and subsequent intellectual changes. In R. K. Parker (Ed.), *The preschool in action: Exploring early childhood programs.* Boston: Allyn & Bacon.

Palti, H., Mansbach, I., Pridan, H., Adler, B., & Palti, Z. (1984). Episodes of illness in breast-fed and bottle-fed infants in Jerusalem. *Journal of Medical Sciences, 20,* 395–399.

Palumbo, F. M., & Dietz, W. H. (1985). Children's television: Its effects on nutrition and cognitive development. *Pediatr. Ann., 14,* 793–801.

Pappas, C. C. (1983). The relationship between language development and brain development. *Journal of Children in Contemporary Society, 16,* 133–169.

Park, D. C., & James, C. Q. (1983). Effect of encoding instructions on children's spatial and color memory: Is there evidence for automaticity? *Child Development, 54,* 61–68.

Park, K. A., & Waters, E. (1989). Security of attachment and preschool friendships. *Child Development, 60,* 1076–1081.

Parke, R. D., & Collmer, C. W. (1975). Child abuse: An interdisciplinary analysis. In E. M. Hetherington (Ed.), *Review of child development research* (Vol. 5). Chicago: Univ. of Chicago Press.

Parke, R. D., Grossman, K., & Tinsley, B. R. (1981). Father-mother-infant interaction in the newborn period: A German-American comparison. In T. Field (Ed.), *Culture and early interactions.* Hillsdale, NJ: Erlbaum.

Parke, R. D., & O'Leary, S. E. (1976). Father-mother-infant interaction in the newborn period: Some findings, some observations and some unresolved issues. In K. F. Riegel, & J. A. Meacham (Eds.), *The developing individual in a changing world: Vol. 2. Social and environmental issues.* Chicago: Aldine.

Parke, R. D., O'Leary, S. E., & West, S. (1972). Mother-father-newborn interaction: Effects of maternal mediation, labor and sex of infant. *Proceedings of the American Psychological Association,* pp. 85–86.

Parke, R. D., & Sawin, D. B. (1975, April). *Infant characteristics and behavior as elicitors of maternal and paternal responsibility in the newborn period.* Paper presented at the meeting of the Society for Research in Child Development, Denver, Colorado.

Parke, R. D., & Slaby, R. G. (1983). The development of aggression. In P. H. Mussen (Ed.), *Handbook of child psychology* (4th ed., Vol. IV, pp. 547–641). New York: Wiley.

Parke, R. D., & Suomi, S. J. (1980). Adult male-infant relationships: Human and nonprimate evidence. In K. Immelman, G. Barlow, M. Main, & L. Petrinovitch (Eds.), *Behavioral development: bielefeld interdisciplinary project.* New York: Cambridge University Press.

Parke, R. D., & Tinsley, B. R. (1981). The father's role in infancy: Determinants of involvement in caregiving and play. In M. E. Lamb (Ed.), *The role of the father in child development* (2nd ed., pp. 429–457). New York: Wiley-Interscience.

Parkhurst, J. T., & Asher, S. R. (1992). Peer rejection in middle school: Subgroup differences in behavior, loneliness, and interpersonal concerns. *Developmental Psychology, 28,* 231–241.

Parmelee, A. H., Jr. (1986). Children's illnesses: Their beneficial effects on behavioral development. *Child Development, 57,* 1–10.

Parmelee, A. H., Wenner, W. H., & Schulz, H. R. (1964). Infant sleep patterns: From birth to 16 weeks of age. *Journal of Pediatrics, 65,* 576.

Parten, M. (1932). Social play among preschool children. *Journal of Abnormal and Social Psychology, 27,* 243–269.

Partnership for the Homeless. (1989). *Moving forward: A national agenda to address homelessness in 1990 and beyond.* New York: Author.

Pascual-Leone, J. (1976). A view of cognition from a formalist's perspective. In K. F. Riegel, & J. Meacham (Eds.), *The developing individual in a changing world* (pp. 89–100). The Hague: Mouton.

Pascual-Leone, J. (1984). Attentional, dialectic, and mental effort. In M. L. Commons, F. A. Richards, & C. Armon (Eds.), *Beyond formal operations.* New York: Plenum.

Pascual-Leone, J., & Smith, J. (1969). The encoding and decoding of symbols by children: A new experimental paradigm and a neo-Piagetian model. *Journal of Experimental Child Psychology, 8,* 328–355.

Patterson, C. J., Kupersmidt, J. B., & Vaden, N. A. (1990). Income level, gender, ethnicity, and household composition as predictors of children's school-based competence. *Child Development, 61,* 485–494.

Patterson, D. (1987). The causes of Down Syndrome. *Scientific American,* 257(2), 52–60.

Patterson, G. R. (1982). *Coercive family processes.* Eugene, OR: Castilia Press.

Paul, D. B. (1991). Enthusiastic claims. *Science, 252,* 142–143.

Pearl, D., Bouthilet, L., & Lazar, J. (Eds.). (1982). *Television and behavior: Ten years of scientific progress and implications for the eighties* (Vols. 1 & 2). Washington, DC: U.S. Government Printing Office.

Pearl, R. (1985). Children's understanding of others' need for help: Effects of problem explicitness and type. *Child Development, 56,* 735–745.

Pearson, J. L., Hunter, A. G., Ensminger, M. E., & Kellam, S. G. (1990). Black grandmothers in multigenerational households: Diversity in family structure and parenting involvement in the Woodlawn community. *Child Development, 61,* 434–442.

Pedersen, E., Faucher, T. A., & Eaton, W. W. (1978). A new perspective on the effects of first grade teachers on children's subsequent adult status. *Harvard Educational Review, 48,* 1–31.

Pederson, D. R., Moran, G., Sitko, C., Campbell, K., Ghesquire, K., & Acton, H. (1990). Maternal sensitivity and the security of infant-mother attachment: A Q-sort study. *Child Development, 61,* 1974–1983.

Pederson, D. R., Rook-Green, A., & Elder, J. L. (1981). The role of action in the development of pretend play in young children. *Developmental Psychology, 17,* 756–759.

Pederson, F. A., Anderson, B. T., & Cain, R. L. (1977). *An approach to understanding linkages between the parent-infant and spouse relationships.* Paper presented at the Society for Research in Child Development, New Orleans, Louisiana.

Pelham, W. E. (1977). Withdrawal of a stimulant drug and concurrent behavioral intervention in the treatment of a hyperactive child. *Behavior Therapy, 8,* 473–479.

Pence, A. R., & Goelman, H. (1987). Silent partners: Parents of children in three types of day care. *Early Childhood Research Quarterly, 2,* 103–118.

Pennington, B. F., Bender, B., Puck, M., Salbenblatt, J., & Robinson, A. (1982). Learning disabilities in children with sex chromosome anomalies. *Child Development, 53,* 1182–1192.

Pennington, B. F., McCabe, L. L., Smith, S. D., Lefly, D. L., Brookman, M. O., Kimberling, W. J., & Lubs, H. A. (1986). Spelling errors in adults with a form of familial dyslexia. *Child Development, 57,* 1001–1013.

Pepler, D. J., & Ross, H. S. (1981). The effects of play on convergent and divergent problem solving. *Child Development, 52,* 1202–1210.

Perrin, D. G., Becker, L. E., Madapallimatum, A., Cutz, E., Bryan, A. C., & Sole, M. J. (1984). Sudden Infant Death Syndrome: Increased carotid-body dopamine and noradrenaline content. *Lancet,* 2(8402), 535–537.

Perris, E. E., Myers, N. A., & Clifton, R. K. (1990). Long-term memory for a single infancy experience. *Child Development, 61,* 1796–1807.

Perry, D. G., Perry, L. C., & Rasmussen, P. (1986). Cognitive social learning mediators of aggression. *Child Development, 57,* 700–711.

Petersen, A. C. (1979). Female pubertal development. In M. Sugar (Ed.), *Female adolescent development.* New York: Brunner/Mazel.

Petersen, A. C., & Taylor, B. (1980). The biological approach to adolescence. In J. Adelson (Ed.), *Handbook of adolescent psychology.* New York: Wiley.

Peterson, L. (1982). An alternative perspective to norm-based explanations of modeling and children's generosity. *Merrill-Palmer Quarterly, 28,* 283–290.

Peterson, L. (1983). Influence of age, task competence, and responsibility focus on children's altruism. *Developmental Psychology, 19,* 141–148.

Petitto, L. A., & Marentette, P. F. (1991). Babbling in the manual mode: Evidence for the ontogeny of language. *Science, 251,* 1493–1496.

Pfeffer, C. R., Plutchik, R., Mizruchi, M. S., & Lipkins, R. (1986). Suicidal behavior in child psychiatric inpatients and outpatients and in nonpatients. *American Journal of Psychiatry, 143,* 733–738.

Phear, W. P., et al. (1983). An empirical study of custody agreements: Joint versus sole legal custody. *Journal of Psychiatry and the Law, 11,* 419–441.

Phillips, D. A. (1987). Socialization of perceived academic competence among highly competent children. *Child Development, 58,* 1308–1320.

Phillips, D., McCartney, K., & Scarr, S. (1987). Child-care quality and children's social development. *Developmental Psychology, 23,* 537–543.

Phillips, D. P. (1977). Motor vehicle fatalities increase just after publicized suicide stories. *Science, 196,* 1464–1465.

Phillips, D. P., & Carstensen, L. L. (1986). Clustering of teenage suicides after television news stories about suicide. *New England Journal of Medicine, 315,* 685–689.

Phillips, D. P., & Paight, D. J. (1987). The impact of televised movies about suicide. A replicative study. *New England Journal of Medicine, 317,* 809–811.

Phillips, H. P. (1960). Problems of translation and meaning in field work. *Human Organization, 18*(4), 184–192.

Phillips, J. L. (1969). *The origins of intellect: Piaget's theory.* San Francisco: W. H. Freeman.

Piaget, J. (1932). *The moral judgment of the child.* New York: Harcourt Brace.

Piaget, J. (1952). *The origins of intelligence in children.* New York: Int'l. Universities Press.

Piaget, J. (1957). Logique et equilibre dans les comportements du sujet. *Etud. Epist. Gen., 2,* 27–118.

Piaget, J. (1960). *The chiid's conception of the world.* London: Routledge.

Piaget, J. (1962). *Play, dreams and imitation in childhood.* New York: Norton.

Piaget J. (1964). Development and learning. In R. E. Ripple, & V. N. Rockcastle (Eds.), *Piaget rediscovered* (pp. 7–20). Ithaca, NY: Cornell School of Education Press.

Piaget, J. (1967). *Six psychological studies.* New York: Random House.

Piaget, J. (1970). Piaget's theory. In P. H. Mussen (Ed.), *Carmichael's manual of child psychology* (Vol. 1, 3rd ed.). New York: John Wiley.

Piaget, J., & Inhelder, B. (1969). *The psychology of the child.* (H. Weaver, Trans.). New York: Basic Books. (Original work published 1967)

Pick, H. L., & Pick, A. D. (1970). Sensory and perceptual development. In P. H. Mussen (Ed.), *Carmichael's manual of child psychology* (3rd ed., Vol. 1, pp. 773–847). New York: Wiley.

Pieterse, M., & Center, Y. (1984). The integration of eight Down's Syndrome children into regular schools. *Australia & New Zealand Journal of Developmental Disabilities, 10*(1), 11- 20.

Pihl, R. O., & Parkes, M. (1977). Hair element content in learning disabled children. *Science, 198,* 204–206.

Pinkel, D., Garner, D. L., Gledhill, B. L., Lake, S., Stephens, D., & Johnson, L. A. (1985). Flow cytometric determination of the proportions of X-chromosome-bearing and Y-chromosome-bearing sperm in samples of purportedly separated bull sperm. *Journal of Animal Science, 60,* 1303–1307.

Pinneau, S. R. (1955). The infantile disorders of hospitalism and anaclitic depression. *Psychological Bulletin, 52,* 429–452.

Pipp, S., & Harmon, R. J. (1987). Attachment as regulation: A commentary. *Child Development, 58,* 648–652.

Plattner, G., Renner, W., Went, J., Beaudett, L., & Viau, G. (1983). Determination of ultrasound scan in the 2nd and 3rd trimesters. *Obstetrics & Gynecology, 61,* 454–458.

Pleck, E. (1987). *The making of social policy against family violence from colonial times to the present.* New York: Oxford University Press.

Plomin, R. (1990). The role of inheritance in Behavior. *Science, 248,* 183–188.

Plomin, R., McClearn, G. E., Pedersen, N. L., Nesselroade, J. R., & Bergeman, C. S. (1988). Genetic influence on childhood family environment perceived retrospectively from the last half of the life span. *Developmental Psychology, 24,* 738–745.

Pope, A. W., Bierman, K. L., & Mumma, G. H. (1991). Aggression, hyperactivity, and inattention-immaturity: Behavior dimensions associated with peer rejection in elementary school boys. *Developmental Psychology, 27,* 663–671.

Posner, J. K. (1982). The development of mathematical knowledge in two West African societies. *Child Development, 53,* 200–208.

Powell, D. (1977, March). *The coordination of preschool socialization: Parent and caregiver relationships in day care settings.* Paper presented at the meeting of the Society for Research in Child Development, New Orleans, LA.

Powell, D. (1978). The interpersonal relationship between parents and caregivers in day care settings. *American Journal of Orthopsychiatry, 48,* 680–689.

Power, M. J., Alderson, M. R., Phillipson, C. M., Schoenberg, E., & Morris, J. N. (1967, October 19). Delinquent schools? *New Society,* pp. 542–543.

Power, T. G. (1981). Sex-typing in infancy: The role of the father. *Infant Mental Health Journal, 2,* 226–240.

Power, T. G., & Chapieski, M. L. (1986). Childrearing and impulse control in toddlers: A naturalistic investigation. *Developmental Psychology, 22,* 271–275.

Powers, S. I., Hauser, S. T., Schwartz, J. M., Noam, G. G., & Jacobson, A. M. (1983). Adolescent ego development and family interaction: A structural-developmental perspective. In H. D. Grotevant, & C. R. Cooper (Eds.), *Adolescent development in the family: New directions for child development* (pp. 5–25). San Francisco: Jossey-Bass.

Poznanski, E., Mokros, H. B., Grossman, J., & Freeman, L. N. (1985). Diagnostic criteria in childhood depression. *American Journal of Psychiatry, 142,* 1168–1173.

Pratkanis, A. R., & Greenwald, A. B. (1985). How shall the self be conceived? *Journal for the Theory of Social Behavior, 15,* 311–328.

Pratt, M. W., Kerig, P., Cowan, P. A., & Cowan, C. P. (1988). Mothers and fathers teaching 3-year-olds: Authoritative parenting and adult scaffolding of young children's learning. *Developmental Psychology, 24,* 832–839.

Preventing crib deaths. (1979, January 27). *Science News,* p. 57.

Price, J. O., Elias, S., Wachtel, S. S., Klinger, K., Dockter, M., Tharapel, A., Shulman, L. P., Phillips, O. P., Meyers, C. M., & Shook, D. (1991). Prenatal diagnosis with fetal cells isolated from maternal blood by multiparameter flow cytometry. *American Journal of Obstetrics & Gynecology, 165,* 1731–1737.

Price-Williams, D., Gordon, W., & Ramirez, M. (1969). Skill and conservation: A study of pottery-making children. *Developmental Psychology, 1,* 769.

Pugliese, M. T., Lifshitz, F., Grad, G., Fort, P., & Marks-Katz, M. (1983). Fear of obesity. *New England Journal of Medicine, 309,* 513–518.

Putallaz, M. (1983). Predicting children's sociometric status from their behavior. *Child Development, 54,* 1417–1426.

Quigley, M. E., Sheehan, K. L., Wilkes, M. M., & Yen, S. S. C. (1979). Effects of maternal smoking on circulating catecholamine levels and fetal heart rates. *American Journal of Obstetrics and Gynecology, 133,* 685–690.

Ra, J. B. (1977). A comparison of preschool children's preferences for television and their parents. *Journal of Social Psychology, 102*(1), 163–164.

Rader, N. (1979, April). *The behavior of pre-crawling infants on the visual cliff with locomotor aids.* Paper presented at the meeting of the Western Psychological Association, San Diego, California.

Radin, N., & Harold-Goldsmith, R. (1989). The involvement of selected unemployed and employed men with their children. *Child Development, 60,* 454–459.

Radke-Yarrow, M., Zahn-Waxler, C., & Chapman, M. (1983). Children's prosocial dispositions and behavior. In P. H. Mussen (Ed.), *Handbook of child psychology* (4th ed., Vol. IV, pp. 469–545). New York: Wiley.

Radziszewska, B., & Rogoff, B. (1991). Children's guided participation in planning imaginary errands with skilled adult or peer partners. *Developmental Psychology, 27,* 381–389.

Rafferty, Y., & Shinn, M. (1991). The impact of homelessness on children. *American Psychologist, 46,* 1170–1179.

Rafman, S. (1974). The infant's reaction to imitation of the mother's behavior by the stranger. In T. Decarie (Ed.), *The infant's reaction to strangers* (pp. 117–148). New York: Int'l. Universities Press.

Raloff, J. (1982, February 6). Childhood lead: Worrisome national levels. *Science News,* p. 88.

Raloff, J. (1992, February 15). Infant growth: A sporadic phenomenon. *Science News,* p. 102.

Ralt, D., Goldenberg, M., Fetterolf, P., Thompson, D., Dor, J., Mashiach, S., Garbers, D. L., & Eisenbach, M. (1991). Sperm attraction to a follicular factor(s) correlates with human egg fertilizability. *Proceedings of the National Academy of Science USA, 88,* 2840–2844.

Ramey, C. (1982). Commentary by Craig T. Ramey. *Monographs of the Society for Research in Child Development, 47*(2–3, Serial No. 195), 142–151.

Ratner, N. B., & Pye, C. (1984). Higher pitch in BT is not universal: Acoustic evidence from Quiche Mayan. *Journal of Child Language, 11,* 515–522.

Rauh, V. A., Achenbach, T. M., Nurcombe, B., Howell, C. T., & Teti, D. M. (1988). Minimizing adverse effects of low birthweight: Four-year results of an early intervention program. *Child Development, 59,* 544–553.

Reaves, J. Y., & Roberts, A. (1983). The effect of type of information on children's attraction to peers. *Child Development, 54,* 1024–1031.

Reed, G. L., & Leiderman, P. H. (1983). Is imprinting an appropriate model for human infant attachment? *International Journal of Behavioral Development, 6,* 51–69.

Reese, H. W., & Lipsitt, L. P. (1970). *Experimental child psychology.* New York: Academic Press.

Reese, H. W., & Overton, W. F. (1970). Models of development and theories of development. In L. R. Goulet, & P. B. Baltes (Eds.), *Life-span developmental psychology: Research and theory* (pp. 115–145). New York: Academic Press.

Reiss, I. L. (1976). *Family systems in America* (2nd ed.). Hinsdale, IL: Dryden Press.

Reissland, N. (1988). Neonatal imitation in the first hour of life: Observations in rural Nepal. *Developmental Psychology, 24,* 464–469.

Reite, M., Kaemingk, K., & Boccia, M. L. (1989). Maternal separation in bonnet monkey infants: Altered attachment and social support. *Child Development, 60,* 473–480.

Remafedi, G., Resnick, M., Blum, R., & Harris, L. (1992). Demography of sexual orientation in adolescents. *Pediatrics, 89,* 714–721.

Reppucci, N. D., & Haugaard, J. J. (1989). Prevention of child sexual abuse: Myth or reality. *American Psychologist, 44,* 1266–1275.

Rescorla, R. A. (1969). Pavlovian conditioned inhibition. *Psychological Bulletin, 72,* 77–94.

Resnick, S. M., Berenbaum, S. A., Gottesman, I. I., & Bouchard, T. J., Jr. (1986). Early hormonal influences on cognitive functioning in congenital adrenal hyperplasia. *Developmental Psychology, 22,* 191–198.

Rest, J. (1968). *Developmental hierarchy in preference and comprehension of moral judgment.* Unpublished doctoral dissertation, University of Chicago.

Restak, R. M. (1982, January/February). Newborn knowledge. *Science, 82,* pp. 58–65.

Reynolds, B. A., & Weiss, S. (1992). Generation of neurons and astrocytes from isolated cells of the adult mammalian central nervous system. *Science, 255,* 1707–1710.

Reynolds, D., Jones, D., & St Leger, S. (1976, July 29). Schools do make a difference. *New Society,* pp. 223–225.

Reynolds, D., & Murgatroyd, S. (1977). The sociology of schooling and the absent pupil: The school as a factor in the generation of truancy. In H. C. M. Carroll (Ed.), *Absenteeism in South Wales: Studies of pupils, their homes and their secondary schools.* Swansea: Univ. of Swansea, Faculty of Educ.

Rheingold, H. L. (1961). The effect of environmental stimulation upon social and exploratory behavior in the human infant. In B. M. Foss (Ed.), *Determinants of infant behavior* (Vol. 1, pp. 143–177). New York: Wiley.

Rheingold, H. L. (1982). Little children's participation in the work of adults, a nascent prosocial behavior. *Child Development, 53,* 114–125.

Rheingold, H. L., & Bayley, N. (1959). The later effects of an experimental modification of mothering. *Child Development, 30,* 363–372.

Rheingold, H. L., & Cook, K. V. (1975). The content of boys' and girls' rooms as an index of parents' behavior. *Child Development, 46,* 459–463.

Rheingold, H. L., Cook, K. V., & Kolowitz, V. (1987). Commands activate the behavior and pleasure of 2-year-old children. *Developmental Psychology, 23,* 146–151.

Rheingold, H. L., & Eckerman, C. O. (1970). The infant separates himself from his mother. *Science, 168,* 78–83.

Rheingold, H. L., Gewirtz, J. L., & Ross, H. W. (1959). Social conditioning of vocalizations in the infant. *Journal of Comparative and Physiological Psychology, 52,* 68–73.

Rice, M. L., Huston, A. C., Truglio, R., & Wright, J. (1990). Words from "Sesame Street": Learning vocabulary while viewing. *Developmental Psychology, 26,* 421–428.

Rice, M. L., & Woodsmall, L. (1988). Lessons from television: Children's word learning when viewing. *Child Development, 59,* 420–429.

Rich, C. L., Sherman, M., & Fowler, R. C. (1990). San Diego Suicide Study: The adolescents. *Adolescence, 25,* 855–865.

Richards, J. E. (1987). Infant visual sustained attention and respiratory sinus arrhythmia. *Child Development, 58,* 488–496.

Richards, M. H., Boxer, A. M., Petersen, A. C., & Albrecht, R. (1990). Relation of weight to body image in pubertal girls and boys from two communities. *Developmental Psychology, 26,* 313–321.

Richards, M. P. M., Dunn, J. F., & Antonis, B. (1977). Caretaking in the first year of life: The role of fathers' and mothers' social isolation. *Child: Care, Health and Development, 3,* 23–26.

Ritts, R. E. (1968). A physician's view of informed consent in human experimentation. *Fordham Law Review, 36,* 631–638.

Ritvo, E. R., Mason-Brothers, A., Freeman, C. P., Jenson, W. R., McMahon, W. M., Petersen, P. B., Jorde, L. B., Mo, A., & Ritvo, A. (1990). The UCLA-University of Utah Epidemiologic Survey of Autism: The etiologic role of rare diseases. *American Journal of Psychiatry, 147,* 1614–1621.

Ritvo, E. R., Spence, M. A., Freeman, B. J., Mason-Brothers, A., Mo, A., & Marazita, M. L. (1985). Evidence for autosomal recessive inheritance in 46 families with multiple incidences of autism. *American Journal of Psychiatry, 142,* 187–192.

Riverside Publishing Company. (1983, November 22). Information release.

Roberts, K. (1988). Retrieval of a basic-level category in prelinguistic infants. *Developmental Psychology, 24,* 21–27.

Roberts, L. (1989). Genome mapping goal now in reach. *Science, 244,* 424–425.

Roberts, W. L. (1986). Nonlinear models of development: An example from the socialization of competence. *Child Development, 57,* 1166–1178.

Robinson, J. P., & Bachman, J. G. (1972). Television viewing habits and aggression. In G. A. Comstock, & E. A. Rubinstein (Eds.), *Television and social behavior, Vol. 3: Television and adolescent aggressiveness* (pp. 372–382). Washington, D.C.: U.S. Government Printing Office.

Roche, A. F., & Davila, G. H. (1972). Late adolescent growth in stature. *Pediatrics, 50,* 874–880.

Roche, J. P. (1986). Premarital sex: Attitudes and behavior by dating stage. *Adolescence, 21,* 107–121.

Rogoff, B., & Waddell, K. J. (1982). Memory for information organized in a scene by children from two cultures. *Child Development, 53,* 1224–1228.

Rohner, R. P., & Pettengill, S. M. (1985). Perceived parental acceptance-rejection and parental control among Korean adolescents. *Child Development, 56,* 524–528.

Rohner, R. P., & Rohner, E. C. (1981). Parental acceptance-rejection and parental control: Cross-cultural codes. *Ethnology, 20,* 245–260.

Rolf, J., & Read, P. B. (1984). Programs advancing developmental psychopathology. *Child Development, 55,* 8–16.

Rondal, J. A. (1985). *Adult-child interaction and the process of language acquisition.* New York: Praeger.

Roopnarine, J. L. (1981). Peer play interaction in a mixed-age preschool setting. *Journal of General Psychology, 104,* 161–166.

Roopnarine, J. L., & Johnson, J. E. (1984). Socialization in a mixed-age experimental program. *Developmental Psychology, 20,* 828–832.

Rose, R. J., & Ditto, W. B. (1983). A developmental-genetic analysis of common fears from early adolescence to early adulthood. *Child Development, 54,* 361–368.

Rose, S. A., Feldman, J. F., & Wallace, I. F. (1988). Individual differences in infants' information processing: Reliability, Stability, and Prediction. *Child Development, 59,* 1177–1197.

Rose, S. A., & Orlian, E. K. (1991). Asymmetries in infant cross-modal transfer. *Child Development, 62,* 706–718.

Rosenblum, L. A., & Harlow, H. F. (1963). Approach-avoidance conflict in the mother surrogate situation. *Psychological Reports, 12,* 83–85.

Rosenkrantz, A. L. (1978). A note on adolescent suicide: Incidence, dynamics and some suggestions for treatment. *Adolescence, 13,* 209–214.

Rosenthal, D., & Quinn, O. W. (1977). Quadruplet hallucinations: Phenotypic variations of a schizophrenic genotype. *Archives of General Psychiatry, 34,* 817–827.

Rosenthal, M. K. (1982). Vocal dialogues in the neonatal period. *Developmental Psychology, 18,* 17–21.

Rosenthal, P. A., & Rosenthal, S. (1984). Suicidal behavior by preschool children. *American Journal of Psychiatry, 141,* 520–525.

Rosenzweig, M. R. (1966). Environmental complexity, cerebral change, and behavior. *American Psychologist, 21,* 321–332.

Ross, H. S., & Goldman, B. M. (1976). Establishing new social relations in infancy. In T. Alloway, L. Krames, & P. Pliner (Eds.), *Advances in communication and affect* (Vol. 4). New York: Plenum.

Rotheram-Borus, M. J., Koopman, C., Haignere, C., & Davies, M. (1991). Reducing HIV sexual risk behaviors among runaway adolescents. *Journal of the American Medical Association, 266,* 1237–1241.

Roupp, R., Travers, J., Glantz, F., Coelen, C., Bache, W. L., O'Neil, C., & Singer, J. (1979). *Children at the center: Final report of the National Day Care Study* (Vol. 1). Cambridge, MA: Abt Books.

Rovee-Collier, C., Schechter, A., Shyi, G. C.-W., & Shields, P. (1992). Perceptual identification of contextual attributes and infant memory retrieval. *Developmental Psychology, 28,* 307–318.

Rowe, D. C., & Plomin, R. (1981). The importance of nonshared (E1) environmental influences in behavioral development. *Developmental Psychology, 17,* 517–531.

Rozin, P., Fallon, A., & Augustoni-Ziskind, M. (1985). The child's conception of food: The development of contamination sensitivity to "disgusting" substances. *Developmental Psychology, 21,* 1075–1079.

Rubenstein, J., & Howes, C. (1976). The effects of peers on toddler interaction with mother and toys. *Child Development, 47,* 597–605.

Rubin, K. H., Fein, G. G., & Vandenberg, B. (1983). Play. In E. M. Hetherington (Ed.), *Handbook of child psychology* (4th ed., Vol. IV, pp. 693–774). New York: Wiley.

Rubin, K. H., Maioni, T. L., & Hornung, M. (1976). Free play behaviors in middle- and lower-class preschoolers: Parten and Piaget revisited. *Child Development, 47,* 414–419.

Rubinson, L., & de Rubertis, L. (1991). Trends in sexual attitudes and behaviors of a college population over a 15-year period. *Journal of Sex*

Education & Therapy, 17, 32–41.

Rubinstein, E. A. (1983). Television and behavior: Research conclusions of the 1982 NIMH report and their policy implications. *American Psychologist, 38,* 820–825.

Rushton, J. P., & Sorrentino, R. M. (Eds.). (1981). *Altruism and helping behavior: Social, personality, and developmental perspectives.* Hillsdale, NJ: Erlbaum.

Russell, G. (1980, July 15–17). *Fathers as caregivers: Possible antecedents and consequences.* Papers presented to a study group on "The Role of the Father in Child Development, Social Policy and the Law," University of Haifa, Haifa, Israel.

Russell, J. A., & Bullock, M. (1986). On the dimensions preschoolers use to interpret facial expressions of emotion. *Developmental Psychology, 22,* 97–102.

Rutter, M. (1983). School effects on pupil progress: Research findings and policy implications. *Child Development, 54,* 1–29.

Rutter, M., & Garmezy, N. (1983). Developmental psychopathology. In P. H. Mussen (Ed.), *Handbook of child psychology* (4th ed., Vol. IV, pp. 775–911). New York: Wiley.

Rutter, M., Maughan, B., Mortimore, P., Ouston, J., & Smith, A. (1979). *Fifteen thousand hours: Secondary schools and their effects on children.* Cambridge, MA: Harvard University Press.

Sackett, G. P., Holm, R. A., & Landesman-Dwyer, S. (1975). Vulnerability for abnormal development: Pregnancy outcomes and sex differences in macaque monkeys. In N. R. Ellis (Ed.), *Aberrant development in infancy* (pp. 59–76). New York: Erlbaum.

Sackett, G. P., Holm, R. A., & Ruppenthal, G. C. (1976). Social isolation rearing: Species differences in behavior of macaque monkeys. *Developmental Psychology, 12,* 283–288.

Sagar, H. A., Schofield, J. W., & Snyder, H. N. (1983). Race and gender barriers: Preadolescent peer behavior in academic classrooms. *Child Development, 54,* 1032–1040.

Sagi, A., & Hoffman, M. L. (1976). Empathic distress in the newborn. *Developmental Psychology, 12,* 175–176.

Sagi, A., Van IJzendoorn, M. H., & Koren-Karie, N. (1991). Primary appraisal of the strange situation: A cross-cultural analysis of preseparation episodes. *Developmental Psychology, 27,* 587–596.

Sagotsky, G., Wood-Schneider, M., & Konop, M. (1981). Learning to cooperate: Effects of modeling and direct instruction. *Child Development, 52,* 1037–1042.

Sainsbury, P., Jenkins, J., & Levey, A. (1980). The social correlates of suicide in Europe. In R. T. D. Farmer, & S. R. Hirsch (Eds.), *The suicide syndrome* (pp. 38–53). London: Croom Helm.

Saltz, E., Campbell, S., & Skotko, D. (1983). Verbal control of behavior: The effects of shouting. *Developmental Psychology, 19,* 461–464.

Saltzstein, H. D. (1983). Critical issues in Kohlberg's theory of moral reasoning. *Monographs of the Society for Research in Child Development, 48*(1–2, Serial No. 200), 108–119.

Sameroff, A. J. (1968). The components of sucking in the human newborn. *Journal of Experimental Child Psychology, 6,* 607–623.

Sampson, E. E. (1962). Birth order, need achievement, and conformity. *Journal of Abnormal and Social Psychology, 64,* 155–159.

Sanson, A., Prior, M., & Kyrios, M. (1990). Contamination of measures in temperament research. *Merrill-Palmer Quarterly, 36,* 179–192.

Santrock, J. W., & Tracy, R. L. (1978). Effects of children's family structure status on the development of stereotypes by teachers. *Journal of Educational Psychology, 70,* 754–757.

Sapienza, C. (1990). Parental imprinting of genes. *Scientific American, 263*(4), 52–60.

Sarason, S. B., & Klaber, M. (1985). The school as a social situation. *Annual Review of Psychology, 36,* 115–140.

Sarlo, G., Jason, L. A., & Lonak, C. (1988). Parents' strategies for limiting children's television viewing. *Psychological Reports, 63,* 435–438.

Savage-Rumbaugh, S., Sevcik, R. A., & Hopkins, W. D. (1988). Symbolic cross-modal transfer in two species of chimpanzees. *Child Development, 59,* 617–625.

Savin-Williams, R. C. (1979). Dominance hierarchies in groups of early adolescents. *Child Development, 50,* 923–935.

Savin-Williams, R. C., & Demo, D. H. (1984). Developmental change and stability in adolescent self-concept. *Developmental Psychology, 20,* 1100–1110.

Saxe, G. B. (1988). The mathematics of child street vendors. *Child Development, 59,* 1415–1425.

Scarborough, H. S. (1990). Very early language deficits in dyslexic children. *Child Development, 61,* 1728–1743.

Scarr, S., & Grajek, S. (1982). Similarities and differences among siblings. In M. E. Lamb, & B. Sutton-Smith (Eds.), *Sibling relationships: Their nature and significance across the lifespan.* Hillsdale, NJ: Erlbaum.

Scarr, S., & McCartney, K. (1983). How people make their own environments: A theory of genotype-environment effects. *Child Development, 54,* 424–435.

Scarr, S., & McCartney, K. (1988). Far from home: An experimental evaluation of the mother-child home program in Bermuda. *Child Development, 59,* 531–543.

Scarr, S., Phillips, D., & McCartney, K. (1989). Working mothers and their families. *American Psychologist, 44,* 1402–1409.

Scarr, S., & Weinberg, R. A. (1976). IQ test performance of black children adopted by white families. *American Psychologist, 31,* 726–739.

Schaefer, E. S. (1959). A circumplex model for maternal behavior. *Journal of Abnormal and Social Psychology, 59,* 226–235.

Schaffer, H. R. (1977). Early interactive development. In H. R. Schaffer (Ed.), *Studies in mother infant interaction.* London: Academic Press.

Schaffer, H. R., & Emerson, P. E. (1964). The development of social attachments in infancy. *Monographs of the Society for Research in Child Development,* (3, Serial No. 94).

Schaie, K. W., & Hertzog, C. (1982). Longitudinal methods. In B. B. Wolman (Ed.), *Handbook of developmental psychology* (pp. 91–115). Englewood Cliffs, NJ: Prentice-Hall.

Schiff, M., Duyme, M., Dumaret, A., & Tomkiewicz, S. (1982). How much could we boost scholastic achievement and IQ scores? A direct answer from a French adoption study. *Cognition, 12,* 165–196.

Schiff, W. (1983). Conservation of length redux: A perceptual-linguistic phenomenon. *Child Development, 54,* 1497–1506.

Schiffman, P. L., Westlake, R. E., Santiago, T. V., & Edelman, N. H. (1980). Ventilatory control in parents of victims of sudden-infant-death syndrome. *New England Journal of Medicine, 302,* 486–491.

Schiller, P. H. (1957). Innate motor action as a basis of learning. In S. H. Schiller (Ed.), *Instinctive behavior.* New York: Int'l. Universities Press.

Schmidt, H. J., & Beauchamp, G. K. (1988). Adult-like odor preferences and aversions in three-year-old children. *Child Development, 59,* 1136–1143.

Schofield, J. W., & Francis, W. D. (1982). An observational study of peer interaction in racially mixed "accelerated" classrooms. *Journal of Educational Psychology, 74,* 722–732.

Schofield, J. W., & Whitley, B. E., Jr. (1983). Peer nomination vs. rating scale measurement of children's peer preferences. *Social Psychology Quarterly, 46,* 242–251.

Schopf, J. W. (1978). The evolution of the earliest cells. *Scientific American, 239*(3), 110–138.

Schrag, P., & Divoky, D. (1975). *The myth of the hyperactive child and other means of child control.* New York: Pantheon.

Schuck, S. Z., Schuck, A., Hallam, E., Mancini, F., & Wells, R. (1971). Sex differences in aggressive behavior subsequent to listening to a radio broadcast of violence. *Psychological Reports, 28,* 931–936.

Schwartz, H. (1978). Abraham Lincoln and cardiac decompensation: A preliminary report. *Western Journal of Medicine, 128*(2), 174–177.

Schwartz, M., & Schwartz, J. (1974). Evidence against a genetical component to performance on IQ tests. *Nature, 248,* 84–85.

Schweinhart, L. J., & Weikart, D. P. (1985). Evidence that good early childhood programs work. Phi *Delta Kappan, 66,* 545–551.

Schweinhart, L. J., & Weikart, D. P. (1986). What do we know so far? A review of the Head Start Synthesis Project. *Young Children, 41,* 49–55.

Scoe, H. F. (1933). Bladder control in infancy and early childhood. *University of Iowa Studies in Child Welfare, V,* No. 4.

Sears, R. R., Maccoby, E. E., & Levin, H. (1957). *Patterns of childrearing.* Evanston, IL: Row, Peterson.

Seidman, E., Rappaport, J., & Davidson, W. S. (1980). Adolescents in legal jeopardy: Initial success and replication of an alternative to the criminal justice system. In R. Ross, & P. Gendreau (Eds.), *Effective correctional treatment.* Toronto: Butterworths.

Seitz, V., Rosenbaum, L. K., & Apfel, N. H. (1985). Effects of family support intervention: A ten-year follow-up. *Child Development, 56,* 376–391.

Seligman, M. E. P., & Maier, S. F. (1967). Failure to escape traumatic shock. *Journal of Experimental Psychology, 74,* 1–9.

Selman, R. L., Schorin, M. Z., Stone, C. R., & Phelps, E. (1983). A naturalistic study of children's social understanding. *Developmental Psychology, 19,* 81–102.

Semmel, M. I., Gottlieb, J., & Robinson, N. M. (1979). Mainstreaming: Perspectives on educating handicapped children in the public schools. In D. C. Berliner (Ed.), *Review of research in education* (Vol. 7, pp. 223–279). Washington, DC: Amer. Educ. Research Assn.

Serbin, L. A., & Sprafkin, C. (1986). The salience of gender and the process of sex typing in three- to seven-year-old children. *Child Development, 57,* 1188–1199.

Sevinc, M., & Turner, C. (1976). Language and the latent structure of cognitive development. *International Journal of Psychology, 11,* 231–250.

Shaffran, R., & Decarie, T. G. (1973). *Short term stability of infants' responses to strangers.* Paper presented at the meeting of the Society for Research in Child Development, Philadelphia, Pennsylvania.

Shafii, M., Carrigan, S., Whittinghill, J. R., & Derrick, A. (1985). Psychological autopsy of completed suicide in children and adolescents. *American Journal of Psychiatry, 142,* 1061–1064.

Shaheen, S. J. (1984). Neuromaturation and behavior development: The case of childhood lead poisoning. *Developmental Psychology, 20,* 542–550.

Shapira, A., & Madsen, M. C. (1974). Between- and within-group cooperation and competition among kibbutz and nonkibbutz children. *Developmental Psychology, 10,* 140–145.

Sharabany, R., & Bar-Tal, D. (1982). Theories of the development of altruism: Review, comparison and integration. *International Journal of Behavioral Development, 5,* 49–80.

Shatz, M., & Gelman R. (1973). The development of communication skills: Modifications in the speech of young children as a function of listener. *Monographs of the Society for Research in Child Development, 38*(5 Serial No. 152).

Shaver, J. P., & Strong, W. (1976). *Facing value decisions: Rationale-building for teachers.* Belmont, CA: Wadsworth.

Shedler, J., & Block, J. (1990). Adolescent drug use and psychological health. *American Psychologist, 45,* 612–630.

Shigetomi, C. C., Hartmann, D. P., & Gelfand, D. M. (1981). Sex differences in children's altruistic behavior and reputations for helpfulness. *Developmental Psychology, 17,* 434–437.

Shoda, Y., Mischel, W., & Peake, P. K. (1990). Predicting adolescent cognitive and self- regulatory competencies from preschool delay of gratification: Identifying diagnostic conditions. *Developmental Psychology, 26,* 978–986.

Short, R. V. (1984). Breast feeding. *Scientific American, 250*(4), 35–41.

Shweder, R. A. (1981). What's there to negotiate? Some questions for Youniss. *Merrill-Palmer Quarterly, 27,* 405–412.

Siegel, O. (1982). Personality development in adolescence. In B. B. Wolman (Ed.), *Handbook of developmental psychology* (pp. 537–548). Englewood Cliffs, NJ: Prentice-Hall.

Siegler, R. S., & Liebert, R. M. (1975). Acquisition of formal scientific reasoning by 10- and 13-year-olds: Designing a factorial experiment. *Developmental Psychology, 11,* 401–402.

Siegler, R. S., & Richards, D. D. (1982). The development of intelligence. In R. J. Sternberg (Ed.), *Handbook of human intelligence* (pp. 897–971). Cambridge, Engl.: Cambridge Univ. Press.

Silber, S. J. (1980). *How to get pregnant.* New York: Charles Scribner's Sons.

Silberner, J. (1985, October 12). Herpes babies. *Science News,* p. 232.

Silberner, J. (1986, October 11). Survival of the fetus. *Science News,* pp. 234–235.

Siman, M. L. (1977). Application of a new model of peer group influence to naturally existing adolescent friendship groups. *Child Development, 48,* 270–274.

Simister, N. E., & Mostov, K. E. (1989). An Fc receptor structurally related to MHC class I antigens. *Nature, 337,* 184–187.

Simon, H. A. (1962). An information processing theory of intellectual development. *Monographs of the Society for Research in Child Development, 27*(2, Serial No. 82).

Simons, R. L., Whitbeck, L. B., Conger, R. D., & Chyi-In, W. (1991). Intergenerational transmission of harsh parenting. *Developmental Psychology, 27,* 159–171.

Sinclair, A. H., Berta, P., Palmer, M. S., Hawkins, J. R., Griffiths, B. L., Smith, M. J., Foster, J. W., Frischauf, A. M., Lovell-Badge, R., & Goodfellow, P. N. (1990). A gene from the human sex-determining region encodes a protein with homology to a conserved DNA-binding motif. *Nature, 346,* 240–244.

Singer, D. G. (1982). Television and the developing imagination of the child. In D. Pearl, L. Bouthilet, & J. Lazar (Eds.), *Television and behavior: Ten years of scientific progress and implications for the eighties* (Vol. 2). Washington, DC: U.S. Government Printing Office.

Singer, D. G. (1983). A time to reexamine the role of television in our lives. *American Psychologist, 38,* 815–816.

Singer, J. L., & Singer, D. G. (1974). *Fostering imaginative play in preschool children: Effects of television viewing and direct adult modeling.* Paper presented at the meeting of the American Psychological Association, New Orleans, Louisiana.

Singer, J. L., & Singer, D. G. (1976). Fostering creativity in children: Can TV stimulate imaginative play? *Journal of Communication, 26*(3), 74–80.

Singer, J. L., & Singer, D. G. (1983a). Psychologists look at television: Cognitive, developmental, personality, and social policy implications. *American Psychologist, 38,* 826–834.

Singer, J. L., & Singer, D. G. (1983b). Implications of childhood television viewing for cognition, imagination, and emotion. In J. Bryant, & D. R. Anderson (Eds.), *Children's understanding of television: Research on attention and comprehension.* New York: Academic Press.

Singer, L. M., Brodzinsky, D. M., Ramsay, D., Steir, M., & Waters, E. (1985). Mother-infant attachment in adoptive families. *Child Development, 56,* 1543–1551.

Sinnott, E. W., Dunn, L. C., & Dobzhansky, T. (1958). *Principles of genetics.* New York: McGraw-Hill.

Sirignano, S. W., & Lachman, M. E. (1985). Personality change during the transition to parenthood: The role of perceived infant temperament. *Developmental Psychology, 21,* 558–567.

Siwolop, S., & Mohs, M. (1985, February). The war on Down Syndrome. *Discover,* pp. 67–73.

Skeels, H. M. (1966). Adult status of children with contrasting early life experiences. *Monographs of the Society for Research in Child Development, 31*(3 Serial No. 105).

Skeels, H. M., Updegraff, R., Wellman, B. L., & Williams, H. M. (1938). A study of environmental stimulation: An orphanage preschool project. *University of Iowa Studies in Child Welfare, 15*(4).

Skinner, B. F. (1969). *Contingencies of reinforcement.* New York: Appleton-Century-Croft.

Slater, A., Morison, V., & Rose, D. (1983). Perception of shape by the new-born baby. *British Journal of Developmental Psychology, 1,* 135–142.

Slaughter-Defoe, D. T., Nakagawa, K., Takanishi, R., & Johnson, D. J. (1990). Toward cultural/ecological perspectives on schooling and achivement in African- and Asian-American children.

Slobin, D. I. (1966). The acquisition of Russian as a native language. In F. Smith, & G. Miller (Eds.), *The genesis of language* (pp. 129–148). Cambridge, Mass.: MIT Press.

Slobin, D. I. (1970). Universals of grammatical development in children. In G. B. Flores d'Arcams, & W. J. M. Levelt (Eds.), *Advances in psycholinguistics*. New York: American Elsevier.

Smith, B. A., Fillion, T. J., & Blass, E. M. (1990). Orally mediated sources of calming in 1- to 3-day-old human infants. *Developmental Psychology, 26,* 731–737.

Smith, H. (1990). *The new Russians*. New York: Random House.

Smith, P. B., & Pederson, D. R. (1988). Maternal sensitivity and patterns of infant-mother attachment. *Child Development, 59,* 1097–1101.

Smith, P. K., & Vollstedt, R. (1985). On defining play: An empirical study of the relationship between play and various play criteria. *Child Development, 56,* 1042–1050.

Smith, S. D., Kimberling, W. J., Pennington, B. F., & Lubs, H. A. (1983). Specific reading disability: Identification of an inherited form through linkage analysis. *Science, 219,* 1345–1347.

Smolucha, F. (1988). *An introduction to Vygotsky's theory of social-cognitive development*. Unpublished manuscript.

Smuts, A. B., & Hagen, J. W. (Eds.). (1985). History and research in child development. *Monographs of the Society for Research in Child Development, 50*(4–5, Serial No. 211).

Snarey, J. R., Reimer, J., & Kohlberg, L. (1985). Development of social-moral reasoning among kibbutz adolescents: A longitudinal cross-cultural study. *Developmental Psychology, 21,* 3–17.

Snow, C. E. (1972). Mothers' speech to children learning language. *Child Development, 43,* 549–565.

Snyderman, M., & Rothman, S. (1987). Survey of expert opinion on intelligence and aptitude testing. *American Psychologist, 42,* 137–144.

Sokol, R. J., Miller, S. I., & Reed, G. (1980). Alcohol abuse during pregnancy: An epidemiologic study. *Alcoholism, 4,* 135–145.

Sommerville, C. J. (1982). *The rise and fall of childhood*. Beverly Hills, CA: Sage Publications.

Sontag, L. W., & Wallace, R. F. (1935). The effect of cigarette smoking during pregnancy upon the fetal heart rate. *American Journal of Obstetrics and Gynecology, 29,* 77–83.

Sorce, J. F., Emde, R. N., Campos, J., & Klinnert, M. D. (1985). Maternal emotional signaling: Its effect on the visual cliff behavior of 1-year-olds. *Developmental Psychology, 21,* 195–200.

Sorensen, R. C. (1973). *Adolescent sexuality in contemporary America*. New York: World.

Sorenson, E. R. (1977, May). Growing up as a Fore is to be "in touch" and free. *Smithsonian,* pp. 107–114.

Sosa, R., Kennell, J., Klaus, M., Robertson, S., & Urrutia, J. (1980). The effect of a supportive companion on perinatal problems, length of labor, and mother-infant interaction. *New England Journal of Medicine, 303,* 597–600.

Spalding, D. A. (1873). Instinct, with original observations on young animals. Macmillan's Magazine, 27, 282–293. *Reprinted in British Journal of Animal Behaviour* (1954), 2, 2–11.

Spearman, C. (1927). *The abilities of man*. New York: Macmillan.

Spelke, E. (1979). Perceiving bimodally specified events in infancy. *Developmental Psychology, 15,* 626–636.

Spelke, E. (1981). The infant's acquisition of knowledge of bimodally specified events. *Journal of Experimental Child Psychology, 31,* 279–299.

Spencer, M. B. (1990). Development of minority children: An introduction. *Child Development, 61,* 267–269.

Spencer, M. B., & Horowitz, F. D. (1973). Racial attitudes and color concept-attitude modification in black and caucasian preschool children. *Developmental Psychology, 9,* 246–254.

Spencer, M. B., & Markstrom-Adams, C. M. (1990). Identity processes among racial and ethnic minority children in America. *Child Development, 61,* 290–310.

Spinetta, J. J., & Rigler, D. (1972). The child-abusing parent: A psychological review. *Psychological Bulletin, 77,* 296–304.

Spitz, R. A. (1945). Hospitalism: An inquiry into the genesis of psychiatric conditions in early childhood. *Psychoanalytic Study of the Child, 1,* 53–74.

Spitz, R. A. (1946). Hospitalism: A follow-up report on investigation described in Volume I, 1945. *Psychoanalytic Study of the Child, 2,* 113–117.

Spock, B. (1968). *Baby and child care*. New York: Pocket Books.

Sprunger, L. W., Boyce, W. T., & Gaines, J. A. (1985). Family-infant congruence: Routines and rhythmicity in family adaptations to a young infant. *Child Development, 56,* 564–572.

Sroufe, L. A. (1979). Socioemotional development. In J. Osofsky (Ed.), *Handbook of infant development* (pp. 462–516). New York: Wiley Interscience.

Sroufe, L. A. (1983). Individual patterns of adaptation from infancy to preschool. In M. Perlmutter (Ed.), *Minnesota Symposium in Child Psychology* (Vol. 16). Hillsdale, NJ: Erlbaum.

Sroufe, L. A., Jacobvitz, D., Mangelsdorf, S., DeAngelo, E., & Ward, M. J., (1985). Generational boundary dissolution between mothers and their preschool children: A relationship systems approach. *Child Development, 56,* 317–325.

St. Peters, M., Fitch, M., Huston, A. C., Wright, J. C., & Eakins, D. J. (1991). Television and families: What do young children watch with their parents? *Child Development, 62,* 1409–1423,

Staats, A. W., & Staats, C. K. (1958). Attitudes established by classical conditioning. *Journal of Abnormal and Social Psychology, 57,* 37–40.

Stagno, S., Reynolds, D. W., Huang, E., Thames, S. D., Smith, R. J., & Alford, C. A. (1977). Congenital cytomegalovirus infection: Occurrence in an immune population. *New England Journal of Medicine, 296,* 1254–1258.

Stallings, J. (1975). Implementation and child effects of teaching practices in Follow Through classrooms. *Monographs of the Society for Research in Child Development, 40*(5, Serial No. 163).

Stanton, A. N., Scott, D. J., & Downham, M. A. P. S. (1980, May 17). Is overheating a factor in some unexpected infant deaths? *Lancet,* pp. 1054–1057.

Starkey, P., Spelke, E. S., & Gelman, R. (1983). Detection of intermodal numerical correspondences by human infants. *Science, 222,* 179–181.

Starr, R. H. (1979). Child abuse. *American Psychologist, 34,* 872–878.

Staub, E. (1971). The use of role playing and induction in children's learning of helping and sharing behavior. *Child Development, 42,* 805–816.

Staub, E. (1978). *Positive social behavior and morality*. New York: Academic Press.

Stavric, B., Klassen, R., Watkinson, B., Karpinski, K., Stapley, R., & Fried, P. (1988). Variability in caffeine consumption from coffee and tea: Possible significance for epidemiological studies. *Food Chem Toxicology, 26,* 111–118.

Stebbins, G. L., & Ayala, F. J. (1985). The evolution of Darwinism. *Scientific American, 253*(1), 72–82.

Stechler, G., & Halton, A. (1982). Prenatal influences on human development. In B. B. Wolman (Ed.), *Handbook of developmental psychology* (pp. 175–189). Englewood Cliffs, NJ: Prentice-Hall.

Steckol, K. F., & Leonard, L. B. (1981). Sensorimotor development and the use of prelinguistic performatives. *Journal of Speech and Hearing Research, 24,* 262–268.

Stein, A. H. (1973). The effects of maternal employment and educational attainment on the sex-typed attributes of college females. *Social Behavior and Personality, 1,* 111–114.

Stein, A. H., & Friedrich, L. K. (1972). Television content and young children's behavior. In J. P. Murray, E. A. Rubinstein, & G. A. Comstock (Eds.), *Television and social behavior, Vol. 2: Television and social learning*. Washington, DC: U.S. Government Printing Office.

Steinberg, L. (1986). Latchkey children and susceptibility to peer pressure: An ecological analysis. *Developmental Psychology, 22,* 433–439.

Steinberg, L., & Dornbusch, S. M. (1991). Negative correlates of part-time employment during adolescence: Replication and elaboration. *Develop-*

mental Psychology, 27, 304–313.

Steinberg, L., Elmen, J. D., & Mounts, N. S. (1989). Authoritative parenting, psychosocial maturity, and academic success among adolescents. *Child Development, 60,* 1424–1426.

Steiner, G. A. (1963). *The people look at television.* New York: Knopf.

Steiner, J. E. (1977). Facial expressions of the neonate infant indicating the hedonics of food-related chemical stimuli. In J. M. Weiffenbach (Ed.), *Taste and development: The genesis of sweet preference.* Washington, D.C.: U.S. Government Printing Office.

Steiner, J. E. (1979). Human facial expressions in response to taste and smell stimulation. In H. Reese & L. Lipsitt (Eds.), *Advances in child development and behavior* (Vol. 13). New York: Academic Press.

Stergachis, A., Scholes, D., Daling, J. R., Weiss, N. S., & Chu, J. (1991). Maternal cigarette smoking and the risk of tubal pregnancy. *American Journal of Epidemiology, 133,* 332–337.

Stern, M., & Hildebrandt, K. A. (1984). Prematurity stereotype: Effects of labeling on adults' perceptions of infants. *Developmental Psychology, 20,* 360–362.

Stern, M., & Hildebrandt, K. A. (1986). Prematurity stereotyping: Effects on mother-infant interaction. *Child Development, 57,* 308–315.

Sternberg, R. J. (1984). *Beyond IQ: A triarchic theory of human intelligence.* New York: Cambridge Univ. Press.

Sternberg, R. J. (1985). Human intelligence: The model is the message. *Science, 230,* 1111–1118.

Sternberg, R. J. (1986). *Intelligence applied.* San Diego, CA: Harcourt Brace.

Stevenson, H. W. (1968). Developmental psychology. In D. L. Sills (Ed.), *International encyclopedia of the social sciences.* New York: Macmillan.

Stevenson, H. W., Stigler, J. W., Lee, S., Lucker, G. W., Kitamura, S., & Hsu, C. (1985). Cognitive performance and academic achievement of Japanese, Chinese, and American children. *Child Development, 56,* 718–734.

Stevenson, H. W., Stigler, J. W., Lucker, G. W., Lee, S., Hsu, C., & Kitamura, S. (1982). Reading disabilities: The case of Chinese, Japanese, and English. *Child Development, 53,* 1164–1181.

Stewart, R. B., Mobley, L. A., Van Tuyl, S. S., & Salvador, M. A. (1987). The firstborn's adjustment to the birth of a sibling: A longitudinal assessment. *Child Development, 58,* 341–355.

Stith, S. M., & Davis, A. J. (1984). Employed mothers and family day-care substitute caregivers: A comparative analysis of infant care. *Child Development, 55,* 1340–1348.

Stocker, C., Dunn, J., & Plomin, R. (1989). Sibling relationships: Links with child temperament, maternal behavior, and family structure. *Child Development, 60,* 715–727.

Stoller, R. J. (1976). Gender identity. In B. J. Sadock, H. I. Kaplan, & A. M. Freedman (Eds.), *The sexual experience.* Baltimore, MD: Williams & Wilkins.

Stoller, R. J. (1985). *Presentations of gender.* New Haven: Yale Univ. Press.

Streissguth, A. P., Aase, J. M., Clarren, S. K., Randels, S. P., LaDue, R. A., & Smith, D. F. (1991). Fetal alcohol syndrome in adolescents and adults. *Journal of the American Medical Association, 265,* 1961–1967.

Streissguth, A. P., Barr, H. M., & Martin, D. C. (1983). Maternal alcohol use and neonatal habituation assessed with the Brazelton Scale. *Child Development, 54,* 1109–1118.

Streissguth, A. P., Barr, H. M., Sampson, P. D., Darby, B. L., & Martin, D. C. (1989). IQ at age 4 in relation to maternal alcohol use and smoking during pregnancy. *Developmental Psychology, 25,* 3–11.

Stringer, C. B., Grun, R., Schwarcz, H. P., & Goldberg, P. (1989). ESR dates for the hominid burial site of Es Skhul in Israel. *Nature, 338,* 756–758.

Subramanian, S. K. (1990). *Problems in intervention: The crisis of teenage pregnancy.* Paper presented at the meeting of the Society for the Study of Social Problems.

Sugarman, S. (1977). A description of communicative development in the prelanguage child. In I. Markova (Ed.), *The social context of language.* London: Wiley.

Sulik, K. K., Johnston, M. C., & Webb, M. A. (1981). Fetal alcohol syndrome: Embryogenesis in mouse model. *Science, 214,* 936–938.

Sullivan-Bolyai, J., Hull, H. F., Wilson, C., & Corey, L. (1983). Neonatal herpes simplex virus infection in King County, Washington: Increasing incidence and epidemiologic correlates. *Journal of the American Medical Association, 250,* 3059–3062.

Sullivan, S. A., & Birch, L. (1990). Pass the sugar, pass the salt: Experience dictates preference. *Developmental Psychology, 26,* 546–551.

Sun, M. (1985). EPA accelerates ban on leaded gas. *Science, 227,* 1448.

Suomi, S. J., & Harlow, H. (1972). Social rehabilitation of isolate-reared monkeys. *Developmental Psychology, 6,* 487–496.

Sussman, N. (1976). Sex and sexuality in history. In B. J. Sadock, H. I. Kaplan, & A. M. Freedman (Eds.), *The sexual experience.* Baltimore, MD: Williams & Wilkins.

Sutton-Smith, B. (1981). *A history of children's play: The New Zealand Playground 1840–1950.* Univ. of Penn. Press.

Sutton-Smith, B. (1985, October). The child at play. *Psychology Today,* pp. 64–65.

Svejda, M. J., Pannabecker, B. J., & Emde, R. N. (1982). Parent-to-infant attachment. A critique of the early "bonding" model. In R. N. Emde, & R. J. Harmon (Eds.), *The development of attachment and affiliative systems* (pp. 83–93). New York: Plenum Press.

Swedo, S. E., Rettew, D. C., Kuppenheimer, M., Lum, D., Dolan, S., & Goldberger, E. (1991). Can adolescent suicide attempters be distinguished from at-risk adolescents? *Pediatrics, 88,* 620–629.

Sylva, K., Bruner, J., & Genova, P. (1976). The role of play in the problem solving of children 3–5 years old. In J. S. Bruner, A. Jolly, & K. Sylva (Eds.), *Play.* New York: Basic Books.

Tager, I. B., Weiss, S. T., Munoz, A., Rosner, B., & Speizer, F. E. (1983). Longitudinal study of the effects of maternal smoking on pulmonary function in children. *New England Journal of Medicine, 309,* 699–703.

Tanner, J. M. (1962). *Growth at adolescence* (2nd ed.). Oxford: Blackwell.

Tanner, J. M. (1968). Earlier maturation in man. *Scientific American, 218*(1), 21–27.

Tanner, J. M. (1969). Growth and endocrinology in the adolescent. In L. I. Gardner (Ed.), *Endocrine and genetic diseases of childhood.* Philadelphia, PA: Saunders.

Tanner, J. M., Whitehouse, R. H., & Takaishi, M. (1966). Standards from birth to maturity for height, weight, height velocity and weight velocity: British children, 1965. *Archives of Disease in Childhood, 41,* 454–471; 613–635.

Taylor, M., & Gelman, S. A. (1989). Incorporating new words into the lexicon: Preliminary evidence for language hierarchies in two-year-old children. *Child Development, 60,* 625–636.

Terasaki, P. I., Gjertson, D., Bernoco, D., Perdue, S., Mickey, M. R., & Bond, J. (1978). Twins with two different fathers identified by HLA. *New England Journal of Medicine, 299,* 590–592.

Terman, L. M. (1925). Mental and physical traits of a thousand gifted children. In L. M. Terman (Ed.), *Genetic studies of genius.* Stanford: Stanford University Press.

Terman, L. M. (1954). Scientists and nonscientists in a group of 800 gifted men. *Psychological Monographs, 68*(7), 1–44.

Tessman, L. H. (1978). *Children of parting parents.* New York: Aronson.

Teti, D. M., & Ablard, K. E. (1989). Security of attachment and infant-sibling relationships: A laboratory study. *Child Development, 60,* 1519–1528.

Thatcher, R. W., Walker, R. A., & Giudice, S. (1987). Human cerebral hemispheres develop at different rates and ages. *Science, 236,* 1110–1113.

Thelen, E. (1986). Treadmill-elicited stepping in seven-month-old infants. *Child Development, 57,* 1498–1506.

Thelen, E. & Fisher, D. M. (1982). Newborn stepping: An explanation for a "disappearing" reflex. *Developmental Psychology, 18,* 760–775.

Thelen, E., & Ulrich, B. D. (1991). Hidden skills. *Monographs of the Society for Research in Child Development, 56*(1, Serial No. 223).

Thomas, A., Chess, S., & Birch, H. (1968). *Temperament and behavior dis-*

orders in children. New York: New York Univ. Press.

Thomas, A., Chess, S., & Birch, H. G. (1970). The origin of personality. *Scientific American, 223*(2), 102–109.

Thomas, D. G., Campos, J. J., Shucard, D. W., Ramsay, D. S., & Shucard, J. (1981). Semantic comprehension in infancy: A signal detection analysis. *Child Development, 52,* 798–803.

Thomas, L. (1982, March). On altruism. *Discover,* pp. 58–59.

Thompson, L. A., Fagan, J. F., & Fulker, D. W. (1991). Longitudinal prediction of specific cognitive abilities from infant novelty preference. *Child Development, 62,* 530–538.

Thompson, R. A. (1988). The effects of infant day care through the prism of attachment theory: A critical appraisal. *Early Childhood Research Quarterly, 3,* 273–282.

Thompson, R. A., Connell, J. P., & Bridges, L. J. (1988). Temperament, emotion, and social interactive behavior in the strange situation: A component process analysis of attachment system functioning. *Child Development, 59,* 1102–1110.

Thompson, S. K. (1975). Gender labels and early sex role development. *Child Development, 46,* 339–347.

Thomsen, D. E. (1983, January 22). NASA to help listen for E.T.'s call. *Science News,* p. 52.

Thorndike, E. L. (1905). *The elements of psychology*. New York: Seiler.

Tieger, T. (1980). On the biological basis of sex differences in aggression. *Child Development, 51,* 943–963.

Timberlake, W., & Farmer-Dougan, V. A. (1991). Reinforcement in applied settings: Figuring out ahead of time what will work. *Psychological Bulletin, 110,* 379–391.

Tolson, T. F. J., & Wilson, M. N. (1990). The impact of two- and three-generational black family structure on perceived family climate. *Child Development, 61,* 416–428.

Torrance, E. P., & Wu, T. (1981). A comparative longitudinal study of the adult creative achievements of elementary school children identified as highly intelligent and as highly creative. *Creative Child and Adult Quarterly, 6,* 71–76.

Tower, R. B., Singer, D. G., Singer, J. L., & Biggs, A. (1979). Differential effects of television programming on preschoolers' cognition, imagination, and social play. *American Journal of Orthopsychiatry, 49,* 265–281.

Trehub, S. E., Schneider, B. A., Morrongiello, B. A., & Thorpe, L. A. (1988). Auditory sensitivity in school-age children. *Journal of Experimental Child Psychology, 46,* 273–285.

Triandis, H. C., & Brislin, R. W. (1984). Cross-cultural psychology. *American Psychologist, 39,* 1006–1016.

Trickett, P. K., & Kuczynski, L. (1986). Children's misbehaviors and parental discipline strategies in abusive and nonabusive families. *Developmental Psychology, 22,* 115–123.

Tronick, E. Z., Morelli, G. A., & Ivey, P. K. (1992). The Efe forager infant and toddler's pattern of social relationships: Multiple and simultaneous. *Developmental Psychology, 28,* 568–577.

Trotter, R. J. (1980, October 11). Born too soon. *Science News,* pp. 234–235.

Tsai, L., Stewart, M. A., & August, G. J. (1981). Implication of sex differences in the familial transmission of infantile autism. *Journal of Autism and Developmental Disorders, 11,* 165–173.

Tseng, W., Ebata, K., Miguchi, M., Egawa, M., & McLaughlin, D. G. (1990). Transethnic adoption and personality traits: A lesson from Japanese orphans returned from China to Japan. *American Journal of Psychiatry, 147,* 330–335.

Turkewitz, G., Moreau, T., & Birch, H. G. (1966). Head position and receptor organization in the human neonate. *Journal of Experimental Child Psychology, 4,* 169–177.

Turkington, C. (1983, May). Child suicide: An unspoken tragedy. *APA Monitor,* p. 15.

Turkington, C. (1986, November). Down syndrome child is frequently educable. *APA Monitor,* p. 22.

Turkington, C. (1987, September). Special talents. *Psychology Today,* pp. 42–46.

Turnbull, C. (1973). The mountain people. *Intellectual Digest, 3*(8), 49–56.

Turnbull, C. M. (1961). Some observations regarding the experiences and behavior of the Bambuti Pygmies. *American Journal of Psychology, 74,* 304–308.

Turner, G., Brookwell, R., Daniel, A., Selikowitz, M., & Zilibowitz, M. (1980). Heterozygous expression of X-linked mental retardation and X-chromosome marker fra(X)(q27). *New England Journal of Medicine, 303,* 662–664.

Turner, P. J. (1991). Relations between attachment, gender, and behavior with peers in preschool. *Child Development, 62,* 1475–1488.

U.S. Conference of Mayors. (1988). *A status report on the Stewart B. McKinney Homeless Assistance Act of 1987*. Washington, DC: Author.

United States Adivsory Board on Child Abuse and Neglect. (1990). *Child abuse and neglect: Critical first steps in response to a national emergency* (stock no. 017–092–00104–5). Washington, DC: U. S. Government Printing Office, Congressional Sales Office.

Valdez-Menchaca, M. C., & Whitehurst, G. J. (1988). The effects of incidental teaching on vocabulary acquisition by young children. *Child Development, 59,* 1451–1459.

Valencia, R. R. (1985). Predicting academic achievement in Mexican-American children using the Kaufman Assessment Battery for children. *Educational and Psychological Research, 5,* 11–17.

van Doorninck, W. J., Caldwell, B. M., Wright, C., & Frankenburg, W. K. (1981). The relationship between twelve-month home stimulation and school achievement. *Child Development, 52,* 1080–1083.

Van IJzendoorn, M. H., & Kroonenberg, P. M. (1988). Cross-cultural patterns of attachment: A meta-analysis of the strange situation. *Child Development, 59,* 147–156.

Van Osdol, W. R., & Shane, D. G. (1982). *An introduction to exceptional children* (3rd ed.). Dubuque, Iowa: William C. Brown.

Vandell, D. L., & Mueller, E. C. (1980). Peer play and friendships during the first two years. In H. C. Foot, A. J. Chapman, & J. R. Smith (Eds.), *Friendship and social relations in children*. New York: Wiley.

Vandenberg, B. (1978). Play and development from an ethological perspective. *American Psychologist, 33,* 724–738.

Vandenberg, B. (1981). Environmental and cognitive factors in social play. *Journal of Experimental Child Psychology, 31,* 169–175.

Vandenberg, B. (1984). Developmental features of exploration. *Developmental Psychology, 20,* 3–8.

Vandiver, R. (1972). *Sources and interrelation of premarital sexual standards and general liberality conservatism*. Unpublished doctoral dissertation, Southern Illinois University.

Vaughn, B. E., Kopp, C. B., & Krakow, J. B. (1984). The emergence and consolidation of self-control from eighteen to thirty months of age: Normative trends and individual differences. *Child Development, 55,* 990–1004.

Vaughn, B. E., & Langlois, J. H. (1983). Physical attractiveness as a correlate of peer status and social competence in preschool children. *Developmental Psychology, 19,* 561–567.

Vaughn, B. E., Lefever, G. B., Seifer, R., & Barglow, P. (1989). Attachment behavior, attachment security, and temperament during infancy. *Child Development, 60,* 728–737.

Vellutino, F. R. (1987). Dyslexia. *Scientific American, 256*(3), 34–41.

Vinter, A. (1986). The role of movement in eliciting early imitations. *Child Development, 57,* 66–71.

Vitz, P. C. (1990). The use of stories in moral development: New psychological reasons for an old education method. *American Psychologist, 45,* 709–720.

Vollrath, D., Foote, S., Hilton, A., Brown, L. G., Beer-Romero, P., Bogan, J. S., & Page, D. C. (1992). The human Y chromosome: A 43-interval map based on naturally occurring deletions. *Science, 258,* 52–59.

Vondracek, F. W., & Lerner, R. M. (1982). Vocational role development in adolescence. In B. B. Wolman (Ed.), *Handbook of developmental psychology* (pp. 602–614). Englewood Cliffs, NJ: Prentice-Hall.

Vuchinich, S., Emery, R. E., & Cassidy, J. (1988). Family members as third parties in dyadic family conflict: Strategies, alliances, and outcomes. *Child Development, 59,* 1293–1302.

Vuchinich, S., Hetherington, E. M., Vuchinich, R. A., & Clingempeel, W. G. (1991). Parent-child interaction and gender differences in early adolescents' adaptation to stepfamilies. *Developmental Psychology, 27,* 618–626.

Vurpillot, E., & Ball, W. A. (1979). The concept of identity and children's selective attention. In G. Hale, & M. Lewis (Eds.), *Attention and cognitive development.* New York: Plenum.

Vygotsky, L. S. (1962). *Thought and language* (E. Hanfmann & G. Vakar, Trans.). Cambridge: Massachusetts Institute of Technology. (Original work published 1934).

Wachs, T. D. (1987). Short-term stability of aggregated and nonaggregated measures of parental behavior. *Child Development, 58,* 796–797.

Waddington, C. H. (1957). *The strategy of the genes.* London: Allen & Unwin.

Wagner, D. A. (1978). Memories of Morocco: The influence of age, schooling, and environment on memory. *Cognitive Psychology, 10,* 1–28.

Wagner, D. A., & Stevenson, H. W. (Eds.). (1982). *Cultural perspectives on child development.* San Francisco: W. H. Freeman.

Waldhauser, F., Weiszenbacher, G., Frisch, H., Zeitlhuber, U., Waldhauser, M., & Wurtman, R. J. (1984). Fall in nocturnal serum melatonin during prepuberty and pubescence. *Lancet, 1*(8373), 362–365.

Walker-Andrews, A. S., & Lennon, E. M. (1985). Auditory-visual perception of changing distance by human infants. Child Development, 56, 544–548.

Walker, E., & Emory, E. (1985). Commentary: Interpretive bias and behavioral genetic research. *Child Development, 56,* 775–778.

Walker, E., & Lewine, R. J. (1990). Prediction of adult-onset schizophrenia from childhood home movies of the patients. *American Journal of Psychiatry, 147,* 1052–1056.

Walker, L. J., de Vries, B., & Bichard, S. L. (1984). The hierarchical nature of stages of moral development. *Developmental Psychology, 20,* 960–966.

Walker, L. J., & Taylor, J. H. (1991a). Family interactions and the development of moral reasoning. *Child Development, 62,* 264–283.

Walker, L. J., & Taylor, J. H. (1991b). Stage transitions in moral reasoning: A longitudinal study of developmental processes. *Developmental Psychology, 27,* 330–337.

Wallach, M. A. (1970). Creativity. In P. H. Mussen (Ed.), *Carmichael's manual of child psychology* (3rd ed., pp. 1211–1272). New York: Wiley.

Wallach, M. A., & Kogan, N. (1965). *Modes of thinking in young children: A study of the creativity-intelligence distinction.* New York: Holt.

Wallach, M. A., & Wing, C. W. (1969). *The talented student: A validation of the creativity-intelligence distinction.* New York: Holt.

Wallerstein, J. S. (1984a). Children of divorce: Preliminary report of a ten-year follow-up of young children. *American Journal of Orthopsychiatry, 54,* 444–458.

Wallerstein, J. S. (1984b). Children of divorce: The psychological tasks of the child. *Annual Progress in Child Psychiatry and Child Development, 1984,* 263–280.

Wallerstein, J. S. (1985). Effect of divorce on children. *The Harvard Medical School Mental Health Letter,* 2(3), 8.

Wallerstein, J. S., & Kelly, J. B. (1975). The effects of parental divorce: Experiences of the preschool child. *Journal of the American Academy of Child Psychiatry, 14,* 600–616.

Wallerstein, J. S., & Kelly, J. B. (1976). The effects of parental divorce: Experiences of the child in later latency. *American Journal of Orthopsychiatry, 46,* 256–269.

Wallerstein, J. S., & Kelly, J. B. (1981). *Surviving the breakup: How children and parents cope with divorce.* New York: Basic Books.

Wallis, C., Booth, C., Ludtke, M., & Taylor, E. (1985, December 9). Children having children. *Time,* pp. 78–90.

Wallis, C., Hull, J. C., Ludtke, M., & Taylor, E. (1987June 22). The child-care dilemma. *Time,* pp. 54–60.

Wallis, C., & Ludtke, M. (1987June 22). Is day care bad for babies? *Time,* p. 63.

Warren, M. P. (1980). The effects of exercise on pubertal progression and reproductive function in girls. *Journal of Clinical Endocrinology and Metabolism, 51,* 1150–1157.

Washburn, S. L., & Hamburg, D. A. (1965). The study of primate behavior. In I. DeVore (Ed.), *Primate behavior: Field studies of monkeys and apes.* New York: Holt.

Wassarman, P. M. (1987). The biology and chemistry of fertilization. *Science, 235,* 553–560.

Waters, E. (1983). The stability of individual differences in infant attachment: Comments on the Thompson, Lamb, and Estes contribution. *Child Development, 54,* 516–520.

Waters, E., Wippman, J., & Sroufe, L. A. (1979). Attachment, positive affect, and competence in the peer group: Two studies in construct validation. *Child Development, 50,* 821–829.

Watkinson, B., & Fried, P. A. (1985). Maternal caffeine use before, during and after pregnancy and effects upon offspring. *Neurobehavioral Toxicology and Teratology, 7,* 9–17.

Watson, J. B. (1970). *Behaviorism* (Rev. ed.). New York: Norton. (Original work published 1924).

Watson, J. B., & Rayner, R. (1920). Conditioned emotional responses. *Journal of Experimental Psychology, 3,* 1–14.

Watson, J. D., & Crick, F. H. C. (1953). Molecular structure of nucleic acids: A structure for deoxyribose nucleic acid. *Nature, 171,* 737–738.

Watson, J. S., & Ramey, C. T. (1969, March). *Reactions to responsive contingent stimulation in early infancy.* Paper presented at the biennial meeting of the Society for Research in Child Development, Santa Monica, California.

Watson, J. S., & Ramey, C. T. (1972). Reactions to response-contingent stimulation in early infancy. *Merrill-Palmer Quarterly, 18,* 219–227.

Webb, E., Campbell, D., Schwartz, R., Sechrest, L. (1966). *Unobtrusive measures: Nonreactive research in the social sciences.* Chicago: Rand McNally.

Weber, G. (1971). *Inner city children can be taught to read: Four successful schools.* Washington, D.C.: Council for Basic Education, Occasional Paper no. 18.

Wehren, A., & De Lisi, R. (1983). The development of gender understanding: Judgments and explanations. *Child Development, 54,* 1568–1578.

Weinberg, R. A. (1989). Intelligence and IQ. *American Psychologist, 44,* 98–104.

Weinstock, A., & Lerner, R. M. (1972). Attitudes of late adolescents and their parents toward contemporary issues. *Psychological Reports, 30,* 239–244.

Weisfeld, G. E. (1982). The nature-nurture issue and the integrating concept of function. In B. B. Wolman (Ed.), *Handbook of developmental psychology* (pp. 208–229). Englewood Cliffs, NJ: Prentice-Hall.

Weisler, A., & McCall, R. B. (1976). Exploration and play. *American Psychologist, 31,* 144–152.

Weisner, T. S., & Wilson-Mitchell, J. E. (1990). Nonconventional family life-styles and sex typing in six-year-olds. *Child Development, 61,* 1915–1933.

Weiss, B. (1982). Food additives and environmental chemicals as sources of childhood behavior disorder. *Journal of the American Academy of Child Psychiatry, 21,* 144, 152.

Weiss, R. (1989, January 21). Predisposition and prejudice. *Science News,* pp. 40–42.

Weist, R. M. (1983). The word order myth. *Journal of Child Language, 10,* 97–106.

Weisz, J. R., Rothbaum, F. M., & Blackburn, T. C. (1984). Standing out and standing in: The psychology of control in America and Japan. *American Psychologist, 39,* 955–969.

Weitzman, N., Birns, B., & Friend, R. (1985). Traditional and nontraditional mothers' communication with their daughters and sons. *Child Development, 56,* 894–898.

Wellman, H. (1983). Metamemory revisited. In M. T. H. Chi (Ed.), *Trends in memory development research* (Vol. 9, pp. 31–51). Basel, Switzerland: Karger.

Wells, G. (1985). Preschool literacy-related activities and success in school. In D. R. Olson, N. Torrance, & A. Hildyard (Eds.), *Literacy, language, and learning: The nature and consequences of reading and writing* (pp. 229–255). New York: Cambridge University Press.

Werry, J. S. (1979). The childhood psychoses. In H. C. Quay, & J. S. Werry (Eds.), *Psychopathological disorders of childhood* (2nd ed.). New York: Wiley.

Wertheimer, M. (1961). Psycho-motor coordination of auditory-visual space at birth. *Science, 134,* 1692.

Wertlieb, D., Weigel, C., Springer, T., & Feldstein, M. (1988). Temperament as a moderator of children's stressful experiences. In S. Chess, A. Thomas, & M. E. Hertzig (Eds.), *Annual progress in child psychiatry and child development* (pp. 238–254). New York: Brunner/Mazel.

West, J. R., Hodges, C. A., & Black, A. C., Jr. (1981). Prenatal exposure to ethanol alters the organization of hippocampal mossy fibers in rats. *Science, 211,* 957–958.

West, M. J., & Rheingold, H. L. (1978). Infant stimulation of maternal instruction. *Infant Behavior and Development, 1,* 205–215.

Whalen, C. K., & Henker, B. (1976). Psychostimulants and children: A review and analysis. *Psychological Bulletin, 83,* 1113–1130.

Whitehurst, G. J. (1982). Language development. In B. B. Wolman (Ed.), *Handbook of developmental psychology* (pp. 367–386). Englewood Cliffs, NJ: Prentice-Hall.

Whitehurst, G. J., Falco, F. L., Lonigan, C. J., Fischel, J. E., DeBaryshe, B. D., Valdez-Menchaca, M. C., & Caulfield, M. (1988). Accelerating language development through picture book reading. *Developmental Psychology, 24,* 552–559.

Whiting, B. B., & Whiting, J. W. M. (1975). *Children of six cultures: A psychocultural analysis.* Cambridge, Mass.: Harvard Univ. Press.

Wickelgren, I. (1989, June 3). Genetic evidence for autism. *Science News,* p. 349.

Wilcox, A. J., Weinberg, C. R., O'Connor, J. F., Baird, D. D., Schlatterer, J. P., Canfield, R. E., Armstrong, E. G., & Nisula, B. C. (1988). Incidence of early loss of pregnancy. *New England Journal of Medicine, 319,* 189–194.

Wilentz, A., Gorman, C., & Hull, J. (1987, March 23). Teen suicide. *Time,* pp. 12–13.

Will, J. A., Self, P. A., & Datan, N. (1976). Maternal behavior and perceived sex of infant. *American Journal of Orthopsychiatry, 46,* 135–139.

Willerman, L., Schultz, R., Rutledge, J. N., & Bigler, E. D. (1991). In vivo brain size and intelligence. *Intelligence, 15,* 223–228.

Williams, D. A., & King, P. (1980b, December 15). Do males have a math gene? *Newsweek,* p. 72.

Williams, D. A., & King, P. (1980a, December 22). It really is a head start. *Newsweek,* p. 54.

Williams, L., & Golenski, J. (1979). Infant behavioral state and speech sound discrimination. *Child Development, 50,* 1243–1246.

Williams, T. M. (Ed.). (1986). *The impact of television: A natural experiment in three communities.* Orlando, FL: Academic Press, Inc.

Wilson, E. O. (1975). *Sociobiology.* Cambridge, Mass.: Belknap Press.

Wilson, R. S. (1983). The Louisville Twin Study: Developmental synchronies in behavior. *Child Development, 54,* 298–316.

Wilson, R. S. (1985). Risk and resilience in early mental development. *Developmental Psychology, 21,* 795–805.

Winer, G. A., Craig, R. K., & Weinbaum, E. (1992). Adults' failure on misleading weight-conservation tests: A developmental analysis. *Developmental Psychology, 28,* 109–120.

Wing, J. K. (1977). *Early childhood autism.* Elmsford, NY: Pergamon Press.

Wolff, P. H. (1966). The causes, controls and organization of behavior in the neonate. *Psychological Issues, 5*(1, Serial No. 17).

Wolock, I., & Horowitz, B. (1984). Child maltreatment as a social problem: The neglect of neglect. *American Journal of Orthopsychiatry, 54,* 530–543.

Woodhead, M. (1988). When psychology informs public policy: The case of early childhood intervention. *American Psychologist, 43,* 443–454.

Woods, M. B. (1972). The unsupervised child of the working mother. *Developmental Psychology, 6,* 14–25.

Wright, H. F. (1967). *Recording and analyzing child behavior.* New York: Harper & Row.

Wroblewski, R., & Huston, A. C. (1987). Televised occupational stereotypes and their effects on early adolescents: Are they changing? *Journal of Early Adolescence, 7,* 283–297.

Wulbert, M., & Dries, R. (1977). The relative efficacy of methylphenidate (Ritalin) and behavior-modification techniques in the treatment of a hyperactive child. *Journal of Applied Behavior Analysis, 10,* 21–31.

Yalom, I. D., Green, R., & Fisk, N. (1973). Prenatal exposure to female hormones: Effect on psychosexual development in boys. *Archives of General Psychiatry, 28,* 554–561.

Yang, K. S. (1986). Chinese personality and its change. In M. H. Bond (Ed.), *The psychology of the Chinese people.* Hong Kong: Oxford University Press.

Yarrow, M. R., Campbell, J. D., & Burton, R. (1968). *Child rearing, an inquiry into research and methods.* San Francisco: Jossey-Bass.

Yarrow, M. R., & Waxler, C. (1977, March). Paper presented at the meeting of the Society for Research in Child Development, New Orleans, Louisiana.

Yates, B. T., & Mischel, W. (1979). Young children's preferred attentional strategies for delaying gratification. *Journal of Personality and Social Psychology, 37,* 286–300.

Yazigi, R. A., Odem, R. R., & Polakoski, K. L. (1991). Demonstration of specific binding of cocaine to human spermatozoa. *Journal of the American Medical Association, 266,* 1956–1959.

Yonas, A., Granrud, C. E., & Pettersen, L. (1985). Infants' sensitivity to relative size information for distance. *Developmental Psychology, 21,* 161–167.

Yonas, A., Pettersen, L., & Granrud, C. E. (1982). Infants' sensitivity to familiar size as information for distance. *Child Development, 53,* 1285–1290.

Young, W. C., Goy, R. W., & Phoenix, C. H. (1964). Hormones and sexual behavior. *Science, 143,* 212–218.

Youngblade, L. M., & Belsky, J. (1992). Parent-child antecedents of 5-year-olds' close friendships: A longitudinal analysis. *Developmental Psychology, 28,* 700–713.

Younger, B. (1990). Infants' detection of correlations among feature categories. *Child Development, 61,* 614–620.

Youngstrom, N. (1991, October). Warning: Teens at risk for AIDS. *The APA Monitor,* pp. 38–39.

Zahn-Waxler, C., Radke-Yarrow, M., Wagner, E., & Chapman, M. (1992). Development of concern for others. *Developmental Psychology, 28,* 126–136.

Zajonc, R. B. (1986). The decline and rise of scholastic aptitude scores: A prediction derived from the confluence model. *American Psychologist, 41,* 862–867.

Zajonc, R. B., & Markus, G. B. (1975). Birth order and intellectual development. *Psychological Review, 82,* 74–88.

Zametkin, A. J., Nordahl, T. E., Gross, M., King, A. C., Semple, W. E., Rumsey, J., Hamburger, S., & Cohen, R. M. (1990). Cerebral glucose metabolism in adults with hyperactivity of childhood onset. *New England Journal of Medicine, 323,* 1361–1366.

Zarbatany, L., Hartmann, D. P., Gelfand, D. M., & Vinciguerra, P. (1985). Gender differences in altruistic reputation: Are they artifactual? *Developmental Psychology, 21,* 97–101.

Zarbatany, L., Hartmann, D. P., & Rankin, D. B. (1990). The psychological functions of preadolescent peer activities. *Child Development, 61,* 1067–1080.

Zelazo, P. R., Kotelchuck, M., Barber, L., & David, J. (1977, March). *Fathers and sons: An experimental facilitation of attachment behaviors.* Paper presented at the meeting of the Society for Research in Child Development, New Orleans, Louisiana.

Zelazo, P. R., Zelazo, N. A., & Kolb, S. (1972). "Walking" in the newborn. *Science, 176,* 314–315.

Zeskind, P. S., & Marshall, T. R. (1988). The relation between variations in pitch and maternal perceptions of infant crying. *Child Development, 59,* 193–196.

Zigler, E., & Turner, P. (1982). Parents and day care workers: A failed partnership? In E. Zigler, & E. Gordon (Eds.), *Day care: Scientific and social policy issues.* Boston, MA: Auburn House.

Zimbardo, P. G. (1979). *Psychology and life* (10th ed.). Glenview, IL: Scott Foresman.

NAME INDEX

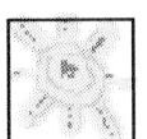

SUBJECT INDEX*

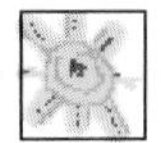

*Italicized page numbers that appear in this index refer to pages on which a running glossary definition of the particular subject can be found.

Acknowledgements

Page 89, Table 3.2, From "Evaluation of the newborn infant—second report," by V. Apgar, D. A. Holaday, L. S. James, & C. Berrien. In *Journal of the American Medical Association,* Vol. 168, pp. 1985–1988. Copyright 1958, American Medical Association. Reprinted by permission.

Page 93, Figure 3.11, From *Science News,* October 11, 1980, p. 234. Reprinted by permission of Evelyn B. Thoman.

Page 94, Figure 3.12, From "Neonatal Mortality Risk in Relation to Birth Weight and Gestational Age: Update," by B. L. Koops, L. J. Morgan, and F. C. Battaglia. In *Journal of Pediatrics,* 1982, Vol. 101, p. 972. Reprinted by permission of C. V. Mosby Company and B. L. Koops.

Page 108, Figure 4.2, From "Some Aspects of Form and Growth," by C. M. Jackson. In *Growth,* © 1929 by Yale University Press. Reprinted by permission of the publisher.

Page 114, Table 4.3, From "The Origin of Personality," by Alexander Thomas, Stella Chess, and Herbert G. Birch. Copyright © 1970 by Scientific American, Inc. All rights reserved.

Page 119, Figure 4.4, From "Sudden Infant Death," by Richard L. Naeye. Copyright © 1980 by Scientific American, Inc. All rights reserved.

Page 139, Figure 5.5, From "Self-Produced Locomotion and the Development of Responsiveness to Linear Perspective and Texture Gradients," by M. Arterberry, A. Yonas, & A. S. Bensen. In *Developmental Psychology,* 1989, Vol. 25, pp. 976–982. Copyright 1985 by the American Psychological Association. Photo courtesy of Albert Yonas, University of Minnesota.

Page 139, Figure 5.6, From "Infants' Sensitivity to Accretion and Deletion of Texture as Information for Depth at an Edge," by C. E. Granrud, et al. In *Child Development,* 1984, Vol. 55, p. 1631. © The Society for Research in Child Development. Reprinted by permission.

Page 140, Figure 5.7, From "Perception of Relational Invariants by Newborns," by S. E. Antell, C. J. Caron, & R. S. Myers. In *Developmental Psychology,* 1985, Vol. 21, p. 943. Copyright 1985 by the American Psychological Association. Reprinted by permission of the author.

Page 140, Figure 5.8, From "A Critical Test of Infant Pattern Preference Models," by J. L. Dannemiller and B. R. Stephens. In *Child Development,* 1988, Vol. 59, p. 212. © The Society for Research in Child Development. Reprinted by permission.

Page 170, Table 6.5, Adapted from "Socioemotional Development," by L. Alan Sroufe. In J. Osofsky (Ed.), *Handbook of Infant Development,* 1979, p. 473. Reprinted by permission of John Wiley & Sons, Inc.

Page 192, Figure 7.4, From "Thorndike and the Problem of Animal Intelligence," by M. E. Bitterman. In *American Psychologist,* 1969, Vol. 24, p. 445. Copyright 1969 by the American Psychological Association. Reprinted by permission of the publisher and author.

Page 193, Figure 7.5, From "Thorndike and the Problem of Animal Intelligence," by M. E. Bitterman. In *American Psychologist,* 1969, Vol. 24, p. 446. Copyright 1969 by the American Psychological Association. Reprinted by permission of the publisher and author.

Page 199, quotation, Reprinted from NEBRASKA SYMPOSIUM ON MOTIVATION, 1962, Marshall R. Jones Ed., by Permission of University of Nebraska Press. Copyright © 1962 by the University of Nebraska Press.

Page 216, Figure 8.1, From "Retrieval of a Basic-Level Category in Prelinguistic Infants," by Kenneth Roberts. In *Developmental Psychology,* 1988, Vol. 24, p. 23. Copyright 1988 by the American Psychological Association. Reprinted by permission of the author.

Page 221, Figure 8.2, From "The Acquisition of Language," by Breyne Arlene Moskowitz. Copyright © 1978 by Scientific American, Inc. All rights reserved.

Page 223, Table 8.1, From R. M. Liebert et al. DEVELOPMENTAL PSYCHOLOGY, 2nd ed. © 1977, pp. 250. Reprinted by permission of Prentice-Hall, Inc., Englewood Cliffs, New Jersey.

Page 225, Table 8.2, From PSYCHOLOGY AND LANGUAGE by Herbert H. Clark and Eve V. Clark. © 1977 by Harcourt Brace Jovanovich, Inc. Reprinted by permission of the publisher.

Page 226, Figure 8.3, From "The Child's Learning of English Morphology," by J. Berko. In *Word,* 1958, Vol. 14, p. 154. Reprinted by permission of the International Linguistic Association.

Page 227, Table 8.3, From Grover J. Whitehurst "Language Development" in HANDBOOK OF DEVELOPMENTAL PSYCHOLOGY, Wolman et al., eds., © 1982, p. 371. Reprinted by permission of Prentice-Hall, Englewood Cliffs, New Jersey.

Page 228, Figure 8.4, From "Intonation and Communicative Intent in Mothers' Speech to Infants: Is the Melody the Message," by Anne Fernald. In *Child Development,* 1989, Vol. 60, pp. 1497–1510. © The Society for Research in Child Development, Inc. Reprinted by permission.

Page 256, Figure 9.2, From OF CHILDREN, Fourth Edition, by Guy R. Lefrancois. © 1983, 1980 by Wadsworth, Inc. Reprinted by permission of the publisher.

Page 263, Figures 9.4–9.5, From "Object Permanence in 3½- and 4½-month old infants," by Renee

Baillargeon. In *Developmental Psychology,* 1987, Vol. 23, p. 656. Copyright 1987 by the American Psychological Association. Reprinted by permission of the author.

Page 264, Figure 9.7, From "Conservation of Length Redux: A Perceptual-Linguistic Phenomenon," by William Schiff. In *Child Development,* 1983, Vol. 54, p. 1499. © The Society for Research in Child Development, Inc. Reprinted by permission.

Page 282, Figure 10.1, From "Information Processing in the Child," by J. Kagan, B. L. Rosman, D. Day, J. Albert, & W. Phillips. In *Psychological Monographs,* 1964, Whole No. 578, p. 22. Copyright 1964 by the American Psychological Association. Reprinted by permission of the author.

Page 288, Figure 10.2, From "Age Differences in Organization and Recall," by C. Liberty and P. A. Ornstein. In *Journal of Experimental Child Psychology,* 1973, Vol. 15, p. 177. Reprinted by permission of Academic Press Inc., and P. A. Ornstein.

Page 296, Figure 10.4, From "Verbal Control of Behavior: The Effects of Shouting," by Eli Saltz, Sarah Campbell, and David Skotko. In *Developmental Psychology,* 1983, Vol. 19, p. 463. Copyright 1983 by the American Psychological Association. Reprinted by permission of the author.

Page 315, Figure 11.3, Copyright 1985 by the Riverside Publishing Company. Reproduced by permission of the publisher.

Page 316, Figure 11.4, Sample item A5 from Raven's Progressive Matrices Test. Reprinted by permission of J. C. Raven Limited.

Page 319, Table 11.4, From "Predictive Value of Infant Tests," by L. D. Anderson. In *Child Development,* 1939, Vol. 10, p. 204. © The Society for Research in Child Development, Inc. Reprinted by permission.

Page 320, Figure 11.5, From *Stability and Change in Human Characteristics,* by B. S. Bloom. Reprinted by permission of John Wiley & Sons, Inc.

Page 336, Table 12.1, From *Socialization and Society,* by J. Clausen, p. 141. Reprinted by permission of the author.

Page 345, Figure 12.1, From "A Circumplex Model for Maternal Behavior," by E. S. Schaefer. In the *Journal of Abnormal and Social Psychology,* 1959, Vol. 59, pp. 226–235. Copyright 1959 by the American Psychological Association. Reprinted by permission of the author.

Page 389, Figure 14.1, From "Growth of Social Play with Peers during the Second Year of Life," by C. O. Eckerman, J. L. Whatley, & S. L. Kutz. In *Developmental Psychology,* 1975, Vol. 11, p. 47. Copyright 1975 by the American Psychological Association. Reprinted by permission of the author.

Page 391, Table 14.1, From "How Children Become Friends," by J. M. Gottman. In *Monographs of the Society for Research in Child Development,* 1983, Vol. 48, pp. 27, 53–54. © The Society for Research in Child Development, Inc. Reprinted by permission.

Page 392, Table 14.2, From "How Children Become Friends," by J. M. Gottman. In *Monographs of the Society for Research in Child Development,* 1983, Vol. 48, pp. 54–55. © The Society for Research in Child Development, Inc. Reprinted by permission.

Page 406, Figure 14.3, From *Disadvantaged Children: Health, Nutrition, and School Failure,* by H. G. Birch and J. D. Gussow, 1970, p. 268. Reprinted by permission of Grune & Stratton, Inc.

Page 413, Figure 14.4, From "Developmental Differences in Responses to a Television Character's Appearance and Behavior," by C. Hoffner, & J. Cantor. In *Developmental Psychology,* 1985, Vol. 21, p. 1067. Copyright 1985 by the American Psychological Association. Reprinted by permission of the author.

Page 433, Table 15.1, Dilemma and pro and con answers from Developmental Hierarchy in Preference and Comprehension of Moral Judgment, by James Rest, Unpublished doctoral dissertation, 1968. Reprinted by permission of the author.

Page 436, Figure 15.3, From "Preschoolers' Moral Actions and Emotions in Prisoner's Dilemma," by D. Matsumoto, N. Haan, G. Yabrove, P. Theodorou, & C. C. Carney. In *Developmental Psychology,* 1986, Vol. 22, p. 665. Copyright 1986 by the American Psychological Association. Reprinted by permission of the author.

Page 455, Table 16.1, From *Two Worlds of Childhood: U.S.A. and U.S.S.R.,* by Urie Bronfenbrenner, 1970. Reprinted by permission of Basic Books, Inc., and George Allen & Unwin, Ltd.

Pages 461–466, Figures 16.1–16.6, Reprinted by permission of Alexander Alland, Columbia University.

Page 478, Figure 17.1, From "Postural Disequilibrium Quantification in Children with Chronic Lead Exposure," by A. Bhattacharya, R. Shukla, R. Bornschein, K. Dietrich, & J. E. Kopke. In *Neurotoxicology,* 1988, Vol. 9, pp. 327–340. Used courtesy of Dr. Amit Bhattacharya.

Page 494, Table 17.2, From "Adult Status of Children with Contrasting Life Experiences," by H. M. Skeels. In *Monographs of the Society for Research in Child Development,* 1966, Vol. 31(3, Serial No. 105). © The Society for Research in Child Development, Inc. Reprinted by permission.

Page 503, Figure 18.1, Adapted from "Growth and Endocrinology in the Adolescent," by J. M. Tanner. In L. I. Gardner (Ed.), *Endocrine and Genetic Diseases of Childhood,* 1969. Adapted by permission of W. B. Saunders Co. and Dr. J. M. Tanner.

Page 505, Figure 18.2, From "Standards From Birth to Maturity for Height, Weight, Height Velocity and Weight Velocity: British Children 1965," by J. M. Tanner, R. H. Whitehouse, & M. Takaishi. In *Archives of Disease in Childhood,* 1966, Vol. 41, 454–471; 613–635. Reprinted by permission.

Page 507, Figure 18.3, From J. M. Tanner, 1962, *Growth at Adolescence;* data from Jones, 1949. By permission of Blackwell Scientific Publications and J. M. Tanner.

Page 514, Figure 18.5, From "Adolescence and Formal Operations," by A. Blasi, & E. C. Hoeffel. In *Human Development,* 1974, Vol. 17, p. 345. Reprinted by permission of S. Karger AG, Basel, Switzerland.

Page 536, Table 19.3, From "Premarital Sex: Attitudes and Behavior by Dating Stage," by John P. Roche. In *Adolescence,* 1986, Vol. 21(No. 81), p. 110. Reprinted by permission.

Page 538, quotation, Copyright 1985, Time, Inc. All rights reserved. Reprinted by permission of TIME.

Photo Credits

3 © Phil Huber, Black Star; **6** The Bettmann Archive; **6** Brown Brothers; **7** Brown Brothers; **13** © Cary Wolinsky, Stock, Boston; **16** © Anthony Jalandoni, Monkmeyer; **17** © Lorraine Rorke, The Image Works; **24** © Jerry Schad, Photo Researchers; **31** © Junebug Clark, Photo Researchers; **39** © Dr. Fred Hecht, The Genetics Center of Southwest Biomedical Research Institute; **40** Brown Brothers; **43** The Bettmann Archive; **47** © Richard Hutchings, Photo Researchers; **50** © Leonard Lee Rue III, Monkmeyer; **56** Brown Brothers; **57** A/P Wide World; **60** © Ray Nelson, Phototake NYC; **65** © Lawrence Migdale, Photo Researchers; **67 (top)** © Evelyn Scolney, Monkmeyer; **67 (lower left)** © G. R. Richardson, Taurus; **67 (lower right)** © Willie L. Hill, Jr., Stock, Boston; **70** Stansbury, Ronsaville, Wood, Inc.; **72** © Lennart Nilsson. All photos originally appeared in *A Child Is Born* by Lennart Nilsson (New York: Dell Publishing) and *Behold Man* by Lennart Nilsson (Boston: Little, Brown and Company); **73** © Alexander Tsiaras, Science Source; **75** © Arleen Lewis; **76** © Dr. Ann Pythkowicz Streissguth, University of Washington; **78** © Chas Cancellare Picture Group; **86** © Mark McKenna; **87** © Arleen Lewis; **91** © Paul Conklin, Monkmeyer; **94** © Mikki Ansin, Taurus; **96** © Hank Morgan, Rainbow; **101** © Rob Nelson, Black Star; **103** © Larry Mulvehill/Science Source and Photo Researchers; **104** © Arleen Lewis; **105** © Lew Merrim, Monkmeyer; **106 (left)** © Pinney, Monkmeyer; **106 (right)** © Arleen Lewis; **107** © Andy Levin, Photo Researchers; **110** Courtesy of Kim Hill; **112 (both photos)** © Arleen Lewis; **115** © Owen Franken, Stock, Boston; **116** © Arleen Lewis; **118** © Milton Feinberg, The Picture Cube; **123** © Elizabeth Crews; **124** Anthony DeCasper, photographer Walter Salinger; **129** © Cary Wolinsky, Stock, Boston; **130** © Jerome Bruner; **131** © Arleen Lewis; **132** © Arleen Lewis; **133** © Renate Hiller, Monkmeyer; **139** Photo courtesy of Albert Yonas, University of Minnesota; **144** © John Dworetzky; **147** © Elizabeth Crews; **150** Harry Harlow, University of Wisconsin Primate Lab; **151** Harry Harlow, University of Wisconsin Primate Lab; **152** © Life Magazine, Time, Inc.; **153** © Erik Hesse; **156** © Erik Hesse; **158** © Steven Baratz, The Picture Cube; **164** © Corroon & Co., Monkmeyer; **165** © Arleen Lewis; **166 (left)** © Julie O'Neil; **166 (middle)** © George Zimball, Monkmeyer; **166 (right)** © Simo Neri-Valentine, Jeroboam; **171** © Susan Arms, Jeroboam; **173** © David Strickler, Monkmeyer; **176** © Lawrence Migdale, Photo Researchers; **183** © Elizabeth Crews; **189** Dr. Ben Harris, J. B. Watson, EXPERIMENTAL INVESTIGATION OF BABIES (1919); **197** © John Rees, Black Star; **199** © Albert Bandura; **201** "Imitation of Facial and Manual Gestures by Human Neonates" by A. N. Meltzoff and M. K. Moore, SCIENCE, vol. 198, pp. 75–78, Fig. 1, October © 1977 The American Association for the Advancement of Science; **205** © Albert Bandura; **209** © Photo Researchers; **212** © Ursula Markus, Photo Researchers; **214** © Carol Lee, The Picture Cube; **217 (left)** © J. R. Holland, Stock, Boston; **217 (middle)** © Mike L. Wannemacher, Taurus; **217 (right)** © George Goodwin, Monkmeyer; **239** © Bob Daemmrich, Stock, Boston; **241** © Yves DeBraine, Black Star; **243** © L. Benedict Jones, The Picture Cube; **246** © Suzanne Szasz, Photo Researchers; **247 (both photos)** © Doug Goodman, Monkmeyer; **248** Erika Stone, Peter Arnold; **250 (both photos)** © Suzanne Chevalier-Skolnikoff; **268** Steve Dworetzky; **273** © James Sugar, Black Star; **284** © Sybil Shackman, Monkmeyer; **286** © Stephen Frisch, Stock, Boston; **287** © Lew Merrim, Monkmeyer; **299** © Elizabeth Crews; **300** © Bettmann; **307** © Mimi Forsyth, Monkmeyer; **312** AP/Wide World; **318** © Bettmann; **321** Courtesy of Marc Bornstein, New York University; **323** © George Goodwin, Monkmeyer; **333** © Junebug Clark, Photo Researchers; **335** © Peter Menzel, Stock, Boston; **337** © Elizabeth Crews; **344** © Ray Ellis, Photo Researchers; **346** © Elizabeth Crews; **365** © Kathy Sloane, Photo Researchers; **376 (left)** © Robert Smith, Black Star; **376 (right)** © J. Berndt, Stock, Boston; **379** © Jean Marc Barey, Photo Researchers; **385** © David R. Frazier, Photo Researchers; **388** © Roy Pinney, Monkmeyer; **390** © Elizabeth Crews; **392** © Jody Drake, Mutrux & Associates; **395 (left)** © Gale Zucker, Stock, Boston; **395 (right)** © Stock, Boston; **397 (top)** © Ed Lettau, Photo Researchers; **397 (bottom)** © H.

Cartier-Bresson, Magnum; **404** © Deni McIntyre, Photo Researchers; **405** © Rick Browne, Stock Boston; **407** © Evan Johnson, Jeroboam; **412** © David Strickler, Monkmeyer; **413** IN ACKNOWLEDGMENTS; **417** © Arleen Lewis; **419** © Edith G. Haun, Stock, Boston; **421** © Arleen Lewis; **424** © Arleen Lewis; **427** © Arleen Lewis; **432** Courtesy of Harvard University News Office; **439** © Rick Kopstein, Monkmeyer; **445** © Scott Rutherford, Black Star; **452** © Frank Wing, Stock, Boston; **453** © Kara Kurith, Discover Magazine, Time, Inc.; **454** © Neil Goldstein, Stock, Boston; **458** © Dr. E. R. Sorenson, National Anthropological Film Center; **461–466** Photos by Peter Tenzer from Alexander Alland, Jr. Collection. © Columbia University Press, 1983. Reprinted by permission. **469** © Richard Hutchings/Science Source, Photo Researchers; **474** © John Lei, Stock, Boston; **480** © David Grossman, Photo Researches; **481** © Bob Daemmrich, The Image Works; **483** © Joe Rodriguez, Black Star; **485 (left)** University of Wisconsin Primate Lab; **485 (right)** University of Wisconsin Primate Lab; **486** © The Bettmann Archive; **491** © Stewart D. Halperin; **501** © Will McIntyre, Photo Researchers; © Ted Spiegel, Black Star; **504** © Larry Miller, Photo Researchers; **506** © Gerard Vandystadt, Photo Researchers; **508** © Charles Gupton, Stock, Boston; **513** © David M. Grossman, Photo Researchers; **521** © Black Star; **525** © Andrew Gottlieb, Monkmeyer; **528** © Lew Merrim, Monkmeyer; **531** © Eric Kroll, Taurus; **533** © Lawrence Migdale, Stock, Boston; **535** © Herve Donnezan, Photo Researchers; **539** © Rhoda Sidney, Monkmeyer.